PRENTICE HALL COURSE 1

MATHEMATICS

Randall I. Charles
Judith C. Branch-Boyd
Mark Illingworth
Darwin Mills
Andy Reeves

Prentice Hall

Needham, Massachusetts
Upper Saddle River, New Jersey

Authors

Series Author

Randall I. Charles, Ph.D., is Professor Emeritus in the Department of Mathematics and Computer Science at San Jose State University, San Jose, California. He began his career as a high school mathematics teacher, and he was a mathematics supervisor for five years. Dr. Charles has been a member of several NCTM committees and is the former Vice President of the National Council of Supervisors of Mathematics. Much of his writing and research has been in the area of problem solving. He has authored more than 75 mathematics textbooks for kindergarten through college.
Scott Foresman-Prentice Hall Mathematics Series Author Kindergarten through Algebra 2

Program Authors

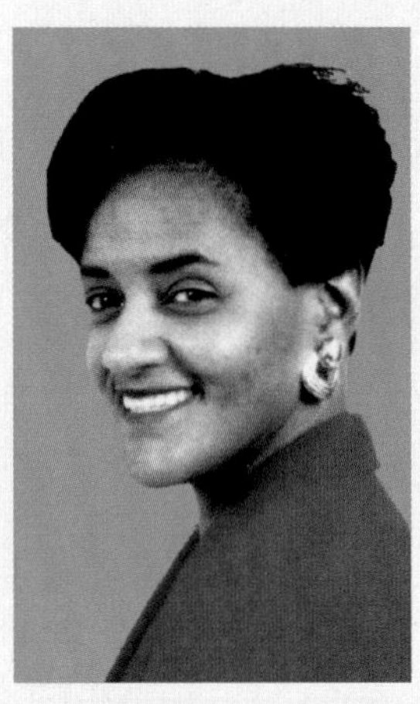

Judith C. Branch-Boyd, Ph.D., is the Area 24 Mathematics Coordinator for the Chicago Public School District. She works with high school teachers to provide quality instruction to students who are mandated to take Algebra, Geometry, and Advanced Algebra-Trigonometry. She also works with middle school and high school teachers to help students transition to Algebra 1. Dr. Branch-Boyd is active in several professional mathematics organizations at the state and national levels, including the National Council of Teachers of Mathematics. She believes,"All children can learn to love mathematics if it is taught with energy!"

ISBN 0-13-063136-1

2 3 4 5 6 7 8 9 10 07 06 05 04 03

Mark Illingworth has taught fifth-graders and enrichment programs for fifteen years. During this time, he received the Christa McAullife sabbatical to develop problem-solving materials and projects for middle-grades math students, and he was granted the Presidential Award for Excellence in Mathematics Teaching. In addition to serving as the district math task force coordinator for the last six years, he has written two of his own books and has contributed to both math and science textbooks at Prentice Hall. Mr. Illingworth has recently shifted from teaching fifth-graders to teaching math to high school students.

Darwin Mills is a mathematics lead teacher for the public schools in Newport News, Virginia and a mathematics adjunct professor at Thomas Nelson Community College in Hampton, Virginia. He has received various teaching awards, including teacher of the year for the 1999–2000 school year and an Excellence in Teaching Award from the College of Wooster, Ohio in 2002. He is a frequent presenter for staff development, especially in the area of graphing calculator usage in the classroom. He believes that all students can learn mathematics if given the proper instruction.

Andy Reeves, Ph.D., teaches at the University of South Florida in St. Petersburg. His career in education spans 30 years and includes seven years as a middle grades teacher. He subsequently served as Florida's K–12 mathematics supervisor and more recently he supervised the publication of the *Mathematics Teacher*, *Mathematics Teaching in the Middle School*, and *Teaching Children Mathematics* for NCTM. Prior to entering education, he worked as an engineer for Douglas Aircraft.

Contributing Author

Denisse R. Thompson, Ph.D., is Associate Professor of Mathematics Education at the University of South Florida. She has particular interests in the connections between literature and mathematics and in the teaching and learning of mathematics in the middle grades. Dr. Thompson contributed to the Reading Math lessons and features.

Reviewers

Course 1 Reviewers

Donna Anderson
Math Supervisor 7–12
West Hartford Public Schools
West Hartford, Connecticut

Nancy L. Borchers
West Clermont Local Schools
Cincinnati, Ohio

Kathleen Chandler
Walnut Creek Middle School
Erie, Pennsylvania

Jane E. Damaske
Lakeshore Public Schools
Stevensville, Michigan

Frank Greco
Parkway South Middle School
Manchester, Missouri

Rebecca L. Jones
Odyssey Middle School
Orlando, Florida

Marylee R. Liebowitz
H. C. Crittenden Middle School
Armonk, New York

Kathy Litz
K. O. Knudson Middle School
Las Vegas, Nevada

Don McGurrin
Wake County Public School System
Raleigh, North Carolina

Ron Mezzadri
K–12 Mathematics Supervisor
Fair Lawn School District
Fair Lawn, New Jersey

Sylvia O. Reeder-Tucker
Prince George's County Math Department
Upper Marlboro, Maryland

Julie A. White
Allison Traditional Magnet Middle School
Wichita, Kansas

Charles Yochim
Bronxville Middle School
Bronxville, New York

Course 2 Reviewers

Cami Craig
Prince William County Public Schools
Marsteller Middle School
Bristow, Virginia

Donald O. Cram
Lincoln Middle School
Rio Rancho, New Mexico

Pat A. Davidson
Jacksonville Junior High School
Jacksonville, Arkansas

Yvette Drew
DeKalb County School System
Open Campus High School
Atlanta, Georgia

Robert S. Fair
K–12 District Mathematics Coordinator
Cherry Creek School District
Greenwood Village, Colorado

Michael A. Landry
Glastonbury Public Schools
Glastonbury, Connecticut

Nancy Ochoa
Weeden Middle School
Florence, Alabama

Charlotte J. Phillips
Wichita USD 259
Wichita, Kansas

Mary Lynn Raith
Mathematics Curriculum Specialist
Pittsburgh Public Schools
Pittsburgh, Pennsylvania

Tammy Rush
Consultant, Middle School Mathematics
Hillsborough County Schools
Tampa, Florida

Judith Russ
Prince George's County Public Schools
Prince George's County, Maryland

Tim Tate
Math/Science Supervisor
Lafayette Parish School System
Lafayette, Louisiana

Dondi J. Thompson
Alcott Middle School
Norman, Oklahoma

Candace Yamagata
Hyde Park Middle School
Las Vegas, Nevada

Course 3 Reviewers

Linda E. Addington
Andrew Lewis Middle School
Salem, Virginia

Jeanne Arnold
Mead Junior High School
Schaumburg, Illinois

Sheila S. Brookshire
A. C. Reynolds Middle School
Asheville, North Carolina

Jennifer Clark
Mayfield Middle School
Putnam City Public Schools
Oklahoma City, Oklahoma

Nicole Dial
Chase Middle School
Topeka, Kansas

Christine Ferrell
Lorin Andrews Middle School
Massillon, Ohio

Virginia G. Harrell
Education Consultant
Hillsborough County, Florida

Jonita P. Howard
Mathematics Curriculum Specialist
Lauderdale Lakes Middle School
Lauderdale Lakes, Florida

Patricia Lemons
Rio Rancho Middle School
Rio Rancho, New Mexico

Susan Noce
Robert Frost Junior High School
Schaumburg, Illinois

Carla A. Siler
South Bend Community School Corp.
South Bend, Indiana

Kathryn E. Smith-Lance
West Genesee Middle School
Camillus, New York

Kathleen D. Tuffy
South Middle School
Braintree, Massachusetts

Patricia R. Wilson
Central Middle School
Murfreesboro, Tennessee

Patricia Young
Northwood Middle School
Pulaski County Special School District
North Little Rock, Arkansas

Content Consultants

Courtney Lewis
Mathematics
Prentice Hall Senior National Consultant
Baltimore, Maryland

Deana Cerroni
Mathematics
Prentice Hall National Consultant
Las Vegas, Nevada

Kimberly Margel
Mathematics
Prentice Hall National Consultant
Scottsdale, Arizona

Sandra Mosteller
Mathematics
Prentice Hall National Consultant
Anderson, South Carolina

Rita Corbett
Mathematics
Prentice Hall Consultant
Elgin, Illinois

Cathy Davies
Mathematics
Prentice Hall Consultant
Laguna Niguel, California

Sally Marsh
Mathematics
Prentice Hall Consultant
Baltimore, Maryland

Addie Martin
Mathematics
Prentice Hall Consultant
Upper Marlboro, Maryland

Rose Primiani
Mathematics
Prentice Hall Consultant
Brick, New Jersey

Loretta Rector
Mathematics
Prentice Hall Consultant
Foresthill, California

Charlotte Samuels
Mathematics
Prentice Hall Consultant
Lafayette Hill, Pennsylvania

Margaret Thomas
Mathematics
Prentice Hall Consultant
Indianapolis, Indiana

Contents in Brief

Chapter 1

Decimals

Student Support

Instant Check System

Diagnosing Readiness, 4

Check Skills You'll Need, 5, 9, 13, 19, 25, 30, 35, 40, 43, 48

Check Understanding, 5, 6, 9, 10, 13, 14, 19, 20, 25, 26, 27, 31, 35, 36, 37, 40, 41, 43, 44, 45, 49

Checkpoint Quiz, 17, 39

Comprehensive Test Prep

Daily Test Prep, 7, 12, 17, 23, 29, 33, 39, 42, 47, 51

Test-Taking Strategies, 53

Cumulative Test Prep, 57

Reading Math

Reading Math, 9, 26, 36, 43

Reading Your Textbook, 18

Understanding Vocabulary, 54

Reading Comprehension, 18, 39, 57

Writing in Math

Daily Writing Practice, 7, 11, 16, 22, 28, 33, 38, 42, 46, 50, 52

Real-World Problem Solving

Strategy: Using a Problem-Solving Plan, 30–33
Sports, 10
Earth Science, 14
Nutrition, 22
Bridges, 46
. . . and more!

Chapter 2

Algebra

Patterns and Variables

Student Support

Instant Check System

Diagnosing Readiness, 62

Check Skills You'll Need, 63, 68, 74, 80, 84, 90, 95, 99, 105

Check Understanding, 64, 65, 69, 70, 74, 75, 76, 80, 84, 85, 90, 91, 92, 95, 96, 99, 100, 101, 106

Checkpoint Quiz, 78, 98

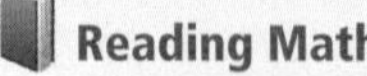

Comprehensive Test Prep

Daily Test Prep, 67, 72, 78, 82, 88, 94, 98, 103, 108

Test-Taking Strategies, 109

Cumulative Test Prep, 113

Reading Math

Reading Math, 63, 84, 86, 100

Reading Algebraic Expressions, 73

Understanding Vocabulary, 110

Reading Comprehension, 67

Writing in Math

Daily Writing Practice, 66, 71, 77, 81, 87, 93, 97, 102, 107

Writing to Compare, 83

Real-World Problem Solving

Strategy: Make a Table and Look for a Pattern, 80–82
Astonomy, 66
Cooking, 77
Biology, 97
Math at Work, 108
. . . and more!

Chapter 3

Number Theory and Fractions

Student Support

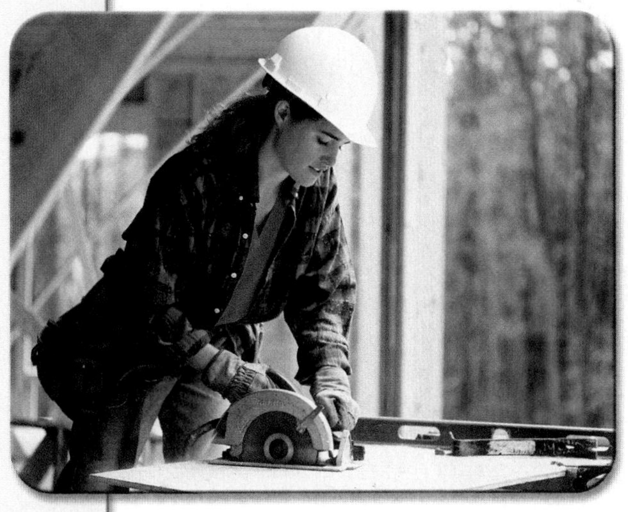

Chapter 4

Adding and Subtracting Fractions

Student Support

Chapter 5

Multiplying and Dividing Fractions

Chapter 6

Ratios, Proportions, and Percents

Student Support

Chapter 7

Data and Graphs

Student Support

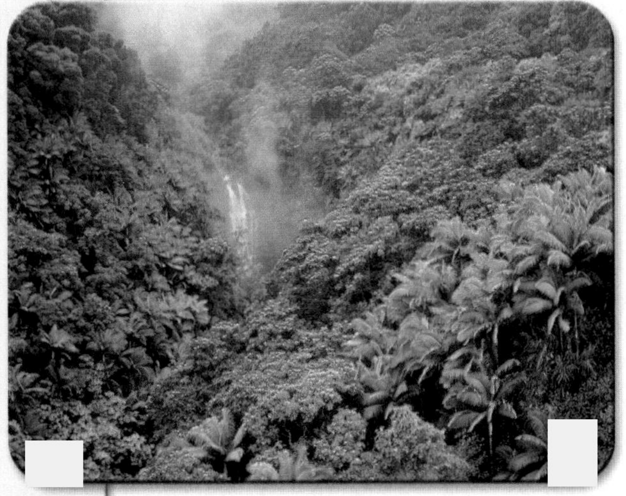

Chapter 8

Tools of Geometry

Student Support

Instant Check System

Diagnosing Readiness, 372

Check Skills You'll Need, 373, 379, 386, 392, 397, 401, 405, 410, 415

Check Understanding, 374, 375, 379, 380, 386, 387, 388, 392, 393, 394, 397, 398, 401, 402, 405, 406, 407, 411, 415, 416, 417

Checkpoint Quiz, 390, 414

Comprehensive Test Prep

Daily Test Prep, 377, 383, 390, 396, 400, 404, 409, 414, 419

Test-Taking Strategies, 421

Cumulative Test Prep, 425

Reading Math

Reading Math, 374, 379, 398

Common Words and Prefixes, 378

Understanding Vocabulary, 422

Reading Comprehension, 377

Writing in Math

Daily Writing Practice, 376, 382, 389, 395, 399, 403, 408, 413, 418

Real-World Problem Solving

Strategy: Use Logical Reasoning, 401–404
Architecture, 389
Games, 394
Science, 399
Math at Work, 400
. . . and more!

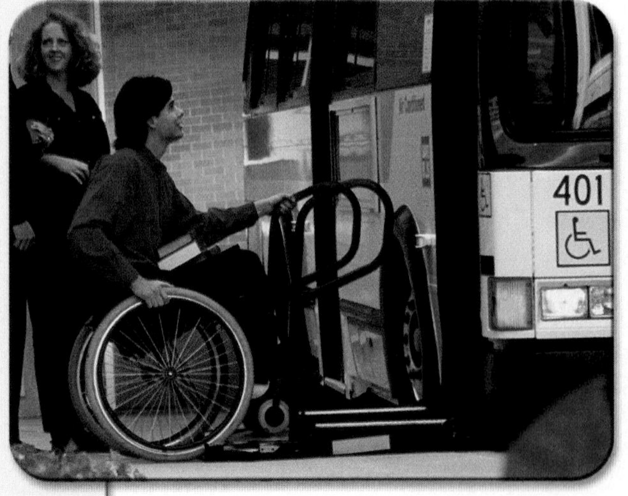

Chapter 9

Geometry and Measurement

Student Support

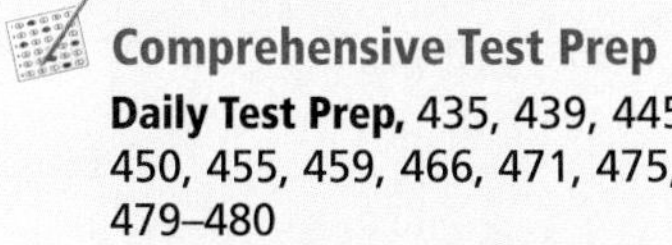

Instant Check System

Diagnosing Readiness, 430

Check Skills You'll Need, 431, 436, 440, 446, 452, 456, 462, 467, 472, 477

Check Understanding, 431, 432, 433, 436, 437, 440, 441, 442, 447, 448, 452, 453, 457, 463, 467, 468, 469, 472, 473

Checkpoint Quiz, 450, 476

Comprehensive Test Prep

Daily Test Prep, 435, 439, 445, 450, 455, 459, 466, 471, 475, 479–480

Test-Taking Strategies, 481

Cumulative Test Prep, 485

Reading Math

Reading Math, 441, 452, 458

Using Concept Maps to Connect Ideas, 460

Understanding Vocabulary, 482

Reading Comprehension, 459, 485

Writing in Math

Daily Writing Practice, 434, 438, 444, 449, 454, 458, 465, 470, 475, 479

Real-World Problem Solving

Strategy: Work Backward, 477–480

Landscaping, 441
Conservation, 447
Archery, 453
Math at Work, 480
. . . and more!

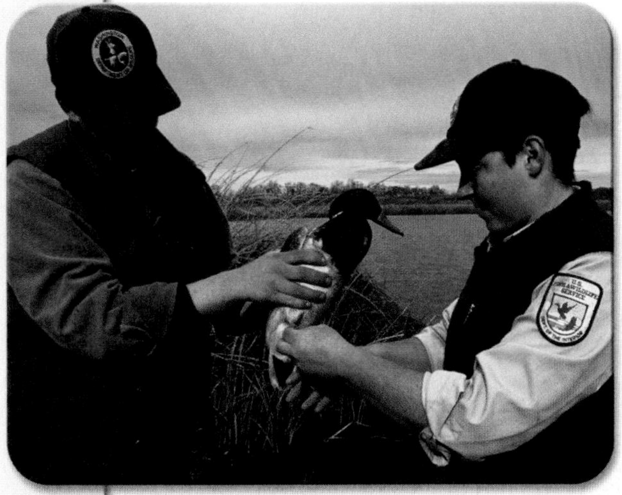

Chapter 10

Integers

Student Support

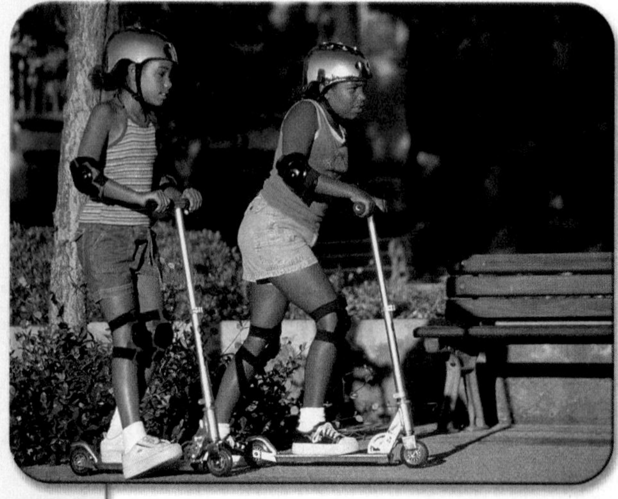

Chapter 11

Exploring Probability

Student Support

Instant Check System

Diagnosing Readiness, 546

Check Skills You'll Need, 547, 553, 558, 563, 568, 574, 580

Check Understanding, 548, 554, 559, 564, 568, 569, 574, 575, 580, 581

Checkpoint Quiz, 562, 578

Comprehensive Test Prep

Daily Test Prep, 551, 557, 562, 566, 573, 577, 583–584

Test-Taking Strategies, 585

Cumulative Test Prep, 589

Reading Math

Reading Math, 550, 577, 581

Understanding Word Problems, 579

Understanding Vocabulary, 586

Reading Comprehension, 562, 589

Writing in Math

Daily Writing Practice, 549, 556, 561, 565, 572, 577, 582, 588

Real-World Problem Solving

Strategy: Simulate a Problem, 563–566

School Fundraising, 548

Baseball, 572

Track and Field, 575

Math at Work, 584

. . . and more!

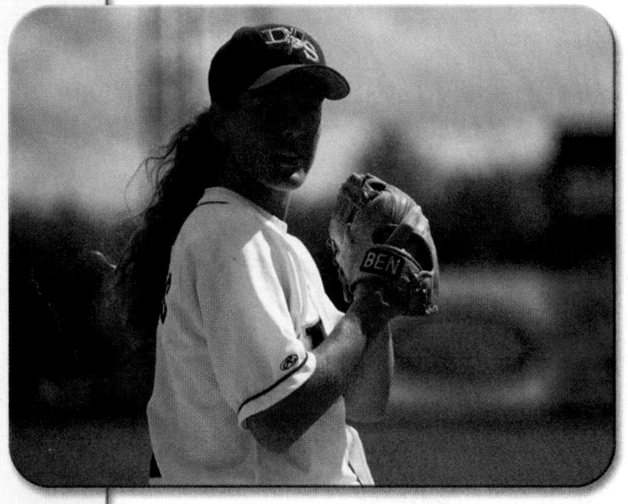

Chapter 12

Algebra

Equations and Inequalities

Student Support

From the Authors

Dear Student,

We have designed this unique mathematics program with you in mind. We hope that Prentice Hall Mathematics will help you make sense of the mathematics you learn. We want to enable you to tap into the power of mathematics.

Examples in each lesson are broken into steps to help you understand how and why math works. Work the examples so that you understand the concepts and the methods presented. Then do your homework. Ask yourself how new concepts relate to old ones. Make connections! As you practice the concepts presented in this text, they will become part of your mathematical power.

The many real-world applications will let you see how you can use math in your daily life and give you the foundation for the math you will need in the future. The applications you will find in every lesson will help you see why it is important to learn mathematics. In addition, the Dorling Kindersley Real-World Snapshots will bring the world to your classroom.

This text will help you be successful on the tests you take in class and on high-stakes tests required by your state. The practice in each lesson will prepare you for the format as well as for the content of these tests.

Ask your teacher questions! Someone else in your class has the same question in mind and will be grateful that you decided to ask it.

We wish you the best as you use this text. The mathematics you learn this year will prepare you for your future as a student and your future in our technological society.

Sincerely,

Randy Charles. Andy Reeves

Darwin E. Mills Mark Illingworth

Judith C. Branch-Boyd

Connect Your Learning

Through Problem Solving, Activities, and the Web

Applications: Real-World Applications

And Over 100 More Topics!
See Real World Applications in the Index, Page 746.

Applications: Careers

Applications: Interdisciplinary Connections

Problem-Solving Strategies

Course 1 Students learn to apply a single problem-solving strategy in each lesson.

Course 2 Students learn to use more than one strategy to solve a problem. They also compare strategies to determine which one is most appropriate in a given situation.

Course 3 Students continue to combine and compare strategies to solve problems. Throughout the text, a greater focus on the strategy *write an equation* helps prepare students for success in algebra.

The problem-solving lessons included in each chapter of *Prentice Hall Mathematics* progress in depth and sophistication within a course and from course to course.

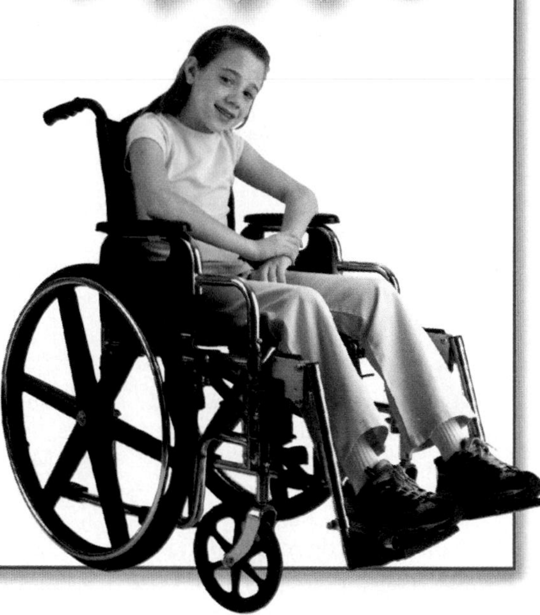

***Prentice Hall Mathematics* contains ample opportunities for you to actively explore mathematics, either working as a whole class, in groups, or individually.**

Activities: Investigations

10–20-minute activities that either introduce or provide practice with lesson concepts

Activities: Real-World Snapshots

20–40-minute activities that apply the math from a chapter to real-world settings

Activities: Chapter Projects

Fun projects that allow you to show off the math you've learned

Activities: Technology

20–40-minute activities that use calculators or software to introduce math concepts

Plus timely calculator and graphing calculator hints

Take It to the Net

Throughout this book, you will find links to the Prentice Hall Web site. Use the Web Code provided with each link to gain direct access to online material.

Here's how to **Take It to the NET**:
- Go to **www.PHSchool.com**.
- Enter the Web Code.
- Click. Go!

For a complete list of online features, use Web Code aak-0099.

Lesson Quiz Web Codes

There is an online quiz for each lesson. Access these quizzes with Web Codes aaa-0101 through aaa-1206 for Lesson 1-1 through Lesson 12-6. *See page 7.*

102 Lesson Quizzes
Web Code format: aba-0204 02 = Chapter 2 04 = Lesson 4

Chapter Resource Web Codes

Chapter	Vocabulary Quizzes *See page 54.*	Chapter Tests *See page 56.*	Dorling Kindersley Real-World Snapshots *See pages 58-59.*	Chapter Projects
1	aaj-0151	aaa-0152	aae-0153	aad-0161
2	aaj-0251	aaa-0252	aae-0253	aad-0261
3	aaj-0351	aaa-0352	aae-0353	aad-0361
4	aaj-0451	aaa-0452	aae-0453	aad-0461
5	aaj-0551	aaa-0552	aae-0553	aad-0561
6	aaj-0651	aaa-0652	aae-0653	aad-0661
7	aaj-0751	aaa-0752	aae-0753	aad-0761
8	aaj-0851	aaa-0852	aae-0853	aad-0861
9	aaj-0951	aaa-0952	aae-0953	aad-0961
10	aaj-1051	aaa-1052	aae-1053	aad-1061
11	aaj-1151	aaa-1152	aae-1153	aad-1161
12	aaj-1251	aaa-1252	aae-1253	aad-1261
End-of-Course		aaa-1254		

Additional Resource Web Codes

Data Updates Use Web Code aag-2041 to get up-to-date government data for use in examples and exercises. *See page 28.*

Math at Work For information about each Math at Work feature, use Web Code aab-2031. *See page 12.*

iTEXT Complete student textbook available online. Includes interactivities and videos.

Using Your Book for Success

Welcome to *Prentice Hall Mathematics, Course 1*. There are many features built into the daily lessons of this text that will help you learn the important skills and concepts you will need to be successful in this course. Look through the following pages for some study tips that you will find useful as you complete each lesson.

Instant Check System™
An *Instant Check System*, built into the text and marked with a ✓, allows you to check your understanding of skills before moving on to the next topic.

✓ Diagnosing Readiness
Complete the *Diagnosing Readiness* exercises to see what topics you may need to review before you begin the chapter.

✓ Check Skills You'll Need
Complete the *Check Skills You'll Need* exercises to make sure you have the skills needed to successfully learn the concepts in the lesson.

✓ Check Understanding
Every lesson includes several *Examples*, each followed by a *Check Understanding* question that you can do on your own to see if you understand the skill being introduced. Check your progress with the answers at the back of the book.

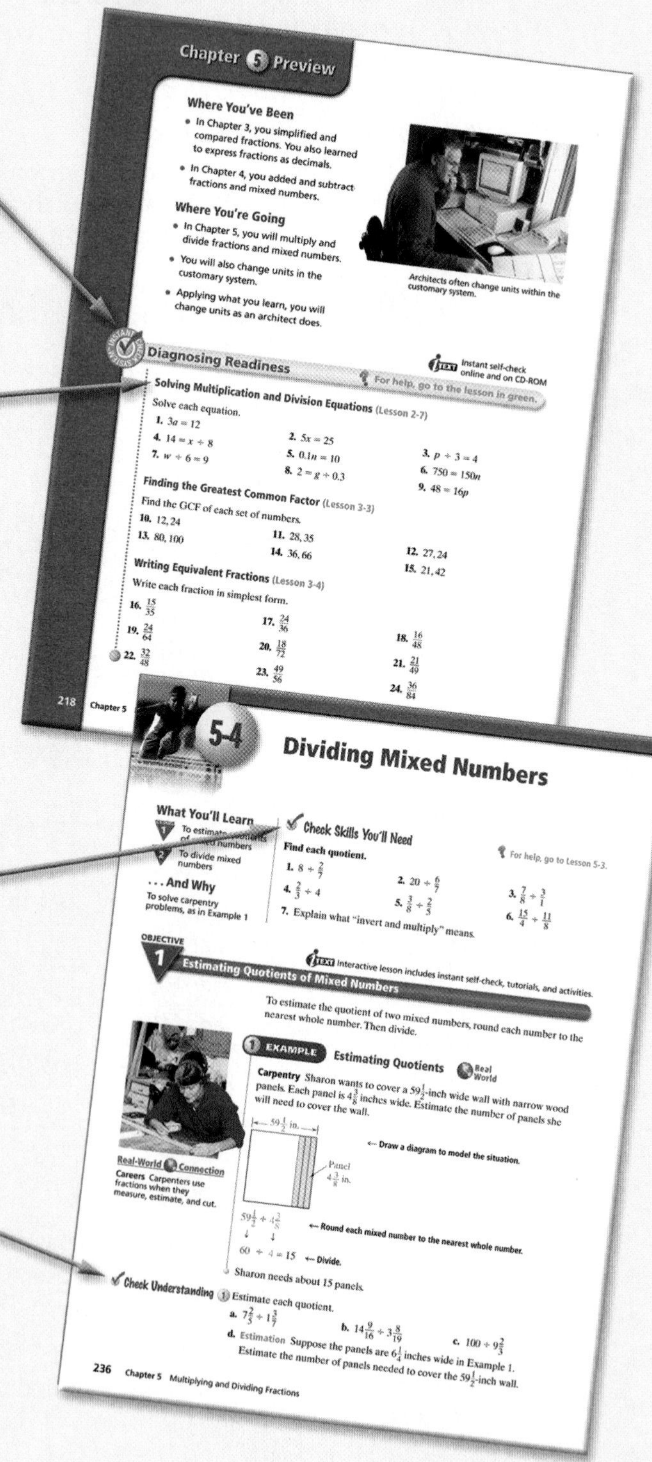

Chapter 5 Preview

Where You've Been
- In Chapter 3, you simplified and compared fractions. You also learned to express fractions as decimals.
- In Chapter 4, you added and subtracted fractions and mixed numbers.

Where You're Going
- In Chapter 5, you will multiply and divide fractions and mixed numbers.
- You will also change units in the customary system.
- Applying what you learn, you will change units as an architect does.

Architects often change units within the customary system.

Diagnosing Readiness

Instant self-check online and on CD-ROM

For help, go to the lesson in green.

Solving Multiplication and Division Equations (Lesson 2-7)
Solve each equation.
1. $3a = 12$ 2. $5x = 25$ 3. $p \div 3 = 4$
4. $14 = x \div 8$ 5. $0.1n = 10$ 6. $750 = 150n$
7. $w \div 6 = 9$ 8. $2 = g \div 0.3$ 9. $48 = 16p$

Finding the Greatest Common Factor (Lesson 3-3)
Find the GCF of each set of numbers.
10. 12, 24 11. 28, 35 12. 27, 24
13. 80, 100 14. 36, 66 15. 21, 42

Writing Equivalent Fractions (Lesson 3-4)
Write each fraction in simplest form.
16. $\frac{15}{35}$ 17. $\frac{24}{36}$ 18. $\frac{16}{48}$
19. $\frac{24}{64}$ 20. $\frac{18}{72}$ 21. $\frac{21}{49}$
22. $\frac{32}{48}$ 23. $\frac{49}{56}$ 24. $\frac{36}{84}$

218 Chapter 5

5-4 Dividing Mixed Numbers

What You'll Learn
1. To estimate quotients of mixed numbers
2. To divide mixed numbers

. . . And Why
To solve carpentry problems, as in Example 1

✓ Check Skills You'll Need
For help, go to Lesson 5-3.
Find each quotient.
1. $8 \div \frac{2}{7}$ 2. $20 \div \frac{6}{7}$ 3. $\frac{7}{8} \div \frac{3}{1}$
4. $\frac{2}{3} \div 4$ 5. $\frac{3}{8} \div \frac{2}{5}$ 6. $\frac{15}{4} \div \frac{11}{8}$
7. Explain what "invert and multiply" means.

OBJECTIVE 1 **Estimating Quotients of Mixed Numbers**

Interactive lesson includes instant self-check, tutorials, and activities.

To estimate the quotient of two mixed numbers, round each number to the nearest whole number. Then divide.

1 EXAMPLE Estimating Quotients Real World

Carpentry Sharon wants to cover a $59\frac{1}{2}$-inch wide wall with narrow wood panels. Each panel is $4\frac{3}{8}$ inches wide. Estimate the number of panels she will need to cover the wall.

$59\frac{1}{2} \div 4\frac{3}{8}$ ← Round each mixed number to the nearest whole number.
$60 \div 4 = 15$ ← Divide.

Sharon needs about 15 panels.

Real-World Connection
Careers Carpenters use fractions when they measure, estimate, and cut.

✓ Check Understanding 1 Estimate each quotient.
a. $7\frac{2}{3} \div 1\frac{3}{7}$ b. $14\frac{9}{16} \div 3\frac{8}{19}$ c. $100 \div 9\frac{2}{3}$
d. Estimation Suppose the panels are $6\frac{1}{4}$ inches wide in Example 1. Estimate the number of panels needed to cover the $59\frac{1}{2}$-inch wall.

236 Chapter 5 Multiplying and Dividing Fractions

Need Help?
Need Help? notes provide a quick review of a concept you need to understand the topic being presented. Look for the green labels throughout the book that tell you where to "Go" for help.

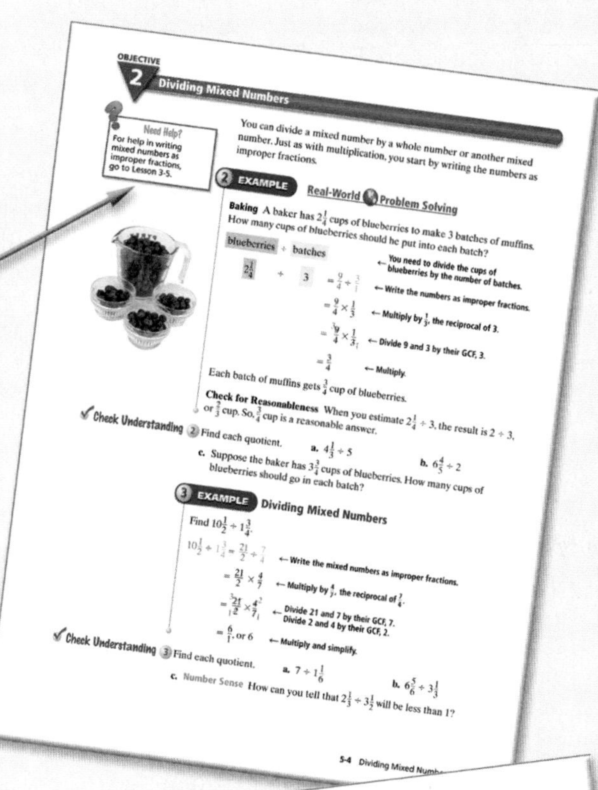
OBJECTIVE 2 Dividing Mixed Numbers

Need Help? For help in writing mixed numbers as improper fractions, go to Lesson 3-5.

You can divide a mixed number by a whole number or another mixed number. Just as with multiplication, you start by writing the numbers as improper fractions.

2 EXAMPLE Real-World Problem Solving

Baking A baker has $2\frac{1}{4}$ cups of blueberries to make 3 batches of muffins. How many cups of blueberries should he put into each batch?

blueberries ÷ batches ← You need to divide the cups of blueberries by the number of batches.

$2\frac{1}{4} \div 3 = \frac{9}{4} \div \frac{3}{1}$ ← Write the numbers as improper fractions.

$= \frac{9}{4} \times \frac{1}{3}$ ← Multiply by $\frac{1}{3}$, the reciprocal of 3.

$= \frac{{}^{3}9}{4} \times \frac{1}{3_1}$ ← Divide 9 and 3 by their GCF, 3.

$= \frac{3}{4}$ ← Multiply.

Each batch of muffins gets $\frac{3}{4}$ cup of blueberries.

Check for Reasonableness When you estimate $2\frac{1}{4} \div 3$, the result is $2 \div 3$, or $\frac{2}{3}$ cup. So, $\frac{3}{4}$ cup is a reasonable answer.

Check Understanding 2 Find each quotient. a. $4\frac{1}{3} \div 5$ b. $6\frac{4}{5} \div 2$

c. Suppose the baker has $3\frac{3}{4}$ cups of blueberries. How many cups of blueberries should go in each batch?

3 EXAMPLE Dividing Mixed Numbers

Find $10\frac{1}{2} \div 1\frac{3}{4}$.

$10\frac{1}{2} \div 1\frac{3}{4} = \frac{21}{2} \div \frac{7}{4}$ ← Write the mixed numbers as improper fractions.

$= \frac{21}{2} \times \frac{4}{7}$ ← Multiply by $\frac{4}{7}$, the reciprocal of $\frac{7}{4}$.

$= \frac{{}^{3}21}{{}_{1}2} \times \frac{4^{2}}{7_{1}}$ ← Divide 21 and 7 by their GCF, 7. Divide 2 and 4 by their GCF, 2.

$= \frac{6}{1}$, or 6 ← Multiply and simplify.

Check Understanding 3 Find each quotient. a. $7 \div 1\frac{1}{6}$ b. $6\frac{5}{6} \div 3\frac{1}{3}$

c. Number Sense How can you tell that $2\frac{1}{3} \div 3\frac{1}{2}$ will be less than 1?

5-4 Dividing Mixed Numb...

More Than One Way
The *More Than One Way* features show you two different methods to solve a problem. By analyzing each student's method, you can think critically about the solution and then choose the method you would use to solve a similar problem.

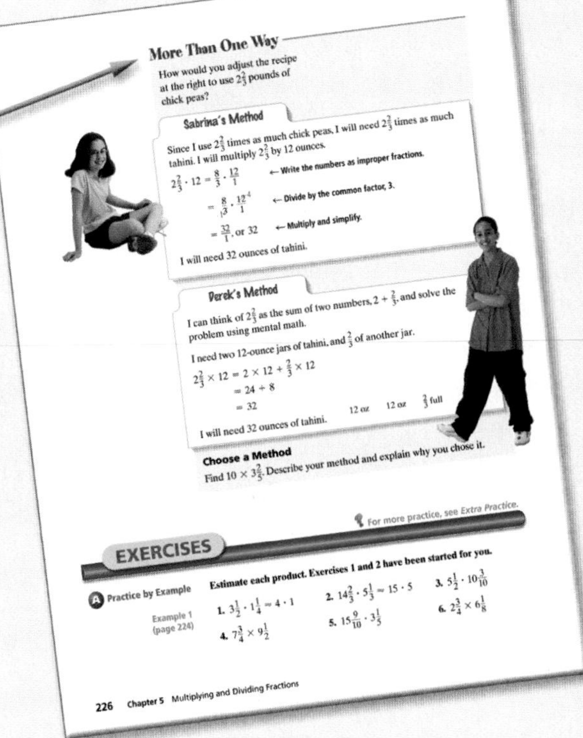
More Than One Way

How would you adjust the recipe at the right to use $2\frac{2}{3}$ pounds of chick peas?

Sabrina's Method

Since I use $2\frac{2}{3}$ times as much chick peas, I will need $2\frac{2}{3}$ times as much tahini. I will multiply $2\frac{2}{3}$ by 12 ounces.

$2\frac{2}{3} \cdot 12 = \frac{8}{3} \cdot \frac{12}{1}$ ← Write the numbers as improper fractions.

$= \frac{8}{{}_{1}3} \cdot \frac{12^{4}}{1}$ ← Divide by the common factor, 3.

$= \frac{32}{1}$, or 32 ← Multiply and simplify.

I will need 32 ounces of tahini.

Derek's Method

I can think of $2\frac{2}{3}$ as the sum of two numbers, $2 + \frac{2}{3}$, and solve the problem using mental math.

I need two 12-ounce jars of tahini, and $\frac{2}{3}$ of another jar.

$2\frac{2}{3} \times 12 = 2 \times 12 + \frac{2}{3} \times 12$

$= 24 + 8$

$= 32$

12 oz 12 oz $\frac{2}{3}$ full

I will need 32 ounces of tahini.

Choose a Method

Find $10 \times 3\frac{2}{5}$. Describe your method and explain why you chose it.

For more practice, see *Extra Practice*.

EXERCISES

A Practice by Example

Example 1 (page 224)

Estimate each product. Exercises 1 and 2 have been started for you.

1. $3\frac{1}{2} \cdot 1\frac{1}{4} \approx 4 \cdot 1$
2. $14\frac{2}{3} \cdot 5\frac{1}{3} \approx 15 \cdot 5$
3. $5\frac{1}{2} \cdot 10\frac{3}{10}$
4. $7\frac{3}{4} \times 9\frac{1}{2}$
5. $15\frac{9}{10} \cdot 3\frac{1}{5}$
6. $2\frac{3}{4} \times 6\frac{1}{8}$

226 Chapter 5 Multiplying and Dividing Fractions

Exercise Sets

Exercises
There are numerous *Exercises* in each lesson that give you the practice you need to master the concepts in the lesson. Each practice set includes the following sections.

A: Practice by Example
The *A: Practice by Example* exercises refer you to the Examples in the lesson, in case you need help completing these exercises.

B: Apply Your Skills
The *B: Apply Your Skills* exercises combine skills from earlier lessons to offer you richer skill exercises and multi-step application problems.

C: Challenge
The *C: Challenge* exercises give you an opportunity to solve problems that extend and stretch your thinking.

Test Prep
The *Test Prep* exercises give you daily practice with the types of test question formats that you will encounter on state and national tests.

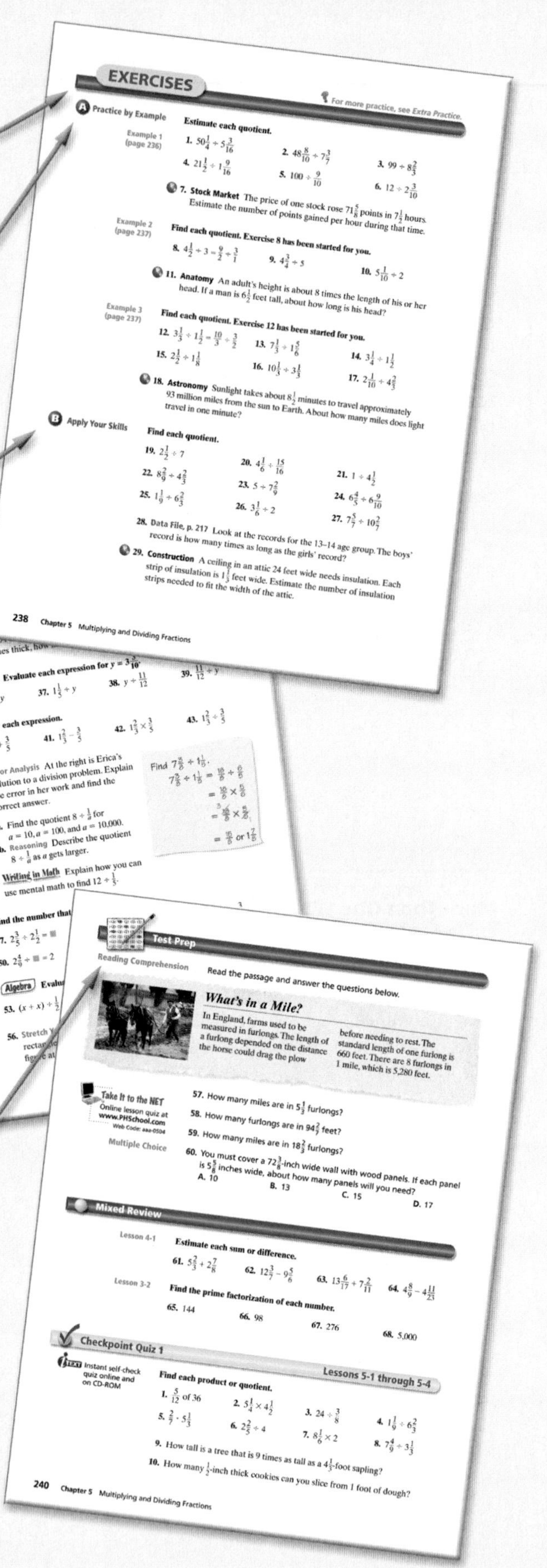

Test-Taking Strategies
Test-Taking Strategies in every chapter teach you strategies to be successful and give you practice in the skills you need to pass state tests and standardized national exams.

Test Prep
In addition to the exercises in every lesson, the *Test Prep* pages in every chapter give you more opportunities to prepare for the tests you will have to take.

Test Item Formats
The *Test Prep* exercises in your book give you the practice you need to answer all types of test questions.

- *Multiple Choice*
- *Gridded Response* (answers are written in a grid)
- *Short Response* (answers are scored with a rubric)
- *Extended Response* (answers are scored with a rubric)
- *Reading Comprehension*

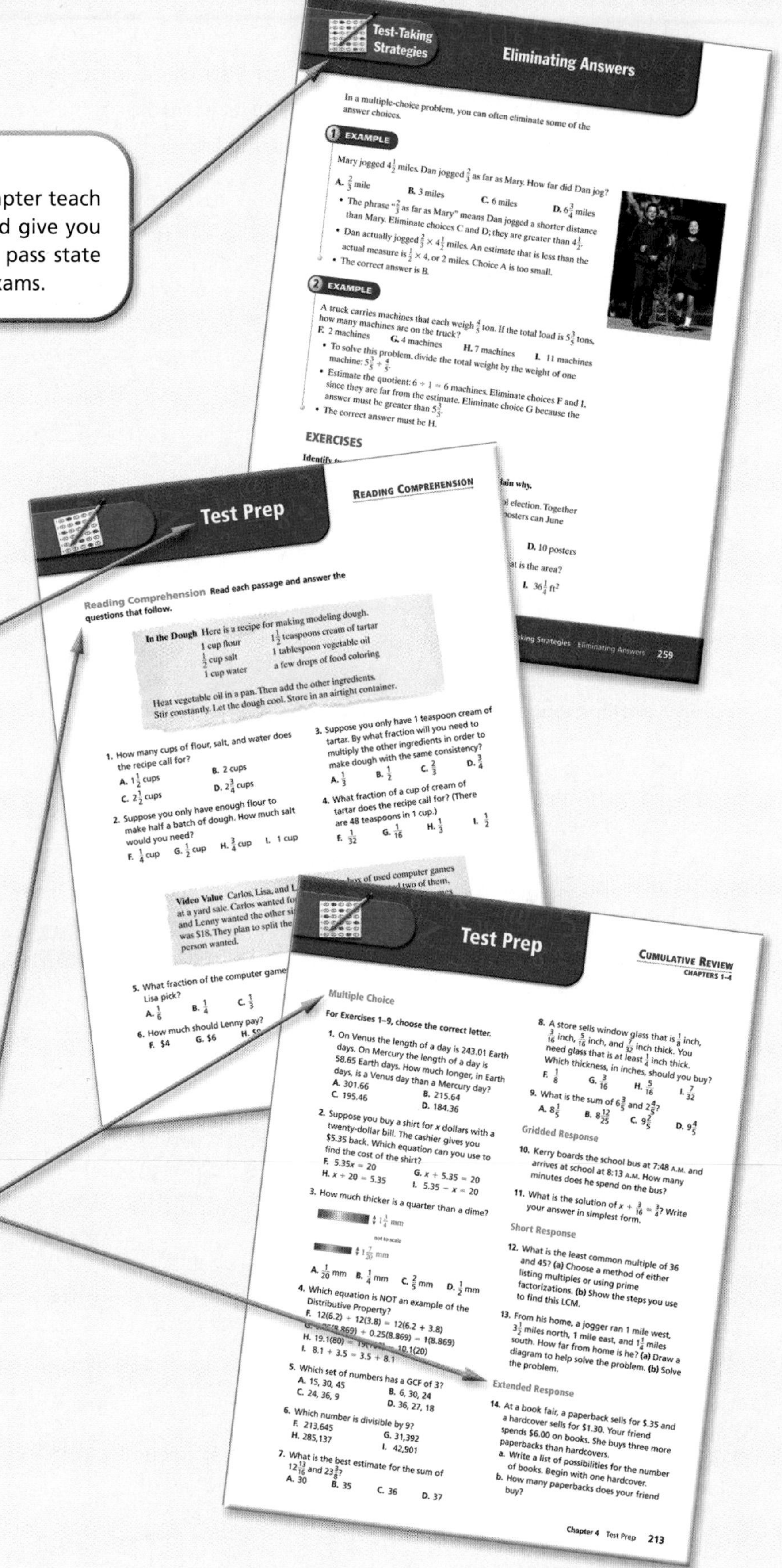

Your *Course 1* text provides even more ways for you to develop your ability to read and write mathematically so that you are successful in this course and on state tests.

New Vocabulary
New Vocabulary is listed for each lesson so you can pre-read the text. As each term is introduced, it is highlighted in yellow.

Reading Math hints
These *hints* help you to use the mathematical notation correctly, understand vocabulary, and translate symbols into everyday English so you can talk about what you've learned.

Reading Math lessons
Reading Math lessons focus on a variety of topics to help you read more effectively, so that you can write, speak, and think mathematically.

Writing in Math lessons
Writing in Math lessons help you write more effectively about the mathematics you are learning.

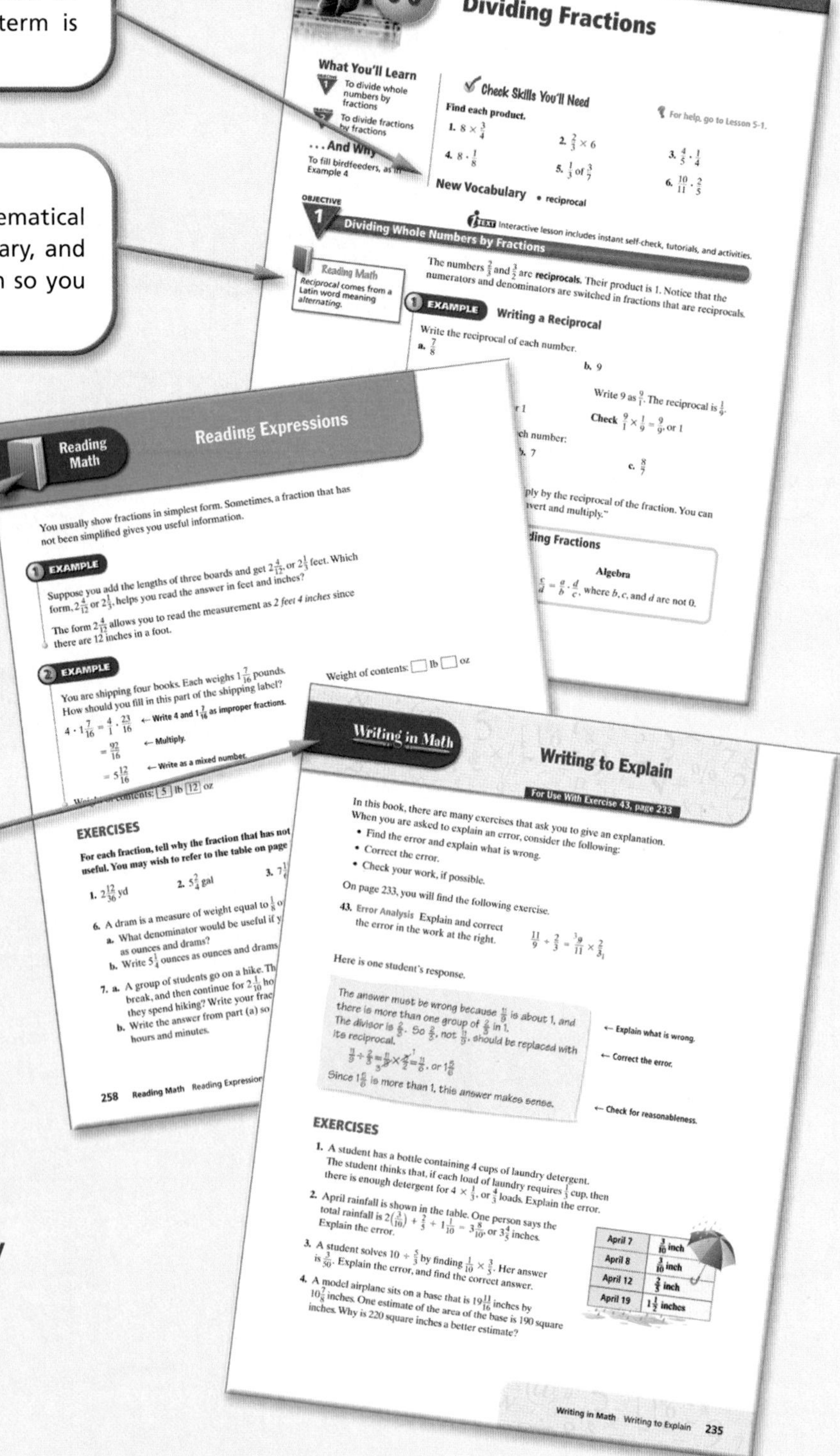

For more help:

- **Reading Math exercises**
  Reading Math exercises in the Chapter Review help you to understand and correctly use the vocabulary presented in the chapter.
- **English/Spanish Illustrated Glossary**
  While you are learning, use this handy reference that contains a written explanation and an illustrated example to help you understand and remember each term.

Dorling Kindersley (DK) Real-World Snapshots

Dorling Kindersley (DK) is an international publishing company that specializes in the creation of high-quality, illustrated information books for children and adults. DK is part of the Pearson family of companies.

Real-World Snapshots
The *Real-World Snapshots* feature applies the exciting and unique graphic presentation style found in Dorling Kindersley books to show you how mathematics is used in real life.

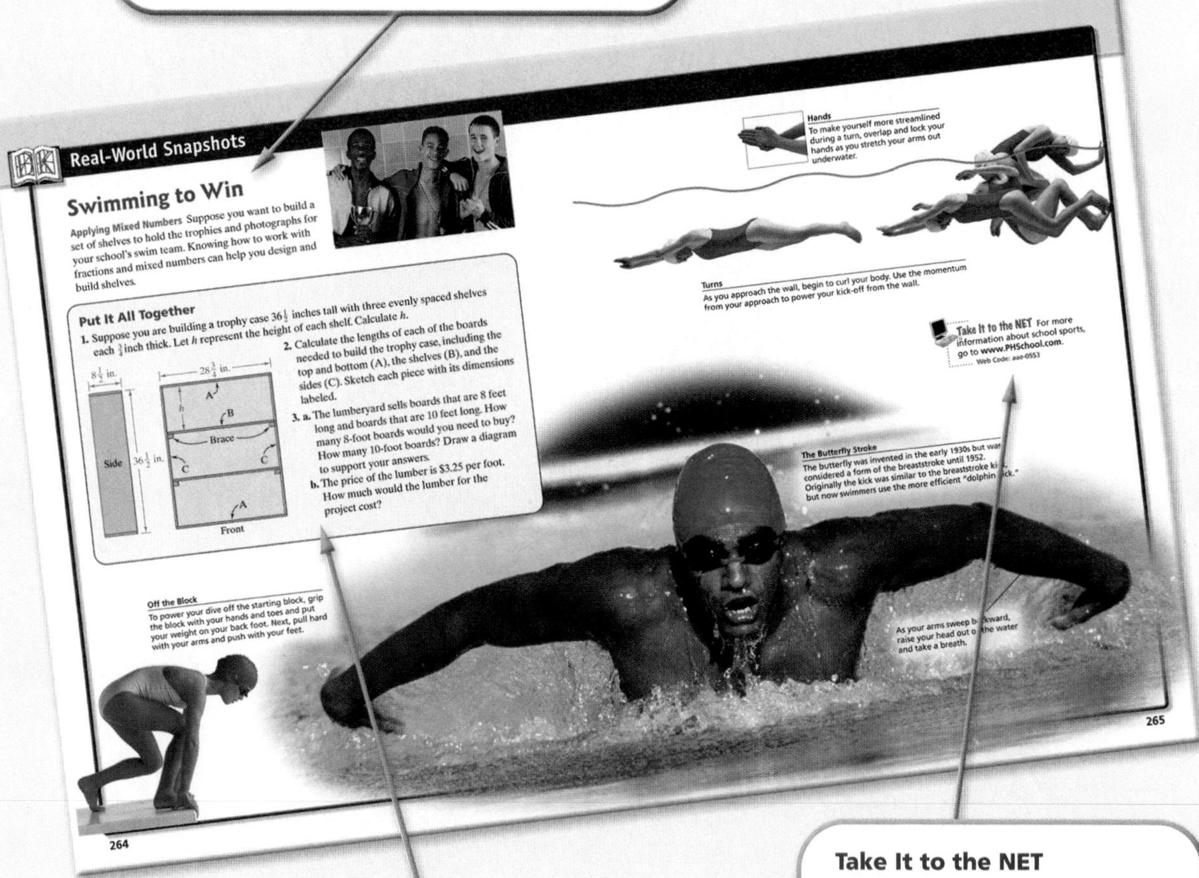

Real-World Snapshots

Swimming to Win

Applying Mixed Numbers Suppose you want to build a set of shelves to hold the trophies and photographs for your school's swim team. Knowing how to work with fractions and mixed numbers can help you design and build shelves.

Put It All Together

1. Suppose you are building a trophy case $36\frac{1}{2}$ inches tall with three evenly spaced shelves each $\frac{3}{4}$ inch thick. Let h represent the height of each shelf. Calculate h.
2. Calculate the lengths of each of the boards needed to build the trophy case, including the top and bottom (A), the shelves (B), and the sides (C). Sketch each piece with its dimensions labeled.
3. a. The lumberyard sells boards that are 8 feet long and boards that are 10 feet long. How many 8-foot boards would you need to buy? How many 10-foot boards? Draw a diagram to support your answers.
   b. The price of the lumber is $3.25 per foot. How much would the lumber for the project cost?

Off the Block
To power your dive off the starting block, grip the block with your hands and toes and put your weight on your back foot. Next, pull hard with your arms and push with your feet.

Hands
To make yourself more streamlined during a turn, overlap and lock your hands as you stretch your arms out underwater.

Turns
As you approach the wall, begin to curl your body. Use the momentum from your approach to power your kick-off from the wall.

Take It to the NET For more information about school sports, go to **www.PHSchool.com**.
Web Code: aae-0553

The Butterfly Stroke
The butterfly was invented in the early 1930s but was considered a form of the breaststroke until 1952. Originally the kick was similar to the breaststroke ki[illegible] but now swimmers use the more efficient "dolphin [illegible]ck."

As your arms sweep b[illegible]kward, raise your head out o[illegible] the water and take a breath.

264

265

Put It All Together
Using data that you gather as well as data from these pages and the Data File, complete the hands-on activities to apply the mathematics you are learning in real-world situations.

Take It to the NET
Enter the Web Code for online information you can use to learn more about the topic of the feature.

CHAPTER 1

Decimals

Lessons

Key Vocabulary

- Associative Properties (pp. 25, 36)
- Commutative Properties (pp. 25, 36)
- compatible numbers (p. 20)
- expanded form (p. 5)
- front-end estimation (p. 20)
- Identity Properties (pp. 25, 36)
- order of operations (p. 48)
- repeating decimal (p. 44)
- standard form (p. 5)
- terminating decimal (p. 44)

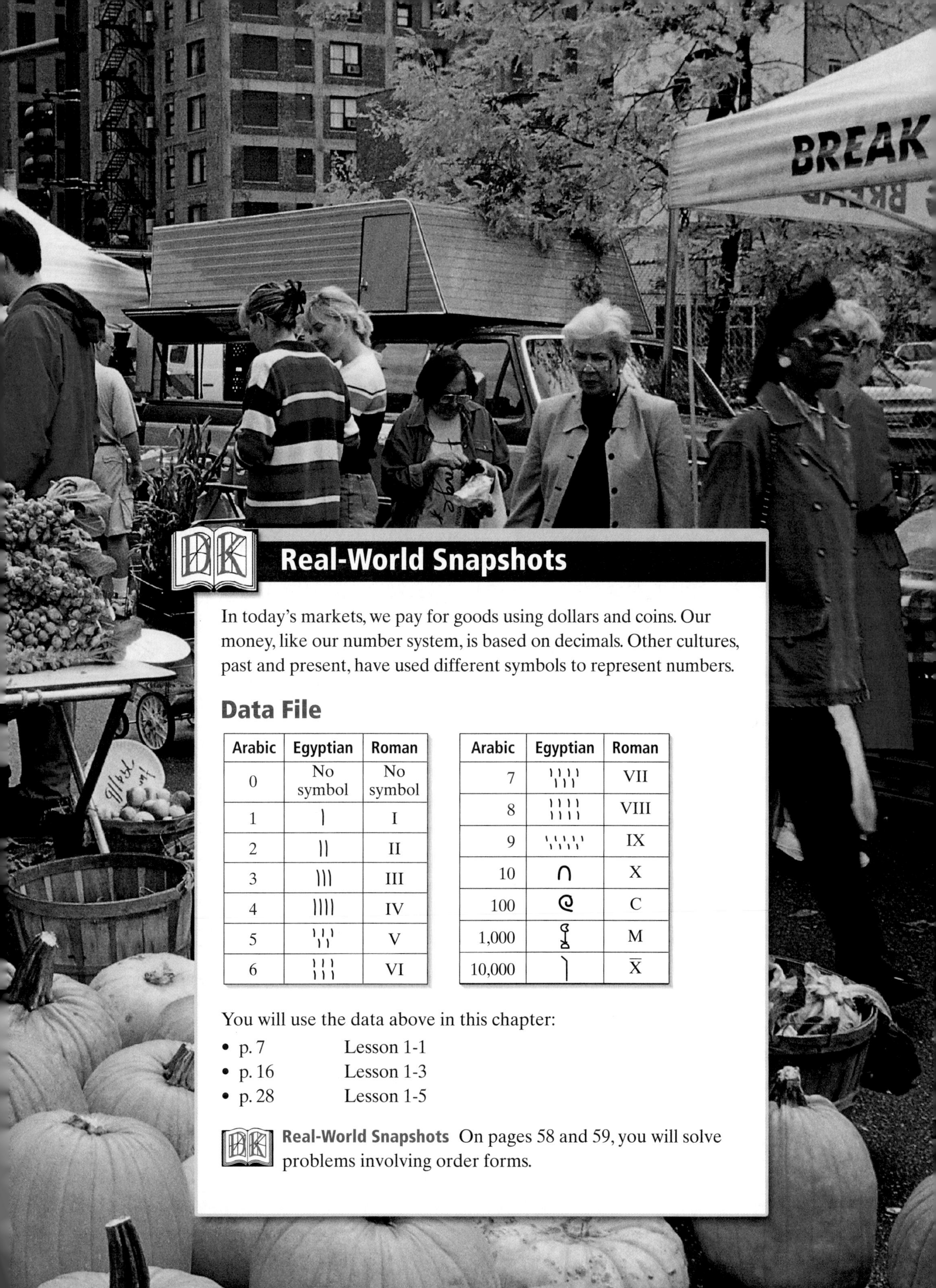

Real-World Snapshots

In today's markets, we pay for goods using dollars and coins. Our money, like our number system, is based on decimals. Other cultures, past and present, have used different symbols to represent numbers.

Data File

Arabic	Egyptian	Roman
0	No symbol	No symbol
1	𓏺	I
2	𓏻	II
3	𓏼	III
4	𓏽	IV
5	𓏾	V
6	𓏿	VI

Arabic	Egyptian	Roman
7	𓐀	VII
8	𓐁	VIII
9	𓐂	IX
10	𓎆	X
100	𓍢	C
1,000	𓆼	M
10,000	𓂭	$\overline{X}$

You will use the data above in this chapter:

- p. 7 Lesson 1-1
- p. 16 Lesson 1-3
- p. 28 Lesson 1-5

Real-World Snapshots On pages 58 and 59, you will solve problems involving order forms.

Chapter 1 Preview

Where You've Been

- In a previous course, you added, subtracted, multiplied, and divided with whole numbers. You also estimated with whole numbers.

Where You're Going

- In Chapter 1, you will add, subtract, multiply, divide, compare, order, and estimate with decimals.
- Applying what you learn, you will perform operations with decimals in the correct order. You will compare decimals so you can find a nonfiction book in a library.

The Dewey Decimal System for nonfiction books assigns each book a number based on its topic.

 Instant self-check online and on CD-ROM

Diagnosing Readiness

 For help, go to the Skills Handbook.

Rounding to the Nearest Ten (Skills Handbook page 655)

Round each number to the nearest ten.

1. 312 **2.** 7,525 **3.** 38

4. 55 **5.** 699 **6.** 1,989

Adding and Subtracting Whole Numbers (Skills Handbook pages 656 and 657)

Add or subtract.

7. 59 + 116 **8.** 182 − 37 **9.** 8,745 + 5,447

10. 4,823 − 1,796 **11.** 9,004 + 996 **12.** 2,049 − 657

Multiplying Whole Numbers (Skills Handbook page 658)

Multiply.

13. 9×83 **14.** 64×71 **15.** 437×100

16. $25 \times 1{,}000$ **17.** 33×14 **18.** 232×8

Dividing Whole Numbers (Skills Handbook page 660)

Divide.

19. $50 \div 10$ **20.** $85 \div 5$ **21.** $1{,}944 \div 27$

22. $256 \div 8$ **23.** $2{,}132 \div 164$ **24.** $1{,}241 \div 17$

1-1 Understanding Whole Numbers

What You'll Learn

OBJECTIVE 1 To write and compare whole numbers

. . . And Why

To compare amounts, as in Exercise 27

Check Skills You'll Need

For help, go to Skills Handbook p. 654.

Write the value of the digit 2 in each number.

1. 28 **2.** 8,672
3. 612,980 **4.** 7,249,800,401

New Vocabulary • standard form • expanded form

OBJECTIVE

 Interactive lesson includes instant self-check, tutorials, and activities.

1 Writing and Comparing Whole Numbers

To work with decimals, you need to understand the *place value* of whole numbers. The **standard form** of a number uses digits and place value. The *place* of the digit 5 in 254 is tens. The *value* of 5 is 5 tens, or 50. A sum that shows the place and value of each digit of a number is its **expanded form**.

Trillions Period			Billions Period			Millions Period			Thousands Period			Ones Period		
Hundreds	Tens	Ones	Hundreds	Tens	Ones	Hundreds	Tens	Ones	Hundreds	Tens	Ones	Hundreds	Tens	Ones
		2,	6	2	3,	6	8	4,	6	0	8,	0	0	0

1 EXAMPLE Writing a Whole Number in Words

Buildings The number in the chart above is the number of pennies you would need to build a stack of pennies as tall as the Sears Tower. Write the number in standard form and in words.

Standard form: 2,623,684,608,000 ← **Use commas to separate the periods.**

Words: First write the number in expanded form.

2,000,000,000,000	+	623,000,000,000	+	684,000,000	+	608,000
2 trillions		623 billions		684 millions		608 thousands

two trillion, six hundred twenty-three billion, six hundred eighty-four million, six hundred eight thousand

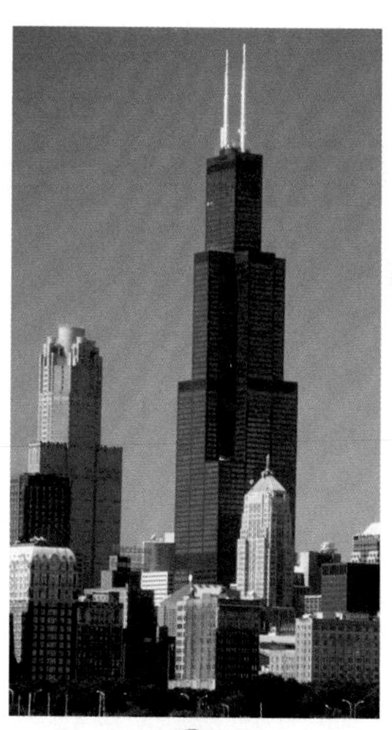

Real-World Connection
The Sears Tower in Chicago is 1,454 feet tall without its antenna towers.

Check Understanding 1 Write the value of $26,236,846,080, in words.

You can use place value to compare and order whole numbers. You can also use a number line to compare whole numbers. The numbers on a number line are in order from least to greatest.

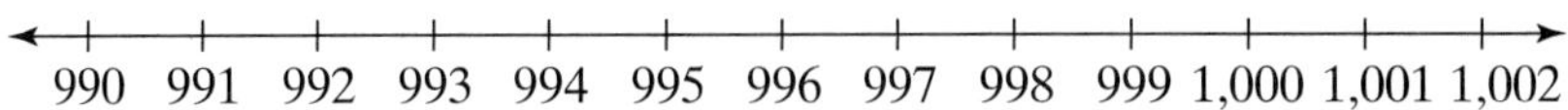

2 EXAMPLE Comparing and Ordering Whole Numbers

Need Help?
To compare numbers, use these symbols.
< is read "is less than."
= is read "is equal to."
> is read "is greater than."

a. Use < or > to complete: 995 ■ 998.

995 is to the left of 998 on the number line above.

So, 995 < 998.

b. Write in order from least to greatest: 12,875; 12,675; 12,695.
Compare the digits starting with the highest place values.

12,875 — **8 is greater than 6, so 12,875 is the greatest number.**
12,675 ← **Compare the tens digit in the remaining numbers. 9 is greater than 7, so 12,695 is the next greatest number.**
12,695

The order from least to greatest is: 12,675; 12,695; 12,875.

2 a. Use < or > to complete: 129,631 ■ 142,832.
b. Write in order from least to greatest: 9,897; 9,987; 9,789.

EXERCISES

Write each number in standard form and in words.

Example 1 (page 5)

1. 20 + 5 **2.** 3,000 + 200 **3.** 500,000 + 8,000 + 300 + 10

4. eight hundred ninety **5.** 7 trillion, 2 million, 31 thousand

Use < or > to complete each statement.

Example 2 (page 6)

6. 366 ■ 36 **7.** 54,001 ■ 54,901 **8.** 8,801 ■ 810

9. 84,123 ■ 9,996 **10.** 29,286 ■ 29,826 **11.** 31,010 ■ 30,101

Write in order from least to greatest.

12. 20,403; 20,304; 23,404; 23,040 **13.** 54,172; 51,472; 57,142; 51,572

14. 7,910; 7,890; 7,901 **15.** 17,444; 18,242; 17,671; 17,414

B Apply Your Skills

Write the value of the digit 4 in each number.

16. 468 **17.** 645,017 **18.** 146,215,020 **19.** 105,034,863

20. 542 **21.** 1,394 **22.** 418,920 **23.** 781,409

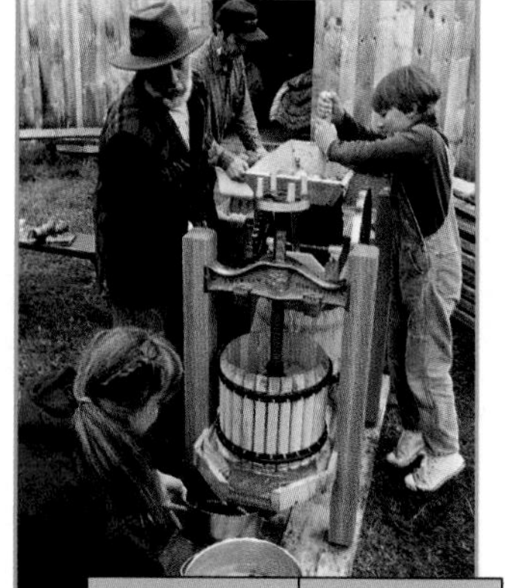

Type of Apple	Cartons
Idared	2,753,000
Empire	2,739,000
Braeburn	2,198,000
McIntosh	3,304,000
York	3,212,000

SOURCE: U.S. Apple Association

Data File, p. 3 The ancient Egyptians did not use a place-value system for their numbers. Instead, they used hieroglyphs to represent numerals.

24. What number is represented at the right?

25. Write 82 and 1,059 using hieroglyphs.

26. **Open-Ended** Write a 5-digit number. Then write it using hieroglyphs.

27. **Apples** Order the apple types from least to greatest number of cartons.

Use < or > to make each sentence true.

28. 60,789 ■ 60,798 ■ 62,532 **29.** 24,891 ■ 18,000 ■ 12,501

30. 42,101 ■ 42,077 ■ 41,963 **31.** 10,455 ■ 11,400 ■ 11,483

32. **Writing in Math** Describe two methods of comparing whole numbers.

Challenge

33. **Research** How many zeros does the number one *quadrillion* have? How many zeros does the number one *quintillion* have?

Test Prep

Multiple Choice

34. What is the value of the digit 2 in 524,065?
A. two **B.** twenty **C.** two thousand **D.** twenty thousand

35. What is the place of the digit 5 in 23,459?
F. ones **G.** tens **H.** hundreds **I.** thousands

36. Which number is NOT greater than 16,374?
A. 16,734 **B.** 17,437 **C.** 16,347 **D.** 16,743

Take It to the NET
Online lesson quiz at
www.PHSchool.com
Web Code: aaa-0101

Mixed Review

Skills Handbook p. 658

Add.

37. 375 + 15 **38.** 120 + 6 **39.** 1,820 + 309 **40.** 2,617 + 1,904

Investigation Exploring Decimal Models

For Use With Lesson 1-2

You can use grid models to represent decimals. If you divide a square into 10 equal parts, each part is *one tenth* of the square.

Tenths Model

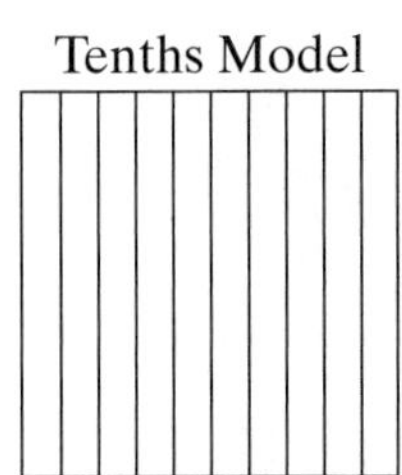

Hundredths Model

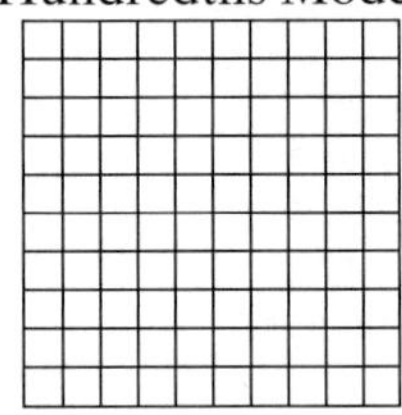

1 EXAMPLE Modeling Decimals

Write a decimal for the model below in words and in numerals.

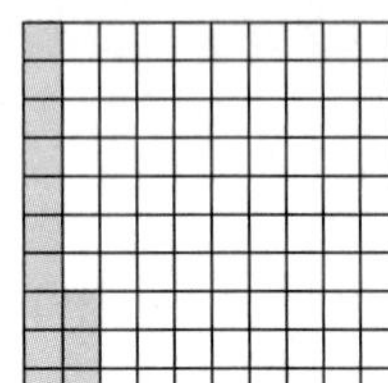

There are 100 squares.
Thirteen squares are shaded.

Words thirteen hundredths

↓

Numerals 0.13

2 EXAMPLE Modeling Equal Decimals

Find the number of hundredths that is equal to five tenths.

Draw a model. Shade five tenths, or 0.5.

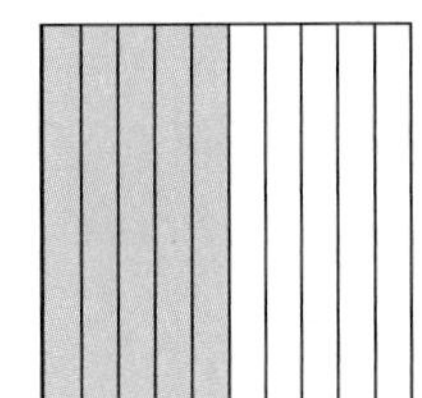

five tenths = 0.5

Divide the model into hundredths. Fifty squares are shaded.

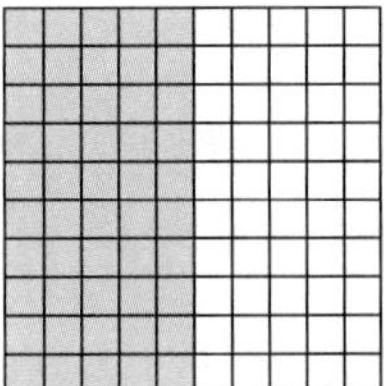

fifty hundredths = 0.50

0.50 is equal to 0.5.

EXERCISES

Write a decimal for each model.

1. 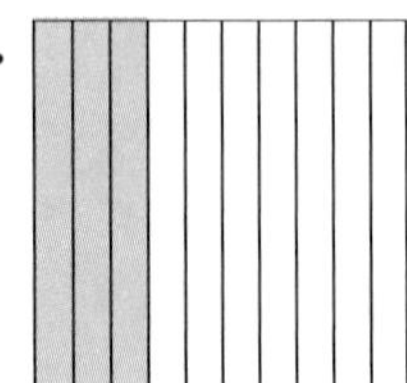

2. 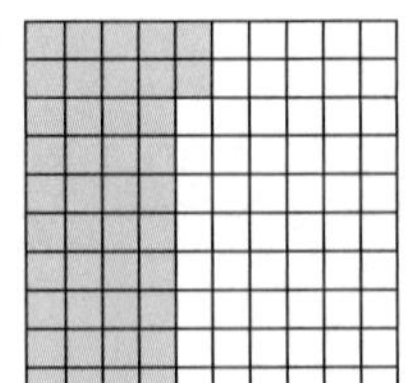

3. 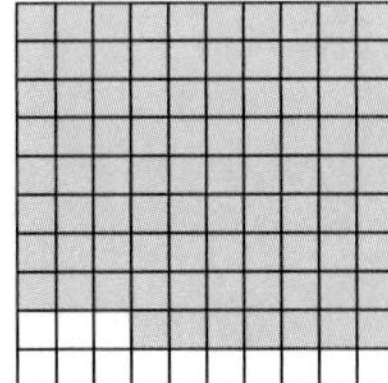

Write a decimal that is equal to each given decimal.

4. sixty hundredths **5.** forty hundredths **6.** eight hundredths

7. 0.2 **8.** 0.9 **9.** 0.7 **10.** 0.40

1-2 Reading and Writing Decimals

What You'll Learn

To read and write decimals

. . . And Why

To read scores in sports, as in Example 3

Check Skills You'll Need

For help, go to Lesson 1-1.

Write each whole number in words.

1. 28 **2.** 8,672

3. 612,980 **4.** 58,026,113

OBJECTIVE

Interactive lesson includes instant self-check, tutorials, and activities.

1 Reading and Writing Decimals

Reading Math

To show that a number is less than 1, a 0 is usually placed to the left of the decimal point.

You can extend the place-value chart to include values for decimal places. You can also write decimals in standard form and in expanded form.

Standard Form		Expanded Form		
0.75	=	0.7	+	0.05
seventy-five hundredths		seven tenths		five hundredths

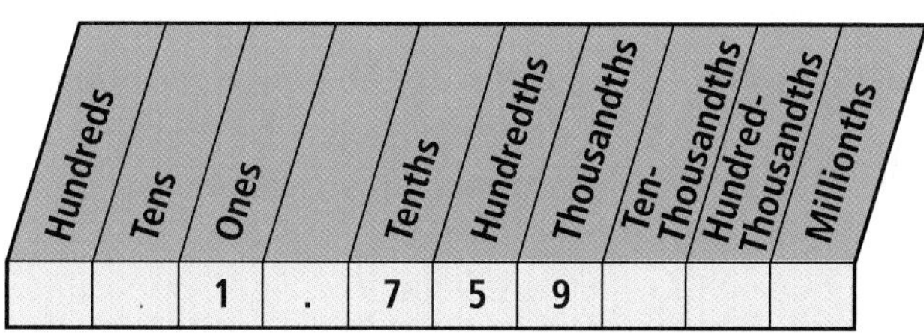

1 EXAMPLE Writing a Decimal in Expanded Form

Real World

Fuel The price of a gallon of gasoline is \$1.759. Write 1.759 from the chart above in expanded form.

	one		seven tenths		five hundredths		nine thousandths
1.759 =	1	+	0.7	+	0.05	+	0.009

Check Understanding 1 Write each number in expanded form.

a. 3.1416 **b.** 0.865 **c.** 37.5

d. **Reasoning** Do you need to include 0.00 in the expanded form of 6.207? Explain.

When you read a decimal that is greater than 1, read the decimal point as "and." Be careful to read "and" for the decimal point only.

2 EXAMPLE Writing a Decimal in Words

Write 20.0408 in words.

20.0408 ← Four decimal places indicate ten-thousandths.

twenty and four hundred eight ten-thousandths

2 Write each decimal in words.

a. 16,702.3   b. 1,670.234   c. 1.67023

Real-World Connection

Blaine Wilson scored nine and five hundred eighty-seven thousandths on the pommel horse.

3 EXAMPLE Writing a Decimal in Standard Form

Sports In the 2000 Olympic Games, the United States men's gymnastics team did not win a medal. Their score was one and thirty-six thousandths points too low. Write this number in standard form.

1 ← Write the whole number part.

1. ← Place the decimal point.

1.■■■ ← Thousandths is 3 places to the right of the decimal point.

1.■ 3 6 ← Place 36 to the far right.

1.036 ← Insert a zero for tenths.

3 a. Refer to the photo caption. Write Blaine Wilson's score in standard form.

b. **Number Sense** In Blaine Wilson's score, which has the greater value, the 5 or the 7? Explain.

EXERCISES

For more practice, see *Extra Practice*.

A Practice by Example

Write each decimal in expanded form.

Example 1 (page 9)

1. 530.34   **2.** 3.004   **3.** 0.23   **4.** 7.5

5. 433.0005   **6.** 1.28   **7.** 93.68   **8.** 130.6

Write each decimal in words.

Example 2 (page 10)

9. 2.3   **10.** 6.02   **11.** 9.5   **12.** 0.006

13. 2.061   **14.** 3.0008   **15.** 0.40   **16.** 50.6003

Example 3 (page 10)

Write each decimal in standard form in Exercises 17–20.

17. forty and nine thousandths

18. six hundred and four millionths

19. **Biology** The diameter of a white blood cell measures twelve ten-thousandths of a centimeter.

20. **Running** A marathon race is twenty-six and two tenths miles long.

B Apply Your Skills

Write each number in expanded form and in words.

21. 8.2 **22.** 91.91 **23.** 91.091 **24.** 1,000,650.02

Money **Write each amount as a decimal part of $1.00 in standard form.**

25. two dimes **26.** five pennies **27.** one quarter **28.** seven nickels

29. **Writing in Math** Describe how the value represented by each "2" in the number 2,222.22 changes as you move from right to left.

30. **Data Analysis** According to the bar graph, sales for Company A were $0.7 million. As a whole number, this value is written $700,000. Write each amount.

a. Company B sales as a decimal
b. Company B sales as a whole number
c. Company C sales as a decimal
d. Company C sales as a whole number

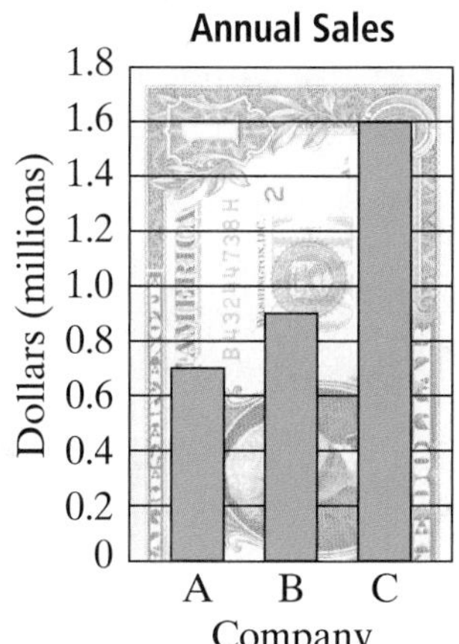

Find the value of the digit 4 in each number.

31. 0.4 **32.** 42.3926

33. 17.55643 **34.** 34,567.89

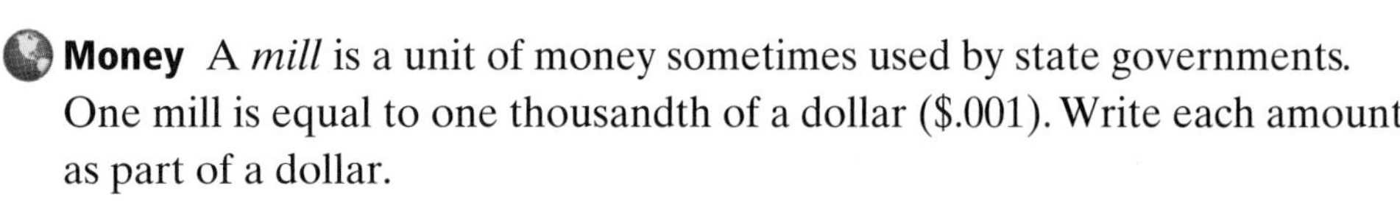

Money A *mill* is a unit of money sometimes used by state governments. One mill is equal to one thousandth of a dollar ($.001). Write each amount as part of a dollar.

35. 6 mills **36.** 207 mills **37.** 53 mills **38.** 328 mills

39. **Heights** Artists use a ratio called the Golden Mean to describe a person's height. Your height from the floor to your waist is usually six hundred eighteen thousandths of your total height. Write this number as a decimal.

C Challenge

40. Extend the place value chart on page 9 to the right.
   a. Write 0.000001 in words.
   b. Write 0.0000001 in words.
   c. **Critical Thinking** What place is to the right of millionths? Explain.

41. **Stretch Your Thinking** A three-digit number's last digit is three times its first digit. Its first digit is twice its second digit. What is the number?

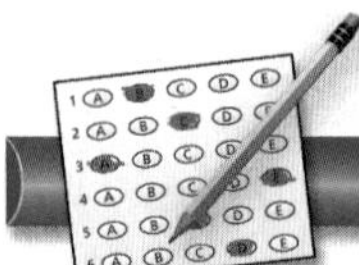

Test Prep

Multiple Choice

42. What is the value of the digit 1 in 94.107?
   A. ten B. one C. one tenth D. one hundredth

43. What is the place of the digit 3 in 14.038?
   F. tens G. ones H. tenths I. hundredths

44. What is forty thousandths in standard form?
   A. 40,000 B. 40 C. 0.040 D. 0.0040

45. What is one hundred and seven thousandths in standard form?
   F. 107,000 G. 100.007 H. 100.0007 I. 0.107

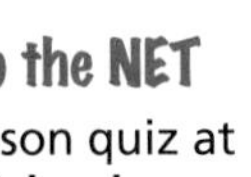
Take It to the NET
Online lesson quiz at **www.PHSchool.com**
Web Code: aaa-0102

Mixed Review

Lesson 1-1

Use < or > to complete each statement.

46. 98,410 ■ 98,140
47. 40,000 ■ 300,009
48. 478,296 ■ 478,269

Math at Work

Accountant

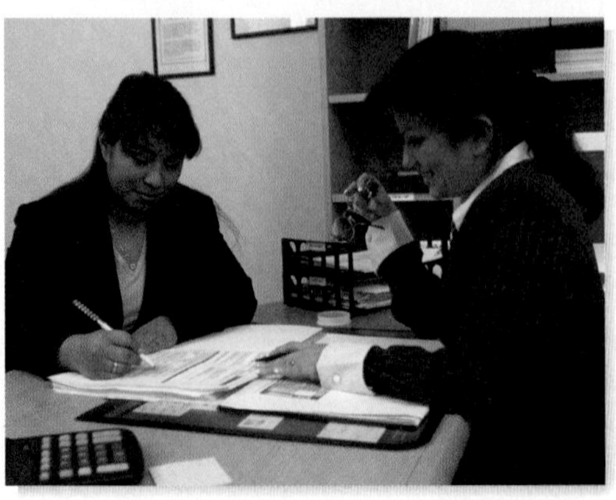

Accountants use mathematics to prepare and analyze financial reports, tax returns, and budgets. They help individuals and companies track financial history and plan for future growth. Accountants' reports help people make good business decisions.

Take It to the NET For more information about accounting, go to **www.PHSchool.com**.
Web Code: aab-2031

1-3 Comparing and Ordering Decimals

What You'll Learn

 To compare decimals using models

 To use place value

. . . And Why

To compare bodies of water, as in Example 4

Check Skills You'll Need

For help, go to Lesson 1-1.

Use < or > to complete each statement.

1. 430 ■ 340 **2.** 2,005 ■ 205

3. 80,020 ■ 8,020 **4.** 473 ■ 347

5. Number Sense Two whole numbers have the same number of digits. To compare them, do you begin with the digits on the left or on the right?

Interactive lesson includes instant self-check, tutorials, and activities.

OBJECTIVE 1 Comparing Decimals Using Models

You can use grid models and number lines to compare and order decimals.

1 EXAMPLE Using Models to Compare Decimals

Draw models for 0.4 and 0.36. Which number is greater?

Use a tenths grid for 0.4.
Use a hundredths grid for 0.36.

0.4

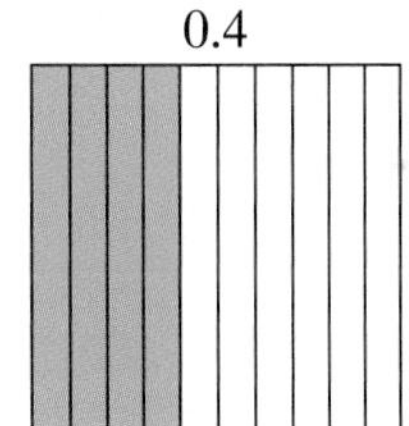

0.36

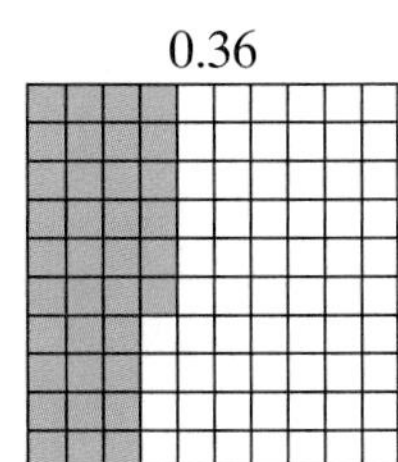

A greater area is shaded for 0.4 than for 0.36, so 0.4 is greater than 0.36.

Check Understanding 1 Draw models for 0.59 and 0.6. Which number is greater?

2 EXAMPLE Ordering Decimals on a Number Line

Order the decimals 2.4, 2.3, 2.17, and 2.43 on a number line.

All the numbers are between 2 and 2.5. Make a number line showing tenths. Then mark the hundredths. Graph the points.

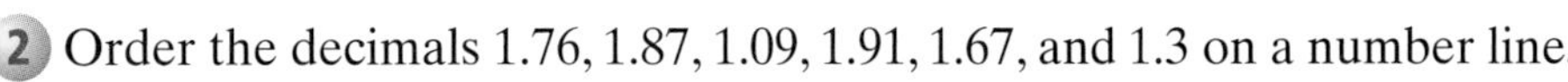

Check Understanding 2 Order the decimals 1.76, 1.87, 1.09, 1.91, 1.67, and 1.3 on a number line.

OBJECTIVE

2 Using Place Value

You can use place value to compare two decimals, just as you do to compare whole numbers.

3 EXAMPLE Comparing Two Decimals

Use <, =, or > to complete the statement 3.18 ■ 3.8.

Write a zero at the end of 3.8 so each number has the same number of decimal places. 3.18 3.80

Compare each digit from left to right. 3.18 3.80

The ones digits are the same.

The tenths digits are different. 1 is less than 8.

Since 1 tenth < 8 tenths, 3.18 < 3.8.

Check Understanding 3 Use <, =, or > to complete each statement.

a. 2.37 ■ 2.7 **b.** 0.56 ■ 0.543 **c.** 1.650 ■ 1.65

d. Reasoning Explain how you can use place value to compare 1.679 and 1.697.

4 EXAMPLE Ordering Decimals

Earth Science Order these bodies of water from least salty to most salty.

Salt per Liter in Major Bodies of Water

Body of Water	Arctic Ocean	Dead Sea	Caspian Sea	Black Sea
Salt per Liter	0.032 kg	0.28 kg	0.013 kg	0.018 kg

SOURCE: Natural Wonders of the World

Write a zero at the end of 0.28. Then compare the digits from left to right.

2 is the greatest tenths digit, so 0.280 is the greatest decimal.

0.032	0.032	← 3 is the greatest hundredths digit, so 0.032 is the second greatest decimal.
0.280	0.280	
0.013	0.013	
0.018	0.018	← 8 is the greatest thousandths digit, so 0.018 is the third greatest decimal.

The decimals from least to greatest are 0.013, 0.018, 0.032, and 0.28.

The bodies of water from least to most salty are the Caspian Sea, the Black Sea, the Arctic Ocean, and the Dead Sea.

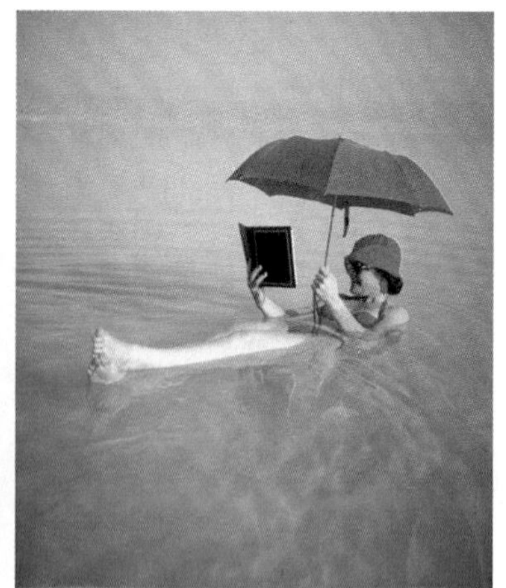

Real-World Connection

People float easily in the salty water of the Dead Sea, which lies between Israel and Jordan.

Check Understanding 4 Order each set of decimals from least to greatest.

a. 2.6, 2.76, 2.076 **b.** 3.059, 3.64, 3.46

More Than One Way

Nutrition Use the table at the right. Order the foods by sodium content from least to greatest.

Food	Sodium
half a bagel	0.19 g
1 corn tortilla	0.04 g
3 pieces of Melba toast	0.12 g
5 crackers	0.195 g
1 slice of wheat bread	0.132 g

Elena's Method

I can use place value and mental math to order the decimals.

0.19 0.04 0.12 0.195 0.132

First, I compare the tenths place in all the numbers. $0 < 1$, so 0.04 is the least number.

Next, I compare the hundredths place in the remaining numbers. $2 < 3 < 9$, so $0.12 < 0.13 < 0.19$.

Finally, I compare 0.19 and 0.195. Since $0.19 = 0.190$ and $0 < 5, 0.19 < 0.195$.

The correct order is 0.04, 0.12, 0.132, 0.19, and 0.195. The foods from least to greatest sodium content are corn tortilla, Melba toast, wheat bread, bagel, and crackers.

Leon's Method

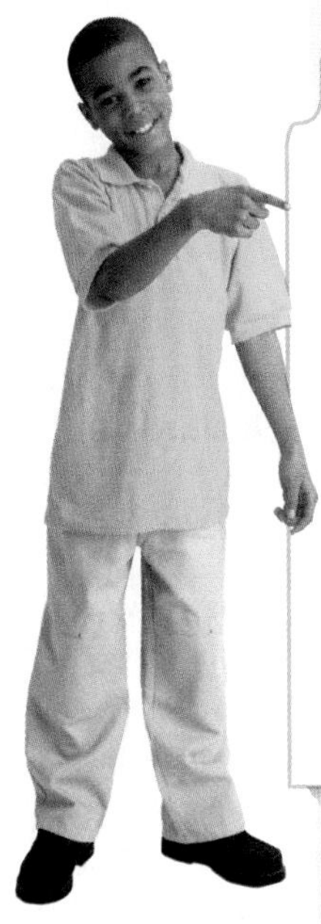

I can order the decimals by graphing them on a number line.

I see that all the numbers are between 0 and 0.2. I'll make a number line marked in hundredths.

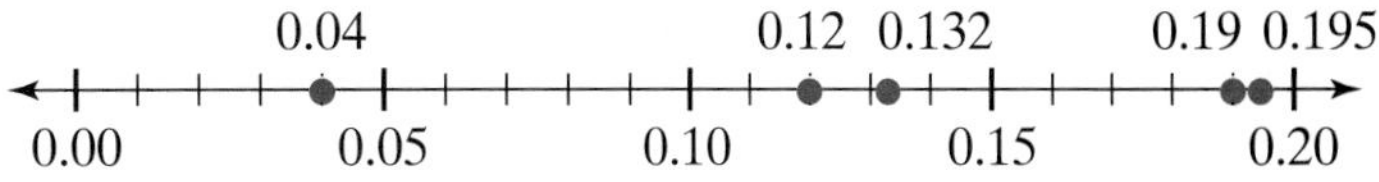

The decimals from least to greatest are 0.04, 0.12, 0.132, 0.19, and 0.195. The foods from least to greatest sodium content are corn tortilla, Melba toast, wheat bread, bagel, and crackers.

Choose a Method

Order the values 0.964, 0.26, 0.576, 0.059, 0.9, 0.96, and 0.264 from least to greatest. Describe your method and explain why you chose it.

EXERCISES

For more practice, see *Extra Practice*.

A Practice by Example

Example 1 (page 13)

Draw models for each pair of decimals. Which number is greater?

1. 0.4 and 0.5 **2.** 0.35 and 0.53 **3.** 0.2 and 0.02

Example 2 (page 13)

Order each set of decimals on a number line.

4. 0.7, 0.2, 0.35, 0.75 **5.** 2.1, 2.53, 2.3, 2.5

6. 6.4, 6.04, 7.6, 6.59, 7.2 **7.** 0.49, 0.34, 0.4, 0.3, 0.38

Example 3 (page 14)

Use <, =, or > to complete each statement.

8. 0.76 ■ 0.78 **9.** 1.42 ■ 1.4 **10.** 2.30 ■ 2.3

11. 0.3 ■ 0.27 **12.** 5.7 ■ 5.70 **13.** 0.048 ■ 0.408

Example 4 (page 14)

Order each set of decimals from least to greatest.

14. 0.5, 0.7, 0.65 **15.** 17.1, 17.7, 13.7

16. 0.503, 0.53, 0.529 **17.** 9.2, 9.02, 9.209, 9.024

B Apply Your Skills

18. 1.79, 2.19, 1.991, 2.185, 1.979 **19.** 5.5506, 5.5660, 5.561, 5.58, 5.665

Year	Time (seconds)
1984	10.97
1988	10.54
1992	10.82
1996	10.94
2000	10.75

SOURCE: *The World Almanac*

20. Population About 11.02 million people live in Jakarta, Indonesia. About 11.7 million people live in Delhi, India. About 11.79 million people live in Karachi, Pakistan. Order the cities from least to greatest population.

21. Open-Ended Write six numbers between 2.2 and 2.222. Order them from least to greatest.

Select all the values on the right that will make each statement true.

22. 4.18 < ■ < 4.25 4.25, 4.17, 4.27, 4.2025, 4.319, 4.198

23. 0.57 < ■ < 0.67 0.6595, 0.5025, 0.6701, 0.6095, 0.62, 0.567

24. Olympics The United States won the women's 100-meter run in all the years listed at the left. Order the times from least to greatest.

25. Writing in Math Alia ran the 100-yard dash in 11.88 seconds. Patty ran it in 11.9 seconds. Who ran faster? Explain how you know.

26. Data File, p. 3 Write $\overline{X}$MCXIV and $\overline{X}$MCXVI as Arabic numerals (standard form). Compare the Roman numerals using <, =, or >.

Challenge

27. **Estimation** Estimate the decimals represented by points A, B, and C.

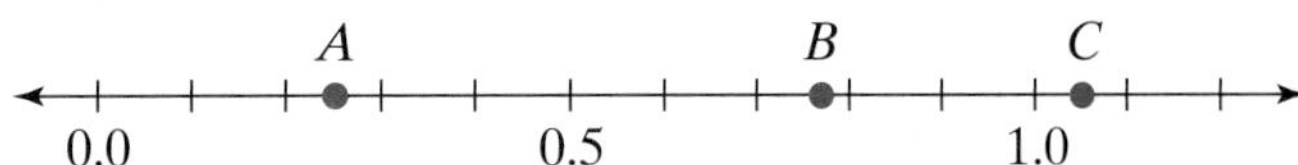

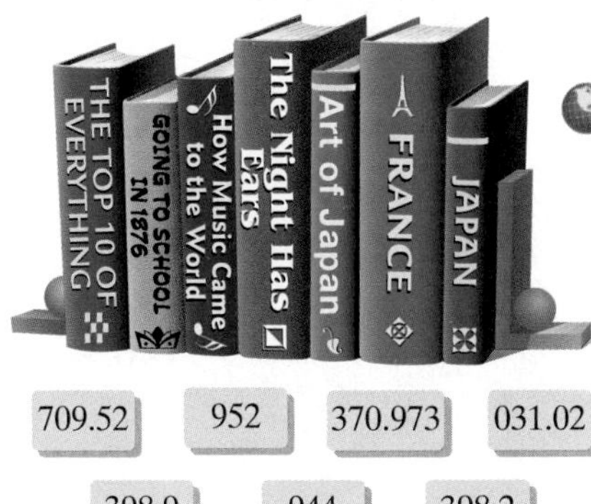

28. **Libraries** The Dewey Decimal System assigns a number to every nonfiction book. These seven books are arranged in the correct order from left to right. Match each label to its book by ordering the labels from least to greatest.

29. Stretch Your Thinking During a scavenger hunt, Team A found 8 more items than Team B. Team C found twice as many items as Team B. Together, the three teams found a total of 72 items. How many items did Team A find?

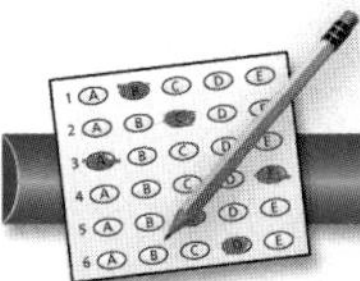

Test Prep

Multiple Choice

30. Which statement is NOT true about the decimals 0.2, 0.4, and 0.6?
    A. $0.2 < 0.4$ and $0.4 < 0.6$ **B.** $0.2 < 0.4$ and $0.6 > 0.2$
    C. $0.2 < 0.6$ and $0.6 < 0.4$ **D.** $0.4 < 0.6$ and $0.6 > 0.2$

31. Which value is NOT between 3.6 and 3.75?
    F. 3.62 **G.** 3.647 **H.** 3.7 **I.** 3.8

Take It to the NET
Online lesson quiz at
www.PHSchool.com
Web Code: aaa-0103

32. Which value is greater than 0.72 and less than 1.29?
    A. 0.7 **B.** 0.999 **C.** 1.3 **D.** 1.9

Mixed Review

Skills Handbook p. 659

Subtract.

33. $152 - 27$ **34.** $34{,}567 - 488$ **35.** $13{,}789 - 3{,}653$

36. $91 - 62$ **37.** $836 - 459$ **38.** $4{,}071 - 2{,}190$

Checkpoint Quiz 1 — Lessons 1-1 through 1-3

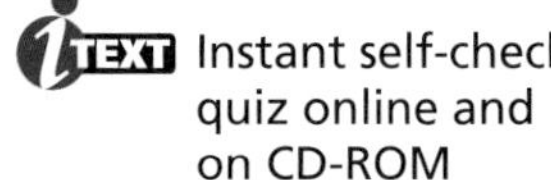

Instant self-check quiz online and on CD-ROM

1. Write 6,080,000,000,405.31 in words.
2. Write 12.035 in expanded form.
3. Write the number four hundred and seven tenths in standard form.
4. Use <, =, or > to complete the statement 1.082 ■ 1.28.
5. Order the numbers 9, 8.7, 9.31, 8.0, and 8.05 from least to greatest.

Reading Math

Reading Your Textbook

For Use With Lesson 1-3

Here are some reading tips to keep in mind as you read this textbook.

- Read carefully. Even little words make a difference in mathematics. Read the graphs, diagrams, and symbols that go with the text. These items contain important mathematical information.
- Learn new vocabulary. Make your own list of new words. Include a definition and example for each word.
- Read with pencil and paper. You should work the steps of each example as you read.

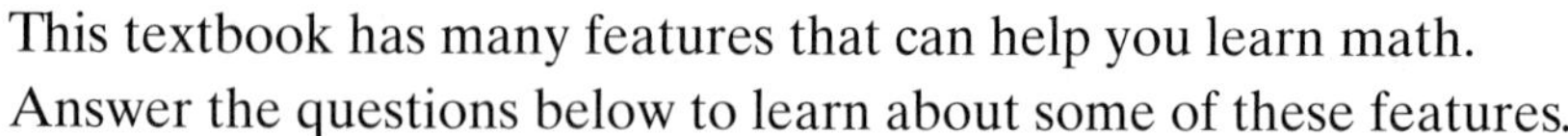

This textbook has many features that can help you learn math. Answer the questions below to learn about some of these features.

EXERCISES

Each lesson begins with What You'll Learn, Check Skills You'll Need, and New Vocabulary features. Find these items for Lesson 1-4 on page 19.

1. **a.** What are the two objectives in Lesson 1-4?
   b. Look through the lesson. On what page does each objective start?
2. **a.** What skills do you need to have before you start the lesson?
   b. Where in your book can you look for help with these skills?
3. What new vocabulary words are introduced in this lesson?

Find the three examples presented in Lesson 1-4, beginning on page 19.

4. Which example shows how to use front-end estimation?
5. Which example shows how to round in estimating a product?
6. Which example shows how to use compatible numbers?

Find the exercises for Lesson 1-4, beginning on page 21.

7. To the left of Exercises 1–7 on page 21, you see "**Example 1 (page 19)**." How could this information help you work these exercises?

1-4 Estimating With Decimals

What You'll Learn

To estimate by rounding and using compatible numbers

To use front-end estimation

. . . And Why

To estimate total costs, as in Example 3

Check Skills You'll Need

For help, go to Skills Handbook p. 655.

Round each number to the nearest ten.

1. 45 **2.** 65,328 **3.** 132,798

Round each number to the nearest thousand.

4. 30,910,067 **5.** 5,555 **6.** 15,345,357

New Vocabulary

- compatible numbers
- front-end estimation

OBJECTIVE

Interactive lesson includes instant self-check, tutorials, and activities.

1 Estimating by Rounding and Using Compatible Numbers

Need Help?
For help with rounding numbers, go to Skills Handbook page 657.

Rounding decimals is similar to rounding whole numbers. You know that 32 rounds down to 30, and 35 and 39 round up to 40.

	Round down:	Round up:	Round up:	
Value < 5, so round down to nearest tenth. →	0.32	0.35	0.39	← **Value ≥ 5, so round up to nearest tenth.**
	↓	↓	↓	
	0.3	0.4	0.4	

1 EXAMPLE Estimate by Rounding

Estimate. First round each decimal to the nearest whole number.

a. $10.93 + 3.25 \rightarrow 11 + 3 = 14$

So, $10.93 + 3.25 \approx 14$. ← **The symbol ≈ means "is approximately equal to."**

b. $15.3 \times 2.6 \rightarrow 15 \times 3 = 45$

So, $15.3 \times 2.6 \approx 45$.

1 Estimate by first rounding to the nearest whole number.

a. 1.16×32.06 **b.** $5.05 - 1.9$ **c.** $18.75 + 93.346$

Another method for estimating uses compatible numbers. **Compatible numbers** are numbers that are easy to compute mentally.

2 EXAMPLE Estimating With Compatible Numbers

a. Estimate 5.21×78.03.

5.21×78.03

$5 \times 80 = 400$ ← Use compatible numbers such as 5 and 80.

$5.21 \times 78.03 \approx 400$

b. Estimate $29.56 \div 4.13$.

$29.56 \div 4.13$

$28 \div 4 = 7$ ← Use compatible numbers such as 28 and 4.

$29.56 \div 4.13 \approx 7$

Check Understanding 2 **a.** **Number Sense** In part (b), why are 28 and 4 compatible numbers?
b. Use compatible numbers to estimate $302.1 - 48.79$.

OBJECTIVE

2 Using Front-End Estimation

To use **front-end estimation,** you add the "front-end digits," estimate the sum of the remaining digits, and adjust the estimate as necessary.

3 EXAMPLE Using Front-End Estimation

Food Use front-end estimation to estimate the total cost of one of each size of popcorn.

Step 1 Add the front-end digits, the dollars.

\$3.98
6.49
9.08
+ 3.47
\$21

Step 2 Look at the cents and adjust the estimate.

\$3.98	→ about \$1
6.49	
9.08	about \$1
+ 3.47	
\$21	about \$2

The total cost is about \$21 + \$2, or \$23.

Check Understanding 3 **a.** Use front-end estimation to estimate the total cost of one small popcorn and two large popcorns.
b. **Reasoning** Find an estimate for the total cost in Example 3 by rounding. Why is front-end estimation a good method when money is involved?

Investigation: Finding an Exact or Estimated Answer

Most problems require an exact answer. Others need only an estimate for the answer. Decide whether each situation needs an exact or estimated answer. Explain your reasoning.

1. the record attendance at a college football game
2. amount of money you plan on spending when shopping
3. amount of money a store cashier earns each hour
4. the time it takes you to get to school
5. **Reasoning** Describe two situations, one that needs only an estimate and one that needs an exact answer. Explain why.

EXERCISES

For more practice, see *Extra Practice*.

A Practice by Example

Example 1 (page 19)

Estimate by first rounding to the nearest whole number.

1. $\begin{array}{r} 35.617 \\ +\ 0.816 \\ \hline \end{array}$ **2.** $\begin{array}{r} 10.581 \\ -\ 1.203 \\ \hline \end{array}$ **3.** $\begin{array}{r} 16.91 \\ \times\ 2.25 \\ \hline \end{array}$ **4.** $\begin{array}{r} 15.3 \\ \times\ 2.6 \\ \hline \end{array}$

5. $15.8 + 38.095$ **6.** $6.501 - 3.999$ **7.** 0.95×22.8

Example 2 (page 20)

Use compatible numbers to estimate. Exercise 8 has been started for you.

8. $46.4 \div 4.75 \rightarrow 45 \div 5 = ?$ **9.** $392 + 193$

10. $653 - 295$ **11.** 27×9.98 **12.** $36.4 \div 6.2$

13. $73.25 \div 9.43$ **14.** 23.3×4.2 **15.** $30.9 \div 5.1$

Example 3 (page 20)

Use front-end estimation to estimate each sum to the nearest dollar.

16. $\begin{array}{r} \$4.89 \\ +\ \$3.97 \\ \hline \end{array}$ **17.** $\begin{array}{r} \$6.15 \\ +\ \$8.86 \\ \hline \end{array}$ **18.** $\begin{array}{r} \$14.65 \\ \$27.29 \\ +\ \$63.85 \\ \hline \end{array}$ **19.** $\begin{array}{r} \$16.81 \\ \$19.94 \\ +\ \$11.49 \\ \hline \end{array}$

B Apply Your Skills

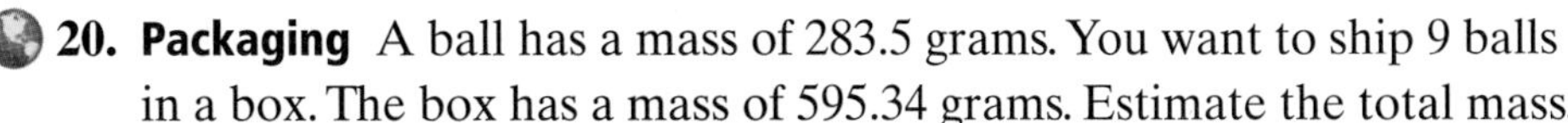

20. Packaging A ball has a mass of 283.5 grams. You want to ship 9 balls in a box. The box has a mass of 595.34 grams. Estimate the total mass.

21. Estimate the total of 3.894 and 5.2.

One Serving	Sugar Content
Orange Juice	0.886 oz
Granola bar	0.273 oz
Grapes	0.529 oz
Milk	0.413 oz
Yogurt	0.98 oz

Nutrition **Use the chart. Estimate to the nearest tenth of an ounce.**

22. About how much sugar is in a serving of orange juice plus a granola bar?

23. If you ate one of every item in the chart, about how much sugar would you have eaten?

24. About how much more sugar is in a serving of yogurt than in a serving of milk?

25. About how much sugar is in the last three items combined?

Round each number to the place of the underlined digit.

26. $1.\underline{3}66$ **27.** $\underline{7}2.418$ **28.** $5.1\underline{2}51$ **29.** $2.31\underline{9}6$

30. $3\underline{0}6.042$ **31.** $1\underline{0}.901$ **32.** $0.3\underline{4}5$ **33.** $\underline{1}4.9$

Estimate each answer by rounding or by using compatible numbers. Describe which method you chose and why.

34. $4.29 + 8.89$ **35.** $11.42 - 7.201$ **36.** $55.1 \div 8.6$

37. $134.8 - 51.95$ **38.** 8.56×9.863 **39.** $23.56 + 33.51$

40. **Writing in Math** The cost for three copies of a book is $38.85. Estimate the cost for one book. Do you think your estimate is higher or lower than the book's actual cost? Explain.

41. **Savings** Suppose you saved $443.75 in one year.
- **a.** Estimate how much you saved each week.
- **b.** **Reasoning** Explain why you chose the method you used in part (a).

42. **Money** This Chinese kwan note is 92.8 centimeters long. The United States dollar bill is 15.6 centimeters long. About how many times as long as a dollar bill is the kwan note?

Real-World Connection

The largest paper money ever printed was the Chinese kwan note, which was used in the fourteenth century.

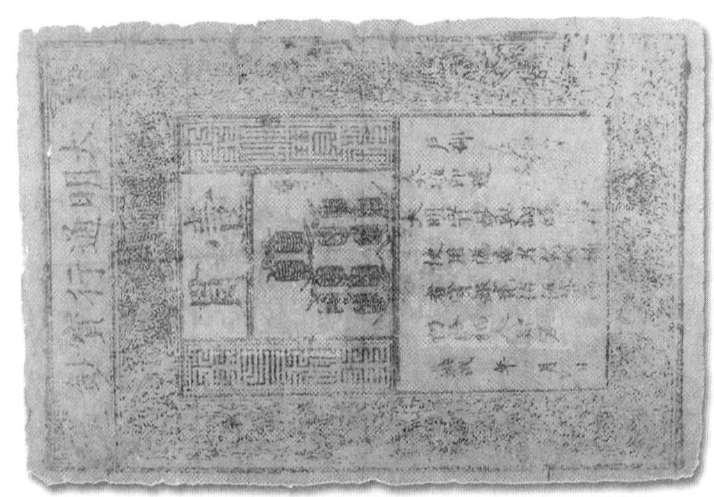

Use "clustering" to estimate each sum. For example, the numbers 4.8, 5.2, and 4.9 cluster around the whole number 5. You can estimate their sum by multiplying 3 and 5 for a total of 15.

43. 5.879 + 6.3 + 5.6 + 6.09

44. \$7.99 + \$8.14 + \$7.85

45. 2.6 + 3.3 + 2.8 + 2.91 + 3.14

46. \$39.81 + \$42 + \$38.06

47. **Open-Ended** A number rounded to the nearest tenth is 10.6. Rounded to the nearest hundredth, it is 10.65. What could the number be?

Need Help?
4 cups = 1 quart
4 quarts = 1 gallon

48. **Writing in Math** Your class is bringing apple juice to the fall school party. You know that 268 people are invited. You think that each person will drink one cup of juice. Explain the steps you would take to estimate how many gallons of apple juice your class should buy.

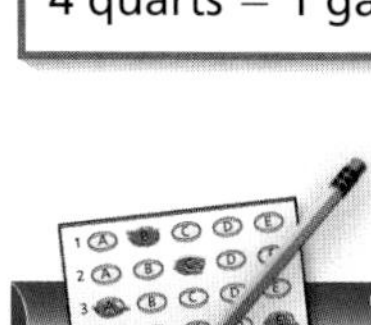

Test Prep

Multiple Choice

49. Between which two numbers is the quotient 18.7 ÷ 5?
A. 2 and 3 **B.** 3 and 4 **C.** 4 and 5 **D.** 5 and 6

50. Which sum has an estimate of \$22?
F. \$4.22 + \$10.85 + \$8.97
G. \$2.80 + \$13.75 + \$4.66
H. \$6.05 + \$7.86 + \$10.22
I. \$15.32 + \$9.63 + \$.45

51. Tom has \$20 to spend. He wants to buy a book for \$7.29, film for \$12.95, marker for \$3.95, and magazine for \$6.25. He can buy some items and have less than \$1.00 left. Which items could he buy?
A. book, marker, and magazine
B. film and magazine
C. book and film
D. film and marker

Take It to the NET
Online lesson quiz at
www.PHSchool.com
Web Code: aaa-0104

52. Yvonne earns \$38.25 in one week by baby-sitting. She earns \$4.75 per hour. Estimate the number of hours she works.
F. 8 **G.** 33.5 **H.** 43 **I.** 200

Mixed Review

Lesson 1-3

Use <, = , or > to complete each statement.

53. 0.112 ■ 0.121

54. 0.0009 ■ 0.001

55. 0.9985 ■ 0.998

Lesson 1-2

Write each decimal in standard form.

56. seven and eight tenths

57. twenty-three hundredths

58. two hundred eight and one tenth

59. thirty-eight ten-thousandths

Investigation

Using Models

For Use With Lesson 1-5

You can use models to add or subtract two decimals.

1 EXAMPLE Modeling Decimal Sums

Draw a model to find each sum.

a. 0.4 + 0.03

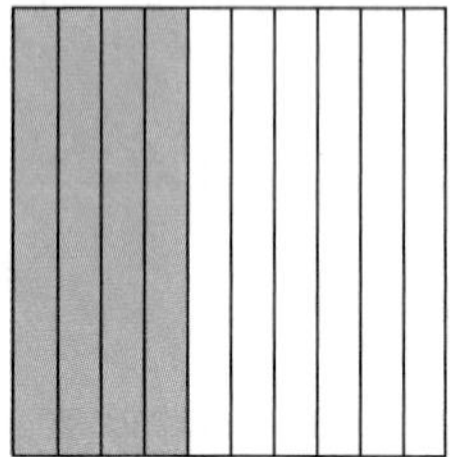

Draw a tenths grid and shade four tenths.

Divide the grid into hundredths. Shade three hundredths.

43 hundredths of the grid are shaded, so 0.4 + 0.03 = 0.43.

b. 0.9 + 0.5

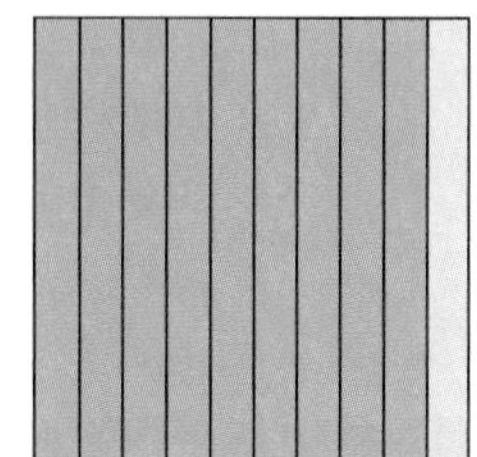

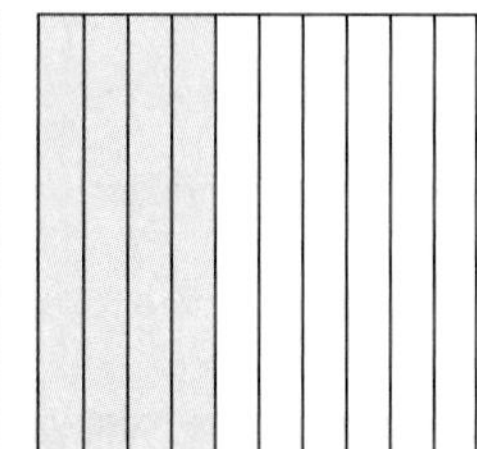

Draw a tenths grid and shade nine tenths. Shade five more tenths. To do this, you need to draw another grid.

The total amount shaded is 14 tenths.

$0.9 + 0.5 = 14 \text{ tenths} = 10 \text{ tenths and } 4 \text{ tenths}$
$= 1 \text{ and } 4 \text{ tenths} = 1.4$

2 EXAMPLE Modeling Decimal Differences

Draw a model to find the difference 1.4 − 0.6.

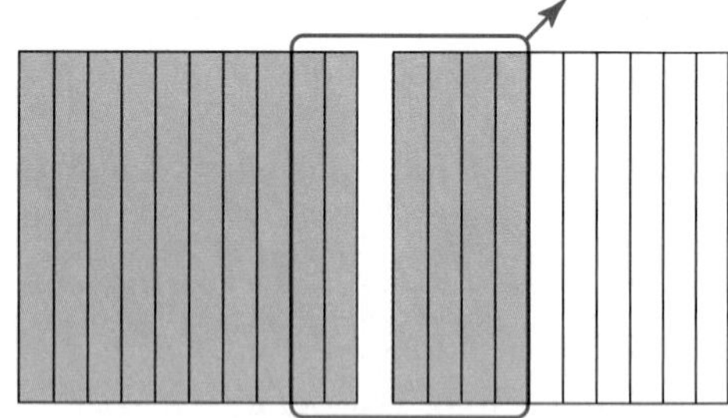

← Remove six tenths from fourteen tenths. Eight tenths remain.

1.4 − 0.6 = 0.8

EXERCISES

Draw a model on grid paper to find each sum or difference.

1. 0.1 + 0.8
2. 0.41 + 0.59
3. 0.06 + 0.55
4. 0.8 + 0.34
5. 1.5 − 1.2
6. 1.2 − 0.7
7. 0.88 − 0.57
8. 1.54 − 0.72

1-5 Adding and Subtracting Decimals

What You'll Learn

 To add decimals

 To subtract decimals

. . . And Why

To find basketball sizes, as in Example 3

✓ Check Skills You'll Need

For help, go to Lesson 1-4.

Round each decimal to the nearest whole number.

1. 8.7	**2.** 9.5	**3.** 4.94
4. 0.92	**5.** 2.982	**6.** 3.090

New Vocabulary

- Commutative Property of Addition
- Associative Property of Addition
- Identity Property of Addition

 Interactive lesson includes instant self-check, tutorials, and activities.

OBJECTIVE 1 Adding Decimals

If you estimate before adding, you can tell if your sum is reasonable.

1 EXAMPLE Finding Decimal Sums

Find the sum 3.026 + 4.7 + 1.38.

Estimate $3.026 + 4.7 + 1.38 \approx 3 + 5 + 1$, or 9

Add.

$$\begin{array}{r} 3.026 \\ 4.700 \\ +\ 1.380 \\ \hline 9.106 \end{array}$$

← **Line up the decimal points.**

← **Write zeros so that all decimals have the same number of digits to the right of the decimal point.**

Check for Reasonableness The sum 9.106 is reasonable since it is close to 9.

✓ **Check Understanding** 1 First estimate and then find the sum 0.84 + 2.0 + 3.32.

Need Help?
An addend is a number that is added to one or more other numbers.

Key Concepts: Properties of Addition

Commutative Property of Addition
Changing the order of the addends does not change the sum.

$$3.6 + 7 = 7 + 3.6$$

Associative Property of Addition
Changing the grouping of the addends does not change the sum.

$$(3.6 + 7) + 3 = 3.6 + (7 + 3)$$

Identity Property of Addition
The sum of 0 and any number is that number.

$$3.6 + 0 = 0 + 3.6 = 3.6$$

You can *simplify* an expression by replacing it with the simplest name for its value. So to simplify 4 + 5, you write 9 for its value.

2 EXAMPLE Using the Properties of Addition

Mental Math Use mental math to find the sum 42 + 13.9 + 58.

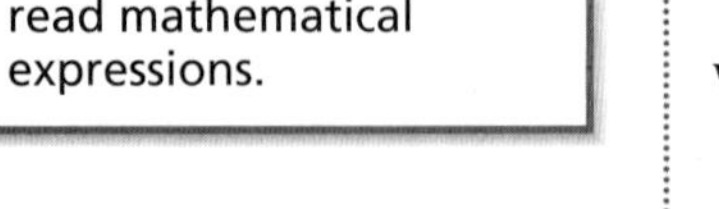

Reading Math
Parentheses ( ) are used to help you read mathematical expressions.

What you think

42 and 58 are easy to add. Adding 42 and 58 gives you 100. Adding 100 and 13.9 gives you 113.9. So, 42 + 13.9 + 58 = 113.9.

Why it works

$42 + 13.9 + 58 = 42 + (58 + 13.9)$ ← **Commutative Property of Addition**

$= (42 + 58) + 13.9$ ← **Associative Property of Addition**

$= 100 + 13.9$ ← **Add inside the parentheses.**

$= 113.9$ ← **Simplify.**

Check Understanding 2 **Mental Math** Use mental math to find each sum.

a. 8.9 + 0 + 5.0 **b.** 74 + 19 + 1 **c.** 5.92 + 0.4 + 3.08

OBJECTIVE 2 Subtracting Decimals

3 EXAMPLE Estimating and Finding a Difference

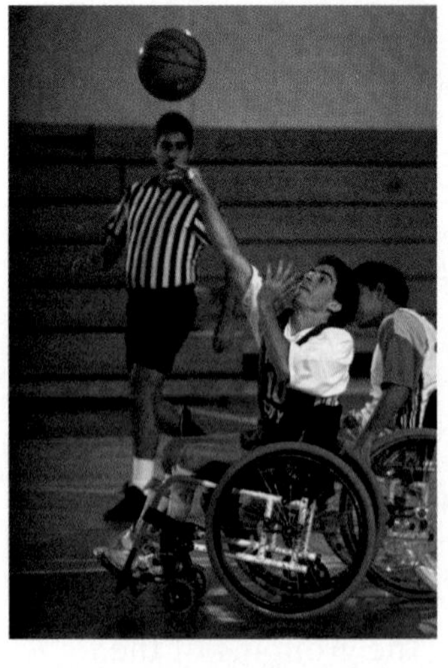

Sports According to the International Basketball Federation, the official distance around a basketball can be no more than 78.0 centimeters. The distance can also be no less than 74.9 centimeters. What is the difference between these distances?

Estimate $78.0 - 74.9 \approx 78 - 75$, or 3

Subtract.

$$\begin{array}{r} \overset{7\ 10}{7\not{8}.\not{0}} \\ -\ 74.9 \\ \hline 3.1 \end{array}$$

← **Rename 8 as 7 and 10 tenths.**
← **Subtract 74.9**
← **Simplify.**

The difference between the distances is 3.1 centimeters.

Check for Reasonableness The difference 3.1 is reasonable since it is close to 3.

Check Understanding 3 First estimate and then find each difference.

a. 2.7 − 0.9 **b.** 14.5 − 6.97 **c.** 0.4 − 0.13

d. Reasoning Use what you know about place value to explain why you should line up the decimal points before adding or subtracting.

4 EXAMPLE Subtracting Decimals From Whole Numbers

Find the difference 50 − 7.86.

Estimate 50 − 7.86 ≈ 50 − 8, or 42

Subtract.

Write a decimal point and two zeros.	Rename 50 as 49 and 10 tenths.	Rename 10 tenths as 9 tenths and 10 hundredths.
$\begin{array}{r} 50.00 \\ -\ 7.86 \\ \hline \end{array}$	$\begin{array}{r} {\scriptstyle 49\ 10} \\ \not{5}\not{0}.\not{0}0 \\ -\ 7.86 \\ \hline \end{array}$	$\begin{array}{r} {\scriptstyle 9} \\ {\scriptstyle 49\ \not{10}\ 10} \\ \not{5}\not{0}.\not{0}\not{0} \\ -\ 7.86 \\ \hline 42.14 \end{array}$

Check for Reasonableness The difference 42.14 is reasonable since it is close to 42.

Check Understanding

4 First estimate and then find each difference.

a. 98 − 6.8 **b.** 40 − 8.32 **c.** 82 − 4.916

EXERCISES

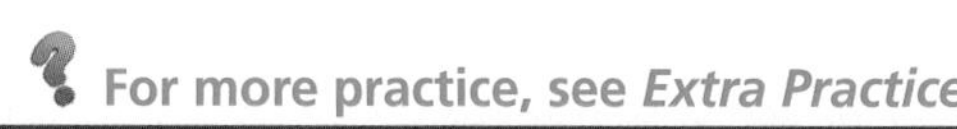
For more practice, see *Extra Practice.*

A Practice by Example

Example 1 (page 25)

First estimate and then find each sum.

1. 0.6 + 3.4 **2.** 6.2 + 0.444 **3.** 8.001 + 0.77

4. 7 + 11.436 + 3.08 **5.** 0.445 + 8.99 + 3 **6.** 0.33 + 1.11 + 3.2

Example 2 (page 26)

Use mental math to find each sum.

7. 0 + 5.7 + 4 **8.** 1.060 + 0 + 2.705 **9.** 8.37 + 1.4 + 2.6

10. 3.21 + 4.33 + 1.67 **11.** 18 + 6.354 + 102 **12.** 7.81 + 5.23 + 0.19

Examples 3, 4 (pages 26, 27)

First estimate and then find each difference.

13. 22.2 − 4.3 **14.** 8.91 − 6.08 **15.** 9.45 − 3.76 **16.** 9.1 − 6.05

17. 0.8 − 0.126 **18.** 4 − 1.29 **19.** 60 − 2.037 **20.** 9 − 0.45

60 m
70 m
80 m
76.80 m
74.08 m
Men s record
Women s record

21. Data Analysis Use the graph at the left. How much greater is the women's world-record discus throw than the men's?

22. **Bicycles** At one store, an 18-speed bicycle costs $174.99. At another store, the same bicycle costs $222.98. What is the difference in prices?

B Apply Your Skills

23. **Money** Jonah had $340.87 in his checking account. He withdrew $52 and wrote a check for $18.72. Find the new balance.

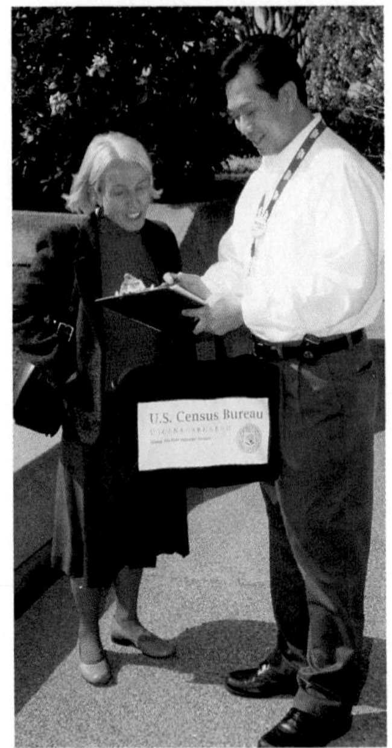

Real-World Connection

Careers Every 10 years, census takers try to count every person in the United States.

24. **Population** In the 2000 Census, the New England states had a total population of about 13.92 million. Find the population of Maine.

State	Population
Connecticut	3.41 million
Maine	■
Massachusetts	6.35 million
New Hampshire	1.24 million
Rhode Island	1.05 million
Vermont	0.61 million

SOURCE: U.S. Census Bureau
Go to **www.PHSchool.com** for a data update.
Web Code: aag-2041

25. **Choose a Method** A hot-dog vendor receives $20 for a $5.25 purchase. Is the vendor most likely to use estimation, mental math, paper and pencil, or a calculator to determine the amount of change? Why?

Use <, =, or > to complete each statement.

26. 0.041 + 0.009 ■ 0.5

27. 0.315 + 0.14 + 0.05 ■ 0.5

28. 6,869.583 + 1,504.222 ■ 8,373.8

29. 97,655.5 − 89,281.7 ■ 8,373.8

Find each missing number. Name the property of addition that you used.

30. 6.37 + ■ + 2.43 = 6.37 + 2.43

31. 0.43 + ■ = 0.43

32. (2.1 + 0.3) + 4 = 2.1 + (■ + 4)

33. ■ + 8.9 = 8.9 + 7.5

34. (6 + 1.1) + ■ = 6 + (1.1 + 5.9)

35. 6.4 + 3.1 = ■ + 6.4

36. (5.6 + 0.4) + 0.1 = (0.4 + 5.6) + ■

37. **Data File, p. 3** Your friend drew the hieroglyph below to show that a pharaoh had 3,290 cattle.
   a. Is he correct? Explain.
   b. How would you correctly write 3,290 as a hieroglyph?

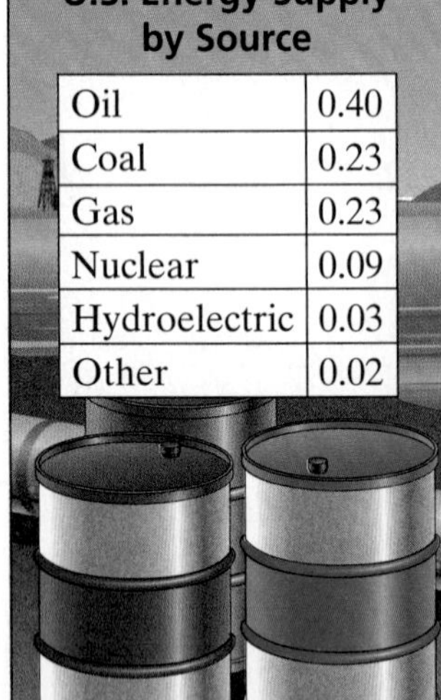

U.S. Energy Supply by Source

Source	
Oil	0.40
Coal	0.23
Gas	0.23
Nuclear	0.09
Hydroelectric	0.03
Other	0.02

SOURCE: Energy Information Administration

Data Analysis **Refer to the data at the left.**

38. Add the numbers in the table. What does this sum represent?

39. **Writing in Math** What part of all the energy is produced from oil and coal? Is it more than half? Explain.

40. **Estimation** Which natural resource produces an amount of energy approximately $\frac{1}{3}$ that of nuclear power?

41. **Modeling** Make a hundredths model showing the part of all energy produced by each natural resource.

 Challenge

T-Shirts and Sweatshirts For Sale

Adult T-shirt (M-XL) \$15.00 (XXL) \$17.95

Adult Sweatshirt (M-XL) \$29.50 (XXL) \$29.95

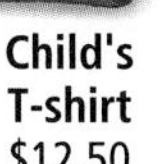

Child's T-shirt \$12.50

Child's Sweatshirt \$16.95

Data Analysis **When you order clothes, you usually pay a shipping charge. Use the information in the charts.**

Shipping Charges

Order Amount	Charge
Under \$25.00	\$3.95
\$25.00 – \$39.99	\$4.95
\$40.00 – \$49.99	\$5.95
\$50.00 – \$74.99	\$6.95
\$75.00 – \$99.99	\$7.95
\$100.00 and over	\$8.95

42. a. A customer orders one adult sweatshirt (size XXL) and three child's T-shirts. What is the amount of the order?

b. Find the shipping charge and the total.

43. A customer orders one adult T-shirt (size M) and one adult sweatshirt (size XL). Find the total cost, including the shipping charge.

Use <, =, or > to complete each statement.

44. 8,863.0024 − 486.2024 ■ 8,373.8

45. 2,562.031 + 4,792.019 ■ 7,354.05

46. Stretch Your Thinking Complete the number square at the right. The sum for each row, column, and diagonal should be 1.47.

0.76		0.58
0.31		

Test Prep

Multiple Choice

47. Which statement is NOT true?
A. 10.3 = 10.30 **B.** 8.39 > 7.98
C. 4.9 < 4.889 **D.** 5.09 < 5.1

48. Which statement represents the Commutative Property of Addition?
F. 1 + 7 = 8 **G.** 2 + 9 = 9 + 2
H. 3 + 6 = 4 + 5 **I.** 10 + 0 = 10

49. At a baseball game, you order nachos for \$4.75 and two drinks for \$3.25 each. You pay with a \$20 bill. How much change will you get?
A. \$8.00 **B.** \$8.75 **C.** \$11.25 **D.** \$12.00

50. Replacing the box with which number will make 0.22 + 0.■8 > 0.5 true?
F. 0 **G.** 1 **H.** 2 **I.** 3

Take It to the NET
Online lesson quiz at **www.PHSchool.com**
Web Code: aaa-0105

Mixed Review

Lesson 1-4

Round each number to the place of the underlined digit.

51. $2\underline{0},567$ **52.** $0.13\underline{2}9$ **53.** $0.\underline{0}93$ **54.** $5.6\underline{1}84$ **55.** $6,4\underline{5}6$

1-6 Using a Problem-Solving Plan

What You'll Learn

To use a plan to solve problems

. . . And Why

To have an organized way to solve problems, as in Example 1

Check Skills You'll Need

For help, go to Skills Handbook, p. 657.

Subtract.

1. 84 − 22 **2.** 75 − 18

3. 91 − 67 **4.** 103 − 21

5. 714 − 637 **6.** 4,758 − 943

OBJECTIVE

Interactive lesson includes instant self-check, tutorials, and activities.

1 Using a Plan to Solve Problems

Some problems require good problem-solving skills. A problem-solving plan like the one below can help you solve more challenging problems.

Key Concepts **A Problem-Solving Plan**

1. Read and understand the problem.
2. Plan how to solve the problem, then solve it.
3. Look back and check to see if your answer makes sense.

1 EXAMPLE Real-World Problem Solving

Olympic Race Skeleton competitors slide headfirst down an ice track on a metal sled. The winner has the fastest total time in two heats, or runs.

At the 2002 Winter Olympics, Tristan Gale won the women's skeleton event. How much faster was Gale's total time than Parsley's?

Women's Skeleton Results

Name	Heat 1 Time (seconds)	Heat 2 Time (seconds)
Tristan Gale	52.26	52.85
Lea Ann Parsley	52.27	52.94
Alex Coomber	52.48	52.89

Read and Understand Determine what you know and what you need to find out.

> Read the problem again. Ask yourself, "What information is given? What information is missing? What am I being asked to find?"

You are asked to find how much faster Gale's total time was than Parsley's. You know the times of each heat for each person.

Plan and Solve Choose a strategy.

> As you learn problem-solving strategies throughout this book, you will decide which one is best for the problem you are trying to solve.

Real-World Connection
Tristan Gale won the gold medal in the first women's skeleton event in Olympic history.

First, find the total time for each competitor. Extend the table.

Women's Skeleton Results

Name	Heat 1 Time (seconds)	Heat 2 Time (seconds)	Total Time (seconds)
Tristan Gale	52.26	52.85	
Lea Ann Parsley	52.27	52.94	
Alex Coomber	52.48	52.89	

To find each competitor's total time, you add.

Gale's total time: $52.26 + 52.85 = 105.11$ seconds

Parsley's total time: $52.27 + 52.94 = 105.21$ seconds

To compare the total times, you subtract.

$105.21 - 105.11 = 0.10$ second

Gale's total time was 0.10 second faster than Parsley's total time.

Look Back and Check Think about how you solved the problem.

> Look back at your work and compare it with the information and question in the problem. Ask yourself, "Is my answer reasonable? Did I check my work?"

You can compare the times in each heat. Gale's time in the first heat was 0.01 second faster. In the second heat her time was 0.09 second faster. So, the answer, 0.10 second, for the total time is reasonable and checks.

Check Understanding 1 How much faster was Parsley's total time than Coomber's?

EXERCISES

For more practice, see *Extra Practice.*

A Practice by Example

Use a problem-solving plan to solve each problem.

Example 1 (page 30)

Need Help?
- Reread the problem.
- Identify the key facts and details.
- Tell the problem in your own words.
- Try a different strategy.
- Check your work.

1. **Entertainment** Three friends go to a baseball game. Each has a hot dog, a bag of roasted peanuts, and a soda. They spend a total of $78 on food and tickets. How much does each person spend?

2. **Shopping** Granola bars cost $2.79 per box. A coupon in last Sunday's paper will save you $.45 on two boxes. How much will two boxes of granola bars cost before tax if you use the coupon?

3. Sasha arrived at the bowling alley at 6:37. Ellen and Rosa had been waiting for her for 8 minutes. Ellen had waited for Rosa for 4 minutes. What time did Ellen arrive at the bowling alley?

4. A scientist used a cylinder as a vase for a rose. Each day, 14 mL of water evaporated. The water level originally read 100 mL. How much water remained after 4 days?

B Apply Your Skills

Choose a strategy to solve each problem.

Strategies
- Draw a Diagram
- Make a Graph
- Make an Organized List
- Make a Table and Look for a Pattern
- Simulate a Problem
- Solve a Simpler Problem
- Try, Check, and Revise
- Use Logical Reasoning
- Work Backward
- Write an Equation

5. It takes Clara 12 minutes to cut a log into 4 pieces. How long will it take her to cut another log that is the same size into 5 pieces?

6. **Fundraising** Chris, Ted, Tim, and Jerry biked in a 10-mile charity race. Tim was last in 39 minutes 6.5 seconds. Ted finished 2 minutes 0.3 second ahead of Tim. Jerry finished 47.8 seconds ahead of Ted. Chris finished 1 minute 57.4 seconds ahead of Jerry. What was Chris's time?

7. **Elections** The candidates for sixth-grade president are Sheresa, Robert, and Bethany. The candidates for secretary are Tim, Ling, Dennis, and Annie. How many different teams of president and secretary are there?

8. A dog trainer has a bag of 70 dog treats. He gives 8 treats each day. How many whole days will the treats last? How many extra treats can he give on the last day?

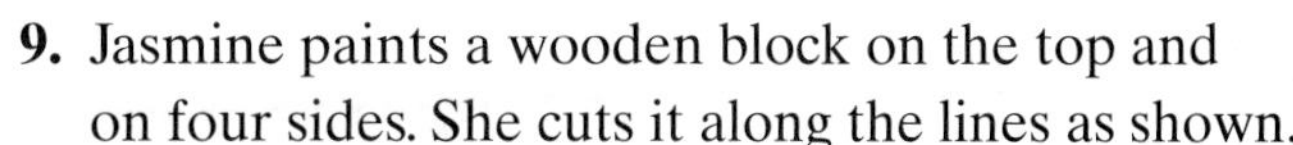

9. Jasmine paints a wooden block on the top and on four sides. She cuts it along the lines as shown.
   a. How many cuts does Jasmine make?
   b. Into how many pieces does she cut the block?
   c. **Writing in Math** How many of the pieces do not have any paint on them? Explain how you know.

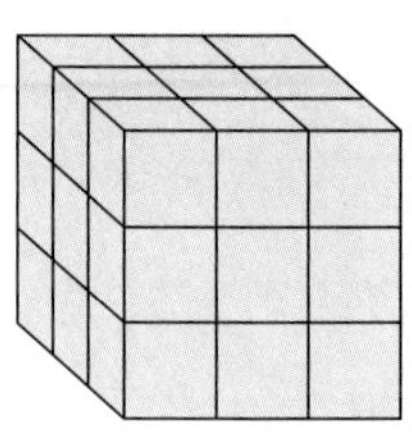

Challenge

10. Each competitor for men's halfpipe snowboarding is judged on two runs. The *greater* of the two scores determines the winner. How would the ranking have changed if the *total* score of both runs were used?

2002 Winter Olympics

Competitor	Scores in Points	
	Run 1	Run 2
Powers (USA)	46.1	32.0
Kass (USA)	42.5	41.5
Thomas (USA)	33.2	42.1
Kratter (Italy)	34.9	42.0
Nakai (Japan)	38.3	40.7
Czeschin (USA)	40.6	40.5

SOURCE: U.S. Ski Team

11. **Stretch Your Thinking** Turn the triangle "upside-down" by sliding one circle at a time to a new location so that it touches 2 other circles. How many moves did you make? (The fewest moves is 3.)

Test Prep

Multiple Choice

12. Which value completes the statement 54 = 3 × ■?
    A. 18 B. 51 C. 57 D. 162

13. In 9 minutes, it will be 11:06. What time is it now?
    F. 2:06 G. 11:15 H. 10:97 I. 10:57

14. The difference 8.7 − 0.368 is closest to which value?
    A. 8.3 B. 8.4 C. 8.7 D. 9

15. Which value completes the statement 3.15 + ■ < 5?
    F. 1.95 G. 1.85 H. 1.84 I. 2.85

Take It to the NET
Online lesson quiz at **www.PHSchool.com**
Web Code: aaa-0106

Mixed Review

Lesson 1-5 **Add or subtract.**

16. 0.8 + 0.5 17. 2.59 − 0.83 18. 0.56 + 0.9 19. 1.8 − 0.09

Lesson 1-2 **Write the value of the digit 3 in each number.**

20. 108.39 21. 38.22 22. 0.523 23. 345.650 24. 0.0293

Investigation Modeling Multiplication of Decimals

For Use With Lesson 1-7

A model can help you understand how to multiply decimals.

1 EXAMPLE Multiplying a Whole Number by a Decimal

Coin Collecting A collector buys two 1942 Mercury dimes. Each coin costs \$.92. Draw a model to find the total cost.

Real-World Connection

Miss Liberty's wings look like the Roman god Mercury. So, the coin was called the "Mercury" dime.

You want to find $0.92 + 0.92$, or 2×0.92.

Shade 92 squares in each of two grids. →

Move 8 hundredths from the second grid to fill the first grid. →

Count the shaded squares in the grids. →

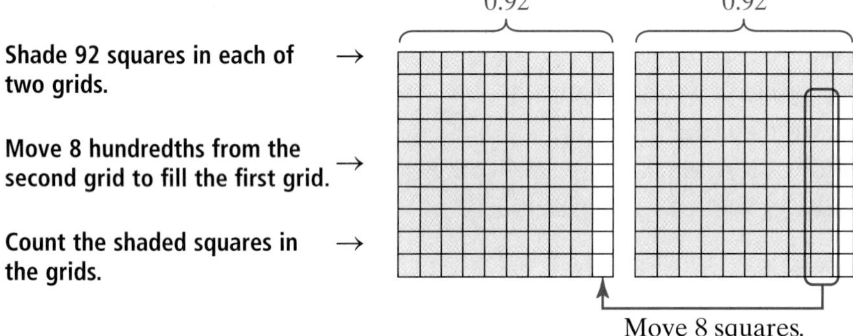

The shaded area is 1 whole and 84 hundredths, or 1.84.
The total cost is \$1.84.

2 EXAMPLE Multiplying Decimals

Draw a model to find the product 0.5×0.4.

Shade 4 *columns* of a grid to represent 0.4. →

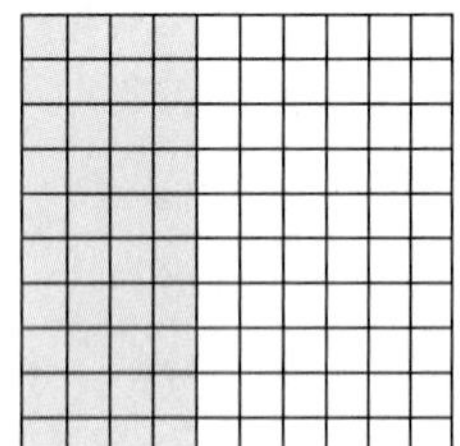

Shade 5 *rows* to represent 0.5. Use a different color or style. →

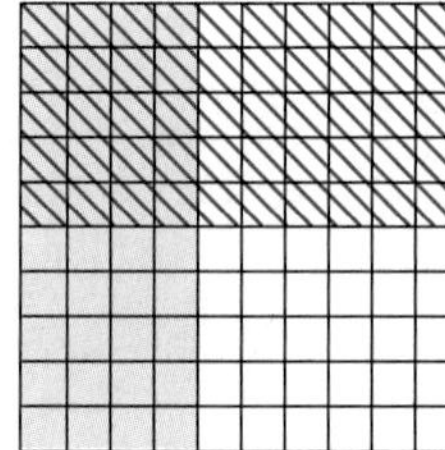

The shadings overlap in 20 squares, representing 20 hundredths, or 0.20.
So, $0.5 \times 0.4 = 0.20$.

EXERCISES

Draw a model on grid paper to find each product.

1. 3×0.9 **2.** 2×0.61 **3.** 0.8×0.5 **4.** 0.7×0.2 **5.** 0.1×0.6

1-7 Multiplying Decimals

What You'll Learn

To multiply decimals

To use the properties of multiplication

. . . And Why

To predict tree growth, as in Example 3

Check Skills You'll Need

For help, go to Skills Handbook, p. 658.

Multiply.

1. 7×21 **2.** 68×12 **3.** 41×527 **4.** $2{,}117 \times 20$

New Vocabulary

- **Commutative Property of Multiplication**
- **Associative Property of Multiplication**
- **Identity Property of Multiplication**

Interactive lesson includes instant self-check, tutorials, and activities.

OBJECTIVE 1 Multiplying Decimals

The model below shows how to find 0.5×1.5. You are finding half of 1.5.

Shade 1.5 grids.

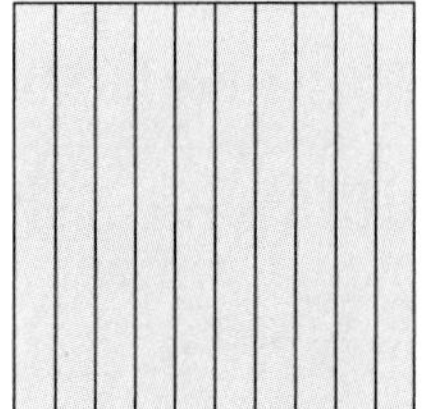

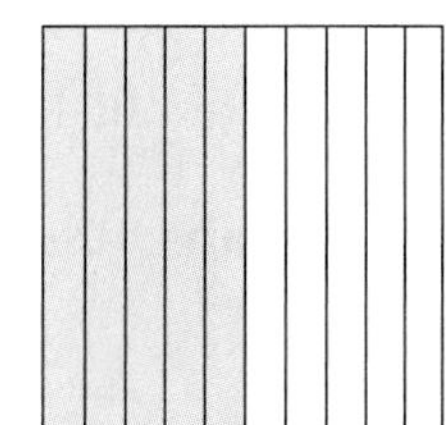

Shade 0.5 of each grid.

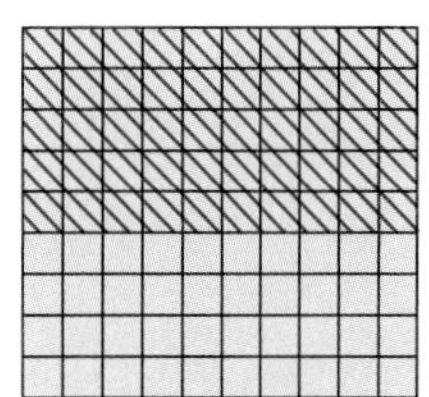

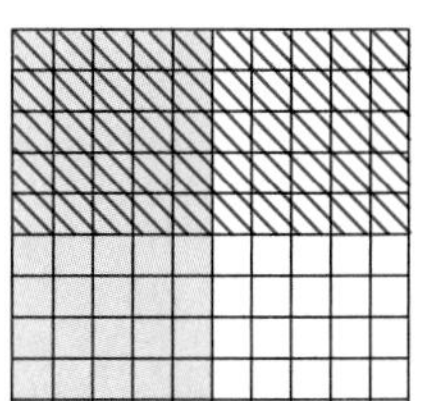

The shadings overlap in 75 squares, or 75 hundredths. So, $0.5 \times 1.5 = 0.75$.

The model also illustrates a pattern. You can add the number of decimal places in the factors to find the number of decimal places in the product.

1 EXAMPLE Multiplying a Whole Number by a Decimal

Find the product 0.47×8.

0.47	←	**2 decimal places**
× 8	←	**+ 0 decimal places**
3.76	←	**2 decimal places**

1 Find each product. **a.** 6×0.13 **b.** 4.37×5

You can indicate multiplication in these three ways: 0.5×1.5, $0.5 \cdot 1.5$, and $0.5(1.5)$.

2 EXAMPLE Multiplying Decimals

Reading Math

Factors are numbers that are multiplied.

Find the product $0.3 \cdot 0.7$.

0.3	←	1 decimal place
× 0.7	←	+1 decimal place
0.21	←	2 decimal places

Check Understanding 2 Find each product. **a.** 0.3(0.2) **b.** $0.9 \cdot 0.14$

c. Number Sense Look at your answers to parts (a) and (b). Both factors are less than 1. How does the product compare to the two factors?

3 EXAMPLE Real-World Problem Solving

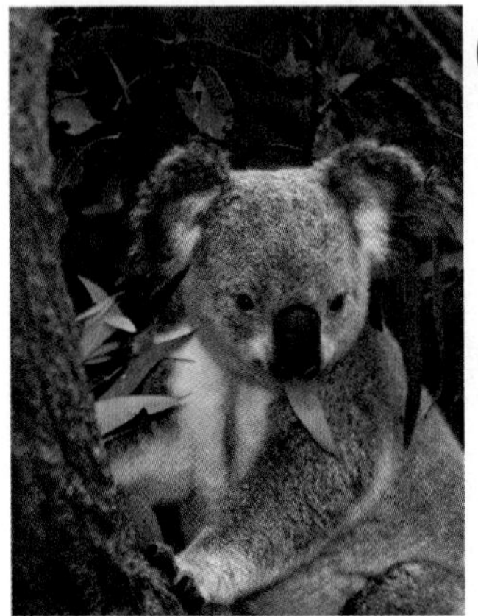

Real-World Connection

The leaves and flowers of eucalyptus trees are the main diet of koala bears.

Growth Prediction A eucalyptus tree grows about 5.45 meters in one year. At that rate of growth, how much will the tree grow in 3.5 years?

Estimate $3.5 \times 5.45 \approx 4 \times 5$, or 20

Multiply.

5.45	←	2 decimal places
× 3.5	←	1 decimal place
2725		
+ 1635		
19.075	←	3 decimal places

The tree will grow about 19.075 meters in 3.5 years.

Check for Reasonableness 19.075 is reasonable since it is close to 20.

Check Understanding 3 Find each product. **a.** 2.4×3.11 **b.** 15.1(3.84)

OBJECTIVE

2 Using the Properties of Multiplication

Key Concepts Properties of Multiplication

Commutative Property of Multiplication

Changing the order of the factors does not change the product.

$4.7 \times 5 = 5 \times 4.7$

Associative Property of Multiplication

Changing the grouping of the factors does not change the product.

$(4.7 \times 5) \times 2 = 4.7 \times (5 \times 2)$

Identity Property of Multiplication

The product of 1 and any number is that number.

$4.7 \times 1 = 1 \times 4.7 = 4.7$

The properties of multiplication can also help you do math mentally.

4 EXAMPLE Using the Properties of Multiplication

Mental Math A customer buys 4 bags of corn. Each bag contains 8 ears of corn that cost \$.25 per ear. Use mental math to find $4(8 \times \$.25)$.

What you think

\$.25 and 4 are easy to multiply. Multiplying \$.25 and 4 gives \$1. Multiplying \$1 and 8 gives \$8. So, $4(8 \times \$.25) = \$8$.

Why it works

$4(8 \times \$.25) = 4 \times (\$.25 \times 8)$ ← **Commutative Property of Multiplication**

$= (4 \times \$.25) \times 8$ ← **Associative Property of Multiplication**

$= \$1 \times 8$ ← **Multiply inside the parentheses.**

$= \$8$ ← **Identity Property of Multiplication**

Real-World Connection

Some people use mental math when making change.

4 Use mental math to find each product.

a. $2(5 \times 2.3)$ **b.** $3.1 \times 1 \times 100$ **c.** $500 \times 0.333(2)$

EXERCISES

Find each product. Exercises 1 and 9 have been started for you.

Example 1 (page 35)

1. $\begin{array}{r} 0.018 \\ \times \quad 4 \\ \hline 72 \end{array}$ **2.** $\begin{array}{r} 1.9 \\ \times \; 9 \\ \hline \end{array}$ **3.** $\begin{array}{r} 31 \\ \times 5.6 \\ \hline \end{array}$ **4.** $\begin{array}{r} 39 \\ \times 0.06 \\ \hline \end{array}$

5. $358(0.7)$ **6.** $0.12(47)$ **7.** $53 \cdot 0.04$ **8.** $0.28 \cdot 92$

Example 2 (page 36)

9. $\begin{array}{r} 0.2 \\ \times 0.7 \\ \hline 14 \end{array}$ **10.** $\begin{array}{r} 0.8 \\ \times 0.4 \\ \hline \end{array}$ **11.** $\begin{array}{r} 0.3 \\ \times 0.5 \\ \hline \end{array}$ **12.** $\begin{array}{r} 0.7 \\ \times 0.9 \\ \hline \end{array}$

13. $0.12(0.96)$ **14.** $0.06(0.18)$ **15.** $0.486 \cdot 0.9$ **16.** $0.03 \cdot 0.574$

Example 3 (page 36)

17. $4.5(230)$ **18.** 1.7×3.702 **19.** $3.2 \cdot 4.5$ **20.** $8.1 \cdot 1.3$

21. $3.3(420)$ **22.** $3.2 \cdot 15.5$ **23.** $4.25 \cdot 6.18$ **24.** 1.2×2.065

25. One pound of tomatoes costs \$1.29. To the nearest cent, how much would 2.75 pounds of tomatoes cost?

Example 4 (page 37)

Use mental math to find each product.

26. $5 \times 0.47 \times 2$ **27.** $(0.7 \times 1) \times 4$ **28.** $25 \cdot 1.3 \cdot 40$

29. $20 \times 1.9(5)$ **30.** $6.8 \cdot 25 \cdot 4$ **31.** $9.5(1 \cdot 100)$

32. $4 \times 0.2 \times 1{,}000$ **33.** $(0.02 \cdot 33)50$ **34.** $5 \times (6.83 \times 0.2)$

35. Money What is the value of 25 rolls of nickels if there are 40 nickels in each roll?

B Apply Your Skills

Find each product.

36. 522×0.5 **37.** 22.76×3 **38.** 0.15×0.31 **39.** 8.42×6.7

Choose a Method **Find each product. Tell whether you would use mental math, paper and pencil, or a calculator.**

40. 16×2.5 **41.** $0.8 \cdot 0.008$ **42.** $60(0.5)$ **43.** $56.37 \cdot 5.29$

44. Nutrition There is 0.2 gram of calcium in 1 serving of cheddar cheese. How much calcium is in 3.25 servings of cheddar cheese?

Passenger cars: 22.0 miles per gallon

Sport utility vehicles (SUV): 17.5 miles per gallon

45. Automobiles The average fuel rates for 2000 are at the left. How much farther could a car travel on 13 gallons of gas than an SUV?

46. Writing in Math Explain how multiplying 0.3×0.4 is like multiplying 3×4. How is it different?

47. Astronomy Mercury is about 36 million miles from the sun. Jupiter is about 13.43 times that distance. About how far is Jupiter from the sun?

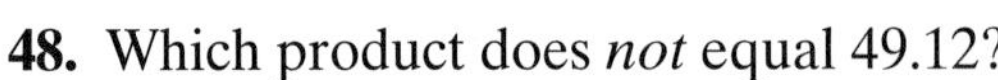

48. Which product does *not* equal 49.12?
A. 15.35×3.2 **B.** 12.8×3.8375 **C.** 16×3.07 **D.** 35.15×2.5

Error Analysis **Estimate to tell if each calculator answer is correct. If incorrect, explain the error.**

49. $0.937 \cdot 24.78$
232.1886

50. $4.52 \cdot 0.615$
2.7798

51. $43.45 \cdot 0.2162$
43.6662

C Challenge

Algebra **Find the value that makes each statement true.**

52. $\blacksquare \div 0.2 = 0.7$ **53.** $\blacksquare \div 0.03 = 0.5$ **54.** $\blacksquare \div 1.6 = 0.04$

55. Stretch Your Thinking Find the least whole number greater than 1,000 whose digits are all different. What is its units digit?

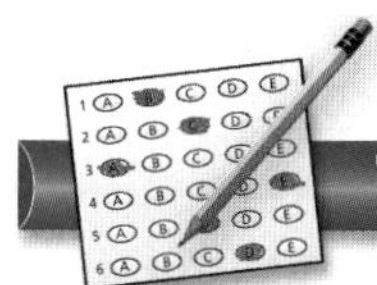

Test Prep

Reading Comprehension Read the passage and answer the questions below.

Calories Burned

Activity	Calories/Minute/ Pound
Dancing	0.05
Jumping rope	0.07
Running	0.10
Playing softball	0.04

Calorie Counter

The energy in food and the energy your body uses are measured in Calories. Not all foods have the same number of Calories. Not all activities use the same number of Calories. Your weight is also a factor. The number of Calories you burn is equal to:

Your weight × Minutes of activity × Calories burned per minute per pound

56. Jim weighs 100 pounds. He jumps rope for 15 minutes and runs for 20 minutes. How many Calories does he burn?

57. Tara weighs 80 pounds and dances for 1 hour 50 minutes. How many Calories does she burn?

58. A 150-lb man plays softball and runs for 30 minutes each. Which sport burns more Calories for him? How much more?

Mixed Review

Lesson 1-3 **Use <, =, or > to complete each statement.**

59. 6.225 ■ 6.25 **60.** 0.156 ■ 0.15 **61.** 17.34 ■ 17.051

Checkpoint Quiz 2 — Lessons 1-4 through 1-7

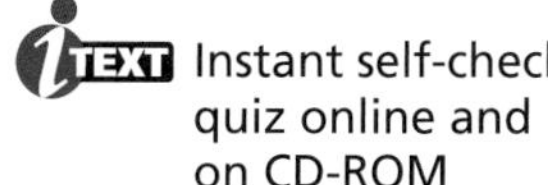

Instant self-check quiz online and on CD-ROM

Estimate each answer.

1. $37.1 - 7.83$ **2.** 4.9×12.2 **3.** $7.94 + 5.29 + 2.08$ **4.** $68.4 \div 8.72$

Find each sum, difference, or product.

5. $1.25 + 6.07$ **6.** $9.06 - 0.8$ **7.** 5.2×6.3 **8.** $1.7 - 0.28$

9. Jo made 7 pounds of cookies. She gave 3.25 pounds to her friends and 0.7 pound each to her three brothers. How much did she have left?

10. **Reasoning** Use properties to justify that $8 \cdot 13.1 \cdot 0.5 = 52.4$.

1-8 Multiplying and Dividing Decimals by 10, 100, and 1,000

What You'll Learn

To multiply and divide decimals by 10, 100, and 1,000

. . . And Why

To use mental math to divide, as in Example 2

✓ Check Skills You'll Need

For help, go to Skills Handbook p. 659.

Multiply or divide.

1. 10×36

2. 100×36

3. $1{,}000 \times 36$

4. $4{,}700 \div 10$

5. $4{,}700 \div 100$

6. $4{,}700 \div 1{,}000$

OBJECTIVE

Interactive lesson includes instant self-check, tutorials, and activities.

1 Multiplying and Dividing by 10, 100, and 1,000

Investigation: Multiplying by 10, 100, and 1,000

1. Multiply.

   a. $2.6 \times 10 = ■$
      $2.6 \times 100 = ■$
      $2.6 \times 1{,}000 = ■$

   b. $0.45 \times 10 = ■$
      $0.45 \times 100 = ■$
      $0.45 \times 1{,}000 = ■$

2. **Patterns** What pattern do you notice in the products? Hint: Think about the direction the decimal point moves and the number of decimal places in the answer.

There are shortcuts for multiplying decimals by 10, 100, and 1,000. You can use these shortcuts to multiply mentally.

1 EXAMPLE Multiplying by 10, 100, or 1,000

Use mental math to find each product.

a. $0.875 \times 100 = 0.87.5$ ← **To multiply a decimal by 100, move the decimal point 2 places to the right.**
$= 87.5$

b. $0.41 \times 1{,}000 = 0.410.$ ← **To multiply a decimal by 1,000, move the decimal point 3 places to the right.**
$= 410$

✓ Check Understanding 1 Use mental math to find each product.

a. $100(3.42)$ **b.** 0.235×10 **c.** $55.2 \cdot 1{,}000$

To divide a number by 10, 100, or 1,000, you can move the decimal point to the left. You may need to insert zeros.

Dividing by 10 moves the point 1 place to the left.	5,700 ÷ 10 = 570 570 ÷ 10 = 57 57 ÷ 10 = 5.7	5,700 ÷ 100 = 57 570 ÷ 100 = 5.7 57 ÷ 100 = 0.57	**Dividing by 100 moves the point 2 places to the left.**

Test-Prep Tip
You can sometimes do mental math faster than you can use a calculator.

2 EXAMPLE Dividing by 10, 100, or 1,000

Use mental math to find the quotient 43 ÷ 1,000.

43 ÷ 1,000 = .043. = 0.043 ← **To divide by 1,000, move the decimal point 3 places to the left.**

Check Understanding 2 Use mental math to find each quotient.

a. 534.2 ÷ 100 **b.** 0.235 ÷ 10 **c.** 55.2 ÷ 1,000

d. **Number Sense** Write a rule to divide by 10,000. Find 7.3 ÷ 10,000.

EXERCISES

For more practice, see *Extra Practice*.

A Practice by Example

Example 1 (page 40)

Use mental math to find each product.

1. 6.2 × 10 **2.** 100 · 2.57 **3.** 10(9.25)

4. 100 × 1.6 **5.** 1,000(4.3) **6.** 1,000 · 0.89

Example 2 (page 41)

Use mental math to find each quotient.

7. 122.9 ÷ 10 **8.** 1.37 ÷ 10 **9.** 161.7 ÷ 100

10. 1.5 ÷ 100 **11.** 2,048.8 ÷ 1,000 **12.** 8.17 ÷ 1,000

B Apply Your Skills

Use <, =, or > to complete each statement.

13. 0.92 · 100 ■ 9.2 · 1,000 **14.** 2.5(0.56 · 4) ■ 0.56 · 10

15. 0.99 ÷ 100 ■ 9.9 ÷ 10 **16.** 88 ÷ 100 ■ 8.8 ÷ 100

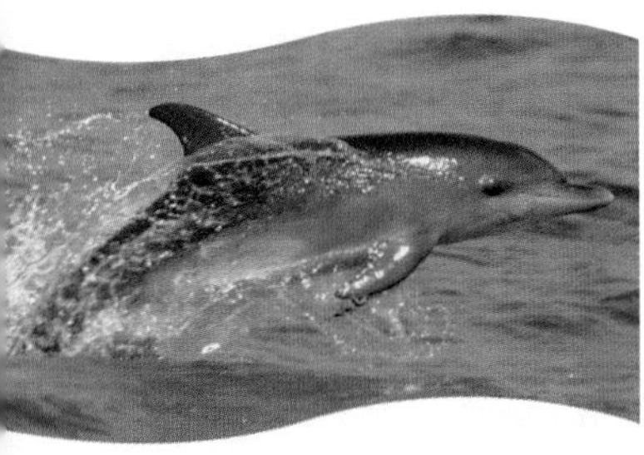

17. Speed Dolphins swim about 27.5 miles per hour. A person can swim about 0.1 times as fast as a dolphin. How fast can a person swim?

18. Packaging Pencils come in packages of 10 each. Packages are packed 20 to a box, and boxes are packed 500 to a carton. How many pencils are in a carton?

True or False? If false, give an example to support your answer.

19. Dividing by 100 is the same as multiplying by 0.1.

20. Multiplying by 0.001 is the same as dividing by 1,000.

21. Changing the order of the factors does not change the product.

22. Any decimal multiplied by 1 is equal to the original decimal.

23. **Writing in Math** Use mental math to find $0.8 \div 100$. Explain your method.

24. Multiply.
a. 572×0.1 **b.** 572×0.01 **c.** 572×0.001 **d.** 572×0.0001
e. **Patterns** What pattern do you notice in your answers to parts (a)–(d)?

C Challenge

25. Find each answer.
a. 52×10 **b.** $52 \div 10$ **c.** 52×0.1 **d.** $52 \div 0.1$
e. **Reasoning** Explain how you solved part (d).
f. Complete: Dividing by 0.1 is the same as multiplying by ■.

26. **Stretch Your Thinking** Six days after the day before yesterday is Monday. What day is today?

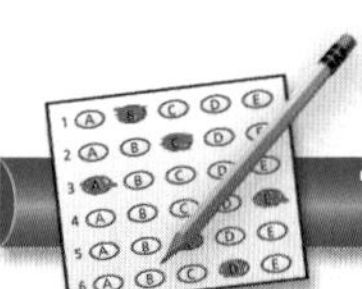

Test Prep

Multiple Choice

27. Which quotient is greatest?
A. $8.31 \div 10$ **B.** $83.1 \div 100$ **C.** $83.1 \div 10$ **D.** $831 \div 1{,}000$

28. Which value is NOT greater than 1?
F. 0.035×10 **G.** 9.8×10 **H.** $67.3 \div 10$ **I.** $452 \div 10$

Online lesson quiz at **www.PHSchool.com**
Web Code: aaa-0108

29. Ten mice weigh 106.7 grams. About how much does one mouse weigh?
A. 1,067 grams **B.** 106.7 grams **C.** 10.67 grams **D.** 1.067 grams

30. Replacing the box with which value will make ■ $\div 10 > 7.19 \times 10$ true?
F. 0.72 **G.** 7.2 **H.** 72 **I.** 720

Mixed Review

Lesson 1-4 **Estimate using rounding or compatible numbers.**

31. $90.88 \div 14.2$ **32.** 6.7×4.1 **33.** 26.50×4

34. $37.6 \div 3.8$ **35.** 86.2×43.9 **36.** $15.2 \div 8.3$

1-9 Dividing Decimals

What You'll Learn

To divide decimals by whole numbers

To divide decimals by decimals

. . . And Why

To find the cost per person, as in Example 1

✔ Check Skills You'll Need

For help, go to Skills Handbook p. 660.

Divide.

1. $30 \div 6$ **2.** $96 \div 3$ **3.** $1{,}212 \div 12$ **4.** $729 \div 27$

Tell whether each quotient has a remainder.

5. $89 \div 8$ **6.** $35 \div 7$ **7.** $98 \div 10$ **8.** $833 \div 4$

New Vocabulary • terminating decimal • repeating decimal

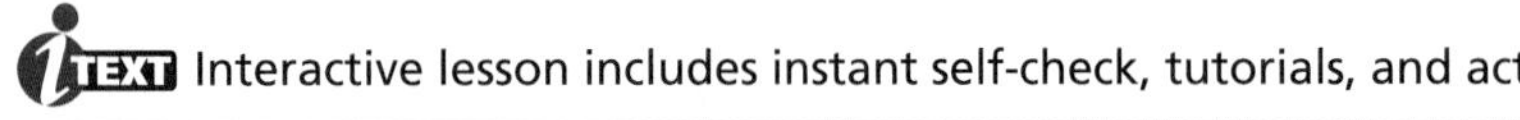
Interactive lesson includes instant self-check, tutorials, and activities.

OBJECTIVE 1 Dividing Decimals by Whole Numbers

Dividing decimals is similar to dividing whole numbers.

1 EXAMPLE Dividing by a Whole Number

Real World

Reading Math

You can rewrite 15 ÷ 3 as follows:

```
    5  ← Quotient
 3)15  ← Dividend
 ↑
 Divisor
```

Entertainment Transportation and tickets to an amusement park cost \$364.20 for 12 friends. How much will each person pay?

Since you are looking for the size of equal groups, you need to divide.

Estimate $364.20 \div 12 \approx 360 \div 12$, or 30

```
      30.35
  12)364.20   ← Divide as with whole numbers.
    − 36↓       Place the decimal point in the
       04       quotient above the decimal
      − 0↓      point in the dividend.
       4 2
     − 3 6↓
         60
       − 60
          0
```

Each person will pay \$30.35 for the transportation and ticket.

Check for Reasonableness 30.35 is reasonable since it is close to 30.

Check Understanding 1 Find each quotient.

a. $9.12 \div 6$ **b.** $8\overline{)385.6}$ **c.** $12\overline{)1.728}$

A **terminating decimal** is a decimal that stops, or terminates. Examples are 0.5 and 1.25. A **repeating decimal** repeats the same digit or group of digits. A bar is drawn over the digits that repeat. You write $1.\overline{27}$ for 1.2727 . . .

2 EXAMPLE Finding a Decimal Quotient

Find each quotient. Identify each as a terminating or repeating decimal.

a. 62 ÷ 8

$$\begin{array}{r} 7.75 \\ 8\overline{)62.00} \\ -56 \\ \hline 60 \\ -56 \\ \hline 40 \\ -40 \\ \hline 0 \end{array}$$

← **Insert zeros when needed.**

Since 7.75 ends, 7.75 is a terminating decimal.

b. 5 ÷ 6

$$\begin{array}{r} 0.833\ldots \\ 6\overline{)5.000} \\ -48 \\ \hline 20 \\ -18 \\ \hline 20 \\ -18 \\ \hline 2 \end{array}$$

← **Insert zeros when needed.**

← **The subtraction 20 − 18 will continue without end. So the digit 2 will keep repeating.**

Since the 3 repeats, $0.8\overline{3}$ is a repeating decimal.

Check Understanding 2 Find each quotient. Identify each as a terminating or repeating decimal.

a. 2 ÷ 3 **b.** 2 ÷ 8 **c.** 2 ÷ 11

OBJECTIVE 2 Dividing Decimals by Decimals

You can use a model to divide a decimal by a decimal.

3 EXAMPLE Modeling Division by Tenths

Draw a model to find 0.8 ÷ 0.2.

You want to know how many groups of 0.2 are in 0.8.

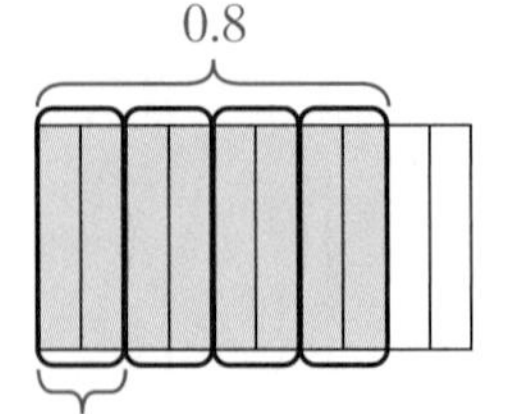

← **Draw a model for 0.8.**

← **Circle groups of 0.2.**

There are 4 groups of 0.2 in 0.8, so 0.8 ÷ 0.2 = 4.

Check Understanding 3 Draw a model to find each quotient.

a. 0.8 ÷ 0.4 **b.** 0.6 ÷ 0.2 **c.** 0.9 ÷ 0.15

d. **Reasoning** In the sentence 1.5 ÷ 0.75 = 2, the divisor, 0.75, represents the size of each group. What does the quotient, 2, represent?

Study the pattern of quotients below.

	Dividend	÷	Divisor	=	Quotient
	0.8	÷	0.4	=	2
Multiply dividend and divisor by 10. →	8	÷	4	=	2
Multiply dividend and divisor by 100. →	80	÷	40	=	2

Note that if you multiply both the dividend and the divisor by the same number, the quotient remains the same.

Key Concepts **Dividing Decimals**

To divide a decimal by a decimal, multiply both the dividend and the divisor by the same number so that the divisor is a whole number.

4 EXAMPLE Dividing a Decimal by a Decimal

Recipes Alika uses 0.5 pound of strawberries in each smoothie. How many smoothies can Alika make with 2.25 pounds of strawberries?

$0.5\overline{)2.25}$

Since the divisor has one decimal place, multiply the dividend and divisor by 10 so that the divisor is a whole number.

$$\begin{array}{r} 4.5 \\ 5\overline{)22.5} \\ -20 \\ \hline 2\,5 \\ -2\,5 \\ \hline 0 \end{array}$$

← **Now divide as with whole numbers. Place the decimal point in the quotient above the decimal point in the dividend.**

Alika can make 4.5 smoothies.

Check Understanding 4 Find each quotient.

a. 0.248 ÷ 0.04 **b.** $0.08\overline{)8.64}$ **c.** $1.25\overline{)38.125}$

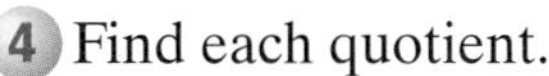

EXERCISES

For more practice, see *Extra Practice*.

A Practice by Example

Example 1 (page 43)

Find each quotient.

1. 328.25 ÷ 13 **2.** $7\overline{)255.5}$ **3.** 237.6 ÷ 33 **4.** $32\overline{)258.24}$

5. $84\overline{)26.46}$ **6.** 144.54 ÷ 6 **7.** $27\overline{)99.36}$ **8.** 38.27 ÷ 43

9. Four friends share a pizza that costs $12.72. How much does each friend owe for his or her share?

Example 2 (page 44)

Find each quotient. Identify each as a terminating or repeating decimal.

10. $9 \div 4$ **11.** $6 \div 11$ **12.** $512 \div 80$ **13.** $19 \div 25$

14. $15 \div 33$ **15.** $3 \div 16$ **16.** $17 \div 20$ **17.** $17 \div 180$

Example 3 (page 44)

Draw a model to find each quotient.

18. $0.6 \div 0.2$ **19.** $1.6 \div 0.8$ **20.** $0.9 \div 0.01$ **21.** $0.3 \div 0.15$

22. A pack of baseball cards costs \$2.75. A friend tells you that each card costs \$.25. Draw a model to find the number of cards in the pack.

Example 4 (page 45)

Find each quotient.

23. $29.5 \div 0.4$ **24.** $8.9\overline{)6.497}$ **25.** $3.1\overline{)10.261}$

26. $16.8 \div 2.4$ **27.** $0.96\overline{)0.144}$ **28.** $10.54 \div 0.17$

B Apply Your Skills

Complete each equation.

29.

■ $\div 0.4 = 2$

30.

$0.9 \div 0.3 =$ ■

31.

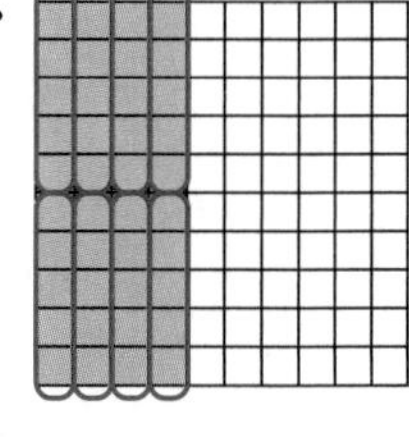

$0.4 \div$ ■ $= 8$

Real-World Connection

The Great Seto Bridge in Japan is six separate bridges with a total length of 9,368 meters.

32. Bridges A bicyclist riding across the Great Seto Bridge can travel 500 meters in 1 minute. A person walking can travel 100 meters in 1 minute. How many minutes shorter is the bicycle trip than the walk?

Find each quotient. Round each answer to the nearest hundredth.

33. $64.97 \div 3.2$ **34.** $10.126 \div 2.3$ **35.** $26.81 \div 3.3$ **36.** $5.637 \div 0.17$

37. Museums Seventeen students each bought two posters at the museum shop. The total cost was \$168.30. What was the price per poster?

38. School Supplies A stack of paper measures 0.9 centimeter thick. Each piece of paper is 0.01 centimeter thick.

a. How many pieces of paper are in the stack?

b. Could each of 25 students get three pieces of paper?

Find each quotient. Identify each as a terminating or repeating decimal.

39. $3.5 \div 0.7$ **40.** $7\overline{)54}$ **41.** $27\overline{)5.4}$

42. $36 \div 0.33$ **43.** $0.59\overline{)0.0649}$ **44.** $1.5\overline{)4.48}$

Gas Mileage Find the gas mileage. Round to the nearest tenth. To find the gas mileage of a vehicle in miles per gallon, divide the number of miles driven by the number of gallons of gas used.

45. A family car travels 367.9 miles on 12.5 gallons of gas.

46. A hybrid car travels 414.3 miles on 6.6 gallons of gas.

C Challenge

47. **Reasoning** Suppose you know a car's gas mileage and the number of miles the car traveled. How would you find the amount of gas used?

48. **Stretch Your Thinking** All of the digits in a certain 4-digit number are different. The first digit is twice the fourth digit. The second digit is twice the first digit. The last digit is twice the third digit. The sum of the digits is 15. What is the number?

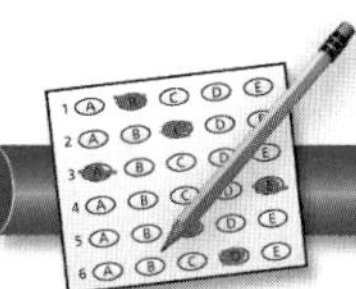

Test Prep

Multiple Choice

49. Which quotient is greatest?
A. $0.075 \div 5$ **B.** $0.75 \div 10$ **C.** $0.625 \div 25$ **D.** $7.5 \div 10$

50. Which quotient is equivalent to three and eight-tenths divided by thirty-two thousandths?
F. $0.032 \div 3.8$ **G.** $0.32 \div 3.8$ **H.** $3.8 \div 0.032$ **I.** $3.8 \div 0.32$

51. The quotient $1.35 \div 0.4$ is nearest which value?
A. 0.3 **B.** 3 **C.** 30 **D.** 300

Take It to the NET
Online lesson quiz at
www.PHSchool.com
Web Code: aaa-0109

52. Regular unleaded gasoline costs $1.259 per gallon. You spent $5 on gasoline. About how many gallons did you buy?
F. 3 gallons **G.** 4 gallons **H.** 5 gallons **I.** 6 gallons

Mixed Review

Lesson 1-7 **Find each product.**

53. 9.07×0.025 **54.** 0.145×0.12 **55.** $8.3 \cdot 5.6$

56. $15(0.87)$ **57.** $(1.013)5$ **58.** $3.0 \cdot 0.7$

1-10 Order of Operations

What You'll Learn

To use the order of operations

. . . And Why

To find the total cost of a purchase, as in Example 2

✓ Check Skills You'll Need

For help, go to Lesson 1-3.

Use <, =, or > to complete each statement.

1. 25.005 ■ 25.0050 **2.** 4.000 ■ 3.999 **3.** 289.1 ■ 289.001

4. 1.382 ■ 1.0385 **5.** 0.0107 ■ 0.070 **6.** 9.0 ■ 9.001

New Vocabulary • **expression** • **order of operations**

Interactive lesson includes instant self-check, tutorials, and activities.

OBJECTIVE

1 Using the Order of Operations

An **expression** is a mathematical phrase containing numbers and operation symbols. The expression $18 + 11 \times 6$ contains two operations. You might ask, "Which operation is performed first, the addition or the multiplication?"

Diane's Work (addition first)	Dana's Work (multiplication first)
$18 + 11 \times 6 \stackrel{?}{=} (18 + 11) \times 6$	$18 + 11 \times 6 \stackrel{?}{=} 18 + (11 \times 6)$
$\stackrel{?}{=} 29 \times 6$	$\stackrel{?}{=} 18 + 66$
$\stackrel{?}{=} 174$ X	$\stackrel{?}{=} 84$ ✓

Only one answer is correct. To make sure everyone gets the same value for an expression, you use the **order of operations.**

Key Concepts **Order of Operations**

1. Do all operations within parentheses first.
2. Multiply and divide in order from left to right.
3. Add and subtract in order from left to right.

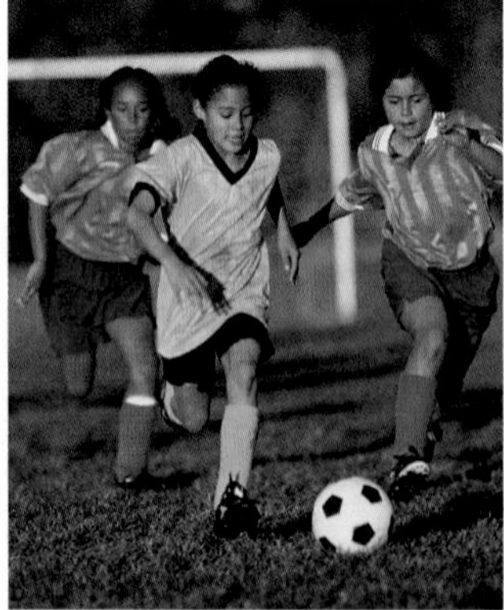

Real-World Connection

Even soccer equipment—shoes with cleats, socks, shin guards—needs to be put on in a certain order.

Based on the order of operations, you multiply before you add.

$$18 + 11 \times 6 = 18 + 66$$
$$= 84$$

So Dana's answer is correct.

1 EXAMPLE Finding the Value of Expressions

Find the value of each expression.

a. $6 + 20.4 \div 2 = 6 + 10.2$ ← **Divide 20.4 by 2.**

$= 16.2$ ← **Add.**

b. $30 - (6 + 2) \times 3 = 30 - 8 \times 3$ ← **Add 6 and 2 within the parentheses.**

$= 30 - 24$ ← **Multiply 8 and 3.**

$= 6$ ← **Subtract 24 from 30.**

Check Understanding 1 Find the value of each expression.

a. $17 - 4 \times 2.25$ **b.** $3.4 + 5 \times 2 - 1.7$ **c.** $(6 + 18) \div 3 \times 2$

d. **Reasoning** Explain when you might add before multiplying.

2 EXAMPLE Writing Expressions

CRAWFORD'S
ITEMS ORDERED
JEANS 2@ $19.95 EACH
DISCOUNT −$5.00
SHIRTS 3@ $15.99 EACH
TAX $4.35
TOTAL

Sales Receipts Suppose you buy the items shown in the store receipt at the left. Write an expression for the total cost, including the tax. Then find the value of the expression.

Words	cost of jeans	−	discount	+	cost of shirts	+	tax	
Expression	2 × $19.95	−	$5.00	+	3 × $15.99	+	$4.35	
	$39.90	−	$5.00	+	$47.97	+	$4.35	← **Multiply.**
		$34.90		+	$47.97	+	$4.35	← **Subtract.**
							$87.22	← **Add.**

The total cost, including tax, is $87.22.

Check Understanding 2 Find the value of $3 \times \$16.95 - \$10.00 + 4 \times \$1.50$.

EXERCISES

A Practice by Example

Find the value of each expression.

Example 1 (page 49)

1. $6 - 2 + 4 \times 2$ **2.** $33 - (14 + 6)$ **3.** $6 \times (2 \times 5)$

4. $4 \times 3 + 20 \div 5$ **5.** $400 \div (44 - 24)$ **6.** $7 \times (4 + 6) \times 3$

Example 2 (page 49)

7. $45 \div 4.5 + 6.2 \times 3$ **8.** $26 + 4.6 - 4 \times 2.4$

9. $14 - (7.6 + 5) \div 2$ **10.** $13 + 5.1 \times 12 - 4.2$

Example 2 (page 49)

11. **Marbles** You buy 1 red rainbow marble at \$.45 each, 3 bumblebee marbles at \$.95 each, and 2 tricolored rainbows at \$.65 each.
   a. Write an expression for the total cost of the marbles you buy.
   b. Find the total cost.

12. **Jobs** You are paid \$4.10 per hour to rake leaves. Your brother is paid \$3.30 per hour.
   a. Write an expression for how much the two of you will earn together if you work 3 hours and your brother works 2 hours.
   b. Find the total amount earned.

B Apply Your Skills

Which operation would you perform first in each expression?

13. $30 - 10 \times 3 \div 5$
14. $63 \div 7 \times (5 - 2)$
15. $12 - 9 \div 3 - 2$

Find the value of each expression.

16. $(63 - 48) \times 10$
17. $18 \div 6 - (5 - 4)$
18. $40 \times 0.1 - (9 - 6)$
19. $(0.1 + 0.9) \times 1 - 1$

Use <, =, or > to complete each statement.

20. $(3 + 6) \times 4$ ■ $3 + 6 \times 4$
21. $6 \times (8 - 2)$ ■ $(8 - 2) \times 6$
22. $2 \times (15 - 3.5)$ ■ $2 \times 15 - 3.5$
23. $62 - 37.3 + 8$ ■ $62 - (37.3 + 8)$
24. $0.8 \div 2 \times 2$ ■ $0.8 \div (2 \times 2)$
25. $3.5 \times 10 \div 5$ ■ $3.5 \times (10 \div 5)$

26. **Writing in Math** Explain the steps you would use to find the value of the expression $8 \div 4 \times 6 + (7 - 5)$.

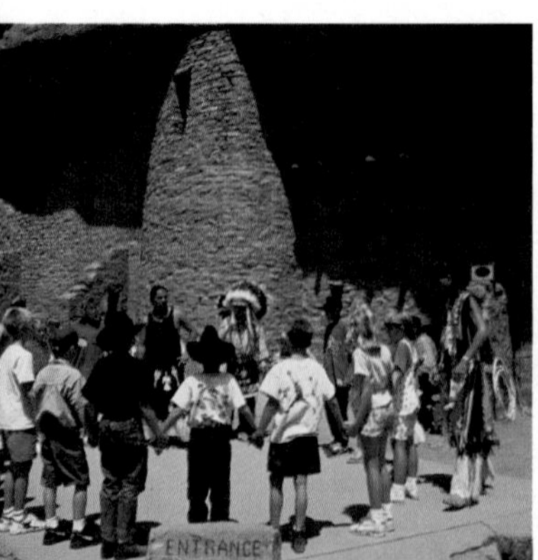

27. **Field Trip** A group of 11 boys and 9 girls go on a field trip to a Native American museum. The cost is \$5 per person. Which expression does *not* show the total amount the group will pay?
   A. $\$5 \times (11 + 9)$
   B. $(\$5 \times 11) + (\$5 \times 9)$
   C. $\$5 \times 11 \times 9$
   D. $\$5 \times 20$

28. **Coins** There are 312 coins of the same type in two stacks. One stack of coins is 15 inches tall. The other stack is 9 inches tall. Find the thickness of one coin to the nearest thousandth of an inch.

Reasoning **Insert parentheses to make each statement true.**

29. $11 - 7 \div 2 = 2$
30. $1 + 2 \times 15 - 4 = 33$
31. $7 - 2 \times 2 - 1 = 9$
32. $5 \times 6 \div 2 + 1 = 10$

Nutrition **Use the chart below for Exercises 33 and 34.**

Food	Serving Size	Protein (grams)
Canned tuna	3 oz	24.4
Rye bread	1 slice	2.3
Cheese pizza	1 slice	7.8

33. About how many grams of protein are in 4 sandwiches (2 slices of rye bread and 3 ounces of tuna each)?

34. About how many grams of protein are in a slice of pizza and a sandwich consisting of 2 slices of rye bread and 2 ounces of tuna?

Challenge

Insert operation symbols to make each statement true.

35. (6 ■ 9) ■ 4 ■ 6 = 10

36. 15 ■ 3 ■ 2 = 10

37. (12 ■ 8) ■ (5 ■ 2) = 11

38. 14 ■ 7 ■ 2 ■ 3 = 7

39. Algebra In the expression (10 − ■) ÷ (▲ − 1), ■ and ▲ represent unknown values.

a. Find the value of the expression if ■ = 4 and ▲ = 3.

b. Find the value of the expression if ■ = 4 and ▲ = 4.

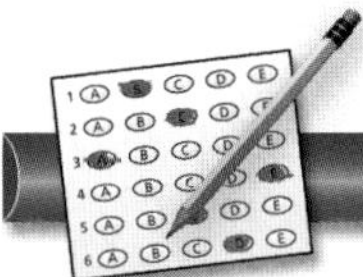

Test Prep

Multiple Choice

40. Find the value of the expression $36 \div 3 - 1 \times 7$.

A. 5 **B.** 9 **C.** 77 **D.** 126

41. Find the value of the expression (\$1.25 × 3) + (\$3.50 ÷ 5).

F. \$3.05 **G.** \$4.45 **H.** \$4.50 **I.** \$21.25

42. Which expression has a value of 0.40?

A. $(0.2 + 0.2) \times (1 - 1)$ **B.** $2 \times 0.1 + 0.1$

C. $0.1 + (0.9 \div 3)$ **D.** $1.4 - 1 \times 0.7$

43. At an amusement park, each person pays \$5 to enter plus \$2 for each ride. While at the park, Jamie goes on 9 rides. Which expression represents the total amount Jamie spends?

F. \$5 + 9 × \$2 **G.** (\$5 + 9) × \$2

H. (\$5 × 9) + \$2 **I.** \$5 × 9 × \$2

Take It to the NET
Online lesson quiz at
www.PHSchool.com
Web Code: aaa-0110

Mixed Review

Lesson 1-8 **Use mental math to find each product or quotient.**

44. $1{,}000 \times 0.035$

45. $4(2.8 \times 25)$

46. $2 \cdot 5.4 \cdot 5$

47. $0.462 \div 100$

48. $1.39 \div 1{,}000$

49. $25.6 \div 10$

Technology

Exploring Order of Operations

For Use With Lesson 1-10

Some calculators use the order of operations in math and some do not. Check the value of $18 + 6 \div 3$ on your calculator.

18 [+] 6 [÷] 3 [=]

If the display is 20, your calculator follows the order of operations.

$18 + (6 \div 3) = 18 + 2 = 20$

If the display is 8, your calculator has added first. You will have to use parentheses as you enter expressions.

18 [+] [(] 6 [÷] 3 [)] [=]

EXAMPLE Using a Calculator

Multiply 1.4 by the sum of 45.2 and 7.5.

Method 1 Use a calculator with ( ) keys.

1.4 [×] [(] 45.2 [+] 7.5 [)] [=] *73.78* ← **Put parentheses around 45.2 + 7.5 so addition will be completed first.**

Method 2 Use a calculator without ( ) keys.

45.2 [+] 7.5 [=] *52.7* ← **Complete the addition first.**

[×] 1.4 [=] *73.78* ← **Then multiply your answer by 1.4.**

EXERCISES

Suppose your calculator does not follow the order of operations. Write a calculator key sequence for each expression and give the value.

1. Subtract 85.4 from 97.5. Then divide by 2.5.

2. Multiply 23.5 by 1.1. Then add 4.75.

3. Divide 7.28 by the sum of 0.14 and 1.86.

4. Divide the sum of 0.72 and 2.79 by 3.

Place parentheses in each number sentence to make it true.

5. $4 \times 8 - 1 = 28$

6. $14 - 9 \times 7 = 35$

7. $4.7 - 2.3 + 2.01 = 4.41$

8. $14.9 - 2.6 + 8.3 = 4$

9. $3.08 \times 3.7 + 2.12 = 13.516$

10. $6.5 + 3.2 \times 7.1 = 68.87$

11. **Writing in Math** Suppose you use a calculator to divide 4.00 by 16. Is it necessary to enter all three digits in 4.00? Explain your answer.

Writing Gridded Responses

Some tests include gridded-response questions. When you find an answer, write the answer at the top of the grid and fill in the matching bubbles below.

EXAMPLE Using the Answer Grid

A fitness trail is 3.4 miles long. You walk 2.7 miles of the trial. How much farther must you walk to finish the trail?

3.4 miles − 2.7 miles = 0.7 mile

You can write the answer as 0.7, .7, or $\frac{7}{10}$. Here are the three ways to enter these answers. You do not include the label in a grid.

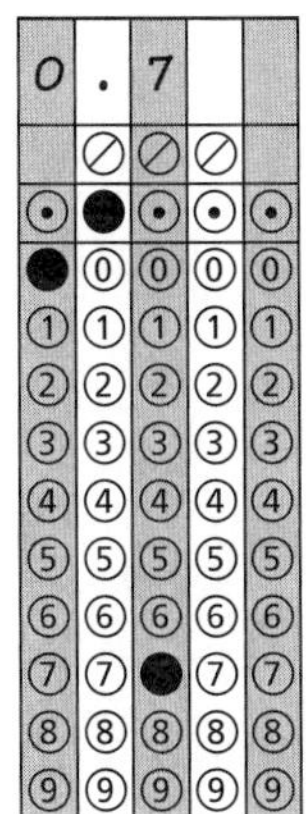

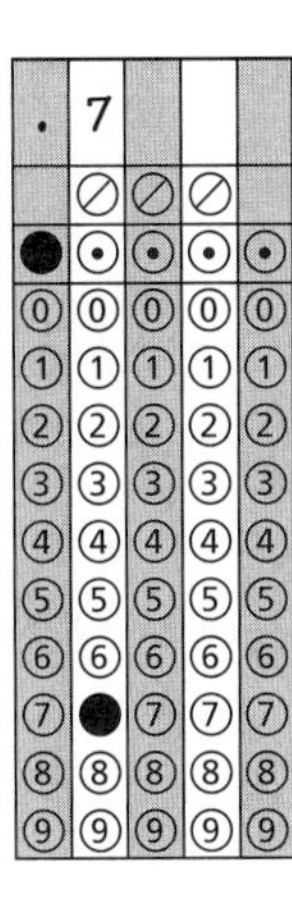

Write a decimal point as part of the answer.

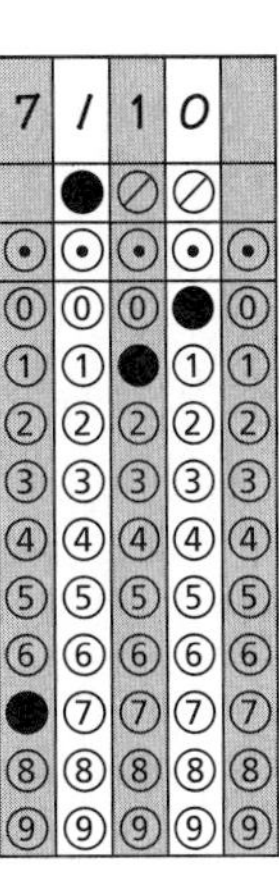

Write a slash with a fraction.

EXERCISES

Write what you would mark on the grid for each answer.

1. 4.6 − 3 **2.** 8 + 2.31 **3.** 0.65 ÷ 5 **4.** 0.75 × 0.02

5. 2.2 × 5 − 11 + 6.6 ÷ 3 **6.** 2.5 ÷ (0.5 × 5) × 1.525

7. What decimal number does the model at the right represent?

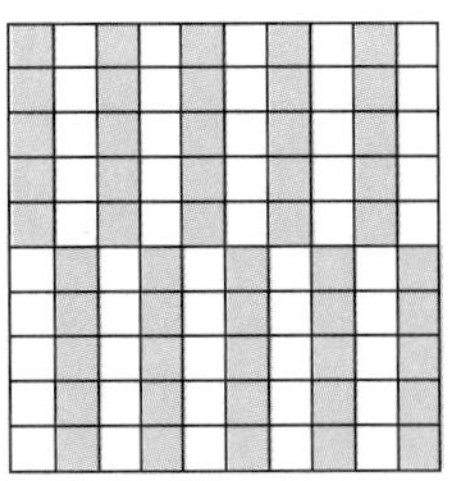

8. A diver received scores of 6.5, 5.5, 6.0, 6.5, and 6.0 in a diving competition. What is the total score?

Chapter Review

Vocabulary

Associative Property of Addition (p. 25)
Associative Property of Multiplication (p. 36)
Commutative Property of Addition (p. 25)
Commutative Property of Multiplication (p. 36)
compatible numbers (p. 20)
expanded form (p. 5)
expression (p. 48)
front-end estimation (p. 20)
Identity Property of Addition (p. 25)
Identity Property of Multiplication (p. 36)
order of operations (p. 48)
repeating decimal (p. 44)
standard form (p. 5)
terminating decimal (p. 44)

Reading Math: Understanding Vocabulary

Choose the correct vocabulary term to complete each sentence.

1. An example of the ? is $5 + 0 = 5$.

2. $(4 + 7) \div 2$ is an example of a(n) ? .

3. 0.5830 is in ? .

4. An example of a(n) ? is $157.\overline{3}$.

5. $5.3 + (6.8 + 8.1) = (5.3 + 6.8) + 8.1$ is an example of the ? .

Take It to the NET
Online vocabulary quiz at **www.PHSchool.com**
Web Code: aaj-0151

Skills and Concepts

1-1, 1-2, and 1-3 Objectives

- To write and compare whole numbers
- To read and write decimals
- To compare decimals using models
- To use place value

You can write decimals in words, in **standard form,** or in **expanded form.** A decimal in expanded form shows the place and value of each digit. You can compare and order decimals using models, a number line, or place value.

Write each number in standard form.

6. six million, four thousand thirty **7.** six and forty-three thousandths

Write each number in words and in expanded form.

8. 525.5 **9.** 5,000,025 **10.** 0.5255 **11.** 5.025

Use <, =, or > to complete each statement.

12. 4,406 ■ 640 **13.** 0.33 ■ 0.35 **14.** 1.838 ■ 1.839 **15.** 0.18 ■ 0.081

Order each set of decimals from least to greatest.

16. 0.52; 0.4; 0.14; 0.06 **17.** 23; 23.2; 23.25; 23.03 **18.** 9.4; 9.24; 9.04; 9.2

1-4 and 1-5 Objectives

- To estimate by rounding and using compatible numbers
- To use front-end estimation
- To add decimals
- To subtract decimals

To estimate, you can round each number or you can use **compatible numbers.** You can also use **front-end estimation** to estimate a sum.

Use rounding, front-end estimation, or compatible numbers to estimate each answer.

19. $337.4 + 20.08$ **20.** $1.741 - 0.81$ **21.** 3.21×1.04 **22.** $6.25 \div 1.25$

Find each sum or difference.

23. $1.6 + 1.8$ **24.** $0.96 - 0.79$ **25.** $4.12 - 0.253$ **26.** $2.01 + 5.39$

1-6 Objective

- To use a plan to solve problems

When solving a problem, be sure to *read and understand* the problem, *plan* how to solve it, *solve* the problem, and then *look back and check* to see if your answer makes sense.

27. Consumer Issues Tacos cost $1.49 each. You can also buy three tacos for $3.99. Matt buys two tacos. Ursula buys one taco. How much money would they have saved if they had bought their tacos together?

1-7, 1-8, and 1-9 Objectives

- To multiply decimals
- To use the properties of multiplication
- To multiply and divide decimals by 10, 100, and 1,000
- To divide decimals by whole numbers
- To divide decimals by decimals

When multiplying decimals, add the decimal places in the factors to place the decimal point in the product. When dividing decimals, you may need to place a decimal point in the quotient.

You can use the **Commutative, Associative,** and **Identity Properties of Multiplication** to help you multiply mentally.

Find each product or quotient.

28. 1.2×29.5 **29.** $12.12 \div 6$ **30.** $38.4 \div 0.08$ **31.** $0.54 \cdot 17$

Use mental math to find each product or quotient.

32. $5 \times 34 \times 0.02$ **33.** $(0.3)(3)(1)$ **34.** $98.127 \div 100$

1-10 Objective

- To use the order of operations

An **expression** is a mathematical phrase containing numbers and operation symbols. You use the **order of operations** to find the value of an expression.

Find the value of each expression.

35. $30 - 5 + 4 \times 3$ **36.** $6 - (27 - 9) \div 3$ **37.** $5.3 \times 8 + 4 \div 2$

Chapter Test

Online chapter test at
www.PHSchool.com
Web Code: aaa-0152

Write each number in standard form.

1. two thousand twenty and twenty-five thousandths
2. one million, four hundred nine thousand, eight hundred thirty-five

Write each decimal in words and in expanded form.

3. 623.7
4. 2.086
5. 89.123

6. Writing in Math Explain why thirteen hundredths are equivalent to one hundred thirty thousandths.

Use <, =, or > to complete each statement.

7. 32.12 ■ 32.42
8. 9.7 ■ 9.70

Order each set of decimals from least to greatest.

9. 8.1, 8.2, 8.08, 8.15, 8.03
10. 1.63, 1.064, 0.163, 1.036, 0.153

Use rounding, front-end estimation, or compatible numbers to estimate each answer.

11. 50.32×22.1
12. 4.63×50.491
13. $98.13 \div 24.27$
14. $4.38 + 2.74 + 1.17$
15. $1.01 + 2.89$
16. $62.85 - 24.12$

17. **DVDs** Five DVDs cost $74.85. Explain whether the best estimate for the cost of one DVD is greater than or less than $14.

First estimate, then find each sum or difference.

18. $3.89 + 15.3$
19. $4.6 - 2.07$
20. $41.2 - 19.8$
21. $53.7 + 28.6$

Use mental math to find each answer.

22. $8.29 + 0 + 0.71$
23. $3.6 + (7.28 + 6.4)$
24. 100×5.2
25. $25 \times 6.7 \times 4$
26. $4.3 \times 1 \times 10$
27. $83.11 \div 1{,}000$

28. **Working** Larry wants to work 2.75 hours each day from Monday through Wednesday. How many hours must he work on Thursday to work a total of 10 hours?

Find each product or quotient.

29. 9.063×24
30. $0.36(1.5)$
31. $21.6 \div 0.06$
32. $10 \div 3$
33. $7 \div 0.14$
34. $6.34 \cdot 1.091$

35. **Pet Food** Zelda spent $6.24 on pet food. The food cost $.24 per cup. How many cups of pet food did Zelda purchase?

36. **Money** What is the value of 18 rolls of quarters if there are 40 quarters in each roll?

Find the value of each expression.

37. $16 \div (4 \times 4)$
38. $8 - 4 \div 2$
39. $5 + (3.3 - 1.6)$
40. $(9 - 1.2 \times 3) \div 4$

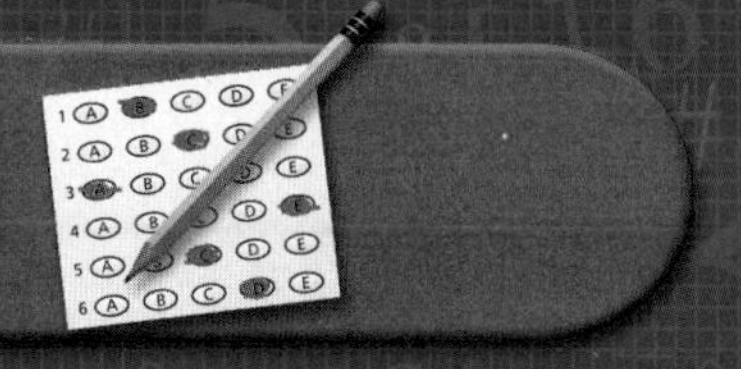

Test Prep

Reading Comprehension **Read each passage below. Then answer the questions based on what you have read.**

Rainfall Hilo, Hawaii, usually receives 129.19 inches of rain each year. Compare that to Phoenix, Arizona, which receives 7.66 inches of rain a year. In Hilo, the wettest month is April, with 15.26 inches of rain, while its driest month is June with 6.2 inches of rain. Phoenix's wettest month is December with 1 inch, and its driest is May with 0.12 inch.

1. In Hilo, how many more inches of rain typically fall in April than in June?
   A. 0.88 inch **B.** 9.06 inches
   C. 15.26 inches **D.** 21.46 inches

2. In July, Phoenix typically gets 0.83 inch of rain. About how many times as much rain falls in July as in May?
   F. 6 **G.** 7 **H.** 8 **I.** 9

3. How many inches of rain does Hilo receive in a typical ten-year period?
   A. 1,291.9 inches **B.** 76.60 inches
   C. 12.919 inches **D.** 0.766 inch

4. Hilo's yearly rainfall is about how many times the yearly rainfall in Phoenix?
   F. 1,040 times **G.** 138 times
   H. 122 times **I.** 16 times

Coins Did you know that some coins contain more pure metal than others? American Gold Eagle coins are 0.9166 gold and Canadian Maple Leaf coins are 0.9999 gold. American Silver Eagle coins are 0.999 silver while the American Platinum Eagle coins are 0.9995 platinum.

5. How might you write the purity of the American Silver Eagle coin in order to compare it with the other coins?
   A. 0.99 **B.** 0.0999
   C. 0.9990 **D.** 0.9999

6. What portion of the American Gold Eagle coin is NOT gold?
   F. 0.0004 **G.** 0.0034
   H. 0.0834 **I.** 0.0934

7. Which of the five coins mentioned contains the greatest portion of pure metal?
   A. American Silver Eagle
   B. American Gold Eagle
   C. Canadian Maple Leaf
   D. American Platinum Eagle

8. How much gold is in an American Gold Eagle coin that weighs 0.1 ounce?
   F. 9.166 ounces **G.** 0.9166 ounce
   H. 0.91660 ounce **I.** 0.09166 ounce

Real-World Snapshots

That's an Order!

Applying Decimals Ancient Mesopotamians bought and traded grain and other items. They developed a writing system to keep track of their goods and money. Today, we use order forms and receipts to purchase items and record the money we spend.

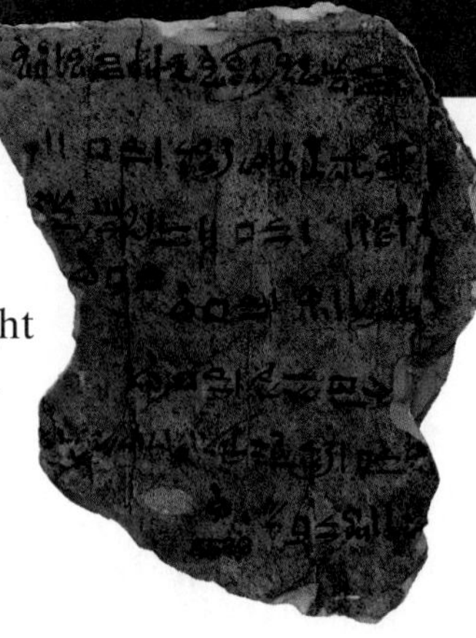

How Much for That Goat?

This piece of limestone shows part of a business deal including a goat worth one deben of copper, an Ancient Egyptian measure of metal. One deben equals 3 ounces.

Put It All Together

1. Find the five missing values in the sample order form. (*Hint:* Some missing values cannot be found without finding others first.)
2. **Open-Ended** Suppose you have a clothing budget of $500.
   a. **Research** Make a list of items you would like to purchase. Find their prices.
   b. Use an order form like the sample. Complete the Quantity, Description, and Unit Price columns for the items on your list. At least four of the values in the Quantity column should be greater than 1.
   c. Find the total for each row by multiplying the quantity by the unit price. Follow the directions on the order form to fill in the rest of the boxes. Make sure you stay within your budget!
   d. Copy your order form onto another sheet of paper. Leave the same boxes blank as in the sample. Trade order forms with another student and find each other's missing values.

Sample Order Form

Quantity	Description	Unit Price	Total
■	20-gallon aquarium	$119.99	$119.99
1	Air pump	$14.95	$14.95
2	Water filter	■	$64.98
3	Tropical fish food	$7.49	$22.47
■	Gravel, one bag	$1.99	■
3	Driftwood decoration	$13.25	$39.75
		Subtotal (Add the totals from above.)	■
		6% Shipping (Multiply subtotal by 0.06.)	$16.44
		Total (Add subtotal and shipping.)	$290.52

Tally Sticks

People have used notched sticks for tallying totals for thousands of years. Larger notches denote greater amounts.

Calculations and More

Handheld calculators, which once took the place of adding machines, perform many mathematical operations. This one can display graphs.

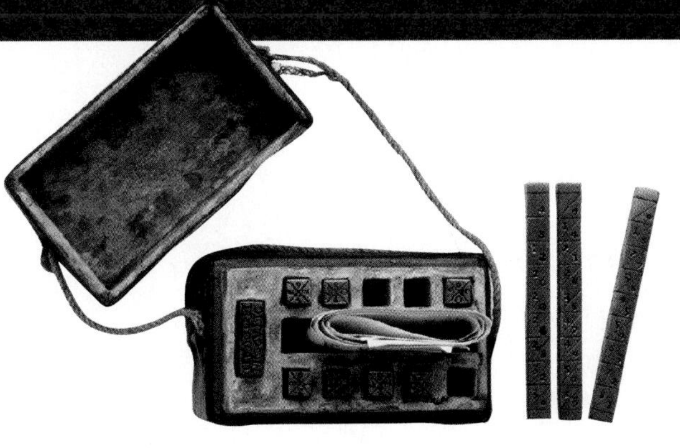

Napier's Rods

You can use Napier's rods to find products. The rods in the photo show multiples of 4, 7, and 9.

Take It to the NET For more information about completing order forms, go to **www.PHSchool.com**.
Web Code: aae-0153

Cuneiform

Ancient Babylonians wrote their numbers in cuneiform, printed with sticks and wedges in clay tablets. The Babylonian number system is sexagesimal, which means it is based on counting 60s. This system remains in our measures of time and angles.

Counting Sheep

The cuneiform characters on this clay tablet are a tally of sheep and goats from an area called Tello, in ancient Mesopotamia.

Algebra

CHAPTER 2

Patterns and Variables

Lessons

Key Vocabulary

- algebraic expression (p. 69)
- base (p. 99)
- Distributive Property (p. 105)
- exponent (p. 99)
- inverse operations (p. 90)
- numerical expression (p. 68)
- power (p. 100)
- Properties of Equality (pp. 90, 91, 95, 96)
- term (p. 63)
- variable (p. 69)

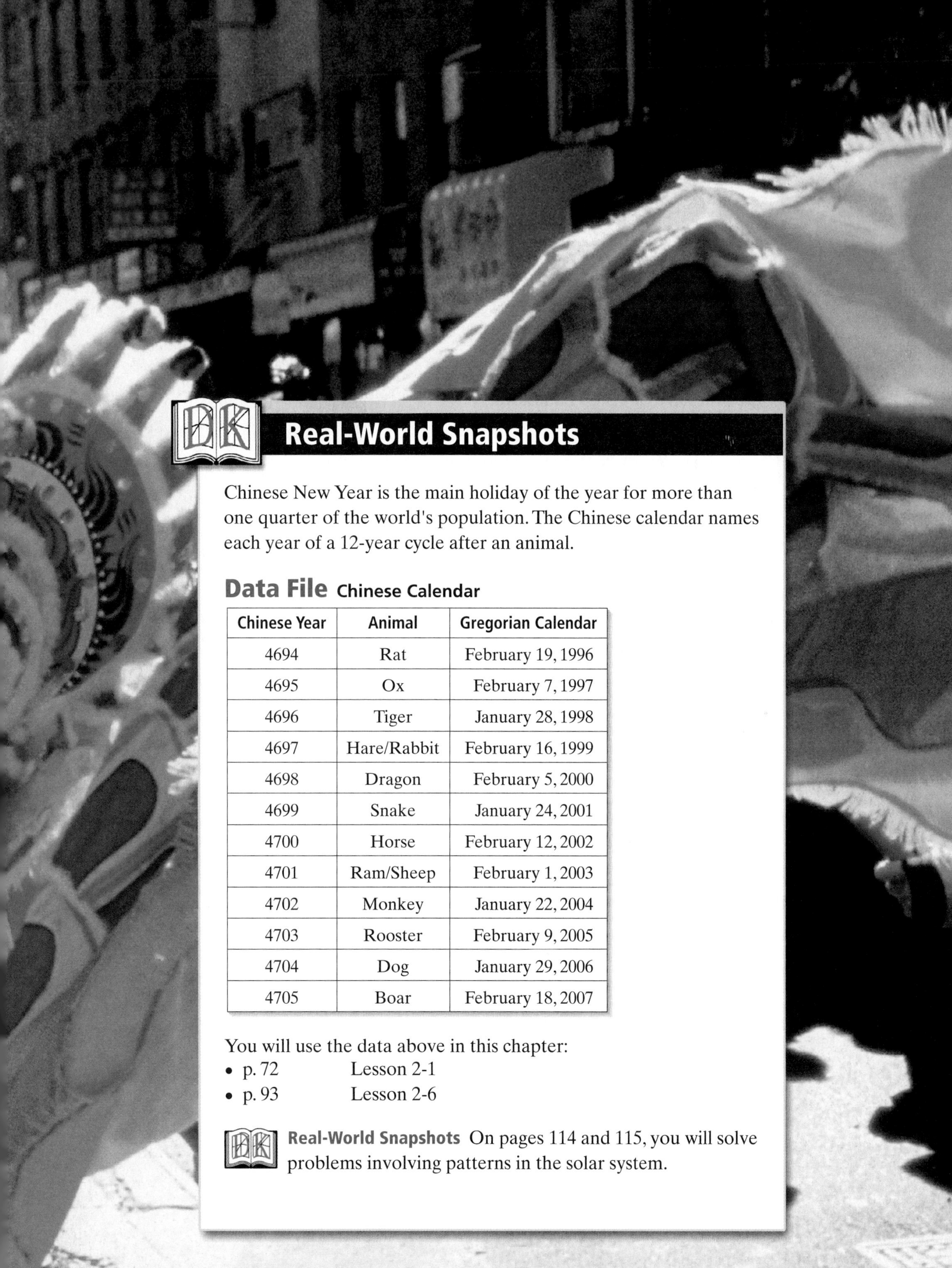

Real-World Snapshots

Chinese New Year is the main holiday of the year for more than one quarter of the world's population. The Chinese calendar names each year of a 12-year cycle after an animal.

Data File Chinese Calendar

Chinese Year	Animal	Gregorian Calendar
4694	Rat	February 19, 1996
4695	Ox	February 7, 1997
4696	Tiger	January 28, 1998
4697	Hare/Rabbit	February 16, 1999
4698	Dragon	February 5, 2000
4699	Snake	January 24, 2001
4700	Horse	February 12, 2002
4701	Ram/Sheep	February 1, 2003
4702	Monkey	January 22, 2004
4703	Rooster	February 9, 2005
4704	Dog	January 29, 2006
4705	Boar	February 18, 2007

You will use the data above in this chapter:

- p. 72 Lesson 2-1
- p. 93 Lesson 2-6

Real-World Snapshots On pages 114 and 115, you will solve problems involving patterns in the solar system.

Chapter 2 Preview

Where You've Been

- In Chapter 1, you learned to compare, order, and estimate with decimals. You used the order of operations to compute with decimals.

Where You're Going

- In Chapter 2, you will learn how to use algebraic expressions to describe words and patterns.
- You will solve one-step equations.
- Applying what you learn, you will continue patterns, such as those found in a sunflower's rings.

The number of seeds in a sunflower's ring are part of the pattern 1, 1, 2, 3, 5, 8, . . .

Instant self-check online and on CD-ROM

Diagnosing Readiness

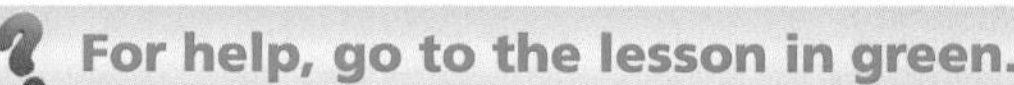

For help, go to the lesson in green.

Estimating With Decimals (Lesson 1-4)

Estimate by first rounding to the nearest whole number.

1. 5.26×9.8 **2.** $3.71 + 2.86$ **3.** $57.35 - 4.92$

Adding and Subtracting Decimals (Lesson 1-5)

First estimate then find each sum or difference.

4. $36.05 + 6.1$ **5.** $36 - 26.5$ **6.** $0.05 + 5.05$

Using Mental Math to Multiply and Divide Decimals (Lesson 1-9)

Find each product or quotient.

7. $3.79 \times 5 \times 20$ **8.** $1{,}000 \times 3.04$ **9.** $157 \div 100$

Using the Order of Operations (Lesson 1-10)

Find the value of each expression.

10. $3 \times 8 + 2.5$ **11.** $36 + 6 \div 2$ **12.** $48.2 - 6.2 \times 5$

Algebra

2-1 Describing a Pattern

What You'll Learn

 To continue a number pattern

 To write a rule for a number pattern

. . . And Why

To find the number of tiles in a pattern, as in Example 1

Check Skills You'll Need

For help, go to Lesson 1-3.

Order each set of decimals from least to greatest.

1. 0.105, 0.0105, 10.5

2. 3.331, 3.1, 3.31

3. 9.06, 9.6, 9.09

4. 20.06, 26.0, 0.602

5. 100.1, 101.0, 100.01

6. 0.99, 0.4, 0.35

New Vocabulary

• term • conjecture

OBJECTIVE

iTEXT Interactive lesson includes instant self-check, tutorials, and activities.

1 Continuing a Number Pattern

Investigation: Recognizing and Extending Patterns

The first three designs in a pattern are shown at the right.

1. Continue the pattern. Sketch the fourth and fifth designs on grid paper.

2. How many squares are in the fourth design? The fifth design?

3. Copy and complete the table.

Design Number	1	2	3	4	5	6	7
Number of Squares	1	5					

4. **Reasoning** Describe how you will find the tenth design in the pattern.

Reading Math

Read the three dots in the pattern 1, 4, 7, 10, . . . as "and so on."

The numbers 1, 4, 7, 10, . . . form a number pattern. Each number in the pattern is a **term.** For example, the third term in this pattern is 7.

The three dots after the number 10 tell you that the pattern continues beyond what is shown.

A **conjecture** is a prediction about what may happen. You can use the terms you know to make a conjecture about how a pattern will continue.

1 EXAMPLE Finding Number Patterns 

Decorating Jacob is creating a pattern of colored tiles for a wall in his bathroom. The first four designs are shown below. How many squares will be in the fifth and sixth designs?

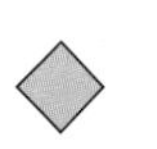 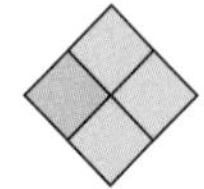 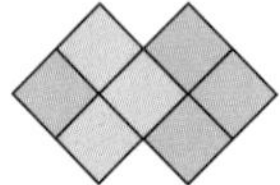 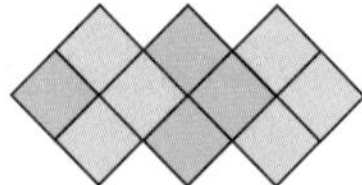

Count the squares in each design. There are 1, 4, 7, and 10 squares. Notice that each design has three more squares than the one before it.

$$1,\ 4,\ 7,\ 10,\ \underset{+3}{13},\ \underset{+3}{16},\ \ldots$$

← **Add 3 to 10 to get the fifth term. Add 3 to 13 to get the sixth term.**

So, the fifth and sixth designs will have 13 and 16 squares.

Check Understanding 1 Write the next two terms in each number pattern.

a. 1, 11, 21, 31, . . . **b.** 56, 48, 40, 32, . . . **c.** 29, 36, 43, 50, . . .

d. **Reasoning** In Example 1, the eighth design will go all the way across Jacob's bathroom wall. How many tiles will be in the eighth design?

OBJECTIVE

2 Writing a Rule for a Number Pattern

One way you can describe a number pattern is to give the first term and the rule. A rule is an explanation of how you go from one term to the next.

2 EXAMPLE Writing Number Patterns From Rules

Write the first six terms in the number pattern described by this rule: *Start with 1 and multiply by 2 repeatedly.*

The first term is 1. ↓

$$1,\ \underset{\times 2}{2},\ \underset{\times 2}{4},\ \underset{\times 2}{8},\ \underset{\times 2}{16},\ \underset{\times 2}{32}$$

← **Multiply each term by 2 to find the next term.**

Check Understanding 2 Write the first six terms in each number pattern.

a. Start with 90 and subtract 15 repeatedly.

b. Start with 1 and multiply by 3 repeatedly.

c. Start with 17 and add 19 repeatedly.

3 EXAMPLE Writing a Rule

Patterns Write the next three terms in each pattern. Then write a rule for the pattern.

a. 53, 49, 45, 41, . . .

−4 −4 −4 −4 −4 −4

53, 49, 45, 41, 37, 33, 29 ← To get from one term to the next, subtract 4.

The rule is *start with 53 and subtract 4 repeatedly.*

b. 1.5, 4.5, 13.5, 40.5, . . .

×3 ×3 ×3 ×3 ×3 ×3

1.5, 4.5, 13.5, 40.5, 121.5, 364.5, 1,093.5 ← To get from one term to the next, multiply by 3.

The rule is *start with 1.5 and multiply by 3 repeatedly.*

Check Understanding 3 Write the next three terms and write a rule to describe each number pattern.

a. 1, 7, 49, 343, . . . **b.** 10.0, 8.8, 7.6, . . . **c.** 256, 128, 64, . . .

EXERCISES

A Practice by Example

Example 1 (page 64)

Write the next two terms in each number pattern.

1. 2, 6, 10, 14, . . .

2. 99, 88, 77, 66, . . .

3. 1, 3, 9, 27, . . .

4. 1, 1.4, 1.8, 2.2, . . .

Example 2 (page 64)

Write the first six terms in each number pattern.

5. Start with 7 and add 4 repeatedly.

6. Start with 512 and divide by 2 repeatedly.

Example 3 (page 65)

Write the next three terms and write a rule for each number pattern.

7. 1, 5, 25, 125, . . .

8. 2, 10, 50, 250, . . .

9. 6,000,000; 600,000; 60,000; . . .

10. $2.85, $5.70, $8.55, . . .

Departures

Red Train	Blue Train
12:51 P.M.	12:17 P.M.
1:51 P.M.	1:02 P.M.
2:51 P.M.	1:47 P.M.
3:51 P.M.	2:32 P.M.

11. Schedules The schedule shows the departure times for two trains.

a. Predict all departure times before 6 P.M. for the Red Train.

b. Predict all departure times before 6 P.M. for the Blue Train.

B Apply Your Skills

Write the fifth term of each number pattern.

12. 1, 8, 64, 512, . . .

13. 18, 15, 12, 9, . . .

14. 0, 17, 34, 51, . . .

15. 0.12, 1.2, 12, 120, . . .

16. 2, 8, 14, 20, . . .

17. 100, 89, 78, 67, . . .

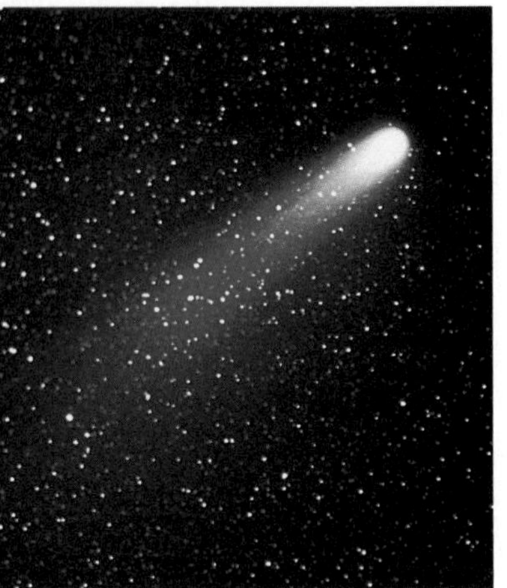

Real-World Connection

Astronomers use patterns to predict the paths of comets.

18. Astronomy Edmond Halley (1656–1742) first saw the comet named for him in 1682. He correctly predicted that it would return about every 76 years.

a. Based on Halley's calculations, when did the comet last appear?

b. When is the comet expected to return next? About how old will you be when that happens?

c. Number Sense Did Halley see the comet a second time? Explain.

Find the missing term.

19. 7, 21, 63, ■, 567

20. 352, ■, 88, 44, 22, 11

21. ■, 180, 144, 108

22. 1, 0.2, 0.04, ■, 0.0016

23. 1.2, 2.4, ■, 9.6, 19.2

24. ■, 91, 83, 75

25. Writing in Math Write a number pattern and its rule.

26. Business A dry cleaner charges $5.00 to clean one item. He offers to clean a second item for $4.50, and a third item for $4.00.

a. If he continues to subtract $.50 for each additional item, how much will it cost to clean six items?

b. If the pattern continues, which item will be cleaned for free?

27. Computers The Difference Engine is a computer designed by Charles Babbage (1791–1871). If you feed it a list of numbers, it will look for a pattern and continue the list, if possible. Why do you think the computer was given this name?

Geometry **Draw the next design in each pattern.**

28.

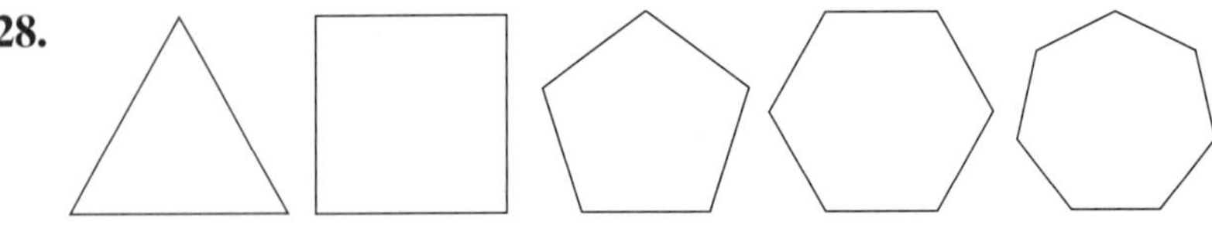

29.

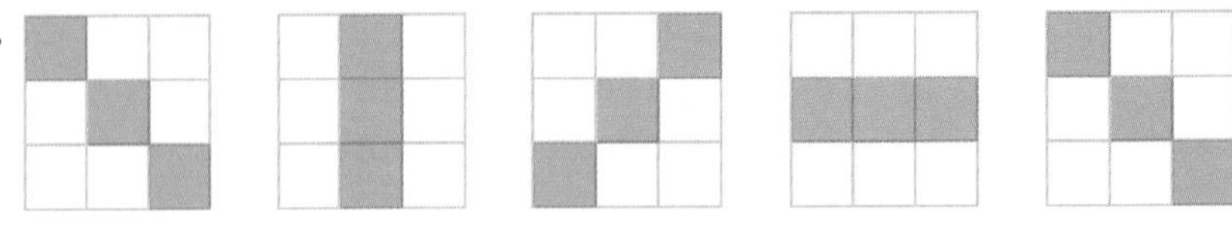

Challenge

30. The number pattern below is called a Fibonacci sequence. Write a rule to describe this number pattern.

1, 1, 2, 3, 5, 8, 13, 21, 34, 55, . . .

31. **Stretch Your Thinking** How many different straight lines can you draw through any two of the points at the right?

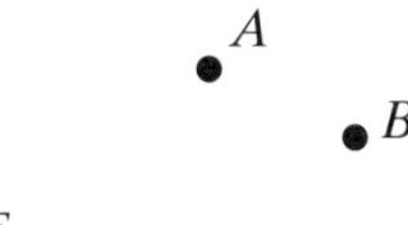

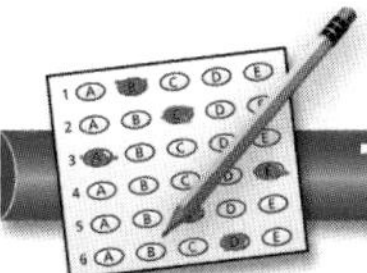

Test Prep

Reading Comprehension

Read the article below and answer Exercises 32 and 33.

Leap Year

It takes about 365.24 days for Earth to orbit the sun. Four years of 365.24 days is about three years with 365 days each, plus a fourth year with 366 days. This fourth year is known as a "leap year."

In a leap year, February has 29 days. A leap year is any year that can be divided by 4, except century years, such as 1500. Only century years that can be divided evenly by 400, such as 1600, are leap years.

32. Which years between 2007 and 2030 will be leap years?

33. Will 2100 be a leap year? Explain.

Multiple Choice

34. What is the value of the missing term? 102, 94, 86, ■, 70, 62, 54.
 A. 76 B. 78 C. 79 D. 80

35. What is the fifth term in the number pattern? 1; 20; 400; 8,000; . . .
 F. 8,400 G. 16,000 H. 80,000 I. 160,000

36. What is the fifth term in the number pattern? 3, 7, 11, 15, . . .
 A. 16 B. 17 C. 18 D. 19

Take It to the NET
Online lesson quiz at
www.PHSchool.com
Web Code: aaa-0201

Mixed Review

Lesson 1-5

First estimate then find each sum or difference.

37. 15.1 − 11.9 38. 1.10 − 0.04 39. 50.2 − 0.99

40. 17.2 − 4.5 41. 2.005 + 2.307 42. 8.01 + 1.7 + 1.09

Algebra

2-2 Variables and Expressions

What You'll Learn

To use variables

To evaluate algebraic expressions

. . . And Why

To describe earnings, as in Example 3

Check Skills You'll Need

For help, go to Lesson 1-10.

Find the value of each expression.

1. $40 - 16 \div 2$
2. $3 \times 5 + 12 \div 3$
3. $7 \times (9.5 - 3.2)$
4. $48 \div (5.8 + 6.2)$

New Vocabulary

- numerical expression
- variable
- algebraic expression
- evaluate

Interactive lesson includes instant self-check, tutorials, and activities.

OBJECTIVE

1 Using Variables

Investigation: Patterns and Algebraic Expressions

1. Copy each diagram. From point *A* on each figure draw a segment to the point or points not connected to *A*.

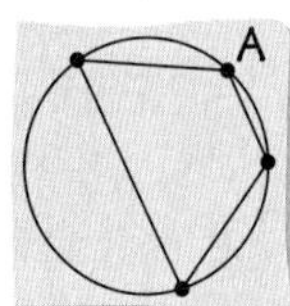

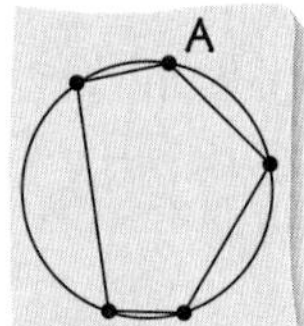

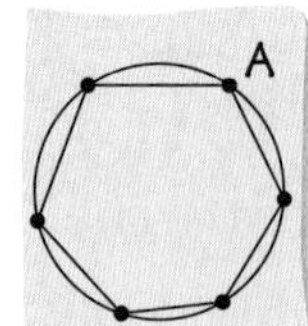

2. Copy and complete the table using your answers to Question 1.

Number of points on circle	4	5	6
Number of segments drawn from *A* to points not connected to *A*	■	■	■

3. a. Extend your table to include 7 points and 8 points on a circle.
   b. Suppose there are *n* points on a circle. How many segments would connect *A* to points not next to *A*?

The following expressions are numerical expressions.

$8 + 5 - 2$ $\qquad 25 \times 4 - 9^2 \times 13$ $\qquad (7 - 6 \div 3) \times 12$

A **numerical expression** is a mathematical phrase with only numbers and operation symbols ($+, -, \times, \div$).

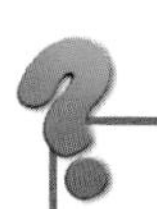

Need Help?
The expression 5*d* means "5 times a number *d*."

The following mathematical expressions have symbols that represent unknown numbers.

$n + 2$ $5d$ $7b - 2$ $12x \div 3$

In the expressions above, *n*, *a*, *b*, and *x* are variables. A **variable** is a symbol that represents one or more numbers. A mathematical expression with one or more variables is an **algebraic expression.**

You can model algebraic expressions using algebra tiles.

A yellow tile represents 1.

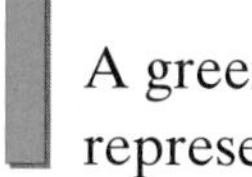

A green tile represents a variable.

1 EXAMPLE From Expressions to Algebra Tiles

Model the expression $5x + 3$ with algebra tiles.

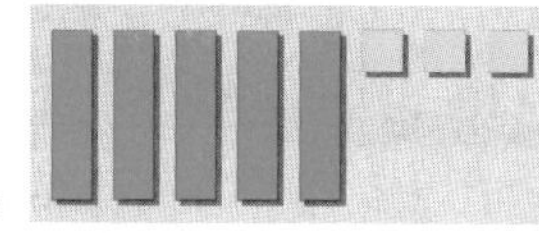

← **5 green tiles represent 5*x*, and 3 yellow tiles represent 3.**

Check Understanding 1 Draw algebra tiles to model each expression.

a. $3x$ **b.** $x + 2$ **c.** $4x + 3$

OBJECTIVE

2 Evaluating Algebraic Expressions

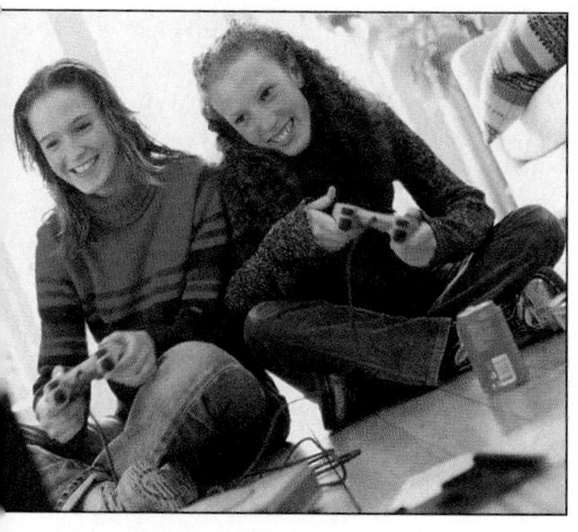

The first screen of a video game usually asks, "How many players?" The number of players is a variable. The game software uses your entry to set up the game.

Similarly, to **evaluate** an algebraic expression, you replace each variable with a number. Use the order of operations to simplify the expression.

2 EXAMPLE Evaluating Algebraic Expressions

Evaluate $2x - 8$ for $x = 11$.

$2x - 8 = 2(11) - 8$ ← **Replace *x* with 11.**

$= 22 - 8$ ← **Multiply 2 and 11.**

$= 14$ ← **Subtract 8 from 22.**

Check Understanding 2 Evaluate each expression for $x = 7$.

a. $3x + 15$ **b.** $5x \div 7$ **c.** $56 - 4x$

d. Reasoning Explain how you used the order of operations to evaluate the expression in part (c).

3 EXAMPLE Real-World Problem Solving

Fundraising The history club sells magazine subscriptions to earn money for a trip to the state capitol. For each subscription, the club earns \$3. The expression $3s$ represents the amount of money the club earns. Complete the table for the given number of subscriptions.

Number of Subscriptions	Dollars Club Earns
s	$3s$
15	■
40	■
65	■

Substitute each number of subscriptions for *s*.

← 3 × 15 = 45

← 3 × 40 = 120

← 3 × 65 = 195

✓ Check Understanding 3 How much will the club earn if they sell 85 subscriptions?

More Than One Way

Jessica and Luis want to make a long-distance call. The call costs 10 cents, plus 4.5 cents for each minute. How much will an 8-minute call cost?

Jessica's Method

To find the cost of the call, I can use the algebraic expression $10 + 4.5m$, with m representing the number of minutes. Then I will evaluate the expression for $m = 8$.

$10 + 4.5m = 10 + 4.5(8)$ ← **Replace *m* with 8.**

$= 10 + 36$ ← **Multiply 4.5 and 8.**

$= 46$ ← **Add 10 and 36.**

The telephone call will cost 46 cents.

Luis's Method

If one minute costs 4.5 cents, then a two-minute call will cost 9 cents, a four-minute call will cost 18 cents, and an eight-minute call will cost 36 cents. I need to add the 10 cents. So the total cost is 36 + 10, or 46 cents.

Choose a Method

Another long-distance plan charges 5 cents per call, plus 4 cents for each minute. Find how much a 10-minute call costs with this plan. Explain why you chose the method you used.

For more practice, see *Extra Practice.*

A Practice by Example

Draw algebra tiles to model each expression.

Example 1 (page 69)

1. $3x + 5$ **2.** $c + 3$ **3.** 8 **4.** $z + 4$

5. $4 + 2x$ **6.** $a + 6$ **7.** $c + c + c$ **8.** $3m + 2$

Example 2 (page 69)

Evaluate each expression for $x = 8$.

9. $x + 12$ **10.** $80 \div x$ **11.** $2x - 3$ **12.** $2(x - 3)$

13. $10 + 2x$ **14.** $12x$ **15.** $42(x - 7)$ **16.** $2x \div 4$

Example 3 (page 70)

17. Rentals The rental fee for a bicycle is \$5, plus \$2 for each hour h the bike is rented. The expression for the total cost is $5 + 2h$. Copy and complete the table for the given number of hours.

Hour	Rental Fee
h	$5 + 2h$
1	■
2	■
3	■

B Apply Your Skills

Evaluate each expression.

18. $24 \div d$ for $d = 3$

19. $p + 8$ for $p = 6$

20. $3r - 2$ for $r = 65$

21. $8b - 12$ for $b = 2.1$

22. $n \div 10$ for $n = 30$

23. $n \div 10$ for $n = 17$

24. $3(2c)$ for $c = 3$

25. $18 - 3y$ for $y = 2.5$

26. $75s$ for $s = 5$

27. $5x - y$ for $x = 12, y = 14$

28. Writing in Math How are numerical and algebraic expressions different? Give examples.

29. Data File, p. 61 Write an expression for finding the Year of the Dog starting with the year 2006.

30. Bricklayer's Formula The formula $N = 7 \times \ell \times h$ gives the number of bricks needed for a wall of length ℓ feet and height h feet. How many bricks are needed for a wall with length 22 feet and height 30 feet?

Copy and complete each table.

31.

x	$x + 6$
1	7
4	■
7	■

32.

x	$7x$
2	■
4	■
6	■

33.

x	$100 - x$
20	■
35	■
50	■

C Challenge

Evaluate each expression.

34. $x + y$ for $x = 12$ and $y = 37$

35. $2r + st$ for $r = 7, s = 30$, and $t = 5$

36. $4m + n$ for $m = 1.5$ and $n = 2.2$

37. $2ab$ for $a = 35$ and $b = 3$

38. $11t - 6v$ for $t = 9$ and $v = 4$

39. $2x + 3y$ for $x = 3$ and $y = 4$

40. **Stretch Your Thinking** A class attended a school fair. For one activity, each of the 25 students in the class got one throw. When the ball hit the target, the class got 12 points toward prizes. They lost 8 points for each miss. The class started with a score of 0 and ended with a score of 0. How many hits and how many misses did the class have?

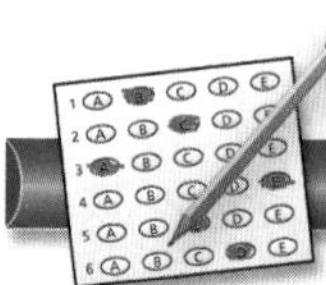

Test Prep

Multiple Choice

41. What is the value of $3p + 6$ when $p = 7$?
A. 7 B. 21 C. 27 D. 45

42. Which number pattern can be described by the rule *start with 1 and multiply by 4 repeatedly*?
F. 1, 3, 5, 7, . . . G. 1, 2, 4, 7, . . . H. 1, 5, 9, 13, . . . I. 1, 4, 16, 64, . . .

Take It to the NET
Online lesson quiz at **www.PHSchool.com**
Web Code: aaa-0202

43. Which of the following numbers can replace x in the expression $4.75x + 1$ and produce a whole number?
A. 2 B. 3 C. 4 D. 5

Mixed Review

Lesson 2-1

Algebra **Write the next two terms in each number pattern.**

44. 32, 35, 38, 41, . . .

45. 729, 243, 81, 27, . . .

46. 101, 97, 93, 89, . . .

Lesson 1-7

Find each product.

47. 2.43×12

48. 4.05×1.5

49. 37.4×0.001

Reading Math

Reading Algebraic Expressions

For Use With Lesson 2-2

To read or evaluate an algebraic expression, you must identify the operations. Sometimes, numbers or variables are placed next to each other without an operation symbol between them.

Expression	Meaning
$3\frac{1}{2}$	You read $3\frac{1}{2}$ as "three and one half." The word *and* translates to addition. So, $3\frac{1}{2}$ means "3 plus $\frac{1}{2}$."
$3n$	In $3n$, multiplication is an unwritten operation. $3n$ means "3 times n."
$\frac{18}{a}$	The fraction bar represents division, so $\frac{18}{a}$ means "18 divided by a."

Sometimes, a slight change in words can greatly affect what an expression means and how to write it.

$n < 3$ means "n is less than 3."

$3 - n$ means "n less than 3" or "3 minus n."

$n - 3$ means "n less 3" or "n minus 3."

EXAMPLE Reading Expressions

Read each of the following.

Expression	**How to read the expression**
a. $7c$	"seven times c"
b. $x > 6.3$	"x is greater than six and three tenths."
c. $\frac{t}{4} + 1$	"t divided by four, plus one"

EXERCISES

1. Write an algebraic expression for the sum of n and 2.

2. Reasoning Is "5 less than 11" the same as "5 less 11"? Explain.

Write each of the following in words as you would read it.

3. $d + 7x$ **4.** $3 \cdot d$ **5.** $6 < z$ **6.** $\frac{a}{9}$

7. $y - 6z$ **8.** $8 < 5w$ **9.** $12 \div r$ **10.** $5\frac{1}{2} - b$

Algebra

2-3 Writing Algebraic Expressions

What You'll Learn

To write algebraic expressions

To use algebraic expressions

. . . And Why

To describe total cost, as in Example 2

Check Skills You'll Need

For help, go to Lesson 2-2.

Evaluate each expression for $a = 7$.

1. $a + 3$ **2.** $a - 6$ **3.** $2a + 1$

4. $7a - 19$ **5.** $6 \cdot (a + 1)$ **6.** $2 + (2a - 5)$

OBJECTIVE

Interactive lesson includes instant self-check, tutorials, and activities.

1 Relating Words to Algebraic Expressions

You can write a word phrase as an algebraic expression.

Operation	Word Phrase	Algebraic Expression
addition	a number plus 45 the sum of a number and 45 45 more than a number	$m + 45$
subtraction	a number minus 6 the difference of a number and 6 6 subtracted from a number	$p - 6$
multiplication	4 times a number the product of 4 and a number	$4k$
division	the quotient of a number and 25 a number divided by 25	$\frac{z}{25}$

1 EXAMPLE From Words to Expressions

Write an expression for each word phrase.

a. 2 more than x

$x + 2$

b. the product of 7 and k

$7 \cdot k$, or $7k$

Check Understanding 1 Write an expression for each word phrase.

a. five divided by y **b.** six times z **c.** m increased by 3.4

Drawing a diagram can help you write an algebraic expression for a real-world situation.

2 EXAMPLE **Real-World Problem Solving**

Bowling When Tai goes bowling on Saturday afternoons, he bowls three games. Shoe rental for the day is $1.75. Use g for the cost of one game. Write an algebraic expression for the total Tai pays when he bowls.

Total Cost			
g	g	g	1.75

Write the cost of 3 games as 3*g*.

The total cost is $3g + 1.75$.

Check Understanding 2 At the end of a space flight, an astronaut's height can temporarily be 2 inches greater than normal. Write an algebraic expression that describes an astronaut's height h after a flight.

OBJECTIVE

2 Using Algebraic Expressions

You can use an algebraic expression to describe the relationship of data in a table.

3 EXAMPLE **From Patterns to Expressions**

Write an expression to describe the relationship of the data in the table.

n	■
1	14
2	15
3	16

$1 + 13 = 14$
$2 + 13 = 15$
$3 + 13 = 16$

Adding 13 to each number in the first column gives you the number in the second column.

The expression $n + 13$ describes the pattern.

Check Understanding 3 Write an expression to describe the relationship of the data in each table.

a.

n	■
2	1
6	3
9	4.5

b.

n	■
2	6
5	9
7	11

Sometimes you will need to decide on what variable to use and state what it represents in a real-world situation.

4 EXAMPLE Real-World Problem Solving

Age Brandon is 5 years older than his sister Ruth. Write an expression using Brandon's age to describe Ruth's age.

Let b = Brandon's age. ← **You don't know Brandon's age, so choose a variable to represent it.**

Since Brandon is older than Ruth, Ruth's age is 5 years *less* than Brandon's age. So, Ruth's age is $b - 5$.

Check Understanding 4 **a.** Brandon is 28 years younger than his father. Write an expression using Brandon's age to describe his father's age.

b. If Brandon is 13, how old is his father?

EXERCISES

For more practice, see *Extra Practice*.

A Practice by Example

Write an expression for each word phrase.

Example 1 (page 74)

1. 34 less than k **2.** 4 plus e **3.** d more than 50

4. 23 times q **5.** 7 decreased by b **6.** b divided by 3

Example 2 (page 75)

Draw a model for each situation. Then write an expression.

7. Boating A paddle boat rents for \$10 plus \$8 per hour. How much does it cost to rent a paddle boat for h hours?

8. You buy one 10-pack of juice boxes. Each juice box contains j ounces. How many ounces of juice did you buy?

Example 3 (page 75)

Write an expression to describe the relationship of the data in each table.

9.

n	■
10	7
12	9
15	12

10.

n	■
1	7
2	14
3	21

11.

n	■
3	5
4.5	6.5
7	9

Example 4 (page 76)

12. a. Jobs Jon and his two brothers make money by doing yardwork for neighbors. The boys split the money equally. Write an expression that describes how much money each boy makes in one day.

b. If they get \$36 for yardwork, how much does each boy receive?

13. a. A bike shop has been in business 20 years longer than a skateboard store across the street. The bike shop is y years old. Write an expression for the number of years the skateboard store has been in business.

b. If the bike shop is 27 years old, how old is the skateboard store?

B Apply Your Skills

Write an expression to describe the relationship of the data in each table.

14.

n	■
42	7
54	9
72	12

15.

n	■
1	11
2	22
3	33

16.

n	■
30	23
45	38
52	45

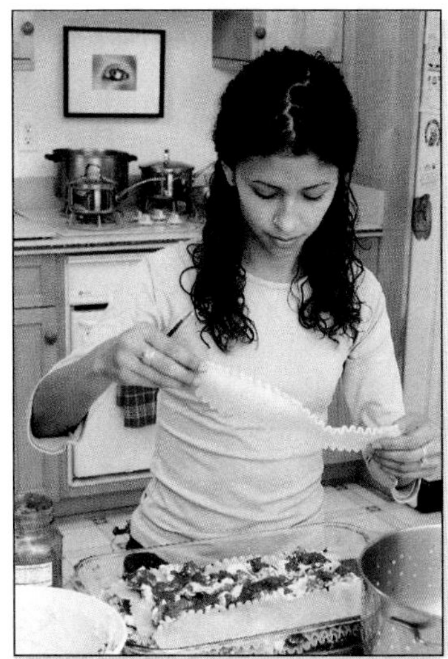

Real-World Connection

A regular-size pan of lasagna weighs about 3 pounds.

17. a. **Cooking** The largest pan of lasagna weighed 3,477 pounds. The length of the pan was ten times its width. Write an algebraic expression for the length of the pan of lasagna in terms of its width w.

b. The lasagna measured 7 feet wide. Evaluate the expression to find the length of the pan of lasagna.

Write an expression for each word phrase.

18. 5 less than the quotient of m and n

19. 12 greater than the product of 3 and j

20. **Buying Paint** Customers in a paint store use the chart at the right to decide how many gallons of paint they need. Write an expression that relates the painted area A in square feet to the number of gallons of paint.

Area sq ft.	Gallons
400	1
800	2
2,000	5
3,200	8

21. **Writing in Math** Describe a situation you could model with $y + 50$.

22. **Zoo** On Saturday, admission to the zoo costs \$3 per person. The Sengs have a coupon for a discount of \$5 off for a family. There are p people in the Seng family. Write an expression for how much the Sengs pay for admission to the zoo if they use the coupon.

C Challenge

23. A store that personalizes T-shirts charges \$20 for a shirt plus \$.75 for each letter. Write an algebraic expression for the total cost of a shirt using n letters.

24. **Stretch Your Thinking** The 4-digit number 2, ■ ■ 5 is a product of a number by itself. What are the two missing digits?

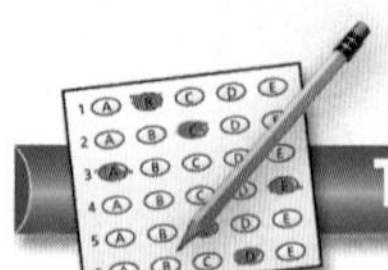

Test Prep

Multiple Choice

25. Which of the following describes the expression uv?
   A. the difference of u and v
   B. the total of u and v
   C. u divided by v
   D. the product of u and v

26. Which of the following does NOT describe the expression $x - 36$?
   F. x minus 36
   G. x less than 36
   H. 36 subtracted from x
   I. 36 less than x

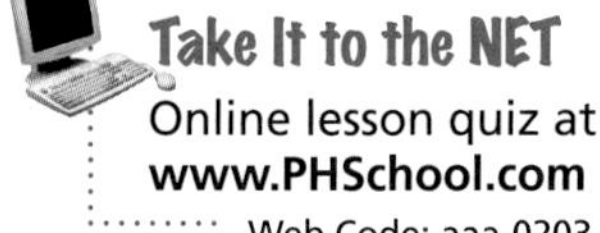

Take It to the NET
Online lesson quiz at
www.PHSchool.com
Web Code: aaa-0203

27. In what order should operations be performed in the expression $36 \times 7 - 12 \div 2 + 3$?
   A. $\times\ -\ \div\ +$
   B. $-\ +\ \times\ \div$
   C. $\div\ \times\ +\ -$
   D. $\times\ \div\ -\ +$

28. If you know the dimensions of a piece of property, which operation will be most useful in finding the perimeter of the property?
   F. addition
   G. subtraction
   H. multiplication
   I. division

Mixed Review

Lesson 1-5

Find each sum.

29. $4.432 + 1.009$ **30.** $2.005 + 12.5$ **31.** $2.449 + 0.7$

Lesson 1-4

Estimate each product by first rounding to the nearest whole number.

32. 2.25×13.76 **33.** 38.1×9.87 **34.** 15.23×3.47

Checkpoint Quiz 1 — Lessons 2-1 through 2-3

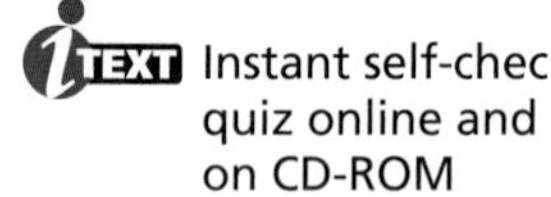

Instant self-check quiz online and on CD-ROM

Write the next three terms and write a rule for each pattern.

1. $1, 6, 36, 216, \ldots$ **2.** $285, 270, 255, 240, \ldots$ **3.** $50, 5, 0.5, 0.05, \ldots$

Evaluate each expression for $x = 7$.

4. $8x$ **5.** $3 \cdot (x - 4)$ **6.** $3x \div 2$

Write an expression for each word phrase.

7. d less than 17 **8.** a times e **9.** 14 divided by q

10. **a.** Each guest receives five party favors. Write an expression that describes the total number of party favors Mrs. Jones bought if three favors are left.
b. If there were 12 guests, how many favors did Mrs. Jones buy?

Extension Using Formulas

For Use With Lesson 2-3

A formula is an equation that shows a relationship between quantities that are represented by variables.

1 EXAMPLE

The formula $d = rt$ relates distance d, rate r, and time t. How far will you travel if you drive with an average speed (rate) of 52 miles per hour for 3 hours?

$d = rt$ ← **Write the formula.**

$d = 52 \cdot 3$ ← **Substitute 52 for *r* and 3 for *t*.**

$d = 156$ ← **Multiply.**

You will travel 156 miles.

2 EXAMPLE

The formula $F = \frac{n}{4} + 37$ relates the number of chirps a cricket makes in one minute n to the approximate outside temperature in Fahrenheit F. Estimate the temperature when a cricket chirps 88 times in one minute.

$F = \frac{n}{4} + 37$ ← **Write the formula.**

$F = \frac{88}{4} + 37$ ← **Substitute 88 for *n*.**

$F = 22 + 37$ ← **Divide.**

$F = 59$ ← **Add.**

The temperature is about 59°F.

EXERCISES

1. Use the formula in Example 2 to estimate the temperature outside if a cricket chirps 104 times in one minute.

2. A plane flies at a speed of about 325 miles per hour. Use the formula $d = rt$ to find how far it travels in 4 hours.

Use the formula $P = 2\ell + 2w$, to find the perimeter of each rectangle.

3. 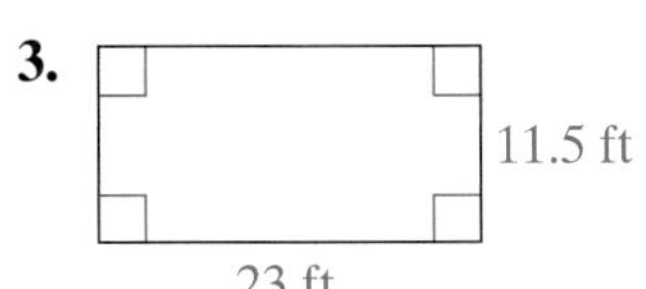

4. 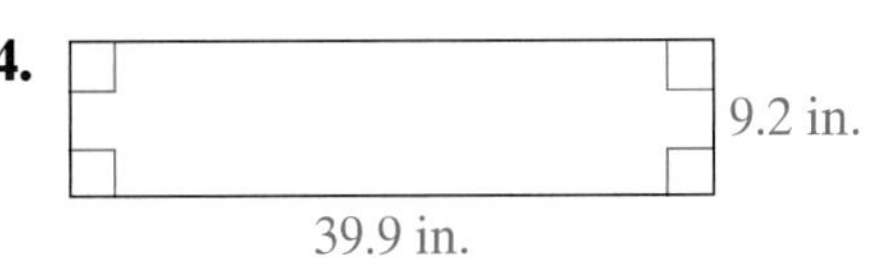

Problem Solving

2-4 Make a Table and Look for a Pattern

What You'll Learn

To solve problems by making a table to find a pattern

. . . And Why

To organize information, as in Example 1

Check Skills You'll Need

For help, go to Lesson 2-1.

Write the next three terms in each number pattern.

1. 1, 4, 16, 64, . . .
2. 7, 14, 21, 28, . . .
3. 7, 14, 28, 56, . . .
4. 88, 79, 70, 61, . . .
5. 1.7, 2.8, 3.9, 5.0, . . .
6. 80, 40, 20, 10, . . .

OBJECTIVE

Interactive lesson includes instant self-check, tutorials, and activities.

1 Solving Problems by Making a Table to Find a Pattern

When to Use This Strategy You can make a table to help you look for a pattern. Then you can use the pattern to solve a problem.

1 EXAMPLE Make a Table to Find a Pattern

A rectangular table seats two people on each end and three on each side. How many seats are available if you push the ends of five tables together?

Read and Understand There are five rectangular tables. Each table seats two people on each end and three on a side.

Plan and Solve To find the number of seats when five tables are pushed together, start by finding the number of seats when there are fewer tables.

1 table → 10 seats

2 tables → 16 seats

3 tables → 22 seats

Number of Tables	1	2	3	4	5
Number of Seats	10	16	22	28	34

Extend the pattern by adding 6 seats for each new table.

There will be 34 seats available.

Look Back and Check Five tables pushed together seat 5×6, or 30, people on the sides and 2 people on each end, or $30 + 2 + 2 = 34$.

Check Understanding **1** **Number Sense** Is the number of available seats for 20 tables pushed together twice the number of seats for ten tables pushed together? Explain.

EXERCISES

For more practice, see *Extra Practice.*

Practice by Example

Example 1 (page 80)

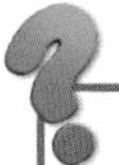

Need Help?
- Reread the problem.
- Identify the key facts and details.
- Tell the problem in your own words.
- Try a different strategy.
- Check your work.

Solve each problem by making a table and looking for a pattern.

1. Suppose a rectangular table seats four people on one side and three on each end. How many seats are available if the ends of seven tables are pushed together?

2. **Savings** A high school student has started a new job. He plans to save \$1 the first week, \$2 the second week, \$4 the third week, and \$8 the fourth week. If this pattern of savings could continue, how much would he save the tenth week?

3. a. Fence posts are 10 feet apart. How many fence posts are required for a straight fence that is 100 feet long?
   b. What if the fence is circular?

4. **Geometry** A figure made from seven identical trapezoids is shown. Find the perimeter of the figure.

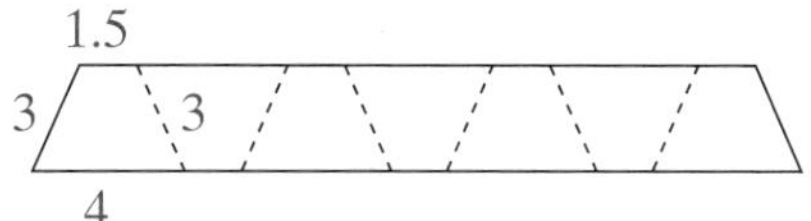

Apply Your Skills

Strategies

Draw a Diagram
Make a Graph
Make an Organized List
Make a Table and Look for a Pattern
Simulate a Problem
Solve a Simpler Problem
Try, Check, and Revise
Use Logical Reasoning
Work Backward
Write an Equation

Choose a strategy to solve the problem.

5. **Cars** A car dealer sells at least 3 cars a day. On Monday morning there are 50 cars on the lot. By Friday evening of that week, what is the greatest number of cars the dealer can expect to have left?

6. **Jobs** Sanjay earns \$13.00 each week from his paper route. He earns \$.15 for each daily paper and \$.35 for each Sunday paper he delivers. He delivers twice as many daily papers as Sunday papers. How many of each type does he deliver each week?

7. **Band** Tia, Lewis, and Jill play trombone. Wendi, Pali, and Nigel play baritone. How many different pairs of a trombone player and a baritone player are there?

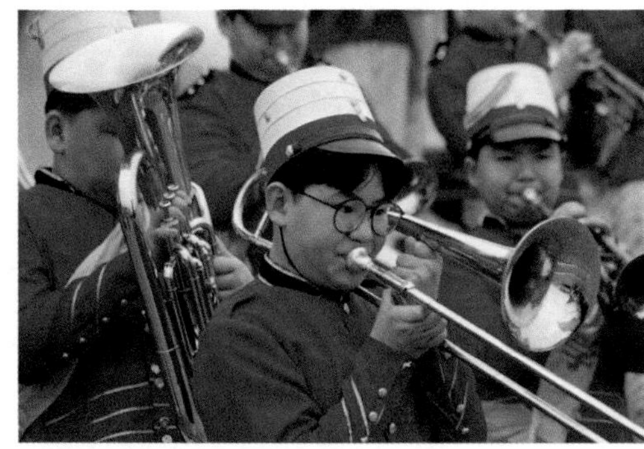

8. **Writing in Math** Your younger brother is pulling his sled up a hill. Each minute he moves forward 20 feet but also slides back 3 feet. Describe how you can determine the time he needs to pull his sled 130 feet forward.

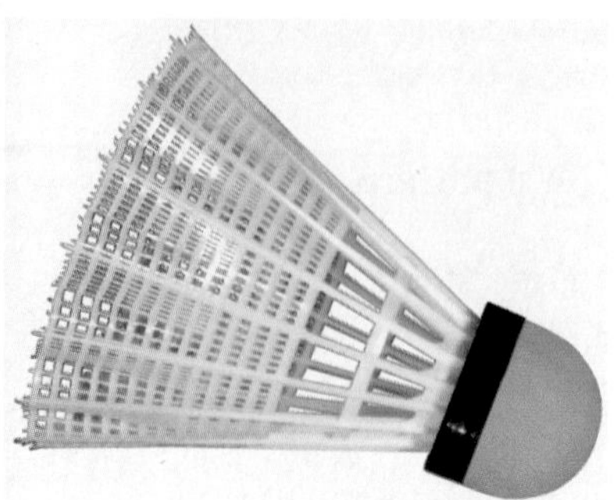

9. **Geometry** This figure is made from a chain of five identical hexagons. All sides are 6 inches. Find the perimeter of the figure.

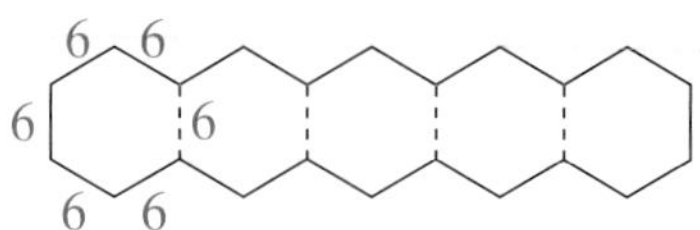

10. **Sports** At the beginning of a single's badminton tournament, 24 players are paired. At the end of each match, the loser is eliminated. How many matches must be played to determine the winner of the tournament?

C Challenge

11. There are 6 ways to add any of the numbers 3, 5, 7, 9, 11, and 12 to get a sum of 20. Numbers may be repeated. One way to get a sum of 20 is $9 + 5 + 3 + 3$. Find four other ways.

12. **Stretch Your Thinking** The sum of three consecutive odd numbers is 387. Find the numbers.

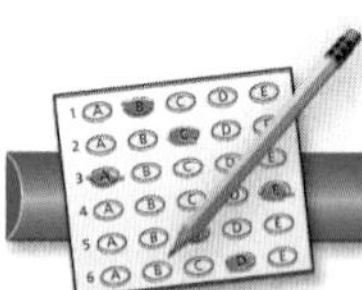

Test Prep

Multiple Choice

13. What is the value of $8x - 6$ when $x = 4$?
A. 16 B. 26 C. 32 D. 38

14. What is the value of $5n + 2$ when $n = 9$?
F. 43 G. 45 H. 47 I. 55

15. For which value of a does $7a - 2$ equal 40?
A. 4 B. 6 C. 10 D. 11

16. Which expression represents x decreased by 4?
F. $x - 4$ G. 4 H. $\frac{x}{4}$ I. $4 - x$

Take It to the NET
Online lesson quiz at
www.PHSchool.com
Web Code: aaa-0204

Mixed Review

Lesson 2-3

Algebra **Write an expression for each word phrase.**

17. 12 times c
18. 9 multiplied by d
19. n more than 4.5
20. 6.8 less than g
21. r less than 13
22. 8.1 decreased by y

Lesson 2-2

Algebra **Evaluate each expression for $x = 6$.**

23. $2x - 9$
24. $x + 15$
25. $4 \cdot (x + 2)$
26. $52.7 - 3x$
27. $4x + 3$
28. $5x - (x + 2)$

Writing to Compare

For Use With Lesson 2-4

When you are asked to compare two methods or concepts, you should
a. Describe each concept. Try to include diagrams to illustrate your descriptions.
b. State any similarities and differences between the two concepts.

EXAMPLE

Compare the following two rules for patterns.

i. Start with 1 and add 2 repeatedly.
ii. Multiply the term number by 2, and subtract 1 to get the next term.

a. Describe each rule.

- The first rule begins with 1; you find the next term by adding 2.
  The pattern is 1, 3, 5, 7, 9, . . .
- In the second rule, the first term is $1 \times 2 - 1 = 1$; the next term is $2 \times 2 - 1 = 3$, and so on.
  The pattern is 1, 3, 5, 7, 9, . . .

b. State any similarities or differences.

- Both rules result in the same pattern: 1, 3, 5, 7, 9, . . .
- The first rule uses the *previous term* to get the next term. The second rule uses the *term number* to get the new term.
- The first rule uses addition; the second rule uses multiplication and subtraction.

EXERCISES

1. Compare the following two rules for number patterns.

i. Start with 1 and add 4 repeatedly.
ii. Multiply the term number by 4, and then subtract 3 to get the term.

2. Compare the following two rules for number patterns.

i. Multiply the term number by itself.
ii. Start with 1. Find the next term by adding 3, and next by adding 5, and so on.

3. Compare "simplifying an expression" and "evaluating an expression."

Algebra

2-5 Using Number Sense to Solve One-Step Equations

What You'll Learn

To use mental math to solve equations

To estimate solutions of equations

. . . And Why

To solve problems using mental math, as in Example 2

For help, go to Lesson 1-5.

Estimate by first rounding to the nearest whole number.

1. $5.3 + 1.07$	**2.** $6.1 - 2.4$
3. $8 - 6.3$	**4.** $12.04 + 3.6$
5. $24 + 0.085$	**6.** $4.5 - 0.106$

New Vocabulary • equation • open sentence • solution

OBJECTIVE

Interactive lesson includes instant self-check, tutorials, and activities.

1 Using Mental Math to Solve Equations

An **equation** is a mathematical sentence that has an equal sign, =. An equation is like a balanced scale. To be in balance, a scale must have weights with the same total on each side. A true equation has equal values on each side of the equal sign.

$8 + 4 = 3 \times 4$

If each side of the equation does not have the same value, the equation is false. Use $\neq$ to indicate that an equation is false.

1 EXAMPLE Deciding If an Equation Is True or False

Is the equation $6 + 13 = 18$ true or false?

$6 + 13 \stackrel{?}{=} 18$ ← **Write the equation.**

19 ← **Add 6 + 13.**

$19 \neq 18$ ← **Compare.**

The equation is false.

Reading Math

Read "$1 \stackrel{?}{=} 2$" as "Does 1 equal 2?" Read "$1 \neq 2$" as "1 does not equal 2."

1 Tell whether each equation is true or false.

a. $7 \times 9 = 63$ **b.** $4 + 5 = 45$ **c.** $70 - 39 = 41$

An equation with one or more variables is an **open sentence.** A **solution** of an equation is the value of the variable that makes the equation true. For example, $x - 15 = 12$ is an open sentence. Since $27 - 15 = 12$, the value 27 is the solution of $x - 15 = 12$.

You can use mental math to find the solution of some equations.

2 EXAMPLE Using Mental Math

Baseball Cards How many baseball cards do you need to add to the 14 cards you already own to have a total of 25 cards? Solve the equation $n + 14 = 25$, which models this situation.

What you think
$11 + 14 = 25$, so the solution is 11.

You need 11 more cards.

Check Understanding 2 **Mental Math** Use mental math to solve each equation.
a. $17 - x = 8$ **b.** $w \div 4 = 20$ **c.** $4.7 + c = 5.9$

OBJECTIVE

2 Estimating Solutions of Equations

3 EXAMPLE Estimating Solutions

Estimation Estimate the solution of each equation.

a. $n - 3.85 = 12.33$

Round 3.85 and 12.33 to the nearest whole number

$3.85 \approx 4 \quad 12.33 \approx 12$

Estimate the solution of $n - 3.85 = 12.16$ by solving $n - 4 = 12$.

Since $16 - 4 = 12$, the solution of $n - 3.85 = 12.33$ is about 16.

b. $12n = 105$

Use compatible numbers: 12 divides 108 without a remainder and 108 is close to 105. Solve $12n = 108$ to estimate the solution of $12n = 105$.

$12n = 108$

$12 \cdot 9 = 108$

The solution of $12n = 105$ is about 9.

3 **Estimation** Estimate the solution of each equation.
a. $y - 6.14 = 23.08$ **b.** $8.2x = 49.3$ **c.** $d - 3.8 = 14.1$

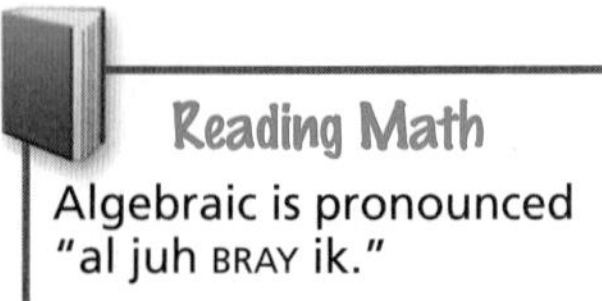

Reading Math

Algebraic is pronounced "al juh BRAY ik."

Many open sentences are true for only one solution. There are some open sentences that are true for every value you use for the variable. The algebraic equations that illustrate the number properties below are true for all values of a, b, and c.

Key Concepts **Number Properties**

Identity Properties

The sum of 0 and any number is that number.

Algebra $0 + a = a$ **Arithmetic** $0 + 9 = 9$

The product of 1 and any number is that number.

Algebra $1 \cdot a = a$ **Arithmetic** $1 \cdot 9 = 9$

Commutative Properties

Changing the order of addends or factors does not change the sum or the product.

Algebra $a + b = b + a$ $a \cdot b = b \cdot a$

Arithmetic $9 + 6 = 6 + 9$ $9 \cdot 6 = 6 \cdot 9$

Associative Properties

Changing the grouping of numbers does not change the sum or the product.

Algebra $a + (b + c) = (a + b) + c$ $a(bc) = (ab)c$

Arithmetic $9 + (6 + 4) = (9 + 6) + 4$ $9 \cdot (6 \cdot 4) = (9 \cdot 6) \cdot 4$

EXERCISES

For more practice, see *Extra Practice*.

Practice by Example

Tell whether each equation is true or false.

Example 1 (page 84)

1. $3 + 50 = 80$ **2.** $4 \times 7 = 28$ **3.** $25 = 35 + 10$

4. $0 \times 5.7 = 5.7$ **5.** $54 \div 9 = 7$ **6.** $3 + 4 + 6 = 3 + 10$

Example 2 (page 85)

Mental Math **Use mental math to solve each equation.**

7. $x + 5 = 7$ **8.** $4x = 32$ **9.** $25 = 25 - x$ **10.** $x + 2 = 6.3$

11. $g \div 4 = 2$ **12.** $p - 6 = 25$ **13.** $x + 14 = 23$ **14.** $1.2 = a + 0.2$

15. Sports A hockey team spends \$75 on chin straps. Each strap costs \$5. Solve the equation $5n = 75$ to find how many straps the team buys.

Example 3 (page 85)

Estimation **Estimate the solution of each equation.**

16. $6d = 75$ **17.** $k + 9.3 = 28.4$ **18.** $p \div 4 = 7.99$

19. $420 = 63n$ **20.** $b - 2.33 = 6.8$ **21.** $w + 12.8 = 68.7$

B Apply Your Skills

Tell whether each equation is true or false.

22. $0 + 3a = 3a$ **23.** $1 \cdot 3a = 3a$ **24.** $3 \cdot 5 + x = 8 + x$

Tell whether the given number is a solution of the equation.

25. $3x + 2x = 10;\ 2$ **26.** $120n = 40;\ 30$ **27.** $b + b = 22;\ 2$

28. Shopping Suppose you spent \$20 for a shirt. You also bought a jacket, but you cannot find the sales receipt. You know that the total amount you spent was \$75. Solve the equation $20 + j = 75$ to find how much you spent on the jacket.

29. Pollution When burned, 18 gallons of gasoline produce about 360 pounds of carbon dioxide. Solve the equation $18n = 360$ to find how much carbon dioxide 1 gallon produces.

30. Writing in Math Write a real-world problem that could be modeled by the equation $x - 7.5 = 1.2$.

Reasoning **Tell whether each equation is true or false. Explain.**

31. $x + 1 = x$ **32.** $3 + x = 1 + 2 + x$

33. $98n = (100 - 2)n$ **34.** $8 + x = x + 8$

Tell which choice, 100, 500, or 1,000, is the best estimate of the solution.

35. $4{,}272 = 53x$ **36.** $n - 89.15 = 326.5$ **37.** $m \div 47 = 8.89$

Real-World Connection

Peanuts are a rich source of protein.

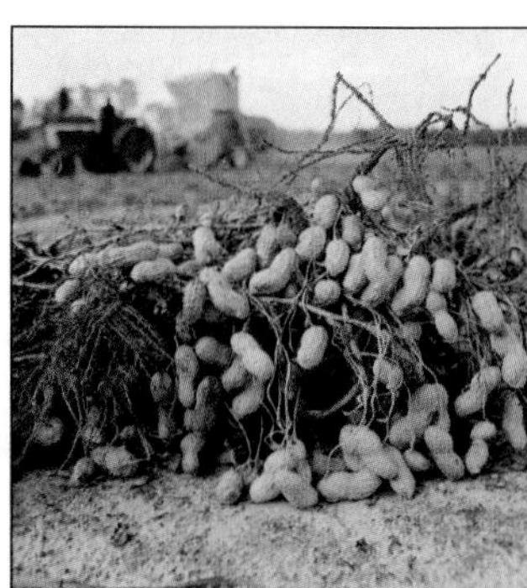

38. You have 1.5 pounds of pecans, a pounds of almonds, and 2.7 pounds of peanuts. You have 6 pounds of nuts altogether. To find how many pounds of almonds you have, solve the equation $1.5 + a + 2.7 = 6$, which models this situation.

39. Error Analysis Your friend claims that the equation $2x = 3x$ is always false. Do you agree with your friend? Explain.

40. Writing in Math Explain how to estimate the solution of the equation $s - 4.87 = 32.42$.

Challenge **Number Sense** **Without solving the equations, tell if each solution is less than, greater than, or equal to 10.**

41. $x + 0.6 = 15$ **42.** $999 = x + 990$ **43.** $10x = 15$

44. $1 = 0.1x$ **45.** $x + 32 = 40$ **46.** $5x = 50$

47. **Stretch Your Thinking** How many different rectangles are in the figure at the right?

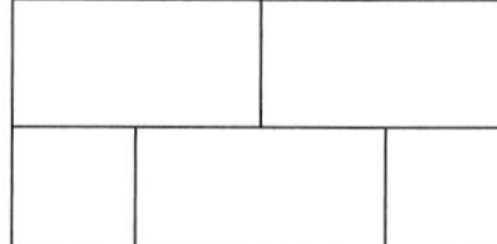

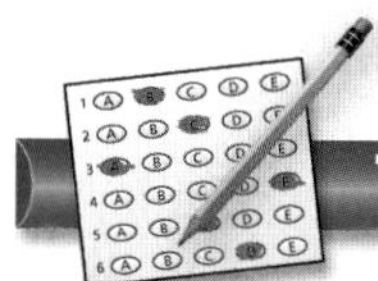

Test Prep

Multiple Choice

48. What is the solution of $n + 62 = 100$?
A. 100 **B.** 62 **C.** 38 **D.** 26

49. What is the solution of $18 = 54 - x$?
F. 72 **G.** 54 **H.** 36 **I.** 18

50. What is the solution of $60 \div n = 4$?
A. 12 **B.** 15 **C.** 64 **D.** 240

Take It to the NET
Online lesson quiz at
www.PHSchool.com
Web Code: aaa-0205

51. What is the solution of $5f = 140$?
F. 5 **G.** 28 **H.** 140 **I.** 700

52. What is the solution of $c \div 4 = 12$?
A. 3 **B.** 8 **C.** 48 **D.** 124

53. Which equation has the solution 22?
F. $2(44) = s$ **G.** $2s = 44$ **H.** $2 \div s = 44$ **I.** $2 = 44s$

Mixed Review

Lesson 2-1

Algebra **Write the next three terms in each number pattern.**

54. 100, 97, 94, 91, . . . **55.** 4, 12, 36, 108, . . .

56. **Algebra** Write the first six terms in the pattern. *Start with 3.2 and multiply by 5 repeatedly.*

Lesson 1-10

Find the value of each expression.

57. $7 \times 8 + 4$ **58.** $2.2 + 3.1 \times 7$ **59.** $9.6 \div 2.4 \times 4$

Investigation: Using Models to Solve Equations

For Use With Lesson 2-6

Models can help you understand the steps you need to follow to solve equations.

1 EXAMPLE Solving Equations by Subtracting

Solve $x + 7 = 15$.

$x + 7 = 15$

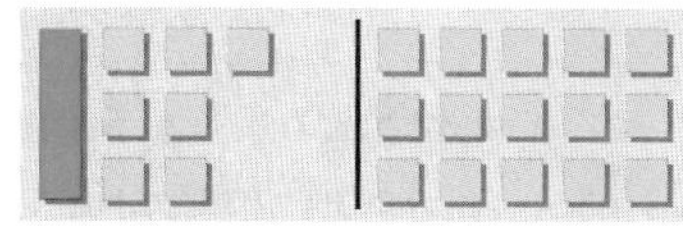

← Model the equation.

$x + 7 = 15$
$\underline{-7} \quad \underline{-7}$

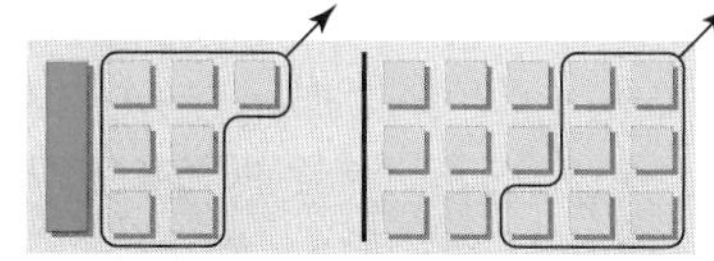

← Remove 7 tiles from each side.

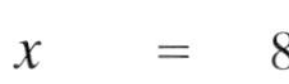

$x = 8$

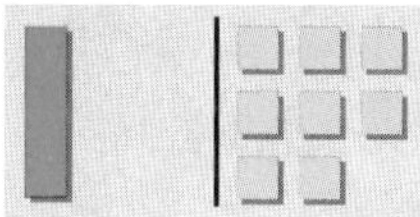

← Find the solution.

2 EXAMPLE Solving Equations by Dividing

Solve $4x = 12$.

$4x = 12$

← Model the equation.

$4x \div 4 = 12 \div 4$

← Divide each side of the equation into 4 equal parts.

$x = 3$

← Find the solution.

EXERCISES

Solve each equation by drawing or using tiles.

1. $x + 2 = 7$

2. $3g = 12$

3. $a + 9 = 12$

4. $5c = 35$

5. $8 = n + 5$

6. $7m = 21$

2-6

Algebra

Solving Addition and Subtraction Equations

What You'll Learn

 To solve equations by subtracting

 To solve equations by adding

. . . And Why

To solve problems involving weights, as in Example 2

Check Skills You'll Need

For help, go to Lesson 2-5.

Use mental math to solve each equation.

1. $3x = 27$ **2.** $4 = 5 - t$ **3.** $x + 4 = 74$

4. $6 \div y = 3$ **5.** $p \div 3 = 3$ **6.** $7x = 21$

New Vocabulary • inverse operations • Subtraction Property of Equality • Addition Property of Equality

OBJECTIVE

Interactive lesson includes instant self-check, tutorials, and activities.

1 Solving Equations by Subtracting

In the equation $x + 4 = 38$, 4 is added to the variable. You undo adding 4 by subtracting 4. Operations that *undo* each other, such as addition and subtraction, are **inverse operations.**

Key Concepts **Subtraction Property of Equality**

If you subtract the same value from each side of an equation, the two sides remain equal.

Arithmetic	Algebra
$2 \cdot 3 = 6$, so $2 \cdot 3 - 4 = 6 - 4$.	If $a = b$, then $a - c = b - c$.

1 EXAMPLE Solving Equations by Subtracting

Solve $x + 4 = 38$.

Get x alone on one side of the equation.

$$x + 4 = 38$$
$$-4 \quad -4$$ ← Subtract 4 from each side to undo the addition and get x by itself.

$$x = 34$$ ← Simplify.

Check $x + 4 = 38$ ← Check your solution in the original equation.

$34 + 4 \stackrel{?}{=} 38$ ← Substitute 34 for x.

$38 = 38$ ✓

 1 Solve $w + 4.3 = 9.1$. Check the solution.

When you solve real-world problems using equations, drawing a diagram first may help you. The model at the right indicates that the whole = part + part.

Whole	
Part	Part

2 EXAMPLE Real-World Problem Solving

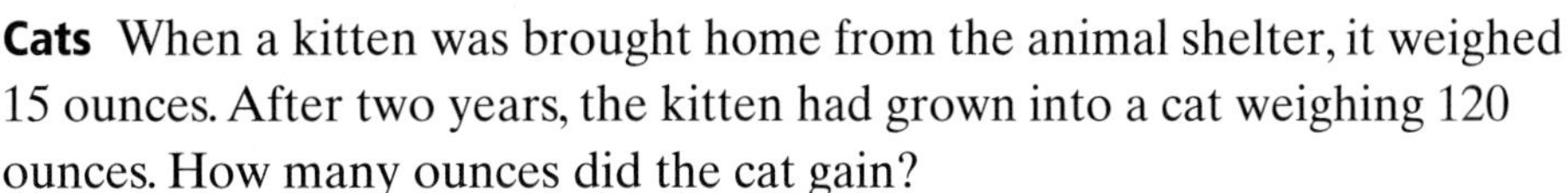

Cats When a kitten was brought home from the animal shelter, it weighed 15 ounces. After two years, the kitten had grown into a cat weighing 120 ounces. How many ounces did the cat gain?

Weight after 2 years	
Original weight	Ounces gained

Let g = the ounces gained.

120	
15	g

The equation $15 + g = 120$ models this situation.

$$15 + g = 120$$

$$\begin{array}{rcl} 15 + g &=& 120 \\ -15 & & -15 \\ \hline g &=& 105 \end{array}$$

← **Subtract 15 from each side to undo the addition.**

← **Simplify.**

The cat gained 105 ounces.

Check Understanding 2 A cat has gained 1.8 pounds since its checkup a year ago. It now weighs 11.6 pounds. How much did it weigh at its checkup last year?

OBJECTIVE

2 Solving Equations by Adding

Just as you can subtract the same amount from each side of an equation, you can add the same amount to each side of an equation.

Key Concepts — Addition Property of Equality

If you add the same value to each side of an equation the two sides remain equal.

Arithmetic	**Algebra**
$2 \cdot 3 = 6$, so $2 \cdot 3 + 4 = 6 + 4$.	If $a = b$, then $a + c = b + c$.

When you have an equation with a number subtracted on one side, add that number to each side of the equation to solve the equations.

3 EXAMPLE Solving Equations by Adding

Solve $c - 12 = 43$.

$c - 12 + 12 = 43 + 12$ ← **Add 12 to undo the subtraction.**

$c = 55$ ← **Simplify.**

Check Understanding 3 Solve each equation.

a. $n - 53 = 28$ **b.** $x - 43 = 12$ **c.** $k - 6.4 = 0$

Another way to model a real-world situation is to start by stating the problem as simply as you can. Then write an equation from your statement.

4 EXAMPLE Real-World Problem Solving

Savings Susan saved \$87.11. Susan's savings are \$9.62 less than Dorinne's savings. How much has Dorinne saved?

Words Susan's savings are \$9.62 less than Dorinne's savings

Let d = Dorinne's savings.

Equation \$87.11 = d − \$9.62

$d - 9.62 = 87.11$ ← **Write the equation.**

$+ 9.62 \quad + 9.62$ ← **Add 9.62 to each side to undo the subtraction.**

$d = 96.73$ ← **Simplify.**

Dorinne has saved \$96.73.

Check Understanding 4 The temperature dropped 9°F between 7 P.M. and midnight. It was 54°F at midnight. Write and solve an equation to find the temperature at 7 P.M.

EXERCISES

For more practice, see *Extra Practice*.

A Practice by Example

Solve each equation. Then check the solution.

Example 1 (page 90)

1. $x + 46 = 72$ **2.** $d + 5 = 53$ **3.** $y + 12 = 64$

4. $n + 17 = 56$ **5.** $m + 1.3 = 2.8$ **6.** $n + 4.5 = 10.8$

7. $k + 8 = 15$ **8.** $2.7 + g = 8.2$ **9.** $2.6 = 1.9 + g$

Example 2 (page 91)

Write and solve an equation. Then check the solution.

10. Biology A hippopotamus can hold its breath for about 15 minutes. A sea otter can hold its breath about 10 minutes less than a hippopotamus. How long can a sea otter hold its breath?

11. Sale Jeans that were on sale last week now cost $29.97. The savings were $4.99. What was the sale price of the jeans?

Example 3 (page 92)

Solve each equation.

12. $x - 16 = 72$ **13.** $x - 5.7 = 5.7$ **14.** $n - 2 = 18$

15. $d - 8 = 40$ **16.** $y - 12 = 23$ **17.** $k - 56 = 107$

18. $5.8 = n - 0.35$ **19.** $0.6 = h - 2.9$ **20.** $q - 8 = 154$

Example 4 (page 92)

21. Biology The height of the female giraffe in one zoo is 14.1 feet. The female is 3.2 feet shorter than the male giraffe. Write and solve an equation to find the male's height.

B Apply Your Skills

Solve each equation.

22. $y + 13.82 = 24$ **23.** $1.5 + x = 9.7$ **24.** $p - 1.23 = 8.77$

25. $0.4 + g = 1.9$ **26.** $n - 10.5 = 11.7$ **27.** $11.4 = h + 5.9$

28. Writing in Math Write a real-world problem that can be solved by writing an equation that contains a variable. Then solve the equation.

29. Estimation Use estimation to check whether 59.4 is a reasonable solution for the equation $x + 27.6 = 31.8$. Explain your answer.

30. You buy a poster and a framing kit. The total cost is $18.95. You have $7.05 left in your wallet. Write and solve an equation to find how much money was in your wallet before these purchases.

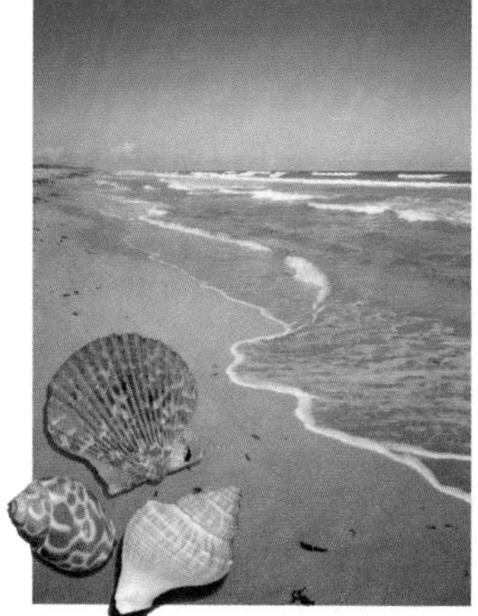

31. National Seashores The area of Cape Canaveral National Seashore in Florida is approximately 57,627 acres. The area of Cape Cod National Seashore in Massachusetts is approximately 14,101 acres smaller. Write and solve an equation to find the approximate area of Cape Cod National Seashore.

32. a. Data File, p. 61 Write and solve an equation to find the last Year of the Monkey prior to 2004.

b. Write and solve an equation to find the next Year of the Dragon.

Challenge

The earliest known number square, the *lo-shu*, was written on a tortoise shell. It may have looked like this drawing.

33. Error Analysis Sonja says the solution to $y - 1{,}214 = 31{,}214$ is 30,000. What is her error?

34. Number Squares In a number square, the sum of the numbers in each row, column, and main diagonal is the same.

a	7	2
1	5	b
8	c	4

a. Find the sum for the square at the right.

b. Use the sum to write and solve equations to find the values of a, b, and c.

35. Stretch Your Thinking A large stepping stone in a garden weighs five times as much as a brick. Together, one brick and one stepping stone weigh 30 pounds. Find the weight of the stepping stone.

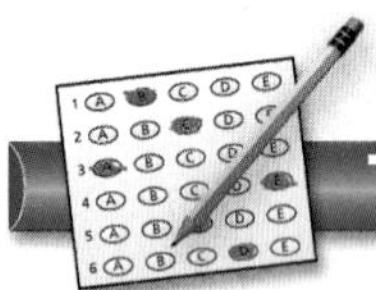

Test Prep

Multiple Choice

36. Which of the following operations would you use to get the variable in $x + 6 = 27$ alone on one side of the equation?

A. Add 6 to both sides. **B.** Subtract 6 from both sides.
C. Add 27 to both sides. **D.** Subtract 27 from both sides.

37. What is the solution of $x - 42 = 17$?

F. 25 **G.** 35 **H.** 49 **I.** 59

38. What is the solution of $n + 16 = 85$?

A. 86 **B.** 83 **C.** 73 **D.** 69

39. What is the solution of $z - 2.71 = 5$?

F. 2.29 **G.** 2.76 **H.** 3.21 **I.** 7.71

40. What is the solution of $86.04 = 57.2 + y$?

A. 143.24 **B.** 29.24 **C.** 29.2 **D.** 28.84

Take It to the NET
Online lesson quiz at
www.PHSchool.com
Web Code: aaa-0206

Mixed Review

Lesson 2-1

41. Algebra Write the first five terms in the number pattern *start with 37 and add 3 repeatedly.*

Lesson 1-10

Find the value of each expression.

42. $24 \div 4 - 2 \times 3$

43. $24 \div 3 - 2 \times 4$

44. $24 \div (3 - 2) \times 4$

45. $(24 \div 3 - 2) \times 4$

Algebra

2-7 Solving Multiplication and Division Equations

What You'll Learn

 To solve equations by dividing

 To solve equations by multiplying

. . . And Why

To split costs equally, as in Example 2

Check Skills You'll Need

For help, go to Lesson 1-4.

Use compatible numbers to estimate each product or quotient.

1. 7.3×1.07 **2.** $6.1 \div 1.1$ **3.** 8×2.3

4. $13.04 \div 3.8$ **5.** $24 \div 3.085$ **6.** 16.1×1.89

New Vocabulary
- **Division Property of Equality**
- **Multiplication Property of Equality**

 Interactive lesson includes instant self-check, tutorials, and activities.

OBJECTIVE 1 Solving Equations by Dividing

You can use the Division Property of Equality to solve equations involving multiplication.

Key Concepts **Division Property of Equality**

If you divide each side of an equation by the same nonzero number, the two sides remain equal.

Arithmetic	Algebra
$4 \times 2 = 8$,	If $a = b$ and $c \neq 0$,
so $4 \times 2 \div 2 = 8 \div 2$.	then $a \div c = b \div c$.

Need Help?
Recall that 4*n* means 4 times *n*. So $4n \div 4 = n$.

1 EXAMPLE Solving Equations by Dividing

Solve $4n = 68$.

$4n \div 4 = 68 \div 4$ ← **Divide each side by 4 to undo the multiplication and get *n* alone on one side.**

$n = 17$ ← **Simplify.**

Check $4n = 68$ ← **Check your solution in the original equation.**

$4 \times 17 \stackrel{?}{=} 68$ ← **Replace *n* with 17.**

$68 = 68$ ✓

 1 Solve each equation. Then check the solution.

a. $9x = 36$ **b.** $10y = 27$ **c.** $0.8p = 32$

2 EXAMPLE Real-World Problem Solving

Buying in Bulk A package of blank CDs costs \$38.88, including tax. Six friends share the CDs and split the cost equally. How much does each friend pay?

Use a diagram to help write an equation.

\$38.88					
c	c	c	c	c	c

Let c = each person's share of the cost of the package of CDs. The equation $6c = 38.88$ models this situation.

$6c = 38.88$ ← **Write the equation.**

$6c \div 6 = 38.88 \div 6$ ← **Divide each side by 6 to undo the multiplication.**

$c = 6.48$ ← **Simplify.**

Each friend's share is \$6.48.

Check Understanding 2 The Pep Club sells greeting cards for a fundraiser. It receives \$.35 profit for each card it sells. The club's total profit is \$302.75. Write and solve an equation to find the number of greeting cards the Pep Club sells.

OBJECTIVE

2 Solving Equations by Multiplying

You can use the Multiplication Property of Equality to solve equations involving division.

Key Concepts **Multiplication Property of Equality**

If you multiply each side of an equation by the same number, the two sides remain equal.

Arithmetic	Algebra
$6 \div 2 = 3$, so $(6 \div 2) \times 2 = 3 \times 2$.	If $a = b$, then $a \cdot c = b \cdot c$.

3 EXAMPLE Solving Equations by Multiplying

Solve $y \div 6.4 = 8$.

$y \div 6.4 \times 6.4 = 8 \times 6.4$ ← **Multiply by 6.4 to undo the division and get y alone.**

$y = 51.2$ ← **Simplify.**

Check Understanding 3 Solve each equation. Then check the solution.

a. $n \div 5 = 40$ **b.** $w \div 1.5 = 10$ **c.** $z \div 0.2 = 7.9$

EXERCISES

For more practice, see *Extra Practice.*

A Practice by Example

Example 1 (page 95)

Solve each equation. Then check the solution.

1. $5a = 100$ **2.** $8k = 76$ **3.** $7n = 11.9$

4. $25h = 450$ **5.** $0.4x = 1$ **6.** $75 = 15c$

7. $16j = 80$ **8.** $2.5g = 17.5$ **9.** $10y = 5$

Example 2 (page 96)

Write and solve an equation for each situation. Then check the solution.

10. Each shelf in a store can hold 24 videos. The store has a total of 8,616 videos. How many shelves are needed for the videos?

11. Geography The area of the Pacific Ocean is about 64,000,000 square miles. This area is about twice the area of the Atlantic Ocean. Find the approximate area of the Atlantic Ocean.

Example 3 (page 96)

Solve each equation. Then check the solution.

12. $q \div 6 = 4$ **13.** $a \div 7 = 63$ **14.** $n \div 2.5 = 3$

15. $y \div 43 = 1{,}204$ **16.** $10 = k \div 20$ **17.** $12 = r \div 9$

18. $n \div 4 = 0.6$ **19.** $t \div 0.3 = 1.4$ **20.** $b \div 11 = 87$

B Apply Your Skills

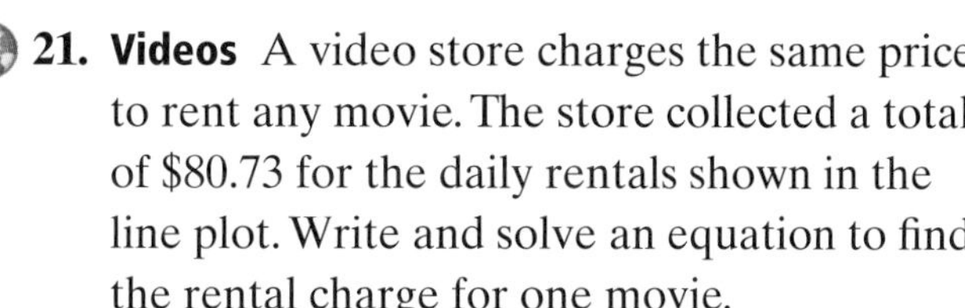

21. Videos A video store charges the same price to rent any movie. The store collected a total of $80.73 for the daily rentals shown in the line plot. Write and solve an equation to find the rental charge for one movie.

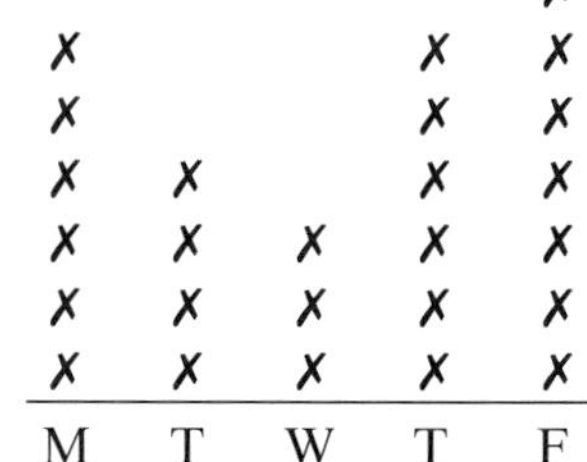

22. Writing in Math Explain what you would do to solve the equation $z \div 48 = 6$.

Solve each equation. Then check the solution.

23. $y \div 1.6 = 0.256$ **24.** $13 = 65x$ **25.** $30 = p \div 30$

26. $5.6k = 19.152$ **27.** $0.02g = 6$ **28.** $h \div 2.4 = 15$

29. Error Analysis Your soccer team scored 41 goals this season. Explain what is wrong with a teammate's claim that he scored half the goals.

30. Biology An adult female elephant's height is about 5.5 times the length of her hind footprint. Use an equation to find the approximate height of an adult female elephant whose hind footprint is 1.5 feet long.

Real-World Connection

After about six months, a baby elephant is too large to stand under its mother.

31. **Measurement** One of the world's largest oil tankers, the *Jahre Viking*, is so long that if 3.5 similar tankers were placed end-to-end, they would measure about 1 mile long. Find the length, in feet, of the *Jahre Viking*. (*Hint*: 1 mile = 5,280 feet)

32. **Stretch Your Thinking** The single-digit numbers in the following expressions have been replaced with the symbols ⊙, △, and ▱. Each symbol represents the same number in all three expressions. Find what number each symbol represents.

▱ − △ = 3　　　⊙ + △ + ▱ = 20　　　⊙ × △ = 30

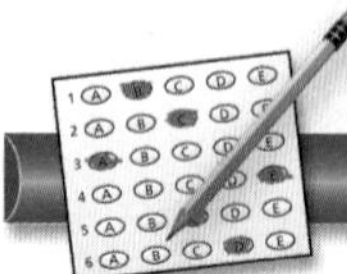

Test Prep

Gridded Response

What is the solution of each equation?

33. $15x = 135$　　**34.** $y \div 15 = 1.5$　　**35.** $4x = 2.8$

36. $1.5 = q \div 3.06$　　**37.** $n \div 3.5 = 2$　　**38.** $8.4 = 0.14k$

Take It to the NET
Online lesson quiz at
www.PHSchool.com
Web Code: aaa-0207

39. About 0.95 of the weight of a watermelon is water. What is the weight of the water in a 13-pound watermelon?

Mixed Review

Lesson 1-3

Use <, =, or > to complete each statement.

40. 6 ■ 1.6　　**41.** 3.4 ■ 3.40　　**42.** 8.05 ■ 5.08

Lesson 1-2

43. Write the decimal eighteen hundredths in standard form.

Checkpoint Quiz 2

Lessons 2-4 through 2-7

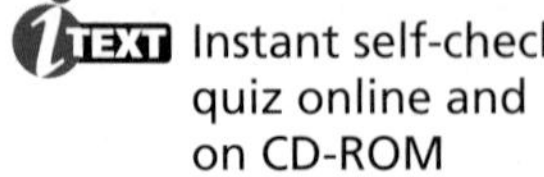

Instant self-check quiz online and on CD-ROM

Solve each equation.

1. $5x = 65$　　**2.** $n - 3.2 = 15$　　**3.** $z + 6 = 8.2$

4. $k \div 4 = 3.6$　　**5.** $14 = 3.2 + y$　　**6.** $28 = 1.4a$

7. $x - 4.8 = 3.6$　　**8.** $23 = 16 + y$　　**9.** $48 = 9.6a$

10. You pay for refreshments at a movie theater with a $10 bill. The refreshments cost $5.73. Use an equation to find how much change you should receive.

2-8 Exponents

What You'll Learn

To use exponents

To simplify expressions with exponents

. . . And Why

To use exponents to write a product, as in Example 1

Check Skills You'll Need

For help, go to Lesson 1-10.

Find the value of each expression.

1. $3 \times 3 + 4 \times 4$ **2.** $1 \times 3 - 1 \times 3$

3. $3.2 \times 4.5 + 4.8$ **4.** $10 \times 10 \times 10 \times 10$

5. $1 \times 1 \times 1$ **6.** $1 + 1 \times 2 - 1$

New Vocabulary • exponent • base • power

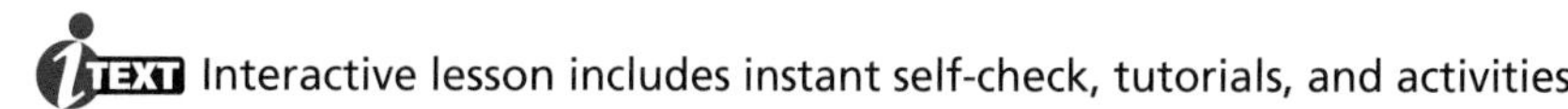
Interactive lesson includes instant self-check, tutorials, and activities.

OBJECTIVE 1 Using Exponents

You can write 625 as a product of factors. $625 = \underbrace{5 \times 5 \times 5 \times 5}_{\text{factors}}$

Reading Math

You read 5^4 as "5 to the fourth power."

The number 5 is used as a factor four times. You can indicate repeated multiplication of the same number by using an exponent. An **exponent** tells you how many times a number, or **base,** is used as a factor.

$$5 \times 5 \times 5 \times 5 = 5^4$$ ← exponent
↑ base

1 EXAMPLE Using Exponents

Write $3 \times 3 \times 3 \times 3$ using an exponent. Name the base and the exponent.

$3 \times 3 \times 3 \times 3 = 3^4$ ← 3^4 means that 3 is used as a factor 4 times.

The base is 3 and the exponent is 4.

Check Understanding 1 Write each expression using an exponent. Name the base and the exponent.

a. 3.94×3.94 **b.** $7 \times 7 \times 7 \times 7$ **c.** $x \cdot x \cdot x$

d. Number Sense Does 5^4 have the same value as 5×4? Explain.

The area of the square is 3×3, or 3^2. You read 3^2 as "three squared."

The volume of the cube is $4 \times 4 \times 4$, or 4^3. You read 4^3 as "four cubed."

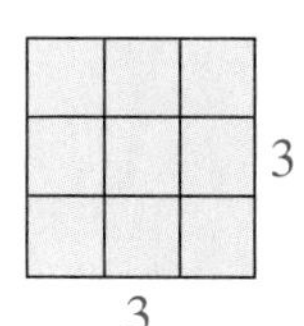

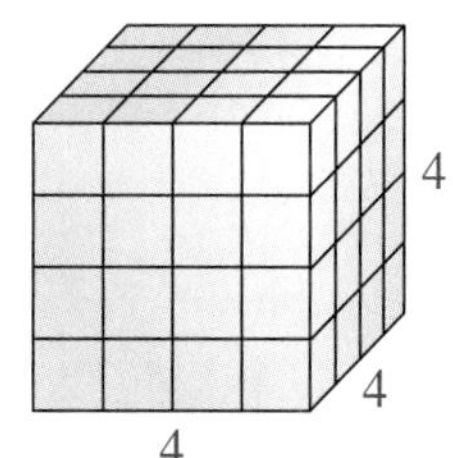

Reading Math

You read 10^{100} as "ten to the hundredth power." 10^{100} is called a *googol.*

A **power** is a number that can be expressed using an exponent. You read 10^5 as "ten to the fifth power." Powers of 10 are used to name the place-value positions in our number system. You can use powers of 10 to write numbers in expanded form.

2 EXAMPLE Writing in Expanded Form

Write the number 9,572 in expanded form using powers of 10.

$9{,}572 = 9{,}000 + 500 + 70 + 2$

$= 9 \times 1{,}000 + 5 \times 100 + 7 \times 10 + 2 \times 1$

$= 9 \times 10^3 + 5 \times 10^2 + 7 \times 10^1 + 2 \times 1$

Check Understanding 2 Write each number in expanded form using powers of 10.

a. 55,607 **b.** 380,254

OBJECTIVE

2 Simplifying Expressions With Exponents

Some calculators have special keys to use with exponents. You can use the x^2 key to square a number. You can use the ^ key to evaluate any power.

3 EXAMPLE Simplifying Powers

2 beads

Simplify each expression.

a. $2^5 = 2 \times 2 \times 2 \times 2 \times 2 = 32$ ← **The base 2 is used as a factor 5 times.**

b. $1.5^3 = 1.5$ ^ 3 = 3.375 ← **Use a calculator.**

Check Understanding 3 Simplify each expression.

a. 10^5 **b.** 3^9 **c.** 1.1^3

d. **Reasoning** Does 2^5 have the same value as 5^2? Explain.

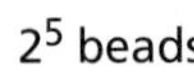

2^5 beads

The order of operations can be extended to include exponents.

Key Concepts **Order of Operations**

1. Do all operations within parentheses first.
2. **Do all work with exponents.**
3. Multiply and divide in order from left to right.
4. Add and subtract in order from left to right.

The phrase **P**lease **E**xcuse **M**y **D**ear **A**unt **S**ally can help you remember the order of operations.

P	**P**arentheses
E	**E**xponents
M, D	**M**ultiplication and **D**ivision in order from left to right
A, S	**A**ddition and **S**ubtraction in order from left to right

4 EXAMPLE Simplifying Expressions

Simplify the expression: $3 \times (7^2 + 18 \div 2)$.

$3 \times (49 + 18 \div 2)$ ← **Simplify 7^2 in parentheses first.**

$3 \times (49 + 9)$ ← **In parentheses, simplify 18 ÷ 2.**

$3 \times (58)$ ← **In parentheses, add 49 + 9.**

174 ← **Multiply 3 and 58.**

Check Understanding 4 Simplify each expression.

a. $2^3 - 6 \div 3$ **b.** $1 + 11^2 - 20 \div 2$ **c.** $5 + (2 + 1)^2$

EXERCISES

For more practice, see *Extra Practice.*

A Practice by Example

Example 1 (page 99)

Write each expression using an exponent. Name the base and exponent.

1. 3×3 **2.** $2 \times 2 \times 2$ **3.** $9 \times 9 \times 9$

4. 100×100 **5.** $12 \times 12 \times 12 \times 12$ **6.** $8.1 \cdot 8.1$

7. $1 \times 1 \times 1 \times 1 \times 1$ **8.** 29 **9.** $n \cdot n \cdot n \cdot n \cdot n \cdot n$

Example 2 (page 100)

Write each number in expanded form using powers of 10.

10. 7,650 **11.** 83,792 **12.** 41,006

13. 60,251 **14.** 400,003 **15.** 7,892,510

Examples 3, 4 (pages 100, 101)

Simplify each expression. Exercise 16 has been started for you.

16. $14^2 = 14 \times 14 = \blacksquare$ **17.** 2^6 **18.** 3^5

19. 25^3 **20.** 2.5^3 **21.** 3^4

22. $4^2 + 5$ **23.** $2^2 + 3^2$ **24.** $(2 + 3)^2$

25. $(3^2 - 1)^2$ **26.** $5(5^2 - 9)$ **27.** $(9 - 7)^3 \times 6$

B Apply Your Skills

Simplify each expression.

28. $37^3 + 1$ **29.** $(37 + 1)^3$ **30.** $(9 + 1)^2 - 1^3$

31. $15^2 - (1 + 13^2) + 5$ **32.** $(10 - 8)^4 \times 3.5$ **33.** $2 \times 3^2 \times 4^2$

34. Number Sense Tell whether the expression $2^2 \cdot 3^2 - 2^3 - 1$ has the same value as the expression $2^2 \cdot (3^2 - 2^3) - 1$. Explain why or why not.

Find the missing exponent that makes each equation true.

35. $40 = 2^{■} \times 5$ **36.** $45 = 5 \times 3^{■}$ **37.** $343 = 7^{■}$ **38.** $144 = 9 \cdot 4^{■}$

39. Patterns Copy the table at the right.
  a. Fill in the missing values.
  b. Writing in Math Explain how the number of zeros in the standard form of a power of 10 relates to the exponent.
  c. Extend and complete the table for 10^7 and 10^8.

Power	Standard Form
10^1	10
10^2	100
10^3	1,000
10^4	■
■	■

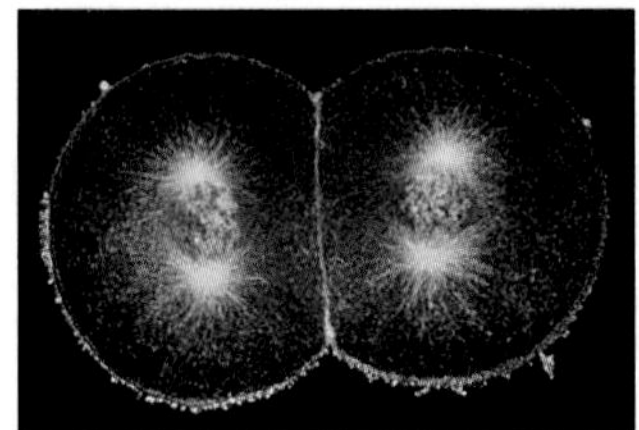

40. Biology Suppose a single-celled animal splits in two after one hour. Each new cell also splits in two after one hour. How many cells will there be after eight hours? Write your answer using an exponent.

41. Astronomy The interior temperature of the sun is about 35,000,000°F. Write this number in expanded form using powers of 10.

42. Science Scientists estimate that Earth is approximately 15×10^9 years old. Write this number in standard form.

43. Copy and complete the table of cubes below.

n^3	1^3	2^3	3^3	4^3	5^3	6^3
Standard Form	1	8	■	■	■	■

Write each product or quotient using an exponent.

44. $5^2 \times 5^3$ **45.** $2^4 \times 2^3$ **46.** $4^5 \div 4^2$ **47.** $10^6 \div 10^1$

Simplify each expression.

48. $(2 \times 3^3 + 1) \div 11$ **49.** $10^2 \times 4 \div 5$ **50.** $(4^2 - 1) \div 3 + 1$

51. $(1 + 6)^2 - (1^2 + 6^2)$ **52.** $100 - (1.8 + 5)^2$ **53.** $2.7(125 \div 5^2)$

54. **Entertainment** The size of the image of a motion picture is related to the distance of the projector from the screen.
  a. **Writing in Math** Describe how the size of the screen is related to the distance the projector is from the screen.
  b. A projector is 25 feet from a screen. How large will the image of the motion picture be?

Distance From Screen	Picture Size
1 unit	1 unit^2
2 units	4 units^2
3 units	9 units^2
4 units	16 units^2

Challenge

55. **Patterns** Copy the pattern at the right.
  a. Extend the pattern three more rows.
  b. Write the sum of each row using an exponent.
  c. What is the sum of the first 20 odd numbers?

$1 = 1$
$1 + 3 = 4$
$1 + 3 + 5 = 9$
$1 + 3 + 5 + 7 = 16$

56. **Stretch Your Thinking** In the equations at the right, ■ represents a one-digit number and ✿ represents a two-digit number. What are the numbers?

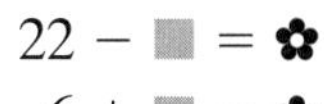

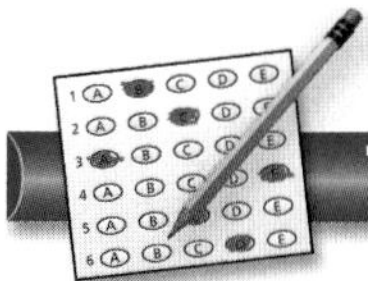

Test Prep

Multiple Choice

57. Which expression is NOT equivalent to $3 \times 3 \times 3 \times 3$?
  A. $(3 + 3)^2 \times 3 \times 3$ B. $3^1 \times 3^3$
  C. $(3 + 3 + 3) \times 3^2$ D. $3^2 \times (3 \times 3)$

58. What is the value of $2^3 \times 3^2$?
  F. 72 G. 54 H. 48 I. 36

59. What is the value of $5 + 6^2 - 1$?
  A. 16 B. 30 C. 40 D. 120

60. What is the value of $2 + (2^4 + 100) \div 2^2$?
  F. 9 G. 11 H. 31 I. 32

Take It to the NET
Online lesson quiz at
www.PHSchool.com
Web Code: aaa-0208

Mixed Review

Lesson 1-7 **Find each product.**

61. 11.23×100 62. 7.005×10 63. $1{,}000 \times 0.88$

64. 1.25×4.5 65. 9.05×3.30 66. 11×0.18

Lesson 1-3 **Use <, =, or > to complete each statement.**

67. 10.0010 ■ 10.01 68. 0.0991 ■ 0.00999 69. 21.1 ■ 21.100

Extension Scientific Notation

For Use With Lesson 2-8

The distance from Earth to the sun is about 150,000,000 kilometers. You can write this number in *scientific notation.*

To write a number in scientific notation, write the number as a product of two factors. The first factor is a number equal to or greater than 1 but less than 10. The second factor is a power of 10.

1 EXAMPLE Changing to Scientific Notation

Write 150,000,000 using scientific notation.

$$150,000,000. = 1.5 \times 10^8$$

Move the decimal point to the left, so that you have a factor greater than or equal to 1 and less than 10.

The exponent, 8, shows that you moved the decimal point 8 places.

2 EXAMPLE Changing to Standard Form

The distance from Earth to the moon is approximately 3.844×10^5 kilometers. Write 3.844×10^5 in standard notation.

$$3.844 \times 10^5 = 384,400.$$

Move the decimal point 5 places to the right. Use zeros to fill places as needed.

EXERCISES

Write each number in scientific notation.

1. 34,000 **2.** 165,000,000,000 **3.** 800,000 **4.** 310,210

5. 22,030,000 **6.** 902,000,000 **7.** 4,000,500,000 **8.** 3,045,250

Write each number in standard form.

9. 3.05×10^2 **10.** 2×10^{11} **11.** 9.037×10^8 **12.** 1×10^9

13. 6.5×10^1 **14.** 4.0201×10^7 **15.** 1.4×10^5 **16.** 7.3×10^2

17. The distance from our sun to the nearest star, Alpha Centauri, is about 42,000,000,000,000 kilometers. Write this distance in scientific notation.

2-9 The Distributive Property

What You'll Learn

To use the Distributive Property

. . . And Why

To find a salary, as in Example 2

✓ Check Skills You'll Need

For help, go to Lesson 1.5.

Use mental math to find each sum.

1. $1.5 + 8.4 + 3.5$

2. $4.4 + 7.3 + 5.6$

3. $8.1 + 5.3 + 9.9$

4. $6.5 + 3.7 + 6.3$

New Vocabulary • **Distributive Property**

OBJECTIVE

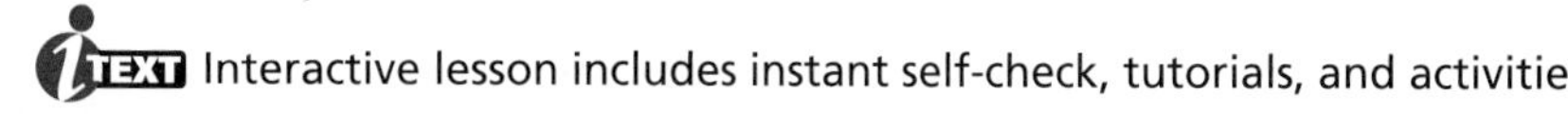

Interactive lesson includes instant self-check, tutorials, and activities.

1 Using the Distributive Property

Investigation: Making Area Models

1. On graph paper, draw rectangles like those shown below.

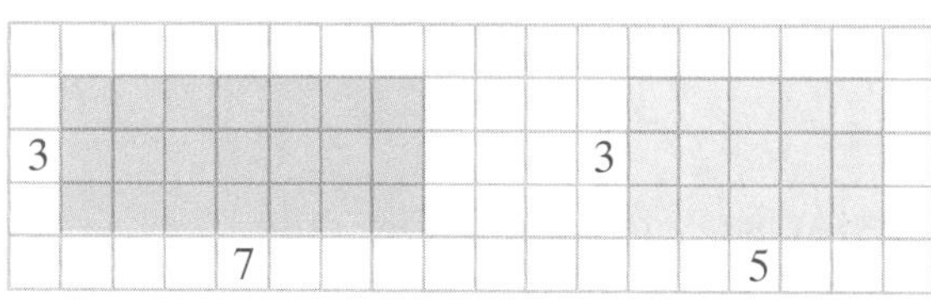

2. a. Count the squares to find the area of each rectangle.
   b. What is the sum of the two areas?
3. a. Cut out the rectangles. Arrange them so that the sides of length 3 touch. What are the length and width of the new rectangle?
   b. Count the squares to find the area of the new rectangle.
4. What do you notice about the results of Questions 2(b) and 3(b)?

The **Distributive Property** shows how multiplication affects an addition or subtraction.

$$3 \times (7 + 5) = (3 \times 7) + (3 \times 5) = 21 + 15 = 36$$

$$9 \times (5 - 2) = (9 \times 5) - (9 \times 2) = 45 - 18 = 27$$

Key Concepts **The Distributive Property**

Arithmetic	Algebra
$8 \times (4 + 6) = (8 \times 4) + (8 \times 6)$	$a(b + c) = ab + ac$
$7 \times (6 - 2) = (7 \times 6) - (7 \times 2)$	$a(b - c) = ab - ac$

You can use the Distributive Property to multiply mentally. To simplify 4×29, you can think of 29 as $(20 + 9)$ or as $(30 - 1)$. Then multiply.

1 EXAMPLE Evaluating Expressions

Simplify 4×29.

What you think

Think of 29 as $30 - 1$. Then multiply by 4: $4 \times 30 = 120$ and $4 \times 1 = 4$. Now subtract the two products: $120 - 4 = 116$.

Why it works

$4 \times 29 = 4 \times (30 - 1)$ ← Write 29 as 30 − 1.

$= (4 \times 30) - (4 \times 1)$ ← Use the Distributive Property.

$= 120 - 4$ ← Simplify within parentheses.

$= 116$ ← Subtract.

Check Understanding 1 Use the Distributive Property to simplify each expression.

a. 3×42 **b.** 5×68

You can use the Distributive Property to multiply a whole number and a decimal.

2 EXAMPLE Real-World Problem Solving

Salary A summer job as an assistant camp counselor pays $6.50 per hour. What is the salary for working 8 hours?

$8 \times 6.50 = 8(6.00 + 0.50)$ ← Write 6.50 as 6.00 + 0.50.

$= (8 \times 6.00) + (8 \times 0.50)$ ← Use the Distributive Property.

$= 48.00 + 4.00$ ← Simplify within parentheses.

$= 52.00$ ← Add.

The salary for working 8 hours is $52.00.

Check Understanding 2 A local video store charges $2.80 for each day a rental is late. What are the late charges if a video is 5 days late?

EXERCISES

For more practice, see *Extra Practice.*

A Practice by Example

Example 1 (page 106)

Use the Distributive Property to simplify each expression. Exercises 1 and 2 have been started for you.

1. $4 \times 18 = 4 \times (10 + 8) = (4 \times ■) + (4 \times ■) = ■ + ■ = ■$

2. $4 \times 18 = 4 \times (20 - 2) = (4 \times ■) - (4 \times ■) = ■ - ■ = ■$

3. 8×28 **4.** 5×63 **5.** 12×34

Example 2 (page 106)

6. Fundraising Your class is selling Earth Day posters for \$2.90 each. On the first day of sales, your class sold 8 posters. How much money did your class collect on the first day of sales?

7. A group of 6 students plan to go to a skating rink. The rink charges \$4.80 per person. Find the total cost for the group.

B Apply Your Skills

Use the Distributive Property to simplify each expression.

8. 7×83 **9.** 3×2.9 **10.** 9×48

11. 5×1.9 **12.** 6×99 **13.** 11×8.7

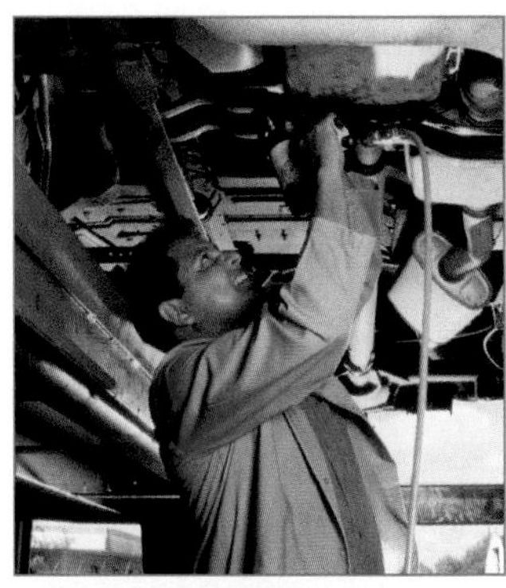

Real-World Connection

Careers Auto mechanics use computers to help diagnose engine problems.

14. Money Mr. Garcia's company pays him 32.5 cents per mile for gasoline and car maintenance when he uses his car for company business. How much money does he receive for driving 40 miles on company business?

15. Fundraising There are 53 people walking in a fundraising event. Each participant walks 5 miles. How many total miles do the participants walk?

16. Gardening Your school's ecology club plants 8 rows of sunflowers in a vacant lot. Each row has 27 plants. Find the total number of sunflowers that the ecology club plants.

17. Writing in Math Describe two ways to find the total area of the rectangle at the right.

C Challenge

Algebra **Copy and complete each equation.**

18. $4(7 - y) = (4 \cdot 7) - (4 \cdot ■)$ **19.** $9(a + b) = (■ \cdot a) + (9 \cdot ■)$

20. Stretch Your Thinking Change two operations in the expression below so that the value of the expression is 35.

$$5 + 5 + 5 + 5 + 5 + 5$$

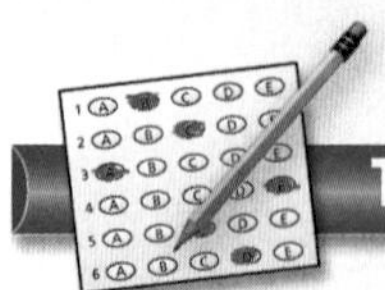

Test Prep

Multiple Choice

21. Which of these expressions is NOT equivalent to 19×12?

A. $(19 \times 10) + (19 \times 2)$ **B.** $(10 \times 12) + (9 \times 12)$
C. $(20 \times 12) - (1 \times 12)$ **D.** $(10 \times 10) + (9 \times 2)$

22. A family is buying carpeting for two rooms. One room measures 15 feet by 17.5 feet and the other is 17.5 feet by 20 feet. Which expression gives the total square feet of carpet that the family is buying?

F. 35×35 **G.** 32.5×37.5 **H.** 17.5×35 **I.** 15×37.5

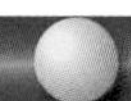

Take It to the NET Online lesson quiz at **www.PHSchool.com** Web Code: aaa-0209

23. Which expression is NOT equivalent to the others?

A. $(3 \times 5) + (2 \times 5)$ **B.** $3 \times (5 + 2)$
C. $(3 + 2) \times 5$ **D.** $(2 + 3) \times 5$

Mixed Review

Lesson 2-5

Tell whether each equation is true or false.

24. $5 \times 3 = 8$ **25.** $0 \times 9.8 = 9.8$ **26.** $1 \times 6.7 = 6.7$

Lesson 2-1

27. **Algebra** Write the next two terms in the following pattern.

1, 2, 4, 8, 16, . . .

28. **Geometry** Draw the next two figures in the pattern.

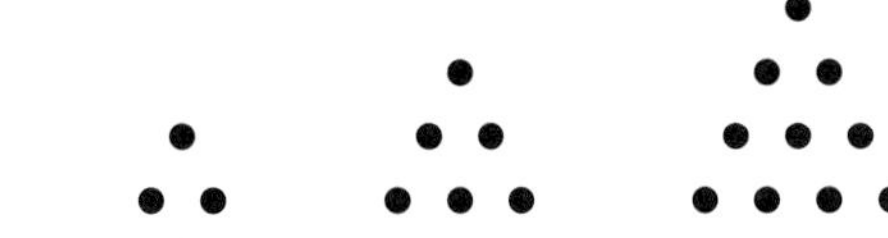

Math at Work

Bicycle Designer

Bicycle designers combine visual, artistic, and mathematical skills to make bicycle designs. They use mathematical patterns to find the size of the wheels, the shape of the frame, the number of gears, and the manner in which these parts will work together.

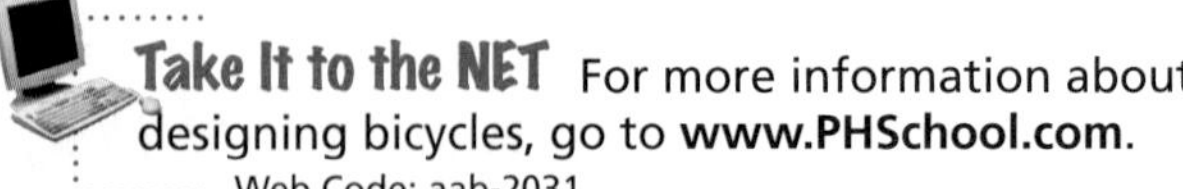

Take It to the NET For more information about designing bicycles, go to **www.PHSchool.com**. Web Code: aab-2031

Test-Taking Strategies

Writing Short Responses

Short-response questions in this textbook are worth 2 points. To receive full credit, you must give the correct answer with units, if needed, and show your work or explain your reasoning.

EXAMPLE

Measurement Jenny stands on a scale. She weighs 104 pounds. Then she steps on the scale while holding her dog. Now the scale reads 121 pounds. Define a variable. Write and solve an equation to find the weight of the dog.

The problem asks you to define a variable, set up an equation, and solve the equation to find the weight of the dog. Below is a scoring guide that shows the number of points awarded for different answers.

Scoring

[2] The equation and solution are correct and all work is shown. The dog weighs 17 pounds.

[1] There is no equation, but there is a method to show that the dog weighs 17 pounds, OR an equation is written and solved. The response may contain minor errors.

[0] There is no response, no work shown, OR the response is completely incorrect.

Three responses are below with the points each received.

2 points	1 point	0 points
Let d = weight of dog. $104 + d = 121$ $104 + d - 104 = 121 - 104$ $d = 17$ The dog weighs 17 pounds.	$121 - 104 = 17$ 17 pounds	27 pounds

EXERCISES

Use Example 1 to answer each question.

1. Why did each response receive the indicated number of points?
2. Write a 2-point response for solving the equation $121 - d = 104$.

Chapter 2

Chapter Review

Vocabulary

Addition Property of Equality (p. 91)
algebraic expression (p. 69)
base (p. 99)
conjecture (p. 64)
Distributive Property (p. 105)
Division Property of Equality (p. 95)
equation (p. 84)
evaluate (p. 69)
exponent (p. 99)
inverse operations (p. 90)
Multiplication Property of Equality (p. 96)
numerical expression (p. 68)
open sentence (p. 85)
power (p. 100)
solution (p. 85)
Subtraction Property of Equality (p. 90)
term (p. 63)
variable (p. 69)

Reading Math: Understanding Vocabulary

Take It to the NET
Online vocabulary quiz at www.PHSchool.com
Web Code: aaj-0251

Fill in the blank.

1. Each number in a number pattern is called a(n) __?__.

2. A(n) __?__ contains one or more variables.

3. In the expression 4^2, the factor 4 is called the __?__.

4. A(n) __?__ is a symbol that stands for a number.

5. A(n) __?__ tells how many times to multiply a factor.

Skills and Concepts

2-1 Objectives

- To continue a number pattern
- To write a rule for a number pattern

Each number in a number pattern is called a **term.** A **conjecture** predicts how a pattern may continue. You can describe a pattern with a rule.

Write the next three terms and write a rule for each number pattern.

6. 2, 6, 18, 54, . . .   **7.** 7, 19, 31, 43, . . .   **8.** 7, 14, 28, 56, . . .

2-2 and 2-3 Objectives

- To use variables
- To evaluate algebraic expressions
- To write algebraic expressions
- To use algebraic expressions

A **numerical expression** contains only numbers and operation symbols. An **algebraic expression** contains at least one **variable.** To **evaluate** an algebraic expression, replace each variable with a number.

Evaluate each expression.

9. $48 \div x$ for $x = 6$ **10.** $c - 7$ for $c = 56$ **11.** $14b$ for $b = 3$

Write an expression for each word phrase.

12. x divided by 12   **13.** 2 times b **14.** h plus k

2-4 Objective

- ▼ To solve problems by making a table to find a pattern

To solve problems involving a progression of data, you can make a table that will help you organize information and find a pattern.

15. Swimming To train for a swim meet, Theresa plans to swim 4 laps each day in the first week, 8 laps each day in the second week, 12 laps each day in the third week, 16 laps each day in the fourth week, and so on. How many laps does she plan to swim each day in the seventh week?

2-5, 2-6, and 2-7 Objectives

- ▼ To use mental math to solve equations
- ▼ To estimate solutions of equations
- ▼ To solve equations by adding and subtracting
- ▼ To solve equations by multiplying and dividing

An **open sentence** is a sentence that contains one or more variables. An **equation** is a mathematical sentence that contains an equal sign. The number that makes an equation true is a **solution.**

Tell whether each equation is true or false.

16. $15 + 25 = 30$ **17.** $21 \div 3 = 7$ **18.** $6 \times 4 = 28$

Mental Math **Use mental math to solve each equation.**

19. $x + 7 = 12$ **20.** $m + 13 = 21$ **21.** $4t = 32$

Solve each equation.

22. $r - 1{,}078 = 4{,}562$ **23.** $m + 8 = 15$ **24.** $756 = p - 254$

25. $78x = 4{,}368$ **26.** $t \div 4 = 32$ **27.** $d - 2.16 = 3.9$

28. $5.6 + x = 7$ **29.** $4.5 = 5n$ **30.** $v \div 3.2 = 19$

2-8 Objectives

- ▼ To use exponents
- ▼ To simplify expressions with exponents

You can use an **exponent** to show how many times a number, or **base,** is used as a factor. A number expressed using an exponent is called a **power.**

Simplify each expression.

31. 2×4^3 **32.** $10^3 \div 5^2$ **33.** $3^2 + 2^3$ **34.** $(5^2 - 1) - 3^2$

2-9 Objective

- ▼ To use the Distributive Property

You can use the **Distributive Property** to simplify an expression.

Use the Distributive Property to simplify each expression.

35. 7×28 **36.** 5×3.4 **37.** 11×57

38. Shopping You go back-to-school shopping and buy five notebooks for \$3.80 each. Find the total cost of the notebooks.

Chapter 2

Chapter Test

Take It to the NET
Online chapter test at
www.PHSchool.com
Web Code: aaa-0252

Write the first six terms in each number pattern described.

1. Start with 10 then multiply by 2 repeatedly.

2. Start with 50 then subtract by 4 repeatedly.

Write the next three terms and write a rule for each number pattern.

3. 6, 10, 14, 18, . . .

4. 64, 32, 16, 8, . . .

5. 78, 69, 60, 51, . . .

6. 4, 12, 36, 108, . . .

Evaluate each expression for $x = 12$.

7. $500 + (x - 8)$

8. $2x - 3$

9. $8 + x \div 2$

Write an algebraic expression for each model.

10. 

11. 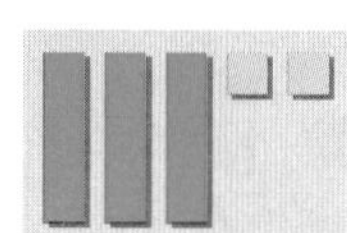

Use algebra tiles or a drawing to model each equation. Then solve.

12. $v + 3 = 8$

13. $3g = 15$

Write an expression for each word phrase.

14. c more than 4

15. 8 less than $3d$

16. Gus is 8 years younger than his brother, Alex. Alex is x years old. Write an algebraic expression that describes how old Gus is.

17. **Writing in Math** Write a word problem that could be described by the expression $d + 4$.

Tell whether each equation is true or false.

18. $6 + 7 \times 3 = 39$

19. $1.5 \times (6 - 4) = 3$

Tell whether the given number is a solution to the equation.

20. $x + 1.5 = 32$; 17

21. $h - 8 = 2$; 28

Solve each equation.

22. $n - 4 = 8.4$

23. $25 + b = 138$

24. $k \div 12 = 3$

25. $11t = 99$

26. **Fundraising** The baseball team sold greeting cards to raise money for uniforms. They received \$.40 profit for each card they sold. Their total profit was \$302. How many cards did the team sell?

27. **Patterns** Look at the pattern below. How many squares will be in the sixth figure?

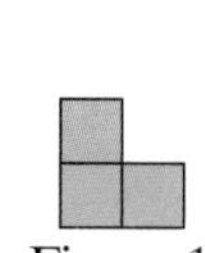
Figure 1

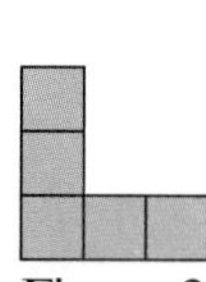
Figure 2

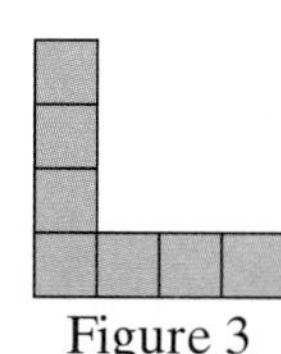
Figure 3

Write each expression using an exponent. Name the base and the exponent.

28. $10 \times 10 \times 10 \times 10$

29. $p \cdot p \cdot p \cdot p \cdot p \cdot p$

Simplify each expression.

30. $4^3 - 1$

31. 2×3^2

32. $150 \div 5^2$

33. $(9 \times 4) - (8 - 6)^4$

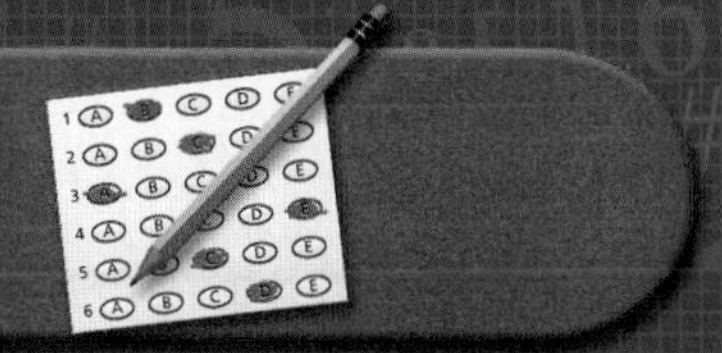

Test Prep

CUMULATIVE REVIEW
CHAPTERS 1–2

Multiple Choice

For Exercises 1–10, choose the correct letter.

1. What is the decimal for fifty-four hundredths?
 A. 0.054 **B.** 0.54 **C.** 5.40 **D.** 54.00

2. Which inequality is NOT a true statement?
 F. $0.04 > 0.01$ **G.** $0.014 < 0.02$
 H. $0.48 < 0.4798$ **I.** $29.6 > 29.06$

3. Which sentence represents the Commutative Property of Multiplication?
 A. $5 \times 2 = 10$
 B. $5 \times (6 + 3) = 5 \times 9$
 C. $5 \times 9 = 9 \times 5$
 D. $(5 \times 6) \times 2 = 5 \times (6 \times 2)$

4. For 4 days, Akiko recorded the number of laps she jogged around a track. The numbers she recorded were 7, 11, 15, and 19. If she continues in the same pattern, how many laps will she jog on the sixth day?
 F. 21 **G.** 23 **H.** 25 **I.** 27

5. Which word phrase does NOT describe the algebraic expression $b - 10$?
 A. ten less than *b* **B.** *b* less ten
 C. *b* less than ten **D.** *b* minus ten

6. Which expression has a value of 13?
 F. $(3 + 2)^2$ **G.** $3 + (2)^2$
 H. $3^2 + 2^2$ **I.** $3^3 + 2^2$

7. Which operation would you use to get the variable in $x - 15 = 40$ alone on one side of the equation?
 A. Subtract 15 from each side.
 B. Subtract *x* from each side.
 C. Add 15 to each side.
 D. Add 40 to each side.

8. What is the value of $2.5c + 2$ when $c = 6$?
 F. 2.56 **G.** 17 **H.** 20 **I.** 256

9. Which expression is NOT equivalent to the others?
 A. $13 \times (20 + 2)$
 B. $13 \times 20 + 13 \times 2$
 C. $(10 + 13) \times (10 + 12)$
 D. $22 \times (10 + 3)$

10. Apples cost $.38 each. You have $4.00. What is the greatest number of apples you can buy?
 F. 5 **G.** 9 **H.** 10 **I.** 11

Gridded Response

11. What is the solution of $x \div 0.15 = 1.2$?

12. Fresh cod sells for $4.86 per pound. You buy two pieces, which cost a total of $12.15. How many pounds of fish did you buy?

13. A sheet of metal has a thickness of 0.004 inches. In inches, how many inches thick is a stack of 100 sheets?

Short Response

14. **a.** Draw the fourth figure in the pattern.
 b. How many white squares will the sixth figure have?

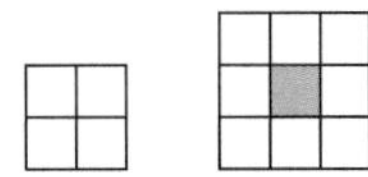
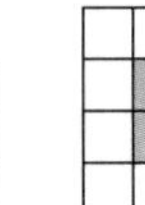

Figure 1 Figure 2 Figure 3

15. How many different sandwiches can you make from the choices of wheat bread, rye bread, or oatmeal bread with a filling of chicken, turkey, cheese, or peanut butter? Explain your method.

It's About Time

Applying Patterns Our day, month, and year are all based on the motion of Earth and the moon. One day is 24 hours long because that's how long it takes Earth to rotate once about its axis. The moon takes one month to orbit Earth, and Earth takes one year to orbit the sun. If we lived on another planet, each of these measures would be different, and we would have different measurements of time.

Earth's Moon

The moon contains almost the same elements, minerals, and rocks as Earth, but it has no water and no atmosphere. The moon orbits Earth in 29 days, 12 hours, 44 minutes, and 3 seconds, on average.

The Last Planet

In 1930, U.S. astronomer Clyde Tombaugh discovered Pluto, the ninth planet in the solar system. During part of Pluto's year its orbit brings it closer to the sun than Neptune.

Pluto

Jupiter

Uranus

Sun

Venus

Mercury

Saturn

Earth

Mars

Measuring Time

The Jantar Mantar observatory, built between 1728 and 1734 in Jaipur, India, includes a giant sundial 27.5 meters high. You climb the steps to read the time, which is accurate to within a few seconds.

The Solar System

All nine planets orbit the sun in the same direction (counterclockwise when viewed from above), and most spin around their axes in the direction, also.

Put It All Together

Planet	Length of Day (Earth hours)	Length of Year (Earth days)
☿ Mercury	1,407.51	87.97
♀ Venus	5,832.61	224.7
⊕ Earth	23.93	365.24
♂ Mars	24.62	686.98
♃ Jupiter	9.93	4,332.71
♄ Saturn	10.23	10,759.3
♅ Uranus	17.23	30,684
♆ Neptune	16.11	60,188.3
♇ Pluto	153.29	90,777.3

Source: *The Cambridge Planetary Handbook*

1. a. How many Mercury years are equivalent to one Earth year? (Give your answer to the nearest whole number.)

b. If you lived on Mercury, how old would you now be in Mercury years?

2. a. If you lived on Jupiter, how many birthdays would you be likely to celebrate in your lifetime? Explain.

b. How many birthdays would you celebrate if you lived on Pluto? Explain.

3. Mars has two moons, Phobos and Deimos. Phobos orbits the planet every 7.5 hours and Deimos every 30.25 hours.

a. **Writing in Math** How might you define a "month" on Mars? Explain.

b. **Reasoning** Do you think a Martian month would be a useful measure of time? Explain.

Take It to the NET For more information about planets, go to **www.PHSchool.com**.
Web Code: aae-0253

CHAPTER 3

Number Theory and Fractions

Lessons

- **3-1** Divisibility and Mental Math
- **3-2** Prime Numbers and Prime Factorization
- **3-3** Greatest Common Factor
- **3-4** Equivalent Fractions
- **3-5** Mixed Numbers and Improper Fractions
- **3-6** Least Common Multiple
- **3-7** Comparing and Ordering Fractions
- **3-8** Fractions and Decimals
- **3-9** Problem Solving: Try, Check, and Revise

Key Vocabulary

- common factor (p. 128)
- common multiple (p. 143)
- composite number (p. 124)
- divisible (p. 119)
- equivalent fractions (p. 134)
- greatest common factor (p. 128)
- improper fraction (p. 139)
- least common denominator (p. 148)
- least common multiple (p. 143)
- mixed number (p. 139)
- prime factorization (p. 124)
- prime number (p. 124)
- simplest form (p. 135)

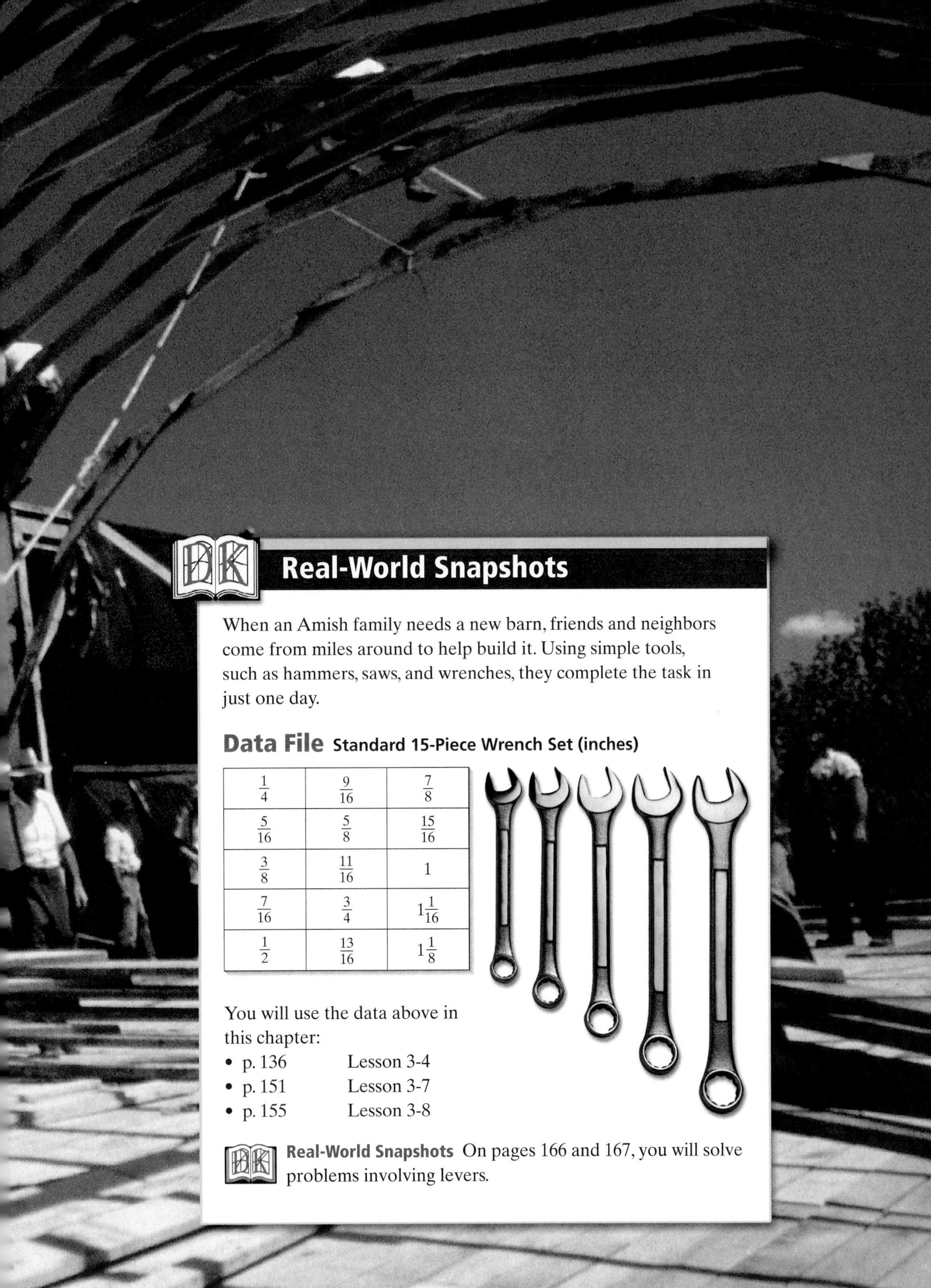

Real-World Snapshots

When an Amish family needs a new barn, friends and neighbors come from miles around to help build it. Using simple tools, such as hammers, saws, and wrenches, they complete the task in just one day.

Data File Standard 15-Piece Wrench Set (inches)

$\frac{1}{4}$	$\frac{9}{16}$	$\frac{7}{8}$
$\frac{5}{16}$	$\frac{5}{8}$	$\frac{15}{16}$
$\frac{3}{8}$	$\frac{11}{16}$	1
$\frac{7}{16}$	$\frac{3}{4}$	$1\frac{1}{16}$
$\frac{1}{2}$	$\frac{13}{16}$	$1\frac{1}{8}$

You will use the data above in this chapter:

- p. 136 Lesson 3-4
- p. 151 Lesson 3-7
- p. 155 Lesson 3-8

Real-World Snapshots On pages 166 and 167, you will solve problems involving levers.

Chapter 3 Preview

Where You've Been

- In Chapter 2, you worked with patterns, variables, and algebraic expressions. You also learned to solve equations.

Where You're Going

- In Chapter 3, you will work with divisibility rules, prime numbers, factors, and fractions.
- You will compare and order fractions and write decimals as fractions and fractions as decimals.
- Applying what you learn, you will see how common factors and multiples are important in everyday functions such as time keeping.

Daily life for many people is divided into hours and minutes.

Instant self-check online and on CD-ROM

Diagnosing Readiness

For help, go to the lesson in green.

Reading and Writing Decimals (Lesson 1-2)

Write each decimal in words.

1. 0.4 **2.** 0.37 **3.** 1.8

4. 0.205 **5.** 20.88 **6.** 0.150

Comparing and Ordering Decimals (Lesson 1-3)

Order the decimals from least to greatest.

7. 4.2, 4.02, 4.21 **8.** 0.3, 0.33, 0.033 **9.** 6.032, 6.302, 6.203

Dividing Decimals (Lesson 1-8)

Find each quotient.

10. $1.6 \div 2$ **11.** $3.85 \div 7$ **12.** $7.6 \div 0.4$

13. $290.4 \div 8$ **14.** $211.2 \div 1.6$ **15.** $583 \div 11$

Exponents (Lesson 2-8)

Write each expression using an exponent.

16. $3 \times 3 \times 3$ **17.** 5×5 **18.** $2 \times 2 \times 2 \times 2 \times 2 \times 2$

3-1 Divisibility and Mental Math

What You'll Learn

To identify numbers divisible by 2, 3, 5, 9, or 10

. . . And Why

To form teams, as in Example 4

✓ Check Skills You'll Need

For help, go to Lesson 2-7.

Solve each equation. Then check the solution.

1. $10x = 490$ **2.** $5x = 205$ **3.** $2x = 83$

4. $725 = 5x$ **5.** $123 = 3x$ **6.** $0.6x = 30$

New Vocabulary
• divisible • even number • odd number

 Interactive lesson includes instant self-check, tutorials, and activities.

OBJECTIVE

1 Using Divisibility Tests

One whole number is **divisible** by a second whole number if the remainder is 0 when the first number is divided by the second number. For example, 84 is divisible by 4, since $84 \div 4 = 21$, with no remainder.

You can use multiplication facts to decide about divisibility.

Need Help?
For help with multiplying whole numbers, go to Skills Handbook page 658.

1 EXAMPLE Using Mental Math for Divisibility

a. Is 56 divisible by 7?

Think Since $56 = 8 \times 7$, 56 is divisible by 7.

b. Is 56 divisible by 4?

Think Since $56 = 8 \times 7 = (4 \times 2) \times 7$, 56 is divisible by 4.

Check Understanding 1 **a.** Is 64 divisible by 6? **b.** Is 93 divisible by 3?

c. Number Sense Since 54 is divisible by 6, explain why 54 is also divisible by 2 and by 3.

Divisibility tests can help you determine divisibility.

Key Concepts **Divisibility of Whole Numbers**

A whole number is divisible by
- 2 if it ends in 0, 2, 4, 6, or 8.
- 3 if the sum of its digits is divisible by 3.
- 5 if it ends in 0 or 5.
- 9 if the sum of its digits is divisible by 9.
- 10 if it ends in 0.

An **even number** is any whole number that ends with a 0, 2, 4, 6, or 8. An **odd number** is a whole number that ends with a 1, 3, 5, 7, or 9.

2 EXAMPLE Divisibility by 2, 5, or 10

Test each number for divisibility by 2, 5, or 10.

a. 715

715 ends with a 5. So, it is divisible by 5, but not by 2 or 10.

b. 1,020

1,020 ends with a 0. So, it is divisible by 2, 5, and 10.

Check Understanding 2 Test each number for divisibility by 2, 5, or 10.

a. 150 **b.** 325 **c.** 1,021 **d.** 2,112

3 EXAMPLE Divisibility by 3

Test 2,571 for divisibility by 3.

$2 + 5 + 7 + 1 = 15$ ← **Find the sum of the digits in 2,571.**

$15 \div 3 = 5$ ← **The sum is divisible by 3.**

So, 2,571 is divisible by 3. (**Check** $2{,}571 \div 3 = 857$)

Check Understanding 3 Test each number for divisibility by 3.

a. 613 **b.** 1,770 **c.** 882

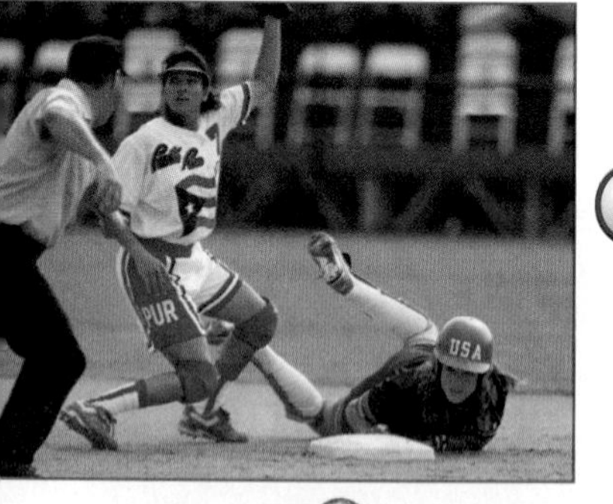

Real-World Connection

Softball became an Olympic medal sport for the first time at the Summer Games in 1996.

To test a number for divisibility by 9, you start by finding the sum of its digits—just as you did with 3.

4 EXAMPLE Divisibility by 9  Real World

Planning One of the activities at a company picnic is a softball tournament. Each team will have exactly 9 players. If 163 people have signed up to play, will everyone who has signed up have a spot on a 9-person team?

If 163 is divisible by 9, then everyone will have a spot on a team.

$1 + 6 + 3 = 10$ ← **Find the sum of the digits in 163.**

$10 \div 9$ has a remainder of 1. ← **The sum is not divisible by 9.**

So, 163 is not divisible by 9. Not everyone will have a spot on a team.

Check Understanding 4 Test each number for divisibility by 9.

a. 225 **b.** 1,655 **c.** 52,371

d. **Reasoning** Explain why a number that is divisible by 9 must also be divisible by 3.

EXERCISES

For more practice, see *Extra Practice*.

A Practice by Example

Example 1 (page 119)

Is the first number divisible by the second? Use mental math.

1. 48 by 4 **2.** 46 by 4 **3.** 63 by 7

4. 122 by 6 **5.** 42 by 6 **6.** 88 by 11

Example 2 (page 120)

Test each number for divisibility by 2, 5, or 10.

7. 48,960 **8.** 2,385 **9.** 928

10. 672 **11.** 202,470 **12.** 53,559

Example 3 (page 120)

Test each number for divisibility by 3.

13. 57 **14.** 92 **15.** 171

16. 962 **17.** 1,956 **18.** 11,160

Example 4 (page 120)

Test each number for divisibility by 9.

19. 1,187 **20.** 2,187 **21.** 17,595

22. 988 **23.** 6,283 **24.** 10,005

25. **Planning** A total of 114 people have signed up to play in a basketball tournament. There are 3 people on each team. Will everyone who has signed up have a spot on a 3-person team? Explain.

B Apply Your Skills

Test each number for divisibility by 2, 3, 5, 9, or 10.

26. 836 **27.** 837 **28.** 840 **29.** 842

30. 621 **31.** 1,086 **32.** 1,110 **33.** 5,555

34. **Writing in Math** Describe how you can use a calculator to tell if one number is divisible by another.

Number Sense **Find the digit that makes each number divisible by 9.**

35. 9,0■5 **36.** ■7,302 **37.** 2■6,555

38. Which numbers between 150 and 200 are divisible by 9?

39. **Time** The number 60 is convenient for timekeeping because it can be easily divided by many numbers. Test 60 for divisibility by 2, 3, 4, 5, 6, 7, 8, 9, or 10.

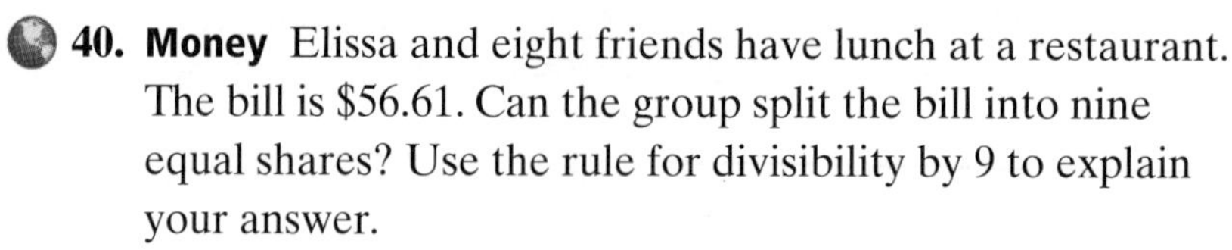

40. **Money** Elissa and eight friends have lunch at a restaurant. The bill is $56.61. Can the group split the bill into nine equal shares? Use the rule for divisibility by 9 to explain your answer.

41. **Patterns** A number pattern begins 6, 12, 18, 24, . . .
   a. Write the next four numbers in the pattern.
   b. Which of the eight numbers are divisible by both 2 and 3?
   c. **Writing in Math** Write a rule for divisibility by 6.

42. If a number is divisible by 2 and 5, is it divisible by 10? Explain.

Challenge

43. **Algebra** Explain why the value of the expression $2n + 1$ is always an odd number. (Assume the variable n is a whole number.)

44. **Stretch Your Thinking** Write all the three-digit numbers containing a 1, 2, and 3. Which of these numbers are divisible by 4?

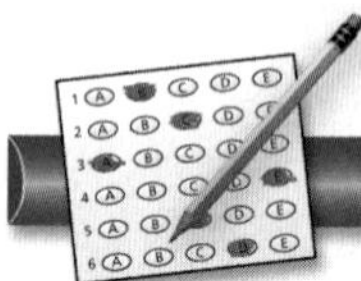

Test Prep

Multiple Choice

45. Which number is NOT divisible by 9?
A. 351 B. 657 C. 753 D. 855

46. Which number is NOT divisible by both 2 and 5?
F. 385,290 G. 621,765 H. 773,270 I. 817,020

Take It to the NET
Online lesson quiz at
www.PHSchool.com
Web Code: aaa-0301

47. Which number is divisible by both 2 and 3?
A. 1,323 B. 1,298 C. 1,230 D. 1,148

Short Response

48. Which two-digit numbers ending in 5 or 7 are divisible by 3? Explain how you can use the rule for divisibility by 3 to help find your answer.

Mixed Review

Lesson 2-6

Algebra **Solve each equation.**

49. $x - 10 = 35$ 50. $y - 8 = 92$ 51. $n - 6.2 = 10$

52. $a - 4.25 = 1.75$ 53. $b - 0.06 = 1.4$ 54. $c - 1.02 = 3.6$

Lesson 2-2

Algebra **Evaluate each expression for $a = 1.5$.**

55. $2(a - 1)$ 56. $10a \div 3$ 57. $1 + 7a$

3-2 Prime Numbers and Prime Factorization

What You'll Learn

 To find factors of a number

 To find the prime factorization

. . . And Why

To find formations for marching, as in Exercise 27

✓ Check Skills You'll Need

For help, go to Lesson 3-1.

Test each number for divisibility by 2, 3, 5, 9, or 10.

1. 990 **2.** 901 **3.** 695

4. 800 **5.** 2,080 **6.** 94,022

New Vocabulary • factor • composite number • prime number • prime factorization

OBJECTIVE

Interactive lesson includes instant self-check, tutorials, and activities.

1 Finding Factors of a Number

Investigation: Modeling Divisibility With Rectangles

1. Use graph paper. Draw as many different rectangles as you can by using exactly 12 squares of the grid at a time. What are the dimensions of each rectangle?
2. How many different rectangles can you draw using 24 squares? Using 25 squares? Using 7 squares?
3. Explain how the number of rectangles that you can draw relates to the divisibility of a number.

Need Help? For help with dividing whole numbers, go to Skills Handbook page 660.

Rules for divisibility can help you find factors. A **factor** is a whole number that divides a nonzero whole number with remainder 0.

1 EXAMPLE Finding Factors

List all the factors of 20.

1×20 ← Write factor pairs. Start with 1.

$2 \times 10, 4 \times 5$ ← 2 and 4 are factors. Skip 3, since 20 is not divisible by 3.

5×4 ← Stop when you repeat factors.

The factors of 20 are 1, 2, 4, 5, 10, and 20.

✓ Check Understanding 1 List all the factors of 42.

A **composite number** is a whole number greater than 1 with more than two factors. For example, 25 is composite since it has three factors: 1, 5, and 25.

A **prime number** is a whole number with exactly two factors, 1 and the number itself. The first ten prime numbers are 2, 3, 5, 7, 11, 13, 17, 19, 23, and 29. The whole numbers 0 and 1 are neither prime nor composite.

2 EXAMPLE Prime or Composite?

Tell whether each number is prime or composite. Explain.

a. 51

Composite; 51 is divisible by 3, so it has more than two factors.

b. 53

Prime; 53 has only two factors, 1 and 53.

Check Understanding 2 Tell whether each number is prime or composite. Explain.

a. 39 **b.** 47 **c.** 63

OBJECTIVE

2 Finding the Prime Factorization of a Number

Writing a composite number as a product of prime numbers gives the **prime factorization** of the number. You can use a *division ladder* or a *factor tree* to find the prime factorization of a composite number.

3 EXAMPLE Prime Factorization

Find the prime factorization of 84.

Method 1 Using a division ladder.

2)84 ← **Divide 84 by the prime number 2. Work down.**
2)42 ← **The result is 42. Since 42 is even, divide by 2 again.**
3)21 ← **The result is 21. Divide by the prime number 3.**
7 ← **The prime factorization is 2 × 2 × 3 × 7.**

Method 2 Using a factor tree.

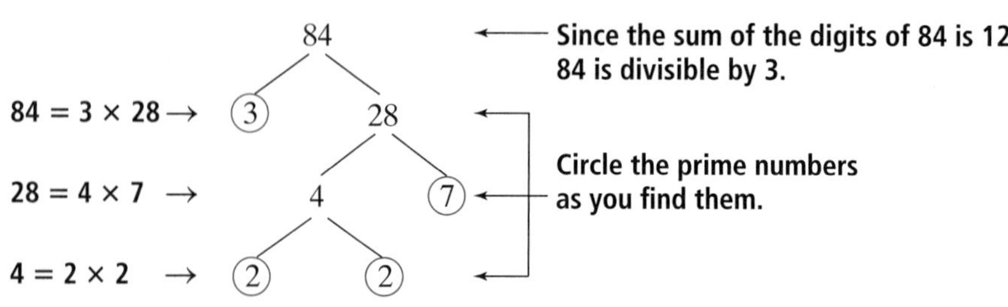

The prime factorization of 84 is $2^2 \times 3 \times 7$.

Check Understanding 3 Find the prime factorization of each number. **a.** 28 **b.** 125

EXERCISES

For more practice, see *Extra Practice*.

A Practice by Example

List the factors of each number.

Example 1 (page 123)

1. 8	**2.** 12	**3.** 18	**4.** 35
5. 28	**6.** 21	**7.** 17	**8.** 60

Example 2 (page 124)

Tell whether each number is prime or composite. Explain.

9. 55	**10.** 51	**11.** 83	**12.** 87
13. 19	**14.** 67	**15.** 57	**16.** 91

Example 3 (page 124)

Find the prime factorization of each number.

17. 32	**18.** 42	**19.** 75	**20.** 400
21. 15	**22.** 45	**23.** 450	**24.** 10,000

B Apply Your Skills

Calculator **Find the number with the given prime factorization.**

25. $7 \times 11 \times 13$

26. $2^3 \times 5^2 \times 7 \times 11$

27. Parades A group has 36 ceremonial guards. When they march, they form rows of equal numbers of guards. What numbers of rows can they make? How many guards will be in each row?

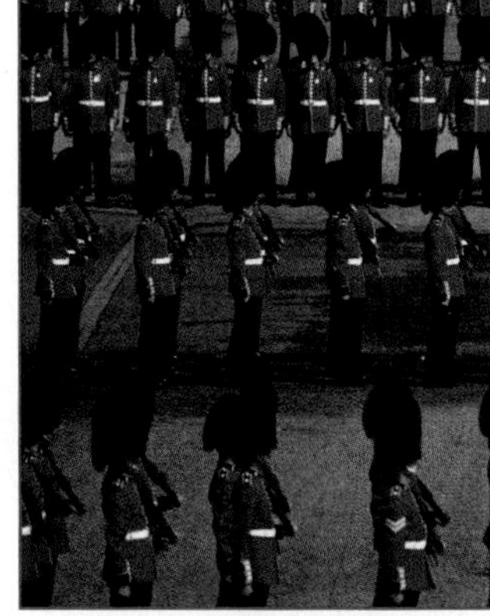

Real-World Connection

In England, the Queen's official birthday is celebrated with a military parade.

Tell whether each number is prime or composite. For each composite number, find the prime factorization.

28. 216	**29.** 135	**30.** 47	**31.** 210
32. 432	**33.** 73	**34.** 765	**35.** 1,089

36.  Writing in Math Explain how you would use divisibility rules to make a factor tree for 864. Then find the prime factorization.

C Challenge

37. Algebra Suppose p is a prime number greater than 2. Does $p + 1$ represent a prime or a composite number? Explain.

38. An *emirp* (*prime* spelled backward) is a number that is a *different* prime when its digits are reversed. The number 13 is the first emirp (13 and 31). Find the other emirps less than 100.

39. Stretch Your Thinking Norma used a total of 192 digits to number the pages of her book, starting with page 1. How many pages are in Norma's book?

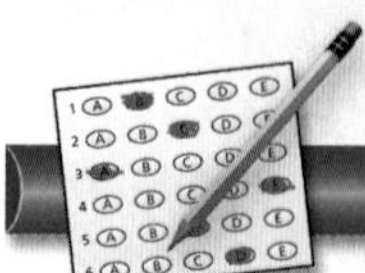

Test Prep

Multiple Choice

40. What is the prime factorization of 48?
A. $12 \cdot 4$ **B.** $6 \cdot 2^4$ **C.** $3 \cdot 2 \cdot 2^2$ **D.** $3 \cdot 2^4$

41. What number has the prime factorization $2^3 \times 3^2 \times 7$?
F. 252 **G.** 336 **H.** 378 **I.** 504

Short Response

42. Make a factor tree for 81. Write the prime factorization.

43. a. Explain why $2^3 \times 5^2 \times 9 \times 11 \times 15$ is NOT a correct prime factorization.
b. Give the correct prime factorization.

Take It to the NET
Online lesson quiz at
www.PHSchool.com
Web Code: aaa-0302

Mixed Review

Lesson 2-7

Algebra **Solve each equation.**

44. $x \div 3 = 12$ **45.** $x \div 10 = 5$ **46.** $30 = y \div 6$

Lesson 1-10

Use <, =, or > to complete each statement.

47. $(8 + 10) \div 2$ ■ $14 \div (2 + 5)$ **48.** $4 + 12 \times 2$ ■ $(6 + 10) \div 2$

49. $3.5 + 2.5 \times 2$ ■ $24 \div 4 + 3$ **50.** $15 - 5 \div 5$ ■ $4 \times 7 \div 2$

Practice Game

Triple Prime Time

Getting Started

- Draw a 4-by-4 grid.
- Arrange the following numbers on your grid, one in each square.
  12, 18, 20, 28, 30, 42, 45, 50, 63, 66, 70, 75, 105, 110, 154, 165
- The host writes the prime numbers **2, 3, 5, 7,** and **11** on separate pieces of paper and puts them in a container.

How to Play

- The host draws a prime number, calls it out, and replaces it.
- Find a number on your grid for which the number called is a factor. Write the number called in that square.
- The host continues to draw slips and call numbers.
- When you record all three prime factors for a square, cross out the square. For example, you can cross out the square with 28 when you record 2, 2, and 7.
- The first player to cross out 4 squares in a row wins.

Extension The Sieve of Eratosthenes

For Use With Lesson 3-2

Eratosthenes (circa 275–194 B.C.) was a Greek scientist. He found a method to identify prime numbers. This method is now known as the "Sieve of Eratosthenes."

Activity

To make the sieve for numbers up to 40, follow these steps.

Step 1 Make a list of whole numbers from 1 to 40. Cross out 1, since it is not prime.

Step 2 Circle 2, the first prime number. Cross out every number divisible by 2, beginning with 4.

~~1~~ (2) 3 ~~4~~ 5 ~~6~~ 7 ~~8~~ 9 ~~10~~
11 ~~12~~ 13 ~~14~~ 15 ~~16~~ 17 ~~18~~ 19 ~~20~~
21 ~~22~~ 23 ~~24~~ 25 ~~26~~ 27 ~~28~~ 29 ~~30~~
31 ~~32~~ 33 ~~34~~ 35 ~~36~~ 37 ~~38~~ 39 ~~40~~

Step 3 The next unmarked number, 3, is prime. Circle it. Cross out every number divisible by 3, beginning with 6. (Some numbers will already be crossed out.)

~~1~~ (2) (3) ~~4~~ 5 ~~6~~ 7 ~~8~~ ~~9~~ ~~10~~
11 ~~12~~ 13 ~~14~~ ~~15~~ ~~16~~ 17 ~~18~~ 19 ~~20~~
~~21~~ ~~22~~ 23 ~~24~~ 25 ~~26~~ ~~27~~ ~~28~~ 29 ~~30~~
31 ~~32~~ ~~33~~ ~~34~~ 35 ~~36~~ 37 ~~38~~ ~~39~~ ~~40~~

Step 4 Circle the next unmarked number, 5. Cross out every number divisible by 5 that is greater than 5.

Step 5 Continue until all numbers have been circled or crossed out. The circled numbers are prime.

EXERCISES

1. **a.** Use the method of the Sieve of Eratosthenes to find the prime numbers between 2 and 100. List them.
   b. *Twin primes* are pairs of prime numbers that differ by 2. For example, 11 and 13 are twin primes. Identify all the twin primes less than 100.

2. **Reasoning** Explain why it is not necessary to cross out numbers divisible by 9.

3. **Algebra** Many prime numbers have the form $6n + 1$, where n is a whole number. Two examples are $6(1) + 1 = 7$ and $6(2) + 1 = 13$. Evaluate $6n + 1$ for each value of n, and identify the result as prime or composite.
   a. $n = 6$ **b.** $n = 8$ **c.** $n = 13$ **d.** $n = 15$

3-3 Greatest Common Factor

What You'll Learn

To find the greatest common factor of two or more numbers

. . . And Why

To equally distribute stamps, as in Example 1

✓ Check Skills You'll Need

For help, go to Lesson 3-2.

Find the prime factorization of each number.

1. 45 **2.** 21 **3.** 99

4. 93 **5.** 39 **6.** 128

7. Error Analysis Explain why the expression $2 \times 3 \times 13 \times 21 \times 31$ is not a correct prime factorization.

New Vocabulary • common factor • greatest common factor (GCF)

OBJECTIVE

Interactive lesson includes instant self-check, tutorials, and activities.

1 Finding the Greatest Common Factor

Suppose a stamp club president equally distributes two different sets of stamps among the club members. One set contains 18 stamps. The other set contains 30 stamps. There are no stamps left undistributed. What is the greatest possible number of club members?

The number of possible club members depends on the common factors of 18 and 30. A factor that two or more numbers share is a **common factor.**

The **greatest common factor (GCF)** of two or more numbers is the greatest factor shared by all the numbers. You can find the GCF of two numbers by listing their factors.

Real-World Connection

Careers Collectors buy and sell rare items including stamps, coins, antiques, and sports memorabilia.

1 EXAMPLE Using Lists of Factors

Find the greatest common factor of 18 and 30.

List the factors of 18 and the factors of 30. Then circle the common factors.

Factors of 18: (1), (2), (3), (6), 9, 18
Factors of 30: (1), (2), (3), 5, (6), 10, 15, 30

← The common factors are 1, 2, 3, and 6.

The greatest common factor (GCF) is 6.

✓ Check Understanding

1 List the factors to find the GCF of each set of numbers.

a. 6, 21 **b.** 18, 49 **c.** 14, 28

d. Number Sense Based on Example 1, no more than six people can share equally 18 stamps from one set and 30 stamps from another set. How many stamps from each set will each person receive?

You can also use a division ladder or factor trees to find the greatest common factor of two or more numbers.

2 EXAMPLE Using a Division Ladder

Use a division ladder to find the GCF of 42 and 56.

2) 42 56 ← **Divide by 2, a common factor of 42 and 56.**
7) 21 28 ← **Divide by 7, a common factor of 21 and 28.**
↑ 3 4 ← **3 and 4 have no common factors.**
Multiply the common factors: $2 \times 7 = 14$.

The GCF of 42 and 56 is 14.

Check Understanding 2 Use a division ladder to find the GCF of each set of numbers.
a. 24, 54 **b.** 18, 27, 36

3 EXAMPLE Using Factor Trees

Use factor trees to find the GCF of 27 and 36.

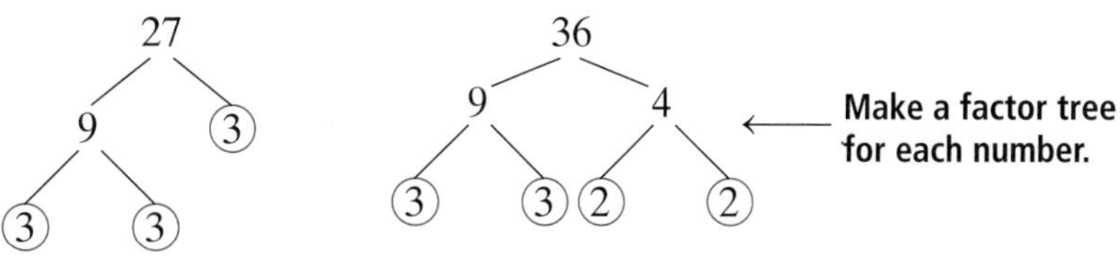

$27 = \boxed{3} \times \boxed{3} \times 3$ ← **Write the prime factorization for each number.**
$36 = \boxed{3} \times \boxed{3} \times 2 \times 2$

↑ ↑ **Identify common factors.**

$3 \times 3 = 9$ ← **Multiply the common factors.**

The GCF of 27 and 36 is 9.

Check Understanding 3 Use factor trees to find the GCF of each set of numbers.
a. 12, 32 **b.** 18, 42

EXERCISES

For more practice, see *Extra Practice*.

A Practice by Example

List the factors to find the GCF of each set of numbers.

Example 1 (page 128)

1. 14, 35 **2.** 24, 45 **3.** 26, 34

4. 30, 35 **5.** 48, 88 **6.** 36, 63

Example 2 (page 129) **Use a division ladder to find the GCF of each set of numbers.**

7. 10, 18 **8.** 24, 60 **9.** 11, 23

10. 27, 30 **11.** 12, 16, 28 **12.** 33, 55, 132

Example 3 (page 129) **Use factor trees to find the GCF of each set of numbers. Exercise 13 has been started for you.**

13. 22, 110 $22 = 2 \times 11$; $110 = 2 \times 5 \times 11$; GCF = ■

14. 20, 60 **15.** 54, 84 **16.** 72, 120

17. 64, 125 **18.** 117, 130 **19.** 45, 150

B Apply Your Skills

Find the GCF of each set of numbers.

20. 300, 450 **21.** 280, 420 **22.** 200, 300, 400

23. 50, 250, 425 **24.** 31, 32, 33 **25.** 16, 60, 90

26. Summer Camp At a camp, 14 counselors and 77 campers will be split into groups for activities. Each group will have the same number of counselors and the same number of campers. At most, how many groups can there be? How many counselors will be in each group? How many campers?

Real-World Connection

Over six million children attend camp in the United States each summer.
SOURCE: National Camp Association

27. Baseball Cards Three friends pool their money to buy baseball cards. Brand A has 8 cards in each pack, Brand B has 12 cards, and Brand C has 15 cards. If they want to split the cards equally, which two brands should they buy? Explain.

28. Writing in Math Suppose several people are going to share equally 24 stamps from one set and 36 stamps from another set. Explain why 9 people cannot share the stamps equally.

Mental Math **Find the GCF of each set of numbers.**

29. 8, 12, 20 **30.** 3, 5, 7 **31.** 30, 50, 70

32. Error Analysis Find and correct the error(s) in the following statement.

Since $36 = 6^2$ and $18 = 3 \cdot 6$, the GCF of 36 and 18 is 6.

33. Reasoning Which number less than 50 has the most factors? List the factors of that number.

C Challenge

34. Stretch Your Thinking Below are three different two-digit numbers. Each is less than 50 and ends in 6. Find the GCF of the numbers.

■6; ■6; ■6

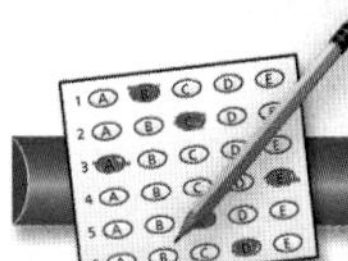

Test Prep

Multiple Choice

35. What is the greatest common factor of 56 and 84?
A. 4 **B.** 12 **C.** 14 **D.** 28

Take It to the NET
Online lesson quiz at **www.PHSchool.com**
Web Code: aaa-0303

36. What are the common factors of 36 and 54?
F. 1, 2, 3, 6, 9 **G.** 1, 2, 3, 4, 6, 9
H. 1, 2, 3, 6, 9, 18 **I.** 1, 2, 4, 6, 9, 18

37. What is the greatest common factor of 60 and 132?
A. 2×3 **B.** $2^2 \times 3$ **C.** 2×3^2 **D.** $2^2 \times 3^2$

Short Response

38. For a field day, 84 girls and 78 boys will be split into teams. Each team will have the same number of girls and the same number of boys.
a. At most, how many teams are possible?
b. How many girls and how many boys will be on each team?

Mixed Review

Lesson 1-10

39. You buy 3 packs of notebook paper at $1.25 each and a binder for $1.50.
a. Write an expression for the total cost of the items you want.
b. Find the total cost.

Lesson 1-2

Write each decimal in words.

40. 0.4 **41.** 0.9 **42.** 0.10 **43.** 0.80

Checkpoint Quiz 1 — Lessons 3-1 through 3-3

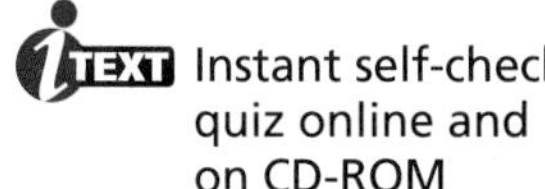

Instant self-check quiz online and on CD-ROM

Test each number for divisibility by 2, 3, 5, 9, or 10.

1. 375 **2.** 1,402 **3.** 240

Find the prime factorization of each number.

4. 48 **5.** 80 **6.** 1,000

Find the GCF of each set of numbers.

7. 45, 80 **8.** 24,72 **9.** 9, 18, 51

10. Make two lists of factors to find all the common factors of 18 and 48.

Investigation

Modeling Fractions

For Use With Lesson 3-4

A fraction describes a part of a set of items, or a part of a whole item. The whole item must be split into equal parts.

$\frac{3}{4}$ ← The numerator shows how many parts are being considered.
← The denominator shows the total number of parts.

1 EXAMPLE Writing Fractions

Write a fraction for each situation.

a. What fraction of the flowers are red?

There are 9 red flowers and 16 flowers altogether. So, $\frac{9}{16}$ of the flowers are red.

b. What fraction of the pie is left?

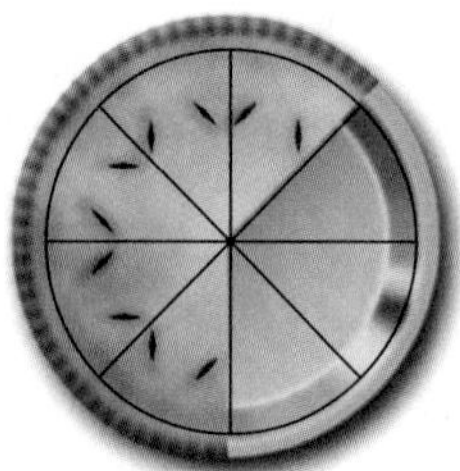

The pie had 8 equal pieces. Five are left. So $\frac{5}{8}$ of the pie is left.

c. On the number line, what fraction describes point *A*?

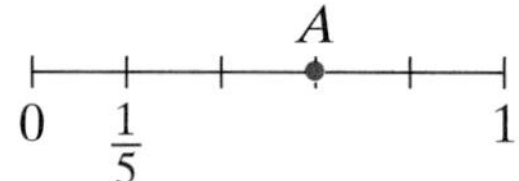

The segment from 0 to 1 is divided into 5 equal parts. So, $\frac{3}{5}$ describes point *A*.

EXERCISES

Name the fraction represented by each model.

1.

2.

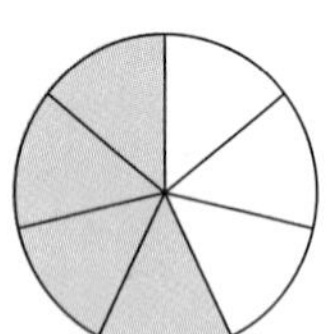

3.
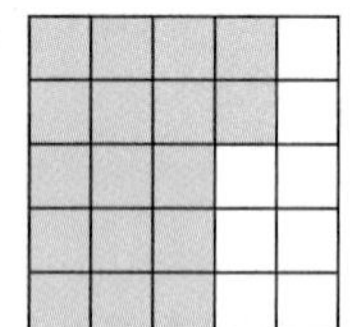

4.
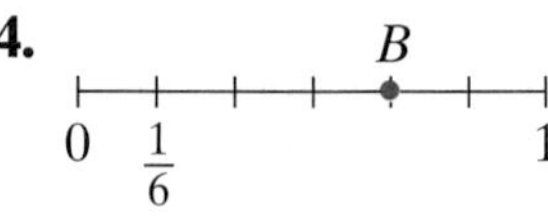

Draw a fraction model for each situation.

5. $\frac{3}{4}$ as part of a set

6. $\frac{4}{7}$ as part of a whole

7. $\frac{5}{8}$ on a number line

8. At the grocery store, you purchase 5 apples and 7 oranges. What fraction of the fruit is apples?

9. **Number Sense** What fraction is represented when all parts of a fraction model are shaded? When no parts are shaded?

The marks on an inch ruler are based on fractions.

2 EXAMPLE Fractions on a Ruler 

Biology Find the length shown for each insect.

a.

The ruler is marked every $\frac{1}{8}$ inch. The insect extends over seven $\frac{1}{8}$-inch spaces.

So, the length of the insect is $\frac{7}{8}$ inch.

b.

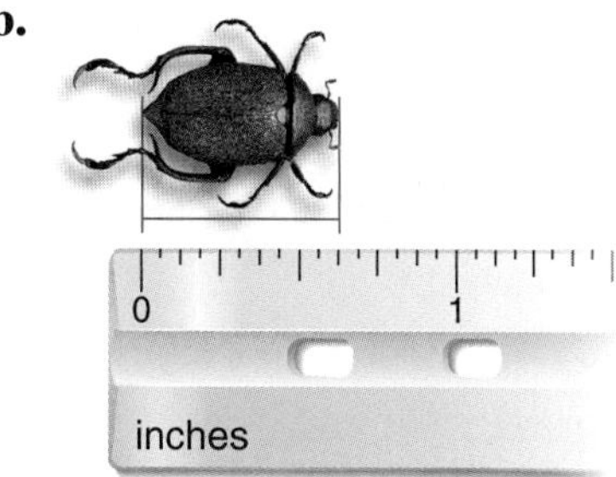

The ruler is marked every $\frac{1}{16}$ inch. The insect extends over ten $\frac{1}{16}$-inch spaces.

So, the length of the insect is $\frac{10}{16}$, or $\frac{5}{8}$ inch.

EXERCISES

Find the length of each segment.

10. 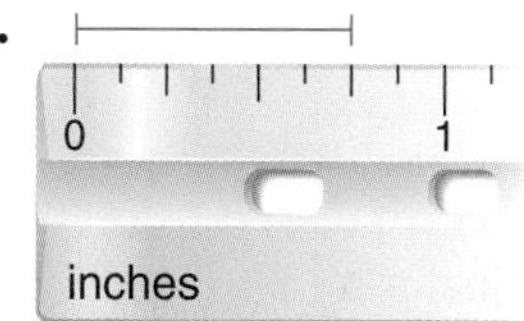

11. 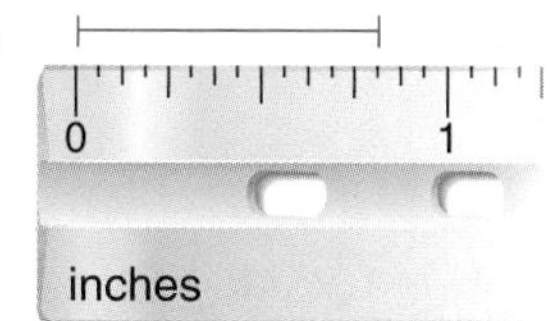

12. 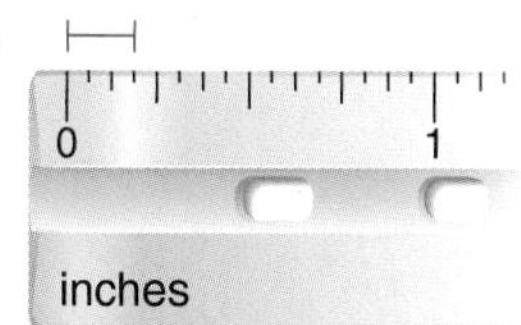

Use a ruler to measure the length of each segment or object. Measure to the nearest sixteenth of an inch.

13. ———

14. ————

15. —————

16. ——

17. 

18. 

19. 

20. 

3-4 Equivalent Fractions

What You'll Learn

To find equivalent fractions

To write fractions in simplest form

. . . And Why

To simplify statistics, as in Exercise 17

✔ Check Skills You'll Need

For help, go to Lesson 3-3.

Find the GCF of each set of numbers.

1. 8, 12
2. 20, 25
3. 12, 30
4. 5, 18
5. 36, 100
6. 7, 21, 28

New Vocabulary • equivalent fractions • simplest form

Interactive lesson includes instant self-check, tutorials, and activities.

OBJECTIVE 1 Finding Equivalent Fractions

The two fraction models at the right have the same amount shaded. **Equivalent fractions** are fractions that name the same amount.

$\frac{2}{3}$ $\frac{4}{6}$

$\frac{2}{3} = \frac{4}{6}$

You form equivalent fractions by multiplying (or dividing) the numerator and denominator of a fraction by the same nonzero number.

1 EXAMPLE Equivalent Fractions

Write three fractions equivalent to $\frac{6}{8}$.

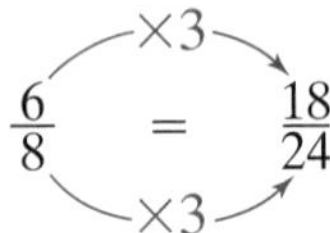

$\frac{6}{8} = \frac{12}{16}$ ← Multiply the numerator and denominator by 2.

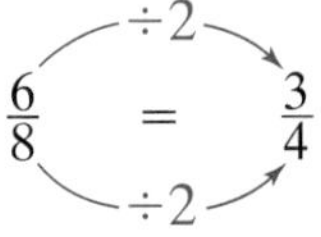

$\frac{6}{8} = \frac{18}{24}$ ← Multiply the numerator and denominator by 3.

$\frac{6}{8} = \frac{3}{4}$ ← Divide the numerator and denominator by 2.

So, $\frac{3}{4} = \frac{6}{8} = \frac{12}{16} = \frac{18}{24}$.

✔ Check Understanding 1 Write three fractions equivalent to each fraction.

a. $\frac{4}{10}$ b. $\frac{5}{8}$ c. $\frac{2}{6}$

OBJECTIVE 2

Writing Fractions in Simplest Form

A fraction is in **simplest form** when the only common factor of the numerator and denominator is 1. For example, $\frac{2}{3}$ is in simplest form, since 2 and 3 have only 1 as a common factor.

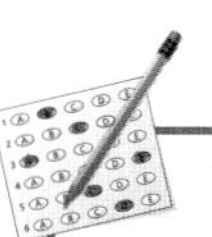

Test-Prep Tip

Some standardized tests may ask you to write a fraction in lowest terms, which is the same as simplest form.

One way to write a fraction in simplest form is to divide both the numerator and denominator by their greatest common factor.

2 EXAMPLE Fractions in Simplest Form

Write $\frac{20}{28}$ in simplest form.

20: 1, 2, 4, 5, 10, 20 ← **List the factors for the numerator and denominator.**

28: 1, 2, 4, 7, 14, 28 ← **Find the greatest common factor.**

$\frac{20}{28} = \frac{5}{7}$ (÷4 numerator and denominator) ← **Divide the numerator and denominator by the GCF.**

The fraction $\frac{20}{28}$ written in simplest form is $\frac{5}{7}$.

Check Understanding 2 Write each fraction in simplest form.

a. $\frac{24}{32}$ **b.** $\frac{14}{49}$ **c.** $\frac{20}{100}$

3 EXAMPLE Real-World  Problem Solving

Pet Foods A pet store stocks 36 different types of cat food, 42 types of dog food, 18 types of bird food, and 24 other pet foods. In simplest form, what fraction of the foods are cat foods?

Add to find the total number of foods: 36 + 42 + 18 + 24 = 120.

Write the fraction.

$\frac{36}{120}$ ← **number of cat foods** / ← **total number of foods**

$\frac{36}{120} = \frac{3}{10}$ (÷12 numerator and denominator) ← **Divide the numerator and denominator by the GCF, 12.**

So, $\frac{3}{10}$ of the foods are cat foods.

Check Understanding 3 **a.** In simplest form, what fraction of the foods are dog foods?

b. **Reasoning** Which two types of foods together make up $\frac{1}{2}$ of the foods? Explain your reasoning.

EXERCISES

For more practice, see *Extra Practice*.

A Practice by Example

Write two fractions equivalent to each fraction.

Example 1 (page 134)

1. $\frac{2}{4}$ 2. $\frac{6}{7}$ 3. $\frac{12}{18}$ 4. $\frac{3}{16}$

5. $\frac{3}{10}$ 6. $\frac{3}{9}$ 7. $\frac{1}{20}$ 8. $\frac{15}{20}$

Example 2 (page 135)

Write each fraction in simplest form.

9. $\frac{4}{6}$ 10. $\frac{10}{35}$ 11. $\frac{10}{20}$ 12. $\frac{40}{50}$

13. $\frac{15}{45}$ 14. $\frac{6}{8}$ 15. $\frac{12}{18}$ 16. $\frac{9}{21}$

Example 3 (page 135)

17. **Sports** Over the last three seasons, a school football team has won 15 out of 25 games. In simplest form, what fraction of their games have they won?

18. **Greeting Cards** A store stocks 50 birthday cards, 10 anniversary cards, and 45 get-well cards. In simplest form, what fraction of the cards are get-well cards?

B Apply Your Skills

State whether each fraction is in simplest form. If it is not, write it in simplest form.

19. $\frac{6}{8}$ 20. $\frac{1}{7}$ 21. $\frac{12}{18}$ 22. $\frac{4}{5}$

23. $\frac{24}{56}$ 24. $\frac{21}{77}$ 25. $\frac{25}{150}$ 26. $\frac{3}{50}$

27. $\frac{15}{135}$ 28. $\frac{17}{51}$ 29. $\frac{10}{65}$ 30. $\frac{120}{150}$

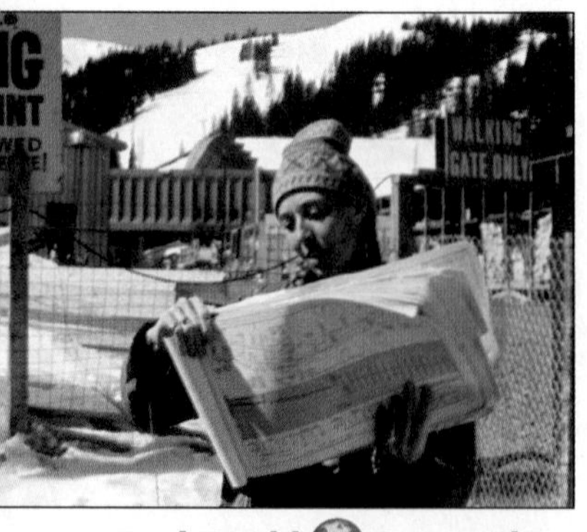

Real-World Connection

Careers Traffic engineers study things that influence traffic conditions, such as traffic volume and signals.

31. **Traffic Planning** Two traffic engineers are writing about the average driving time between two towns. One engineer writes the time as 45, but the other writes it as $\frac{3}{4}$. What could explain the difference?

32. **Data File, p. 117** Indicate which size wrenches are equivalent to $\frac{6}{16}$ inch, $\frac{12}{16}$ inch, and $\frac{30}{32}$ inch.

33. **Writing in Math** How can you use the GCF of the numerator and the denominator to write a fraction in simplest form?

Name the fractions modeled and determine if they are equivalent.

34. 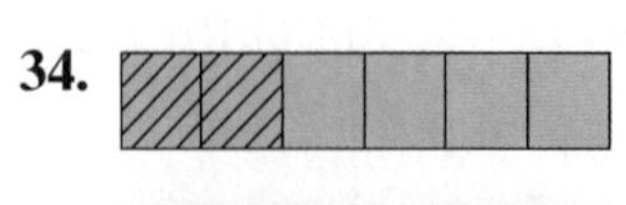
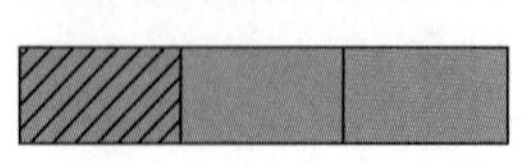

35. 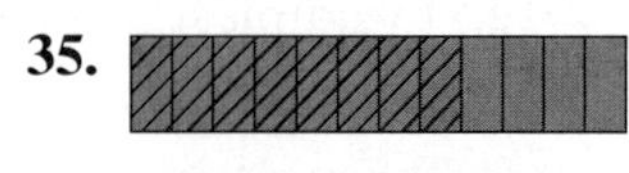
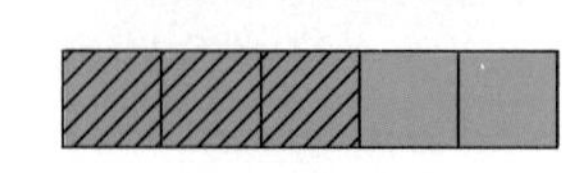

36. 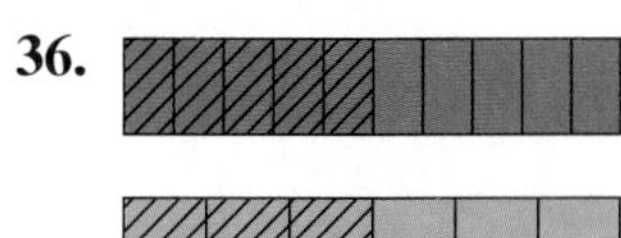
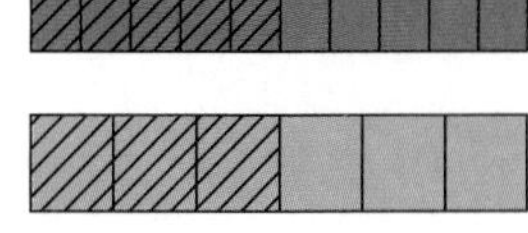

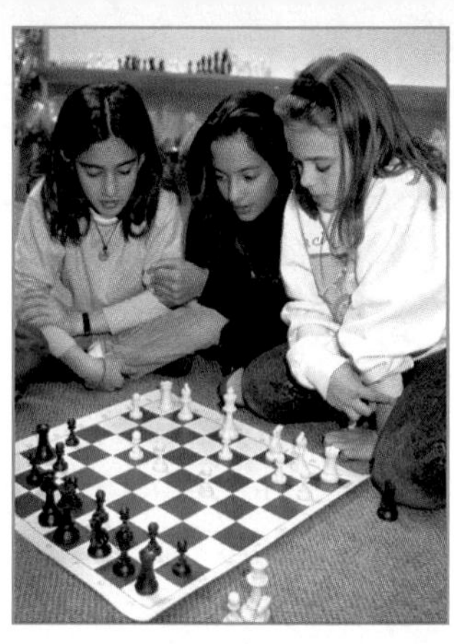

37. **Games** On a chessboard, 32 of the squares are white. At the start of a game, each player places half of her 16 pieces on white squares. What fraction of the white squares have pieces on them?

38. **Open-Ended** Choose from the numbers 2, 3, 4, 6, 12, 18, and 24. Write three pairs of equivalent fractions.

C Challenge

39. a. **Algebra** Evaluate $\frac{2a}{3a}$ for $a = 1, 2, 5,$ and 10. Write each result as a fraction.
    b. When a is a nonzero whole number, what do you think is the simplest form for $\frac{2a}{3a}$? Explain.

40. **Stretch Your Thinking** A fraction greater than $\frac{1}{8}$ and less than $\frac{1}{4}$ is in simplest form. Its denominator is four more than its numerator. What is the fraction?

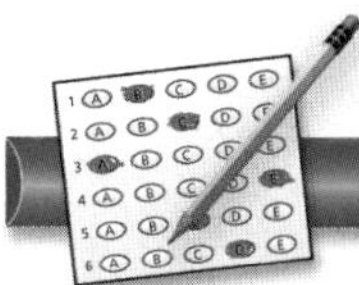

Test Prep

Gridded Response

41. How do you write $\frac{80}{100}$ as a fraction in simplest form?

42. The length of a segment is $\frac{3}{8}$ inch. How do you write the length as a fraction with 16 as its denominator?

43. In simplest form, what fraction of an hour is 40 minutes?

44. Samantha made 45 out of 75 free throw attempts. In simplest form, what fraction of her attempts did she make?

45. A newsstand stocks 21 different newspapers and 35 different magazines. In simplest form, what fraction represents the portion that is newspapers?

Mixed Review

Lesson 3-3 **Find the GCF of each set of numbers.**

46. 48, 56 47. 15, 21 48. 42, 72 49. 300, 450

Lesson 2-7 **Algebra** **Solve each equation. Check your solution.**

50. $4x = 36$ 51. $6x = 5.4$ 52. $20x = 1$ 53. $0.5x = 10$

Technology

Simplifying Fractions

For Use With Lesson 3-4

You can use a fraction calculator to simplify a fraction. The calculator divides the numerator and denominator by a common factor and rewrites the fraction. Repeat the process until the fraction is in simplest form.

EXAMPLE

Use a fraction calculator to simplify $\frac{9}{27}$.

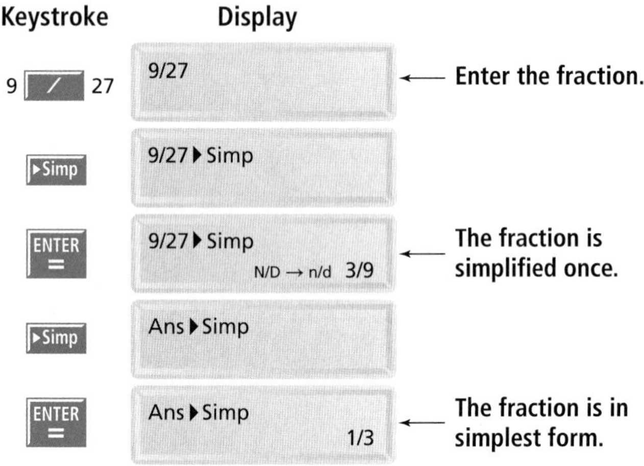

In simplest form, $\frac{9}{27} = \frac{1}{3}$.

EXERCISES

Use a fraction calculator to simplify each fraction.

1. $\frac{18}{51}$ **2.** $\frac{21}{49}$ **3.** $\frac{102}{387}$ **4.** $\frac{35}{56}$

5. $\frac{20}{65}$ **6.** $\frac{17}{68}$ **7.** $\frac{12}{15}$ **8.** $\frac{28}{32}$

9. $\frac{12}{30}$ **10.** $\frac{45}{75}$ **11.** $\frac{24}{32}$ **12.** $\frac{12}{96}$

13. $\frac{35}{45}$ **14.** $\frac{14}{63}$ **15.** $\frac{40}{48}$ **16.** $\frac{105}{180}$

17. $\frac{92}{132}$ **18.** $\frac{39}{117}$ **19.** $\frac{126}{324}$ **20.** $\frac{200}{385}$

21. **Writing in Math** Explain how you know whether the calculator does or does not use the greatest common factor (GCF) when simplifying.

3-5 Mixed Numbers and Improper Fractions

What You'll Learn

 To write numbers as improper fractions

 To write fractions as mixed numbers

. . . And Why

To convert measurements, as in Example 2

For help, go to Lesson 3-4.

Write each fraction in simplest form.

1. $\frac{9}{27}$ **2.** $\frac{18}{27}$ **3.** $\frac{20}{64}$ **4.** $\frac{3}{51}$ **5.** $\frac{36}{40}$

6. Explain how to write 35 minutes as a fraction of an hour.

New Vocabulary • proper fraction • improper fraction • mixed number

OBJECTIVE

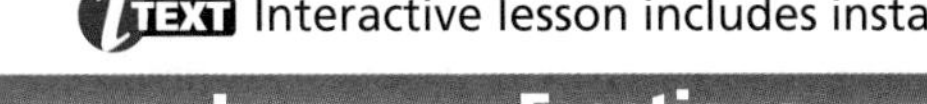

1 Writing Mixed Numbers as Improper Fractions

Investigation: Comparing Numerators and Denominators

1. Which fractions below are less than 1? Equal to 1? Greater than 1?

$\frac{4}{4}$ 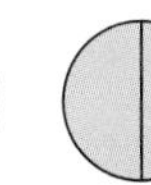 $\frac{5}{2}$ 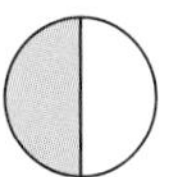 $\frac{1}{6}$ 

$\frac{1}{2}$ $\frac{11}{8}$ 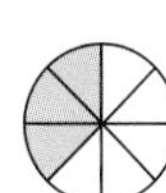 $\frac{3}{3}$ 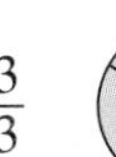 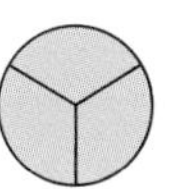

2. Explain how comparing the numerator to the denominator shows whether a fraction is less than, equal to, or greater than 1.

3. Use a ruler to draw a line segment for each length.

a. $1\frac{3}{8}$ inches **b.** $2\frac{3}{4}$ inches **c.** $3\frac{5}{8}$ inches

d. How many eighths are there in each measurement? Explain.

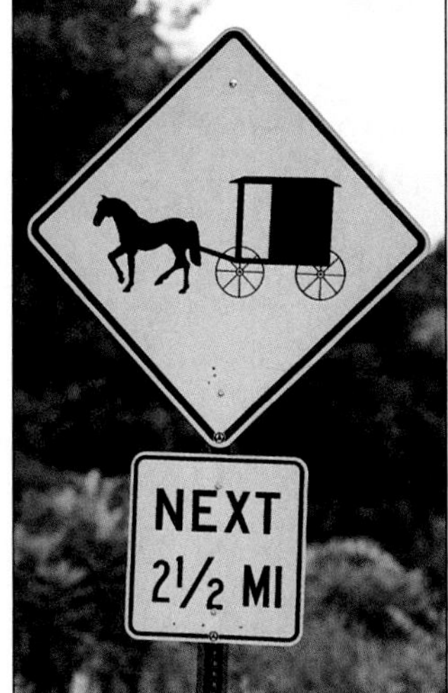

	Examples		
A **proper fraction** has a numerator that is less than its denominator.	$\frac{1}{2}$	$\frac{3}{8}$	$\frac{4}{5}$
An **improper fraction** has a numerator that is greater than or equal to its denominator.	$\frac{5}{2}$	$\frac{11}{8}$	$\frac{5}{5}$
A **mixed number** shows the sum of a whole number and a proper fraction: $2\frac{1}{2} = 2 + \frac{1}{2}$.	$2\frac{1}{2}$	$1\frac{3}{8}$	$1\frac{1}{5}$

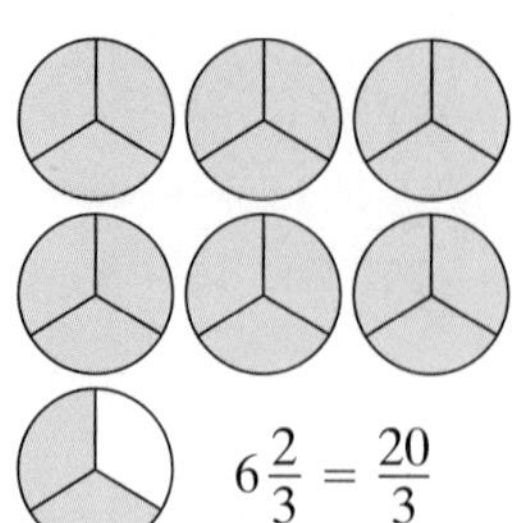
$6\frac{2}{3} = \frac{20}{3}$

1 EXAMPLE Writing Mixed Numbers as Improper Fractions

Write $6\frac{2}{3}$ as an improper fraction.

Multiply the whole number by the denominator. (6 × 3 thirds is 18 thirds.) → $6\frac{2}{3} = \frac{(6 \times 3) + 2}{3}$ ← **Add the numerator. (There are 2 more thirds.)**

$= \frac{20}{3}$ ← **Write as an improper fraction.**

Check Understanding 1 Write $3\frac{4}{7}$ as an improper fraction.

2 EXAMPLE Real-World Problem Solving

Engines A mechanic needs $3\frac{1}{4}$ gallons of oil to fill a diesel engine. How many quarts will the mechanic need? (*Hint:* 1 quart $= \frac{1}{4}$ gallon)

Change $3\frac{1}{4}$ to an improper fraction.

$$3\frac{1}{4} = \frac{3 \times 4 + 1}{4} = \frac{13}{4}$$

Since there are 13 fourths in $3\frac{1}{4}$, the mechanic will need 13 quarts of oil.

Check Understanding 2 **Reasoning** What does the denominator in the improper fraction $\frac{7}{1}$ represent?

OBJECTIVE

2 Writing Improper Fractions as Mixed Numbers

Use division to write an improper fraction as a mixed number.

3 EXAMPLE Writing Improper Fractions as Mixed Numbers

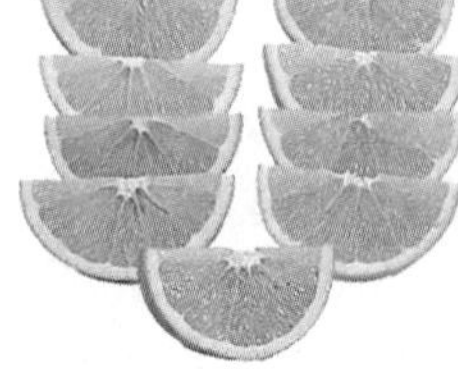

Each orange slice is $\frac{1}{6}$ of an orange. How many oranges are represented by 9 slices?

Write $\frac{9}{6}$ as a mixed number. Begin by dividing 9 by 6.

$6\overline{)9}$ with quotient 1 ← **The quotient represents one whole orange.**

-6

3 ← **The remainder represents three slices.**

$\frac{9}{6} = 1\frac{3}{6}$ ← **Express the remainder as a fraction.**

$= 1\frac{1}{2}$ ← **Simplify.**

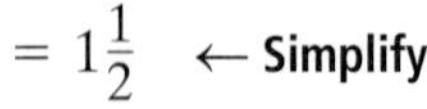

Check Understanding 3 Write each improper fraction as a mixed number in simplest form.

a. $\frac{40}{9}$ **b.** $\frac{32}{6}$ **c.** $\frac{23}{4}$ **d.** $\frac{30}{18}$

EXERCISES

For more practice, see *Extra Practice.*

A Practice by Example

Examples 1, 2 (page 140)

Write each mixed number as an improper fraction. Exercise 1 has been started for you.

1. $3\frac{5}{6} = \frac{(3 \times 6) + 5}{6} = \blacksquare$ **2.** $1\frac{2}{9}$ **3.** $4\frac{3}{5}$

4. $1\frac{4}{15}$ **5.** $7\frac{1}{7}$ **6.** $21\frac{1}{3}$ **7.** $5\frac{1}{2}$

8. $1\frac{3}{11}$ **9.** $3\frac{3}{8}$ **10.** $2\frac{1}{16}$ **11.** $3\frac{1}{4}$

12. Engines Your family car needs $1\frac{1}{4}$ gallons of oil. How many $\frac{1}{4}$'s are in $1\frac{1}{4}$?

Example 3 (page 140)

Write each improper fraction as a mixed number in simplest form.

13. $\frac{17}{5}$ **14.** $\frac{10}{4}$ **15.** $\frac{27}{12}$ **16.** $\frac{9}{4}$

17. $\frac{21}{14}$ **18.** $\frac{18}{11}$ **19.** $\frac{21}{10}$ **20.** $\frac{16}{12}$

B Apply Your Skills

Write each mixed number as an improper fraction. Write each improper fraction as a mixed number in simplest form.

21. $4\frac{5}{7}$ **22.** $\frac{68}{8}$ **23.** $\frac{106}{5}$ **24.** $11\frac{13}{15}$

25. $\frac{232}{12}$ **26.** $15\frac{1}{10}$ **27.** $1\frac{11}{12}$ **28.** $\frac{80}{9}$

Find the length of each segment. Write mixed numbers in simplest form.

29.

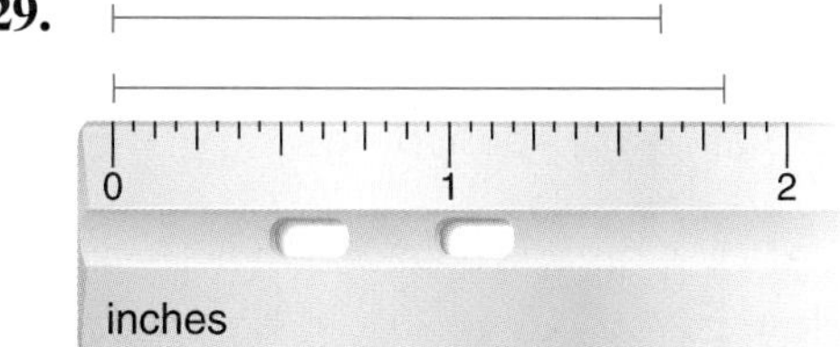

30.

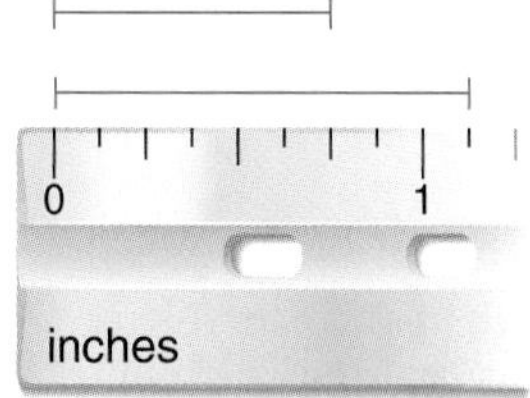

Reading Math

Most fraction names end in *-ths* or *-rds.*

Write each number as an improper fraction and as a mixed number.

31. 33 halves **32.** 7 fifths **33.** 106 fourths

34. 2 and 3 fifths **35.** 8 and 7 ninths **36.** 6 and 3 sevenths

37. Food A caterer plans to serve two slices of melon to each of 50 guests. She estimates getting 12 slices from each melon. Write the number of melons she will use as a mixed number. How many whole melons does she need?

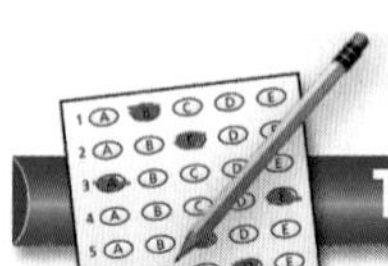

Challenge

38. **Open-Ended** Find a number that is between $\frac{6}{4}$ and $\frac{7}{4}$. Write your answer as an improper fraction and as a mixed number.

39. **Stretch Your Thinking** Replace each ■ with either the number 5 or an addition sign to get the sum shown.

■ ■ ■ ■ ■ ■ ■ ■ ■ ■ = 1,165

Test Prep

Reading Comprehension

Read the passage and answer the questions below.

Gifts From the Sea

Pearls are the only gems that come from the sea. They are also the only gems made by living things—mollusks.

The largest pearl was found in the Philippines in 1934. It was $9\frac{1}{2}$ inches long with a diameter of $5\frac{1}{2}$ inches. The pearl weighed 14 pounds 1 ounce.

40. Which improper fraction represents the diameter of the pearl?

A. $5\frac{1}{2}$ inches B. $\frac{7}{2}$ inches C. $\frac{11}{2}$ inches D. $\frac{19}{2}$ inches

41. Which number represents the weight of the pearl in pounds? (*Hint:* There are 16 ounces in a pound.)

F. $1\frac{1}{4}$ G. $1\frac{14}{16}$ H. $14\frac{1}{16}$ I. $14\frac{1}{4}$

Short Response

42. a. A number pattern begins $1\frac{1}{2}, 2\frac{1}{4}, 3, 3\frac{3}{4}, 4\frac{1}{2}, \ldots$ Write the next three numbers in the pattern.
b. Explain your reasoning.

Take It to the NET
Online lesson quiz at
www.PHSchool.com
Web Code: aaa-0305

43. A chef cuts his spice cakes into 16 servings each.
a. How many cakes should he prepare in order to serve 150 people?
b. What part of a cake will be left over?

Mixed Review

Lesson 2-5

Tell whether each equation is true or false.

44. $48 \div 6 = 8$ 45. $0.7 + 0.8 = 15$ 46. $1.8 = 5.4 \div 3$

Lesson 2-2

Algebra **Evaluate each expression for $x = 7$.**

47. $3x + 5$ 48. $42 \div x$ 49. $(x + 3) - 4$

3-6 Least Common Multiple

What You'll Learn

To find the least common multiple of numbers

. . . And Why

To find when three trains will arrive at a station, as in Example 2

Check Skills You'll Need

For help, go to Lesson 3-3.

Find the prime factorization of each number.

1. 80	**2.** 32	**3.** 95
4. 500	**5.** 208	**6.** 625

New Vocabulary • common multiple • least common multiple (LCM)

 Interactive lesson includes instant self-check, tutorials, and activities.

OBJECTIVE 1 Finding the Least Common Multiple

Peg gets a haircut every four weeks. Pam gets a haircut every six weeks at the same time and place as Peg. If Peg meets Pam while getting a haircut, when would they meet again?

You can list *multiples* of 4 and 6 to answer this question. A **multiple** of a number is the product of that number and a nonzero whole number.

$6 \times 1 = 6$
$6 \times 2 = 12$
$6 \times 3 = 18$
$6 \times 4 = 24$
$6 \times \blacksquare =$ multiple of 6

A number that is a multiple of each of two or more numbers is a **common multiple.** The **least common multiple (LCM)** of two or more numbers is the least multiple that is common to all the numbers.

Real-World Connection

Americans spend $45 billion on haircuts and hair care each year.

1 EXAMPLE Finding the LCM Using Lists of Multiples

Find the least common multiple of 4 and 6.

multiples of 4: 4, 8, (12), 16, 20, (24)
multiples of 6: 6, (12), 18, (24)

← **List multiples of each number. 12 and 24 are common multiples.**

The least common multiple is 12.

Check Understanding 1 **a.** List multiples to find the LCM of 10 and 12.
b. **Number Sense** Name the first five common multiples of 4 and 6.

REGULAR SERVICE	EVERY
YELLOW LINE	8 MIN
GREEN LINE	10 MIN
PURPLE LINE	20 MIN

2 EXAMPLE LCM From Prime Factorizations

Scheduling Suppose the three trains in the table have just arrived together. In how many minutes will they arrive together again?

Write the prime factorizations for 8, 10, and 20. Then circle each different factor where it appears the greatest number of times.

$8 = \boxed{2 \times 2 \times 2}$ ← **2 appears three times.**

$10 = 2 \times \boxed{5}$ ← **5 appears once.**

$20 = 2 \times 2 \times 5$ ← **Don't circle 5 again.**

$2 \times 2 \times 2 \times 5 = 40$ ← **Multiply the circled factors.**

The LCM of 8, 10, and 20 is 40. So, it will be 40 minutes until the trains again arrive at the same time.

Check Understanding 2 Use prime factorizations to find the LCM of: 25, 35, and 50.

More Than One Way

Find the LCM of 20, 30, and 45.

Michael's Method

I can use the prime factorizations of 20, 30, and 45 to find the LCM.

$20 = \boxed{2 \times 2} \times \boxed{5}$ ← **2 appears twice. 5 appears once.**

$30 = 2 \times 3 \times 5$ ← **Don't circle 2 or 5 again.**

$45 = \boxed{3 \times 3} \times 5$ ← **3 appears twice.**

$2 \times 2 \times 3 \times 3 \times 5 = 180$ ← **Multiply the circled factors.**

The LCM of 20, 30, and 45 is 180.

Amanda's Method

The greatest number is 45. I will list the multiples of 45 until I find one that is also a multiple of 20 and 30.

45, 90, 135, 180

90 is a multiple of 30, but not of 20.

← **180! That's a multiple of both 20 and 30.**

So, the LCM of 20, 30, and 45 is 180.

Choose a Method

Find the LCM of 6, 9, and 10. Explain which method you chose and why.

EXERCISES

For more practice, see *Extra Practice*.

A Practice by Example

Example 1 (page 143)

List multiples to find the LCM of each pair of numbers.

1. 4, 9 **2.** 5, 6 **3.** 12, 15 **4.** 10, 16

5. 14, 21 **6.** 20, 30 **7.** 25, 75 **8.** 8, 10

Example 2 (page 144)

Use prime factorizations to find the LCM of each set of numbers. Exercise 9 has been started for you.

9. 16, 24; $16 = 2 \times 2 \times 2 \times 2$; $24 = 2 \times 2 \times 2 \times 3$; LCM = ■

10. 9, 21 **11.** 18, 24 **12.** 75, 100

13. 8, 14 **14.** 22, 55 **15.** 18, 108

B Apply Your Skills

16. Travel Two ships sail between New York and London. One ship makes the round trip in 12 days. The other ship takes 16 days. They both leave London today. When will both ships leave London together again?

17. Business During a promotion, a music store gives a free CD to every fifteenth customer and a free DVD to every fortieth customer. Which customer will be the first to get both a free CD and a free DVD?

Find the LCM of each set of numbers.

18. 7, 10 **19.** 7, 12 **20.** 7, 14

21. 35, 45 **22.** 22, 25 **23.** 60, 100

24. 4, 7, 20 **25.** 6, 8, 16 **26.** 30, 50, 200

27. $2^2 \times 7, 2 \times 7^2$ **28.** $2^3 \times 7, 2^2 \times 3, 2 \times 3^2 \times 5$

29. Recycling City recycling trucks pick up plastic from a collection bin every 3 days and glass every 5 days.
- **a.** Suppose both items are picked up today. In how many days will both items again be picked up on the same day?
- **b.** Suppose both items are picked up on a Monday. In how many days will they be picked up together on a Sunday?

30. Writing in Math What is the LCM for two numbers that have no common factors greater than 1? Give examples and explain your reasoning.

31. Number Sense A number *N* has both 8 and 10 as factors.
- **a.** Name three other factors of the number *N*, other than 1.
- **b.** What is the smallest the number *N* could be?

32. **Fitness** Suppose you lift weights every third day and swim every fourth day. If you do both activities today, when will you again do both activities on the same day?

33. **Algebra** The LCM of 3 and 6 is 6. The LCM of 5 and 10 is 10. The LCM of x and $2x$ is ■.

C Challenge

Find the LCM of each set of numbers.

34. 3, 8, 12, 15 **35.** 4, 7, 12, 21 **36.** 25, 50, 125, 200

37. 2, 3, 5, 7, 11 **38.** $2^2, 2^4, 2^5$ **39.** 100, 200, 300, 400

40. **Stretch Your Thinking** A gross is a dozen dozens. How many items are in a gross? Write "a dozen dozens" using an exponent.

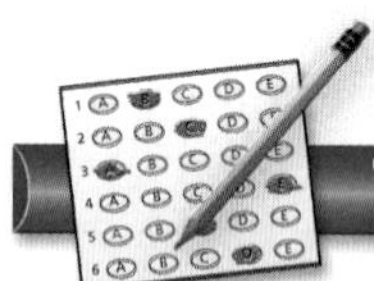

Test Prep

Multiple Choice

41. What is the least common multiple of 24 and 28?
A. 4 **B.** 84 **C.** 168 **D.** 336

42. The least common multiple of 20 and another number is 80. What is the other number?
F. 10 **G.** 16 **H.** 40 **I.** 160

Take It to the NET
Online lesson quiz at www.PHSchool.com
Web Code: aaa-0306

43. What is the least common multiple of 20 and 30?
A. $2 \times 3 \times 5$ **B.** $2^2 \times 3 \times 5$ **C.** $2^2 \times 3^2 \times 5$ **D.** $2^2 \times 3 \times 5^2$

Short Response

44. Folders are sold in packs of 6. Stickers are sold in packs of 10. What is the least number of folders and stickers you can buy so that so you have a sticker for each folder? Explain your reasoning.

Mixed Review

Lesson 1-3

Order each set of decimals on a number line.

45. 0.51, 0.3, 0.49, 0.37, 0.6 **46.** 9.2, 9.28, 9.13, 9.25, 9.26

Lesson 2-8

Write each expression using an exponent. Name the base and the exponent.

47. $5 \times 5 \times 5$ **48.** $4 \times 4 \times 4 \times 4$ **49.** $7 \times 7 \times 7$

50. $2 \times 2 \times 2 \times 2 \times 2$ **51.** 12×12 **52.** 1.5×1.5

Learning Vocabulary

For Use With Lesson 3-6

You can learn new vocabulary by building your own index-card word list.

- Write the term. Then, write the definition.
- Include any math symbols related to the term.
- Give an example that shows how the term is used.
- Give a nonexample showing how the term might *not* apply.

EXAMPLE

Make an index card for the vocabulary term *greatest common factor* (*GCF*).

Index card	
Greatest Common Factor (GCF)	← Write the term.
Definition: The GCF of two or more numbers is the greatest factor shared by all the numbers.	← Write the definition.
Example: The GCF of 12 and 20 is 4.	← Give an example using numbers.
Nonexample: 2 is a common factor of 12 and 20, but is not the GCF.	← Give a nonexample.

Sometimes you can use the everyday meaning of the word as a connection to the mathematical meaning.

A *factor in a decision* forms part of the decision.
A *greatest common factor* is the largest "part" some numbers have in common.

A *composite picture* is a picture made up of many parts.
A *composite number* is a number with more than two factors.

EXERCISES

Make an index card for each vocabulary term. List any helpful everyday meanings.

1. least common multiple

2. equivalent fractions

3. exponent

4. prime number

5. divisible

6. improper fraction

3-7 Comparing and Ordering Fractions

What You'll Learn

 To compare fractions

 To order fractions

. . . And Why

To solve carpentry problems, as in Example 2

Check Skills You'll Need

For help, go to Lesson 3-4.

Write two fractions equivalent to each given fraction.

1. $\frac{3}{7}$
2. $\frac{7}{21}$
3. $\frac{8}{40}$
4. $\frac{2}{3}$
5. $\frac{10}{12}$
6. $\frac{25}{150}$
7. $\frac{6}{8}$
8. $\frac{40}{100}$
9. $\frac{8}{5}$

New Vocabulary • least common denominator (LCD)

OBJECTIVE 1

Comparing Fractions

Interactive lesson includes instant self-check, tutorials, and activities.

Investigation: Comparing Fractions

1. Look at the fraction models below. In each pair, tell whether the top model is less than, equal to, or greater than the bottom model.

a. b. c.

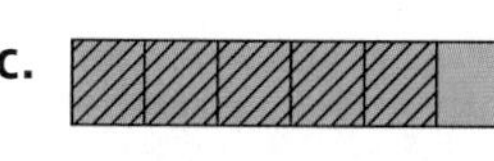

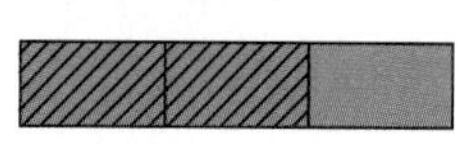

d. e. f.

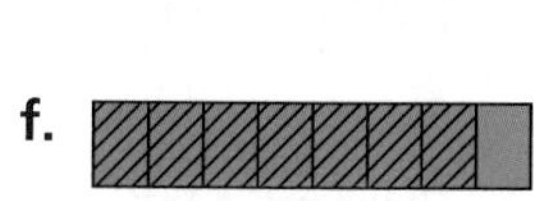

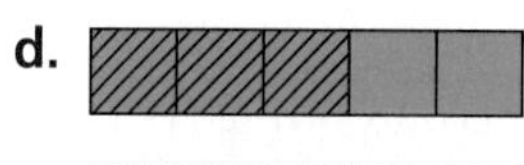

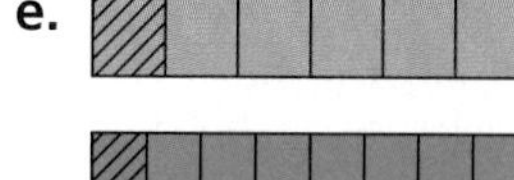

2. Describe a rule to compare fractions with the same denominator.
3. Describe a rule to compare fractions with the same numerator.

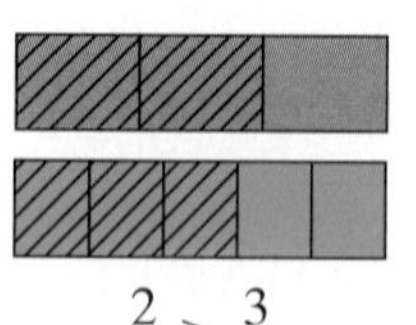

$\frac{2}{3} > \frac{3}{5}$

Which is greater: $\frac{2}{3}$ of an hour or $\frac{3}{5}$ of an hour? Models like those at the left can help you decide. To compare fractions without using models, you can find equivalent fractions that have the same denominator.

Sometimes it is easiest to use the least common denominator. The **least common denominator (LCD)** of two or more fractions is the least common multiple (LCM) of their denominators.

1 EXAMPLE Comparing Fractions With Unlike Denominators

Compare $\frac{5}{6}$ and $\frac{3}{4}$. Use <, =, or >.

Method 1 Multiply denominators to find a common denominator.
Use 6×4, or 24, as a common denominator.

$\frac{5}{6} = \frac{20}{24}$ (×4) $\frac{3}{4} = \frac{18}{24}$ (×6) ← **Find equivalent fractions and compare.**

$\frac{20}{24} > \frac{18}{24}$. So, $\frac{5}{6} > \frac{3}{4}$.

Method 2 Use the least common denominator.
The least common multiple of 6 and 4 is 12. Use 12 as the LCD.

$\frac{5}{6} = \frac{10}{12}$ $\frac{3}{4} = \frac{9}{12}$ ← **Find equivalent fractions and compare.**

$\frac{10}{12} > \frac{9}{12}$. So, $\frac{5}{6} > \frac{3}{4}$.

Check Understanding 1 Compare each pair of fractions. Use <, =, or >.

a. $\frac{6}{8}$ ■ $\frac{7}{9}$ **b.** $\frac{6}{10}$ ■ $\frac{9}{15}$ **c.** $\frac{2}{3}$ ■ $\frac{3}{5}$

d. **Number Sense** Use the common denominator 60 to compare $\frac{2}{3}$ and $\frac{3}{5}$. How many minutes are in $\frac{2}{3}$ of an hour? In $\frac{3}{5}$ of an hour? Which is greater?

Real-World Connection

Careers Carpenters cut, fit, and assemble wood used in the construction of structures.

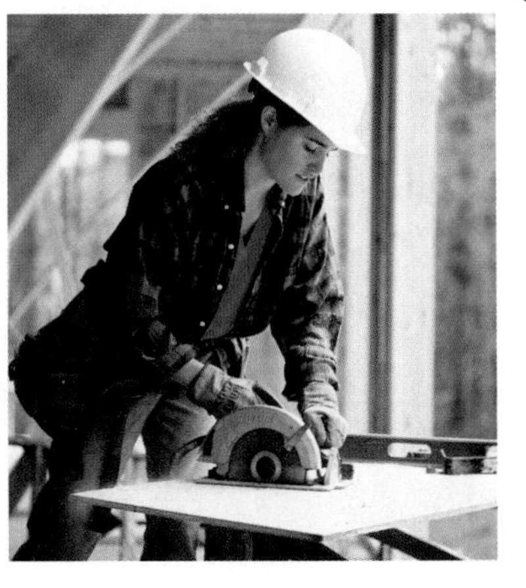

2 EXAMPLE Comparing Mixed Numbers

Carpentry "Measure twice, cut once" is the carpenters' motto. A carpenter needs a piece of lumber that is at least $6\frac{27}{32}$ inches wide. Is a $6\frac{3}{4}$-inch piece wide enough?

Since the whole numbers are the same, compare $\frac{27}{32}$ and $\frac{3}{4}$.

$\frac{27}{32} = \frac{27}{32}$ $\frac{3}{4} = \frac{24}{32}$ ← **Write equivalent fractions. Use the LCD 32.**

$\frac{27}{32} > \frac{24}{32}$. So, $6\frac{27}{32} > 6\frac{3}{4}$. ← **Compare fractions and mixed numbers.**

The $6\frac{3}{4}$-inch piece is not wide enough.

Check Understanding 2 Compare each pair of mixed numbers using <, =, or >.

a. $4\frac{2}{5}$ ■ $4\frac{3}{7}$ **b.** $1\frac{2}{3}$ ■ $1\frac{6}{11}$ **c.** $2\frac{12}{21}$ ■ $2\frac{4}{7}$

d. **Number Sense** In Example 2, would a $6\frac{7}{8}$-inch piece of lumber be wide enough? Explain.

OBJECTIVE

2 Ordering Fractions

To order fractions with like denominators, you can compare numerators.

To order fractions with unlike denominators, first write the fractions with common denominators.

3 EXAMPLE Ordering Fractions

Order from least to greatest: $\frac{3}{8}, \frac{2}{5}$, and $\frac{1}{4}$.

Any multiple of 8 is also a multiple of 4. So, you can multiply 8×5 to find a common multiple. A common multiple of 8, 5, and 4 is 40.

$\frac{3}{8} = \frac{15}{40}$ $\frac{2}{5} = \frac{16}{40}$ $\frac{1}{4} = \frac{10}{40}$ ← **Write equivalent fractions.**

$10 < 15 < 16$ ← **Arrange the numerators in order.**

$\frac{10}{40} < \frac{15}{40} < \frac{16}{40}$. So, $\frac{1}{4} < \frac{3}{8} < \frac{2}{5}$.

✓ Check Understanding 3 Order $2\frac{5}{6}, 2\frac{4}{5}$, and $2\frac{2}{3}$ from least to greatest.

EXERCISES

For more practice, see *Extra Practice*.

A Practice by Example

Compare each pair of numbers. Use <, =, or >.

Example 1 (page 149)

1. $\frac{3}{5}$ ■ $\frac{5}{8}$
2. $\frac{3}{4}$ ■ $\frac{3}{5}$
3. $\frac{1}{2}$ ■ $\frac{7}{16}$
4. $\frac{3}{5}$ ■ $\frac{12}{20}$
5. $\frac{5}{7}$ ■ $\frac{5}{6}$
6. $\frac{3}{11}$ ■ $\frac{1}{4}$
7. $\frac{2}{9}$ ■ $\frac{4}{15}$
8. $\frac{15}{16}$ ■ $\frac{7}{8}$
9. $\frac{9}{24}$ ■ $\frac{3}{8}$

Example 2 (page 149)

10. $3\frac{1}{8}$ ■ $3\frac{1}{4}$
11. $7\frac{2}{3}$ ■ $7\frac{4}{6}$
12. $8\frac{7}{10}$ ■ $8\frac{3}{5}$
13. $2\frac{11}{16}$ ■ $2\frac{13}{16}$
14. $5\frac{4}{6}$ ■ $5\frac{5}{7}$
15. $3\frac{1}{4}$ ■ $3\frac{1}{5}$
16. Tim ran $1\frac{3}{4}$ miles. Naomi ran $1\frac{7}{10}$ miles. Who ran farther?

Example 3 (page 150)

Order each set of numbers from least to greatest.

17. $\frac{2}{3}, \frac{5}{6}, \frac{3}{4}$
18. $\frac{5}{8}, \frac{3}{4}, \frac{1}{2}$
19. $\frac{1}{8}, \frac{7}{40}, \frac{3}{10}$
20. $3\frac{2}{3}, 3\frac{2}{5}, 3\frac{7}{15}$
21. $2\frac{8}{9}, 2\frac{5}{6}, 2\frac{11}{12}$
22. $6\frac{7}{12}, 6\frac{2}{3}, 6\frac{1}{5}$

B Apply Your Skills

23. **Shopping** Two sports drinks have the same price. The cherry-flavored drink is $12\frac{9}{20}$ ounces. The blueberry-flavored drink is $12\frac{7}{16}$ ounces. Assuming you like both flavors, which drink is the better buy?

24. **Construction** Plywood comes in a variety of thicknesses for different uses. Put these thicknesses in order from least to greatest.

$$\frac{3}{4}\text{ inch}, \frac{3}{8}\text{ inch}, \frac{1}{2}\text{ inch}, \frac{1}{4}\text{ inch}, \frac{5}{8}\text{ inch}$$

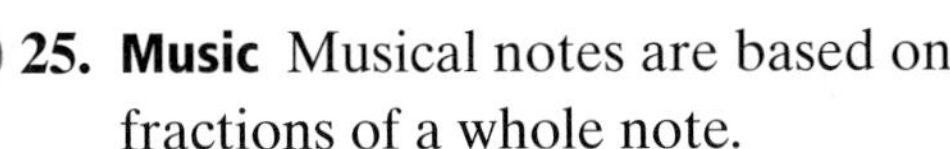

25. **Music** Musical notes are based on fractions of a whole note.
   a. Order the fractions shown from greatest to least.
   b. Redraw the note symbols so they are in order.
   c. **Patterns** Do the symbols change in a pattern? Explain.

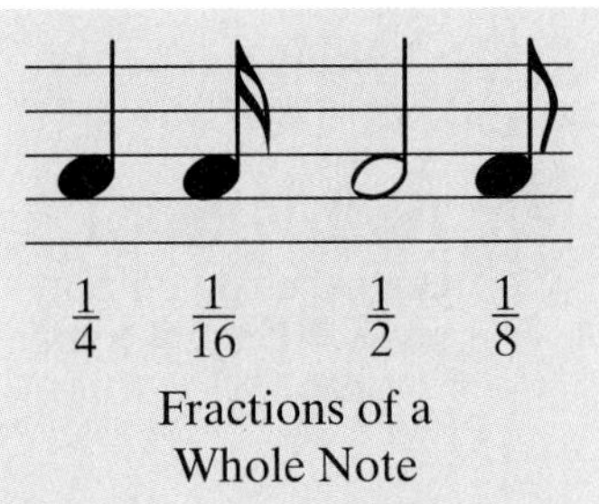

Fractions of a Whole Note

Number Sense **Without using a common denominator, compare each pair of fractions using <, =, or >. Explain your reasoning.**

26. $\frac{3}{7} \blacksquare \frac{3}{8}$ 27. $\frac{11}{16} \blacksquare \frac{11}{12}$ 28. $\frac{1}{8} \blacksquare \frac{1}{18}$

Mental Math **Compare each pair of numbers. Use <, =, or >.**

29. $\frac{1}{15} \blacksquare \frac{1}{20}$ 30. $\frac{3}{4} \blacksquare \frac{3}{2}$ 31. $\frac{2}{45} \blacksquare \frac{1}{30}$

Determine if each statement is true or false.

32. $\frac{13}{14} > \frac{25}{28}$ 33. $\frac{21}{45} > \frac{4}{9}$ 34. $\frac{2}{11} < \frac{15}{100}$ 35. $\frac{9}{3} < \frac{13}{4}$

36. **Data File, p. 117** If a $\frac{7}{16}$-inch wrench is too big for a bolt, and a $\frac{5}{16}$-inch wrench is too small, what size wrench should you try on the bolt?

37. **Writing in Math** Write a rule to compare fractions that have the same numerator. Give examples, such as $\frac{7}{11}$ and $\frac{7}{12}$.

C Challenge

Order each set of numbers from least to greatest.

38. $\frac{3}{2}, \frac{9}{7}, \frac{8}{5}, \frac{13}{10}$ 39. $\frac{11}{10}, \frac{21}{20}, \frac{12}{10}, \frac{23}{10}$ 40. $\frac{55}{45}, \frac{60}{50}, \frac{50}{40}, \frac{65}{55}$

41. **Algebra** Find a whole number x so that $\frac{2}{3} < \frac{x}{8} < 1$.

42. **Stretch Your Thinking** Copy the diagram. Fill in the squares with the digits 1–9. The sum of the numbers in each indicated row, column, and diagonal must be 15.

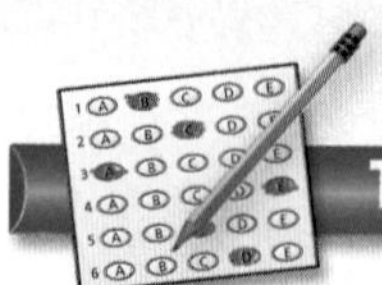

Test Prep

Multiple Choice

43. Which set of fractions is NOT in order from least to greatest?

A. $\frac{3}{8}, \frac{3}{9}, \frac{5}{12}$ **B.** $\frac{1}{2}, \frac{7}{12}, \frac{5}{6}$ **C.** $\frac{2}{3}, \frac{3}{4}, \frac{4}{5}$ **D.** $\frac{2}{9}, \frac{3}{10}, \frac{4}{11}$

44. What is the order of $\frac{7}{20}, \frac{15}{40}, \frac{10}{30}$ from least to greatest?

F. $\frac{7}{20}, \frac{10}{30}, \frac{15}{40}$ **G.** $\frac{10}{30}, \frac{7}{20}, \frac{15}{40}$ **H.** $\frac{15}{40}, \frac{10}{30}, \frac{7}{20}$ **I.** $\frac{15}{40}, \frac{10}{30}, \frac{7}{20}$

Short Response

45. a. What mixed number is halfway between $1\frac{1}{8}$ and $1\frac{3}{8}$?
b. Show your answer on a number line.

Take It to the NET
Online lesson quiz at
www.PHSchool.com
Web Code: aaa-0307

46. Use the lengths shown for each side of the triangle at the right. Put the lengths in order from least to greatest. Explain your reasoning.

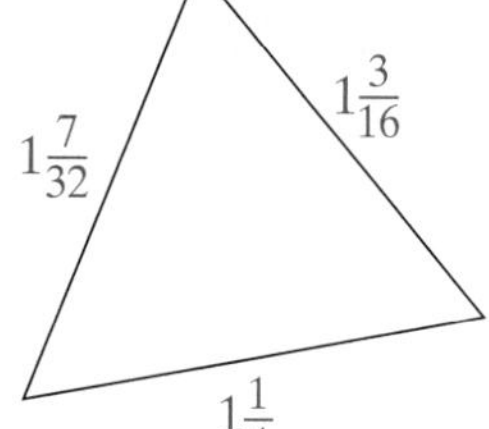

Mixed Review

Lesson 3-5 **Write each mixed number as an improper fraction.**

47. $5\frac{2}{3}$ **48.** $1\frac{8}{9}$ **49.** $1\frac{15}{21}$ **50.** $13\frac{1}{4}$

Lesson 3-4 **Write each fraction in simplest form.**

51. $\frac{18}{42}$ **52.** $\frac{16}{36}$ **53.** $\frac{36}{132}$ **54.** $\frac{36}{153}$

Checkpoint Quiz 2 — Lessons 3-4 through 3-7

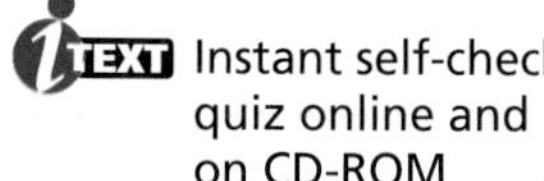

Instant self-check quiz online and on CD-ROM

Write each fraction in simplest form.

1. $\frac{8}{12}$ **2.** $\frac{21}{28}$ **3.** $\frac{16}{64}$

4. Write $3\frac{1}{5}$ as an improper fraction. **5.** Write $\frac{13}{8}$ as a mixed number.

6. Find the least common multiple of 4, 5, and 12.

7. Order these fractions from least to greatest: $\frac{3}{16}, \frac{1}{8}, \frac{1}{3}$.

Compare. Use <, =, or >.

8. $\frac{5}{8}$ ■ $\frac{5}{6}$ **9.** $3\frac{2}{3}$ ■ $3\frac{7}{12}$ **10.** $\frac{13}{16}$ ■ $\frac{4}{5}$

3-8 Fractions and Decimals

What You'll Learn

 To write decimals as fractions

 To write fractions as decimals

. . . And Why

To convert measurements, as in Example 2

✓ Check Skills You'll Need

For help, go to Lesson 1-9.

Find each quotient. Identify each as a terminating or a repeating decimal.

1. $3 \div 2$ **2.** $2 \div 3$ **3.** $8 \div 5$

4. $3 \div 8$ **5.** $3 \div 10$ **6.** $24 \div 100$

7. $36 \div 150$ **8.** $25 \div 125$ **9.** $16 \div 5$

OBJECTIVE

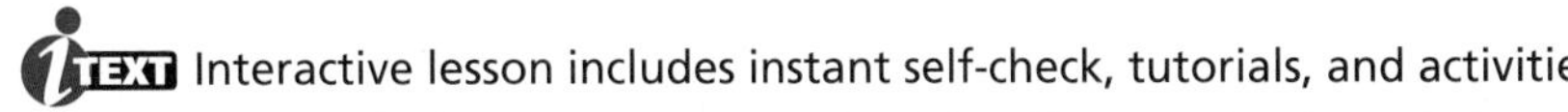

Interactive lesson includes instant self-check, tutorials, and activities.

1 Writing Decimals as Fractions

To write a decimal as a fraction, write the fraction as you would say the decimal. Then simplify.

1 EXAMPLE Writing Decimals as Fractions

Reading Math

Reading 0.225 as "two hundred twenty-five thousandths" can help you write 0.225 as a fraction.

a. Write 0.225 as a fraction in simplest form.

$0.225 = \frac{225}{1,000}$ ← **Use the place value of the 5 to write a fraction.**

$\frac{225}{1,000} \overset{\div 25}{\underset{\div 25}{=}} \frac{9}{40}$ ← **Simplify. The GCF of 225 and 1,000 is 25.**

So, $0.225 = \frac{9}{40}$.

b. Write 2.06 as a mixed number in simplest form.

$2\frac{6}{100} \overset{\div 2}{\underset{\div 2}{=}} 2\frac{3}{50}$ ← **Write "two and six hundredths" as a mixed number. Then simplify.**

So, $2.06 = 2\frac{3}{50}$.

Check Understanding 1 Write each decimal as a fraction or mixed number in simplest form.

a. 0.6 **b.** 0.35 **c.** 5.08 **d.** 7.405

e. Reasoning How does saying or writing the decimal in words help you to write the decimal as a fraction?

OBJECTIVE

2 Writing Fractions as Decimals

A fraction indicates division. To write a fraction as a decimal, divide the numerator by the denominator.

2 EXAMPLE Writing a Fraction as a Decimal

Construction A construction worker wants to drill a hole with a diameter that is no more than 0.6 inch. Can she use a $\frac{5}{8}$-inch drill bit?

To write $\frac{5}{8}$ as a decimal, divide 5 by 8.

$$\begin{array}{r} 0.625 \\ 8\overline{)5.000} \\ \underline{4\,8} \\ 20 \\ \underline{16} \\ 40 \\ \underline{40} \\ 0 \end{array}$$

← **$\frac{5}{8}$ = 0.625**

Since $0.625 > 0.6$, the $\frac{5}{8}$-inch drill bit is too big.

Check Understanding 2 **a.** Write $\frac{9}{20}$ as a decimal.

b. **Reasoning** Explain how to write $2\frac{3}{4}$ as a decimal.

3 EXAMPLE Repeating Decimals

Need Help?

For help with repeating decimals, go to Lesson 1-8.

Write $\frac{4}{11}$ as a decimal.

Method 1 Divide.

$$\begin{array}{r} 0.3636 \\ 11\overline{)4.0000} \\ \underline{3\,3} \\ 70 \\ \underline{66} \\ 40 \\ \underline{33} \\ 70 \\ \underline{66} \\ 4 \end{array}$$

← **The digits 3 and 6 repeat.**

$\frac{4}{11} = 0.\overline{36}$

Method 2 Use a calculator.

4 ÷ 11 = 0.363636364

The calculator rounds the last digit in the display to 4. Look for the repeated digits: 3636. . .

$\frac{4}{11} = 0.\overline{36}$

Check Understanding 3 Write each fraction as a decimal. Use a bar to show repeating digits.

a. $\frac{2}{3}$ **b.** $\frac{1}{6}$ **c.** $\frac{5}{9}$ **d.** $\frac{4}{3}$

e. **Number Sense** Examine the fractions $\frac{2}{3}$, $\frac{3}{3}$, $\frac{4}{3}$, $\frac{5}{3}$, and $\frac{6}{3}$. Explain when a denominator of 3 will result in a repeating decimal.

For more practice, see *Extra Practice.*

A Practice by Example

Write each decimal as a fraction or mixed number in simplest form.

Example 1 (page 153)

1. 0.3 **2.** 0.8 **3.** 0.75 **4.** 0.04

5. 0.15 **6.** 0.17 **7.** 0.008 **8.** 5.5

9. 4.25 **10.** 3.149 **11.** 5.075 **12.** 8.32

Examples 2, 3 (page 154)

Write each fraction or mixed number as a decimal.

13. $\frac{2}{5}$ **14.** $\frac{3}{4}$ **15.** $\frac{3}{8}$ **16.** $\frac{9}{10}$

17. $\frac{5}{6}$ **18.** $\frac{7}{15}$ **19.** $\frac{11}{8}$ **20.** $\frac{10}{9}$

21. $4\frac{7}{10}$ **22.** $1\frac{1}{9}$ **23.** $2\frac{7}{12}$ **24.** $5\frac{3}{20}$

B Apply Your Skills

25. Shopping You order $1\frac{1}{4}$ pounds of cheese at a deli. What decimal number should the digital scale show?

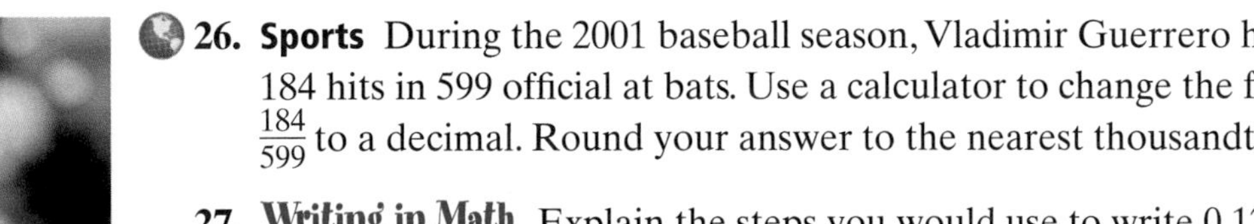

26. Sports During the 2001 baseball season, Vladimir Guerrero had 184 hits in 599 official at bats. Use a calculator to change the fraction $\frac{184}{599}$ to a decimal. Round your answer to the nearest thousandth.

27. Writing in Math Explain the steps you would use to write 0.125 as a fraction in simplest form.

28. Data File, p. 117 Which wrenches measure 0.375 inch, 0.4375 inch, and 0.8125 inch?

State whether each fraction is less than, equal to, or greater than 0.75.

29. $\frac{7}{8}$ **30.** $\frac{4}{5}$ **31.** $\frac{21}{28}$ **32.** $\frac{11}{15}$

Write each measurement as a mixed number and as a decimal.

33. four and three-fourths pounds

34. five and seven-eighths inches

Order each set of numbers from least to greatest.

35. $\frac{7}{8}$, 0.8, 0.87 **36.** 1.65, $1\frac{2}{3}$, $1\frac{3}{5}$, 1.7

37. Stocks Until 2001, stock prices were reported as mixed numbers. Find the dollar amounts represented by $6\frac{5}{8}$ and $8\frac{1}{2}$.

Challenge

Match each number with its location on the number line.

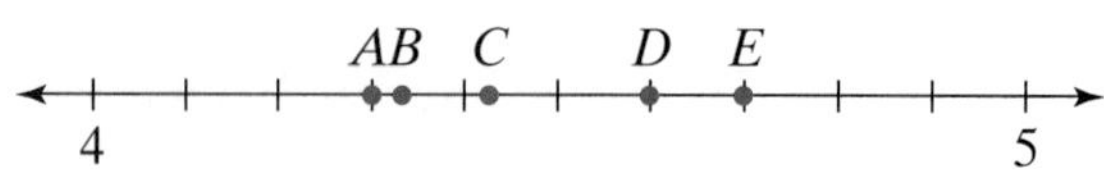

38. $4\frac{3}{5}$ **39.** 4.3 **40.** 4.43 **41.** $4\frac{1}{3}$ **42.** 4.7

43. Write the decimal $0.0\overline{3}$ as a fraction. (*Hint*: How is the decimal different than $\frac{1}{3} = 0.\overline{3}$?)

44. **Stretch Your Thinking** Copy and fill in both blanks with the same digit to make the equation true. $\frac{\blacksquare 6}{125} = 0.\blacksquare 08$

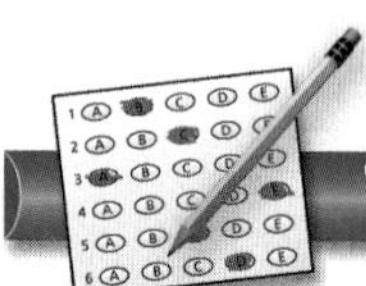

Test Prep

Multiple Choice

45. A carton of juice contains 1 liter, or about 33.8 fluid ounces. What is 33.8 as a mixed number in simplest form?

A. $33\frac{4}{5}$ **B.** $33\frac{8}{10}$ **C.** $33\frac{9}{10}$ **D.** $34\frac{4}{5}$

46. Which decimal is equivalent to $\frac{8}{15}$?

F. 0.53 **G.** $0.5\overline{3}$ **H.** 0.54 **I.** 0.6

47. On a digital scale, some sliced ham weighs 1.38 pounds. Which amount is nearest this weight?

A. $1\frac{1}{4}$ pounds **B.** $1\frac{1}{3}$ pounds **C.** $1\frac{3}{8}$ pounds **D.** $1\frac{1}{2}$ pounds

Short Response

48. Three paint brushes have widths of $\frac{1}{2}$ inch, $\frac{3}{8}$ inch, and $\frac{3}{4}$ inch.

a. Which brush is the least wide?

b. Justify your answer.

Mixed Review

Lesson 2-9

Use the Distributive Property to simplify each expression.

49. 3×42 **50.** 9×68 **51.** 7×2.9 **52.** 4×9.1

Lesson 1-6

Choose a strategy to solve each problem.

53. Delino lives 0.5 mile from the bus stop. How many miles does he walk going to and from the bus stop five days a week for 36 weeks?

54. **Gardening** Your uncle is planting a row of tomato plants along his back fence. The fence is 30 feet long. If he places the plants 30 inches apart, how many plants does he have room for?

3-9 Try, Check, and Revise

What You'll Learn

To solve problems by trying, checking, and revising

. . . And Why

To solve a problem involving different prices, as in Example 1

Check Skills You'll Need

For help, go to Lesson 2-1.

Write the next three terms in each pattern.

1. 2, 4, 6, 8, . . .

2. 2, 4, 8, 16, . . .

3. 2, 6, 18, . . .

4. 100, 95, 90, . . .

5. 1, 6, 11, 16, . . .

6. 1, 1, 2, 3, 5, 8, . . .

OBJECTIVE

Interactive lesson includes instant self-check, tutorials, and activities.

1 Solving Problems by Trying, Checking, and Revising

When to Use This Strategy You can use this strategy when the solution to a problem involves several related numbers.

To use this strategy, first *try* to make a reasonable estimate of the solution. Then *check* against the given information. If your estimate is incorrect, *revise* it to make it more reasonable. Keep trying, checking, and revising until you find the correct answer.

1 EXAMPLE Real-World Problem Solving

Entertainment Movie tickets cost \$7 for adults and \$4 for children. On Friday the total sales from 120 tickets was \$720. How many adult tickets were sold?

Read and Understand Adult tickets cost \$7. Child tickets cost \$4. The theater collected \$720 by selling 120 tickets. You need to find how many adult tickets were sold.

Plan and Solve To help determine how many adult tickets were sold, try, check, and revise a reasonable combination of numbers.

Try: Since 120 tickets were sold, try 40 adult tickets and 80 child tickets.

You can organize your data in a table.

Adult Tickets	Child Tickets	Total Sales
$40 \times \$7 = \$280$	$80 \times \$4 = \$320$	$\$280 + \$320 = \$600$

Check: With 40 adult tickets, the total sales of \$600 is too low.

Since \$600 is too low, increase the number of tickets that are more expensive.

Revise: Increase the number of adult tickets. Keep a total of 120 tickets.

Adult Tickets	Child Tickets	Total Sales
$50 \times \$7 = \$350$	$70 \times \$4 = \$280$	\$630
$90 \times \$7 = \$630$	$30 \times \$4 = \$120$	\$750

You can see that 50 adult tickets is too low, and 90 adult tickets is too high. But the total sales of \$750 with 90 adult tickets is close to \$720. Revise once more. Try 80 adult tickets.

Adult Tickets	Child Tickets	Total Sales
$80 \times \$7 = \$560$	$40 \times \$4 = \$160$	\$720

Look Back and Check With 80 adult tickets and 40 child tickets, the number of tickets sold is equal to 120 and the total sales are \$720.

Check Understanding 1 If the theater collected \$540 by selling 120 tickets at the same prices as those in Example 1, how many adult tickets were sold?

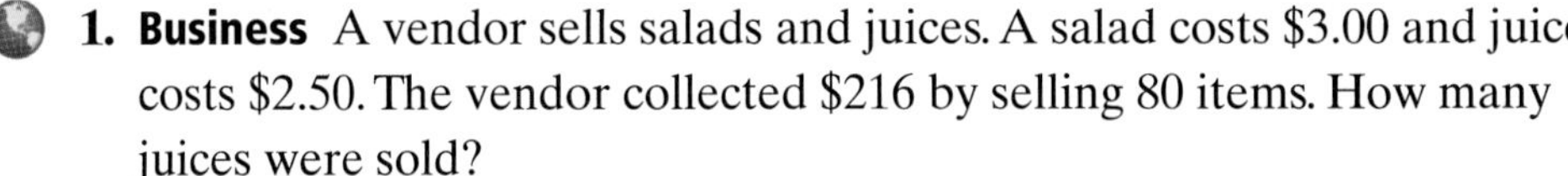

EXERCISES

For more practice, see *Extra Practice*.

A Practice by Example

Solve each problem by trying, checking, and revising.

Example 1 (page 157)

1. **Business** A vendor sells salads and juices. A salad costs \$3.00 and juice costs \$2.50. The vendor collected \$216 by selling 80 items. How many juices were sold?

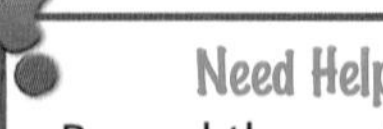

Need Help?
- Reread the problem.
- Identify the key facts and details.
- Tell the problem in your own words.
- Try a different strategy.
- Check your work.

2. **Pet Care** A rectangular turtle cage is made with 40 feet of wire fence. The length is 6 feet more than the width. What are the length and width of the turtle cage?

3. The Kinjo family has two children. The sum of their ages is 27. They were born 5 years apart. How old are the two children?

4. **Sports** The junior high school soccer team played a total of 24 games. They won 6 more games than they lost. They tied in 4 games. How many games did they win?

5. Split the face of the clock at the right into two halves so that the sum of the clock's numbers in each of the halves is equal.

B Apply Your Skills **Choose a strategy to solve each problem.**

6. **Music** Wayne gives piano and voice lessons. Piano lessons are 30 minutes long and voice lessons are 45 minutes long. Wayne spent a total of $4\frac{1}{2}$ hours giving 8 different lessons. How many piano lessons did Wayne give?

7. Trains leave Farmville for Lexinburg every 40 minutes. The first train leaves at 5:00 A.M. What is the departure time closest to 12:35 P.M.?

8. **Money** Suppose you save quarters and dimes in a jar. Last night you counted $6.75. The number of dimes is one more than the number of quarters. How many quarters are there?

Strategies

- Draw a Diagram
- Make a Graph
- Make an Organized List
- Make a Table and Look for a Pattern
- Simulate a Problem
- Solve a Simpler Problem
- Try, Check, and Revise
- Use Logical Reasoning
- Work Backward
- Write an Equation

9. **Fundraising** A school sells T-shirts and sweatshirts. T-shirts sell for $10 each, and sweatshirts sell for $15 each. The school collects $1,120 by selling 100 items. How many sweatshirts did the school sell?

10. **Writing in Math** Rearrange the boxes so that the weight of each pile is equal. Explain the steps you took in trying, checking, and revising.

1 lb	4 lb	7 lb
2 lb	5 lb	8 lb
3 lb	6 lb	9 lb

C Challenge

11. Place the digits 2, 3, 4, 6, and 8 in a copy of the figure below so the product is the same in both directions. Find the product.

12. **Stretch Your Thinking** The puzzle below is a cryptarithm. Each letter represents a different digit. Find a value for each letter. (*Hint:* What is the only possible value for M?)

$$\begin{array}{r} \text{FUN} \\ +\ \ \text{IS} \\ \hline \text{MATH} \end{array}$$

13. Carnivals A game at a carnival involves throwing bean bags through target holes for different numbers of points. The object of the game is to score exactly 50 points. What are the different ways you can score exactly 50 points?

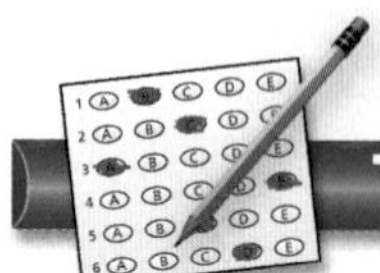

Test Prep

Multiple Choice

14. What is 0.24 as a fraction in simplest form?

A. $\frac{1}{4}$ **B.** $\frac{6}{25}$ **C.** $\frac{12}{50}$ **D.** $\frac{24}{100}$

15. Which number is both a factor and a multiple of 26?

F. 1 **G.** 13 **H.** 26 **I.** 52

Take It to the NET
Online lesson quiz at
www.PHSchool.com
Web Code: aaa-0309

16. Which of the following numbers is a prime number?

A. 9 **B.** 16 **C.** 23 **D.** 57

Short Response

17. Order from least to greatest: $\frac{7}{20}, \frac{7}{32}, \frac{8}{25}, \frac{3}{11}$.

Mixed Review

Lesson 3-7

Compare each pair of numbers. Use <, =, or >.

18. $\frac{3}{4} \blacksquare \frac{7}{8}$ **19.** $\frac{1}{5} \blacksquare \frac{4}{20}$ **20.** $\frac{4}{7} \blacksquare \frac{3}{6}$

21. $2\frac{3}{5} \blacksquare \frac{13}{5}$ **22.** $\frac{10}{8} \blacksquare \frac{5}{2}$ **23.** $6\frac{1}{3} \blacksquare 5\frac{5}{3}$

Lesson 2-6

Algebra **Solve each equation.**

24. $x + 35 = 90$ **25.** $x + 0.6 = 0.92$ **26.** $5 = x + 3.1$

27. $x + 8 = 18.5$ **28.** $1.2 = x + 0.05$ **29.** $x + 2.4 = 2.7$

Lesson 2-3

Algebra **Write an expression for each word phrase.**

30. 6 times r **31.** 3 less than p **32.** 15 more than y

Writing Extended Responses

An extended-response question in this book is worth a total of 4 points. To get full credit, you must show your work and explain your reasoning.

EXAMPLE

Mary plans to fence 80 square feet of her backyard for her dog. She wants the length and width to be whole numbers (in feet). What dimensions can she use? Tell how you know that you have found all possible pairs.

Here are four responses with the points each received.

4 points

1 ft by 80 ft, 2 ft by 40 ft, 4 ft by 20 ft, 5 ft by 16 ft, and 8 ft by 10 ft

These are all the pairs because there are no other whole numbers that divide 80 without a remainder.

The 4-point response shows all of the correct whole-number factors of 80 and the student's explanation of why the answer is complete.

3 points

8 and 10, 4 and 20, 5 and 14, 2 and 40, 1 and 80

There are no other whole numbers that divide 80 with no remainder, so this must be the answer.

The 3-point response has one error and the student's explanation of why the answer is complete.

2 points

8 ft by 10 ft, 1 ft by 80 ft, 2 ft by 40 ft, 5 ft by 16 ft, and 4 ft by 20 ft

The 2-point response gives all pairs of factors but does not have an explanation.

1 point

2 and 40, 1 and 80, 8 and 10

The 1-point response is missing some pairs and does not have an explanation.

EXERCISES

Use the example above to answer each question.

1. Read the 3-point response. What error did the student make?
2. Read the 1-point response. Which dimensions are missing?

Chapter Review

Vocabulary

common factor (p. 128)
common multiple (p. 143)
composite number (p. 124)
divisible (p. 119)
equivalent fractions (p. 134)
even number (p. 120)
factor (p. 123)
greatest common factor (p. 128)
improper fraction (p. 139)
least common denominator (p. 148)
least common multiple (p. 143)
mixed number (p. 139)
odd number (p. 120)
prime factorization (p. 124)
prime number (p. 124)
proper fraction (p. 139)
simplest form (p. 135)

Reading Math: Understanding Vocabulary

Choose the vocabulary term from the column on the right that best completes each sentence.

1. Fractions that represent the same amount are _?_.
2. The number $5\frac{1}{8}$ is a(n) _?_.
3. The _?_ of 42 is $2 \times 3 \times 7$.
4. Every _?_ is divisible by 2.
5. The numbers 2, 3, 5, 7, and 11 are _?_.

A. prime factorization
B. equivalent fractions
C. even number
D. mixed number
E. prime numbers

Take It to the NET
Online vocabulary quiz at www.PHSchool.com
Web Code: aaj-0351

Skills and Concepts

3-1 and 3-2 Objectives

- To identify numbers divisible by 2, 3, 5, 9, and 10
- To find factors of a number
- To find the prime factorization of a number

A **prime number** has exactly two factors, 1 and the number itself.
A **composite number** has more than two whole-number factors. Writing a composite number as a product of prime numbers is the **prime factorization** of the number.

Test each number for divisibility by 2, 3, 5, 9, or 10.

6. 207 **7.** 585 **8.** 756 **9.** 3,330

Find the prime factorization of each number.

10. 28 **11.** 51 **12.** 100 **13.** 250

3-3 Objective

- To find the greatest common factor of two or more numbers

The **greatest common factor (GCF)** of two or more numbers is the greatest factor shared by all the numbers.

Find the GCF of each set of numbers.

14. 18, 28 **15.** 12, 62 **16.** 25, 35 **17.** 16, 40

3-4 and 3-5 Objectives

- To find equivalent fractions
- To write fractions in simplest form
- To write mixed numbers as improper fractions
- To write improper fractions as mixed numbers

Equivalent fractions are fractions that name the same amount. A fraction is in **simplest form** when the only common factor of the numerator and the denominator is 1. A **mixed number** shows the sum of a whole number and a fraction. An **improper fraction** has a numerator that is greater than or equal to its denominator.

State whether each fraction is in simplest form. If not, write it in simplest form. Then, write two other equivalent fractions for each fraction.

18. $\frac{5}{20}$ **19.** $\frac{4}{6}$ **20.** $\frac{1}{4}$ **21.** $\frac{2}{9}$

Write each number as an improper fraction or a mixed number.

22. $4\frac{2}{3}$ **23.** $8\frac{1}{5}$ **24.** $\frac{13}{3}$ **25.** $\frac{58}{6}$

3-6 Objective

- To find the least common multiple

A number that is a multiple of each of two or more numbers is a **common multiple.** The **least common multiple** is abbreviated **LCM.**

Find the LCM of each set of numbers.

26. 2, 10 **27.** 6, 9 **28.** 12, 22 **29.** 10, 20, 35

3-7 and 3-8 Objectives

- To compare fractions
- To order fractions
- To write decimals as fractions
- To write fractions as decimals

To compare fractions with unlike denominators, find equivalent fractions that have a common denominator. To write a fraction as a decimal, divide the numerator by the denominator. Write a fraction for a decimal just as you would say the decimal.

Order the numbers from least to greatest.

30. $\frac{1}{2}, \frac{1}{4}, \frac{1}{6}$ **31.** $2\frac{4}{15}, 2\frac{1}{3}, 22\frac{2}{5}$ **32.** $\frac{17}{40}, \frac{7}{20}, \frac{5}{16}$

Write each number as a fraction in simplest form or as a decimal.

33. $\frac{6}{32}$ **34.** $6\frac{5}{24}$ **35.** 0.06 **36.** 4.52

3-9 Objective

- To solve problems by trying, checking, and revising

You can try, check, and revise when you solve a problem that uses several related numbers.

37. Catering The caterer at a banquet prepared twice as many chicken dinners as turkey dinners. A total of 114 dinners were prepared. How many chicken dinners were prepared?

38. Film Rich bought 7 rolls of film, some with 36 exposures and some with 24 exposures. He can take 192 pictures in all. How many of each type of film did he buy?

Chapter Test

Test each number for divisibility by 2, 3, 5, 9, or 10.

1. 70 **2.** 405 **3.** 628 **4.** 837

Tell whether each number is prime or composite.

5. 19 **6.** 39 **7.** 51 **8.** 67

Find the prime factorization of each number.

9. 72 **10.** 80 **11.** 120

Find the GCF of each set of numbers.

12. 24, 36 **13.** 20, 25, 30 **14.** 7, 19

15. For a writing workshop, 15 coaches and 35 students will be split into groups, each with the same number of coaches and the same number of students. At most, how many groups can there be?

16. Find the length of each segment.

a.
b.
c.

0 1 2
inches

17. Lawns Today, two neighbors water their lawns. One neighbor waters her lawn every four days. The other neighbor waters his lawn every three days. In how many days will they next water their lawns on the same day?

18. Write two fractions equivalent to each.

a. $\frac{6}{18}$ **b.** $\frac{9}{24}$ **c.** $\frac{18}{20}$ **d.** $\frac{60}{100}$

19. Write $\frac{34}{51}$ in simplest form.

20. Writing in Math Explain how to use prime factorizations to find the LCM of two numbers. Include an example.

Write as a mixed number and as an improper fraction.

21. one and two thirds **22.** five and four fifths

23. eight and one sixth **24.** three and one half

Find the LCM for each set of numbers.

25. 4, 8 **26.** 6, 11 **27.** 10, 12, 15

Compare each set of numbers using <, =, or >.

28. $1\frac{2}{5} \blacksquare 1\frac{1}{5}$ **29.** $\frac{15}{4} \blacksquare \frac{17}{5}$

30. $\frac{7}{14} \blacksquare \frac{1}{2}$ **31.** $2\frac{3}{5} \blacksquare 2\frac{7}{11}$

32. Order from least to greatest: $1\frac{5}{6}, 1\frac{7}{9}, \frac{35}{36}, 1\frac{3}{4}$.

33. Fitness Lee jogged $\frac{1}{2}$ mile, Orlando jogged $\frac{2}{3}$ mile, and Holden jogged $\frac{3}{8}$ mile. Who jogged the longest distance?

Write each decimal as a fraction in simplest form. Write each fraction as a decimal.

34. 0.04 **35.** $\frac{17}{40}$ **36.** 3.875

37. $\frac{8}{9}$ **38.** 2.14 **39.** $\frac{6}{11}$

40. Field Trips Students at Gale Middle School are going to a museum. The entrance fee is $1.75 per student and $3.25 per adult. The bus fee is $189 per bus. Each bus holds 44 people. Find the cost for 182 students and 14 adults.

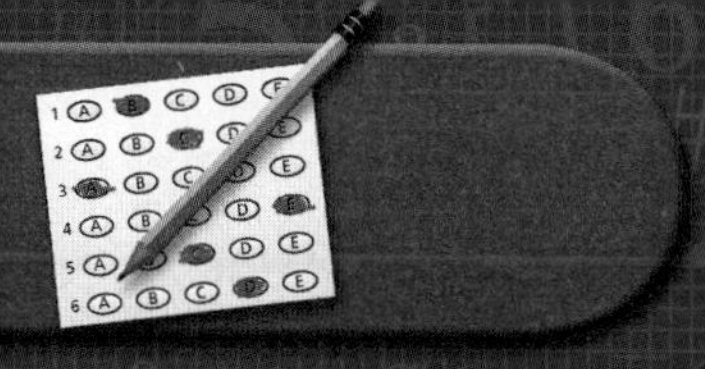

Test Prep

Reading Comprehension **Read each passage and answer the questions that follow.**

16	3	2	*a*
5	*b*	11	*c*
d	6	7	*e*
f	15	14	1

Sum Art Artists have often used mathematics in their work. The artist M. C. Escher used math ideas in many of his drawings. In the early sixteenth century, Albrecht Dürer included a 4×4 number square in one of his engravings, *Melancholia.* A number square has numbers arranged so that each row, column, and main diagonal has the same sum. Part of Dürer's number square is shown at the left.

1. What must be the sum of each row, column, and diagonal in Dürer's number square?
A. 21 **B.** 23
C. 34 **D.** 38

2. What numbers do *a* and *f* represent?
F. 13 and 6 **G.** 14 and 4
H. 14 and 3 **I.** 13 and 4

3. What is the sum of $b + c$?
A. 15 **B.** 16
C. 17 **D.** 18

4. Two squares next to each other contain the year that Dürer made the engraving. In what year did Dürer engrave *Melancholia*?
F. 715 **G.** 911
H. 1112 **I.** 1514

Something to Prove One of the most famous unsolved math problems is Goldbach's Conjecture. In 1742, Christian Goldbach made the conjecture that every even number greater than 2 can be written as the sum of two prime numbers. For example, $6 = 3 + 3$ and $10 = 3 + 7$. Today, mathematicians are still trying to prove Goldbach's Conjecture.

5. To which of the following numbers does Goldbach's Conjecture apply?
A. 1 **B.** 2
C. 3 **D.** 4

6. Which of the following illustrates Goldbach's Conjecture for 100?
F. $100 = 35 + 65$ **G.** $100 = 37 + 63$
H. $100 = 39 + 61$ **I.** $100 = 41 + 59$

7. Which of the following does NOT illustrate Goldbach's Conjecture for 30?
A. $30 = 7 + 23$ **B.** $30 = 21 + 9$
C. $30 = 11 + 19$ **D.** $30 = 17 + 13$

8. Which of the following odd numbers would NOT be used to illustrate Goldbach's Conjecture?
F. 5 **G.** 7
H. 9 **I.** 11

Real-World Snapshots

Lifting With Levers

Applying Fractions The simplest machines have only a few moving parts and can be powered by hand. For example, you can use a lever like the one in the diagram below to help lift a heavy load. If you know the distances a and b in the diagram, and the weight of a load, you can find the force needed to lift the load.

Levers in Nature

The pincer of a fiddler crab is a Class 3 lever.

How to Measure Force

force = $\frac{a}{b}$ × weight of load

Put It All Together

Data File **Use the information on these two pages and on page 117 to answer these questions.**

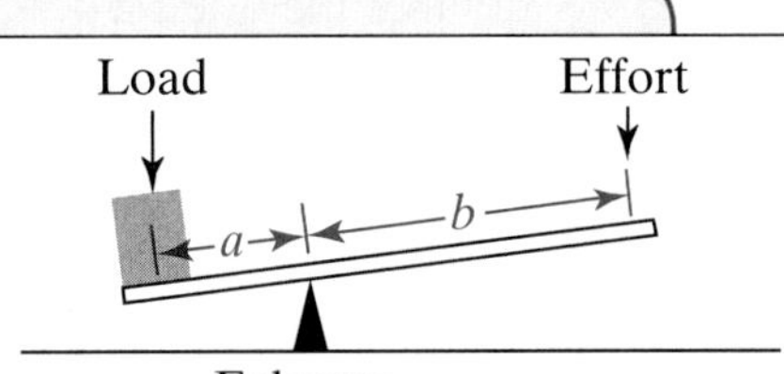

Fulcrum, or pivot point

a = distance from fulcrum to load
b = distance from fulcrum to effort

1. **a.** Suppose $a = 3$ and $b = 6$. Find the fraction of the load the force will be.
   b. How much force would it take to lift 100 pounds?

Lever	Muscle Multiplier	Great Lifter	Load Lifter	Extra Muscle	Effort Less	Lever Greatness
a	6	4	5	10	8	5
b	10	6	8	15	14	9

2. The table shows the values of a and b in feet for six different levers.
   a. Use the force formula to write the fraction of the load required to work each lever. Write each fraction in simplest form.
   b. List the levers in order from least to most force required. Which levers need the same force?
   c. Convert each of the fractions to a decimal. Round to the nearest hundredth. Use the decimals to check the order of your list.
3. **Open-Ended** Make up your own set of levers.
   a. Choose a and b for six levers (make a less than b).
   b. Make a table to record the data about your levers. Name each lever.
   c. Exchange tables with a classmate. Write the fraction of the load required by each lever (in simplest form). Arrange the levers in order from least to most force required.
4. **Reasoning** For the levers on this page, $a < b$. What would happen if $a > b$? Can you think of a use for such a lever?
5. **Writing in Math** What class of lever is a wrench? Explain.

Levers in Playgrounds

A seesaw is a Class 1 lever. The fulcrum is between the load (one child) and the effort (the other child). The load and effort positions change as the seesaw rocks.

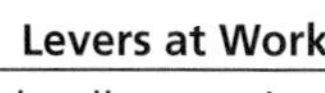

Levers at Work

A wheelbarrow is a Class 2 lever. The load (the hay) is between the fulcrum (the front wheel) and the effort (the girl in green).

Take It to the NET For more information about levers, go to **www.PHSchool.com**.
Web Code: aae-0353

Three Classes of Levers

Class 1 Lever
Pliers

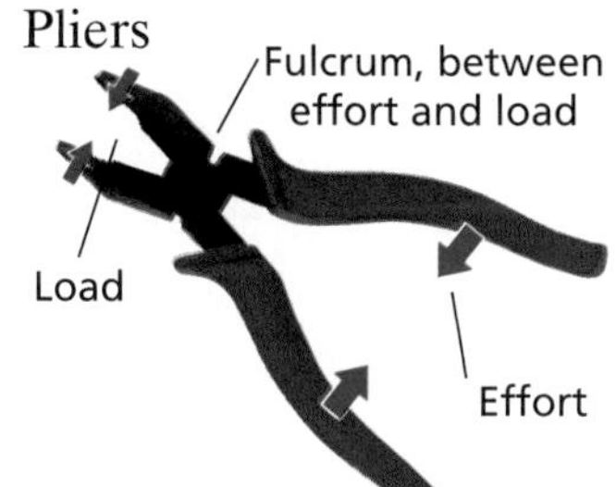

Class 2 Lever
Nutcrackers

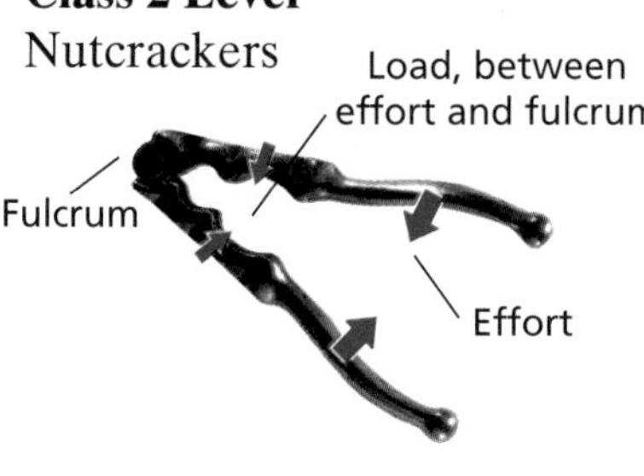

Class 3 Lever
Tongs

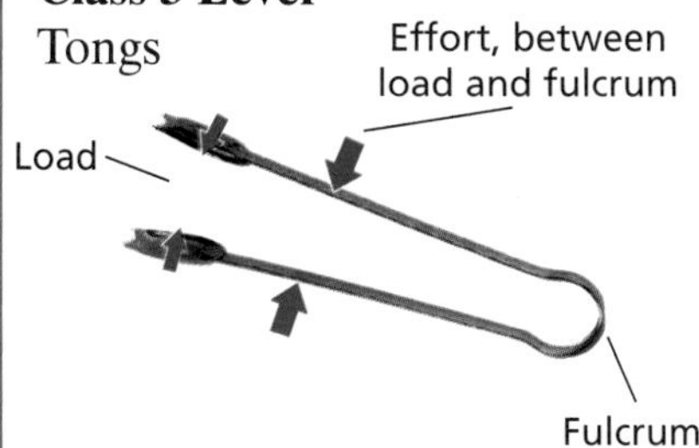

Levers at Home

When you use a hammer to remove a nail, it acts as a Class 1 lever. The fulcrum (the head of the hammer) is between the load (the nail) and the effort (your hand).

CHAPTER 4

Adding and Subtracting Fractions

Lessons

- **4-1** Estimating Sums and Differences
- **4-2** Fractions With Like Denominators
- **4-3** Fractions With Unlike Denominators
- **4-4** Adding Mixed Numbers
- **4-5** Subtracting Mixed Numbers
- **4-6** Equations With Fractions
- **4-7** Measurement: Elapsed Time
- **4-8** Problem Solving: Draw a Diagram

Key Vocabulary

- benchmark (p. 171)
- elapsed time (p. 202)

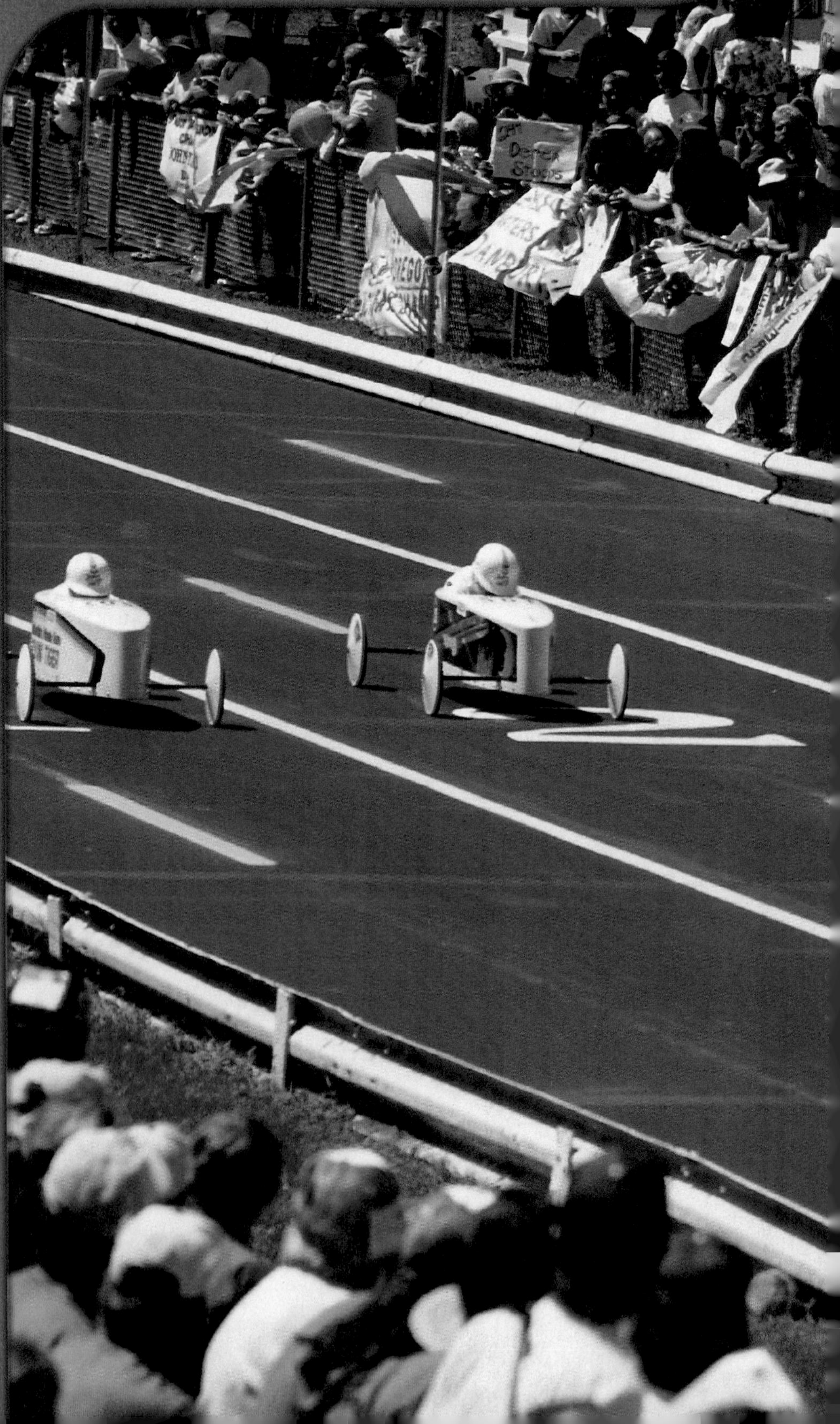

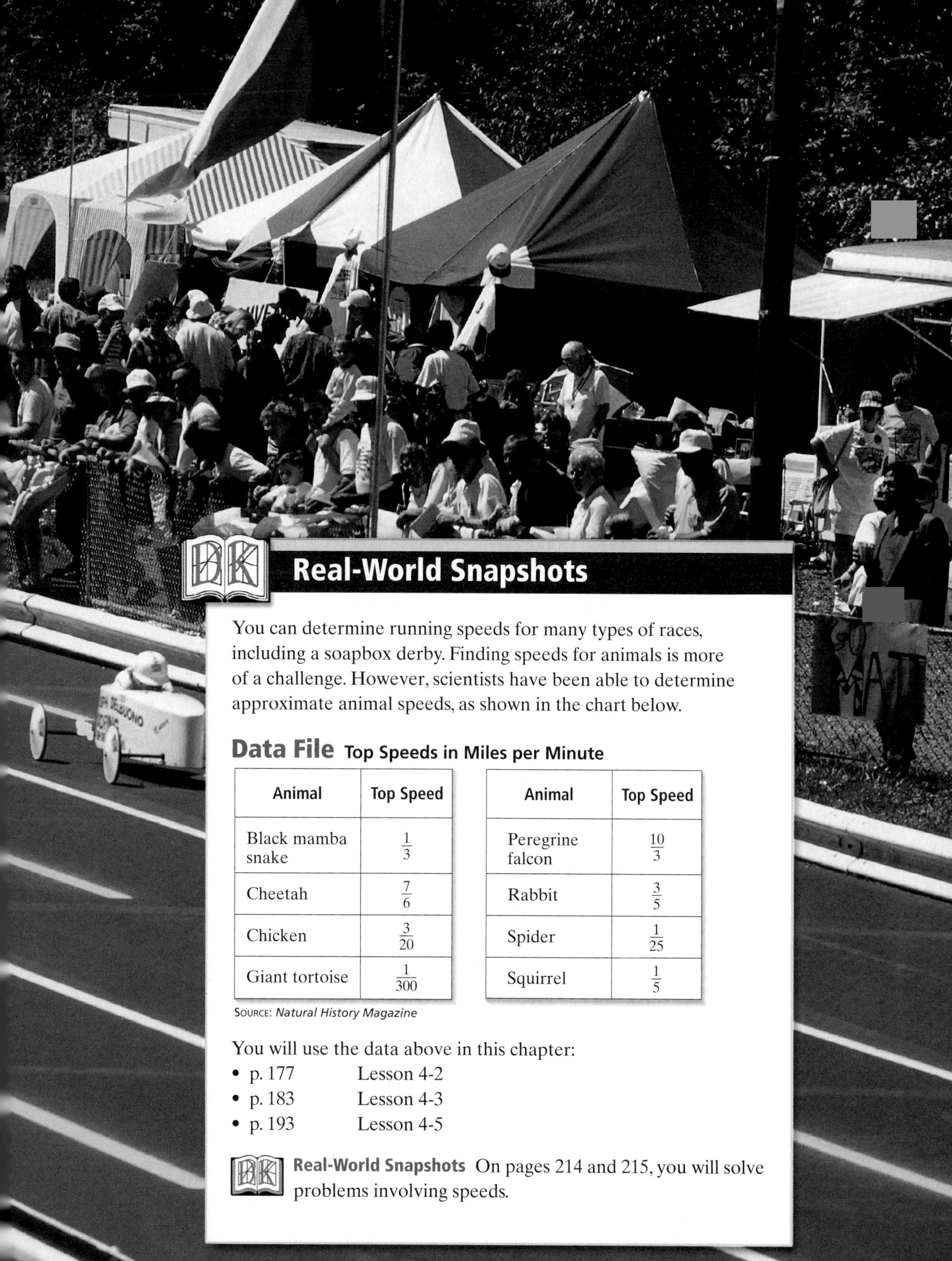

Real-World Snapshots

You can determine running speeds for many types of races, including a soapbox derby. Finding speeds for animals is more of a challenge. However, scientists have been able to determine approximate animal speeds, as shown in the chart below.

Data File Top Speeds in Miles per Minute

Animal	Top Speed
Black mamba snake	$\frac{1}{3}$
Cheetah	$\frac{7}{6}$
Chicken	$\frac{3}{20}$
Giant tortoise	$\frac{1}{300}$

Animal	Top Speed
Peregrine falcon	$\frac{10}{3}$
Rabbit	$\frac{3}{5}$
Spider	$\frac{1}{25}$
Squirrel	$\frac{1}{5}$

SOURCE: *Natural History Magazine*

You will use the data above in this chapter:

- p. 177 Lesson 4-2
- p. 183 Lesson 4-3
- p. 193 Lesson 4-5

Real-World Snapshots On pages 214 and 215, you will solve problems involving speeds.

Chapter 4 Preview

Where You've Been

- In Chapter 1, you learned to add, subtract, and estimate using decimals.
- In Chapter 2, you learned to solve equations.
- In Chapter 3, you learned to write and compare fractions and mixed numbers.

Where You're Going

- In Chapter 4, you will add and subtract fractions and mixed numbers.
- You will also solve equations with fractions.
- Applying what you learn, you will find elapsed time.

Pilots calculate elapsed time to determine if a flight is on schedule.

 Instant self-check online and on CD-ROM

Diagnosing Readiness

For help, go to the lesson in green.

Estimating With Decimals (Lesson 1-4)

Round each decimal to the nearest hundredth.

1. 2.58796 **2.** 1.98637 **3.** 6.219054

Finding Equivalent Fractions (Lesson 3-5)

Write each fraction in simplest form.

4. $\frac{5}{10}$ **5.** $\frac{6}{15}$ **6.** $\frac{12}{16}$

Writing Mixed Numbers and Improper Fractions (Lesson 3-6)

Write each improper fraction as a mixed number.

7. $\frac{87}{9}$ **8.** $\frac{21}{4}$ **9.** $\frac{15}{2}$

Write each mixed number as an improper fraction.

10. $8\frac{2}{3}$ **11.** $5\frac{3}{4}$ **12.** $16\frac{7}{9}$

Finding the Least Common Multiple (Lesson 3-7)

Find the LCM of each pair of numbers.

13. 8, 18 **14.** 5, 16 **15.** 14, 30

Estimating Sums and Differences

What You'll Learn

To estimate sums and differences

. . . And Why

To estimate the difference of two measurements, as in Example 2

Check Skills You'll Need

For help, go to Lesson 3-7.

Compare each pair of fractions using <, =, or >.

1. $\frac{3}{5}$ ■ $\frac{2}{5}$ **2.** $\frac{5}{7}$ ■ $\frac{5}{6}$ **3.** $\frac{2}{3}$ ■ $\frac{16}{24}$

4. $\frac{8}{9}$ ■ $\frac{9}{8}$ **5.** $\frac{15}{18}$ ■ $\frac{5}{8}$ **6.** $\frac{23}{24}$ ■ $\frac{71}{72}$

New Vocabulary
- benchmark

OBJECTIVE

Interactive lesson includes instant self-check, tutorials, and activities.

1 Estimating Sums and Differences

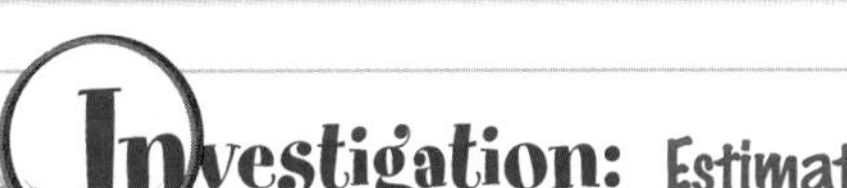

Investigation: Estimating Fractions

You can use 0 and 1 and the fractions $\frac{1}{4}$, $\frac{1}{2}$, and $\frac{3}{4}$ as *benchmarks* as you estimate fractions.

Estimate the shaded part of each figure using 0, $\frac{1}{4}$, $\frac{1}{2}$, $\frac{3}{4}$, and 1.

1. 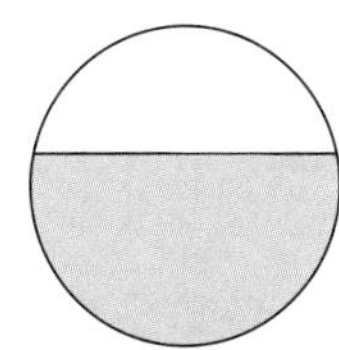

2. 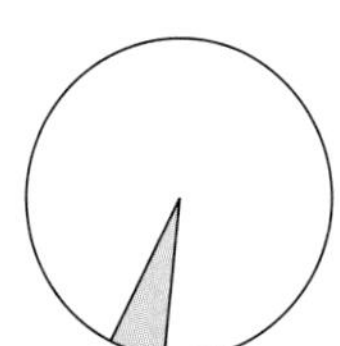

3. 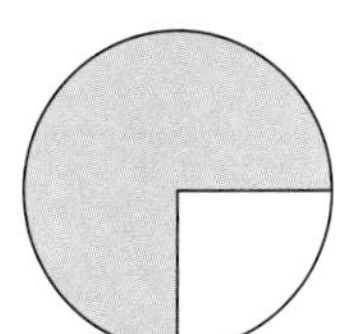

A **benchmark** is a number that is close to a fraction and is easy to use when you estimate. The benchmarks 0, $\frac{1}{2}$, and 1 are particularly useful when estimating sums and differences of fractions. The following table will help you determine which benchmarks to use when estimating.

Description	Examples	Benchmark
Numerator is close to 0. Denominator is not close to 0.	$\frac{1}{8}, \frac{3}{16}, \frac{2}{25}, \frac{9}{100}$	0
Numerator is about one half of denominator.	$\frac{3}{8}, \frac{9}{16}, \frac{11}{25}, \frac{52}{100}$	$\frac{1}{2}$
Numerator and denominator are close to each other.	$\frac{7}{8}, \frac{14}{16}, \frac{23}{25}, \frac{95}{100}$	1

Determine the benchmark for each fraction. Then estimate the sum or difference using the benchmarks $0, \frac{1}{2}$, and 1.

1 EXAMPLE Estimating Sums and Differences

Estimate.

a. $\frac{7}{12} + \frac{4}{5}$

$\frac{7}{12} + \frac{4}{5}$

$\approx \frac{1}{2} + 1$ ← **Replace each fraction with a benchmark.**

$= 1\frac{1}{2}$ ← **Simplify.**

b. $\frac{9}{10} - \frac{1}{7}$

$\frac{9}{10} - \frac{1}{7}$

$\approx 1 - 0$

$= 1$

Check Understanding 1 Estimate each sum or difference. **a.** $\frac{5}{6} + \frac{3}{7}$ **b.** $\frac{12}{13} - \frac{2}{25}$

You can round mixed numbers to the nearest whole number. The diagram below shows how to round $7\frac{9}{16}$ inches and $6\frac{1}{8}$ inches.

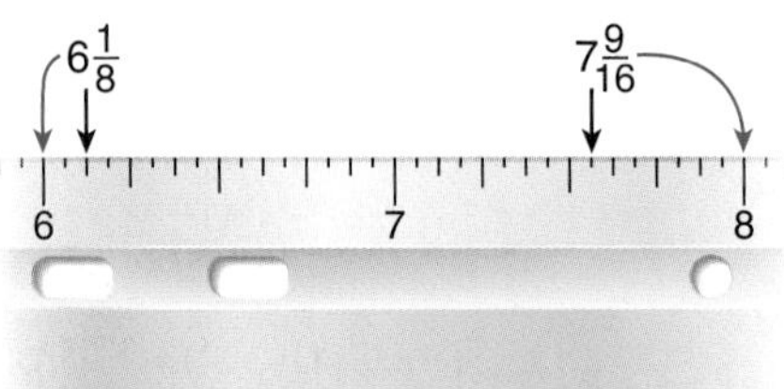

You can round before estimating the sum or difference of two mixed numbers. If a mixed number has a fraction of $\frac{1}{2}$, round up.

2 EXAMPLE Estimating With Mixed Numbers

Measurement Dave's hand span is $7\frac{9}{16}$ inches. Galina's hand span is $6\frac{1}{8}$ inches. Estimate the difference between their hand spans.

Estimate $7\frac{9}{16} - 6\frac{1}{8}$.

$7\frac{9}{16} \approx 8$ ← **Since $\frac{9}{16} > \frac{1}{2}$, round to 8.**

$6\frac{1}{8} \approx 6$ ← **Since $\frac{1}{8} < \frac{1}{2}$, round to 6.**

$8 - 6 = 2$ ← **Estimate by finding the difference.**

Dave's hand span is about 2 inches greater than Galina's hand span.

Check Understanding 2 **Travel** It takes $3\frac{3}{4}$ hours to drive to the beach. It takes $8\frac{1}{2}$ hours to drive to the mountains. Estimate the difference in driving times.

EXERCISES

For more practice, see *Extra Practice*.

A Practice by Example

Example 1 (page 172)

Estimate each sum or difference. Use the benchmarks 0, $\frac{1}{2}$, and 1.

1. $\frac{5}{13} + \frac{4}{25}$
2. $\frac{17}{19} - \frac{2}{13}$
3. $\frac{70}{85} + \frac{32}{51}$
4. $\frac{11}{20} - \frac{2}{15}$
5. $\frac{9}{16} - \frac{18}{37}$
6. $\frac{5}{16} + \frac{7}{15}$

Example 2 (page 172)

Estimate each sum or difference.

7. $4\frac{2}{9} + 6\frac{13}{27}$
8. $9\frac{7}{15} - 3\frac{1}{2}$
9. $22\frac{1}{9} - 16\frac{9}{11}$
10. $22\frac{8}{14} - 17\frac{3}{7}$
11. $76\frac{6}{23} - 45\frac{1}{5}$
12. $84\frac{3}{36} + 41\frac{7}{8}$

13. **Life Science** In an experiment, a kudzu plant is $1\frac{1}{12}$ feet tall. Over time, the plant grows to $4\frac{7}{12}$ feet. About how much did the plant grow?

B Apply Your Skills

Choose a benchmark for each measurement. Use 0, $\frac{1}{2}$, or 1.

14. $\frac{1}{8}$ inch
15. $\frac{4}{8}$ inch
16. $\frac{15}{16}$ inch
17. $\frac{3}{8}$ inch
18. $\frac{11}{16}$ inch
19. $\frac{3}{16}$ inch

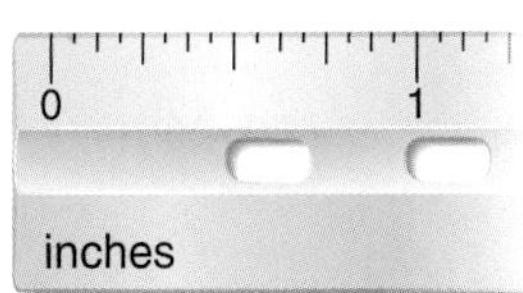

20. a. Measurement Use the table. About how much did each person grow during the summer?
    b. Who grew the most?

Heights (inches)

Person	June	Sept.
Jocelyn	$61\frac{7}{8}$	$62\frac{1}{4}$
Carlos	$60\frac{3}{4}$	$61\frac{5}{8}$
Amanda	$59\frac{1}{8}$	$60\frac{5}{8}$

21. Error Analysis Your friend says that when you estimate the sum of two fractions, the estimate must be a fraction. Do you agree? Explain.

22. Writing in Math Why does it make sense to round a mixed number to the nearest whole number before adding or subtracting? Could you round to the nearest $\frac{1}{2}$ instead?

23. **Coins** Use the table at the left to estimate the total width of the coins in the picture below.

U.S. Coins

Coin	Diameter (inches)
Dime	$\frac{11}{16}$
Penny	$\frac{3}{4}$
Nickel	$\frac{13}{16}$
Quarter	$\frac{15}{16}$

Challenge

Estimation **Use estimation to compare. Use < or >.**

24. $14\frac{9}{10} - \left(8\frac{1}{7} + 1\frac{8}{9}\right) \blacksquare 14\frac{9}{10} - 8\frac{1}{7} + 1\frac{8}{9}$

25. $\left(13\frac{5}{8} - 10\frac{2}{5}\right) - 2\frac{1}{3} \blacksquare 13\frac{5}{8} - \left(10\frac{2}{5} - 2\frac{1}{3}\right)$

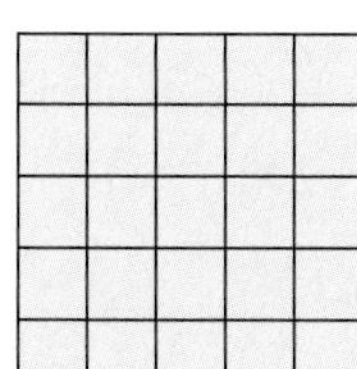

26. Number Sense You estimate $\frac{5}{8} + \frac{9}{16} + \frac{17}{32}$ using the benchmarks 0, $\frac{1}{2}$, and 1. Is the estimate less than or greater than the actual sum? Explain.

27. Stretch Your Thinking Divide the grid at the left into eight squares. The squares do not need to be the same size. There can be no overlaps and no space can be left over.

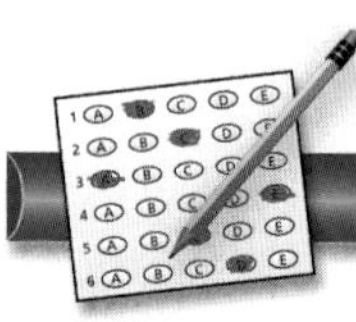

Test Prep

Short Response

28. Which number is closest to 5?

A. $4\frac{3}{4}$ B. $4\frac{2}{6}$ C. $4\frac{7}{8}$ D. $4\frac{1}{3}$

29. Which number is closest to $\frac{1}{2}$?

F. $\frac{3}{4}$ G. $\frac{3}{8}$ H. $\frac{3}{9}$ I. $\frac{3}{10}$

30. Which is the best estimate of $1\frac{8}{9} - \frac{17}{20}$?

A. 0 B. $\frac{1}{2}$ C. 1 D. $1\frac{1}{2}$

Take It to the NET
Online lesson quiz at
www.PHSchool.com
Web Code: aaa-0401

31. Which is the best estimate of $\frac{5}{11} + \frac{12}{13}$?

F. 0 G. $\frac{1}{2}$ H. 1 I. $1\frac{1}{2}$

Short Response

32. Fabric costs $7.00 per yard. Suppose you need $1\frac{5}{8}$ yards of solid-colored fabric and $\frac{3}{4}$ yard of print fabric for a quilt. **(a)** What is the best estimate of the total amount of fabric you need? **(b)** About how much will the fabric cost? Justify your answer.

Mixed Review

Lesson 3-8 **Write each fraction as a decimal.**

33. $\frac{47}{1{,}000}$ **34.** $\frac{4}{5}$ **35.** $\frac{3}{500}$ **36.** $\frac{17}{20}$ **37.** $\frac{1}{8}$

Lesson 2-3 Algebra **Write an algebraic expression for each word phrase.**

38. 10 more than g **39.** 20 times h **40.** 5 less than m

41. 12 added to s **42.** r decreased by 6 **43.** 14 divided by t

4-2 Fractions With Like Denominators

What You'll Learn

To add fractions

To subtract fractions

. . . And Why

To solve problems involving measurement, as in Exercise 28

Check Skills You'll Need

For help, go to Lesson 3-5.

Write each fraction in simplest form.

1. $\frac{10}{40}$
2. $\frac{8}{24}$
3. $\frac{16}{20}$
4. $\frac{12}{15}$
5. $\frac{8}{12}$
6. $\frac{9}{12}$
7. $\frac{20}{24}$
8. $\frac{12}{28}$
9. $\frac{15}{35}$

OBJECTIVE

Interactive lesson includes instant self-check, tutorials, and activities.

1 Adding Fractions

Investigation: Modeling Like Denominators

A pizza has 8 equal slices. You eat 2 and a friend eats 3.

1. a. Write a fraction for the amount of pizza you eat. Do not simplify your answer. Then write a fraction for the amount of the pizza your friend eats.
   b. Write a fraction for the total eaten.
   c. When you add fractions, do you add the denominators? Explain.

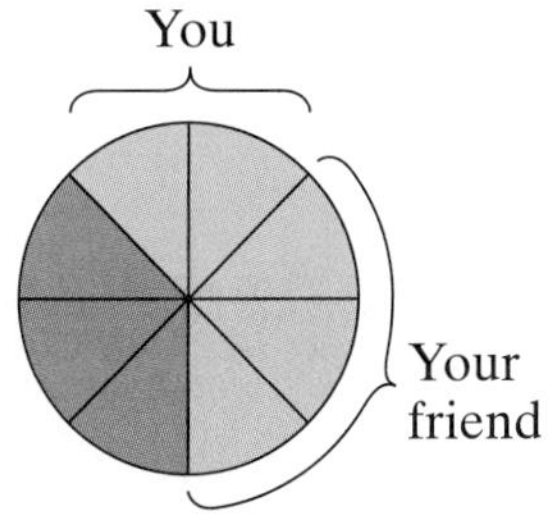

To add fractions with like denominators, add the numerators and keep the same denominator.

1 EXAMPLE Adding With Like Denominators

Find $\frac{4}{15} + \frac{7}{15}$.

$\frac{4}{15} + \frac{7}{15} = \frac{4 + 7}{15}$ ← **The fractions have like denominators. Add the numerators. The denominator stays the same.**

$= \frac{11}{15}$ ← **Simplify the numerator.**

Check Understanding 1 Add. **a.** $\frac{1}{6} + \frac{4}{6}$ **b.** $\frac{2}{5} + \frac{1}{5}$

If the sum of fractions results in an improper fraction, rename the improper fraction as a mixed number.

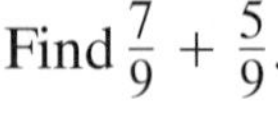

Sums Greater Than 1

Need Help?
For help with writing an improper fraction as a mixed number, go to Lesson 3-6.

Find $\frac{7}{9} + \frac{5}{9}$.

$\frac{7}{9} + \frac{5}{9} = \frac{7+5}{9}$ ← **Add the numerators. The denominator remains the same.**

$= \frac{12}{9}$ ← **Simplify the numerator.**

$= 1\frac{3}{9}$ ← **Write as a mixed number.**

$= 1\frac{1}{3}$ ← **Divide the numerator and denominator by the GCF, 3.**

2 Find each sum. **a.** $\frac{5}{16} + \frac{13}{16}$ **b.** $\frac{11}{20} + \frac{17}{20}$

c. **Number Sense** Explain how you could recognize when your answer needs to be written in simplest form.

OBJECTIVE

2 Subtracting Fractions

To subtract fractions with like denominators, subtract the numerators and keep the same denominator. Write the answer in simplest form.

Subtracting With Like Denominators

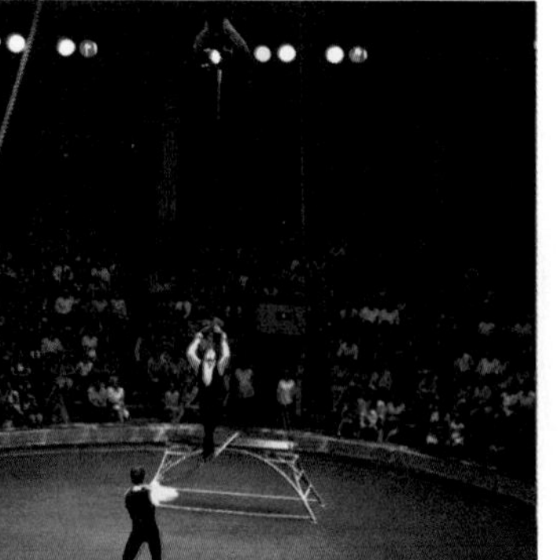

Circus There are 10 sections in a circular seating area for a circus. Three sections are empty. Just before the show begins, a large group completely fills one section. How much of the seating area is empty?

Three sections out of ten means $\frac{3}{10}$. One section out of 10 means $\frac{1}{10}$. The number of sections empty is $\frac{3}{10} - \frac{1}{10}$.

$\frac{3}{10} - \frac{1}{10} = \frac{3-1}{10}$ ← **Subtract the numerators. The denominator remains the same.**

$= \frac{2}{10}$ ← **Simplify the numerator.**

$= \frac{1}{5}$ ← **Write the fraction in simplest form.**

In the circus, $\frac{1}{5}$ of the sections are empty.

3 Find each difference. **a.** $\frac{3}{5} - \frac{2}{5}$ **b.** $\frac{3}{4} - \frac{1}{4}$

c. Suppose you are building a tree house. A board is $\frac{11}{12}$ foot. You need $\frac{7}{12}$ foot of the board for a brace. How much is left after you cut off the piece you need?

EXERCISES

For more practice, see *Extra Practice.*

A Practice by Example

Find each sum.

Examples 1, 2 (pages 175, 176)

1. $\frac{1}{4} + \frac{1}{4}$ **2.** $\frac{2}{5} + \frac{3}{5}$ **3.** $\frac{2}{9} + \frac{4}{9}$ **4.** $\frac{1}{6} + \frac{3}{6}$

5. $\frac{2}{3} + \frac{2}{3}$ **6.** $\frac{9}{10} + \frac{7}{10}$ **7.** $\frac{2}{3} + \frac{2}{3}$ **8.** $\frac{4}{5} + \frac{3}{5}$

Find each difference.

Example 3 (page 176)

9. $\frac{17}{18} - \frac{5}{18}$ **10.** $\frac{15}{20} - \frac{3}{20}$ **11.** $\frac{4}{5} - \frac{3}{5}$ **12.** $\frac{6}{7} - \frac{3}{7}$

13. $\frac{5}{9} - \frac{2}{9}$ **14.** $\frac{9}{16} - \frac{3}{16}$ **15.** $\frac{8}{12} - \frac{5}{12}$ **16.** $\frac{17}{24} - \frac{7}{24}$

17. Spiders A typical garden spider is $\frac{7}{8}$ inch long. A typical black widow spider is $\frac{3}{8}$ inch long. How much longer is the garden spider?

18. Office Supplies White correction fluid is sold in a $\frac{7}{10}$-ounce bottle. Blue correction fluid is sold in a $\frac{6}{10}$-ounce bottle. You buy one bottle of each color. How much more white correction fluid than blue do you get?

B Apply Your Skills

Write an addition or subtraction sentence for each model.

19. 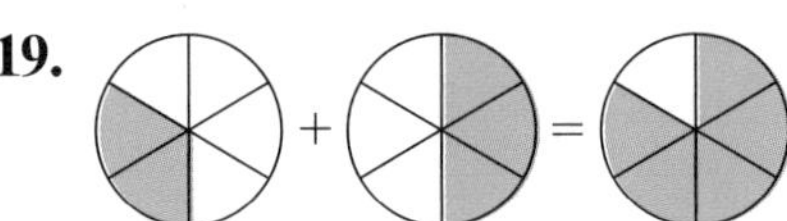

20. 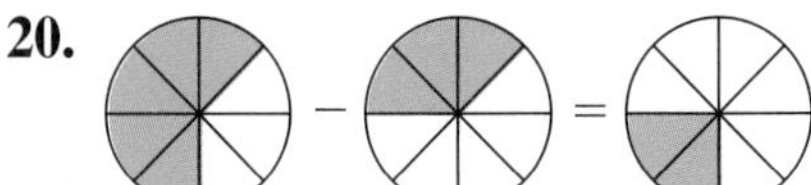

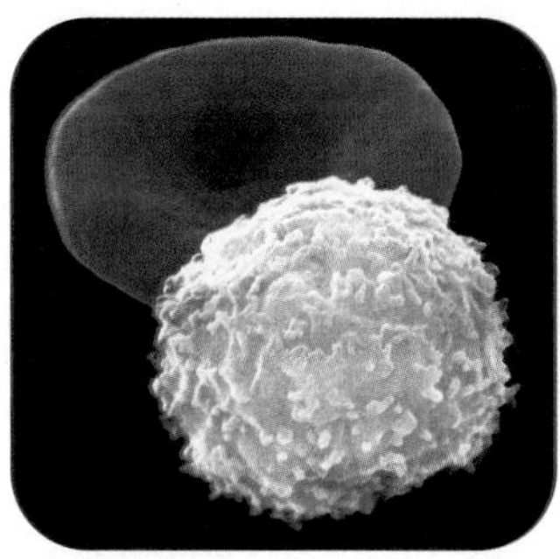

Most cells in your blood are red blood cells, white blood cells, or platelets.

21. Biology Plasma makes up $\frac{11}{20}$ of your blood. Blood cells make up the other $\frac{9}{20}$. How much more of your blood is plasma than blood cells?

22. Data File, p. 169 How much faster is the running speed of a rabbit than the running speed of a squirrel?

Find each sum.

23. $\frac{1}{20} + \frac{3}{20} + \frac{5}{20}$ **24.** $\frac{27}{100} + \frac{41}{100} + \frac{3}{100}$ **25.** $\frac{4}{15} + \frac{1}{15} + \frac{7}{15}$

26. Error Analysis One of your classmates says $\frac{3}{5} + \frac{1}{5} = \frac{4}{10}$. Explain the error and find the correct sum.

27. Writing in Math Explain how to find the sum of $\frac{5}{9}$ and $\frac{7}{9}$.

28. Rainfall Suppose it rains $\frac{3}{8}$ inch on Friday and $\frac{7}{8}$ inch on Saturday.

a. What is the total rainfall during the two days?

b. What is the difference in rainfall for the two days?

Challenge

PEANUT SAUCE

2 cups chopped onion
1 tablespoon peanut oil
$\frac{1}{4}$ tablespoon cayenne
$\frac{1}{4}$ teaspoon ground ginger
1 ripe banana
1 cup tomato juice
$\frac{1}{2}$ cup apple or apricot juice
$\frac{1}{2}$ cup peanut butter
$\frac{1}{2}$ teaspoon salt

Algebra **Replace each ■ with a number to make the equation true.**

29. $\frac{3}{5} + \frac{■}{5} = \frac{4}{5}$ **30.** $\frac{■}{10} - \frac{1}{10} = 0$ **31.** $\frac{7}{12} - \frac{■}{12} = \frac{1}{6}$

32. Recipes Use the recipe card shown at the left for peanut sauce.

a. To make the sauce spicier, you decide to double the amount of cayenne. How much cayenne should you use?

b. You decide to use equal amounts of apple and apricot juices. In simplest form, how much of each type of juice should you use?

33. Stretch Your Thinking In a jar, 26 out of 27 marbles are the same weight. One marble weighs less. You have a scale to find the odd marble. What is the least number of weighings you need to find the marble?

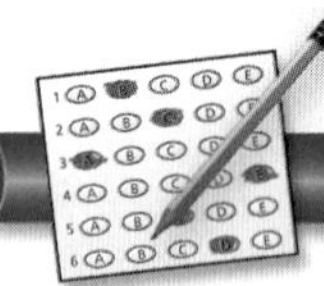

Test Prep

Multiple Choice

34. What is the sum of $\frac{9}{16}$ and $\frac{3}{16}$?

A. $\frac{3}{4}$ **B.** $\frac{2}{3}$ **C.** $\frac{11}{16}$ **D.** $\frac{9}{16}$

35. What is the difference of $\frac{35}{60}$ and $\frac{11}{60}$?

F. $\frac{4}{15}$ **G.** $\frac{2}{5}$ **H.** $\frac{3}{4}$ **I.** $\frac{5}{6}$

36. Two students explore a cove along an old road. One student explores $\frac{1}{8}$ mile of the cove. The other explores $\frac{3}{8}$ mile of the cove at the opposite end. Together, how much of the cove do they explore?

A. $\frac{1}{8}$ mile **B.** $\frac{3}{8}$ mile **C.** $\frac{1}{2}$ mile **D.** $\frac{3}{4}$ mile

Take It to the NET
Online lesson quiz at
www.PHSchool.com
Web Code: aaa-0402

Short Response

37. In an archery tournament, a team hits the target 9 times out of 12 in the first round. **(a)** What fraction of the team's arrows did NOT hit the target? **(b)** Explain how you found your answer.

Mixed Review

Lesson 3-4 **Write two fractions equivalent to each fraction.**

38. $\frac{3}{8}$ **39.** $\frac{1}{6}$ **40.** $\frac{2}{5}$ **41.** $\frac{7}{10}$

Lesson 2-8 **Simplify each expression.**

42. $3^2 + 5.1$ **43.** $500 \div 10^2$ **44.** $6^2 \times 10^3$

Investigation Modeling Unlike Denominators

For Use With Lesson 4-3

In Lesson 4-2, you added and subtracted fractions that had like denominators. To add or subtract fractions such as $\frac{5}{8}$ and $\frac{1}{4}$, first you must write the fractions using like denominators.

EXAMPLE

Use models to find each sum or difference.

a. $\frac{5}{8} + \frac{1}{4}$

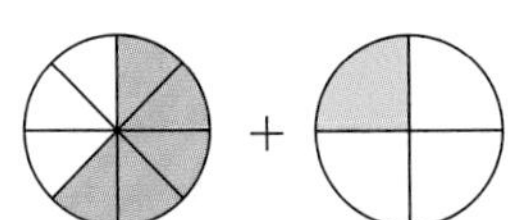

$\frac{5}{8}$ $\frac{1}{4}$

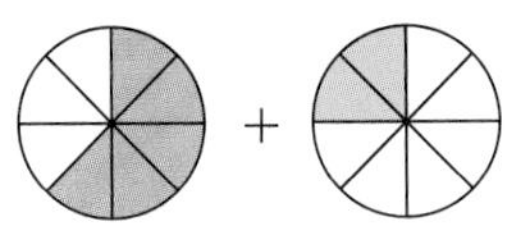

$\frac{5}{8}$ $\frac{2}{8}$

← Change the model for $\frac{1}{4}$ so that it has the same number of sections as the model for $\frac{5}{8}$.

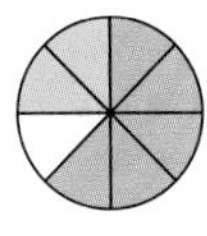

$\frac{7}{8}$

← Add $\frac{2}{8}$ to the model for $\frac{5}{8}$.

b. $\frac{5}{6} - \frac{2}{3}$

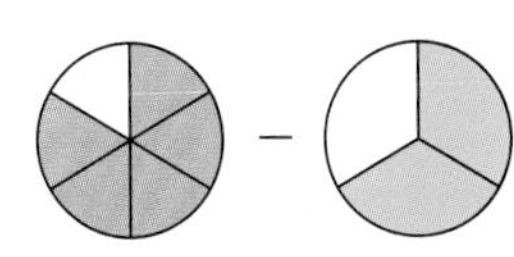

$\frac{5}{6}$ $\frac{2}{3}$

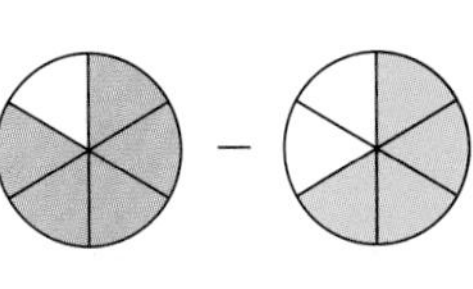

$\frac{5}{6}$ $\frac{4}{6}$

← Change the model for $\frac{2}{3}$ so that it has the same number of sections as the model for $\frac{5}{6}$.

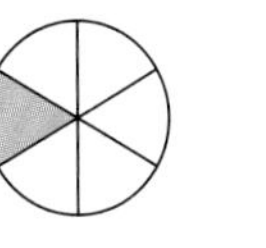

$\frac{1}{6}$

← Take away $\frac{4}{6}$ from the model for $\frac{5}{6}$.

EXERCISES

Use models to find each sum or difference.

1. 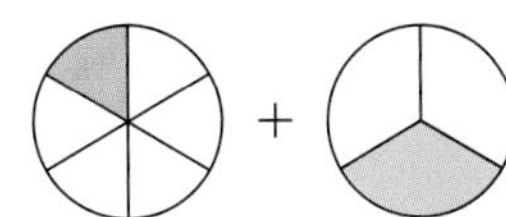

2. 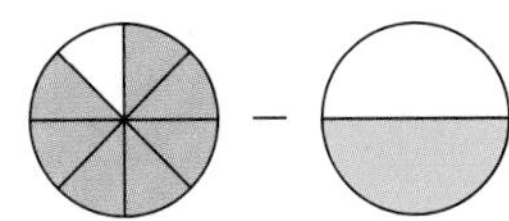

3. 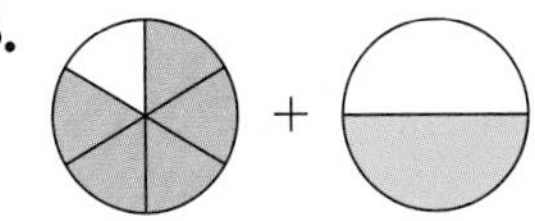

Draw models to find each sum or difference.

4. $\frac{1}{8} + \frac{3}{4}$

5. $\frac{2}{3} - \frac{1}{6}$

6. $\frac{1}{2} + \frac{3}{8}$

7. $\frac{5}{6} - \frac{1}{3}$

8. $\frac{1}{2} + \frac{1}{3}$

9. $\frac{5}{8} - \frac{1}{2}$

4-3 Fractions With Unlike Denominators

What You'll Learn

To add fractions

To subtract fractions

. . . And Why

To find survey results, as in Example 2

✓ Check Skills You'll Need

For help, go to Lesson 3-6.

Find the LCM.

1. 6, 9 **2.** 12, 18 **3.** 5, 24

4. 40, 48 **5.** 30, 75 **6.** 4, 6, 15

7. Explain your method for finding the LCM of 8 and 12.

Interactive lesson includes instant self-check, tutorials, and activities.

OBJECTIVE

1 Adding Fractions

When the denominators of fractions are different, you can use fraction models, or you can write equivalent fractions with the same denominator to add the fractions.

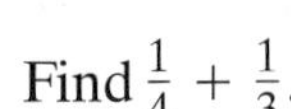

1 EXAMPLE Adding Fractions With Unlike Denominators

Find $\frac{1}{4} + \frac{1}{3}$.

Method 1 Model $\frac{1}{4} + \frac{1}{3}$.

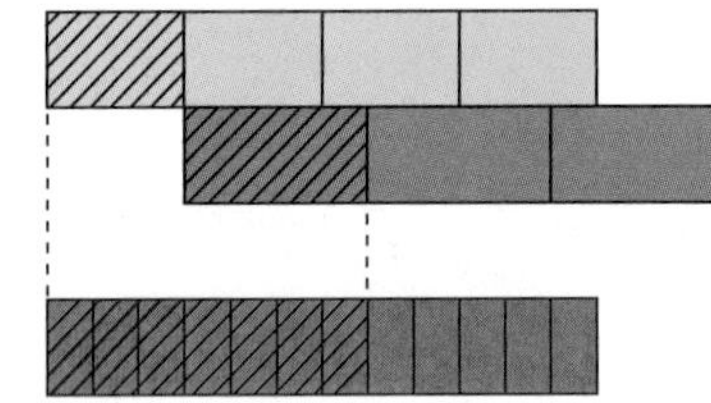

← Use the fraction model for $\frac{1}{4}$.

← Use the fraction model for $\frac{1}{3}$.

$\frac{1}{4} + \frac{1}{3} = \frac{7}{12}$

Method 2 Use a common denominator.

$$\frac{1}{4} \rightarrow \frac{1 \times 3}{4 \times 3} \rightarrow \frac{3}{12}$$

$$+\frac{1}{3} \rightarrow \frac{1 \times 4}{3 \times 4} \rightarrow +\frac{4}{12}$$

← The LCD is 12. Write the fractions with the same denominator.

$$\frac{7}{12}$$

← Add the numerators.

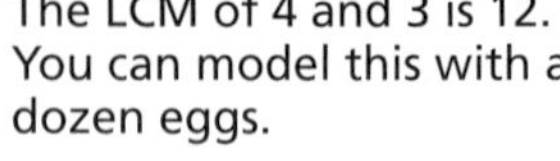

Real-World Connection

The LCM of 4 and 3 is 12. You can model this with a dozen eggs.

Check Understanding **1** Find $\frac{3}{5} + \frac{1}{10}$. Use a model or a common denominator.

2 EXAMPLE Real-World Problem Solving

Real-World Connection

The oven, or kiln, used for ceramics can reach a temperature of over 2,000°F.

Art Class Students in art class completed a survey about their favorite activity. Ceramics is the favorite of $\frac{2}{5}$ of the students. Drawing is the favorite of $\frac{3}{8}$ of the students. What fraction of the students chose either ceramics or drawing as their favorite art class activity?

Add $\frac{2}{5}$ and $\frac{3}{8}$ to find the fraction of students who chose ceramics or drawing.

$$\begin{array}{r} \frac{2}{5} \\ +\frac{3}{8} \\ \hline \end{array} \rightarrow \begin{array}{c} \frac{2 \times 8}{5 \times 8} \\ \frac{3 \times 5}{8 \times 5} \end{array} \rightarrow \begin{array}{r} \frac{16}{40} \\ +\frac{15}{40} \\ \hline \frac{31}{40} \end{array}$$

← The LCD is 40. Write the fractions with the same denominator.

← Add the numerators.

The favorite art activity of $\frac{31}{40}$ of the students is either ceramics or drawing.

Check Understanding 2 You exercise $\frac{3}{4}$ hour on Monday and $\frac{2}{3}$ hour on Tuesday. How long did you exercise on Monday and Tuesday?

OBJECTIVE

2 Subtracting Fractions

You can subtract fractions that have unlike denominators.

3 EXAMPLE Subtracting Fractions

Find $\frac{1}{2} - \frac{1}{3}$.

Method 1 Model $\frac{1}{2} - \frac{1}{3}$.

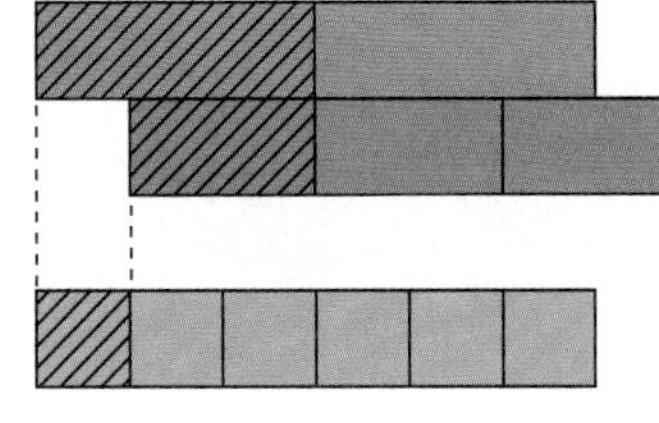

← Use the fraction model for $\frac{1}{2}$.

← Use the fraction model for $\frac{1}{3}$.

$\frac{1}{2} - \frac{1}{3} = \frac{1}{6}$

Method 2 Use a common denominator.

$$\begin{array}{r} \frac{1}{2} \\ -\frac{1}{3} \\ \hline \end{array} \rightarrow \begin{array}{c} \frac{1 \times 3}{2 \times 3} \\ \frac{1 \times 2}{3 \times 2} \end{array} \rightarrow \begin{array}{r} \frac{3}{6} \\ -\frac{2}{6} \\ \hline \frac{1}{6} \end{array}$$

← The LCD is 6. Write the fractions with the same denominator.

← Add the numerators.

Check Understanding 3 Find $\frac{3}{4} - \frac{5}{8}$. Use a model or common denominators.

4 EXAMPLE Real-World Problem Solving

Parks A property owner donates $\frac{1}{4}$ acre to increase the size of a park next to his house to $\frac{5}{6}$ acre. Find the area of the park before the donation.

Subtract $\frac{1}{4}$ from $\frac{5}{6}$ to find the original size of the park.

Estimate Use benchmarks to estimate: $\frac{5}{6} - \frac{1}{4} \approx 1 - \frac{1}{2}$, or $\frac{1}{2}$.

$$\begin{array}{r} \frac{5}{6} \\ -\frac{1}{4} \\ \hline \end{array} \rightarrow \begin{array}{c} \frac{5 \times 2}{6 \times 2} \\ \frac{1 \times 3}{4 \times 3} \end{array} \rightarrow \begin{array}{r} \frac{10}{12} \\ -\frac{3}{12} \\ \hline \frac{7}{12} \end{array}$$

← **The LCD is 12. Write the fractions with the same denominator.**

← **Subtract the numerators.**

The park was originally $\frac{7}{12}$ acre.

Check for Reasonableness The answer $\frac{7}{12}$ is close to the estimate $\frac{1}{2}$.

Check Understanding 4 Suppose you have $\frac{3}{5}$ yard of felt. You use $\frac{1}{2}$ of the felt for a display. How much felt do you have left?

EXERCISES

For more practice, see *Extra Practice*.

A Practice by Example

Find each sum. Exercises 1 and 2 have been started for you.

Example 1 (page 180)

1. $\frac{2}{5} + \frac{1}{2}$

Use a model.

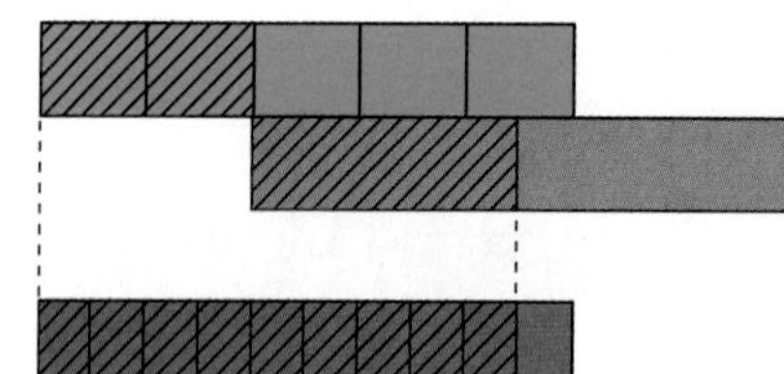

2. $\frac{1}{10} + \frac{2}{5}$

Use the LCD.

$$\begin{array}{r} \frac{1}{10} \\ +\frac{2}{5} \\ \hline \end{array} \rightarrow \begin{array}{c} \frac{1}{10} \\ \frac{2 \times 2}{5 \times 2} \end{array} \rightarrow \begin{array}{r} \frac{1}{10} \\ +\frac{4}{10} \\ \hline \blacksquare \end{array}$$

3. $\frac{1}{3} + \frac{1}{6}$

4. $\frac{1}{6} + \frac{1}{2}$

5. $\frac{8}{9} + \frac{5}{6}$

6. $\frac{5}{6} + \frac{1}{4}$

Example 2 (page 181)

7. Corky's house is $\frac{7}{10}$ mile farther from school than Diane's house is. Diane lives $\frac{7}{8}$ mile from school. How far from school does Corky live?

8. Suppose you have two goldfish. One goldfish weighs $\frac{1}{6}$ ounce and the other weighs $\frac{1}{3}$ ounce. How much do the goldfish weigh together?

Example 3 (page 181)

Find each difference. Exercises 9 and 10 have been started for you.

9. $\frac{2}{3} - \frac{5}{12}$

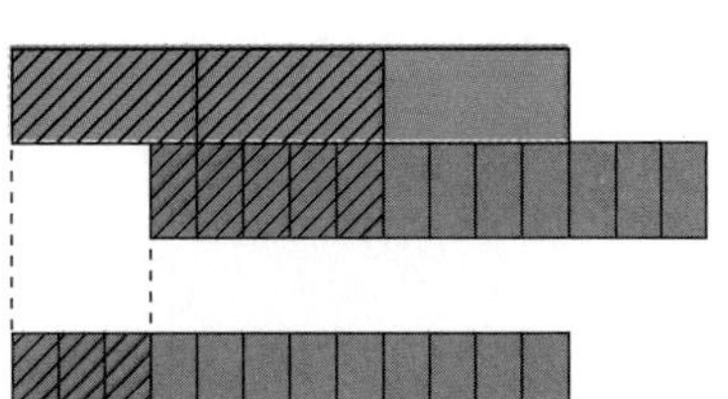

10. $\frac{7}{12} - \frac{1}{4}$

$$\begin{array}{r}\frac{7}{12}\\ -\ \frac{1}{4}\\ \hline\end{array} \rightarrow \frac{1 \times 3}{4 \times 3} \rightarrow \begin{array}{r}\frac{7}{12}\\ -\ \frac{3}{12}\\ \hline \blacksquare\end{array}$$

11. $\frac{13}{16} - \frac{1}{4}$ **12.** $\frac{17}{20} - \frac{2}{5}$ **13.** $\frac{9}{10} - \frac{3}{5}$ **14.** $\frac{3}{4} - \frac{1}{12}$

Example 4 (page 182)

15. Cooking A cook blends $\frac{1}{3}$ cup crushed raspberries into $\frac{3}{4}$ cup sugar for a sauce. How much more sugar than raspberries does the cook use?

16. Leftovers Suppose you have $\frac{3}{4}$ pound cooked salmon. You eat $\frac{1}{8}$ pound for dinner. How much salmon do you have for leftovers?

B Apply Your Skills

Find each sum or difference.

17. $\frac{1}{3} + \frac{2}{5}$ **18.** $\frac{13}{16} - \frac{1}{4}$ **19.** $\frac{4}{5} - \frac{1}{2}$ **20.** $\frac{3}{4} + \frac{1}{3}$

21. $\frac{3}{5} + \frac{3}{20}$ **22.** $\frac{7}{10} - \frac{1}{4}$ **23.** $\frac{5}{6} - \frac{1}{2}$ **24.** $\frac{3}{10} + \frac{1}{4}$

Real-World Connection

Central Florida is known as the "lightning capital" of the United States.

25. Weather A weather reporter records the rainfall as $\frac{3}{10}$ inch between 9:00 and 10:00 and $\frac{7}{8}$ inch between 10:00 and 11:00.

a. Estimation Estimate the total rainfall between 9:00 and 11:00.

b. What is the total rainfall between 9:00 and 11:00?

26. Writing in Math To add $\frac{5}{6}$ and $\frac{7}{12}$, you can use the LCD, 12, or another common denominator, such as 72. Find the sum each way. Which do you prefer, and why?

27. Data File, p. 169 How much faster in miles per minute is the speed of a rabbit than the speed of a chicken?

Mental Math Simplify by using mental math.

28. $\frac{2}{3} + \frac{1}{6} - \frac{1}{6}$ **29.** $\frac{9}{10} - \frac{7}{8} + \frac{1}{10}$ **30.** $\frac{4}{5} - \left(\frac{1}{10} + \frac{1}{10}\right)$

C Challenge

Use any method to add and subtract.

31. $\frac{5}{8} + \frac{9}{12} + \frac{1}{2}$ **32.** $\frac{11}{30} - \frac{1}{5} - \frac{1}{6}$ **33.** $\frac{2}{5} + \frac{1}{2} - \frac{1}{10}$

34. Stretch Your Thinking How can you cut an 8-foot by 3-foot board into two pieces so that both pieces together cover a 12-foot by 2-foot hole?

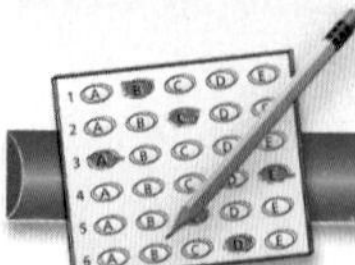

Test Prep

Gridded Response

Find each sum or difference.

35. $\frac{9}{16} + \frac{4}{32}$
36. $\frac{2}{5} + \frac{3}{10}$
37. $\frac{16}{24} - \frac{1}{2}$
38. $\frac{3}{4} - \frac{3}{8}$
39. $\frac{9}{12} + \frac{4}{16}$
40. $\frac{8}{12} - \frac{4}{9}$

Take It to the NET
Online lesson quiz at
www.PHSchool.com
Web Code: aaa-0403

41. A package of sliced ham weighs $\frac{1}{2}$ pound. Another package of ham weighs $\frac{1}{8}$ pound. What is the total weight in pounds of both packages?

Mixed Review

Lesson 3-3 **List the factors to find the GCF of each set of numbers.**

42. 16, 64 **43.** 33, 121 **44.** 40, 72 **45.** 60, 210

Lesson 2-6 **Solve each equation. Then check the solution.**

46. $x + 5 = 2$ **47.** $x - 12 = 4$ **48.** $x - 0.5 = 1.6$

Lesson 1-8 **Use mental math to find each product.**

49. 10×4.9 **50.** $100(3.14)$ **51.** $1{,}000 \cdot 0.72$

Checkpoint Quiz 1

Lessons 4-1 through 4-3

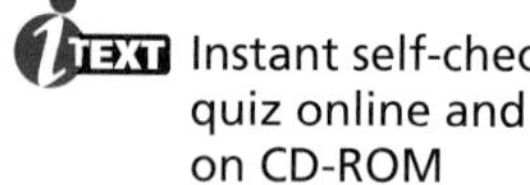

Instant self-check quiz online and on CD-ROM

Estimate each sum or difference. Use the benchmarks 0, $\frac{1}{2}$, and 1.

1. $\frac{8}{9} + \frac{5}{16}$ **2.** $\frac{12}{13} - \frac{1}{9}$

Find each sum or difference.

3. $\frac{3}{10} + \frac{9}{10}$ **4.** $\frac{5}{6} - \frac{1}{3}$ **5.** $\frac{7}{12} + \frac{2}{3}$

6. $\frac{9}{10} - \frac{1}{3}$ **7.** $\frac{1}{7} + \frac{5}{14}$ **8.** $\frac{17}{20} - \frac{3}{20}$

9. In a class, $\frac{1}{6}$ of the students have blue eyes and $\frac{7}{9}$ of the students have brown eyes. Find how much more of the class has brown eyes than blue eyes.

10. Cereal Suppose you are still hungry after eating $\frac{2}{3}$ cup wheat flakes, so you eat $\frac{1}{2}$ cup corn flakes. How much cereal do you eat that morning?

4-4 Adding Mixed Numbers

What You'll Learn

To add mixed numbers

To add mixed numbers with renaming

. . . And Why

To solve problems involving animals, as in Example 2

Check Skills You'll Need

For help, go to Lesson 3-5.

Write each improper fraction as a mixed number in simplest form.

1. $\frac{9}{2}$ **2.** $\frac{10}{3}$ **3.** $\frac{8}{6}$

4. $\frac{15}{6}$ **5.** $\frac{7}{4}$ **6.** $\frac{25}{10}$

7. Explain how to simplify $\frac{36}{15}$.

OBJECTIVE

Interactive lesson includes instant self-check, tutorials, and activities.

1 Adding Mixed Numbers

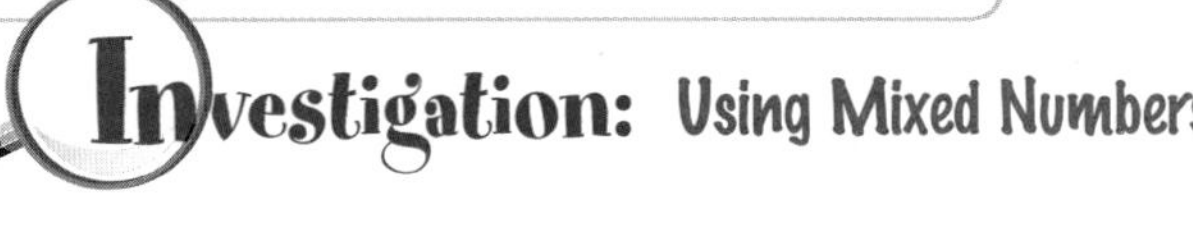

Investigation: Using Mixed Numbers

Cut string into lengths of $1\frac{3}{8}$ inches, $2\frac{1}{4}$ inches, $1\frac{7}{8}$ inches, $3\frac{1}{8}$ inches, and $5\frac{3}{4}$ inches. Place two of the pieces end to end.

1. a. **Estimation** Estimate the total length of the two pieces.
   b. Find the actual length by adding. Check your sum by measuring the total length of the two pieces.
2. Repeat for several different pairs of pieces.

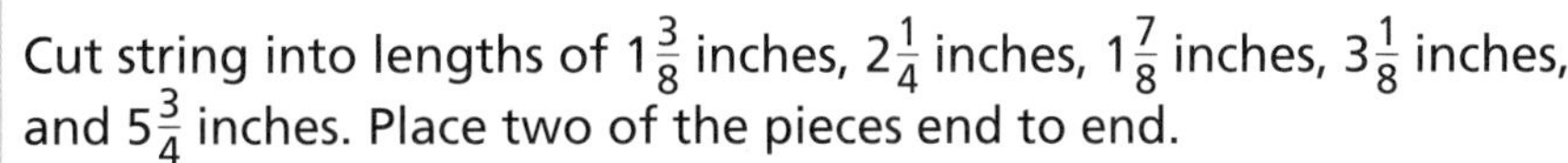

You can find the sum of mixed numbers by adding the whole number and fraction parts separately. Then combine the two parts to find the total.

1 EXAMPLE Adding Mixed Numbers Mentally

Mental Math Find $10\frac{1}{5} + 6\frac{2}{5}$.

$10 + 6 = 16$ ← **Add the whole numbers.**

$\frac{1}{5} + \frac{2}{5} = \frac{3}{5}$ ← **Add the fractions.**

$16 + \frac{3}{5} = 16\frac{3}{5}$ ← **Combine the two parts.**

Check Understanding 1 **Reasoning** In Example 1, does it matter whether you add the whole numbers or the fractions first to get the correct answer? Explain.

Real-World Connection

The top speed of a giant tortoise is about $\frac{1}{6}$ miles per hour.

2 EXAMPLE Real-World Problem Solving

Turtles A giant tortoise traveled $8\frac{1}{3}$ yards and stopped. Then it traveled $6\frac{1}{2}$ yards. Find the total distance the giant tortoise traveled.

Find $8\frac{1}{3} + 6\frac{1}{2}$.

Estimate $8\frac{1}{3} + 6\frac{1}{2} \approx 8 + 7 = 15$

$$\begin{array}{r} 8\frac{1}{3} \\ +\ 6\frac{1}{2} \\ \hline \end{array} \rightarrow \begin{array}{r} 8\frac{2}{6} \\ +\ 6\frac{3}{6} \\ \hline 14\frac{5}{6} \end{array}$$

← The LCD is 6. Write the fractions with the same denominator.

← Add the whole numbers. Then add the fractions.

The giant tortoise traveled a total of $14\frac{5}{6}$ yards.

Check for Reasonableness The answer $14\frac{5}{6}$ is close to the estimate of 15.

Check Understanding 2 **a.** Some students spent $2\frac{1}{3}$ hours on Friday and $3\frac{4}{5}$ hours on Saturday working on a science project. How long did the students work?

b. Estimation Use estimation to check the reasonableness of your sum.

OBJECTIVE

2 Adding Mixed Numbers With Renaming

The sum of the fraction parts may be an improper fraction. If so, rename it as a mixed number. Then write the answer in simplest form.

3 EXAMPLE Adding Mixed Numbers

Find $15\frac{5}{6} + 3\frac{1}{2}$.

$$\begin{array}{r} 15\frac{5}{6} \\ +\ 3\frac{1}{2} \\ \hline \end{array} \rightarrow \begin{array}{r} 15\frac{5}{6} \\ +\ 3\frac{3}{6} \\ \hline 18\frac{8}{6} \end{array}$$

← The LCD is 6. Write $\frac{1}{2}$ as $\frac{3}{6}$.

← Add the whole numbers. Then add the fractions.

$= 18 + 1\frac{2}{6}$ ← Rename $\frac{8}{6}$ as $1\frac{2}{6}$.

$= 19\frac{2}{6}$ ← Add the whole numbers.

$= 19\frac{1}{3}$ ← Simplify.

Check Understanding 3 Find each sum. **a.** $3\frac{5}{6} + 5\frac{11}{12}$ **b.** $12\frac{3}{8} + 6\frac{3}{4}$ **c.** $7\frac{3}{5} + 13\frac{2}{3}$

4 EXAMPLE Real-World Problem Solving

Hours at Practice

Total	
$2\frac{1}{2}$ Monday	$1\frac{3}{4}$ Tuesday

Sports Practice A sports team practiced for $2\frac{1}{2}$ hours on Monday and for $1\frac{3}{4}$ hours on Tuesday. How long did the team practice?

Find $2\frac{1}{2} + 1\frac{3}{4}$.

$$\begin{array}{r} 2\frac{1}{2} \\ +\ 1\frac{3}{4} \\ \hline \end{array} \rightarrow \begin{array}{r} 2\frac{2}{4} \\ +\ 1\frac{3}{4} \\ \hline 3\frac{5}{4} \end{array}$$

← The LCD is 4. Write $\frac{1}{2}$ as $\frac{2}{4}$.

← Add the whole numbers. Then add the fractions.

$= 3 + 1\frac{1}{4}$ ← Rename $\frac{5}{4}$ as $1\frac{1}{4}$.

$= 4\frac{1}{4}$ ← Add the whole numbers.

The team practiced for $4\frac{1}{4}$ hours.

Check Understanding 4 **Number Sense** One recipe uses $1\frac{3}{4}$ cups of milk. Another recipe uses $1\frac{1}{2}$ cups of milk. You have 3 cups of milk at home. Do you have enough milk to make both recipes? Explain.

EXERCISES

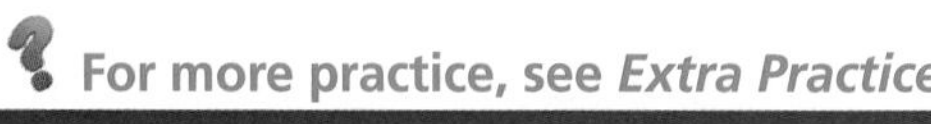

Mental Math **Find each sum.**

Example 1 (page 185)

1. $1 + 2\frac{1}{6}$
2. $2\frac{2}{3} + 4$
3. $3\frac{5}{7} + 1\frac{1}{7}$
4. $8\frac{1}{5} + 3\frac{2}{5}$

Example 2 (page 186)

5. **Apples** You have $1\frac{3}{4}$ pounds of red apples and $2\frac{1}{2}$ pounds of golden apples. How many pounds of apples do you have?

Examples 3, 4 (pages 186, 187)

Find each sum. Exercise 6 has been started for you.

6. $11\frac{1}{3} + 6\frac{7}{9}$ $\quad \begin{array}{r} 11\frac{1}{3} \\ +\ 6\frac{7}{9} \\ \hline \end{array} \rightarrow \begin{array}{r} \blacksquare \\ +\ 6\frac{7}{9} \\ \hline \end{array}$
7. $8\frac{5}{6} + 2\frac{1}{3}$
8. $5\frac{2}{3} + 4\frac{1}{2}$
9. $2\frac{3}{4} + 1\frac{5}{8}$
10. $4\frac{5}{8} + 1\frac{1}{4}$
11. $3\frac{1}{3} + 2\frac{5}{6}$
12. $1\frac{1}{2} + 3\frac{5}{6}$
13. **Soccer** Suppose you play $12\frac{3}{8}$ minutes during the first half of a soccer game and $8\frac{3}{4}$ minutes during the second half. How many total minutes do you play?

B **Apply Your Skills**

Mental Math **Compare using <, =, or >.**

14. $5\frac{8}{9} + 7\frac{5}{6}$ ■ 13

15. $17\frac{3}{5} + 12\frac{7}{10}$ ■ $29\frac{1}{2}$

16. $7\frac{1}{6} + 3\frac{6}{18}$ ■ 11

17. $4\frac{5}{13} + 5\frac{4}{9}$ ■ $10\frac{12}{13}$

Careers Oceanographers study water, plants, and animals in the ocean.

18. a. **Tides** At low tide, the water is $4\frac{11}{12}$ feet deep. At high tide, the water depth increases by $2\frac{3}{4}$ feet. How deep is the water at high tide?
    b. The next day, the depth is $5\frac{1}{2}$ feet at low tide. The depth increases the same amount as the day before. What is the water depth at high tide?

19. Writing in Math Explain how you can use mental math to find the sum $5\frac{1}{3} + 3\frac{4}{5} + 3\frac{2}{3} + 6\frac{1}{5}$.

20. Number Sense Is the sum of two mixed numbers *always*, *sometimes*, or *never* a mixed number? Give examples to support your answer.

21. **News Articles** In a newspaper, an article is $1\frac{1}{4}$ inches long. Another article is $2\frac{7}{8}$ inches long. How much space is needed for both articles?

Find each sum.

22. $4\frac{7}{8} + 5\frac{3}{16} + 3\frac{1}{8}$

23. $6\frac{7}{24} + 2\frac{7}{12} + 2\frac{2}{24}$

24. $11\frac{2}{3} + 4\frac{7}{9} + 1\frac{5}{9}$

25. **Fabric** Suppose you need the amounts of fabric shown in the table to make a flag. How much total fabric do you need?

Fabric Colors

Color	Length (yards)
Red	$3\frac{1}{4}$
White	$5\frac{1}{2}$
Blue	$4\frac{1}{4}$

26. a. **Dogs** You walk your dog $1\frac{1}{8}$ miles to your friend's house, $1\frac{3}{4}$ miles to the park, and 1 mile back to your house. How far do you walk your dog?
    b. Suppose a friend claims to walk a dog twice as far as you do. How far does your friend walk?

C **Challenge**

Find each sum.

27. $5\frac{1}{2} + 2\frac{3}{4} + 5\frac{3}{8}$

28. $7\frac{1}{3} + 7\frac{1}{6} + 7\frac{1}{9}$

29. $4\frac{2}{3} + 3\frac{5}{9} + 6$

30. Stretch Your Thinking Copy the diagram. Write the numbers $1\frac{1}{3}, 1\frac{2}{3}, 2, 2\frac{1}{3}, 2\frac{2}{3}$, and 3 in the circles so that the sum of the numbers along each side of the triangle is 6.

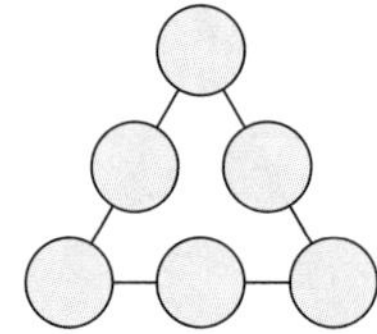

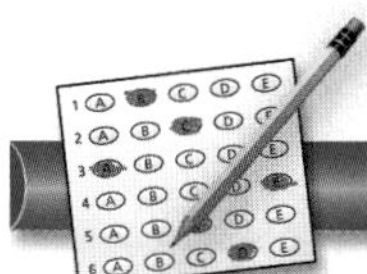

Test Prep

Multiple Choice

31. What is the sum of $2\frac{2}{3}$ and $1\frac{7}{8}$?

A. $3\frac{9}{11}$ B. $4\frac{9}{11}$ C. $4\frac{13}{24}$ D. $4\frac{14}{24}$

32. What is the sum of $9\frac{1}{10}$ and $1\frac{2}{5}$?

F. $10\frac{3}{15}$ G. $10\frac{2}{50}$ H. $10\frac{1}{10}$ I. $10\frac{1}{2}$

Take It to the NET
Online lesson quiz at **www.PHSchool.com**
Web Code: aaa-0404

33. Which two numbers have a sum of $15\frac{3}{8}$?

A. $8\frac{1}{4}$ and $7\frac{3}{16}$ B. $8\frac{1}{8}$ and $7\frac{1}{4}$ C. $8\frac{1}{2}$ and $7\frac{1}{8}$ D. $8\frac{1}{3}$ and $7\frac{2}{5}$

Short Response

34. Ruth's house is near a park that has a $2\frac{3}{10}$-mile rollerblading path. Ruth rollerblades $1\frac{1}{4}$ miles from her house to the park. She goes once around the path and then rollerblades home.

a. What is the total distance she rollerblades?

b. Explain how you found your answer.

Mixed Review

Lesson 3-9

35. Vacation Pedro's family drives 600 miles on a two-day vacation. The second day they drive 120 miles less than the first day. How many miles did they drive the first day?

Lesson 2-8

Evaluate each expression.

36. $2^3 \times 3^2 + 5$ **37.** $500 \div 10^2$ **38.** $6^2 \times 10^3$

Practice Game

That's Some Sum!

How to Play

- Draw a square game board and divide it into 16 smaller squares. Write fractions in half of the squares and mixed numbers in the other half.
- Player 1 circles any two numbers and then finds their sum. The sum is added to the player's score.
- Player 2 circles two different numbers, finds the sum, and adds it to his or her score. Players take turns until all numbers have been chosen.
- Any answer may be challenged. If the answer is correct, the challenger loses a turn. If the challenger corrects the answer, that sum is added to the challenger's score. The other player's turn is over without any change to his or her score.
- The player with the greater total score wins.

4-5 Subtracting Mixed Numbers

What You'll Learn

To subtract mixed numbers

To subtract mixed numbers with renaming

. . . And Why

To subtract two weights, as in Example 1

Check Skills You'll Need

For help, go to Lesson 3-5.

Write each improper fraction as a mixed number in simplest form.

1. $\frac{3}{2}$ **2.** $\frac{8}{3}$ **3.** $\frac{23}{5}$

4. $\frac{20}{8}$ **5.** $\frac{15}{6}$ **6.** $\frac{24}{10}$

7. Explain the steps you used to write $\frac{24}{10}$ as a mixed number in simplest form.

OBJECTIVE

 Interactive lesson includes instant self-check, tutorials, and activities.

1 Subtracting Mixed Numbers

To subtract mixed numbers, first you may need to write the fractions with a common denominator. Then subtract the whole numbers and the fraction parts separately.

1 EXAMPLE Real-World Problem Solving

Real-World Connection

Male cubs grow to an adult weight of 600 pounds.

Lions At birth, one lion cub weighs $3\frac{3}{4}$ pounds. Another cub in the same litter weighs $2\frac{5}{8}$ pounds. How much more does the heavier cub weigh?

To calculate the difference in weights, find $3\frac{3}{4} - 2\frac{5}{8}$.

$$\begin{array}{r} 3\frac{3}{4} \\ -\,2\frac{5}{8} \\ \hline \end{array} \quad \rightarrow \quad \begin{array}{r} 3\frac{6}{8} \\ -\,2\frac{5}{8} \\ \hline 1\frac{1}{8} \end{array}$$

← The LCD is 8. Write $\frac{3}{4}$ as $\frac{6}{8}$.

← Subtract the whole numbers. Then subtract the fractions.

The heavier cub weighs $1\frac{1}{8}$ pounds more than the other cub.

Check for Reasonableness Round each mixed number: $3\frac{7}{8} \approx 4$; $2\frac{3}{4} \approx 3$. Then subtract: $4 - 2 = 2$. The answer $1\frac{5}{8}$ is close to the estimate. So, the answer is reasonable.

Check Understanding 1

a. A supporting wedge for a window is $2\frac{3}{16}$ inches wide and $2\frac{7}{8}$ inches long. How much longer is the wedge than it is wide?

b. Reasoning In Example 1, could you use 32 as the common denominator? Explain your answer.

OBJECTIVE

2 Subtracting Mixed Numbers by Renaming

Sometimes you need to rename whole numbers or fractions in order to subtract from them. Here is how to rename $3\frac{1}{4}$.

Need Help?
For help writing mixed numbers as improper fractions, go to Lesson 3-5.

$3\frac{1}{4} = 2\frac{5}{4}$

$$3\frac{1}{4} = 2 + 1\frac{1}{4} = 2 + \frac{5}{4} = 2\frac{5}{4}$$

2 EXAMPLE Renaming Whole Numbers

Find $7 - 2\frac{5}{8}$.

Write 7 as a mixed number. Use 8 for the denominator since you must subtract $\frac{5}{8}$.

$$\begin{array}{r} 7 \\ -\,2\frac{5}{8} \\ \hline \end{array} \;\rightarrow\; \begin{array}{r} 6\frac{8}{8} \\ -\,2\frac{5}{8} \\ \hline 4\frac{3}{8} \end{array}$$

← Rename 7 as $6 + 1 = 6 + \frac{8}{8}$, or $6\frac{8}{8}$.

← Subtract the whole numbers. Then subtract the fractions.

Check Understanding 2 Find each difference. **a.** $5 - 3\frac{2}{3}$ **b.** $10 - 4\frac{1}{4}$

3 EXAMPLE Renaming Mixed Numbers

Distance (miles)

Moth $11\frac{1}{6}$	
$5\frac{2}{3}$ Bee	■ Difference

Biology In one hour, a bee can fly $5\frac{2}{3}$ miles and a moth can fly $11\frac{1}{6}$ miles. How much farther can the moth fly in one hour?

To answer the question, find $11\frac{1}{6} - 5\frac{2}{3}$. Since $\frac{1}{6} < \frac{2}{3}$, rename $11\frac{1}{6}$.

Estimate $11\frac{1}{6} - 5\frac{2}{3} \approx 11 - 6 = 5$

$$\begin{array}{r} 11\frac{1}{6} \\ -\,5\frac{2}{3} \\ \hline \end{array} \;\rightarrow\; \begin{array}{r} 10\frac{7}{6} \\ -\,5\frac{4}{6} \\ \hline \end{array}$$

← Rename $11\frac{1}{6}$ as $10 + 1\frac{1}{6} = 10\frac{7}{6}$.

← The LCD is 6. Write $\frac{2}{3}$ as $\frac{4}{6}$.

$= 5\frac{3}{6}$ ← Subtract.

$= 5\frac{1}{2}$ ← Simplify.

Check for Reasonableness The answer $5\frac{1}{2}$ is close to the estimate of 5.

The moth can fly $5\frac{1}{2}$ miles farther than the bee.

Check Understanding 3 **Number Sense** How can you use benchmarks to tell whether you will have to rename before subtracting?

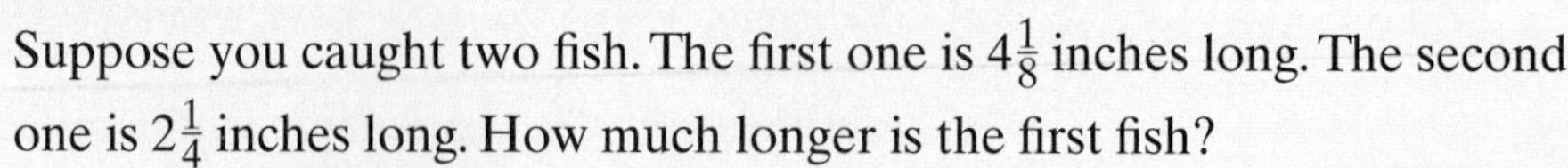

More Than One Way

Suppose you caught two fish. The first one is $4\frac{1}{8}$ inches long. The second one is $2\frac{1}{4}$ inches long. How much longer is the first fish?

Leon's Method

I need to subtract the lengths. Since $\frac{1}{8} < \frac{1}{4}$, I will rename $4\frac{1}{8}$.

$$\begin{array}{r} 4\frac{1}{8} \\ -\,2\frac{1}{4} \\ \hline \end{array} \rightarrow \begin{array}{r} 3\frac{9}{8} \\ -\,2\frac{2}{8} \\ \hline 1\frac{7}{8} \end{array}$$

← **Rename $4\frac{1}{8}$ as $3 + 1\frac{1}{8} = 3\frac{9}{8}$.**

← **The LCD is 8. Write $\frac{1}{4}$ as $\frac{2}{8}$.**

← **Find the difference.**

The first fish is $1\frac{7}{8}$ inches longer than the second one.

Lauren's Method

I need to subtract the lengths. I will change both mixed numbers to improper fractions with the same denominator.

$4\frac{1}{8} - 2\frac{1}{4} = \frac{33}{8} - \frac{9}{4}$ ← **Write as improper fractions.**

$= \frac{33}{8} - \frac{18}{8}$ ← **Rename as equivalent fractions with a like denominator.**

$= \frac{15}{8}$, or $1\frac{7}{8}$ ← **Subtract. Write the difference in simplest form.**

The first fish is $1\frac{7}{8}$ inches longer than the second one.

Choose a Method

Find $10\frac{1}{3} - 7\frac{8}{9}$. Describe your method and explain your choice.

EXERCISES

For more practice, see *Extra Practice*.

A Practice by Example

Example 1 (page 190)

Find each difference. Exercise 1 has been started for you.

1. $\begin{array}{r} 12\frac{3}{4} \\ -\,10\frac{3}{8} \\ \hline \end{array} \rightarrow \begin{array}{r} 12\frac{6}{8} \\ -\,10\frac{3}{8} \\ \hline \end{array}$

2. $7\frac{3}{4} - 6\frac{2}{5}$

3. $2\frac{5}{8} - 1\frac{1}{4}$

4. $9\frac{4}{5} - 4\frac{4}{15}$

5. $21\frac{3}{8} - 11\frac{1}{4}$

6. $15\frac{11}{12} - 11\frac{1}{2}$

7. $12\frac{1}{4} - 4\frac{1}{8}$

8. $3\frac{2}{3} - 1\frac{1}{6}$

9. You spend $2\frac{2}{3}$ hours reading and $1\frac{1}{2}$ hours watching a movie. How much more time did you spend reading than watching a movie?

Example 2 (page 191)

Find each difference. Exercise 10 has been started for you.

10. $\begin{array}{r} 4 \\ -2\frac{3}{4} \\ \hline \end{array} \rightarrow \begin{array}{r} 3\frac{4}{4} \\ -2\frac{3}{4} \\ \hline \end{array}$

11. $\begin{array}{r} 23 \\ -19\frac{5}{8} \\ \hline \end{array}$

12. $\begin{array}{r} 32 \\ -16\frac{1}{2} \\ \hline \end{array}$

Example 3 (page 191)

13. $10\frac{1}{10} - 3\frac{2}{5}$ **14.** $3\frac{3}{8} - 1\frac{3}{4}$ **15.** $4\frac{5}{12} - 1\frac{3}{4}$ **16.** $6\frac{1}{5} - 2\frac{2}{3}$

17. Science You and your partner are growing bean plants for a science project. After one week, one plant is $7\frac{7}{8}$ inches tall and another plant is $5\frac{15}{16}$ inches tall. Find the difference in the heights of the two plants.

B Apply Your Skills

Find each difference.

18. $9\frac{2}{3} - 5\frac{2}{3}$ **19.** $1 - \frac{1}{6}$ **20.** $3 - 1\frac{2}{3}$ **21.** $12\frac{3}{4} - 10\frac{1}{4}$

22. $5\frac{7}{9} - 2\frac{1}{9}$ **23.** $8 - 3\frac{5}{11}$ **24.** $5\frac{1}{5} - 4\frac{4}{5}$ **25.** $9\frac{1}{8} - 6\frac{3}{4}$

26. **Data File, p. 169** Find the difference in the swooping speed of a peregrine falcon and the running speed of a cheetah.

27. Writing in Math Explain how you can use mental math to find $12\frac{1}{4} - 10\frac{3}{4}$.

28. On Monday, the snowfall in the mountains was $15\frac{3}{4}$ inches. On Tuesday, the snowfall was $18\frac{1}{2}$ inches. What was the difference in snowfall?

Olympics Use the table for Exercises 29–31.

29. How much farther did Heike Drechsler jump in 1992 than in 2000?

30. Which two jumps were closest in length? Explain.

31. Find the difference between the longest and the shortest winning jumps shown.

Women's Olympic Long Jump Winners

Year	Winner, Country	Distance
1984	Anisoara Stanciu, Romania	22 ft 10 in.
1988	Jackie Joyner-Kersee, U.S.A.	24 ft $3\frac{1}{2}$ in.
1992	Heike Drechsler, Germany	23 ft $5\frac{1}{4}$ in.
1996	Chioma Ajunwa, Nigeria	23 ft $4\frac{1}{2}$ in.
2000	Heike Drechsler, Germany	22 ft $11\frac{1}{4}$ in.

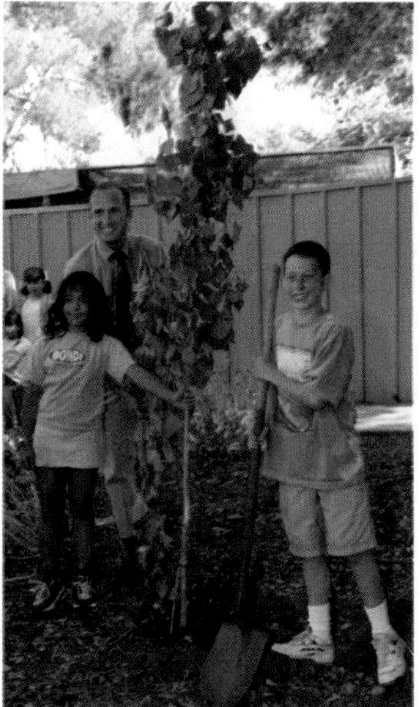

32. Gardening Carlos plants a spruce tree in a garden of a new school. The height of the tree when he plants it is $3\frac{1}{2}$ feet. He measures the tree two years later. It is $4\frac{3}{8}$ feet tall. How much has the tree grown?

C Challenge

Algebra **Solve each equation.**

33. $x = 9\frac{4}{7} - \frac{13}{14}$

34. $x = 6\frac{3}{16} - 2\frac{2}{3}$

35. $x + 3\frac{1}{2} = 4\frac{3}{4}$

36. **Stretch Your Thinking** Fill in each □ with one of the digits 4, 5, 6, 7, 8, or 9 to find the least possible whole number difference. Use each digit only once.

$$\begin{array}{r} \square\square\square \\ -\ \square\square\square \\ \hline \end{array}$$

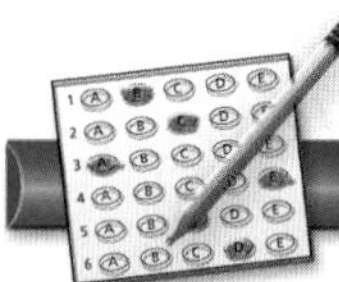

Test Prep

Reading Comprehension Read the passage and answer the questions below.

Time of Day

Latitude	Jun. 21	Dec. 21
20°N	$13\frac{1}{5}$ h	$10\frac{4}{5}$ h
40°N	$14\frac{1}{2}$ h	$9\frac{1}{6}$ h
60°N	$18\frac{1}{2}$ h	$5\frac{1}{2}$ h

The tilt of Earth's axis affects the length of daylight in a given region throughout the year. Latitude, the measure of the distance from the equator toward the poles, also affects the length of daylight. In the Northern Hemisphere, June 21 is sometimes referred to as the "longest day of the year." December 21 is the "shortest day of the year." The table shows the number of daylight hours for some latitudes in the Northern Hemisphere.

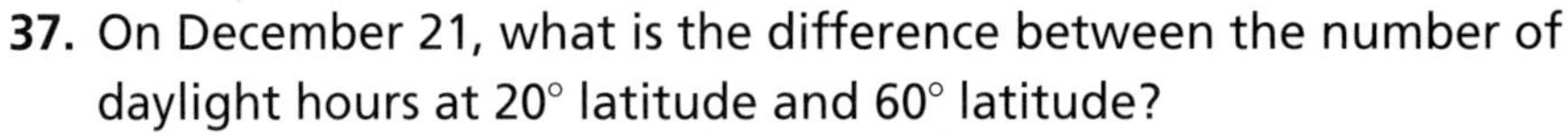

37. On December 21, what is the difference between the number of daylight hours at 20° latitude and 60° latitude?

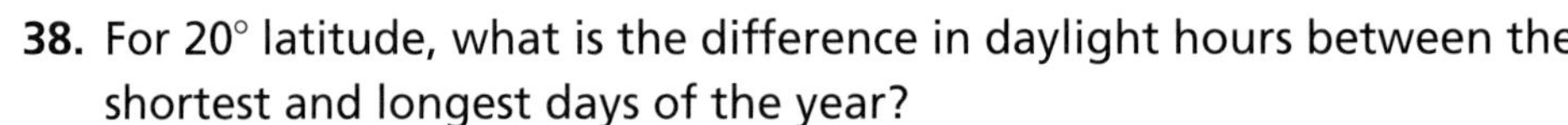

38. For 20° latitude, what is the difference in daylight hours between the shortest and longest days of the year?

Take It to the NET
Online lesson quiz at
www.PHSchool.com
Web Code: aaa-0405

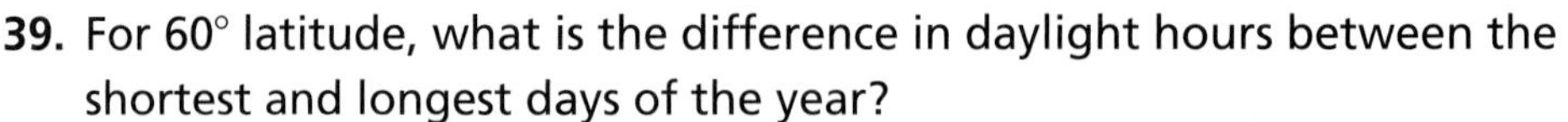

39. For 60° latitude, what is the difference in daylight hours between the shortest and longest days of the year?

Mixed Review

Lesson 4-2 **Find each sum or difference.**

40. $\frac{10}{15} + \frac{7}{15}$

41. $\frac{9}{10} + \frac{6}{10}$

42. $\frac{21}{24} - \frac{5}{24}$

43. $\frac{23}{25} - \frac{3}{25}$

44. $\frac{11}{18} + \frac{5}{18}$

45. $\frac{9}{28} - \frac{3}{28}$

Lesson 3-4 **Write each fraction in simplest form.**

46. $\frac{15}{25}$

47. $\frac{16}{56}$

48. $\frac{36}{54}$

49. $\frac{8}{4}$

Understanding Word Problems

For Use With Lesson 4-5

Some problems contain **too much information.** You need to decide which information is necessary for solving the problem. You can use the problem-solving plan you learned in Lesson 1-6. Start by asking yourself, "What do I know?" and "What do I need to find out?"

Track Team Each member of the track team runs 15 miles each week. On Monday, Celine runs $2\frac{7}{8}$ miles. She runs $3\frac{1}{4}$ miles on Tuesday and $2\frac{1}{2}$ miles on Wednesday. She runs 11 miles per hour. How many more miles does she need to run?

Read and Understand Read for understanding. Summarize the problem.

What do I know?
- The team runs 15 miles each week.
- Celine has already run $2\frac{7}{8}$, $3\frac{1}{4}$, and $2\frac{1}{2}$ miles.
- Celine runs 11 miles per hour.

What do I need to find out?
- How many miles must Celine run on Thursday and Friday?

What information is not needed?
- How fast Celine runs is not needed to solve the problem.

EXERCISES

For each word problem, answer the questions "What do I know?" and "What do I need to find out?" Identify any information not needed to solve the problem.

1. **Dressmaking** A dressmaker sends 250 dresses to several stores. The same number of dresses are sent to each store. The dressmaker charges \$59 for each dress. How much money does the dressmaker receive?

2. Carey worked $3\frac{3}{4}$ hours on Monday. Ricky worked $4\frac{1}{2}$ hours on Monday and 2 hours on Tuesday. Who worked more hours on Monday? How many more?

Algebra

4-6 Equations With Fractions

What You'll Learn

To use mental math to solve equations

To solve equations with fractions

. . . And Why

To find the missing amount, as in Example 3

Check Skills You'll Need

For help, go to Lesson 2-6.

Solve each equation.

1. $17 + x = 43$

2. $x - 123 = 145$

3. $4.2 + x = 8$

4. $10.7 = x - 8.2$

5. $2.5 = 2.5 + x$

6. $x - 5 = 9.2$

Interactive lesson includes instant self-check, tutorials, and activities.

OBJECTIVE

1 Using Mental Math to Solve Equations

Investigation: Exploring Differences

1. Write your age in years and months. Use $\frac{1}{12}$ to represent each month. For example, write 11 years 4 months as $11\frac{4}{12}$ years.

2. a. In how many years will you be $14\frac{11}{12}$ years old?
   b. Reasoning Explain how you found your answer.

You can sometimes use mental math to solve equations that involve fractions or mixed numbers.

1 EXAMPLE Using Mental Math in Equations

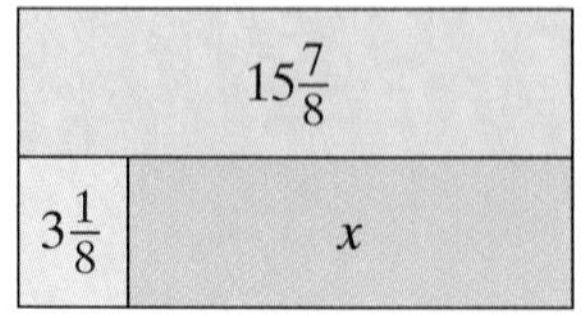

Solve $x + 3\frac{1}{8} = 15\frac{7}{8}$ using mental math.

$12 + 3 = 15$

$\frac{6}{8} + \frac{1}{8} = \frac{7}{8}$ ← **Use mental math to find missing whole number and missing fraction.**

$x = 12\frac{6}{8}$ ← **Combine the two parts.**

$= 12\frac{3}{4}$ ← **Simplify.**

Check Understanding 1 Solve each equation using mental math.

a. $5\frac{5}{6} - x = 2\frac{1}{6}$ **b.** $14\frac{1}{4} + x = 25\frac{1}{2}$ **c.** $x - 1\frac{3}{8} = 1\frac{3}{8}$

OBJECTIVE

2 Solving Equations With Fractions

You can use inverse operations to get the variable alone on one side of the equation. Write the answer in simplest form.

2 EXAMPLE Solving Equations With Fractions

Solve $x - \frac{1}{3} = \frac{5}{6}$.

$$x - \frac{1}{3} = \frac{5}{6}$$
$$+\frac{1}{3} \quad +\frac{1}{3}$$ ← Add $\frac{1}{3}$ to each side.

$$x = \frac{5}{6} + \frac{1}{3}$$ ← Write the sum.

$$= \frac{5}{6} + \frac{2}{6}$$ ← The LCD is 6. Write $\frac{1}{3}$ as $\frac{2}{6}$.

$$= \frac{7}{6}, \text{ or } 1\frac{1}{6}$$ ← Simplify.

Check Understanding 2 Solve each equation. **a.** $n + \frac{1}{3} = \frac{11}{12}$ **b.** $\frac{2}{5} + a = \frac{13}{20}$

3 EXAMPLE Real-World  Problem Solving

Rainfall During the first week of January, a rain gauge collected $\frac{1}{2}$ inch of rain. By the end of the month, the rain gauge showed that the total January rainfall was $2\frac{3}{5}$ inches. How much rain fell after the first week of January?

Words	rainfall in 1st week of January	+	rainfall after the first week of January	=	total rainfall in January

Let r = the rainfall in inches during the remainder of January.

Equation	$\frac{1}{2}$	+	r	=	$2\frac{3}{5}$

$$\frac{1}{2} + r = 2\frac{3}{5}$$
$$-\frac{1}{2} \quad -\frac{1}{2}$$ ← Subtract $\frac{1}{2}$ from each side.

$$r = 2\frac{3}{5} - \frac{1}{2}$$ ← Write the difference.

$$= 2\frac{6}{10} - \frac{5}{10}$$ ← The LCD is 10. Write each fraction with a denominator of 10.

$$= 2\frac{1}{10}$$ ← Subtract.

The January rainfall after the first week was $1\frac{4}{5}$ inches.

Check Understanding 3 You drive a nail that is $2\frac{3}{8}$ inches long through a wooden block. The nail extends beyond the board by $\frac{5}{8}$ inches. How thick is the wooden block?

EXERCISES

For more practice, see *Extra Practice*.

A Practice by Example

Example 1 (page 196)

Mental Math Solve each equation using mental math.

1. $x + 4\frac{2}{5} = 7\frac{4}{5}$
2. $a + 6\frac{1}{3} = 20\frac{2}{3}$
3. $c - \frac{3}{10} = 6\frac{9}{10}$
4. $7\frac{1}{5} = 2\frac{3}{5} + n$
5. $4\frac{3}{8} = k - 7\frac{1}{8}$
6. $12\frac{5}{6} = s + 2\frac{5}{6}$

Example 2 (page 197)

Solve each equation.

7. $x = \frac{2}{7} + \frac{5}{6}$
8. $\frac{2}{5} - \frac{1}{9} = x$
9. $x - \frac{5}{6} = \frac{7}{8}$
10. $\frac{5}{24} + g = \frac{1}{3}$
11. $\frac{4}{9} = y - \frac{2}{5}$
12. $t - \frac{7}{9} = \frac{1}{3}$

Example 3 (page 197)

Write and solve an equation for each situation.

13. **Reading** You read $\frac{1}{3}$ of a book one week and $\frac{1}{4}$ of the book the following week. How much of the book have you read?
14. Your frog won second place in a jumping contest. The jump was $\frac{2}{3}$ foot less than the winning jump of $11\frac{1}{2}$ feet. How far did your frog jump?

B Apply Your Skills

Solve each equation.

15. $\frac{2}{3} = n + \frac{11}{12}$
16. $y - 2\frac{8}{9} = \frac{5}{6}$
17. $3\frac{1}{5} = x - \frac{12}{25}$
18. $\frac{5}{8} = a + \frac{1}{3}$
19. $k + 4\frac{5}{6} = 2\frac{1}{4}$
20. $9\frac{7}{8} = b - \frac{3}{4}$

Write and solve an equation for each situation.

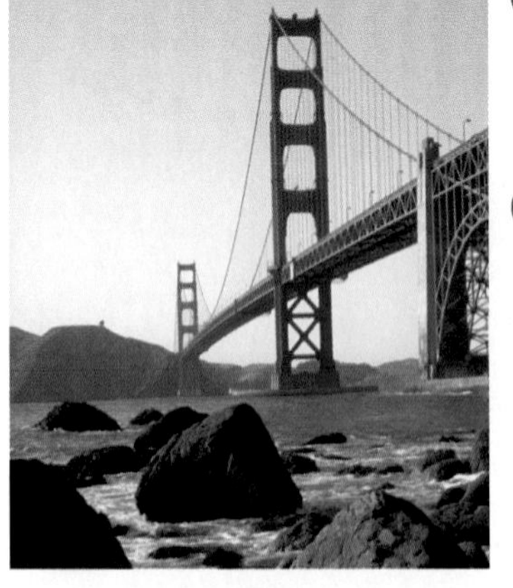

Real-World Connection

The total length of the steel wires used in the cables of the Golden Gate Bridge would circle Earth three times.

21. **Bridges** The Brooklyn Bridge in New York is approximately $\frac{3}{10}$ mile long. The Golden Gate Bridge in California is approximately $\frac{1}{2}$ mile longer than the Brooklyn Bridge. How long is the Golden Gate Bridge?

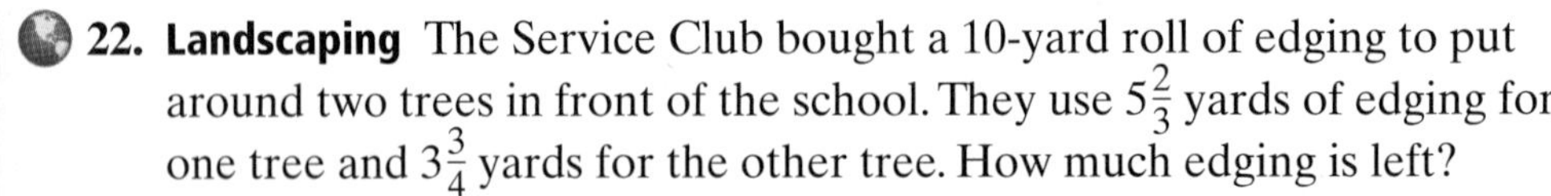

22. **Landscaping** The Service Club bought a 10-yard roll of edging to put around two trees in front of the school. They use $5\frac{2}{3}$ yards of edging for one tree and $3\frac{3}{4}$ yards for the other tree. How much edging is left?
23. Your teacher asks your class to name a primary color. If $\frac{2}{5}$ of the class chooses blue and $\frac{1}{3}$ of the class chooses yellow, what fraction of the class chooses red?
24. **Patterns** Solve each equation.
    a. $\frac{1}{3} + x = \frac{1}{2}$
    b. $\frac{1}{4} + x = \frac{1}{3}$
    c. $\frac{1}{5} + x = \frac{1}{4}$
    d. **Writing in Math** Predict the solution of $\frac{1}{9} + x = \frac{1}{8}$. Explain your reasoning.

25. a. **Mental Math** Without computing, do you think the relay team at the right beat their best time of 6 minutes for this 1600-meter relay? Explain.
b. Find the team's total time.

Relay Times (minutes)

Kim	$1\frac{1}{2}$
Alison	$1\frac{3}{8}$
Laura	$1\frac{3}{4}$
Jamie	$1\frac{1}{4}$

26. You have a rope that is $18\frac{1}{2}$ feet long to use for a tug-of-war. The team captains agree to shorten the rope by cutting off $3\frac{3}{4}$ feet. Now how long is the rope?

C Challenge

27. **Number Sense** Which variable, m or n, has the greater value?

$$m - \frac{3}{4} = \frac{37}{50} \qquad n - \frac{4}{5} = \frac{37}{50}$$

28. **Stretch Your Thinking** If one girl eats $\frac{1}{2}$ apple in $\frac{1}{2}$ minute, how many apples do two girls eat in two minutes?

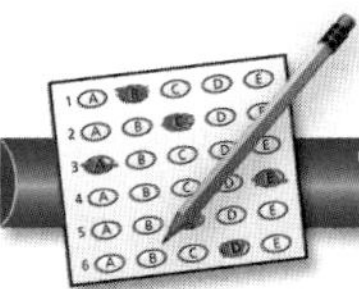

Test Prep

Multiple Choice

29. What is the solution of $\frac{4}{5} + x = 4\frac{3}{10}$?
A. $3\frac{1}{2}$ B. $3\frac{7}{10}$ C. $4\frac{1}{2}$ D. $5\frac{1}{10}$

30. A roll of wrapping paper is 84 inches long. You cut lengths of $23\frac{1}{2}$ inches and $15\frac{1}{4}$ inches to wrap two gifts. How much paper is left?
F. $38\frac{3}{4}$ inches G. $45\frac{1}{4}$ inches H. $46\frac{1}{4}$ inches I. $75\frac{3}{4}$ inches

31. A baby weighed $6\frac{3}{16}$ pounds at birth and gained $2\frac{1}{8}$ pounds. What is the weight of the baby?
A. $4\frac{1}{16}$ pounds B. $8\frac{1}{4}$ pounds C. $8\frac{5}{16}$ pounds D. $9\frac{5}{16}$ pounds

Extended Response

Online lesson quiz at www.PHSchool.com
Web Code: aaa-0406

32. You buy the following vegetables: $2\frac{1}{2}$ pounds of onions, $1\frac{7}{8}$ pounds of corn, and 1 pound of carrots. You buy the following fruit: $1\frac{3}{8}$ pounds of apples, $2\frac{5}{8}$ pounds of grapes, and $1\frac{1}{4}$ pounds of bananas. Do you buy more vegetables or more fruit? How much more? Justify your answer.

Mixed Review

Lesson 4-3 **Find each sum or difference.**

33. $\frac{5}{6} - \frac{7}{12}$ 34. $\frac{2}{5} + \frac{3}{10}$ 35. $\frac{1}{4} + \frac{2}{3}$ 36. $\frac{4}{5} - \frac{1}{2}$

Lesson 3-7 **Order each set of numbers from least to greatest.**

37. $\frac{1}{2}, \frac{2}{3}, \frac{4}{7}, \frac{3}{10}$ 38. $\frac{3}{4}, \frac{4}{3}, \frac{1}{9}, \frac{11}{12}$ 39. $\frac{2}{11}, \frac{0}{5}, \frac{5}{9}, \frac{8}{7}$

Technology Computing With a Fraction Calculator

For Use With Lesson 4-6

You can use a fraction calculator to add and subtract fractions. Use the / key, which indicates division, for the fraction bar.

1 EXAMPLE

Find $\frac{5}{6} - \frac{3}{8}$.

Enter 5 / 6 − 3 / 8 = *11/24.*

$\frac{5}{6} - \frac{3}{8} = \frac{11}{24}$

You can also use a fraction calculator to add or subtract mixed numbers. Use the UNIT key to enter the whole number. If you do not use the unit key, the calculator will interpret $1\frac{3}{4}$ as $\frac{13}{4}$.

2 EXAMPLE

Find $1\frac{3}{4} + 3\frac{1}{2}$.

Enter 1 UNIT 3 / 4 + 3 UNIT 1 / 2 = *21/4.*

To rename this number, press 2nd $a^b/_c$ = *5⌴1/4.*

In simplest form, $1\frac{3}{4} + 3\frac{1}{2} = 5\frac{1}{4}$.

EXERCISES

Use a fraction calculator to find each sum or difference.

1. $\frac{3}{4} - \frac{2}{5}$
2. $\frac{5}{8} + \frac{1}{4}$
3. $\frac{9}{10} - \frac{1}{5}$
4. $\frac{8}{9} + \frac{1}{12}$
5. $\frac{11}{12} - \frac{3}{8}$
6. $\frac{4}{5} + \frac{1}{20}$
7. $\frac{3}{10} - \frac{2}{9}$
8. $\frac{22}{25} + \frac{9}{100}$
9. $\frac{5}{9} - \frac{2}{5}$
10. $\frac{2}{3} + \frac{4}{5}$
11. $9\frac{3}{4} + 3\frac{3}{4}$
12. $5\frac{3}{8} + 8\frac{1}{8}$
13. $11\frac{8}{9} - 7\frac{1}{2}$
14. $6\frac{9}{10} + 2\frac{1}{12}$
15. $18\frac{5}{12} - 9\frac{1}{2}$
16. $1\frac{1}{10} + 8\frac{1}{12}$
17. $13\frac{5}{12} - 5\frac{1}{3}$
18. $4\frac{1}{4} + 2\frac{1}{3}$
19. $14\frac{3}{10} - 3\frac{1}{2}$
20. $7\frac{8}{9} - 3\frac{1}{6}$

21. ***Writing in Math*** How can you use a fraction calculator to simplify an improper fraction?

4-7 Measuring Elapsed Time

What You'll Learn

To add and subtract measures of time

To read and use schedules

. . . And Why

To read bus schedules, as in Example 4

Check Skills You'll Need

For help, go to Lesson 3-4.

Write an equivalent fraction with a denominator of 60.

1. $\frac{4}{15}$ **2.** $\frac{3}{12}$ **3.** $\frac{1}{5}$

4. $\frac{2}{6}$ **5.** $\frac{2}{3}$ **6.** $\frac{7}{12}$

New Vocabulary • elapsed time

OBJECTIVE

iTEXT Interactive lesson includes instant self-check, tutorials, and activities.

1 Adding and Subtracting Measures of Time

Investigation: Exploring Elapsed Time

1. a. What time does Clock 1 show?
   b. What time does Clock 2 show?
2. Reasoning How much time has passed between the times shown on Clock 1 and Clock 2?
3. Draw a third clock showing the time 40 minutes after Clock 2.

Clock 1

Clock 2

The standard unit of time is the second (s). You use equivalent units to change from one unit of time to another.

Units of Time	
second (s)	
minute (min)	1 min = 60 s
hour (h)	1 h = 60 min
day	1 day = 24 h
week (wk)	1 wk = 7 days
year (yr)	1 yr ≈ 52 wk

1 EXAMPLE Writing Equivalent Times

How many seconds are equivalent to 1 minute 20 seconds?

1 minute 20 seconds = 60 s + 20 s ← **One minute is equivalent to 60 seconds.**
= 80 s ← **Simplify.**

So, 1 minute 20 seconds is equivalent to 80 seconds.

✔ Check Understanding 1 How many days are equivalent to 4 weeks 3 days?

The time between two events is called **elapsed time.** To find elapsed time, you can subtract hours and minutes.

2 EXAMPLE Calculating Elapsed Time

Test-Prep Tip
A drawing of a clock face can help you compute elapsed time.

Find the elapsed time between 1:45 P.M. and 5:27 P.M.

To find the elapsed time, subtract 1:45 from 5:27.

5:27 → 5 h 27 min → 4 h 87 min ← **Rename 5 h 27 min as 4 h 87 min.**
1:45 → 1 h 45 min → − 1 h 45 min
3 h 42 min ← **Subtract.**

The elapsed time is 3 hours 42 minutes.

✔ Check Understanding 2 Find the elapsed time between 7:25 A.M. and 8:12 A.M.

To find elapsed time between a morning and an afternoon or between an evening and the next morning, add 12 hours to the later time.

3 EXAMPLE Real-World Problem Solving

School How long is a school day that goes from 8:15 A.M. to 3:25 P.M.?

Since 3:25 P.M. is later than 8:15 A.M., you need to add 12 hours to 3:25.

3:25 → 3 h 25 min ← **Add 12 to the later time.**
12 h

15:25 → 15 h 25 min
8:15 → − 8 h 15 min ← **Subtract the earlier time.**
7 h 10 min ← **Subtract.**

The school day that goes from 8:15 A.M. to 3:25 P.M. is 7 h 10 min long.

✔ Check Understanding 3 **a.** Find the elapsed time between 10:00 A.M. and 7:15 P.M.
b. **Reasoning** Explain why you add 12 in Example 3.

OBJECTIVE

2 Reading and Using Schedules

You think about elapsed time when reading and using schedules.

4 EXAMPLE Reading and Using a Schedule

Yellow Bus Line Buses Run Every 30 Minutes Monday–Friday	
Leave Willson St.	Arrive Kagy Blvd.
7:20 A.M.	7:45 A.M.
7:50 A.M.	8:15 A.M.
. . .	. . .
11:20 P.M.	11:45 P.M.

Bus Schedules Use the bus schedule at the left. Suppose you arrive at the Willson Street bus stop 5 minutes after the 11:50 A.M. bus leaves.

a. How long will you wait for the next bus?

The bus runs every 30 minutes. You will wait 30 − 5 min, or 25 minutes.

b. How long is the bus ride?

Using the first run, the elapsed time is 7:45 A.M − 7:20 A.M., or 25 min.

c. When will you arrive at Kagy Boulevard?

11:50 + 30 min = 11:80 min ← **Find when the next bus leaves.**
= 11 h 80 min
= 12 h 20 min

The next bus will leave at 12:20 P.M. The trip takes 25 minutes. So, you will arrive at 12:20 + 25 min or 12:45 P.M.

4 It is a 5-minute walk from the bus stop on Kagy Boulevard to a gym. Which bus should you take from Willson Street to get to the gym by 6:00 P.M.?

EXERCISES

For more practice, see *Extra Practice*.

Example 1 (page 202)

For each time, write an equivalent time using only the smaller unit.

1. 1 h 30 min **2.** 2 min 59 s **3.** 8 h 2 min

4. 5 min 36 s **5.** 3 wk 5 days **6.** 2 days 17 h

Example 2 (page 202)

Find the elapsed time between each pair of times.

7. from 2:25 P.M. to 3:35 P.M. **8.** from 8:25 A.M. to 10:52 A.M.

9. from 5:25 P.M. to 11:11 P.M. **10.** from 9:28 A.M. to 11:07 A.M.

11. from 11:25 A.M. to 2:45 P.M. **12.** from 8:30 P.M. to 7:39 A.M.

Example 3 (page 202)

13. How long is a car parked on the street if it arrives at 10:25 P.M. and leaves at 8:12 A.M.?

Example 4 (page 203)

Use the train schedule for Exercises 14–16.

Train Schedule

Station	Train A	Train B
Fairview	8:15 A.M.	8:42 A.M.
Huntville	8:26 A.M.	8:55 A.M.
Rush City	8:34 A.M.	9:04 A.M.
Grayland	8:45 A.M.	9:19 A.M.

14. Which train takes less time to travel from Fairview to Grayland?

15. How long do you wait for the train if you get to Rush City at 8:35 A.M.?

16. How long does it take to get to Grayland from Huntville on Train B?

B Apply Your Skills

Time Zones The map below shows the time zones in the continental United States. Find the time for each city if it is 12:00 noon in Denver.

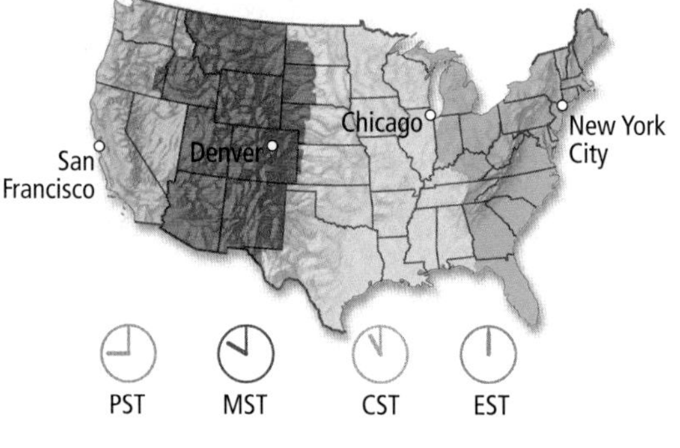

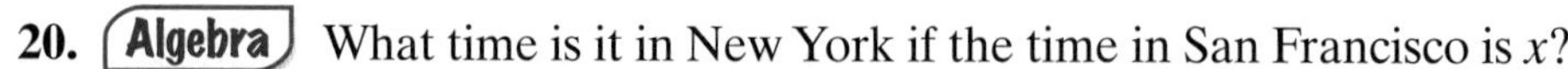

17. Chicago

18. New York City

19. San Francisco

20. Algebra What time is it in New York if the time in San Francisco is x?

21. Writing in Math Explain how it can be Monday in one part of the United States and Tuesday in another part of the United States.

Real-World Connection

Careers Clowns often make balloon animals at children's parties.

22. Clowns A clown wants to perform a 45-minute show at each of three birthday parties on the same Saturday. The first party must begin at 10:00 A.M. and he needs to leave the third party by 2:15 P.M. He wants to leave one hour between each party. Make a schedule for the clown.

C Challenge

23. Find the elapsed time from Sunday at 10:50 P.M. to Tuesday at 6:12 A.M.

24. Find the elapsed time from Saturday at 7:15 A.M. to Sunday at 3:05 P.M.

25. Stretch Your Thinking Draw a square. Then, without lifting your pencil, draw three line segments that divide it into four identical squares.

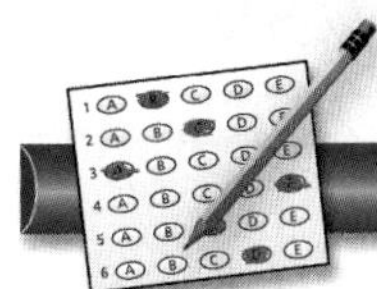

Test Prep

Multiple Choice

26. How many minutes are in 3 h 25 min?
A. 28 min **B.** 75 min **C.** 105 min **D.** 205 min

27. What is the elapsed time between 4:25 A.M. and 7:24 A.M.?
F. 2 h 1 min **G.** 2 h 59 min **H.** 3 h 1 min **I.** 3 h 59 min

28. Jack has 2 hours of homework. He will take one 30-minute break. To finish by 9:30 P.M., what is the latest time he can begin?
A. 6:00 P.M. **B.** 6:30 P.M. **C.** 7:00 P.M. **D.** 7:30 P.M.

Short Response

29. You make a list of things to do before a party that starts today at 4:00 p.m.

a. If you follow the list in order, at what time should you begin?

b. Which activities must you do in order? Can any be done at the same time? Revise the list.

c. Use the revised list of part (b) to make a new schedule. Allow yourself an extra 25 min before the party.

Decorate room (1 h)
Mix cake (40 min)
Bake cake (35 min)
Cool cake (45 min)
Frost cake (20 min)
Shower and dress (25 min)

Take It to the NET
Online lesson quiz at
www.PHSchool.com
Web Code: aaa-0407

Mixed Review

Lesson 2-6

Solve each equation.

30. $a + 14 = 31$ **31.** $t - 8 = 28$ **32.** $b - 2.4 = 5.1$

33. $5.3 - c = 9.1$ **34.** $15 = w + 9$ **35.** $23 = d - 16$

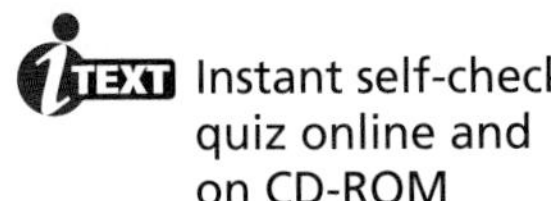

Checkpoint Quiz 2

Lessons 4-4 through 4-7

iTEXT Instant self-check quiz online and on CD-ROM

Find each sum or difference.

1. $2\frac{1}{2} + 3\frac{1}{8}$ **2.** $9\frac{1}{2} - 4\frac{3}{4}$ **3.** $6\frac{1}{3} + 8\frac{1}{2}$ **4.** $7\frac{5}{9} - 1\frac{2}{3}$

Solve each equation.

5. $a + \frac{2}{6} = \frac{5}{6}$ **6.** $p - \frac{5}{9} = \frac{2}{3}$ **7.** $\frac{1}{5} + b = \frac{1}{2}$ **8.** $h + \frac{2}{3} = \frac{12}{15}$

9. Find the elapsed time between 8:42 A.M. and 3:29 P.M.

10. Find the elapsed time between 6:35 P.M. and 4:18 A.M.

4-8 Draw a Diagram

What You'll Learn

To solve problems by drawing a diagram

... And Why

To solve sports-related problems, as in Example 1

✓ Check Skills You'll Need

For help, go to Lesson 4-1.

Estimate each sum or difference.

1. $3\frac{1}{12} + 2\frac{3}{4}$
2. $15\frac{1}{5} - 5\frac{3}{10}$
3. $1\frac{1}{3} + 9\frac{7}{12}$
4. $5\frac{1}{8} - 2\frac{4}{5}$
5. $7\frac{1}{6} + 12\frac{1}{5}$
6. $18\frac{7}{8} - 17\frac{5}{15}$

OBJECTIVE

Interactive lesson includes instant self-check, tutorials, and activities.

1 Solving Problems by Drawing a Diagram

When to Use This Strategy Sometimes it is hard to picture a word problem. By drawing a diagram, you can make a problem easier to solve.

1 EXAMPLE Real-World Problem Solving

Sports A volleyball tournament will be held on a soccer field that is 110 yards long and 80 yards wide. The game area for each volleyball court allows space for the court and a safety zone around it. Each game area is 25 yards long by 15 yards wide. How many game areas will fit on the field?

Read and Understand The field is 110 yards by 80 yards. Each game area is 25 yards by 15 yards. You are asked to find how many will fit on the field.

Plan and Solve To help decide, first ***draw a diagram*** of the field. Then show how many game areas that are 25 yards by 15 yards fit on the field.

Mark off 7 game areas along the length of the field and 3 game areas along the width of the field. Since $3 \times 7 = 21$, you can fit 21 in the field.

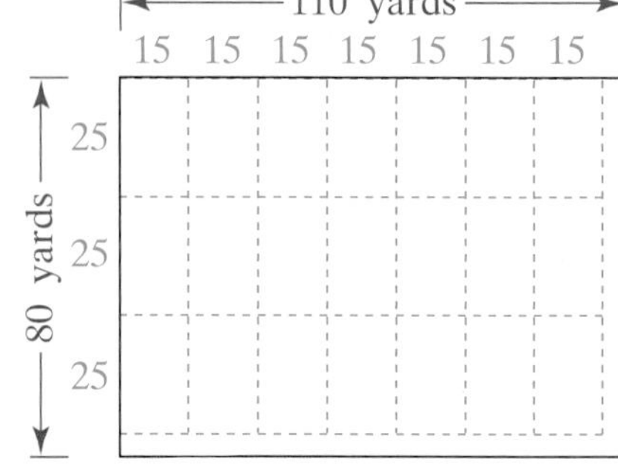

Look Back and Check Check the answer by dividing the area of the field by the area of a game area. Use the formula area = length × width.

$$\frac{\text{area of the field}}{\text{area of a game area}} \rightarrow \frac{110 \text{ yards} \times 80 \text{ yards}}{25 \text{ yards} \times 15 \text{ yards}} \rightarrow \frac{8{,}800 \text{ square yards}}{375 \text{ square yards}} \approx 23.$$

Twenty-one courts is a reasonable answer.

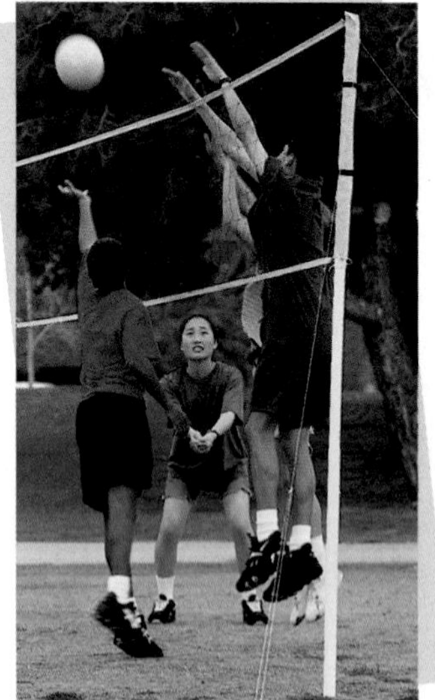

Real-World Connection

Outdoors, volleyball is played on grass or sand courts.

✓ Check Understanding ① A gymnastics floor exercise mat is 14 yards by 14 yards. How many floor exercise mats are needed to cover a soccer field?

EXERCISES

For more practice, see *Extra Practice.*

Ⓐ Practice by Example

Example 1 (page 206)

> **Need Help?**
> - Reread the problem.
> - Identify the key facts and details.
> - Tell the problem in your own words.
> - Try a different strategy.
> - Check your work.

Solve each problem by drawing a diagram.

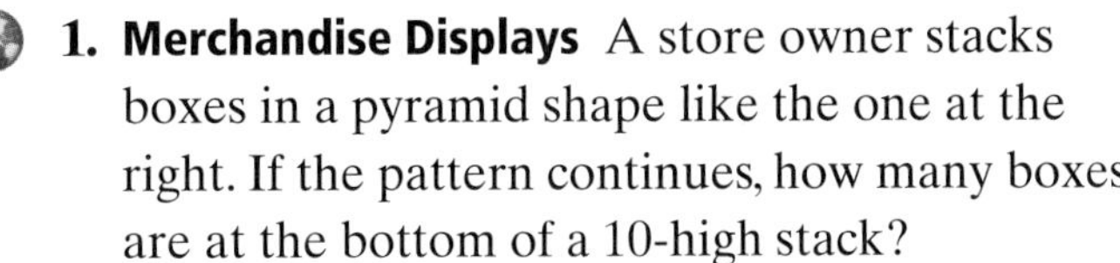

1. **Merchandise Displays** A store owner stacks boxes in a pyramid shape like the one at the right. If the pattern continues, how many boxes are at the bottom of a 10-high stack?

2. Each side of a square game board measures 16 inches.
   a. What is the perimeter of the game board?
   b. A 2-inch square is cut from each corner of the board. What is the perimeter of the new game board?

3. **Carpentry** A bookcase is made from wood that is $\frac{3}{4}$ inch thick. The bookcase has four shelves. Each shelf is $12\frac{1}{2}$ inches tall. Find the total height of the bookcase.

4. **Gardening** A rectangular garden is 2 feet by $1\frac{1}{2}$ feet. A landscaper plants flowers $\frac{1}{2}$ foot apart along the edges and at the corners of the garden. How many plants does the landscaper need?

Ⓑ Apply Your Skills

> **Strategies**
> Draw a Diagram
> Make a Graph
> Make an Organized List
> Make a Table and Look for a Pattern
> Simulate a Problem
> Solve a Simpler Problem
> Try, Check, and Revise
> Use Logical Reasoning
> Work Backward
> Write an Equation

Choose a strategy to solve each problem.

5. **Lighting** Lights are placed every $1\frac{3}{4}$ feet along both sides of a 14-foot driveway. How many lights are needed?

6. **Tiles** An artist uses a tile design on a wall that is 6 feet by 10 feet. Tiles are placed at the border on all four sides. Each tile is a square that measures 0.5 foot on a side. How many tiles does the artist need for the entire border?

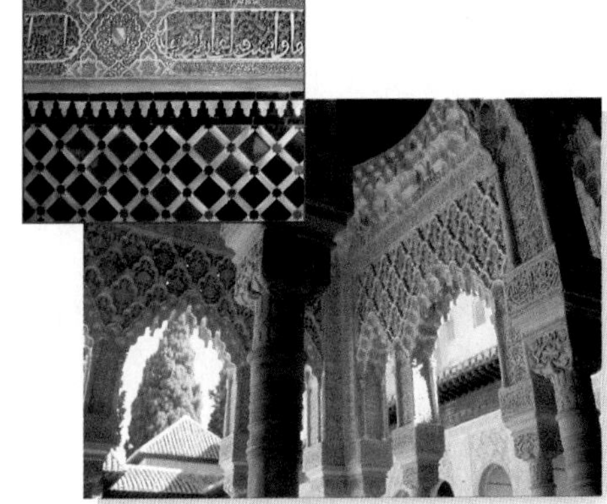

The Alhambra in Spain has intricate tile designs.

7. a. The lengths of three rods are 4 cm, 6 cm, and 9 cm. Arrange these rods to measure 11 cm.
   b. **Writing in Math** Explain the problem-solving strategy you used to solve the problem.

Real-World Connection

Careers A gymnastics instructor keeps a close watch over the student.

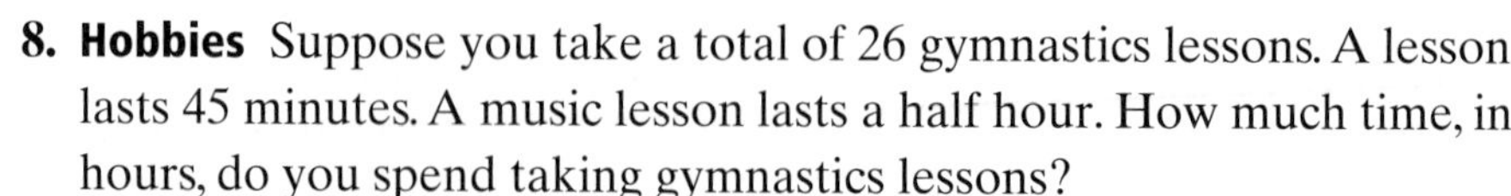

8. **Hobbies** Suppose you take a total of 26 gymnastics lessons. A lesson lasts 45 minutes. A music lesson lasts a half hour. How much time, in hours, do you spend taking gymnastics lessons?

9. To celebrate its opening day, a store gives a free gift to every fifteenth customer. The store manager expects about 100 customers each hour. About how many gifts will the store give out in its 12-hour day?

10. **Patterns** Predict the next figure in the pattern and draw it.

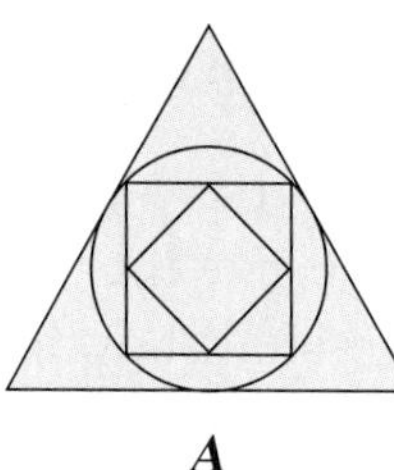

A

B

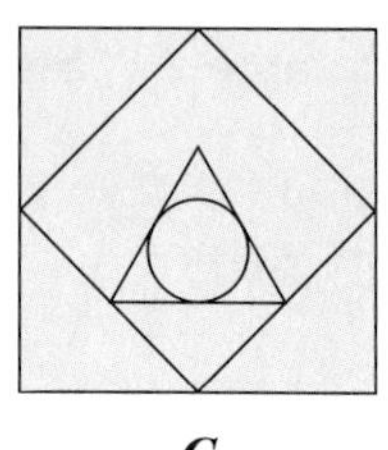

C

Challenge

11. **Stretch Your Thinking** The sum of the digits in a 3-digit number is 6. Digits may be repeated. How many such 3-digit numbers are possible?

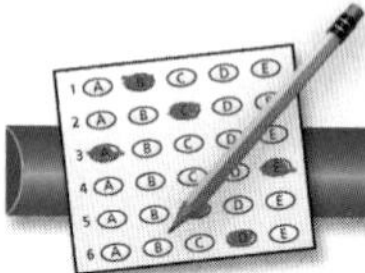

Test Prep

Multiple Choice

12. What is the difference between $9\frac{1}{2}$ and $2\frac{3}{4}$?

A. $6\frac{1}{4}$ B. $6\frac{3}{4}$ C. $7\frac{1}{8}$ D. $7\frac{1}{4}$

13. What is the sum of $\frac{3}{5}$ and $\frac{3}{4}$?

F. $\frac{3}{10}$ G. $\frac{9}{20}$ H. $\frac{2}{3}$ I. $\frac{17}{20}$

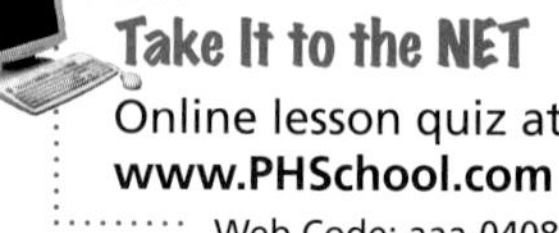

Take It to the NET
Online lesson quiz at
www.PHSchool.com
Web Code: aaa-0408

14. What is the difference between $\frac{11}{15}$ and $\frac{1}{3}$?

A. $\frac{2}{5}$ B. $\frac{8}{15}$ C. $\frac{1}{2}$ D. $\frac{5}{6}$

Short Response

15. You have 24 feet of fencing for a rectangular dog pen. Each side must be a whole number of feet. List all possible dimensions for the dog pen. Which dimensions give your dog the most area?

Mixed Review

Lesson 4-6

Algebra **Solve each equation.**

16. $x - \frac{7}{10} = 4\frac{1}{2}$ 17. $x + 2\frac{1}{3} = 5\frac{5}{6}$ 18. $x - 3\frac{1}{4} = 2\frac{3}{5}$

Lesson 4-4

Find each sum.

19. $4\frac{1}{16} + 9\frac{7}{8}$ 20. $1\frac{1}{2} + 3\frac{1}{4}$ 21. $2\frac{1}{5} + 5\frac{1}{2}$

Reading-Comprehension Questions

Reading-comprehension questions are based on a passage that gives facts. Read the directions and questions. Then read the passage. Look for information that helps answer the questions.

EXAMPLE

Desert Area Deserts cover about $\frac{1}{5}$ of Earth's land surface. A *desert* is an area of land where less than 10 inches of rain or snow falls per year.

The Sahara Desert is the largest desert, covering about $3\frac{1}{2}$ million square miles. The Sahara Desert gets about 8 inches of rain each year.

Antarctica consists largely of desert. It is about 5 million square miles in area. Antarctica contains $\frac{7}{10}$ of the world's fresh water. The South Pole lies in the middle of the continent, and gets less than 1 inch of snow each year.

How much larger is Antarctica than the Sahara Desert?

What is the question asking? the difference in area between Antarctica and the Sahara Desert

Identify the information you need. Antarctica is about 5 million square miles in area. The Sahara Desert is about $3\frac{1}{2}$ million square miles.

Solve the problem

Difference in areas, in million square miles:

$$\begin{array}{r} 5 \\ -\ 3\frac{1}{2} \\ \hline \end{array} \rightarrow \begin{array}{r} 4\frac{2}{2} \\ -\ 3\frac{1}{2} \\ \hline 1\frac{1}{2} \end{array}$$

Antarctica is about $1\frac{1}{2}$ million square miles larger than the Sahara Desert.

EXERCISES

Use the passage above to answer Exercises 1 and 2.

1. How much more rain does the Sahara Desert get in a year than the South Pole?

2. Rain forests cover about $\frac{3}{50}$ of Earth's land surface. What fraction of Earth is covered by either desert or rain forest?

Chapter 4 Chapter Review

Take It to the NET
Online vocabulary quiz at www.PHSchool.com
Web Code: aaj-0451

Vocabulary

benchmark (p. 171) **elapsed time** (p. 202)

Reading Math: Understanding Vocabulary

Choose the vocabulary term that completes each sentence.

1. A(n) _?_ is a value that you use as an estimate for a fraction.
2. The time between two events is called _?_.

Skills and Concepts

4-1 Objective

- To estimate sums and differences

A **benchmark** is a number that is close to a fraction and easy to estimate with. You can use the benchmarks 0, $\frac{1}{2}$, or 1 to estimate sums and differences of fractions.

To estimate sums and differences of mixed numbers, round to the nearest whole number.

Estimate each sum or difference. Use the benchmarks 0, $\frac{1}{2}$, and 1.

3. $\frac{8}{9} + \frac{3}{7}$
4. $\frac{5}{8} - \frac{3}{12}$
5. $\frac{4}{5} + \frac{1}{6}$
6. $\frac{23}{35} - \frac{4}{7}$

Estimate each sum or difference.

7. $4\frac{1}{7} + 9\frac{7}{14}$
8. $24\frac{11}{16} - 15\frac{1}{4}$
9. $8\frac{5}{6} + 6\frac{3}{8}$
10. $45\frac{33}{35} - 40\frac{2}{7}$
11. You need $1\frac{1}{3}$ cups of lemon juice and $4\frac{3}{4}$ cups of water to make lemonade. Estimate the amount of lemonade you will make.

4-2 and 4-3 Objectives

- To add fractions (like denominators)
- To subtract fractions (like denominators)
- To add fractions (unlike denominators)
- To subtract fractions (unlike denominators)

To add or subtract fractions, you may need to write each fraction using a common denominator. Then add or subtract the numerators.

Find each sum or difference.

12. $\frac{2}{5} + \frac{5}{5}$
13. $\frac{7}{8} - \frac{3}{8}$
14. $\frac{3}{20} + \frac{9}{20}$
15. $\frac{25}{36} - \frac{5}{36}$
16. $\frac{1}{8} + \frac{3}{4}$
17. $\frac{4}{5} - \frac{3}{10}$
18. $\frac{17}{24} - \frac{7}{12}$
19. $\frac{11}{15} + \frac{1}{2}$
20. You rode your bicycle $\frac{2}{3}$ mile to school and $\frac{1}{5}$ mile to a friend's house. How far did you ride your bicycle?

4-4 and 4-5 Objectives

- To add mixed numbers
- To add mixed numbers with renaming
- To subtract mixed numbers
- To subtract mixed numbers with renaming

You can add or subtract mixed numbers by first adding or subtracting the whole numbers and then adding or subtracting the fraction parts.

Find each sum or difference.

21. $3 + 4\frac{1}{8}$ **22.** $9\frac{8}{9} + 7\frac{4}{9}$ **23.** $35\frac{1}{5} - 28\frac{7}{10}$

24. Your sister is 10 years old and $54\frac{1}{3}$ inches tall. Her doctor says she will grow about $2\frac{1}{2}$ inches during the next year and about $2\frac{3}{4}$ inches the year after that. About how tall will your sister be when she is 12 years old?

4-6 Objectives

- To use mental math to solve equations with fractions
- To solve equations with fractions

You can use mental math or the properties of inverse operations to solve equations involving fractions or mixed numbers.

Solve each equation.

25. $\frac{5}{7} = p + \frac{2}{7}$ **26.** $q + \frac{5}{8} = \frac{3}{4}$ **27.** $\frac{2}{3} = t - \frac{4}{9}$

28. $4\frac{2}{3} = x + 1\frac{1}{3}$ **29.** $k - 2\frac{1}{6} = 8\frac{8}{9}$ **30.** $13\frac{3}{5} + h = 20$

4-7 Objectives

- To add and subtract measures of time
- To read and use schedules

The time between two events is called **elapsed time.** You may need to rewrite hours and minutes before you can add or subtract time.

Find the elapsed time between each pair of times.

31. from 8:15 A.M. to 11:56 A.M. **32.** from 9:33 P.M. to 6:21 A.M.

33. You start doing things on your to-do list at 6:00 P.M. If you take a 25-minute break while doing homework, at what time will you complete your list?

Eat dinner	40 min
Homework	55 min
Walk dog	10 min

4-8 Objective

- To solve problems by drawing a diagram

You can draw diagrams to make problems easier to understand and solve.

Solve each problem by drawing a diagram.

34. Hobbies Baseball cards are $2\frac{1}{2}$ inches by $3\frac{1}{2}$ inches. How many baseball cards fit on a bulletin board that is 45 inches long and 36 inches wide?

35. You want a plant at each corner and every 2 feet along the border of a square patio. The patio is 12 feet long. How many plants do you need?

Chapter 4

Chapter Test

Estimate each sum or difference. Use the benchmarks 0, $\frac{1}{2}$, or 1.

1. $\frac{18}{35} + \frac{14}{16}$ **2.** $\frac{7}{50} + \frac{9}{16}$ **3.** $\frac{9}{10} + \frac{2}{26}$

4. How much did Sophia's hair grow during the month of May?

Sophia's Hair Length

May 1	$8\frac{1}{8}$ in.
May 31	$8\frac{5}{16}$ in.

Estimate each sum or difference.

5. $6\frac{5}{6} + 2\frac{1}{9}$ **6.** $11\frac{6}{7} - 3\frac{7}{9}$ **7.** $10\frac{5}{12} - 5\frac{1}{8}$

8. Lumber You need $\frac{3}{8}$ foot of lumber to fix a fence and $\frac{3}{4}$ foot of lumber to fix a shed. How much lumber do you need?

Find each sum or difference.

9. $\frac{4}{5} + \frac{2}{5}$ **10.** $\frac{11}{13} - \frac{7}{13}$ **11.** $\frac{4}{7} + \frac{6}{7}$

12. $1\frac{13}{15} - \frac{2}{3}$ **13.** $\frac{9}{20} + \frac{4}{5}$ **14.** $\frac{3}{4} - \frac{3}{8}$

15. $3\frac{3}{4} - 2\frac{8}{10}$ **16.** $8\frac{1}{5} + 4\frac{1}{6}$ **17.** $5\frac{4}{9} + 7\frac{3}{5}$

Find each sum.

18. $\frac{1}{7} + \frac{2}{7} + \frac{5}{7}$ **19.** $\frac{4}{12} + \frac{2}{12} + \frac{5}{12}$

20. Dan ran $\frac{5}{6}$ mile. Sol ran $\frac{7}{8}$ mile.
- **a.** How much farther did Sol run than Dan?
- **b.** What combined distance did they run?

21. Writing in Math Explain how you could mentally solve the equation $x - 7\frac{4}{5} = 3\frac{1}{10}$.

Solve each equation.

22. $\frac{6}{9} = \frac{1}{3} + g$ **23.** $y - \frac{4}{5} = \frac{11}{20}$

24. $4\frac{3}{4} + v = 17\frac{1}{8}$ **25.** $13\frac{2}{3} = k - 10\frac{7}{9}$

Use the table for Exercises 26–28.

Spruce Tree	Length of Cone (inches)
White	$1\frac{5}{8}$
Norway	$5\frac{1}{2}$
Black	$\frac{7}{8}$
Red	$1\frac{1}{4}$

26. Find the difference in length between the shortest and longest cones.

27. Estimation Which two cones differ in length by about $\frac{1}{2}$ inch?

28. What is the difference in length between the Red and White Spruce tree cones?

How many minutes are in each amount of time?

29. 5 h 47 min **30.** 23 h 8 min

31. Find the elapsed time between 6:33 A.M. and 7:20 P.M.

32. Trees The roots of a tree reach $18\frac{1}{2}$ feet into the ground. A bird's nest is $6\frac{3}{4}$ feet from the top of the tree. The distance from the top of the tree to the bottom of the roots is 60 feet. How far above the ground is the bird's nest?

Test Prep

CUMULATIVE REVIEW
CHAPTERS 1–4

Multiple Choice

For Exercises 1–9, choose the correct letter.

1. On Venus the length of a day is 243.01 Earth days. On Mercury the length of a day is 58.65 Earth days. How much longer, in Earth days, is a Venus day than a Mercury day?

A. 301.66 **B.** 215.64
C. 195.46 **D.** 184.36

2. Suppose you buy a shirt for x dollars with a twenty-dollar bill. The cashier gives you $5.35 back. Which equation can you use to find the cost of the shirt?

F. $5.35x = 20$ **G.** $x + 5.35 = 20$
H. $x \div 20 = 5.35$ **I.** $5.35 - x = 20$

3. How much thicker is a quarter than a dime?

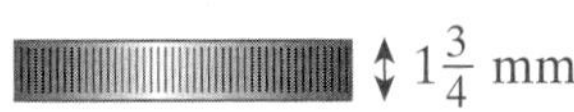

$1\frac{3}{4}$ mm

$1\frac{7}{20}$ mm

A. $\frac{1}{20}$ mm **B.** $\frac{1}{4}$ mm **C.** $\frac{2}{5}$ mm **D.** $\frac{1}{2}$ mm

4. Which equation is NOT an example of the Distributive Property?

F. $12(6.2) + 12(3.8) = 12(6.2 + 3.8)$
G. $0.75(8.869) + 0.25(8.869) = 1(8.869)$
H. $19.1(80) = 19(100) - 10.1(20)$
I. $8.1 + 3.5 = 3.5 + 8.1$

5. Which set of numbers has a GCF of 3?

A. 15, 30, 45 **B.** 6, 30, 24
C. 24, 36, 9 **D.** 36, 27, 18

6. Which number is divisible by 9?

F. 213,645 **G.** 31,392
H. 285,137 **I.** 42,901

7. What is the best estimate for the sum of $12\frac{13}{16}$ and $23\frac{3}{8}$?

A. 30 **B.** 35 **C.** 36 **D.** 37

8. A store sells window glass that is $\frac{1}{8}$ inch, $\frac{3}{16}$ inch, $\frac{5}{16}$ inch, and $\frac{7}{32}$ inch thick. You need glass that is at least $\frac{1}{4}$ inch thick. Which thickness, in inches, should you buy?

F. $\frac{1}{8}$ **G.** $\frac{3}{16}$ **H.** $\frac{5}{16}$ **I.** $\frac{7}{32}$

9. What is the sum of $6\frac{3}{5}$ and $2\frac{4}{5}$?

A. $8\frac{1}{5}$ **B.** $8\frac{12}{25}$ **C.** $9\frac{2}{5}$ **D.** $9\frac{4}{5}$

Gridded Response

10. Kerry boards the school bus at 7:48 A.M. and arrives at school at 8:13 A.M. How many minutes does he spend on the bus?

11. What is the solution of $x + \frac{3}{16} = \frac{3}{4}$? Write your answer in simplest form.

Short Response

12. What is the least common multiple of 36 and 45? **(a)** Choose a method of either listing multiples or using prime factorizations. **(b)** Show the steps you use to find this LCM.

13. From his home, a jogger ran 1 mile west, $3\frac{1}{2}$ miles north, 1 mile east, and $1\frac{1}{4}$ miles south. How far from home is he? **(a)** Draw a diagram to help solve the problem. **(b)** Solve the problem.

Extended Response

14. At a book fair, a paperback sells for $.35 and a hardcover sells for $1.30. Your friend spends $6.00 on books. She buys three more paperbacks than hardcovers.

a. Write a list of possibilities for the number of books. Begin with one hardcover.
b. How many paperbacks does your friend buy?

Fast Fractions

Applying Mixed Numbers People love to race. Some races, like the Iditarod, the Tour de France, and the Paris–Dakar Rally, last days or even weeks. Other races can be over in a flash. The fastest runners can finish a 100-meter race in 10 or 11 seconds.

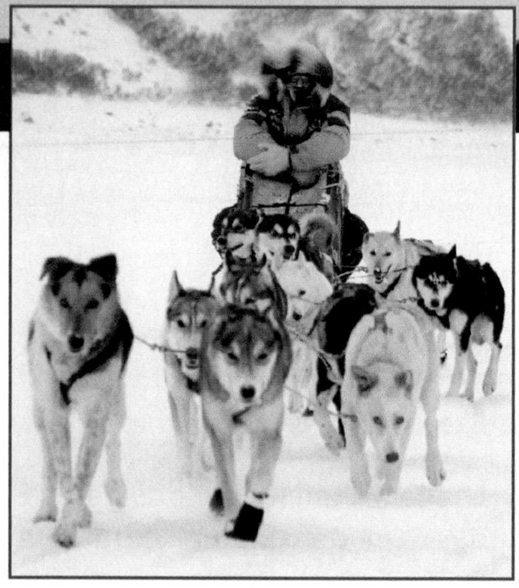

The Iditarod

The Iditarod is a dog sled race over at least 1,049 miles in Alaska. The fastest sled drivers, or mushers, finish in about 10 days.

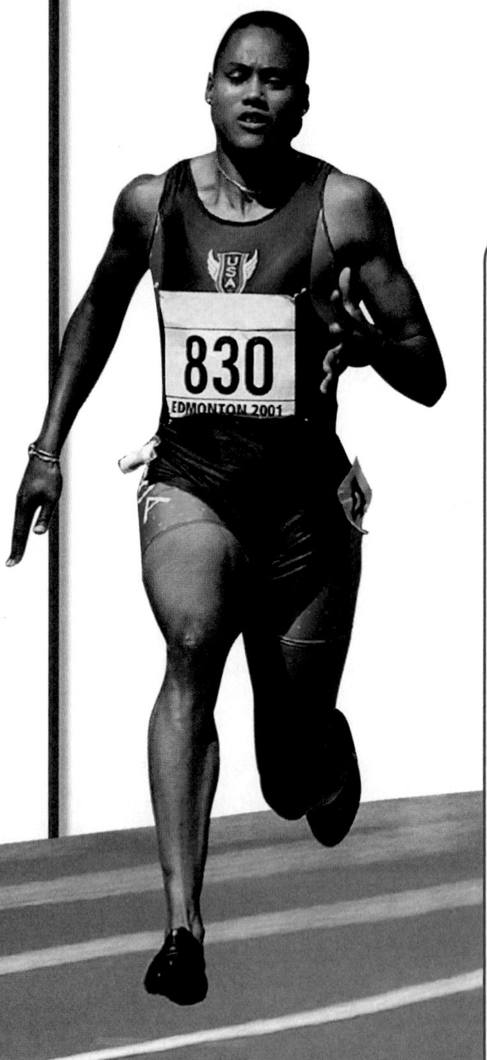

Marion Jones

Marion Jones won three gold medals and two bronze medals at the 2000 Olympic Summer Games in Sydney, Australia.

Put It All Together

What You'll Need

- 3 number cubes

How to Play

- Work in a group. The goal of the game is to "run" each of four quarter-mile sections of a one-mile track.
- Roll three number cubes. Write a mixed number that includes a proper fraction. If all three numbers are the same, roll again.
- Take turns until each group member has times for each quarter-mile section of the track.
- If you roll the same three numbers more than once, you must make a different mixed number with them each time. If that is not possible, roll again.

1. Order your times from least to greatest.
2. a. **Estimation** Estimate the total time for each group member. Who do you think has the fastest time? Explain.
   b. Find your total time. Write your answer in simplest form.
   c. Compare your total to the totals for the others in your group. Who won the race?
3. **Number Sense** The record time for "running" this track is 4.95 minutes. Is it possible to beat this time? Explain.
4. **Data File** Pick one of the animals from page 169. How long would it take the animal to "run" the track? Who runs faster, you or the animal? Explain.

Take It to the NET For more information about racing, go to **www.PHSchool.com**.
Web Code: aae-0453

Speed Skater

Catherine Raney of the 2002 U.S. Olympic team skated between 20 and 25 miles per hour during the women's 5,000-meter final.

Tour de France

The Tour de France bicycle race lasts about three weeks and covers about 2,000 miles.

CHAPTER 5

Multiplying and Dividing Fractions

Lessons

Key Vocabulary

- reciprocal (p. 230)

Real-World Snapshots

Track and field meets include events such as hurdles, relay races, high jump, long jump, and pole vault. Times are measured using decimals. Lengths and heights are measured using decimals or fractions.

Data File Junior Olympic Records for Long Jump

	Distance (feet)	
Age Group	**Boys**	**Girls**
10 and under	$15\frac{19}{24}$	$14\frac{29}{48}$
11–12	$18\frac{7}{16}$	$18\frac{5}{48}$
13–14	$21\frac{5}{8}$	$18\frac{23}{48}$
15–16	$24\frac{1}{8}$	$20\frac{3}{16}$
17–18	$24\frac{15}{16}$	$20\frac{7}{8}$

SOURCE: USA Track & Field. Go to **www.PHSchool.com** for a data update.

You will use the data above in this chapter:

- p. 227 Lesson 5-2
- p. 238 Lesson 5-4
- p. 256 Lesson 5-8

Real-World Snapshots On pages 264 and 265, you will solve problems involving carpentry.

Chapter 5 Preview

Where You've Been

- In Chapter 3, you simplified and compared fractions. You also learned to express fractions as decimals.
- In Chapter 4, you added and subtracted fractions and mixed numbers.

Where You're Going

- In Chapter 5, you will multiply and divide fractions and mixed numbers.
- You will also change units in the customary system.
- Applying what you learn, you will change units as an architect does.

Architects often change units within the customary system.

Instant self-check online and on CD-ROM

Diagnosing Readiness

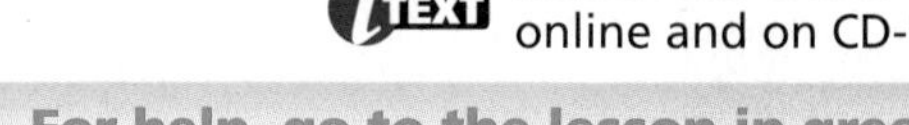

For help, go to the lesson in green.

Solving Multiplication and Division Equations (Lesson 2-7)

Solve each equation.

1. $3a = 12$ **2.** $5x = 25$ **3.** $p \div 3 = 4$

4. $14 = x \div 8$ **5.** $0.1n = 10$ **6.** $750 = 150n$

7. $w \div 6 = 9$ **8.** $2 = g \div 0.3$ **9.** $48 = 16p$

Finding the Greatest Common Factor (Lesson 3-3)

Find the GCF of each set of numbers.

10. 12, 24 **11.** 28, 35 **12.** 27, 24

13. 80, 100 **14.** 36, 66 **15.** 21, 42

Writing Equivalent Fractions (Lesson 3-4)

Write each fraction in simplest form.

16. $\frac{15}{35}$ **17.** $\frac{24}{36}$ **18.** $\frac{16}{48}$

19. $\frac{24}{64}$ **20.** $\frac{18}{72}$ **21.** $\frac{21}{49}$

22. $\frac{32}{48}$ **23.** $\frac{49}{56}$ **24.** $\frac{36}{84}$

Multiplying Fractions

What You'll Learn

To multiply two fractions

To multiply fractions by whole numbers

. . . And Why

To compare lengths, as in Example 4

✓ Check Skills You'll Need

For help, go to Lesson 3-4.

Write each fraction in simplest form.

1. $\frac{5}{10}$ **2.** $\frac{9}{15}$ **3.** $\frac{28}{42}$

4. $\frac{90}{100}$ **5.** $\frac{18}{24}$ **6.** $\frac{36}{48}$

7. Is $\frac{9}{16}$ in simplest form? Explain.

Interactive lesson includes instant self-check, tutorials, and activities.

OBJECTIVE

1 Multiplying Two Fractions

Investigation: Modeling Multiplication of Fractions

Suppose you and your friend order a half-vegetable, half-cheese pizza. You like vegetable; your friend likes cheese.

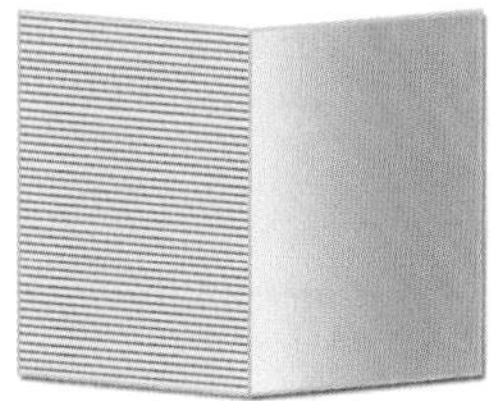

1. Use a rectangular piece of paper to represent the pizza. Fold it in half as shown. Shade one of the two parts to represent your half.

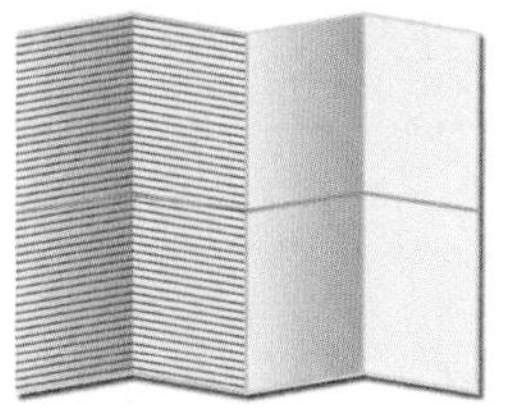

2. Refold the paper. Then fold it in half two more times. How many slices of pizza are there?

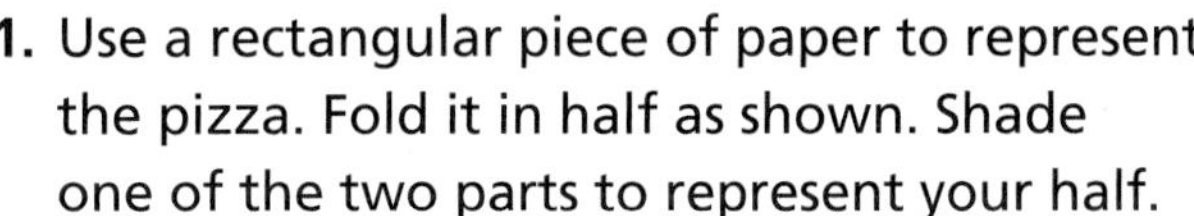

3. Suppose you eat $\frac{3}{4}$ of your half. Draw an X on three of the four slices in your half. What fraction of the whole pizza have you eaten?
4. The third model represents $\frac{3}{4} \times \frac{1}{2}$. Use a model to find $\frac{1}{2} \times \frac{1}{2}$.

You can model the multiplication of fractions by shading parts of a rectangle. This type of model is an area model. The model at the right shows $\frac{5}{6} \times \frac{1}{2} = \frac{5}{12}$.

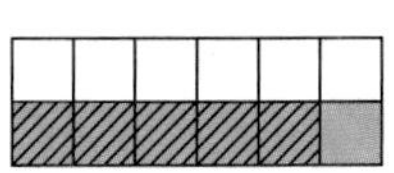

1 EXAMPLE Modeling Fraction Multiplication

Draw a model to find the product $\frac{3}{5} \times \frac{1}{2}$.

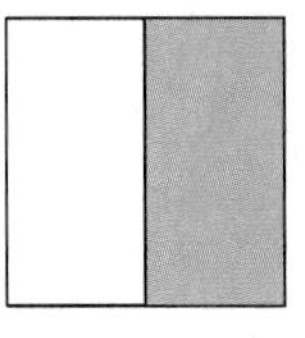

← Divide a rectangle in half. Shade one of the halves.

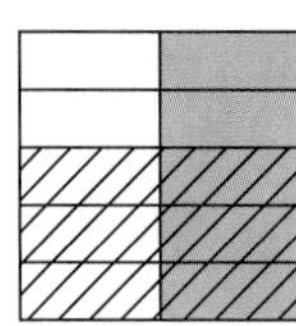

← Divide each half into fifths. Use diagonal lines to shade three of the fifths.

$\frac{3}{5} \times \frac{1}{2} = \frac{3}{10}$

Check Understanding 1 Draw a model to find the product of $\frac{1}{3} \times \frac{2}{5}$.

Example 1 shows that $\frac{3}{5} \times \frac{1}{2} = \frac{3}{10}$. You can get this product by multiplying the numerators and multiplying the denominators.

Key Concepts — Multiplying Fractions

Arithmetic	Algebra
$\frac{3}{4} \times \frac{1}{2} = \frac{3 \times 1}{4 \times 2} = \frac{3}{8}$	$\frac{a}{b} \cdot \frac{c}{d} = \frac{ac}{bd}$, where b and d are not zero.

2 EXAMPLE Multiplying Two Fractions

Need Help?
For help with simplifying fractions, go to Lesson 3-4.

Find the product $\frac{3}{8} \cdot \frac{2}{5}$.

$\frac{3}{8} \cdot \frac{2}{5} = \frac{3 \cdot 2}{8 \cdot 5}$ ← Multiply the numerators. ← Multiply the denominators.

$= \frac{6}{40}$ ← Find the two products.

$= \frac{3}{20}$ ← Simplify.

Check Understanding 2 Find each product. **a.** $\frac{3}{5} \cdot \frac{1}{4}$ **b.** $\frac{2}{9} \times \frac{5}{7}$

c. **Reasoning** How is adding $\frac{3}{8}$ and $\frac{5}{8}$ different from multiplying the two fractions? Explain.

Sometimes you can simplify before multiplying fractions.

$\frac{3}{8} \cdot \frac{2}{5} = \frac{3}{{}_4\not{8}} \cdot \frac{\not{2}^1}{5}$ ← Divide 8 and 2 by their GCF, 2.

$= \frac{3 \cdot 1}{4 \cdot 5}$ ← Multiply the numerators and the denominators.

$= \frac{3}{20}$ ← Simplify.

OBJECTIVE

2 Multiplying Fractions by Whole Numbers

To multiply a fraction by a whole number, write the whole number as an improper fraction with a denominator of 1. Then multiply the two fractions.

3 EXAMPLE Multiplying Fractions by Whole Numbers

Reading Math
The word *of* usually indicates multiplication.

Find $\frac{3}{4}$ of 20.

$\frac{3}{4} \times 20 = \frac{3}{4} \times \frac{20}{1}$ ← **$\frac{3}{4}$ of 20 means $\frac{3}{4} \times 20$. Write 20 as $\frac{20}{1}$.**

$= \frac{3}{{}_1\not{4}} \times \frac{\not{20}^5}{1}$ ← **Simplify first. Divide 20 and 4 by their GCF, 4.**

$= \frac{15}{1}$ ← **Multiply the numerators and the denominators.**

$= 15$ ← **Simplify.**

Fifteen prizes have been won.

Check Understanding 3 Find each product. **a.** $\frac{4}{5}$ of 7 **b.** $24 \cdot \frac{5}{9}$

4 EXAMPLE Real-World Problem Solving

Measurement Students in art class are using ribbon to decorate a bulletin board. A piece of green ribbon is $\frac{5}{6}$ yard long. A piece of yellow ribbon is nine times as long. How long is the piece of yellow ribbon?

Draw a diagram to help see how these lengths relate to each other.

Find the length of the yellow ribbon by multiplying 9 and $\frac{5}{6}$.

$9 \cdot \frac{5}{6} = \frac{9}{1} \cdot \frac{5}{6}$ ← **Write 9 as $\frac{9}{1}$.**

$= \frac{{}^3\not{9}}{1} \cdot \frac{5}{\not{6}_2}$ ← **Divide 9 and 6 by their GCF, 3.**

$= \frac{15}{2}$ ← **Multiply the numerators and the denominators.**

$= 7\frac{1}{2}$ ← **Write as a mixed number.**

The yellow ribbon is $7\frac{1}{2}$ yards long.

Check Understanding 4 Juanita lives $\frac{3}{4}$ mile from school. Carlota lives 6 times as far away from school as Juanita. How far from school does Carlota live?

EXERCISES

For more practice, see *Extra Practice*.

A Practice by Example

Example 1 (page 220)

Draw a model to find each product.

1. $\frac{1}{4} \times \frac{1}{3}$
2. $\frac{1}{2} \times \frac{3}{4}$
3. $\frac{1}{5} \cdot \frac{5}{8}$
4. $\frac{2}{3} \cdot \frac{2}{5}$

Find each product. Exercise 5 has been started for you.

Example 2 (page 220)

5. $\frac{1}{2} \times \frac{3}{8} = \frac{1 \times 3}{2 \times 8}$
6. $\frac{5}{11} \times \frac{2}{7}$
7. $\frac{3}{4} \times \frac{11}{12}$
8. $\frac{2}{9} \times \frac{4}{8}$
9. $\frac{4}{9} \cdot \frac{3}{10}$
10. $\frac{3}{5} \cdot \frac{2}{3}$
11. $\frac{4}{11}$ of $\frac{5}{8}$
12. $\frac{9}{10}$ of $\frac{2}{5}$
13. $\frac{7}{15}$ of $\frac{3}{4}$

Find each product. Exercise 14 has been started for you.

Examples 3, 4 (page 221)

14. $\frac{3}{8} \times 5 = \frac{3}{8} \times \frac{5}{1}$
15. $\frac{11}{14}$ of 28
16. $\frac{5}{12} \cdot 30$
17. $\frac{7}{9}$ of 21
18. $\frac{1}{6} \cdot 6$
19. $\frac{3}{10} \times 45$

20. **Fitness** For gym class, you run $\frac{3}{4}$ of a mile. Your gym teacher runs that distance 3 times, since she teaches 3 classes. How far does she run?

B Apply Your Skills

Mental Math **Find each product.**

21. $\frac{1}{4} \cdot 44$
22. $\frac{2}{7}$ of 63
23. $\frac{1}{12} \times 60$
24. $\frac{4}{5}$ of 50
25. $\frac{1}{6}$ of 72
26. $\frac{3}{8}$ of 24
27. $\frac{5}{9}$ of 81
28. $\frac{7}{10}$ of 80

29. **Writing in Math** Explain how you can divide by common factors before you multiply to find $\frac{2}{3} \cdot \frac{4}{5} \cdot \frac{3}{4}$.

30. **Food** At the movies you eat all but $\frac{1}{3}$ of a box of popcorn. Your friend eats $\frac{2}{3}$ of what is left. What fraction of the popcorn does your friend eat? Who eats more? How much more?

Algebra **Evaluate each expression for $x = \frac{2}{3}$.**

31. $15x$
32. $\frac{3}{2}x$
33. $\frac{9}{10}x$
34. $\frac{2}{3}x$

35. **Landscaping** Suppose $\frac{3}{5}$ of your yard will be grass and the rest will be plants. You plant flowers in $\frac{3}{4}$ of the plant area. What portion of the yard will have flowers?

36. **Monuments** The length of a side at the base of the Washington Monument is about $\frac{1}{10}$ of its height. The monument is about 555 feet tall. Find the length of a side at the base.

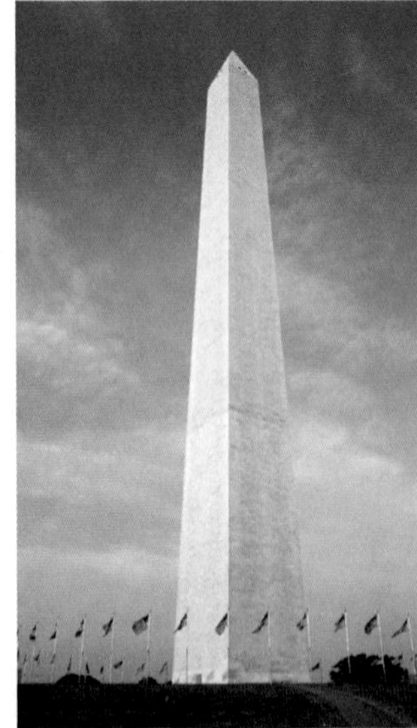

Real-World Connection

The Washington Monument is the largest masonry structure in the world.

C Challenge

37. **Budgets** Suppose the graph describes Paul's monthly spending. He makes \$2,712 a month. How much does he spend each month on his rent and his car combined?

Other $\frac{5}{8}$

Rent $\frac{1}{4}$

Car $\frac{1}{8}$

38. **Stretch Your Thinking** In a three-digit number, the sum of its ones digit and tens digit is ten. Its tens digit is twice its hundreds digit, and its hundreds digit is twice its ones digit. What is the number?

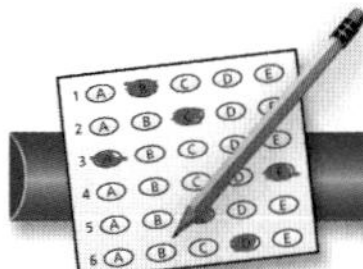

Test Prep

Multiple Choice

39. What is $\frac{3}{7}$ of 35?

A. $\frac{1}{15}$ B. $\frac{3}{5}$ C. 5 D. 15

40. What is the product of $\frac{5}{6}$ and $\frac{14}{15}$?

F. $\frac{2}{9}$ G. $\frac{2}{3}$ H. $1\frac{1}{2}$ I. $4\frac{1}{2}$

41. Which product is NOT equal to the others?

A. $\frac{4}{25} \cdot 20$ B. $\frac{4}{25} \cdot \frac{1}{20}$ C. $\frac{4}{5} \cdot \frac{4}{1}$ D. $\frac{20}{1} \cdot \frac{4}{25}$

Extended Response

42. You buy several items on sale. You buy a shirt for $\frac{4}{5}$ of its original cost of \$21, jeans for $\frac{3}{4}$ of their original cost of \$40, and shoes for $\frac{9}{10}$ of their original cost of \$27.

a. How much money do you save on your shopping trip?

b. What fraction of the total original cost do you pay? Explain in words how you found your answer.

Take It to the NET
Online lesson quiz at **www.PHSchool.com**
Web Code: aaa-0501

Mixed Review

Lesson 4-3

Find each sum or difference.

43. $\frac{5}{6} + \frac{1}{3}$ 44. $\frac{4}{5} - \frac{1}{2}$ 45. $\frac{7}{9} - \frac{3}{5}$ 46. $\frac{3}{10} + \frac{5}{8}$

47. $\frac{7}{8} - \frac{5}{12}$ 48. $\frac{3}{4} + \frac{1}{6}$ 49. $\frac{2}{3} + \frac{1}{2}$ 50. $\frac{2}{3} - \frac{3}{7}$

Lesson 3-2

Tell whether each number is prime or composite. Explain.

51. 119 52. 10,101 53. 61 54. 135,792

55. 231 56. 97 57. 441 58. 157

5-2 Multiplying Mixed Numbers

What You'll Learn

To estimate products of mixed numbers

To multiply mixed numbers

. . . And Why

To find how far a person can ski, as in Example 3

✓ Check Skills You'll Need

For help, go to Lesson 4-1.

Estimate each sum or difference.

1. $3\frac{6}{7} - 2\frac{1}{3}$

2. $5\frac{2}{3} + 7\frac{1}{5}$

3. $11\frac{3}{4} + 17\frac{5}{9}$

4. $6\frac{5}{6} + 1\frac{1}{7}$

5. $8\frac{7}{9} - 2\frac{6}{7}$

6. $7\frac{5}{8} - 1\frac{2}{3}$

OBJECTIVE

 Interactive lesson includes instant self-check, tutorials, and activities.

1 Estimating Products of Mixed Numbers

To estimate the product of mixed numbers, round the mixed numbers to the nearest whole number and then multiply. If the fraction part of a mixed number is $\frac{1}{2}$ or greater, round up.

1 EXAMPLE Estimating Products

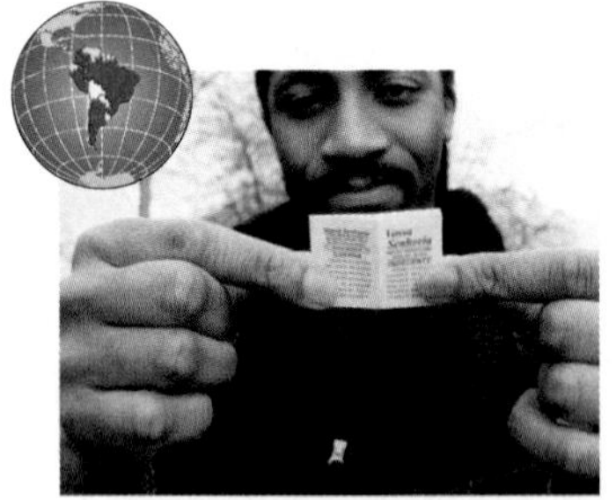

Real-World Connection

The smallest newspaper in circulation is the Brazilian *Vossa Senhoria.* It measures 0.98 inch by 1.38 inches!

Newspapers One of the smallest newspapers ever printed had a page size of $1\frac{1}{4}$ inches wide by $2\frac{3}{4}$ inches long. Estimate the area of a page.

Step 1 Round the length and width to the nearest whole numbers.

Original size: $1\frac{1}{4}$ in. by $2\frac{3}{4}$ in. → Rounded size: 1 in. by 3 in.

Step 2 Multiply to estimate the area.

$$\text{Area} = \text{length} \times \text{width}$$
$$\approx 3 \times 1$$
$$= 3$$

The area of a page is about 3 square inches.

1 Estimate each product.

a. $5\frac{5}{6} \times 6\frac{4}{9}$ **b.** $7\frac{11}{16} \cdot 7\frac{1}{5}$ **c.** $12\frac{1}{2} \times 10\frac{2}{3}$

d. **Reasoning** Suppose you want to estimate the product of $82\frac{5}{7}$ and $\frac{1}{8}$. Explain why $80 \cdot \frac{1}{8}$ is a better estimate than $83 \cdot 0$.

OBJECTIVE

2 Multiplying Mixed Numbers

To find the product of mixed numbers, write each mixed number as an improper fraction before multiplying.

2 EXAMPLE Multiplying Using Improper Fractions

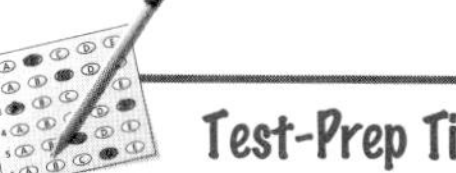

Test-Prep Tip

Estimate first and then check your computation to determine if your answer is reasonable.

Find the product $2\frac{2}{3} \times 3\frac{1}{4}$.

Estimate $2\frac{2}{3} \times 3\frac{1}{4} \approx 3 \times 3$, or 9

$2\frac{2}{3} \times 3\frac{1}{4} = \frac{8}{3} \times \frac{13}{4}$ ← **Write the mixed numbers as improper fractions.**

$= \frac{{}^{2}\not{8}}{3} \times \frac{13}{\not{4}_{1}}$ ← **Divide 8 and 4 by their GCF, 4.**

$= \frac{26}{3}$, or $8\frac{2}{3}$ ← **Multiply the numerators and the denominators. Then write as a mixed number.**

Check for Reasonableness $8\frac{2}{3}$ is near the estimate of 9.

Check Understanding 2 Find each product.

a. $1\frac{1}{4} \times 2\frac{3}{4}$ **b.** $7\frac{1}{3} \times 3\frac{3}{4}$ **c.** $10\frac{4}{5} \cdot 1\frac{2}{3}$

3 EXAMPLE Real-World Problem Solving

Skiing A student can ski cross-country $3\frac{1}{2}$ miles in one hour. Her instructor can ski cross-country $1\frac{1}{3}$ times as far in the same amount of time. How far can the instructor ski in one hour?

Student

$4\frac{1}{2}$ miles

Instructor

The diagram at the left shows the distance that the instructor skis in one hour, which is $1\frac{1}{3}$ times as far as the student skis.

number of miles the instructor skis $= 1\frac{1}{3} \times$ number of miles the student skis

$= 1\frac{1}{3} \times 3\frac{1}{2}$

$= \frac{4}{3} \times \frac{7}{2}$ ← **Write the mixed numbers as improper fractions.**

$= \frac{{}^{2}\not{4}}{3} \times \frac{7}{\not{2}_{1}}$ ← **Divide 4 and 2 by their GCF, 2.**

$= \frac{14}{3}$, or $4\frac{2}{3}$ ← **Multiply the numerators and the denominators. Then write as a mixed number.**

The instructor can ski $4\frac{2}{3}$ miles in one hour.

Check Understanding 3 How many miles can the student ski in $\frac{3}{4}$ hour?

More Than One Way

How would you adjust the recipe at the right to use $2\frac{2}{3}$ pounds of chick peas?

HUMMUS

1 lb chick peas
12 oz tahini
1 tbsp lemon juice
2 cloves garlic
Chop garlic and mix.
Add paprika, salt, cumin to taste.

Sabrina's Method

Since I use $2\frac{2}{3}$ times as much chick peas, I will need $2\frac{2}{3}$ times as much tahini. I will multiply $2\frac{2}{3}$ by 12 ounces.

$2\frac{2}{3} \cdot 12 = \frac{8}{3} \cdot \frac{12}{1}$ ← **Write the numbers as improper fractions.**

$= \frac{8}{{}_1\cancel{3}} \cdot \frac{\cancel{12}^4}{1}$ ← **Divide by the common factor, 3.**

$= \frac{32}{1}$, or 32 ← **Multiply and simplify.**

I will need 32 ounces of tahini.

Derek's Method

I can think of $2\frac{2}{3}$ as the sum of two numbers, $2 + \frac{2}{3}$, and solve the problem using mental math.

I need two 12-ounce jars of tahini, and $\frac{2}{3}$ of another jar.

$$2\frac{2}{3} \times 12 = 2 \times 12 + \frac{2}{3} \times 12$$
$$= 24 + 8$$
$$= 32$$

12 oz 12 oz $\frac{2}{3}$ full

I will need 32 ounces of tahini.

Choose a Method

Find $10 \times 3\frac{2}{5}$. Describe your method and explain why you chose it.

EXERCISES

For more practice, see *Extra Practice*.

Practice by Example

Example 1 (page 224)

Estimate each product. Exercises 1 and 2 have been started for you.

1. $3\frac{1}{2} \cdot 1\frac{1}{4} \approx 4 \cdot 1$

2. $14\frac{2}{3} \cdot 5\frac{1}{3} \approx 15 \cdot 5$

3. $5\frac{1}{2} \cdot 10\frac{3}{10}$

4. $7\frac{3}{4} \times 9\frac{1}{2}$

5. $15\frac{9}{10} \cdot 3\frac{1}{5}$

6. $2\frac{3}{4} \times 6\frac{1}{8}$

Examples 2, 3 (page 225)

Find each product. Exercise 7 has been started for you.

7. $7\frac{1}{2} \cdot 8\frac{2}{3} = \frac{15}{2} \cdot \frac{26}{3}$ **8.** $5\frac{1}{3} \times 2\frac{1}{4}$ **9.** $3\frac{1}{9} \cdot 3\frac{3}{8}$

10. $2\frac{4}{5} \times 12\frac{1}{2}$ **11.** $1\frac{1}{3} \cdot 10\frac{1}{2}$ **12.** $3\frac{1}{5} \cdot 1\frac{7}{8}$

13. $3\frac{5}{9} \times 4\frac{1}{2}$ **14.** $1\frac{5}{8} \times 2\frac{2}{3}$ **15.** $3\frac{3}{4} \times 5\frac{1}{3}$

16. Estimate the area of a folder that measures $9\frac{3}{8}$ inches by $11\frac{3}{4}$ inches.

B Apply Your Skills

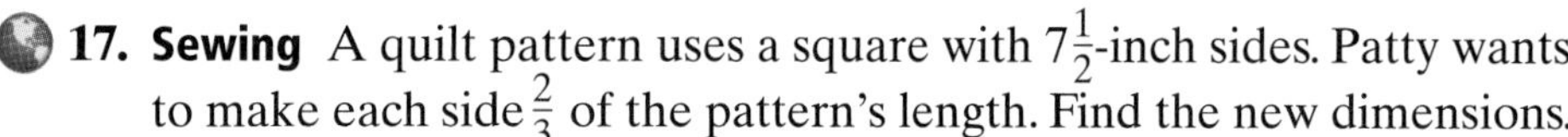

17. Sewing A quilt pattern uses a square with $7\frac{1}{2}$-inch sides. Patty wants to make each side $\frac{2}{3}$ of the pattern's length. Find the new dimensions.

18. a. A mother is $1\frac{3}{8}$ times as tall as her daughter. The girl is $1\frac{1}{3}$ times as tall as her brother. The mother is how many times as tall as her son?

b. If the son is $2\frac{1}{2}$ feet tall, how tall is his mother?

Exercise 18

Algebra **Evaluate each expression for $x = 5\frac{1}{3}$.**

19. $9x$ **20.** $2\frac{5}{8} \cdot x$ **21.** $3x + 2$ **22.** $7\frac{1}{2}x + 5\frac{1}{4}x$

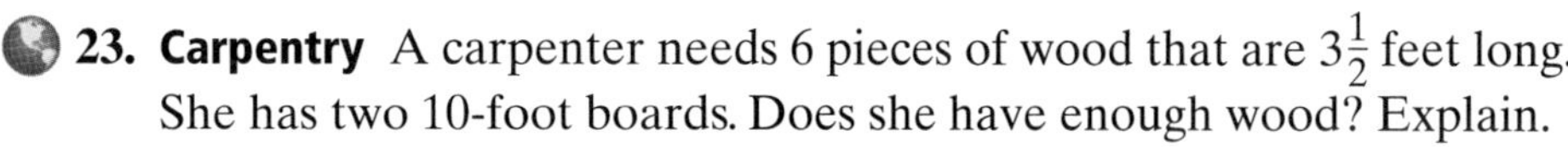

23. Carpentry A carpenter needs 6 pieces of wood that are $3\frac{1}{2}$ feet long. She has two 10-foot boards. Does she have enough wood? Explain.

24. Data File, p. 217 The women's world outdoor long-jump record is about $1\frac{1}{5}$ the distance of the 15–16-year-old girls' record. Find the distance of this record to the nearest foot.

25. Construction A "2-by-4" board is $1\frac{1}{2}$ inches thick. How high is a stack of four boards?

Find each product.

26. $15\frac{1}{2} \times 3\frac{5}{8}$ **27.** $12\frac{1}{10} \cdot 8\frac{2}{3}$ **28.** $5\frac{3}{4} \cdot 8\frac{1}{12}$

29. $2\frac{7}{8} \cdot 17\frac{1}{3}$ **30.** $5\frac{5}{12} \times 4\frac{2}{5}$ **31.** $5\frac{1}{5} \cdot 5\frac{5}{6}$

32. Writing in Math Describe some items that have an area you can find by multiplying mixed numbers.

C Challenge

33. Design An artist is planning to make a painting that is $1\frac{3}{4}$ feet by $2\frac{5}{8}$ feet. The size of the painting may change depending on the available space. What size will the painting be if its length and width are increased to $1\frac{1}{3}$ of their original sizes?

34. Stretch Your Thinking Every 15 minutes a cell divides into 2 cells. At 12:00 P.M., there are 256 cells. At what time were there 32 cells?

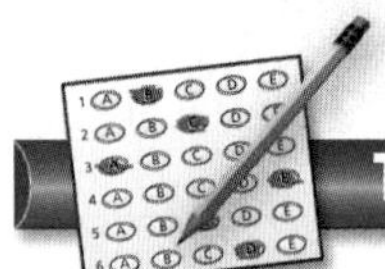

Test Prep

Multiple Choice

35. What is $3\frac{3}{4} \times 5\frac{1}{3}$?

A. 12 **B.** $15\frac{1}{4}$ **C.** 20 **D.** 24

36. Which of the following is NOT equal to $8 \times 4\frac{1}{6}$?

F. $8 \times \frac{25}{6}$ **G.** $\frac{8}{3} \times \frac{25}{2}$ **H.** $\frac{100}{3}$ **I.** $4 \times 8\frac{1}{6}$

Take It to the NET
Online lesson quiz at
www.PHSchool.com
Web Code: aaa-0502

37. Which number multiplied by $4\frac{1}{3}$ gives a product closest to 12?

A. $1\frac{1}{5}$ **B.** $2\frac{1}{5}$ **C.** $3\frac{1}{5}$ **D.** $4\frac{1}{5}$

Short Response

38. Suppose Andrew earns \$6.25 an hour. He works $4\frac{1}{2}$ hours per day, 5 days per week. **(a)** How much money does he earn in 2 weeks? **(b)** Explain in words how you found your answer.

Mixed Review

Lesson 4-4 **Find each sum.**

39. $3\frac{2}{5} + 4\frac{1}{5}$ **40.** $2\frac{1}{6} + 1\frac{5}{6}$ **41.** $5\frac{3}{8} + 2\frac{1}{4}$

42. $7\frac{5}{12} + 6\frac{3}{4}$ **43.** $8\frac{1}{6} + 3\frac{1}{2}$ **44.** $1\frac{2}{3} + 4\frac{2}{9}$

Lesson 3-6 **Find the LCM of each set of numbers.**

45. 6, 15 **46.** 35, 40 **47.** 10, 20, 50 **48.** 15, 18, 24

Practice Game

Estimate That Product!

What You'll Need

- 20 cards or paper slips, each with a fraction or mixed number
- fraction calculator (optional)

How to Play

- One student acts as the game host. Two students are the players.
- The host shuffles the cards and then turns over two cards.
- Players have 10 seconds to write an estimate for the product.
- The host finds the product. The host also computes the difference between each player's estimate and the actual product.
- The player with the estimate closer to the actual product earns 1 point. If there is a tie, each player gets 1 point.
- The first player to earn 5 points wins.

Fraction Division

For Use With Lesson 5-3

Suppose you serve three large cheese quesadillas at a party. You divide the three quesadillas into eighths. How many pieces do you have?

You can use circle models to represent each quesadilla.

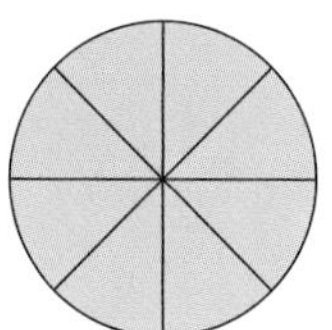 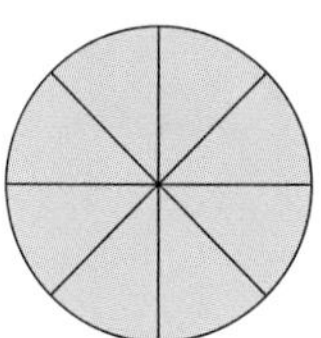 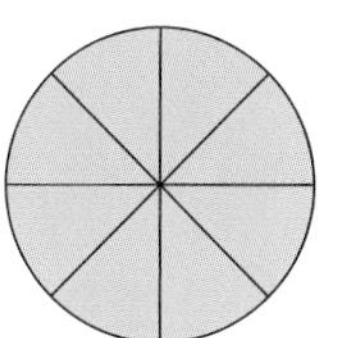

Each circle is divided into eighths. You see that there are 24 pieces.

So, $3 \div \frac{1}{8} = 24$.

Activity

1. **a.** Draw 3 circles. Divide each circle in half. How many halves are there?
   b. What is $3 \div \frac{1}{2}$?

2. Divide 4, 5, and 6 circles into halves. Copy and complete the table.

Number of Circles	Fraction	Number of Pieces	Division Problem
3	$\frac{1}{2}$	■	$3 \div \frac{1}{2} =$ ■
4	$\frac{1}{2}$	■	■
5	$\frac{1}{2}$	■	■
6	$\frac{1}{2}$	■	■

3. **a.** **Patterns** How do the number of pieces relate to the number of circles in the table?
   b. What happens when you divide a number by $\frac{1}{2}$?

4. **Number Sense** How are dividing by $\frac{1}{2}$ and multiplying by 2 related? Explain.

EXERCISES

Find each quotient.

5. $4 \div \frac{1}{3}$ **6.** $5 \div \frac{1}{3}$ **7.** $4 \div \frac{1}{4}$ **8.** $5 \div \frac{1}{4}$

5-3 Dividing Fractions

What You'll Learn

To divide whole numbers by fractions

To divide fractions by fractions

. . . And Why

To fill birdfeeders, as in Example 4

Check Skills You'll Need

For help, go to Lesson 5-1.

Find each product.

1. $8 \times \frac{3}{4}$ **2.** $\frac{2}{3} \times 6$ **3.** $\frac{4}{5} \cdot \frac{1}{4}$

4. $8 \cdot \frac{1}{8}$ **5.** $\frac{1}{3}$ of $\frac{3}{7}$ **6.** $\frac{10}{11} \cdot \frac{2}{5}$

New Vocabulary • reciprocal

Interactive lesson includes instant self-check, tutorials, and activities.

OBJECTIVE 1

Dividing Whole Numbers by Fractions

The numbers $\frac{2}{3}$ and $\frac{3}{2}$ are **reciprocals.** Their product is 1. Notice that the numerators and denominators are switched in fractions that are reciprocals.

Reading Math
Reciprocal comes from a Latin word meaning *alternating.*

1 EXAMPLE Writing a Reciprocal

Write the reciprocal of each number.

a. $\frac{7}{8}$

The reciprocal is $\frac{8}{7}$.

Check $\frac{7}{8} \times \frac{8}{7} = \frac{56}{56}$, or 1

b. 9

Write 9 as $\frac{9}{1}$. The reciprocal is $\frac{1}{9}$.

Check $\frac{9}{1} \times \frac{1}{9} = \frac{9}{9}$, or 1

1 Write the reciprocal of each number.

a. $\frac{3}{4}$ **b.** 7 **c.** $\frac{8}{7}$

To divide by a fraction, multiply by the reciprocal of the fraction. You can remember this by thinking "invert and multiply."

Key Concepts **Dividing Fractions**

Arithmetic	Algebra
$\frac{3}{5} \div \frac{1}{3} = \frac{3}{5} \times \frac{3}{1}$	$\frac{a}{b} \div \frac{c}{d} = \frac{a}{b} \cdot \frac{d}{c}$, where b, c, and d are not 0.

2 EXAMPLE Using Reciprocals to Divide by a Fraction

Find $12 \div \frac{8}{9}$.

$12 \div \frac{8}{9} = 12 \times \frac{9}{8}$ ← Multiply 12 by $\frac{9}{8}$, the reciprocal of $\frac{8}{9}$.

$= \frac{12}{1} \times \frac{9}{8}$ ← Write 12 as $\frac{12}{1}$.

$= \frac{^{3}\cancel{12}}{1} \times \frac{9}{\cancel{8}_{2}}$ ← Divide 12 and 8 by their GCF, 4.

$= \frac{27}{2}$ ← Multiply.

$= 13\frac{1}{2}$ ← Write as a mixed number.

Check Understanding 2 Find each quotient.

a. $8 \div \frac{3}{4}$ b. $7 \div \frac{2}{9}$ c. $12 \div \frac{8}{7}$

OBJECTIVE

2 Dividing Fractions by Fractions

In the diagram at the right, a rectangle is divided into seven pieces. There are two groups of $\frac{3}{7}$ in $\frac{6}{7}$.

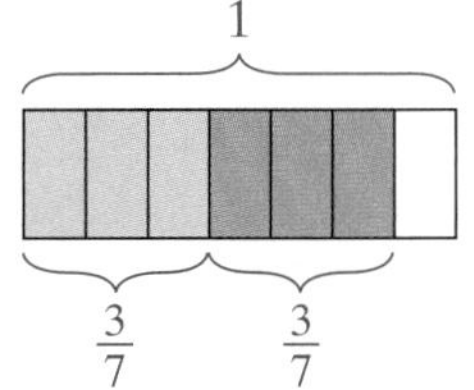

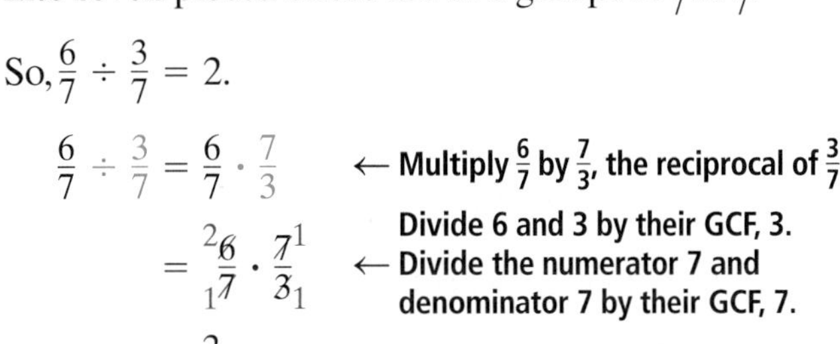

So, $\frac{6}{7} \div \frac{3}{7} = 2$.

$\frac{6}{7} \div \frac{3}{7} = \frac{6}{7} \cdot \frac{7}{3}$ ← Multiply $\frac{6}{7}$ by $\frac{7}{3}$, the reciprocal of $\frac{3}{7}$.

$= \frac{^{2}\cancel{6}}{_{1}\cancel{7}} \cdot \frac{\cancel{7}^{1}}{\cancel{3}_{1}}$ ← Divide 6 and 3 by their GCF, 3. Divide the numerator 7 and denominator 7 by their GCF, 7.

$= \frac{2}{1}$, or 2 ← Multiply and simplify.

3 EXAMPLE Dividing a Fraction by a Fraction

Find $\frac{5}{10} \div \frac{5}{6}$.

$\frac{5}{10} \div \frac{5}{6} = \frac{5}{10} \times \frac{6}{5}$ ← Multiply by $\frac{6}{5}$, the reciprocal of $\frac{5}{6}$.

$= \frac{^{1}\cancel{5}}{_{5}\cancel{10}} \times \frac{\cancel{6}^{3}}{\cancel{5}_{1}}$ ← Divide 5 and 5 by their GCF, 5. Divide 10 and 6 by their GCF, 2.

$= \frac{3}{5}$ ← Multiply.

Check Understanding 3 Find each quotient.

a. $\frac{9}{16} \div \frac{3}{4}$ b. $\frac{5}{8} \div \frac{5}{6}$ c. $\frac{8}{15} \div \frac{2}{3}$

d. **Number Sense** Without dividing, how can you tell whether $\frac{2}{3} \div \frac{1}{4}$ is greater than or less than 2?

To divide a fraction by a whole number, first write the whole number as an improper fraction with a denominator of 1.

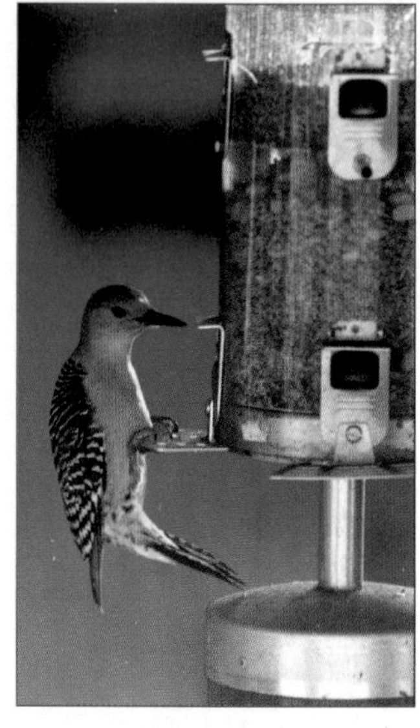

4 EXAMPLE Dividing a Fraction by a Whole Number 

Feeding Birds Suppose you plan to put the same amount of seed in three feeders. You have $\frac{7}{8}$ pound of seed. How much seed will each feeder get?

The $\frac{7}{8}$ pound of seed must be distributed evenly among three feeders, so divide $\frac{7}{8}$ by 3.

$\frac{7}{8} \div 3 = \frac{7}{8} \div \frac{3}{1}$ ← **Write 3 as $\frac{3}{1}$.**

$= \frac{7}{8} \times \frac{1}{3}$ ← **Multiply by $\frac{1}{3}$, the reciprocal of $\frac{3}{1}$.**

$= \frac{7}{24}$ ← **Multiply.**

Each feeder will get $\frac{7}{24}$ pound of seed.

Check Understanding 4 Find each quotient. **a.** $\frac{3}{8} \div 12$ **b.** $\frac{11}{15} \div 110$

c. Your art teacher must cut $\frac{5}{6}$ yard of fabric into five equal pieces for his students. How much fabric does each student get?

EXERCISES

 For more practice, see *Extra Practice*.

A Practice by Example

Write the reciprocal of each number.

Example 1 (page 230)

1. $\frac{2}{5}$ **2.** $\frac{1}{7}$ **3.** 11 **4.** $\frac{5}{3}$ **5.** $\frac{4}{11}$

Example 2 (page 231)

Find each quotient. Exercise 6 has been started for you.

6. $5 \div \frac{3}{8} = 5 \times \frac{8}{3}$ **7.** $4 \div \frac{3}{5}$ **8.** $5 \div \frac{5}{16}$

9. $7 \div \frac{3}{5}$ **10.** $9 \div \frac{4}{9}$ **11.** $6 \div \frac{2}{5}$ **12.** $8 \div \frac{3}{7}$

Example 3 (page 231)

13. $\frac{8}{9} \div \frac{1}{3}$ **14.** $\frac{1}{4} \div \frac{1}{4}$ **15.** $\frac{11}{2} \div \frac{3}{4}$ **16.** $\frac{1}{5} \div \frac{1}{4}$

17. $\frac{4}{9} \div \frac{2}{3}$ **18.** $\frac{9}{2} \div \frac{1}{2}$ **19.** $\frac{8}{9} \div \frac{4}{5}$ **20.** $\frac{3}{4} \div \frac{1}{8}$

Example 4 (page 232)

21. $\frac{3}{4} \div 3$ **22.** $\frac{1}{2} \div 5$ **23.** $\frac{11}{3} \div 4$ **24.** $\frac{5}{12} \div 15$

25. **Construction** Sam has $\frac{3}{4}$ ton of stones to divide evenly among four sidewalks. How much stone will be used in each sidewalk?

B Apply Your Skills

Find each quotient.

26. $\frac{4}{3} \div \frac{5}{3}$ **27.** $11 \div \frac{121}{10}$ **28.** $\frac{9}{8} \div 4$ **29.** $\frac{11}{9} \div 3$

30. $2 \div \frac{9}{7}$ **31.** $\frac{5}{3} \div \frac{4}{3}$ **32.** $\frac{15}{8} \div \frac{9}{5}$ **33.** $8 \div \frac{15}{6}$

Geography **Use the table at the right.**

Country	Portion of South America's Population
Brazil	$\frac{1}{2}$
Colombia	$\frac{1}{8}$
Argentina	$\frac{1}{10}$
Peru	$\frac{3}{40}$

34. About how many times more people live in Argentina than in Peru?

35. About how many times more people live in Brazil than in Colombia?

36. The population of Brasilia, the capital of Brazil, is about $\frac{1}{85}$ of the population of Brazil. What fraction of the total population of South America lives in Brasilia?

Algebra **Evaluate each expression for $x = \frac{5}{6}$ and $n = 3$.**

37. $30 \div x$ **38.** $\frac{3}{5} \div x$ **39.** $x \div 2$

40. $\frac{n}{5} \div \frac{1}{3}$ **41.** $\frac{51}{16} \div n$ **42.** $\frac{1}{3} \div \frac{5}{n}$

43. **Error Analysis** Explain and correct the error in the work at the right.

$$\frac{11}{9} \div \frac{2}{3} = \frac{{}^{3}9}{11} \times \frac{2}{3_{1}} = \frac{6}{11}$$

> **Writing in Math**
> For help with writing to explain, as in Exercise 43, see p. 235.

44. **Measurement** How many $\frac{1}{4}$ inches are in $\frac{1}{2}$ foot? Draw a diagram that shows the problem and your solution.

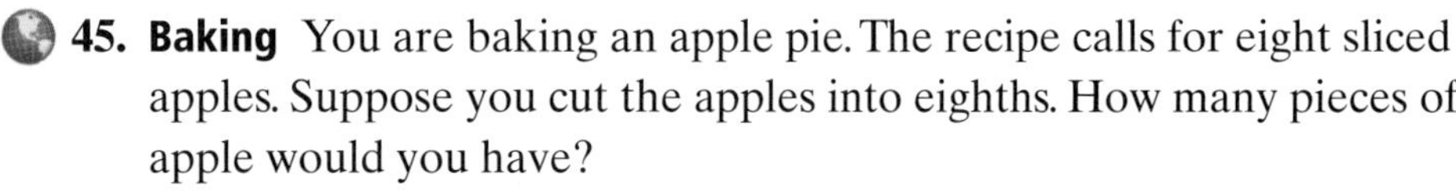

45. **Baking** You are baking an apple pie. The recipe calls for eight sliced apples. Suppose you cut the apples into eighths. How many pieces of apple would you have?

46. **Writing in Math** How are dividing by 2 and dividing by $\frac{1}{2}$ different? Include a diagram.

Find the number that completes each equation.

47. $\frac{3}{2} \div \frac{1}{2} = \blacksquare$ **48.** $\frac{3}{2} \div \blacksquare = 3$ **49.** $\frac{3}{2} \div \blacksquare = \frac{3}{4}$

50. **Baking** A recipe for a loaf of banana bread requires $\frac{2}{3}$ cup of vegetable oil. You have 3 cups of oil but need 1 cup for a different recipe. How many loaves of banana bread can you make with the rest of the oil?

Challenge

Simplify each expression.

51. $\left(\frac{2}{7} \times \frac{2}{7}\right) \div \frac{2}{7}$ **52.** $\left(\frac{2}{7}\right)^2 \div \frac{2}{7}$ **53.** $\left(\frac{2}{7}\right)^2 \div 2^2$ **54.** $\left(\frac{2}{7}\right)^2 \div \left(\frac{1}{7}\right)^2$

55. **Stretch Your Thinking** The numerator of a fraction is a two-digit prime number. The denominator is four more than the numerator. Three of the digits are the same prime number. What is the fraction?

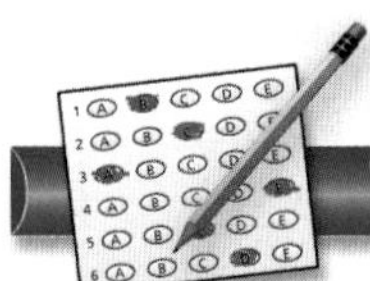

Test Prep

Multiple Choice

The table shows the different weights of the same object on Earth, on the moon, and on Venus.

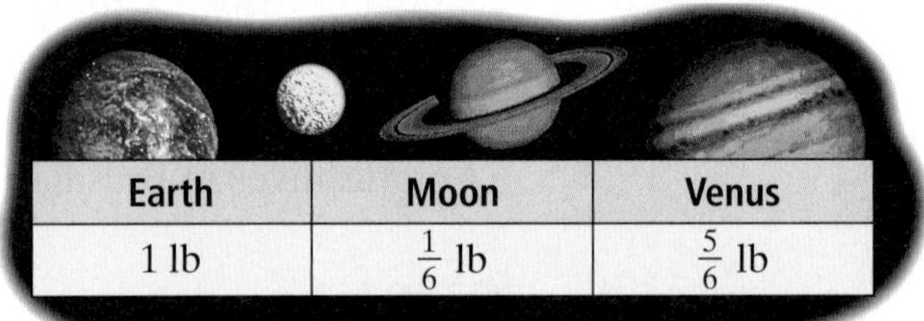

Earth	Moon	Venus
1 lb	$\frac{1}{6}$ lb	$\frac{5}{6}$ lb

56. How many pounds would a 186-pound astronaut weigh on Venus?
A. 31 **B.** 155 **C.** 186 **D.** 365

Take It to the NET
Online lesson quiz at
www.PHSchool.com
Web Code: aaa-0503

57. Suppose you weigh *m* pounds on the moon. Which expression represents your weight on Venus?
F. $\frac{1}{5}m$ **G.** $1\frac{1}{5}m$ **H.** $5m$ **I.** $6m$

58. If Ezra weighs 150 pounds on Earth, what is his weight on the moon?
A. 20 lb **B.** 25 lb **C.** 30 lb **D.** 35 lb

Short Response

59. Jaime bought a carton of juice containing 192 fluid ounces, or 24 cups of juice. **(a)** If a serving is $\frac{3}{4}$ cup, how many servings of juice are in the carton? **(b)** Explain in words how you found your answer.

Mixed Review

Lesson 5-2 **Find each product.**

60. $3\frac{3}{8} \times 2\frac{2}{9}$ **61.** $8\frac{1}{3} \times 2\frac{2}{5}$ **62.** $5\frac{1}{3} \cdot 8\frac{1}{4}$ **63.** $4\frac{1}{2} \cdot 3\frac{1}{3}$

Lesson 3-1 **Test each number for divisibility by 2, 3, 5, 9, or 10.**

64. 1,250 **65.** 372 **66.** 55,600 **67.** 445

Writing in Math

Writing to Explain

For Use With Exercise 43, page 233

In this book, there are many exercises that ask you to give an explanation. When you are asked to explain an error, consider the following:

- Find the error and explain what is wrong.
- Correct the error.
- Check your work, if possible.

On page 233, you will find the following exercise.

43. **Error Analysis** Explain and correct the error in the work at the right.

$$\frac{11}{9} \div \frac{2}{3} = \frac{{}^{3}\cancel{9}}{11} \times \frac{2}{\cancel{3}_1} = \frac{6}{11}$$

Here is one student's response.

The answer must be wrong because $\frac{11}{9}$ is about 1, and there is one group of $\frac{2}{3}$ in 1. ← **Explain what is wrong.**

The divisor is $\frac{2}{3}$. So $\frac{2}{3}$, not $\frac{11}{9}$, should be replaced with its reciprocal. ← **Correct the error.**

$$\frac{11}{9} \div \frac{2}{3} = \frac{11}{{}_{3}\cancel{9}} \times \frac{\cancel{3}^{1}}{2} = \frac{11}{6}, \text{ or } 1\frac{5}{6}$$

Since $1\frac{5}{6}$ is more than 1, this answer makes sense. ← **Check for reasonableness.**

EXERCISES

1. A student has a bottle containing 4 cups of laundry detergent. The student thinks that, if each load of laundry requires $\frac{1}{3}$ cup, then there is enough detergent for $4 \times \frac{1}{3}$, or $\frac{4}{3}$ loads. Explain the error.

2. April rainfall is shown in the table. One person says the total rainfall is $2\left(\frac{3}{10}\right) + \frac{2}{5} + 1\frac{1}{10} = 3\frac{8}{10}$, or $3\frac{4}{5}$ inches. Explain the error.

April 7	$\frac{3}{10}$ inch
April 8	$\frac{3}{10}$ inch
April 12	$\frac{2}{5}$ inch
April 19	$1\frac{1}{2}$ inches

3. A student solves $10 \div \frac{5}{3}$ by finding $\frac{1}{10} \times \frac{3}{5}$. Her answer is $\frac{3}{50}$. Explain the error, and find the correct answer.

4. A model airplane sits on a base that is $19\frac{11}{16}$ inches by $10\frac{7}{8}$ inches. One estimate of the area of the base is 190 square inches. Why is 220 square inches a better estimate?

5-4 Dividing Mixed Numbers

What You'll Learn

To estimate quotients of mixed numbers

To divide mixed numbers

. . . And Why

To solve carpentry problems, as in Example 1

Check Skills You'll Need

For help, go to Lesson 5-3.

Find each quotient.

1. $8 \div \frac{2}{7}$ **2.** $20 \div \frac{6}{7}$ **3.** $\frac{7}{8} \div \frac{3}{1}$

4. $\frac{2}{3} \div 4$ **5.** $\frac{3}{8} \div \frac{2}{5}$ **6.** $\frac{15}{4} \div \frac{11}{8}$

7. Explain what "invert and multiply" means.

Interactive lesson includes instant self-check, tutorials, and activities.

OBJECTIVE 1 Estimating Quotients of Mixed Numbers

To estimate the quotient of two mixed numbers, round each number to the nearest whole number. Then divide.

Real-World Connection

Careers Carpenters use fractions when they measure, estimate, and cut.

1 EXAMPLE Estimating Quotients

Real World

Carpentry Sharon wants to cover a $59\frac{1}{2}$-inch wide wall with narrow wood panels. Each panel is $4\frac{3}{8}$ inches wide. Estimate the number of panels she will need to cover the wall.

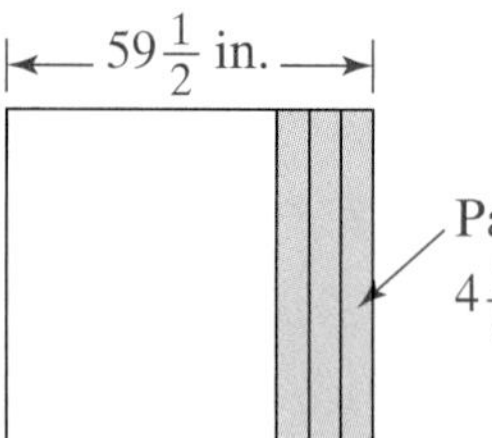

← **Draw a diagram to model the situation.**

$59\frac{1}{2} \div 4\frac{3}{8}$ ← **Round each mixed number to the nearest whole number.**

$\downarrow \quad \downarrow$

$60 \div 4 = 15$ ← **Divide.**

Sharon needs about 15 panels.

Check Understanding 1 Estimate each quotient.

a. $7\frac{2}{5} \div 1\frac{3}{7}$ **b.** $14\frac{9}{16} \div 3\frac{8}{19}$ **c.** $100 \div 9\frac{2}{3}$

d. **Estimation** Suppose the panels are $6\frac{1}{4}$ inches wide in Example 1. Estimate the number of panels needed to cover the $59\frac{1}{2}$-inch wall.

OBJECTIVE

2 Dividing Mixed Numbers

Need Help?
For help in writing mixed numbers as improper fractions, go to Lesson 3-5.

You can divide a mixed number by a whole number or another mixed number. Just as with multiplication, you start by writing the numbers as improper fractions.

2 EXAMPLE Real-World Problem Solving

Baking A baker has $2\frac{1}{4}$ cups of blueberries to make 3 batches of muffins. How many cups of blueberries should he put into each batch?

blueberries ÷ batches ← You need to divide the cups of blueberries by the number of batches.

$2\frac{1}{4} \div 3 = \frac{9}{4} \div \frac{3}{1}$ ← Write the numbers as improper fractions.

$= \frac{9}{4} \times \frac{1}{3}$ ← Multiply by $\frac{1}{3}$, the reciprocal of 3.

$= \frac{^{3}\cancel{9}}{4} \times \frac{1}{\cancel{3}_{1}}$ ← Divide 9 and 3 by their GCF, 3.

$= \frac{3}{4}$ ← Multiply.

Each batch of muffins gets $\frac{3}{4}$ cup of blueberries.

Check for Reasonableness When you estimate $2\frac{1}{4} \div 3$, the result is $2 \div 3$, or $\frac{2}{3}$ cup. So, $\frac{3}{4}$ cup is a reasonable answer.

Check Understanding 2 Suppose the baker has $3\frac{3}{4}$ cups of blueberries. How many cups of blueberries should go in each batch to make 3 batches of muffins?

3 EXAMPLE Dividing Mixed Numbers

Find $10\frac{1}{2} \div 1\frac{3}{4}$.

$10\frac{1}{2} \div 1\frac{3}{4} = \frac{21}{2} \div \frac{7}{4}$ ← Write the mixed numbers as improper fractions.

$= \frac{21}{2} \times \frac{4}{7}$ ← Multiply by $\frac{4}{7}$, the reciprocal of $\frac{7}{4}$.

$= \frac{^{3}\cancel{21}}{_{1}\cancel{2}} \times \frac{\cancel{4}^{2}}{\cancel{7}_{1}}$ ← Divide 21 and 7 by their GCF, 7. Divide 2 and 4 by their GCF, 2.

$= \frac{6}{1}$, or 6 ← Multiply and simplify.

Check Understanding 3 Find each quotient.

a. $7 \div 1\frac{1}{6}$ **b.** $6\frac{5}{6} \div 3\frac{1}{3}$ **c.** $8\frac{3}{4} \div 2\frac{1}{2}$

d. **Number Sense** How can you tell that $2\frac{1}{3} \div 3\frac{1}{2}$ will be less than 1?

EXERCISES

For more practice, see *Extra Practice.*

A Practice by Example

Example 1 (page 236)

Estimate each quotient.

1. $50\frac{1}{4} \div 5\frac{3}{16}$ **2.** $48\frac{8}{10} \div 7\frac{3}{7}$ **3.** $99 \div 8\frac{2}{3}$

4. $21\frac{1}{2} \div 1\frac{9}{16}$ **5.** $100 \div \frac{9}{10}$ **6.** $12 \div 2\frac{3}{10}$

7. Stock Market The price of one technology stock rose $71\frac{5}{8}$ points in $7\frac{1}{2}$ hours. Estimate the number of points gained per hour during that time.

Example 2 (page 237)

Find each quotient. Exercise 8 has been started for you.

8. $4\frac{1}{2} \div 3 = \frac{9}{2} \div \frac{3}{1}$ **9.** $4\frac{3}{4} \div 5$ **10.** $5\frac{1}{10} \div 2$

11. Anatomy An adult's height is about 8 times the length of his or her head. If a man is $6\frac{1}{2}$ feet tall, about how long is his head?

Example 3 (page 237)

Find each quotient. Exercise 12 has been started for you.

12. $3\frac{1}{3} \div 1\frac{1}{2} = \frac{10}{3} \div \frac{3}{2}$ **13.** $7\frac{1}{3} \div 1\frac{5}{6}$ **14.** $3\frac{1}{4} \div 1\frac{1}{2}$

15. $2\frac{1}{2} \div 1\frac{1}{8}$ **16.** $10\frac{1}{3} \div 3\frac{1}{3}$ **17.** $2\frac{1}{10} \div 4\frac{2}{3}$

18. Astronomy Sunlight takes about $8\frac{1}{2}$ minutes to travel approximately 93 million miles from the sun to Earth. About how many miles does light travel in one minute?

B Apply Your Skills

Find each quotient.

19. $2\frac{1}{2} \div 7$ **20.** $4\frac{1}{6} \div \frac{15}{16}$ **21.** $1 \div 4\frac{1}{2}$

22. $8\frac{2}{9} \div 4\frac{2}{3}$ **23.** $5 \div 7\frac{2}{9}$ **24.** $6\frac{4}{5} \div 6\frac{9}{10}$

25. $1\frac{1}{9} \div 6\frac{2}{3}$ **26.** $3\frac{1}{6} \div 2$ **27.** $7\frac{5}{7} \div 10\frac{2}{7}$

28. Data File, p. 217 Look at the records for the 13–14 age group. The boys' record is how many times as long as the girls' record?

29. Construction A ceiling in an attic 24 feet wide needs insulation. Each strip of insulation is $1\frac{1}{3}$ feet wide. Estimate the number of insulation strips needed to fit the width of the attic.

Estimation **Estimate each quotient.**

30. $121 \div 9\frac{7}{8}$ **31.** $210 \div 3\frac{1}{4}$ **32.** $12\frac{5}{8} \div 1\frac{1}{8}$ **33.** $9\frac{21}{32} \div 2\frac{1}{4}$

Real-World Connection

About 30 percent of U.S. households planted flower bulbs in 2001.

34. Gardening A gardener is building a border for a garden with a row of red bricks. The row is $136\frac{1}{2}$ inches long. Each brick is $10\frac{1}{2}$ inches long.
- **a.** How many bricks does the gardener need?
- **b.** If each brick costs $.35, how much will the border cost?

35. Books A bookstore has a shelf that is $37\frac{1}{2}$ inches long. If each book is $1\frac{1}{4}$ inches thick, how many books can fit on the shelf?

Algebra **Evaluate each expression for $y = 3\frac{3}{10}$.**

36. $11 \div y$ **37.** $1\frac{1}{5} \div y$ **38.** $y \div \frac{11}{12}$ **39.** $\frac{11}{12} \div y$

Simplify each expression.

40. $1\frac{2}{3} + \frac{3}{5}$ **41.** $1\frac{2}{3} - \frac{3}{5}$ **42.** $1\frac{2}{3} \times \frac{3}{5}$ **43.** $1\frac{2}{3} \div \frac{3}{5}$

44. Error Analysis At the right is Erica's solution to a division problem. Explain the error in her work and find the correct answer.

Find $7\frac{3}{8} \div 1\frac{1}{5}$.

$7\frac{3}{8} \div 1\frac{1}{5} = \frac{18}{8} \div \frac{6}{5}$

$= \frac{18}{8} \times \frac{5}{6}$

$= \frac{\overset{3}{\cancel{18}}}{8} \times \frac{5}{\underset{1}{\cancel{6}}}$

$\frac{15}{8}$, or $1\frac{7}{8}$

45. a. Find the quotient $8 \div \frac{1}{a}$ for $a = 10, a = 100$, and $a = 10{,}000$.
b. Reasoning Describe the quotient $8 \div \frac{1}{a}$ as a gets larger.

46. Writing in Math Explain how you can use mental math to find $12 \div \frac{1}{5}$.

Find the number that completes each equation.

47. $2\frac{3}{5} \div 2\frac{1}{2} = \blacksquare$ **48.** $2\frac{3}{5} \div \blacksquare = 1$ **49.** $\blacksquare \div \frac{1}{2} = 1\frac{3}{4}$

50. $2\frac{4}{9} \div \blacksquare = 2$ **51.** $\blacksquare \div 2 = 3\frac{1}{8}$ **52.** $4\frac{1}{2} \div 1\frac{1}{3} = \blacksquare$

Challenge

Algebra **Evaluate each expression for $x = 1\frac{1}{3}$.**

53. $(x + x) \div \frac{1}{2}$ **54.** $(x + 1) \div 1\frac{1}{2}$ **55.** $x^2 \div 4$

56. Stretch Your Thinking How many rectangles can you find in the figure at the right?

Test Prep

Reading Comprehension Read the passage and answer the questions below.

What's in a Mile?

In England, farms used to be measured in furlongs. The length of a furlong depended on the distance the horse could drag the plow before needing to rest. The standard length of one furlong is 660 feet. There are 8 furlongs in 1 mile, which is 5,280 feet.

Take It to the NET
Online lesson quiz at **www.PHSchool.com**
Web Code: aaa-0504

57. How many miles are in $5\frac{1}{3}$ furlongs?

58. How many furlongs are in $94\frac{2}{7}$ feet?

59. How many miles are in $18\frac{2}{3}$ furlongs?

Multiple Choice

60. You must cover a $72\frac{3}{8}$-inch wide wall with wood panels. If each panel is $5\frac{5}{8}$ inches wide, about how many panels will you need?
A. 10 **B.** 13 **C.** 15 **D.** 17

Mixed Review

Lesson 4-1 **Estimate each sum or difference.**

61. $5\frac{2}{3} + 2\frac{7}{8}$ **62.** $12\frac{3}{7} - 9\frac{5}{6}$ **63.** $13\frac{6}{17} + 7\frac{2}{11}$ **64.** $4\frac{8}{9} - 4\frac{11}{23}$

Lesson 3-2 **Find the prime factorization of each number.**

65. 144 **66.** 98 **67.** 276 **68.** 5,000

Checkpoint Quiz 1 — Lessons 5-1 through 5-4

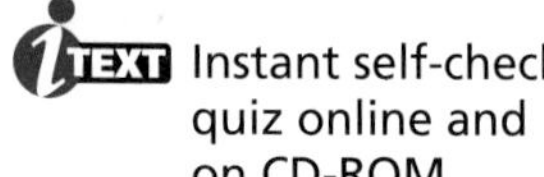

Instant self-check quiz online and on CD-ROM

Find each product or quotient.

1. $\frac{5}{12}$ of 36 **2.** $5\frac{1}{4} \times 4\frac{1}{2}$ **3.** $24 \div \frac{3}{8}$ **4.** $1\frac{1}{9} \div 6\frac{2}{3}$

5. $\frac{2}{7} \cdot 5\frac{1}{3}$ **6.** $2\frac{2}{5} \div 4$ **7.** $8\frac{1}{6} \times 2$ **8.** $7\frac{4}{9} \div 3\frac{1}{3}$

9. How tall is a tree that is 9 times as tall as a $4\frac{1}{3}$-foot sapling?

10. How many $\frac{1}{2}$-inch thick cookies can you slice from 1 foot of dough?

Technology Using a Calculator for Fractions

For Use With Lesson 5-4

Many calculators do not have fraction keys. You can still use a calculator without fraction keys to check your computations with fractions by changing the fractions to decimals. The example below is for a calculator that follows the order of operations.

Round repeating decimals to several decimal places. When you compute with rounded decimals, results may be slightly different.

EXAMPLE Mixed Numbers to Decimals

a. Check $2\frac{3}{8} \times 4\frac{7}{10} = 11\frac{13}{80}$.

Change the fraction part of each mixed number to a decimal by dividing the numerator by the denominator. Then add the whole number.

$2\frac{3}{8}$ $\times$ $4\frac{7}{10}$ $\stackrel{?}{=}$ $11\frac{13}{80}$

2 [+] 3 [÷] 8 [=] 2.375   4 [+] 7 [÷] 10 [=] 4.7   11 [+] 13 [÷] 80 [=] 11.1625

2.375 [×] 4.7 [=] 11.1625 ← **Use a calculator to find 2.375 × 4.7.**

Since $2.375 \div 4.7 = 11.1625$ and $11\frac{13}{80} = 11.1625$, the answer checks.

b. Check $2\frac{2}{7} \div 1\frac{1}{3} = 1\frac{5}{7}$.

Find the decimal equivalent of each fraction to three decimal places.

$2\frac{2}{7}$ $\div$ $1\frac{1}{3}$ $\stackrel{?}{=}$ $1\frac{5}{7}$

2 [+] 2 [÷] 7 [=] 2.285...   1 [+] 1 [÷] 3 [=] 1.333...   1 [+] 5 [÷] 7 [=] 1.714...

2.285 [÷] 1.333 [=] 1.715 ← **Use a calculator to find 2.285 ÷ 1.333.**

Since 1.715 is very close to 1.714, the answer $1\frac{5}{7}$ checks.

EXERCISES

Write a decimal number sentence to check each fraction sentence. Round repeating decimals to three decimal places.

1. $3\frac{1}{5} \times 1\frac{3}{4} = 5\frac{3}{5}$

2. $9\frac{3}{10} - 3\frac{2}{5} = 5\frac{9}{10}$

3. $6\frac{1}{2} \div 1\frac{3}{5} = 4\frac{1}{16}$

4. $2\frac{5}{7} + 7\frac{1}{2} = 10\frac{3}{14}$

5-5 Solving Fraction Equations by Multiplying

Algebra

What You'll Learn

To solve fraction equations

. . . And Why

To solve measurement problems, as in Example 3

Check Skills You'll Need

For help, go to Lesson 5-1.

Find each product.

1. $\frac{1}{3} \times \frac{7}{10}$ **2.** $\frac{2}{3} \cdot \frac{9}{22}$ **3.** $\frac{3}{7} \times \frac{14}{15}$

OBJECTIVE

Interactive lesson includes instant self-check, tutorials, and activities.

1 Solving Fraction Equations

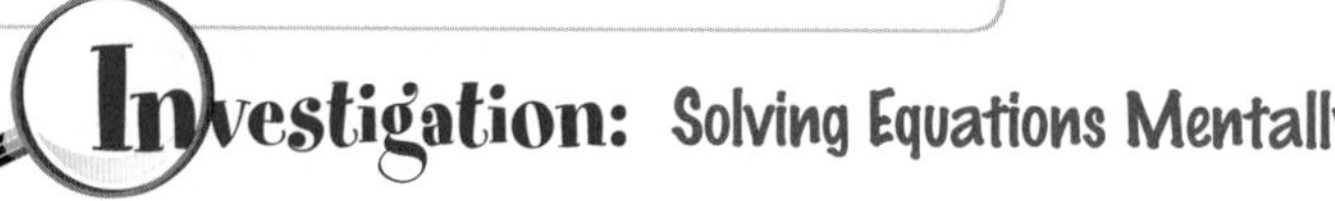

Investigation: Solving Equations Mentally

1. Use mental math to find each numerator.

   a. $\frac{■}{4} = 5$ b. $\frac{■}{3} = 12$ c. $\frac{■}{10} = 10$ d. $\frac{■}{10} = 100$

2. How can you find the value of each numerator from the other two numbers in the equation?

The Multiplication Property of Equality says that multiplying each side of an equation by the same number does not change the equation.

1 EXAMPLE Solving Equations by Multiplying

Solve $\frac{x}{8} = 20$.

$\frac{x}{8} = 20$

$8 \cdot \frac{x}{8} = 8 \cdot 20$ ← **Multiply each side by 8.**

$\frac{^{1}8}{1} \cdot \frac{x}{8_{1}} = 160$ ← **Write 8 as $\frac{8}{1}$. Simplify.**

$\frac{x}{1} = 160$ ← **Multiply the numerators and the denominators.**

$x = 160$ ← **Simplify.**

Check Understanding 1 Solve. **a.** $\frac{x}{2} = 15$ **b.** $\frac{n}{6} = 12$

To solve $\frac{2}{3}x = 8$, multiply each side by $\frac{3}{2}$, since $\frac{3}{2} \cdot \frac{2}{3} = 1$.

2 EXAMPLE Using Reciprocals to Solve Equations

Solve $\frac{2}{3}x = 8$. Check the solution.

$\frac{2}{3}x = 8$

$\frac{3}{2} \cdot \left(\frac{2}{3}x\right) = \frac{3}{2} \cdot (8)$ ← **Multiply each side by $\frac{3}{2}$, the reciprocal of $\frac{2}{3}$.**

$1 \cdot x = 12$ ← **Multiply.**

$x = 12$ ← **Simplify.**

Check $\frac{2}{3}x = 8$ ← **Start with the original equation.**

$\frac{2}{3}(12) \stackrel{?}{=} 8$ ← **Replace *x* with 12.**

$8 = 8$ ✓ ← **The solution checks.**

Check Understanding 2 Solve each equation. Check the solution.

a. $\frac{9}{10}x = 18$ **b.** $\frac{4}{5}x = 20$ **c.** $\frac{7}{8}x = 42$

3 EXAMPLE Writing and Solving Equations

Spelling Bee Students are making banners to support friends in a national spelling bee. They have 6 yards of material. Each banner takes $\frac{5}{8}$ yard of material. How many banners can they make?

Words yards per banner × number of banners = total yards

Let b = number of banners.

Equation $\frac{5}{8} \times b = 6$

$\frac{5}{8}b = 6$ ← **Write the equation.**

$\frac{5}{8}b = \frac{6}{1}$ ← **Write 6 as $\frac{6}{1}$.**

$\frac{8}{5} \cdot \left(\frac{5}{8}b\right) = \frac{8}{5} \cdot \frac{6}{1}$ ← **Multiply each side by $\frac{8}{5}$, the reciprocal of $\frac{5}{8}$.**

$1 \cdot b = \frac{48}{5}$ ← **Multiply.**

$b = 9\frac{4}{5}$ ← **Write as a mixed number.**

The students can make 9 banners.

Real-World Connection

The first national spelling bee was held in 1925. Today more than 10 million students participate in local spelling bees.

3 Beth needs boards that are $\frac{3}{4}$ foot long. She has a board that is 8 feet long. How many $\frac{3}{4}$-foot sections can she cut from it?

EXERCISES

For more practice, see *Extra Practice*.

Practice by Example

Solve each equation. Check the solution.

Example 1 (page 242)

1. $\frac{x}{3} = 12$
2. $\frac{a}{7} = 8$
3. $\frac{j}{12} = 27$
4. $\frac{s}{5} = 35$
5. $\frac{v}{4} = 11$
6. $\frac{p}{9} = 9$
7. $\frac{x}{15} = 3$
8. $\frac{t}{2} = 75$
9. $\frac{r}{12} = 1.5$

Example 2 (page 243)

10. $\frac{1}{2}m = 6$
11. $\frac{2}{3}r = 10$
12. $\frac{3}{5}n = 9$
13. $\frac{7}{8}p = 21$
14. $\frac{4}{5}y = 8$
15. $\frac{5}{9}z = 30$

Example 3 (page 243)

Write an equation for each problem. Then solve the equation.

16. **Costumes** Each ballerina's costume needs $\frac{5}{6}$ yard of ribbon trim. Joy has 9 yards of ribbon. How many costumes can she trim?
17. **Coin Collecting** Gerald's nickel collection weighs $7\frac{1}{2}$ times as much as his brother's nickel collection. If Gerald has 3 pounds of nickels, how many pounds of nickels does his brother have?

Apply Your Skills

Solve each equation. Check the solution.

18. $11 = \frac{x}{5}$
19. $\frac{9}{10}k = 18$
20. $7 = \frac{n}{7}$
21. $\frac{7}{8}b = \frac{1}{2}$
22. $\frac{3}{20}x = 5$
23. $\frac{3}{4}y = \frac{3}{8}$
24. $2\frac{2}{5}p = 10$
25. $\frac{1}{6}m = \frac{3}{20}$
26. $\frac{2}{7}n = \frac{1}{14}$
27. **Writing in Math** In the equation $\frac{3}{5}k = 11$, how can you tell k is greater than 11 without solving?

Write an equation for each problem. Then solve the equation.

28. **Shopping** You buy a shirt and a pair of pants. The price of the shirt is $\frac{5}{6}$ the price of the pants. The shirt costs \$12.50. How much do the pants cost?
29. **Running** Andrew and Keith are training for a marathon. On a given day, Andrew runs 12 miles, which is $\frac{8}{5}$ the distance Keith runs. How far does Keith run?
30. **Architecture** The Sears Tower in Chicago is about 1,450 feet tall, which is $\frac{29}{25}$ as tall as the Empire State Building in New York City. How tall is the Empire State Building?

Travel **Refer to the map.**

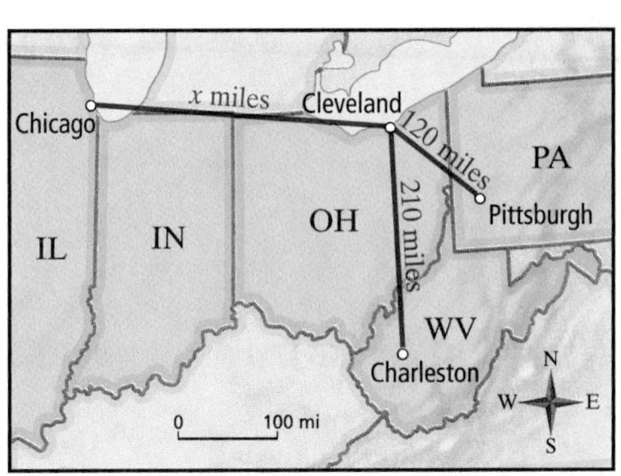

31. The distance from Cleveland to Pittsburgh is about $\frac{2}{5}$ the distance from Cleveland to Chicago. About how far is Cleveland from Chicago?

32. Cleveland to Charleston is about how many times as far as Cleveland to Pittsburgh?

C Challenge

Solve each equation. Check the solution.

33. $\frac{1}{4}w = 2\frac{1}{2}$ **34.** $2\frac{5}{8}y = 10\frac{1}{2}$ **35.** $6\frac{4}{9}p = 9\frac{2}{3}$

36. **Stretch Your Thinking** You have 48 yellow blocks and 40 green blocks. What is the greatest number of identical towers that you can build using all 88 blocks?

Test Prep

Multiple Choice

37. What is the value of x in the equation $\frac{3}{4}x = 12$?
A. 6 **B.** 9 **C.** 16 **D.** 48

38. If $15 = d - 7$, what is the value of $3d$?
F. 8 **G.** 22 **H.** 45 **I.** 66

39. What is the value of t in the equation $\frac{3}{8}t = 6$?
A. $\frac{1}{16}$ **B.** $2\frac{1}{4}$ **C.** 16 **D.** $48\frac{1}{3}$

Short Response

40. Pedro bikes $3\frac{1}{3}$ times as far as Pat, and Pat bikes $\frac{1}{5}$ as far as Jen. **(a)** If Pedro rides 8 miles a day, how far does Jen ride? **(b)** Explain in words how you found your answer.

Mixed Review

Lesson 4-5 **Find each difference.**

41. $15\frac{6}{9} - 13\frac{5}{12}$ **42.** $23\frac{2}{3} - 4\frac{1}{2}$ **43.** $26 - 4\frac{1}{9}$

Lesson 3-8 **Write each decimal as a fraction or mixed number in simplest form.**

44. 0.375 **45.** 0.09 **46.** 2.125

Problem Solving

5-6 Solve a Simpler Problem

What You'll Learn

To solve problems by solving a simpler problem

. . . And Why

To tile a floor, as in Example 1

Check Skills You'll Need

For help, go to Lesson 5-4.

Find each quotient.

1. $5\frac{1}{2} \div 3\frac{2}{3}$ **2.** $1\frac{1}{3} \div 3\frac{3}{5}$ **3.** $18 \div 1\frac{4}{5}$

4. $1\frac{12}{13} \div 2\frac{10}{13}$ **5.** $56 \div 8\frac{3}{4}$ **6.** $4\frac{1}{6} \div 4\frac{6}{11}$

OBJECTIVE

Interactive lesson includes instant self-check, tutorials, and activities.

1 Solving a Simpler Problem

When to Use This Strategy Using simpler numbers can help you develop a plan for solving a difficult problem.

1 EXAMPLE Real-World Problem Solving

$17\frac{1}{2}$ ft

$13\frac{3}{4}$ ft

Tiling You are to tile a $17\frac{1}{2}$-foot by $13\frac{3}{4}$-foot rectangular floor with square tiles $1\frac{1}{4}$-foot on each side. How many tiles do you need?

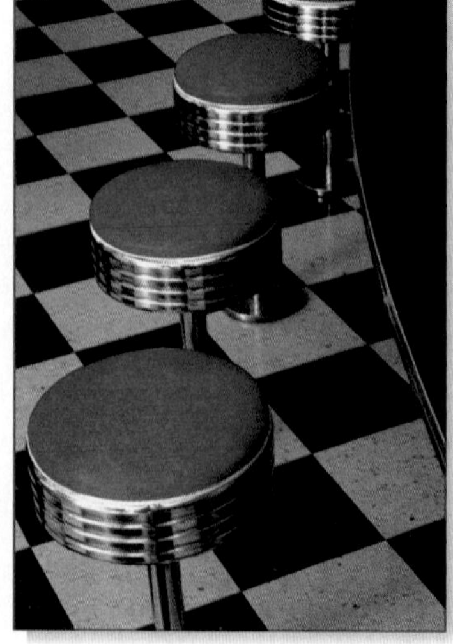

Read and Understand The rectangular floor is $17\frac{1}{2}$ feet long and $13\frac{3}{4}$ feet wide. Each tile is a square with sides $1\frac{1}{4}$ feet long. You must find how many tiles are needed to cover the floor.

Plan and Solve To help you decide how many tiles are needed, ***solve a simpler problem.*** Replace $17\frac{1}{2}$ with 18, $13\frac{3}{4}$ with 14, and $1\frac{1}{4}$ with 1.

Simpler Problem A rectangular floor is 18 feet by 14 feet. How many 1-foot by 1-foot tiles do you need to cover the floor?

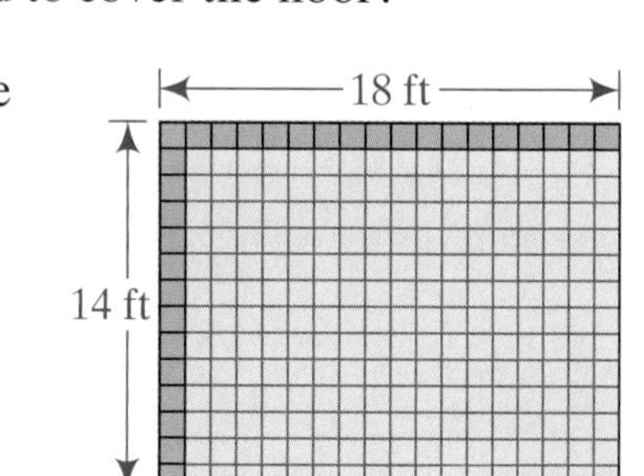

Step 1 For one row of tiles to cover the length of the room, you need

$18 \div 1 = 18$ tiles.

Step 2 For enough rows to cover the width of the room, you need

$14 \div 1 = 14$ rows.

So, you need $14 \times 18 = 252$ tiles.

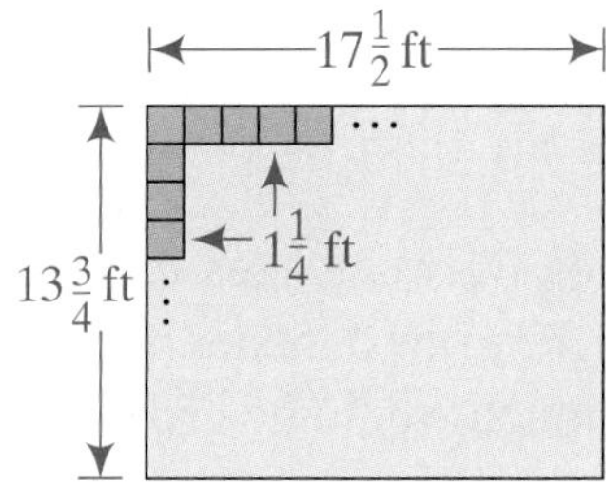

Solving the simpler problem helps you understand what operations and steps to use. Now solve the *original problem,* using the same steps.

Step 1 Divide to find the number of tiles in a row to cover the length of the room.

$$17\frac{1}{2} \div 1\frac{1}{4} = \frac{35}{2} \div \frac{5}{4} = \frac{^{7}\cancel{35}}{_{1}\cancel{2}} \cdot \frac{\cancel{4}^{2}}{\cancel{5}_{1}} = 14 \text{ tiles}$$

Step 2 Divide to find the number of rows to cover the width of the room.

$$13\frac{3}{4} \div 1\frac{1}{4} = \frac{55}{4} \div \frac{5}{4} = \frac{^{11}\cancel{55}}{_{1}\cancel{4}} \cdot \frac{\cancel{4}^{1}}{\cancel{5}_{1}} = 11 \text{ rows}$$

So, the floor will have 11 rows of tiles with 14 tiles per row. You need $11 \times 14 = 154$ tiles.

Look Back and Check The sides of each tile are slightly longer than 1 foot, so you will need fewer than $17\frac{1}{2}$ tiles along the length of the floor and fewer than $13\frac{3}{4}$ tiles along the width. It is reasonable that you need 14 tiles for the length and 11 rows for the width. The answer checks.

Check Understanding 1 Each of 12 people from Company A gives a business card to each of 17 people from Company B. Each person from Company B gives a card to each person from Company A. How many cards are given?

EXERCISES

For more practice, see *Extra Practice.*

A Practice by Example

Example 1 (pages 246–247)

Solve each problem by first solving a simpler problem.

1. On a school day, Jose spends $5\frac{1}{4}$ hours in classes. Each class lasts $\frac{3}{4}$ hour. How many classes does he have?

2. A grandfather clock sounds a chime every 15 minutes. How many times in a 30-day month does the clock chime?

3. **Sewing** A tailor has a section of material that is $28\frac{1}{2}$ feet long. He wants to cut it into pieces that are each $1\frac{1}{2}$ feet long. How many cuts will he have to make?

4. **Decorating** Nadine wants to cover a wall of her dining room with glass tiles. The wall is 8 feet by 8 feet, and the tiles are 16 inches by 16 inches. How many tiles will she need?

5. **Baking** A baking pan of brownies measures 9 inches by 12 inches. How many $1\frac{1}{2}$-inch by $1\frac{1}{2}$-inch brownies can be cut from this batch?

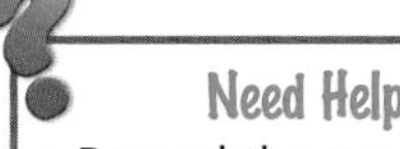

Need Help?
- Reread the problem.
- Identify the key facts and details.
- Tell the problem in your own words.
- Try a different strategy.
- Check your work.

B Apply Your Skills

Strategies

Draw a Diagram
Make a Graph
Make an Organized List
Make a Table and Look for a Pattern
Simulate a Problem
Solve a Simpler Problem
Try, Check, and Revise
Use Logical Reasoning
Work Backward
Write an Equation

Choose a strategy to solve each problem.

6. **Fundraising** The pep club sells shirts with the school logo. The shirts come with long sleeves or short sleeves. The color choices are orange, green, purple, and blue. How many different styles are there?

7. Between the ages of 5 and 10, Brian grew 27 inches. Between ages 10 and 15, he grew 9 inches. Between ages 15 and 20, he grew 3 inches.
   a. If Brian could continue to grow this way, how much would he grow between ages 20 and 25?
   b. At age 5, Brian was 30 inches tall. Based on your answer to part (a), what would his height be at age 25?

5 years 10 years 15 years 20 years

8. Find two consecutive odd numbers whose product is 399. (*Hint*: 11 and 13 are consecutive odd numbers.)

9. **Biology** Two rats, Squeaky and Moe, are running through a 50-foot maze. Both run 10 feet in 10 seconds.
   - Squeaky's path has a food bin every 2 feet. She takes 3 seconds to eat at each bin.
   - Moe's path has a food bin every 5 feet. He takes 5 seconds to eat at each bin.

   a. Which rat will finish first?
   b. **Writing in Math** Explain how you solved this problem.

10. **Estimation** You spend \$12.50 a year for a pass to school events. If you attend 7 events, is your cost more or less than \$1.50 per event?

11. **Weaving** Jamal makes wall hangings and sells them for \$4.95 per square foot. How much will he charge for a 4-foot by 4-foot hanging?

12. **Music** A chorus teacher can arrange singers in rows of 10, 12, or 15 with no one left over. What is the least possible number of singers in the chorus?

13. Roz, David, and Chris all have chores. Roz sets the table every 5 days. David sets the table every day. Chris sets the table every 6 days. On May 9, they all set the table. In which month will they all set the table on the same day next?

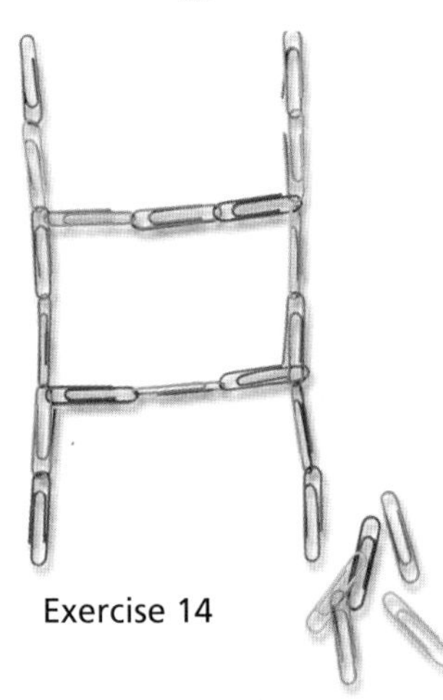

Exercise 14

14. **Crafts** Meghan is making a paper clip ladder like the one at the left. The legs of the ladder must extend above the top rung and below the bottom rung. Each rung is three clips. To make a ladder with 15 rungs, how many paper clips will Meghan need?

15. **Stretch Your Thinking** In a two-digit prime number, the ones digit is four less than its tens digit. The number can be made by reversing the digits of another prime number. What is the number?

Test Prep

Multiple Choice

16. Which of the following is NOT a whole number?

A. $24 \div 8$ B. $24 \div \frac{6}{7}$ C. $24 \div \frac{5}{6}$ D. $24 \div \frac{1}{3}$

17. Which of the following is greater than x for $x > 0$?

F. $x \div \frac{16}{17}$ G. $x \div \frac{112}{97}$ H. $x \div \frac{7}{7}$ I. $x \div 11$

18. If $y = \frac{3}{4}$, which of the following is NOT a whole number?

A. $y \div \frac{1}{8}$ B. $(y + 1) \div 7$ C. $12 \div y$ D. $9 \div \left(y - \frac{1}{2}\right)$

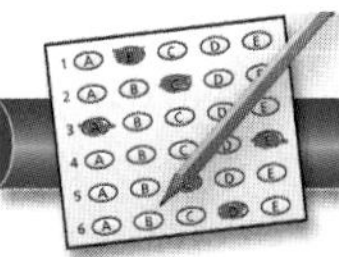

Take It to the NET
Online lesson quiz at **www.PHSchool.com**
Web Code: aaa-0506

19. Which of the following is equivalent to $\frac{9}{8} \div \frac{3}{4}$?

F. $\frac{27}{32}$ G. $\frac{8}{9} \cdot \frac{3}{4}$ H. $\frac{9 \div 4}{8 \div 3}$ I. $\frac{9 \div 3}{8 \div 4}$

Short Response

20. A bus arrives at the bus depot every half-hour from 6:00 A.M. until 7:00 P.M. every day. **(a)** How many times in a week does a bus stop at the depot? **(b)** Explain in words how you found your answer.

Mixed Review

Lesson 4-6

Algebra **Solve each equation.**

21. $x - \frac{1}{2} = 2$
22. $y + \frac{1}{5} = 7$
23. $m - \frac{4}{7} = \frac{8}{21}$
24. $w - \frac{3}{4} = 3\frac{3}{4}$
25. $b + 2\frac{1}{3} = 4\frac{1}{3}$
26. $8\frac{1}{4} + g = 9\frac{1}{2}$

Lesson 3-3

Find the GCF of each set of numbers.

27. 12, 30
28. 75, 50
29. 12, 16
30. 28, 32

5-7 The Customary System

What You'll Learn

To choose an appropriate unit of measurement

. . . And Why

To choose a unit for capacity, as in Example 3

Check Skills You'll Need

For help, go to Lesson 3-7.

Compare each pair of numbers. Use <, =, or >.

1. $\frac{1}{2}$ ■ $\frac{1}{3}$

2. $\frac{5}{6}$ ■ $\frac{5}{7}$

3. 4 ■ $3\frac{1}{4}$

4. 5 ■ $\frac{1}{50}$

5. $\frac{5}{8}$ ■ $\frac{2}{3}$

6. $9\frac{4}{8}$ ■ $9\frac{2}{4}$

TEXT Interactive lesson includes instant self-check, tutorials, and activities.

OBJECTIVE 1 Choosing Appropriate Units of Measurement

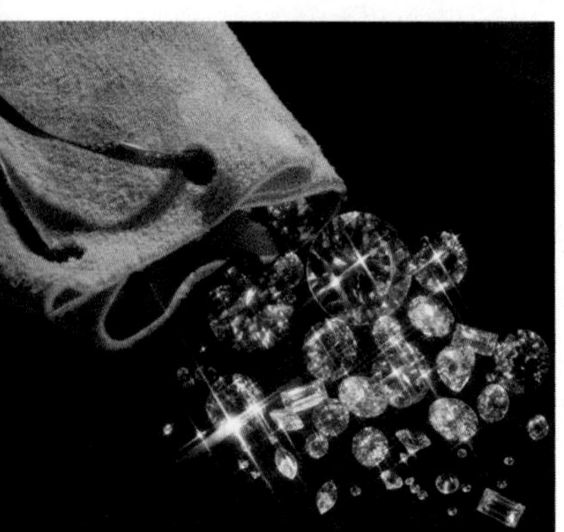

Real-World Connection

There are several kinds of ounces. Jewelers measure the weights of precious stones or metals in troy ounces.

The customary system of measurement was established in 1824. Today, it is still used by the United States and some other countries. Unlike the metric system, the customary system does not use a base unit and prefixes. Each unit has a separate name.

Customary Units of Measure

	Name	Symbol	Approximate Comparison
Length	inch	in.	Length of soda bottle cap
	foot	ft	Length of an adult male's foot
	yard	yd	Length across a door
	mile	mi	Length of 14 football fields
Weight	ounce	oz	Weight of a slice of bread
	pound	lb	Weight of a loaf of bread
	ton	t	Weight of two grand pianos
Capacity	fluid ounce	fl oz	Amount in a mouthful of mouthwash
	cup	c	Amount of milk in a single-serving carton
	pint	pt	Amount in a container of cream
	quart	qt	Amount in a bottle of fruit punch
	gallon	gal	Amount in a large can of paint

You can describe 128 ounces of juice as 16 cups, 8 pints, 4 quarts, or 1 gallon. Usually the most appropriate name is the one with the smallest number.

Quantity	Measurement	Less Helpful Measurement
Weight of a person	160 pounds	2,560 ounces
Distance from home to school	About 1 mile	About 63,360 inches

1 EXAMPLE Choosing a Unit of Length

Flagpoles Choose an appropriate customary unit of measure to describe the height of a flagpole.

The unit "mile" is too large and "inches" is too small. Use feet or yards.

Check Understanding 1 Choose an appropriate unit for each length. Explain.

a. length of a pencil

b. length of an adult whale

c. **Reasoning** Explain why inches are *not* an appropriate unit of measure for the distance from your home to school.

2 EXAMPLE Choosing a Unit of Weight

Ice What customary unit describes the weight of a bag of ice?

The customary units that describe weight are ounces, pounds, and tons. The weight of a bag of ice is best described in pounds.

Check Understanding 2 Choose an appropriate unit for each weight. Explain.

a. weight of a refrigerator

b. weight of an ice cube

You use a unit of capacity to describe amounts of liquid. Some sample units of capacity are shown below.

1 fluid ounce 1 cup 1 pint 1 quart 1 gallon

3 EXAMPLE Choosing a Unit of Capacity

Beverages Choose an appropriate customary unit of measure to describe the amount of lemonade in a pitcher.

The customary units that describe capacity are fluid ounces, cups, pints, quarts, and gallons. The capacity of a pitcher is best described in quarts.

Check Understanding 3 Choose an appropriate unit for each capacity. Explain.

a. gasoline in a tanker truck

b. serving of yogurt

c. water in a bathtub

d. bottle of cough syrup

Investigation: Customary Units

Make a study card for each customary unit found on page 250.

On your card, record the name of the unit, its symbol, and 3 or 4 examples.

pound (lb)
- bag of carrots
- regular size box of cereal
- 3 large apples

EXERCISES

For more practice, see *Extra Practice*.

A Practice by Example

Choose an appropriate unit for each length. Explain.

Example 1 (page 251)

1. length of a back yard
2. distance to the moon
3. length of a car's license plate
4. width of a photograph

Choose an appropriate unit for each weight. Explain.

Example 2 (page 251)

5. bag of oranges
6. package of chewing gum
7. bowling ball
8. pickup truck

Choose an appropriate unit for each capacity. Explain.

Example 3 (page 251)

9. sample-size bottle of shampoo
10. bowl of soup
11. gasoline in a lawnmower
12. tube of toothpaste

B Apply Your Skills

Compare using <, ≈, or >.

13. your shower water ■ 2 pints
14. a raindrop ■ 1 fluid ounce
15. weight of a pencil ■ 6 ounces
16. height of a tree ■ 0.5 mile

17. **Prehistoric Creatures** In 2001, scientists discovered the fossil of a huge crocodile. This crocodile was more than 40 feet long and weighed over 10 tons. A Nile crocodile can weigh $\frac{3}{4}$ ton. How many times as heavy as the Nile crocodile was the prehistoric crocodile?

18. **Writing in Math** What is the difference when you measure in fluid ounces or ounces? Explain.

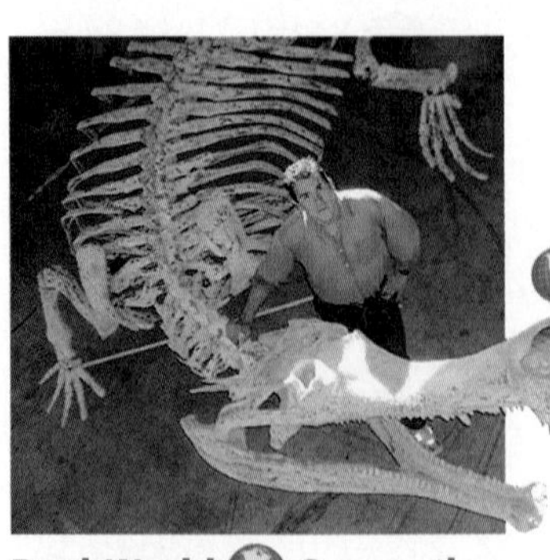

Real-World Connection

This prehistoric crocodile was discovered in Africa.

19. Algebra Jill is 5 feet 1 inch tall. The expression $12x + y$ can be used to find her height in inches. Which variable represents the number of feet? Explain.

20. **Stretch Your Thinking** The product of two mixed numbers x and y is 10. If $x = \blacksquare\frac{2}{3}$ and $y = \blacksquare\frac{3}{4}$, find x and y.

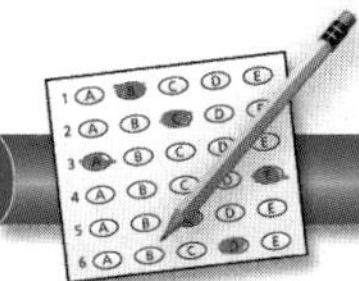

Test Prep

Gridded Response

For gridded responses, write mixed numbers as improper fractions or decimals. For the mixed number $3\frac{4}{5}$, you must grid 19/5 or 3.8. Simplify each expression. Show the answer you would use for a gridded response.

21. $\frac{21}{25} \times \frac{10}{27}$

22. $1\frac{7}{9} \div 5\frac{1}{3}$

23. $4\frac{2}{5} \cdot \frac{2}{11}$

Take It to the NET
Online lesson quiz at
www.PHSchool.com
Web Code: aaa-0507

24. Jai alai is a game played in Cuba, Spain, Mexico, and the United States. The ball, or *pelota,* weighs $4\frac{1}{2}$ ounces. How many ounces are in 16 *pelotas?*

25. Sally plans to make bows from 200 yards of ribbon. If she needs $1\frac{1}{6}$ yards of ribbon for each bow, how many bows can she complete?

Mixed Review

Lesson 5-5

Algebra **Solve each equation. Check the solution.**

26. $\frac{1}{2}x = 36$

27. $\frac{2}{5}z = \frac{8}{15}$

28. $4m = \frac{10}{3}$

Lesson 4-7

Find the elapsed time between each pair of times.

29. 9:30 A.M. and 11:29 A.M.

30. 8:15 A.M. and 2:30 P.M.

Checkpoint Quiz 2 — Lessons 5-5 through 5-7

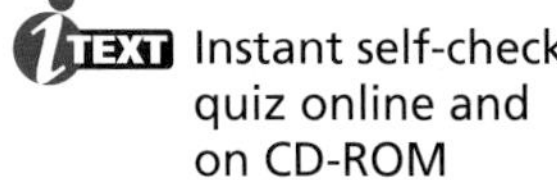

Instant self-check quiz online and on CD-ROM

1. Solve $\frac{2}{3}x = 7$.

2. Solve $\frac{1}{3} = \frac{5}{6}h$.

Choose an appropriate unit for each measurement.

3. distance from school to a park

4. weight of your gym shoes

5. A 25-mile course has markers at the start, the end, and every $\frac{1}{2}$ mile. How many markers are there?

5-8 Changing Units in the Customary System

What You'll Learn

To change units of measurement

To compute with units

. . . And Why

To determine a person's growth, as in Example 3

Check Skills You'll Need

For help, go to Lesson 5-1.

Find each product.

1. $\frac{1}{2} \times 51$ **2.** $\frac{3}{4} \cdot 14$ **3.** $\frac{2}{3} \times 36$

4. $\frac{5}{6} \times \frac{11}{13}$ **5.** $\frac{2}{3} \cdot \frac{9}{16}$ **6.** $\frac{2}{3} \times 1\frac{1}{9}$

7. Draw an area model to find the product $\frac{3}{8} \times \frac{1}{3}$.

OBJECTIVE

Interactive lesson includes instant self-check, tutorials, and activities.

1 Changing Units of Measurement

To solve many problems, you must change units of measurement. To do this, you need to know how the units are related.

Conversions for Customary Units

Length	Weight	Capacity
12 in. = 1 ft	16 oz = 1 lb	8 fl oz = 1 cup
36 in. = 1 yd	2,000 lb = 1 T	2 cups = 1 pt
3 ft = 1 yd		4 cups = 1 qt
5,280 ft = 1 mi		2 pt = 1 qt
		4 qt = 1 gal

1 EXAMPLE Changing Units of Length

Real World

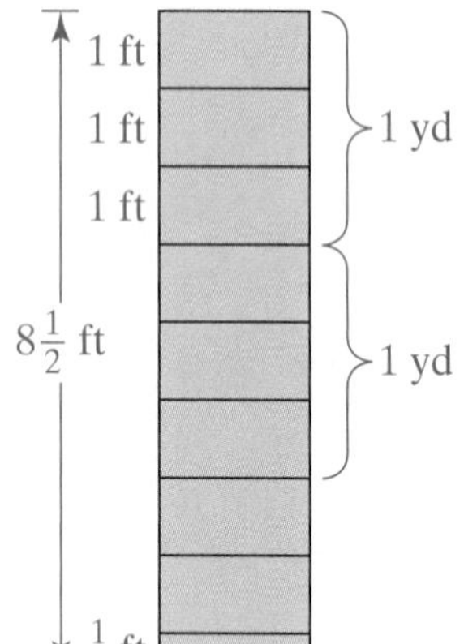

Costume Design Suppose you need $8\frac{1}{2}$ feet of fabric to make a costume. Fabric is sold in yards. How many yards of fabric should you buy?

Since 3 feet = 1 yard, you need to find how many groups of 3 feet there are in $8\frac{1}{2}$ feet. This is shown by the diagram at the left.

$8\frac{1}{2}$ ft $= \left(8\frac{1}{2} \div 3\right)$ yd ← **Divide $8\frac{1}{2}$ by 3.**

$= \left(\frac{17}{2} \times \frac{1}{3}\right)$ yd ← **Multiply by $\frac{1}{3}$, the reciprocal of 3.**

$= \frac{17}{6}$ yd, or $2\frac{5}{6}$ yd

You should buy $2\frac{5}{6}$ yards of fabric.

Check Understanding 1 Complete each statement. **a.** 45 in. = ■ ft **b.** $56\frac{1}{3}$ in. = ■ ft

c. Sewing How many feet of fabric are in $2\frac{1}{2}$ yards of fabric?

In Example 1, the goal was to go from a smaller unit (feet) to a larger unit (yards). To do this, you divided. Here are some rules to keep in mind.

Start With	Convert	Get
Many small units ⟶	Divide ⟶	A few large units
A few large units ⟶	Multiply ⟶	Many small units

2 EXAMPLE Changing Units of Weight and Capacity

a. Find the number of pounds in 28 ounces.

$28 \text{ oz} = (28 \div 16) \text{ lb}$ ← **Divide to go from a smaller unit to a larger unit.**

$= \left(\frac{^7\cancel{28}}{1} \times \frac{1}{\cancel{16}_4}\right) \text{ lb}$ ← **Multiply by 16, the reciprocal of $\frac{1}{16}$.**

$= \frac{7}{4} \text{ lb, or } 1\frac{3}{4} \text{ lb}$ ← **Multiply and simplify.**

b. Find the number of quarts in $2\frac{1}{2}$ gallons.

$2\frac{1}{2} \text{ gal} = \left(2\frac{1}{2} \times 4\right) \text{ qt}$ ← **Multiply to go from a larger unit to a smaller unit.**

$= \left(\frac{9}{_1\cancel{2}} \times \frac{\cancel{4}^2}{1}\right) \text{ qt}$ ← **Write the numbers as improper fractions.**

$= \frac{18}{1} \text{ lb, or } 18 \text{ qt}$ ← **Multiply and simplify.**

Check Understanding 2 Complete each statement. **a.** 13 c = ■ pt **b.** $2\frac{1}{4}$ t = 7 lb

OBJECTIVE 2

Computing With Units

Sometimes you need to rename units before you subtract or after you add.

3 EXAMPLE Computing With Units

Growth At age 12, Robert Wadlow was 6 feet 11 inches tall. At age 19, he was 8 feet 7 inches tall. How much did he grow from age 12 to age 19?

Think: 8 ft 7 in. = 7 ft + 1 ft + 7 in. ← **Write 8 ft as 7 ft + 1 ft.**

= 7 ft + 12 in. + 7 in. ← **Rename 1 ft as 12 in.**

= 7 ft 19 in. ← **Combine 12 in. and 7 in.**

Now subtract:

$$\begin{array}{r} 8 \text{ ft } \ 7 \text{ in.} \\ -\ 6 \text{ ft } 11 \text{ in.} \\ \hline \end{array} \rightarrow \begin{array}{r} 7 \text{ ft } 19 \text{ in.} \\ -\ 6 \text{ ft } 11 \text{ in.} \\ \hline 1 \text{ ft } \ 8 \text{ in.} \end{array}$$

Robert grew 1 foot 8 inches between the ages of 12 and 19.

Check Understanding 3 Your baby cousin was 6 pounds 8 ounces at birth. She gained 1 pound 9 ounces. How much does she weigh now?

EXERCISES

For more practice, see *Extra Practice*.

A Practice by Example

Examples 1, 2 (pages 254, 255)

Complete each statement.

1. 6 lb = ■ oz

2. 3 mi = ■ ft

3. $5\frac{1}{2}$ ft = ■ in.

4. 5,500 lb = ■ t

5. $27\frac{1}{4}$ c = ■ pt

6. 40 in. = ■ ft

7. Nature In parts of Alaska, moose cause traffic jams. An adult moose weighs about 1,000 pounds. How many tons does an adult moose weigh?

Example 3 (page 255)

Add or subtract.

8. 6 gal 3 qt + 4 gal 1 qt

9. 4 ft 10 in. + 1 ft 9 in.

10. 8 qt 1 pt − 6 qt 1 pt

11. Maria bought 2 pounds of ricotta cheese. She used 15 ounces to make manicotti. How much does she have left to make a ricotta cheese pie?

B Apply Your Skills

Use <, =, or > to complete each statement.

12. 91 in. ■ 8 ft

13. $3\frac{1}{2}$ lb ■ 56 oz

14. $1\frac{1}{2}$ t ■ 4,000 lb

15. 3 lb ■ 50 oz

16. 18 fl oz ■ 2 c

17. 4 ft ■ 66 in.

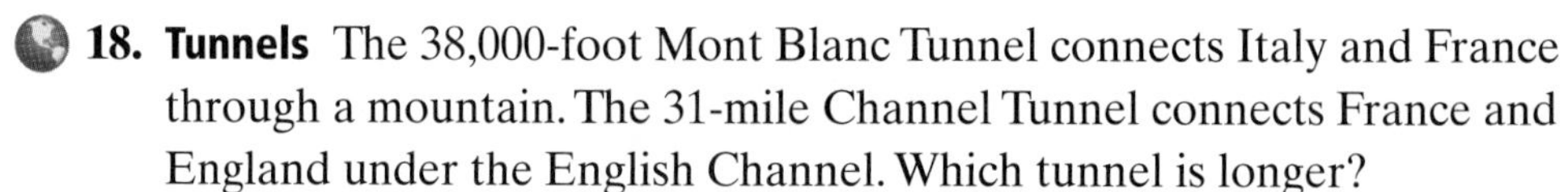

18. Tunnels The 38,000-foot Mont Blanc Tunnel connects Italy and France through a mountain. The 31-mile Channel Tunnel connects France and England under the English Channel. Which tunnel is longer?

19. Writing in Math Describe a situation in daily life in which you need to change from one unit of measure to another.

Complete each statement.

20. 42 in. = ■ ft

21. 30,000 lb = ■ t

22. 105,600 ft = ■ mi

23. $4\frac{1}{4}$ pt = ■ fl oz

24. 880 yd = ■ mi

25. $3\frac{1}{2}$ yd = ■ in.

26. Data File, p. 217 How much farther in inches would the 15–16-year-old Junior Olympic record holder for boys need to jump to match the world record of $29\frac{3}{8}$ feet?

27. Costume Design A costume designer is making a costume for a figure skater. To make the legs, she needs two strips of fabric that are each 34 inches long. How many yards of fabric does she need to make the legs?

Real-World Connection

Careers Costume designers use measurements involving mixed numbers.

C Challenge

Add or subtract.

28. 6 yd 1 ft 7 in. + 1 ft 11 in.

29. 8 gal 5 fl oz − 3 c 7 fl oz

30. 2 t − 15 lb 8 oz

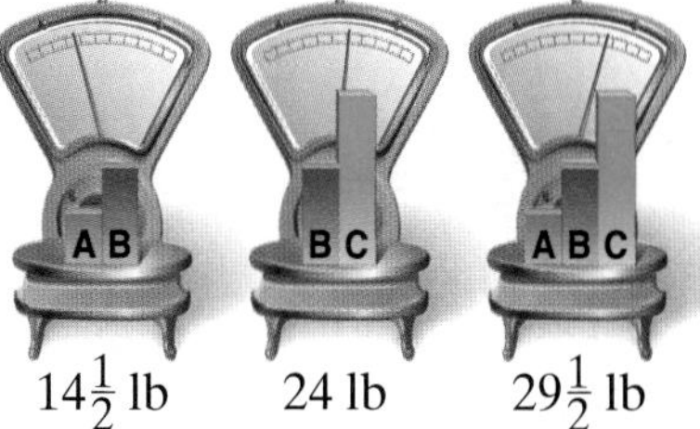

31. Stretch Your Thinking Use the drawings to find the weight of each block.

32. Algebra The equation $3x = y$ can be used to convert feet to yards or yards to feet. Which variable is feet and which is yards? Explain.

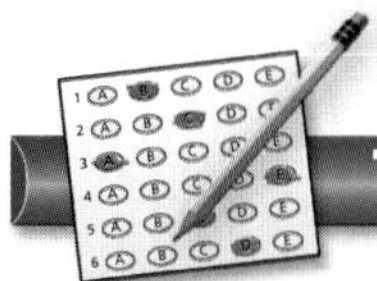

Test Prep

Reading Comprehension

Read the passage and answer the questions below.

Latest News From the American Heart Association

The American Heart Association recommends that an adult eat about 6 ounces of cooked poultry, fish, or lean red meat each day.

Meat, fish, and poultry are the major contributors of iron, zinc, and B vitamins in most American diets.

Take It to the NET
Online lesson quiz at
www.PHSchool.com
Web Code: aaa-0508

33. What is the weight of a single serving of red meat in pounds?

34. Five adults share a $2\frac{1}{2}$-pound roast chicken for dinner. Each adult eats about the same amount. Should they eat the whole chicken? Explain in words how you found your answer.

Mixed Review

Lesson 4-5

Write each difference in simplest form.

35. $8\frac{4}{7} - 3\frac{5}{14}$

36. $4\frac{3}{8} - 1\frac{5}{16}$

37. $7\frac{2}{9} - 5\frac{5}{6}$

Lesson 3-5

Write each improper fraction as a mixed number in simplest form.

38. $\frac{49}{5}$

39. $\frac{17}{3}$

40. $\frac{49}{6}$

41. $\frac{51}{4}$

Reading Math

Reading Expressions

You usually show fractions in simplest form. Sometimes, a fraction that has not been simplified gives you useful information.

1 EXAMPLE

Suppose you add the lengths of three boards and get $2\frac{4}{12}$, or $2\frac{1}{3}$ feet. Which form, $2\frac{4}{12}$ or $2\frac{1}{3}$, helps you read the answer in feet and inches?

The form $2\frac{4}{12}$ allows you to read the measurement as *2 feet 4 inches* since there are 12 inches in a foot.

2 EXAMPLE

You are shipping four books. Each weighs $1\frac{7}{16}$ pounds.
How should you fill in the shipping information at the right?

Weight of contents: ☐ lb ☐ oz

$4 \cdot 1\frac{7}{16} = \frac{4}{1} \cdot \frac{23}{16}$ ← **Write 4 and $1\frac{7}{16}$ as improper fractions.**

$= \frac{92}{16}$ ← **Multiply.**

$= 5\frac{12}{16}$ ← **Write as a mixed number.**

Weight of contents: [5] lb [12] oz

EXERCISES

For each fraction, tell why the fraction that has not been simplified is useful. You may wish to refer to the table on page 250.

1. $2\frac{12}{36}$ yd **2.** $5\frac{2}{4}$ gal **3.** $7\frac{15}{60}$ min **4.** $5\frac{7}{12}$ ft **5.** $59\frac{32}{100}$ dollars

6. A dram is a measure of weight equal to $\frac{1}{8}$ ounce.

a. What denominator would be useful if you wish to write $5\frac{1}{4}$ ounces as ounces and drams?

b. Write $5\frac{1}{4}$ ounces as ounces and drams.

7. a. A group of students go on a hike. They travel for $1\frac{1}{6}$ hours, take a break, and then continue for $2\frac{1}{10}$ hours. How much time, in hours, do they spend hiking? Write your fraction with a denominator of 60.

b. Write the answer from part (a) so that it can be read as hours and minutes.

Test-Taking Strategies

Eliminating Answers

In a multiple-choice problem, you can often eliminate some of the answer choices.

1 EXAMPLE

Mary jogged $4\frac{1}{2}$ miles. Dan jogged $\frac{2}{3}$ as far as Mary. How far did Dan jog?

A. $\frac{2}{3}$ mile **B.** 3 miles **C.** 6 miles **D.** $6\frac{3}{4}$ miles

- The phrase "$\frac{2}{3}$ as far as Mary" means Dan jogged a shorter distance than Mary. Eliminate choices C and D; they are greater than $4\frac{1}{2}$.
- Dan actually jogged $\frac{2}{3} \times 4\frac{1}{2}$ miles. An estimate that is less than the actual measure is $\frac{1}{2} \times 4$, or 2 miles. Choice A is too small.
- The correct answer is B.

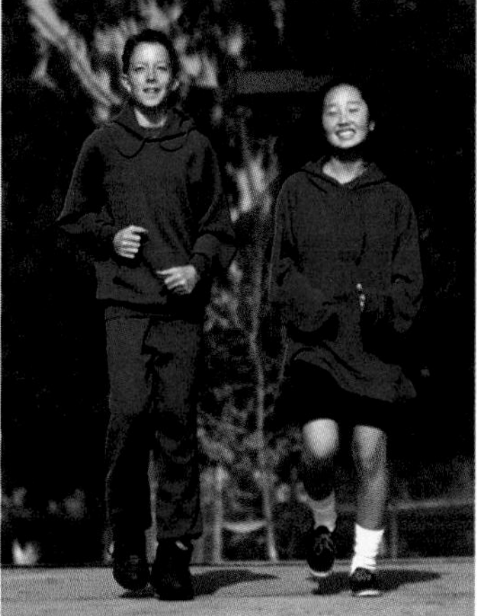

2 EXAMPLE

A truck carries machines that each weigh $\frac{4}{5}$ ton. If the total load is $5\frac{3}{5}$ tons, how many machines are on the truck?

F. 2 machines **G.** 4 machines **H.** 7 machines **I.** 11 machines

- To solve this problem, divide the total weight by the weight of one machine: $5\frac{3}{5} \div \frac{4}{5}$.
- Estimate the quotient: $6 \div 1 = 6$ machines. Eliminate choices F and I, since they are far from the estimate. Eliminate choice G because the answer must be greater than $5\frac{3}{5}$.
- The correct answer must be H.

EXERCISES

Identify two choices you can easily eliminate and explain why.

1. June and Franklin are making posters for the school election. Together they can make a poster in $\frac{3}{4}$ of an hour. How many posters can June make in 6 hours?

   A. 4 posters **B.** 6 posters **C.** 8 posters **D.** 10 posters

2. Mike is planting a garden that is $5\frac{1}{3}$ feet by $6\frac{3}{4}$ feet. What is the area?

   F. $24\frac{1}{3}$ square feet **G.** 30 square feet

   H. 36 square feet **I.** $36\frac{1}{4}$ square feet

Chapter Review

Take It to the NET
Online vocabulary quiz at www.PHSchool.com
Web Code: aaa-0551

Vocabulary

reciprocal (p. 230)

Skills and Concepts

5-1 and 5-2 Objectives

- To multiply two fractions
- To multiply fractions by whole numbers
- To estimate products of mixed numbers
- To multiply mixed numbers

To multiply fractions, multiply the numerators and then multiply the denominators.

To multiply with mixed numbers, first write the mixed numbers as improper fractions. Then multiply the fractions.

Estimate each product.

1. $3\frac{1}{3} \times 4\frac{1}{8}$ **2.** $5\frac{2}{3} \cdot 1\frac{5}{6}$ **3.** $8\frac{3}{8} \times 9\frac{11}{15}$ **4.** $7\frac{10}{23} \cdot 12\frac{3}{16}$

Find each product.

5. $\frac{1}{2} \cdot \frac{3}{5}$ **6.** $\frac{12}{13} \times \frac{1}{18}$ **7.** $\frac{7}{9} \cdot \frac{18}{35}$ **8.** $\frac{5}{8} \times 24$

9. $25 \cdot \frac{7}{10}$ **10.** $5\frac{1}{6} \times \frac{3}{4}$ **11.** $3\frac{1}{3} \times 2\frac{2}{25}$ **12.** $4\frac{5}{11} \cdot 4\frac{9}{14}$

13. Dessert A recipe for fruit salad calls for $\frac{2}{3}$ cup peaches. How many cups of peaches do you need to make $\frac{1}{2}$ of the original recipe?

5-3 and 5-4 Objectives

- To divide whole numbers by fractions
- To divide fractions by fractions
- To estimate quotients of mixed numbers
- To divide mixed numbers

Two numbers are **reciprocals** if their product is 1. The numbers $\frac{2}{3}$ and $\frac{3}{2}$ are reciprocals, as are $\frac{1}{5}$ and 5. To divide by a fraction, multiply by the reciprocal of the fraction.

To divide mixed numbers, first write the numbers as improper fractions. Then multiply by the reciprocal of the divisor.

Estimate each quotient.

14. $2\frac{1}{5} \div 2\frac{1}{3}$ **15.** $8\frac{2}{3} \div 3\frac{2}{11}$ **16.** $12\frac{2}{7} \div 3\frac{5}{9}$ **17.** $13\frac{1}{2} \div 7\frac{5}{16}$

Find each quotient.

18. $8 \div \frac{1}{2}$ **19.** $4 \div \frac{12}{17}$ **20.** $\frac{3}{11} \div \frac{3}{5}$ **21.** $\frac{5}{6} \div \frac{15}{16}$

22. $\frac{4}{7} \div \frac{2}{5}$ **23.** $\frac{18}{25} \div 9$ **24.** $3\frac{3}{4} \div 1\frac{13}{15}$ **25.** $4\frac{1}{7} \div 1\frac{1}{3}$

5-5 Objective

▼ To solve fraction equations

To solve equations in which a variable is multiplied by a fraction, multiply both sides of the equation by the reciprocal of the fraction.

If the variable is multiplied by a mixed number, write the mixed number as an improper fraction. Then solve.

Solve each equation.

26. $\frac{m}{6} = 16$ **27.** $\frac{2}{5}x = 10$ **28.** $\frac{3}{8}k = \frac{3}{4}$ **29.** $\frac{6}{7}y = \frac{9}{14}$

30. $\frac{5}{6}z = 3\frac{1}{3}$ **31.** $\frac{4}{5}w = 1\frac{3}{5}$ **32.** $\frac{2}{3}x = 4\frac{4}{5}$ **33.** $5a = 1\frac{3}{10}$

5-6 Objective

▼ To solve problems by solving a simpler problem

Solving a similar, simpler problem can help you see how to solve a more complicated problem.

Solve the problem by first solving a simpler problem.

34. A fire alarm rings 20 times. It pauses for 1 second between rings. Each ring is 3 seconds long. How long does the ringing last?

5-7 and 5-8 Objectives

▼ To choose an appropriate unit of measurement

▼ To change units of measurement

▼ To compute with units

When trying to decide what unit of measurement to use, first decide whether you are measuring length, weight, or capacity. Then choose the unit in that category that best describes what you are measuring.

These conversions can help you change measurements.

Length	Weight	Capacity
12 inches = 1 foot 3 feet = 1 yard 5,280 feet = 1 mile	16 ounces = 1 pound 2,000 pounds = 1 ton	8 fluid ounces = 1 cup 2 cups = 1 pint 2 pints = 1 quart 4 quarts = 1 gallon

Choose an appropriate unit for each measurement.

35. weight of a car **36.** the capacity of a can of soda

Complete each statement.

37. 880 in. = ▪ ft **38.** $2\frac{1}{2}$ gal = ▪ c **39.** 12,000 lb = ▪ t

Use <, =, or > to complete each statement.

40. 3 yd ▪ 9 ft **41.** 1,800 lb ▪ $\frac{3}{4}$ t **42.** 68 fl oz ▪ 2 qt

Chapter Test

Take It to the NET
Online chapter test at
www.PHSchool.com
Web Code: aaa-0552

Estimate each product.

1. $4\frac{2}{3} \times 1\frac{2}{7}$
2. $5\frac{3}{4} \cdot 7\frac{4}{9}$
3. $2\frac{1}{2} \cdot \frac{11}{19}$
4. $9\frac{1}{8} \times 2\frac{5}{6}$

Find each product.

5. $\frac{3}{8}$ of 32
6. $\frac{5}{6} \cdot \frac{12}{25}$
7. $\frac{7}{9} \cdot 5\frac{4}{7}$
8. $3\frac{1}{3} \times 2\frac{3}{4}$

9. **Cabin Design** A log cabin has walls made up of 12 logs lying horizontally on top of one another. If each log is $\frac{3}{4}$ foot thick, how tall is each wall?

10. Jolene weighs 96 pounds. Jolene's father weighs $1\frac{7}{8}$ as much as she does. How much does her father weigh?

Find each quotient.

11. $15 \div \frac{9}{11}$
12. $\frac{2}{5} \div \frac{8}{25}$
13. $\frac{5}{7} \div 25$
14. $6\frac{3}{4} \div 4\frac{1}{2}$

Estimate each quotient.

15. $10\frac{4}{17} \div 4\frac{5}{9}$
16. $30\frac{2}{7} \div 15\frac{1}{10}$

17. **Encyclopedias** A set of encyclopedias fills a shelf. Each volume is $1\frac{1}{4}$ inches wide and the shelf is $27\frac{1}{2}$ inches long. How many volumes are in the set of encyclopedias?

Solve for *x*.

18. $\frac{1}{3}x = 5$
19. $\frac{2}{3}x = \frac{7}{24}$
20. $\frac{1}{3}x = 3\frac{1}{7}$
21. $\frac{x}{3} = 8$

22. How many miles are in 63,360 inches?

23. How many gallons are in $36\frac{1}{2}$ quarts?

24. Instead of walking from school to the grocery store, Scott walked 2 miles to the video store. His walk was $\frac{5}{6}$ of the distance to the grocery store. How far from school is the grocery store?

25. **a.** What is the area of the square? Use the formula area = side × side.
    b. How many squares with sides of length 2 inches will fill the square?

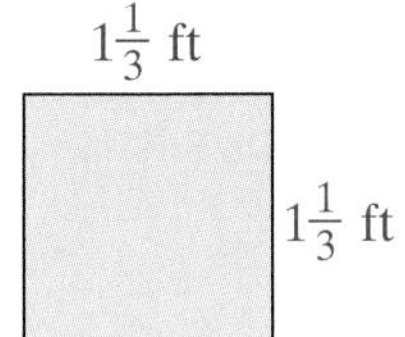

26. There are $1\frac{1}{3}$ times as many women as there are men at a party. If there are 18 men, how many people are at the party?

Complete each statement.

27. $5\frac{3}{4}$ ft = ■ yd
28. 150 lb = ■ oz

Use <, =, or > to complete each statement.

29. 15 qt ■ $3\frac{1}{2}$ gal
30. 16 fl oz ■ 1 pt

31. **Writing in Math** Explain how you can use the Distributive Property to find $7\frac{2}{5} \times 5$.

32. **Match the object in the left column with the most appropriate unit of measurement.**

A. weight of an airplane	I. ounces
B. length of a soccer field	II. pounds
C. amount of water in a bathtub	III. tons
	IV. fluid ounces
D. amount of mouthwash in one mouthful	V. quarts
	VI. gallons
E. weight of a mouse	VII. inches
F. length of a person's foot	VIII. yards
	IX. miles

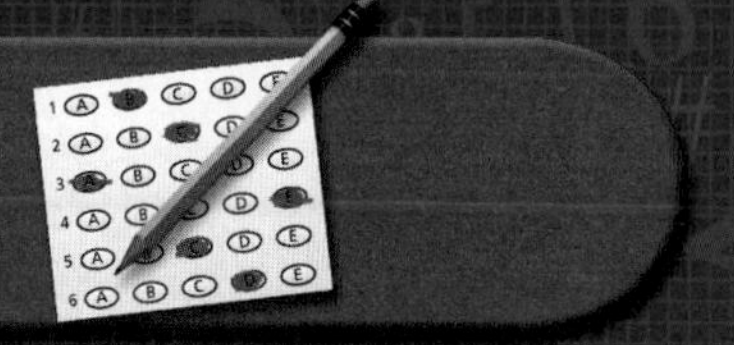

Test Prep

Reading Comprehension **Read each passage and answer the questions that follow.**

In the Dough Here is a recipe for making modeling dough.

1 cup flour	$1\frac{1}{2}$ teaspoons cream of tartar
$\frac{1}{2}$ cup salt	1 tablespoon vegetable oil
1 cup water	a few drops of food coloring

Heat vegetable oil in a pan. Then add the other ingredients. Stir constantly. Let the dough cool. Store in an airtight container.

1. How many cups of flour, salt, and water does the recipe call for?

A. $1\frac{1}{2}$ cups **B.** 2 cups **C.** $2\frac{1}{2}$ cups **D.** $2\frac{3}{4}$ cups

2. Suppose you only have enough flour to make half a batch of dough. How much salt would you need?

F. $\frac{1}{4}$ cup **G.** $\frac{1}{2}$ cup **H.** $\frac{3}{4}$ cup **I.** 1 cup

3. Suppose you only have 1 teaspoon cream of tartar. By what fraction will you need to multiply the other ingredients in order to make dough with the same consistency?

A. $\frac{1}{3}$ **B.** $\frac{1}{2}$ **C.** $\frac{2}{3}$ **D.** $\frac{3}{4}$

4. What fraction of a cup of cream of tartar does the recipe call for? (There are 48 teaspoons in 1 cup.)

F. $\frac{1}{32}$ **G.** $\frac{1}{16}$ **H.** $\frac{1}{3}$ **I.** $\frac{1}{2}$

Video Value Carlos, Lisa, and Lenny found a box of used computer games at a yard sale. Carlos wanted four of the games, Lisa wanted two of them, and Lenny wanted the other six. The price for the box of computer games was $18. They plan to split the cost according to how many games each person wanted.

5. What fraction of the computer games did Lisa pick?

A. $\frac{1}{6}$ **B.** $\frac{1}{4}$ **C.** $\frac{1}{3}$ **D.** $\frac{2}{3}$

6. How much should Lenny pay?

F. $4 **G.** $6 **H.** $9 **I.** $12

7. How much should Lisa pay?

A. $3 **B.** $4 **C.** $6 **D.** $8

8. What fraction of the computer games did Lenny and Carlos pick together?

F. $\frac{2}{3}$ **G.** $\frac{3}{4}$ **H.** $\frac{5}{6}$ **I.** $\frac{7}{8}$

Real-World Snapshots

Swimming to Win

Applying Mixed Numbers Suppose you want to build a set of shelves to hold the trophies and photographs for your school's swim team. Knowing how to work with fractions and mixed numbers can help you design and build shelves.

Put It All Together

1. Suppose you are building a trophy case $36\frac{3}{4}$ inches tall with three evenly spaced shelves each $\frac{3}{4}$ inch thick. Let h represent the height of each shelf. Calculate h.

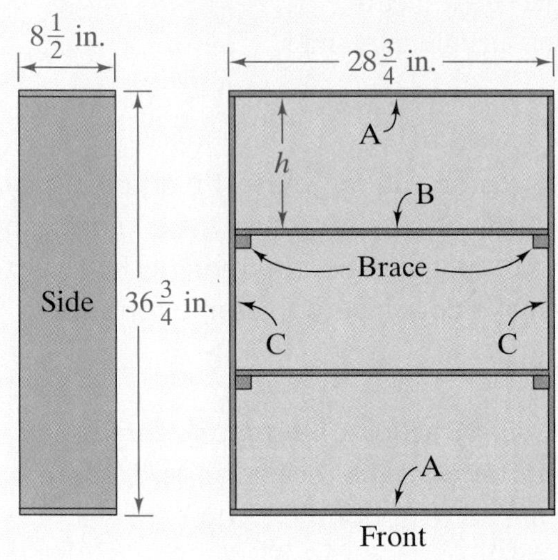

2. Calculate the lengths of each of the boards needed to build the trophy case, including the top and bottom (A), the shelves (B), and the sides (C). Sketch each piece with its dimensions labeled.
3. a. The lumberyard sells boards that are 8 feet long and boards that are 10 feet long. How many 8-foot boards would you need to buy? How many 10-foot boards? Draw a diagram to support your answers.
   b. The price of the lumber is $3.25 per foot. How much would the lumber for the project cost?

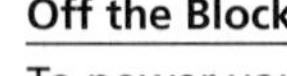

Off the Block

To power your dive off the starting block, grip the block with your hands and toes and put your weight on your back foot. Next, pull hard with your arms and push with your feet.

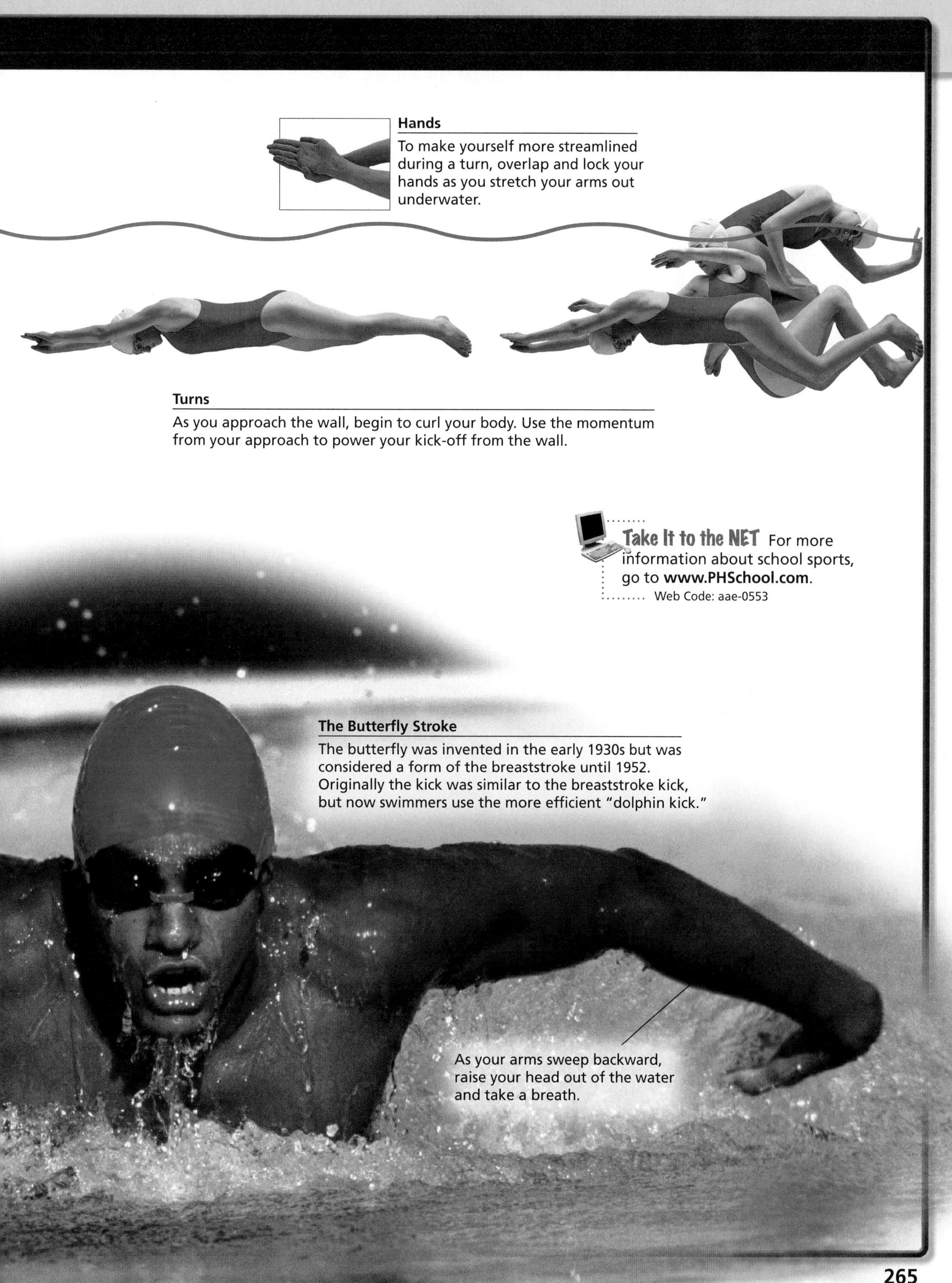
Hands
To make yourself more streamlined during a turn, overlap and lock your hands as you stretch your arms out underwater.
Turns
As you approach the wall, begin to curl your body. Use the momentum from your approach to power your kick-off from the wall.
Take It to the NET For more information about school sports, go to www.PHSchool.com.
Web Code: aae-0553
The Butterfly Stroke
The butterfly was invented in the early 1930s but was considered a form of the breaststroke until 1952. Originally the kick was similar to the breaststroke kick, but now swimmers use the more efficient "dolphin kick."
As your arms sweep backward, raise your head out of the water and take a breath.

CHAPTER 6

Ratios, Proportions, and Percents

Lessons

Key Vocabulary

- cross products (p. 283)
- equal ratios (p. 270)
- percent (p. 294)
- proportion (p. 278)
- rate (p. 273)
- ratio (p. 269)
- scale (p. 288)
- unit price (p. 274)
- unit rate (p. 273)

Real-World Snapshots

Evidence of dinosaurs has been found throughout the world. These dinosaur tracks were discovered in the Painted Desert near Cameron, Arizona. The heights of dinosaurs and other animals are usually proportional to the lengths of their tracks.

Data File Animal Tracks

Animal	Track	Track Size (inches)	Animal Height (feet)
Beaver		7	2 to $3\frac{3}{5}$
Grizzly bear		12	$5\frac{3}{5}$ to $9\frac{1}{5}$
Moose		$6\frac{1}{4}$	$7\frac{9}{10}$ to $10\frac{1}{5}$
Norway rat		$\frac{5}{8}$	$\frac{3}{10}$ to 1
Striped skunk		$1\frac{1}{2}$	$\frac{9}{10}$ to $1\frac{1}{5}$

SOURCE: Mammals of the World

You will use the data above in this chapter:

- p. 271 Lesson 6-1
- p. 291 Lesson 6-5
- p. 302 Lesson 6-7

Real-World Snapshots On pages 316 and 317, you will solve problems involving scale drawings of dinosaurs.

Chapter 6 Preview

Where You've Been

- In Chapter 1, you learned to multiply, compare, order and estimate with decimals.
- In Chapter 3, you learned to write decimals as fractions and fractions as decimals, and to simplify fractions using prime factorization.

Muralists use proportions to enlarge their sketches to create paintings.

Where You're Going

- In Chapter 6, you will write ratios, use unit rates, recognize and solve proportions, and use a scale to determine actual dimensions.
- You will find and estimate percents.
- Applying what you learn, you will use a map to find distances. You will also use proportions to enlarge photo sizes.

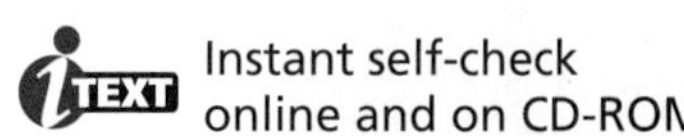

Instant self-check online and on CD-ROM

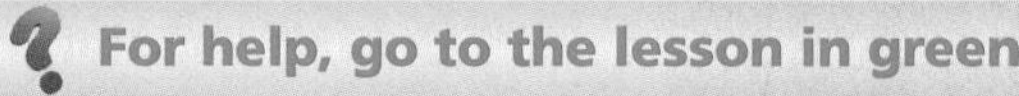

Diagnosing Readiness

For help, go to the lesson in green.

Solving Equations by Multiplying or Dividing (Lesson 2-7)

Solve for n.

1. $n \div 3 = 6$ **2.** $5n = 35$ **3.** $n \div 8 = 6$ **4.** $n \div 11 = 12$

5. $3 \times n = 72$ **6.** $\frac{n}{7} = 6$ **7.** $6n = 54$ **8.** $n \times 4 = 64$

Simplifying Fractions (Lesson 3-4)

Write each fraction in simplest form.

9. $\frac{10}{25}$ **10.** $\frac{20}{44}$ **11.** $\frac{34}{51}$ **12.** $\frac{27}{81}$

Comparing Fractions (Lesson 3-7)

Compare. Use $<$, $=$, or $>$.

13. $\frac{7}{9} \blacksquare \frac{3}{4}$ **14.** $\frac{2}{3} \blacksquare \frac{3}{5}$ **15.** $\frac{12}{9} \blacksquare \frac{12}{15}$ **16.** $\frac{24}{48} \blacksquare \frac{1}{2}$

Multiplying and Dividing Fractions (Lessons 5-1 and 5-3)

Find the product or quotient.

17. $\frac{4}{7} \times \frac{2}{3}$ **18.** $\frac{12}{14} \times \frac{7}{12}$ **19.** $\frac{7}{9} \div \frac{1}{5}$ **20.** $\frac{11}{12} \div \frac{2}{9}$

6-1 Ratios

What You'll Learn

To write ratios

. . . And Why

To compare amounts in a recipe, as in Example 1

Check Skills You'll Need

For help, go to Lesson 3-4.

Write each fraction in simplest form.

1. $\frac{4}{12}$ **2.** $\frac{18}{27}$ **3.** $\frac{14}{63}$ **4.** $\frac{3}{48}$

New Vocabulary • ratio • equal ratios

OBJECTIVE

Interactive lesson includes instant self-check, tutorials, and activities.

1 Writing Ratios

A recipe for 6 cups of party mix calls for 4 cups of cereal and 2 cups of pretzels. You can compare amounts like these using ratios. A **ratio** is a comparison of two numbers by division. Each number in a ratio is called a *term*.

The table below shows three ways to write the ratio of cups of party mix to cups of pretzels. All three ratios are read "six to two."

	Ways to Write a Ratio		
Statement	**In Words**	**With a Symbol**	**As a Fraction**
6 cups party mix to 2 cups pretzels	6 to 2	6 : 2	$\frac{6}{2}$

1 EXAMPLE Three Ways to Write a Ratio

Real World

PARTY MIX
Makes 6 cups
4 cups cereal
2 cups pretzels
3 tbsp Worcestershire sauce

Recipes Use the party-mix recipe at the left. Write each ratio in three ways.

a. amount of cereal to amount of pretzels

The recipe calls for 4 cups of cereal and 2 cups of pretzels.

cereal to pretzels → 4 to 2 or 4:2 or $\frac{4}{2}$

b. amount of cereal to amount of party mix

The recipe calls for 4 cups of cereal and makes 6 cups of party mix.

cereal to party mix → 4 to 6 or 4:6 or $\frac{4}{6}$

Check Understanding 1 Use the recipe in Example 1. Write each ratio in three ways.

a. pretzels to cereal **b.** pretzels to party mix

Two ratios that name the same number are **equal ratios.** You can find equal ratios by multiplying or dividing each term of a ratio by the same nonzero number.

2 EXAMPLE Writing Equal Ratios

Write two different ratios equal to $\frac{4}{6}$.

Two ratios equal to 4:6 are 2:3 and 12:18.

Check Understanding 2 Write two different ratios equal to each ratio.

a. $\frac{10}{35}$ **b.** 12:3 **c.** 8 to 22

d. **Number Sense** Use the definition of ratio to explain why $\frac{9}{5}$ is a ratio but $1\frac{4}{5}$ is not a ratio.

Just as with fractions, you can write ratios in simplest form. Divide the terms of the ratio by their greatest common factor (GCF).

Need Help?
For help finding the greatest common factor (GFC), go to Lesson 3-3.

3 EXAMPLE Ratios in Simplest Form

Write the ratio of bats to balls in simplest form.

There are 8 bats and 12 balls, so the ratio of bats to balls is 8 to 12.

$$\frac{8}{12} \underset{\div 4}{\overset{\div 4}{=}} \frac{2}{3}$$ ← **Write the ratio in simplest form.**

In simplest form, the ratio of bats to balls is 2 to 3.

Check Understanding 3 Write each ratio in simplest form.

a. 4:20 **b.** 50 to 45 **c.** $\frac{39}{3}$

d. Suppose you use 3 cups of popcorn kernels to make 24 quarts of popcorn. Write the ratio of kernels to the amount of popcorn the kernels can make in simplest form.

EXERCISES

For more practice, see *Extra Practice.*

A Practice by Example

Example 1 (page 269)

A drama club sells 35 student tickets, 24 adult tickets, and 11 senior citizen tickets. Write each ratio in three ways.

1. student tickets to adult tickets **2.** adult tickets to senior citizen tickets

3. senior citizen tickets to total number of tickets

Example 2 (page 270)

Write two different ratios equal to each ratio.

4. 6 to 18 **5.** $\frac{4}{14}$ **6.** 8:10 **7.** $\frac{30}{40}$

Example 3 (page 270)

Write each ratio in simplest form.

8. $\frac{6}{15}$ **9.** 40:30 **10.** 42 to 50 **11.** $\frac{14}{42}$

12. 9 to 81 **13.** 75:15 **14.** 8:36 **15.** 18 to 12

B Apply Your Skills

Find the value that makes the ratios equal.

16. 6 to 9, ■ to 3 **17.** 10:1, ■:70 **18.** $\frac{■}{20}$, $\frac{50}{50}$

19. 32:90, 16:■ **20.** $\frac{18}{3}$, $\frac{54}{■}$ **21.** ■ to 25, 9 to 5

22. $\frac{72}{24}$, $\frac{■}{6}$ **23.** ■ to 96, 4 to 6 **24.** 50:150, 75:■

25. **Writing in Math** Explain the steps you would use to rewrite 48:56 as 6:7.

26. **Data File, p. 267** Write the ratio of a striped skunk's track size to a grizzly bear's track size in simplest form.

27. **Cats and Dogs** The average adult cat has 30 teeth. The average adult dog has 42 teeth. Write the ratio of cat's teeth to dog's teeth in simplest form.

Use the picture. Write each ratio in three ways.

28. cups to bowls **29.** coasters to blue cups

30. coasters to cups **31.** yellow cups to blue bowls

32. coasters to total number of items

33. **Open-Ended** Write a ratio of the number of vowels to the number of consonants in your first name.

Challenge

Write each comparison in simplest form. (*Hint:* Use the GCF.)

34. 15 : 10 : 5 **35.** 32 : 20 : 8 **36.** 18 : 30 : 57 **37.** $8x : 16x : 4x$

38. **Stretch Your Thinking** For the figure at the left, which three toothpicks should you remove so that exactly three squares remain?

39. Each digit from 1 through 9 is used once on the left side of this pair of equal ratios. Complete with the missing digits.

$$\frac{9,\blacksquare 76}{\blacksquare 2,34\blacksquare} = \frac{4}{5}$$

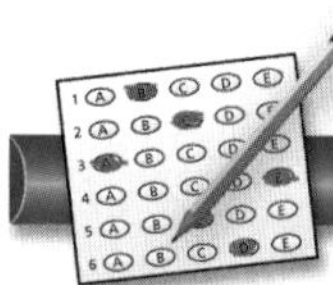

Test Prep

Reading Comprehension Read the passage and answer the questions below. Write each ratio in simplest form.

Sign on the Dotted Line

Autographs from famous people are sometimes worth big money. Stephen King's autograph is worth \$60. Nomar Garciaparra's autograph is worth \$35. Denzel Washington's autograph is worth \$25, and Albert Einstein's autograph is worth \$900.

Button Gwinnett signed the Declaration of Independence, and his autograph recently sold for \$85,000.

Take It to the NET
Online lesson quiz at **www.PHSchool.com**
Web Code: aaa-0601

40. the price of Denzel Washington's autograph to Nomar Garciaparra's

41. the price of Stephen King's autograph to Albert Einstein's

42. the price of Denzel Washington's autograph to Button Gwinnett's

Multiple Choice

43. A bookstore sells 24 paperbacks, 6 hardcovers, 38 magazines, and 5 calendars. What is the ratio of magazines sold to paperbacks sold?

A. 24 : 38 **B.** 19 to 31 **C.** $\frac{19}{12}$ **D.** 12 : 24

Mixed Review

Lesson 5-1 **Write each product in simplest form.**

44. $\frac{2}{5} \times \frac{3}{7}$ **45.** $\frac{3}{4} \times \frac{5}{8}$ **46.** $\frac{1}{6}$ of $\frac{3}{5}$ **47.** $\frac{3}{16} \cdot \frac{16}{21}$

Lesson 4-8 **48.** A garden is enclosed by a fence that has 9 posts on each side. How many posts are there in all?

6-2 Unit Rates

What You'll Learn

 To find unit rates

 To use unit rates

. . . And Why

To compare unit prices, as in Example 3

Check Skills You'll Need

For help, go to Lesson 6-1.

Write each ratio in simplest form.

1. $\frac{48}{12}$
2. $\frac{36}{9}$
3. $\frac{75}{15}$
4. $\frac{42}{7}$
5. $\frac{125}{5}$
6. $\frac{52}{4}$

New Vocabulary
- rate
- unit rate
- unit price

 Interactive lesson includes instant self-check, tutorials, and activities.

OBJECTIVE

1 Finding a Unit Rate

A **rate** is a ratio that compares two quantities measured in different units. The rate $\frac{150 \text{ heartbeats}}{2 \text{ minutes}}$ compares heartbeats to minutes. The rate for one unit of a given quantity is called the **unit rate.**

$$\frac{150 \text{ heartbeats}}{2 \text{ minutes}} \rightarrow 150 \div 2 = 75$$

The unit rate is 75 heartbeats per minute.

Suppose a box of wheat crackers holds 6 servings and has a total of 420 Calories. You want to find the number of Calories in 1 serving.

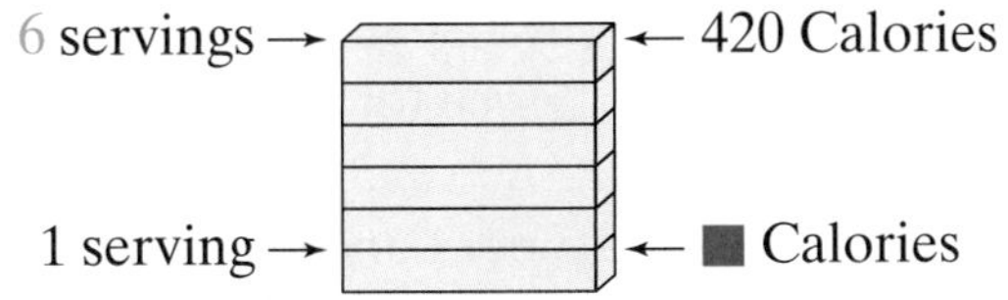

The model shows that total Calories ÷ number of servings = Calories per serving.

1 EXAMPLE Finding a Unit Rate

Find the unit rate for 420 Calories in 6 servings.

$$\frac{\text{Calories} \rightarrow}{\text{servings} \rightarrow} \frac{420}{6} = 70$$ ← Divide the first quantity by the second quantity.

The unit rate is $\frac{70 \text{ Calories}}{1 \text{ serving}}$, or 70 Calories per serving.

Check Understanding 1 Find the unit rate for each situation.

a. 66 pages read in 2 hours

b. \$2.37 for 3 pounds of grapes

c. **Reasoning** Which of the following rates, $\frac{36 \text{ inches}}{3 \text{ feet}}$ or $\frac{12 \text{ inches}}{1 \text{ foot}}$, is a unit rate? Explain how you know.

OBJECTIVE

2 Using Unit Rates

You can use unit rates to solve problems.

2 EXAMPLE Using a Unit Rate

Travel A car travels 25 miles on 1 gallon of gas. How far can the car travel on 8 gallons of gas?

Write the unit rate as a ratio. Then find an equal ratio.

$$\frac{25 \text{ miles}}{1 \text{ gallon}} \overset{\times 8}{=} \frac{200 \text{ miles}}{8 \text{ gallons}}$$ ← **Multiply each term by 8.**

The car can travel 200 miles on 8 gallons of gas.

Check Understanding 2 Write the unit rate as a ratio. Then find an equal ratio.

a. You earn \$5.25 in 1 hour. How much do you earn in 5 hours?

b. You type 25 words in 1 minute. How many words can you type in 10 minutes?

A unit rate that gives the cost per unit is a **unit price.** Unit prices help you compare costs.

3 EXAMPLE Comparing Unit Prices

Comparison Shopping Two sizes of sports drink bottles are shown. Which size is the better buy? Round each unit price to the nearest cent.

Divide to find the unit price for each size.

$$\frac{\text{price} \rightarrow \$1.20}{\text{size} \rightarrow 24 \text{ oz}} = \$.05 \text{ per ounce}$$

$$\frac{\text{price} \rightarrow \$1.29}{\text{size} \rightarrow 32 \text{ oz}} \approx \$.04 \text{ per ounce}$$

The better buy costs less per ounce. Since \$.04 is less than \$.05, the 32-ounce bottle is the better buy.

Check Understanding 3 Find each unit price. Round to the nearest cent. Then determine the better buy.

a. yogurt: 6 ounces for \$.68
32 ounces for \$2.89

b. phone call: 3 minutes for \$.42
15 minutes for \$1.35

c. **Reasoning** Explain how unit pricing helps you compare costs in a grocery store.

EXERCISES

For more practice, see *Extra Practice*.

A Practice by Example

Example 1 (page 273)

Find the unit rate for each situation. Exercise 1 has been started for you.

1. 210 heartbeats in 3 minutes: $\frac{\text{210 heartbeats}}{\text{3 minutes}} \rightarrow 210 \div 3 = \blacksquare$

2. 92 desks in 4 classrooms

3. \$19.50 for 3 T-shirts

4. 45 miles in 5 hours

5. \$29.85 for 3 presents

Example 2 (page 274)

Write the unit rate as a ratio. Then find an equal ratio.

6. The cost is \$6.75 for 1 item. Find the cost of 8 items.

7. There are 3 feet in 1 yard. Find the number of feet in 15 yards.

8. There are 9 players per team. Find the number of players on 7 teams.

9. There are 45 students per bus. Find the number of students on 5 buses.

Example 3 (page 274)

Comparison Shopping Find each unit price. Round to the nearest cent. Then determine the better buy.

10. crackers: 16 ounces for \$2.39
20 ounces for \$3.19

11. bagels: 3 for \$2.85
5 for \$4.00

12. juice: 48 ounces for \$2.07
32 ounces for \$1.64

13. apples: 3 pounds for \$1.89
1 pound for \$.79

B Apply Your Skills

For Exercises 14–18, tell which unit rate is greater.

14. Carlos earns \$44.55 in 9 hours. Maggie earns \$51 in 12 hours.

15. Dylan reads 60 pages in 2 hours. Terry reads 99 pages in 3 hours.

16. Damian types 110 words in 5 minutes. Heather types 208 words in 8 minutes.

17. Janelle bikes 18 miles in 2 hours. Nicole bikes 33 miles in 3 hours.

18. Tanya scores 81 points in 9 games. Todd scores 132 points in 12 games.

19. Jump Rope Crystal jumps 255 times in 3 minutes. The United States record for 11-year-olds is 864 jumps in 3 minutes.

a. Find Crystal's unit rate for jumps per minute.

b. Find the record-holder's unit rate for jumps per minute.

c. How many more times did the record-holder jump per minute?

20. Writing in Math Explain how a car's speed is an example of a unit rate.

Challenge **Air Travel** **A commercial airplane flies 2,750 miles in 5 hours. Find each unit rate. Round your answer to the nearest tenth if necessary.**

21. miles per hour **22.** miles per minute **23.** miles per second

24. **Stretch Your Thinking** Tina is two inches taller than Jay. Tim is 5 inches shorter than Cole. Cole is 1 inch shorter than Tina. Who is shortest?

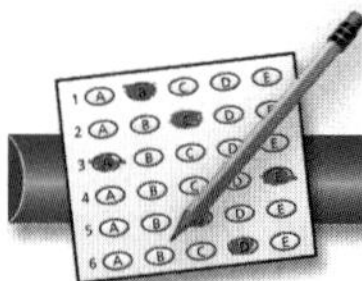

Test Prep

Multiple Choice

25. You earn \$4.75 per hour babysitting. How much will you earn in 4 hours?

A. \$17 **B.** \$18 **C.** \$19 **D.** \$20

26. There are 54 students and 18 computers. What is the unit rate of students to computers?

F. $\frac{\text{6 students}}{\text{2 computers}}$ **G.** $\frac{\text{3 students}}{\text{1 computer}}$ **H.** $\frac{\text{5 students}}{\text{1 computer}}$ **I.** $\frac{\text{1 student}}{\text{5 computers}}$

Take It to the NET
Online lesson quiz at
www.PHSchool.com
Web Code: aaa-0602

27. Which of these is a unit rate?

A. $\frac{\text{3 pages}}{\text{5 minutes}}$ **B.** $\frac{\text{2 miles}}{\text{8 minutes}}$ **C.** $\frac{\$2.00}{\text{1 pound}}$ **D.** $\frac{\text{80 miles}}{\text{90 hours}}$

28. Which is the best buy?

F. \$6.59 for 6 muffins **G.** \$2.00 for 2 muffins
H. \$7.20 for 8 muffins **I.** \$3.00 for 4 muffins

29. The cost for 2 pounds of fish is \$7.98. Which of the following is the unit price of the fish?

A. 1 pound for \$2.99 **B.** 3 pounds for \$11.97
C. 4 pounds for \$19.96 **D.** 5 pounds for \$23.95

Short Response

30. A car travels 279.9 miles on 9.8 gallons of gasoline. **(a)** Estimate the car's miles per gallon. **(b)** Explain how you found your estimate.

Mixed Review

Lesson 5-4 **Find each quotient.**

31. $2\frac{1}{5} \div 1\frac{5}{6}$ **32.** $6\frac{1}{2} \div 2\frac{1}{6}$ **33.** $5\frac{1}{8} \div 2\frac{1}{2}$

34. $4\frac{2}{3} \div 1\frac{3}{4}$ **35.** $6\frac{1}{4} \div 2\frac{1}{2}$ **36.** $2\frac{2}{5} \div 7\frac{1}{5}$

Lesson 5-1 **Find each product.**

37. $\frac{1}{7} \times \frac{1}{2}$ **38.** $\frac{2}{5} \times \frac{4}{5}$ **39.** $\frac{10}{11} \cdot \frac{5}{6}$

Reading a Math Lesson

For Use With Lesson 6-2

When you read a math lesson, keep the purpose in mind. Here are some strategies you can use to help you understand the important ideas of a math lesson.

Focus Before you read a lesson:

- Read the objective headings in the red bars. These headings let you know what topics will be covered.
- Write questions for each objective heading. Ask for information you think is important.

Read When you read a new section:

- Try to answer your questions.
- Ask yourself how the ideas connect with earlier ideas in the book.
- If necessary, read the lesson or section again.

Reflect After you read a section:

- Make up your own example. Explain it to a friend, or write out the explanation.

EXAMPLE

Write questions for the objective headings of Lesson 6-2.

- What is a unit rate?
- How do I find a unit rate?
- How are rates and ratios alike? How are they different?

EXERCISES

1. Answer the questions that were posed for Lesson 6-2 in the example.
2. Look ahead to Lesson 6-3. The title is "Understanding Proportions." The objective headings are "Testing Ratios" and "Completing Proportions."
   a. Write a question for each objective heading.
   b. Read Lesson 6-3. Answer your questions.
   c. How does this lesson relate to any earlier lessons in the book?

Algebra

6-3 Understanding Proportions

What You'll Learn

To test ratios

To complete proportions

. . . And Why

To find driving distances, as in Example 2

Check Skills You'll Need

For help, go to Lesson 3-7.

Compare each pair of fractions using <, =, or >.

1. $\frac{3}{5}$ ■ $\frac{7}{9}$
2. $\frac{1}{3}$ ■ $\frac{5}{15}$
3. $\frac{4}{9}$ ■ $\frac{2}{3}$
4. $\frac{14}{35}$ ■ $\frac{14}{25}$
5. $\frac{8}{48}$ ■ $\frac{1}{8}$
6. $\frac{36}{42}$ ■ $\frac{18}{21}$

New Vocabulary • proportion

 Interactive lesson includes instant self-check, tutorials, and activities.

OBJECTIVE 1

Testing Ratios

Investigation: Using Proportional Reasoning

Suppose you make lemonade by adding a powdered mix to water. The more powdered mix you add, the stronger the lemonade will be.

1. Order these glasses of lemonade from strongest to weakest.
   A. 8 ounces of water 1 scoop of mix **B.** 8 ounces of water 2 scoops of mix **C.** 8 ounces of water $1\frac{1}{2}$ scoops of mix
2. Order these glasses of lemonade from strongest to weakest.
   A. 8 ounces of water 1 scoop of mix **B.** 9 ounces of water 1 scoop of mix **C.** 10 ounces of water 1 scoop of mix
3. Two of the three glasses below have the same strength. Find them, and explain how you know they have the same strength.
   A. 8 ounces of water 1 scoop of mix **B.** 10 ounces of water 1 scoop of mix **C.** 16 ounces of water 2 scoops of mix

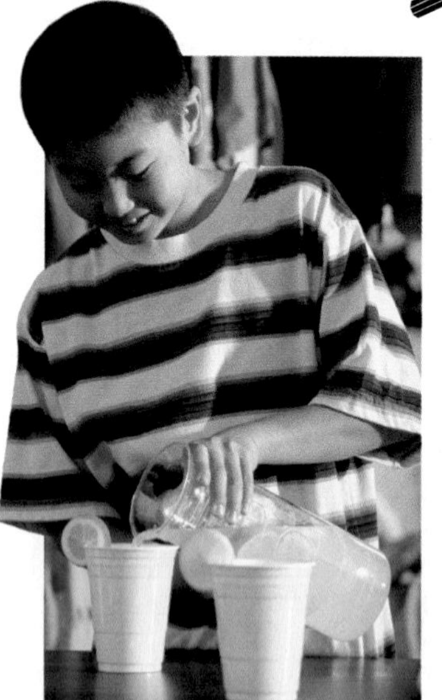

Real-World Connection

You can change the strength of lemonade by adjusting the ratio of water to powdered mix.

When two ratios are equal, you can write them as a proportion.

Key Concepts — Proportions

A **proportion** is an equation stating that two ratios are equal.

Examples:

$\frac{1}{2} = \frac{4}{8}$; $\frac{27}{18} = \frac{9}{6}$

A way to show that two ratios can form a proportion is to show that the ratios are equivalent.

1 EXAMPLE Recognizing Proportions

Do the ratios in each pair form a proportion?

a. $\frac{9}{10}, \frac{27}{30}$

$$\frac{9}{10} \overset{?}{=} \frac{27}{30} \quad (\times 3 \text{ numerator and denominator})$$

$$\frac{9}{10} = \frac{27}{30}$$ ← **Compare ratios.**

$\frac{9}{10}$ and $\frac{27}{30}$ form a proportion.

b. $\frac{72}{81}, \frac{7}{9}$

$$\frac{72}{81} \overset{?}{=} \frac{7}{9} \quad (\div 9)$$ ← **72 ÷ 9 = 8, not 7**

Compare ratios. → $$\frac{72}{81} \neq \frac{7}{9}$$

$\frac{72}{81}$ and $\frac{7}{9}$ do *not* form a proportion.

Check Understanding 1 Do the ratios in each pair form a proportion?

a. $\frac{2}{5}, \frac{8}{20}$ **b.** $\frac{12}{52}, \frac{4}{14}$ **c.** $\frac{8}{5}, \frac{36}{20}$

OBJECTIVE

2 Completing Proportions

You can sometimes use a unit rate to complete a proportion.

2 EXAMPLE Completing a Proportion 

Cars A hybrid car can travel 260 miles using 5 gallons of gas. How many miles can the car travel using 8 gallons of gas?

Write a proportion that compares miles driven to gallons of gas used.

$$\frac{260}{5} = \frac{\blacksquare}{8}$$ (miles → numerators ← miles; gallons → denominators ← gallons)

The denominators 5 and 8 are not easy to relate by multiplication, so find a unit rate for 260 miles and 5 gallons.

$$\frac{260}{5} = \frac{52}{1} \quad (\div 5)$$ ← **Find an equivalent fraction with denominator 1.**

52 miles per gallon × 8 gallons = 416 miles

The car can travel 416 miles using 8 gallons of gas.

Real-World Connection

A hybrid car uses both gas and electricity for fuel. Hybrids were introduced to the U.S. in 1999.

2 Find the value that completes each proportion.

a. $\frac{12}{4} = \frac{\blacksquare}{5}$ **b.** $\frac{3}{9} = \frac{2}{\blacksquare}$

More Than One Way

A package of 50 blank CDs is \$25. However, the store ran out of 50-packs. The manager agrees to sell you packages of 12 at the same unit price. How much should a 12-pack of CDs cost?

Jessica's Method

First I'll set up a proportion.

$$\frac{50 \text{ CDs}}{\$25} = \frac{12 \text{ CDs}}{\blacksquare \text{ dollars}}$$

In the first ratio, I can divide 50 by 2 to get 25. I'll do the same thing to the second ratio.

$$\div 2 \quad \frac{50}{\$25} = \frac{12}{\$6} \quad \div 2$$

A pack of 12 blank CDs should cost \$6.

Michael's Method

I know that \$25 is the cost of a 50-pack of blank CDs. I'll find the unit rate for the cost of one CD.

$$\$25 \div 50 = \$.50$$

Each CD costs \$.50. I'll multiply to find the price of 12 CDs.

$$12 \times \$.50 = \$6$$

A pack of 12 blank CDs should cost \$6.

Choose a Method

An ad says "3 videos for \$18." At the same rate, how much will 5 videos cost? Describe your method, and explain why you chose it.

EXERCISES

For more practice, see *Extra Practice*.

A Practice by Example

Do the ratios in each pair form a proportion?

Example 1 (page 279)

1. $\frac{1}{2}, \frac{50}{100}$ **2.** $\frac{10}{20}, \frac{30}{40}$ **3.** $\frac{4}{12}, \frac{6}{8}$ **4.** $\frac{42}{6}, \frac{504}{72}$

5. $\frac{9}{11}, \frac{63}{77}$ **6.** $\frac{72}{27}, \frac{8}{3}$ **7.** $\frac{16}{27}, \frac{4}{9}$ **8.** $\frac{3}{2}, \frac{22}{16}$

Example 2 (page 279)

Find the value that completes each proportion.

9. $\frac{7}{35} = \frac{21}{\blacksquare}$ **10.** $\frac{12}{4} = \frac{\blacksquare}{28}$ **11.** $\frac{57}{\blacksquare} = \frac{19}{38}$ **12.** $\frac{2}{4} = \frac{\blacksquare}{52}$

13. $\frac{\blacksquare}{20} = \frac{11}{55}$ **14.** $\frac{8}{32} = \frac{\blacksquare}{40}$ **15.** $\frac{\blacksquare}{190} = \frac{3}{114}$ **16.** $\frac{38}{\blacksquare} = \frac{2}{6}$

17. Earth Science A glacier moves about 12 inches every 36 hours. About how far does the glacier move in 90 hours?

B Apply Your Skills

Do the ratios in each pair form a proportion?

18. $\frac{93}{60}, \frac{62}{40}$ **19.** $\frac{18}{9}, \frac{6}{3}$ **20.** $\frac{10}{15}, \frac{3}{5}$ **21.** $\frac{10}{16}, \frac{5}{8}$ **22.** $\frac{24}{54}, \frac{8}{18}$

23. Photos A photo 5 inches wide and 7 inches long is enlarged. The new photo is 10 inches wide. What is the length of the enlarged photo?

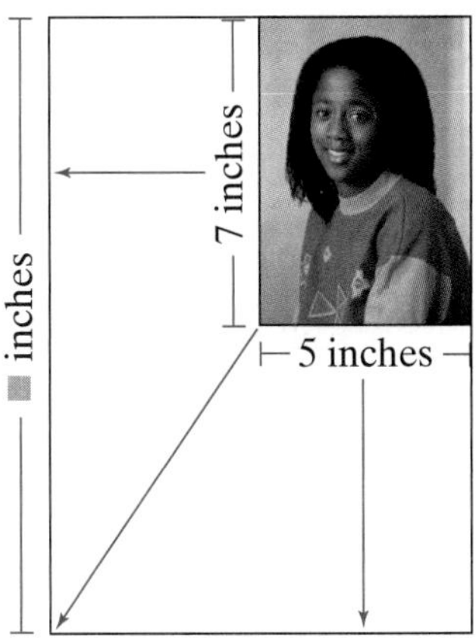

24. Yogurt A flavor of frozen yogurt has 64 Calories in 2 ounces. How many Calories are in 5 ounces?

25. Gas Mileage A car can travel 54 miles on 3 gallons of gas. How far can the car travel on 8 gallons of gas?

26. Architecture Blueprints like the one at the left represent actual dimensions. In a blueprint, suppose 1 inch represents 3 feet. The kitchen in the blueprint is 6 inches long and 4.75 inches wide. What are the kitchen's actual dimensions?

Real-World Connection

Careers Architects create blueprints when designing buildings or bridges.

Find the values of each variable.

27. $\frac{42}{g} = \frac{7}{10}$ **28.** $\frac{25}{6} = \frac{d}{30}$ **29.** $\frac{z}{12} = \frac{56}{4}$ **30.** $\frac{60.5}{6} = \frac{f}{3}$

31. Writing in Math Explain why the ratios $\frac{\$.37}{1 \text{ stamp}}$ and $\frac{\$1.85}{5 \text{ stamps}}$ do not form a proportion.

C Challenge

32. Babysitting Suppose you charge \$7 to babysit for 2 hours. Last night you earned \$17.50. How long did you babysit?

33. Solve the first proportion for y. Use that value of y to solve the second proportion for x.

$$\frac{y}{15} = \frac{54}{30} \qquad \frac{y}{9} = \frac{x}{5}$$

34. Stretch Your Thinking Change two operations in the expression below to make the value of the expression equal to 27.

$$7 + 7 + 7 + 7 + 7 + 7$$

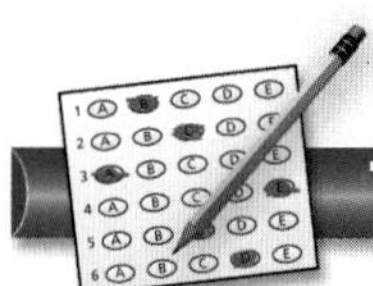

Test Prep

Multiple Choice

Take It to the NET
Online lesson quiz at **www.PHSchool.com**
Web Code: aaa-0603

35. What value makes $\frac{\blacksquare}{12} = \frac{6}{18}$ true?

A. 2 **B.** 4 **C.** 5 **D.** 9

36. If 2 ounces of cheese has 230 Calories, how many Calories are in 5 ounces of cheese?

F. 500 **G.** 550 **H.** 575 **I.** 615

37. Which pair of ratios do NOT form a proportion?

A. $\frac{4}{32}$ and $\frac{1}{8}$ **B.** $\frac{9}{4}$ and $\frac{3}{2}$ **C.** $\frac{16}{80}$ and $\frac{1}{5}$ **D.** $\frac{21}{42}$ and $\frac{9}{18}$

Short Response

38. Youth soccer teams in Hopkinton have 22 players and 3 coaches each. How many coaches are needed for 198 players? **(a)** Write a proportion to find the number of coaches. **(b)** Solve your proportion.

Mixed Review

Lesson 5-8

Complete each statement.

39. 80 oz = $\blacksquare$ lb **40.** 2 mi = $\blacksquare$ ft **41.** 3 pt = $\blacksquare$ c

Lesson 4-5

Find each difference.

42. $7\frac{1}{2} - 6\frac{1}{4}$ **43.** $7\frac{2}{9} - 5\frac{1}{3}$ **44.** $4\frac{1}{4} - 1\frac{1}{2}$ **45.** $9\frac{1}{6} - 4\frac{2}{3}$

Math at Work

Help-Desk Technician

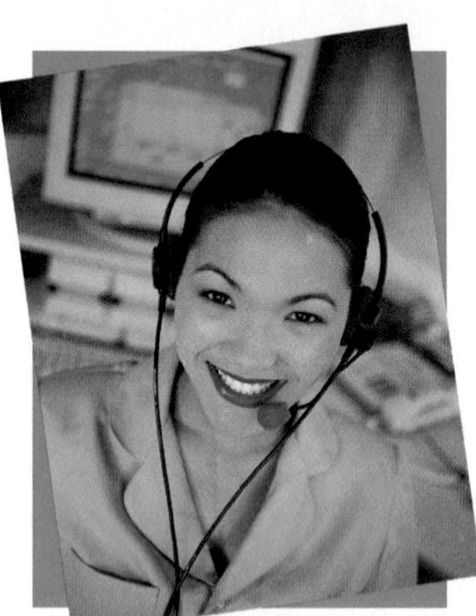

Do you enjoy helping your family and friends with their computer-related questions? If so, a career as a help-desk technician might be for you. Help-desk technicians provide computer support to people who have hardware and software questions. Help-desk technicians are valued by companies that make computer products because they understand customers' questions and concerns.

Help-desk technicians must be able to apply logical-reasoning and problem-solving skills in order to assist their customers.

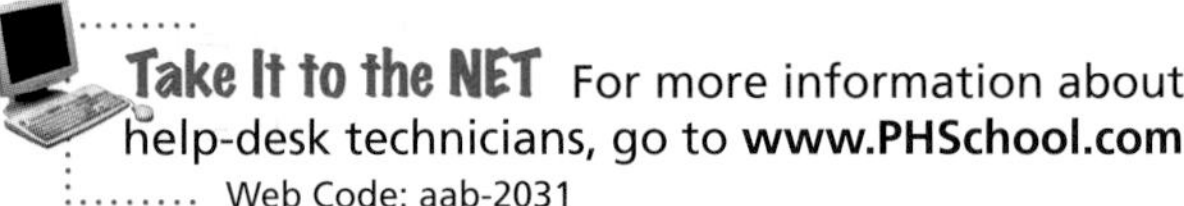

Take It to the NET For more information about help-desk technicians, go to **www.PHSchool.com**.
Web Code: aab-2031

6-4 Using Cross Products

What You'll Learn

To identify proportions

To solve proportions

. . . And Why

To find the cost of school supplies, as in Example 3

Check Skills You'll Need

For help, go to Lesson 6-3.

Complete each proportion.

1. $\frac{5}{8} = \frac{\blacksquare}{16}$ **2.** $\frac{4}{12} = \frac{2}{\blacksquare}$ **3.** $\frac{3}{\blacksquare} = \frac{15}{35}$

4. $\frac{6}{18} = \frac{4}{\blacksquare}$ **5.** $\frac{9}{12} = \frac{\blacksquare}{144}$ **6.** $\frac{\blacksquare}{60} = \frac{14}{15}$

New Vocabulary • cross products

OBJECTIVE 1

Interactive lesson includes instant self-check, tutorials, and activities.

1 Using Cross Products to Identify Proportions

Investigation: Identifying Proportions

1. Simplify each ratio. Which pairs of ratios form proportions?

a. $\frac{15}{20} \stackrel{?}{=} \frac{12}{16}$ **b.** $\frac{8}{12} \stackrel{?}{=} \frac{9}{15}$ **c.** $\frac{6}{16} \stackrel{?}{=} \frac{9}{24}$ **d.** $\frac{5}{15} \stackrel{?}{=} \frac{4}{10}$

2. For each pair of ratios above, find the products of the blue numbers. Then find the products of the red numbers.

3. a. What do you notice about the products for the pairs of ratios that form proportions?

b. What do you notice about the products for the pairs of ratios that do not form proportions?

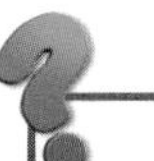

Need Help?
Go to Lesson 2-7 to review the Multiplication Property of Equality.

You can use the Multiplication Property of Equality to show an important property of proportions.

$$\frac{3}{4} = \frac{15}{20}$$ ← Start with a proportion.

$$\frac{3}{4} \times \frac{4}{1} \times \frac{20}{1} = \frac{15}{20} \times \frac{4}{1} \times \frac{20}{1}$$ ← Multiply each side by the values in the denominators.

$$\frac{3}{{}_1\not{4}} \times \frac{\not{4}^1}{1} \times \frac{20}{1} = \frac{15}{{}_1\not{20}} \times \frac{4}{1} \times \frac{\not{20}^1}{1}$$ ← Divide the common factors.

$$(3 \times 20) = (15 \times 4)$$ ← Multiply and divide by 1.

$$60 = 60$$ ← The products are equal.

The products 20×3 and 4×15 are called *cross products.*

You can find the **cross products** of two ratios by multiplying the denominator of each ratio by the numerator of the other ratio. The cross products of a proportion are *always* equal.

$\frac{3}{4} = \frac{15}{20}$ ← **Start with a proportion.**

$3 \times 20 = 4 \times 15$ ← **Multiply the numerator of each ratio by the denominator of the other ratio.**

$60 = 60$ ← **The cross products are equal.**

1 EXAMPLE Using Cross Products

Does each pair of ratios form a proportion?

a. $\frac{3}{9}, \frac{6}{18}$

b. $\frac{10}{7}, \frac{30}{14}$

a.		b.
$\frac{3}{9} \stackrel{?}{=} \frac{6}{18}$	← **Write a possible proportion.** →	$\frac{10}{7} \stackrel{?}{=} \frac{30}{14}$
$3 \times 18 \stackrel{?}{=} 9 \times 6$	← **Write the cross products.** →	$10 \times 14 \stackrel{?}{=} 7 \times 30$
$54 = 54$	← **Multiply.** →	$140 \neq 210$

The ratios $\frac{3}{9}$ and $\frac{6}{18}$ form a proportion.

The ratios $\frac{10}{7}$ and $\frac{30}{14}$ do *not* form a proportion.

Check Understanding 1 Do the ratios $\frac{2}{4}$ and $\frac{8}{16}$ form a proportion? Explain.

OBJECTIVE

2 Solving Proportions

To solve a proportion that contains a variable, you find the value of the variable that makes the equation true.

2 EXAMPLE Solving Proportions Using Cross Products

Solve $\frac{x}{9} = \frac{4}{6}$.

$\frac{x}{9} = \frac{4}{6}$ ← **Start with the proportion.**

$x \cdot 6 = 9 \cdot 4$ ← **Write the cross products.**

$6x = 36$ ← **Multiply.**

$\frac{6x}{6} = \frac{36}{6}$ ← **Divide each side by 6.**

$x = 6$ ← **Simplify.**

Check Understanding 2 Solve each proportion.

a. $\frac{6}{8} = \frac{n}{20}$ **b.** $\frac{9}{12} = \frac{3}{x}$ **c.** $\frac{2}{8} = \frac{t}{20}$

3 EXAMPLE Real-World Problem Solving

School Supplies A student buys 6 drawing pencils for \$3.90. How much will the student have to pay for 10 pencils?

Write a proportion that compares that number of pencils to their cost. Let c = the cost of the pencils.

$$\frac{6}{3.90} = \frac{10}{c}$$ ← Write a proportion. (pencils → 6, cost (\$) → 3.90; 10 ← pencils, c ← cost (\$))

$$6 \cdot c = 3.90 \cdot 10$$ ← Write the cross products.

$$6c = 39$$ ← Multiply.

$$\frac{6c}{6} = \frac{39}{6}$$ ← Divide each side by 6.

$$c = 6.5$$ ← Simplify.

The student will have to pay \$6.50 for 10 drawing pencils.

Check Understanding 3
a. If 5 notebooks cost \$7.50, how much do 3 notebooks cost?
b. **Estimation** If 7 pens cost \$5.53, about how much will 4 pens cost?

EXERCISES

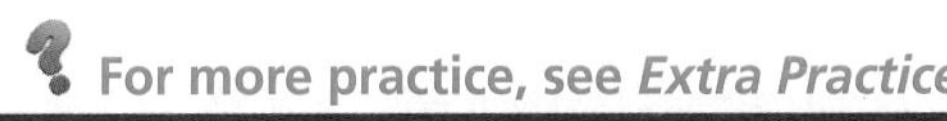
For more practice, see *Extra Practice*.

A Practice by Example

Does each pair of ratios form a proportion? Exercise 1 has been started for you.

Example 1 (page 284)

1. $\frac{3}{18}, \frac{1}{6}$ → $\frac{3}{18} \stackrel{?}{=} \frac{1}{6}$ → $3 \times 6 \stackrel{?}{=} ■ \times ■$ → ?

2. $\frac{4}{12}, \frac{3}{9}$ 3. $\frac{32}{80}, \frac{4}{10}$ 4. $\frac{5}{7}, \frac{8}{10}$ 5. $\frac{6}{2}, \frac{8}{5}$

Example 2 (page 284)

Solve each proportion.

6. $\frac{10}{3} = \frac{c}{12}$ 7. $\frac{12}{n} = \frac{4}{21}$ 8. $\frac{3}{11} = \frac{15}{a}$ 9. $\frac{16}{27} = \frac{4}{m}$

10. $\frac{h}{2} = \frac{3}{16}$ 11. $\frac{25}{4} = \frac{p}{8}$ 12. $\frac{9}{28} = \frac{18}{t}$ 13. $\frac{k}{17} = \frac{20}{68}$

Example 3 (page 285)

Write and solve a proportion for each exercise.

14. **Groceries** Three quarts of milk cost \$2.97. How much will 7 quarts of milk cost?

15. **Cooking** A recipe for 10 ounces of fondue requires 8 ounces of cheese. How much cheese is needed to make 36 ounces of fondue?

B Apply Your Skills

Does each pair of ratios form a proportion?

16. $\frac{93}{6}, \frac{62}{4}$ **17.** $\frac{25}{6}, \frac{4}{30}$ **18.** $\frac{7}{2}, \frac{77}{22}$

Solve each proportion.

19. $\frac{b}{9} = \frac{3}{27}$ **20.** $\frac{96}{144} = \frac{n}{12}$ **21.** $\frac{7}{2} = \frac{77}{w}$

22. $\frac{25}{6} = \frac{d}{30}$ **23.** $\frac{72}{c} = \frac{8}{3}$ **24.** $\frac{42}{g} = \frac{7}{10}$

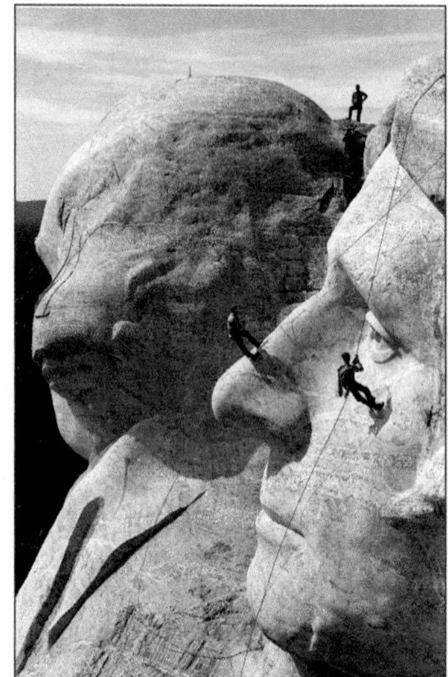

Real-World Connection

The carvings of Washington, Jefferson, Roosevelt, and Lincoln are 80 times larger than life-size.

25. Sculpture The carvings at Mount Rushmore National Memorial in South Dakota are each 60 feet from chin to forehead.

a. If the typical distance from a man's chin to the top of his head is 9 inches, and the typical distance between the pupils of his eyes is 2.5 inches, what is the approximate distance between the pupils in the carving of George Washington's head?

b. **Reasoning** Do you need to convert feet to inches or inches to feet before you solve this proportion? Explain.

26. Printing Your friend is having a poster printed from a photograph that is 4 inches wide by 6 inches tall. If the poster is 22 inches wide, how tall will the poster be if it is proportional to the photograph?

27. Schools There are 221 students and 13 teachers at Hampton School. To keep the same student-to-teacher ratio, how many teachers are needed for 272 students?

28. Basketball Darrin makes 3 free throws for every 5 he attempts. If he attempts 80 free throws in a season, how many is he expected to make?

Solve each proportion. Round to the nearest hundredth if necessary.

29. $\frac{5{,}280 \text{ feet}}{1.609 \text{ kilometers}} = \frac{f}{10 \text{ kilometers}}$ **30.** $\frac{c}{100 \text{ inches}} = \frac{30.48 \text{ centimeters}}{12 \text{ inches}}$

31. $\frac{168 \text{ hours}}{7 \text{ days}} = \frac{h}{365 \text{ days}}$ **32.** $\frac{907.18 \text{ kilograms}}{2{,}000 \text{ pounds}} = \frac{2 \text{ kilograms}}{p}$

33. Writing in Math Explain how you can determine if the ratios $\frac{45}{50}$ and $\frac{18}{20}$ form a proportion.

34. a. **Data File, p. 267** Write the ratio of the beaver's maximum height to the moose's maximum height. Then write the ratio of the beaver's track size to the moose's track size.

b. Does the ratio of their maximum heights form a proportion with the ratio of their track sizes? Explain.

35. Crafts In 10 hours, a weaver makes 4 baskets. In 48 hours, another weaver makes 18 baskets. Are they working at the same pace? Explain.

Challenge **Solve each proportion.**

36. $\frac{7}{9} = \frac{3.5}{r}$ **37.** $\frac{t}{15} = \frac{6.75}{2.25}$ **38.** $\frac{2}{5} = \frac{a}{2}$

39. Stretch Your Thinking Solve for x and y: $\frac{x}{3} = \frac{8}{12} = \frac{14}{y}$.

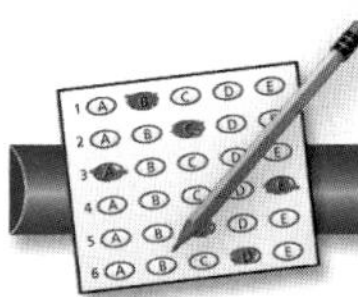

Test Prep

Multiple Choice

40. A basketball team's wins to losses ratio is 4 to 3. What record could the team have?

A. 12 wins and 10 losses **B.** 16 wins and 9 losses
C. 16 wins and 12 losses **D.** 30 wins and 40 losses

41. Matt can type 216 words in 6 minutes. Lya can type 128 words in 4 minutes. Which statement is true?

F. Matt can type faster than Lya.
G. Lya can type faster than Matt.
H. Matt can type 88 more words than Lya during the same time period.
I. Matt and Lya working at the same time need 10 minutes to type 344 words.

Take It to the NET
Online lesson quiz at
www.PHSchool.com
Web Code: aaa-0604

42. Which ratio forms a proportion with $\frac{16}{64}$?

A. $\frac{1}{4}$ **B.** $\frac{4}{8}$ **C.** $\frac{14}{48}$ **D.** $\frac{64}{16}$

Extended Response

43. A cable television channel charges $21 for 6 movies. A movie store charges $22.50 for 10 DVD rentals.

a. Find the unit rate for the cable offer and the DVD offer.
b. How much do you save per movie if you choose the DVD offer?
c. Reasoning Do the ratios of cost to number of movies form a proportion? Explain.

Mixed Review

Lesson 5-3 **Find each quotient.**

44. $4 \div \frac{4}{5}$ **45.** $\frac{4}{5} \div 4$ **46.** $\frac{4}{5} \div \frac{1}{5}$ **47.** $\frac{4}{5} \div 5$

Lesson 2-4 **48.** You have sweaters that are white, blue, green, and yellow. You have pants that are blue, black, and tan. How many combinations of pants and sweaters do you have?

6-5 Scale Drawings

What You'll Learn

 To find the scale of a drawing

 To find actual dimensions

. . . And Why

To find map distances, as in Example 2

✓ Check Skills You'll Need

For help, go to Lesson 6-4.

Solve each proportion.

1. $\frac{6}{30} = \frac{4}{x}$
2. $\frac{15}{21} = \frac{y}{35}$
3. $\frac{5}{z} = \frac{145}{174}$
4. $\frac{5}{m} = \frac{12.5}{5}$
5. $\frac{n}{16} = \frac{4.5}{72}$
6. $\frac{49}{t} = \frac{4.2}{9}$

New Vocabulary • scale

OBJECTIVE 1

Interactive lesson includes instant self-check, tutorials, and activities.

1 Finding the Scale of a Drawing

Investigation: Enlarging a Design

1. Use a metric ruler to find the length of the sides of a green and gold square in each design.

Original Design

Enlarged Design

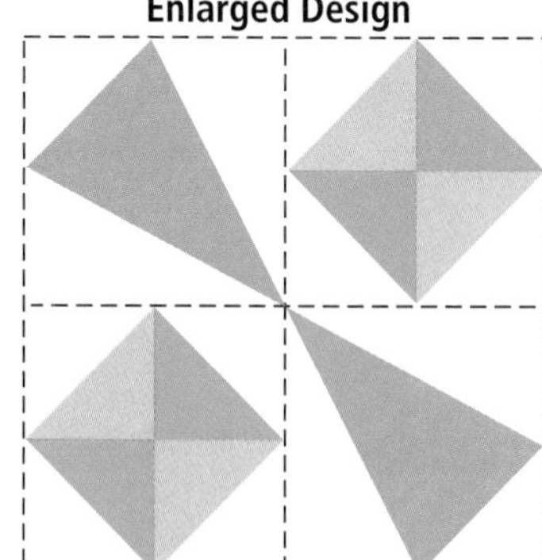

2. Find the ratio of the length of a side in the enlarged design to the length in the original design.
3. Enlarge the original design using a ratio of 3 centimeters (new design) to 1 centimeter (original design).

A **scale** is the ratio that compares a length in a drawing or model to the length in the original object. You write a scale in simplest form.

The scale of the original design to the enlarged design above is 1 to 2 or $\frac{1}{2}$.

1 EXAMPLE Finding the Scale of a Drawing

In the drawing, the height of the goat is 3 centimeters. The actual height of the goat is 90 centimeters. What is the scale of the drawing?

drawing height → / actual height → $\frac{3 \text{ centimeters}}{90 \text{ centimeters}} = \frac{1}{30}$ ← **Divide each measure by the GCF, 3.**

The scale is 1 centimeter to 30 centimeters, or 1:30.

Check Understanding 1 The length of a drawing of an object is 6 inches. The length of the actual object is 84 inches. What is the scale of the drawing?

OBJECTIVE

2 Finding Actual Dimensions

Mapmakers and architects make scale drawings. They apply the same scale ratio to each length in an object to create a drawing that is smaller than actual size. You can use the scale to calculate actual distances.

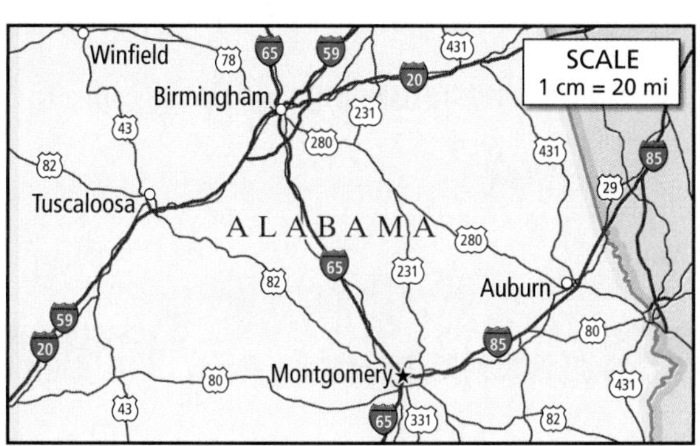

2 EXAMPLE Finding Distances on a Map

Maps Use the map and scale above to find the actual distance from Winfield to Auburn.

Reading Math

The scale on a map sometimes uses "=" to indicate the ratio: 1 cm = 20 mi.

Step 1 Use a metric ruler to measure the distance from Winfield to Auburn on the map. The distance is 6 centimeters.

Step 2 Write the scale as a ratio: $\frac{1 \text{ centimeter}}{20 \text{ miles}}$.

Step 3 Find the number of miles represented by 6 centimeters.

Let y = the actual distance from Winfield to Auburn.

$\frac{1 \text{ cm}}{20 \text{ mi}} = \frac{6 \text{ cm}}{y \text{ mi}}$ ← **map distances** / ← **actual distances**

$1y = 20 \cdot 6$ ← **Write the cross products.**

$y = 120$ ← **Multiply.**

The actual distance from Winfield to Auburn is about 120 miles.

Check Understanding 2 Find the distance from Winfield to Montgomery.

 Real-World Problem Solving

Real-World Connection

The White House contains 132 rooms on 6 floors.

Architecture Gwen uses a scale of 1 inch : 10 feet to build a model of the White House. The White House is 58 feet tall. How tall will her model be?

$\frac{\text{model (in.)}}{\text{actual (ft)}} \rightarrow \frac{1}{10}$ ← Write the scale as a ratio.

$\frac{1}{10} = \frac{h}{58}$ ← Use h to represent the model height. ← actual heights

$1 \cdot 58 = 10 \cdot h$ ← Write the cross products.

$58 = 10h$ ← Multiply.

$\frac{58}{10} = \frac{10h}{10}$ ← Divide each side by 10.

$5.8 = h$ ← Simplify.

Gwen's model will be 5.8 inches tall.

Check Understanding 3 The White House is 170 feet long. How long will Gwen's model be?

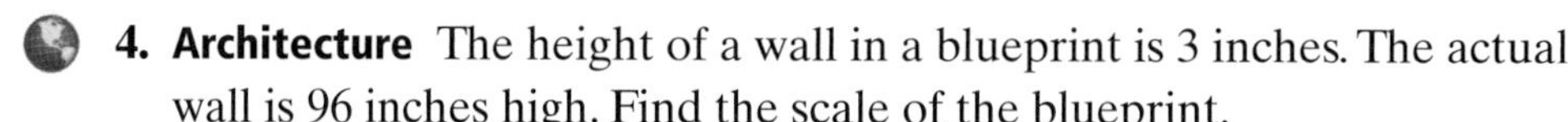

EXERCISES

For more practice, see *Extra Practice*.

A Practice by Example

Write each scale as a ratio. Exercise 1 has been started for you.

Example 1 (page 289)

1. a 4-foot-tall model of a 100-foot-tall building → $\frac{4 \text{ feet}}{100 \text{ feet}} = \frac{1}{\blacksquare}$

2. a 10-inch-long drawing of a 40-inch-long table

3. a 15-foot-long model of a 300-foot-long fence

4. Architecture The height of a wall in a blueprint is 3 inches. The actual wall is 96 inches high. Find the scale of the blueprint.

Example 2 (page 289)

Geography Find the actual distance between each pair of cities. Use a metric ruler to measure. Round to the nearest mile.

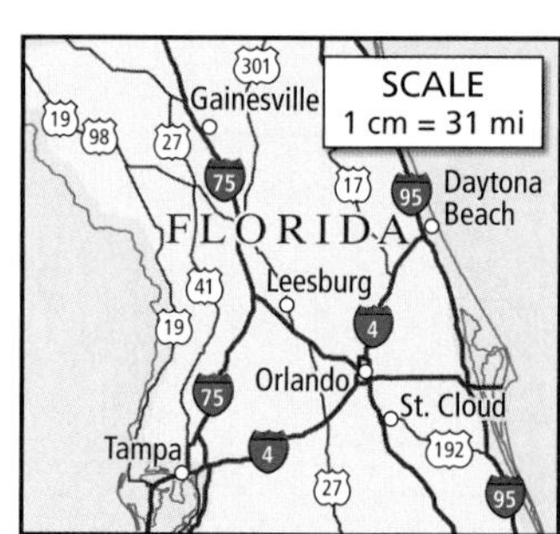

5. Gainesville to Leesburg

6. Gainesville to Orlando

7. Tampa to Daytona Beach

8. St. Cloud to Daytona Beach

Example 3 (page 290)

Suppose you are making a model of each item. Use a scale of 1 inch : 9 inches to find the length or height of your model.

9. A chair is 36 inches tall.

10. A whale is 468 inches long.

11. A lizard is 12 inches long.

12. A stop sign is 117 inches tall.

B Apply Your Skills

Map Scales Use a map scale of 1 centimeter : 100 kilometers. How many centimeters on the map represent each actual distance?

13. 125 kilometers

14. 80 kilometers

15. 4,000 kilometers

16. 170 kilometers

17. 800 kilometers

18. 2,500 kilometers

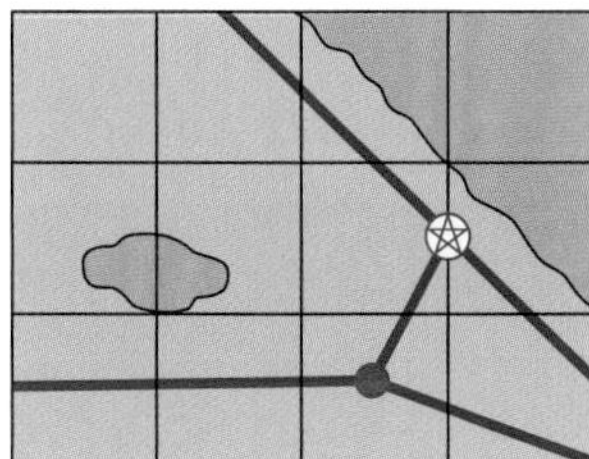

19. a. **Maps** Suppose you redraw the map at the left using a scale of 0.5 centimeter : 1 centimeter. Does your drawing enlarge or reduce the size of the map? Explain how you know.

b. Redraw the map using the scale of 0.5 centimeter : 1 centimeter.

20. Data File, p. 267 The drawing of each track in the table has been scaled to fit the table.

a. Write the scale of a Norway rat.

b. Draw a full-size moose track.

21. **Toy Design** From head to tail, the length of a *Tyrannosaurus rex* was about 40 feet. You want to design a toy of this dinosaur with a scale of 1 inch : 8 feet. How long is your toy?

22. Writing in Math When you find actual distances on a map, would you expect to get exact or approximate answers? Explain.

C Challenge

Model Cars The table below shows toy car measurements and actual car measurements. Copy and complete the table. Use the ratio $\frac{\text{length of toy car}}{\text{length of real car}}$.

	Part	Toy Size	Actual Size
	Car	3 in.	120 in.
23.	Door handle	■	5 in.
24.	Headlight	■	8 in.
25.	Front bumper	0.18 ft	■
26.	Rear window	■	4.5 ft

27. **Stretch Your Thinking** In the problem at the right, replace five of the digits with zeros so that the sum is 1,111.

$$\begin{array}{r} 111 \\ 333 \\ 777 \\ +\,999 \\ \hline \end{array}$$

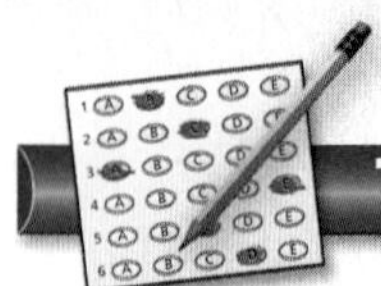

Test Prep

Multiple Choice

28. A scale model of an airplane is 7.5 inches long. The scale used to make the model is 1 inch : 5 feet. How long is the original airplane?
A. 1.5 inches **B.** 5 feet **C.** 37.5 inches **D.** 37.5 feet

Take It to the NET
Online lesson quiz at
www.PHSchool.com
Web Code: aaa-0605

29. Measure the boat. The scale is 1 cm : 3 m.
What is a reasonable length for the actual boat?
F. 2.5 centimeters **G.** 7.5 centimeters
H. 2.5 meters **I.** 7.5 meters

Short Response

30. Aaron is building a model train set. The rails of his model's track are 1.5 inches apart. The actual train's rails are 57 inches apart. The actual locomotive is 76 feet long. How long should Aaron's locomotive be? Write and solve a proportion to find the model's length.

Mixed Review

Lesson 5-4 **Estimate each quotient.**

31. $10 \div 4\frac{3}{4}$ **32.** $7\frac{3}{4} \div 2\frac{1}{8}$ **33.** $13\frac{1}{2} \div 6\frac{6}{7}$ **34.** $99\frac{4}{5} \div 19\frac{5}{8}$

Lesson 5-1 **Find each product.**

35. $\frac{5}{16}$ of 32 **36.** $\frac{3}{4} \times 10$ **37.** $\frac{9}{10} \cdot 55$ **38.** $\frac{4}{5}$ of 100

Checkpoint Quiz 1 — Lessons 6-1 through 6-5

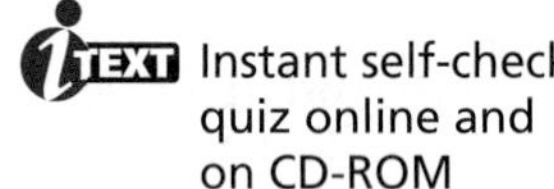
Instant self-check quiz online and on CD-ROM

1. Write 18 : 40 in two other ways.

2. A cereal box is \$.19 per ounce. How much does a 15-ounce box cost?

3. Two movie tickets cost \$7. What is the cost of five tickets?

Do the ratios in each pair form a proportion?

4. $\frac{6}{45}, \frac{2}{18}$ **5.** $\frac{4}{7}, \frac{30}{42}$ **6.** $\frac{8}{12}, \frac{30}{45}$

Solve each proportion.

7. $\frac{21}{36} = \frac{7}{n}$ **8.** $\frac{54}{c} = \frac{9}{13}$ **9.** $\frac{x}{18} = \frac{\$6.30}{7}$

10. A beverage cup is 6 inches tall. The beverage cup on a restaurant billboard is 18 feet tall. Write the scale as a ratio in simplest form.

Modeling Percents

For Use With Lesson 6-6

In Lesson 6-6, you will learn about *percents*, which are ratios that compare numbers to 100. You can model percents with 10-by-10 grids because each grid has 100 squares. The portion of the grid that represents the percent is shaded. You can use the symbol % to write percents.

EXAMPLE Using a Percent Model

What percent of the grid is shaded?

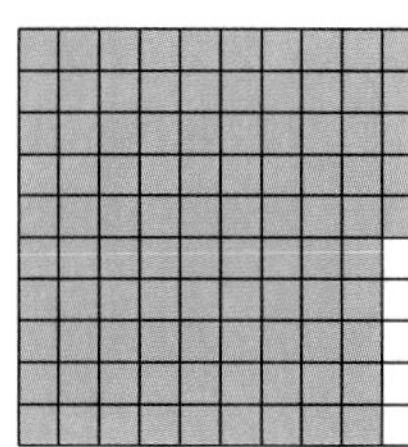

amount shaded → 95 squares / the whole → 100 squares ← Use a fraction to represent the shaded portion of the grid.

$\frac{95}{100} = 95\%$ ← Write the numerator of the fraction followed by %.

95% of the grid is shaded.

EXERCISES

What percent of each grid is shaded?

1. 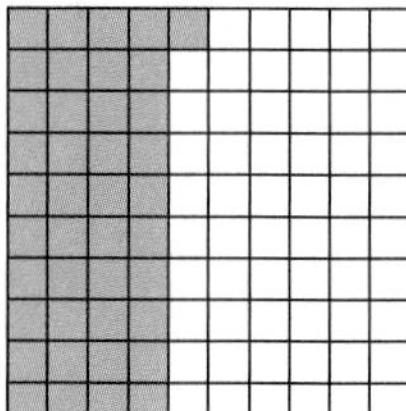

2. 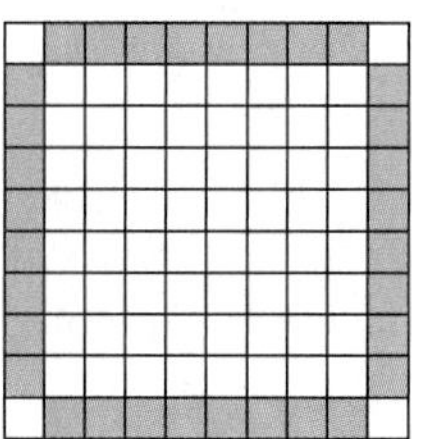

3. 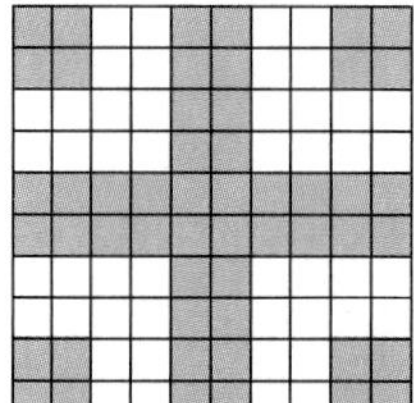

4. a. What percent of the grid at the right is shaded?

b. What percent of the grid at the right is *not* shaded?

c. **Writing in Math** Explain how you found your answer to part (b).

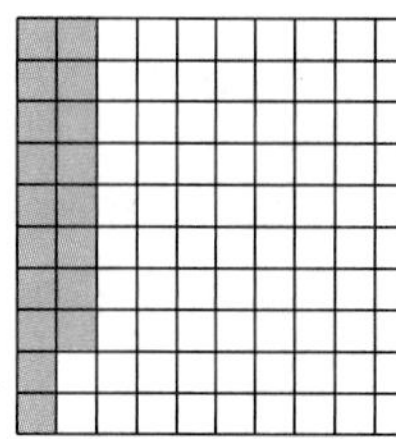

Use a 10-by-10 square grid to model each percent.

5. 5% **6.** 100% **7.** 75% **8.** 37%

6-6 Percents, Fractions, and Decimals

What You'll Learn

1. To write percents as decimals and fractions

2. To write decimals and fractions as percents

. . . And Why

To describe percents with survey data, as in Example 5

✓ Check Skills You'll Need

For help, go to Lesson 3-4.

Write each fraction in simplest form.

1. $\frac{48}{200}$ **2.** $\frac{50}{125}$

3. $\frac{39}{52}$ **4.** $\frac{28}{84}$

5. What fraction is modeled at the right? Write the fraction with a denominator of 100.

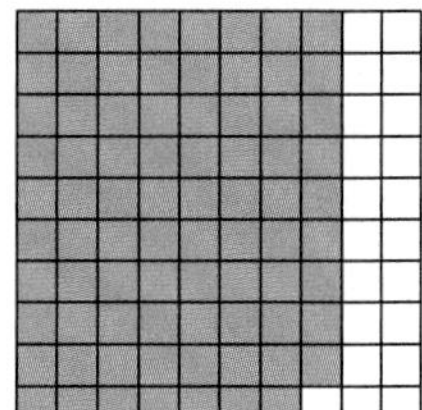

New Vocabulary • percent

Interactive lesson includes instant self-check, tutorials, and activities.

OBJECTIVE 1 Writing Percents as Decimals and Fractions

Reading Math
Read 49% as "49 percent."

A **percent** is a ratio that compares a number to 100. The symbol for percent is %. If 49 out of 100 students are girls, you can say that 49% of the students are girls. You can write any percent as a decimal.

1 EXAMPLE Writing Percents as Decimals

Write each percent as a decimal.

a. 36%

$36\% = \frac{36}{100}$

$= 0.36$

b. 5%

$5\% = \frac{5}{100}$

$= 0.05$

← **Write each percent as a fraction with a denominator of 100.** →

← **Divide.** →

✓ Check Understanding **1** Write each percent as a decimal.
a. 18% **b.** 2% **c.** 25%

When writing percents as fractions, write the fractions in simplest form.

2 EXAMPLE Writing Percents as Fractions

Write 36% as a fraction in simplest form.

$36\% = \frac{36}{100}$ ← **Write the percent as a fraction with a denominator of 100.**

$= \frac{9}{25}$ ← **Write the fraction in simplest form.**

✔ Check Understanding 2 Write each percent as a fraction in simplest form.

a. 4%   b. 55%   c. 75%

d. **Mental Math** Write 20% as a fraction in simplest form.

OBJECTIVE

2 Writing Decimals and Fractions as Percents

To write a percent as a decimal, as in Example 1, you divide by 100. To write a decimal as a percent, you multiply by 100. Remember that multiplying by 100 is the same as moving the decimal point two places to the right.

3 EXAMPLE Writing Decimals as Percents

Write each decimal as a percent.

a. 0.43   0.43 ⟶ 43%

b. 0.07   0.07 ⟶ 7%

← **Move each decimal point two places to the right.**

✔ Check Understanding 3 Write each decimal as a percent.

a. 0.52   b. 0.05   c. 0.5

d. **Reasoning** Explain how you could write 72% as a decimal by moving a decimal point.

When the denominator of a fraction is a factor of 100, you can use equal ratios to convert the fraction to a percent.

4 EXAMPLE Writing Fractions as Percents

Real-World Connection

Careers Primary care physicians see the same patients on a regular basis.

Doctors According to a news article, 6 of every 25 doctors in the United States are women. As a fraction, *6 of every 25* is written $\frac{6}{25}$. Write $\frac{6}{25}$ as a percent.

$$\frac{6}{25} \overset{\times 4}{=} \frac{24}{100}$$

← **Find the fraction with denominator 100 that is equal to $\frac{6}{25}$.**

$$\frac{24}{100} = 24\%$$

← **Write as a percentage.**

Twenty-four percent of the doctors in the United States are women.

✔ Check Understanding 4 a. The same article also stated that 1 of every 20 neurosurgeons in the United States is a woman. Write the fraction $\frac{1}{20}$ as a percent.

b. **Number Sense** List all possible denominators that are factors of 100.

Sometimes the denominator of a fraction is not a factor of 100. In this case, convert the fraction to a decimal. Then write the decimal as a percent.

5 EXAMPLE Percents with Repeating Decimals

Surveys The makers of Grin toothpaste took the survey shown at the right. What percent of the 75 people surveyed say they prefer Grin toothpaste over Brand X?

What Brand of Toothpaste Do You Prefer?	
Grin	40
Brand X	30
No preference	5

Out of 75 people surveyed, 40 prefer Grin.

$\frac{40}{75}$ ← **Write a fraction to represent 40 of 75.**

40 ÷ 75 = 0.533333333 ← **Use a calculator.**

0.533333333 ← **Move the decimal point two places to the right.**

$\approx 53.\overline{3}\%$ ← **Write as a percent.**

About 53% of the people surveyed prefer Grin toothpaste.

Check Understanding 5 Refer to the survey above. What percent of the people surveyed say they have no preference?

EXERCISES

For more practice, see *Extra Practice*.

A Practice by Example

Example 1 (page 294)

Write each percent as a decimal.

1. 15% **2.** 22% **3.** 82% **4.** 63% **5.** 10%

6. 40% **7.** 3% **8.** 7% **9.** 12% **10.** 100%

Example 2 (page 294)

Write each percent as a fraction in simplest form.

11. 70% **12.** 88% **13.** 5% **14.** 33% **15.** 14%

16. 15% **17.** 75% **18.** 18% **19.** 2% **20.** 42%

Examples 3, 4 (page 295)

Write each decimal or fraction as a percent.

21. 0.17 **22.** 0.08 **23.** 0.98 **24.** 0.22 **25.** 0.44

26. $\frac{19}{20}$ **27.** $\frac{27}{50}$ **28.** $\frac{1}{4}$ **29.** $\frac{19}{25}$ **30.** $\frac{7}{25}$

31. School Play Three of every five students who tried out for the school play made the cast list. Write the fraction $\frac{3}{5}$ as a percent.

Example 5
(page 296)

Write each fraction as a percent. Round to the nearest whole percent.

32. $\frac{1}{6}$ **33.** $\frac{4}{15}$ **34.** $\frac{7}{9}$ **35.** $\frac{15}{24}$ **36.** $\frac{14}{45}$

37. Quality Control A shipment of 30 radios is packed incorrectly. Two of the radios arrive damaged. What percent is damaged?

B Apply Your Skills

Copy and complete the table below. Write each fraction in simplest form.

	38.	39.	40.	41.	42.	43.
Fraction	$\frac{11}{50}$	$\frac{39}{50}$	$\frac{22}{25}$	■	■	$\frac{4}{5}$
Decimal	■	0.78	■	0.45	■	■
Percent	22%	■	■	■	42%	■

Real-World Connection
The paradise parrot once lived in Australia. It has been extinct since the early 1900's.

44. Biology Ninety-nine percent of all kinds of plants and animals that have ever lived are now extinct. Write ninety-nine percent as a fraction and as a decimal.

45. Geography About $\frac{7}{10}$ of Earth's surface is covered by water. Write $\frac{7}{10}$ as a decimal and as a percent.

Write each decimal or fraction as a percent. Round to the nearest percent if necessary.

46. $\frac{3}{8}$ **47.** $\frac{5}{6}$ **48.** $\frac{4}{11}$ **49.** $\frac{9}{20}$ **50.** $\frac{17}{30}$

51. $0.\overline{5}$ **52.** $0.\overline{3}$ **53.** $0.\overline{45}$ **54.** $0.\overline{60}$ **55.** 0.7

56. Fuel Gauge Use the fuel gauge at the right to estimate how full the fuel tank is.

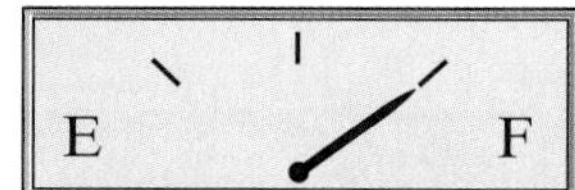

57. Suppose you answer 29 questions correctly on a 40-question test. What percent of the questions are correct?

58. **Writing in Math** Explain how to write a decimal as a percent.

C Challenge

Number Sense **Use the whole numbers 1 through 100 and find the percent of numbers in each category.**

59. multiples of 3 **60.** odd numbers **61.** prime numbers

62. Stretch Your Thinking When a three-digit number is divided by the sum of the digits of the number, the quotient is 26. What is the least number for which this is true?

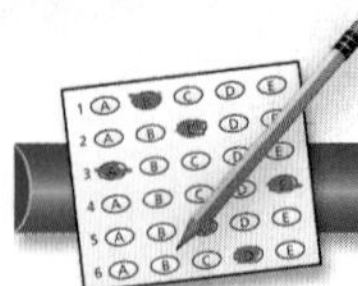

Test Prep

Multiple Choice **Use the graph at the right.**

What's in Lunch Bags?

Fruit
Sandwiches
Cookies
Chips
Cake
0 5 10 15 20 25
Percent

63. Which decimal is equivalent to the percent of lunch bags that contain cake?

A. 0.05 **B.** 0.10
C. 0.15 **D.** 0.50

64. Which of the following can you NOT conclude from the graph?

F. About one fourth of lunch bags contain fruit.
G. Almost 10% of lunch bags contain a peanut butter and jelly sandwich.
H. Fruit is in almost twice as many lunch bags as cookies.
I. More students take fruit than all other items combined.

65. In what percent of lunch bags are you likely to find fruit?

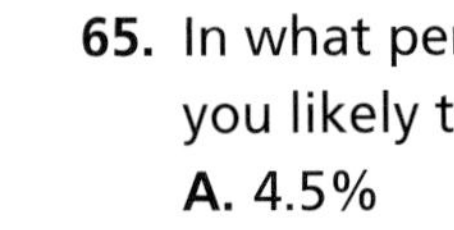

A. 4.5% **B.** 13%
C. 23% **D.** 90%

Take It to the NET
Online lesson quiz at
www.PHSchool.com
Web Code: aaa-0606

Short Response

66. Suppose you answer 32 questions correctly on a 45-question test.

a. If the passing grade is 70%, did you pass?
b. Justify your answer.

Mixed Review

Lesson 5-5

67. **Algebra** A package of soy nuts weighs $\frac{3}{8}$ pound and costs $1.65.

a. Write an equation to determine the cost of 1 pound of soy nuts. Then solve and check your equation.
b. Explain how you could estimate the cost of 1 pound without solving an equation.

Lesson 5-2

Estimate each product.

68. $2\frac{3}{4} \times 5\frac{1}{4}$ **69.** $6\frac{1}{8} \times 3\frac{3}{8}$ **70.** $4\frac{5}{8} \times 2\frac{2}{3}$ **71.** $3\frac{1}{2} \cdot 5\frac{1}{3}$

72. Estimate the area of a floor that measures 11 feet 10 inches by 9 feet 2 inches.

Algebra

6-7 Finding a Percent of a Number

What You'll Learn

To use proportions with percents

To use decimals with percents

. . . And Why

To find a part of a whole, as in Example 1

Check Skills You'll Need

For help, go to Lesson 6-4.

Solve each proportion.

1. $\frac{x}{42} = \frac{3}{7}$
2. $\frac{m}{12} = \frac{6}{9}$
3. $\frac{6}{45} = \frac{2}{n}$
4. $\frac{54}{c} = \frac{9}{13}$
5. $\frac{8}{10} = \frac{68}{y}$
6. $\frac{92}{100} = \frac{q}{250}$
7. Explain how you would solve the proportion $\frac{39}{100} = \frac{x}{140}$.

Interactive lesson includes instant self-check, tutorials, and activities.

OBJECTIVE 1 Using Proportions With Percents

A Little League team won 80% of the 30 games it played. You can write a proportion to find how many games the team won. This model is helpful in setting up a proportion to find 80% of 30.

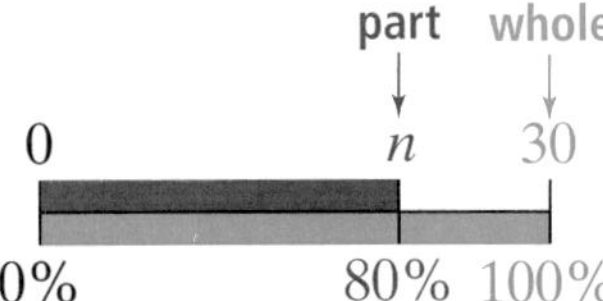

$\frac{n}{30} = \frac{80}{100}$ ← The part n corresponds to 80 in the diagram.
← The whole 30 corresponds to 100.

Real-World Connection

Over 3 million players participate in Little League Baseball.

1 EXAMPLE Using a Proportion — Real World

Baseball A Little League team played 30 games and won 80% of its games. Use a proportion to find the number of games the team wins.

Let n represent the number of wins.

$$\frac{n}{30} = \frac{80}{100} \quad \begin{matrix}\leftarrow \text{part} \\ \leftarrow \text{whole}\end{matrix}$$

$$100 \times n = 80 \times 30 \quad \leftarrow \text{Write the cross products.}$$

$$100n = 2{,}400 \quad \leftarrow \text{Multiply.}$$

$$n = 24 \quad \leftarrow \text{Divide each side by 100.}$$

The team won 24 games.

Check Understanding 1 Brendan has read 60% of a novel that has 80 pages. Use a proportion to find the number of pages Brendan has read.

OBJECTIVE

2 Using Decimals With Percents

You can find a percent of a number by using a decimal.

2 EXAMPLE Using a Decimal

Find 22% of 288.

$22\% = 0.22$ ← **Write 22% as a decimal.**

$0.22 \times 288 = 63.36$ ← **Multiply.**

So, 22% of 288 is 63.36.

Check Understanding 2 Find each answer. **a.** 12% of 91 **b.** 18% of 121

The percents in the table below are commonly found in real-world situations. You can change these to decimals or percents and then use mental math to calculate with them.

Test-Prep Tip
Memorizing the table at the right can help you find percents quickly on tests.

Equivalent Expressions for Mental Math

Percent	10%	20%	25%	50%	75%	80%
Fraction	$\frac{1}{10}$	$\frac{1}{5}$	$\frac{1}{4}$	$\frac{1}{2}$	$\frac{3}{4}$	$\frac{4}{5}$
Decimal	0.1	0.2	0.25	0.5	0.75	0.8

3 EXAMPLE Using Mental Math

Surveys Suppose 25% of 80 students in a survey said they have vacationed in Florida. Find the number of students who have vacationed in Florida.

What you think

25% is equivalent to $\frac{1}{4}$; $\frac{1}{4} \times 80 = 20$. Twenty students have vacationed in Florida.

Why it works

$25\% = \frac{25}{100}$

$= \frac{1}{4}$ ← **Write 25% as a fraction in simplest form.**

$\frac{1}{4} \times 80 = \frac{1}{4} \times \frac{80}{1}$ ← **Multiply 80 by $\frac{1}{4}$. Rewrite 80 as $\frac{80}{1}$.**

$= \frac{80}{4}$ ← **Simplify.**

$= 20$ ← **Divide.**

Check Understanding 3 Use mental math to find each of the following.
a. 10% of 56 **b.** 75% of 12 **c.** 50% of 36

EXERCISES

For more practice, see *Extra Practice*.

A Practice by Example

Example 1 (page 299)

Find each answer. Exercise 1 has been started for you.

1. 18% of 40 $\rightarrow \frac{18}{100} = \frac{n}{40}$ **2.** 42% of 70 **3.** 8% of 210

4. 70% of 185 **5.** 11% of 600 **6.** 15% of 90 **7.** 65% of 240

Example 2 (page 300)

Find each answer.

8. 7% of 50 **9.** 18% of 170 **10.** 44% of 165

11. 43% of 61 **12.** 55% of 91 **13.** 30% of 490

Example 3 (page 300)

Find each answer using mental math.

14. 20% of 180 **15.** 80% of 40 **16.** 75% of 480 **17.** 25% of 50

18. Dance Suppose 50% of the 178 dancers at a school for the performing arts prefer modern dance. How many dancers prefer modern dance?

B Apply Your Skills

19. Vision In the United States, about 46% of the population wear glasses or contact lenses.

a. In a group of 85 people, how many people would you expect to wear glasses or contact lenses?

b. Writing in Math Explain how you found your answer to part (a).

c. Open-Ended How many people in your classroom would you expect to wear glasses or contact lenses?

20. Data File, p. 267 Which animal's track is 10% of the length of the moose track?

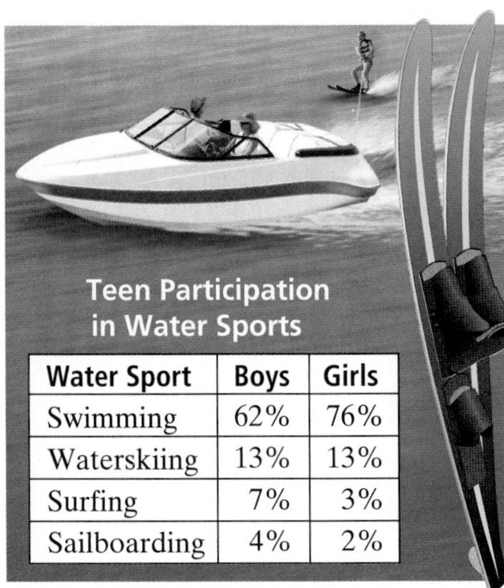

Teen Participation in Water Sports

Water Sport	Boys	Girls
Swimming	62%	76%
Waterskiing	13%	13%
Surfing	7%	3%
Sailboarding	4%	2%

Recreation Use the survey at the left. Suppose 200 boys and 200 girls were surveyed. Find the number of boys or girls who participated in each water sport.

21. girls in swimming **22.** boys in waterskiing

23. boys in surfing **24.** girls in surfing

25. girls in sailboarding **26.** boys in swimming

Money ***Simple interest*** **on a bank account is found by multiplying the original investment (I), the yearly interest rate (r), and the time in years (t). Find the simple interest of each below.**

27. $I = \$500, r = 1\%, t = 2$ **28.** $I = \$1{,}000, r = 3\%, t = 4$

29. $I = \$895, r = 5\%, t = 2$ **30.** $I = \$4{,}500, r = 2\%, t = 3$

You can use a calculator to find percents. Some calculators have a percent key. If yours does not, then enter your percent as a decimal.

SAMPLE Find 58% of 165.

58 [%] [×] 165 [=] 95.7 OR 0.58 [×] 165 [=] 95.7

31. Find 33% of 31. **32.** Find 91% of 234. **33.** Find 12% of 88.

Challenge

34. Store A is selling all books and posters at 60% off the marked price. Store B is selling the same items at $\frac{2}{3}$ off. Which store is offering the greatest discount rate? Explain your thinking.

35. **Stretch Your Thinking** Identical sweatshirts are being sold in two different stores. In the first store, the sale price is 20% off the regular price of \$25. In the second store, the sale price is 30% off the regular price of \$30. Which sweatshirt is the better buy? Explain.

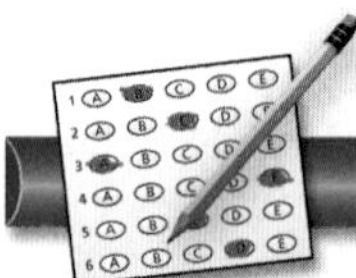

Test Prep

Gridded Response

Use the table below for Exercises 36–39. Estimate, to the nearest whole number, the number of letters to expect in each passage.

Frequency of Vowels in Written Passages

Letter	A	E	I	O	U
Frequency	8%	13%	6%	8%	3%

Take It to the NET
Online lesson quiz at
www.PHSchool.com
Web Code: aaa-0607

36. number of E's in a passage of 300 letters

37. number of A's in a passage of 1,400 letters

38. number of U's in a passage of 235 letters

39. number of I's in a passage of 695 letters

Mixed Review

Lesson 6-1 **Write each ratio in simplest form.**

40. $\frac{10}{45}$ **41.** 36 : 90 **42.** 18 to 21 **43.** $\frac{100}{150}$

44. 24 : 40 **45.** $\frac{55}{30}$ **46.** 336 : 36 **47.** 729 to 540

Lesson 3-5 **Write each improper fraction as a mixed number.**

48. $\frac{23}{4}$ **49.** $\frac{15}{6}$ **50.** $\frac{32}{12}$ **51.** $\frac{42}{5}$

6-8 Estimating With Percents

What You'll Learn

To estimate with percents

. . . And Why

To estimate a tip, as in Example 2

Check Skills You'll Need

For help, go to Lesson 5-1.

Find each product.

1. $\frac{1}{8}$ of 240
2. $\frac{3}{4}$ of 160
3. $\frac{4}{5}$ of 2,500
4. $\frac{2}{7}$ of 1,400

OBJECTIVE

Interactive lesson includes instant self-check, tutorials, and activities.

1 Estimating With Percents

When you go shopping, you want to know if you have enough money to purchase an item. You can use mental math to estimate prices.

1 EXAMPLE Estimating Sales Tax

Real World

Sales Tax Suppose you buy the scarf at the left. The sales tax rate is 6%. Estimate the sales tax and the total cost.

$9.99

$14.99

Method 1

The scarf costs about \$15.

6% of $15 = 0.06 \times 15$ ← **Write 6% as 0.06.**

$= 0.90$ ← **Multiply to find the tax.**

$15 + 0.90 = 15.90$ ← **Find the sum of the price and the tax.**

The cost of the scarf, including tax, is about \$15.90.

Method 2

The scarf costs about \$15. The sales tax rate is 6%, or 6 cents for every dollar.

\$15 × 6 cents/dollar = 90¢, or \$.90.

\$15 + \$.90 = \$15.90

The cost of the scarf, including tax, is about \$15.90.

Check Understanding 1

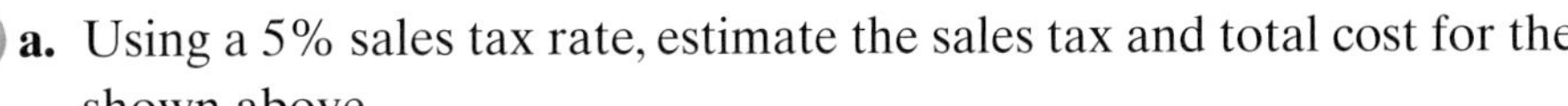

a. Using a 5% sales tax rate, estimate the sales tax and total cost for the hat shown above.

b. **Reasoning** When estimating tax, would it be better to round a price like \$34.48 up to \$35, or down to \$34? Explain your choice.

2 EXAMPLE Estimating a Tip

Dining Out Suppose you and two friends eat at a restaurant. Estimate a 15% tip for a bill of \$26.22.

What you think

The bill is about \$26.
I can break apart 15% into 10% and 5%.
Since 10% of \$26 is \$2.60, 5% is half of \$2.60, or \$1.30.
A 15% tip is about \$2.60 + \$1.30, or \$3.90.

Why it works

$15\% \times \$26 = (10\% + 5\%) \times \$26$	← Replace 15% with 10% + 5%.
$= (10\% \times \$26) + (5\% \times \$26)$	← Distributive Property
$= \$2.60 + (5\% \times \$26)$	← Find 10% × \$26.
$= \$2.60 + \left(\frac{1}{2} \times 10\% \times \$26\right)$	← Replace 5% with $\frac{1}{2}$ × 10%.
$= \$2.60 + \$1.30$	← Simplify inside the parentheses.
$= \$3.90$	← Add.

Check Understanding 2 Estimate a 15% tip for a bill of \$41.63.

3 EXAMPLE Estimating a Sale Price

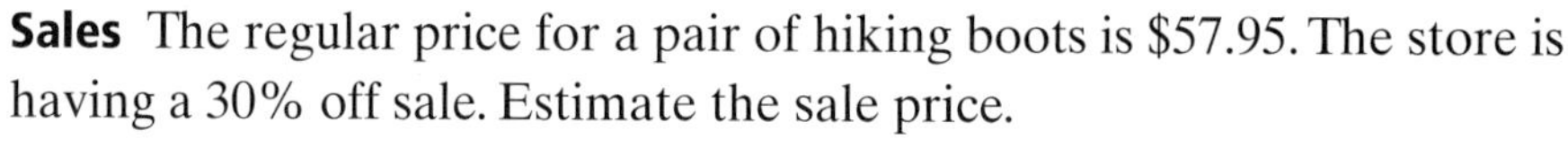

Sales The regular price for a pair of hiking boots is \$57.95. The store is having a 30% off sale. Estimate the sale price.

What you think

The regular price of the boots is about \$60. If the price is 30% off, you pay 100% − 30%, or 70% of the regular price.

70% of \$60 = \$42

The sale price is about \$42.

Why it works

The sale price is 30% off the regular cost.

$30\% \times \$60 = 0.3 \times \$60$	← Write 30% as 0.3.
$= \$18$	← Simplify.

Subtract the amount off the regular price to find the sale price.

\$60 − \$18 = \$42

3 **a.** A baseball glove is on sale for 40% off the original price of \$40.19. Estimate the sale price of the glove.

b. **Number Sense** Is the estimated sale price of the boots in Example 3 a high estimate or a low estimate? Explain how you know.

EXERCISES

For more practice, see *Extra Practice*.

A Practice by Example

Example 1 (page 303)

Using a sales tax rate of 7%, estimate the sales tax and total cost for each item.

1. a board game that costs \$27.60

2. a bicycle that costs \$129

3. a dictionary that costs \$14.59

4. a DVD that costs \$19.95

Example 2 (page 304)

Estimate a 15% tip for each bill amount.

5. \$41.90

6. \$8.60

7. \$79.10

8. \$40.60

Example 3 (page 304)

Estimate the sale price of each item.

9. 40% off a necklace for \$42

10. 50% off a sofa for \$789

11. 70% off a shirt for \$16.99

12. 90% off a jacket for \$68

B Apply Your Skills

Sales Tax **Use the sales tax rate table. Estimate the sales tax and total cost of each item below in each state.**

State Sales Tax

State	Tax
Florida	6%
Georgia	4%
Massachusetts	5%
Tennessee	7%

SOURCE: *The World Almanac*

13. in-line skates: \$75

14. calculator: \$18.50

15. erasers: \$.79

16. birthday card: \$2.99

17. sneakers: \$64.45

18. diary: \$5.29

Estimate each amount.

19. 50% of 89

20. 10% of 302

21. 30% of 295

22. 1% of 512

23. 25% of 59

24. 90% of 49

25. **Writing in Math** Suppose 5% tax on a restaurant bill is \$4.36. Explain how you can use this to find a 20% tip and a 15% tip.

26. **Jobs** Micah received the following tips. Estimate the value of each.
a. 20% of \$14.20
b. 10% of \$24.75
c. 15% of \$19.70
d. Which tip was the greatest value?

C Challenge

27. By the age of 2, a child's height is usually about 50% of his or her full adult height. Estimate the adult height of a 2-year-old whose height is 2 feet 9 inches.

28. **Stretch Your Thinking** What is the least number that has factors of 1, 2, 3, 4, 5, 6, 7, and 8?

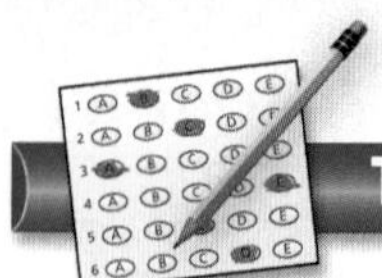

Test Prep

Multiple Choice

29. What is 20% of 128?
A. 2,600 **B.** 260 **C.** 130 **D.** 26

30. Kate estimates 15% of a bill and leaves a $3 tip. What is the amount of the bill?
F. $.20 **G.** $.45 **H.** $20.00 **I.** $45.00

31. Which value is greatest?
A. 25% of 81 **B.** 40% of 63 **C.** 70% of 49 **D.** 85% of 35

Extended Response

Online lesson quiz at **www.PHSchool.com**
Web Code: aaa-0608

32. Alabama has a 4% sales tax. Mississippi has a 7% sales tax. In Alabama, you can buy a camera on sale for $72.72. In Mississippi, you can buy the same camera for 20% off the regular price of $89.99.
(a) At which store would you pay less for a new camera?
(b) Explain your reasoning.

Mixed Review

Lesson 5-6

Solve the problem by first solving a simpler problem.

33. Benito's digital watch beeps every 30 minutes. How many times does it beep in the month of May?

Lesson 4-7

How many minutes are in each amount of time?

34. 1 h 15 min **35.** 2 h 10 min **36.** 5 h 45 min **37.** 6 h 20 min

Lesson 3-2

Use prime factorization to find the LCM of each set of numbers.

38. 12, 40 **39.** 18, 60 **40.** 8, 24, 36 **41.** 9, 30, 40

Checkpoint Quiz 2 Lessons 6-6 through 6-8

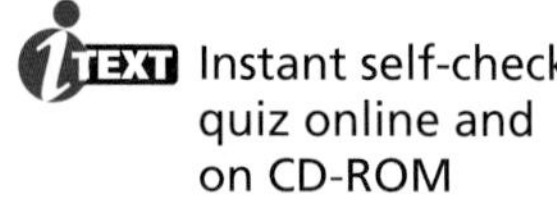

Instant self-check quiz online and on CD-ROM

1. Write 74% as a decimal and as a fraction in simplest form.

2. Write $\frac{21}{25}$ as a percent.

3. Using a sales tax rate of 5%, estimate the sales tax and total cost for a calendar that costs $14.95.

Find each percent.

4. 44% of 250 **5.** 25% of 72

6-9 Write an Equation

What You'll Learn

To solve problems by writing an equation

. . . And Why

To find the regular price of an item, as in Example 1

✓ Check Skills You'll Need

For help, go to Lesson 2-7.

Solve for *x*.

1. $9x = 45$
2. $x \div 15 = 6$
3. $12x = 54$
4. $\frac{x}{8} = 7.25$
5. $5.5x = 121$
6. $2.25x = 450$

OBJECTIVE 1 Solving Problems by Writing an Equation

When to Use This Strategy Writing an equation is a way to organize the information needed to solve a problem.

1 EXAMPLE Real-World Problem Solving

Real-World Connection

The Tour de France is an annual 3,300-kilometer bicycle race. Lance Armstrong won in 1999, 2000, 2001, and 2002.

Discount A bicycle is on sale for \$139.93. This is 30% off the regular price. What is the regular price of the bicycle?

Read and Understand The sale price of the bicycle, \$139.93, is 30% off the regular price. You need to find the regular price.

Plan and Solve You will pay 100% − 30%, or 70% of the regular price.

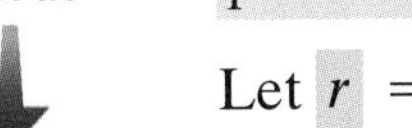

Words	percent you pay	times	regular price	equals	sale price
	Let r = the regular price.				
Equation	70%	×	r	=	\$139.93

$0.7r = 139.93$ ← **Write 70% as a decimal.**

$\frac{0.7r}{0.7} = \frac{139.93}{0.7}$ ← **Divide each side by 0.7 to find *r*.**

$r = \$199.90$ ← **Simplify.**

The regular price of the bicycle is \$199.90.

Look Back and Check The regular price is about \$200. The sale price is about 70% of \$200, or \$140. This is close to the sale price, \$139.93.

✓ Check Understanding 1 A sleeping bag is on sale for \$29.97. This is 25% off the original price. What is the regular price of the sleeping bag?

EXERCISES

For more practice, see *Extra Practice.*

A Practice by Example

Solve each problem by writing an equation.

Example 1 (page 307)

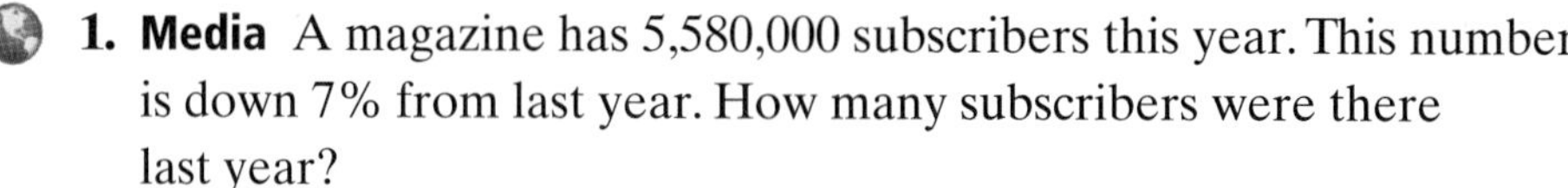

1. Media A magazine has 5,580,000 subscribers this year. This number is down 7% from last year. How many subscribers were there last year?

Need Help?

- Reread the problem.
- Identify the key facts and details.
- Tell the problem in your own words.
- Try a different strategy.
- Check your work.

2. A "light" popcorn has 120 Calories per serving. This is 25% fewer Calories than a serving of the regular popcorn. How many Calories does each serving of the regular popcorn have?

3. The sign at the entrance of a store reads, "30% off all winter apparel! Discount reflected at the register." The price tag of a coat is missing. The register rings up a price before tax of $55.93. What was the regular price of the coat?

4. A boat is on sale for 15% off. Its sale price is $1,700. What is the regular price of the boat?

B Apply Your Skills

Choose a strategy to solve each problem.

5. Sales What is the regular price of the snowboard at the right? The sale price is 20% off the regular price.

Using the sale price that is given, find the regular price for each item at a 20%-off sale.

6. kite: $16 **7.** yo-yo: $12

8. radio: $13.72 **9.** puzzle: $10.60

10. stationery: $7.56 **11.** CD: $11.96

Strategies

Draw a Diagram
Make a Graph
Make an Organized List
Make a Table and Look for a Pattern
Simulate a Problem
Solve a Simpler Problem
Try, Check, and Revise
Use Logical Reasoning
Work Backward
Write an Equation

12. Sales The regular price of a mountain bike is $175.

a. What is the price of the bike with a 10% discount?

b. What is the price of the bike with the 10% discount followed by a 2% discount for paying in cash?

c. **Writing in Math** Is a 10% discount followed by a 2% discount the same as a 12% discount? Explain.

13. Population According to the U.S. Census Bureau, the population of Illinois was 12,419,293 in the year 2000. Of the population, 26% was younger than 18 years of age. To the nearest hundred thousand, how many individuals in Illinois were *not* younger than 18 in the year 2000?

14. **Pennies** The height of 16 pennies is shown at the right. How tall is a stack of 50 pennies?

15. With 1,000,018,176 pennies, you could make five blocks of pennies, each the size of a school bus. Combined, the five blocks would weigh 3,125 tons. How much would two bus-sized blocks of pennies weigh?

Challenge

16. **Depreciation** A new car decreases in value by about 15% each year. Suppose you buy a new car this year for $15,500.
   a. What will be the value of the car after 1 year? 2 years? 5 years?
   b. Will the value of the car ever be zero? Explain.

17. **Stretch Your Thinking** How can you cut a bagel into eight equal pieces with just three cuts?

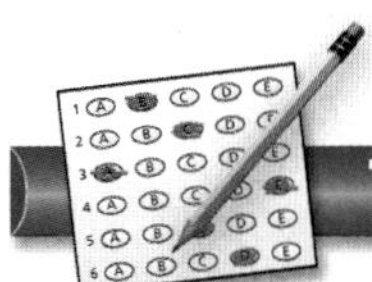

Test Prep

Multiple Choice

18. A pair of sandals is on sale for 65% off the regular price of $8.99. What is the sale price?

A. $3.15 B. $4.05 C. $5.84 D. $14.84

19. A restaurant bill is $15.50. What is the total cost with a 15% tip?

F. $2.33 G. $15.65 H. $17.83 I. $18.00

Take It to the NET
Online lesson quiz at
www.PHSchool.com
Web Code: aaa-0609

20. What is the solution of $24x = 120$?

A. 30 B. 20 C. 5 D. $\frac{4}{3}$

Short Response

21. Earrings at Store A are on sale for 25% off. Earrings at Store B are "Buy 3, Get 1 Free." The least expensive item is the free one. Suppose the regular prices of the earrings you like are $4.65, $5.75, $4.35, and $5.25 at each store. **(a)** At which store do you get a better bargain? **(b)** Explain your reasoning.

Mixed Review

Lesson 6-2

Do the ratios in each pair form a proportion?

22. $\frac{8}{5}, \frac{11}{7}$ 23. $\frac{45}{81}, \frac{5}{9}$ 24. $\frac{3}{23}, \frac{6}{50}$

Lesson 5-5

Algebra **Solve each equation. Check the solution.**

25. $\frac{a}{4} = 11$ 26. $\frac{b}{12} = 3$ 27. $\frac{1}{4}c = 5$ 28. $\frac{2}{3}d = 6$

Extension

Percents Under 1% or Over 100%

For Use With Lesson 6-9

Percents, like the ones modeled at the right, can be less than 1% or greater than 100%. Any fraction less than $\frac{1}{100}$ is less than 1%. Any fraction greater than $\frac{100}{100}$ is greater than 100%.

The examples below show you how to work with these percents.

0.5%

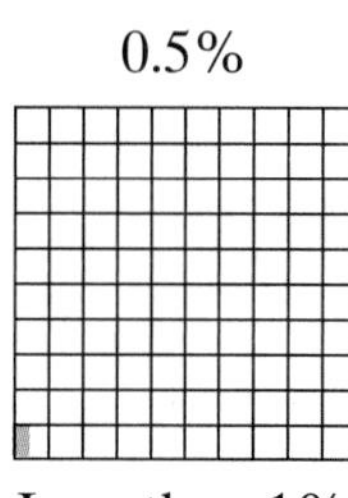

Less than 1%

105%

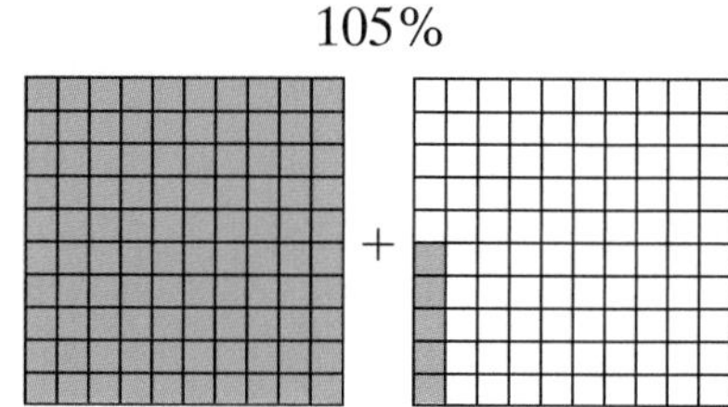

Greater than 100%

1 EXAMPLE Writing a Percent as a Decimal or Fraction

Write 0.4% as a decimal and as a fraction in simplest form.

000.4 ← **Move the decimal point two places to the left.**

0.004

$0.4\% = \frac{0.4}{100}$ ← **Write the percent as a fraction.**

$= \frac{4}{1,000}$ ← **Rewrite the fraction without a decimal.**

$= \frac{1}{250}$ ← **Write the fraction in simplest form.**

As a decimal, 0.4% is 0.004. As a fraction, 0.4% is $\frac{1}{250}$.

2 EXAMPLE Finding a Percent of a Number

Nutrition A vitamin supplement provides 150% of the Suggested Daily Value (SDV) of vitamin C. The SDV is 60 milligrams. How many milligrams of vitamin C are in the vitamin supplement?

$150\% \text{ of } 60 = 1.50 \times 60$ ← **Move the decimal point two places to the left.**

$= 90$

The vitamin supplement contains 90 milligrams of vitamin C.

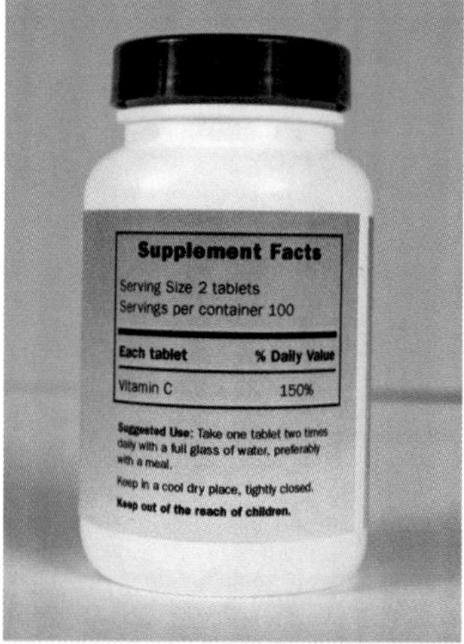

EXERCISES

Write each percent as a decimal and as a fraction in simplest form.

1. 0.2% **2.** 0.75% **3.** 110% **4.** 250%

Find each percent.

5. 400% of 5 **6.** 150% of 18 **7.** 0.5% of 300 **8.** 0.25% of 12

Test-Taking Strategies

Work Backward

The problem-solving strategy ***work backward*** is useful when taking multiple-choice tests. Work backward by testing each choice in the original problem. You will eventually find the correct answer.

EXAMPLE

A fruit stand is selling 8 bananas for $1.00. At this rate, how much will 20 bananas cost?

A. $1.50 **B.** $2.00 **C.** $2.50 **D.** $3.00

Use mental math to test the choices that are easy to use.

$2.00 is twice $1.00. Twice 8 is only 16, so choice B is not the answer.

$3.00 is three times $1.00. Three times 8 is 24, so choice D is not the answer.

Since 20 is between 16 and 24, the cost must be between $2.00 and $3.00. The answer is C.

EXERCISES

1. In the example, how much do 6 bananas cost?
   A. $.25 **B.** $.50 **C.** $.75 **D.** $1.00

2. The telephone company charged Omar for an overseas phone call. The rate was $2.40 for the first minute and $.55 for each additional minute. His bill was $6.80. For how many additional minutes was Omar charged?
   F. 7 **G.** 8 **H.** 9 **I.** 10

3. At the copy center, it costs $4.00 to print 100 copies. At this rate, how much will 450 copies cost?
   A. $16.00 **B.** $18.00 **C.** $20.00 **D.** $22.00

4. What method should NOT be used to find 88% of 40?
   F. 0.88×40 **G.** $\frac{88}{100} \times 40$ **H.** $\frac{n}{40} = \frac{88}{100}$ **I.** $\frac{40}{n} = \frac{88}{100}$

5. Anjeli collected 15 postcards. Some of the cards cost $.79 and some cost $1.19. She spent a total of $14.25. How many postcards of each price did she buy?
   A. 5 for $.79 each, 10 for $1.19 each
   B. 6 for $.79 each, 9 for $1.19 each
   C. 9 for $.79 each, 6 for $1.19 each
   D. 10 for $.79 each, 5 for $1.19 each

6. 40% of what number is 236?
   F. 5.9 **G.** 94.4 **H.** 590 **I.** 9,440

Chapter 6

Chapter Review

Vocabulary

cross products (p. 283)
equal ratios (p. 270)
percent (p. 294)
proportion (p. 278)
rate (p. 273)
ratio (p. 269)
scale (p. 288)
unit price (p. 274)
unit rate (p. 273)

Choose the vocabulary term from the column on the right that best completes the sentence.

1. The _?_ on a map may tell you 1 inch = 250 miles.
2. Two equal ratios can be written as a _?_.
3. You can use a _?_ to compare a part to a part.
4. An example of a _?_ is 25 miles per hour.
5. You can use a _?_ to compare a number to 100.

A. percent
B. proportion
C. rate
D. ratio
E. scale
F. unit rate

Take It to the NET
Online vocabulary quiz at www.PHSchool.com
Web Code: aaj-0651

Skills and Concepts

6-1 Objective

▼ To write ratios

A **ratio** compares two quantities by division. To write a ratio in simplest form, divide both numbers by their GCF. **Equal ratios** name the same number.

A jar contains 8 tacks, 15 bolts, and 23 nails. Write each ratio in three ways.

6. bolts to nails **7.** bolts to tacks **8.** nails to tacks **9.** bolts to total

Write each ratio in simplest form.

10. 8 to 32 **11.** $\frac{18}{30}$ **12.** 24 ft : 8 yd **13.** $\frac{45 \text{ boys}}{54 \text{ girls}}$

6-2 Objectives

▼ To find unit rates
▼ To use unit rates

A **rate** is a ratio that compares quantities measured in different units. A **unit rate** has a denominator of 1. To find a unit rate, divide the numerator by the denominator. A **unit price** gives the cost per unit.

14. You run 1 mile in 8 minutes. How long does it take to run 5 miles?

15. You earn $400 in 32 hours. How much do you earn in 1 hour?

16. Bread A loaf of bread costs $3.09 for 32 ounces or $1.40 for 24 ounces. Find each unit price and then determine the better buy.

6-3 and 6-4 Objectives

- To test ratios
- To complete proportions
- To identify proportions
- To solve proportions

A **proportion** is an equation stating that two ratios are equal.

Do the ratios in each pair form a proportion?

17. $\frac{2}{5}, \frac{1}{3}$ **18.** $\frac{6}{16}, \frac{21}{56}$ **19.** $\frac{15}{9}, \frac{5}{3}$ **20.** $\frac{3}{8}, \frac{9}{16}$

21. There are 944 marbles in a bag. If 3 out of 8 marbles are yellow, how many marbles are yellow?

6-5 Objectives

- To find the scale of a drawing
- To find dimensions

A **scale** is a ratio that compares a length on a model to an actual length.

Ships The *S.S. United States,* a passenger ship built in an American shipyard, is 990 feet long. Find the length of a model with the given scale.

22. 1 foot : 10 feet **23.** 3 inches : 20 feet **24.** 2 inches : 15 feet

6-6 and 6-7 Objectives

- To write percents as decimals and fractions
- To write decimals and fractions as percents
- To use proportions with percents
- To use decimals with percents

A **percent** is a ratio that compares a number to 100.

Write each percent as a fraction in simplest form and as a decimal.

25. 30% **26.** 25% **27.** 56% **28.** 12%

29. There are 200 students in your class, and 30% of them joined the school band. How many students in your class joined the band?

30. If 3 out of 5 children enjoy swimming, what percent like to swim?

6-8 Objective

- To estimate with percents

You can use mental math to estimate percents.

Estimate each amount.

31. 20% of 48 **32.** 6% of $19.99 **33.** 15% of $38.56

34. A game costs $18.95 and the sales tax is 7%. Estimate the total cost.

6-9 Objective

- To solve problems by writing an equation

You can write an equation to solve a problem.

35. Jobs You work every Monday, Friday, and Saturday for 4 hours each day. If you earn $7 per hour, how many weeks will it take to save $252?

36. Suppose you buy six comic books with the same price. You hand the clerk $20 and receive $3.50 in change. How much does each book cost?

Chapter Test

You have 3 nickels, 11 dimes, and 5 quarters in your pocket. Write each ratio in three ways.

1. nickels to quarters
2. dimes to nickels
3. dimes to total coins
4. quarters to dimes
5. Find the ratio of the shaded region to the unshaded region in simplest form. Use the figure below.

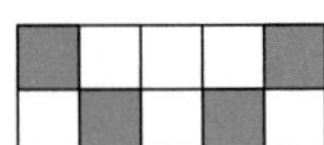

Write three ratios equal to each ratio.

6. 3 to 2
7. $\frac{3}{18}$
8. 6:8
9. **Cars** A car can go 28 miles per gallon of gas. How far can it travel with 8 gallons of gas?
10. A 6-ounce juice costs $.96. An 8-ounce juice costs $1.12. Which juice is the better buy?

Do the ratios in each pair form a proportion?

11. $\frac{5}{3}, \frac{15}{9}$
12. $\frac{3}{4}, \frac{4}{5}$
13. $\frac{8}{12}, \frac{12}{18}$

Solve each proportion.

14. $\frac{4}{5} = \frac{x}{25}$
15. $\frac{6}{4} = \frac{9}{m}$
16. $\frac{a}{25} = \frac{3}{10}$
17. **Groceries** A grocery store sells 6 pounds of apples for $4. How much will 8 pounds of apples cost? Round your answer to the nearest cent.
18. **Writing in Math** The ratio of girls to boys in a class is 5 to 6. Can there be 15 boys in the class? Explain why or why not.

Maps Use a map scale of 1 inch : 30 miles to find each actual distance.

19. 3 inches
20. 6 inches
21. 0.5 inches
22. A scale model of a tiger is 1.5 feet long. If the actual length is 9 feet, what scale is used?

Write each percent as a decimal and a fraction.

23. 25%
24. 6%
25. 98%

Write each decimal or fraction as a percent. If necessary, round to the nearest percent.

26. 0.48
27. 0.02
28. $\frac{1}{10}$
29. $\frac{3}{15}$
30. $\frac{5}{6}$
31. $0.\overline{9}$

Find each percent.

32. 5% of 200
33. 80% of 8
34. 2% of 50
35. Suppose 86% of 50 people at a law firm like their job. How many people like their job?

Estimate a 15% tip for each bill amount.

36. $32.04
37. $48.76
38. $12.83
39. **Sales Tax** Suppose you buy a DVD for $12.98. The sales tax is 7%. Estimate the total cost.
40. **Sales** A pair of sneakers is on sale for 25% off the regular price. The regular price is $89.96. What is the sale price?
41. **Sales** A dress is on sale for $32.88. This is 40% off of the regular price. Find the regular price.

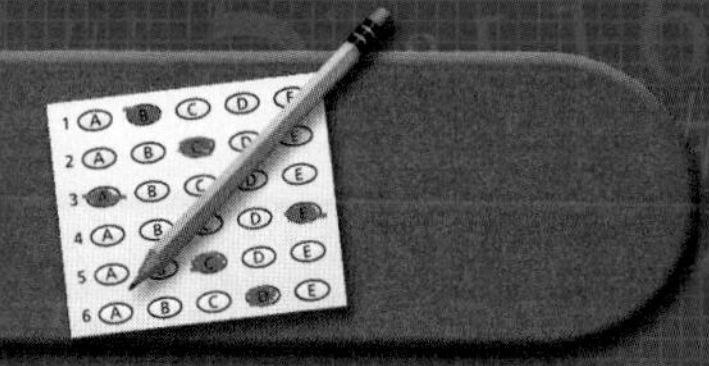

Test Prep

Cumulative Review
Chapters 1–6

Multiple Choice

Choose the correct letter.

1. Find the product of $\frac{2}{9}$ and $\frac{5}{7}$.
   A. $\frac{10}{63}$ B. $\frac{5}{31}$ C. $\frac{14}{45}$ D. $3\frac{3}{14}$

2. Which could you use to describe how to find $1\frac{3}{4}$ divided by $\frac{1}{2}$?
   F. Multiply $\frac{1}{2}$ and $\frac{7}{4}$. G. Multiply $\frac{1}{2}$ and $\frac{4}{7}$.
   H. Multiply $\frac{4}{7}$ and 2. I. Multiply $\frac{7}{4}$ and 2.

3. You bought a 12-count variety pack of dried fruit. Each bag of dried fruit contains c ounces. How many ounces of dried fruit did you buy?
   A. $c \div 12$ B. $12 \div c$
   C. $c + 12$ D. $12c$

4. Which statement is false?
   F. $\frac{8}{10} = \frac{32}{40}$ G. $\frac{1}{3} = \frac{12}{36}$
   H. $\frac{24}{42} = \frac{28}{49}$ I. $\frac{13}{14} = \frac{169}{196}$

5. Which decimal represents the portion of the model that is NOT shaded?

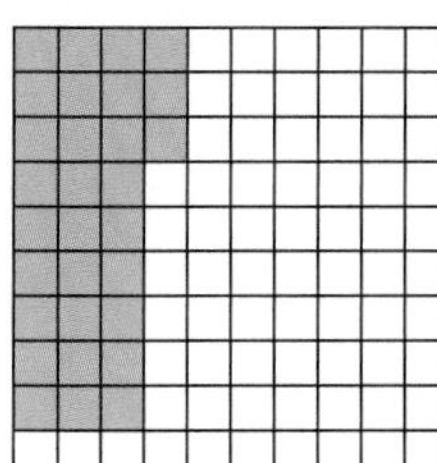

   A. 0.3 B. 0.33 C. 0.67 D. 0.7

6. Which of the following numbers is divisible by 2, 3, 5, 9, and 10?
   F. 1,350 G. 1,010 H. 945 I. 120

7. Choose an appropriate unit for measuring the length of a driveway.
   A. inches B. feet C. miles D. tons

8. Solve $x - \frac{1}{10} = \frac{1}{2}$ for x.
   F. $\frac{1}{10}$ G. $\frac{1}{6}$ H. $\frac{2}{5}$ I. $\frac{3}{5}$

9. At a car dealer, $\frac{2}{5}$ of the vehicles sold during the year were minivans. What percent of the vehicles sold were minivans?
   A. 2.5% B. 20% C. 25% D. 40%

Gridded Response

10. A bank teller spends about 8 minutes helping each customer. How long does the teller spend with 7 customers?

11. Solve $\frac{k}{9} = \frac{2}{5}$ for k. Write your answer as an improper fraction.

12. Find the product of $7\frac{5}{6}$ and $2\frac{1}{2}$. Write your answer as a decimal rounded to the nearest hundredth.

Short Response

13. Summer vacation is 68 days long and $\frac{3}{4}$ of vacation has gone by. How many days are left? Explain how you found your answer.

Extended Response

14. Your dinner bill comes to $19.68. Estimate your total cost for dinner with a 5% tax and a 20% tip. Justify your reasoning.

15. A customer service agent gets a phone call about every 12 minutes in a 7-hour work day. How many calls does she get in a 5-day work week? Explain how you found your answer.

Prehistoric Giants

Applying Proportions Dinosaurs first appeared on Earth about 230 million years ago and died out about 65 million years ago. Today, scientists study dinosaur remains to learn more about them. For example, scientists can calculate the size of a dinosaur by measuring bones they have found. Then they use proportions to estimate the dimensions of other bones.

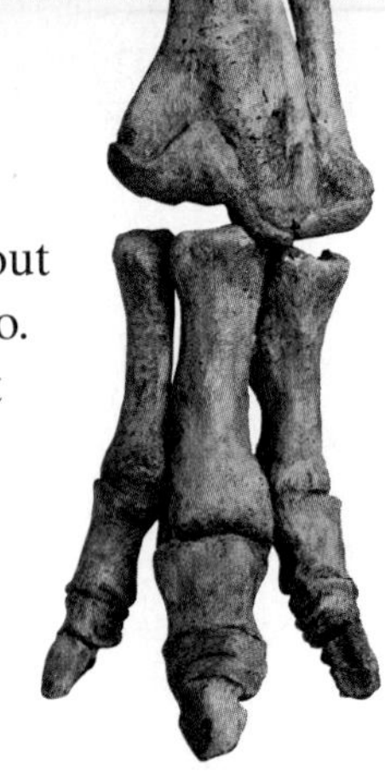

Fossilized Bones

Skeletons of animals that die in soft earth or mud can become fossils. Over time, the skeleton sinks and mud covers it. The mud turns to stone, preserving the skeleton.

Put It All Together

Data File Use the information on these two pages and on page 267 to answer these questions.

Materials centimeter ruler, poster board

Dinosaur Measurements (centimeters)

Body Part	Math Book Length	Actual Length	Poster Length
Height	■	■	■
Leg	■	■	■
Foot	■	■	■
Neck	■	■	■

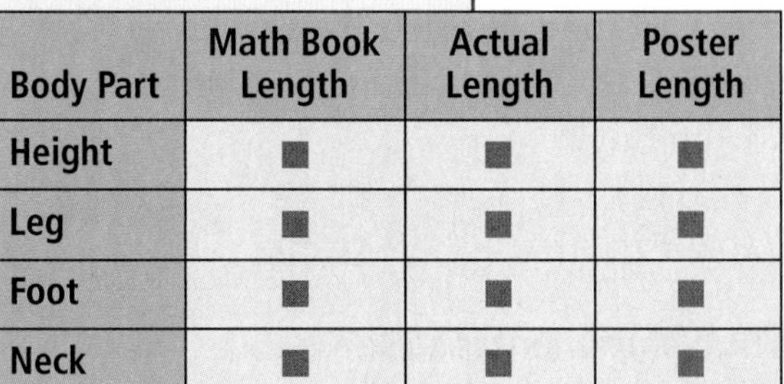

1. Copy the table.
  a. Measure the dinosaur in the photo. Complete the first column of the table.
  b. Measure the height of one of the people in the photo. Then measure your own height (in centimeters). Use the measurements to estimate the scale of the photo.
  c. Use your scale to estimate the actual dimensions of the dinosaur. Complete the second column of the table.

2. a. Open-Ended Choose a large object such as your family's car, your bicycle, your bed, or a desk in your classroom. Measure at least four different parts of the object in centimeters.
  b. Choose a scale that will allow a drawing of both the dinosaur and your object to fit on (and cover as much as possible of) the poster board. Write the scale in a corner of the poster board.
  c. Calculate the poster dimensions for the dinosaur and the object. Complete the third column of your table.
  d. Use the dimensions from part (c) to draw the dinosaur and the object on the poster board.

3. Research Choose an animal from the table on page 267. Find out what the animal looks like. Calculate its size using the scale for your poster. If possible, add a drawing of it to your poster.

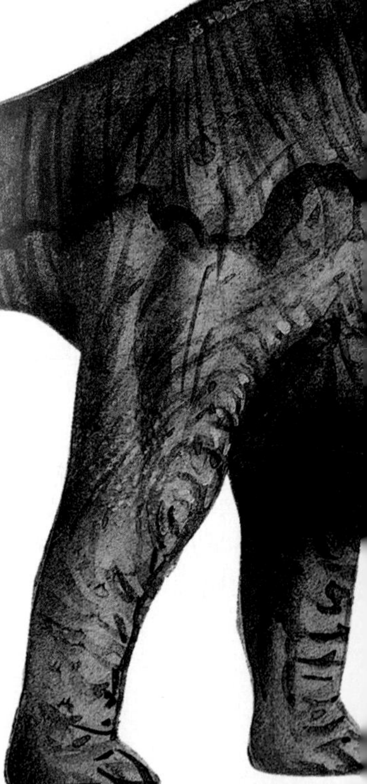

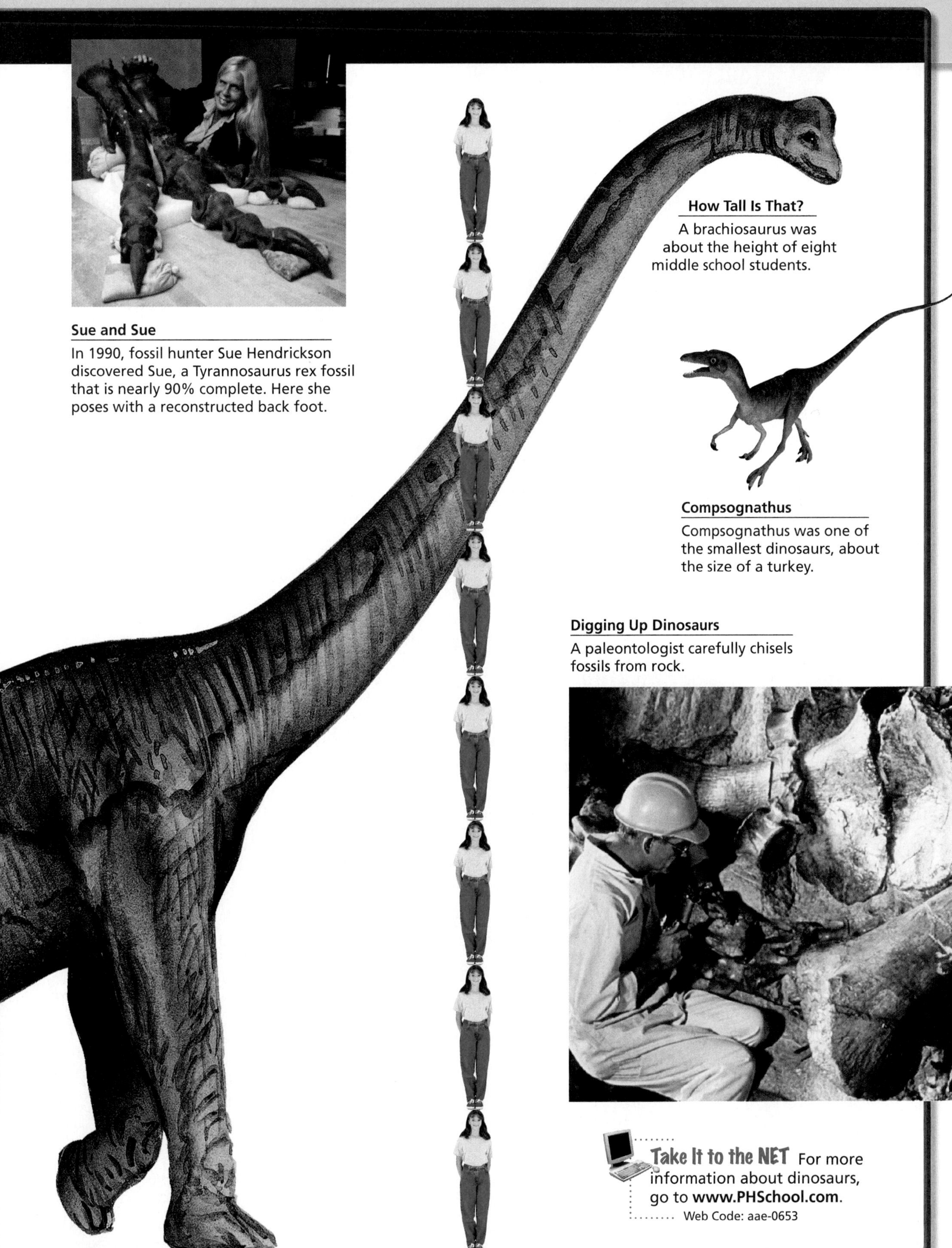

Sue and Sue

In 1990, fossil hunter Sue Hendrickson discovered Sue, a Tyrannosaurus rex fossil that is nearly 90% complete. Here she poses with a reconstructed back foot.

How Tall Is That?

A brachiosaurus was about the height of eight middle school students.

Compsognathus

Compsognathus was one of the smallest dinosaurs, about the size of a turkey.

Digging Up Dinosaurs

A paleontologist carefully chisels fossils from rock.

Take It to the NET For more information about dinosaurs, go to **www.PHSchool.com.**

Web Code: aae-0653

CHAPTER 7

Data and Graphs

Lessons

Key Vocabulary

- bar graph (p. 335)
- cell (p. 347)
- circle graph (p. 341)
- frequency table (p. 326)
- histogram (p. 336)
- line graph (p. 336)
- line plot (p. 327)
- mean (p. 322)
- median (p. 323)
- mode (p. 323)
- outlier (p. 322)
- range (p. 327)
- spreadsheet (p. 347)
- stem-and-leaf plot (p. 352)

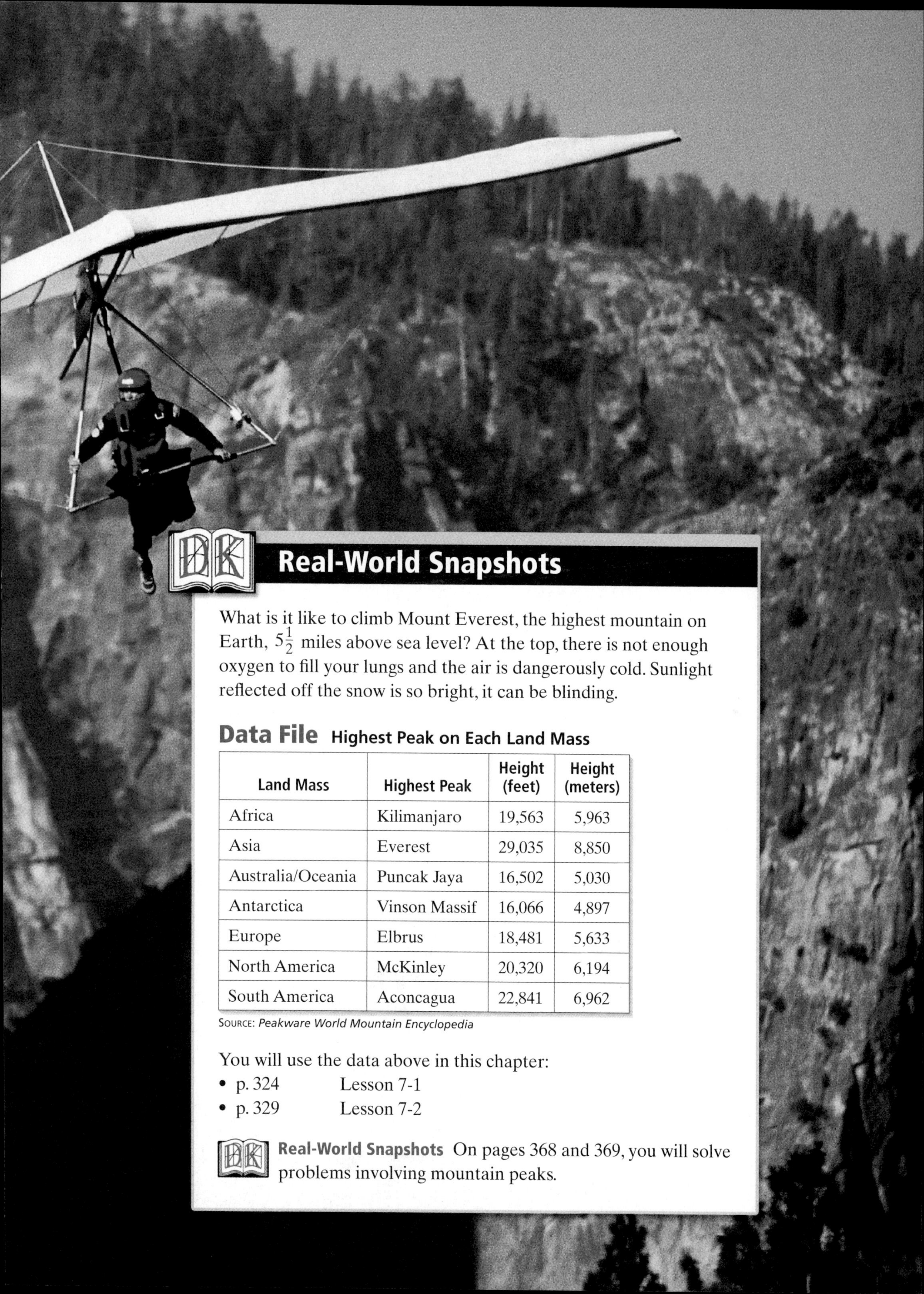

Real-World Snapshots

What is it like to climb Mount Everest, the highest mountain on Earth, $5\frac{1}{2}$ miles above sea level? At the top, there is not enough oxygen to fill your lungs and the air is dangerously cold. Sunlight reflected off the snow is so bright, it can be blinding.

Data File Highest Peak on Each Land Mass

Land Mass	Highest Peak	Height (feet)	Height (meters)
Africa	Kilimanjaro	19,563	5,963
Asia	Everest	29,035	8,850
Australia/Oceania	Puncak Jaya	16,502	5,030
Antarctica	Vinson Massif	16,066	4,897
Europe	Elbrus	18,481	5,633
North America	McKinley	20,320	6,194
South America	Aconcagua	22,841	6,962

SOURCE: *Peakware World Mountain Encyclopedia*

You will use the data above in this chapter:

- p. 324 Lesson 7-1
- p. 329 Lesson 7-2

Real-World Snapshots On pages 368 and 369, you will solve problems involving mountain peaks.

Chapter 7 Preview

Where You've Been

- In Chapter 1, you learned to order decimals. You also learned to add, subtract, multiply, and divide decimals.
- In Chapter 6, you learned to use ratios, proportions, and percents.

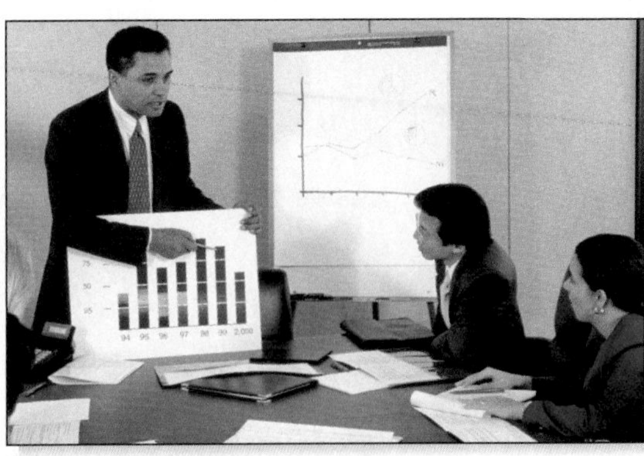

Businesses use graphs to organize and display the number of product sales.

Where You're Going

- In Chapter 7, you will find the mean, median, mode, and range of a set of data. You will also organize, display, and graph data.
- Applying what you learn, you will use a graph to keep track of the number of DVDs rented at a movie rental store.

Instant self-check online and on CD-ROM

Diagnosing Readiness

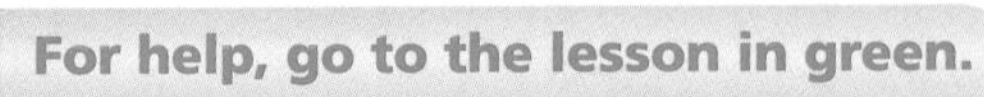

Ordering Decimals (Lesson 1-3)

Order from least to greatest.

1. 0.12, 0.13, 0.45, 0.35, 0.21

2. 45.1, 44, 46.01, 45.01

3. 102, 133, 124.32, 99.9, 100.80

4. 0.99, 2.5, 7.04, 4.9, 0.22

Adding Decimals (Lesson 1-5)

Find each sum.

5. $13.2 + 23.6 + 26.3$

6. $152.3 + 143.6 + 128$

7. $49.0 + 22.2 + 11.22 + 23.4$

8. $6.09 + 1.5 + 4.68 + 13.6$

Subtracting Decimals (Lesson 1-5)

Find each difference.

9. $109.55 - 89.34$

10. $10.42 - 9.36$

11. $75 - 73.2$

Dividing Decimals (Lesson 1-8)

Find each quotient.

12. $142.03 \div 10$

13. $361.6 \div 16$

14. $100.75 \div 25$

Exploring the Mean

For Use With Lesson 7-1

Work Together Activity

1. Write the full first name of each student in your class on strips of grid paper. Use one box for each letter. See the samples below.

2. Arrange the strips in order, based on the lengths of the names. Then use the data to make a graph, as shown below.

Length of First Names

5	6	7	8	9	10
	✗				
✗	✗		✗		✗

Number of Letters

3. a. What is the number of letters in the shortest name?
b. How many letters are in the longest name?

4. Writing in Math What is a typical length of a name of a classmate? Explain how you determined your choice(s).

5. Suppose you were to make a new name for each classmate. You must use as many letters from the strips as possible. Each name must be the same length. Here is a way to find out how many letters will be in each name:
a. Find the total number of letters in the names of your classmates.
b. Divide this sum by the number of names. If necessary, round to the nearest whole number.

6. The number you found in Question 5 is the average, or *mean,* length of a name of a classmate.
a. How does the mean compare to the lengths of the shortest and longest names?
b. How does the mean compare to the typical length you found in Question 4?

7-1 Mean, Median, and Mode

What You'll Learn

 To find the mean

 To find the median and the mode

. . . And Why

To find a mean test score, as in Example 1

For help, go to Lesson 1-8.

Find each quotient. Round to the nearest hundredth if necessary.

1. $330 \div 12$ **2.** $255.5 \div 6$ **3.** $237.4 \div 4$

4. $\frac{29.5}{5}$ **5.** $\frac{68.4}{8}$ **6.** $\frac{9.261}{3}$

New Vocabulary • mean • outlier • median • mode

Interactive lesson includes instant self-check, tutorials, and activities.

1 Finding the Mean

One way to describe a set of numbers is to find the mean. The **mean** of a set of data is the sum of the data divided by the number of data items.

1 EXAMPLE **Finding the Mean**  Real World

> **Reading Math**
> Another word for mean is *average*.

Grades Alena took four tests in science class. She scored 81, 77, 92, and 89. Find her mean test score.

$81 + 77 + 92 + 89 = 339$ ← **Add the test scores.**

$\frac{339}{4} = 84.75$ ← **Divide by the number of test scores.**

Alena's mean test score is 84.75.

Check for Reasonableness The mean must be between the least score, 77, and the greatest score, 92. So, the answer 84.75 is reasonable.

Check Understanding 1 Find the mean of each data set.

a. 3, 2, 8, 4, 2, 3, 1, 5 **b.** 12, 23, 19, 32, 26

c. 4, 16, 20, 40 **d.** 5, 15, 75, 105, 85

e. Reasoning Using the data set from part (d), find the mean of the numbers without the value 105. What do you notice?

An **outlier** is a data item that is far apart from the rest of the data. If a data set has an outlier, then the mean may not describe the data very well. For example, the mean of 1, 2, 6, and 47 is 14. This is much greater than the mean of 1, 2, and 6, which is 3.

OBJECTIVE

2 Finding the Median and the Mode

The **median** is the middle number in a set of ordered data.

4 7 9 13 25
↑
median

When there is an even number of data items, you can find the median by adding the two middle numbers and dividing by 2.

Real-World Connection

Careers A biologist studies the origins, structures, and activities of living organisms.

2 EXAMPLE Real-World Problem Solving

Biology A biologist studying the ecology of a river makes a weekly fish count. The results are 19, 18, 22, 23, 20, 24, 23, 20, 34, and 19. Find the median number of fish.

18, 19, 19, 20, 20, 22, 23, 23, 24, 34 ← **Order the data.**

18, 19, 19, 20, 20, 22, 23, 23, 24, 34 ← **Since there are 10 items (an even number), use the two middle values.**

$\frac{20 + 22}{2} = \frac{42}{2} = 21$ ← **Find the mean of 20 and 22.**

The median number of fish is 21.

Check Understanding 2 Find the median of each data set.

a. 86, 90, 88, 84, 102, 95, 7 **b.** 8, 42, 13, 7, 50, 91

You can also describe data by the mode. The **mode** is the data item(s) that appears most often. *If all data items occur the same number of times, there is no mode.* The mode is especially useful when the data are not numerical.

3 EXAMPLE Finding the Mode

The favorite lunches of 15 students are shown. What is the mode?

Favorite Lunch
hamburger, pizza, taco, pizza, spaghetti, taco, spaghetti, hamburger, hamburger, pizza, taco, pizza, pizza, spaghetti, taco

Group the data.

pizza, pizza, pizza, pizza, pizza

hamburger, hamburger, hamburger

taco, taco, taco, taco

spaghetti, spaghetti, spaghetti

Pizza occurs most often. It is the mode.

Check Understanding 3 Find the mode of the following data.

orange, banana, apple, orange, apple, apple, orange, apple

EXERCISES

For more practice, see *Extra Practice*.

A Practice by Example

Example 1 (page 322)

Find the mean of each data set. Exercise 1 has been started for you.

1. 12, 9, 11, 8, 9, 12, 9; $\frac{12 + 9 + 11 + 8 + 9 + 12 + 9}{7} = \blacksquare$

2. 14, 16, 28, 17, 20

3. 3, 2, 0, 2, 2, 3, 3, 1

4. 121, 95, 115, 92, 113, 108, 99, 97

5. 2.4, 1.8, 3.5, 2.3, 6.5

Example 2 (page 323)

Find the median of each data set.

6. 500, 450, 475, 450, 500

7. 0, 1, 1, 1, 0, 1, 1, 0, 0, 0

8. $\frac{3}{4}, \frac{1}{2}, \frac{5}{8}, \frac{3}{8}, \frac{1}{16}$

9. 14.1, 20.7, 24.3, 16.0, 20.8

10. **Temperatures** The daily high temperatures (°F) for one week are 86, 78, 92, 79, 87, 77, and 91. Find the median high temperature.

Example 3 (page 323)

Find the mode of each data set.

11. 8, 7, 8, 9, 8, 7

12. 15, 12, 17, 13, 20, 19

13. 95, 80, 91, 92, 94, 94, 98

14. 23, 24, 23, 25, 26, 24, 21

B Apply Your Skills

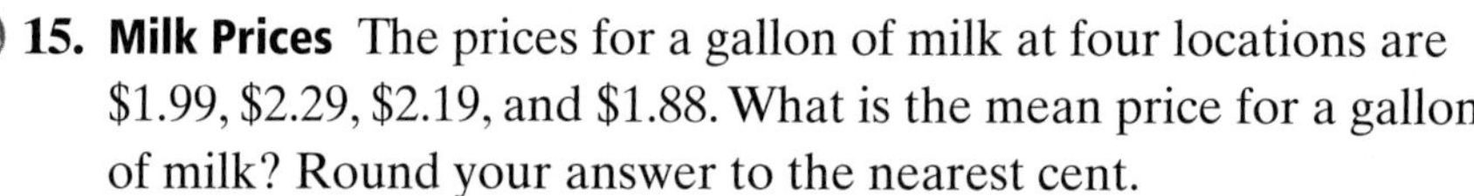

15. **Milk Prices** The prices for a gallon of milk at four locations are \$1.99, \$2.29, \$2.19, and \$1.88. What is the mean price for a gallon of milk? Round your answer to the nearest cent.

16. **Data File, p. 319** Use the data for the highest peaks on each land mass.
    a. Find the mean and median heights in feet of the highest peaks.
    b. Which peaks are taller than the mean?
    c. Which peaks are taller than the median?

Find the mean, median, and mode of each data set.

17. $12\frac{1}{2}$, 15, $13\frac{1}{2}$, 11, 13

18. 8, $7\frac{8}{10}$, $7\frac{1}{10}$, 9, $8\frac{3}{10}$, $7\frac{8}{10}$

19. **Writing in Math** The mean gas mileage (miles per gallon) for the family car is 23.5. How will the mean change if the next gas mileage reading is 27.3? 18.9? 23.5? Explain.

20. **Number Sense** The median of four numbers is 48. If three of the numbers are 42, 51, and 52, what is the other number?

21. **Books** The page lengths of five books are 198, 240, 153, 410, and 374. What is the median?

Challenge

22. Algebra The mean of 22, 19, 25, and x is 23. Find x.

23. **Stretch Your Thinking** Three purple and three white beads are arranged on a string, forming a circular bracelet. How many different patterns are possible?

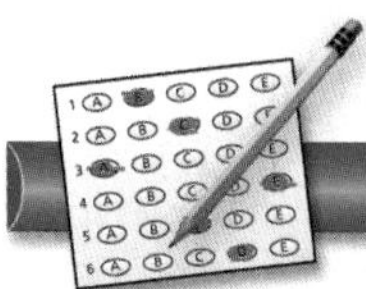

Test Prep

Reading Comprehension Read the passage below and answer the questions that follow.

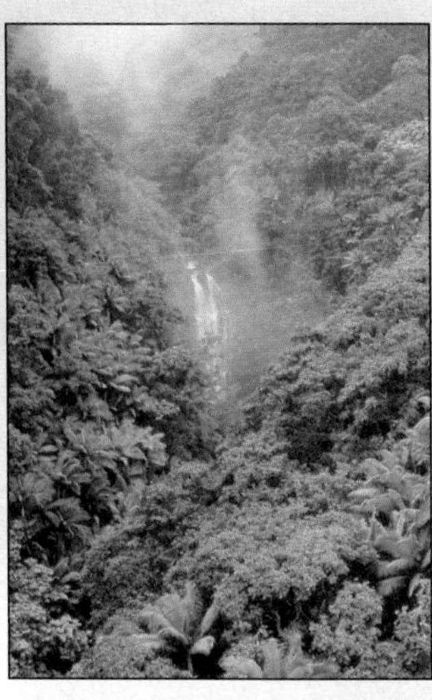

The Hawaiian Rain Forest

Tropical wet climates are found near the equator. With year-round heat and heavy rainfall, vegetation grows lush and green. Dense rain forests grow in these rainy climates.

In the United States, only Hawaii has a tropical wet climate. In some parts of Hawaii, rainfall is very heavy—over 400 inches per year on the windward side of the Hawaiian island of Kauai.

The table shows the monthly rainfall for one year at a reporting station in Hawaii.

Rainfall in Hawaii

Month	Rainfall (in.)
January	21
February	7
March	8
April	68
May	20
June	12
July	18
August	5
September	5
October	13
November	6
December	11

24. Find the mean and the median of the rainfall data in the table.

25. Find the mode. Does it represent the data well? Explain.

26. One year earlier, the total rainfall for April was 11 inches. Find the mean and the median using 11 inches, instead of 68 inches, for April.

Take It to the NET
Online lesson quiz at
www.PHSchool.com
Web Code: aaa-0701

Mixed Review

Lesson 6-6 **Write each fraction as a decimal and as a percent.**

27. $\frac{11}{20}$ **28.** $\frac{13}{25}$ **29.** $\frac{1}{50}$ **30.** $\frac{1}{80}$

Lesson 5-5 Algebra **Solve each equation. Check the solution.**

31. $\frac{a}{8} = 20$ **32.** $\frac{3}{4}b = 1$ **33.** $\frac{c}{10} = 3$ **34.** $\frac{6}{7}d = 6$

7-2 Organizing and Displaying Data

What You'll Learn

To organize data by making a frequency table

To make a line plot and find the range

. . . And Why

To organize data about DVDs, as in Example 2

✔ Check Skills You'll Need

For help, go to Lesson 7-1.

Find the mode of the data set.

1. red, blue, green, blue, green, blue, red, red, green, green, blue

Find the mean, median, and mode of each data set.

2. 5, 8, 6, 4, 5, 6, 7, 3, 4, 4

3. 1.5, 0, 3, 0, 2, 0, 8.5, 1

New Vocabulary • frequency table • line plot • range

OBJECTIVE

 Interactive lesson includes instant self-check, tutorials, and activities.

1 Making a Frequency Table

A **frequency table** is a table that lists each item in a data set with the number of times the item occurs.

1 EXAMPLE Making a Frequency Table

A student made the list at the left to show her classmates' favorite colors. Organize the data by making a frequency table. What is the mode?

Favorite Colors	
Blue	Blue
Purple	Red
Red	Orange
Blue	Yellow
Blue	Green
Yellow	Blue
Green	Yellow
Purple	Blue

Favorite Color

Color	Tally	Frequency
Blue	~~IIII~~ I	6
Green	II	2
Orange	I	1
Purple	II	2
Red	II	2
Yellow	III	3

Make a tally mark for each color chosen.

The number of tally marks in each row is the frequency.

Since most students selected blue as their favorite color, the mode is blue.

✔ Check Understanding 1 The first initial of the names of 15 students are listed below.

A J B K L C K D L S T D V P L

a. Organize the data by making a frequency table. What is the mode?

b. **Reasoning** Explain why you cannot find the mean of the data in Example 1.

OBJECTIVE

2 Making a Line Plot and Finding the Range

A **line plot** is a graph that shows the shape of a data set by stacking X's above each data value on a number line.

2 EXAMPLE Making a Line Plot  Real World

Business Suppose your cousin works at Uptown Movie Rental. His manager asks him to keep track of the number of DVDs rented by each customer. Make a line plot to display the data shown below.

3 5 1 2 2 1 4 1 4 2 3
3 4 1 5 2 6 2 2 4 3 1 4

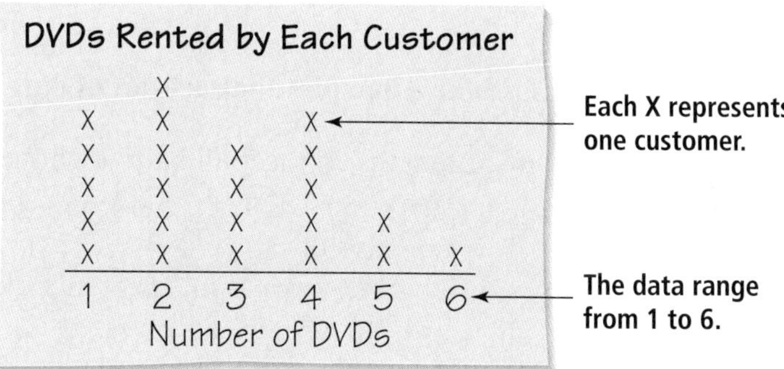

✓ **Check Understanding** 2 Make a line plot of the number of phone calls made by employees in one day: 2, 3, 0, 7, 1, 1, 9, 8, 2, 8, 1, 2, 8, 7, 1, 8, 6, 1.

Real-World Connection

Mount Everest is nearly 5.5 miles above sea level.

The **range** of a data set is the difference between the least and greatest values.

3 EXAMPLE Finding the Range  Real World

Geography In 1849 and 1850, six different surveyors made the following measurements of the height of Mount Everest.

28,990 ft; 28,992 ft; 28,999 ft; 29,002 ft; 29,005 ft; 29,026 ft

What is the range of the measurements?

$29{,}026 - 28{,}990 = 36$ ← **Subtract the least from the greatest value.**

The range of measurements is 36 feet.

✓ **Check Understanding** 3 Find the range for each data set.

a. 36, 21, 9, 34, 36, 10, 4, 35, 5, 30, 28, 27, 5, 10

b. 0.12, 0.11, 0.16, 0.15, 0.20, 0.18, 0.24, 0.7

c. **Reasoning** If two sets of data have the same range do they also have the same median? Explain your reasoning.

For more practice, see *Extra Practice.*

A Practice by Example

Example 1 (page 326)

Organize each set of data by making a frequency table.

1. days in each month:

31 28 31 30 31 30 31 31 30 31 30 31

2. vehicles in a parking lot:

pick-up	compact	compact	mid-size
compact	SUV	mid-size	SUV
mid-size	compact	station wagon	pick-up
compact	compact	mid-size	pick-up
compact	mid-size	SUV	compact
compact	compact	mid-size	station wagon

Example 2 (page 327)

Make a line plot for each set of data.

3. lengths of baseball bats (inches):

30 29 31 28 29 29 30 32 30 29 28 30 30

4. lengths of words in a sentence (letters):

7 2 6 1 7 6 9 1 8 4 2 3 10

Example 3 (page 327)

Find the range for each data set.

5. land areas of the seven midwestern states: shown in the table at the right

6. ages of the first ten U.S. Presidents when they took office: 57, 61, 57, 57, 58, 57, 61, 54, 68, 51

7. heights of trees (meters): 2.3, 1.8, 3.4, 2.5, 2.9, 3.1, 3.2, 3.5, 2.8, 2.7, 2.6, 2.7, 2.2

8. prices of new CD players: $145, $219, $359, $270, $162, $349

Land Areas of Midwestern States (square miles)	
Illinois	55,646
Indiana	35,936
Iowa	55,965
Michigan	56,959
Minnesota	79,548
Ohio	41,004
Wisconsin	54,424

B Apply Your Skills

9. Social Studies A town in Wales is named Llanfairpwllgwyngyllgogerychwyrndrobwllllantysiliogogogoch.

a. Make a frequency table for the letters that make up the name of the Welsh town.

b. **Writing in Math** Use the mean, median, or mode to describe the data recorded in your frequency table. Explain your choice.

10. Concert Tickets The prices of tickets for a concert are $45, $36, $30, $41, $25, $20, $44, $38, and $34. Find the range.

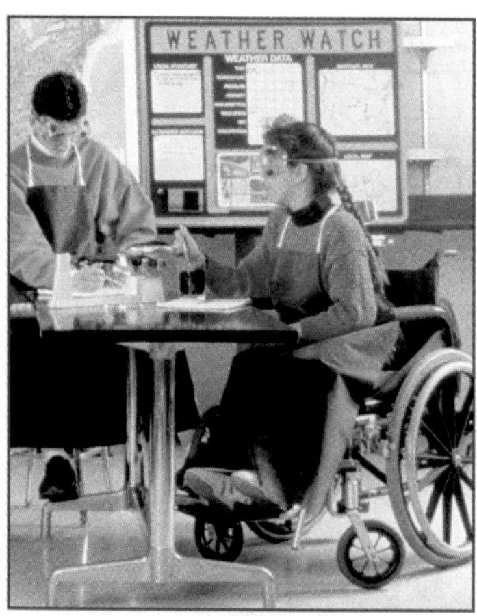

Real-World Connection

Science grades often include students' lab work.

Use the line plot at the right for Exercises 11–13.

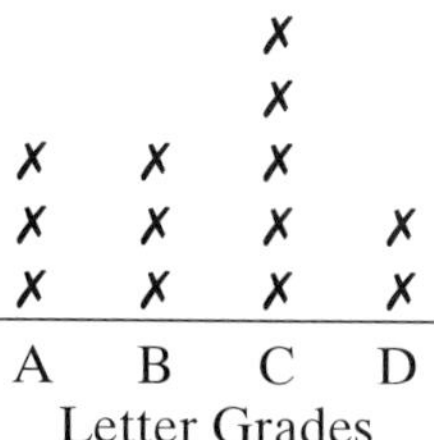

11. What information is displayed?

12. How many test grades are recorded?

13. How many students received a grade of C or better?

14. Speed Limits On a highway, the minimum speed allowed is 40 miles per hour and the maximum speed is 65 miles per hour. What is the range of speeds allowed on the highway?

Draw a line plot for each frequency table.

15.

Number	Tally	Frequency
1	IIII	4
2	I	1
3	III	3
4	III	3
5	I	1
6	I	1
7	I	1
10	I	1

16.

Number	Tally	Frequency
15	I	1
17	I	1
18	I	1
19	II	2
20	IIII	4
21	II	2
22	II	2
24	I	1

17. Siblings The line plot at the right shows the number of siblings (brothers and sisters) that each student has.

a. Find the median and mode.

b. Reasoning Would it make sense to use the mean to describe these data? Why or why not?

c. How many siblings do the 19 students have?

0: X X X X
1: X X X X X X X
2: X X X X X
3: X X
4: X

Correct Answers on Quiz

Number Correct	Tally	Frequency
20	II	2
19	II	2
18	~~IIII~~	5
17	~~IIII~~ I	6
16	II	2
15	II	2
14	III	3

18. The frequency table at the left shows the number of correct answers for each student on a 20-question quiz.

a. What is the mean number of correct answers?

b. What score is the median?

c. What score is the mode?

d. What is the range of the number of correct answers?

19. Data File, p. 319 What is the range in meters of the highest peaks on each land mass?

20. Open-Ended Make two sets of data with the same range but different means.

Challenge

Use the frequency table for Exercises 21 and 22.

Number of Pets Owned

Pet	Tally	Frequency
Bird	𝍸 ||	7
Cat	𝍸 𝍸 𝍸	15
Dog	𝍸 𝍸 𝍸 |||	18
Fish	𝍸 ||||	9
Hamster	|||	3
Other	𝍸	5

21. What percent of the pets are dogs?

22. Half of the pet owners surveyed had one pet and the other half had two pets. How many pet owners are represented in this survey?

23. **Stretch Your Thinking** Henry, Curtis, and Leon were trying to guess the number of buttons in a jar. Henry guessed 113, Curtis guessed 119, and Leon guessed 120. One of the guesses was correct, one missed by 6, and one missed by 1. Who guessed the correct number of buttons?

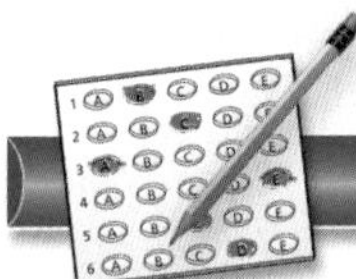

Test Prep

Multiple Choice

Use the results of a 10-point quiz shown at the right.

Quiz Scores		
8	5	9
7	8	6
10	10	8
8	7	10

24. What is the range of the quiz scores?
A. 10 **B.** 9 **C.** 5 **D.** 4

Take It to the NET
Online lesson quiz at
www.PHSchool.com
Web Code: aaa-0702

25. What is the mean? Median? Mode?
F. 7; 8; 10 **G.** 5; 6; 9 **H.** 8; 8; 8 **I.** 8; 8; 10

Short Response

26. **a.** Make a line plot of the quiz scores.
b. How many grades are greater than 7?

Mixed Review

Lesson 6-4

Use a map scale of 1 cm : 100 km to find the actual distance for each map distance given below.

27. 5 cm **28.** 1.8 cm **29.** 8.3 cm **30.** 0.9 cm

Lesson 5-1

Find each product.

31. $\frac{3}{5} \times \frac{1}{2}$ **32.** $\frac{5}{8} \times \frac{3}{10}$ **33.** $\frac{1}{4} \times \frac{8}{9}$ **34.** $\frac{3}{16} \times \frac{32}{33}$

Reading Math

Reading Graphs

For Use With Lesson 7-2

When you read a graph, pay attention to the following.

- **Type of Graph** *Bar graphs* show comparisons. *Line graphs* show trends over time. *Circle graphs* describe the parts that make up the whole.
- **Title** This tells the information you will find in the graph.
- **Labels on the Axes** These tell what the data on each axis represent. Use the numbers on an axis to determine the scale of the graph.

EXAMPLE

Identify the parts on the graph at the right. What can you learn from the data?

- Type of graph: The graph is a bar graph and shows comparisons.
- Title: The title is "Students Enrolled in Band."
- Labels on the axes: The horizontal axis gives the year. The vertical axis gives the number of students. The scale counts by 5.
- Summary: The graph shows that each year more students were enrolled in band.

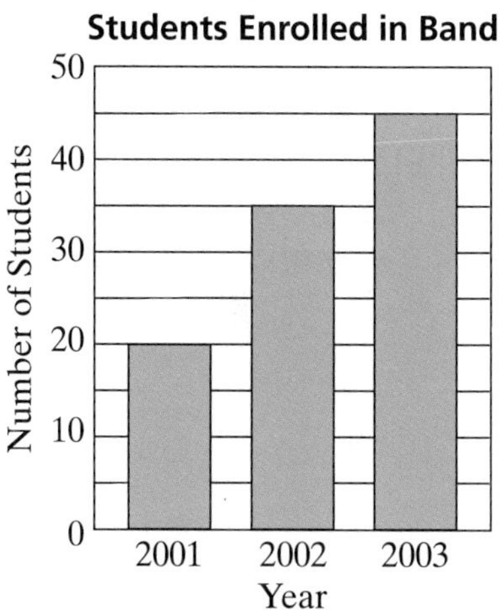

EXERCISES

Use the graph at the right for Exercises 1–4.

Money Collected for Community Project

Money Collected: $100, $200, $300

Year: '94, '96, '98, '00, '02

1. What type of graph is shown?
2. What is the title of the graph?
3. **a.** Describe the axes.
   b. What scale is used on the vertical axis?
4. What can you learn from the graph?

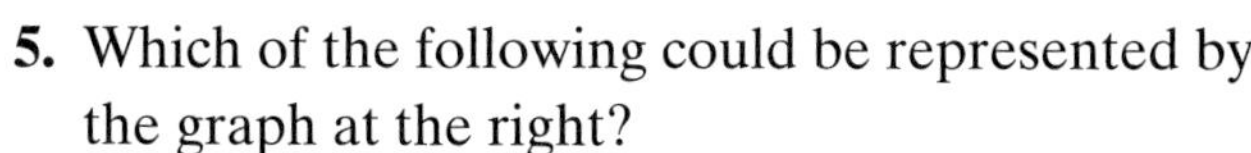

5. Which of the following could be represented by the graph at the right?
   A. the number of brothers and sisters students have
   B. the ages of students in the class
   C. the number of days absent from school in one week
6. Based on your answer from Exercise 5, write labels for the axes and write a title for the graph.

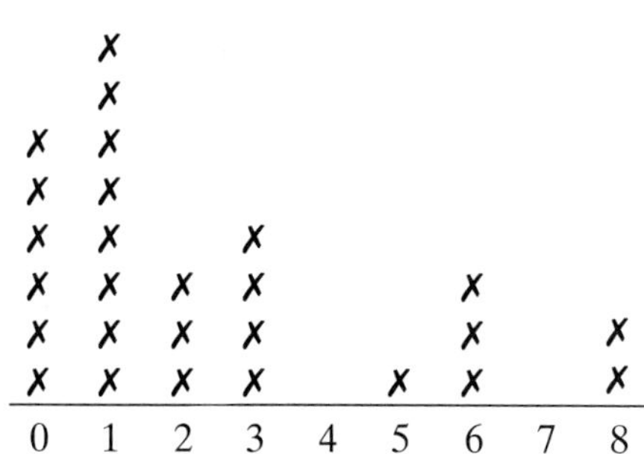

Problem Solving

7-3 Make an Organized List

What You'll Learn

To solve a problem by making an organized list

. . . And Why

To keep track of exercise data, as in Example 1

✓ Check Skills You'll Need

For help, go to Lesson 2-1.

Write the next three terms in each number pattern.

1. 7, 14, 21, 28, …
2. 1, 4, 7, 10, …
3. 88, 79, 70, 61, …
4. 4, 12, 36, 108, …

OBJECTIVE

 Interactive lesson includes instant self-check, tutorials, and activities.

1 Solving Problems By Making an Organized List

When to Use This Strategy An organized list can help you analyze data.

1 EXAMPLE Using an Organized List

Real World

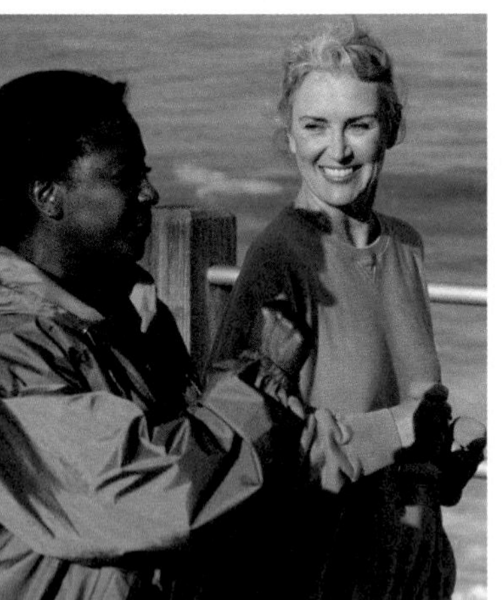

Running Tara wants to walk in a charity event. In her first week of training, she walks three miles each day. Each week after that she adds $\frac{3}{4}$ mile to her daily distance. In which week of training does Tara walk six miles per day?

Read and Understand During the first week of training, Tara walks three miles each day. Each week, she walks an additional $\frac{3}{4}$ mile every day. You need to find the week when her daily walk will be six miles.

Plan and Solve Make an organized list that shows week and distance. Stop when the distance reaches six miles.

Week	Distance (miles/day)
1	3
2	$3 + \frac{3}{4} = 3\frac{3}{4}$
3	$3\frac{3}{4} + \frac{3}{4} = 4\frac{1}{2}$
4	$4\frac{1}{2} + \frac{3}{4} = 5\frac{1}{4}$
5	$5\frac{1}{4} + \frac{3}{4} = 6$

Tara walks six miles per day during her fifth week of training.

Look Back and Check You can check by working backward. In five weeks there were 4 increases of $\frac{3}{4}$ mile. $4 \times \frac{3}{4} = 3$. So, the total increase was 3 miles. The 3-mile increase plus the original 3 miles per day = 6 miles.

✓ Check Understanding 1 Suppose you plan to read a novel. Every day, you want to read two more pages than you did the day before. If you read just one page on the first day, on what day will you reach page 64?

EXERCISES

For more practice, see *Extra Practice.*

A Practice by Example

Solve each problem by making an organized list.

Example 1 (page 332)

1. **Making Change** How many ways can you make 25 cents using pennies, nickels, and dimes?

2. A baseball team has six pitchers (players A, B, C, D, E, and F) and three catchers (players G, H, and I). How many pitcher-catcher pairs can the coach choose from? An organized list has been started for you.

Pitcher – Catcher
A – G
A – H
A – I

3. Find the smallest number that meets all of these conditions.
   - When you divide the number by 7, the remainder is 1.
   - When you divide the number by 9, the remainder is 7.
   - When you divide the number by 11, the remainder is 10.

Need Help?
- Reread the problem.
- Identify the key facts and details.
- Tell the problem in your own words.
- Try a different strategy.
- Check your work.

B Apply Your Skills

Choose a strategy to solve each problem.

4. How many triangles are in the figure at the right?

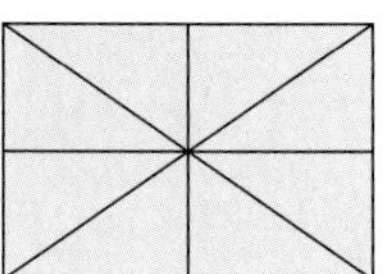

5. **Saving** Your plan is to save \$1 the first week, \$2 the second week, \$4 the third week, \$8 the fourth week, \$16 the fifth week, and so on.
   a. List the total amount you will have saved after each of the first 6 weeks.
   b. **Writing in Math** How can you use the amount saved in a given week to predict the total saved by that week?

Strategies

Draw a Diagram
Make a Graph
Make an Organized List
Make a Table and Look for a Pattern
Simulate a Problem
Solve a Simpler Problem
Try, Check, and Revise
Use Logical Reasoning
Work Backward
Write an Equation

6. **Patterns** The numbers 1, 3, 6, 10, . . . are called *triangular numbers* because of the following pattern.

   a. What number can you add to 10 to get the next triangular number?
   b. What are the next two triangular numbers after 10?

C Challenge

7. **Clocks** A clock chimes once at 1:00, twice at 2:00, and so on. The clock also chimes once at 1:30, 2:30, and so on. How many times will the clock chime from 12 A.M. Monday through 11:59 P.M. Tuesday?

8. **Stretch Your Thinking** You open a book to two facing pages. The product of the two page numbers is 600. Find the page numbers.

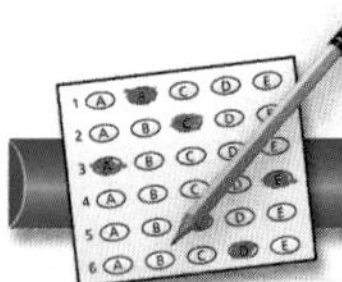

Test Prep

Multiple Choice

9. A bank account is opened with d dollars. Each month, \$3 is deposited. How much money was deposited to the account in one year?
   A. $3d$ B. $d + 3$ C. $d + 12$ D. $d + 36$

Take It to the NET
Online lesson quiz at
www.PHSchool.com
Web Code: aaa-0703

10. Which of the following is NOT equivalent to the other three?
    F. 3^4 G. 27×3 H. $6 \cdot 13$ I. 9^2

11. Which equation has the solution $m = 2$?
    A. $10m = 5$ B. $2 - m = 0$ C. $m + 1 = 1$ D. $3m = 5$

Short Response

12. Suppose you have 1 nickel, 1 dime, and 1 quarter. Explain how you would find the different amounts of money that can be made using one or more coins by using an organized list.

Mixed Review

Lesson 5-7 **Choose the heavier weight.**

13. 14 oz or 1 lb
14. 34 oz or 3 lb
15. $\frac{1}{4}$ lb or 8 oz

Lesson 5-3

Algebra **Find each quotient for $x = \frac{3}{4}$. Write the answer in simplest form.**

16. $15 \div x$
17. $x \div 12$
18. $\frac{9}{16} \div x$
19. $x \div \frac{15}{16}$

Checkpoint Quiz 1 — Lessons 7-1 through 7-3

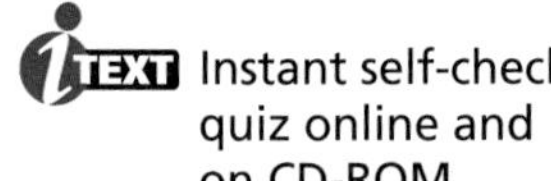

Instant self-check quiz online and on CD-ROM

1. Find the mean, median, mode, and range of the following data.

   40 30 42 31 16 30 33 18 30

Use the line plot for Exercises 2 and 3.

2. Find the median.
3. Find the mode.

High Temperatures

Temperature (°C)	17	18	19	20	21	22	23	24	25	26
X marks	x	x x	x	x	x x x x	x x x		x x		x

4. **Nutrition** The grams of fat per serving for 25 breakfast cereals are 0, 1, 1, 3, 1, 1, 2, 2, 0, 3, 1, 3, 2, 0, 1, 0, 2, 1, 1, 0, 0, 0, 2, 1, and 0. Make a frequency table of the data.

5. How many ways can you make \$.50 with nickels, dimes, and/or quarters?

7-4 Bar Graphs and Line Graphs

What You'll Learn

To make bar graphs

To make line graphs

. . . And Why

To display nutrition data in a graph, as in Example 1

Check Skills You'll Need

For help, go to Lesson 7-2.

Make a line plot for each set of data.

1. 5, 6, 7, 8, 6, 5, 8, 7, 10, 9, 8, 8, 7, 5, 12
2. 1.3, 1.2, 1.0, 1.0, 1.1, 1.4, 1.3, 1.0, 1.2, 1.2, 1.3, 1.0
3. 13, 17, 10, 21, 17, 15, 15

New Vocabulary • bar graph • histogram • line graph

Interactive lesson includes instant self-check, tutorials, and activities.

OBJECTIVE 1 Making Bar Graphs

A **bar graph** uses vertical or horizontal bars to display numerical information. You can use a bar graph to compare amounts.

1 EXAMPLE Making a Bar Graph

Real World

Nutrition Make a bar graph to display the data at the left.

Calcium Content

Food Item (1 cup)	Calcium (mg)
Milk	300
Yogurt	250
Cottage Cheese	150
Ice Cream	200
Broccoli	80
Dried Beans	90

SOURCE: Carnegie Mellon University Health Services

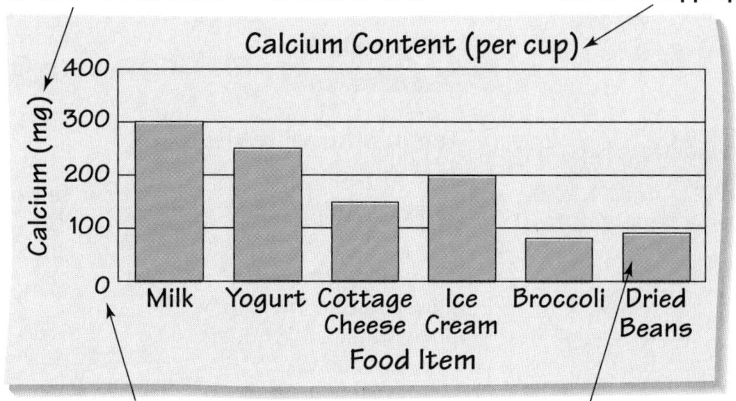

Check Understanding 1 Make a bar graph to display the data below.

Allowance Each Week					
Amount of Money ($)	3	4	5	6	7
Number of Students	10	21	34	12	6

A **histogram** is a bar graph that shows the frequency of each data item. Histograms often combine data into equal-sized intervals.

2 EXAMPLE **Making a Histogram** 

Intervals	Hours of Battery Life
8–11	11, 9, 8
12–15	12, 14, 15, 15
16–19	19, 17
20–23	22, 24, 21

Batteries Make a histogram to display the data at the left.

Step 1 Make a frequency table.

Hours	Tally	Frequency
8–11	|||	3
12–15	||||	4
16–19	||	2
20–23	|||	3

Step 2 Make a histogram.

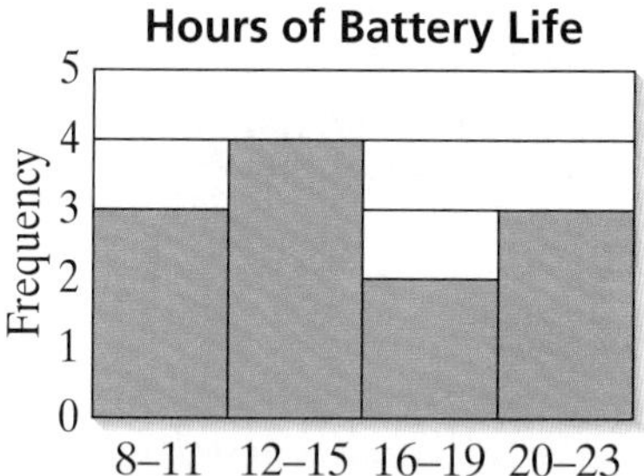

Check Understanding 2 In Example 2, which interval contains the median?

OBJECTIVE

2 Making Line Graphs

A **line graph** uses a series of line segments to show changes in data. Usually, a line graph shows changes over time.

3 EXAMPLE **Making a Line Graph** 

Temperatures Throughout the Day	
Time	Temperature
8 A.M.	62°F
10 A.M.	70°F
12 P.M.	78°F
2 P.M.	81°F
4 P.M.	76°F
6 P.M.	74°F

Temperature Use the data at the left to make a line graph.

Choose a scale. The data range from 62 to 81. Mark 60 to 85 in units of 5.

Draw and label the axes.

The break symbol means that the values between 0 and 60 are not shown.

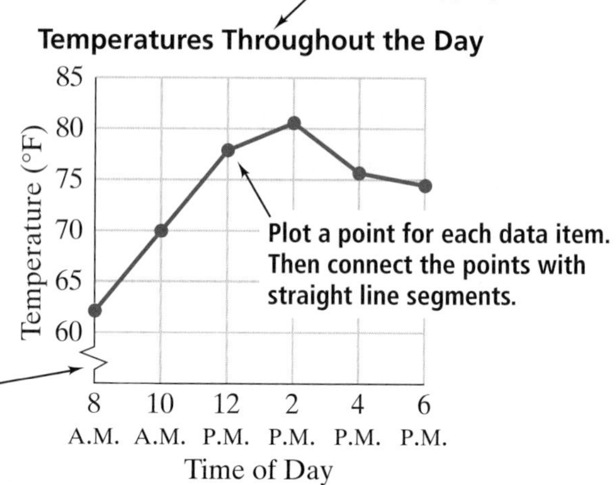

Check Understanding 3 Use the table at the right to make a line graph.

Ticket Sales				
Week	1	2	3	4
Tickets Sold	22	35	33	46

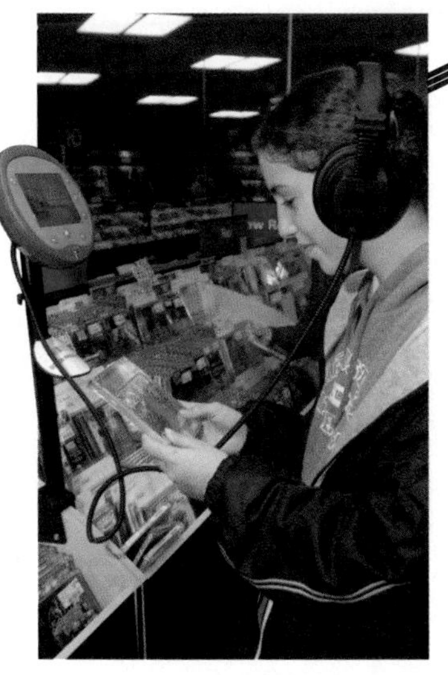

Investigation: Graphing and Reporting Survey Results

1. Write a survey question such as one of the following.
   - What is your favorite type of music?
   - How many hours do you spend watching television each week?
   - How many pets do you have?
2. Have each classmate answer your survey question.
3. Organize your data into a graph of your choice.
4. Write a paragraph to summarize the data you collected. Describe the mean, median, mode, and range, if possible.

EXERCISES

For more practice, see *Extra Practice*.

A Practice by Example

Example 1 (page 335)

Budgets **Use the table at the right.**

1. Make a bar graph to display the planned budgets.
2. Make a bar graph to display the actual budgets.

Monthly Budget

Cost Item	Planned	Actual
Dining Out	$40	$28
Clothes	$35	$42
Concerts	$18	$6
Movies	$22	$22

Example 2 (page 336)

Make a histogram of the data from each table.

3. **Time Spent on Homework**

Intervals	Minutes
0–59	30, 25, 45
60–119	107, 78, 65, 90
120–179	135
180–239	185

4. **Plant Height**

Intervals	Inches
0–24	7, 8, 19, 3, 4, 5
25–49	43, 29, 26
50–74	61
75–99	78, 84

Example 3 (page 336)

5. **Hot Lunches** Make a line graph of the data below.

Students Buying Hot Lunch

Day	Mon.	Tue.	Wed.	Thur.	Fri.
Number of Students	125	143	165	48	183

B Apply Your Skills

6. **Prime Ministers** Make a bar graph to show how many years each prime minister was in office.

Meir (Israel)
5 years

Gandhi (India)
18 years

Thatcher (UK)
11 years

Bruntland (Norway)
13 years

7. **Business** A store tracks the number of customers it has each day.
   a. Make a line graph of the data. Monday: 134, Tuesday: 94, Wednesday: 113, Thursday: 146, Friday: 181, Saturday: 234
   b. What trend does your line graph show?

8. **Data Collection** Make a line graph showing the amount of time you spent on homework for each day of one week.

9. a. Make a histogram using each set of data below.
   b.  Writing in Math Compare the histograms. Do you think the data is better represented using 3 or 4 intervals? Explain your reasoning.

Age of Contestants

Intervals	Years
20–34	21, 28, 25
35–49	39, 36
50–64	57, 55

Age of Contestants

Intervals	Years
20–29	21, 28, 25
30–39	39, 36
40–49	
50–59	57, 55

C Challenge

10. a. **Airports** Which would you use to display the data at the right, a bar graph or a line graph? Explain your answer.
    b. Draw the graph.

11. **Stretch Your Thinking** How many four-digit whole numbers can you make using the digits 1, 4, 6, and 9 if you use each digit only once in each number?

World's Busiest Airports, 2001

Airport	Passengers (millions)
Atlanta	76
Chicago O'Hare	67
Los Angeles	62
London	61
Tokyo	59
Dallas-Ft. Worth	55

SOURCE: Airports Council International

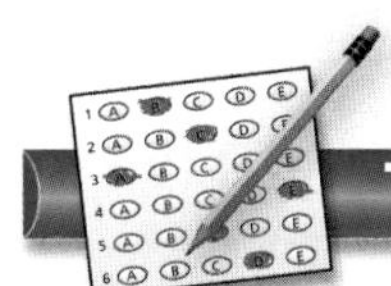

Test Prep

Gridded Response

For Exercises 12–15, use the graph showing electoral votes.

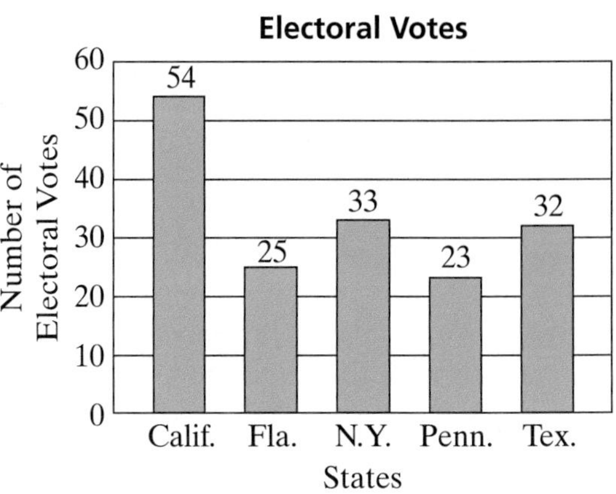

12. How many votes do these five states have in all?

13. What is the range?

14. How many more votes does Texas have than Florida?

15. To be elected President, a candidate needs 270 electoral votes. Suppose a candidate wins the five states above. How many more electoral votes would the candidate need to be elected?

Take It to the NET
Online lesson quiz at
www.PHSchool.com
Web Code: aaa-0704

Mixed Review

Lesson 6-7 **Estimate the sale price of each item.**

16. sandals on sale for 30% of \$18 **17.** boots on sale for 80% of \$62

18. stereo on sale for 60% of \$210 **19.** hair clip on sale for 40% of \$9.95

Lesson 6-1 **Write three ratios equal to each given ratio.**

20. 3:5 **21.** 5 to 9 **22.** $\frac{48}{80}$ **23.** 12:15

Practice Game

Bar Graph Race

What You'll Need
- two number cubes
- graph labeled as shown at the right

How to Play
- Player A chooses a sum from 2 to 12. Player B then chooses two of the remaining sums. Player A then chooses one of the remaining sums.
- Roll the two number cubes. If a player's sum appears, that player fills in one unit on the graph above that sum.
- Roll the two number cubes again until one player's bar reaches a frequency of six. That player is the winner.

Sample Gameboard

Frequency: 1 2 3 4 5 6

Sum: 2 3 4 5 6 7 8 9 10 11 12

Player A (7 or 8) Player B (5 or 6)

Double Bar and Line Graphs

For Use With Lesson 7-4

You can plot two data sets on the same graph to compare them more easily.

EXAMPLE Graphing Two Sets of Data

Sales A bookstore tracks sales of cooking and travel books. Make a double bar graph and a double line graph of the data at the right.

Use a different color for each data set in the double bar graph and double line graph.

Books Sold Each Month

Month	Jan.	Feb.	Mar.	Apr.
Cooking	86	98	112	110
Travel	100	106	88	102

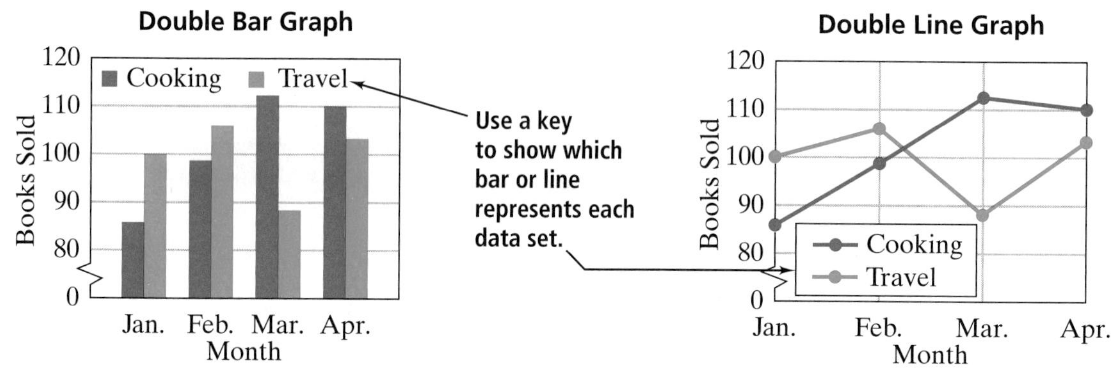

EXERCISES

Use the example above for Exercises 1 and 2.

1. Which graph shows most clearly how book sales increased from January to February?

2. Which graph shows most clearly the differences in sales between the two types of books?

Use the table at the right for Exercises 3 and 4.

3. Make a double bar graph to show the differences between the numbers of endangered plants and animals.

4. Make a double line graph to show how the numbers of endangered plants and animals change over time.

Number of Endangered Species in the U.S.

Year	1980	1985	1990	1995	2000
Plants	50	93	179	432	592
Animals	174	207	263	324	379

7-5 Circle Graphs

What You'll Learn

OBJECTIVE 1 To read and make circle graphs

. . . And Why

To compare parts of a whole, as in Example 2

Check Skills You'll Need

For help, go to Lesson 6-6.

Find each percent.

1. 35% of 280
2. 52% of 200
3. 25% of 384
4. 11% of 800
5. 75% of 820
6. 85% of 160

New Vocabulary

- circle graph

Interactive lesson includes instant self-check, tutorials, and activities.

OBJECTIVE

1 Reading and Making Circle Graphs

Investigation: Exploring Circle Graphs

Make a circle graph of the data below about children's sources of income.

Allowance	Doing Chores	Earned Outside the Home	Gifts
54%	20%	10%	16%

1. Cut a strip of paper slightly more than 100 mm (10 cm) long with a tab at the end as shown.

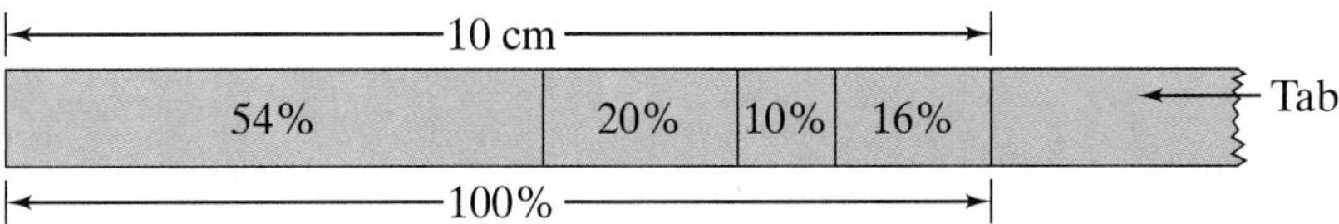

Each millimeter represents 1% of the strip. Mark the strip with lines that represent the percents in the table.

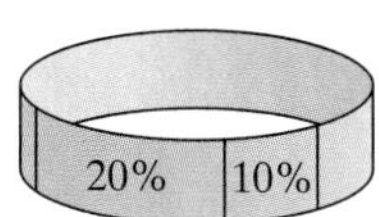

2. Form a ring with the strip. Line up the beginning of the strip with the 100% line and tape the ends. This is your "percent ring."

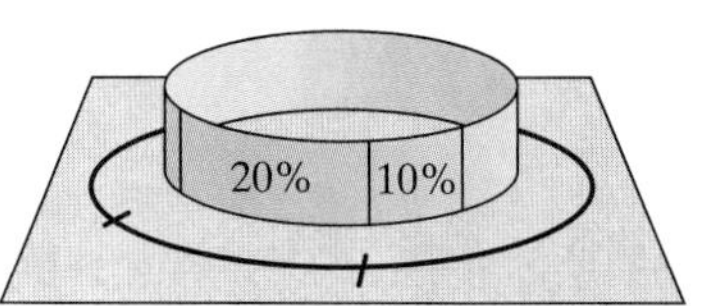

3. Use a compass. Draw a circle slightly larger than your percent ring. Place a dot in the center of the circle.

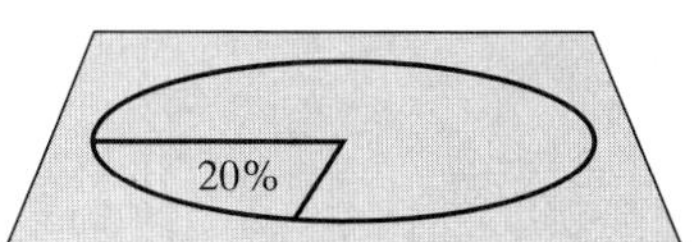

4. Use your percent ring to mark the percents around the edge of the circle. Use a ruler to connect the marks to the center of the circle.

A **circle graph** is a graph of data where the entire circle represents the whole. Each wedge in the circle represents part of the whole.

Reading Math

A circle graph is often called a pie chart. Each wedge of a circle graph is like a "piece of the pie."

1 EXAMPLE Reading a Circle Graph

Apples Use the circle graph.

Where Do All the Apples Go?

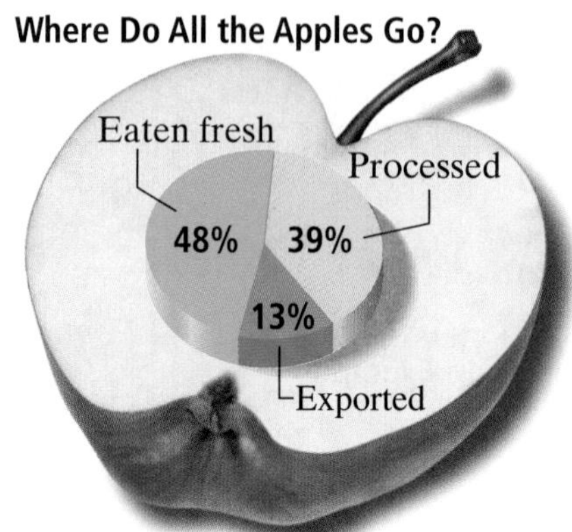

a. For what purpose are 48% of apples used?

48% are eaten fresh.

b. What percent of apples are exported?

13% are exported.

Check Understanding 1 **a.** According to the graph, how are 39% of apples used?
b. What percent of apples are not exported?

2 EXAMPLE Making a Circle Graph

Sports In 2001, the Seattle Mariners stole a total of 174 bases. Make a circle graph of the data.

Stolen Bases by Seattle Mariners

Player	Total
Ichiro Suzuki	56
Mark McLemore	39
Mike Cameron	34
Other players combined	45
Total number of stolen bases	174

First, use a calculator to change the data to percents of the total. Round to the nearest percent.

$\frac{56}{174} \approx 32\%$ $\quad\frac{39}{174} \approx 22\%$

$\frac{34}{174} \approx 20\%$ $\quad\frac{45}{174} \approx 26\%$

Use number sense to divide the circle.

$32\% \approx \frac{1}{3}$ $\quad$ 22% is slightly less than $\frac{1}{4}$ of the circle.

$26\% \approx \frac{1}{4}$ $\quad$ 20% is what is left over.

Stolen Bases by Seattle Mariners

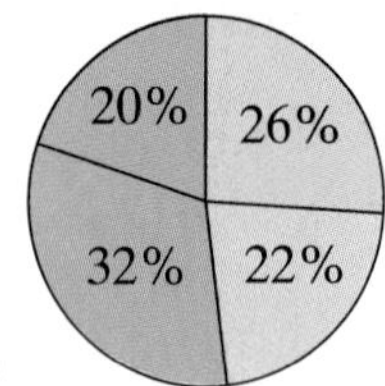

Ichiro Suzuki
Mark McLemore
Mike Cameron
Other players

Label the divided circle with each percent. You can also use a different color for each player. Add a title.

Check Understanding 2 Of 50 students surveyed, 13 preferred hot lunch, 9 packed lunch, 6 ate at the salad bar, and 22 bought sandwiches. Make a circle graph of the data.

More Than One Way

Four NASA space shuttles flew 14 missions from 2000 through 2002. Draw a graph for the following data: *Atlantis*, 5 missions; *Columbia*, 1 mission; *Discovery*, 3 missions; *Endeavour*, 5 missions.

I can make a bar graph to display the data.

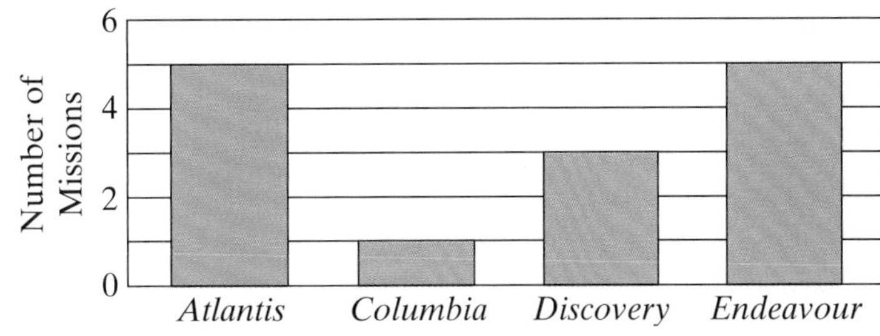

Jessica's Method

I can make a circle graph to display the data.

Space Shuttle Missions, 2000–2002

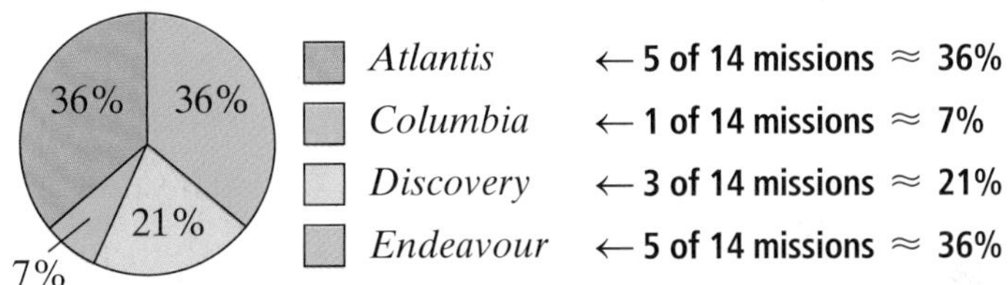

Choose a Method

Of 25 students, 6 ride to school in a car, 14 ride a bus, 1 rides a bike, and 4 walk. Draw a graph to display the data. Explain your choice of graph.

EXERCISES

For more practice, see *Extra Practice*.

Practice by Example

Example 1 (page 342)

Use the graph at the right for Exercises 1–3.

Favorite Sport

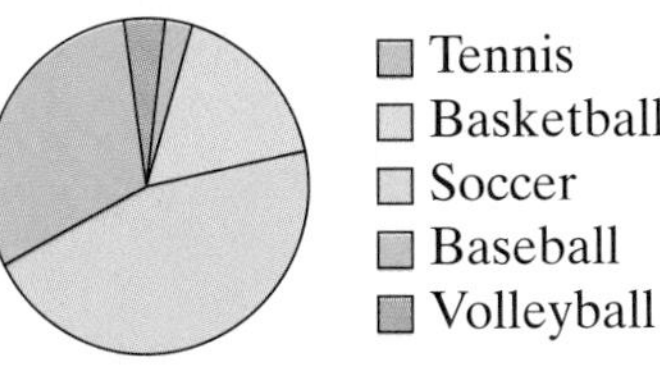

1. Which sport is the least popular?
2. Which is more popular, basketball or tennis?
3. List the sports from least to most popular.

Example 2 (page 342)

Sketch a circle graph for the given percents.

4. 10%, 40%, 50%

5. 5%, 14%, 33%, 48%

6. 12%, 26%, 62%

7. 12%, 34%, 21%, 33%

B Apply Your Skills

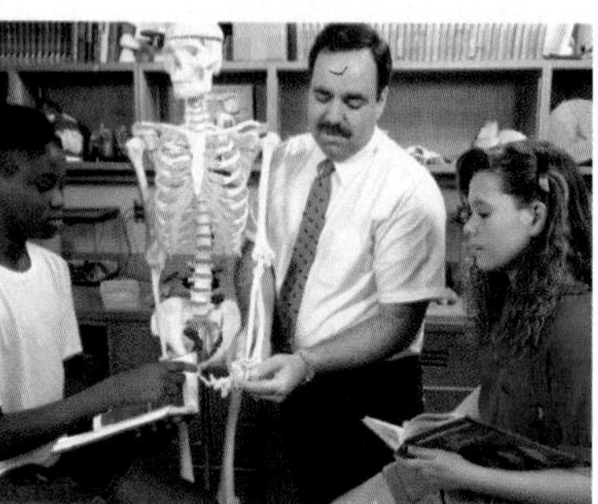

Real-World Connection

Bone is made up of calcium, phosphorus, oxygen, hydrogen, and many other elements.

8. Science The human body is made up of 21 chemical elements. Use the table at the right to make a circle graph.

Human Body Composition

Element	Percent
Oxygen	65
Carbon	18
Hydrogen	10
Nitrogen	3
Other	4

9. Data Collection List the things you do on a Saturday. Estimate the hours you spend on each activity. Write each time as a percent of a 24-hour day. Make a circle graph.

10. Taxes The table below shows that taxes make up a large part of the price of gasoline. Make two circle graphs to compare gasoline taxes to the mean price of gasoline in the United States and the United Kingdom.

Taxes on One Gallon of Gasoline

Country	Price (including tax)	Tax
United States	$1.64	$.38
United Kingdom	$4.57	$3.48

Sketch a circle graph for each set of fractions.

11. $\frac{1}{2}, \frac{1}{3}, \frac{1}{6}$

12. $\frac{3}{4}, \frac{1}{10}, \frac{1}{10}, \frac{1}{20}$

13. $\frac{3}{8}, \frac{1}{8}, \frac{4}{10}, \frac{1}{10}$

14. Surveys A group of 100 students were asked how they like to spend their free time. Of those surveyed, 53% said they like to go to the mall, 80% said they like to watch TV, 72% said they like to play outside, and 34% said they like to search the Internet.

a. Writing in Math Explain why you cannot use a circle graph to display the data.

b. What kind of graph could you use to display these data?

15. Customers A video arcade recorded the ages of customers for a 1-hour period. The results are shown in the line plot.

a. Draw a circle graph.

b. What percent of the customers are older than 15?

c. Reasoning Can you find the percent of customers who are 11 years old? Explain.

Customer Ages at Video Arcade

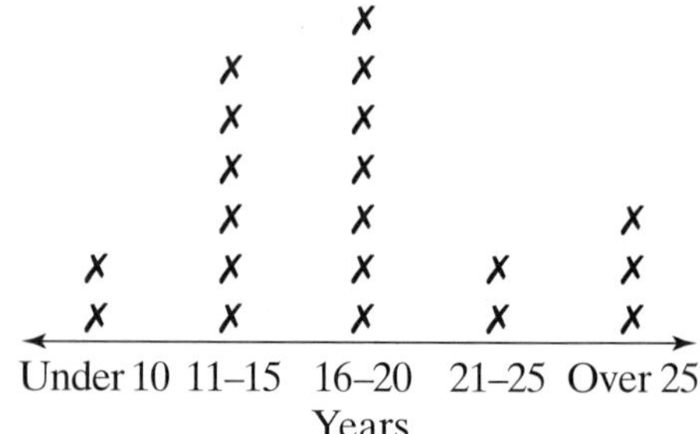

Use the graph at the right for Exercises 16 and 17.

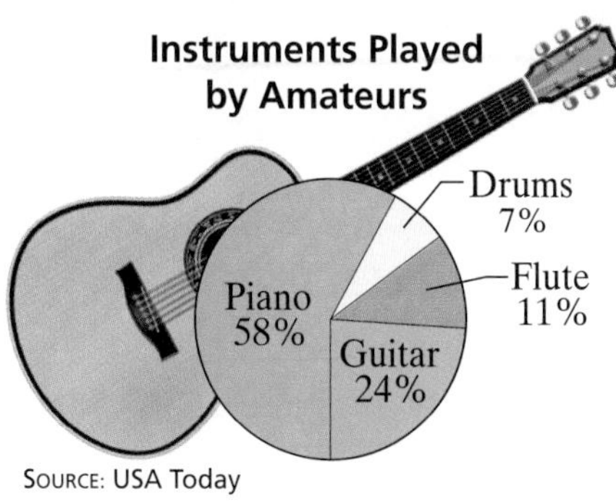

16. What instrument do more amateur musicians play than any other?

17. About what percent play the guitar?

C Challenge

18. Fundraising A class collected 700 coins to donate to charity.

a. How many quarters were donated?

b. How many more nickels were donated than quarters?

c. How much money was donated?

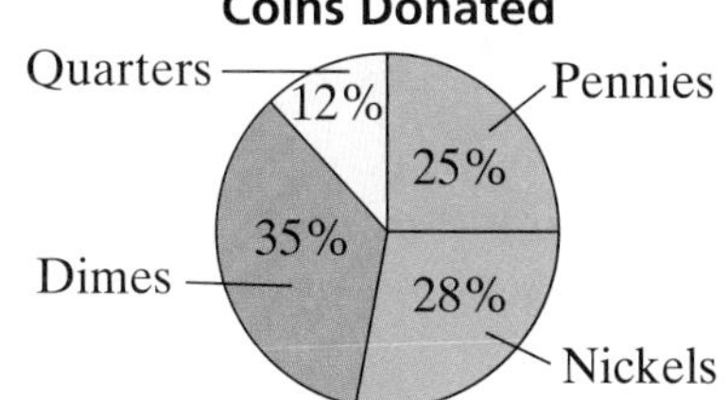

19. Stretch Your Thinking Eve sells candles. Each day, she sells 3 more candles than the day before. If she sold 24 candles on the sixth day, how many candles did she sell on the first day?

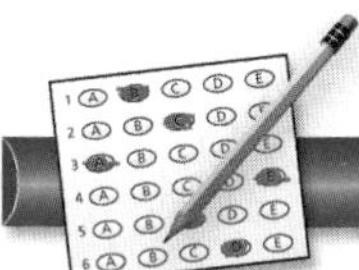

Test Prep

Multiple Choice

Use the circle graph.

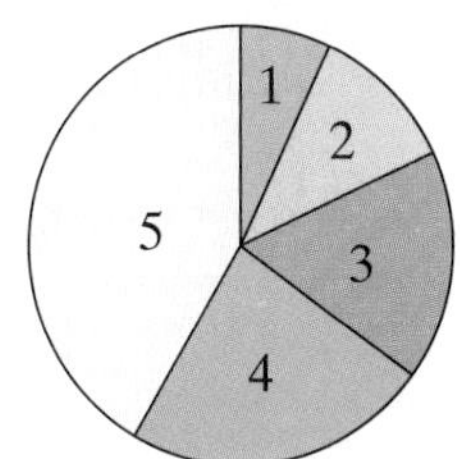

20. How many teachers do the greatest number of students have?

A. 1 **B.** 2 **C.** 4 **D.** 5

21. How many teachers do about 25% of students have?

F. 2 **G.** 3 **H.** 4 **I.** 5

Short Response

22. Do more than half of the students have 5 teachers? Explain your reasoning.

Mixed Review

Lesson 6-8 **Find each percent.**

23. 15% of 80 **24.** 25% of 120 **25.** 82% of 200 **26.** 1% of 125

Lesson 5-2 **Algebra** **Evaluate each expression for $x = 3\frac{3}{4}$.**

27. $8x$ **28.** $\frac{2}{5}x$ **29.** $\frac{4}{3}x$ **30.** $x + 2\frac{1}{2}$

Writing to Persuade

For Use With Lesson 7-5

To persuade others to see things in a certain way, you should

- Identify your audience and your goal.
- Collect data.
- Decide how to display your information.

EXAMPLE

You think the school mascot should be changed and you know many students agree with you.

Identify the Audience and Goal You want to persuade the school administration that students want the school mascot to be changed.

Collect Data You survey the 394 students in your school.

Should the School Change Its Mascot?

Category	Strongly disagree	Disagree	No opinion	Agree	Strongly agree
Number of Students	79	63	51	159	42

Display the Information You decide to make a table and a circle graph of the data. You combine *agree* and *strongly agree* to emphasize the numbers of students that want to change the mascot.

Agree + Strongly Agree: $\frac{159 + 42}{394} \approx 51\%$

Should the School Change Its Mascot?

Category	Disagree or strongly disagree	No opinion	Agree or strongly agree
Number of Students	142	51	201
Percent of Students	36%	13%	51%

Change the School Mascot?

EXERCISE

1. You would like macaroni and cheese on the school lunch menu more often. You collect the data at the right. Identify your audience. Make a display of your information.

Should the School Cafeteria Offer Macaroni and Cheese Twice a Week?

Category	Strongly disagree	Disagree	No opinion	Agree	Strongly agree
Number of Students	20	35	125	195	125

Algebra

7-6 Using Spreadsheets to Organize Data

What You'll Learn

 OBJECTIVE 1 To read data in a spreadsheet

 OBJECTIVE 2 To write formulas for a spreadsheet

. . . And Why

To find the recording time of CDs, as in Example 1

Check Skills You'll Need

For help, go to Lesson 2-3.

Write an expression for each word phrase.

1. 5 times x

2. 7 less than b

3. 52 decreased by x

4. a divided by 9

5. the product of x and y

6. the quotient of a and b

New Vocabulary • spreadsheet • cell

OBJECTIVE 1

Interactive lesson includes instant self-check, tutorials, and activities.

Reading Data in a Spreadsheet

A **spreadsheet** is a table made up of rows and columns used to organize data. A **cell** is a box in a spreadsheet where a particular row and column meet. A computer spreadsheet is an electronic table that is especially useful when you need to repeat calculations.

1 EXAMPLE Using a Spreadsheet  Real World

Music The spreadsheet shows the lengths of 15 CDs from five different categories. Identify the value in cell B5 and tell what this number represents.

Column B

	A	B	C	D	E
1	Music Type	Disc 1 (min)	Disc 2 (min)	Disc 3 (min)	Mean Length (min)
2	Rock/Pop	40	44	45	
3	Rap	48	53	55	
4	Country	32	34	30	
5	Classical	45	54	51	
6	Jazz	41	53	44	

Row 5

Cell B5

The value in cell B5 is 45. This means the first classical CD is 45 minutes long.

Check Understanding 1 **a.** What is the value in cell D4? What does this number represent?

b. What cells are in row 2? What do the numbers in these cells represent?

OBJECTIVE

2 Writing Formulas for a Spreadsheet

Need Help?
These operation symbols are used in spreadsheets:
+ addition
− subtraction
* multiplication
/ division

A computer automatically enters a value in a cell of a spreadsheet when you assign a formula to that cell. A formula is a statement of a mathematical relationship. An "=" sign tells the computer that an expression is a formula.

2 EXAMPLE Formulas in a Spreadsheet

The spreadsheet below gives the numbers of cans three classrooms collected during two weeks of a food drive. Write a formula for cell D2 that will calculate the total number of cans collected by Room 105.

	A	B	C	D
1	Room Number	Week 1 (cans)	Week 2 (cans)	Total (cans)
2	105	389	416	■ ← Add the entries in cells B2 and C2.
3	106	592	462	■
4	107	481	493	■
5		■	■	■

The formula that should go in cell D2 is = B2 + C2.

Check Understanding 2 **a.** Write a formula for cell B5 that will calculate the total number of cans collected in Week 1.

b. For cell D5, write a formula that will calculate the total number of cans collected by all three classrooms.

EXERCISES

For more practice, see *Extra Practice.*

A Practice by Example

Reading Math
A *bug* is a flaw in a computer program.

Use the spreadsheet below for Exercises 1–10.

Four groups of students made videos and received scores for originality, effort, and quality.

	A	B	C	D	E	F
1	Group	Originality	Effort	Quality	Total	Mean Score
2	Red	90	85	80	■	■
3	Orange	90	90	60	■	■
4	Yellow	95	100	75	■	■
5	Green	65	80	80	■	■

Example 1 (page 347)

Identify the cell(s) that indicate each category.

1. Effort **2.** Mean Score **3.** Green **4.** Total

Write the value for the given cell.

5. C4 **6.** C5 **7.** B4 **8.** B2

Example 2 (page 348)

Write a formula to find each quantity.

9. the total in cell E4

10. the mean score in cell F4

B Apply Your Skills

Wages Suppose your cousin works at a part-time job and earns $7 per hour. The spreadsheet shows a typical schedule for a week.

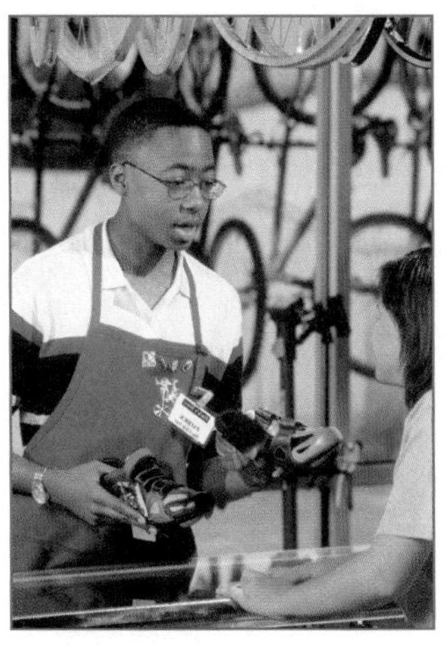

	A	B	C	D	E
1	Day	Time In (P.M.)	Time Out (P.M.)	Hours Worked	Amount Earned
2	9/15	3	8	■	■
3	9/17	4	8	■	■
4	9/19	3	6	■	■
5			Total:	■	■

11. Write a formula for cell D2 and calculate the value in cell D2.

12. Write a formula for cell E2 and calculate the value in cell E2.

13. Write a formula for cell E5.

14. Writing in Math Spreadsheets have a "fill down" function that copies formulas into the cell(s) below and automatically updates the cell references to the corresponding row. How could you use the "fill down" function in the spreadsheet above?

C Challenge

15. Number Sense In Example 2, what will happen to the value in cell D4 if each of the following occurs?
a. The value in cell C4 increases.
b. The value in cell B4 decreases.

16. Stretch Your Thinking A palindrome, such as 54,345, reads the same forward and backward. A certain palindrome has three digits. Its first digit is twice its middle digit. The sum of its digits is 10. What is the palindrome?

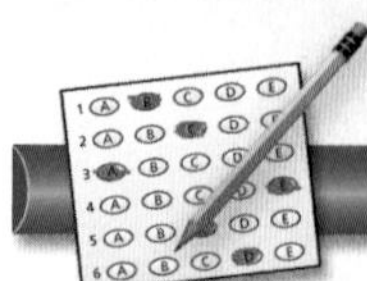

Test Prep

Multiple Choice

Use the spreadsheet at the right.

	A	B	C	D
1	Type of Seat	Tickets Sold	Ticket Price	Total
2	Balcony	36	$13.00	■
3	Mezzanine	105	$18.50	■
4	Front row	10	$26.50	■
5			TOTAL:	■

17. What formula can you use in cell D2?
    A. = B2 + C2
    B. = B2 – C2
    C. = B2 * C2
    D. = B2/C2

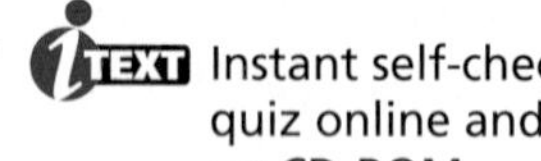

Take It to the NET
Online lesson quiz at **www.PHSchool.com**
Web Code: aaa-0706

18. What is the value in cell D3?
    F. $86.50 **G.** $58.00 **H.** $123.50 **I.** $1,942.50

Short Response

19. What is the value in cell D5? Explain your answer.

Mixed Review

Lesson 6-10

Find each percent.

20. 11% of 200
21. 3% of 150
22. 20% of 50

Lesson 6-9

23. You need $1\frac{1}{2}$ cups of water and milk for a recipe. You have $\frac{2}{3}$ cup of milk. How much water do you need? Solve by writing and solving an equation.

Checkpoint Quiz 2 — Lessons 7-4 through 7-6

*i*TEXT Instant self-check quiz online and on CD-ROM

Use the spreadsheet below for Exercises 1–4.

	A	B
1	Fundraiser	Collected ($)
2	Book sale	200
3	Car wash	125
4	Food stand	325
5	Paper drive	150
6	TOTAL:	■

1. Draw a bar graph of the data.
2. Draw a circle graph of the data.
3. Write a formula for cell B6.
4. How much money was collected from the fundraisers?
5. Suppose your bank account balance is $37 in January, $40 in February, $55 in March, and $15 in April. Draw a line graph of the data.

Technology Making a Graph From a Spreadsheet

For Use With Lesson 7-6

You can use spreadsheet programs to make circle, line, and bar graphs. Enter and highlight the data you want to graph. Use the menu to choose the type of graph and labels. Finally, insert the labels.

EXAMPLE

Sierra makes a table showing how she spends her time on weekdays. She enters the data in the spreadsheet below. Sierra then chooses a circle graph because it shows the portion of her weekday spent on each activity.

	A	B
1	Activity	Number of Hours
2	School	7
3	Homework	2
4	Recreation	4
5	Eating	3
6	Sleeping	8

How Sierra Spends Her Time on Weekdays

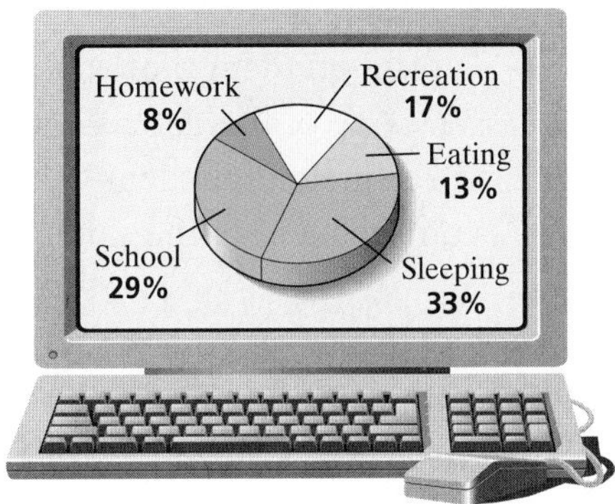

EXERCISES

Enter the data below in a spreadsheet. Then use the program to make a graph of the data. Explain why you chose to make each type of graph.

1. **Ages of Customers at Freddy's Restaurant**

Age	Under 12	12–18	19–30	31–50	Over 50
Number of People	80	120	60	30	70

2. **How Theo Spends His Weekly Allowance**

Category	Food	School	Fun	Savings	Other
Amount Spent	$4	$5	$6	$2	$1

3. **How Often People Need to Search for Keys**

Category	Never	Once a year	Once a month	Once a week	Once a day
Number of Responses	31	15	23	9	2

7-7 Stem-and-Leaf Plots

What You'll Learn

To use a stem-and-leaf plot

. . . And Why

To describe wage data, as in Example 2

✓ Check Skills You'll Need

For help, go to Lesson 7-1.

Find the median of each data set.

1. 23, 32, 32, 15, 26, 52, 38, 44

2. 15, 10, 15, 21, 32, 48, 10, 15

3. 125, 213, 325, 100, 212, 125, 216

4. 6.7, 5.8, 8.9, 3.5, 4.6, 5.8, 3.8, 2.5

New Vocabulary

- stem-and-leaf plot

OBJECTIVE

iTEXT Interactive lesson includes instant self-check, tutorials, and activities.

1 Using a Stem-and-Leaf Plot

A **stem-and-leaf plot** is a graph that uses the digits of each number to show the shape of the data. Each data value is broken into a "stem" on the left and a single-digit "leaf" on the right. To read the data, combine the stem with each leaf in the same row.

stem → 5 | 8 ← leaf

1 EXAMPLE Reading a Stem-and-Leaf Plot

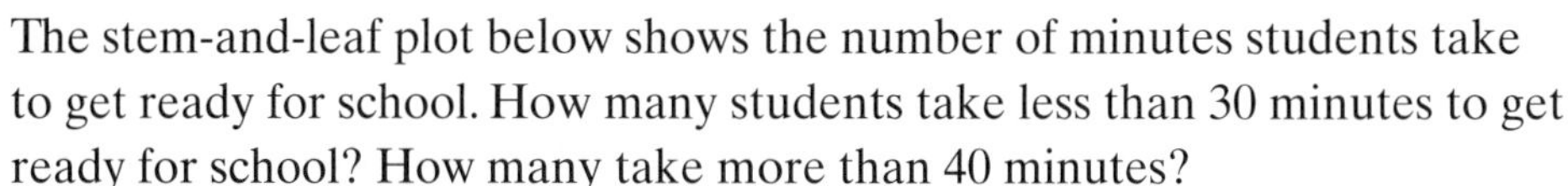

The stem-and-leaf plot below shows the number of minutes students take to get ready for school. How many students take less than 30 minutes to get ready for school? How many take more than 40 minutes?

Times to Get Ready for School (minutes)

Stem	Leaf
2	3 3 5 7 8 8
3	3 4 5 7 7 7 9
4	0 0 2 3 3 5
5	8

Key: 2 | 3 means 23 minutes

6 students take less than 30 minutes. Their times are 23, 23, 25, 27, 28, and 28.

5 students take more than 40 minutes. Their times are 42, 43, 43, 45, and 58.

Six students take less than 30 minutes to get ready for school. Five students take more than 40 minutes.

Check Understanding 1

a. How many students take 37 minutes?

b. What is the range of the data?

c. Reasoning What advantage does a stem-and-leaf plot have compared to an ordered list of values?

2 EXAMPLE Making a Stem-and-Leaf Plot

Hourly Wages	
$8.20	$7.00
$7.30	$8.90
$7.20	$8.30
$8.00	$7.00
$7.70	$7.60
$8.10	$8.70
$8.10	$7.30
$7.20	$10.50
$7.60	$8.50
$6.50	$6.80

Hourly Wages The data at the left shows hourly wages for a group of people. Make a stem-and-leaf plot of the data.

Step 1 Write the stems in order. Use the whole number part. Draw a vertical line to the right of the stems.

stems →
```
 6 |
 7 |
 8 |
 9 |
10 |
```

Step 2 Write the leaves in order. Use the values in the tenths place because there is no nonzero digit in the hundredths place.

```
 6 | 5 8                    ← leaves
 7 | 0 0 2 2 3 3 6 6 7
 8 | 0 1 1 2 3 5 7 9
 9 |
10 | 5
```

Step 3 Choose a title and include a legend to explain what your stems and leaves represent.

Hourly Wages ($)

```
 6 | 5 8
 7 | 0 0 2 2 3 3 6 6 7
 8 | 0 1 1 2 3 5 7 9
 9 |
10 | 5
```

Key: 6 | 5 means $6.50 ← key

2 Make a stem-and-leaf plot of the data: 137, 125, 145, 123, 181, 132, 155, 141, 140, 133, 138, 127, 150, 126, 124, 130, 125, 138, 144, 121, and 136. (*Hint:* Use the one's digit for the leaves.)

EXERCISES

For more practice, see *Extra Practice.*

Example 1 (page 352)

Use the stem-and-leaf plot at the right.

Number of Seconds Customers on Hold

```
0 | 7 8 8 8 9 9
1 | 0 2 2 3 4 5 5 5 6 7 7
```

Key: 0 | 7 means 7 seconds

1. What does "0 | 8" represent?
2. How many entries have a value of 15?
3. How many customers were on hold for 11 seconds?
4. How many customers waited less than 9 seconds?

Example 2 (page 353)

Make a stem-and-leaf plot for each set of data.

5. heights of tomato plants (inches):

   27 40 31 33 35 33 26 36 41 29 30 36

6. test scores (percents):

   93 76 85 85 68 81 84 89 84 91 97 95 86 64

7. number of jelly beans in a scoop:

   47 28 38 47 58 34 76 35 32 45 53 43 35 27

B Apply Your Skills

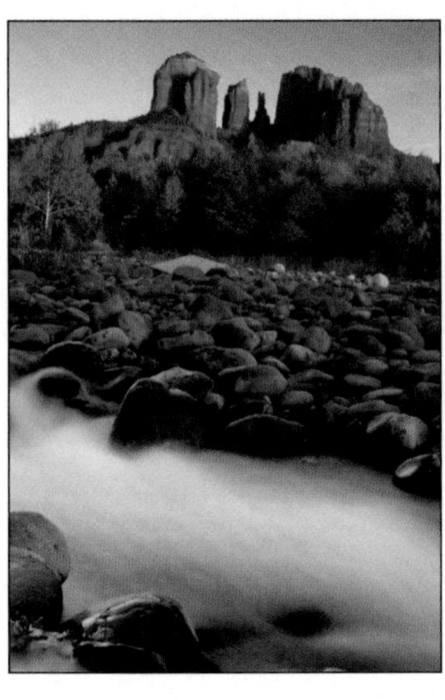

8. **Population** The table at the right shows the populations of nine states.
   a. Make a stem-and-leaf plot.
   b. **Reasoning** Would it be easier to make a stem-and-leaf plot if the state populations were written out (for example: 5,456,453 for Arizona)? Explain your answer.

State	Population (millions)
Arizona	5.5
Colorado	4.5
Indiana	6.2
Kentucky	4.1
Maryland	5.5
Minnesota	5.0
Oregon	3.5
Tennessee	5.8
Wisconsin	5.4

SOURCE: U.S. Census Bureau. Go to **www.PHSchool.com** for a data update. Web Code: aag-2041

9. **Writing in Math** Explain how you can find the median and mode for the data in a stem-and-leaf plot.

10. **Heights** The heights of nine people are given below.

    5 ft 10 in.   4 ft. 11 in.   5 ft 4 in.
    5 ft 6 in.   6 ft. 7 in.   5 ft 7 in.
    6 ft 10 in.   5 ft. 8 in.   5 ft 1 in.

    a. Make a stem-and-leaf plot.
    b. Find the median.
    c. Find the mode.
    d. Are there any outliers? If so, what are they?

11. The ages of 18 people are shown below.

    21 12 15 13 35 24 16 23 40
    9 19 12 15 13 12 20 11 12

    a. Make a stem-and-leaf plot.
    b. Make a line plot.
    c. **Reasoning** Which plot shows the mode most clearly?
    d. **Reasoning** Which plot shows the number of people in their teens most clearly? Explain your answer.

12. a. **Data Collection** Choose a paragraph from a book and record the number of letters in each word.
    b. Make a stem-and-leaf plot.
    c. Use the plot to find the median length word in the paragraph.

Challenge

13. A data set has a least value of 17.26 and a greatest value of 17.89.
    a. What is the range of the data?
    b. Explain how you would display the data using a stem-and-leaf plot.

14. **Stretch Your Thinking** Draw the figure at the right without lifting your pencil from the paper and without retracing any line.

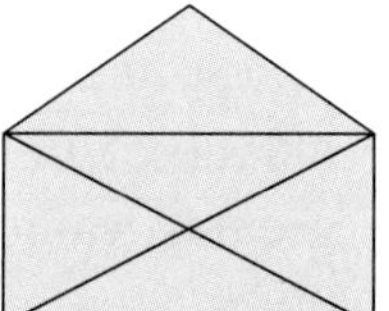

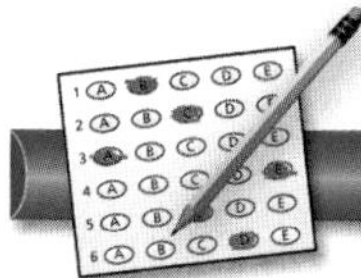

Test Prep

Multiple Choice

Use the stem-and-leaf plot below.

4	0 9
5	2 4 4 5 9
6	3 7 7 7 8 8 9
7	2 4 6

Key: 4 | 0 means 40

15. What is the mode?
    A. 7 B. 54
    C. 67 D. 68

Take It to the NET
Online lesson quiz at
www.PHSchool.com
Web Code: aaa-0707

16. How many data items are greater than 67?
    F. 3 G. 6
    H. 10 I. 17

17. What is the median of the data?
    A. 17 B. 54 C. 62 D. 77

Short Response

18. Which measure would be easiest to find from a stem-and-leaf plot, mean, median, or range? Justify your answer.

Mixed Review

Lesson 6-9

Algebra **Solve each problem by writing an equation.**

19. On the first Wednesday of every month, a department store offers a 10% discount on any item in the store. How much is the regular price if the sale price of a jacket is $54?

20. Before tax, your restaurant dinner plus a 15% tip totals $13.80. What was the cost of the meal alone?

Lesson 6-4

Determine whether each pair of ratios forms a proportion.

21. $\frac{45}{100}, \frac{4}{10}$

22. $\frac{24}{56}, \frac{3}{7}$

23. $\frac{105}{49}, \frac{36}{16}$

Solve each proportion.

24. $\frac{9}{5} = \frac{c}{11}$

25. $\frac{8}{m} = \frac{3}{20}$

26. $\frac{7}{10} = \frac{5}{x}$

Extension Box-and-Whisker Plots

For Use With Lesson 7-7

A *box-and-whisker plot* is a graph that describes a data set along a number line. It shows the greatest value, the least value, and quartiles.

Quartiles divide the data into four equal parts. The *middle quartile* is the median of the data. The *lower quartile* is the median of the lower half of the data. The *upper quartile* is the median of the upper half of the data.

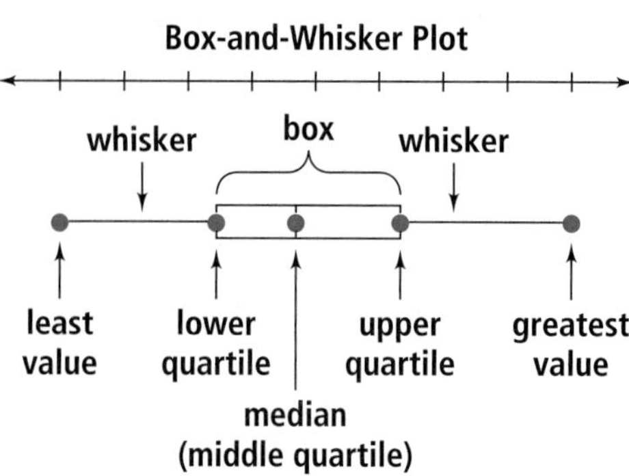

1 EXAMPLE Finding Quartiles

Find the middle, lower, and upper quartiles for the data below.

Home Runs Hit by Barry Bonds

Year	1993	1994	1995	1996	1997	1998	1999	2000	2001	2002
Home Runs	46	37	33	42	40	37	34	49	73	46

Step 1 Find the median of the data.

33 34 37 37 40 42 46 46 49 73 ← **Order the data.**

$\frac{40 + 42}{2} = 41$ ← **Find the median.**

The median of the data is 41, so the middle quartile is 41.

Step 2 Find the median of the lower half of the data and the upper half of the data.

33 34 37 37 40 ← **List the lower half of the data.**

The median of the lower half of the data is 37, so the lower quartile is 37.

42 46 46 49 73 ← **List the upper half of the data.**

The median of the upper half of the data is 46, so the upper quartile is 46.

EXERCISES

Find the middle, lower, and upper quartiles for the data below.

1. 6 8 7 6 5 8 5 6 4 8 7 5 4 7 6 8 6 7

2. 12 24 18 35 30 45 42 21 17 25

2 EXAMPLE Making a Box-and-Whisker Plot

Make a box-and-whisker plot for the data in Example 1.

Step 1 Find the least value and greatest value.

33 34 37 37 40 42 46 46 49 73 ← **Order the data.**

The least value is 33 and the greatest value is 73.

Step 2 Draw a number line that shows the range of the data. Below the number line, plot the least value, greatest value, and quartiles found in Example 1.

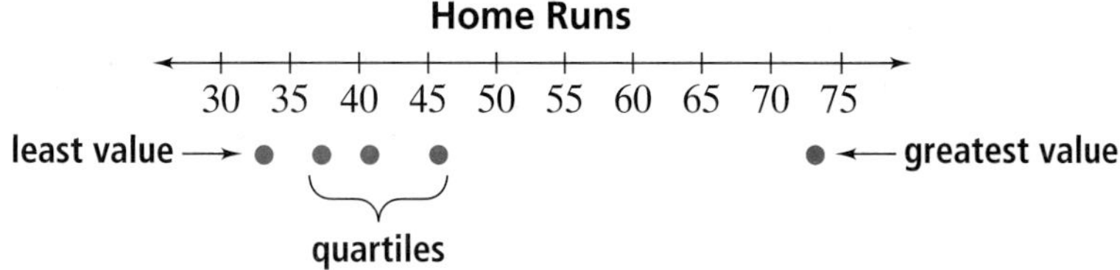

Step 3 Draw a box through each quartile as shown.

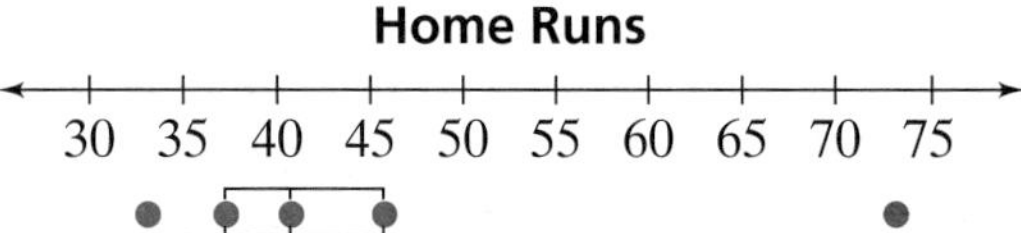

Step 4 Connect the least and the greatest values to the box to make the whiskers.

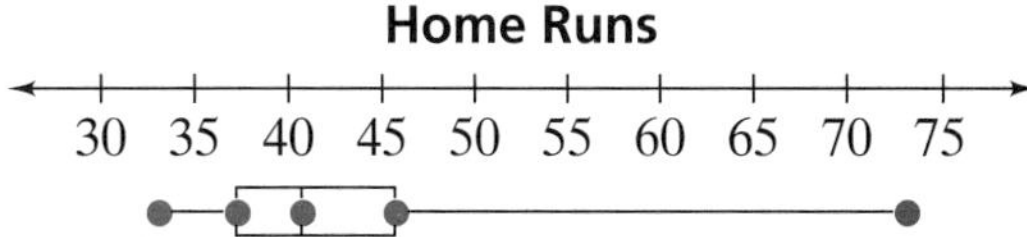

EXERCISES (continued)

Make a box-and-whisker plot for each data set.

3. The heights of eight students in a class are listed below in inches.

58 67 63 60 61 60 64 66

4. The birth weights of 12 kittens are listed below in grams.

114 112 110 113 121 115 117 106 115 108 116 114

Misleading Graphs and Statistics

What You'll Learn

To identify misleading graphs

To identify misleading statistics

. . . And Why

To look at graphs critically, as in Example 1

Check Skills You'll Need

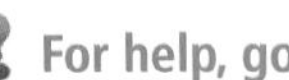
For help, go to Lesson 7-1.

Find the mean for each set of data. Round to the nearest tenth.

1. 21, 25, 52, 58, 64, 71, 71, 82

2. 8, 9, 11, 12, 13, 13, 18, 24

3. 111, 121, 131, 141, 151

4. 3, 10, 85, 87, 98, 99

5. Without finding each median, in which of the sets of data above do you expect the greatest difference between the mean and the median? Explain.

OBJECTIVE

Interactive lesson includes instant self-check, tutorials, and activities.

1 Identifying Misleading Graphs

Data is often presented to influence you. As you look at data displays, consider these questions: Is the information shown accurately? Is the presentation trying to influence you?

1 EXAMPLE Misleading Line Graphs

Real World

Politics Each month residents of a town were asked, "Do you think the mayor is doing a good job?" The results are shown below.

a. What impression is given by the mayor's graph?

The graph suggests only a slight drop in support for the mayor.

b. Why is the graph misleading?

The vertical scale uses unequal intervals. So, the drop from 70% to 40% does not look so large.

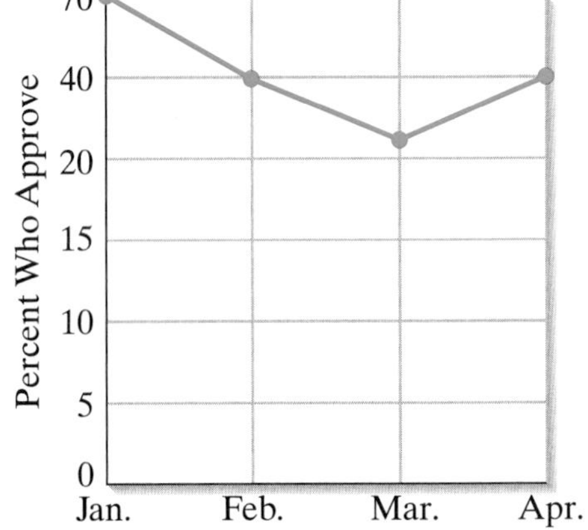

Check Understanding 1 Redraw the graph so that it is not misleading.

Bar graphs and histograms create a misleading impression if the vertical scale does not start at 0.

2 EXAMPLE Misleading Bar Graphs

Real World

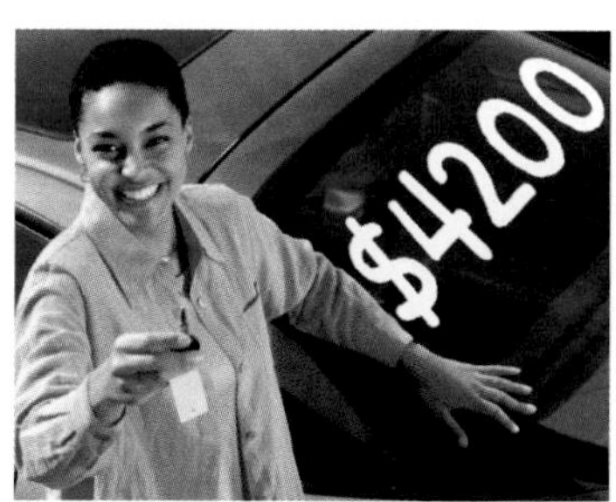

Advertising An auto dealer made the graph at the right.

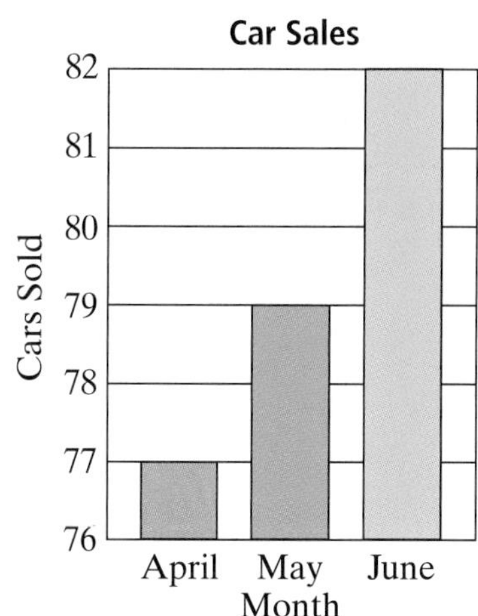

a. What impression is given by the graph?

It looks like there was a dramatic increase in sales.

b. Why is the graph misleading?

The vertical scale does not begin at 0. So, you are looking just at the top of the graph.

Check Understanding 2 Use the graph in Example 2.

a. How many times as tall is the bar for June compared to the bar for May?
b. How many more cars were sold in June than in May?
c. Redraw the graph so that it is not misleading.

OBJECTIVE

2 Identifying Misleading Statistics

The mean is a statistic that can be misleading. This is because the mean can be distorted by outliers.

3 EXAMPLE Real-World Problem Solving

Sports Five players on a professional basketball team have a mean salary of $2.2 million. Their five salaries are shown at the right. Why might the mean salary be misleading?

Players' Salaries
$7,200,000
$1,200,000
$1,000,000
$800,000
$800,000

Only one person makes more than the mean of $2.2 million. The $7.2 million salary is an outlier and greatly increases the mean.

Check Understanding 3 **a.** Find the players' mean salary in Example 3 without the outlier.
b. **Reasoning** In Example 3, which would better describe the basketball player's salaries, the median or the mode? Explain.

The median is often used to describe data sets that have outliers. Salaries and home prices are typical examples.

EXERCISES

For more practice, see *Extra Practice*.

A Practice by Example

Examples 1, 2 (pages 358, 359)

Decide if each graph is misleading. If a graph is misleading, answer the following.

a. What impression is given by the graph?
b. Why is the graph misleading?
c. Redraw the graph so that it is not misleading.

1.

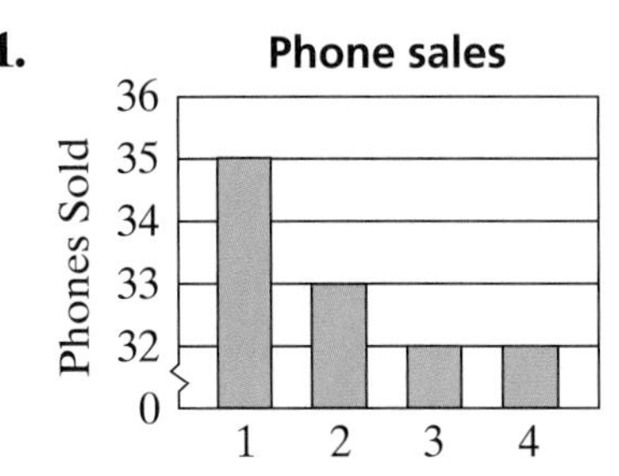

2.

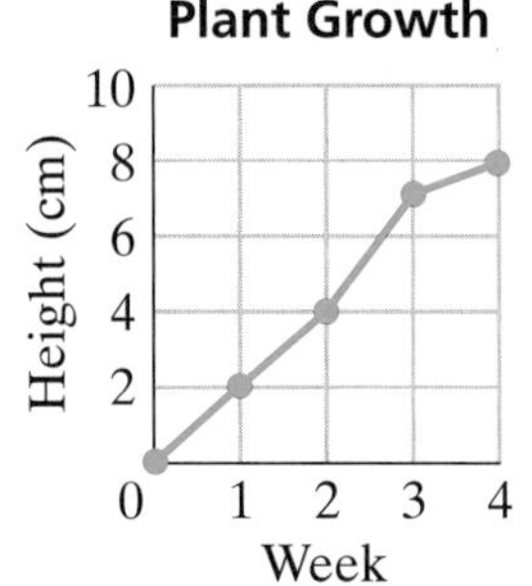

3.

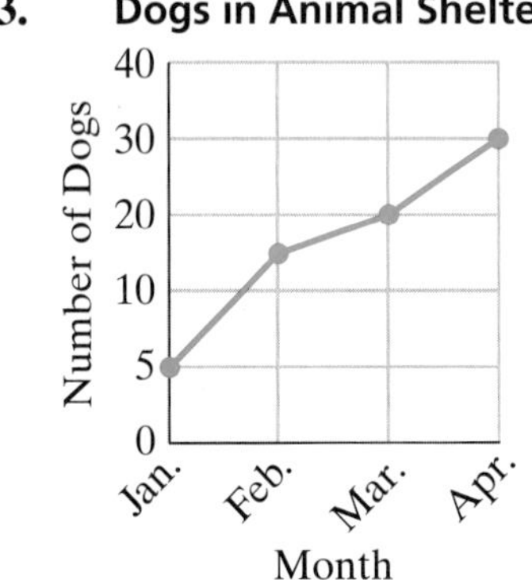

4.

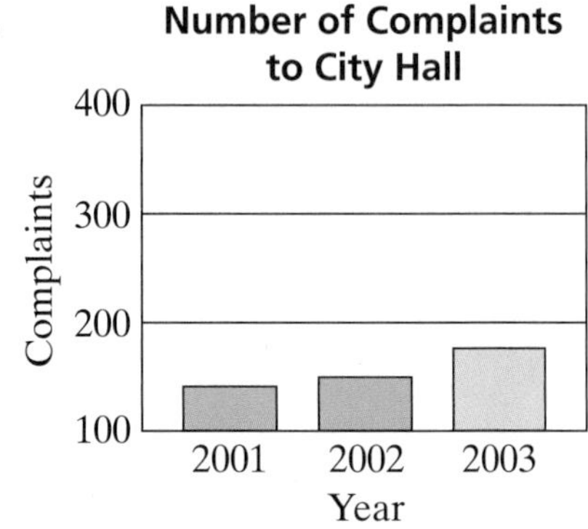

Example 3 (page 359)

5. Bowling Jill and Allen bowl a match of three games. Their scores are shown at the right.

a. Jill claims she won the match. How can she support her claim?

b. Allen claims he won the match. How can he support his claim?

Bowling Scores

Game	Jill	Allen
1	96	75
2	60	81
3	75	75

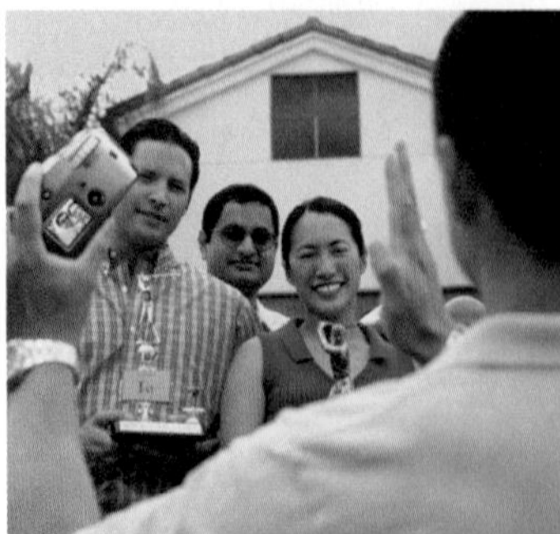

6. Cameras A salesman wants to convince you to buy a digital camera. The prices of cameras available are

$138 $138 $138 $179 $189 $198 $219 $249 $449.

Would the salesman use the mean, median, or mode to encourage you to look at the cameras? Explain your answer.

7. Tests Bill scored 100%, 100%, 90%, 70%, and 60% on five quizzes.

a. Which makes his grades look the highest, the mean, the median, or the mode?

b. Which measure should his teacher use to convince Bill to study harder for the exam?

B Apply Your Skills

8. **Election Results** Two graphs of the same election results are shown. Which graph might be presented by Candidate A? Which might be presented by Candidate B? Explain.

I. 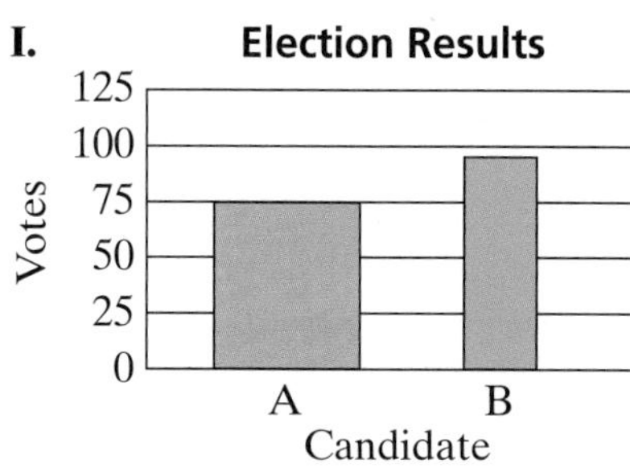

II. 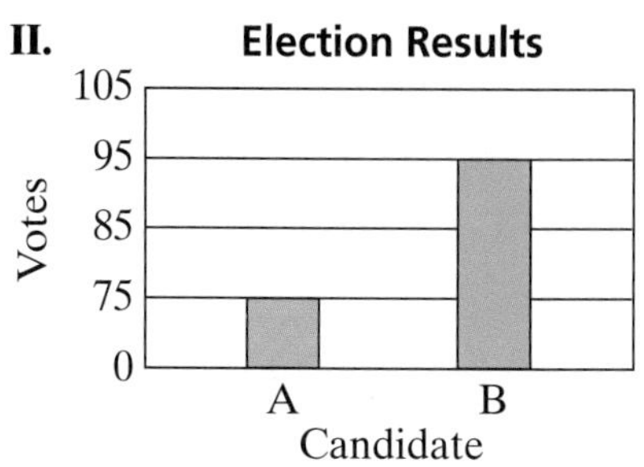

9. **Reasoning** How does the impression of a line graph change when you make thc horizontal axis shorter but keep the vertical scale the same?

Money Pledged to a Public Radio Station

Year	Amount Pledged
1997	$34,096
1998	$39,021
1999	$41,132
2000	$42,209
2001	$44,172
2002	$45,071
2003	$45,759

Fundraising Use the table at the left.

10. Draw a line graph showing that the money pledged appeared to increase greatly from 1997 to 2003.

11. Draw a line graph showing that the money pledged appeared to increase slowly from 1997 to 2003.

12. **Writing in Math** Explain how you drew the graphs in Exercises 11 and 12 to get the desired results.

13. **Track and Field** In successive track meets, Andre jumps the following distances.

11 ft 5 in. 11 ft 8 in. 12 ft 1 in. 11 ft 10 in. 12 ft 1 in.

a. Draw a line graph that shows Andre's jumps increasing sharply.
b. Draw a line graph that shows Andre's jumps increasing slightly.
c. Explain whether these graphs are misleading.

C Challenge

14. Use the data at the right.
a. Make a bar graph using a scale that makes it seem as if there is not much difference in the number of votes for apples and oranges.
b. Make a bar graph using a scale that makes it seem as if there is a significant difference in the number of votes for apples and oranges.

Favorite Juice

Juice	Number of Votes
Orange	30
Grapefruit	6
Apple	21
Grape	15
Cherry	10
Tropical mix	5
Mixed berry	18

15. Which number could you remove from this list so that the mean and the median are the same?

0 7 12 14 19

16. **Stretch Your Thinking** A number is as much greater than 36 as it is less than 94. What is the number?

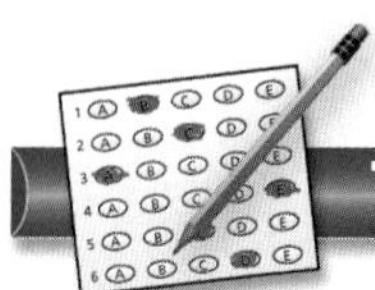

Test Prep

Multiple Choice

Use the graph below.

Favorite Types of Automobiles

Type of Automobile	Number of Responses
SUVs	25
Sports Cars	21
Vans	22

(Vertical axis "Number of Responses" runs from 20 to 25; horizontal axis "Type of Automobile".)

17. How many people like sports cars?
A. 21 **B.** 22 **C.** 23 **D.** 24

18. How many people selected a favorite type of automobile?
F. 25 **G.** 65 **H.** 67 **I.** 68

19. What percent of people prefer an automobile other than an SUV?
A. 67% **B.** 63% **C.** 50% **D.** 43%

Short Response

20. Explain why the bar graph is misleading.

Mixed Review

Lesson 7-1

Find the mean, median, and mode of each data set.

21. 5, 6, 8, 9, 10, 4, 6

22. 600, 550, 475, 520, 500

23. 15, 14, 15, 12, 11, 13

24. 4.5, 4, 4.5, 5.5, 6, 6.5

Lesson 5-6

25. Tara wants to tile the floor of a 13-foot by 12-foot room with 8-inch by 8-inch tiles.
a. How many tiles will she need?
b. Explain how you solved part (a).

Answering the Question Asked

When answering a question, be sure to answer the question that is asked. Read the question carefully and identify the answer that you are asked to find. Some answer choices are answers to related questions, so you have to be careful.

1 EXAMPLE

In Mrs. Sanchez's class, students received the scores shown in the line plot. How many students took the test?

A. 9 **B.** 19 **C.** 20 **D.** 28

The question asks for the number of students who took the test. The total number of scores is $4 + 4 + 4 + 1 + 6 + 9 = 28$. The answer is D.

The number of students who scored 20 points is 9. The mode is 20. The median is 19. But none of these are what is asked for.

Student Scores

					✗
					✗
					✗
				✗	✗
				✗	✗
✗	✗	✗		✗	✗
✗	✗	✗		✗	✗
✗	✗	✗		✗	✗
✗	✗	✗	✗	✗	✗
15	16	17	18	19	20

Score

2 EXAMPLE

The stem-and-leaf plot shows the heights of 11 students in inches. What is the median height?

A. 60 in. **B.** 62 in. **C.** 63 in. **D.** 64 in.

The question asks for the median height. For eleven data items, the sixth is the median. The sixth height is 62 in. The correct answer is B.

The mode is 60 in. The mean is 63 in. Answer D is the average of 57 in. and 71 in., or 64 in. But none of these are what is asked for.

Heights of Students

Stem	Leaf
5	7 8
6	0 0 1 2 3 4 7
7	0 1

Key: 5 | 8 means 58 inches

EXERCISES

1. In Example 1, what is the mean?
   A. 17 **B.** 17.5 **C.** 18 **D.** 19

2. In Example 2, how tall is the tallest student who is less than 70 in. tall?
   F. 60 in. **G.** 67 in. **H.** 70 in. **I.** 71 in.

3. In Example 2, what is the range of the data?
   A. 14 in. **B.** 57 in. **C.** 64 in. **D.** 71 in.

Chapter 7 Chapter Review

Vocabulary

bar graph (p. 335)
cell (p. 347)
circle graph (p. 341)
frequency table (p. 326)
histogram (p. 336)
line graph (p. 336)
line plot (p. 327)
mean (p. 322)
median (p. 323)
mode (p. 323)
outlier (p. 322)
range (p. 327)
spreadsheet (p. 347)
stem-and-leaf plot (p. 352)

Reading Math: Understanding Vocabulary

Choose the correct vocabulary term to complete each sentence. Not all choices will be used.

1. A(n) __?__ is a way to organize data by listing each item in a data set with the number of times it occurs.
2. To calculate the __?__ of a set of data, divide the sum of the values by the number of values in the set.
3. A(n) __?__ of a data set is much greater or much less than the other data values.
4. On the computer, you can use a(n) __?__ to organize data in a table made up of rows and columns.
5. A(n) __?__ typically shows changes over time.

A. mean
B. mode
C. frequency table
D. median
E. line graph
F. spreadsheet
G. outlier

Take It to the NET
Online vocabulary quiz at www.PHSchool.com
Web Code: aaj-0751

Skills and Concepts

7-1 Objectives
- To find the mean
- To find the median and the mode

The **mean** of a set of data is the sum of the values divided by the number of data items. The **median** is the middle value when data are arranged in numerical order. The **mode** is the value or item that appears most often.

Find the mean, median, and mode of each data set.

6. 34, 49, 63, 43, 50, 50, 26
7. 3, 7, 1, 9, 9, 5, 8

7-2 Objectives
- To organize data by making a frequency table
- To make a line plot and find the range

A **frequency table** lists each item in a data set with the number of times the item occurs. A **line plot** displays a data set by stacking X's above each data value on a number line.

8. Make a frequency table showing the number of times each vowel occurs in the paragraph above. Consider *y* a vowel.
9. Make a line plot showing the number of time the words *the*, *and*, *a*, and *of* appear in the paragraph above.

7-3 Objective

- To solve problems by making an organized list

You can make a list to organize possible solutions to a problem.

10. Clothes Kayla spends $48 on gym clothes. She buys at least one of each item. Shorts cost $16, T-shirts cost $8, and socks cost $2 a pair. How many ways can Kayla spend $48 on her gym clothes?

7-4 and 7-5 Objectives

- To make bar graphs
- To make line graphs
- To read and make circle graphs

A **bar graph** is used to compare amounts. A key identifies data that are compared. A **line graph** shows how an amount changes over time. A **circle graph** compares parts to a whole.

11. Tickets Make a line graph to display the cost of tickets shown in the table.

12. Make a bar graph to display the data you used in Exercise 11.

13. Books Use the data in the table below to make a circle graph.

Ticket Prices

Year	Price
1970	$10
1975	$15
1980	$20
1985	$25
1990	$30

Favorite Types of Books

Mysteries	Biographies	Fiction	Humor
22%	13%	55%	10%

7-6 Objectives

- To read data in a spreadsheet
- To write formulas for a spreadsheet

You use a **spreadsheet** to organize and analyze data. A **cell** is the spreadsheet box where a row and column meet. A formula is a set of mathematical instructions.

	A	B	C	D	E
1	Date	Kite Sales ($)	String Sales ($)	Book Sales ($)	Total Sales ($)
2	9/9/03	50	8	145	■
3	9/10/03	75	6	125	■

14. Which cells indicate kite sales?

15. Write the formula for cell E2.

7-7 and 7-8 Objectives

- To use a stem-and-leaf plot
- To identify misleading graphs
- To identify misleading statistics

A **stem-and-leaf plot** orders data and lets you see the values and frequencies.

16. Make a stem-and-leaf plot of the data: 507, 301, 479, 367, 543, 388, 512, 479, 483, 379, 548, 341, 399, and 465.

Which measure best describes the data—the mean, median, or mode?

17. 72, 67, 62, 77, 82

18. 1, 1.5, 4.5, 8, 4.5, 12

Chapter Test

1. Find the mean, median, mode, and range of the data set: 31, 20, 31, 51, and 27.

2. Use the circle graph.
   a. How do *most* students get to school?
   b. What method do students use *least*?
   c. **Writing in Math** Why might a circle graph be better for displaying these data than a bar graph?

How Students Get to School

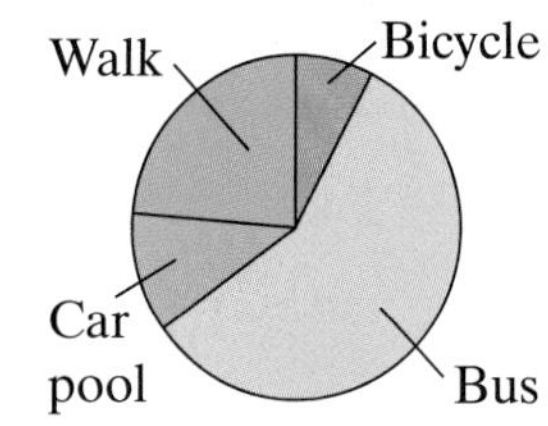

3. The following spreadsheet shows three quiz scores for two students. Write the formulas for cells E2 and E3.

	A	B	C	D	E
1	Student	Q 1	Q 2	Q 3	Mean
2	Yori	81	95	88	■
3	Sarah	78	81	87	■

4. Make a stem-and-leaf plot for these state fair pumpkin weights (pounds): 288, 207, 210, 212, 226, 233, 212, 218, 247, 262, 269, 203, and 271.

5. **Enrollment** Use the bar graph below. Which grade level has the least number of students enrolled?

Public School Enrollment

Grade Level: High School, Middle School, Elementary, Preschool

0 4 8 12 16

Enrollment (millions)

SOURCE: U.S. Department of Education. Go to **www.PHSchool.com** for a data update. Web Code: aag-2041

6. The numbers of children in 15 families are 1, 3, 2, 1, 3, 1, 2, 6, 2, 3, 3, 4, 3, 4, and 5.
   a. Make a frequency table.
   b. Make a line plot.

7. **Coins** How many ways can you have \$1.05 with only dimes, nickels, and quarters?

8. **Reading** Use the data to make a circle graph.

Amount of Time Adults Think They Spend Reading for Pleasure	
Too much	7%
Too little	73%
About right	16%
Don't know	4%

SOURCE: Gallup Organization

9. **Profits** A business has weekly profits of \$5,000, \$3,000, \$2,000, \$2,500, and \$5,000. Why is using the mode to describe this data set misleading?

10. **Hot Lunches** Use the line graph below. What is the median number of students buying hot lunch?

Students Buying Hot Lunch

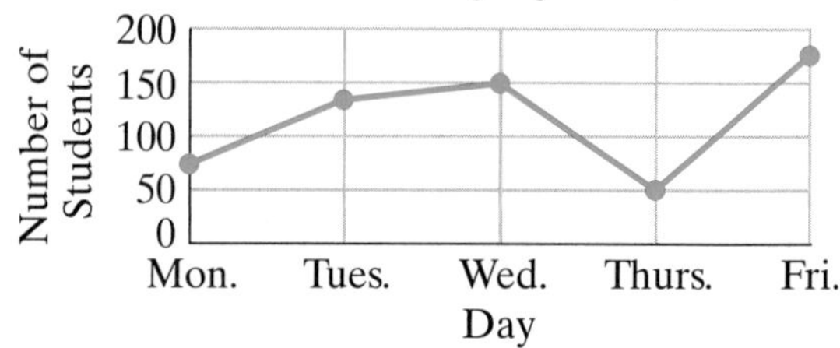

Use the stem-and-leaf plot for Exercises 11 and 12.

11. Find the range.

12. Find the median.

```
5 | 0 2 6
6 | 1 3 6 7
7 | 4 8 9
8 | 0 1
```

Key: 5 | 0 means 5.0

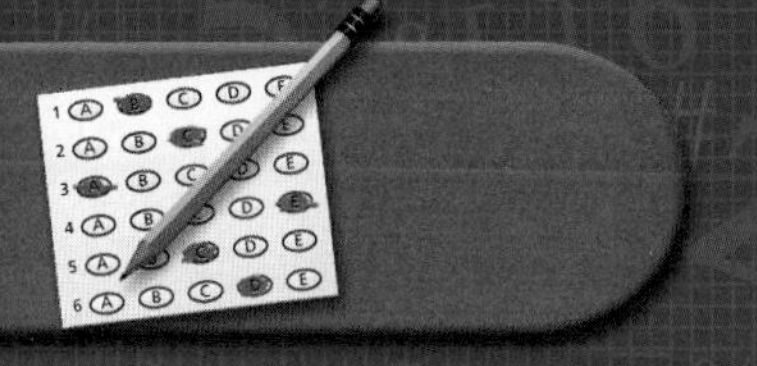

Test Prep

Reading Comprehension **Read each passage and answer the questions that follow.**

Age of Leadership In 1787 twelve of the original thirteen states sent delegates to Philadelphia to work on forming a government for our new country. In all, 55 delegates attended. You probably know some of their names: James Madison (36 years old), Alexander Hamilton (32), George Washington (55), and Benjamin Franklin (the oldest delegate, at 81).

1. What is the mean age of the delegates mentioned in the passage?
A. 32 **B.** 45 **C.** 51 **D.** 55

2. What is the median age of the delegates mentioned?
F. 32 **G.** 5.5 **H.** 51 **I.** 55

3. The mean age of all of the delegates was 42. What was the sum of the ages of all 55 delegates?
A. 2,106 years **B.** 2,310 years
C. 2,501 years **D.** 2,525 years

4. Franklin was in poor health and did not attend many of the meetings. Suppose a 60-year-old delegate replaced him. How would that affect the mean and the median ages of the four delegates mentioned in the passage?
F. The mean would be lower.
G. The median would be lower.
H. The mean and the median would both be lower.
I. Neither the mean nor the median would change.

Math in Space The first American astronaut to circle Earth was John Glenn. In 1962, Glenn made three orbits at an average speed of 17,544 miles per hour. He traveled a total distance of 75,679 miles. This was only a short trip into space. Soon astronauts would be looking beyond Earth orbit to the moon, about 240,000 miles away.

5. Based on the passage, about how far did Glenn travel in one orbit around Earth?
A. 25 miles **B.** 17,544 miles
C. 25,000 miles **D.** 52,632 miles

6. About how long did an average orbit take?
F. 1.5 hours **G.** 4.3 hours
H. 10 hours **I.** 13 hours

7. At Glenn's rate of travel, about how long would it take to reach the moon?
A. 10 hours **B.** 14 hours
C. 24 hours **D.** 38 hours

8. *Apollo 11* took about 3 days to go from Earth orbit to moon orbit. About how fast was *Apollo 11*'s average speed?
F. 80,000 mi/h **G.** 17,544 mi/h
H. 10,000 mi/h **I.** 3,333 mi/h

A Peak Experience

Applying Data Analysis Earth's highest natural features, its great mountains, dwarf even the tallest structures made by humans. The air at the top of Mt. Everest, in the Himalayan mountains, is three times thinner than the air at sea level. Because of the thin air, numbing cold, and unpredictable weather, it takes even the most experienced climbers many weeks to reach the top of Mt. Everest.

Mt. Aconcagua is the highest peak in South America at 6,960 meters.

Mt. Elbrus is Europe's highest peak at 5,633 meters.

Mt. Everest towers over volcanoes like Mt. Kilimanjaro, Fujiyama, and Mt. Vesuvius.

Mt. Kilimanjaro, in Tanzania, rises to 5,895 meters.

Fujiyama is Japan's highest peak at 3,776 meters.

Mt. Vesuvius, in Italy, is 1,277 meters high.

It's All Relative

Although Kilimanjaro is 2,955 meters shorter than Everest, it is still 40 times as tall as the Great Pyramid in Egypt.

Volcanic Storm

Mount St. Helens, a volcano in Washington state, erupted on May 18, 1980, throwing huge clouds of ash into the sky. Before the eruption, the summit was 2,950 meters high. Afterward, it was about 400 meters lower.

Mt. Cook is New Zealand's highest peak at 3,754 meters.

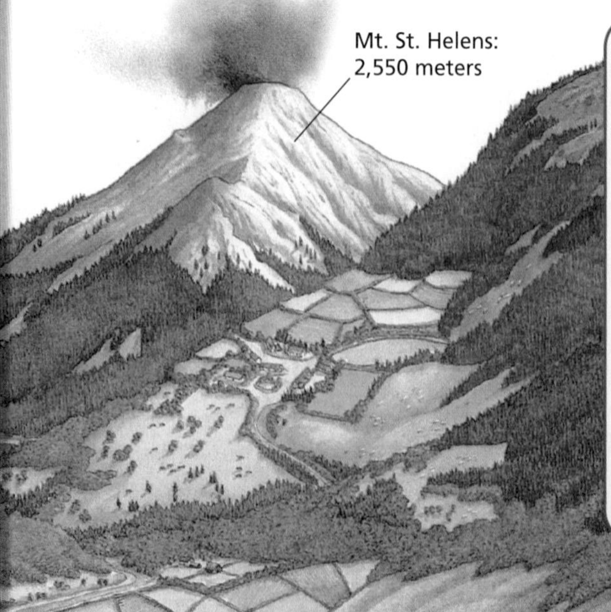

Put It All Together

Data File Use the information on these two pages and on page 319 to answer these questions.

1. a. Write the names of the mountain peaks in the table on page 319 in order from highest to lowest elevation.
   b. Graph the data on a number line. Label each point with the name of the mountain.
   c. Insert data points and labels for New Zealand's highest mountain, Mt. Cook, and the Matterhorn, in the European Alps.
2. How tall is Hawaii's Mauna Kea?

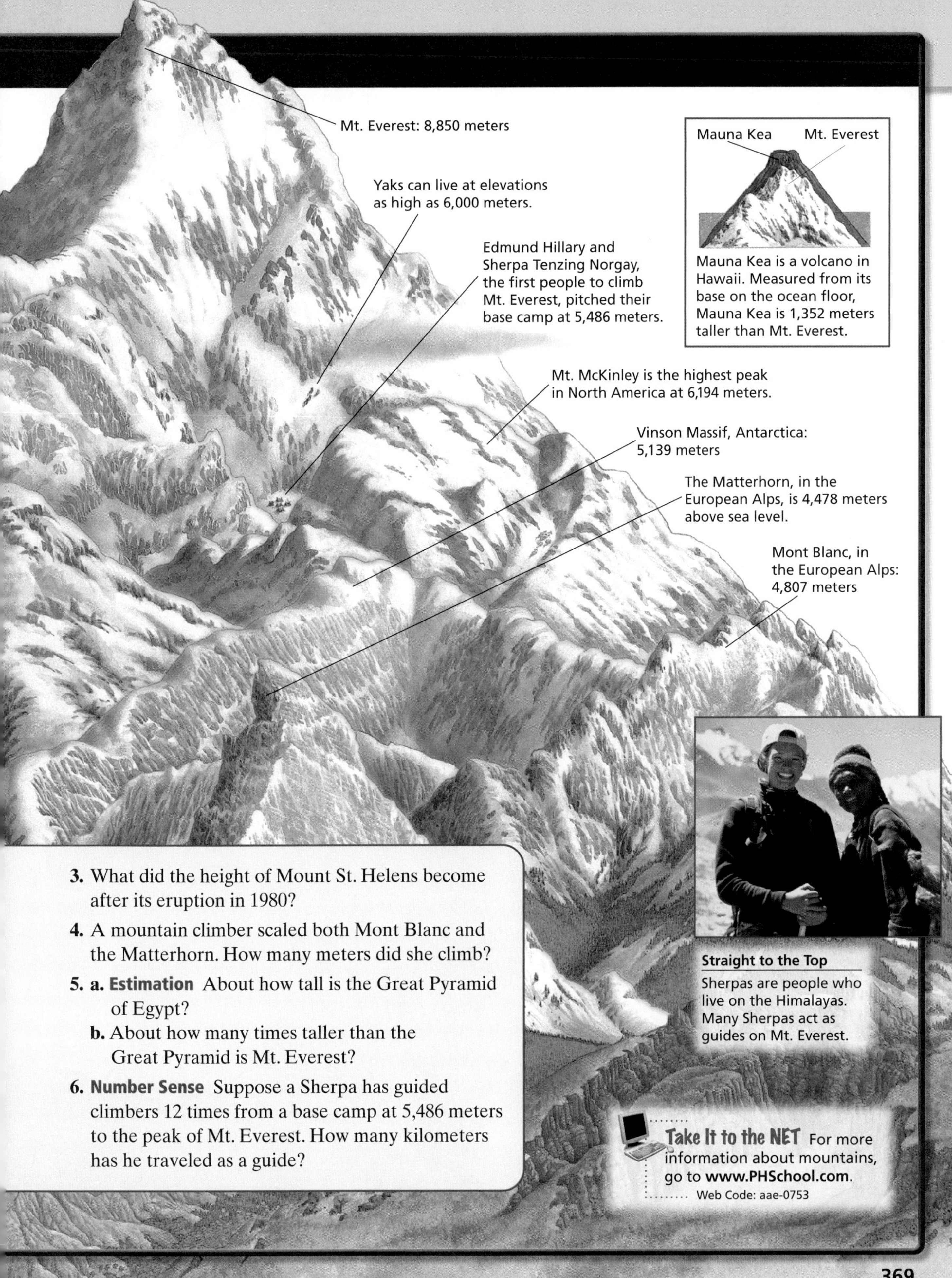

Straight to the Top
Sherpas are people who live on the Himalayas. Many Sherpas act as guides on Mt. Everest.

3. What did the height of Mount St. Helens become after its eruption in 1980?
4. A mountain climber scaled both Mont Blanc and the Matterhorn. How many meters did she climb?
5. a. **Estimation** About how tall is the Great Pyramid of Egypt?
   b. About how many times taller than the Great Pyramid is Mt. Everest?
6. **Number Sense** Suppose a Sherpa has guided climbers 12 times from a base camp at 5,486 meters to the peak of Mt. Everest. How many kilometers has he traveled as a guide?

Take It to the NET For more information about mountains, go to **www.PHSchool.com**.
Web Code: aae-0753

CHAPTER 8

Tools of Geometry

Lessons

Key Vocabulary

- angle (p. 379)
- collinear (p. 374)
- congruent angles (p. 387)
- line (p. 373)
- line symmetry (p. 410)
- parallel lines (p. 374)
- point (p. 373)
- polygon (p. 397)
- quadrilateral (p. 398)
- ray (p. 373)
- reflection (p. 416)
- rotation (p. 416)
- segment (p. 373)
- similar figures (p. 406)
- translation (p. 415)

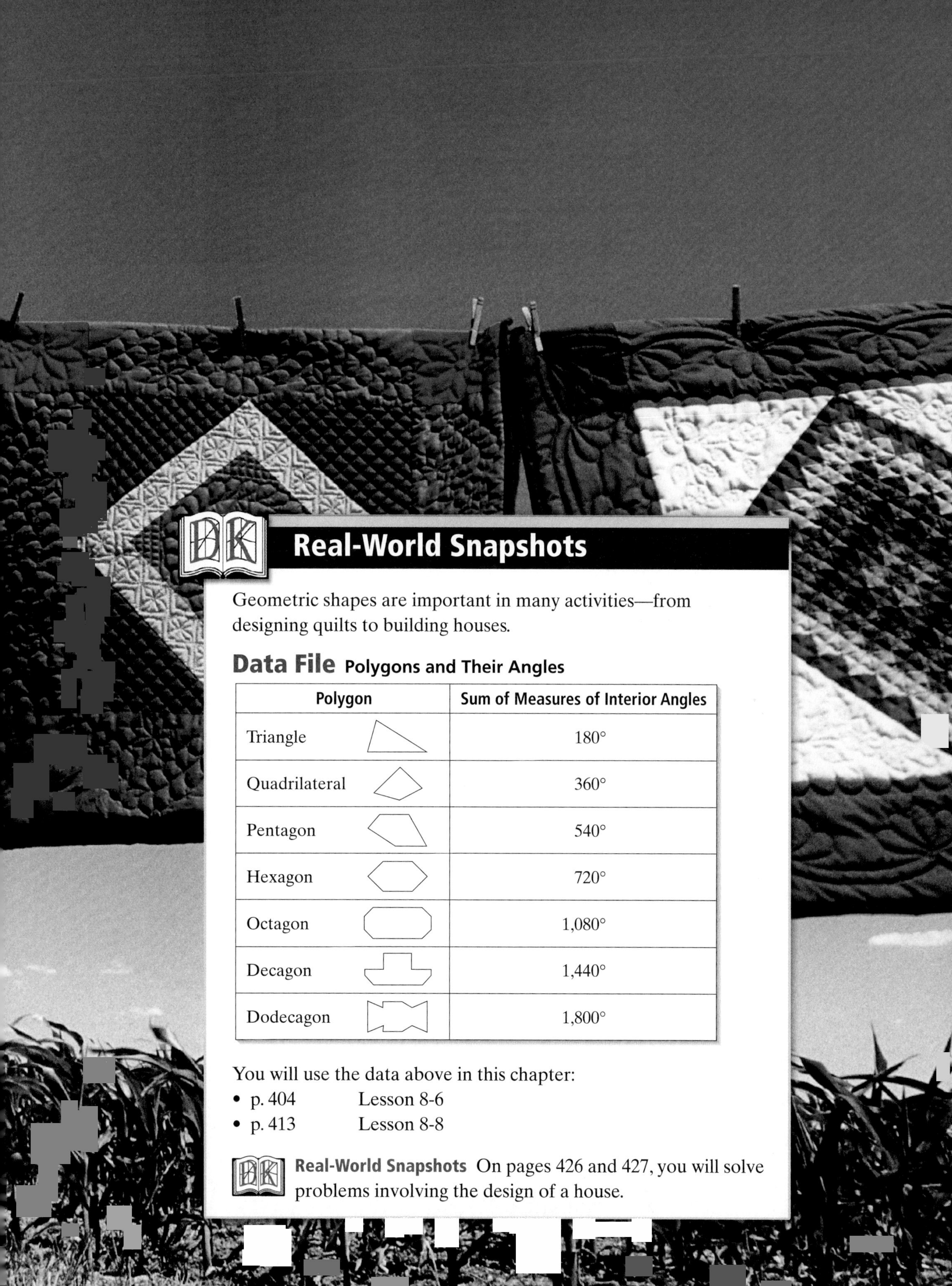

Real-World Snapshots

Geometric shapes are important in many activities—from designing quilts to building houses.

Data File Polygons and Their Angles

Polygon	Sum of Measures of Interior Angles
Triangle	180°
Quadrilateral	360°
Pentagon	540°
Hexagon	720°
Octagon	1,080°
Decagon	1,440°
Dodecagon	1,800°

You will use the data above in this chapter:

- p. 404 Lesson 8-6
- p. 413 Lesson 8-8

Real-World Snapshots On pages 426 and 427, you will solve problems involving the design of a house.

Chapter 8 Preview

Where You've Been

- In Chapter 2, you solved one-step equations by using number sense, subtracting, and adding.
- In Chapter 6, you learned to recognize and solve proportions.

Where You're Going

- In Chapter 8, you will learn how to identify points, lines, and planes.
- You will also find the measurements of angles and sides of figures. You will identify and classify figures and learn about congruency, similarity, and symmetry.
- You will identify geometric figures in real-world situations, such as garden mazes.

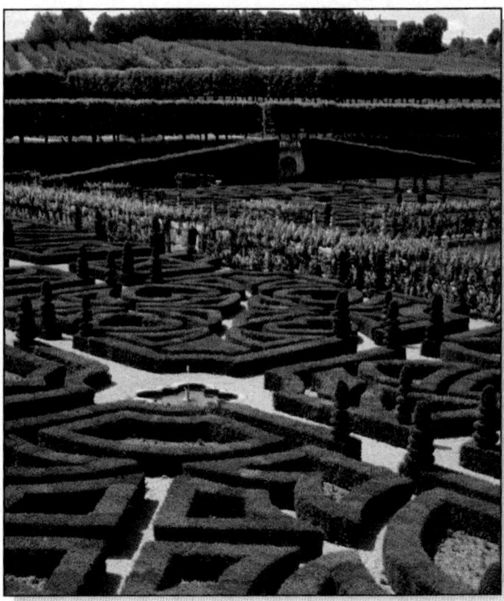

Geometric shapes are used in this garden maze in Versailles, France.

Instant self-check online and on CD-ROM

Diagnosing Readiness

For help, go to the lesson in green.

Using Number Sense to Solve One-Step Equations (Lesson 2-5)

Use mental math to solve each equation.

1. $a + 9 = 18$ **2.** $y \div 3 = 3$ **3.** $11k = 44$ **4.** $c - 5 = 5$

Solving Equations by Subtracting (Lesson 2-6)

Solve each equation. Then, check the solution.

5. $0.23 + x = 1.5$ **6.** $p + 120.5 = 180$ **7.** $62.9 + b = 90$

Solving Equations by Adding (Lesson 2-6)

Solve each equation. Then, check the solution.

8. $d - 13 = 4.5$ **9.** $g - 22 = 11.3$ **10.** $c - 0.45 = 11.62$

Recognizing Proportions (Lesson 6-3)

Do the ratios in each pair form a proportion?

11. $\frac{3}{4}, \frac{18}{24}$ **12.** $\frac{11}{12}, \frac{121}{144}$ **13.** $\frac{16}{20}, \frac{64}{100}$

14. $\frac{12}{15}, \frac{24}{30}$ **15.** $\frac{5}{8}, \frac{15}{20}$ **16.** $\frac{4}{9}, \frac{16}{36}$

8-1 Points, Lines, Segments, and Rays

What You'll Learn

To name points, lines, segments, and rays

To identify parallel, intersecting, and skew lines

. . . And Why

To identify parallel streets on a map, as in Example 3

✓ Check Skills You'll Need

For help, go to Lesson 3-4.

Find the length of each segment. Measure to the nearest $\frac{1}{16}$ inch.

1. ______________________________

2. ______________________

3. ____________________________________

New Vocabulary

• point • line • segment • ray • collinear • plane • intersecting lines • parallel lines • skew lines

OBJECTIVE

Interactive lesson includes instant self-check, tutorials, and activities.

1 Naming Points, Lines, Segments, and Rays

You can locate a star in the sky if you can find the group, or constellation, to which it belongs. The stars in such constellations are like points that can be connected to form a picture.

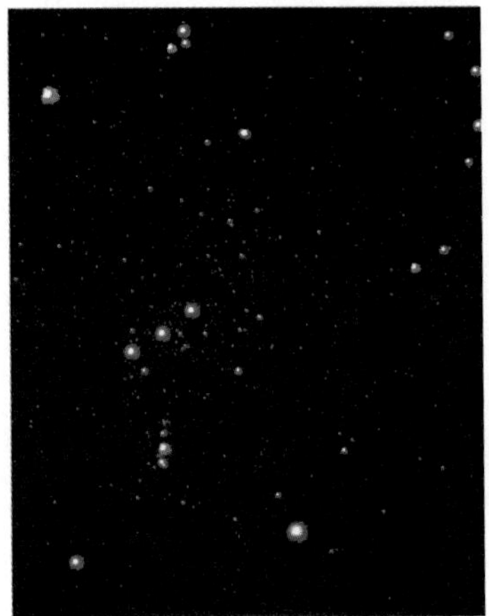

Real-World Connection

To find the constellation Orion, the hunter, look for the three stars in a row that form the belt.

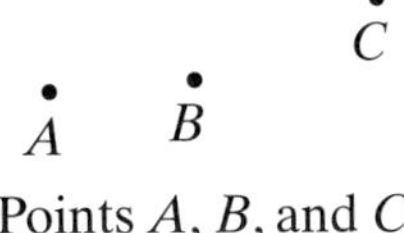

Points A, B, and C

A **point** is a location in space. It has no size. You name a point with a capital letter.

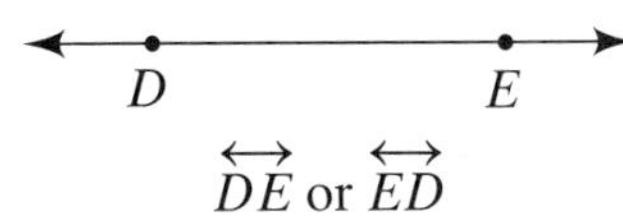

$\overleftrightarrow{DE}$ or $\overleftrightarrow{ED}$

A **line** is a series of points that extends in two opposite directions without end. It has no thickness. Use any two points on a line to name it. Read $\overleftrightarrow{DE}$ as "line DE."

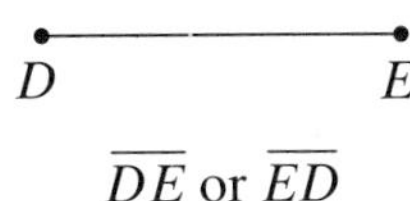

$\overline{DE}$ or $\overline{ED}$

A **segment** is part of a line with two endpoints. You name a segment by its endpoints. Read $\overline{DE}$ as "segment DE."

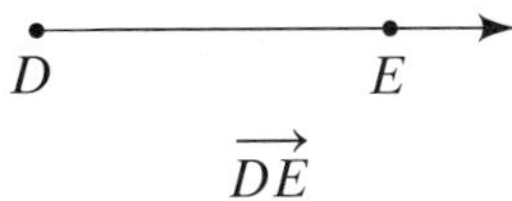

$\overrightarrow{DE}$

A **ray** consists of one endpoint and all the points of a line on one side of the endpoint. To name a ray, use its endpoint first and then any other point on the ray. Read $\overrightarrow{DE}$ as "ray DE."

1 EXAMPLE Naming Lines, Segments, and Rays

Name each line, segment, and ray.

a. 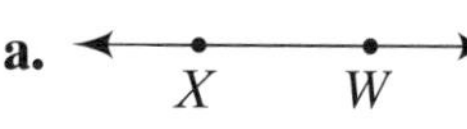

b. F ——— G

c. 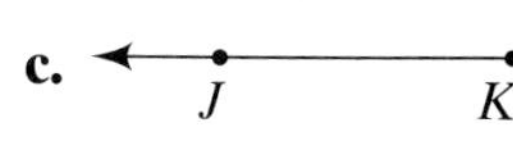

$\overleftrightarrow{XW}$, or line XW $\overline{FG}$, or segment FG $\overrightarrow{KJ}$, or ray KJ

Check Understanding 1 Use the figure at the right.

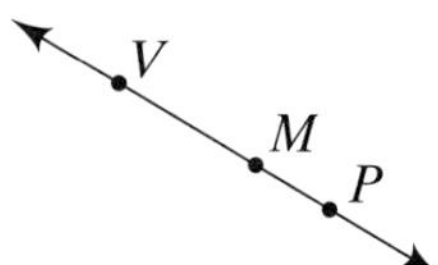

a. Give two names for the line.
b. Name three segments.
c. **Reasoning** How is $\overrightarrow{VM}$ different from $\overrightarrow{MV}$?

Reading Math

Co means "together with." So *collinear* means "together with points on the same line."

Points on the same line are **collinear.** If you cannot draw one line through all the points, the points are *noncollinear.*

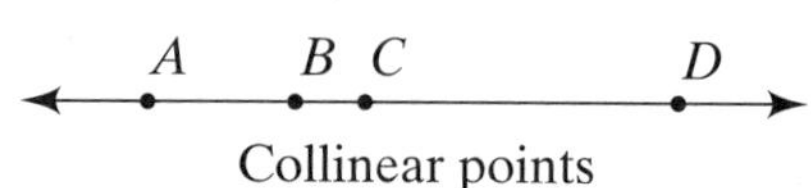

Collinear points

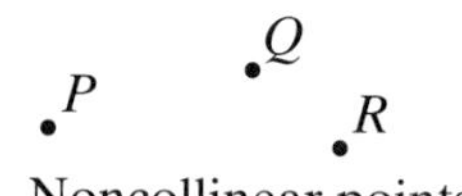

Noncollinear points

2 EXAMPLE Collinear and Noncollinear Points

Name three collinear points.

Points L, Q, and T are collinear.

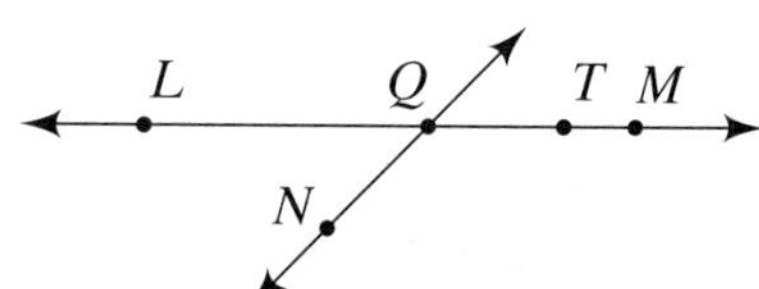

Check Understanding 2 a. Name a different set of three collinear points.
b. Name three points that are noncollinear.

OBJECTIVE

2 Identifying Parallel, Intersecting, and Skew Lines

A **plane** is a flat surface that extends indefinitely in all directions and has no thickness.

Two lines that lie in the same plane are either intersecting or parallel. **Intersecting lines** have exactly one point in common. **Parallel lines** have no points in common.

Skew lines are lines that lie in different planes. They are not parallel and do not intersect.

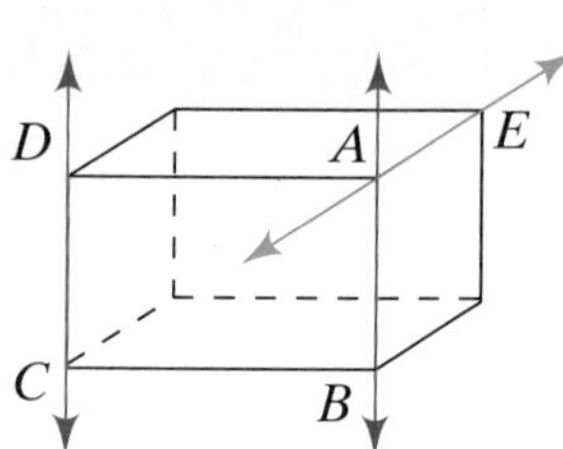

Plane $ABCD$

$\overleftrightarrow{AB}$ is parallel to $\overleftrightarrow{DC}$.

$\overleftrightarrow{AE}$ intersects $\overleftrightarrow{AB}$.

$\overleftrightarrow{AE}$ and $\overleftrightarrow{DC}$ are skew.

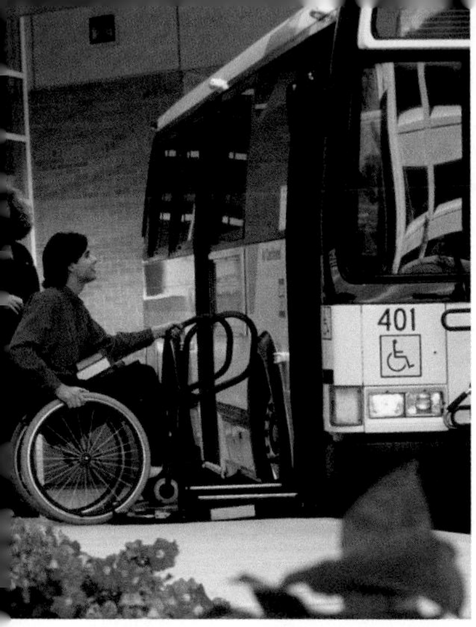

Real-World Connection

Use of public transportation requires map-reading skills.

3 EXAMPLE — Real-World Problem Solving

Maps Are the indicated lines on the map parallel or intersecting?

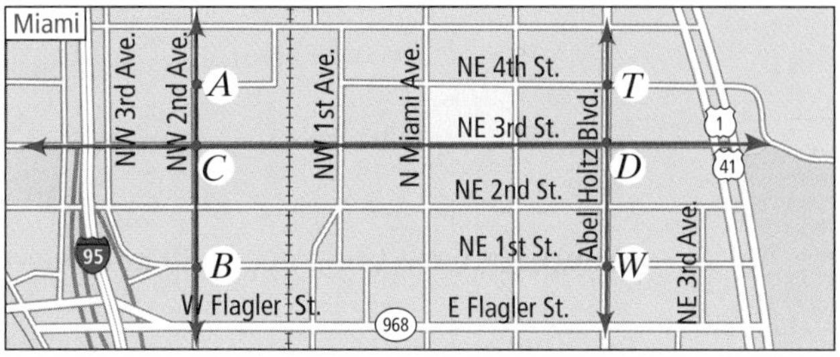

a. $\overleftrightarrow{AB}$ and $\overleftrightarrow{CD}$

$\overleftrightarrow{AB}$ and $\overleftrightarrow{CD}$ are intersecting.

b. $\overleftrightarrow{AB}$ and $\overleftrightarrow{TW}$

$\overleftrightarrow{AB}$ and $\overleftrightarrow{TW}$ are parallel.

Check Understanding 3

a. Name two other streets on the map that are parallel.
b. Name two other streets on the map that intersect.
c. **Reasoning** Can streets on this map represent skew lines? Explain.

EXERCISES

For more practice, see *Extra Practice.*

A Practice by Example

Example 1 (page 374)

Match each figure with its name.

1. 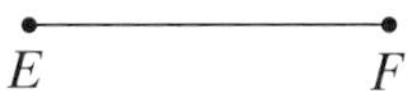

2. 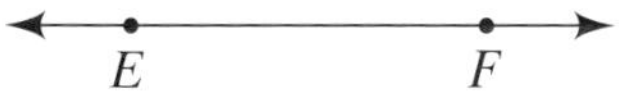

3. 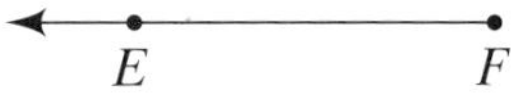

4. 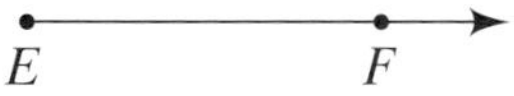

A. $\overleftrightarrow{EF}$ **B.** $\overline{EF}$ **C.** $\overrightarrow{EF}$ **D.** $\overrightarrow{FE}$

Name each segment, ray, or line.

5. 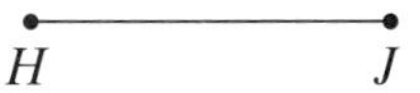

6. 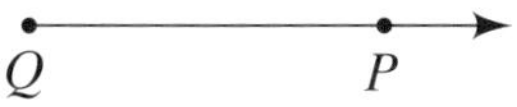

7. 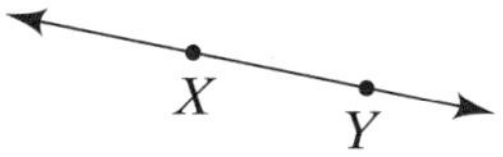

8. 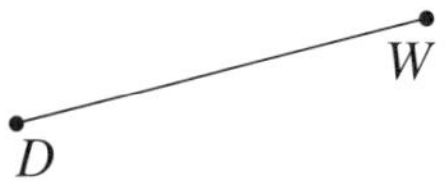

9. 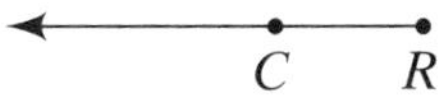

10. 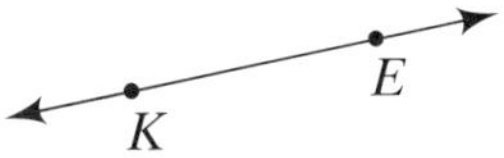

11. 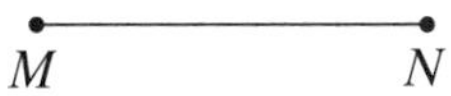

12. 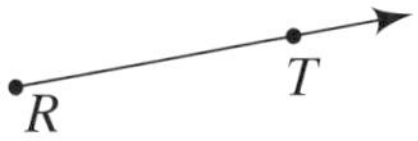

Example 2 (page 374)

Use the diagram at the right for Exercises 13–17.

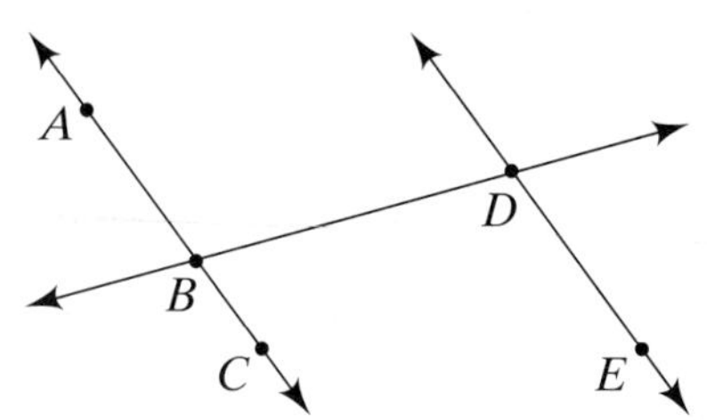

13. Name three collinear points.

14. Name three noncollinear points.

15. Name four noncollinear points.

Complete each sentence with *collinear* or *noncollinear.*

16. Points B and D are ■.

17. Points B, D, and E are ■.

Example 3 (page 375)

Use the diagram below. Name each of the following.

18. a line parallel to $\overline{PQ}$

19. two skew lines

20. a segment parallel to $\overline{SW}$ and $\overline{RV}$

21. a segment that intersects $\overline{SW}$ and $\overline{RV}$

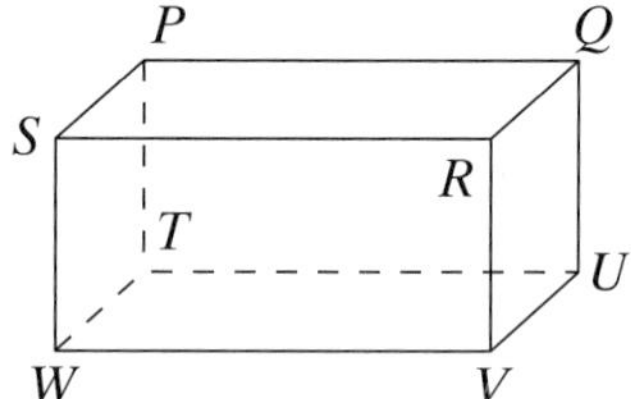

B Apply Your Skills

Use *sometimes, always,* or *never* to complete each sentence.

22. Four points are _?_ collinear.

23. A ray _?_ has two endpoints.

24. A segment _?_ has two endpoints.

25. A line _?_ has two endpoints.

26. Skew lines _?_ intersect.

27. Parallel lines _?_ intersect.

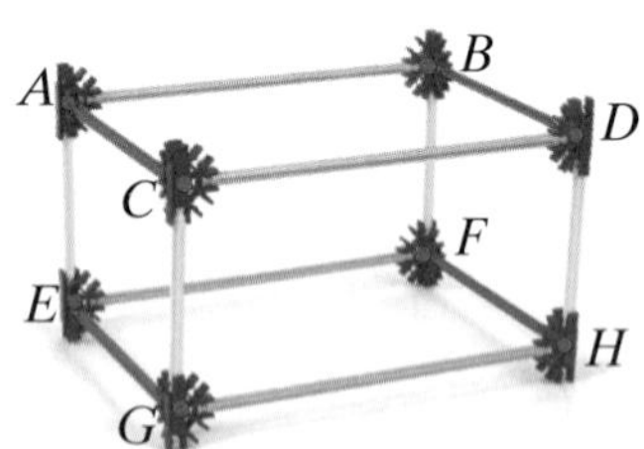

Use the diagram at the left. Name each of the following.

28. the segments that intersect $\overline{GH}$

29. a line parallel to $\overleftrightarrow{AB}$

30. the points collinear to A

31. a segment skew to $\overline{AC}$

32. **Writing in Math** Explain why a line segment is represented as $\overline{AB}$ and a line is represented as $\overleftrightarrow{AB}$.

C Challenge

33. **Planning** A map shows a park at point A and a pool at point B.

a. How many straight roads could go through point A?

b. How many straight roads could the town construct to connect the park at point A and the pool at point B?

34. **Stretch Your Thinking** Find a four-digit number where the first digit is one third the second, the first and second digits add up to the third, and the last digit is three times the second.

Test Prep

Reading Comprehension Read the passage and answer the questions below.

Eclipses

Earth is about 248,550 miles from the moon and 93,000,000 miles from the sun. The diameter of Earth is about 7,910 miles. The moon's diameter is about 2,220 miles. The diameter of the sun is about 865,000 miles. A solar eclipse occurs when the moon comes between the sun and Earth. A lunar eclipse occurs when Earth comes between the moon and the sun.

35. Using geometric terms, describe the position of the moon, Earth, and sun during a solar eclipse.

36. How much greater is the diameter of Earth than the diameter of the moon?

Multiple Choice

Use the diagram at the right.

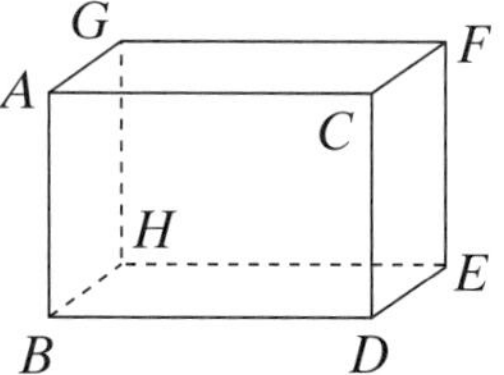

37. Which segment is skew to $\overline{AB}$?

A. $\overline{AC}$ **B.** $\overline{DC}$ **C.** $\overline{CF}$ **D.** $\overline{BD}$

38. Which segment intersects $\overline{AG}$?

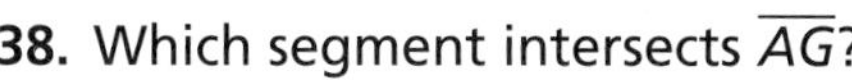

F. $\overline{CF}$ **G.** $\overline{DE}$ **H.** $\overline{BD}$ **I.** $\overline{AC}$

Take It to the NET
Online lesson quiz at **www.PHSchool.com**
Web Code: aaa-0801

39. Which segment is parallel to $\overline{CF}$ and skew to $\overline{AB}$?

A. $\overline{GF}$ **B.** $\overline{DE}$ **C.** $\overline{BD}$ **D.** $\overline{DC}$

Mixed Review

Lesson 7-1 **Find the median of each data set.**

40. 5, 6, 8, 9, 10, 4, 7

41. 600, 550, 475, 520, 500

42. 22, 23, 25, 26, 28, 21

43. 130, 145, 156, 150, 129

Lesson 6-6 **Write each percent as a fraction in simplest form.**

44. 70%

45. 55%

46. 12%

47. 5%

48. 125%

49. 1%

Reading Math: Common Words and Prefixes

For Use With Chapter 8

Here are two strategies to help you learn new vocabulary words.

Make Connections to Common English Words

Common meanings of words can help you understand their meanings in mathematics.

- You watch a *segment*, or part, of a television show. In mathematics, a segment is part of a line.
- Two roads meet at an *intersection* and share a piece of the road. Intersecting lines meet and share a common point.

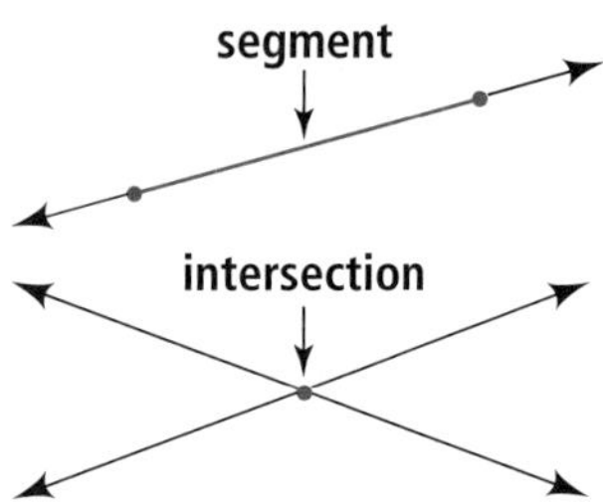

Know Important Prefixes and Root Words

Many mathematics terms are based on Greek or Latin words. Prefixes and root words can help you understand the meaning of a new term.

- *Para* means "alongside." So, *parallel* lines are lines alongside each other.
- *Poly* means "many" and *gon* means "angle." So, a *polygon* means a figure with many angles.
- *Bi* means "two" and *sectus* means "to cut." *Bisect* means to cut something into two equal parts.

Dictionaries often include the root words and prefixes of terms.

EXERCISES

Use the common meaning of each word to help you write the mathematics meaning. Check your meaning with the definition in the Glossary.

1. reflection

2. rotation

Use the root words and prefixes of each word to help you write the mathematics meaning. Check your meaning for each word with the definition in the Glossary.

3. hexagon (*Hex* means "six" and *gon* means "angle.")

4. quadrilateral (*Quadri* means "four" and *latus* means "side.")

8-2 Angles

What You'll Learn

OBJECTIVE 1 To measure and classify angles

. . . And Why

To measure angles related to sports, as in Example 1

Check Skills You'll Need

For help, go to Lesson 8-1.

Use the diagram at the right.

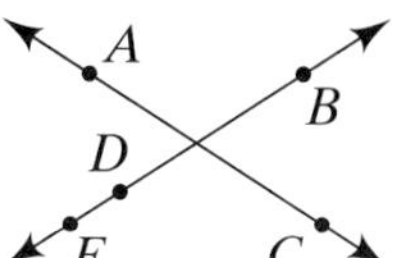

1. Name a line, a segment, and a ray.
2. Are points B, C, and E collinear? Explain.

New Vocabulary

- angle
- vertex
- degree
- acute angle
- right angle
- obtuse angle
- straight angle
- perpendicular lines

OBJECTIVE

Interactive lesson includes instant self-check, tutorials, and activities.

1 Measuring and Classifying Angles

Reading Math

The plural of *vertex* is *vertices*.

An **angle** has two sides and a vertex. The sides are rays, and the **vertex** is their common endpoint. The angle at the right may be called $\angle Y$, $\angle XYZ$, $\angle ZYX$, or $\angle 1$.

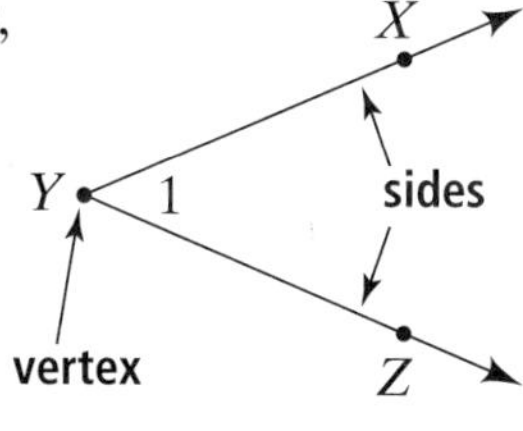

Angles are measured in units called **degrees.** Use the symbol ° for degrees. You can use a *protractor* to find the measure of an angle.

1 EXAMPLE Real-World Problem Solving

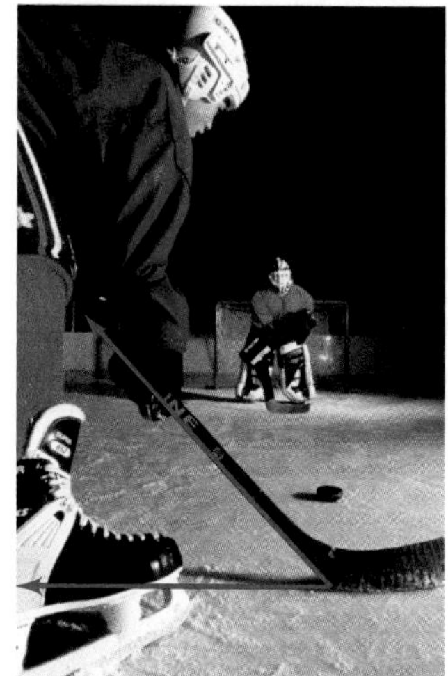

Ice Hockey Measure the angle the hockey stick forms with the ground.

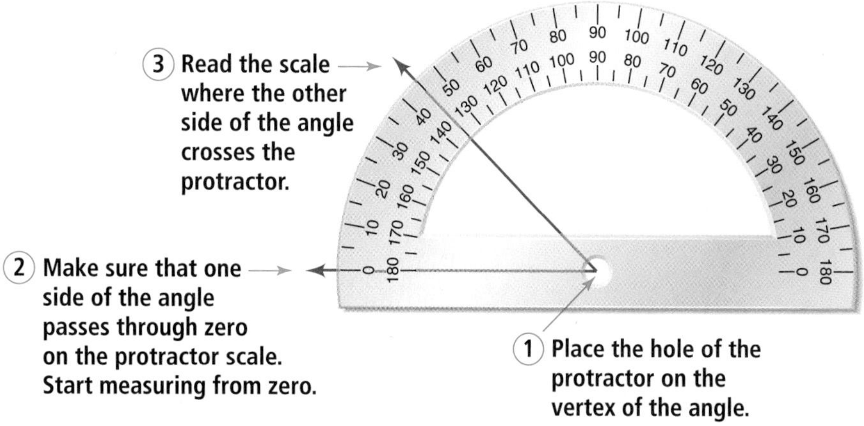

3 Read the scale where the other side of the angle crosses the protractor.

2 Make sure that one side of the angle passes through zero on the protractor scale. Start measuring from zero.

1 Place the hole of the protractor on the vertex of the angle.

The angle measure is 45°.

Check Understanding 1

a. Use a protractor to measure the angle at the right.

b. **Reasoning** Will an angle that measures 100° be greater than or less than the angle formed by a corner of a piece of paper?

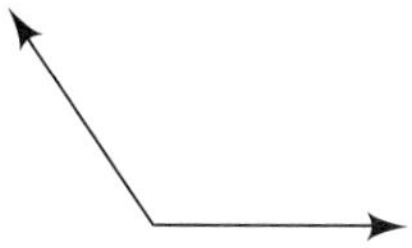

You can use measures to classify angles.

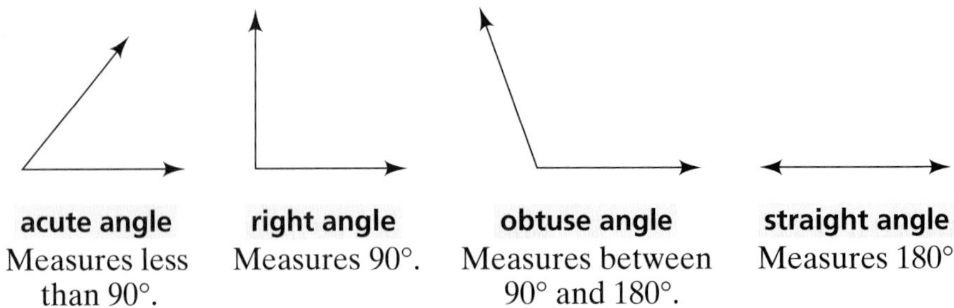

acute angle Measures less than 90°.

right angle Measures 90°.

obtuse angle Measures between 90° and 180°.

straight angle Measures 180°.

> **Test-Prep Tip**
> When you see a right-angle symbol, remember that the angle measures 90°.

Lines that intersect to form right angles are called **perpendicular lines.** The symbol ⌐ on the diagram shows that $\angle AED$ is a right angle and that $\overleftrightarrow{AB}$ is perpendicular to $\overleftrightarrow{CD}$.

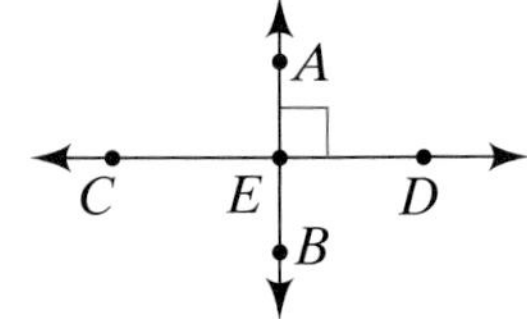

2 EXAMPLE Classifying Angles

Classify each angle as *acute, right, obtuse,* or *straight.*

a. acute

b. obtuse

c. 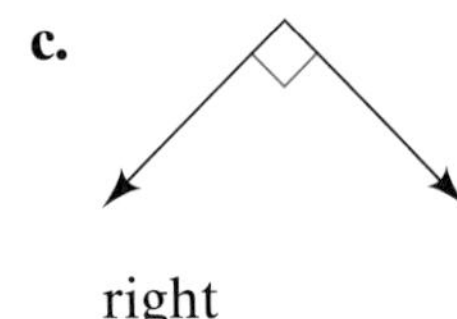

right

2 **a.** **Estimation** Estimate the measure of the angle.
b. Classify the angle as *acute, right, obtuse,* or *straight.*

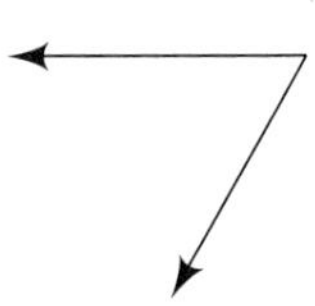

More Than One Way

Use a protractor to measure the angle.

Elena's Method

I place the center point of the protractor on the vertex of the angle. Then I turn the protractor so that 0° lines up with the inside scale for one side of the angle. The second side crosses the inside scale at 50°.

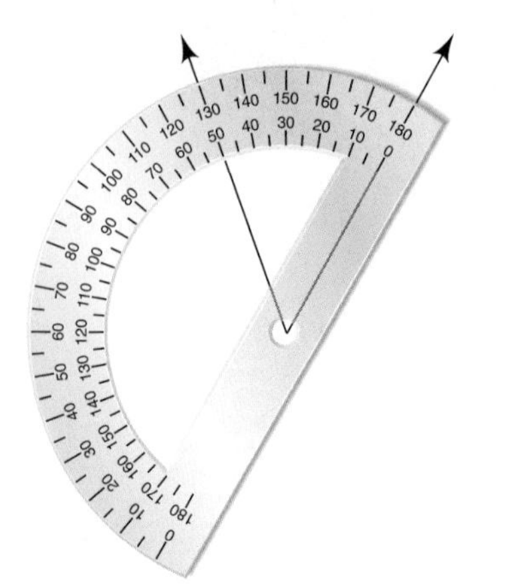

The angle measures 50°.

Zack's Method

I place the center hole of the protractor on the vertex of the angle. I read the scale where each side intersects the protractor. Then I find the difference between the two scale readings.

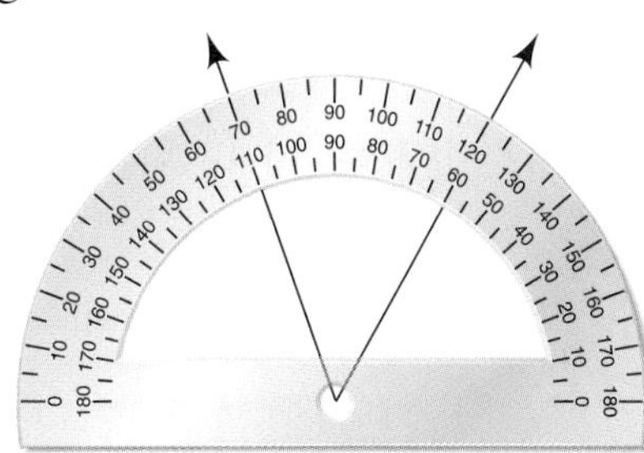

Since $120 - 70 = 50$, the angle measures 50°.

Choose a Method

Measure the angle. Describe your method.

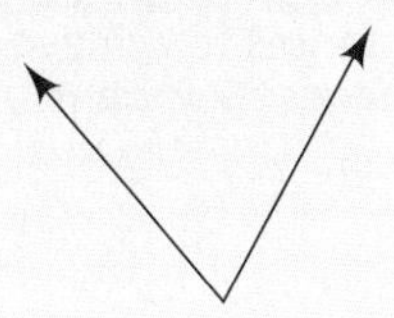

EXERCISES

For more practice, see *Extra Practice.*

A Practice by Example

Example 1 (page 379)

Measurement **Use a protractor to measure each angle.**

1. 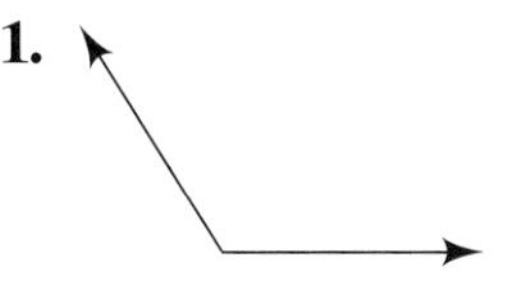

2. 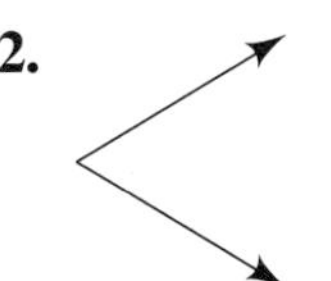

3. 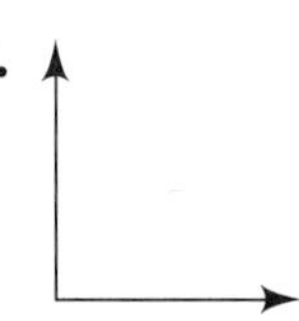

4. 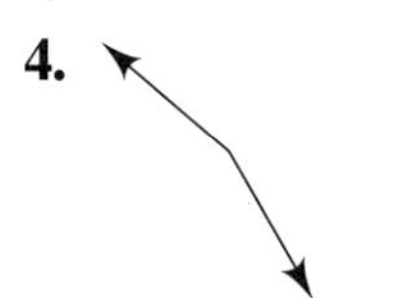

5. 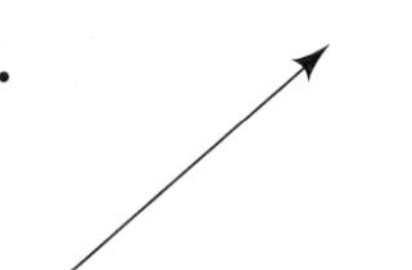

6. 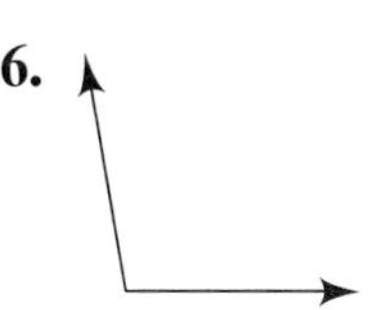

Example 2 (page 380)

Classify each angle as *acute, right, obtuse,* or *straight.*

7.

8. 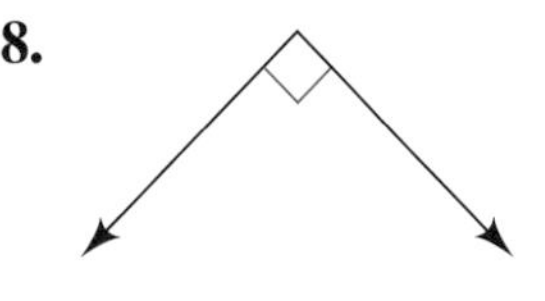

9.

B Apply Your Skills

Use a protractor to draw angles with the following measures.

10. 30° **11.** 135° **12.** 90°

13. 45° **14.** 120° **15.** 60°

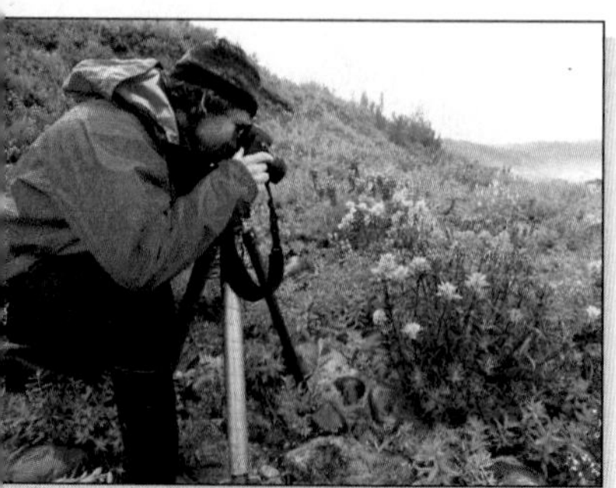

Real-World Connection

Careers Professional photographers use a variety of lenses to achieve the images they want.

16. Photography A 35-mm camera lens has a 45° viewing angle. What kind of angle is this?

17. Reasoning Does increasing the lengths of the sides of an angle change the measurement of the angle? Explain.

18. Open-Ended Describe examples of perpendicular lines in your classroom.

19. Writing in Math Explain how to fold a piece of paper so that the crease lines form four right angles.

Use the figure at the right for Exercises 20–24.

20. Estimation Estimate the measure of each angle. Then measure each angle with a protractor.

a. $\angle AGB$ **b.** $\angle BGD$

c. $\angle BGF$ **d.** $\angle EGB$

e. $\angle AGE$ **f.** $\angle DGF$

21. Name all the obtuse angles. **22.** Name all the right angles.

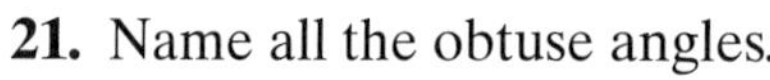

23. Name all the straight angles. **24.** Name all the acute angles.

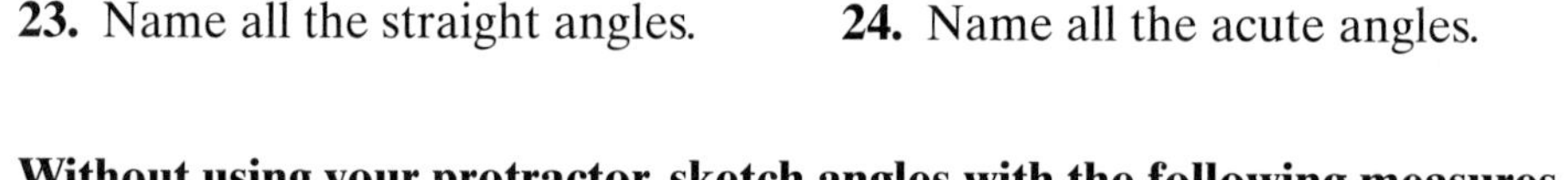

Without using your protractor, sketch angles with the following measures. Then use your protractor to see how close you are.

25. 30° **26.** 60° **27.** 120°

C Challenge

Clocks Classify the angle formed by the minute and hour hands of a clock at each of the following times.

28. 1:00 **29.** 5:00 **30.** 6:00 **31.** 9:00

32. Navigation You are facing north. If you turn 270° counterclockwise, which direction will you face?

33. Stretch Your Thinking Find the missing numbers if each number after the first two is the sum of the two preceding numbers.

■, 8, ■, ■, ■, 56.5

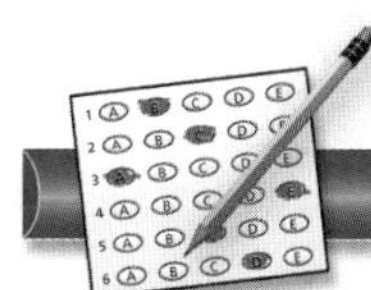

Test Prep

Multiple Choice

Use the diagram at the right for Exercises 34–35.

34. Which measure is NOT a measure of one of the angles shown at the right?

A. 60° **B.** 90°
C. 120° **D.** 150°

35. How many pairs of angles appear to have the same measure?

F. 1 **G.** 2 **H.** 3 **I.** 4

36. Which angle in the figure at the right has the greatest measure?

A. $\angle ABC$ **B.** $\angle CBD$
C. $\angle ABD$ **D.** $\angle ABE$

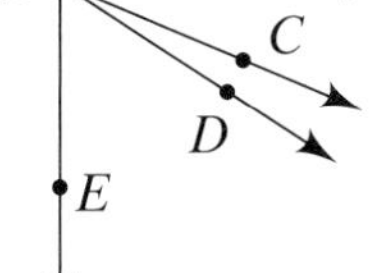

37. Which of the following is NOT correct?

F. A 43° angle is obtuse.
G. An 89° angle is acute.
H. A 90° angle is right.
I. A 180° angle is straight.

Take It to the NET
Online lesson quiz at
www.PHSchool.com
Web Code: aaa-0802

Short Response

38. a. How many angles with vertex X are in the figure at the right?
b. List each angle.

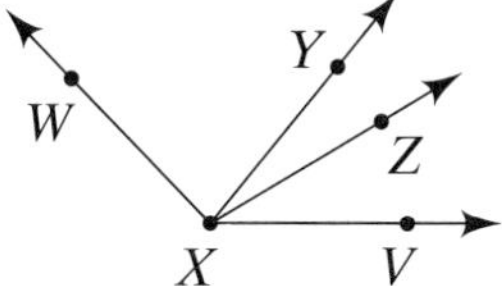

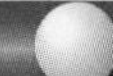

Mixed Review

Lesson 7-3

39. You want to buy a sweatshirt. Color choices are red, black, white, or green. Each color comes in crew neck or V-neck. How many choices do you have? Make an organized list to find the solution.

Lesson 5-7

Choose an appropriate unit for each measurement.

40. length of a soccer field

41. width of this page

42. distance from Miami, Florida to Austin, Texas

43. width of your hand

Lesson 5-4

44. You have a gallon of fruit punch and paper cups that hold a serving of $\frac{3}{4}$ cup of liquid. Do you have enough punch for 25 servings? Explain why or why not. (*Hint:* 1 gallon = 16 cups)

Basic Constructions

For Use With Lesson 8-2

A *perpendicular bisector* is a line that is perpendicular to another segment and passes through that segment's *midpoint.* You can use a compass and straightedge to construct a perpendicular bisector.

1 EXAMPLE

Use a compass and straightedge to construct the perpendicular bisector of $\overline{AB}$.

A B

Step 1 Open the compass to more than half the length of $\overline{AB}$. Put the tip of the compass point at A. Draw a part of a circle, or *arc*, that intersects $\overline{AB}$.

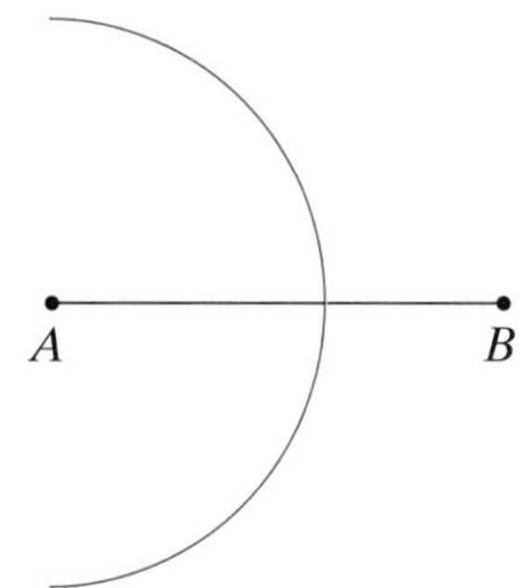

Step 2 Keep the compass open to the same width. Put the tip of the compass at B. Draw another arc that intersects $\overline{AB}$. Label the points of intersection of the two arcs C and D.

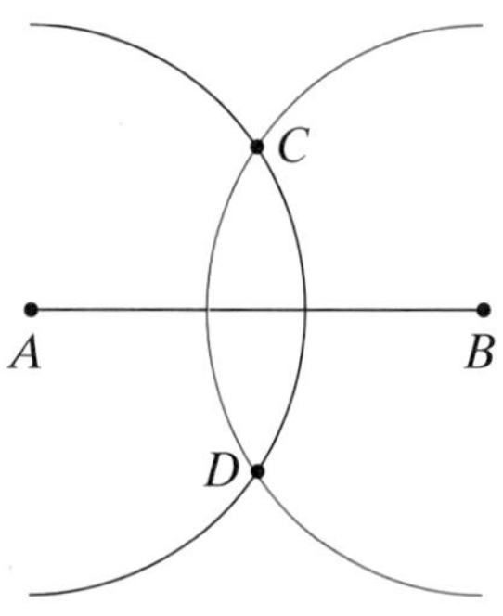

Step 3 Draw $\overleftrightarrow{CD}$. Label the intersection of $\overleftrightarrow{CD}$ and $\overline{AB}$ point M.

$\overleftrightarrow{CD}$ intersects $\overline{AB}$ at its midpoint M.

$\overleftrightarrow{CD}$ is the perpendicular bisector of $\overline{AB}$.

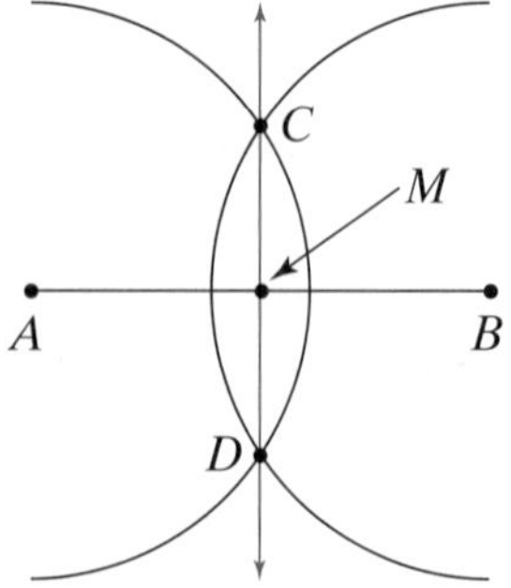

An *angle bisector* is a ray that divides an angle into two congruent angles.

2 EXAMPLE

Use a compass and straightedge to construct the angle bisector of $\angle E$.

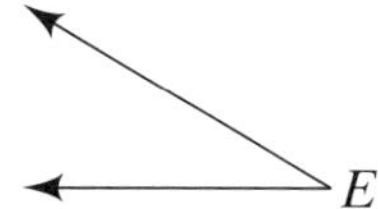

Step 1 Put the tip of the compass at E. Draw an arc that intersects both sides of $\angle E$. Label the points of intersection F and G.

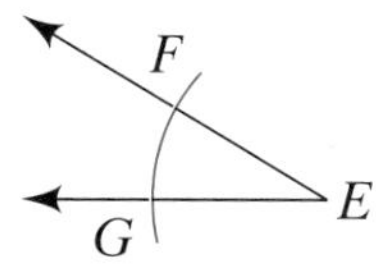

Step 2 Place the tip of the compass at F. Draw a large arc.

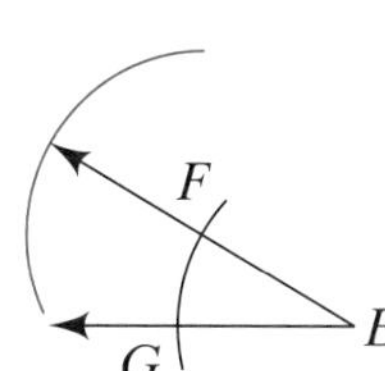

Step 3 Keep the compass open to the same width, and place the tip at G. Draw another large arc. Label the point of intersection of the two large arcs H.

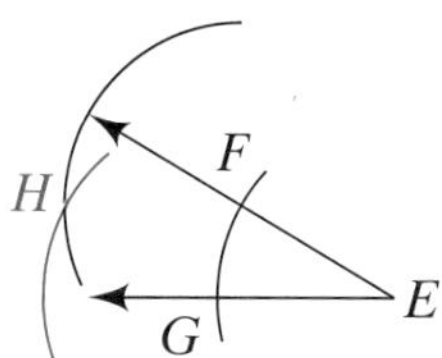

Step 4 Draw $\overrightarrow{EH}$.

$\overrightarrow{EH}$ divides $\angle FEG$ into two congruent angles, $\angle FEH$ and $\angle HEG$.

$\overrightarrow{EH}$ is the angle bisector of $\angle FEG$.

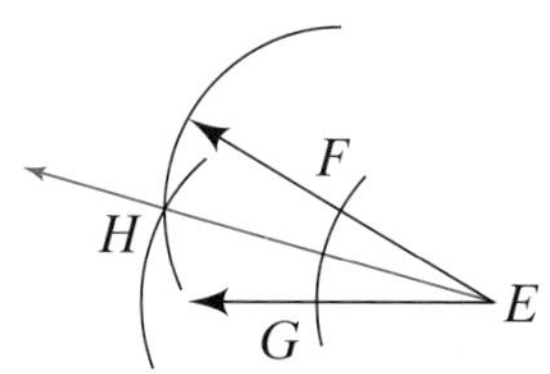

EXERCISES

1. Draw $\overline{JK}$ two inches long. Then construct the perpendicular bisector of $\overline{JK}$.

2. Draw an acute angle and construct its bisector.

3. Draw an obtuse angle and construct its bisector.

4. **Writing in Math** Explain how you can use what you know about perpendicular bisectors and angle bisectors to construct a 90° angle and a 45° angle.

8-3 Special Pairs of Angles

What You'll Learn

To find complements and supplements

To identify special pairs of angles

. . . And Why

To use angles in carpentry, as in Example 3

Check Skills You'll Need

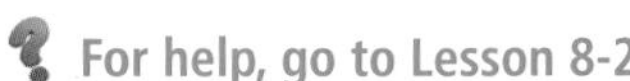

Use a protractor to draw each angle.

1. 30° **2.** 60° **3.** 45° **4.** 120°

New Vocabulary

- complementary angles
- supplementary angles
- vertical angles
- congruent angles
- transversal
- interior angles
- exterior angles

OBJECTIVE

TEXT Interactive lesson includes instant self-check, tutorials, and activities.

1 Finding the Complement and Supplement of an Angle

If the sum of the measures of two angles is 90°, the angles are **complementary angles.** If the sum of the measures of two angles is 180°, the angles are **supplementary angles.**

Complementary angles

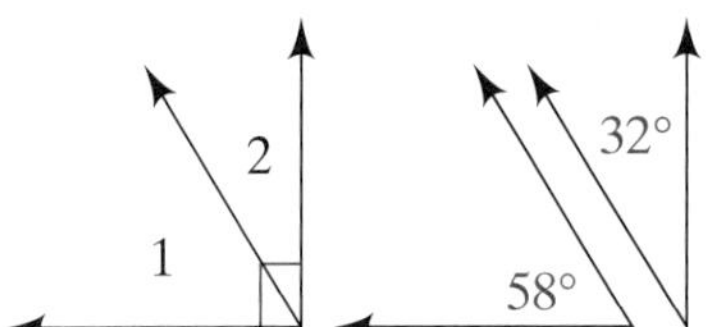

Two angles, the sum of whose measures is 90°

Supplementary angles

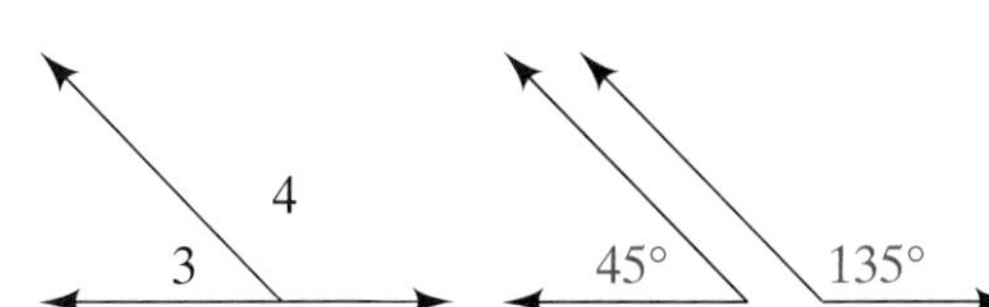

Two angles, the sum of whose measures is 180°

1 EXAMPLE Finding the Complement of an Angle

Algebra Find the value of x.

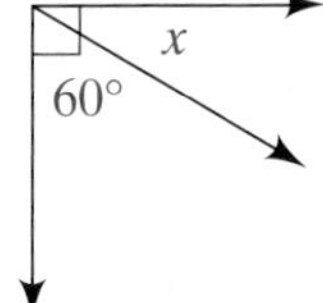

Let x = measure of the angle's complement.

$x + 60° = 90°$ ← **The angles are complementary.**

$x + 60° - 60° = 90° - 60°$ ← **Subtract 60° from each side.**

$x = 30°$ ← **Simplify.**

Check Understanding 1 Find the value of x.

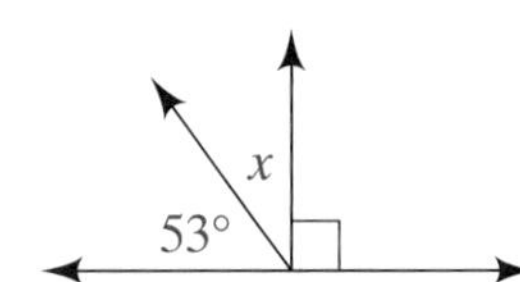

2 EXAMPLE Using Diagrams

Algebra Find the value of x.

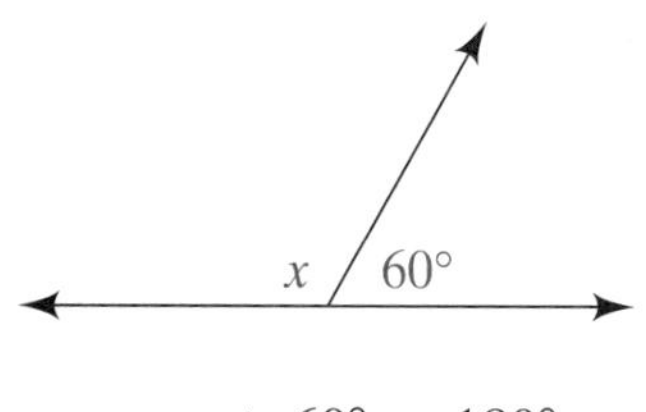

$x + 60° = 180°$ ← **The angles are supplementary.**

$x + 60° - 60° = 180° - 60°$ ← **Subtract 60° from each side.**

$x = 120°$ ← **Simplify.**

Check Understanding 2 Find the value of x.

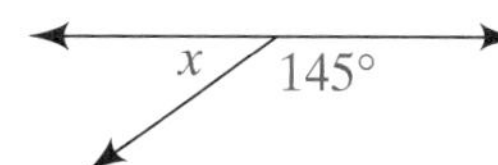

OBJECTIVE 2 Identifying Special Pairs of Angles

Investigation: Angle Measures

1. Measure each numbered angle in the figure at the right.
2. Which angles are supplementary?
3. Which angles have the same measure?

Real-World Connection

The ladder's brace forms a transversal with the sides of the ladder. Notice the interior angles formed by the sides and the brace.

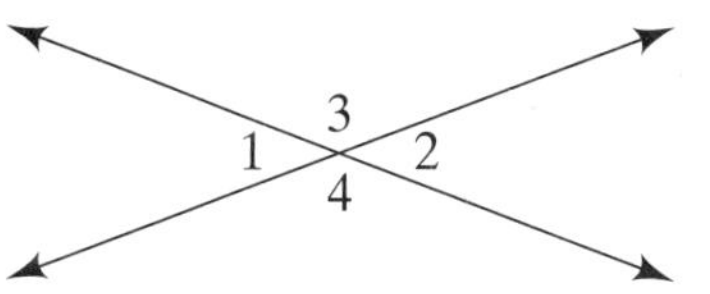

Vertical angles are formed by two intersecting lines. In the drawing at the right, angles 1 and 2 are vertical angles. So are angles 3 and 4. Vertical angles have equal measures. Angles with equal measures are **congruent angles.**

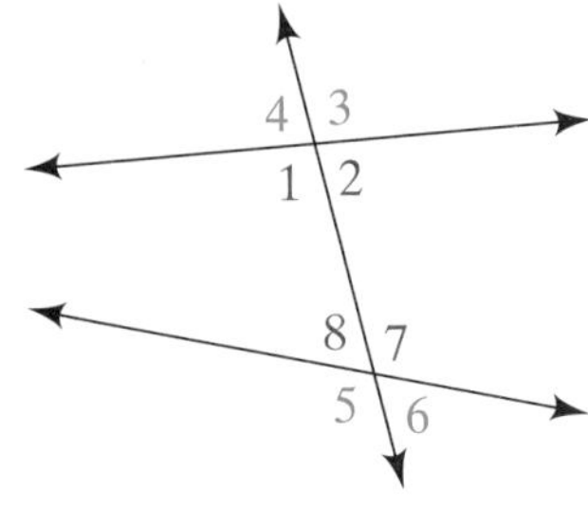

A **transversal** crosses two or more lines at different points. **Interior angles** are on either side of a transversal between a pair of lines. Angles 1, 2, 7, and 8 are interior angles. **Exterior angles** are on either side of a transversal outside of a pair of lines. Angles 3, 4, 5, and 6 are exterior angles.

3 EXAMPLE Real-World Problem Solving

Carpentry The boards that hold this door together are two parallel lines and a transversal. Identify the angles described below.

a. a pair of acute vertical angles $\angle 2$ and $\angle 4$

b. two supplementary interior angles $\angle 3$ and $\angle 5$

Check Understanding 3 Use the diagram above to identify each of the following.
a. a pair of obtuse vertical angles **b.** a pair of supplementary angles

EXERCISES

For more practice, see *Extra Practice*.

A Practice by Example

Examples 1 and 2 (pages 386, 387)

Find the complement and the supplement of each angle measure.

1. 12° **2.** 45° **3.** 83° **4.** 68° **5.** 4°

Find the value of *x* in each figure.

6.
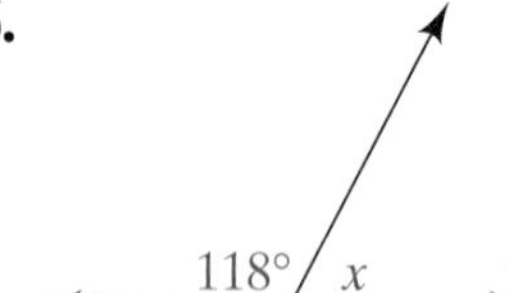

7.
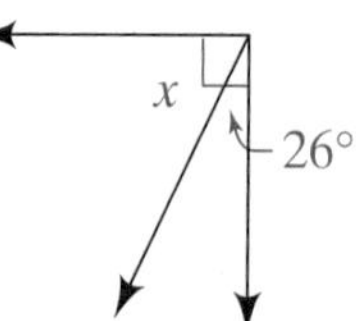

8.
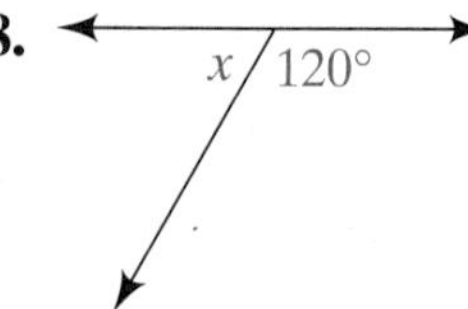

Example 3 (page 388)

Use the diagram at the right to identify each of the following.

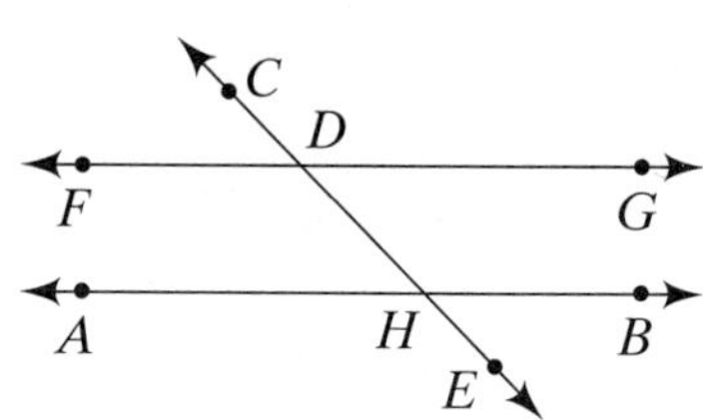

9. a transversal

10. two exterior angles

11. two interior angles

12. a pair of obtuse vertical angles

B Apply Your Skills

Complete each sentence with *sometimes, always,* or *never.*

13. Two acute angles are __?__ complementary.

14. Two obtuse angles are __?__ complementary.

15. Two obtuse angles are __?__ supplementary.

16. Two right angles are __?__ supplementary.

Algebra **Find the value of x in each figure.**

17.

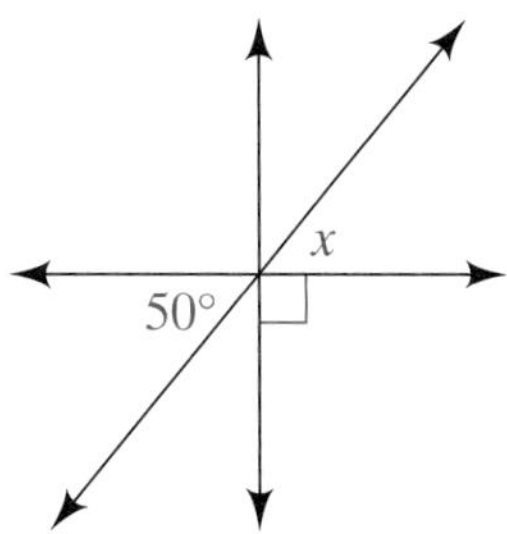

18.

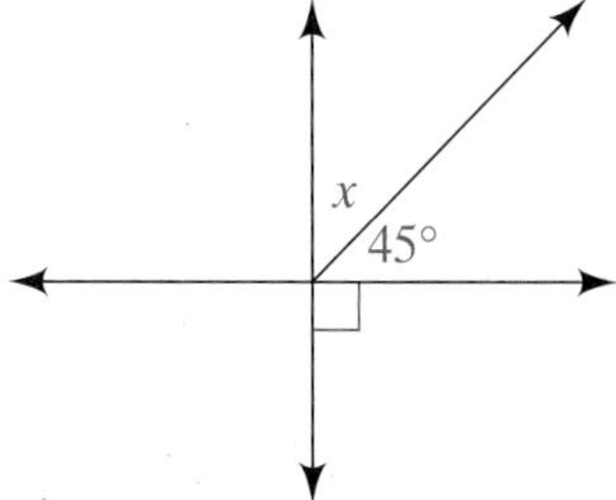

19.

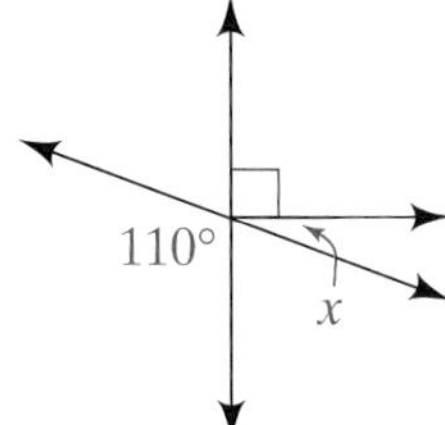

20.

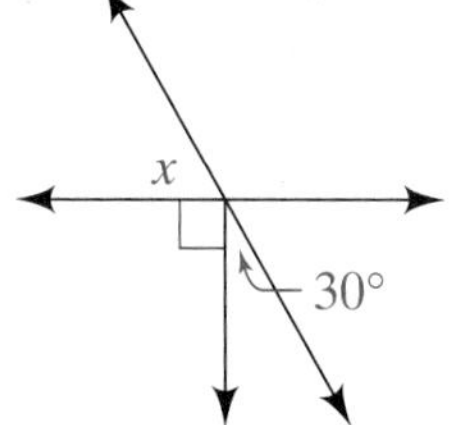

21. Architecture Before renovations, the Leaning Tower of Pisa stood at an angle of about 5° with a vertical line. What is the measure of the acute angle that the tower made with the ground? What is the measure of the obtuse angle?

22. Writing in Math Explain how to draw a pair of supplementary angles without a protractor.

23. Reasoning An angle measures 115°. Explain why you cannot find both a complement and a supplement of the angle.

C Challenge

24. Stretch Your Thinking A number has four digits. The sum of the first and last digits is twice the second digit. The second digit is 2 less than the third digit. The last digit is twice the first digit. Some of the digits are alike. What is the number?

25. Food The pizza is cut into unequal slices. One slice forms an angle whose measure is 65°. Find the measure of the angles formed by the other two slices.

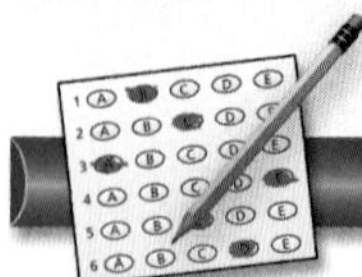

Test Prep

Multiple Choice

Use the diagram at the right.

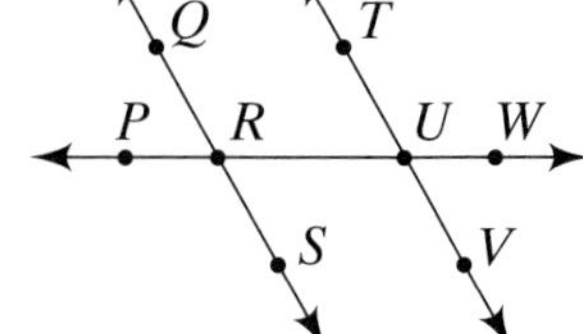

26. Which angle appears to be obtuse?
A. ∠*URS** **B.** ∠*PRS*
C. ∠*TUR* **D.** ∠*WUV*

27. Which pair of angles is supplementary?
F. ∠*TUW*, ∠*PRS* **G.** ∠*WUR*, ∠*PRS*
H. ∠*TUW*, ∠*QRU* **I.** ∠*WUV*, ∠*TUW*

28. Which lines appear to be parallel?
A. $\overleftrightarrow{QS}$, $\overleftrightarrow{PW}$ **B.** $\overleftrightarrow{TV}$, $\overleftrightarrow{PW}$ **C.** $\overleftrightarrow{QS}$, $\overleftrightarrow{RW}$ **D.** $\overleftrightarrow{TV}$, $\overleftrightarrow{QS}$

Take It to the NET
Online lesson quiz at
www.PHSchool.com
Web Code: aaa-0803

29. Which points are noncollinear?
F. *Q, R, S* **G.** *Q, R, U* **H.** *T, U, V* **I.** *R, U, W*

Mixed Review

Lesson 7-4

30. Draw a bar graph to display the data at the right.

City	Annual Precipitation
Los Angeles, CA	about 15 in.
Atlanta, GA	about 50 in.
Miami, FL	about 55 in.
Phoenix, AZ	about 8 in.
Duluth, MN	about 30 in.

SOURCE: *World Almanac 2000*

Lesson 6-7

Find each answer.

31. 5% of 100 **32.** 30% of 50

33. 12% of 80 **34.** 75% of 42

Checkpoint Quiz 1 — Lessons 8-1 through 8-3

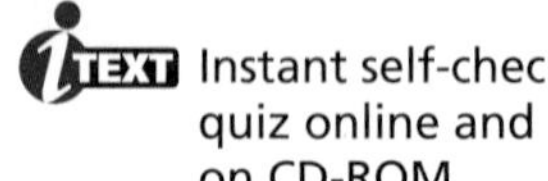

Instant self-check quiz online and on CD-ROM

Use the figure to name the following.

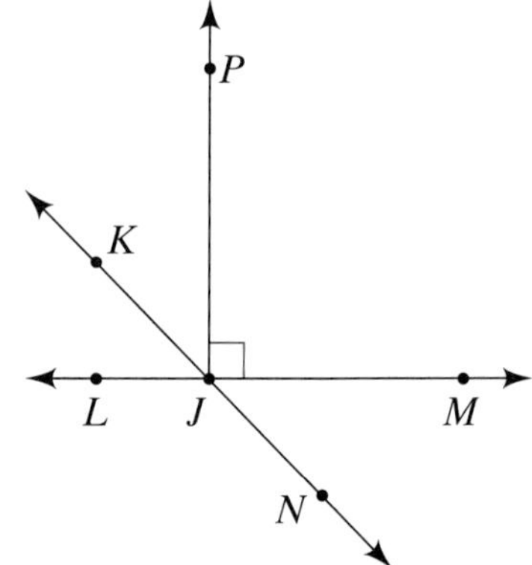

1. two lines **2.** two rays

3. a right angle **4.** an acute angle

5. an obtuse angle **6.** a straight angle

7. a pair of vertical angles

8. an angle congruent to ∠*MJN*

9. a pair of complementary angles

10. a pair of supplementary angles

Technology

Investigating Angles in a Triangle

For Use With Lesson 8-3

Geometry software is a fun way to investigate relationships among angles of a triangle. You can indicate "measure of angle A" with $m\angle A$.

Activity

Step 1 Draw a triangle. Label the vertices A, B, and C.

Step 2 Measure the three interior angles.

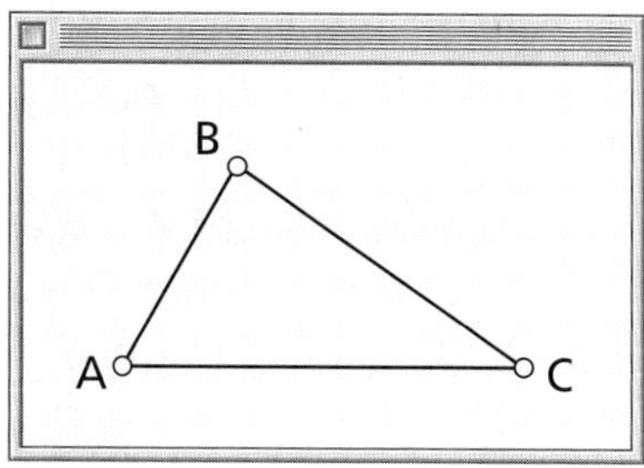

$m\angle BAC = 60.14°$

$m\angle ABC = 85.84°$

$m\angle BCA = 34.02°$

Step 3 Make a table to show the angles, their measures, and the sum of the measures.

Angle	Measurements
∠A	60.14°
∠B	85.84°
∠C	34.02°
	sum 180°

EXERCISES

1. Change the shape of the triangle by dragging A, B, or C. Make a new column in your table and find the sum of the angle measures. What happens to the sum of the angle measures?

2. What seems to be true about the sum of the measures of the interior angles of a triangle?

3. Extend one side of a triangle to make an *exterior angle of a triangle* as shown at the right.

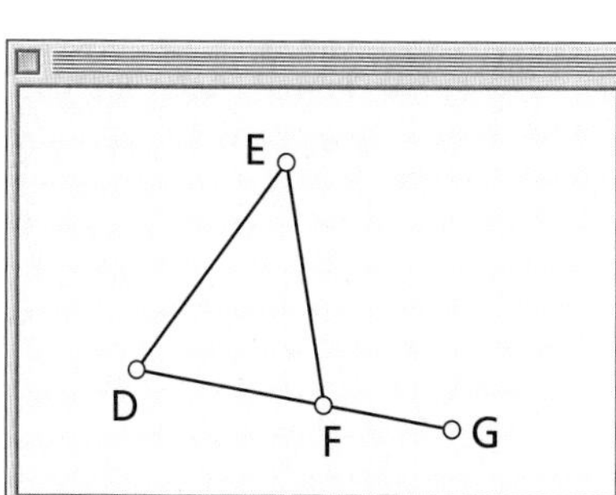

a. What is the measure of $\angle EFG$?

b. What is the sum of the measures of $\angle D$ and $\angle E$?

c. Change the shape of the triangle. Find the measure of $\angle EFG$ and the sum of the measures of $\angle D$ and $\angle E$ again.

d. What seems to be true of an exterior angle and the sum of the two angles of a triangle not adjacent to the exterior angle?

8-4 Classifying Triangles

What You'll Learn

To classify triangles by their angles

To classify triangles by their sides

. . . And Why

To identify triangles in game pieces, as in Example 4

✓ Check Skills You'll Need

For help, go to Lesson 8-2.

Classify each angle as *acute*, *right*, *obtuse*, or *straight*.

1. 45° **2.** 105° **3.** 60° **4.** 100°

5. 90° **6.** 1° **7.** 179° **8.** 180°

New Vocabulary

- acute triangle
- obtuse triangle
- right triangle
- congruent segments
- equilateral triangle
- isosceles triangle
- scalene triangle

OBJECTIVE

TEXT Interactive lesson includes instant self-check, tutorials, and activities.

1 Classifying Triangles by Angles

A *triangle* is a closed figure with three sides. The sides of every closed figure meet only at their endpoints. The sum of the measures of the angles of a triangle is 180°.

You can classify triangles by angle measures.

Classifying by Angles

acute triangle

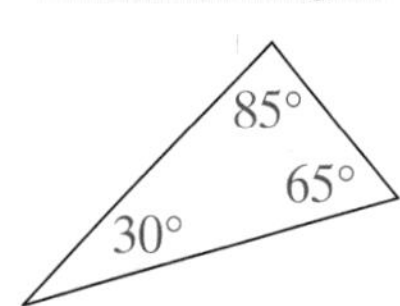

Three acute angles

obtuse triangle

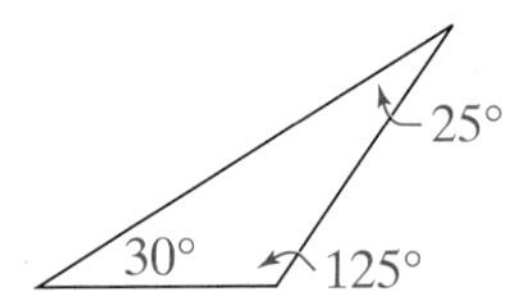

One obtuse angle

right triangle

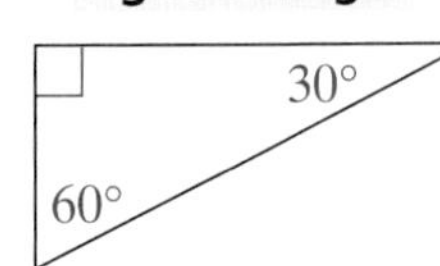

One right angle

1 EXAMPLE Classifying Triangles by Angles

Classify each triangle by its angles.

a.

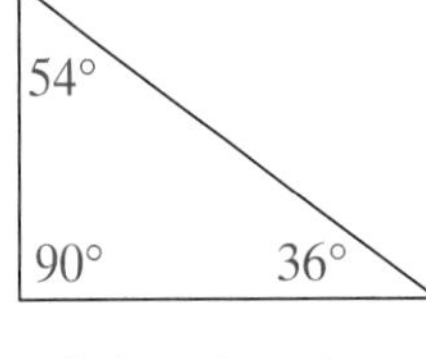

right triangle

b.

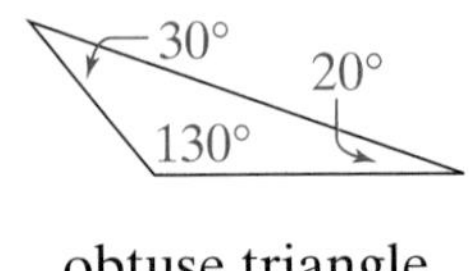

obtuse triangle

c.

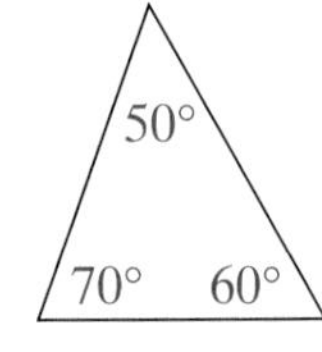

acute triangle

✓ **Check Understanding** 1 **a.** Classify the triangle at the right by its angles.

b. A triangle has three equal angles. Classify the triangle by its angles.

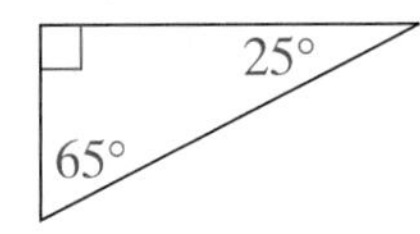

2 EXAMPLE Finding an Angle's Measure

Algebra Find the value of x in the triangle at the left.

$x + 20° + 90° = 180°$ ← **A right angle measures 90°.**

$x + 110° = 180°$ ← **Add 20° and 90°.**

$x + 110° - 110° = 180° - 110°$ ← **Subtract 110° from each side.**

$x = 70°$ ← **Simplify.**

Check Understanding 2 Two angles of a triangle measure 58° and 72°. What is the measure of the third angle?

OBJECTIVE

2 Classifying Triangles by Sides

Segments that have the same length are **congruent segments.** You can classify triangles by the number of congruent segments or sides. Tick marks are often used to indicate congruent sides of a figure.

Real-World Connection

This sign means "falling rocks."

Classifying by Sides

equilateral triangle	isosceles triangle	scalene triangle
	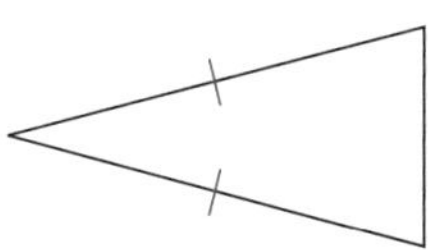	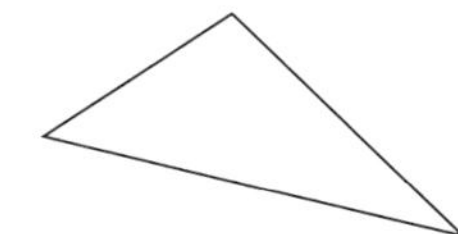
Three congruent sides	At least two congruent sides	No congruent sides

You can sometimes classify a triangle in more than one way. For example, every equilateral triangle is also an isosceles triangle. When classifying triangles, use the most precise name.

3 EXAMPLE Classifying Triangles by Sides

Classify each triangle by its sides.

a. 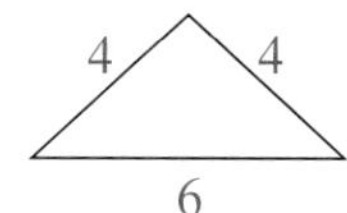

isosceles triangle

b. 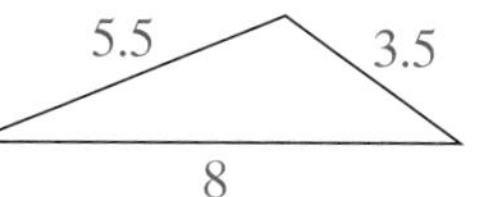

scalene triangle

c. 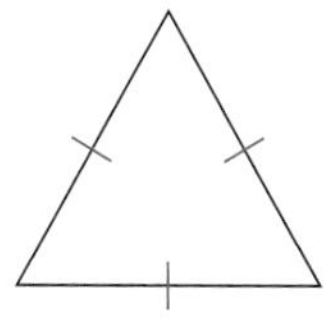

equilateral triangle

Check Understanding 3 **a.** Classify the triangle at the right by its sides.

b. The sides of a triangle have lengths 5, 10, and 12 units. Classify it by its sides.

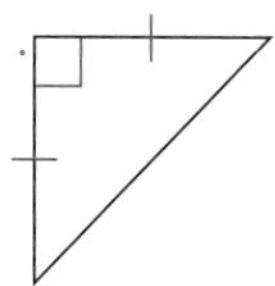

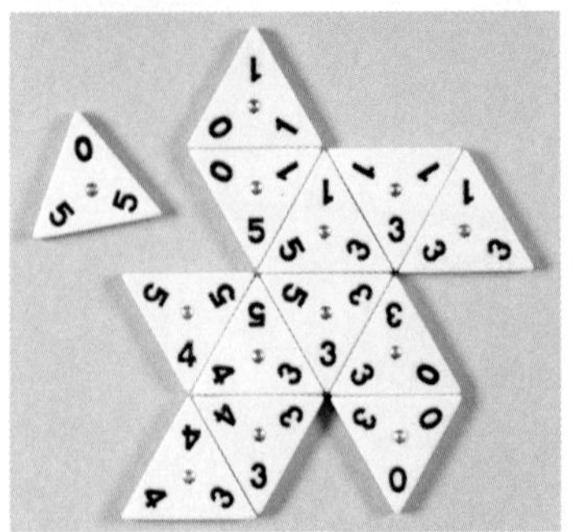

Real-World Connection

Triominoes is a game played by matching numbers.

A triangle can be classified by both its angle measures and by the number of congruent sides it has.

4 EXAMPLE Real-World Problem Solving

Games Name the triangle formed by each triomino by its angles and its sides.

The triangle has three acute angles. It is acute.

The triangle has three congruent sides. It is equilateral.

Check Understanding 4 Name the triangle shown at the right by its angles and its sides.

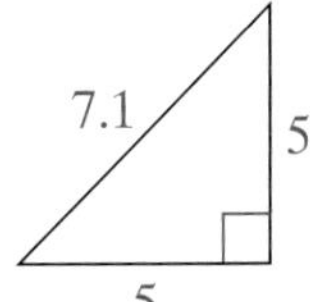

EXERCISES

For more practice, see *Extra Practice.*

A Practice by Example

Example 1 (page 392)

Classify each triangle by its angles.

1. 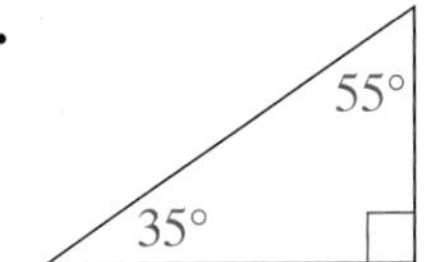

2. 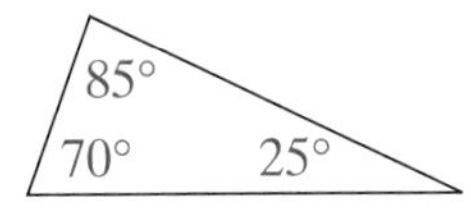

3. 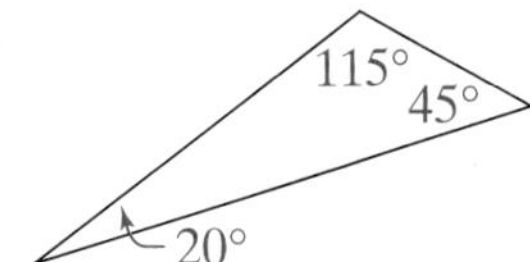

Example 2 (page 393)

Algebra Find the value of x.

4. 15°, 60°, x

5. 14°, x, 76°

6. x, 60°, 61°

7.

8. 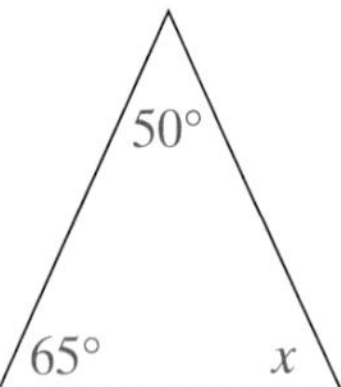

9. 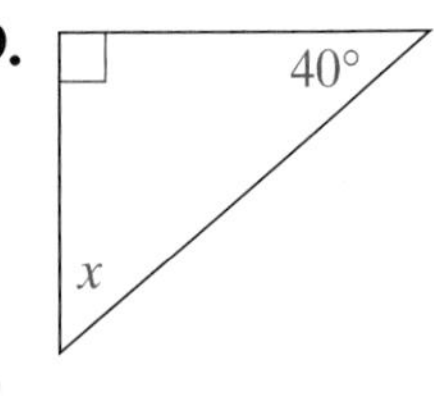

Example 3 (page 393)

Classify each triangle by its sides.

10. 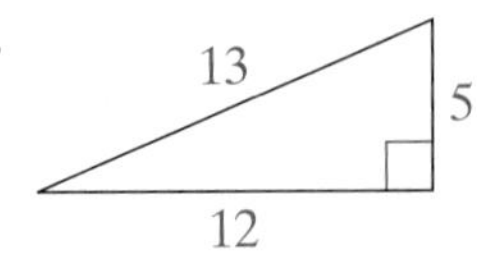

11. 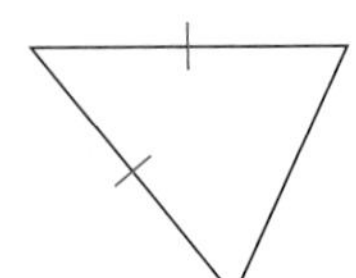

12. 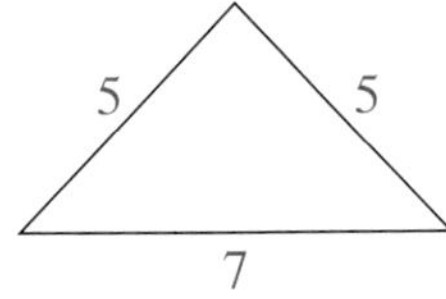

13. triangle with sides 3, 3, 5

14. triangle with sides 6, 9, 4

15. triangle with sides 11, 11, 11

Example 4 (page 394)

Name each triangle by its angles and its sides.

16. 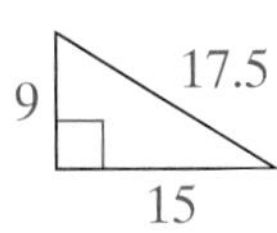

17. 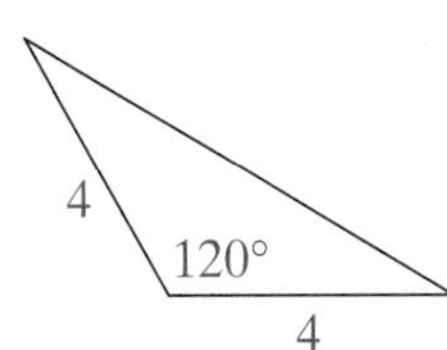

18. 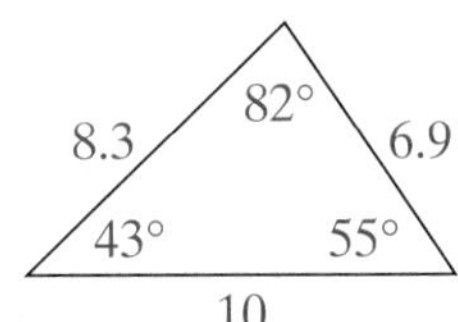

B Apply Your Skills

19. a. Drafting Find the side lengths and angle measures of each drafting triangle at the right.

b. Classify each triangle according to its angle measures.

c. Classify each triangle according to its sides.

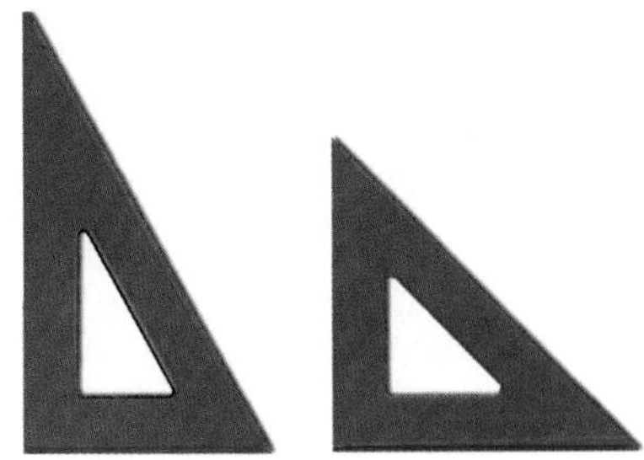

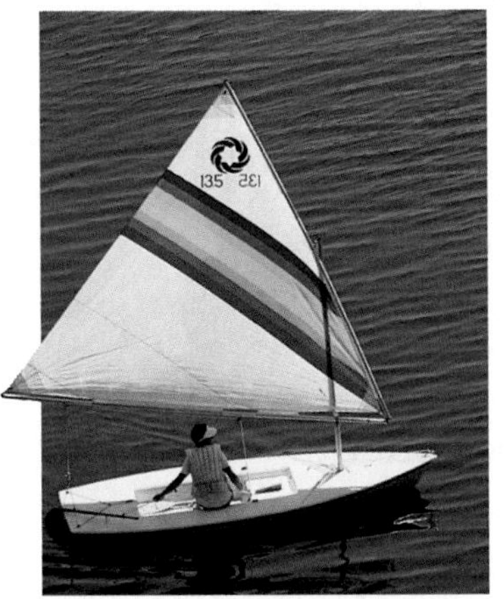

Real-World Connection

Triangular sails are used on sport sailing craft because they are easy to operate.

20. Sailing A triangular sail allows a boat to sail in any direction, even into the wind. Judging by appearance, give all names possible for the triangle in the photo.

21. Writing in Math Explain why you need to know the measures of all three angles of a triangle before you can name it by its angles.

Measure the angles and sides of each triangle. Then name each triangle by its angles and its sides.

22. 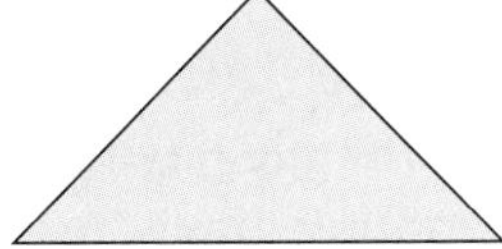

23. 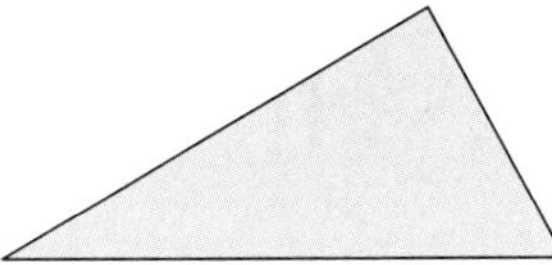

24. 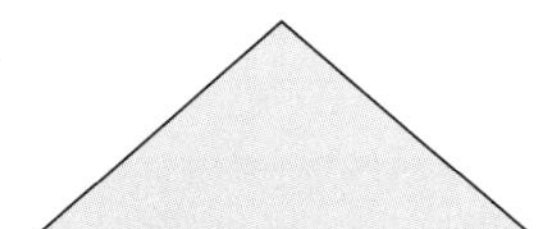

25. 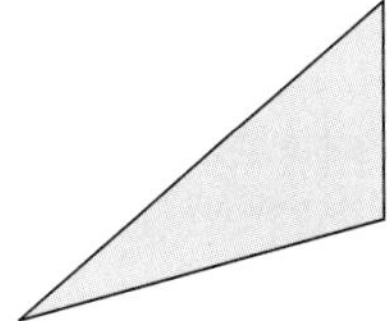

Sketch each triangle.

26. an acute isosceles triangle

27. an obtuse scalene triangle

28. an acute scalene triangle

29. a right scalene triangle

30. Reasoning Every equilateral triangle is also *equiangular*. That is, each of its angles has the same measure. Use the sum of the measures of the angles of a triangle to find the measure of each angle of an equilateral triangle.

31. **Reasoning** Cut out three narrow strips of paper measuring 2, 3, and 6 inches long. Is it possible to construct a triangle with these sides? If not, why not?

32. **Stretch Your Thinking** Nathan is weighing blocks and balls. Each of the blocks weighs the same and each of the balls weighs the same. The weight of 4 blocks and 1 ball is the same as the weight of 2 blocks and 2 balls. Which is heavier, a block or a ball? How much heavier?

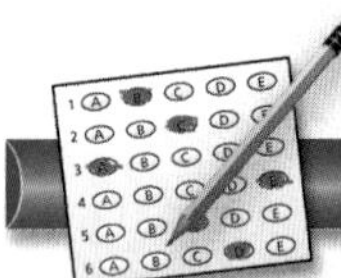

Test Prep

Multiple Choice

Choose the best description for triangles with the following angle measures and side lengths.

33. angle measures: 45°, 45°, 90°; side lengths: 4 cm, 4 cm, and 5.7 cm
    - A. right isosceles
    - B. acute isosceles
    - C. right scalene
    - D. acute scalene

34. angle measures: 60°, 60°, 60°; side lengths: 6 in., 6 in., 6 in.
    - F. acute isosceles
    - G. obtuse isosceles
    - H. acute equilateral
    - I. obtuse equilateral

Take It to the NET
Online lesson quiz at www.PHSchool.com
Web Code: aaa-0804

35. angle measures: 120°, 30°, 30°; side lengths: 8 m, 6 m, 6 m
    - A. acute isosceles
    - B. obtuse isosceles
    - C. acute scalene
    - D. obtuse scalene

Extended Response

36. Sketch an answer to each question. If not possible, explain.
    - a. Can an isosceles triangle have three sides of equal length?
    - b. Can an obtuse triangle have three sides of equal length?

Mixed Review

Lesson 7-5

37. The graph shows the results of a survey. Two hundred people were asked to choose their favorite dessert.
    - a. How many people prefer pie?
    - b. How many prefer ice cream?
    - c. How many more people preferred ice cream than cake?

Favorite Dessert

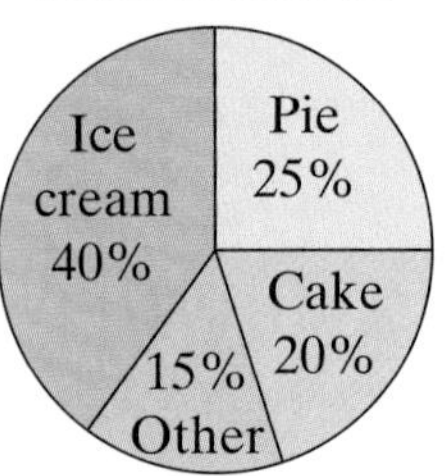

Lesson 6-5

A map has a scale of 1 in. : 12 mi. How many miles equal each of these lengths on the map?

38. 3 in. 39. 5.5 in. 40. 0.5 in. 41. $1\frac{1}{4}$ in.

8-5 Exploring and Classifying Polygons

What You'll Learn

 To identify polygons

 To classify quadrilaterals

. . . And Why

To identify polygons in sports, as in Example 2

Check Skills You'll Need

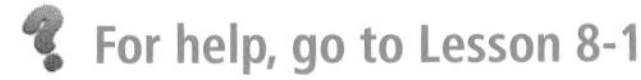
For help, go to Lesson 8-1.

Name each of the following.

1. two segments parallel to $\overline{AB}$
2. two segments skew to $\overline{DE}$
3. two segments intersecting $\overline{BG}$

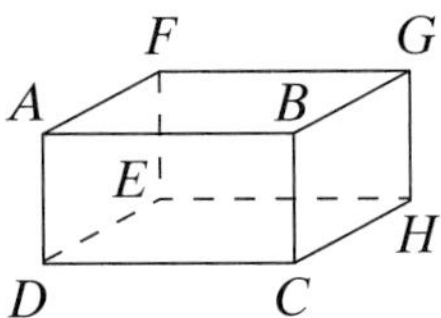

New Vocabulary • polygon • quadrilateral • trapezoid • parallelogram • rectangle • rhombus • square

OBJECTIVE

1 Identifying Polygons

A **polygon** is a closed figure that has three or more line segments that do not cross. See the examples below.

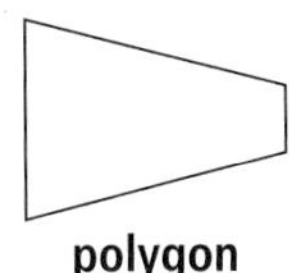
polygon

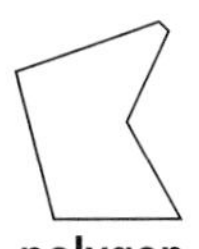
polygon

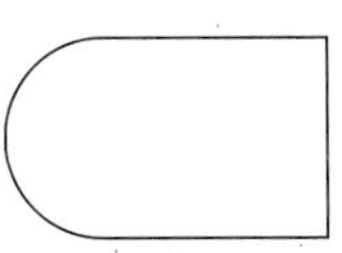
not a polygon

not a polygon

Polygon	Number of Sides
Triangle	3
Quadrilateral	4
Pentagon	5
Hexagon	6
Octagon	8
Decagon	10

To name a polygon, just count the number of sides.

1 EXAMPLE Identifying Polygons

Identify each polygon according to the number of sides.

a.

pentagon

b.

octagon

c.

quadrilateral

 Name each polygon according to the number of sides.

a.

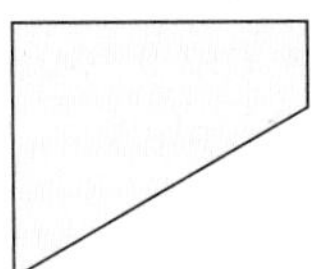

b.

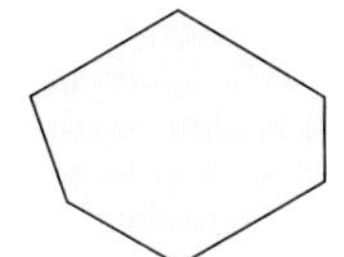

c.

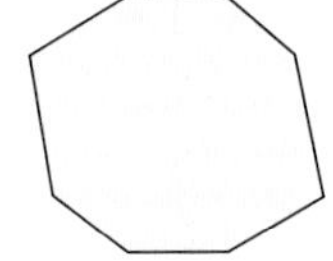

OBJECTIVE

2 Classifying Quadrilaterals

Any polygon with four sides is called a **quadrilateral.** Some have special names depending on whether they have *one* or *two* pairs of parallel lines.

Reading Math
Arrows on a drawing indicate parallel sides.

A **trapezoid** has exactly one pair of parallel lines.

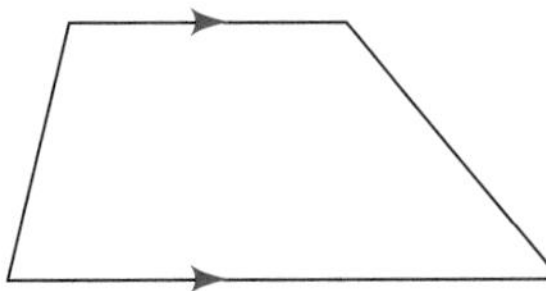

A **parallelogram** has two pairs of parallel lines.

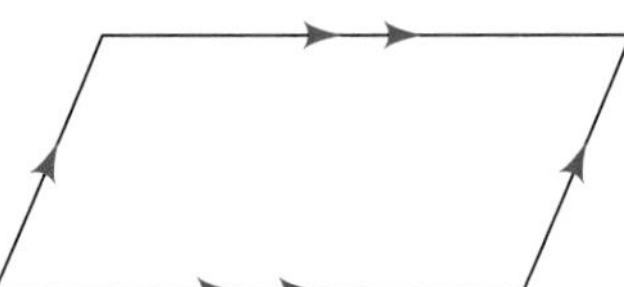

There are three special types of parallelograms.

A **rectangle** has four right angles.

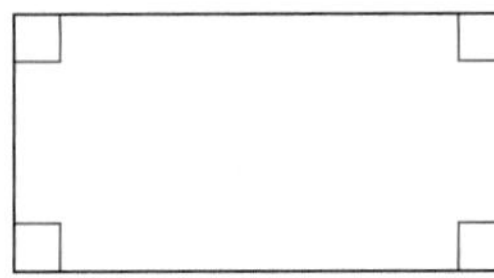

A **rhombus** has four congruent sides.

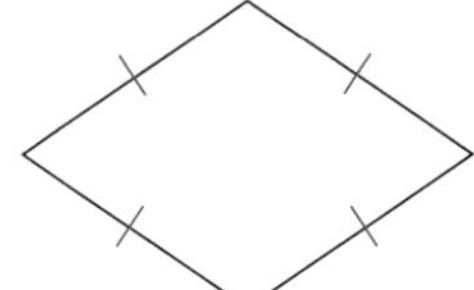

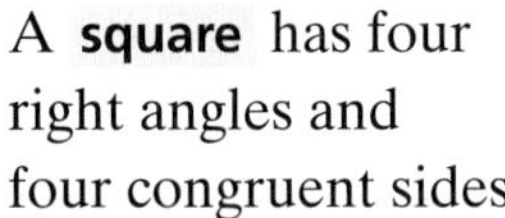

A **square** has four right angles and four congruent sides.

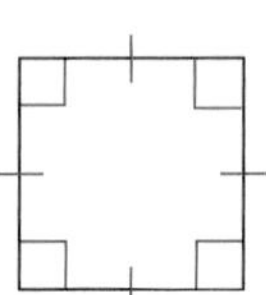

2 EXAMPLE Real-World Problem Solving

Baseball A baseball diamond is a quadrilateral. Write all of its possible names. Which is the best name? Explain.

Both pairs of opposite sides are parallel. It is a parallelogram.

The four angles are right angles. It is a rectangle.

The four sides are congruent. It is a rhombus.

This quadrilateral is best described as a square, because a square has four right angles and four congruent sides.

✓ Check Understanding 2

a. Write all the possible names for the quadrilateral at the right.
b. Which is the best name? Explain.
c. **Reasoning** Draw a rhombus and a square. Is every square a rhombus? Explain.

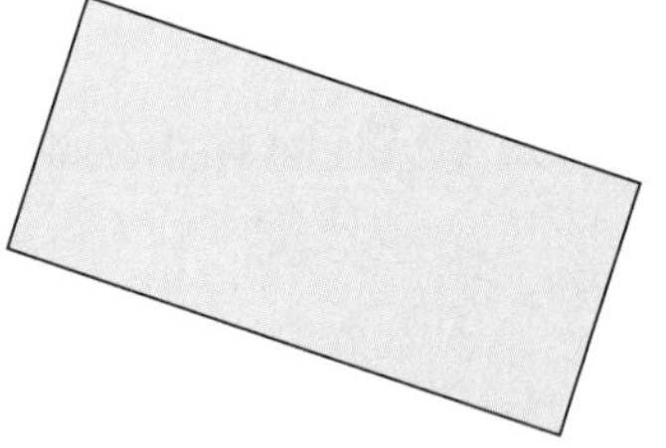

EXERCISES

For more practice, see *Extra Practice.*

A Practice by Example

Example 1 (page 397)

Identify each polygon according to the number of sides.

1. 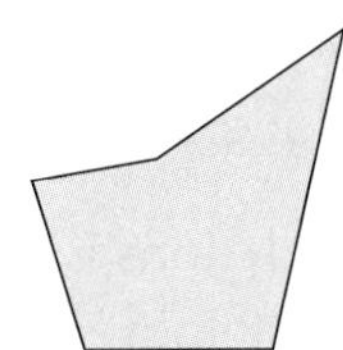

2. 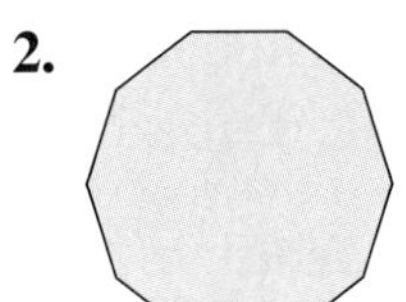

3. 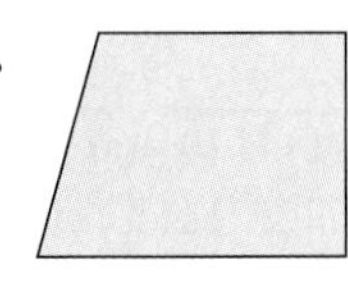

Example 2 (page 398)

Write all the possible names for each quadrilateral. Then give the best name.

4. 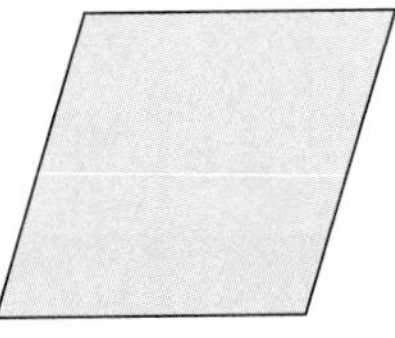

5. 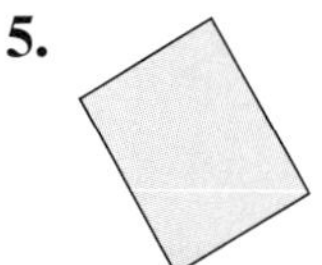

6. 

B Apply Your Skills

Use graph paper to draw an example of each quadrilateral.

7. a parallelogram
8. a rectangle
9. a rhombus
10. a trapezoid
11. a quadrilateral with only one right angle

Real-World Connection

Scientists use the Raft of Treetops in rain forests.

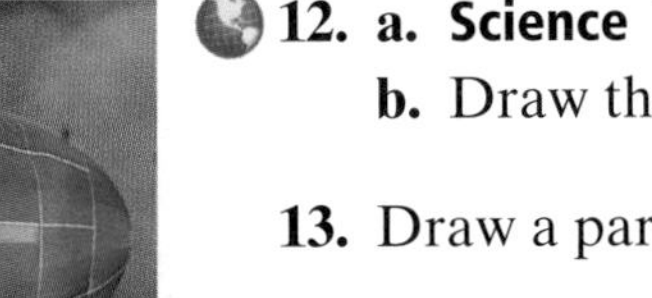

12. **a. Science** What shape is the Raft of Treetops platform at the left?
    b. Draw the polygon. Divide it into a quadrilateral and two triangles.

13. Draw a parallelogram that has a 30° angle.

Complete each sentence with *all, some,* or *no.*

14. _?_ quadrilaterals are squares.
15. _?_ trapezoids are parallelograms.
16. _?_ rhombuses are quadrilaterals.
17. _?_ squares are rectangles.

18. **Writing in Math** Describe the difference between a figure that is *not* a polygon and one that is a polygon.

C Challenge

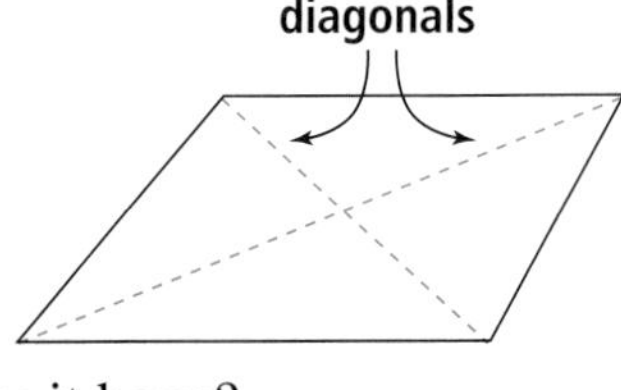

19. **Patterns** A *diagonal* of a polygon is a segment that connects two vertices that are not next to each other. As shown at the right, a quadrilateral has two diagonals.
    a. Draw a pentagon. How many diagonals does it have?
    b. Draw a hexagon. How many diagonals does it have?
    c. Without drawing, predict the number of diagonals in an octagon.

20. **Stretch Your Thinking** Use the figure at the left. Which six sides of the small squares can you remove to leave only two squares?

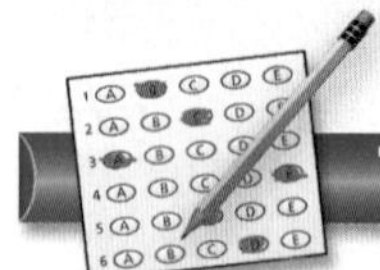

Test Prep

Multiple Choice

21. Which name does NOT appear to describe quadrilateral *RSTU?*

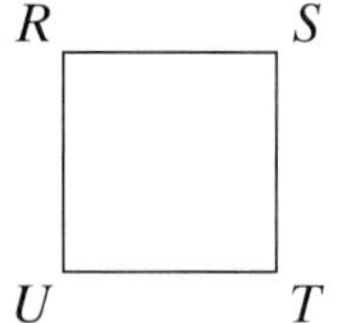

A. square **B.** rhombus
C. trapezoid **D.** parallelogram

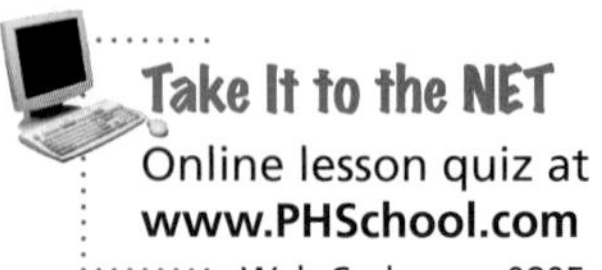

Take It to the NET
Online lesson quiz at **www.PHSchool.com**
Web Code: aaa-0805

22. Which of the following polygons is NOT a quadrilateral?
F. trapezoid **G.** parallelogram **H.** rhombus **I.** pentagon

Short Response

23. Draw each of the following figures. Give the best name for each.
a. a quadrilateral with exactly one pair of parallel sides
b. a quadrilateral with four congruent sides and no right angles

Mixed Review

Lesson 7-6

24. What value is in cell B2?

25. Which cell has the value 92?

26. Write a formula that will calculate the value in cell D3.

	A	B	C	D
1	Student	Test 1	Test 2	Mean
2	Antwon	90	70	■
3	Bianca	82	92	■

Lesson 6-6

What percent of each grid is shaded?

27.

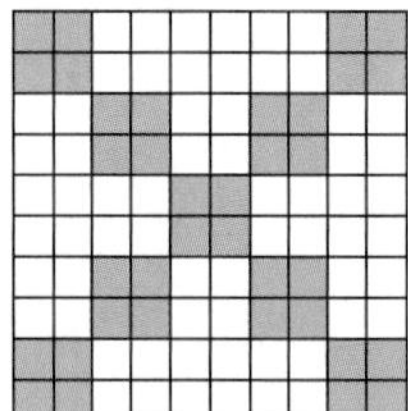

28.

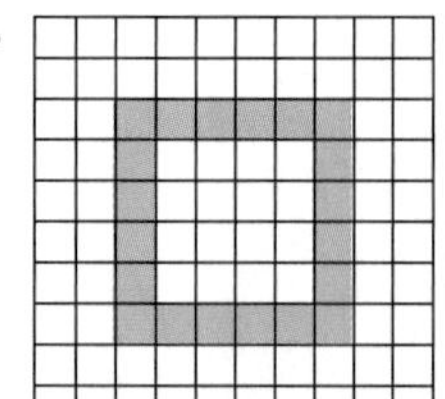

Math at Work

Cartoonist

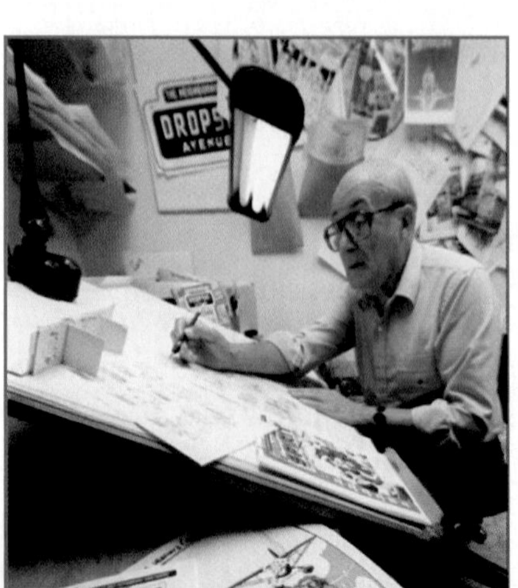

If you enjoy reading comics and draw well, a career as a cartoonist may be right for you. Some cartoonists produce comic strips meant for amusement. Others create illustrations for articles, books, or advertisements. Cartoonists use lines, angles, measures, and perspective to create cartoons.

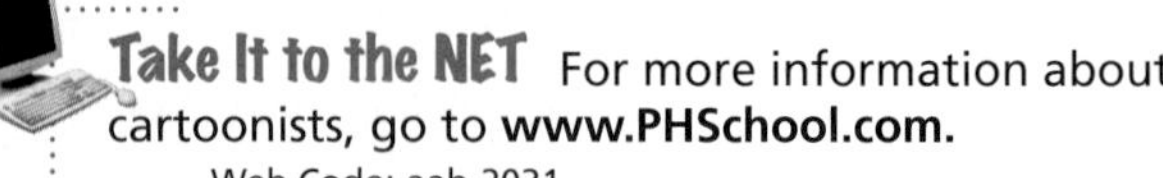

Take It to the NET For more information about cartoonists, go to **www.PHSchool.com.**
Web Code: aab-2031

8-6 Use Logical Reasoning

What You'll Learn

OBJECTIVE 1 To solve problems using logical reasoning

. . . And Why

To use reasoning to solve puzzles, as in Example 1

✓ Check Skills You'll Need

For help, go to Lesson 7-2.

Organize each set of data by making a frequency table.

1. goals in hockey games: 3, 2, 0, 0, 1, 2, 3, 3, 1, 1, 4, 2, 0
2. test scores: 75, 100, 80, 80, 82, 85, 90, 90, 100, 80, 85, 90
3. water temperatures (°F): 80, 80, 82, 82, 85, 87, 88, 89, 87, 88

OBJECTIVE

Interactive lesson includes instant self-check, tutorials, and activities.

1 Solving Problems Using Logical Reasoning

When to Use This Strategy You can ***use logical reasoning*** when you are given a series of clues or when you are playing a game.

1 EXAMPLE Real-World Problem Solving

	a	b	c
a	R	A	Y
b	A	R	E
c	Y	E	A

Puzzles The word square at the left shows three words read the same across and down. Use the clues below to complete the word square at the right.

a. Continues without end in opposite directions
b. Thought
c. Reports of recent events
d. Not difficult

	a	b	c	d
a				
b				
c				
d				

Read and Understand The goal is to complete a word square using the given clues.

Plan and Solve Copy the 4-by-4 grid. Fill in the words using the clues. The word "line" goes in row (a) and column (a). Complete the word square.

	a	b	c	d
a	L	I	N	E
b	I			
c	N			
d	E			

Look Back and Check Check that the words match the clues and that they all read the same across and down.

	a	b	c	d
a	L	I	N	E
b	I	D	E	A
c	N	E	W	S
d	E	A	S	Y

✓ Check Understanding 1 Use these clues to complete a 4-by-4 word square.

a. This and _?_ **b.** Prefix meaning "six"
c. Plural of "axis" **d.** Chore

2 EXAMPLE Real-World Problem Solving

Hobbies Anna, Bob, and Carlos each collect one of the following: sports cards, stamps, and coins. Bob's cousin collects stamps. Carlos had lunch with the coin and the stamp collectors. Decide what each person collects.

Read and Understand The problem gives clues about the hobbies of Anna, Bob, and Carlos. The goal is to match each person with their hobby.

Plan and Solve Make a table. Use the clues and record your conclusions.

- Bob's cousin collects stamps. ⟶
- Carlos had lunch with the coin and stamp collectors. ⟶

	Cards	Stamps	Coins
Anna		Yes	
Bob		No	
Carlos	Yes	No	No

- Carlos must be the card collector. Anna must collect stamps.
- Complete the table. Bob must collect coins.

	Cards	Stamps	Coins
Anna	No	Yes	No
Bob	No	No	Yes
Carlos	Yes	No	No

Look Back and Check Reread the problem. Make sure your solution matches all the facts given.

Check Understanding 2 Janna, Georgine, and Tanika were born in Jamaica, Peru, and France. Janna has never been to France. Tanika plays softball with the girl from Jamaica, but not with the one who came from France. Where was each girl born?

EXERCISES

For more practice, see *Extra Practice*.

A Practice by Example

Example 1 (page 401)

In each exercise, use the clues to complete a 4-by-4 word square.

1. a. Results of adding
b. One of something
c. 5,280 feet
d. __?__-and-leaf plot

2. a. Unit of mass
b. Uncommon
c. Measurement in square units
d. Average

Example 2 (page 402)

Solve each problem using logical reasoning.

3. Amy, Bill, and Chuck each have one bicycle. One bicycle is blue, one is green, and the other is red. Amy's brother rides a red bike. Chuck's bike is neither red nor green. Which bicycle does each person own?

Need Help?

- Reread the problem.
- Identify the key facts and details.
- Tell the problem in your own words.
- Try a different strategy.
- Check your work.

4. Jane, Aldo, and Michelle play guitar, keyboards, and drums. Jane is the friend of the guitar player. Aldo lives next door to the drummer and works with the guitar player. Match each person with his or her instrument.

5. **Track and Field** In a race at the track meet, Sue outran Keisha. Debbie beat Alma but lost to Keisha. Who finished first?

6. **Occupations** Jake, Amelia, Camille, and Lamar each have an occupation represented by one of the objects below. Jake and Lamar did not go to medical school. Camille and Lamar buy the artist's paintings and listen to the musician's performances. Amelia does not play an instrument. What is each person's occupation?

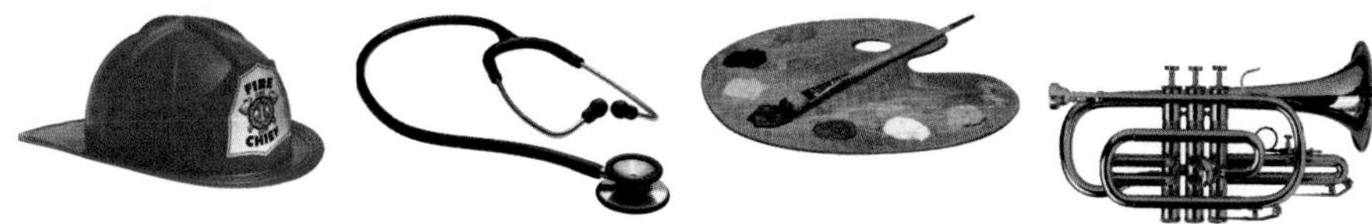

B Apply Your Skills

Use any standard strategy to solve each problem. Show your work.

Strategies

- Draw a Diagram
- Make a Graph
- Make an Organized List
- Make a Table and Look for a Pattern
- Simulate a Problem
- Solve a Simpler Problem
- Try, Check, and Revise
- Use Logical Reasoning
- Work Backward
- Write an Equation

7. **Collections** Your friend decides to sort his collection of baseball cards. When he tries to put the cards in equal piles of two, he has one card left over. He also has one left over when he sorts the cards in piles of three or piles of four. But when he puts them in piles of seven, he has none left over. What is the least possible number of cards in your friend's collection?

8. **Survey** You ask 130 high school students how they earn money. Forty-five students babysit, 32 bag groceries, 28 do yard work, and 12 have after school office jobs. Each student who works does only one kind of job, except for 15 who babysit and also do yard work.
   a. How many students babysit, do yard work, or do both?
   b. How many students do not have a job?

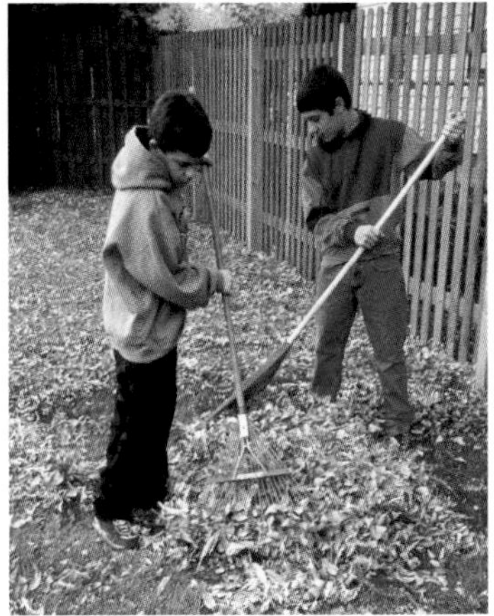

9. **Writing in Math** Find the missing numbers and describe the pattern.

   65, 63, 66, 62, 67, 61, ■, ■, 69, 59 . . .

10. **Sports** There are 20 students on the intramural tennis team. Eight students play only singles, and eight students play both singles and doubles. How many students play only doubles?

11. a. **Geometry** Draw a quadrilateral. Draw a segment to divide the quadrilateral into two triangles. Use your diagram to find the sum of the measures of the angles of a quadrilateral.
   b. Draw a pentagon and a hexagon. Draw segments to divide each figure into the least possible number of triangles. Use your diagram to find the sum of the measures of the angles of a pentagon and a hexagon.
   c. Use your answers in parts (a) and (b) to predict the sums of the measures of the angles of a seven-sided figure and an octagon.
   d. **Data File, p. 371** Are your results the same as those in the table?

Challenge

12. **Lemonade** To make lemonade, you need 3 cups of water for every 2 cups of lemon juice. You want to make 10 gallons of lemonade. How many cups of lemon juice do you need?

13. **Stretch Your Thinking** Marcus makes 3 flower arrangements in 4 hours. At this rate, how long will it take him to make 5 flower arrangements?

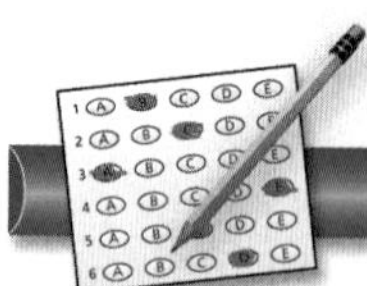

Test Prep

Multiple Choice

14. These are geomlets:

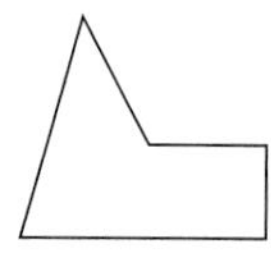 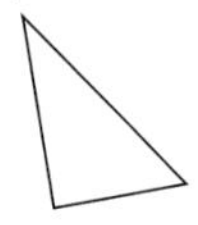 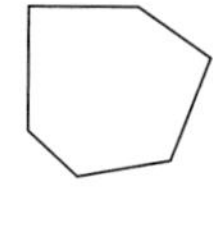

These are not geomlets:

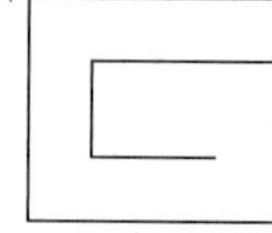 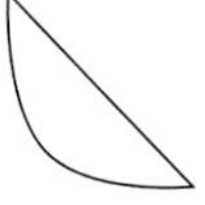 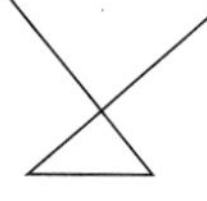

Which of these is a geomlet?

A. 
B. 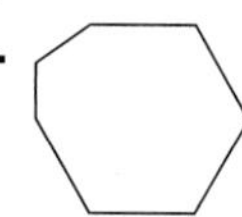
C. 
D. 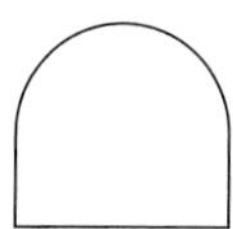

Take It to the NET
Online lesson quiz at
www.PHSchool.com
Web Code: aaa-0806

15. What day of the week is 263 days from Monday?
F. Monday G. Wednesday H. Friday I. Sunday

Short Response

16. The sum of two numbers is 4.2. Their product is 4.4. Find the numbers. Explain how you found your answer.

Mixed Review

Lesson 7-7

Make a stem-and-leaf plot of the data.

17. 33, 42, 16, 45, 14, 28, 37, 16, 23, 33, 25, 16

Lesson 5-8

Complete each statement.

18. 8,800 lb = ■ t ■ lb

19. 18 qt = ■ gal ■ qt

8-7 Congruent and Similar Figures

What You'll Learn

 To identify congruent figures

 To identify similar figures

. . . And Why

To identify similar figures in architecture, as in Example 3

Check Skills You'll Need

For help, go to Lesson 8-4.

Classify each triangle by its sides.

1. 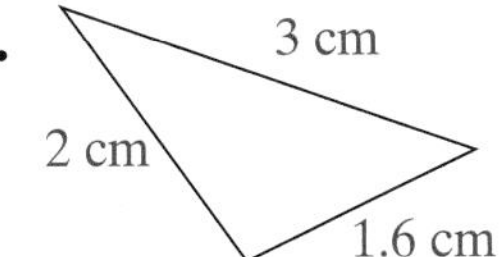

2. 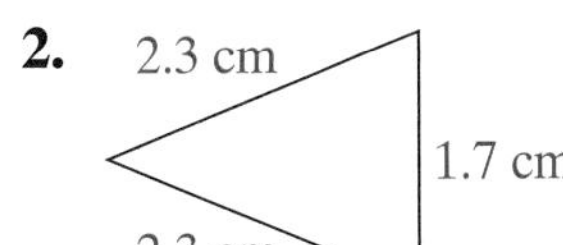

3. 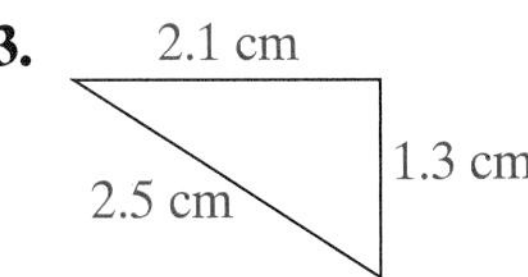

New Vocabulary
- congruent figures
- similar figures

OBJECTIVE 1 Identifying Congruent Figures

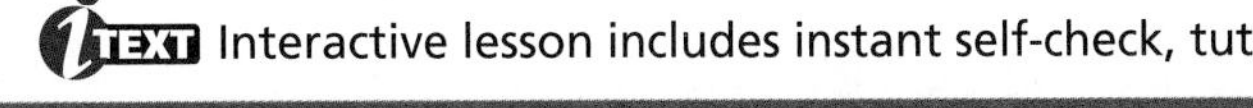

Congruent figures have the same size and shape. Congruent figures have congruent *corresponding sides* and congruent *corresponding angles*.

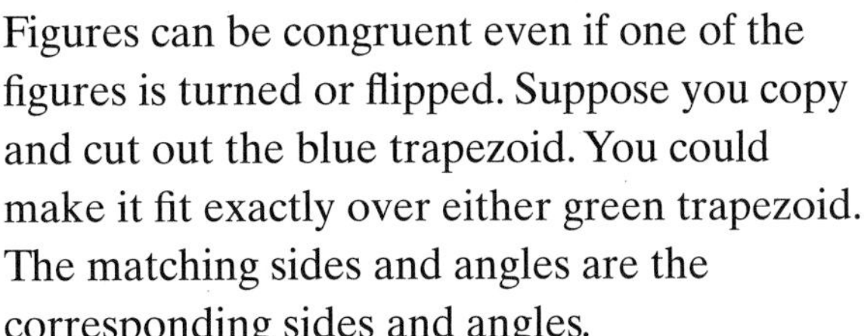

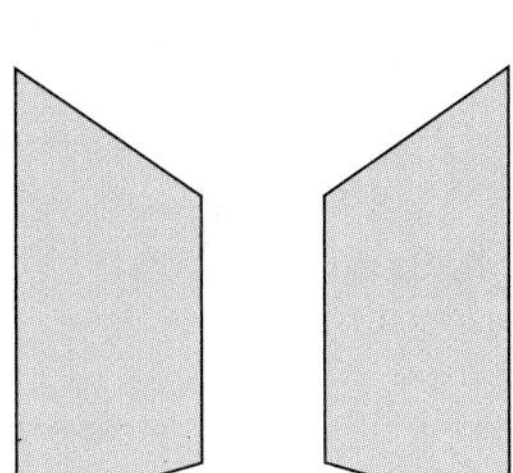

Figures can be congruent even if one of the figures is turned or flipped. Suppose you copy and cut out the blue trapezoid. You could make it fit exactly over either green trapezoid. The matching sides and angles are the corresponding sides and angles.

Real-World Connection

Notice the congruent triangles in this bridge in Pittsburgh, Pennsylvania.

1 EXAMPLE Identifying Congruent Figures

Tell whether each triangle is congruent to triangle PQR.

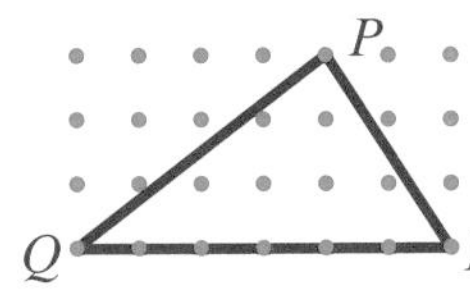

a. congruent

b. 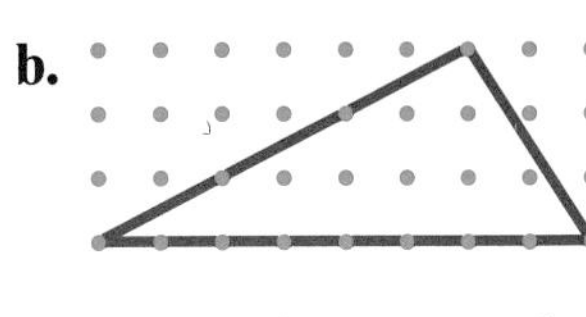

not congruent

Check Understanding

1 Are the two trapezoids congruent to the given trapezoid?

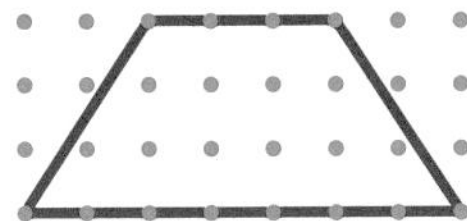

a. 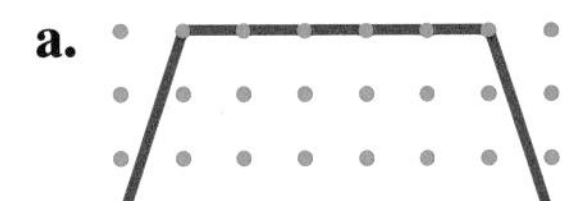

b. 

OBJECTIVE

2 Identifying Similar Figures

Investigation: Comparing Triangles

- Draw four identical triangles on dot paper and cut them out.
- Arrange the four cutout triangles to form a larger triangle that has the same shape as the original triangles. (None of the cutout triangles should overlap.)

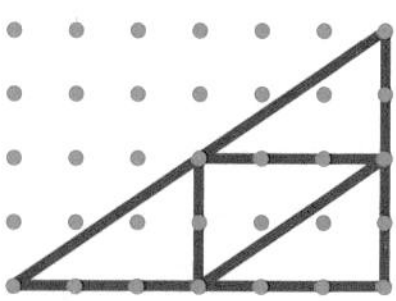

1. How do the lengths of the sides of one of the original triangles and the lengths of the sides of the larger triangle compare?
2. How do the angles of one of the original triangles compare with the angles of the larger triangle?

Similar figures have the same shape, but not necessarily the same size. Corresponding angles of similar figures are congruent. Corresponding sides of similar figures are proportional. Two right triangles are similar if the ratios of two pairs of corresponding sides are congruent.

2 EXAMPLE Identifying Similar Figures

Need Help?
For help with finding proportions, go to Lesson 6-2.

Which triangles appear to be similar to triangle DEF? Confirm your answer by finding whether the corresponding sides are proportional. Use ratios of the longer side to the shorter side.

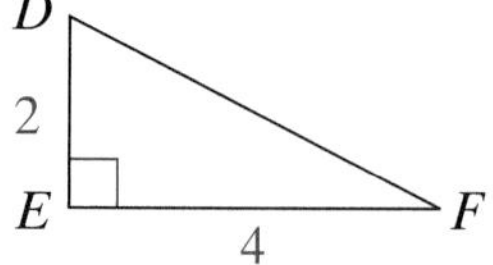

a. 1, 2

Appear similar

$\frac{2}{1} = \frac{4}{2}$

Similar

b.

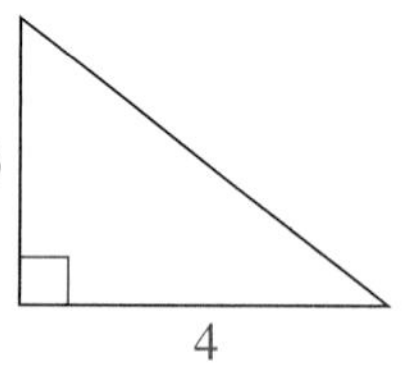

Do not appear similar

$\frac{4}{3} \neq \frac{4}{2}$

Not similar

c.

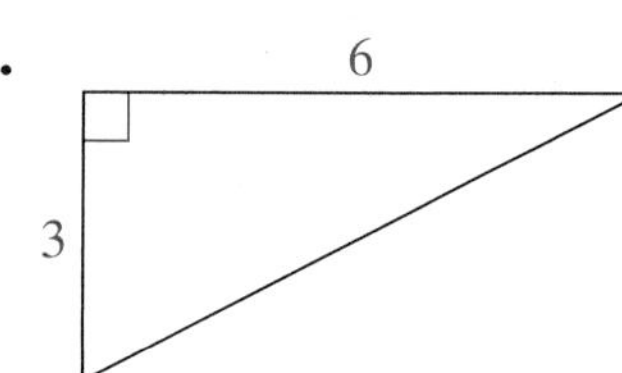

Appear similar

$\frac{6}{3} = \frac{4}{2}$

Similar

Check Understanding 2 Which triangle appears to be similar to triangle DEF in Example 2?

a.

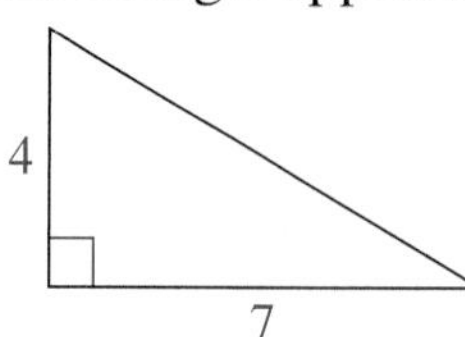

b.

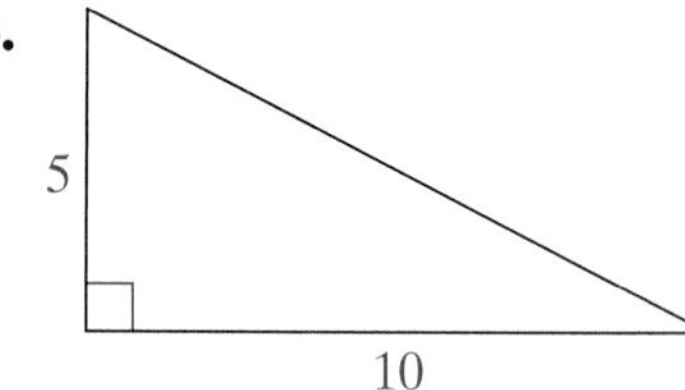

If the angles of two triangles are congruent, then the triangles are similar. The sides must also be congruent for the triangles to be congruent.

3 EXAMPLE **Real-World Problem Solving**

Architecture Are the triangles ABC and CDE congruent or similar? Explain.

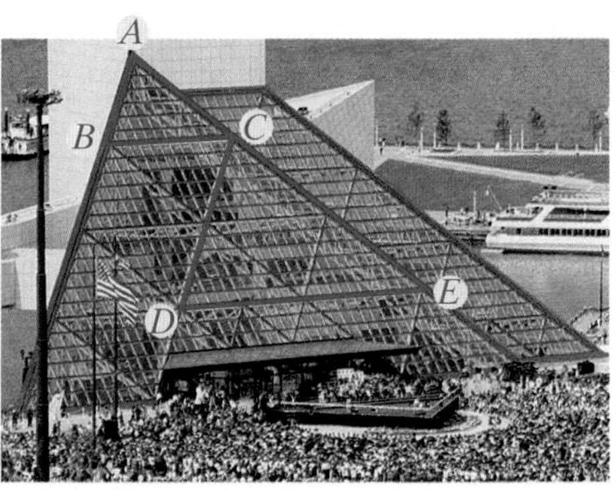

The Rock and Roll Hall of Fame in Cleveland, Ohio.

Triangles ABC and CDE are not congruent because their corresponding sides are not congruent.

Triangles ABC and CDE appear to be similar because their corresponding angles are congruent.

Check Understanding 3 Are the figures *congruent* or *similar*? Explain.

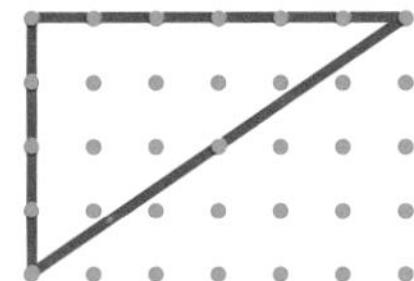

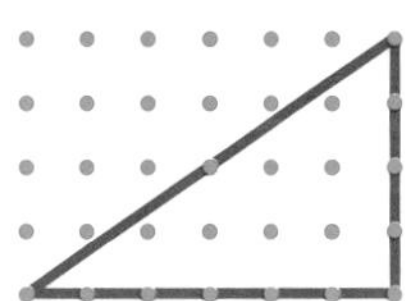

EXERCISES

A Practice by Example

Example 1 (page 405)

For each figure, tell whether it is congruent to trapezoid $ABDC$.

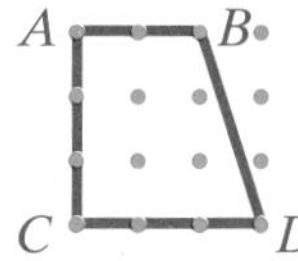

1. 

2.

3.

4.

5.

Example 2 (page 406)

Which rectangles appear to be similar to rectangle $MNOP$? Confirm your answer by finding whether corresponding sides are proportional.

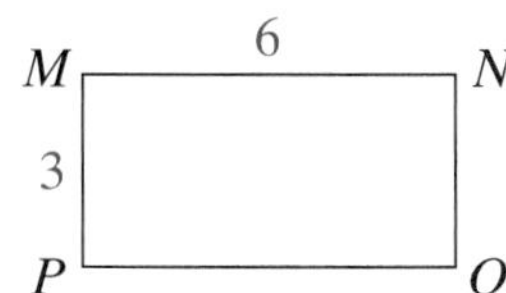

6. 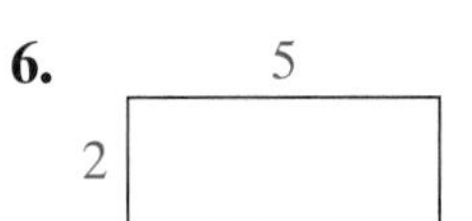

7. 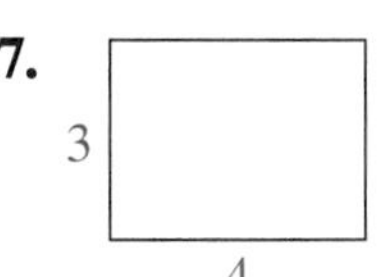

8. 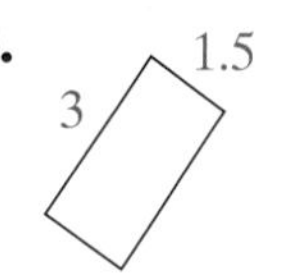

9. 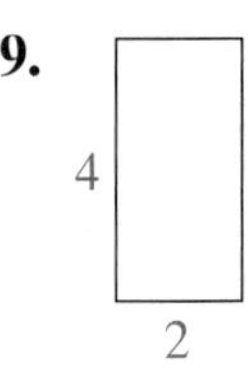

Example 3 (page 407)

Tell whether the triangles are *congruent* or *similar*.

10.  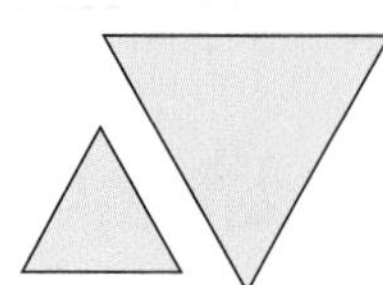

11. 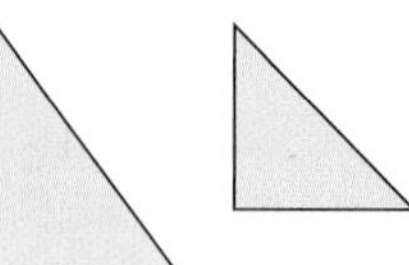

12. 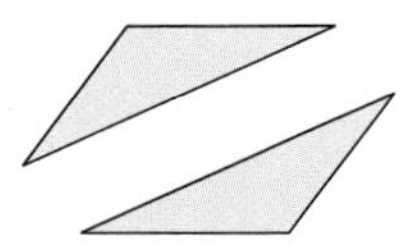

13. Home Repairs Suppose you are replacing a window. Should the replacement be congruent to or similar to the original? Explain.

B Apply Your Skills

Match the congruent triangles. Choose A., B., or C.

14. 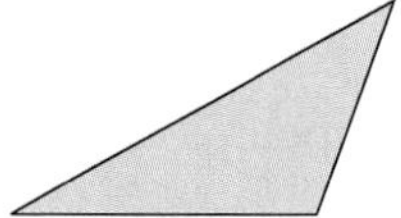

15. 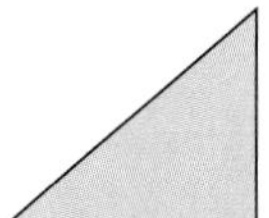

16. 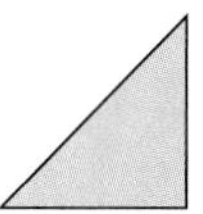

A. 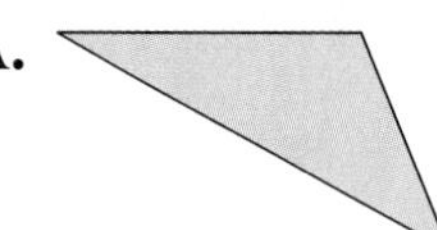

B. 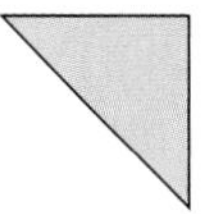

C. 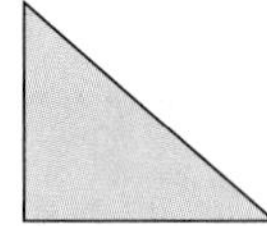

17. List the pairs of figures that are similar.

A. 2, 4

B. 2, 2

C. 3, 2, 2, 3

D. 1, 2, 2, 1

E. 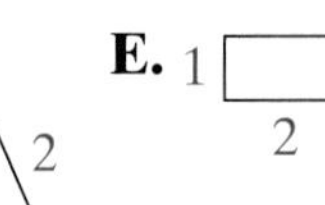

F. 2, 3

G. 3, 2

H. 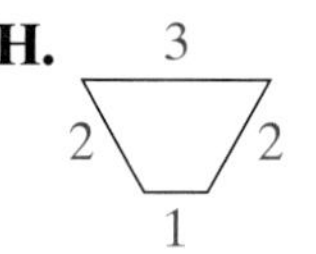

I. 3, 4

J. 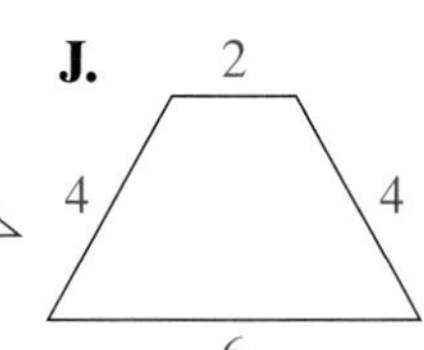

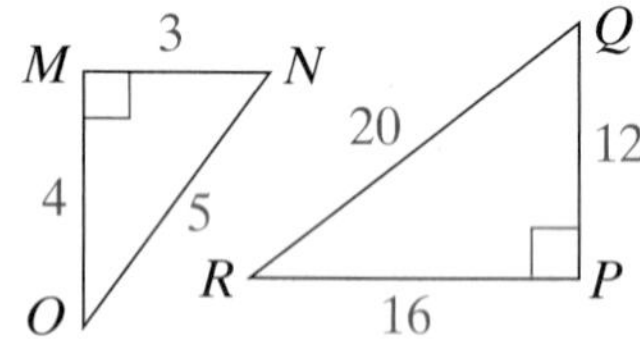

18. Triangles MNO and PQR are similar.

a. List the pairs of congruent angles.

b. Write the proportions for the proportional sides.

19. a. Draw five rhombuses that are not congruent.

b. Are all rhombuses similar? Explain.

20. Writing in Math Are congruent figures always similar figures? Explain.

Algebra **Each pair of figures is congruent. Find *x*.**

21. 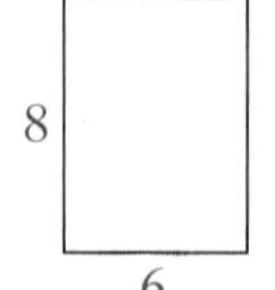

22. 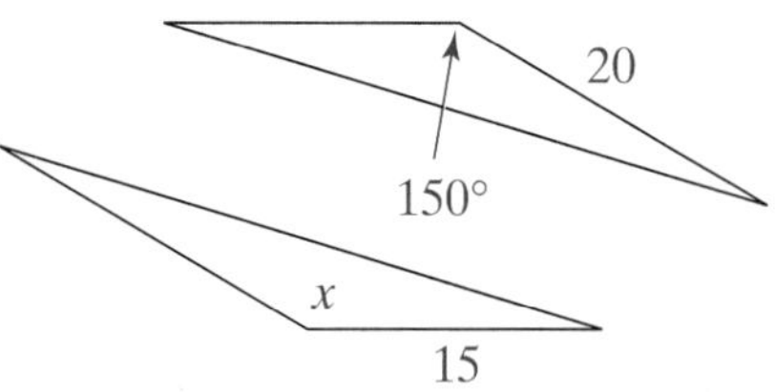

Challenge

23. **Patterns** How many congruent triangles are in the figure at the right? How many similar triangles?

24. **Stretch Your Thinking** One-sixth of a fraction is the same as one-half of one-fourth. What is the fraction?

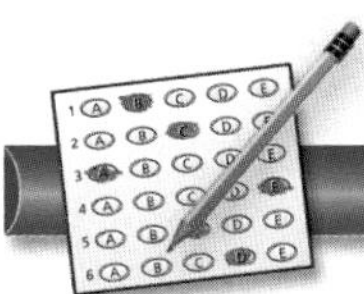

Test Prep

Multiple Choice

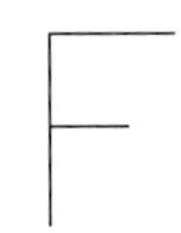

25. Which figure below is NOT congruent to the figure at the left?

A. 
B. 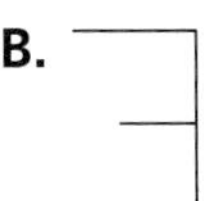
C. 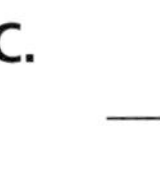
D. 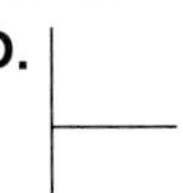

26. Which figure appears to be congruent to triangle *PQR*?

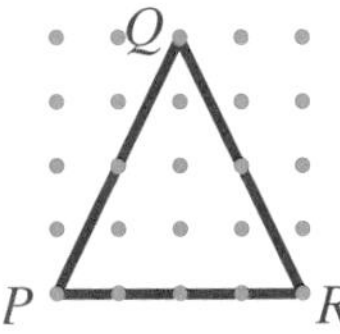

F.  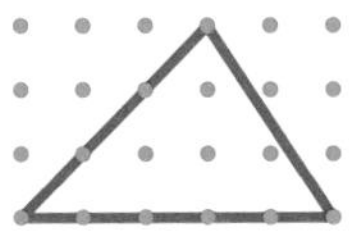
G. 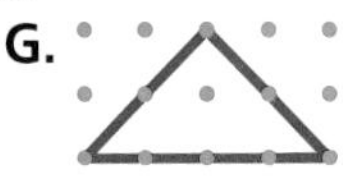
H. 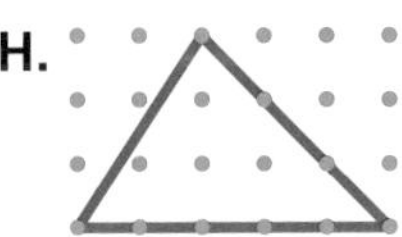
I. 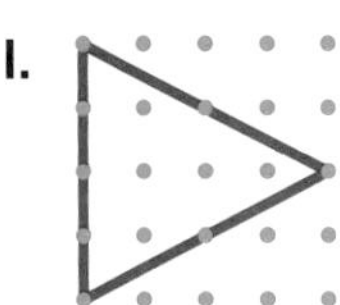

Take It to the NET
Online lesson quiz at
www.PHSchool.com
Web Code: aaa-0807

Short Response

27. Use the similar figures at the right. Find the lengths of $\overline{AB}$ and $\overline{BC}$. Explain how you found your answers.

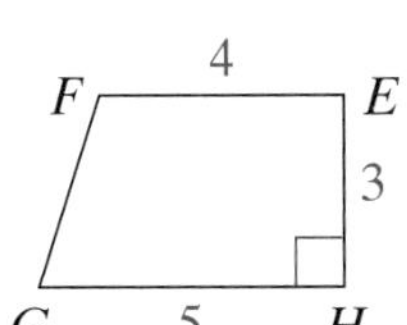

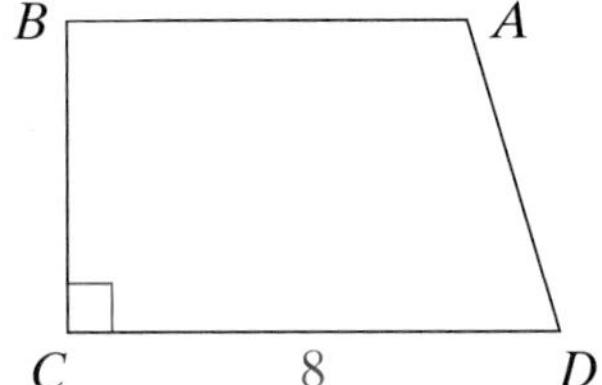

Mixed Review

Lesson 7-4

28. Make a line graph from the data in the table.

Net Profit per Week

Week	1	2	3	4	5
Store A	$1,500	$800	$700	$950	$1,000

Lesson 6-6

Write each fraction as a percent.

29. $\frac{90}{120}$
30. $\frac{2}{5}$
31. $\frac{4}{10}$
32. $\frac{55}{88}$
33. $\frac{7}{8}$
34. $\frac{15}{25}$
35. $\frac{1}{4}$
36. $\frac{7}{35}$

8-8 Line Symmetry

What You'll Learn

To find lines of symmetry

... And Why

To find a line of symmetry in nature, as in Example 2

Check Skills You'll Need

For help, go to Lesson 8-7.

Are the two figures congruent?

1. 

2. 

New Vocabulary • line symmetry • line of symmetry

OBJECTIVE

Interactive lesson includes instant self-check, tutorials, and activities.

1 Finding the Lines of Symmetry

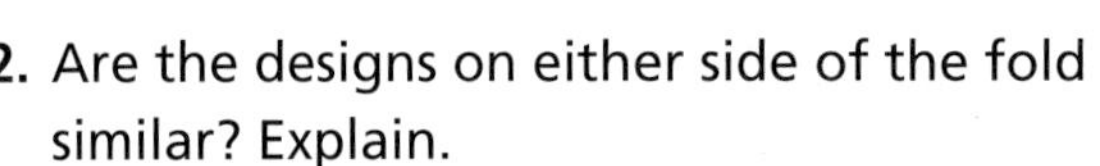

Investigation: Symmetry

1. Fold a sheet of paper in half. Draw a design on one side of the fold line. With the paper still folded, cut out your design. Do not cut along the fold. Unfold the paper.

2. Are the designs on either side of the fold similar? Explain.
3. Fold another sheet of paper in half twice such that the fold lines intersect each other at right angles. Cut out a design on the corner that includes the fold lines. Unfold the paper.

4. How many similar shapes did you form?

Real-World Connection The two butterfly wings are similar. Their shapes are symmetric.

You often see symmetry in nature like the butterfly at the left. You can also find symmetrical designs in fabrics, flags, architecture, and art. Symmetry is appealing to the eye.

A figure has **line symmetry** if a line can be drawn through the figure so that each half is a mirror image of the other. This line is a **line of symmetry.** If you fold a drawing on its line of symmetry, the two sides match.

1 EXAMPLE Testing for Line Symmetry

For each figure, is the dashed line a line of symmetry? Explain.

a.

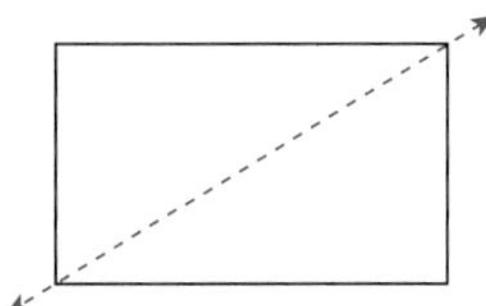

No, if you fold the figure along the line, the two parts do not match.

b.

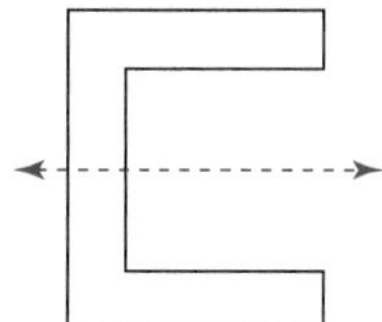

Yes, if you fold the figure along the line, the two parts match.

✓ Check Understanding 1 Is the red dashed line in the figure a line of symmetry? Explain.

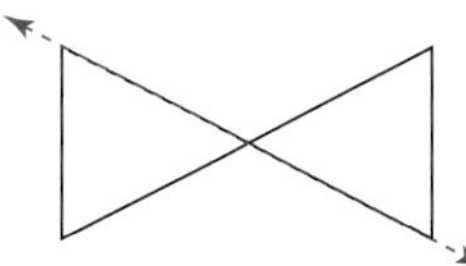

Some figures have more than one line of symmetry.

2 EXAMPLE Real-World Problem Solving

Nature How many lines of symmetry does each figure have? Draw them.

a.

The leaf has one line of symmetry.

b.

The snowflake has 12 lines of symmetry.

✓ Check Understanding 2 How many lines of symmetry does each figure have? Trace the figure and draw the lines of symmetry.

a.

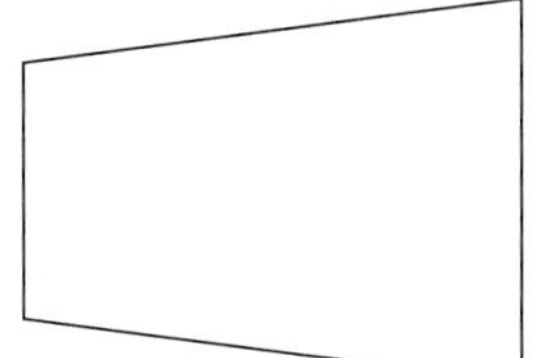

b.

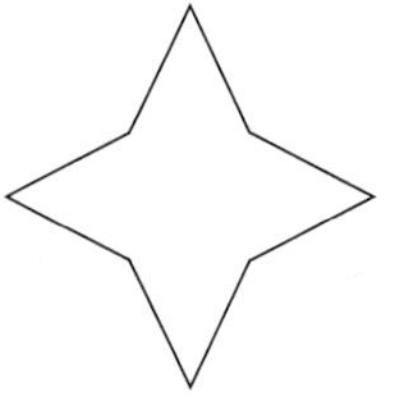

c. Reasoning How many lines of symmetry does a circle have? Explain your reasoning.

EXERCISES

 For more practice, see *Extra Practice*.

A Practice by Example

Example 1 (page 411)

Is the dashed line in each figure a line of symmetry? Explain.

1. 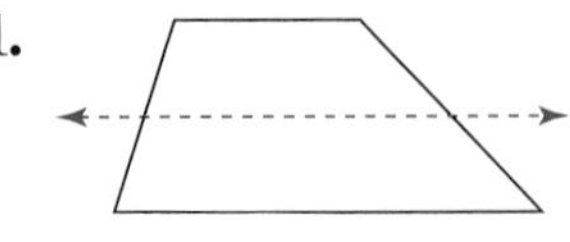

2. 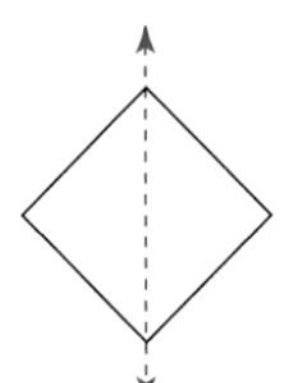

3. 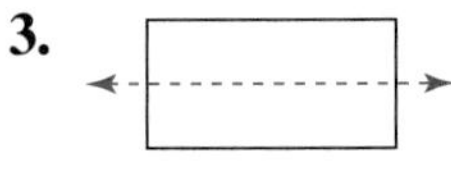

4. 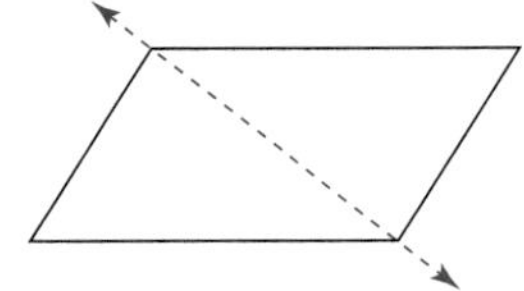

5. 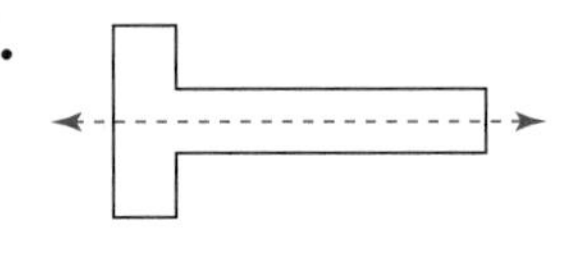

6. 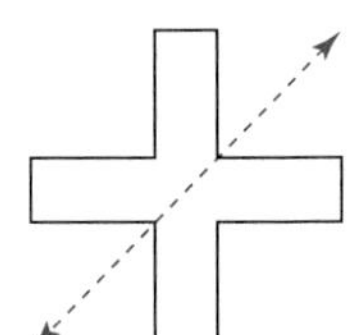

Example 2 (page 411)

How many lines of symmetry does each figure have? Trace the figure and draw the lines of symmetry.

7. 

8. 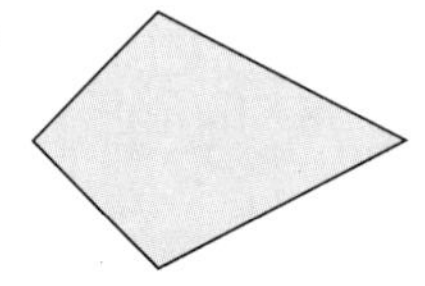

9. 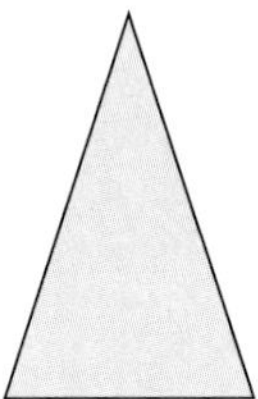

Tell whether each design has line symmetry.

10. 

11. 

12. 

B Apply Your Skills

13. Which capital letters have at least one line of symmetry?

A B C D E F G H J K L M

N O P Q R S T U V W X Y Z

14. Open-Ended The word CODE has a horizontal line of symmetry. Find another word that has a horizontal line of symmetry.

15. Open-Ended The word MOW has a vertical line of symmetry, when written vertically. Find another word that has a vertical line of symmetry when written vertically.

Nature Tell how many lines of symmetry each object has.

16. 

17. 

18. a. Trace the figure at the right and draw all lines of symmetry.
    b. **Data File, page 371** Find the value of x.

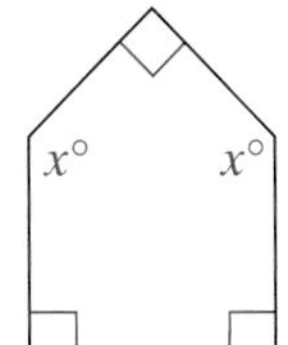

19. **Reasoning** How many lines of symmetry does a square have? Draw a diagram to support your answer.

20. a. Draw a scalene, an equilateral, and an isosceles triangle. Draw all lines of symmetry for each triangle.
    b. **Writing in Math** Describe the lines of symmetry of the three types of triangles.

21. a. **Flags** How many lines of symmetry are in each flag?

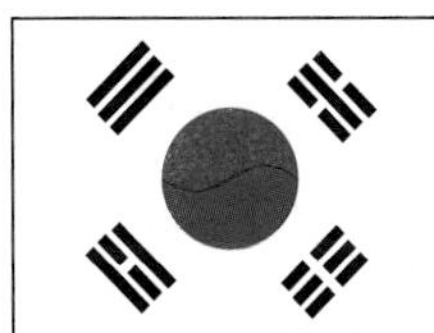

    b. **Open-Ended** Design a flag that has at least one line of symmetry.
    c. **Open-Ended** Design a flag that has no lines of symmetry.

C Challenge

Copy each figure on dot paper. Complete the figure so that the dashed line is a line of symmetry.

22. 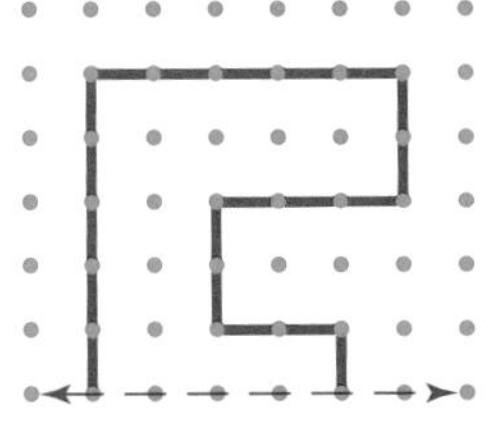

23. 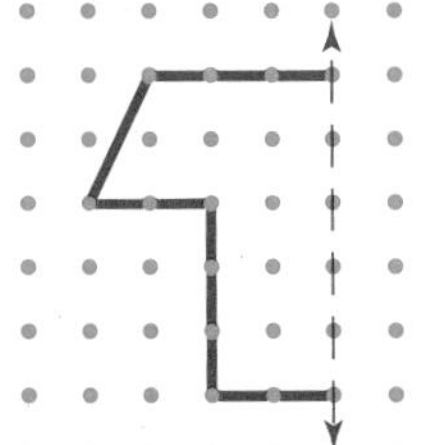

24. 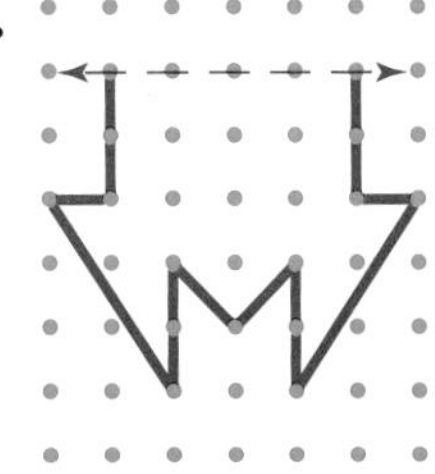

25. **Stretch Your Thinking** A quadrilateral has one obtuse angle, one acute angle, and two right angles. What kind of quadrilateral is it?

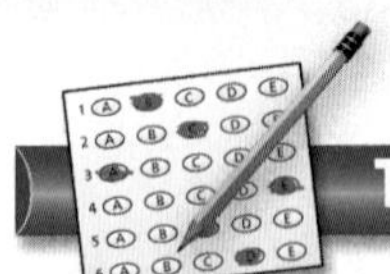

Test Prep

Gridded Response

26. How many lines of symmetry does a nonsquare rectangle have?

27. How many lines of symmetry does a rhombus have?

Take It to the NET
Online lesson quiz at
www.PHSchool.com
Web Code: aaa-0808

28. How many lines of symmetry does a trapezoid with two 60° angles have?

29. How many lines of symmetry does the word BOOK have?

Mixed Review

Lesson 8-1

Use the diagram to name each of the following.

30. a different name for $\overline{AB}$

31. three noncollinear points

32. three rays

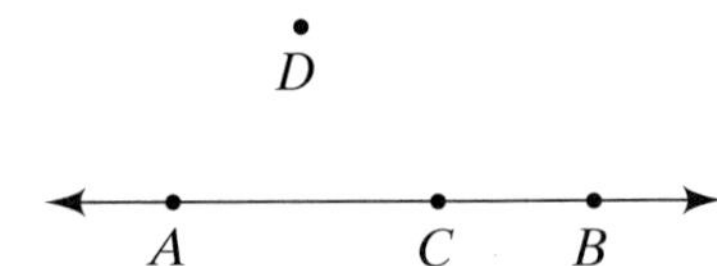

Checkpoint Quiz 2

Lessons 8-4 through 8-8

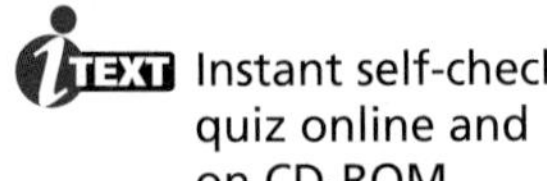

Instant self-check quiz online and on CD-ROM

Classify a triangle with the given angle measures.

1. 20°, 60°, 100°
2. 40°, 50°, 90°
3. 60°, 60°, 60°

Classify a triangle with the given side lengths.

4. 8, 9, and 8 units
5. 3, 4, and 5 units
6. 10, 10, and 10 units

7. How many lines of symmetry does a square have?

8. Fred, Matt, and Alison are a teacher, an artist, and a writer, though not necessarily in that order. Alison is the sister of the teacher. Matt has never met the teacher or the artist. Match each person to his or her job.

Use the figures below for Exercises 9 and 10.

9. Which figures are similar?

10. Which figures are congruent?

A. B. C. D. E.

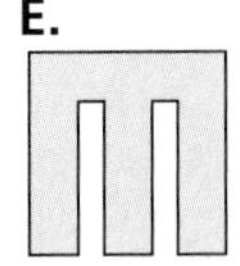

8-9 Transformations

What You'll Learn

To identify and draw translations and reflections

To identify rotations

. . . And Why

To find rotations in nature, as in Example 3

Check Skills You'll Need

For help, go to Lesson 8-8.

Trace each figure and draw the lines of symmetry.

1. 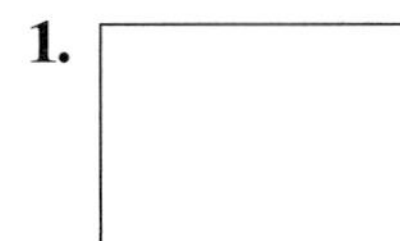

2. 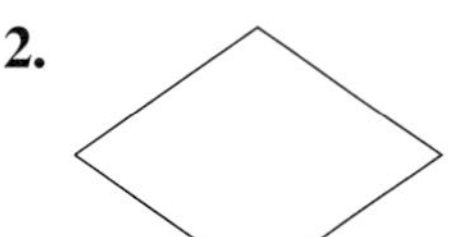

3. 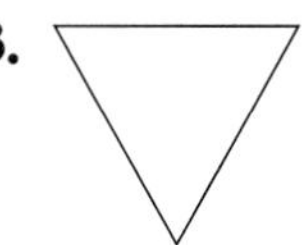

New Vocabulary

- image
- translation
- reflection
- line of reflection
- rotation
- center of rotation

Interactive lesson includes instant self-check, tutorials, and activities.

OBJECTIVE 1 Drawing Translations and Reflections

Real-World Connection
Quilters often translate one design to make a pattern.

A *transformation* of a figure is a change in its position, shape, or size. The new figure is the **image** of the original. Three types of transformations change only the position of the figure. They are *translations*, *reflections*, and *rotations*.

A **translation,** or *slide*, is a transformation that moves every point of a figure the same distance and in the same direction.

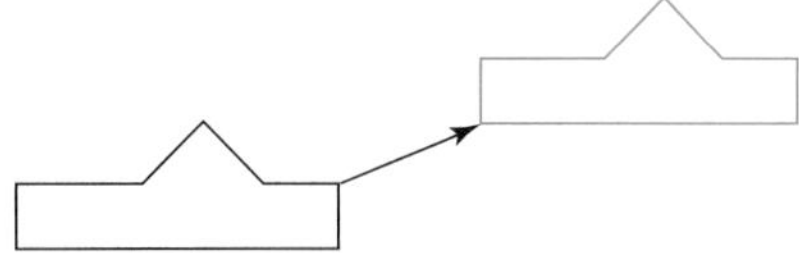

The blue figure is the image of the black figure after a translation.

1 EXAMPLE Identifying Translations

Is the second figure a translation of the first figure?

a.

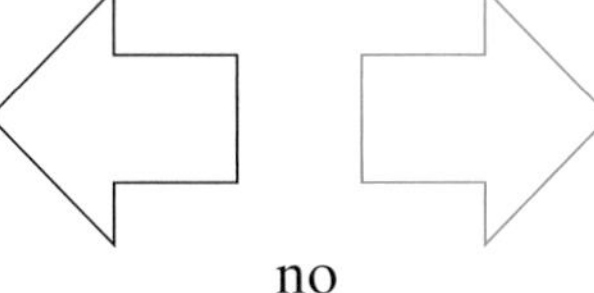

no

b.

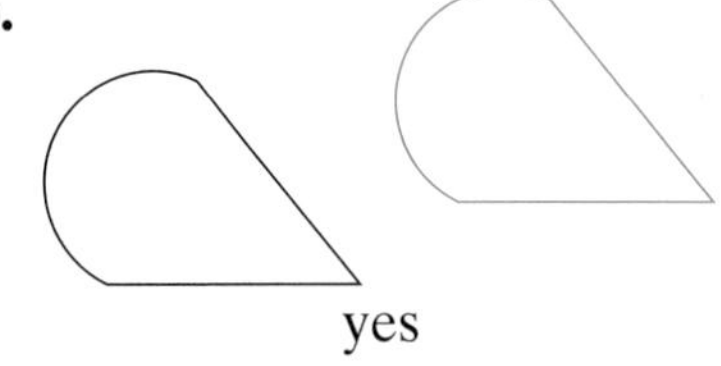

yes

Check Understanding **1** Is the second figure a translation of the first figure?

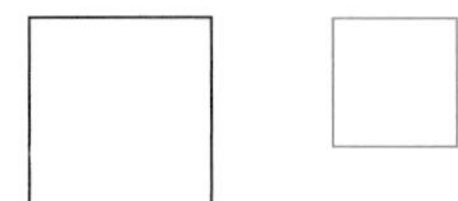

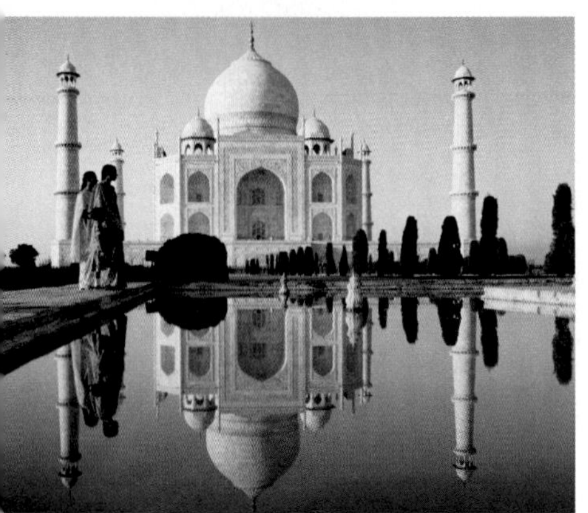

Real-World Connection

The reflecting pool gives an image of the Taj Mahal.

Another way to change the position of a figure is to reflect it. A **reflection,** or *flip,* is a transformation that flips a figure over a line. This line is the **line of reflection.** The new figure is a mirror image of the original.

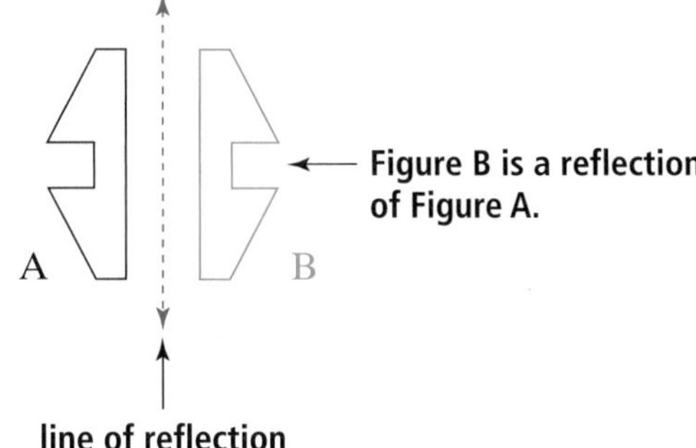

2 EXAMPLE Drawing Reflections

Draw the reflection of Figure A over the line of reflection.

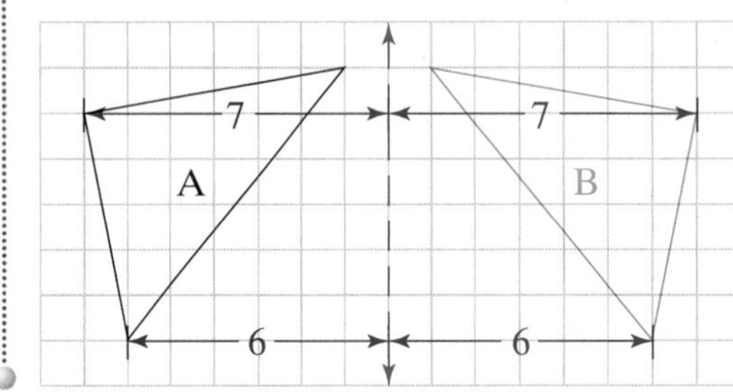

Use the grid to locate vertices equidistant from the line of reflection.

Then connect the vertices.

Check Understanding 2 Copy each figure and draw its reflection over the given line of reflection.

a.

b.

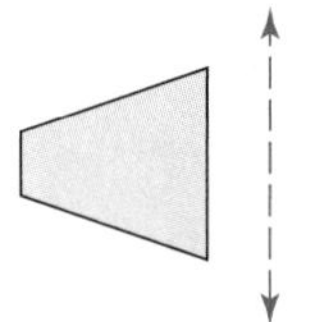

OBJECTIVE 2 Identifying Rotations

A **rotation,** or *turn,* is a transformation that turns a figure about a point. This point stays fixed and is called the **center of rotation.**

The letter P is being rotated around the center of rotation. Each image is congruent to the original letter P.

You can describe a rotation using degrees. The letter P has been rotated clockwise 90°, 180°, and 270°.

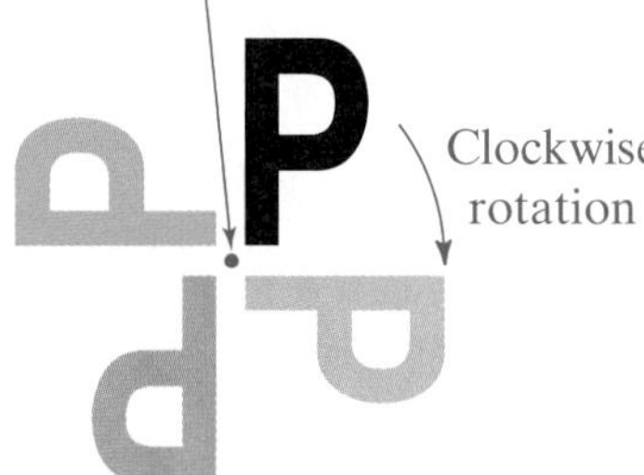

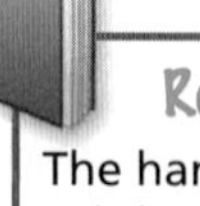

Reading Math

The hands of a clock rotate clockwise.

3 EXAMPLE Real-World Problem Solving

Nature Through how many degrees can you rotate the flower so that the image and the original flower are in the same position?

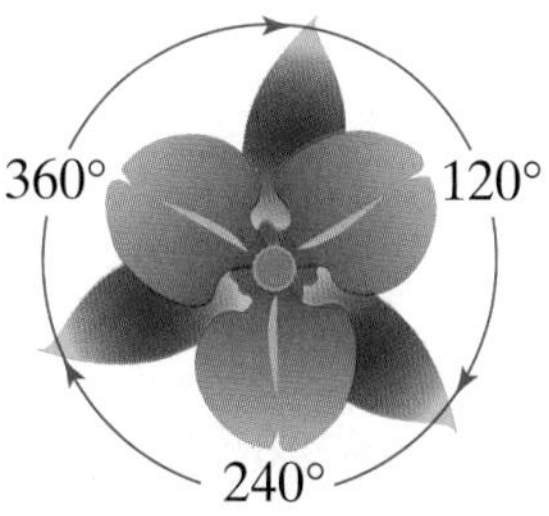

The image matches the original flower after rotations of 120°, 240°, and 360°.

Check Understanding 3 Tell whether each figure is a rotation of the first shape below.

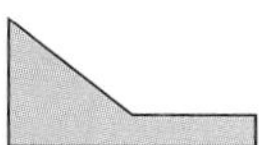

a.  **b.** 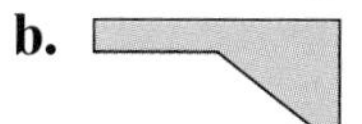 **c.** 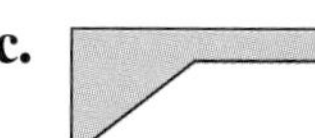

EXERCISES

For more practice, see *Extra Practice.*

A Practice by Example

Example 1 (page 415)

Is the second figure a translation of the first figure?

1. 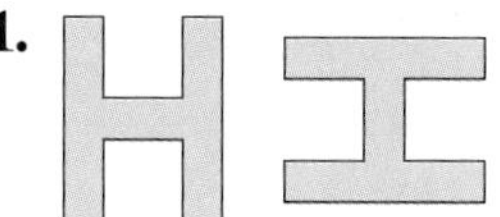 **2.**  **3.** 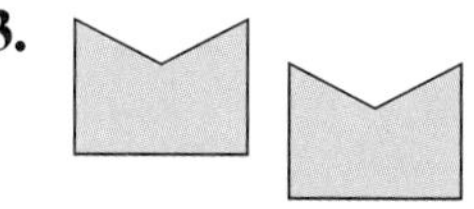

Example 2 (page 416)

Copy each diagram on graph paper and draw its reflection over the given line of reflection.

4. 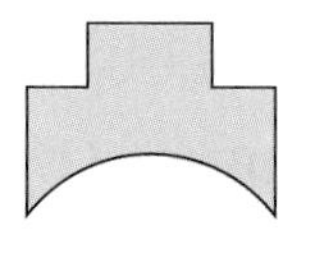 **5.** 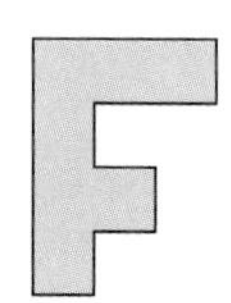 **6.** 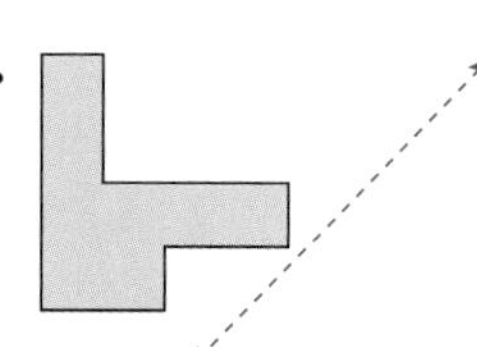

7. 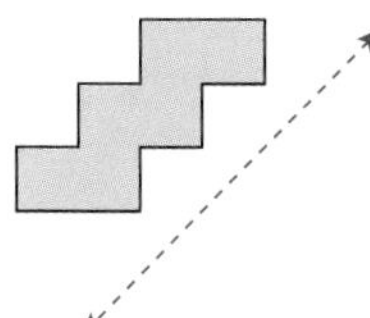 **8.**  **9.** 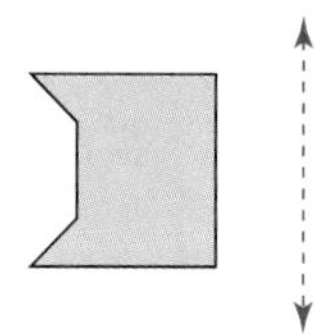

Example 3 (page 417)

Tell whether each figure is a rotation of the shape at the left.

R

10.  **11.**  **12.**  **13.** 

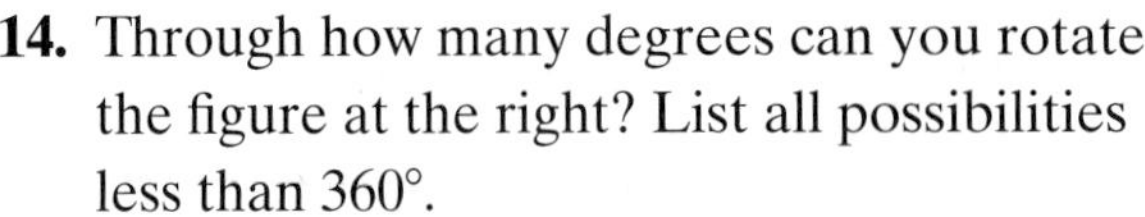

14. Through how many degrees can you rotate the figure at the right? List all possibilities less than 360°.

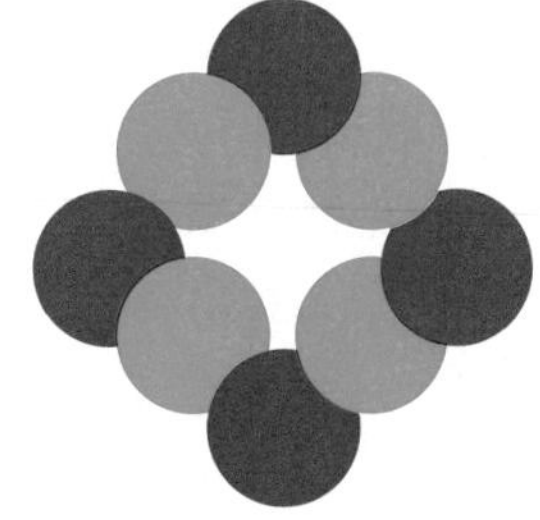

B **Apply Your Skills**

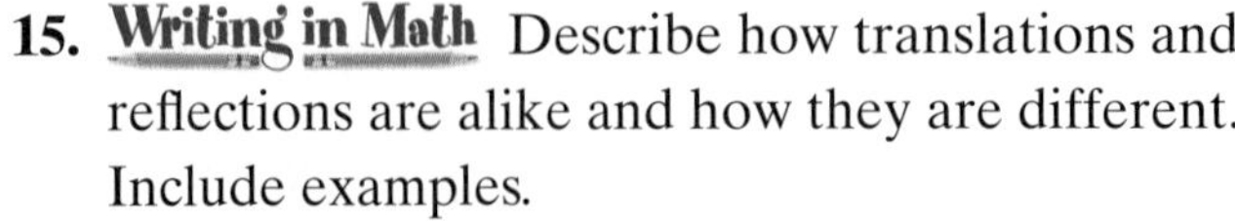

15. **Writing in Math** Describe how translations and reflections are alike and how they are different. Include examples.

16. **Windmills** Describe the type of transformation the blades of a windmill make.

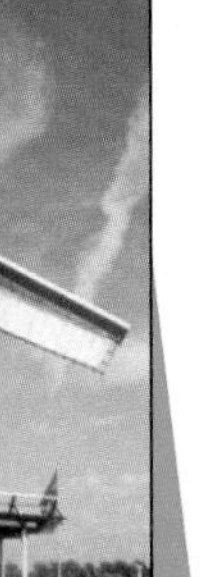

Real-World Connection

Windmills capture the energy of the wind.

Tell whether each pair of figures is a translation or a reflection.

17. 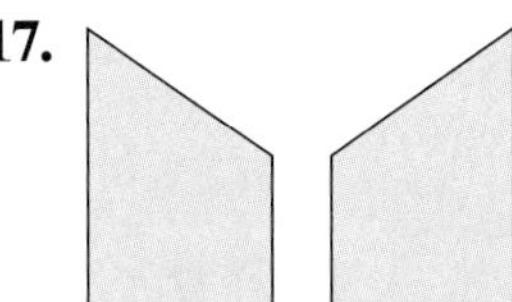

18. 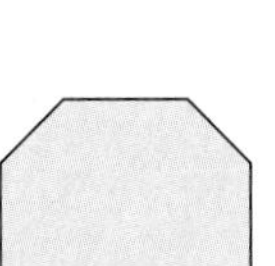

19. 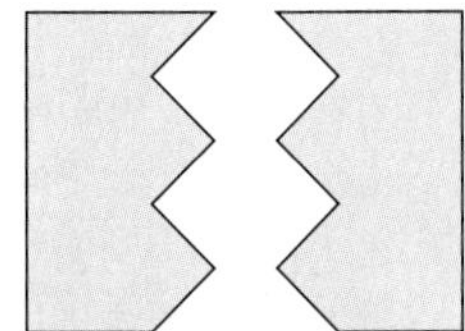

Make three copies of the figure below for Exercises 20–22.

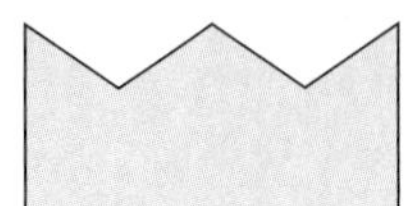

20. Draw a 90° clockwise rotation of the figure.

21. Draw a translation of the figure.

22. Draw a line of reflection below the figure. Than draw the reflection of the figure over the line.

23. What clockwise rotation of a figure will produce the same image as a counterclockwise rotation of 180°?

Copy the figures onto graph paper. Then draw the line of reflection.

24. 

25. 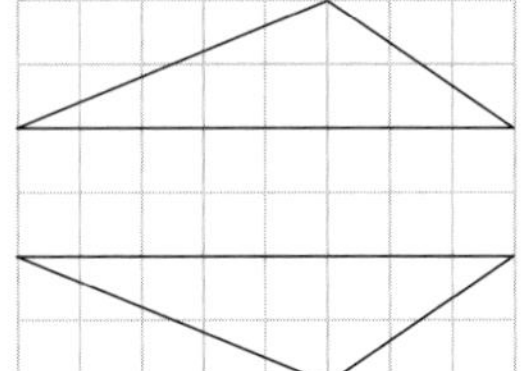

26. **Interior Design** Describe a translation of the figure in the fabric.

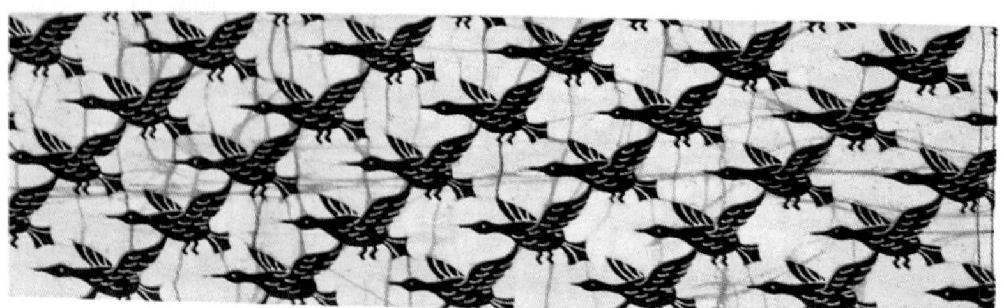

C Challenge

State the least number of degrees you must rotate the figure so the image fits exactly over the original figure shown.

27. 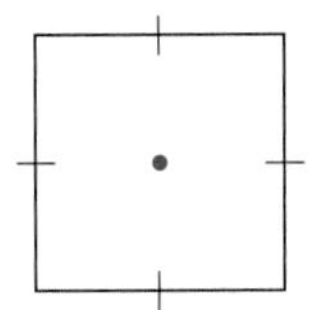

28. 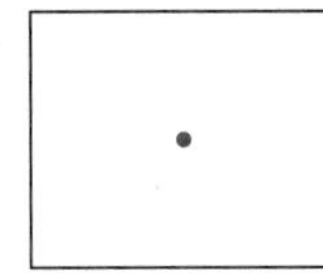

29. 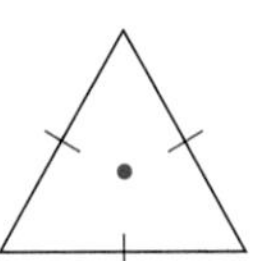

30. Open-Ended Design a pattern that consists of translations, reflections, and rotations of one basic figure.

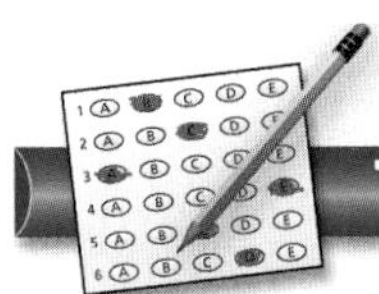

Test Prep

Multiple Choice

Use the figure at the right for Exercises 31–33.

31. Which choice shows a translation of the figure?

A. B. 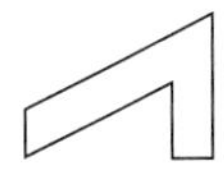 C. 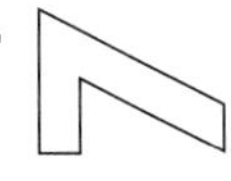 D. 

32. Which choice shows a reflection of the figure over a vertical line?

F.  G.  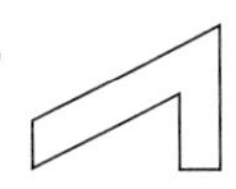 H. 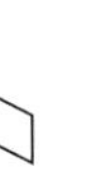 I.

Take It to the NET
Online lesson quiz at
www.PHSchool.com
Web Code: aaa-0809

33. Which choice shows a rotation of the figure?

A.  B. 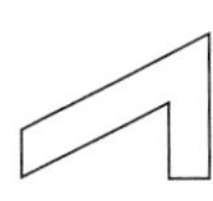 C. 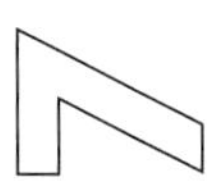 D. 

Extended Response

34. Draw a parallelogram that is not a rectangle. Show its reflection over a vertical line and a 90° clockwise rotation.

Mixed Review

Lesson 6-7

Estimate the sales tax and total cost for each item. The sales tax rate is 8%.

35. a magazine that costs \$3.75

36. a snowboard that costs \$119

Lesson 4-6

Solve each equation.

37. $x + 5\frac{2}{9} = 14\frac{1}{3}$

38. $27\frac{1}{2} = x + 5\frac{3}{4}$

39. $25 - 17\frac{2}{3} = x$

Extension Tessellations

For Use With Lesson 8-9

A *tessellation* is a pattern of repeated, congruent shapes. It covers a surface without gaps or overlaps. You can make a tessellation using just one figure, or several different figures that fit together. The M. C. Escher tessellation at the right uses three shapes: a bird, a sting ray, and a turtle.

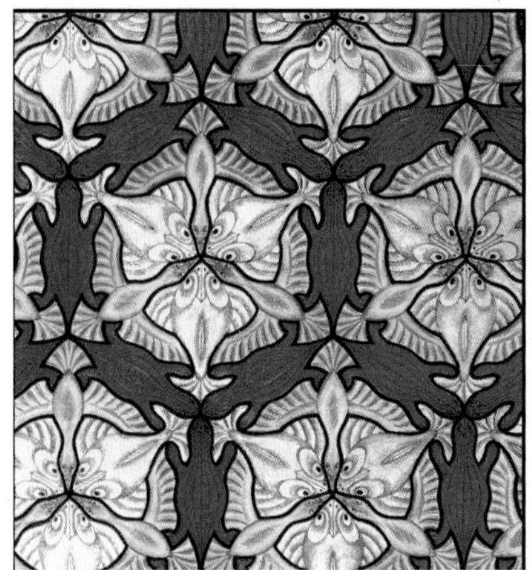

EXAMPLE

Can you use this one figure to make a tessellation? Use a drawing to explain.

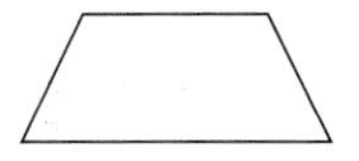

Yes. In the drawing at the right, the figure covers the surface with no gaps or overlaps.

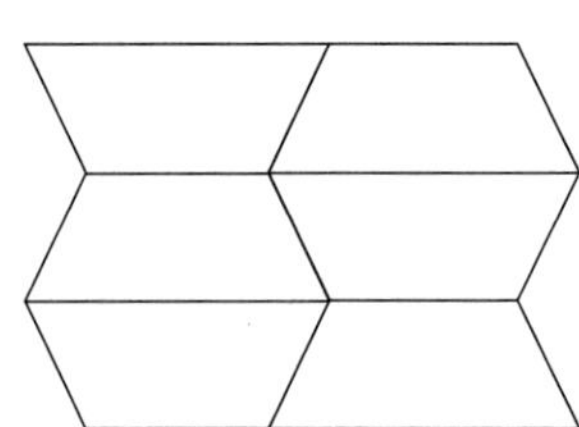

Activity

Make a tessellation.

a. Draw a $1\frac{1}{2}$-inch square and cut it out.

b. Inside the square, draw a trapezoid and a triangle with one side of each shape on the side of the square.

c. Cut out the figures and move each to the opposite side of the square. Tape them in place.

d. Trace the figure repeatedly to make a tessellation.

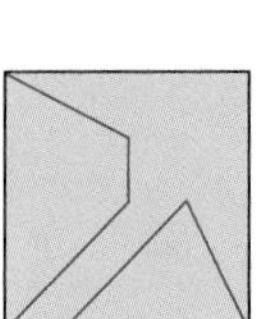

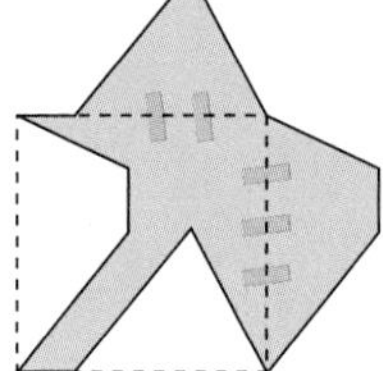

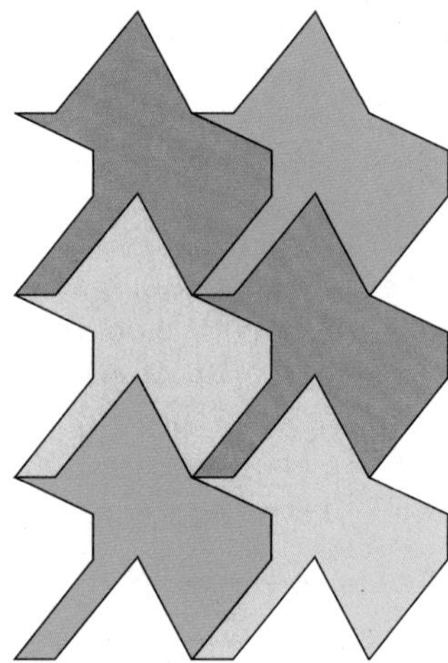

EXERCISES

1. Repeat the Activity using two other shapes inside the square.

Does each figure tessellate? Use a drawing to support your answer.

2.

3.

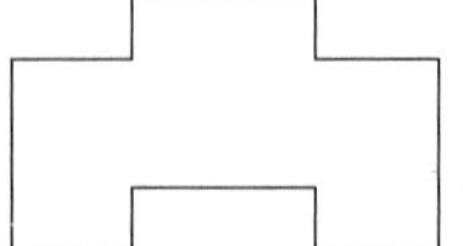

4.

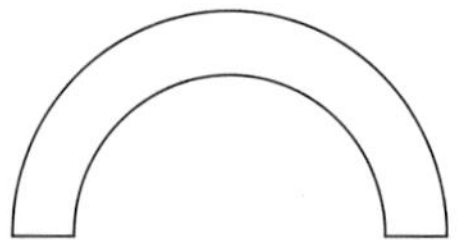

5.

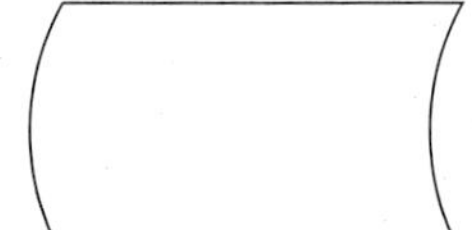

Drawing a Diagram

Often, you can find a solution to a problem more easily if you draw a diagram to show the information in the problem.

1 EXAMPLE

$\overleftrightarrow{MN}$ and $\overleftrightarrow{RS}$ intersect at point W. List two pairs of vertical angles.

Step 1 Draw a diagram of the intersecting lines to visualize the information.

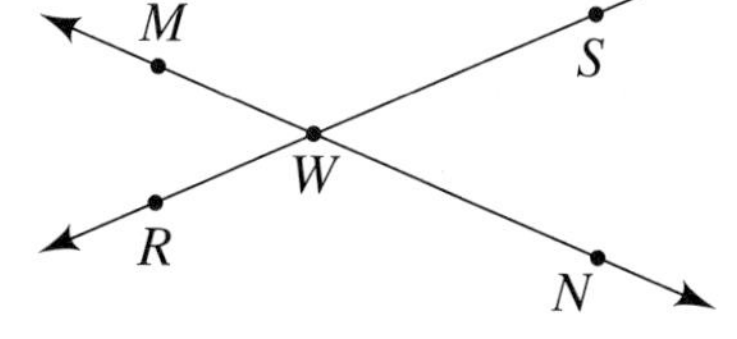

Step 2 List the pairs of vertical angles in your diagram.

$\angle MWS$ and $\angle RWN$ form vertical angles.
$\angle RWM$ and $\angle NWS$ form vertical angles.

2 EXAMPLE

Rectangle A and rectangle B share an edge of 16 inches. The shorter side of rectangle A is 8 inches. The longer side of rectangle B is 34 inches. Are the two rectangles similar?

Step 1 Draw a diagram of the two rectangles to visualize the information.

A | 16 in. | B

8 in. | 34 in.

Step 2 Use a proportion to determine whether the rectangles are similar.

Shorter side of A → / **Longer side of A →** $\frac{8}{16} \stackrel{?}{=} \frac{16}{34}$ **← Shorter side of B** / **← Longer side of B**

$$\frac{8}{16} \neq \frac{8}{17}$$

The sides are not proportional, so the two rectangles are not similar.

EXERCISES

Draw a diagram to solve each problem.

1. $\overleftrightarrow{AF}$ and $\overleftrightarrow{DT}$ intersect at K. List two pairs of adjacent angles.

2. a. How many different types of quadrilaterals can two congruent isosceles right triangles form if they share a side?

b. Name these quadrilaterals.

Chapter Review

Vocabulary

acute angle (p. 380)
acute triangle (p. 392)
angle (p. 379)
center of rotation (p. 416)
collinear (p. 374)
complementary angles (p. 386)
congruent angles (p. 387)
congruent figures (p. 405)
congruent segments (p. 393)
degrees (p. 379)
equilateral triangle (p. 393)
exterior angles (p. 387)
image (p. 415)
interior angles (p. 387)
intersecting lines (p. 374)
isosceles triangle (p. 393)
line (p. 373)
line of reflection (p. 416)
line of symmetry (p. 410)
line symmetry (p. 410)
obtuse angle (p. 380)
obtuse triangle (p. 392)
parallel lines (p. 374)
parallelogram (p. 398)
perpendicular lines (p. 380)
plane (p. 374)
point (p. 373)
polygon (p. 397)
quadrilateral (p. 398)
ray (p. 373)
rectangle (p. 398)
reflection (p. 416)
rhombus (p. 398)
right angle (p. 380)
right triangle (p. 392)
rotation (p. 416)
scalene triangle (p. 393)
segment (p. 373)
similar figures (p. 406)
skew lines (p. 374)
square (p. 398)
straight angle (p. 380)
supplementary angles (p. 386)
translation (p. 415)
transversal (p. 387)
trapezoid (p. 398)
vertex (p. 379)
vertical angles (p. 387)

Reading Math: Understanding Vocabulary

Choose the correct term to complete each sentence.

1. The measure of an (acute, obtuse) angle is between 90° and 180°.
2. An (isosceles, equilateral) triangle has three congruent sides.
3. Lines that intersect to form right angles are (skew, perpendicular).
4. A (rectangle, rhombus) always has four right angles.
5. A (ray, line) extends in two opposite directions without end.

Take It to the NET
Online vocabulary quiz at **www.PHSchool.com**
Web Code: aaj-0851

Skills and Concepts

8-1 Objectives

- To name points, lines, segments, and rays
- To identify parallel, intersecting, and skew lines

A **point** has no size, only location. A **line** continues without end in opposite directions. A **segment** is part of a line and has two endpoints. A **ray** is part of a line and has one endpoint.

If a line can be drawn through a set of points, the points are **collinear.** **Parallel lines** are lines in the same plane that do not intersect. **Skew lines** lie in different planes.

6. Name three collinear points.
7. Name two parallel lines.
8. Name two rays with endpoint B.

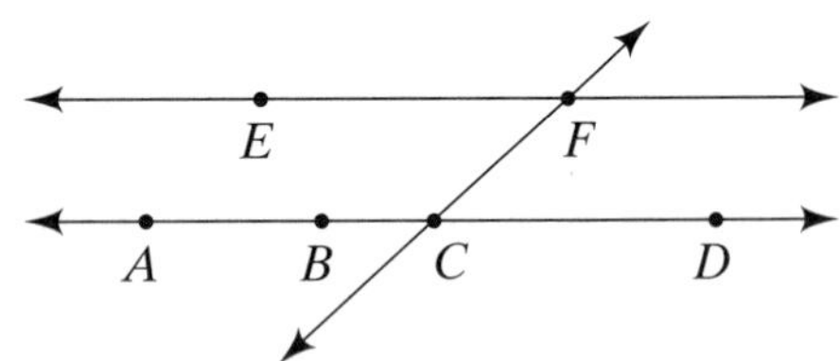

8-2 and 8-3 Objectives

- ▼ To measure and classify angles
- ▼ To find complements and supplements
- ▼ To identify special pairs of angles

Two rays with a common endpoint form an **angle.** Angles are classified as **acute, right, obtuse,** or **straight. Congruent angles** have the same measure.

Two intersecting lines form two pairs of **vertical angles.** The sum of the measures of two **complementary angles** is 90°. The sum of the measures of two **supplementary angles** is 180°.

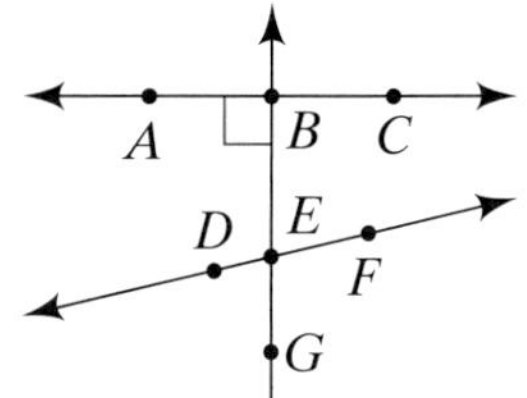

Name each of the following.

9. a pair of vertical angles

10. a transversal

11. two congruent angles

12. an acute angle

8-4 and 8-5 Objectives

- ▼ To classify triangles by their angles
- ▼ To classify triangles by their sides
- ▼ To identify types of polygons
- ▼ To classify quadrilaterals

You can classify a triangle by its angles as **acute, obtuse,** or **right.** You can classify a triangle by its sides as **scalene, isosceles,** or **equilateral.**

Polygons with four sides are called **quadrilaterals.** Three special types of **parallelograms** are the **rhombus, rectangle,** and **square.**

Give the best name for each polygon.

13. 

14. 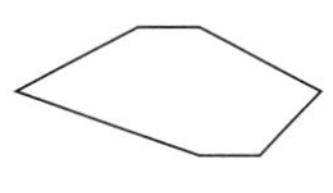

15. 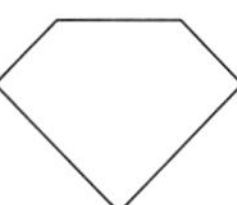

8-6 Objective

- ▼ To solve problems using logical reasoning

You can *use logical reasoning* when you are given a series of clues to solve a problem.

16. Of 26 students, 3 read *The Yearling* and *Where the Red Fern Grows*, 11 students read only the first book, and 7 students read neither book. How many students read only the second book?

8-7, 8-8, and 8-9 Objectives

- ▼ To identify congruent figures
- ▼ To identify similar figures
- ▼ To find lines of symmetry
- ▼ To identify and draw translations and reflections
- ▼ To identify rotations

Congruent figures have the same size and shape. **Similar** figures have the same shape, but not necessarily the same size. **Translations, reflections,** and **rotations** are transformations that change the position of a figure.

Do the triangles appear to be congruent or similar?

17. 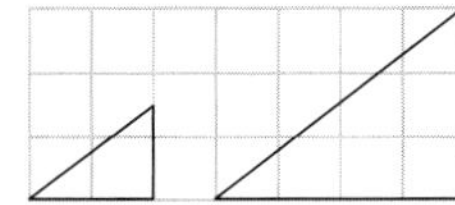

18. 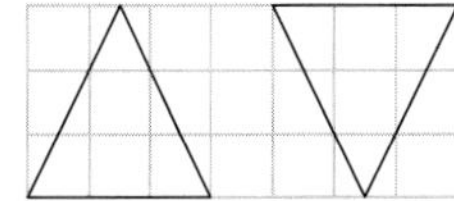

19. Draw a translation and a reflection of the figure shown.

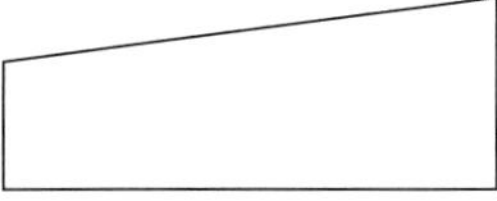

Chapter 8 Chapter Test

1. Draw three noncollinear points. Label them X, Y, and Z. Draw $\overleftrightarrow{XY}$ and $\overline{YZ}$.

Measure each angle. Then classify it as *acute, right, obtuse,* or *straight.*

2. 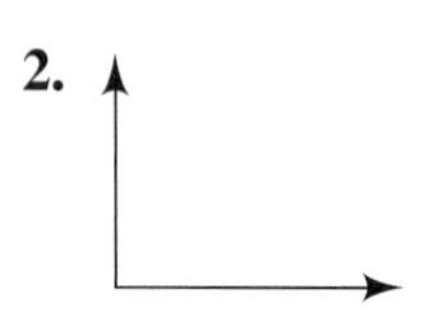

3. 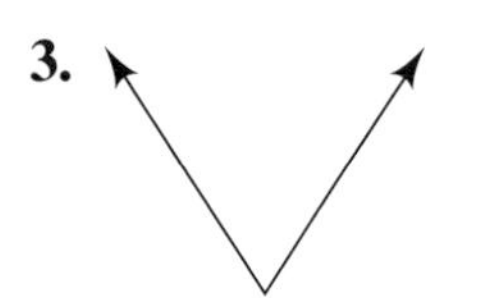

4. 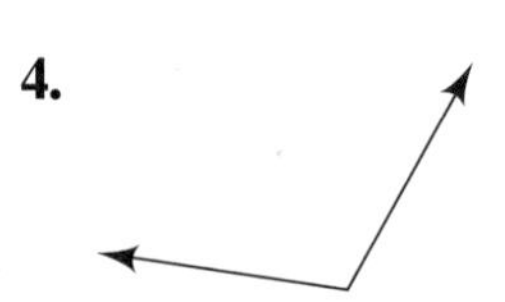

5. 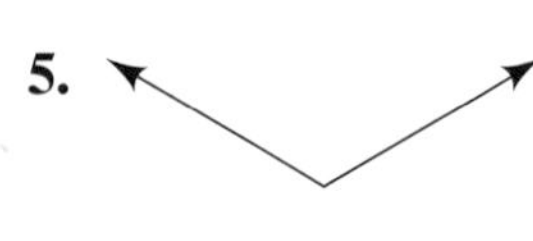

Find the measure of the complement and supplement of each angle.

6. 72°

7. 42°

Classify each triangle as *acute, right,* or *obtuse.*

8. 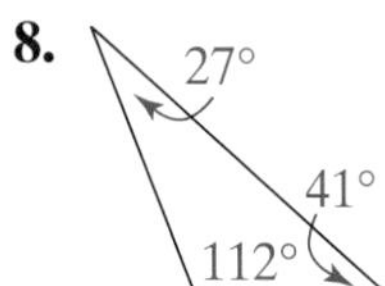

9. 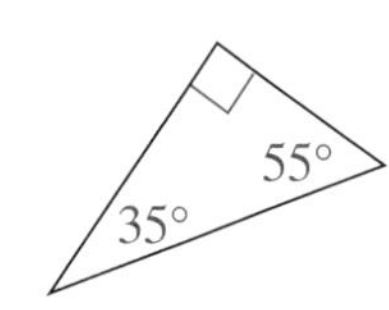

Classify each triangle as *scalene, isosceles,* or *equilateral.*

10. 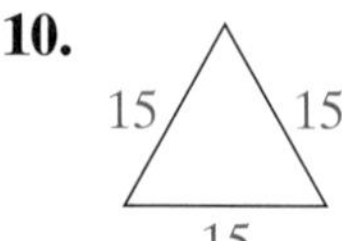

11. 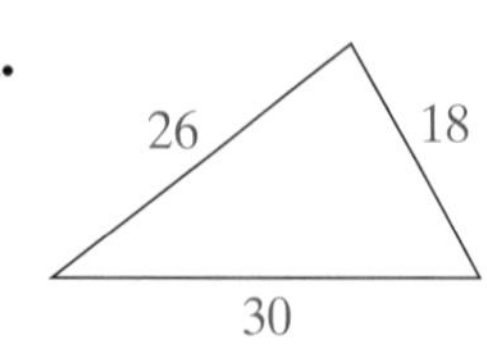

12. Draw a quadrilateral with the given number of lines of symmetry.
    a. 0 b. 1 c. 2 d. 4

13. **Pizza** Who ate the pizza? Al says, "I didn't. Neither did Bob." Bob says, "Cathie ate it. Al didn't." Cathie says, "I didn't eat it. Bob did!" If the person who ate the pizza lied, and the others told the truth, then who ate the pizza? Explain.

Write the best name for each figure.

14. 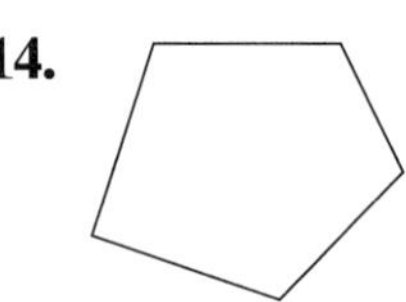

15. 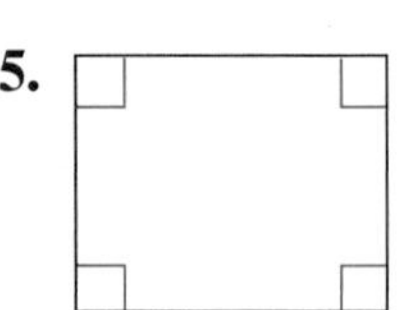

16. 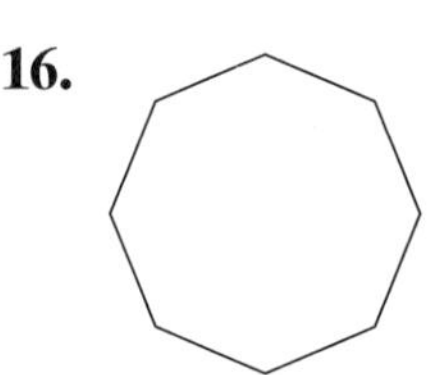

17. 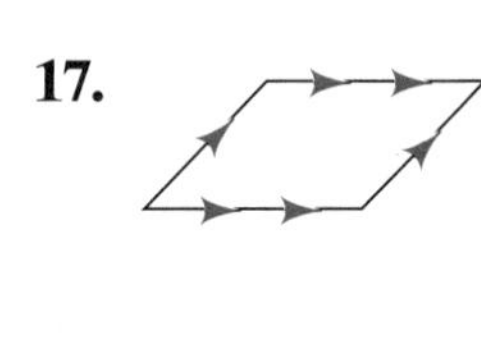

18. Writing in Math Describe how congruent figures and similar figures are alike and how they are different.

How many lines of symmetry does each quadrilateral have?

19. 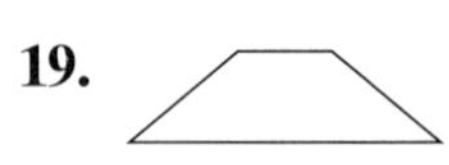

20. 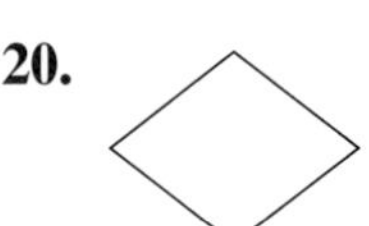

Use the shape below for Exercises 21–22.

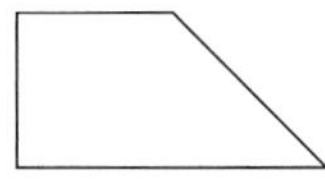

21. Draw a translation of the shape.

22. Draw a reflection of the shape. Show the line of reflection.

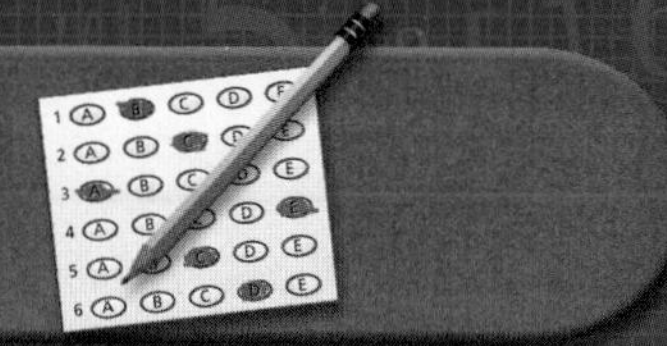

Test Prep

Multiple Choice

Choose the best answer.

1. What information does the circle graph below NOT tell you about Jen?

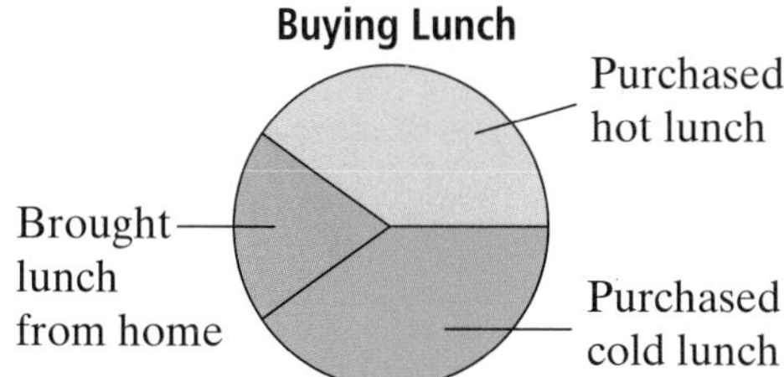

   A. Jen purchased lunch more often than she brought it from home.
   B. Jen purchased hot lunches about as often as cold lunches.
   C. Jen brought lunch from home more often than she purchased cold lunch.
   D. Jen purchased hot lunch more often than she brought lunch from home.

2. A hot air balloon is 2,250 feet in the air. It is scheduled to land at 3:30 P.M. It descends 90 feet every minute. When should the balloonist start descending?
   F. 3:55 P.M. G. 3:05 P.M.
   H. 2:55 P.M. I. 2:45 P.M.

3. In order to conclude that *MNOP* is a rhombus, what do you need to know?

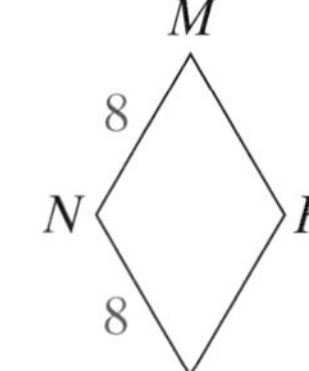

   A. $\overline{MO}$ is perpendicular to $\overline{NP}$.
   B. $\overline{MO}$ has length 8.
   C. $\overline{MP}$ and $\overline{PO}$ have length 8.
   D. $\overline{NP}$ and $\overline{MO}$ are congruent.

4. Which set of decimals is ordered from least to greatest?
   F. 0.2, 0.02, 0.22 G. 0.15, 0.51, 1.05
   H. 0.24, 0.3, 0.05 I. 0.49, 0.4, 0.05

5. The Amazon River in South America carries one sixth of Earth's water that flows into oceans. About what percent is this?
   A. 17% B. 12.5% C. 10% D. 6%

6. Which is ordered from least to greatest?
   F. $\frac{3}{7}, \frac{5}{7}, \frac{7}{11}$ G. $\frac{1}{4}, \frac{1}{2}, \frac{2}{5}$
   H. $\frac{1}{3}, \frac{2}{3}, \frac{4}{5}$ I. $\frac{1}{8}, \frac{2}{5}, \frac{3}{10}$

Gridded Response

7. $31.2 \times ■ = 0.0312$. What is ■?

8. What is the value of $3 + 4 \times 2^3$?

9. What is the degree measurement of a supplement of a 32° angle?

10. The greatest angle in a right triangle measures __?__ degrees.

Short Response

11. Which of the mean, median, mode, or range is the greatest for these data? Explain.
    81, 70, 95, 73, 74, 91, 86, 74

12. Bagels cost $6 per dozen. Find the cost of 5 bagels. Show your work.

Extended Response

13. Are the two triangles below similar? Justify your answer.

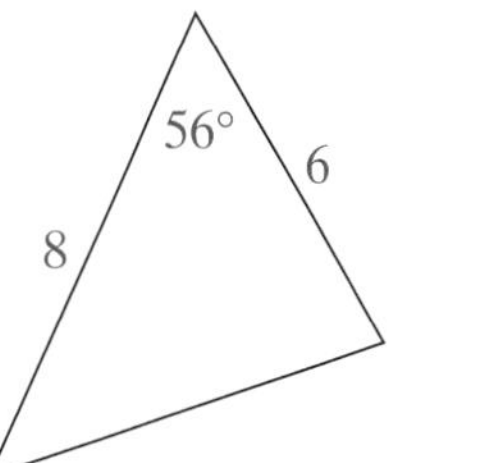

Building Outside the Box

Applying Geometry Before your home was built, it was probably drawn as a two-dimensional plan, or blueprint. A blueprint lets an architect experiment on paper with different ideas. The architect can discuss these ideas with the owner before construction begins. A blueprint also gives clear directions to a contractor on what to build. Most houses and apartments are rectangles with rectangular rooms, but they can be any shape.

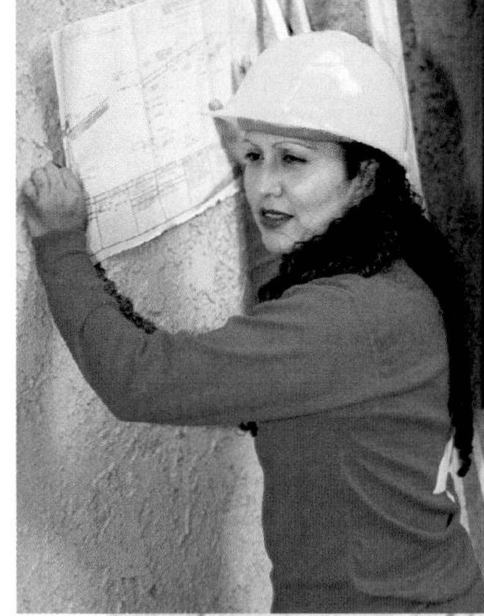

Using a Blueprint

Builders read blueprints and translate the two-dimensional notes into three-dimensional buildings. A builder refers to a blueprint many times a day during the building process.

Reading a Blueprint

A blueprint shows the layout of individual floors of your home in $\frac{1}{4}$-inch to 1-foot scale. It includes the dimensions of each room and closet and provides a key so you know what various symbols mean.

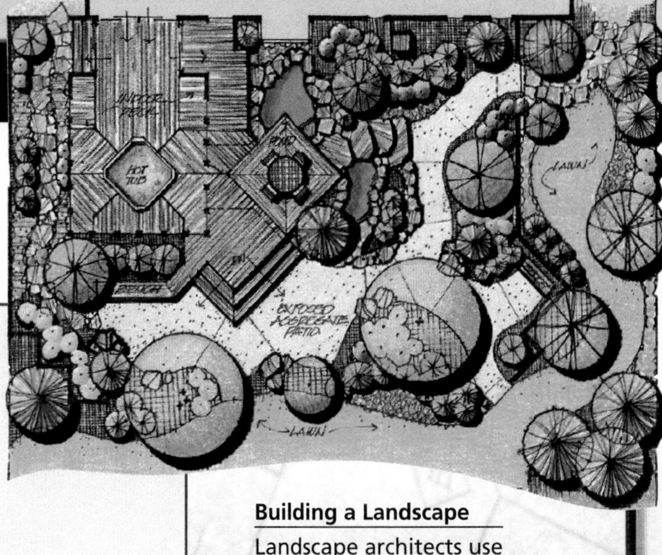

Building a Landscape

Landscape architects use flowers, bushes, and trees to make a pleasing environment around a building.

Put It All Together

Materials ruler

1. The blueprint shows a home where no room is rectangular.
   a. What shape is the home?
   b. Identify the shape of each room.

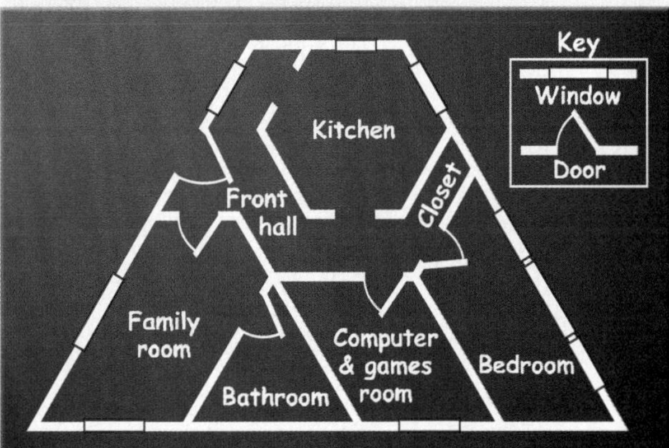

2. **Open-Ended** Suppose you are designing your own home. Make a list of the rooms you would like to include. Feel free to include rooms for hobbies or other special interests.
3. Make a rough sketch of the home, showing the shape and location of each room.
   - Use at least five different shapes from this chapter.
   - Include at least two rooms that are congruent to each other. Make one a translation or rotation of the other.
   - Remember to include hallways and doorways so that people can get into the rooms!
4. Use a ruler to make a final drawing of your design. Show windows and doors using the key in the blueprint. Label the rooms. Add furniture to your drawing if you wish.
5. **Writing in Math** Why do you think homes usually have rectangular rooms?

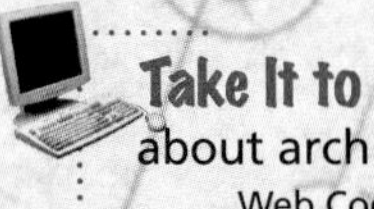

Take It to the NET For more information about architecture, go to **www.PHSchool.com**.
Web Code: aae-0853

CHAPTER 9

Geometry and Measurement

Lessons

Key Vocabulary

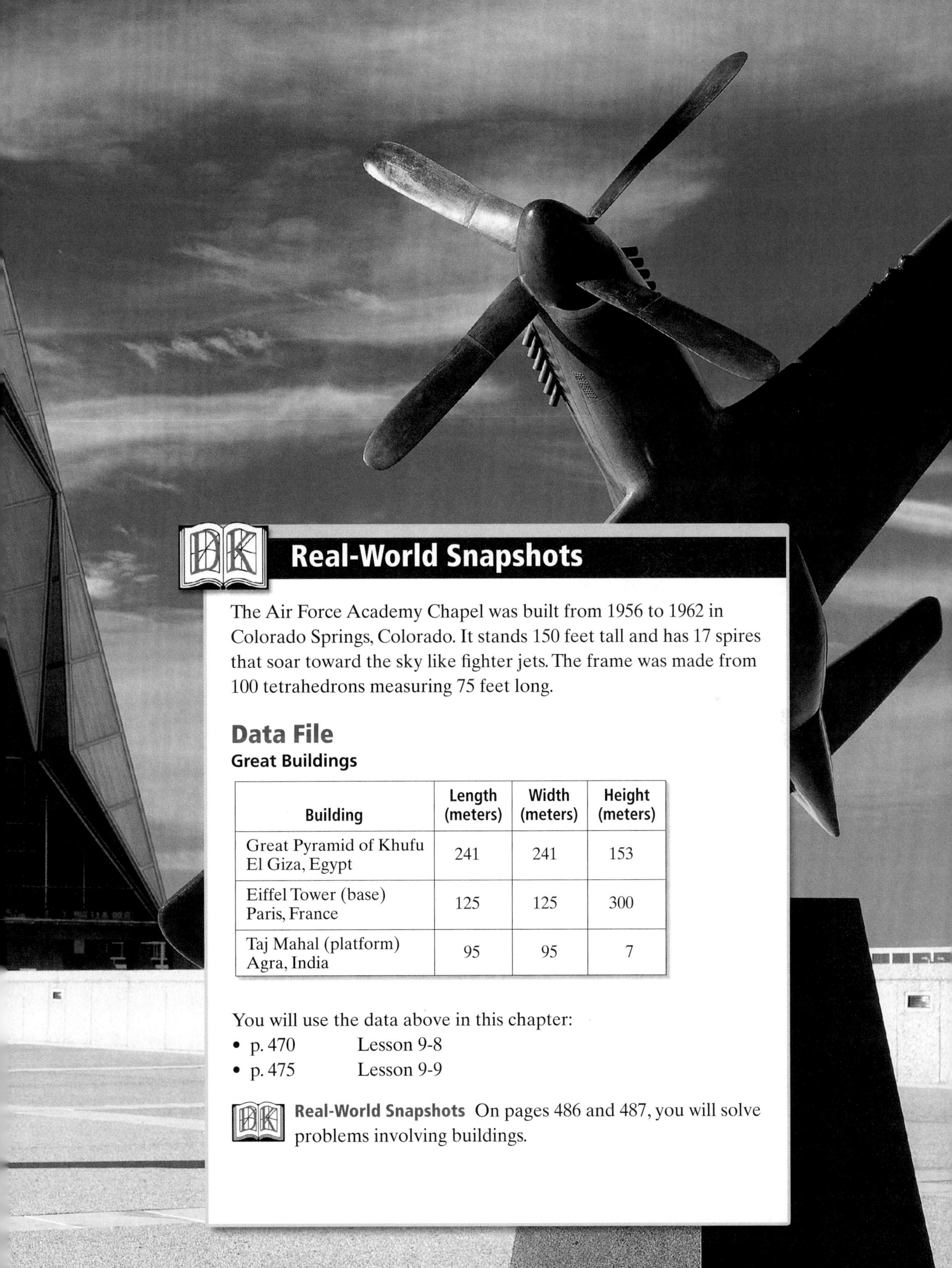

Real-World Snapshots

The Air Force Academy Chapel was built from 1956 to 1962 in Colorado Springs, Colorado. It stands 150 feet tall and has 17 spires that soar toward the sky like fighter jets. The frame was made from 100 tetrahedrons measuring 75 feet long.

Data File

Great Buildings

Building	Length (meters)	Width (meters)	Height (meters)
Great Pyramid of Khufu El Giza, Egypt	241	241	153
Eiffel Tower (base) Paris, France	125	125	300
Taj Mahal (platform) Agra, India	95	95	7

You will use the data above in this chapter:

- p. 470 Lesson 9-8
- p. 475 Lesson 9-9

Real-World Snapshots On pages 486 and 487, you will solve problems involving buildings.

Chapter 9 Preview

Where You've Been

- In Chapter 5, you worked with the customary system of measurement.
- In Chapter 8, you classified angles and polygons.

Where You're Going

- In Chapter 9, you will use the metric system of measurement and compare different units.
- Applying what you learn, you will identify three-dimensional figures as seen in architecture.

Teepees are shaped like pyramids or cones.

Instant self-check online and on CD-ROM

Diagnosing Readiness

For help, go to the lesson in green.

Choosing Appropriate Units of Measurement (Lesson 5-7)

Choose an appropriate unit for each measurement.

1. weight of a newborn baby
2. capacity of a train's oil car
3. distance to the sun
4. length of your hand

Changing Units (Lesson 5-8)

Complete each statement.

5. ■ oz = 9 lb
6. 46 in. = ■ ft
7. $7\frac{1}{4}$ c = ■ pt
8. 4,500 lb = ■ t
9. ■ pt = 13 qt
10. 7,920 ft = ■ mi

Use <, =, or > to complete each statement.

11. 14 ft ■ 4 yd
12. $2\frac{1}{2}$ gal ■ 11 qt
13. 5 c ■ 37 fl oz
14. 3 yd ■ 108 ft
15. $14\frac{1}{4}$ lb ■ 9,000 t
16. 65 c ■ $16\frac{1}{4}$ qt

Classifying Polygons (Lessons 8-4 and 8-5)

Classify each triangle and quadrilateral. Classify each triangle by its sides.

17. 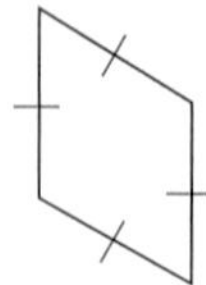

18. 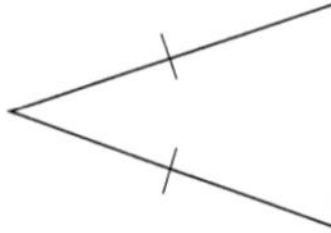

19. 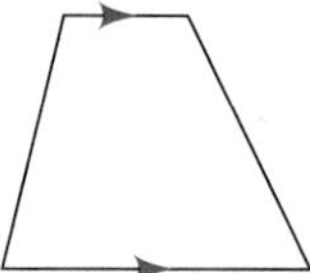

9-1 Metric Units of Length, Mass, and Capacity

What You'll Learn

 To use metric units of length

 To choose units for mass and capacity

. . . And Why

To choose appropriate units of mass, as in Example 3

For help, go to Lesson 5-7.

Choose an appropriate unit for each measurement.

1. the weight of a baseball
2. the weight of your desk
3. the length of a gymnasium
4. the capacity of a juice box

New Vocabulary • metric system • meter • mass • gram • capacity • liter

 Interactive lesson includes instant self-check, tutorials, and activities.

OBJECTIVE 1 Using Metric Units of Length

In Chapter 5, you worked with units in the customary system such as yards, pounds, and gallons. The **metric system** of measurement is a decimal system. It uses prefixes to relate the sizes of units to standard units. The table at the left shows the most common prefixes.

Metric Prefixes

Prefix	Meaning
kilo-	1,000
centi-	$\frac{1}{100}$ or 0.01
milli-	$\frac{1}{1,000}$ or 0.001

The standard unit of length in the metric system is the **meter (m).** A meter is a little longer than a yard.

Metric Units of Length

Unit	Relationship to a Meter	Example
kilometer (km)	1 km = 1,000 meters	2.5 times around an indoor track
meter (m)	1 meter	height of a doorknob from the floor
centimeter (cm)	1 cm = 0.01 meter	thickness of a CD case
millimeter (mm)	1 mm = 0.001 meter	thickness of a CD

1 EXAMPLE Choosing a Unit of Length

Choose an appropriate metric unit of length for a pencil.

A pencil is much shorter than a meter but much longer than a millimeter. The most appropriate unit of measure is centimeters.

 1 Choose an appropriate metric unit of length for a city block.

2 EXAMPLE Using a Metric Ruler

Find the length of the segment in millimeters and in centimeters.

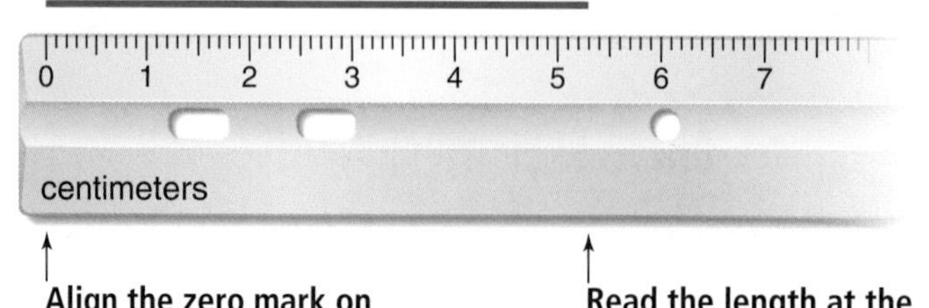

Align the zero mark on the ruler with one end of the segment.

Read the length at the other end of the segment.

The length of the segment is 53 millimeters, or 5.3 centimeters.

Check Understanding 2 Use a metric ruler to find each length in millimeters and in centimeters.

a. ———

b. ——————

c. ————————————

OBJECTIVE 2 Choosing Units for Mass and Capacity

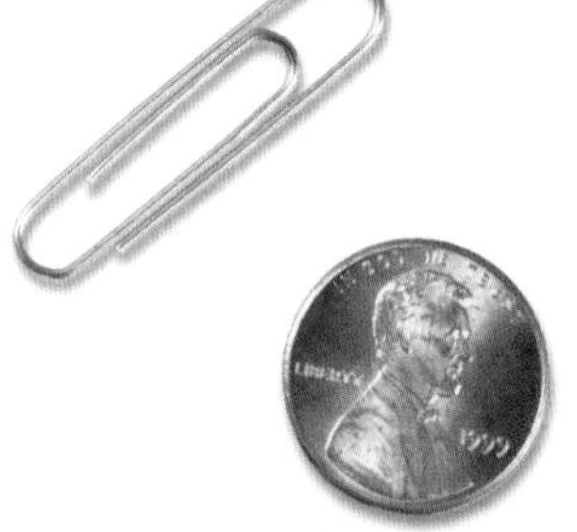

Real-World Connection

The mass of a small paperclip is 1 gram. The mass of a penny is about 2.5 grams.

Solids are sometimes measured in units of mass. **Mass** is a measure of the amount of matter in an object. The standard unit of mass is the **gram (g).**

Unit of Mass	Relationship to a Gram	Example
kilogram (kg)	1 kg = 1,000 grams	mass of 4 videocassettes
gram (g)	1 gram	mass of a small paper clip
milligram (mg)	1 mg = 0.001 gram	mass of an eyelash

3 EXAMPLE Choosing a Unit of Mass

Choose an appropriate metric unit of mass.

a. a pea

A pea has about the same mass as a paperclip. The appropriate unit of measure is grams.

b. a baby

The mass of a baby is much greater than the mass of a paperclip. The appropriate unit of measure is kilograms.

Check Understanding 3 Choose an appropriate metric unit of mass.

a. a car

b. a desk

c. a robin's feather

d. a pencil shaving

Liquids are measured by units of capacity. **Capacity** is a measure of the amount of liquid an object holds. The standard unit of capacity is the **liter (L).** A liter is a little more than a quart.

Unit of Capacity	Relationship to a Liter	Example
kiloliter (kL)	1 kL = 1,000 liters	water to fill 2 or 3 bathtubs
liter (L)	1 liter	a bottle of juice
milliliter (mL)	1 mL = 0.001 liter	2 dewdrops

Choosing a Unit of Capacity

Choose an appropriate metric unit of capacity.

a. a bottle cap

A bottle cap holds about 10 to 20 drops of water. The appropriate unit of measure is milliliters.

b. a swimming pool

The capacity of a swimming pool is much greater than the capacity of a bottle of juice. The appropriate unit of measure is kiloliters.

4 Choose an appropriate metric unit of capacity.

a. a car's fuel tank **b.** a pond **c.** a test tube

EXERCISES

For more practice, see *Extra Practice*.

A Practice by Example

Example 1 (page 431)

Choose an appropriate metric unit of length.

1. width of a highway
2. length of an eyelash
3. height of your desk
4. width of your finger
5. width of your classroom door
6. distance across the state of Ohio

Example 2 (page 432)

Use a metric ruler to find each length in millimeters and in centimeters.

7. ———— **8.** ———————— **9.** ————————

10. ————————————————————————————

Example 3 (page 432)

Choose an appropriate metric unit of mass.

11. a garbage can
12. a pin
13. a chair
14. a pay phone
15. a potato
16. a shirt button

Example 4 (page 433)

Choose an appropriate metric unit of capacity.

17. a watering can **18.** a juice box **19.** a large lake

20. a pail of sand **21.** a bottle of lotion **22.** a glass of milk

B Apply Your Skills

Complete the following.

23. 1 g = ■ kg **24.** 1 mL = ■ L **25.** ■ cm = 1 m

26. ■ L = 1 kL **27.** 1 m = ■ mm **28.** ■ g = 1 mg

Is each measurement reasonable? Explain.

29. A sidewalk is 30 kilometers wide.

30. A ladybug has a mass of 4 kilograms.

31. A giraffe is 550 centimeters tall.

32. A car has a mass of 1,200 kilograms.

33. A cow produces 500 kiloliters of milk each day.

***True* or *False*? If false, explain why.**

34. 1,000 mg = 1 g **35.** 100 kg = 100,000 g

36. 10 L = 1,000 mL **37.** 1 mm = 10 cm

38. Error Analysis Explain and correct the error in each statement.
  a. A tennis ball has a mass of about 58 milliliters.
  b. A dime has a capacity of about 2.5 grams.

39. Writing in Math Explain the difference between mass and capacity. Give an example of each.

40. Estimation The width of a door is about 1 meter. How can you estimate the length of a wall that contains the door?

State whether each item is best measured in terms of mass or capacity.

41. a bottle of lamp oil **42.** a newspaper

43. a bag of oranges **44.** water in a fish tank

Open-Ended **Name two items for which each unit might be used.**

45. milligram **46.** centimeter **47.** kilogram

Challenge 48. **Science** The deciliter (dL) is sometimes used in medical laboratory testing. The prefix *deci-* means $\frac{1}{10}$, or 0.1. Complete the following.

a. 15 L = ■ dL **b.** 49 dL = ■ L **c.** 273 dL = ■ L

49. **Reasoning** Ancient Egyptians based measures of length on the cubit, palm, and digit. The cubit (forearm) was the length from the elbow to the fingers. The palm was the width of the palm excluding the thumb. The digit was the width of the finger. List some advantages and disadvantages of using such a system of measurement.

50. **Stretch Your Thinking** Gerri started with the number 15. She multiplied by 3, divided by some number, and then added 10. The result was 15. By what number did Gerri divide?

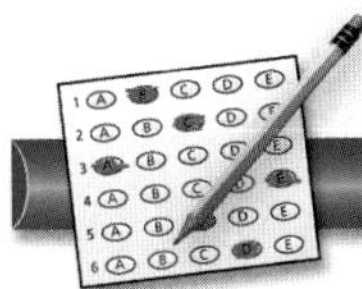

Test Prep

Multiple Choice

51. Which of the following items would NOT be best measured in terms of mass?

A. bread **B.** a box of rice **C.** orange juice **D.** popcorn

Take It to the NET
Online lesson quiz at
www.PHSchool.com
Web Code: aaa-0901

52. Which should be used to measure a baseball bat's length?

F. millimeter **G.** centimeter **H.** meter **I.** kilometer

53. Which should be used to measure a backpack's mass?

A. milligram **B.** centimeter **C.** gram **D.** kilogram

Short Response

54. You have two 650-milliliter bottles of lotion.

a. Will the lotion from the two bottles fit in a 1-liter container?

b. Explain in words how you found your answer.

Mixed Review

Lesson 8-3 **Find the complement and the supplement of each angle.**

55. 44° **56.** 16° **57.** 81° **58.** 62.5°

Lesson 6-3 **Find the value that completes each proportion.**

59. $\frac{4}{5} = \frac{68}{■}$ **60.** $\frac{10}{13} = \frac{■}{65}$ **61.** $\frac{288}{■} = \frac{6}{11}$ **62.** $\frac{■}{162} = \frac{2}{3}$

63. **Consumer Issues** Three pounds of peaches cost $5.67. You need 18 pounds of peaches to make pies for a bake sale. How much will you spend on peaches? Write and solve a proportion.

9-2 Converting Units in the Metric System

What You'll Learn

To convert metric measurements

. . . And Why

To find distances, as in Example 2

✓ Check Skills You'll Need

For help, go to Lesson 1-8.

Use mental math to find each product or quotient.

1. 39×100 **2.** $530 \div 10$ **3.** 57.4×10

4. $0.7 \div 10$ **5.** $143 \div 100$ **6.** $0.98 \times 1{,}000$

Interactive lesson includes instant self-check, tutorials, and activities.

OBJECTIVE 1 Converting Metric Measurements

You can rewrite one metric unit as another metric unit by multiplying or dividing by a power of 10. Multiply to change from larger units to smaller units. Divide to change from smaller units to larger units.

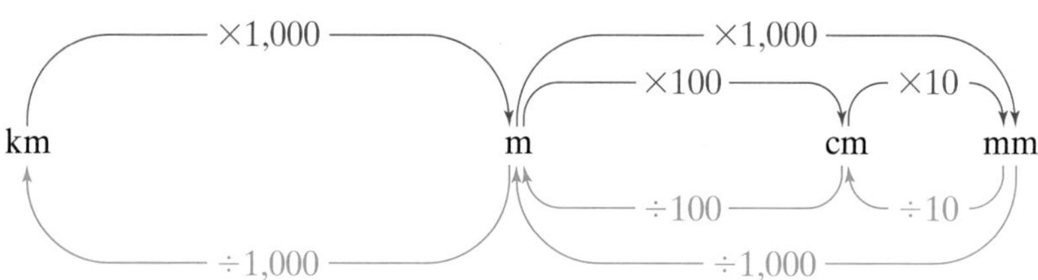

You can think of converting to smaller units as creating many small units from a larger unit. To do this, you must multiply. You should end up with more smaller units than you had larger units.

1 EXAMPLE Converting to Smaller Units

Convert 3.2 meters to centimeters.

The meter is a larger unit than the centimeter. To convert meters to centimeters, multiply by 100.

$3.2 \times 100 = 3.20$ ← **To multiply by 100, move the decimal point 2 places to the right.**

$3.2 \text{ m} = 320 \text{ cm}$

1 Convert each measurement.

a. 15 centimeters to millimeters **b.** 837 kilometers to meters

c. Number Sense Which measurement is greater: 500 millimeters or 5 meters? Explain.

You can think of converting to larger units as combining many small units. To do this, you must divide. You should end up with fewer larger units than you had smaller units.

2 EXAMPLE Converting to Larger Units

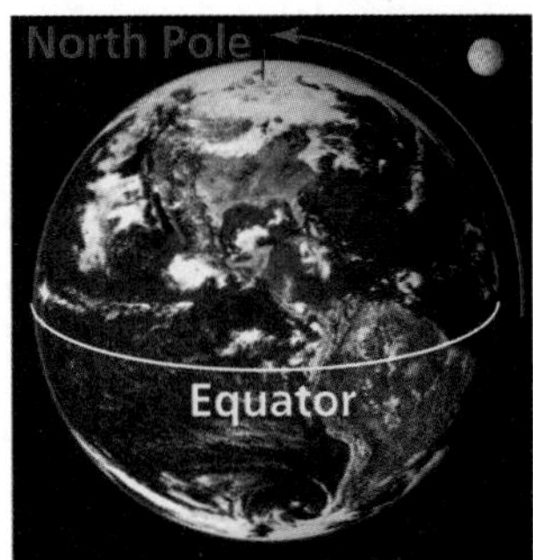

Geography The distance from the equator to the North Pole along Earth's surface is approximately 10,000,000 meters. What is the approximate distance in kilometers?

The meter is a smaller unit than the kilometer. So to convert meters to kilometers, divide by 1,000.

10,000,000 ÷ 1,000 = 10,000.000 ← **To divide by 1,000, move the decimal point 3 places to the left.**

The equator is about 10,000 kilometers from the North Pole.

Check Understanding 2 Convert each measurement.

a. 0.5 centimeter to meters **b.** 75 millimeters to centimeters

c. A sprinter runs 60,000 meters each week to train for a 400-meter race. How many kilometers does the sprinter run each week?

You can also convert grams or liters to related units.

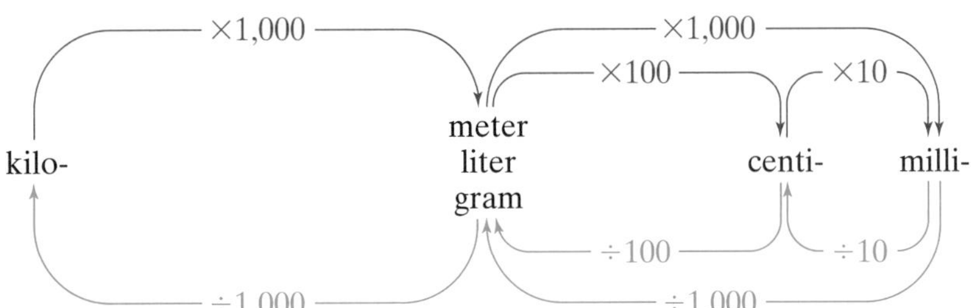

3 EXAMPLE Converting Units of Mass or Capacity

Complete each statement.

a. 0.035 kg = ■ g

To convert kilograms to grams, multiply by 1,000.

0.035 × 1,000 = 0.035. → 35 grams ← **To multiply by 1,000, move the decimal point 3 places to the right.**

b. 325 cL = ■ L

To convert centiliters to liters, divide by 100.

325 ÷ 100 = 3.25. → 3.25 liters ← **To divide by 100, move the decimal point 2 places to the left.**

Check Understanding 3 Complete each statement.

a. 15 mg = ■ g **b.** 386 L = ■ kL **c.** 8.2 cg = ■ g

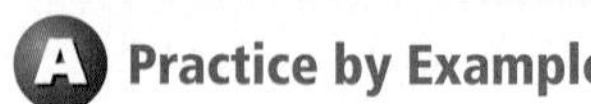

EXERCISES

For more practice, see *Extra Practice*.

A Practice by Example

Example 1 (page 436)

Convert each measurement. Exercise 1 has been started for you.

1. 1.3 kilometers to meters
$1.3 \times 1{,}000 = \blacksquare$

2. 83 grams to centigrams

3. 6,000 meters to centimeters

4. 0.5 liter to milliliters

5. 65 kilograms to grams

6. 59 centimeters to millimeters

Example 2 (page 437)

Convert each measurement. Exercise 7 has been started for you.

7. 206 centimeters to meters
$206 \div 100 = \blacksquare$

8. 142 liters to kiloliters

9. 83 milligrams to grams

10. 7.5 millimeters to centimeters

11. 6,900 milliliters to liters

12. 0.31 centigram to grams

13. Animals One of the world's longest dogs measured 240 centimeters. How many meters long was this dog?

Example 3 (page 437)

Complete each statement.

14. 3,070 mm = ■ m

15. 586 cg = ■ g

16. 0.61 km = ■ m

17. 0.04 m = ■ cm

18. 4,500 g = ■ mg

19. 6.4 kL = ■ L

20. 150 cL = ■ L

21. 120 mg = ■ g

22. 35,000 L = ■ mL

B Apply Your Skills

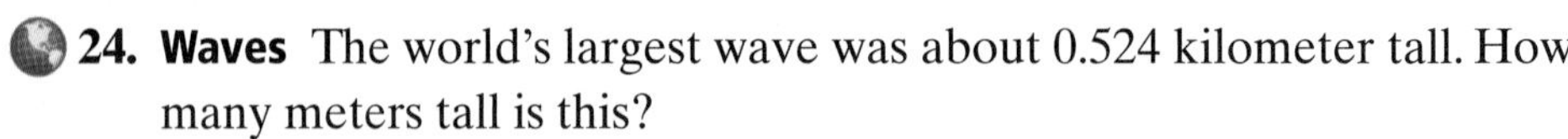

23. Physics Light travels at approximately 299,792,458 meters per second. Approximately how many kilometers does light travel in one second?

Real-World Connection

The height of this wave is about 5 meters.

24. Waves The world's largest wave was about 0.524 kilometer tall. How many meters tall is this?

Convert each measurement to meters, liters, or grams.

25. 8 kL

26. 7,000 mg

27. 0.24 km

28. 34,000 cm

29. 0.07 cL

30. 52 kg

31. 8.6 mm

32. 41.5 cg

34. **Algebra** You have x kilograms of peaches. Write an expression for how many grams of peaches you have.

34. **Writing in Math** When you convert metric measurements, how do you decide whether to multiply or divide?

Challenge

Complete each statement.

35. 1.2 kL = ■ mL **36.** ■ km = 300,000 cm **37.** ■ mL = 0.5 kL

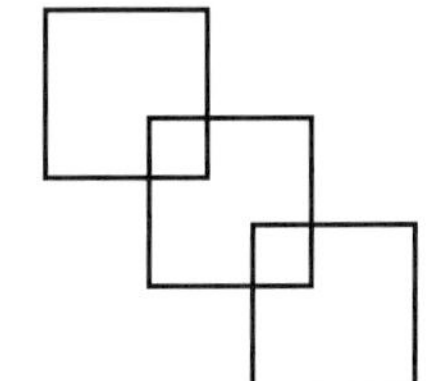

38. **Stretch Your Thinking** Draw the three squares at the right without lifting your pencil from the paper, retracing, or crossing any lines.

39. **Nutrition** A cup of whole milk has 8.5 grams of fat. A cup of skim milk has 400 milligrams of fat. Find the difference in fat content per cup.

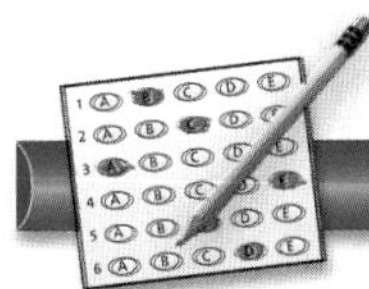

Test Prep

Multiple Choice

40. Which is NOT equivalent to the others?
A. 355.5 cm **B.** 35.55 m **C.** 0.03555 km **D.** 35,550 mm

41. Which mass is least?
F. 1,560 mg **G.** 13.2 kg **H.** 30,000 cg **I.** 7,428 g

42. Which container could hold 80,000 milliliters?
A. 0.5-kiloliter drum **B.** 500-milliliter beaker
C. 48-liter fuel tank **D.** 2-liter bottle

Extended Response

Take It to the NET
Online lesson quiz at
www.PHSchool.com
Web Code: aaa-0902

43. A bottle is supposed to contain 1 liter of juice. The table shows several quality control test measurements.
a. Write each measurement in liters.
b. Which measurement is closest to 1 liter?

Test #	Measurement
1	1,002.3 mL
2	100.1 cL
3	0.000997 kL

Mixed Review

Lesson 8-4

Name each triangle by its angles and its sides.

44. 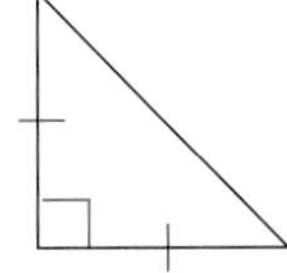

45. 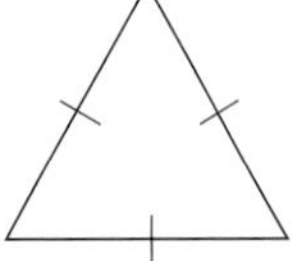

46. 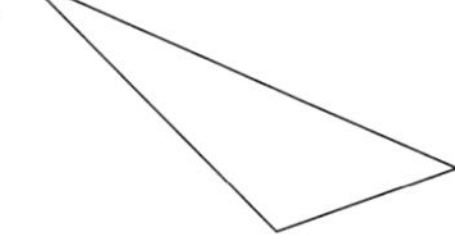

Lesson 6-5

Write each scale as a ratio in simplest form.

47. a 2-foot model of a 122-foot field

48. a 7-inch model of a 40-inch oven

9-3 Perimeters and Areas of Rectangles

What You'll Learn

 To estimate areas

 To find perimeters and areas of rectangles

. . . And Why

To install a fence, as in Example 2

Check Skills You'll Need

For help, go to Lesson 2-8.

Simplify each expression.

1. 16×7.5 **2.** 1.6^2 **3.** $2 \times (4 + 7)$

4. $2 \times 5.8 + 2 \times 9.1$ **5.** $7.2 + 7.2 + 1.3$ **6.** $\left(\frac{40}{4}\right)^2$

7. Use the order of operations to explain how to simplify $2 + (5^2 - 3)$.

New Vocabulary • area • perimeter

OBJECTIVE

 Interactive lesson includes instant self-check, tutorials, and activities.

1 Estimating Areas of Irregular Shapes by Using Squares

The **area** of a figure is the number of square units the figure contains. You can estimate the area of any figure by using a grid and counting the number of squares it covers.

1 EXAMPLE Estimating the Area of an Irregular Shape

Gary South Bend Fort Wayne INDIANA Indianapolis Columbus Evansville

Estimate the area of the state of Indiana. Each square represents 5,760 square kilometers.

Count squares that are full, almost full, about half full, or almost empty.

13 ← Thirteen squares are full.

2 ← Two squares are almost full, and two are almost empty.

$\left(3 \times \frac{1}{2}\right) = 1\frac{1}{2}$ ← Three squares are about half full.

$16\frac{1}{2}$ ← Total number of squares

About $16\frac{1}{2}$ or 16.5 squares are covered. Each square represents 5,760 square kilometers. So, the area of Indiana is about $16.5 \times 5,760$, or 95,040 square kilometers.

Check Understanding **1** Estimate the area of the lake. Each square represents 9 square miles.

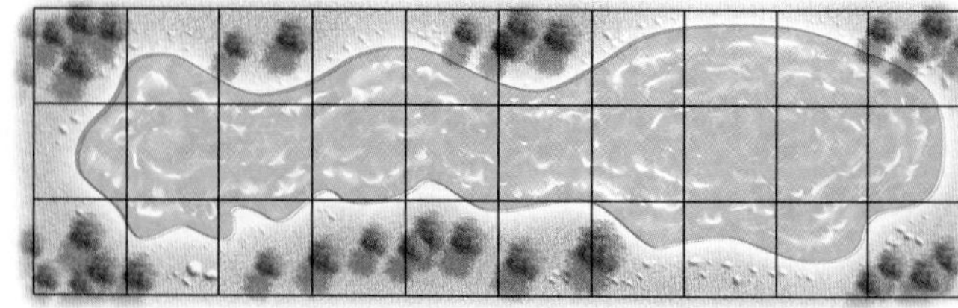

OBJECTIVE

2 Finding Perimeters and Areas of Rectangles

The **perimeter** of a figure is the distance around the figure. You can find the perimeter P of a rectangle by adding each length ℓ and width w. You can use the sum of lengths and widths to develop a formula for the perimeter of a rectangle.

$$P = \ell + \ell + w + w$$

$$= 2\ell + 2w \quad \leftarrow \text{Add the 2 lengths } \ell \text{ and add the 2 widths } w.$$

$$= 2(\ell + w) \quad \leftarrow \text{Use the Distributive Property.}$$

You can find the area A of a rectangle by multiplying the length ℓ and the width w.

Key Concepts **Perimeter and Area of a Rectangle**

$P = 2(\ell + w)$

$A = \ell \times w$

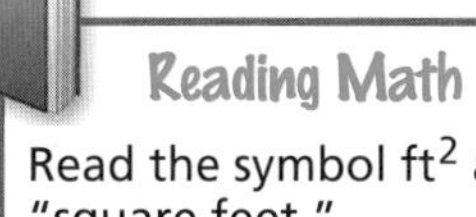

Reading Math

Read the symbol ft^2 as "square feet."

Common units for length and width are feet (ft), yards (yd), and meters (m). Common units for area are square feet (ft^2), square yards (yd^2), and square meters (m^2).

2 EXAMPLE Finding Perimeter and Area

Real-World Connection

A gardener needs to know the area of a garden to determine available space for plants.

Landscaping Mr. Vostal is planting a garden and installing a fence around his rectangular backyard. Find the perimeter and area of his backyard.

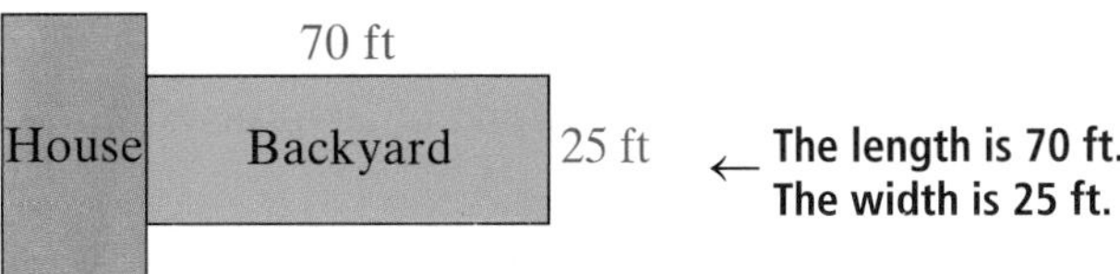

← The length is 70 ft. The width is 25 ft.

$P = 2(\ell + w)$ ← Use the formula for perimeter.

$= 2(70 + 25)$ ← Substitute 70 for ℓ and 25 for w.

$= 2 \times 95$ ← Add.

$= 190$ ← Multiply.

$A = \ell \times w$ ← Use the formula for area.

$= 70 \times 25$ ← Substitute 70 for ℓ and 25 for w.

$= 1{,}750$ ← Multiply.

The perimeter is 190 feet. The area is 1,750 square feet.

Check Understanding 2 Find the perimeter and area of a rectangle with a length of 8 feet and a width of 5 feet.

A square is a rectangle with four sides of equal length. The perimeter of a square is 4 times the length of its side s, or $4s$. The area is $s \times s$, or s^2.

Key Concepts **Perimeter and Area of a Square**

Perimeter: $P = 4s$

Area: $A = s^2$

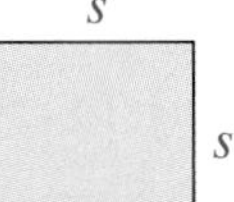

3 EXAMPLE Finding the Area of a Square

The perimeter of a square is 32 centimeters. Find its area.

Use the perimeter formula.

$$P = 4s$$
$$32 = 4s$$
$$\frac{32}{4} = \frac{4s}{4}$$
$$8 = s$$

Use the area formula.

$$A = s^2$$
$$= 8^2$$
$$= 64$$

The area of the square is 64 square centimeters, or 64 cm^2.

3 Find the area of each square given the side s or the perimeter P.

a. $s = 7$ inches **b.** $P = 24$ feet

More Than One Way

Leon and Lauren run laps around the school playground. The playground is 310 feet long and 215 feet wide. How many laps should Leon and Lauren run around the playground to run about 1 mile?

Leon's Method

I can draw a model of the playground and label each side. Then I'll add the four sides to find the length of one lap.

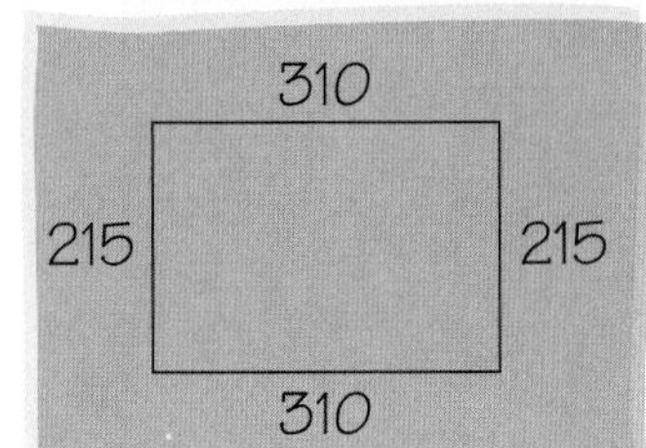

$310 + 215 + 310 + 215 = 1{,}050$

So, each lap I run is 1,050 feet. Since 1 mile contains 5,280 feet, I must divide to find the number of laps I should run.

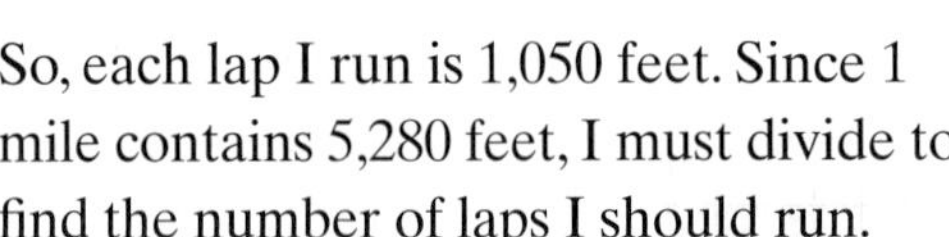

$5{,}280 \div 1{,}050 \approx 5$

I should run 5 laps around the playground to run about 1 mile.

Lauren's Method

I can use the formula for perimeter. I'll substitute 310 feet for the length and 215 feet for the width.

$$\begin{aligned} P &= 2(\ell + w) \\ &= 2(310 + 215) \\ &= 2 \times 525 \\ &= 1{,}050 \end{aligned}$$

The perimeter of the playground is 1,050 feet. There are 5,280 feet in a mile. To find the number of laps I should run, I'll divide.

$$5{,}280 \div 1{,}050 \approx 5$$

I should run 5 laps around the playground to run about 1 mile.

Choose a Method

Baseball diamonds have the shape of a square. Major League diamonds are 90 feet on each side. Little League baseball diamonds are 60 feet on each side. What is the difference in running distance for a home run (once around the diamond) in each league? Describe your method.

EXERCISES

For more practice, see *Extra Practice.*

A Practice by Example

Example 1 (page 440)

Estimate the area of each figure. Each square represents 1 square inch.

1. 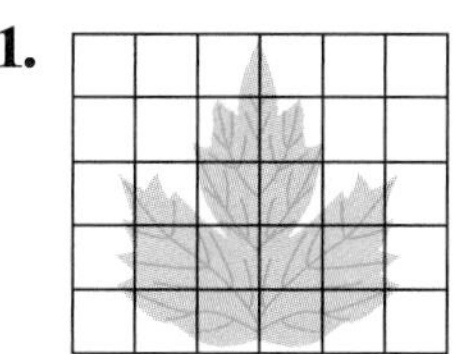

2. 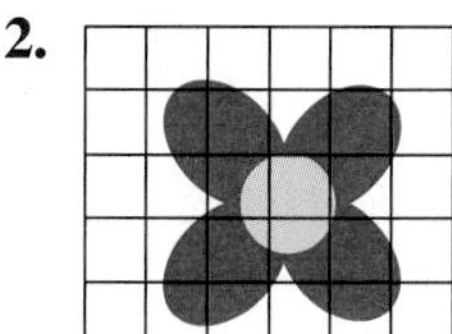

3. 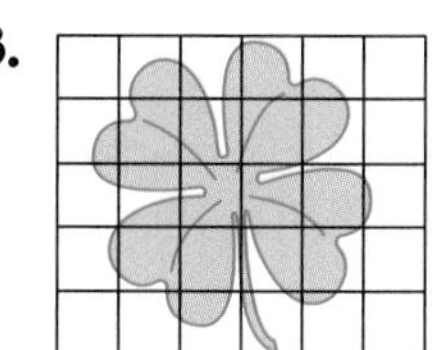

Estimate the area of each figure. Each square represents 4 square feet.

4. 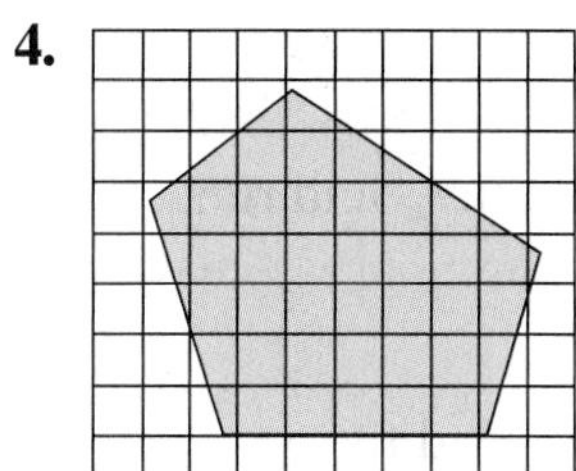

5. 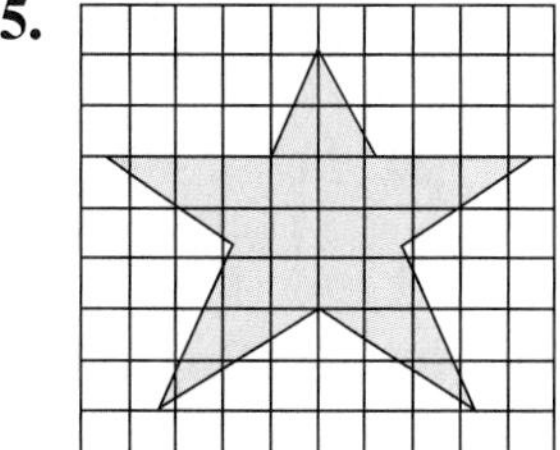

6. 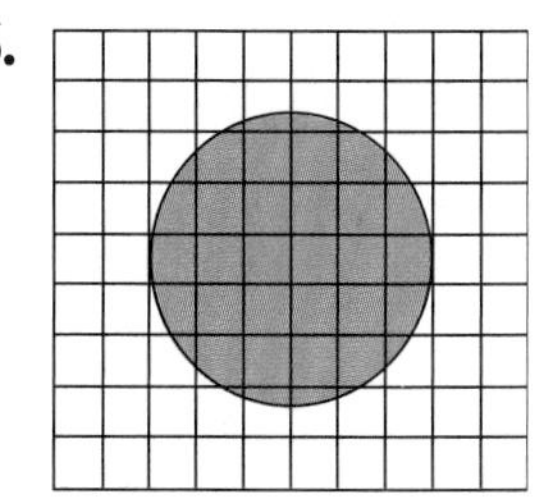

Find the perimeter and area of each rectangle.

7. 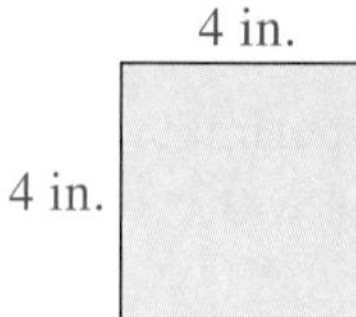

8. 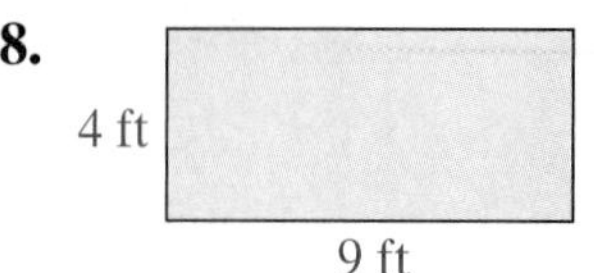

9. 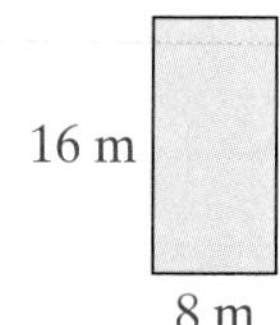

10. ℓ = 12 in., w = 7 in.

11. ℓ = 8 ft, w = 5 ft

12. ℓ = 13 in., w = 9.5 in.

13. ℓ = 1.5 m, w = 0.25 m

Example 3 (page 442)

Find the area of each square given the side s or the perimeter P.

14. s = 2 yd

15. s = 5 m

16. s = 14.2 ft

17. P = 20 cm

18. P = 48 in.

19. P = 10 mm

B Apply Your Skills

20. **Open-Ended** On graph paper, trace your hand with your fingers spread apart. Estimate the area of your hand.

21. **Stamps** The world's smallest stamp, shown at the left, measured 0.31 inch by 0.37 inch. Find the area of the stamp.

Real-World Connection
The world's smallest stamp was issued in Colombia from 1863 to 1866.

Use a centimeter ruler to measure the length and width of each rectangle to the nearest millimeter. Then find the perimeter and area.

22. 

23. 

24. 

25. a. Draw and label as many rectangles as you can with a perimeter of 24 units. Use only whole units.
 b. Find the area of each rectangle. Record your data in a table like the one shown below.

Length	Width	Perimeter	Area
11 units	1 unit	24 units	11 square units

 c. What do you notice about the rectangle with the greatest area?

26. **Number Sense** A rectangle has a length of 4.5 inches and a width of 3 inches. How would the areas change if you doubled both dimensions?

27. **Writing in Math** Suppose you know the area of a rectangle. Can you then find its perimeter? Use examples to explain why or why not.

28. **Recreation** The area of a rectangular swimming pool is 32 square meters. One side is 4 meters. What is the perimeter of the pool?

Find the perimeter and area of each rectangle.

29. $\ell = 2.8$ m, $w = 4.4$ m

30. $\ell = 5.6$ ft, $w = 8.7$ ft

31. $\ell = \frac{3}{4}$ in., $w = \frac{4}{5}$ in.

32. $\ell = 2\frac{1}{3}$ in., $w = 4\frac{1}{6}$ in.

C Challenge

33. **Reasoning** How many square feet are in a square yard? How many square inches are in a square yard? Justify your answer using diagrams.

34. **Stretch Your Thinking** At a food store, $\frac{1}{2}$ of the customers paid for their purchases by check. Of the remaining customers, $\frac{2}{3}$ paid with a credit card, and the rest paid cash. What fraction of the customers paid cash?

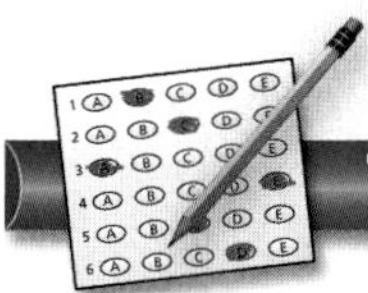

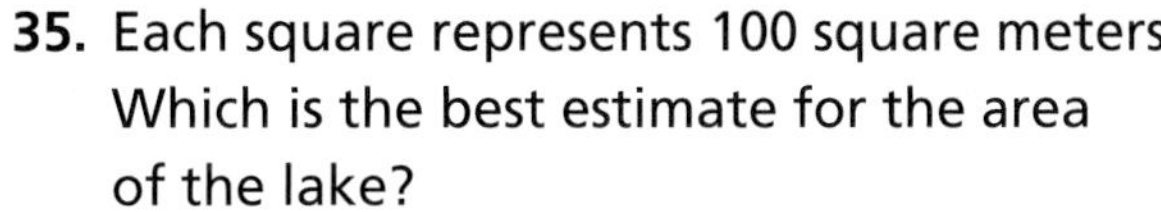

Test Prep

Multiple Choice

35. Each square represents 100 square meters. Which is the best estimate for the area of the lake?

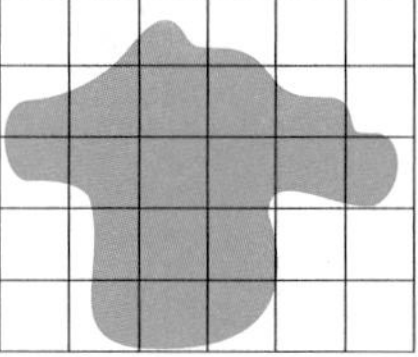

A. 14.5 m^2
B. 150 m^2
C. 1,400 m^2
D. 3,000 m^2

Take It to the NET
Online lesson quiz at
www.PHSchool.com
Web Code: aaa-0903

36. A square has an area of 25 square meters. What is its perimeter?
F. 5 meters
G. 6.25 meters
H. 20 meters
I. 25 meters

37. Wanda would like a garden with an area of 18 square feet. Her garden space is 6 feet long. How wide should she make the garden?
A. 3 feet
B. 48 feet
C. 54 feet
D. 108 feet

Short Response

38. The area of a movie screen is 576 square feet. The ratio of the area of the screen to its width is 16 : 1. **(a)** Write a proportion to find the width of the screen. **(b)** Solve your proportion.

Mixed Review

Lesson 6-6

Write each fraction as a percent.

39. $\frac{3}{4}$

40. $\frac{17}{25}$

41. $\frac{13}{20}$

42. $\frac{2}{5}$

43. $\frac{23}{50}$

Lesson 6-5

44. A map's scale is 1 centimeter : 10 kilometers. How many centimeters on the map represent an actual distance of 25 kilometers?

9-4 Areas of Parallelograms and Triangles

What You'll Learn

To find the areas of parallelograms and triangles

To find the areas of complex figures

. . . And Why

To find the area of a plot of land, as in Example 2

Check Skills You'll Need

For help, go to Lesson 8-5.

Write all the possible names for each quadrilateral. Then give the best name.

1. 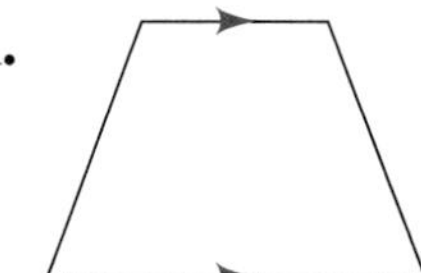

2. 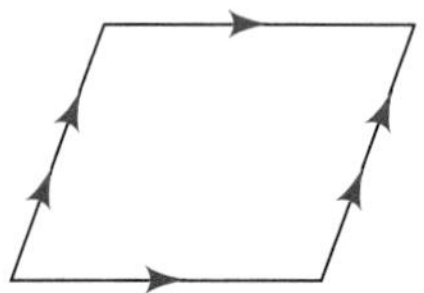

3. 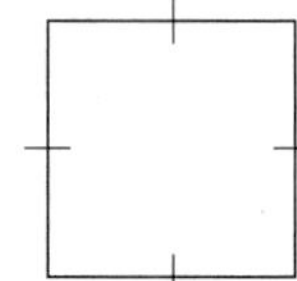

New Vocabulary

- base of a parallelogram
- height of a parallelogram
- base of a triangle
- height of a triangle

Interactive lesson includes instant self-check, tutorials, and activities.

OBJECTIVE

1 Finding the Areas of Parallelograms and Triangles

Investigation: Comparing Areas

- On graph paper, draw a parallelogram that is not a rectangle. Draw a perpendicular segment from one vertex to the base.

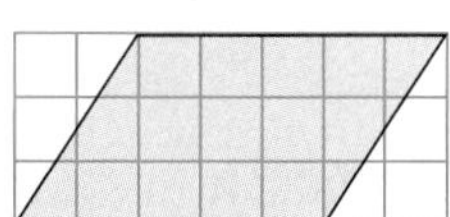

- Cut out the parallelogram. Cut along the perpendicular segment. Rearrange the two figures to form a rectangle.

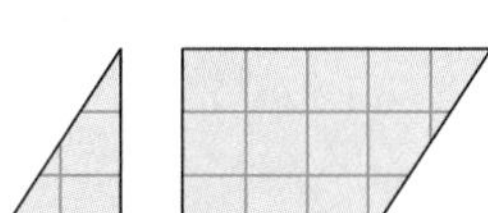

1. a. What is the area of the rectangle?

b. What do you think was the area of the original parallelogram?

c. Repeat this activity. Make two different-sized parallelograms. Are the results similar?

Any side can be considered the **base of a parallelogram.** The **height of a parallelogram** is the perpendicular distance from one base to another. The area of a parallelogram is the product of the base and the height.

Key Concepts — Area of a Parallelogram

$A = b \times h$

1 EXAMPLE Finding the Area of a Parallelogram

Find the area of the parallelogram.

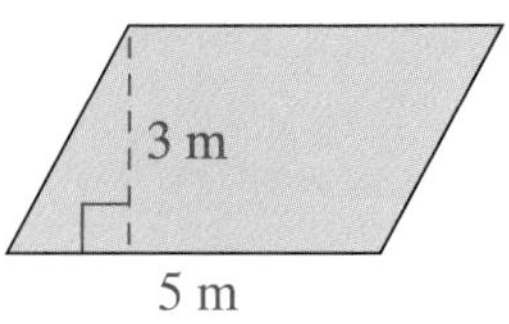

$A = b \times h$ ← Use the formula for the area of a parallelogram.

$= 5 \times 3$ ← Substitute 5 for *b* and 3 for *h*.

$= 15$ ← Simplify.

The area of the parallelogram is 15 square meters.

Check Understanding 1 Find the area of each parallelogram given the base *b* and the height *h*.

a. $b = 14$ m, $h = 5$ m **b.** $b = 30$ ft, $h = 17.3$ ft

Any side can be the **base of a triangle.** The **height of a triangle** is the length of the perpendicular segment from a vertex to the base opposite that vertex.

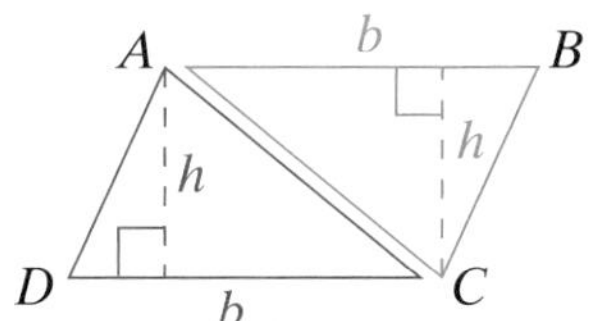

The area of a triangle is half of the area of a parallelogram with the same base length and height.

Key Concepts Area of a Triangle

$A = \frac{1}{2}b \times h$

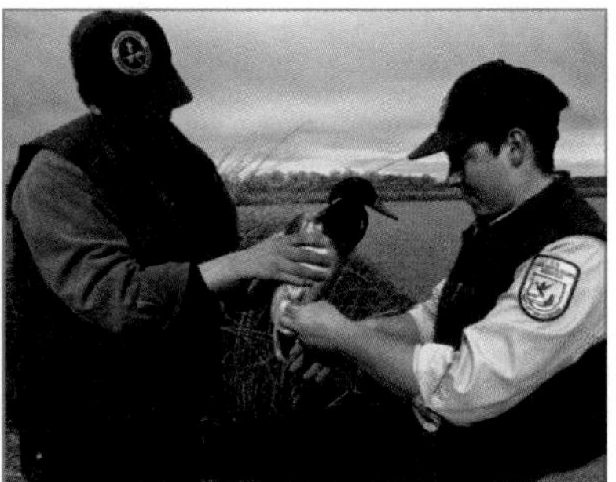

Real-World Connection

Conservation groups buy land to preserve its natural state.

2 EXAMPLE Finding the Area of a Triangle

Conservation A conservation group plans to buy a triangular plot of land. A diagram of the plot is shown at the right. What is the area of the plot?

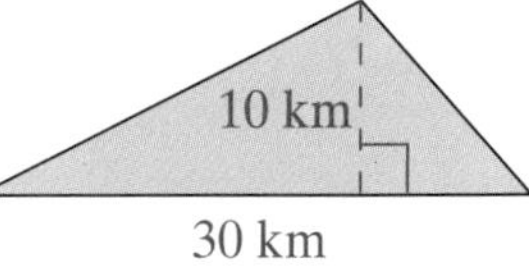

$A = \frac{1}{2}b \times h$ ← Use the formula for the area of a triangle.

$= \frac{1}{2} \times 30 \times 10$ ← Substitute 30 for *b* and 10 for *h*.

$= 150$ ← Simplify.

The area of the plot is 150 square kilometers.

Check Understanding 2 **a.** A triangle has a base of 30 meters and a height of 17.3 meters. Find its area.

b. **Number Sense** Suppose the base of the triangular plot of land in Example 2 were doubled. How would the area of the plot change?

OBJECTIVE

2 Finding the Areas of Complex Figures

Sometimes it helps to split a figure into smaller polygons. Then you can find the area of each polygon and add.

3 EXAMPLE Finding the Area of a Complex Figure

Find the area of the figure below.

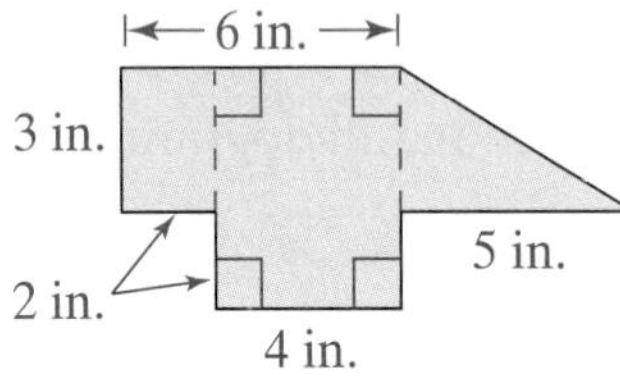

← **Split the polygon into two rectangles and a triangle, as shown by the dashed lines.**

Area of smaller rectangle: $3 \times 2 = 6$, or 6 in.^{2}

Area of larger rectangle: $5 \times 4 = 20$, or 20 in.^{2} ← **Find the area of each polygon.**

Area of triangle: $\frac{1}{2}(5 \times 3) = \frac{1}{2} \times 15$, or 7.5 in.^{2}

The total area is $6 + 20 + 7.5$, or 33.5 square inches.

Check Understanding 3 **a.** Find the area of the complex figure at the right.

b. Reasoning Show another way to split the figure in Example 3 to find the area.

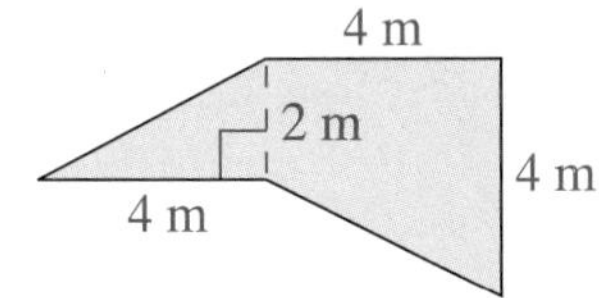

EXERCISES

Find the area of each parallelogram. Exercise 1 has been started for you.

Example 1 (page 447)

1. 3 ft, 8 ft

$A = b \times h = 8 \times 3$

2.

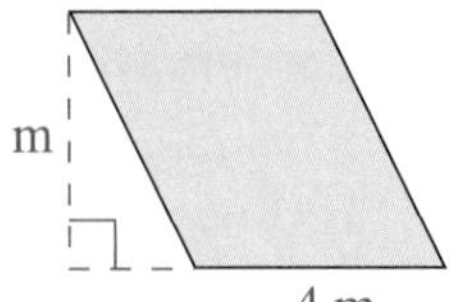

3.

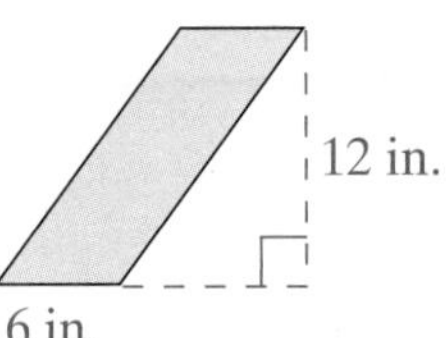

Find the area of each triangle. Exercise 4 has been started for you.

Example 2 (page 447)

4.

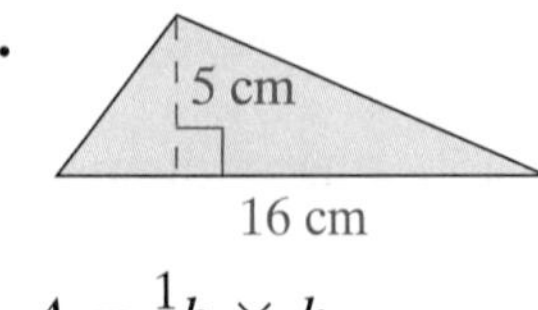

$A = \frac{1}{2}b \times h$

$= \frac{1}{2} \times 16 \times 5$

5.

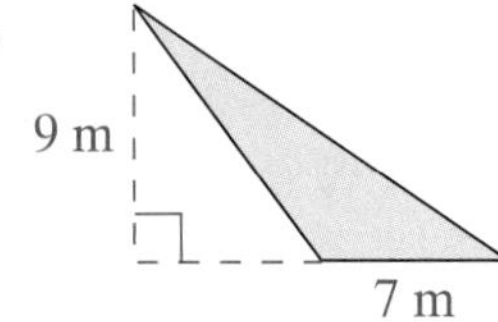

6.

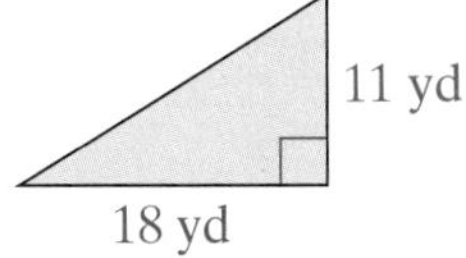

7. **Art** Kaitlyn is sprinkling glitter on a card. The area where she has applied the glue is a triangle with a base of 5 centimeters and a height of 10 centimeters. How large is the area she plans to glitter?

Example 3 (page 448)

Find the area of each complex figure.

8. 9.

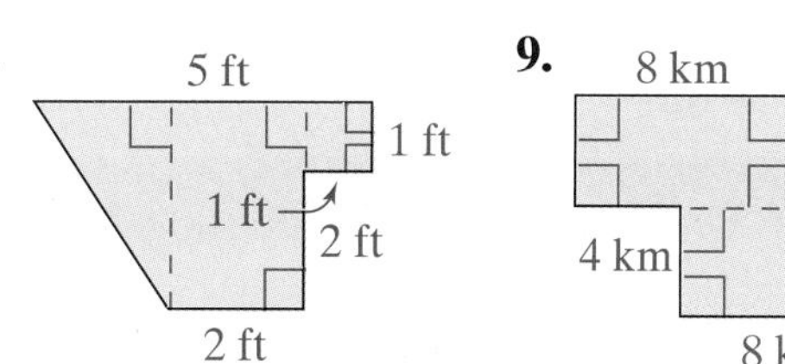

10.

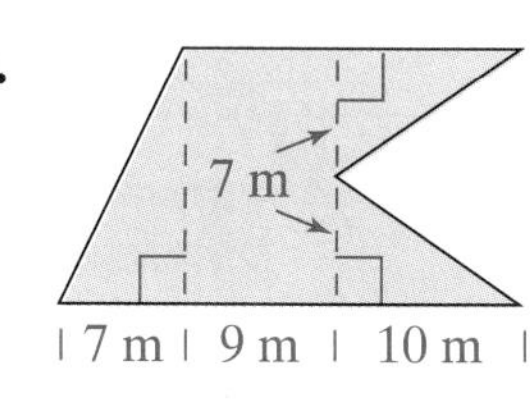

B Apply Your Skills

11. **Food** A triangular cracker has a base length of 4 centimeters and a height of 3.5 centimeters. What is the area of the cracker?

Real-World Connection

Parking spaces are sometimes shaped like parallelograms.

12. **Parking** Each space at the left has a base of 8.5 feet and a height of 22 feet. Find the area of a parking space.

Find the area of each figure.

13.

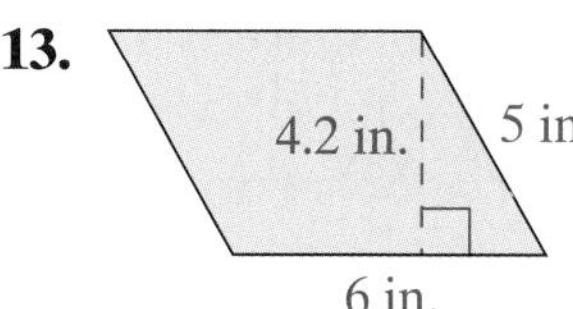

14.

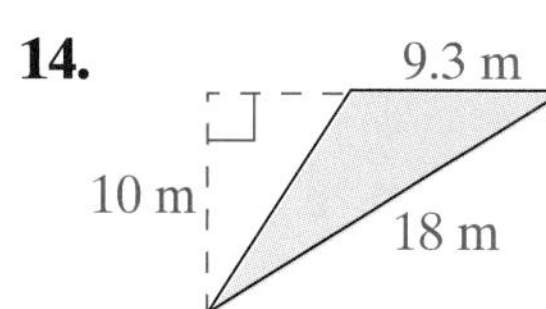

15.

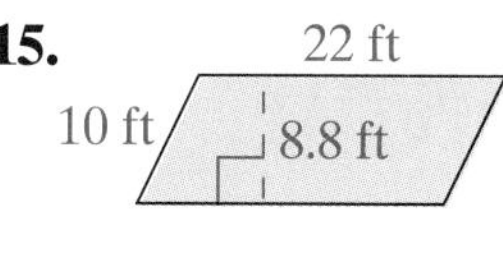

16.

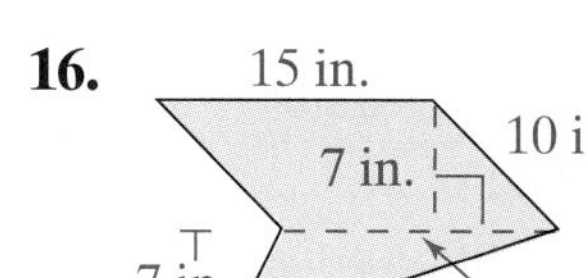

17.

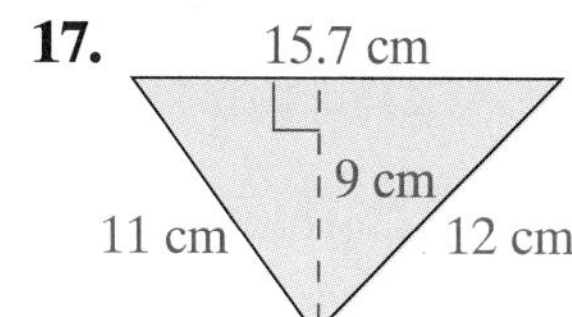

18.

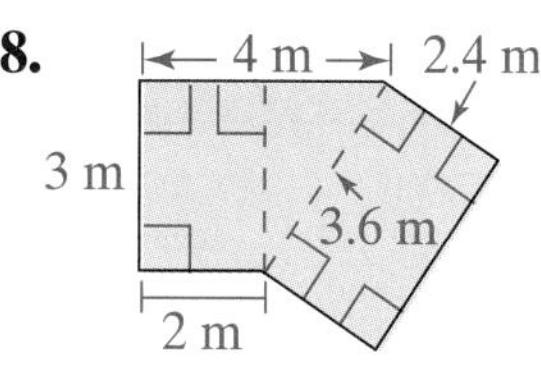

Find the area of a parallelogram and a triangle with the given dimensions.

19. $b = 4$ ft, $h = 9$ ft

20. $b = 20$ yd, $h = 34$ yd

21. $b = 3.5$ m, $h = 7$ m

22. $b = 5.3$ ft, $h = 6.5$ ft

23. **Number Sense** Two parallelograms have the same base length. The height of the first is half the height of the second. What is the ratio of the area of the smaller parallelogram to the area of the larger one?

24. **Writing in Math** Suppose you know the perimeter and the height of an equilateral triangle. Explain how you would find the area of the triangle.

25. **Algebra** A parallelogram has an area of 66 square inches and a base length of 5 inches. What is the height of the parallelogram?

Challenge

26. Draw the trapezoid at the right. Split it into two triangles with 3-centimeter heights. Then find the area of the trapezoid.

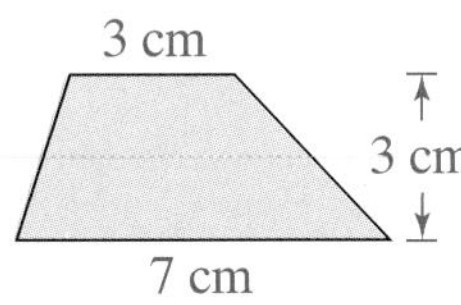

27. **Stretch Your Thinking** An 8-foot wide walkway surrounds a rectangular pool that is 20 feet by 30 feet. Find the area of the walkway.

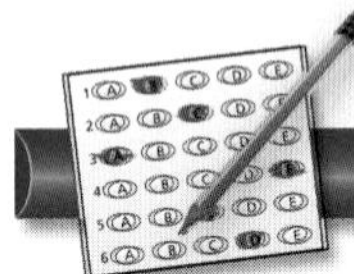

Test Prep

Multiple Choice

28. What is the area of the figure at the right in square feet?
A. 7 B. 8 C. 9 D. 10

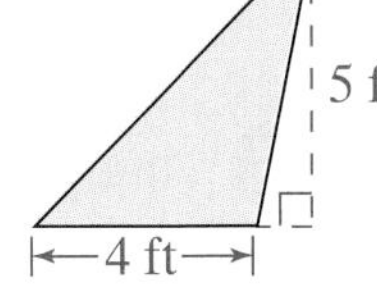

29. A parallelogram has a height of 6 inches and a base length of 8.5 inches. What is its area?
F. 2.5 $in.^2$ G. 14.5 $in.^2$ H. 25.5 $in.^2$ I. 51 $in.^2$

Take It to the NET
Online lesson quiz at www.PHSchool.com
Web Code: aaa-0904

30. A triangle has an area of 42 square meters and a base length of 7 meters. What is the height of the triangle?
A. 6 m B. 7 m C. 12 m D. 14 m

Short Response

31. The area of a rectangular space is 128 square feet.
a. Find all the possible pairs of whole-number dimensions in feet.
b. Explain which pair allows enough space for a car to park.

Mixed Review

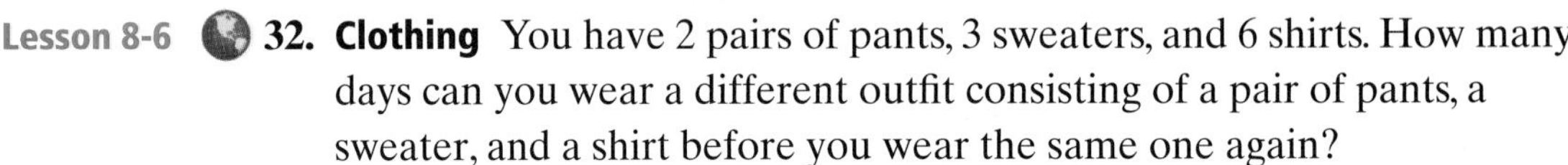

Lesson 8-6

32. **Clothing** You have 2 pairs of pants, 3 sweaters, and 6 shirts. How many days can you wear a different outfit consisting of a pair of pants, a sweater, and a shirt before you wear the same one again?

Lesson 6-7

Find each answer.

33. 50% of 492 34. 35% of 84 35. 15% of 120 36. 11% of 500

Checkpoint Quiz 1 — Lessons 9-1 through 9-4

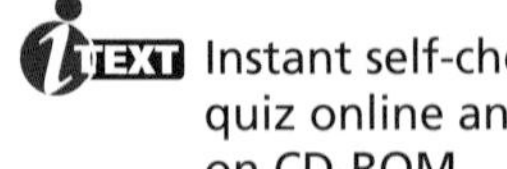

Instant self-check quiz online and on CD-ROM

Convert each measurement to meters, liters, or grams.

1. 62 milliliters 2. 4.3 kilograms 3. 178 centimeters

Find the area of a figure with the given dimensions.

4. square: $s = 8.5$ cm 5. triangle: $b = 4$ mi, $h = 9$ mi

Exploring Circles

For Use With Lesson 9-5

Recall that the perimeter of a figure is the distance around the figure. In Lesson 9-3, you learned the formula for the perimeter of a rectangle and a square. In this Investigation, you will explore the distance around a circle.

Activity

Materials: several circular objects, metric tape measure

1. Find several circular objects, such as a can or a wastebasket.

2. Copy the table shown below.

Object	Distance around the circle	Distance across the circle	$\frac{\text{Distance around the circle}}{\text{Distance across the circle}}$

3. Measure the longest distance across each circle to the nearest tenth. Record the results in your table.

4. Measure the distance around each circle by wrapping the tape measure around the outside of each circle. Measure to the nearest tenth. Record the results in your table.

5. **Calculator** Find the ratio $\frac{\text{distance around the circle}}{\text{distance across the circle}}$ for each circle to the nearest tenth. Record the results in your table.

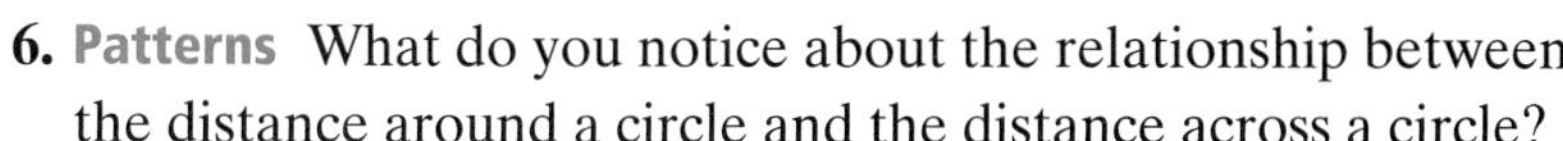

6. **Patterns** What do you notice about the relationship between the distance around a circle and the distance across a circle?

7. **Algebra** Suppose the distance across a circle is x. Write an expression to find the distance around the circle.

8. a. In the diagram at the right, the distance across the circle is the same as the side length of a square. Use your expression from Exercise 7 to estimate the distance around the circle.

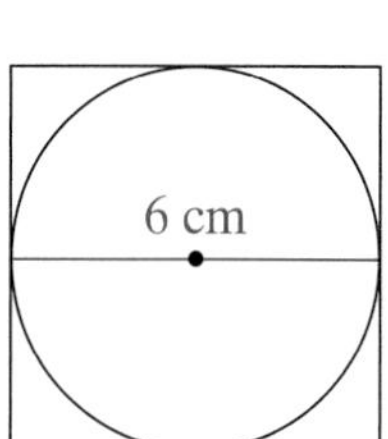

b. Find the perimeter of the square.

c. What is the difference between the distance around the circle and the perimeter of the square?

9-5 Circles and Circumference

What You'll Learn

To identify parts of a circle

To find circumference

. . . And Why

To find the circumference of an archery target, as in Example 3

Check Skills You'll Need

For help, go to Lesson 1-7.

Find each product.

1. 2×3.14 **2.** 3.14×8 **3.** 3.14×50

4. $2 \times 3.14 \times 35$ **5.** 3.14×12 **6.** $2 \times 3.14 \times 10$

New Vocabulary

- circle
- radius
- chord
- diameter
- circumference

Interactive lesson includes instant self-check, tutorials, and activities.

OBJECTIVE 1 Identifying Parts of a Circle

A **circle** is the set of points in a plane that are the same distance from a given point called the *center*. A circle is named after its center point.

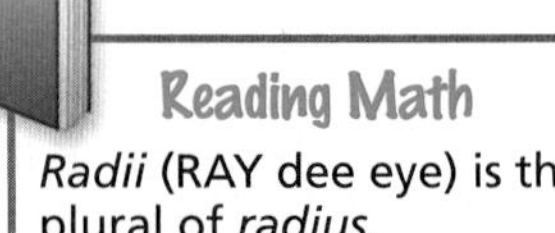

Reading Math

Radii (RAY dee eye) is the plural of *radius.*

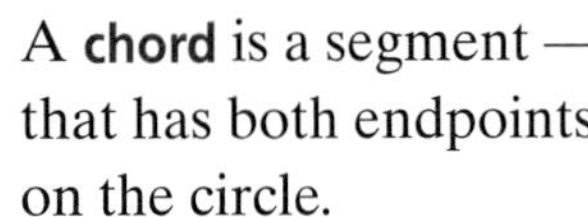

1 EXAMPLE Identifying Parts of a Circle

a. List the radii shown in circle P.

The radii are $\overline{PA}$, $\overline{PB}$, $\overline{PC}$, and $\overline{PD}$.

b. List the chords shown in circle P.

The chords are $\overline{AB}$, $\overline{BC}$, $\overline{CD}$, $\overline{DA}$, $\overline{AC}$, and $\overline{BD}$.

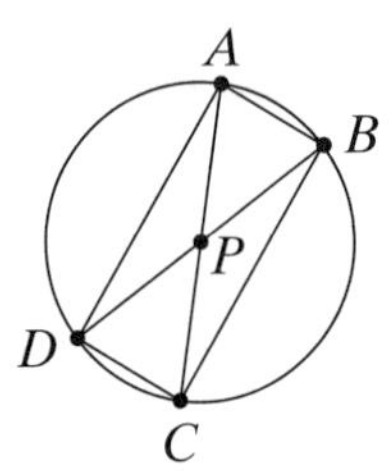

Check Understanding 1 List the diameters shown in circle P.

In Example 1, the diameter $\overline{AC}$ consists of two radii $\overline{PA}$ and $\overline{PC}$. So, the length of a diameter of a circle is twice the length of a radius. Of course, this means that the radius is half the length of a diameter!

2 EXAMPLE Finding Radius and Diameter

Amusement Parks The diameter of a Ferris wheel is 250 feet. How long is its radius?

$r = \frac{1}{2} \times 250$ ← **The radius is half the diameter.**

$= 125$ ← **Simplify.**

The radius of the Ferris wheel is 125 feet.

Check Understanding 2 Find the unknown length for a circle with the given dimension.

a. $d = 8$ cm, $r = ■$ **b.** $r = 10$ in., $d = ■$

OBJECTIVE

2 Finding Circumference

The distance around a circle is its **circumference.** The ratio of the circumference C of a circle to its diameter d is the same for *every* circle. The symbol π (read "pi") represents this ratio. So, $\pi = \frac{C}{d}$.

Pi is a nonrepeating, nonterminating decimal. Two approximations for π are 3.14 and $\frac{22}{7}$. Use $\frac{22}{7}$ when measurements are a multiple of 7 or use fractions. You can also use the π key on a calculator.

You can rewrite the relationship $\pi = \frac{C}{d}$ as $C = \pi \times d$, or πd.

Key Concepts **Circumference of a Circle**

$C = \pi d$

$C = 2\pi r$

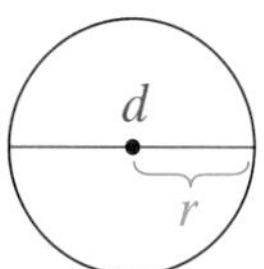

3 EXAMPLE Finding the Circumference of a Circle

Archery A regulation archery target has a circle with a 48-inch diameter. Find the circumference of a regulation target to the nearest inch.

$C = \pi d$ ← **Use the formula for the circumference of a circle.**

$= \pi \times 48$ ← **Substitute 48 for *d*.**

≈ 150.79645 ← **Use a calculator.**

The circumference of a regulation target is about 151 inches.

Check Understanding 3 Find the circumference of a circle with a diameter of 5.8 centimeters. Round to the nearest centimeter.

EXERCISES

For more practice, see *Extra Practice*.

A Practice by Example

Example 1 (page 452)

List each of the following for circle Q.

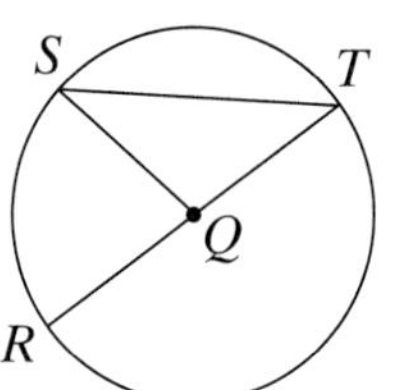

1. three radii **2.** one diameter **3.** two chords

Example 2 (page 453)

Find the unknown length for a circle with the given dimension.

4. $r = 35$ mi, $d = ■$ **5.** $d = 6.8$ yd, $r = ■$

6. $r = 18$ ft, $d = ■$ **7.** $d = 0.25$ km, $r = ■$

Example 3 (page 453)

Find the circumference of each circle. Round to the nearest unit. Exercise 8 has been started for you.

8. 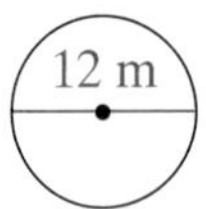

$C = \pi d$
$C = \pi(12)$

9. 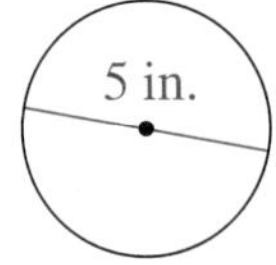

10. 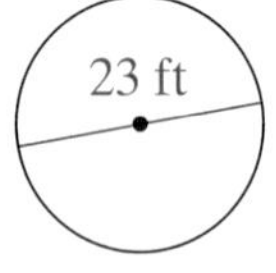

11. 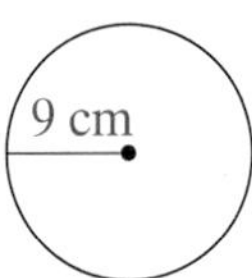

12. 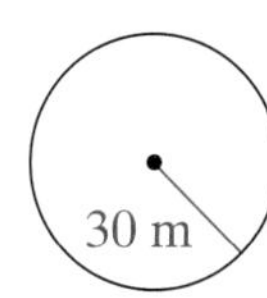

13. 

14. Tanks A circular water tank has a radius of 3.9 meters. What is the circumference of the tank?

B Apply Your Skills

Find the circumference of each circle with the given radius or diameter. Use $\frac{22}{7}$ for π.

15. $d = 28$ mi **16.** $r = 7$ ft **17.** $d = 14$ m **18.** $r = \frac{5}{8}$ mi

19. Hoops A dog trainer uses hoops with diameters of 24 and 30 inches. What is the difference between their circumferences? Use 3 for π.

Find the radius and diameter of a circle with the given circumference. Round to the nearest tenth.

20. 192 ft **21.** 1,273 m **22.** 3.75 in. **23.** 12.4 mi

24. Writing in Math A pebble got stuck in a bicycle's tire and left a mark in the track made by the tire every 69 inches. Explain how you would find the circumference of the tire.

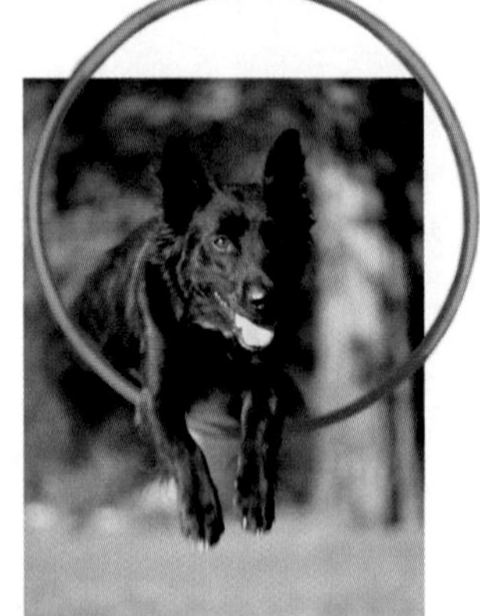

Real-World Connection
Dogs can jump through hoops that are only a little larger than their bodies.

25. **Math in the Media** Read the cartoon below.

Foxtrot *by Bill Amend*

a. Use the value of π from the cartoon to find the circumference of a circle with a diameter of 48 inches.

b. **Reasoning** How many more pumpkins are needed to finish the "pumpkin pi"? Explain your answer.

C Challenge

26. **Bicycles** The diameter of a bicycle wheel is 3 feet. How far will the bicycle travel when the wheel makes one full turn?

27. **Stretch Your Thinking** You fold a square sheet of paper in half. Then you cut along the fold. The perimeter of each of the rectangles formed is 18 inches. What was the area of the original square sheet of paper?

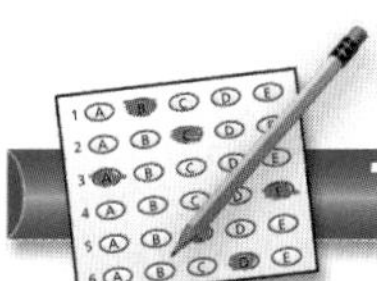

Test Prep

Gridded Response

28. What is the radius of a circle with a diameter of 8.46 kilometers? Round to the nearest hundredth kilometer.

29. The diameter of a circle is 2.24 centimeters. What is the circumference of the circle to the nearest hundredth centimeter?

Take It to the NET
Online lesson quiz at
www.PHSchool.com
Web Code: aaa-0905

30. The circumference of the circle is 11 meters. What is the diameter of the circle to the nearest tenth meter?

31. The circumference of a circle is 48 inches. Suppose the radius of the circle is doubled. What is the new circumference to the nearest inch?

Mixed Review

Lesson 7-1 **Find the median of each data set.**

32. 50, 20, 42, 45, 48, 50

33. 8.0, 7.5, 6.6, 7.8, 7.5

Lesson 6-8

34. Estimate a 15% tip for a $35.90 restaurant bill.

9-6 Area of a Circle

What You'll Learn

To find the area of a circle

. . . And Why

To find the area of a mirror, as in Example 2

✓ Check Skills You'll Need

For help, go to Lesson 2-8.

Simplify each expression.

1. 7^2 **2.** 5^2 **3.** $(7 - 3)^2$

4. $(6 + 4)^2$ **5.** $9 + 3^2$ **6.** 12^2

OBJECTIVE

Interactive lesson includes instant self-check, tutorials, and activities.

1 Finding the Area of a Circle

Suppose you cut a circle into equal-sized wedges. You can rearrange the wedges into a figure that resembles a parallelogram.

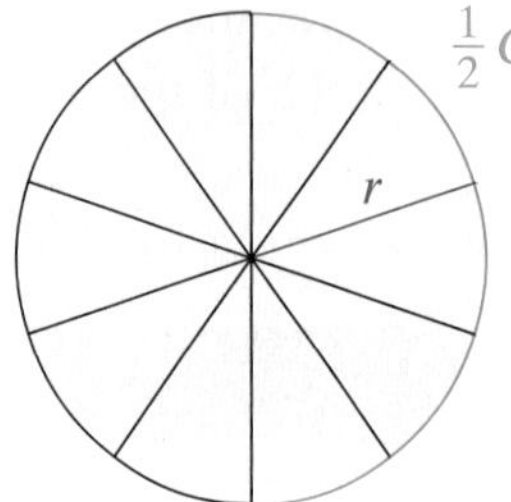

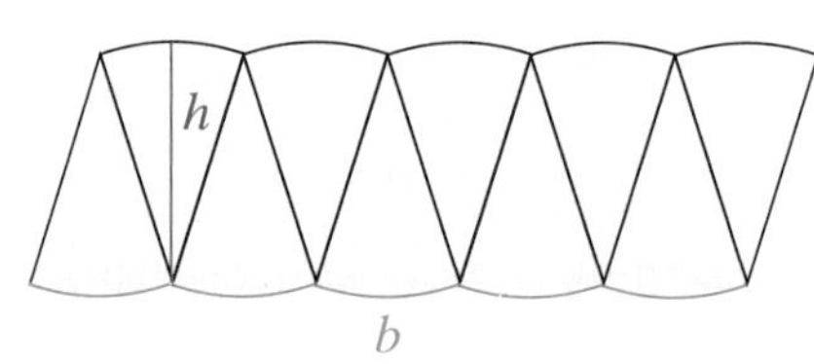

The base of the parallelogram is half the circumference of the circle, or πr. The height of the parallelogram is the same length as the circle's radius.

Need Help?
For help finding the area of a parallelogram, go to Lesson 9-4.

$A = b \times h$ ← **Use the formula for the area of a parallelogram.**

$= \pi r \times r$ ← **Substitute πr for b and r for h.**

$= \pi r^2$ ← **Simplify.**

This suggests a formula for the area of a circle.

Key Concepts **Area of a Circle**

$A = \pi r^2$

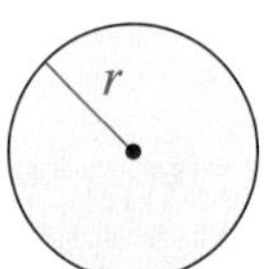

When you are estimating to check for reasonableness, you can use 3 for the value of π.

1 EXAMPLE Finding the Area of a Circle

Find the area of the circle at the right.

5 ft

Estimate Use 3 for π. So, $A \approx 3 \times 5^2$, or 75 square feet.

$A = \pi r^2$ ← **Use the formula for the area of a circle.**

$= \pi \times 5^2$ ← **Substitute 5 for *r*.**

≈ 78.539816 ← **Use a calculator.**

≈ 78.5 ← **Round to the nearest tenth.**

The area is about 78.5 square feet.

Check for Reasonableness The estimate, 75 square feet, is close to 78.5 square feet. So the answer is reasonable.

Check Understanding 1 Find the area of each circle. Round to the nearest tenth.

a.

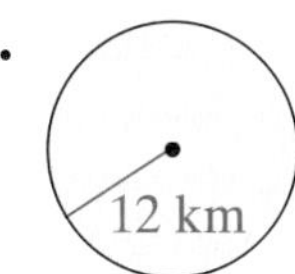

b.

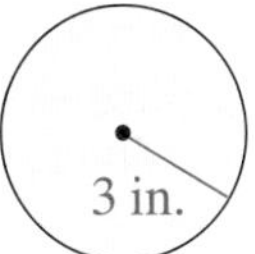

c.

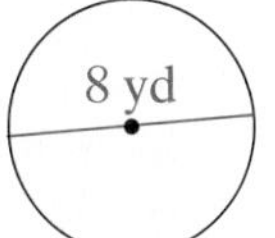

When the radius or diameter of a circle is a multiple of 7 or a fraction, you might want to use $\frac{22}{7}$ for π.

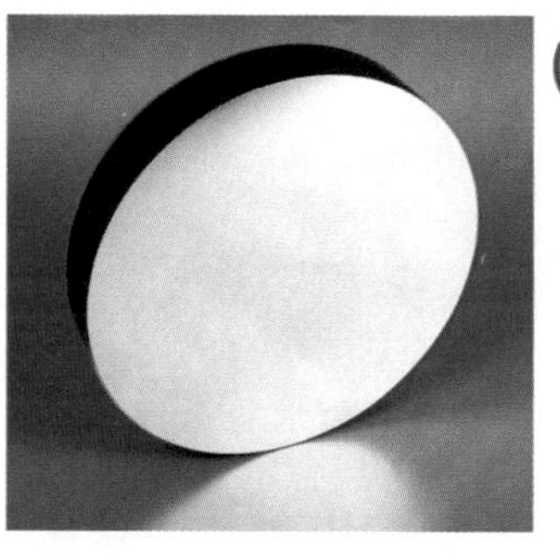

Real-World Connection

Circular mirrors are used to build telescopes.

2 EXAMPLE Real-World Problem Solving

Mirrors Find the area of the circular mirror at the left with a diameter of 14 inches. Use $\frac{22}{7}$ for π.

The radius is half of the diameter, or 7 inches.

$A = \pi r^2$ ← **Use the formula for the area of a circle.**

$\approx \frac{22}{7} \times 7^2$ ← **Use $\frac{22}{7}$ for π and 7 for *r*.**

$= \frac{22}{{}_1\cancel{7}} \times \cancel{49}^7$ ← **Divide 7 and 49 by their GCF, 7.**

$= 154$ ← **Multiply.**

The area of the mirror is about 154 square inches.

Check Understanding 2 Find the area of each circle. Use $\frac{22}{7}$ for π.

a.

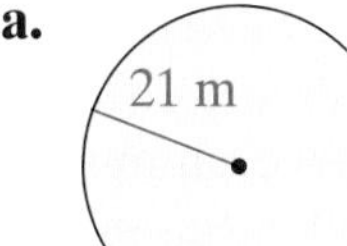

b.

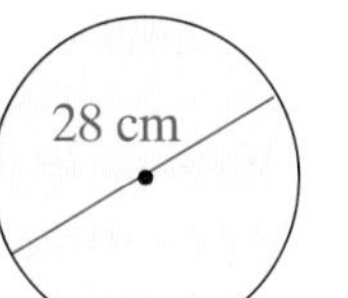

c.

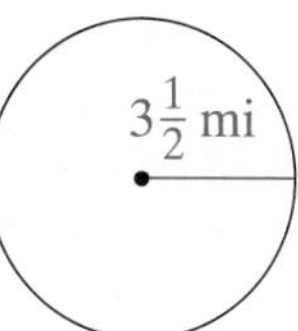

d. Find the area of a 14-inch large pizza. Use $\frac{22}{7}$ for π.

EXERCISES

For more practice, see *Extra Practice.*

A Practice by Example

Example 1
page 457

Find the area of each circle. Round to the nearest tenth. Exercise 1 has been started for you.

1. 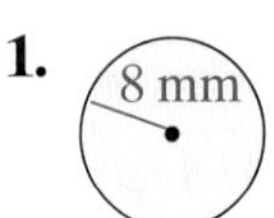

$A = \pi r^2$
$= \pi \times 4^2$

2. 25 in.

3. 37 ft

4. 26 km

5. 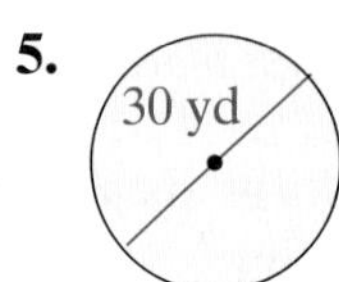

6. 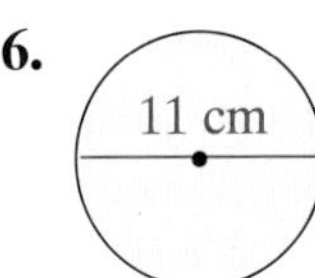

Example 2
page 457

Find the area of each circle. Use $\frac{22}{7}$ for π.

7. $2\frac{1}{3}$ mm

8. 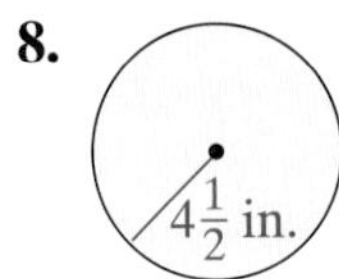

9. 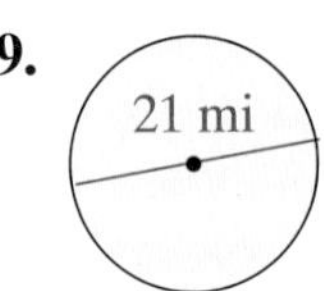

10. Camping Campers arrange stones in a circle around their campfire site. The circle has a diameter of 14 feet. Find the area of the site.

B Apply Your Skills

Mental Math **Estimate the area of each circle. Use 3 for π.**

11. $r = 2$ in. **12.** $d = 6$ mm **13.** $r = 20$ cm **14.** $d = 16$ ft

Find the area of each circle to the nearest tenth. Use 3.14 for π.

15. $r = 1.1$ mi **16.** $d = 2.4$ cm **17.** $r = 0.5$ m **18.** $d = 13.7$ ft

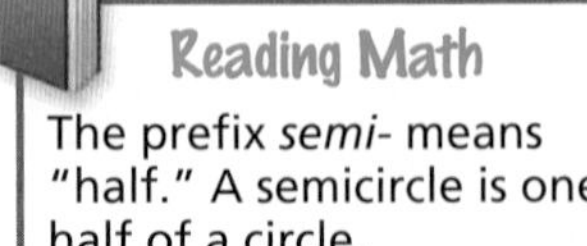

Reading Math

The prefix *semi-* means "half." A semicircle is one half of a circle.

19. Games The hopscotch drawing at the right is composed of squares and a semicircle. Suppose the side lengths of each square are 2 feet. Find the area of the hopscotch drawing.

7 8
6
4 5
3
2
1

20. Communications You can pick up the radio signal for station WAER FM 88 in Syracuse, New York, within a 45-mile radius of the station. What is the approximate area of the broadcast region? Use 3.14 for π.

21. Writing in Math Which is larger: a pan with a radius of 10 inches, or a pan with the same depth and a diameter of 18 inches? Explain.

22. Find the area of a circle with a circumference of 31.4 units.

Challenge **Find the area of each yellow region to the nearest square unit. Use 3.14 for π.**

23. 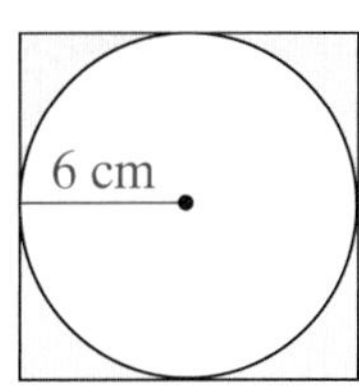

24. 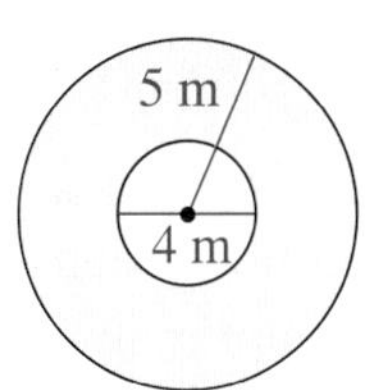

25. 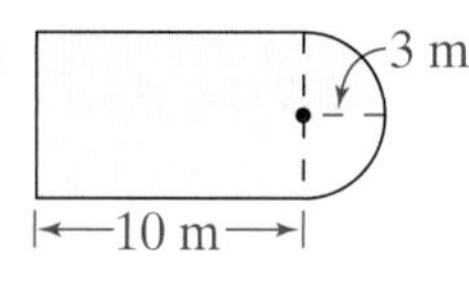

26. **Stretch Your Thinking** The diameter of a circle is tripled. How does this affect the area of the circle?

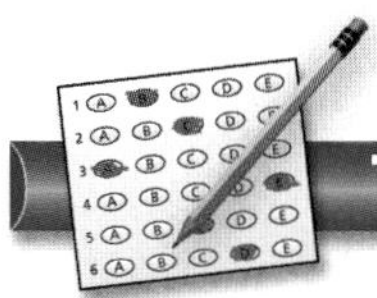

Test Prep

Reading Comprehension Read the passage and answer the questions below.

Follow the Sun

The Aztecs used their accurate knowledge of astronomy and mathematics to make a calendar called the Sun Stone. They carved the calendar on a circular stone 3.6 meters in diameter. The Aztecs began working on the calendar in 1427 and completed the work in 1479. The center circle of the stone shows the face of Tonatiuh, the Aztec sun god. The 20 squares in the second ring name the 20 days of each Aztec month. There were 18 Aztec months.

Take It to the NET
Online lesson quiz at **www.PHSchool.com**
Web Code: aaa-0906

27. Find the area of the Sun Stone. Use 3.14 for π.

28. How long did it take the Aztecs to complete the calendar?

29. How many days were in the Aztec calendar?

Multiple Choice

30. Which is the best value for the area of a circle with a diameter of 5.8 yards?
A. 18 yd^2 **B.** 26 yd^2 **C.** 36 yd^2 **D.** 108 yd^2

Mixed Review

Lesson 8-8 **How many lines of symmetry does each figure have?**

31. 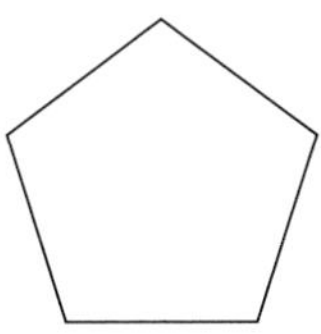

32. 

33. 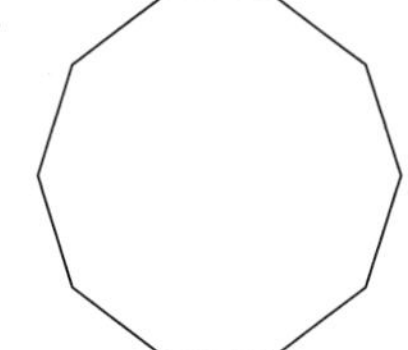

Reading Math Using Concept Maps to Connect Ideas

For Use With Lesson 9-6

One way to show connections among ideas is to draw a diagram called a concept map. The lines in a concept map connect related ideas.

EXAMPLE

Make a concept map with the terms from Chapter 8 related to transformations.

center of rotation
reflection
rotation
translation
transformation
line of reflection

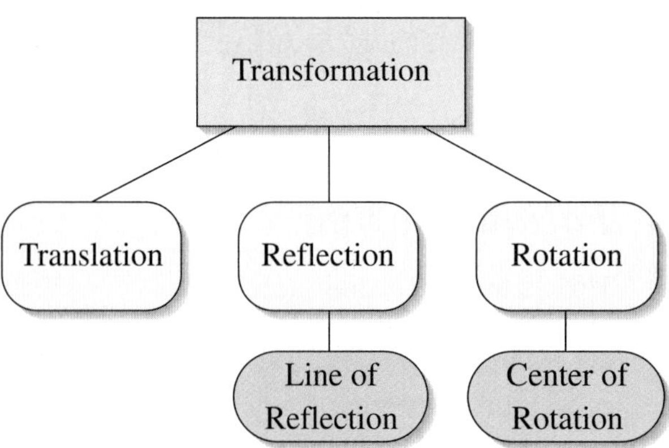

EXERCISES

1. Copy the concept map at the right. Fill in the ovals using the terms listed below. Include area formulas on your concept map.

area	triangle
parallelogram	rectangle
square	base
height	length
width	side
perpendicular	right angle

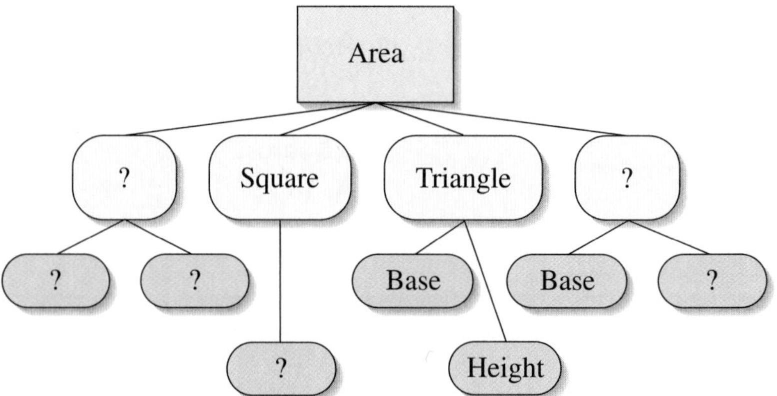

2. Use the list below to make a concept map for circles.

circle	circumference
radius	area of a circle
diameter	π

Investigation Views of Three-Dimensional Objects

For Use With Lesson 9-7

Stack 6 blocks as shown at the right. The number of blocks you can "see" depends on how you look at the stack. The *front view*, the *right side view*, and the *top view* of the stack of blocks are shown below.

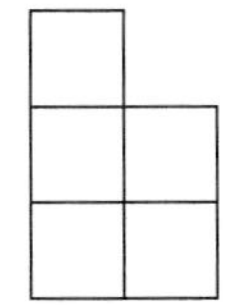

Front View

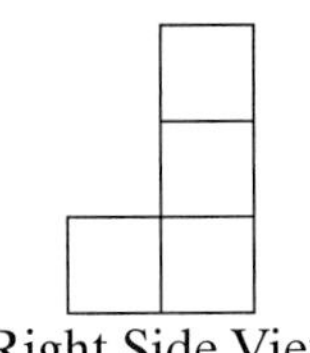

Right Side View

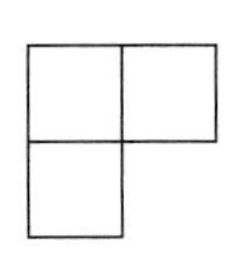

Top View

EXAMPLE

Use the drawings below. How many blocks are possible in the stack?

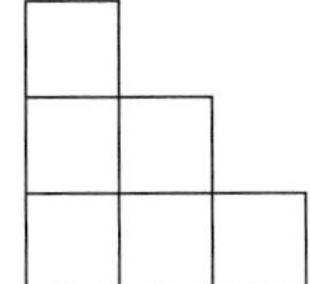

Front View

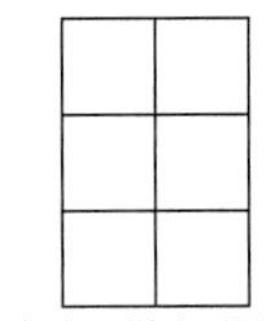

Right Side View

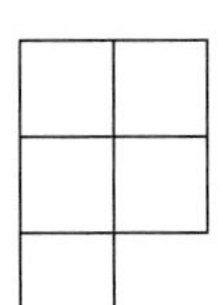

Top View

Use blocks to make a stack that matches each view. Count the blocks.

Two possible stacks have 10 and 11 blocks.

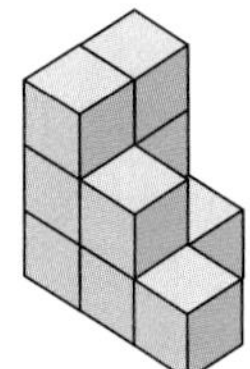

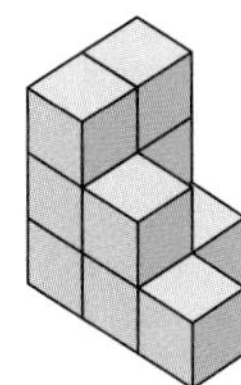

EXERCISES

Draw the front, right side, and top views of each figure.

1. 

2. 

3. 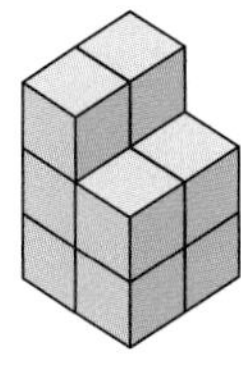

Use the drawings below. How many blocks are possible in the stack for each?

4. 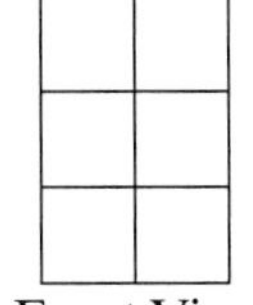

Front View

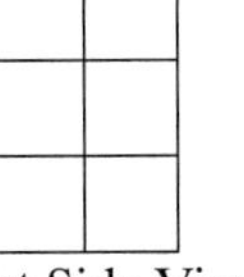

Right Side View

Top View

5. 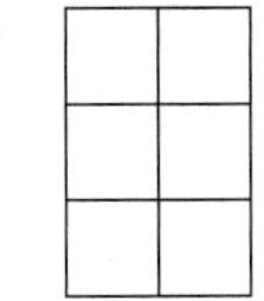

Front View

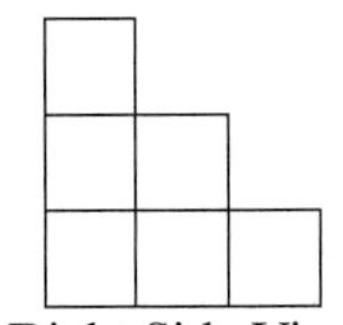

Right Side View

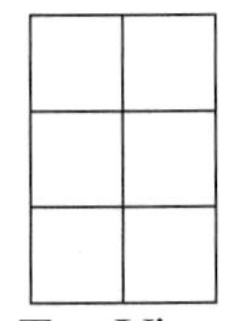

Top View

9-7 Three-Dimensional Figures and Spatial Reasoning

What You'll Learn

To identify three-dimensional figures

. . . And Why

To identify building shapes, as in Example 2

Check Skills You'll Need

For help, go to Lesson 8-5.

Identify each type of polygon according to the numbers of sides.

1.
2.
3.

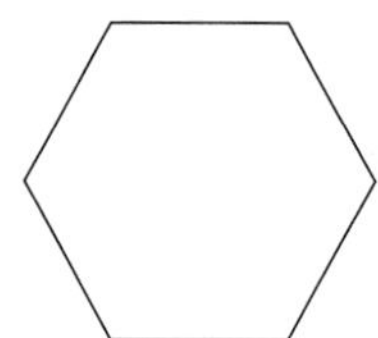

New Vocabulary • three-dimensional figure • faces • prism • cube • pyramid • cylinder • cone • sphere • net

Interactive lesson includes instant self-check, tutorials, and activities.

OBJECTIVE 1 Identifying Three-Dimensional Figures

Three-dimensional figures make up the world around you from your school building to your pencil. A **three-dimensional figure** is a figure that does not lie in a plane. It has three dimensions: length, width, and height.

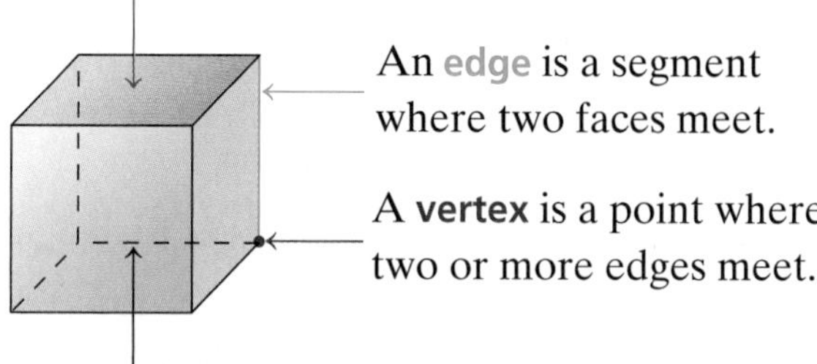

A **prism** is a three-dimensional figure with two parallel and congruent faces that are polygons. These faces are called bases. The prism above is a **cube.** All of its faces are congruent.

Base Shape	Name of Prism
Triangle	Triangular Prism
Rectangle	Rectangular Prism
Pentagon	Pentagonal Prism
Hexagon	Hexagonal Prism
Heptagon	Heptagonal Prism
Octagon	Octagonal Prism

← **You name a prism by the shape of its bases.**

1 EXAMPLE Naming Prisms

Name the prism shown.

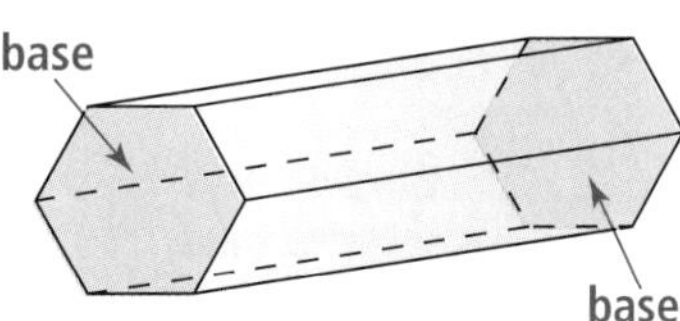

Each base is a hexagon. So the figure is a hexagonal prism.

Check Understanding 1 Name each prism.

a. 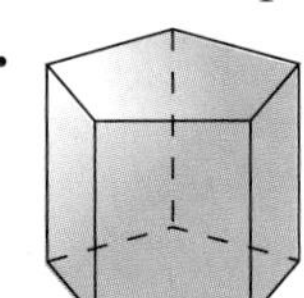

b.

c. 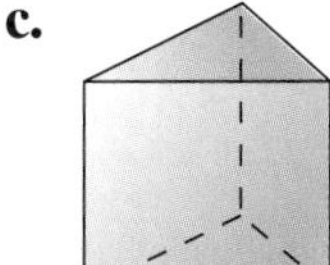

d. **Reasoning** In a prism, what shape is any face that is not the base?

A **pyramid** is a three-dimensional figure with one polygon for a base. All of the other faces are triangles. You name a pyramid by its base.

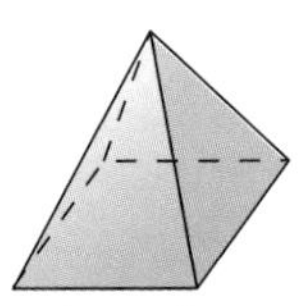

rectangular pyramid

Other three dimensional figures do not use polygons for bases.

Test-Prep Tip

When naming a 3-D figure, notice the shape of its base, and whether or not its faces meet at one vertex.

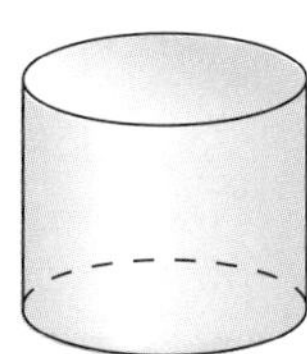

A **cylinder** has two congruent parallel bases that are circles.

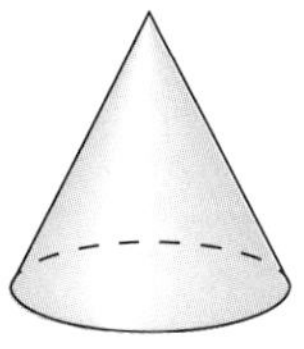

A **cone** has one circular base and one vertex.

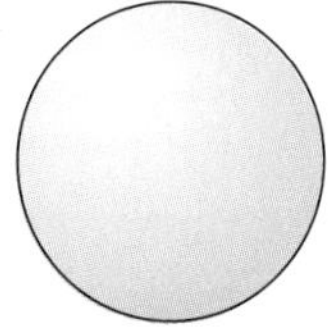

A **sphere** has no base.

2 EXAMPLE Identifying Three-Dimensional Figures

Museum The American Museum of Natural History in New York City is shown at the right. Name one of the three-dimensional figures in the photo.

One of the figures in the photo is a sphere.

Check Understanding 2 **a.** Name another three-dimensional figure in the photo.

b. **Reasoning** How are a cylinder and a cone alike? How are they different?

Investigation: Making Three-Dimensional Figures

A **net** is a pattern that you can fold to form a three-dimensional figure.

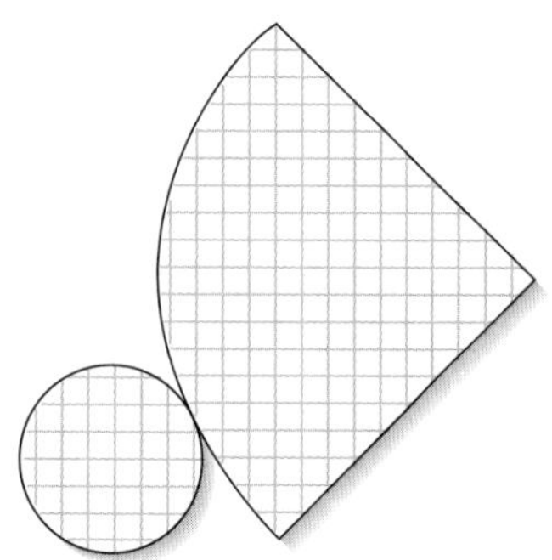

1. a. Name the three-dimensional figure you can form from the net shown.
   b. Copy the net onto graph paper. Cut, fold, and tape it to check your answer to part (a).

2. **Spatial Reasoning** Draw a net that will fold to form each given figure.
   a. rectangular prism   b. cylinder

EXERCISES

For more practice, see *Extra Practice.*

Practice by Example

Example 1 (page 463)

Name each prism.

1. 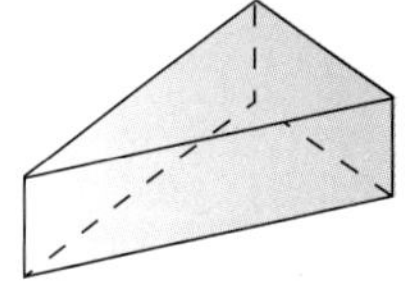

2. 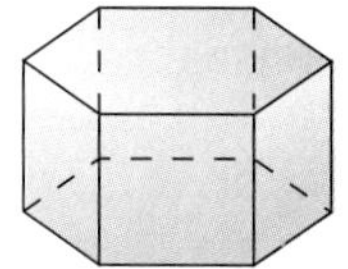

3. 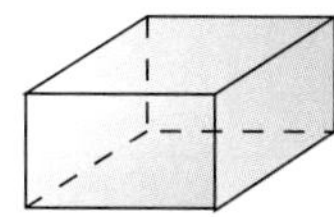

4. 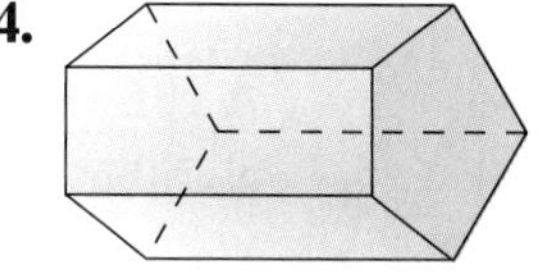

5. 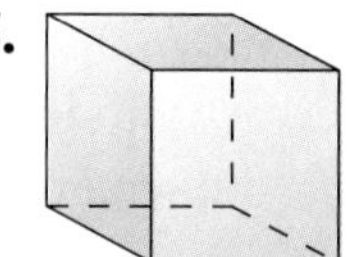

6. 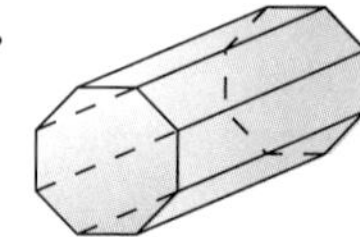

Example 2 (page 463)

Name each figure.

7. 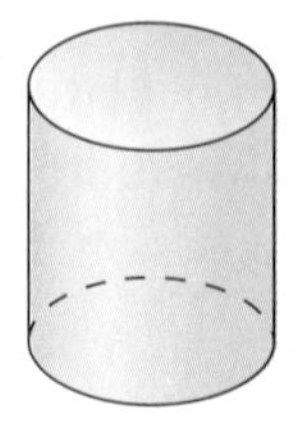

8. 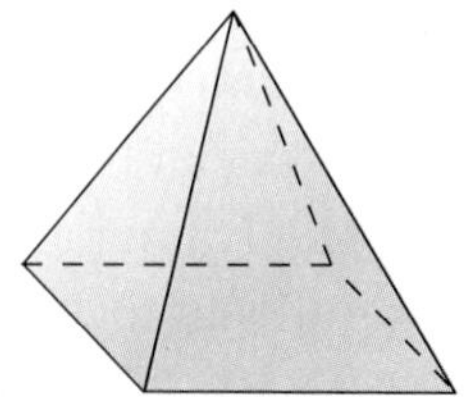

9. 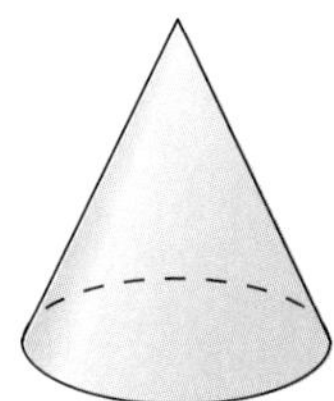

10. 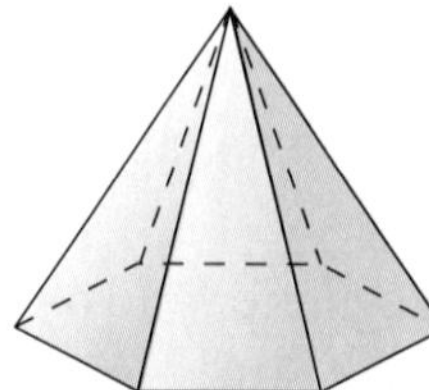

11. 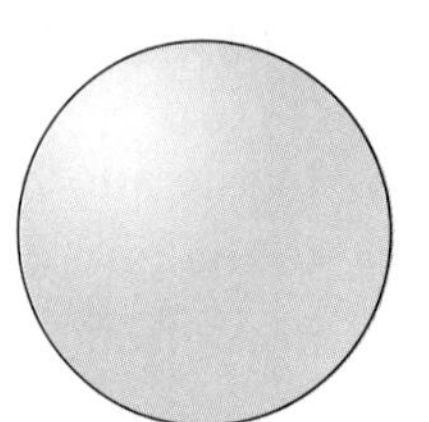

12. 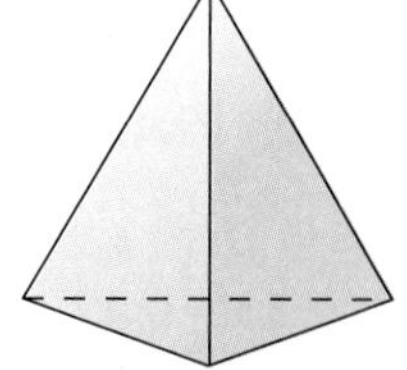

B Apply Your Skills **Structures** **Name the three-dimensional figure in each photo.**

13. 

14. 

15. 

16. 

Sketch each three-dimensional figure on graph paper.

17. rectangular prism
18. cone
19. hexagonal prism
20. cylinder
21. triangular pyramid
22. cube

23. **Writing in Math** Describe the shape of a square pyramid.

24. Name the figure. Then find the number of faces, vertices, and edges in the figure.

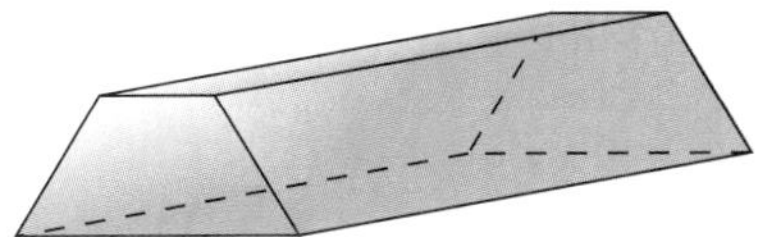

Art **You can use translations to draw three-dimensional figures.**

Step 1	**Step 2**	**Step 3**	**Step 4**
Draw a figure on graph paper.	Translate the figure.	Connect each vertex with its image.	Use dashes for hidden lines.

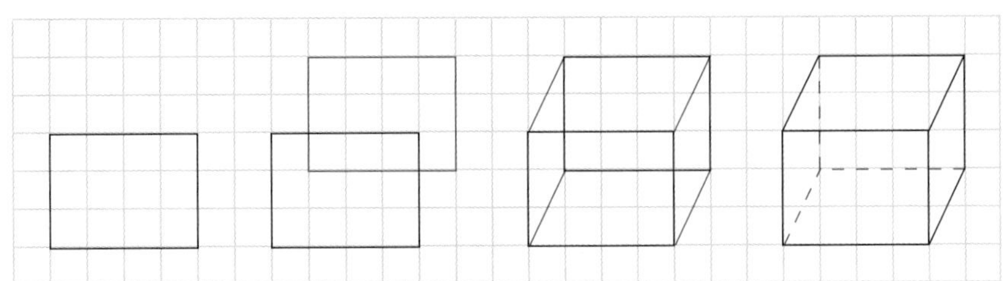

25. Start with a triangle. Draw a three-dimensional figure.

26. Start with a pentagon. Draw a three-dimensional figure.

C Challenge

27. Describe the translation used in the example above. Redraw the rectangle. Use a different translation to draw the figure.

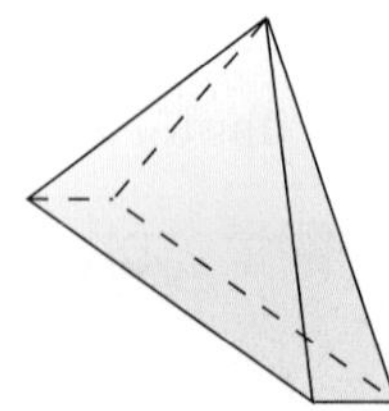

28. Algebra The formula $F + V - E = 2$ shows the relationship between the faces (F), the vertices (V), and the edges (E) of prisms and pyramids. Use the figure shown at the left to verify the formula.

29. **Stretch Your Thinking** The figure at the right has an area of 180 square inches and consists of 5 congruent squares. Rearrange the squares to make a figure with a perimeter of 60 inches.

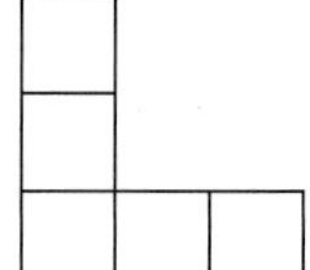

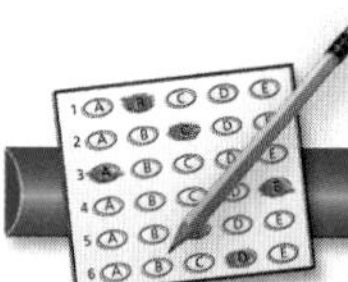

Test Prep

Multiple Choice

30. Which figure does NOT have a rectangular face?
   A. cube
   B. triangular prism
   C. rectangular pyramid
   D. cone

31. Which figure is a square pyramid?

F. 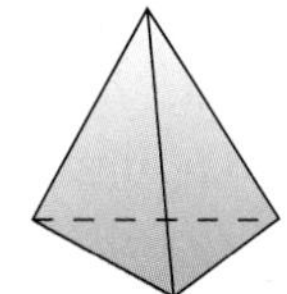
G. 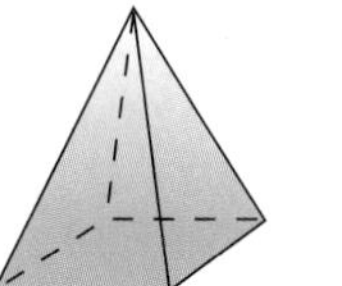
H.
I. 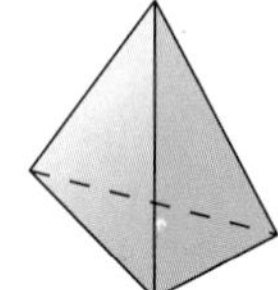

Take It to the NET
Online lesson quiz at
www.PHSchool.com
Web Code: aaa-0907

32. Which figure has more than five faces (including bases)?
   A. square pyramid
   B. triangular prism
   C. triangular pyramid
   D. rectangular prism

33. How many edges does a pentagonal pyramid have?
   F. 5
   G. 8
   H. 10
   I. 13

Mixed Review

Lesson 8-9

Copy each diagram on graph paper and draw its reflection over the given line of reflection.

34. 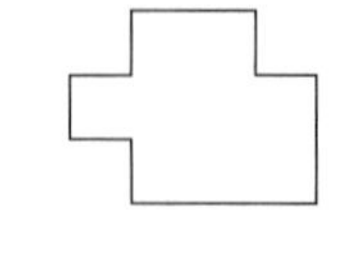

35. 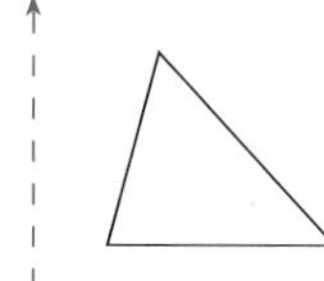

36. 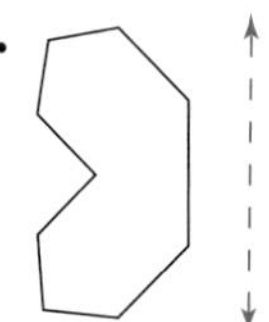

Lesson 6-9

Solve each problem by writing an equation.

37. If the sales tax is 6%, how much tax do you pay for a $15.99 CD?

38. A T-shirt that costs $20 is 30% off. What is the sale price of a $20 T-shirt?

9-8 Surface Areas of Prisms and Cylinders

What You'll Learn

To find the surface area of a prism

To find the surface area of a cylinder

. . . And Why

To find the surface area of a juice box, as in Example 2

✔ Check Skills You'll Need

For help, go to Lesson 9-6.

Find the area of each circle. Round to the nearest tenth.

1.
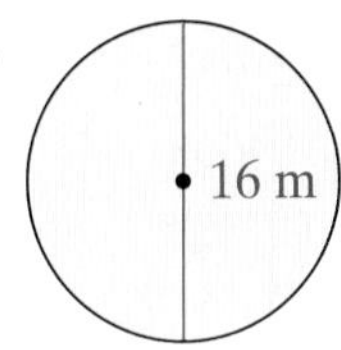

2.
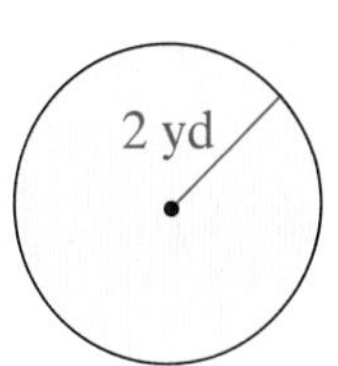

3.
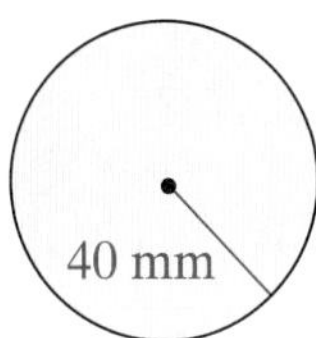

New Vocabulary

- surface area

OBJECTIVE

Interactive lesson includes instant self-check, tutorials, and activities.

1 Finding the Surface Area of a Prism

A *net* is a pattern you can fold to form a three-dimensional figure. Package designers use nets like the one below to make boxes.

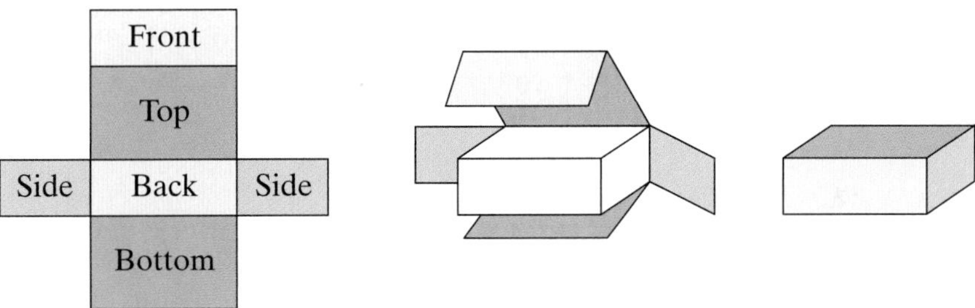

1 EXAMPLE Drawing a Net

Draw a net for the triangular prism at the left.

Step 1 Draw one base.

Step 2 Draw one face that connects the two bases.

Step 3 Draw the other base.

Step 4 Draw the remaining faces.

Back

Left side | Bottom | Right side

Front

✔ Check Understanding 1 Draw a net for a cube.

The **surface area** of a three-dimensional figure is the sum of the areas of its surfaces. You can use nets to find the surface area of a prism.

2 EXAMPLE Finding the Surface Area of a Prism

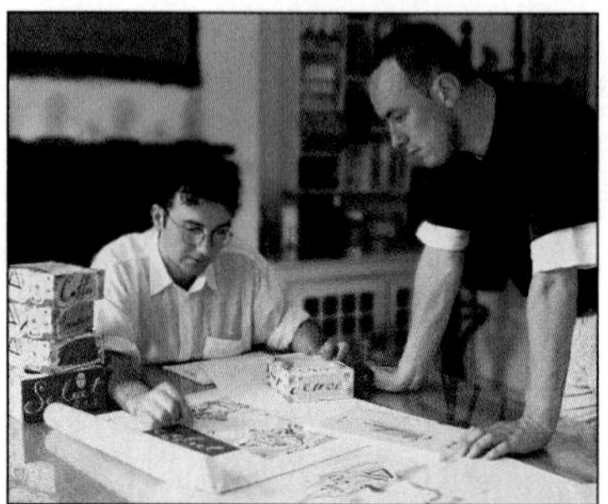

Real-World Connection

Careers Package designers design attractive and cost-efficient packages.

Package Design Find the surface area of the juice box at the right.

Step 1 Draw and label a net for the prism.

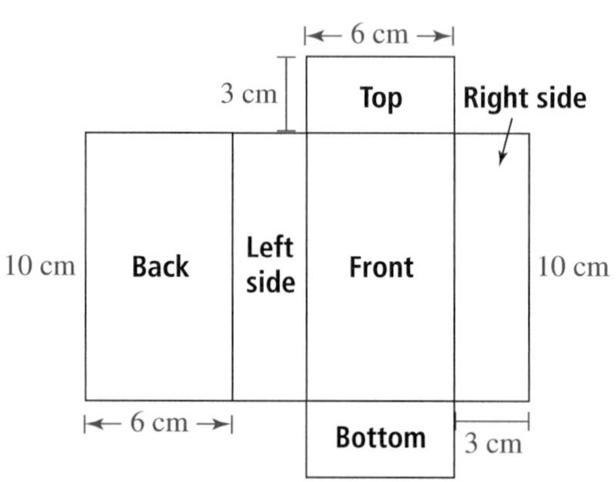

Step 2 Find and add the areas of all the rectangles.

	Top		Back		Left		Front		Right		Bottom
	3×6	+	10×6	+	10×3	+	10×6	+	10×3	+	3×6
=	18	+	60	+	30	+	60	+	30	+	18
=	216										

The surface area of the juice box is 216 square centimeters.

Check Understanding 2 Find the surface area of each prism.

a.

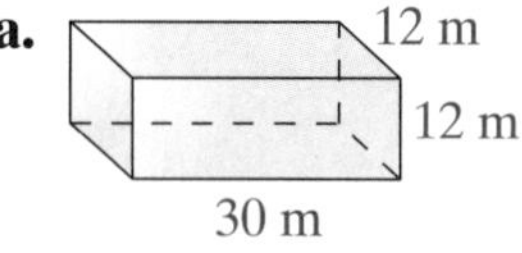

b.

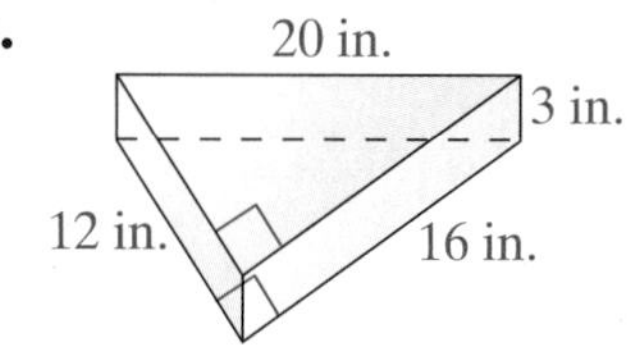

OBJECTIVE

2 Finding the Surface Area of a Cylinder

If you carefully peel a label off of a can of vegetables, you will see that the label is a rectangle.

The width of the rectangle is the height of the can.

The base length of the rectangle is the circumference of the can.

Suppose you draw a net of the cylinder that is the actual vegetable can. You will see that the can is a rectangle and two circles.

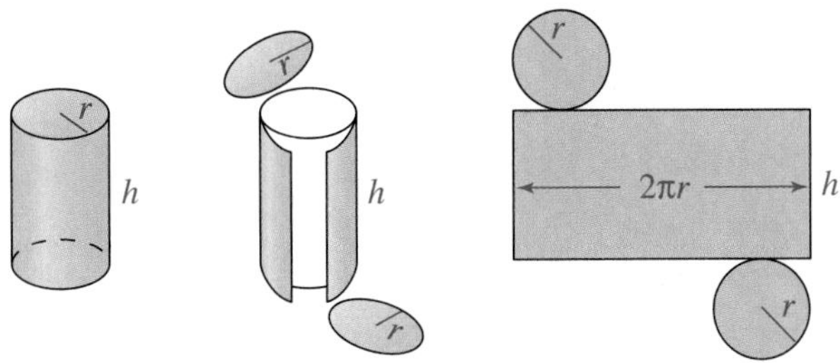

You can find the surface area of a cylinder by finding the area of its net.

3 EXAMPLE Finding the Surface Area of a Cylinder

Find the surface area of the cylinder. Round to the nearest tenth.

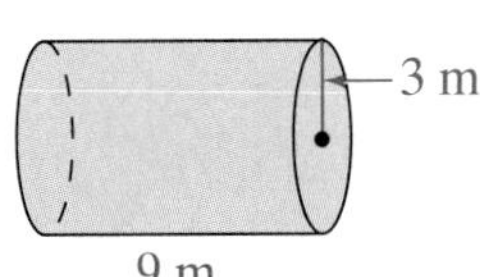

Step 1 Draw and label a net for the cylinder.

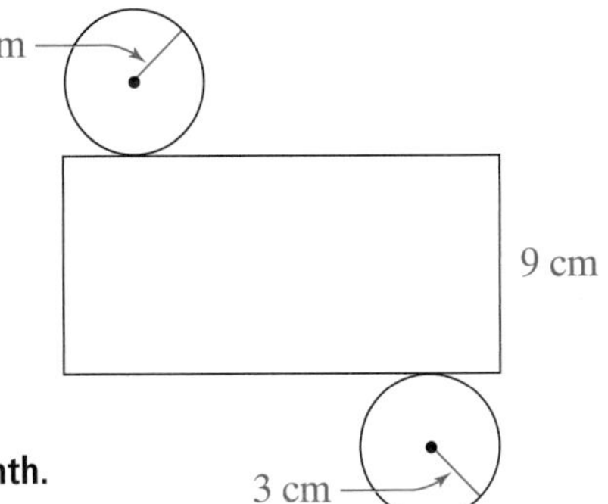

Step 2 Find the area of one circle.

$A = \pi r^2$ ← **Use the formula.**

$= \pi \times 3^2$ ← **Substitute 3 for *r*.**

≈ 28.274333 ← **Use a calculator.**

≈ 28.3 ← **Round to the nearest tenth.**

Need Help?
The formula for the circumference of a circle is $C = \pi d$.

Step 3 Find the area of the rectangle.

$A = l \times w$ ← **Use the formula.**

$= \pi d \times h$ ← **The length of the rectangle is the circumference of the circle. The width of the rectangle is the height of the cylinder.**

$= \pi(6) \times 9$ ← **Substitute 6 for *d* and 9 for *h*.**

≈ 169.64600 ← **Use a calculator.**

≈ 169.6 ← **Round to the nearest tenth.**

Step 4 Add the areas of the rectangles and the two circles.

$28.3 + 169.6 + 28.3 = 226.2$

The surface area of the cylinder is about 226.2 square centimeters.

Check Understanding 3 **a.** **Reasoning** Explain how the formula S.A. $= 2\pi r^2 + C \times h$ can be used to find the surface area of the cylinder at the right.

b. Find the surface area of the cylinder to the nearest square inch.

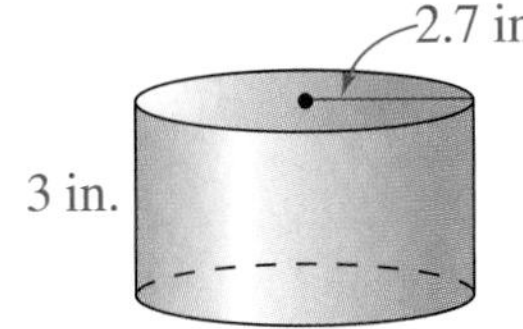

EXERCISES

For more practice, see *Extra Practice*.

A Practice by Example

Example 1 (page 467)

Draw a net for each three-dimensional figure.

1. 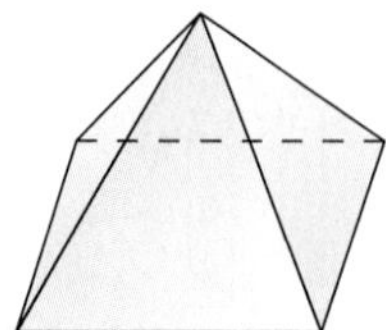

2. 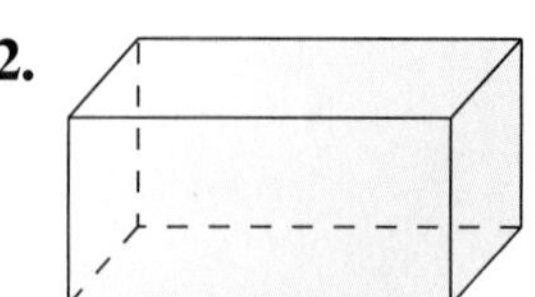

3. 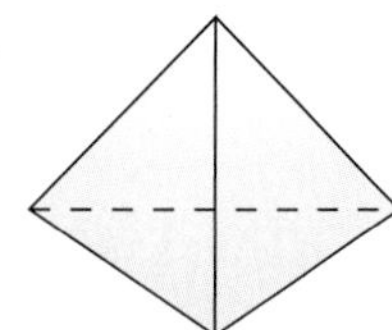

Example 2 (page 468)

Find the surface area of each prism.

4. 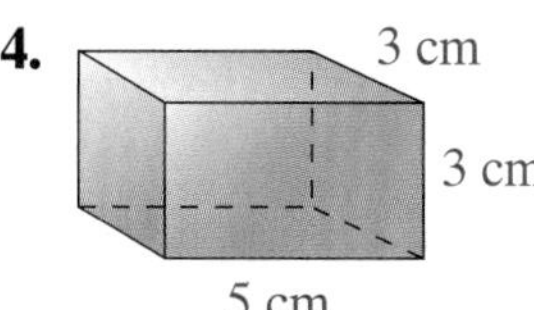

5. 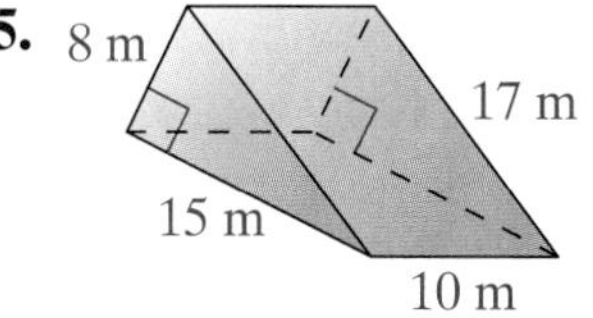

6. 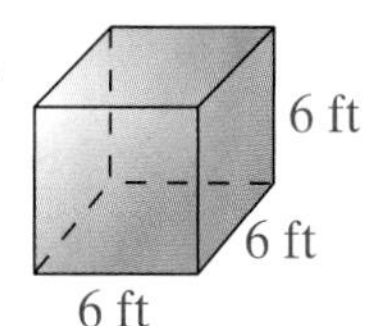

7. 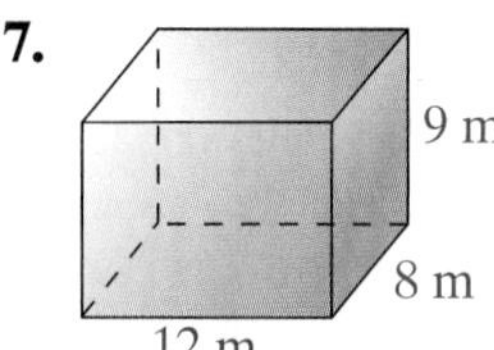

8. 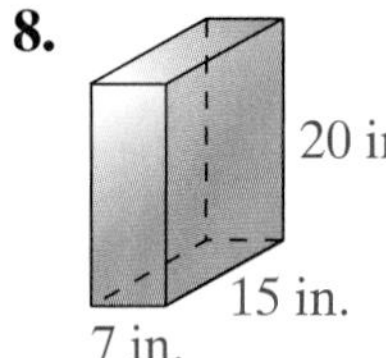

9. 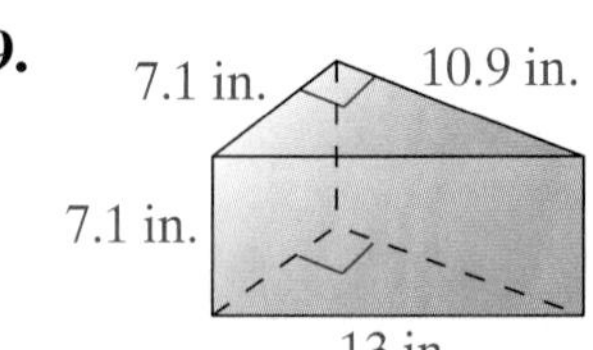

Example 3 (page 469)

Find the surface area of each cylinder. Round to the nearest tenth.

10. 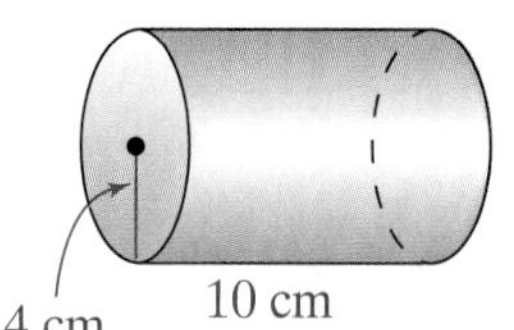

11. 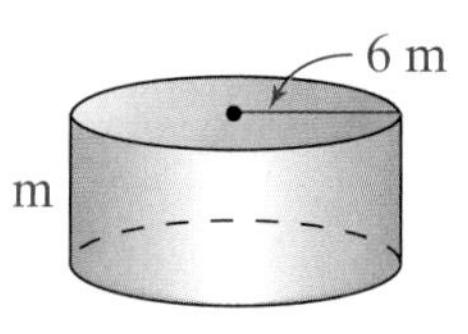

12. 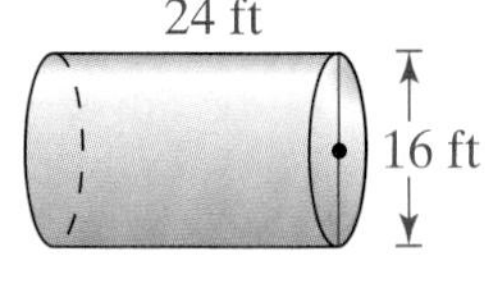

B Apply Your Skills

Household Objects Find the surface area of each object.

13. 

14. 

15. 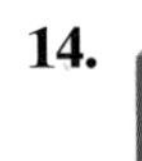 **Writing in Math** Suppose each dimension of a rectangular prism is doubled. How is the surface area affected?

16. **Data File, p. 429** Find the surface area of the base of the Eiffel Tower and the Taj Mahal platform.

Find the surface area of a rectangular prism with the given dimensions.

17. $\ell = 2.2$ m, $w = 3$ m, $h = 11$ m

18. $\ell = 5$ in., $w = 6.3$ in., $h = 8$ in.

Find the surface area of each figure. A small cube measures 1 cm on a side.

19. 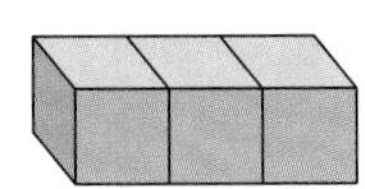

20. 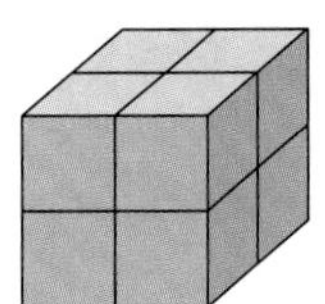

21. 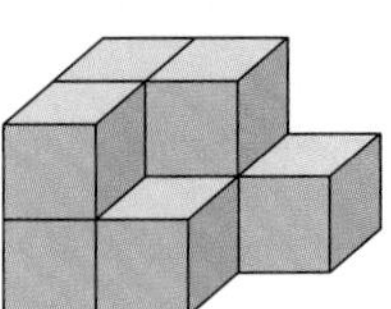

C Challenge

22. **Reasoning** The surface area of a cube is 54 square inches. What is the length of each edge?

23. **Stretch Your Thinking** Terri's cube has a surface area of 6 square centimeters. Each edge of Quinn's cube is twice as long as each edge of Terri's cube. What is the surface area of Quinn's cube?

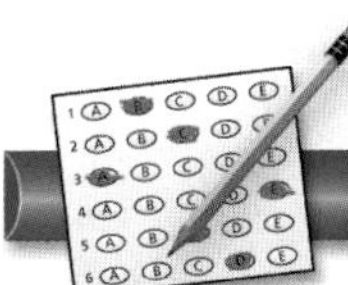

Test Prep

Multiple Choice

24. What is the surface area of the cylinder at the right?

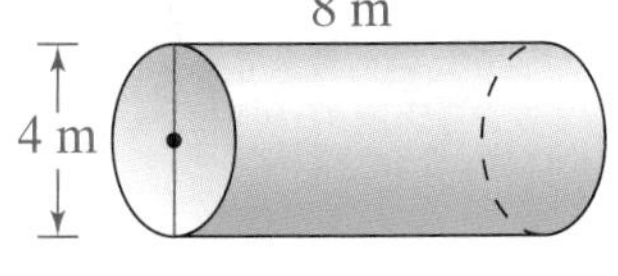

A. 12 square meters **B.** 25 square meters
C. 50 square meters **D.** 75 square meters

Take It to the NET
Online lesson quiz at **www.PHSchool.com**
Web Code: aaa-0908

25. What is the surface area of a cube whose sides are s units long?
F. s^2 **G.** $3s^2$ **H.** $6s^2$ **I.** s^3

26. Which of the following CANNOT be the dimensions of the piece of wrapping paper used to wrap the box?

4 in.
9 in.
15 in.

A. 20 by 28 inches **B.** 36 by 18 inches
C. 40 by 10 inches **D.** 24 by 24 inches

Short Response

27. **a.** What is the surface area of the triangular prism at the right.
b. Explain how you found your answer.

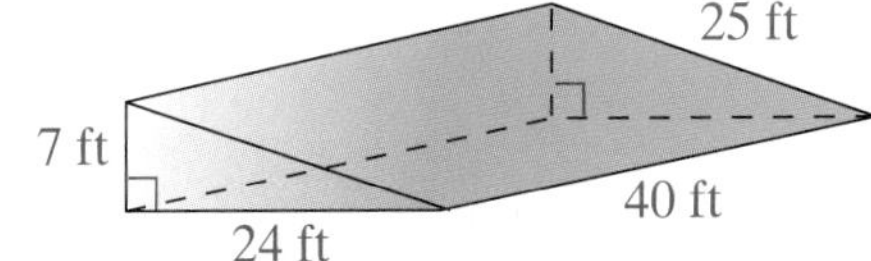

Mixed Review

Lesson 9-3 **Find the area of each square given the side *s* or the perimeter *P*.**

28. $s = 7$ km **29.** $s = 12.6$ in. **30.** $P = 36$ ft **31.** $P = 18$ yd

Lesson 9-1 **Choose an appropriate metric unit of measure.**

32. capacity of a pond **33.** capacity of a thimble **34.** mass of a pencil

9-9 Volumes of Rectangular Prisms and Cylinders

What You'll Learn

To find the volume of a rectangular prism

To find the volume of a cylinder

. . . And Why

To find the volume of a fish tank, as in Example 2

Check Skills You'll Need

For help, go to Lesson 9-4.

Find the area of each figure.

1.

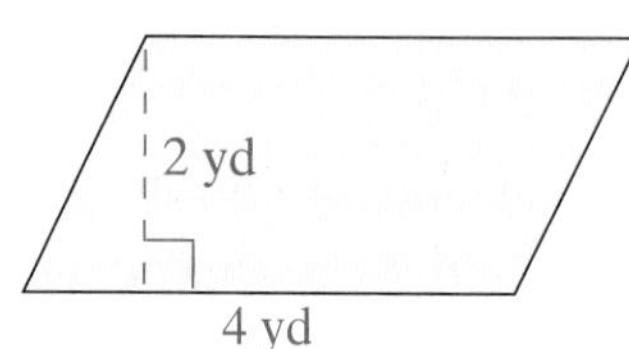

2.

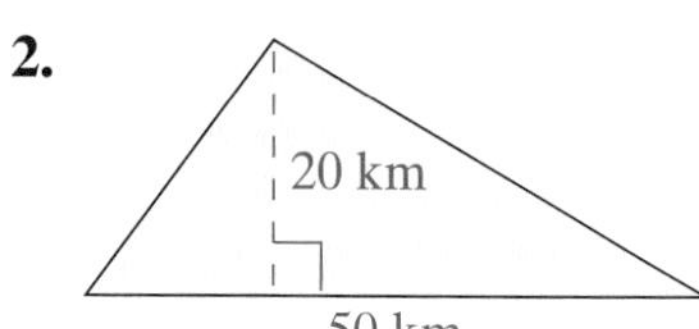

New Vocabulary • volume • cubic unit

Interactive lesson includes instant self-check, tutorials, and activities.

OBJECTIVE 1

Finding the Volume of a Rectangular Prism

The **volume** of a three-dimensional figure is the number of cubic units needed to fill the space inside the figure. A **cubic unit** is the amount of space in a cube that measures 1 unit long by 1 unit wide by 1 unit high.

1 EXAMPLE Counting Cubes to Find Volume

Find the volume of the rectangular prism.

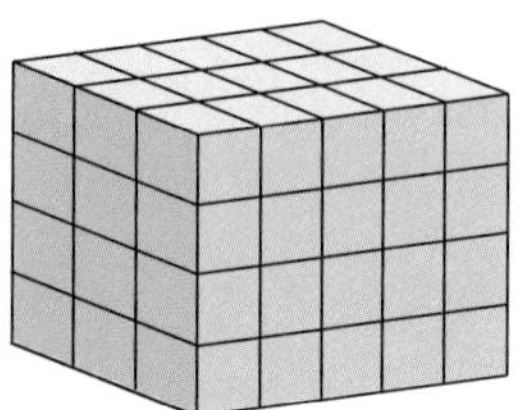

Each layer of the prism is 3 cubes by 5 cubes. This equals 3×5, or 15 cubes. The prism is 4 layers tall. So, the prism has a total of 4×15, or 60 cubes.

The volume of the prism is 60 cubic units.

Check Understanding 1 Use the rectangular prism at the right.

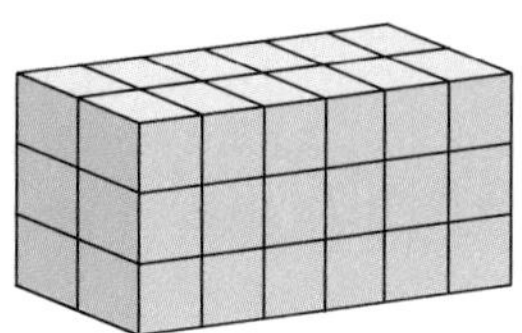

a. What is the volume of one layer?

b. What is the volume of the entire prism?

c. Number Sense How would the volume change if the number of layers were doubled?

Key Concepts Volume of a Prism

Volume = Area of Base × height

$V = B \times h$

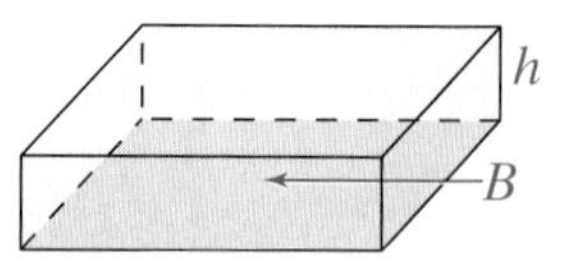

For a rectangular prism, the area of a base is $\ell \times w$. So, the volume formula becomes $V = \ell \times w \times h$. Common cubic units used in measuring volume are cubic centimeters (cm^3), cubic inches, (in.^3), and cubic feet (ft^3).

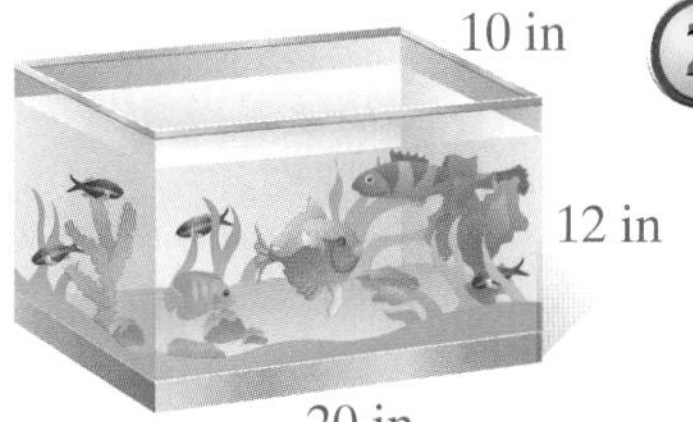

2 EXAMPLE **Finding the Volume of a Prism** 

Fish Tanks Find the volume of the fish tank shown at the left.

$V = \ell \times w \times h$ ← **Use the formula for the volume of a rectangular prism.**

$= 20 \times 10 \times 12$ ← **Substitute 20 for ℓ, 10 for w, and 12 for h.**

$= 2{,}400$ ← **Multiply.**

The volume is about 2,400 cubic centimeters, or 2,400 cm^3.

Check Understanding **2** Find the volume of a rectangular prism with a length of 8 meters, a width of 7 meters, and a height of 10 meters.

OBJECTIVE

2 Finding the Volume of a Cylinder

The formula $V = B \times h$ applies to cylinders as well as to prisms. Since the base of the cylinder is a circle, use $A = \pi r^2$ to find the area of the base. Then multiply by the height to find the volume of the cylinder.

3 EXAMPLE **Finding the Volume of a Cylinder** 

Food Find the volume of the can of Parmesan cheese at the left. Round to the nearest tenth.

Step 1 Find the area of the base.

Area of Base $= \pi \times r^2$ ← **Use $A = \pi r^2$ to find the area of the base.**

$= \pi \times 1.4^2$ ← **Substitute 1.4 for r.**

≈ 6.1575216 ← **Use a calculator.**

≈ 6.158 ← **Round to the nearest thousandth.**

Step 2 Find the volume.

Volume $= B \times h$

$\approx 6.158 \times 6$ ← **Substitute 6.158 for B and 6 for h.**

$= 36.948$ ← **Multiply.**

The volume is about 36.9 cubic inches, or 36.9 in.^{3}.

Check Understanding **3** Find the volume of a cylinder with a radius of 4 inches and a height of 9 inches. Round to the nearest tenth.

For more practice, see *Extra Practice.*

A Practice by Example

Example 1 (page 472)

Find the volume of each rectangular prism.

1\.

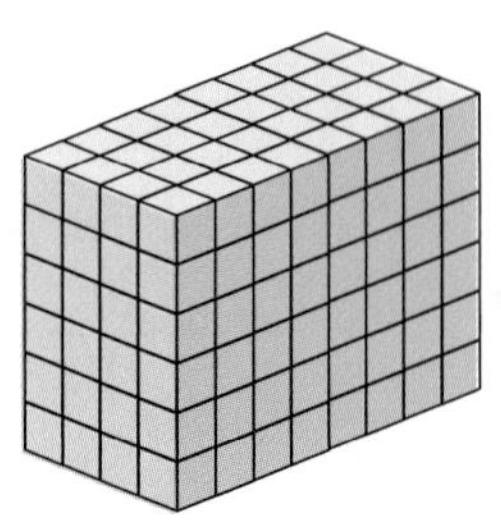

2\.

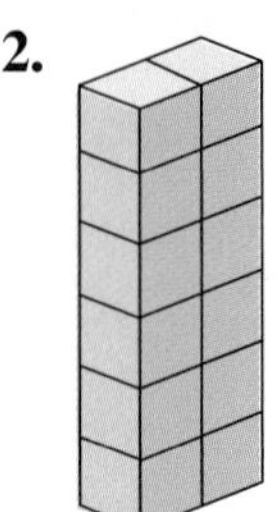

3\.

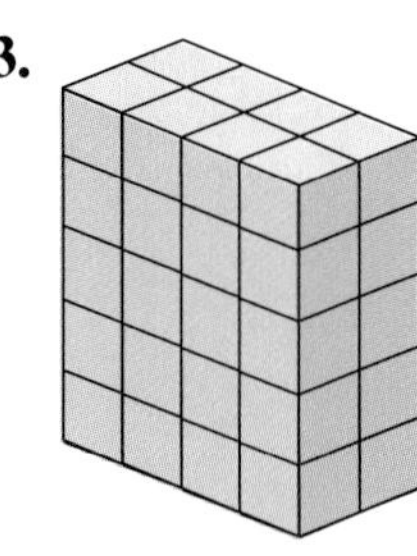

Example 2 (page 473)

Find the volume of each rectangular prism.

4\.

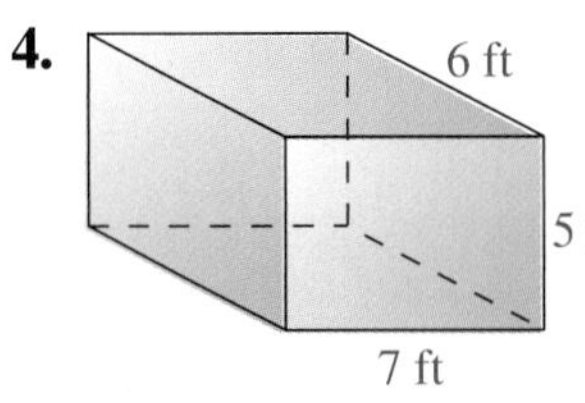

5\.

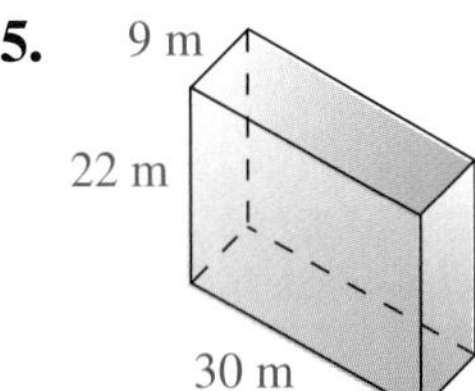

6\.

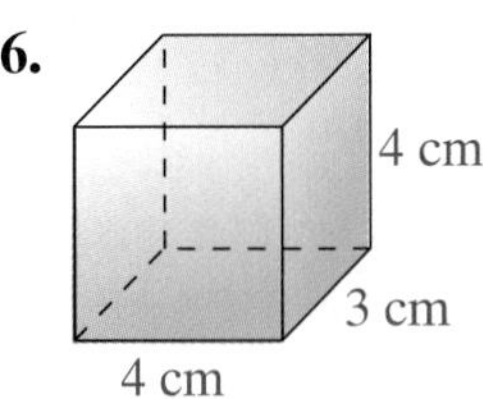

7\.

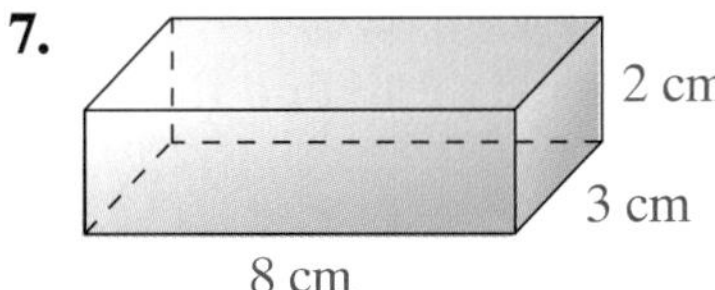

8\.

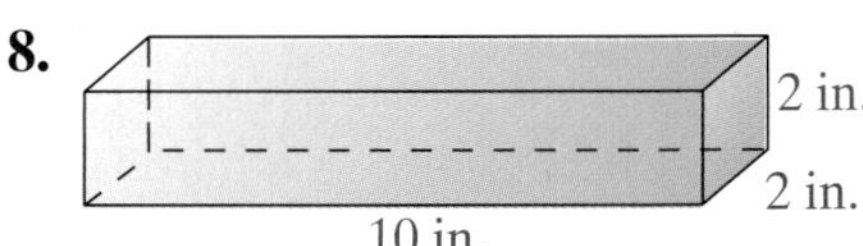

Example 3 (page 473)

Find the volume of each cylinder. Round to the nearest tenth. Exercise 9 has been started for you.

9\.

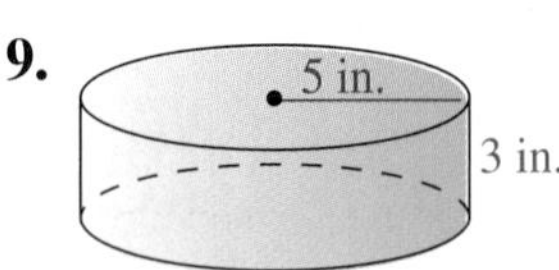

$V = B \times h$

$V = \pi(5^2) \times 3$

10\.

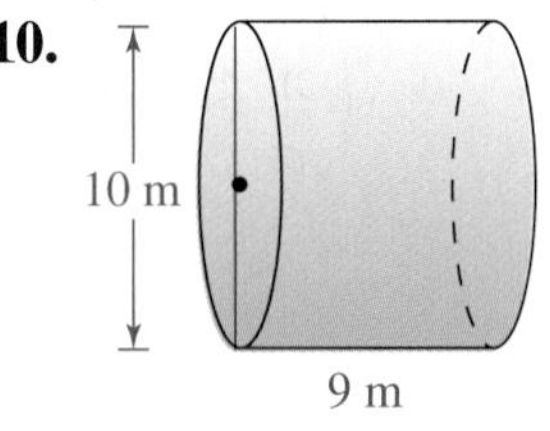

11\.

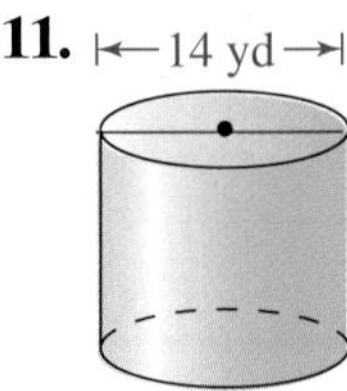

12\.

13\.

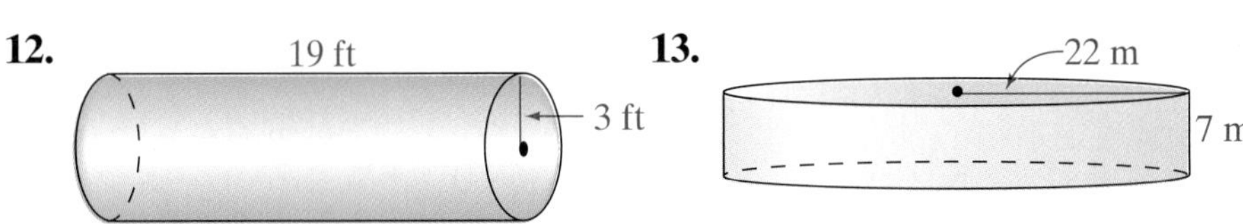

B Apply Your Skills

14\. **Architecture** The shape of a monument is a hexagonal prism. The area of the base is 5.4 square feet and the height is 13 feet. Find the volume.

15\. **Straws** A straw has the shape of a cylinder. Find the volume of a straw with a radius of 3 millimeters and a height of 200 millimeters.

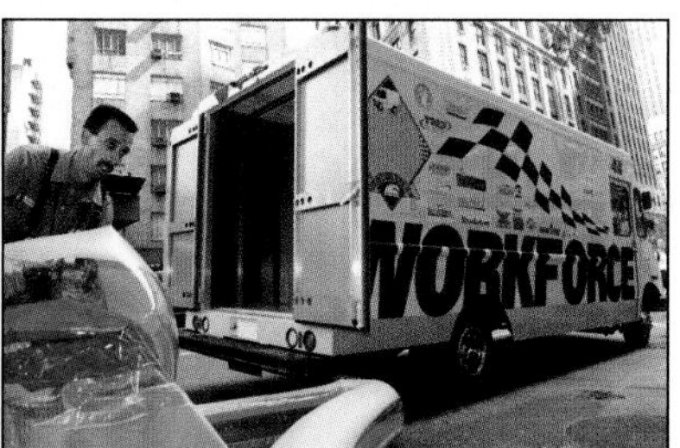

Real-World Connection

A competition for Delivery Driver of the Year tested driver's skills in Manhattan.

16. **Trucks** A rectangular truck bed has a length of 20 feet, a width of 8 feet, and a height of 7 feet. A cylindrical truck tank has a radius of 3.5 feet and a length of 22 feet. Find each volume to the nearest tenth.

17. **Number Sense** How would the volume of a cube change if its dimensions were doubled? What if the dimensions were halved?

18. **Writing in Math** Two rectanglar prisms have the same base area. The second prism has twice the height of the first prism. How do their volumes compare? How do you know?

19. **Data File, p. 429** Find the volume of the Great Pyramid of Khufu using the formula Volume $= \frac{1}{3} \times$ length $\times$ width $\times$ height.

Find the volume of each prism or cylinder with the given dimensions. Round to the nearest hundredth, if necessary.

20. $\ell = 6$ m, $w = 4.3$ m, $h = 11$ m
21. $\ell = 3.2$ ft, $w = 2$ ft, $h = 9.4$ ft
22. $r = 8.1$ cm, $h = 4$ cm
23. $r = 2.4$ in., $h = 5.4$ in.

24. **Reasoning** One ton of coal fills a bin that is 3 feet by 4 feet by 4 feet. Find the dimensions of a bin that would hold 2 tons of coal.

C Challenge

25. **Swimming Pools** A swimming pool is 24 meters long and 16 meters wide. The average depth of the water is 2.5 meters. How many 2-liter bottles of water would be needed to fill the pool? (*Hint:* 1 m^3 = 1,000 L)

26. **Algebra** Find the height of a cylinder with a volume of 85 cubic feet and a radius of 2.6 feet.

27. **Stretch Your Thinking** Items at a garage sale cost $1, $2, and $5. Marty spent $21. He bought one more $2 item than $1 items. He bought twice as many $2 items as $5 items. How many of each item did he buy?

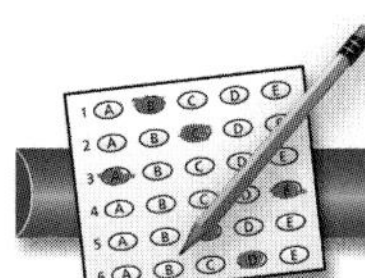

Test Prep

Multiple Choice

28. A cylinder has a radius of 7 feet and a height of 14 feet. What is its approximate volume in square feet?
A. 294 **B.** 333 **C.** 686 **D.** 2,150

29. A rectangular prism is 2 meters long, 50 centimeters wide, and 1 meter high. What is its volume?
F. 1 cubic meter
G. 100 cubic centimeters
H. 100 cubic meters
I. 10,000 cubic centimeters

30. Each cube of the rectangular prism at the right measures 1 inch on each edge. If the top level of cubes is removed, what is the volume of the remaining prism?

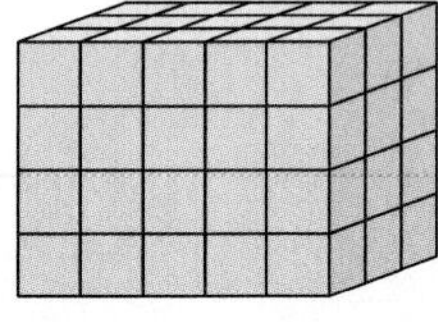

A. 40 cubic inches
B. 45 cubic inches
C. 48 cubic inches
D. 60 cubic inches

Extended Response

31. a. Find all possible rectangular prisms that have a volume of 18 cubic centimeters and whole-number dimensions.
b. For which dimensions does the prism have the most surface area?

Mixed Review

Lesson 9-6

32. **Pets** A dog is tied to a post with a 10-foot rope. The dog gets exercise by running in a circle. (Assume that the rope does not wrap around the post.) What is the circumference of the circle the dog makes? Round to the nearest tenth.

Lesson 9-3

Find the area of each square with the given perimeter.

33. 12 m
34. 24 ft
35. 34 cm
36. 25 in.

Checkpoint Quiz 2

Lessons 9-5 through 9-9

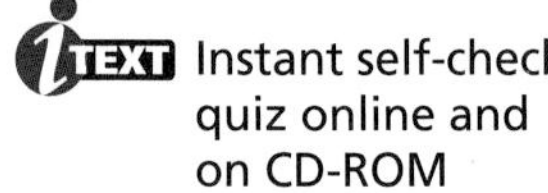

Name each figure.

1. 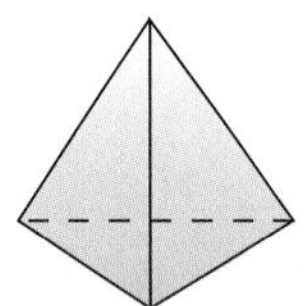
2. 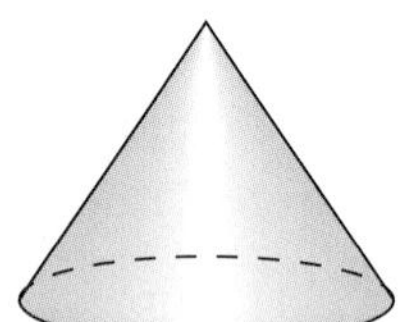
3. 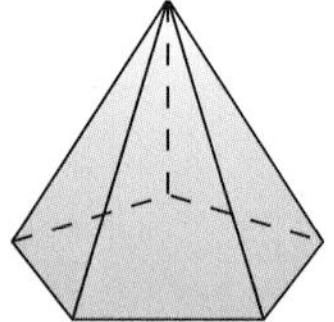
4. 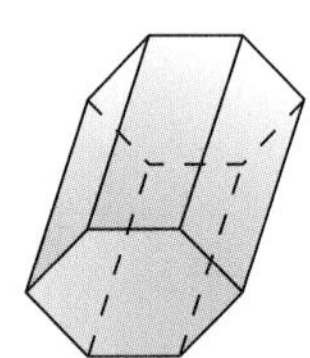

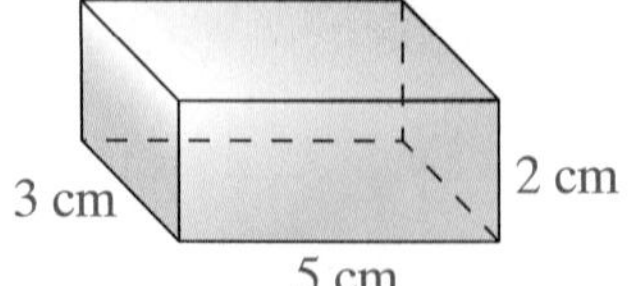

Use the rectangular prism at the left for Exercises 5 and 6.

5. Find the surface area.
6. Find the volume.

Use the cylinder at the right for Exercises 7–10. Use 3.14 for π. Round to the nearest tenth.

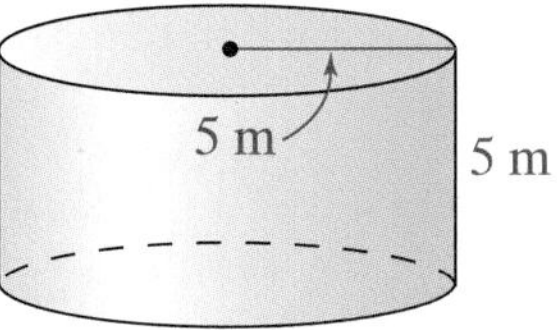

7. Find the circumference of the circular base.
8. Find the area of the circular base.
9. Find the surface area.
10. Find the volume.

9-10 Work Backward

What You'll Learn

To solve problems by working backward

. . . And Why

To solve problems involving money, as in Example 1

Check Skills You'll Need

For help, go to Lesson 1-10.

Find the value of each expression.

1. $3 \times (5 + 7)$
2. $36 \div 3 - 5$
3. $68 \div 4 - 8$
4. $(9 + 8) \times 4$
5. $14 + (13 \times 7)$
6. $105 - 13 \times 7$

OBJECTIVE

 Interactive lesson includes instant self-check, tutorials, and activities.

1 Solving Problems by Working Backward

When to Use This Strategy Some problems involve a series of steps that lead to a final result. If you are asked to find the initial amount, you can ***work backward*** from the final result by using inverse operations.

1 EXAMPLE Real-World Problem Solving

Zoo Luis went to the zoo for a school trip. He paid \$5 for admission. He spent \$14 at the souvenir shop. When he got home, he had \$18 left. How much money did he start with?

Read and Understand You know how much money Luis had when he got home. You know how much he spent. You want to know how much he had when he started.

Plan and Solve To find the amount Luis had when he started, begin with the amount he had at the end. Then work backward.

To undo the amounts that Luis spent, add.

\$18 ← **Luis had \$18 left at the end.**

\$18 + \$5 = \$23 ← **He spent \$5 on admission. Add.**

\$23 + \$14 = \$37 ← **He spent \$14 at the souvenir shop. Add.**

Luis started with \$37.

Look Back and Check Read the problem again. Start with \$37. Subtract the amounts as Luis spends money in the problem. \$37 − \$5 − \$14 = \$18. The answer checks. ✔

Real-World Connection

Natural habitats in zoos help protect some endangered species.

Check Understanding 1 A teacher lends 7 pencils to her students in the morning, collects 5 before lunch, and gives out 3 after lunch. At the end of the day, she has 16 pencils. How many pencils did the teacher have at the start of the day?

EXERCISES

For more practice, see *Extra Practice*.

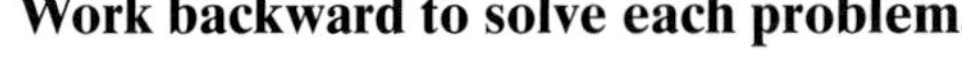

A Practice by Example

Work backward to solve each problem.

Example 1 (page 477)

1. You divide a number by 2, add 7, and then multiply by 5. The result is 50. What is the number?

Need Help?
- Reread the problem.
- Identify the key facts and details.
- Tell the problem in your own words.
- Try a different strategy.
- Check your work.

2. **Shopping** Brenda spent half her money at a store in the mall. At another store, she spent half her remaining money and $6 more. She had $2 left. How much did Brenda have when she arrived at the mall?

3. **Money** The checkbook shows amounts subtracted from an account (checks) and amounts added (deposits). How much was in the account before the $25 check was written?

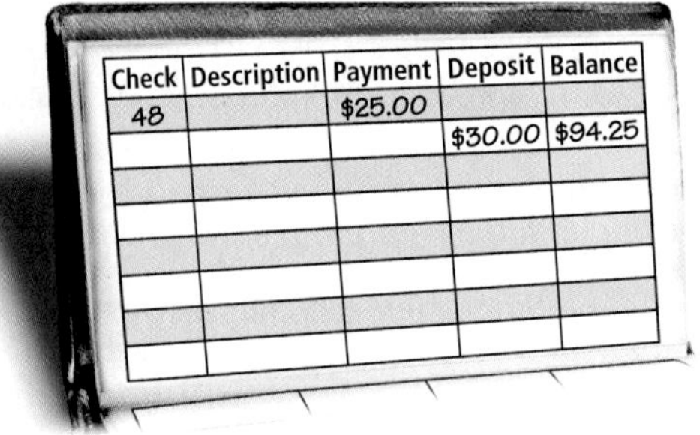

Check	Description	Payment	Deposit	Balance
48		$25.00		
			$30.00	$94.25

B Apply Your Skills

Use any strategy to solve each problem. Show your work.

Strategies
- Draw a Diagram
- Make a Graph
- Make an Organized List
- Make a Table and Look for a Pattern
- Simulate a Problem
- Solve a Simpler Problem
- Try, Check, and Revise
- Use Logical Reasoning
- Work Backward
- Write an Equation

4. **Entertainment** At the Plex Cinema, every 15th customer gets a free ticket. Every 10th customer gets free popcorn. Of 418 ticket buyers, how many received both prizes?

5. **Baking** Henry bakes some muffins. He eats two. He puts half of the muffins away. He divides the remaining muffins among his 3 sisters. Each sister receives 3 muffins. How many muffins did Henry bake?

6. **Hobbies** Kai sold half his baseball cards to Ana, half of the remaining cards to Joe, and the last 10 to Chip. How many cards were sold?

7. **Transportation** A local bus picked up 3 passengers at its first stop. At every stop thereafter, it picked up 2 more passengers than at the previous stop. How many passengers got on at the fifth stop?

Use any strategy to solve each problem. Show your work.

8. **a.** **Money** Taesha has $1.35 in nickels and dimes. She has a total of 15 coins. How many of each coin does she have?

b. **Writing in Math** Explain how you solved this problem.

9. **Biology** A bacterial population doubles in size every 6 minutes. After 2 hours, the population is 8,000. When was the population 4,000?

10. **Calendar** Jeffrey's birthday is circled below. His cousin Marianne was born in the same year and turns 12 on April 19. What day of the week does Marianne turn 12?

March						
S	M	T	W	T	F	S
1	2	3	4	5	6	7
8	9	10	11	12	13	14
15	16	17	18	19	20	21
22	23	24	25	26	(27)	28
28	30	31				

11. **Health** Of 25 students, 11 need a dental check-up and 17 need an eye exam. Five students don't need either. How many students need both a dental check-up and an eye exam?

Challenge

12. **Box** A has 9 green balls and 4 red balls. Box B has 12 green balls and 5 red balls. Suppose you want the fraction of green balls in Box A to equal the fraction of red balls in Box B. How many green balls must you move from Box A to Box B?

13. **Stretch Your Thinking** Suppose you have 4 lengths of chain with 3 links each. How should you cut and rejoin only 3 links so that the 4 lengths form one circular chain with 12 links?

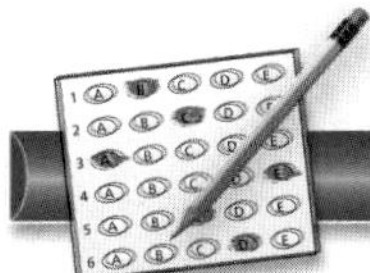

Test Prep

Multiple Choice

14. The diameter of a circle is 8 meters. What is the approximate circumference of the circle?

A. 4 meters **B.** 12 meters **C.** 24 meters **D.** 32 meters

15. The ratio of the circumferences of two circles is 1 : 2. What is the ratio of the radii of the circles?

F. 1 : 2 **G.** 1 : 4 **H.** 1 : 5 **I.** 1 : 10

Take It to the NET
Online lesson quiz at
www.PHSchool.com
Web Code: aaa-0910

16. A circular mirror has a diameter of 12 inches. What is the circumference of the mirror? Round to the nearest inch. Use 3.14 for π.

A. 24 inches **B.** 38 inches **C.** 113 inches **D.** 452 inches

Short Response

17. The diameter of a bicycle's wheel is 28 inches. About how many times does each wheel make a complete turn when the bicycle travels 1,000 feet?

Mixed Review

Lesson 9-2

Convert each measurement.

18. 2.4 kilometers to meters

19. 452 milligrams to centigrams

20. 26,400 liters to kiloliters

21. 0.79 meter to centimeters

Lesson 7-5

Sketch a circle graph for the given percents.

22. 25%, 30%, 45%

23. 3%, 37%, 50%, 10%

Lesson 7-3

Solve each problem by making an organized list.

24. Use each of the digits 2, 3, 4, and 5 exactly once. How many 4-digit numbers can you form?

25. How many ways can you divide 12 books among 3 people? Each person must have at least 1 book.

Math at Work

Event Planner

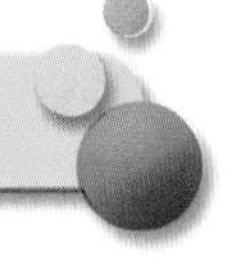

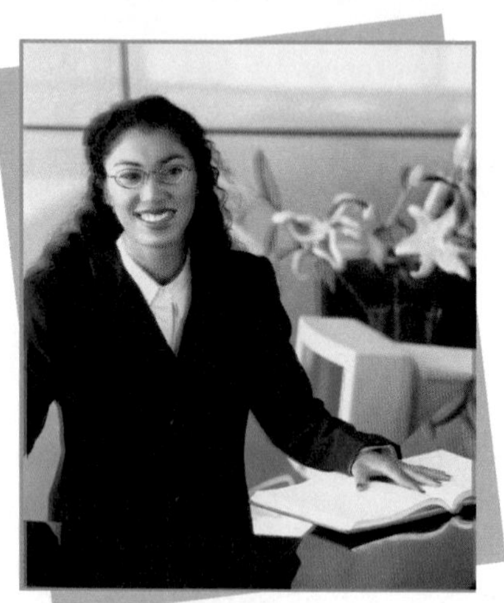

Event planners organize and arrange all the details for parties, business meetings, and other group activities. Their responsibilities include finding the place, choosing the menu, and decorating the tables for an event.

Geometry is useful to event planners as they determine dimensions for room sizes, arrange rectangular or circular tables, and plan serving areas.

Take It to the NET For more information on event planners, go to **www.PHSchool.com**.
Web Code: aab-2031

Using Estimation

Estimating may help you find an answer, check an answer, or eliminate one or more answer choices.

1 EXAMPLE

The diameter of a circular plate is 9 inches. Find its area to the nearest tenth.

A. 14.1 square inches **B.** 28.3 square inches **C.** 63.6 square inches **D.** 254.3 square inches

Since the diameter is 9 inches, the radius is 4.5 inches, or about 5 inches.

$A = \pi r^2$

$\approx 3 \times 5^2$ ← **Substitute 3 for π and 5 for r.**

$= 3 \times 25$, or 75 square inches ← **Simplify.**

Only choice C is close to the estimate, so the correct answer is C.

2 EXAMPLE

Eve has 50 feet of edging. What is the diameter of the largest flowerbed she can make? Round to the nearest tenth.

F. 15.7 feet **G.** 15.9 feet **H.** 157.1 feet **I.** 159.2 feet

$C = \pi d$ ← **Use the formula for the circumference of a circle.**

$50 \approx 3d$ ← **Estimate by substituting 50 for C and 3 for π.**

$\frac{50}{3} \approx \frac{3d}{3}$ ← **Divide each side by 3.**

16.7 feet $\approx d$ ← **Simplify. Round to the nearest tenth.**

You can eliminate choices H and I because they are not near the estimate.

EXERCISES

Estimate each answer. Then tell which answer choice(s) you can eliminate.

1. What value is closest to the area of a circle with a 3-inch radius?
   A. 9 square inches **B.** 19 square inches **C.** 28 square inches **D.** 113 square inches
2. To the nearest inch, find the circumference of a circle with a 3-inch radius.
   F. 9 inches **G.** 19 inches **H.** 28 inches **I.** 113 inches
3. To the nearest tenth, how many more square inches of pizza are in a pizza with a 14-inch diameter than in a pizza with a 12-inch diameter?
   A. 13 square inches **B.** 39.3 square inches **C.** 40.8 square inches **D.** 163.3 square inches

Chapter Review

Vocabulary

area (p. 440)
base of a parallelogram (p. 446)
base of a triangle (p. 447)
capacity (p. 433)
chord (p. 452)
circle (p. 452)
circumference (p. 453)
cone (p. 463)
cube (p. 462)
cubic unit (p. 472)
cylinder (p. 463)
diameter (p. 452)
faces (p. 462)
gram (p. 432)
height of a parallelogram (p. 446)
height of a triangle (p. 447)
liter (p. 433)
mass (p. 432)
meter (p. 431)
metric system (p. 431)
net (p. 464)
perimeter (p. 441)
prism (p. 462)
pyramid (p. 463)
radius (p. 452)
sphere (p. 463)
surface area (p. 468)
three-dimensional figure (p. 462)
volume (p. 472)

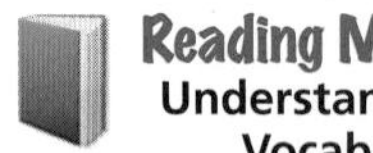

Choose the vocabulary term that best completes each sentence.

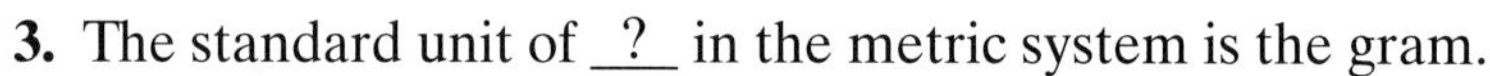

1. A rectangular prism has three pairs of congruent and parallel _?_.
2. A _?_ is a three-dimensional figure with one base.
3. The standard unit of _?_ in the metric system is the gram.
4. A _?_ is a segment that has one endpoint on the circle.
5. _?_ is the number of cubic units inside a three-dimensional figure.

Skills and Concepts

9-1 and 9-2 Objectives

- To choose metric units for length, mass, and capacity
- To convert metric measurements

The standard units of measurement in the **metric system** are the **meter (m),** the **gram (g),** and the **liter (L).** You can convert one metric unit to another by multiplying or dividing by a power of 10.

Complete each statement.

6. 0.3 kg = ■ g
7. 150 cm = ■ m
8. 57,000 mL = ■ L

9-3 and 9-4 Objectives

- To estimate areas
- To find perimeters and areas of rectangles
- To find the areas of parallelograms and triangles
- To find the areas of complex figures

The **area** of a figure is the number of square units inside the figure. The formula for the area of a parallelogram is $A = b \times h$. The formula for the area of a triangle is $A = \frac{1}{2}b \times h$.

Find the perimeter and the area of each figure.

9. 6 ft, 7 ft, 8 ft

10. 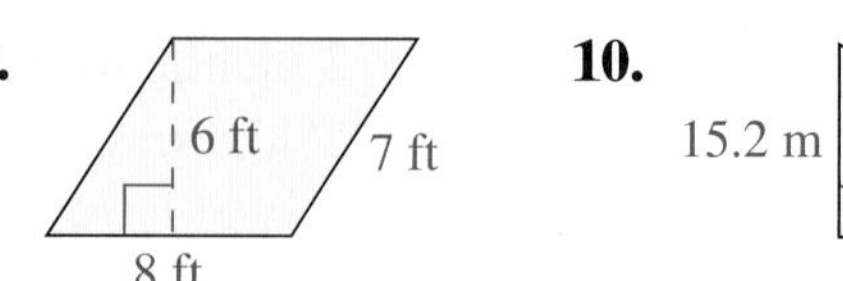

11. 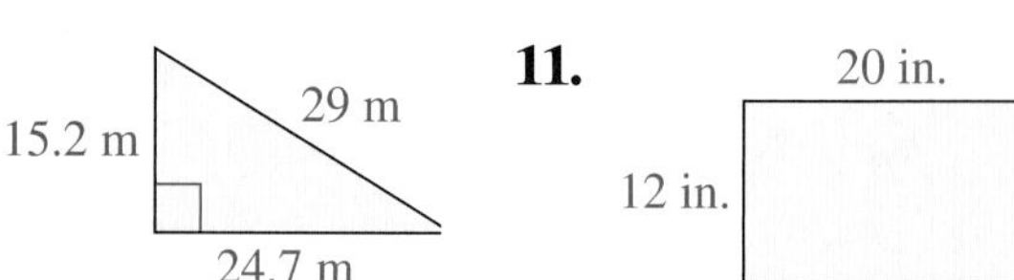

9-5 and 9-6 Objectives

- To identify parts of a circle
- To find circumference
- To find the area of a circle

A **circle** has three kinds of segments: **radius, chord,** and **diameter.** The distance around a circle is the **circumference.** The symbol π represents the ratio $\frac{\text{circumference}}{\text{diameter}}$.

Circumference: $C = \pi d$ or $C = 2\pi r$ Area: $A = \pi r^2$

Use circle *O* for Exercises 12–16. Use 3.14 for π.

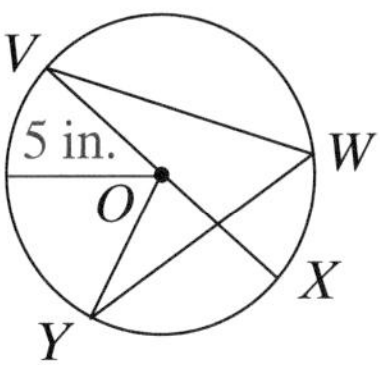

12. Name three chords. **13.** Name a diameter.

14. Name three radii. **15.** Find the circumference.

16. Find the area of the circle to the nearest square inch.

9-7 Objective

- To identify three-dimensional figures

A **prism** is a **three-dimensional figure** with two parallel and congruent **faces** that are polygons. A **pyramid** has triangular faces and one base that is a polygon. You name a prism or a pyramid by the shape of its bases.

Name each figure.

17. 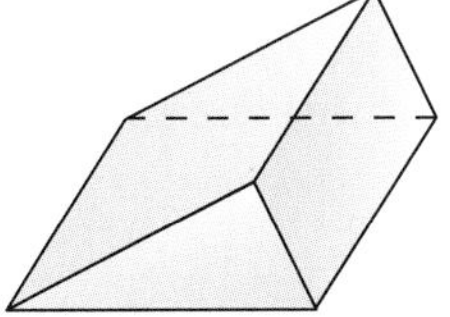

18. 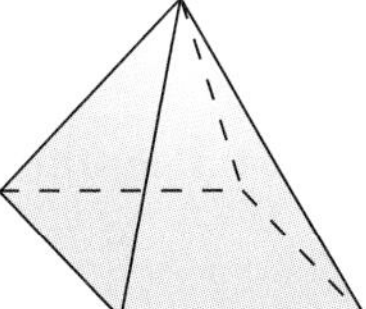

19. 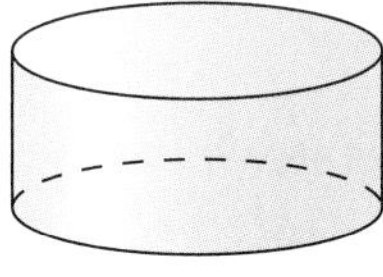

9-8 and 9-9 Objectives

- To find the surface area of a prism
- To find the surface area of a cylinder
- To find the volume of a rectangular prism
- To find the volume of a cylinder

The **surface area** of a three-dimensional figure is the sum of the areas of all its faces. The **volume** of a three-dimensional figure is the number of cubic units needed to fill the space inside the figure. The formula for the volume of a prism or a cylinder is $V = B \times h$, where B is the area of the base.

Find the surface area and volume of each figure.

20. 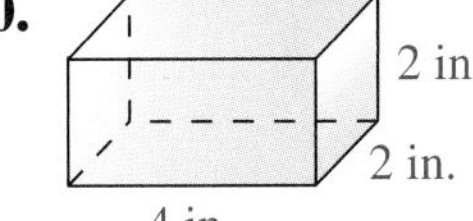

21. 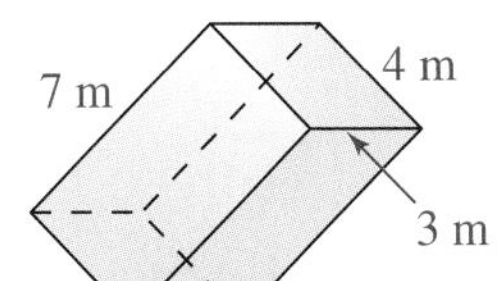

22. 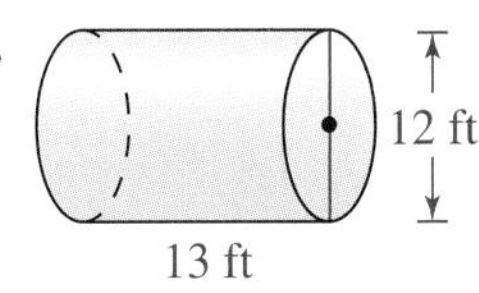

9-10 Objective

- To solve problems by working backward

Some problems involve a series of steps that lead to an end result. To find the initial amount, you can work backward.

23. Travel Tina's family is planning a trip to visit relatives. It will take six hours of driving. Her family will also make two 45-minute stops. If they want to arrive at 4:30 P.M., at what time should they leave?

Chapter Test

Choose an appropriate metric unit for each measurement.

1. length of a car
2. capacity of a cup
3. length of a skateboard
4. mass of a boat

Convert each measurement.

5. 672 millimeters to centimeters
6. 25,040 milliliters to liters
7. 35.1 kilograms to grams
8. 125 liters to kiloliters
9. 42.9 meters to centimeters

Estimate the area of each figure. Each square represents 4 square centimeters.

10. 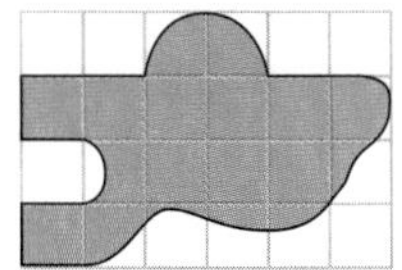

11. 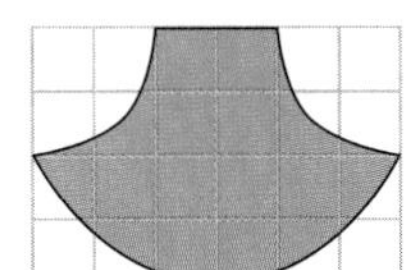

Find the area of each figure.

12. 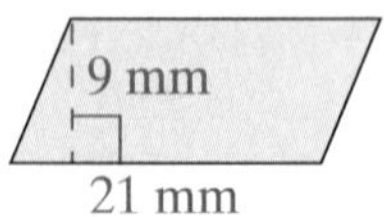

13. 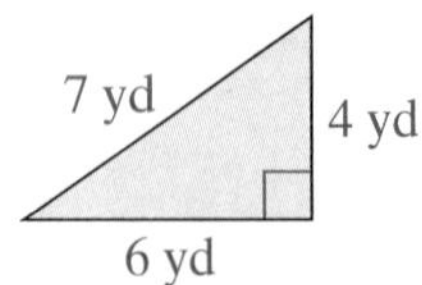

14. 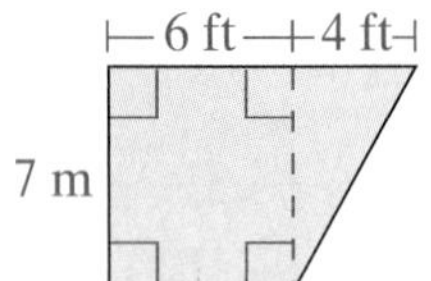

15. 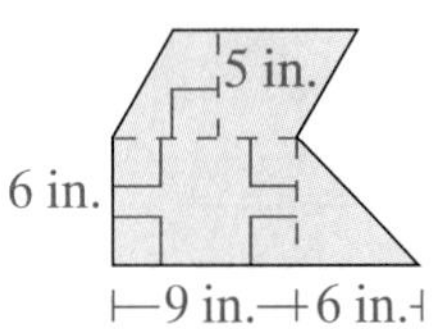

16. **Writing in Math** Which is larger: a pie plate with a radius of 5 inches, or a pie plate with a diameter of 9 inches? Explain.

Find the circumference and area of each circle. Round to the nearest tenth.

17. 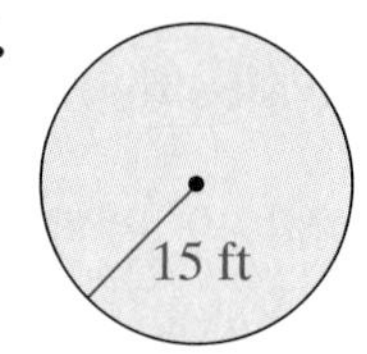

18. 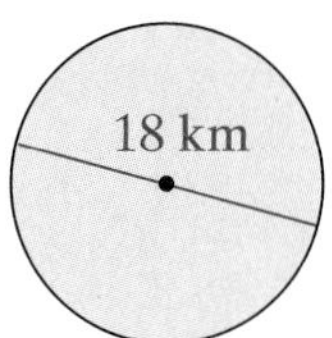

19. **Food** A rectangular cracker has a length of 5 centimeters and an area of 20 square centimeters. Find its perimeter.

20. **Manufacturing** A factory fills cans with tomato juice. A can has a radius of 2 inches and a height of 8 inches. Find its volume.

Find the surface area of each figure.

21. 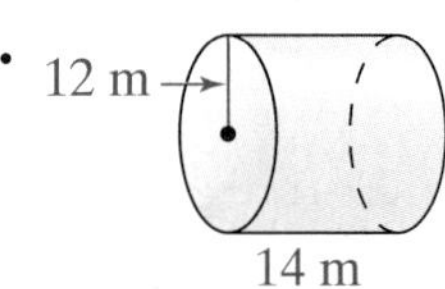

22. 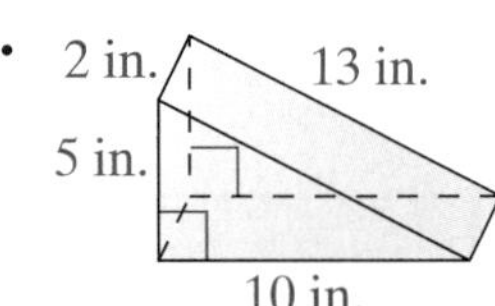

Find the volume of each figure.

23. 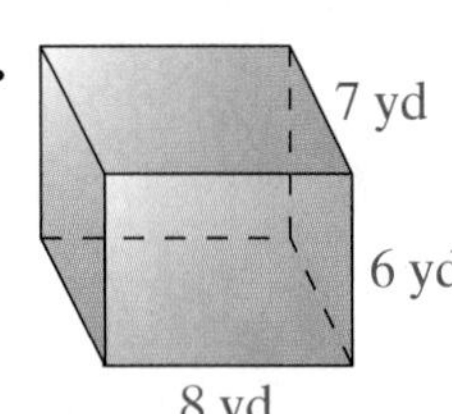

24. 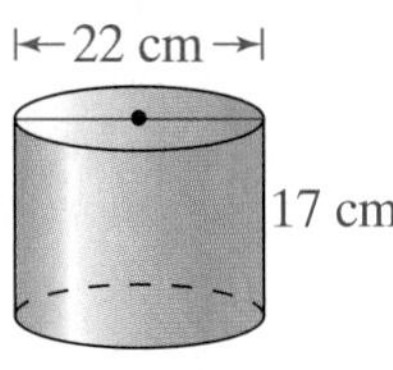

25. Suppose you add 2 to a number, subtract 5, and then multiply by 3. The result is 24. What is the number?

26. The volume of a rectangular prism is 504 square centimeters. The area of the base is 72 square centimeters. Find the height of the prism.

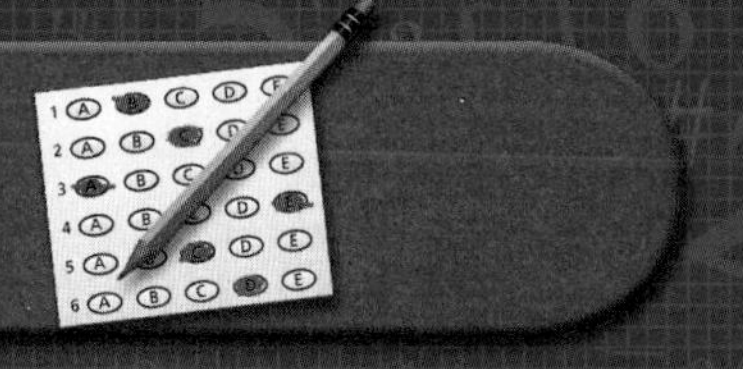

Test Prep

Reading Comprehension **Read each passage below. Then answer each question based on what you have read.**

Clock Face The Clock Tower of the Palace of Westminster in London—what people often call "Big Ben"—is about 316 feet tall. The tower has four sides, each with a large clock. Each clock face is a circle about 22 feet in diameter. The minute hands are about 12 feet long, measuring from the center of the clock face to the tip of the hand. The Clock Tower can be seen from many parts of the city.

1. Which expression represents the circumference of the circle that the tip of one of the minute hands traces out in an hour?
A. 6π **B.** $10\ \pi$ **C.** 12π **D.** 24π

2. If the minute hand were twice as long, how much farther would it travel every hour?
F. half as far **G.** the same distance
H. twice as far **I.** four times as far

3. Which expression represents the area of one of the clock faces?
A. $10 \cdot 10 \cdot \pi$ **B.** $11 \cdot 11 \cdot \pi$
C. $20 \cdot 20 \cdot \pi$ **D.** $22 \cdot 22 \cdot \pi$

4. If the radius of the clock face were twice as long, how many times greater would the area of the face be?
F. the same **G.** two times
H. four times **I.** eight times

Mountain Math It takes about $1\frac{1}{2}$ hours to get from Al's house to Mount Monadnock. First you go west 40 miles on the state highway. Then you turn right and go north another 30 miles, and you're there. On a clear day you can see the tallest buildings in Al's hometown from the top of the mountain.

5. Which choice below does NOT correctly identify a point in this diagram?

A. *Q* is Al's house. **B.** *R* is Al's house.
C. *P* is at the right turn. **D.** *Q* is the mountain.

6. How long will it take Al to get to Mount Monadnock if he drives at a rate of 56 miles per hour for the whole trip?
F. 1 hour **G.** 1.25 hours
H. 1.5 hours **I.** 1.75 hours

7. How many miles is the trip from Al's house to Mount Monadnock?
A. 30 miles **B.** 40 miles
C. 50 miles **D.** 70 miles

8. The odometer on Al's car shows how many miles the car travels. If the odometer shows 12,350 miles as Al leaves home, what will it show after a round trip to the mountain?
F. 12,000 miles **G.** 12,490 miles
H. 12,520 miles **I.** 12,900 miles

Real-World Snapshots

The Shape of Buildings to Come

Applying Measurement When architects design office or apartment buildings, they know that people will want as many windows as possible. The footprint, or area that a building covers, has a lot to do with the arrangement of the windows. For example, a large square building may have inside rooms with no windows. Architects can change the shape of the footprint to make more outside walls.

Let the Sun in

This modern glass building connects two Victorian-era office buildings.

Straw-Bale Construction

College students in Wisconsin designed and built this straw-bale house. Wheat, oats, barley, rice, rye, and flax are all desirable straws for bale walls.

Biosphere 2

Originally constructed as a miniature Earth, Biosphere 2 is now a research facility. It covers 3.15 acres and includes five different environments: a coastal desert, a marsh, a grassy plain, a rain forest, and an ocean.

Rain forest
Grassy plain
Ocean
Kitchen

Put It All Together

Materials graph paper

Footprint using 4 squares

1. Draw three rectangular footprints that you can make using 16 squares. Find each area and perimeter.
2. **Open-Ended** Draw several non-rectangular footprints that use 16 squares. Be creative! Find each perimeter.
3. **a.** Use 16 squares. Draw a square footprint with an open area in the center.
   b. Find the outside perimeter. Find the inside perimeter. Then find the total perimeter.
   c. Reasoning Why might an architect use a design like this for a building? Explain.
4. Consider all the footprints you have drawn. What arrangement of 16 squares gives the greatest total perimeter? The least total perimeter?
5. Buildings A, B, and C at the right are rectangular.
   a. Copy and complete the table. Calculate the volume and total exposed area of each building. (Include the top and four sides, but not the base.) How does the shape affect the surface area?
   b. Which shape gives the most space for windows? Which gives the least? Explain.

Building Entry

These binoculars are four stories tall and made from steel tubing and cement. Each barrel is a conference room with a circular skylight at the top.

A

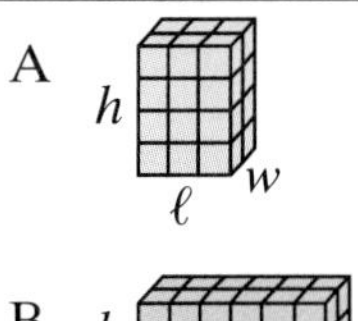

B

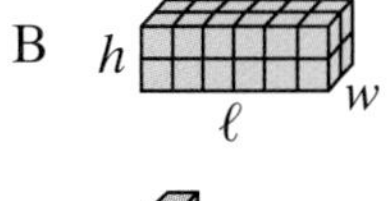

C

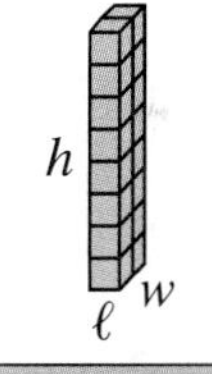

Building Data

Building	ℓ	w	h	Volume	Exposed Surface Area
A	3	2	4	■	■
B	6	2	2	■	■
C	1	3	8	■	■

Take It to the NET For more information about architecture, go to **www.PHSchool.com**.
Web Code: aae-0953

Algebra

CHAPTER 10

Integers

Lessons

Key Vocabulary

- absolute value (p. 492)
- coordinate plane (p. 518)
- function (p. 527)
- integers (p. 491)
- opposites (p. 491)
- ordered pair (p. 518)
- origin (p. 518)
- quadrants (p. 518)

Real-World Snapshots

A forest fire burns at temperatures between 440°F and 2,060°F. As you get closer to the center of Earth, the temperature gets even hotter than a forest fire.

Data File

Selected Earth Temperatures

Location	Temperature (°F)	Elevation (feet)
Vostok Station, Antarctica	−129 (record low)	11,220
Colossal Cave, Arizona	70 (constant)	3,660
El Azizia, Libya	136 (record high)	367
Land surface (average)	47.3	2,559
Sea surface (average)	60.9	0
Upper mantle	932	Above −2,196,480
Lower mantle	3,632	−2,900,000 to −2,196,480
Outer core	9,032	−5,100,000 to −2,900,000
Inner core	12,632	Below −5,100,000

SOURCE: National Oceanic and Atmospheric Administration, *Glossary of Geology*

You will use the data above in this chapter:

- p. 500 Lesson 10-2
- p. 507 Lesson 10-3

Real-World Snapshots On pages 542 and 543, you will solve problems involving elevation.

Chapter 10 Preview

Where You've Been

- In Chapter 1, you added, subtracted, multiplied, and divided decimal numbers greater than or equal to 0.
- In Chapters 4 and 5, you did the same for fractions.

Where You're Going

- In Chapter 10, you will add, subtract, multiply, and divide integers.
- You will graph in the coordinate plane.
- You will see how businesses and stock markets use integers.
- Applying what you learn, you use positive and negative integers in problems related to the weather.

Meteorologists use integers every day to report the temperature.

iTEXT Instant self-check online and on CD-ROM

Diagnosing Readiness

 For help, go to the lesson in green.

Algebra Solving Addition and Subtraction Equations (Lesson 2-6)

Solve each equation.

1. $a - 31 = 8$ **2.** $b + 12 = 43$ **3.** $c - 16 = 84$

4. $d + 13 = 92$ **5.** $e - 23 = 8$ **6.** $f + 45 = 163$

Algebra Solving Multiplication and Division Equations (Lesson 2-7)

Solve each equation.

7. $7g = 42$ **8.** $h \div 6 = 11$ **9.** $8j = 32$

10. $k \div 9 = 8$ **11.** $16m = 240$ **12.** $n \div 14 = 18$

Comparing and Ordering Fractions (Lesson 3-7)

Compare each pair of numbers. Use <, =, or >.

13. $\frac{1}{3} \blacksquare \frac{2}{5}$ **14.** $\frac{3}{4} \blacksquare \frac{2}{3}$ **15.** $\frac{2}{16} \blacksquare \frac{1}{8}$

Order each set of numbers from least to greatest.

16. $\frac{1}{8}, \frac{1}{3}, \frac{1}{12}$ **17.** $\frac{4}{9}, \frac{5}{6}, \frac{7}{12}$ **18.** $\frac{1}{4}, \frac{6}{7}, \frac{1}{2}$

10-1 Using a Number Line

What You'll Learn

To graph integers on a number line

To compare and order integers

. . . And Why

To compare game scores, as in Example 5

Check Skills You'll Need

For help, go to Lesson 3-7.

Compare each pair of numbers. Use <, =, or >.

1. $\frac{3}{2}$ ■ $\frac{7}{10}$
2. $2\frac{2}{3}$ ■ $\frac{8}{3}$
3. $1\frac{7}{5}$ ■ $2\frac{1}{10}$

Order each set of numbers from least to greatest.

4. $\frac{14}{9}, \frac{4}{3}, \frac{8}{5}$
5. $\frac{1}{4}, \frac{2}{5}, \frac{3}{6}$
6. $\frac{3}{8}, \frac{4}{5}, \frac{6}{15}$

New Vocabulary • opposites • integers • absolute value

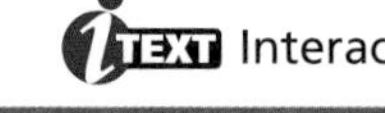
Interactive lesson includes instant self-check, tutorials, and activities.

OBJECTIVE 1 Graphing Integers on a Number Line

Suppose you play tug-of-war with the team on the left shown below. Your team begins by gaining 2 feet. The position of the flag is positive 2 feet, or +2. The expression +2 is usually written simply as 2.

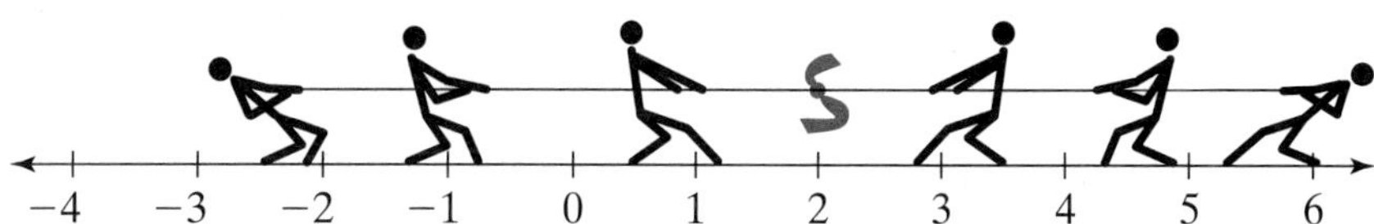

If, instead, your team begins by losing 2 feet, the position of the flag would be negative 2 feet, or −2. These positions can be graphed on a number line.

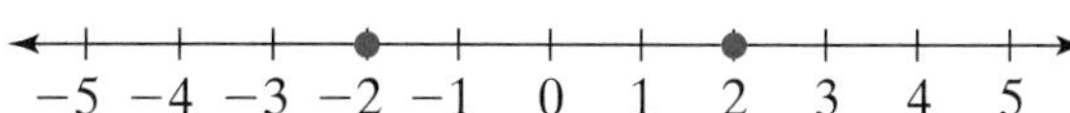

The numbers 2 and −2 are opposites. Two numbers are **opposites** if they are the same distance from 0 on a number line but in opposite directions. **Integers** are the set of positive whole numbers, their opposites, and 0. The opposite of 0 is 0.

Real-World Connection

The "smoke" that makes a performance exciting is actually dry ice.

1 EXAMPLE Representing Situations With Integers

Real World

Dry Ice Dry ice is composed of pressurized carbon dioxide that has a freezing point of 190 degrees below zero Fahrenheit. Use an integer to represent the freezing point of dry ice.

−190°F ← **An integer less than 0 is represented as negative.**

Check Understanding 1 The altitude of New Orleans, Louisiana, is 8 feet below sea level. Use an integer to represent this altitude.

Calculator Hint

You can use the (–) key or the +/– key on your calculator to express an opposite.

2 EXAMPLE Identifying Opposites

Name the opposite of 3.

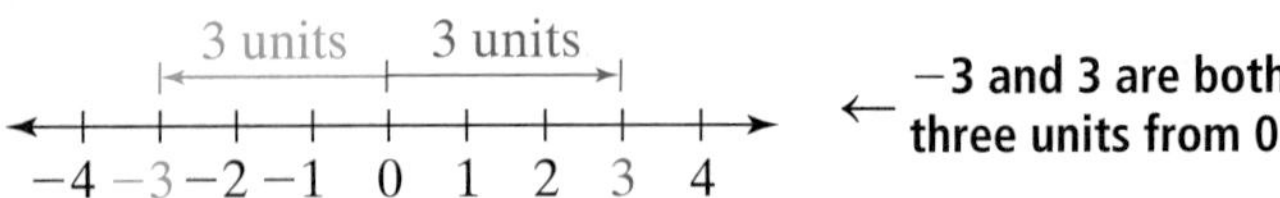

The opposite of 3 is −3.

Check Understanding 2 Name the opposite of −5.

The **absolute value** of a number is its distance from 0 on a number line. You write "the absolute value of negative 3" as $|-3|$. Opposites have the same absolute value.

3 EXAMPLE Finding Absolute Values

Find $|-4|$ and $|2|$.

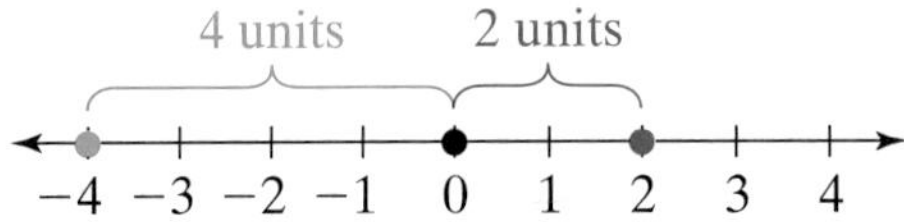

Since −4 is four units from 0, $|-4| = 4$. Since 2 is two units from 0, $|2| = 2$.

Check Understanding 3 **a.** Find $|-1|$. **b.** Find $|7|$. **c.** Find $|-9|$.

OBJECTIVE

2 Comparing and Ordering Integers

Reading Math

As you read from left to right on a horizontal number line, the integers become greater.

You can use a number line to compare integers.

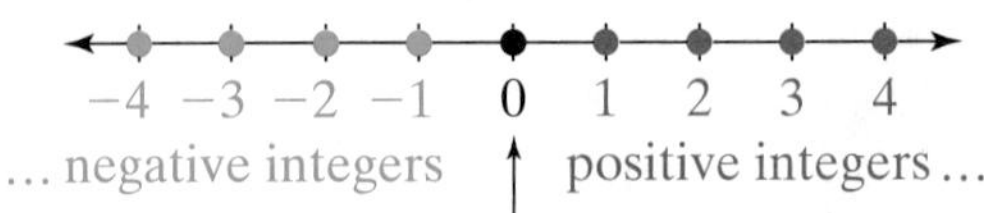

4 EXAMPLE Comparing Integers

Compare −4 and −6.

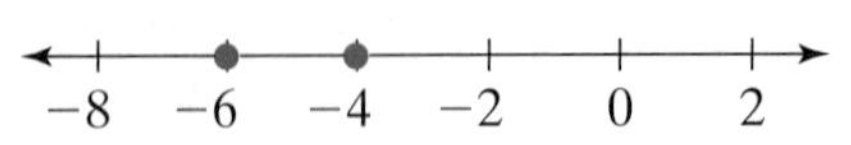

Since −6 is to the left of −4 on the number line, $-6 < -4$.

Check Understanding 4 Compare using < or >. **a.** 5 ■ −3 **b.** −12 ■ 9

You can also use a number line to help you order integers from least to greatest.

5 EXAMPLE Ordering Integers 

Games In a trivia game, points are deducted for incorrect answers. Four teams participate in the game. Order the scores from least to greatest.

Tigers	−200
Bulldogs	+300
Lions	−400
Spartans	+100

Use one hundred as the number line unit.

−400 −300 −200 −100 0 100 200 300 400

−400, −200, 100, 300 ← **Write the scores in order from left to right.**

In order from least to greatest, the scores are −400, −200, 100, and 300.

Check Understanding 5 Order these scores from least to greatest: −25, 100, −50, 75.

EXERCISES

For more practice, see *Extra Practice*.

A Practice by Example

Use an integer to represent each situation.

Example 1 (page 491)

1. earnings of \$15 **2.** 14°F below zero **3.** a debt of \$25

Example 2 (page 492)

Name the opposite of each integer.

4. 13 **5.** −8 **6.** 150 **7.** −1

Example 3 (page 492)

Find each absolute value.

8. $|-4|$ **9.** $|17|$ **10.** $|-65|$ **11.** $|0|$

Example 4 (page 492)

Compare using < or >.

12. 2 ■ −12 **13.** −9 ■ −17 **14.** −23 ■ −4 **15.** −7 ■ 0

Example 5 (page 493)

16. Weather The coldest temperatures on record for five Alaskan cities are −62°F, −70°F, −54°F, −75°F, and −56°F. Write the temperatures in order from coldest to warmest.

  **17. Time Line** A time line is a number line that shows dates.

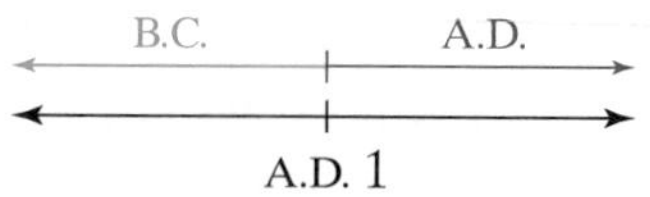

Draw a time line from 2000 B.C. to A.D. 2000. Mark the time line in intervals of 500 years. Then place the following events on the time line.

776 B.C.	First Olympic Games held.
1600 B.C.	Stonehenge is completed.
A.D. 1492	Columbus lands in America.
1190 B.C.	The city of Troy falls to Greek warriors.
A.D. 1971	First microcomputer introduced.
A.D. 1565	Oldest settlement in North America started at St. Augustine.

Real-World Connection

Microchips used in computers are made of silicon, the same material that makes up ordinary beach sand.

Write an integer that represents each situation. Then graph the integer on a number line.

18. You climb 3 flights of stairs.

19. You spend \$7 for a gift.

20. The temperature falls 10 degrees.

21. You earn \$6 babysitting.

Name two numbers that have the given number as their absolute value.

22. 3

23. 22

24. 101

25. 2,004

26. **Writing in Math** Can the absolute value of a number ever be negative? Explain your reasoning.

27. Weather List the following temperatures from least to greatest.

- Normal body temperature is about 37°C.
- An average winter day on the polar ice cap is −25°C.
- The warmest day on record in Canada was 45°C.
- Ski resorts make artificial snow at 0°C, the temperature at which water freezes.
- The coldest day on record in Texas was −31°C.

28. Divers Dean dives 17 feet below the surface of Canyon Lake. Janet dives 25 feet below the lake's surface. Who dives farther below the lake's surface?

29. Starting at the fourth floor, an elevator goes down 3 floors and then up 8 floors. At which floor does the elevator stop?

Compare using <, =, or >.

30. $|-9| \blacksquare |8|$

31. $|13| \blacksquare |-13|$

32. $|0| \blacksquare |-4|$

C Challenge

33. **Number Sense** Compare using $<$ or $>$.

a. If $a > b$, then the opposite of a ■ the opposite of b.

b. If $a < b$, then the opposite of a ■ the opposite of b.

34. **Reasoning** Explain how to locate 225 on the number line below.

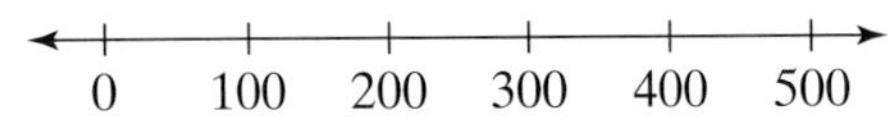

35. **Stretch Your Thinking** In a tug-of-war game, four sixth graders can tug as hard as five fifth graders. Two fifth graders and one sixth grader can tug as hard as one dog. One dog and three fifth graders compete against four sixth graders. Who will win?

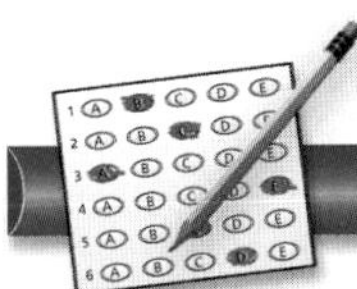

Test Prep

Multiple Choice

36. Which statement is NOT true?

A. $-9 < -7$ **B.** $-3 < 5$ **C.** $-5 > -3$ **D.** $-2 < 6$

37. When multiplied by $\frac{1}{3}$, which number has a product that is an integer?

F. 5 **G.** 6 **H.** 7 **I.** 8

38. Order -2, 4, 0, and -6 from least to greatest.

A. 4, 0, -2, -6 **B.** -6, 4, 0, -2 **C.** 0, -2, 4, -6 **D.** -6, -2, 0, 4

Short Response

39. Write three numbers that are between -4 and -6. Are all of these numbers integers? Explain.

Mixed Review

Lesson 9-4

Find the area of each parallelogram.

40.

41.

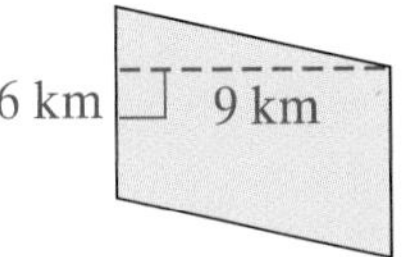

42.

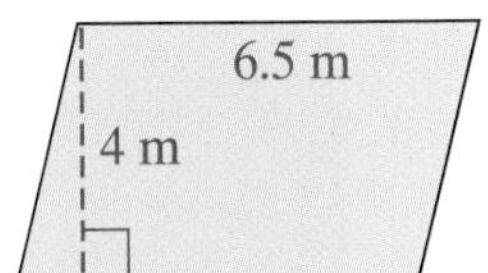

Lesson 7-4

Use the data in the table at the right.

43. Which waterfall has the greatest height? the least height?

44. Which waterfalls are between 2,000 feet and 2,500 feet?

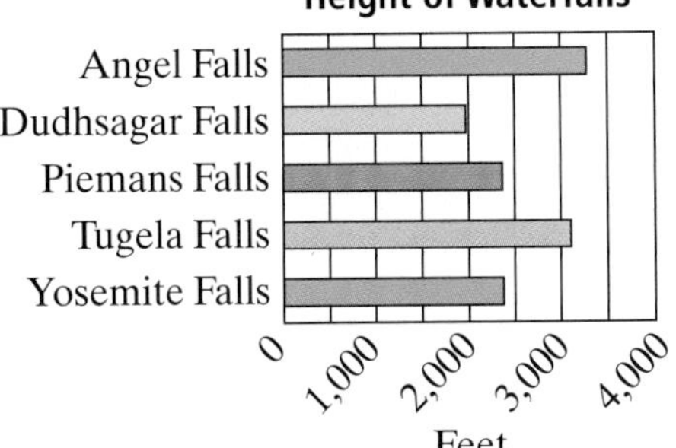

Investigation Modeling Addition of Integers

For Use With Lesson 10-2

Activity

1. Find 5 + 2. Show 5 "+" chips. Then add 2 "+" chips. There are 7 "+" chips. So, 5 + 2 = 7.

2. Find −5 + (−2). Show 5 "−" chips. Then add 2 "−" chips. There are 7 "−" chips. So, −5 + (−2) = −7.

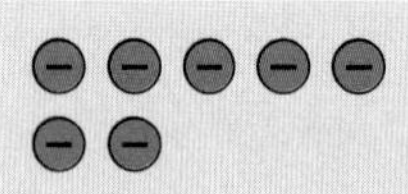

To add integers with different signs, use zero pairs. These chips ⊕ ⊖ are a *zero pair* because ⊕ + ⊖ = 0. Removing a zero pair does not change the sum.

3. Find 5 + (−2). Show 5 "+" chips. Then add 2 "−" chips. Pair the "+" and "−" chips. Remove the pairs. There are 3 "+" chips left. So, 5 + (−2) = 3.

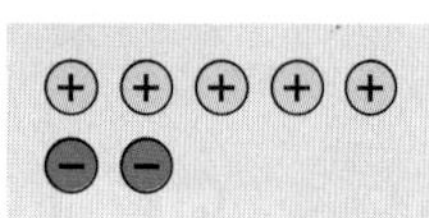

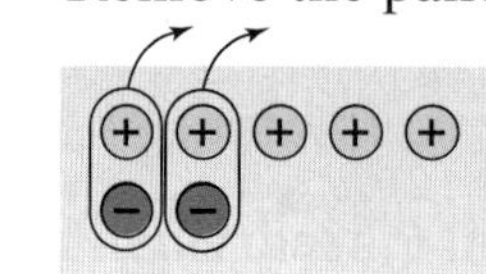

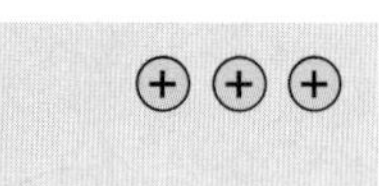

4. Find −5 + 2. Show 5 "−" chips. Then add 2 "+" chips. Pair "+" and "−" chips. Remove the pairs. There are 3 "−" chips left. So, −5 + 2 = −3.

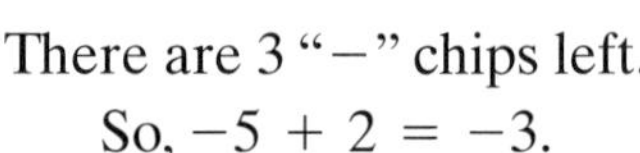

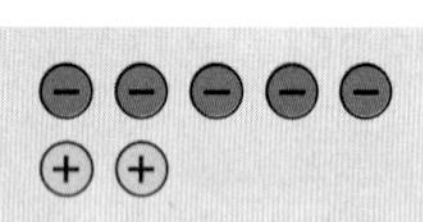

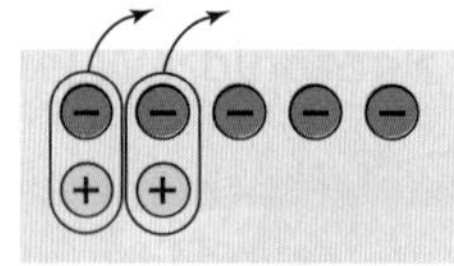

EXERCISES

Use chips or mental math to help you add the following integers.

1. 4 + 5 **2.** 6 + (−3) **3.** −2 + (−3) **4.** −2 + 2

5. 13 + (−8) **6.** −4 + 3 **7.** −7 + (−2) **8.** 8 + (−11)

9. Write a rule for adding each of the following: (a) two positive integers, (b) two negative integers, and (c) two integers with different signs.

10-2 Adding Integers

What You'll Learn

To add integers with the same signs

To add integers with different signs

. . . And Why

To determine the result of a contest, as in Example 5

Check Skills You'll Need

For help, go to Lesson 10-1.

Find each absolute value.

1. $|-15|$ **2.** $|-12|$ **3.** $|-8|$ **4.** $|8|$

5. Is the absolute value of a negative number always less than the absolute value of a positive number? Explain your reasoning.

Interactive lesson includes instant self-check, tutorials, and activities.

OBJECTIVE 1 Adding Integers With the Same Sign

You can use a number line to model the addition of integers. You start at 0, facing the positive direction. You move forward for a positive integer or backward for a negative integer. Here is how to find $3 + 2$.

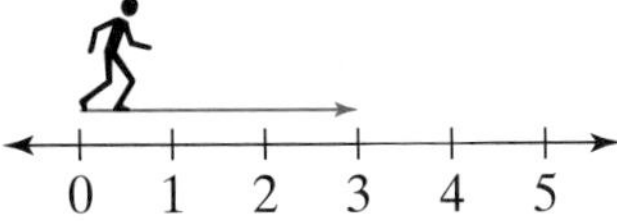

Start at 0. Face the positive direction. Move forward 3 units for 3.

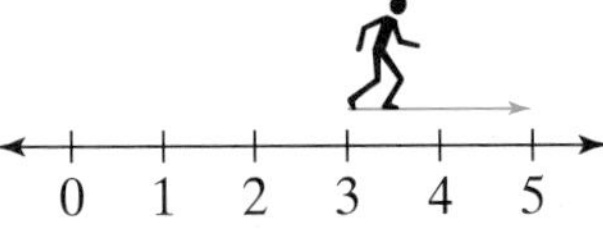

Then move forward 2 more units for 2. You stop at 5.

So, $3 + 2 = 5$. Notice that the sum of two positive integers is positive.

1 EXAMPLE Using a Number Line

Reading Math

Parentheses are used in $-3 + (-2)$ to show that a negative number is being added.

Find $-3 + (-2)$.

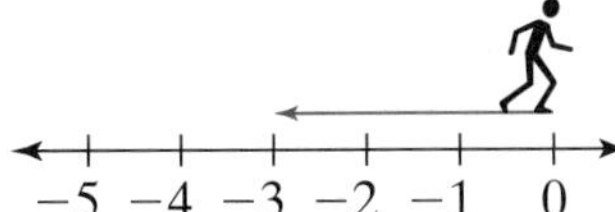

Start at 0. Face the positive direction. Move backward 3 units for −3.

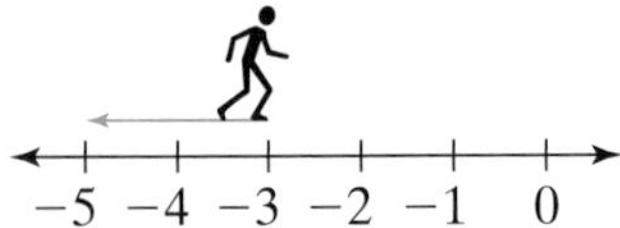

Then move backward 2 more units for −2. You stop at −5.

So, $-3 + (-2) = -5$.

Check Understanding 1 Find each sum. Use a number line.

a. $-1 + (-3)$ **b.** $2 + 10$ **c.** $(-5) + (-4)$

d. Number Sense The sum of two negative integers is _?_.

Key Concepts — Adding Integers With the Same Sign

The sum of two positive integers is positive. The sum of two negative integers is negative.

Examples: $2 + 3 = 5$ $\qquad$ $-2 + (-3) = -5$

2 EXAMPLE — Adding Integers With the Same Sign

Find each sum.

a. $9 + 18$

$9 + 18 = 27$

↑ **The sum of two positive integers is positive.**

b. $-3 + (-7)$

$-3 + (-7) = -10$

↑ **The sum of two negative integers is negative.**

 **2** Find each sum. **a.** $7 + 9$ **b.** $-9 + (-12)$

OBJECTIVE 2 Adding Integers With Different Signs

You can also use a number line to model the addition of integers with different signs. Here is how to find $3 + (-2)$.

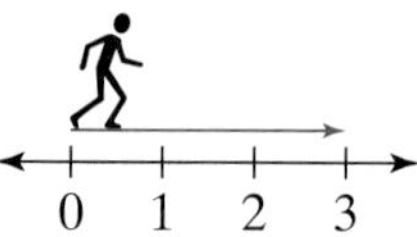

Start at 0, and face the positive direction. Move forward 3 units for 3.

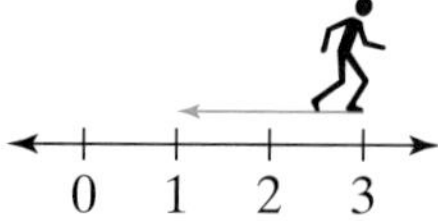

Then move backward 2 units for −2. You stop at 1.

So, $3 + (-2) = 1$.

3 EXAMPLE — Using a Number Line

Find $-3 + 2$. Use a number line.

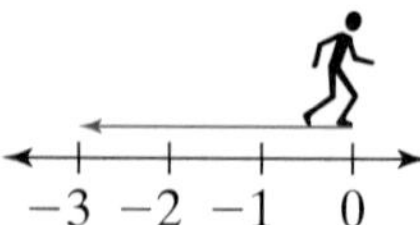

Start at 0, and face the positive direction. Move backward 3 units for −3.

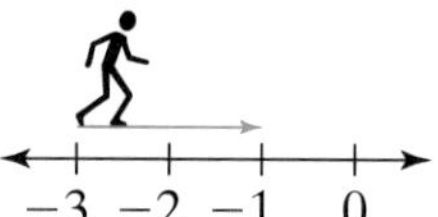

Then move forward 2 units for 2. You stop at −1.

So, $-3 + 2 = -1$.

 **Check Understanding** **3** Use a number line to find each sum. **a.** $4 + (-1)$ **b.** $-1 + 4$

Consider the following:

$3 - 2 = 1 \rightarrow 3 + (-2) = 1$

$4 - 1 = 3 \rightarrow 4 + (-1) = 3$

As you can see, adding integers with different signs is related to subtraction.

Need Help?
Positive 3 can be written as +3 or 3. In either case, its sign is positive.

Key Concepts **Adding Integers With Different Signs**

To add integers with different signs, first find the absolute value of each integer. Then, subtract the lesser absolute value from the greater. The sum has the sign of the integer with the greater absolute value.

Examples: $2 + (-3) = -1$ $\quad -2 + 3 = 1$

4 EXAMPLE Adding Integers With Different Signs

a. Find $8 + (-5)$.

$|8| = 8$
$|-5| = 5$ ← Find the absolute values of the integers.

$8 - 5 = 3$ ← Subtract the absolute values.

$8 + (-5) = 3$ ← The sum has the sign of the integer with the greater absolute value.

b. Find $-9 + 6$.

$|-9| = 9$
$|6| = 6$ ← Find the absolute values of the integers.

$9 - 6 = 3$ ← Subtract the absolute values.

$-9 + 6 = -3$ ← The sum has the sign of the integer with the greater absolute value.

Check Understanding 4 Find each sum.

a. $7 + (-10)$ **b.** $-11 + 4$ **c.** $12 + (-3)$

d. **Number Sense** How can you tell whether a sum will be positive or negative before adding?

5 EXAMPLE Real-World Problem Solving

Real-World Connection
The world record for a frog jumping three times is 21 feet $5\frac{3}{4}$ inches.

Frog Jumping Contest Suppose you enter your frog in a jumping contest. The judge records each jump. A jump toward the finish line is a positive number. A jump away from the finish line is a negative number.

Your frog jumps 4 feet toward the finish line. Then he jumps 6 feet away. What is the result of these jumps?

$|4| = 4$ and $|-6| = 6$ ← Find the absolute value of each integer.

$6 - 4 = 2$ ← Subtract the absolute values.

$4 + (-6) = -2.$ ← Since −6 has the greater absolute value, the sum is negative.

The result of the frog's jumps is −2 feet.

Check Understanding 5 **Reasoning** What would have been the result if the frog jumped 4 feet away from the finish line and then 6 feet toward it?

EXERCISES

For more practice, see *Extra Practice.*

A Practice by Example

Example 1 (page 497)

Use a number line to find each sum.

1. $3 + 7$ **2.** $-8 + (-1)$ **3.** $-7 + (-7)$

4. $-3 + (-5)$ **5.** $6 + 5$ **6.** $-4 + (-4)$

Example 2 (page 498)

Find each sum.

7. $-31 + (-16)$ **8.** $-12 + (-9)$ **9.** $13 + 29$

10. $91 + 28$ **11.** $-47 + (-41)$ **12.** $-51 + (-9)$

Example 3 (page 498)

Use a number line to find each sum.

13. $-5 + 9$ **14.** $-8 + 3$ **15.** $7 + (-7)$

16. $6 + (-4)$ **17.** $-3 + 5$ **18.** $8 + (-1)$

Example 4 (page 499)

Find each sum.

19. $16 + (-5)$ **20.** $-48 + 78$ **21.** $89 + (-176)$

22. $23 + (-15)$ **23.** $-8 + 72$ **24.** $18 + (-39)$

Example 5 (page 499)

25. A submarine is 64 feet below sea level. The submarine then rises 19 feet. What integer describes the position of the submarine?

26. **Football** A football team gains 6 yards on one play. On the next play, the team loses 11 yards. What is the result of these two plays?

B Apply Your Skills

Find each sum.

27. $-6 + (-11) + 7$ **28.** $(-8) + 12 + (-5)$

29. $8 + (-1) + (-6)$ **30.** $-2 + 6 + (-3)$

31. Open-Ended Write an addition exercise involving a positive integer and a negative integer with each type of sum.
a. negative **b.** zero **c.** positive

32. **Money** Suppose you earn \$12 on Saturday, spend \$8 on Monday, and earn \$7 on Friday. How much money do you have for the weekend?

33. **Office Buildings** Suppose the mail center of the Hancock Tower is on the 15th floor. A clerk delivers mail by going up 5 floors, down 3 floors, and then down another 4 floors. Where is the clerk in relation to the mail center?

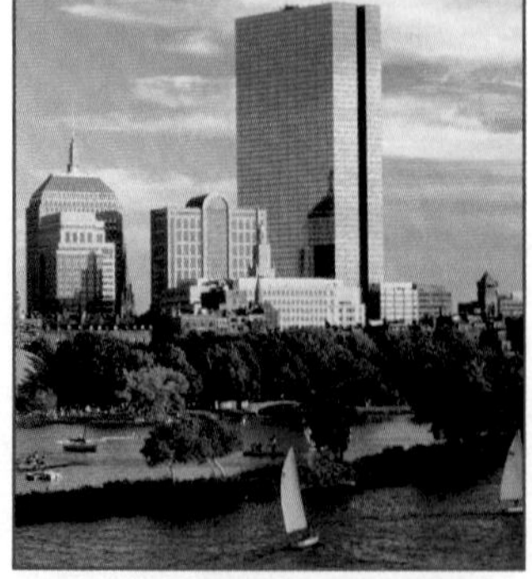

Real-World Connection

The Hancock Tower in Boston has 62 floors.

Compare. Write <, =, or >.

34. $-7 + (-3) \blacksquare 7 + 3$

35. $5 + (-5) \blacksquare -1 + 1$

36. **Writing in Math** Explain how to find the sum of -41 and 48.

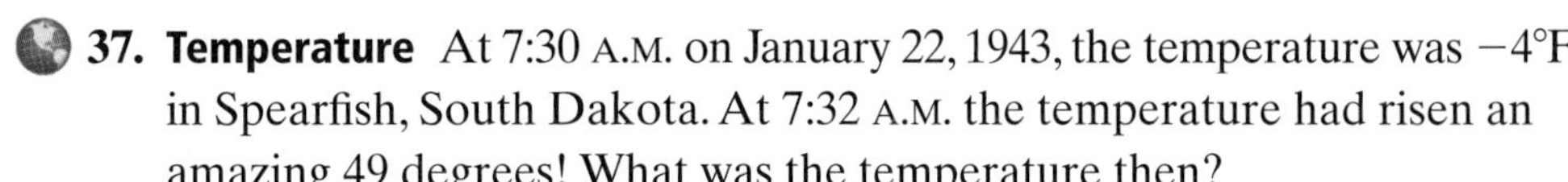

37. Temperature At 7:30 A.M. on January 22, 1943, the temperature was -4°F in Spearfish, South Dakota. At 7:32 A.M. the temperature had risen an amazing 49 degrees! What was the temperature then?

Challenge

38. Puzzles Copy the square at the right. Place the integers $-4, -3, -2, -1, 0, 1, 2, 3$, and 4 in the boxes so that the vertical, horizontal, and diagonal sums are 0.

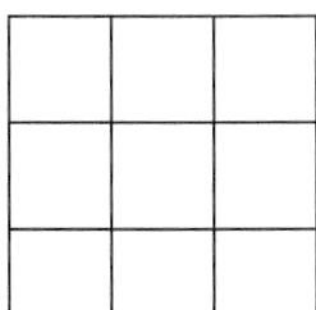

39. Stretch Your Thinking A four-digit number is a multiple of 9. The first two digits are the same and the last two digits are 58. What is the number?

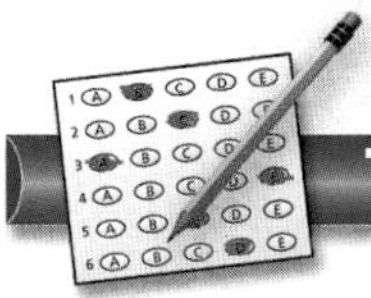

Test Prep

Multiple Choice

40. Which expression has a sum of -8?
A. $-12 + (-4)$ **B.** $-11 + 3$ **C.** $-5 + 3$ **D.** $9 + (-1)$

Take It to the NET
Online lesson quiz at
www.PHSchool.com
Web Code: aaa-1002

41. Which expresson does NOT have a sum of -3?
F. $-4 + 1$ **G.** $-2 + (-1)$ **H.** $7 + (-10)$ **I.** $6 + (-3)$

42. At 6:00 A.M., the temperature was -10°F. Four hours later the temperature had risen 21 degrees. What was the temperature then?
A. -31°F **B.** -11°F **C.** 11°F **D.** 31°F

Short Response

43. The top of a mountain is 425 feet above sea level. The base of the mountain is 654 feet below sea level. **(a)** What is the height of the mountain? **(b)** Draw a diagram to justify your answer.

Mixed Review

Lesson 9-5

Name each of the following for circle *J* at the right.

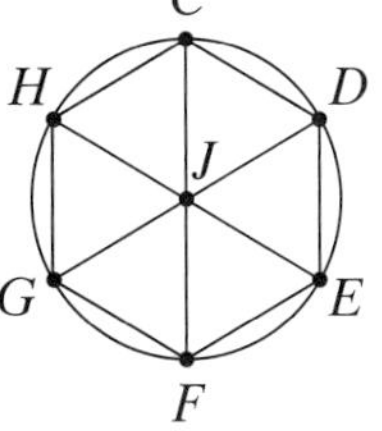

44. radii

45. diameters

46. chords

47. central angles

Lesson 9-4

48. Find the area of a triangle with a base of 12 cm and a height of 6 cm.

Investigation Modeling Subtraction of Integers

For Use With Lesson 10-3

Activity

1. Find $5 - 2$. Show 5 "+" chips. Take away 2 "+" chips. There are 3 "+" chips. So, $5 - 2 = 3$.

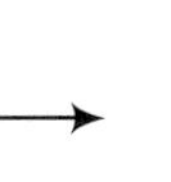

2. Find $-5 - (-2)$. Show 5 "−" chips. Take away 2 "−" chips. There are 3 "−" chips. So, $-5 - (-2) = -3$.

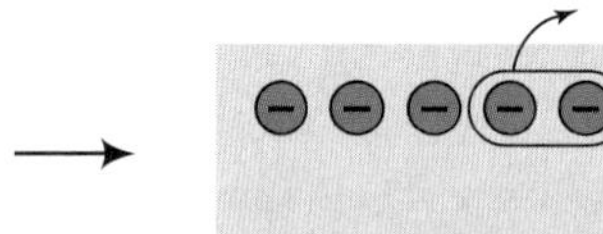

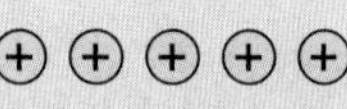

Remember that ⊕ and ⊖ are a zero pair. Sometimes you need to insert zero pairs in order to subtract.

3. Find $5 - (-2)$. Show 5 "+" chips. Insert two zero pairs. Then take away 2 "−" chips. There are 7 "+" chips left. So, $5 - (-2) = 7$.

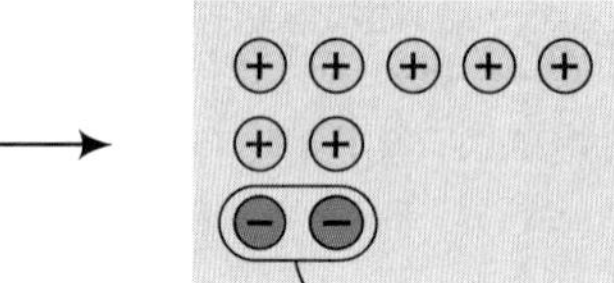
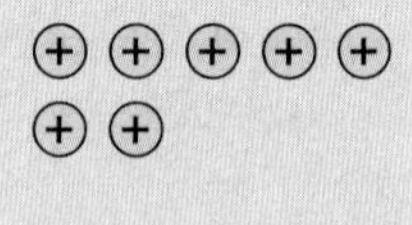

4. Find $-5 - 2$. Show 5 "−" chips. Insert two zero pairs. Then take away 2 "+" chips. There are 7 "−" chips left. So, $-5 - 2 = -7$.

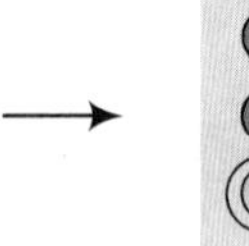
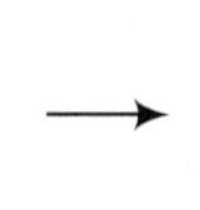
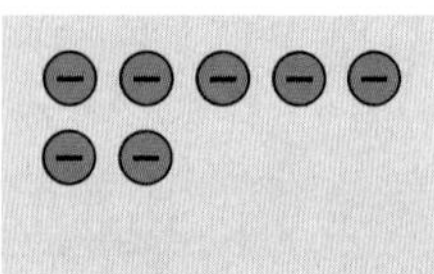

EXERCISES

Use chips or mental math to help you subtract the following integers.

1. $8 - 6$ **2.** $-4 - (-3)$ **3.** $5 - 8$ **4.** $-3 - 7$

5. $-6 - 2$ **6.** $5 - (-9)$ **7.** $-8 - (-13)$ **8.** $-5 - (-8)$

10-3 Subtracting Integers

Algebra

What You'll Learn

 To subtract integers

 To solve equations with integers

. . . And Why

To find a change in depth, as in Example 3

Check Skills You'll Need

For help, go to Lesson 2-6.

Solve each equation.

1. $a + 15 = 32$ **2.** $b + 13 = 44$ **3.** $c + 16 = 23$

4. $d + 88 = 88$ **5.** $105 + e = 263$ **6.** $f + 315 = 495$

7. Estimate the value of x if $x + 26.8 = 65$.

OBJECTIVE

 Interactive lesson includes instant self-check, tutorials, and activities.

1 Subtracting Integers

On a number line, the subtraction operation tells you to turn around and face the negative direction. Here is how to find $3 - 2$ using a number line.

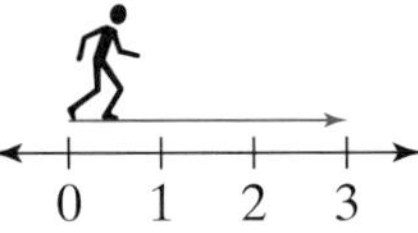

Start at 0. Face the positive direction. Move forward 3 units for 3.

The subtraction sign tells you to turn around.

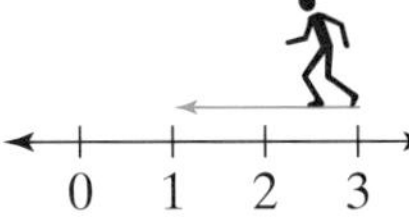

Then move forward 2 units for 2. You stop at 1.

So, $3 - 2 = 1$.

1 EXAMPLE Using a Number Line to Subtract Integers

Reading Math

$3 - (-2)$ is read "3 minus negative 2."

Find $3 - (-2)$.

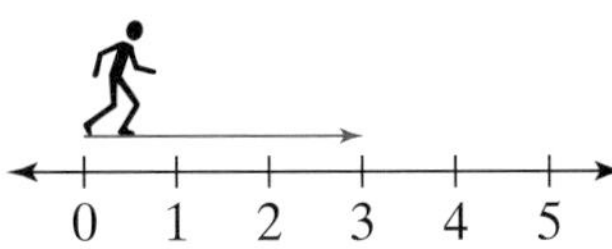

Start at 0. Face the positive direction. Move forward 3 units for 3.

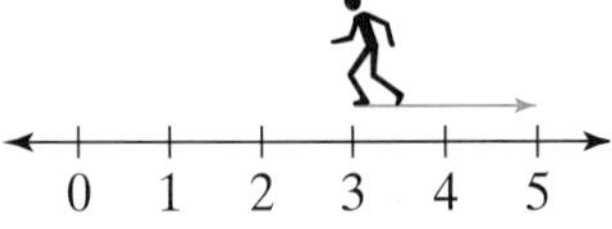

For subtraction, turn around. Then move backward 2 units for −2. You stop at 5.

So, $3 - (-2) = 5$.

Check Understanding 1 Use a number line for each subtraction.

a. $4 - 1$ **b.** $4 - (-1)$ **c.** $3 - (-5)$

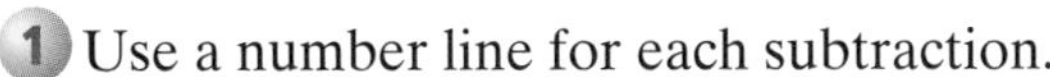

d. Number Sense What seems to happen when you subtract a negative?

There are similarities between addition and subtraction sentences.

$$3 + (-2) = 1 \rightarrow 3 - 2 = 1$$

Subtracting an integer gives the same result as adding its opposite.

Key Concepts | **Subtracting Integers**

You subtract an integer by adding its opposite.

Examples:

$10 - 6 = 10 + (-6)$	$10 - (-6) = 10 + (-6)$
$-10 - 6 = -10 + (-6)$	$-10 - (-6) = 10 + 6$

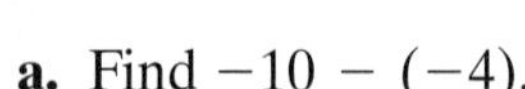

2 EXAMPLE Subtracting Integers

Need Help?
For help adding integers, go to Lesson 10-2.

a. Find $-10 - (-4)$.

$-10 - (-4) = -10 + 4$ ← **To subtract −4, add its opposite, 4.**

$= -6$ ← **Simplify.**

b. Find $-2 - 7$.

$-2 - 7 = -2 + (-7)$ ← **To subtract 7, add its opposite, −7.**

$= -9$ ← **Simplify.**

Check Understanding 2 Find each difference.

a. $9 - (-3)$ **b.** $-6 - (-2)$ **c.** $-3 - 5$

d. **Number Sense** How can you tell that the difference of two numbers will be positive or negative without doing the computation?

Real-World Connection
Alvin has a safe diving depth of about 13,000 feet.

3 EXAMPLE Real-World Problem Solving

Submarines The research submarine *Alvin* was 1,500 feet below sea level (−1,500). It then moved to 1,872 feet below sea level (−1,872). How many feet did *Alvin* descend?

Find $-1{,}872 - (-1{,}500)$.

$-1{,}872 - (-1{,}500) = 1{,}872 + 1{,}500$ ← **To subtract −1,500, add its opposite.**

$= -372$ ← **Simplify.**

Alvin is 372 feet farther below sea level.

Check Understanding 3 Suppose *Alvin* then moved to a position of 1,250 feet below sea level (−1,250). How many feet did it move?

OBJECTIVE

2 Solving Equations With Integers

You can solve addition and subtraction equations using integers. You can write either of the following to solve $t + 9 = 5$.

$$\begin{array}{rr} t + 9 = & 5 \\ -\ 9 & -\ 9 \\ \hline \end{array} \qquad \text{or} \qquad t + 9 - 9 = 5 - 9$$

4 EXAMPLE Solving Equations With Integers

Solve each equation.

a. $t + 9 = 5$

$t + 9 - 9 = 5 - 9$ ← **Subtract 9 from each side.**

$t = 5 + (-9)$ ← **To subtract 9, add its oppposite.**

$t = -4$ ← **Simplify.**

b. $a - 7 = -12$

$a - 7 + 7 = -12 + 7$ ← **Add 7 to each side.**

$a = -5$ ← **Simplify.**

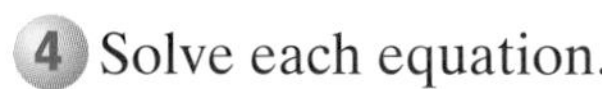

Check Understanding 4 Solve each equation. **a.** $b + 14 = 8$ **b.** $c - 15 = -5$

EXERCISES

For more practice, see *Extra Practice*.

A Practice by Example

Use a number line. Find each difference.

Example 1 (page 503)

1. $6 - (-2)$ **2.** $5 - 3$ **3.** $-4 - (-1)$

4. $-1 - (-1)$ **5.** $7 - (-2)$ **6.** $-4 - 3$

Example 2 (page 504)

Find each difference.

7. $-9 - 7$ **8.** $81 - 106$ **9.** $12 - (-17)$

10. $43 - (-21)$ **11.** $-24 - (-12)$ **12.** $-25 - (-57)$

Example 3 (page 504)

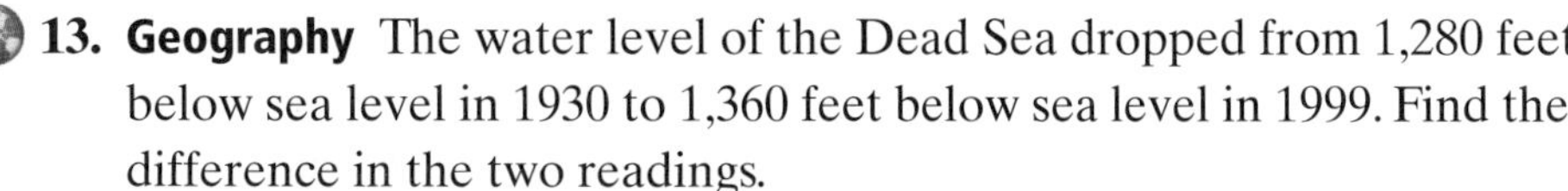

13. Geography The water level of the Dead Sea dropped from 1,280 feet below sea level in 1930 to 1,360 feet below sea level in 1999. Find the difference in the two readings.

14. Bank Accounts You have a balance of \$13 in your bank account. You write a check for \$17. What is the balance in your account?

Example 4 (page 505)

Solve each equation.

15. $t + 12 = 9$
16. $v - 6 = -4$
17. $-3 + c = -8$
18. $12 + r = -11$
19. $w - 18 = -13$
20. $s - 16 = -25$

B Apply Your Skills

Subtract.

21. $17 - 18$
22. $55 - (-81)$
23. $-18 - 13 - 12$
24. $54 - (-81)$
25. $23 - (-18)$
26. $16 - 28 - (-38)$

27. **Bank Accounts** You receive a \$150 check, a \$300 bill, a \$250 bill, an \$80 check, and a \$105 check. By how much will your bank account change when you deposit the checks and pay the bills?

28. **Time Zones** Greenwich, England is located on the 0° meridian, also called the prime meridian. Standard time all over the world is computed in relation to Greenwich Mean Time (GMT). The table at the right indicates the number of hours from the GMT for each city. Suppose it is 1:30 P.M. in Greenwich. Find the time for each city.

City	Hours from GMT
Cairo, Egypt	+2
Honolulu, Hawaii	−10
Lima, Peru	−5
London, England	0
Los Angeles, U.S.A.	−8
Paris, France	+1
Sydney, Australia	+10
Tokyo, Japan	+9
Washington, D.C., U.S.A.	−5

29. **Writing in Math** Explain how to find the difference $-15 - 26$.

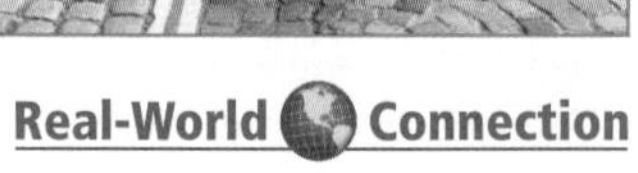

Real-World Connection

This home is divided by the prime meridian. The two sides of the house are in different time zones.

30. **Hiking** A hiker is at the top of Lost Mine Peak. The elevation of the peak is 6,850 feet. The beginning of the Lost Mine trail has an elevation of 5,600 feet. What is the trail's change in elevation?

Determine whether each statement is *always, sometimes,* or *never* true.

31. (positive integer) − (negative integer) = (negative integer)
32. (positive integer) − (positive integer) = (positive integer)
33. (any integer) − (its opposite) = zero

34. **Entertainment** After the first round in a game show, a contestant has 250 points. At the end of the second round, the contestant has −300 points. How did the score change during the second round?

35. **Golf** In golf, par represents an average score. Suppose you are 2 under par at the end of 9 holes. At the end of 18 holes, you are 5 under par. What was your score on the last 9 holes?

36. **Number Sense** Is the subtraction of integers commutative? In other words, is $a - b$ equal to $b - a$ for all integer values of a and b? Explain.

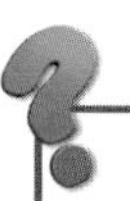

Need Help?
The range is the difference between the greatest and the least value in a set of data.

37. **Data File, p. 489** Find the difference between the record low and the record high temperatures.

Find the range for each set of data.

38. $-3, 12, -6, -15, 8$

39. $25, 31, 20, 0, -3, -18$

40. $13, 29, -32, 8, 30, -19, -4, 3$

Challenge

Compare using <, =, or >.

41. $|8 - (-2)| \blacksquare |8| - |-2|$

42. $|-4 + 8| \blacksquare |-4| + |8|$

43. $|-3 + (-1)| \blacksquare |-3| + |-1|$

44. **Reasoning** Suppose your friend says that she has discovered a new method that can be used to subtract integers. Below is the subtraction of $6 - 8$ using her method.

$$6 - 8 = 6 - (6 + 2) = (6 - 6) - 2 = 0 - 2 = -2$$

Is your friend's method correct? Explain her method in words. Test the method with other numbers.

45. **Stretch Your Thinking** Tomorrow will not be Monday or Friday. Today is not Tuesday or Wednesday. Yesterday was not Thursday or Sunday. What day was yesterday?

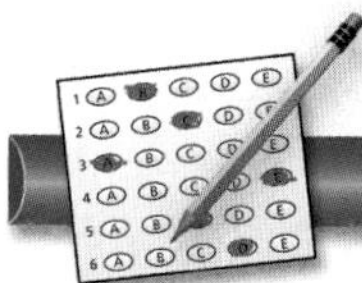

Test Prep

Multiple Choice

46. Which expression does NOT have a difference of -5?
A. $10 - 15$ **B.** $-2 - 7$ **C.** $-7 - (-2)$ **D.** $-4 - 1$

47. The low temperature for a city is -8°F. The high temperature on the same day is 12°F. What is the range in temperatures for that day?
F. -20°F **G.** -4°F **H.** 4°F **I.** 20°F

Take It to the NET
Online lesson quiz at **www.PHSchool.com**
Web Code: aaa-1003

48. You have \$40 in your bank account. You deposit \$12 and then later withdraw \$23. How much money do you have in your account?
A. $-$\$29 **B.** $-$\$5 **C.** \$5 **D.** \$29

Short Response

49. During a winter storm, the temperature fell to 7°F below zero. By noon, the temperature was 8°F above zero. **(a)** Explain how you would find the number of degrees the temperature rose. **(b)** Find how much the temperature rose.

Mixed Review

Lesson 8-1 **Name each of the following using the diagram at the right.**

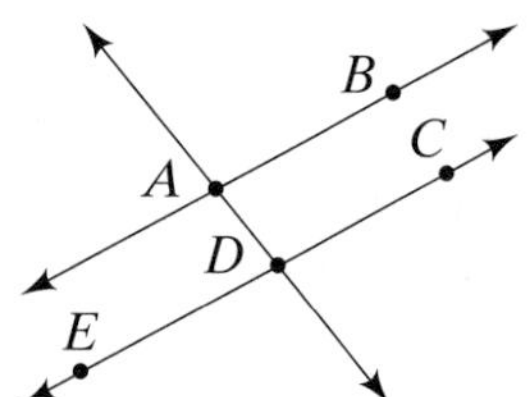

50. three noncollinear points

51. three rays

52. three segments

Lesson 7-6 **The spreadsheet gives the number of cars parked in two parking lots for a three-day county fair.**

53. Write a formula that will calculate the total cars parked in the two lots on Friday.

54. Write a formula that will calculate the total cars parked in Lot X for the three days.

55. Write a formula that will calculate the total cars parked in the two lots for the three days.

	A	B	C	D
1	Day	Lot X (cars)	Lot Y (cars)	
2	Fri.	89	112	
3	Sat.	205	226	
4	Sun.	195	176	
5				

Practice Game

A Race to the End

What You'll Need

- game board
- two different-colored number cubes
- two different-colored place markers

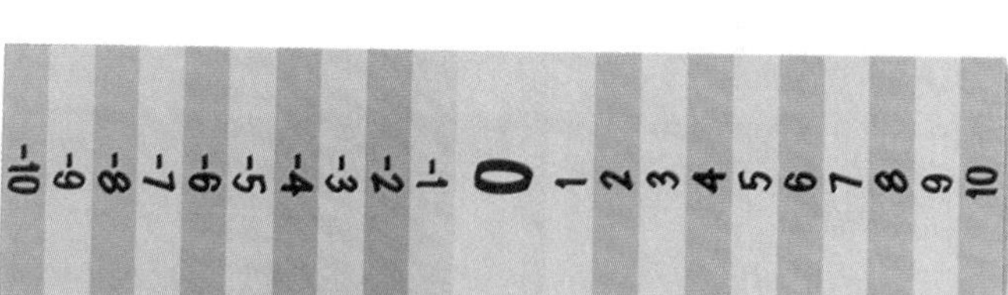

How to Play

- Each of two players places his or her marker on 0.
- Designate one cube to represent positive integers and the other cube to represent negative integers.
- One player rolls the two number cubes.
- The player adds the integers shown on the cubes and then moves his or her marker the number of spaces and direction indicated by the sum.
- Players take turns rolling the number cubes and moving their markers.
- The first player who reaches or goes past either end of the board wins.

10-4 Multiplying Integers

Algebra

What You'll Learn

To multiply integers

. . . And Why

To find the change in stock prices, as in Example 3

✓ Check Skills You'll Need

For help, go to Lesson 10-2.

Find each sum.

1. $-4 + (-4)$ **2.** $32 + 32$

3. $-14 + (-14)$ **4.** $-45 + (-45)$

5. $81 + 81$ **6.** $-23 + (-23)$

OBJECTIVE

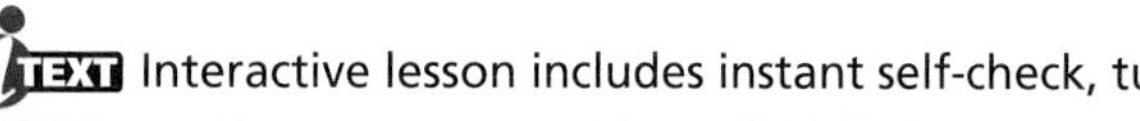

Interactive lesson includes instant self-check, tutorials, and activities.

1 Multiplying Integers

Recall that multiplication can be thought of as repeated addition. You can use a number line to multiply integers. Always start at 0.

3×2 means three groups of 2 each: $3 \times 2 = 6$.

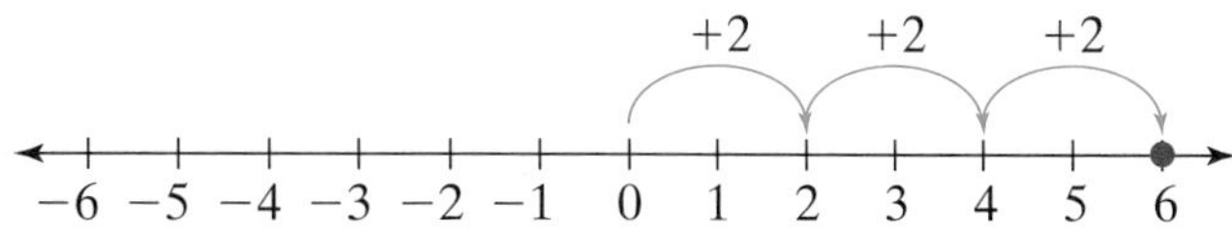

$3 \times (-2)$ means three groups of -2 each: $3 \times (-2) = -6$.

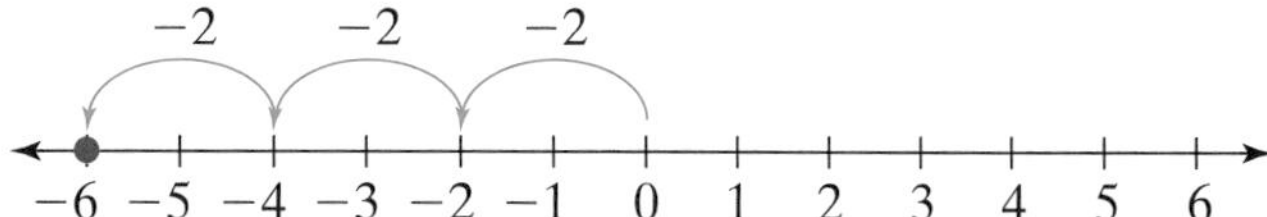

Recall that the integers 3 and -3 are opposites. You can think of -3×2 as the *opposite* of three groups of 2 each. Therefore, $-3 \times 2 = -6$.

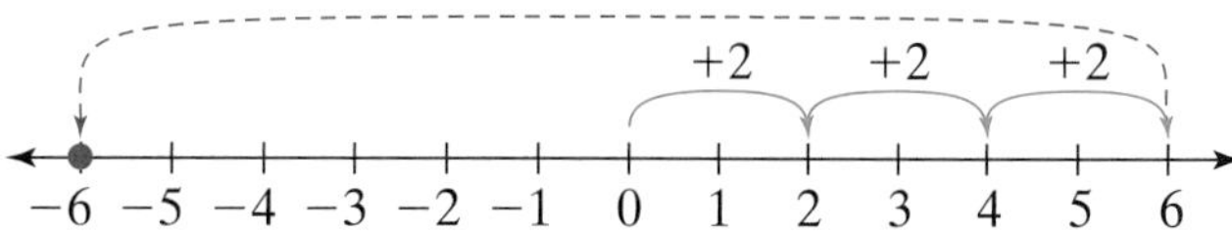

You can think of $-3 \times (-2)$ as the *opposite* of three groups of -2 each. Since $3 \times (-2) = -6$, then $-3 \times (-2) = 6$.

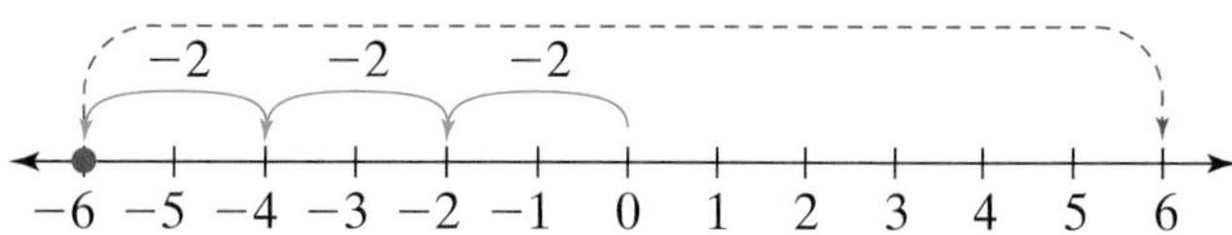

Real-World Connection

Skydivers multiply time (positive) times their rate of descent (negative) to determine when to open their parachutes.

1 EXAMPLE Using a Number Line to Multiply Integers

Use a number line to find $4 \times (-3)$.

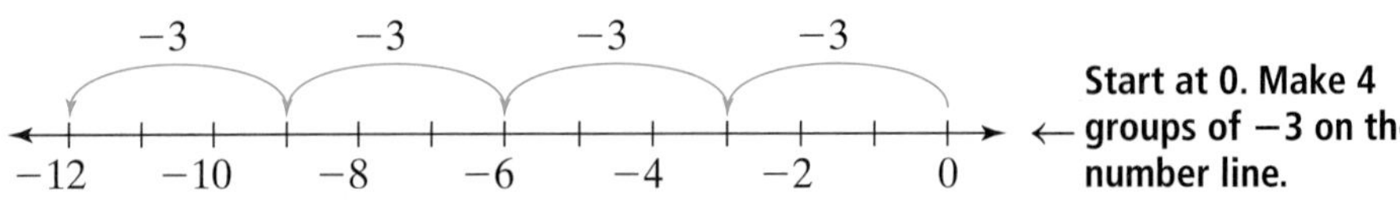

← **Start at 0. Make 4 groups of −3 on the number line.**

The sum of 4 groups of -3 is -12. So, $4 \times (-3) = -12$.

Check Understanding 1 Use a number line to find each product.

a. $3 \times (-4)$ **b.** $-3 \times (-4)$ **c.** -4×3

To multiply integers without using a number line, remember the following rules.

Key Concepts Multiplying Integers

The product of two integers with the *same* sign is positive.
The product of two integers with *different* signs is negative.

Examples: $4 \times 5 = 20$ $4 \times (-5) = -20$

$-4 \times (-5) = 20$ $-4 \times 5 = -20$

2 EXAMPLE Multiplying Integers

a. Find $6 \times (-2)$.

$6 \times (-2) = -12$ ← **different signs, negative product**

b. Find $-5 \times (-2)$.

$-5 \times (-2) = 10$ ← **same signs, positive product**

Check Understanding 2 Find each product.

a. -6×7 **b.** $-9 \times (-3)$ **c.** $5 \times (-3)$

3 EXAMPLE Real-World Problem Solving

Stock Market A share of stock fell \$2 in value each day for five days. Write an integer to express the change in the stock's value over the five days.

$(-2) \times 5 = -10$ ← **Use a negative number to represent a stock losing value.**

The amount, −\$10, expresses the change in the stock's value.

Check Understanding 3 Over four hours, the temperature drops 5°F each hour. What is the total drop in temperature?

Here is a summary of how to determine the sign of the products of integers.

Multiplication of Integers

positive	×	positive	=	positive
negative	×	negative	=	positive
positive	×	negative	=	negative
negative	×	positive	=	negative

EXERCISES

For more practice, see *Extra Practice*.

A Practice by Example

Example 1 (page 510)

Use a number line to find each product.

1. 6×3 **2.** $-4 \times (-2)$ **3.** $5 \times (-2)$ **4.** 2×7

Examples 2, 3 (page 510)

Find each product.

5. -3×5 **6.** $11 \times (-2)$ **7.** 7×12 **8.** $(-4) \times 5$

9. $-6 \times (-9)$ **10.** $15 \times (-4)$ **11.** $-25 \times (-5)$ **12.** -16×4

13. Suppose you want to withdraw $5 from your savings account each week for 4 weeks. What integer expresses the total change to your account?

B Apply Your Skills

14. A temperature that is first recorded at $-2°$F falls three degrees per hour. What is the temperature at the end of four hours?

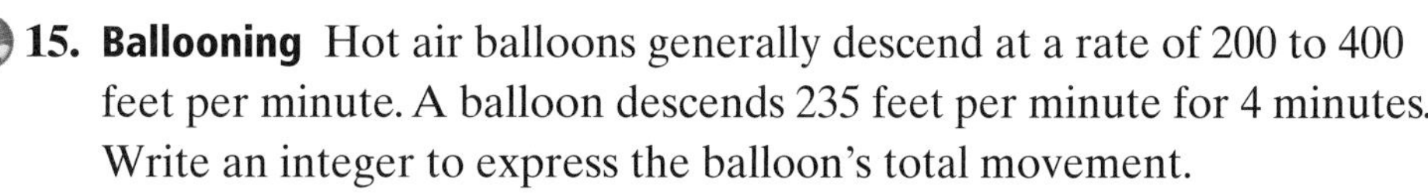

15. Ballooning Hot air balloons generally descend at a rate of 200 to 400 feet per minute. A balloon descends 235 feet per minute for 4 minutes. Write an integer to express the balloon's total movement.

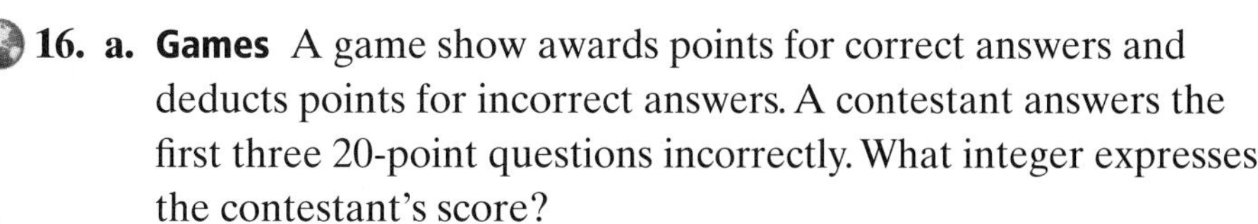

16. a. Games A game show awards points for correct answers and deducts points for incorrect answers. A contestant answers the first three 20-point questions incorrectly. What integer expresses the contestant's score?

b. The contestant then gets the next four 10-point questions correct. Write an integer to express the final score.

17. Number Sense Is the product of three negative integers positive or negative? What is the product of four negative integers?

Real-World Connection

Most hot air balloons fly at an altitude of 1,000 to 1,500 feet.

Find each product.

18. $5 \times 22 \times 2$ **19.** $12 \times (-12) \times (-1)$ **20.** $5 \times (-8) \times 4$

21. $-3 \times (-4) \times (-5)$ **22.** $-6 \times 8 \times (-2)$ **23.** $7 \times 3 \times (-3)$

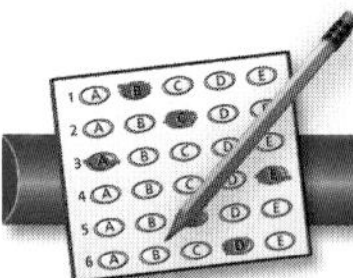

C Challenge

24. **Reasoning** When you add a positive and negative integer, sometimes you get a positive result and sometimes you get a negative result. Is this true for multiplying a positive and negative integer? Explain.

25. **Stretch Your Thinking** Find the value of the expression below. Then change one of the operation symbols in the expression so that the new value is four times the original value.

$$81 - 12 - 13 - 14 - 15 - 17$$

26. Copy and complete the pyramid at the right so that each number represents the product of the two numbers directly beneath it.

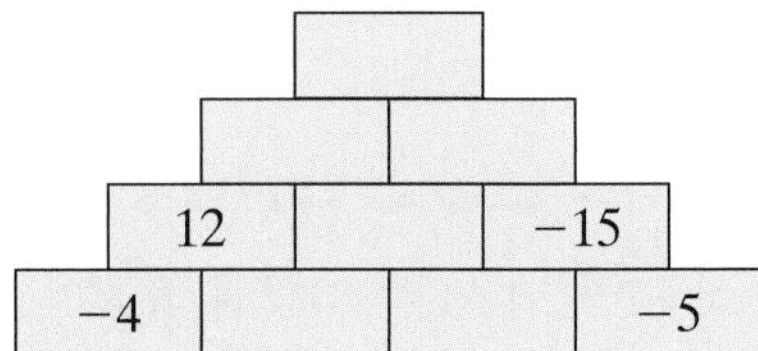

Test Prep

Multiple Choice

27. What is the product of −6 and −8?
A. −48 B. −14 C. 14 D. 48

Take It to the NET
Online lesson quiz at
www.PHSchool.com
Web Code: aaa-1004

28. Which expression does NOT have a value of −24?
F. -8×3 G. $-12 \times (-2)$ H. $6 \times (-4)$ I. $24 \times (-1)$

29. Which expression has the greatest product?
A. $-4 \times (-8)$ B. -2×25 C. $4 \times (-12)$ D. 6×5

Short Response

30. Suppose you spent $12 to go to a football game. Then you earned $6 each day for three days.
a. Write an expression that represents this situation.
b. Simplify your expression.

Mixed Review

Lesson 9-7 **Identify the three-dimensional figures.**

31.  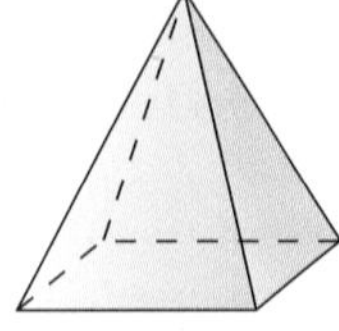
32.  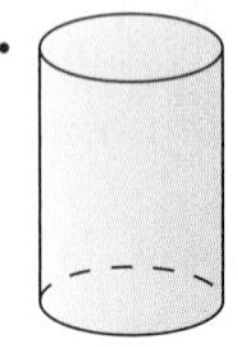
33. 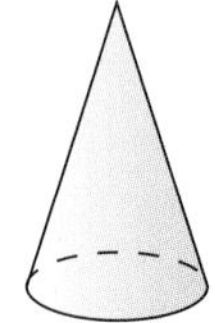
34. 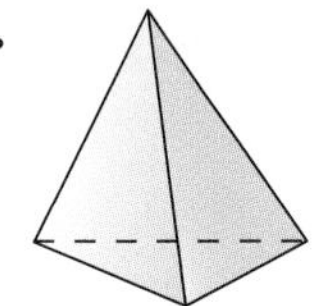

Lesson 8-3 **Find the complement and the supplement of each angle.**

35. 50° 36. 19° 37. 67° 38. 81°

10-5 Dividing Integers

What You'll Learn

 To divide integers

 To solve equations

. . . And Why

To find an average rate of change, as in Example 3

Check Skills You'll Need

For help, go to Lesson 2-7.

Solve each equation.

1. $q \div 8 = 72$

2. $3r = 24$

3. $s \div 6 = 42$

4. $18x = 108$

5. $y \div 6 = 90$

6. $22z = 66$

OBJECTIVE

 Interactive lesson includes instant self-check, tutorials, and activities.

1 Dividing Integers

Investigation: Connecting Division to Multiplication

Copy and complete each of the following.

i.	ii.	iii.
$3 \times 4 = 12$	$3 \times (-4) = -12$	$-3 \times (-4) = 12$
$12 \div 4 = ■$	$-12 \div (-4) = ■$	$12 \div (-4) = ■$
$12 \div 3 = ■$	$-12 \div 3 = ■$	$12 \div (-3) = ■$

1. What is the sign of the quotient of two numbers with the same sign?
2. What is the sign of the quotient of two numbers with different signs?

Since $4 \times 3 = 12$, we know that $12 \div 3 = 4$. So the rules for finding the sign of a quotient when dividing two integers are similar to the rules for finding a product when multiplying integers.

Key Concepts — Dividing Integers

The quotient of two integers with the *same* sign is positive.
The quotient of two integers with *different* signs is negative.

Examples: $20 \div 4 = 5$ $\quad$ $20 \div (-4) = -5$
$-20 \div (-4) = 5$ $\quad$ $-20 \div 4 = -5$

1 EXAMPLE Dividing Integers

a. Find $-15 \div (-3)$.

$-15 \div (-3) = 5$ ← **same signs, positive quotient**

b. Find $-24 \div 8$.

$-24 \div 8 = -3$ ← **different signs, negative quotient**

Check Understanding 1 Find each quotient. **a.** $-24 \div 6$ **b.** $-36 \div (-2)$

OBJECTIVE

2 Solving Equations

You can solve multiplication and division equations with integers using the same methods you used to solve equations with whole numbers.

2 EXAMPLE Solving Equations with Integers

a. Solve $-3n = -18$.

$-3n = -18$

$\frac{-3n}{-3} = \frac{-18}{-3}$ ← **Divide each side by −3.**

$n = 6$ ← **Simplify.**

b. Solve $\frac{m}{5} = -7$.

$\frac{m}{5} = -7$

$5 \times \frac{m}{5} = 5 \times -7$ ← **Multiply each side by 5.**

$m = -35$ ← **Simplify.**

Check Understanding 2 Solve each equation. **a.** $-6z = 36$ **b.** $\frac{u}{7} = -4$

You can use division of integers to find an average rate of change.

3 EXAMPLE Real-World  Problem Solving

Weather The temperature changed from 0 degrees to −56 degrees over 4 hours. Find the average rate of change in degrees per hour.

Words	total change	divided by	number of hours	equals	average change per hour

Let r = the average rate of change in degrees per hour.

Equation	−56	÷	4	=	r

$-56 \div 4 = r$

$-14 = r$ ← **Simplify.**

The temperature changed at an average rate of −14 degrees per hour.

Real-World Connection

Careers Meteorologists analyze and predict changes in the weather.

Check Understanding 3 The value of a share of stock decreased \$20 over the last 5 days. What integer represents the average decrease in stock value each day?

EXERCISES

For more practice, see *Extra Practice*.

A Practice by Example

Example 1 (page 513)

Find each quotient.

1. $18 \div 6$
2. $-25 \div (-5)$
3. $10 \div 2$
4. $-15 \div 3$
5. $-12 \div 4$
6. $100 \div (-20)$
7. $64 \div 8$
8. $156 \div -13$

Example 2 (page 514)

Solve each equation.

9. $-4y = -64$
10. $\frac{s}{5} = -6$
11. $7h = -84$
12. $\frac{k}{3} = 12$

Example 3 (page 514)

Represent each rate of change with a unit rate.

13. decreases \$15 over 5 days
14. climbs 72 stairs in 4 minutes
15. sinks 160 feet in 20 seconds
16. loses 36 pounds over 12 weeks

17. **Weather** Over three hours, the temperature decreased 6 degrees. Find the average rate of change in degrees per hour.

B Apply Your Skills

Find the mean for each set of data.

18. $-4, -1, 0, 3, 7$
19. $-12, -9, -2, 8, 15, 19$
20. $-24, -13, -5, 10$
21. $-8, -7, -5, -3, 3, 5, 7, 8$

22. **Stocks** The value of a share of stock decreased \$30 over the last 5 days. What integer represents the average decrease in stock value each day?

23. **Scuba Diving** Suppose a scuba diver is 100 feet below sea level. The diver rises to the surface at a rate of 25 feet per minute. Use integers to write an expression that represents the time it takes the diver to reach the surface.

Simplify each expression.

24. $14 + 63 \div (-7)$
25. $(-10) \div 2 - 12$
26. $4 + (-2) \div (-1)$
27. $3 + 5 \times (-2) - (-4) \div (-2)$
28. $28 - 14 \div (-2)$
29. $6 \times (-3) + 4 \div (-2)$

30. **Writing in Math** Explain how you know without computing that the quotient $-400 \div 25$ is greater than or less than 0.

Challenge

31. Reasoning Is the division of integers commutative? Give examples to support your answer.

32. Number Sense Is the mean of five negative numbers positive or negative? Explain your reasoning.

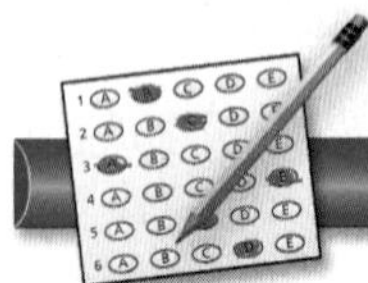

Test Prep

Gridded Response

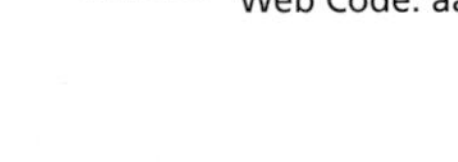

Take It to the NET
Online lesson quiz at
www.PHSchool.com
Web Code: aaa-1005

33. What integer represents a rise of 500 feet per minute for 10 minutes?

34. What is the solution to $-5x = -80$?

35. What is the mean of 14, 6, −8, −12, and 10?

36. What is the range of 19, −5, 0, −15, 27 and 9?

Mixed Review

Lesson 9-9

Find the volume of each rectangular prism.

37.

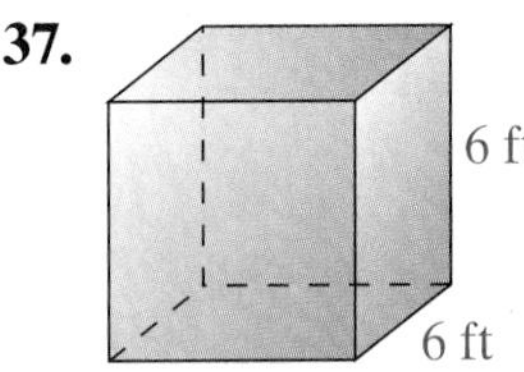

38.

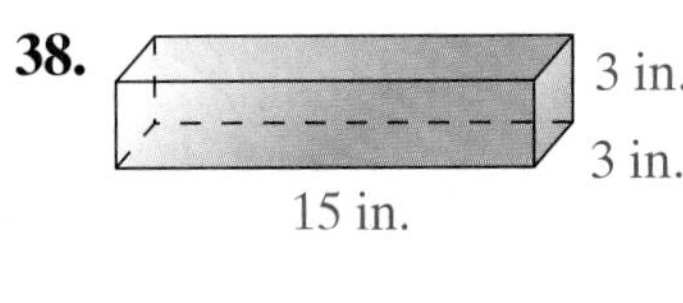

39.

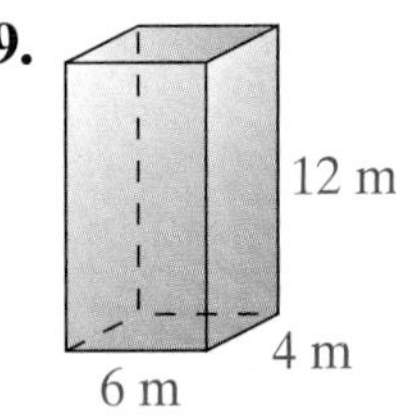

Lesson 9-8

Find the surface area of each rectangular prism with the given dimensions.

40. $\ell = 5$ cm, $w = 3$ cm, $h = 4$ cm

41. $\ell = 9$ in., $w = 6$ in., $h = 7$ in.

Checkpoint Quiz 1 — Lessons 10-1 through 10-5

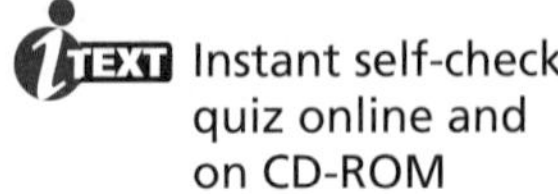

Instant self-check quiz online and on CD-ROM

Find each answer.

1. $-8 + 5$

2. $-4 - (-2)$

3. $-10 + (-2)$

4. $-9 + 3$

5. $-10 - 2$

6. $12 \times (-3)$

7. -8×2

8. $14 \div (-2)$

9. $-21 \div (-3)$

10. What integer represents a change of −2 degrees per hour for 10 hours?

Reading Math: Understanding Word Problems

For Use With Lesson 10-4

Some problems contain *too little information.* You can use the problem-solving plan to decide if you have enough information to solve a problem. Ask yourself, "What do I know?" and "What do I need to find out?"

EXAMPLE

Elevators in a building travel an average of 1,000 feet per minute. From the first floor, a messenger takes an elevator to floors in this order: 7, 5, and 1. About how many minutes does the messenger spend on the elevator?

Read and Understand Read for understanding. Summarize the problem.

What do I know?
- The elevators travel about 1,000 feet per minute.
- The messenger has traveled:
  $7 - 1 = 6$, or 6 floors up;
  $5 - 7 = -2$, or 2 floors down;
  $1 - 5 = -4$, or 4 floors down.

What do I need to find out?
- How many minutes did the messengers spend on elevators?

Do I have enough information to solve the problem? If not, what is missing?
No. I need to know the height of a floor, in feet.

Read and Understand is the first step in problem solving. Here it helps you identify that the problem cannot be solved.

EXERCISES

For each problem, write answers for "What do I know?" and "What do I need to find out?" Identify any missing information.

1. A.J. bought three shirts for a total of \$48. How much did A.J. pay for each shirt?

2. A distributor shipped 3,000 CDs to several stores. All stores received the same number of CDs. How many CDs did each store receive?

3. The formula for converting degrees Celsius to degrees Fahrenheit is $F = \frac{9}{5}C + 32$. Convert 150°C to degrees Fahrenheit.

10-6 Graphing in the Coordinate Plane

Algebra

What You'll Learn

To name coordinates

To graph points on a coordinate plane

. . . And Why

To name the coordinates on a map, as in Example 3

Check Skills You'll Need

For help, go to Lesson 10-1.

Graph each integer on a number line.

1. −2 **2.** 3 **3.** 0

4. −6 **5.** −1 **6.** −4

New Vocabulary
- coordinate plane
- quadrants
- origin
- ordered pair

OBJECTIVE

 Interactive lesson includes instant self-check, tutorials, and activities.

1 Naming Coordinates

Reading Math

The plural of *axis* is *axes.*

The **coordinate plane** is formed by the intersection of two number lines. The plane is divided into four regions, called **quadrants.** The **origin** is the place where the two number lines intersect.

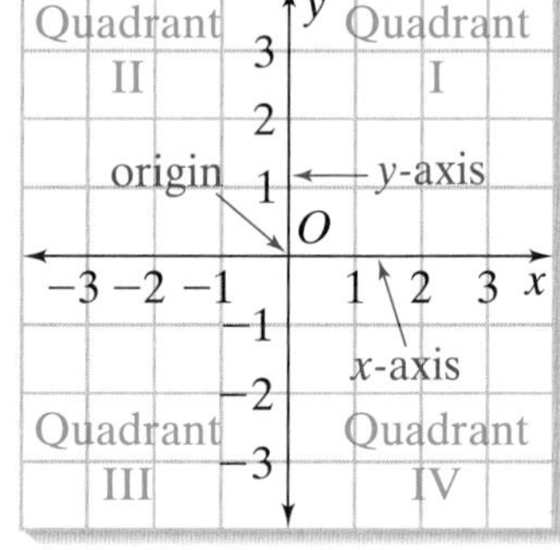

An **ordered pair** is a pair of numbers that describes the location of a point in a coordinate plane. The ordered pair (0, 0) describes the origin.

The x-coordinate tells how far to move left or right along the x-axis. → x y ← The y-coordinate tells how far to move up or down along the y-axis.

1 EXAMPLE Naming Coordinates

Find the coordinates of point B.

Point B is 3 units to the left of the y-axis. So, the x-coordinate is −3. Point B is 2 units above the x-axis. So, the y-coordinate is 2.

The coordinates of point B are (−3, 2).

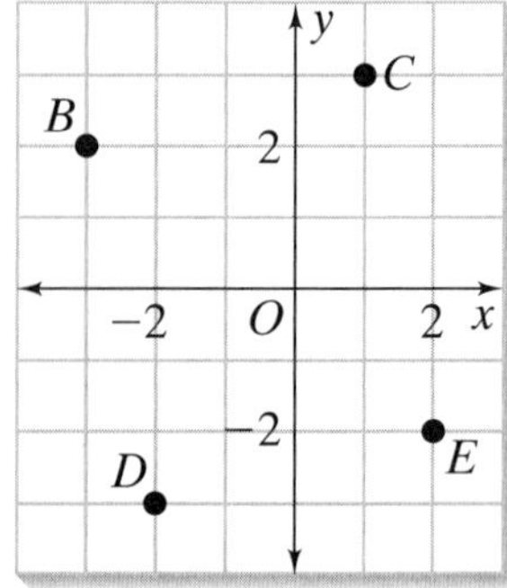

Check Understanding 1 Find the coordinates of each point in the coordinate plane.

a. C **b.** D **c.** E

OBJECTIVE

2 Graphing Points on a Coordinate Plane

You can graph points given their coordinates. You move right from the origin to graph a positive x-coordinate and left from the origin to graph a negative x-coordinate. You move up from the x-axis to graph a positive y-coordinate and down from the x-axis to graph a negative y-coordinate.

2 EXAMPLE Graphing Ordered Pairs

a. Graph the ordered pair with coordinates $(3, -2)$.

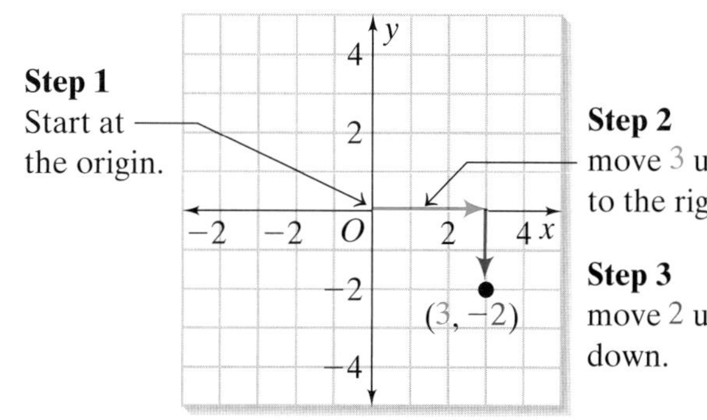

Check Understanding 2 Graph each point in a coordinate plane.

a. $(-4, -4)$ **b.** $(-3, 2)$ **c.** $(1, -2)$

3 EXAMPLE Using Map Coordinates

Test-Prep Tip
Look back at your answer. Make sure it checks in the original problem.

Maps A student drew this a map of certain locations in relationship to his home.

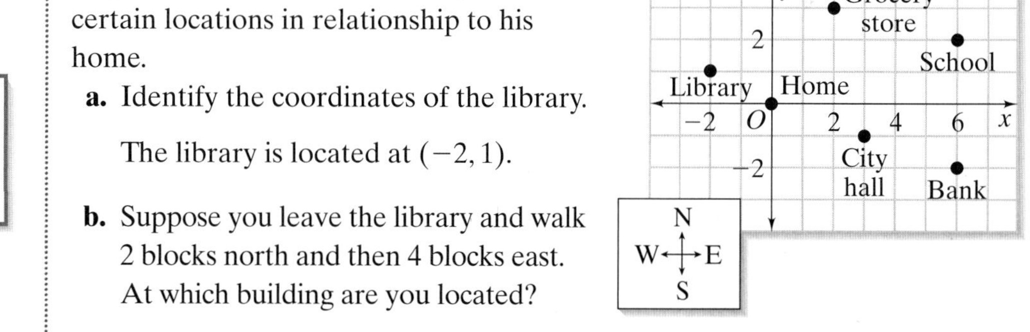

a. Identify the coordinates of the library.

The library is located at $(-2, 1)$.

b. Suppose you leave the library and walk 2 blocks north and then 4 blocks east. At which building are you located?

You are at the grocery store.

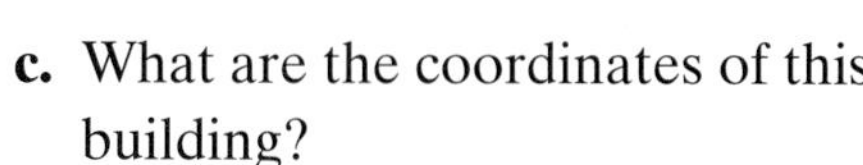

c. What are the coordinates of this building?

The coordinates of the grocery store are $(2, 3)$.

Check Understanding 3 Suppose you leave the library and walk 2 blocks south and then 5 blocks east.

a. At which building are you located?

b. What are the coordinates of the building?

EXERCISES

For more practice, see *Extra Practice.*

A Practice by Example

Example 1 (page 518)

Find the coordinates of each point at the right.

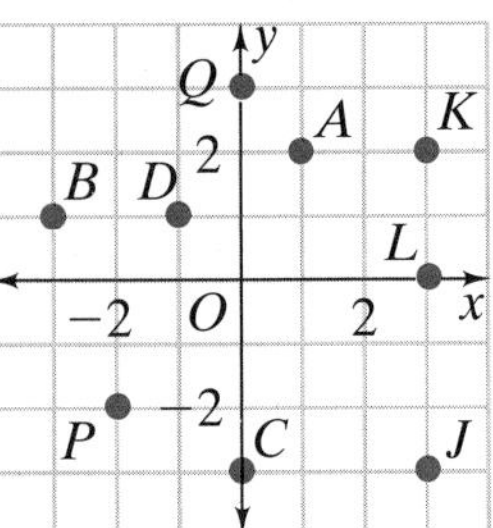

1. B **2.** D

3. K **4.** Q

Name the point with the given coordinates in the coordinate plane at the right.

5. $(1, 2)$ **6.** $(-2, -2)$

7. $(3, -3)$ **8.** $(0, -3)$

Example 2 (page 519)

Graph each point on a coordinate plane.

9. $(1, 5)$ **10.** $(-5, -3)$ **11.** $(2, -4)$

12. $(-2, 3)$ **13.** $(1, -4)$ **14.** $(-5, 5)$

Example 3 (page 519)

Use the map at the right.

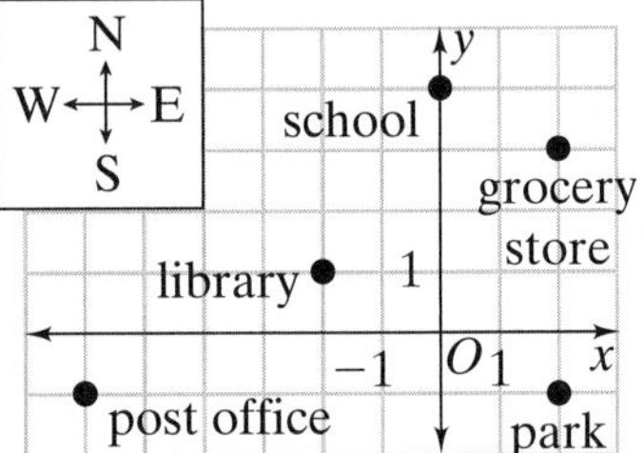

15. If you travel 2 units north of the library and 4 units east, where are you located?

16. Find the coordinates of each building.
a. the post office **b.** school

B Apply Your Skills

Graph each point on a coordinate plane.

17. $(0, 3)$ **18.** $(-4, 0)$ **19.** $(-4, -2)$ **20.** $(5, 3)$

21. Your cousin is located at $(-5, -2)$. He rides his scooter 3 blocks west and then 1 block south to the park. What are the coordinates of the park?

22. A police car begins at $(-2, 8)$. It travels 10 blocks south and 6 blocks east to the court house. What are the coordinates of the court house?

23. **Writing in Math** Describe how you would locate the following points on a coordinate plane.
a. $(0, -8)$ **b.** $(-6, 3)$

24. **Geometry** A symmetrical four-pointed star has eight corner points. Seven of the points are $(-1, 1)$, $(0, 3)$, $(1, 1)$, $(3, 0)$, $(1, -1)$, $(0, -3)$, $(-1, -1)$. What are the coordinates of the missing point?

Real-World Connection

When riding a scooter, wear a helmet and other safety gear to minimize the risk of injury.

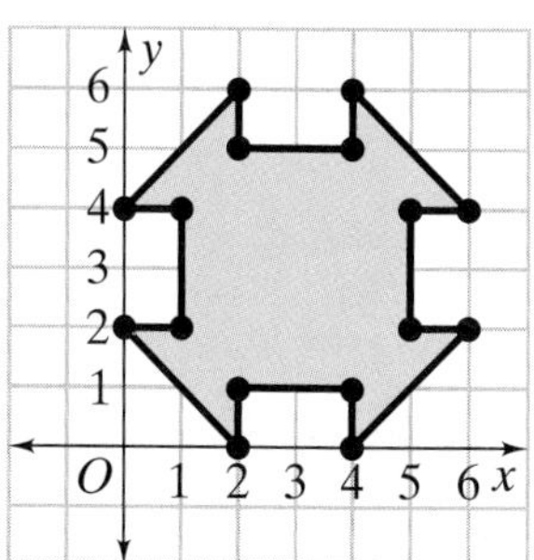

25. **Quilt Making** Quilt designers use coordinate grids to design patterns. Find the coordinates of the pattern points at the left.

26. **Writing in Math** What do all points located on the x-axis have in common? What do all points located on the y-axis have in common? Explain.

27. **Reasoning** Is the order of the coordinates in an ordered pair important? Explain.

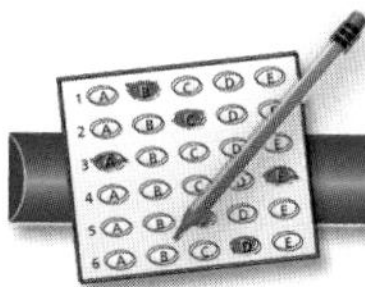

Challenge

28. An oil tanker is located at (8, −8). Another oil tanker is located at (14, −8). How far apart are the two tankers?

29. **Stretch Your Thinking** Suppose you make corn muffins. Your family eats $\frac{1}{3}$ of them. You give $\frac{1}{4}$ of the remaining muffins to a friend. You have 9 muffins left. How many muffins did you make?

Test Prep

Reading Comprehension Read the following passage and answer the questions below.

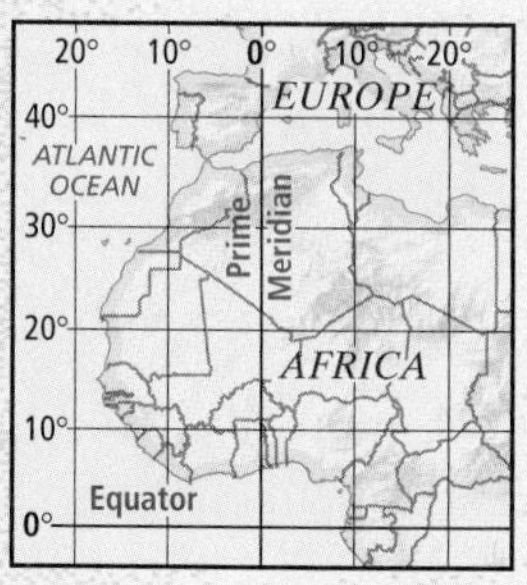

Where on Earth Are You?

Geographers have given Earth a coordinate system so that locations can be described easily. Imagine a coordinate plane wrapped around the planet. The horizontal axis is the equator, and the vertical axis is the prime meridian.

Distances on Earth's coordinate system are measured in degrees. Degrees north or south of the equator are called degrees of latitude. Degrees east or west of the prime meridian are called degrees of longitude.

30. On Earth's coordinate system, what is the vertical axis?

31. On Earth's coordinate system, what is the horizontal axis?

32. On what continent is the location 20° N latitude, 20° E longitude?

33. On what continent is the location 45° N latitude, 5° E longitude?

Take It to the NET
Online lesson quiz at
www.PHSchool.com
Web Code: aaa-1006

Mixed Review

Lesson 9-6

34. What is the circumference and area of a circle with radius of 6 millimeters?

Lesson 7-8

35. Distances of 10 feet, 23 feet, 16 feet, 55 feet, and 21 feet have a mean of 25 feet. Is this statistic misleading? Explain.

Extension

Reflections in the Coordinate Plane

For Use With Lesson 10-6

The grid at the right shows four congruent parallelograms.

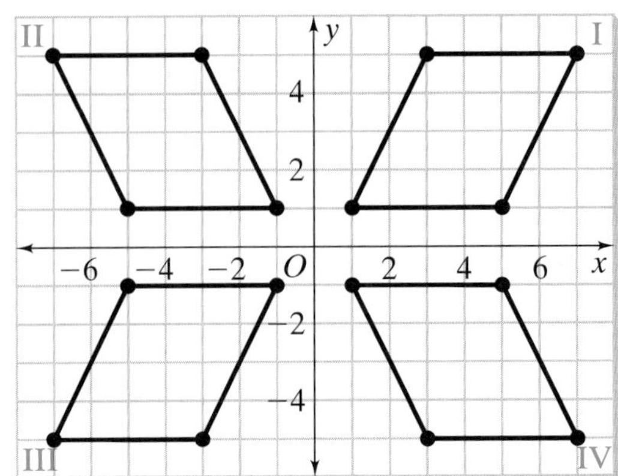

1 EXAMPLE

List the ordered pairs of the vertices of the parallelogram that are in Quadrants I and II. Find a pattern.

Quadrant I	
x	y
1	1
3	5
7	5
5	1

Quadrant II	
x	y
−1	1
−3	5
−7	5
−5	1

All corresponding x-coordinates are opposites and all corresponding y-coordinates are the same.

2 EXAMPLE

List the ordered pairs of the vertices of the parallelogram that are in Quadrants I and IV. Find a pattern.

Quadrant I	
x	y
1	1
3	5
7	5
5	1

Quadrant IV	
x	y
1	−1
3	−5
7	−5
5	−1

All corresponding x-coordinates are the same and all corresponding y-coordinates are opposites.

EXERCISES

Plot the given points and connect them in order. Reflect the figure over the y-axis. Then reflect the original figure over the x-axis.

1. $(2, 2), (4, 6), (6, 2), (2, 2)$
2. $(-1, -1), (-1, -6), (-7, -6), (-1, -1)$
3. $(1, -1), (4, -1), (4, -3), (3, -4), (2, -4), (1, -3), (1, -1)$

10-7 Applications of Integers

What You'll Learn

To find profit and loss

To draw and interpret graphs

. . . And Why

To find profit or loss for a business, as in Example 1

Check Skills You'll Need

For help, go to Lesson 10-2.

Find each sum.

1. 12 + 26	**2.** 18 + (−9)	**3.** 41 + (−54)
4. −19 + (−9)	**5.** −32 + 18	**6.** 26 + (−32)
7. −18 + (−13)	**8.** −25 + (−34)	**9.** −16 + 42

Interactive lesson includes instant self-check, tutorials, and activities.

OBJECTIVE 1 Finding Profit and Loss

Businesses keep track of money they receive and money they spend. Money received is called *income*. Money spent is called *expenses*.

A balance is a company's profit or loss. To find a balance, add the income (positive numbers) and the expenses (negative numbers).

A positive balance means that there is a profit. A negative balance means that there is a loss.

1 EXAMPLE Finding Profit or Loss

Real World

Small Business Find Flower Mania's profit or loss for February.

Income and Expenses for Flower Mania

Month	Income	Expenses
Jan.	$11,917	−$14,803
Feb.	$12,739	−$9,482
Mar.	$11,775	−$10,954
Apr.	$13,620	−$15,149

Careers Small business owners make up more than 90% of all businesses in the United States.

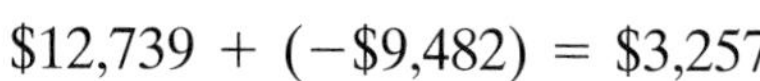

$12,739 + (−$9,482) = $3,257 ← **Add income and expenses for February.**

Flower Mania had a profit of $3,257 for February.

Check Understanding 1 Find the profit or loss for each period.

a. January **b.** March **c.** April **d.** January through April

OBJECTIVE

2 Drawing and Interpreting Graphs

You can use line graphs to look at the trends of monthly balances.

2 EXAMPLE Drawing and Interpreting Graphs

Real World

Business Draw a line graph of the monthly profits and losses for Hobby Town. In which month did the greatest profit occur?

Profit/Loss for Hobby Town; by Month					
Month	Profit/Loss	Month	Profit/Loss	Month	Profit/Loss
Jan.	−$1,917	May	−$150	Sept.	−$417
Feb.	−$682	June	$250	Oct.	−$824
Mar.	$303	July	$933	Nov.	$1,566
Apr.	$781	Aug.	$1,110	Dec.	$1,945

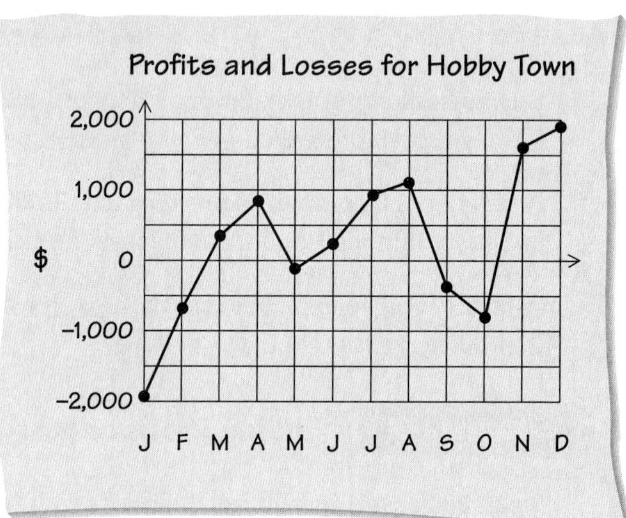

The balances vary from −$1,917 to $1,945. So make a scale from −$2,000 to $2,000. Use intervals of $500.

Hobby Town had the greatest profit in December.

Real-World Connection Many hobby shops provide lessons.

Check Understanding 2 In which month did the greatest loss occur?

EXERCISES

For more practice, see *Extra Practice*.

A Practice by Example

Example 1 (page 523)

Look at the data for Rad's Books. Find the profit or loss for each period.

1. Week 1 **2.** Week 2

3. Week 3 **4.** Week 4

Income and Expenses for Rad's Books

Week	Income	Expenses
Week 1	$4,257	−$6,513
Week 2	$3,840	−$2,856
Week 3	$4,109	−$3,915
Week 4	$3,725	−$4,921

Example 2 (page 524)

5. The table at the right gives the income and expenses for several days.
   a. Find the profit or loss for each day.
   b. Draw a line graph to show the profits and losses.
   c. On what day was the profit the greatest? The least?

Day	Income	Expenses
Mon.	$94	–$85
Tues.	$78	–$60
Wed.	$13	–$22
Thurs.	$90	–$73
Fri.	$37	–$49
Sat.	$15	–$16

B Apply Your Skills

6. a. **Accounting** Determine the balance after each transaction of the checking account shown below.
   b. What was the greatest balance? The least?

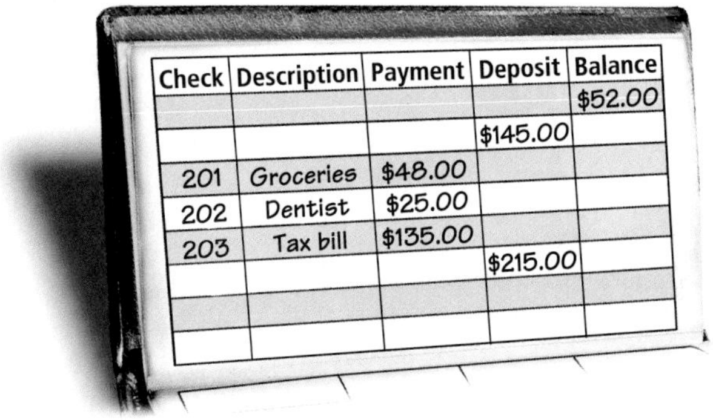

Check	Description	Payment	Deposit	Balance
				$52.00
			$145.00	
201	Groceries	$48.00		
202	Dentist	$25.00		
203	Tax bill	$135.00		
			$215.00	

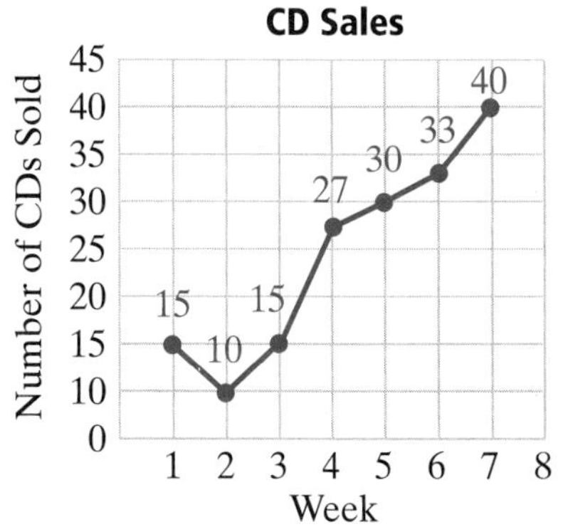

CD Sales

Number of CDs Sold: 45, 40, 35, 30, 25, 20, 15, 10, 0
Week: 1 2 3 4 5 6 7 8
15, 10, 15, 27, 30, 33, 40

Use the line graph at the left for Exercises 7–11.

7. How many CDs were sold in the first week?

8. How many CDs were sold in the fifth week?

9. How many more CDs were sold in the sixth week than were sold in the second week?

10. In which two weeks were the same number of CDs sold?

11. Which week showed a drop in the number of CDs sold?

Population **Use the table for Exercises 12–14.**

City	1950	1960	1970	1980	1990	2000
Miami, Fla.	249	292	335	347	359	362
Oakland, Calif.	385	368	362	339	372	399
Rochester, N.Y.	322	319	296	242	232	220

12. Graph the data on the same grid. Use a different line for each city.

13. Which city shows a positive trend in population? A negative trend?

14. During which decade were the populations of Miami and Rochester equal?

15. **Writing in Math** Explain how you can determine whether a company has made a profit.

16. You receive a total of \$125 for your birthday. You spend \$20 on a sweater, \$15 on a CD, \$8 on a book, \$12 on a pair of sunglasses, and \$35 on a bicycle helmet. How much money do you have left?

C Challenge

17. The table at the right shows the population of the United States every twenty years from 1900 to 2000. Make a graph of the data. Then use the graph to predict the population in 2010.

Year	Population (in millions)
1900	76
1920	106
1940	132
1960	179
1980	227
2000	281

18. **Stretch Your Thinking** A number is divided by 8. When 7 is subtracted from the doubled quotient, the answer is -1. What is the number?

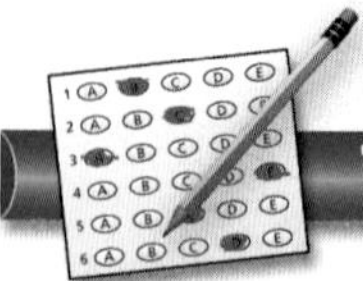

Test Prep

Multiple Choice

19. What is the difference between the average low surface temperature of Earth of $-89°C$ and the average high surface temperature of 58°C?
A. 13°C **B.** 31°C **C.** 147°C **D.** 174°C

20. Suppose you earn \$15 each time you cut your neighbor's lawn. You cut the lawn 18 times. How much money do you earn?
F. \$3 **G.** \$33 **H.** \$180 **I.** \$270

Take It to the NET
Online lesson quiz at
www.PHSchool.com
Web Code: aaa-1007

21. What is the profit or loss for income of \$7,892 and expenses of \$1,698?
A. \$6,194 loss **B.** \$6,194 profit **C.** \$9,590 loss **D.** \$9,590 profit

Extended Response

22. Jordan bought a DVD for \$5. He sold it for \$10, and then bought it back for \$15. Finally, he sold it for \$20. Did Jordan make money, or lose money? How much money did he make or lose?

Mixed Review

Lesson 8-2 **Classify each angle as *acute*, *obtuse*, *right*, or *straight*.**

23. 15° 24. 123° 25. 54° 26. 90°

27. 173° 28. 180° 29. 175° 30. 45°

Lesson 2-6 **Solve each equation.**

31. $d + 25 = 39$ 32. $n - 13 = 74$

Algebra

10-8 Graphing Functions

What You'll Learn

To make a function table

To graph functions

. . . And Why

To find the points scored in a game, as in Example 3

Check Skills You'll Need

For help, go to Lesson 2-2.

Evaluate the expression for $x = 3$.

1. $8 + x$ **2.** $4x$ **3.** $18 \div x$ **4.** $21 - x$

5. $42 \div x$ **6.** $x + 47$ **7.** $79 - x$ **8.** $11x$

New Vocabulary

- **function**

Interactive lesson includes instant self-check, tutorials, and activities.

OBJECTIVE 1

Making a Function Table

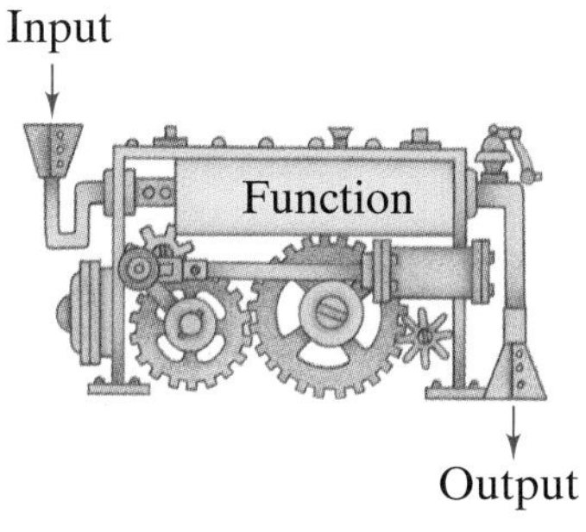

Imagine you have a machine. You can put any number, or input, into the machine. The machine will perform an operation on the number and provide a result, or output. A **function** is a rule that assigns exactly one output value to each input value.

Suppose you tell the machine to multiply by 4. A function table, like the one at the right, shows the input and output values.

Input	Output
3	12
-7	-28

1 EXAMPLE Completing a Function Table

Complete the function table if the rule is Output $=$ Input $\cdot (-2)$.

Input	Output	
-1	2	← **Multiply -1 by -2. Place 2 in the Output column.**
1	-2	← **Multiply 1 by -2. Place -2 in the Output column.**
3	-6	← **Multiply 3 by -2. Place -6 in the Output column.**

Check Understanding **1** Complete the function table given the rule.

a. Rule:
Output $=$ Input $\div 4$

Input	Output
16	■
-24	■
36	■

b. Rule:
Output $=$ Input $- 8$

Input	Output
-6	■
-1	■
4	■

OBJECTIVE

2 Graphing Functions

You can write the function rule in Example 1 using variables.

$$\text{Output} = \text{Input} \cdot (-2)$$
$$y = x \cdot (-2) \text{ or } y = -2x$$

You can show function relationships on the coordinate plane. Graph the input (x) on the horizontal axis. Graph the output (y) on the vertical axis.

2 EXAMPLE Graphing a Function

Make a table and graph the function $y = x + 3$.

Input (x)	Output (y)
−2	1
−1	2
0	3
1	4
2	5

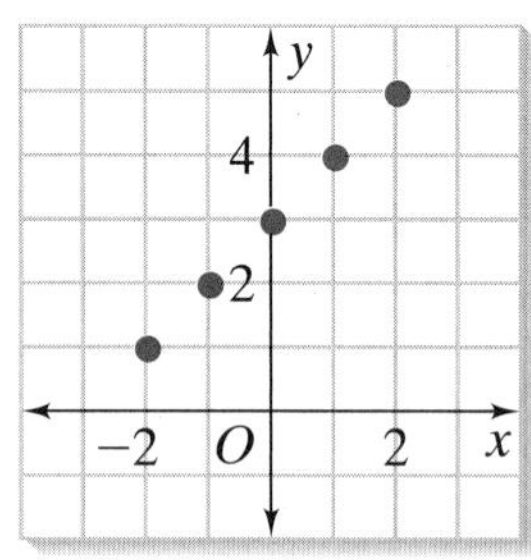

Check Understanding 2 Make a table and graph the function $y = x - 3$.

In Example 2, the points lie along a line. This type of function is a *linear function.* When you graph functions, you can join the points with a line. In real-world situations you can use the line to see trends or make predictions.

3 EXAMPLE Real-World Problem Solving

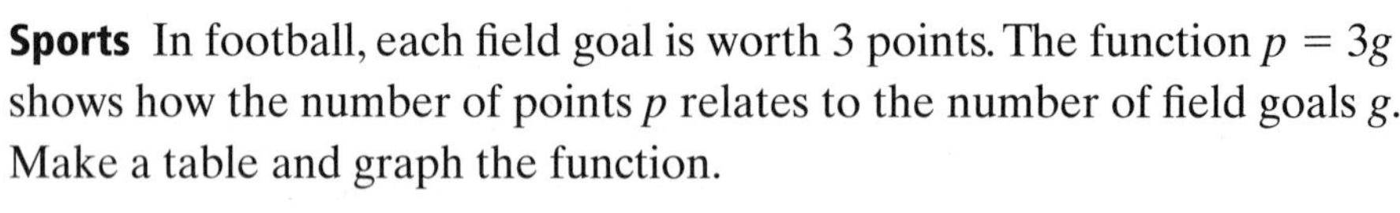

Sports In football, each field goal is worth 3 points. The function $p = 3g$ shows how the number of points p relates to the number of field goals g. Make a table and graph the function.

Field goals	Points
1	3
2	6
3	9
4	12

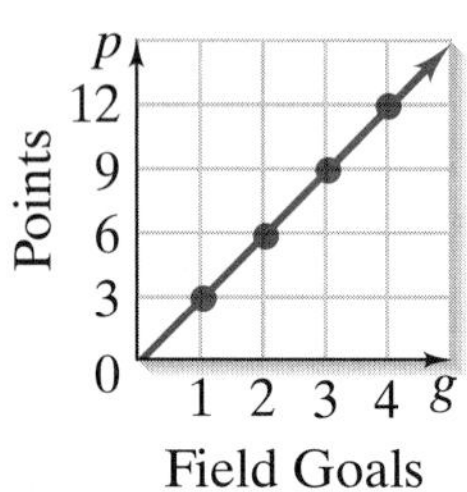

Check Understanding 3 Suppose a car is driven at a steady rate of 45 miles per hour. The function $d = 45t$ shows how time t relates to distance d. Make a table and graph the function.

More Than One Way

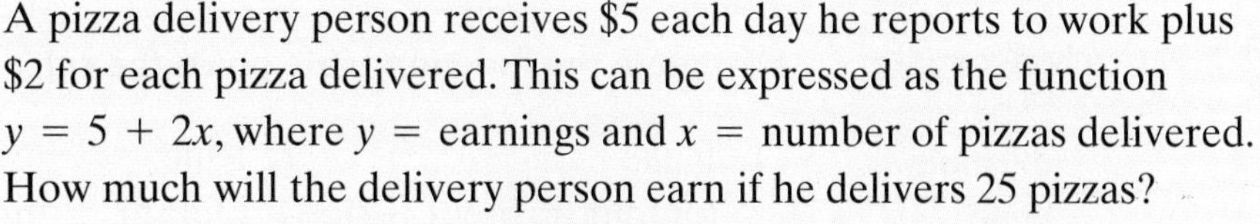

A pizza delivery person receives \$5 each day he reports to work plus \$2 for each pizza delivered. This can be expressed as the function $y = 5 + 2x$, where y = earnings and x = number of pizzas delivered. How much will the delivery person earn if he delivers 25 pizzas?

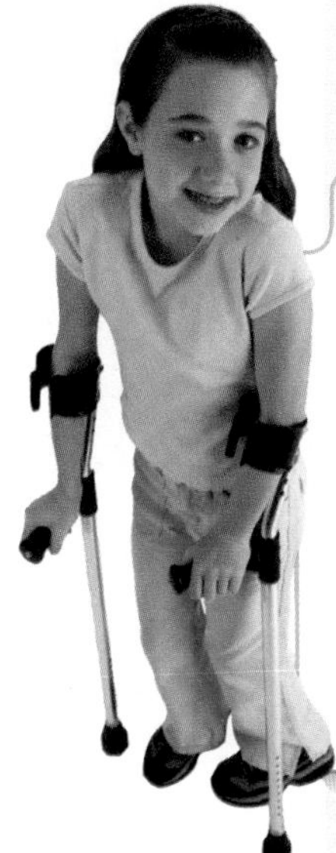

Jessica's Method

I can evaluate the equation to find the amount the delivery person earns. To do this, I replace x with the 25 pizzas delivered.

$y = 5 + 2x$ ← **Write the equation.**

$y = 5 + 2(25)$ ← **Substitute 25 for x.**

$y = 55$

The delivery person will earn \$55 for delivering 25 pizzas.

Leon's Method

If I make a table and a graph, I can look at the graph to tell how much the delivery person earns for delivering different numbers of pizzas.

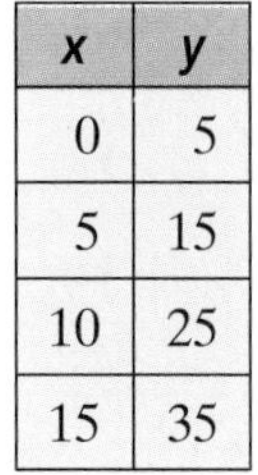

x	y
0	5
5	15
10	25
15	35

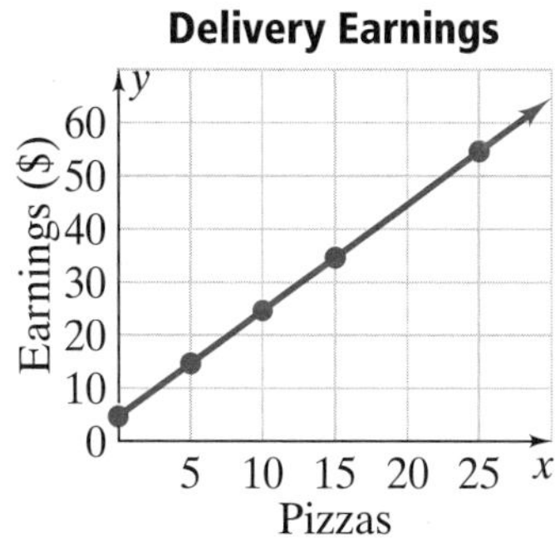

All the points lie on a line, so I can use the graph to find the amount earned for 25 pizzas delivered. The y-value for $x = 25$ is 55. So the delivery person earned \$55.

Choose a Method

Tracy is a member of a discount CD club. Paying an annual fee of \$30 allows her to buy CDs for \$4 each. The function $y = 30 + 4x$ models this situation. If Tracy buys 15 CDs during the year, what will be her total cost? Describe your method and explain why you chose it.

EXERCISES

For more practice, see *Extra Practice*.

A Practice by Example

Example 1 (page 527)

Complete the function table given the rule.

1. Rule:
Output = Input + 4

Input	Output
−5	■
8	■
31	■

2. Rule:
Output = Input − 4

Input	Output
−2	■
5	■
14	■

3. Rule:
Output = Input · (−8)

Input	Output
−3	■
4	■
9	■

Examples 2, 3 (page 528)

Make a table and graph each function. Use x values −2, −1, 0, 1, 2.

4. $y = x + 2$

5. $y = x - 2$

6. $y = 2x$

7. $y = \frac{x}{2}$

8. $y = \frac{x}{2} + 1$

9. $y = -\frac{x}{2}$

10. Library Suppose each day a library book is over due, the fine is $.25. The function $f = 0.25d$ shows how the number of days d, relates to the fine f. Make a table and graph the function.

B Apply Your Skills

Make a table and graph each function. Use x values −2, −1, 0, 1, 2.

11. $y = 2x + 1$

12. $y = 2x - 1$

13. $y = -2x + 1$

14. $y = -2x - 1$

15. $y = 3x + 4$

16. $y = -4x + 3$

17. Suppose you buy T-shirts for $9 each. You have a coupon that gives you $2 off your total purchase. The function $p = 9t - 2$ shows how price p relates to the number of T-shirts t. Find the final price of seven T-shirts.

18. Sports A store sells kicking tees by mail for $3 each. There is a shipping charge of $5 no matter how many tees are ordered. Make a table to find the total price for the purchase of 2, 3, 4, and 5 tees.

Complete each function table. Then write a rule for the function.

19.

Input	Output
3	5
4	6
5	7
6	■
7	■

20.

Input	Output
10	2
15	3
20	4
25	■
30	■

21. **Business** Suppose you want to start a cookie business. You know that it will cost \$600 to buy the oven and materials you need. You decide to charge \$.75 for each cookie. The function $p = 0.75C - 600$ relates profit p to the number of cookies sold C.
   a. What will your profit or loss be if you sell 400 cookies? 500 cookies?
   b. How many cookies must you sell to break even?

Make a table and graph each function.

22. $y = 2x - 12$
23. $y = 4x - 13$
24. $y = 0.5x + 1$
25. $y = 3x - 6$

Writing in Math **Tell whether each function is *linear* or *not linear.* Explain your answers.**

26. $y = x$

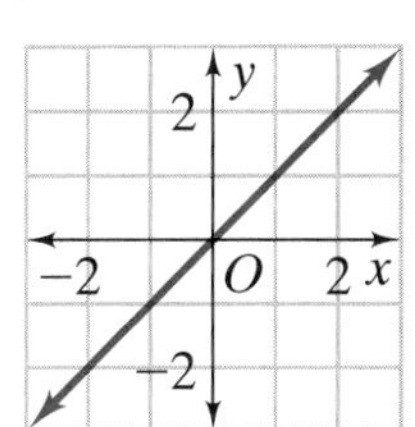

27. $y = x^2$

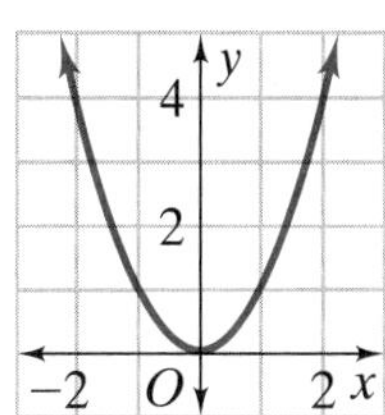

28. $y = \frac{1}{x}$

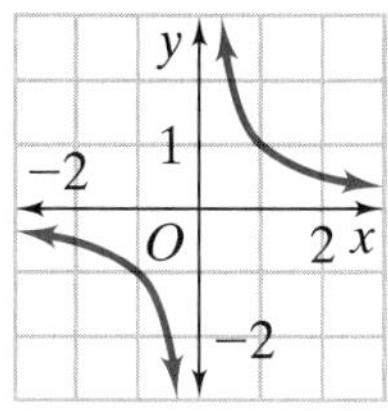

C Challenge

29. **Business** Three companies offer to sew your team name, TIGERS, on your team uniforms. Pro Lettering charges \$2 per letter. Uniforms-R-Us charges \$1 per letter plus a fee of \$5 per uniform. Speedy Lettering charges a fee of \$12 per uniform for any amount of letters. Which graph shows the fees of the company that would charge the least per uniform?

A.

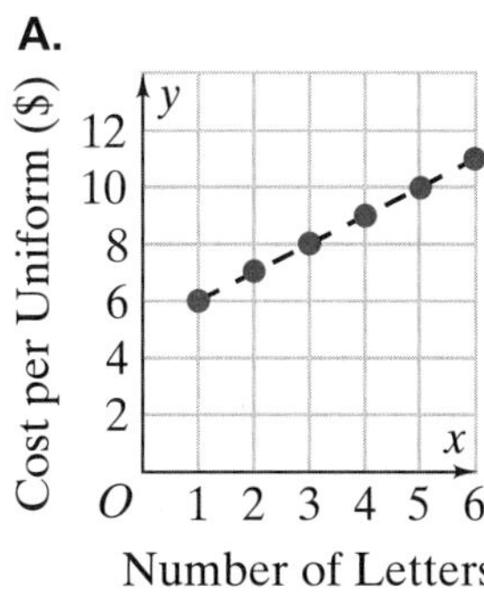

B.

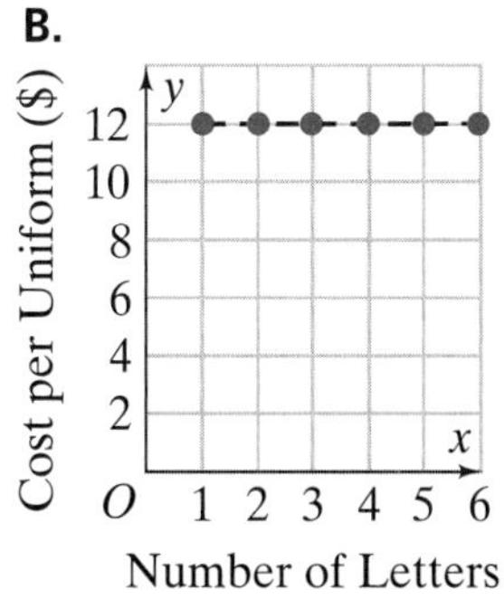

C.

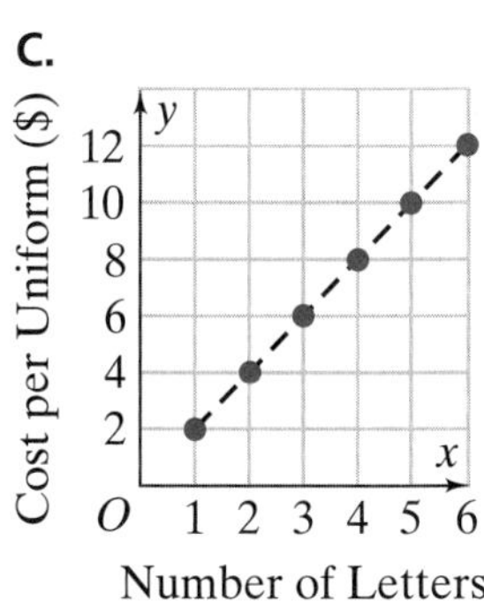

30. **a.** Graph $y = -2x$ and $y = -x^2$ on the same grid.
   b. What points do the graphs have in common?
   c. Describe how the graphs are different.

31. **Stretch Your Thinking** A fraction's numerator is 3 less than its denominator. Its reciprocal is 4 times its value. It is greater than 0. What is the fraction?

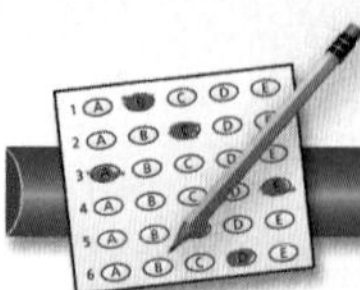

Test Prep

Multiple Choice

32. Which rule could define a function with an input of 4 and an output of 9?

A. Subtract 5. **B.** Multiply by 2. **C.** Add 5. **D.** Divide by 3.

33. Use the function table at the right to find the value of y when $x = 6$.

F. 9 **G.** 10.5 **H.** 13.5 **I.** 15

x	y
2	5
3	7.5
4	10
5	12.5

Take It to the NET
Online lesson quiz at **www.PHSchool.com**
Web Code: aaa-1008

34. What is the input of a function whose rule is *subtract 3* and whose output is 5?

A. −2 **B.** 2 **C.** 8 **D.** 15

Short Response

35. Do the graphs of the functions $y = x + 2$ and $y = x - 2$ have any points in common? Explain.

Mixed Review

Lesson 9-10

Solve the problem by working backward.

36. Suppose your family is planning a trip to a resort. It will take 5 hours of driving. Your family is planning to make three $\frac{1}{2}$ hour stops. They want to arrive at 3:30 P.M. What time should they plan to leave?

Lesson 7-7

Use the stem-and-leaf plot for Exercises 37–40.

Stem	Leaf
1	3 7
2	5 5 8 9
3	1 2
4	9

Key: 1 | 3 means 13

37. What is the lowest value?

38. What is the median?

39. What is the mode?

40. Find the range.

Checkpoint Quiz 2 — Lessons 10-6 through 10-8

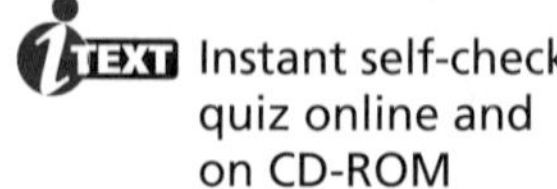

Instant self-check quiz online and on CD-ROM

Graph each point on a coordinate plane.

1. $(-6, 2)$

2. $(0, -6)$

3. Use the table to find the profit or loss for Monday through Wednesday.

Day	Income	Expenses
Monday	\$948	–\$1,285
Tuesday	\$523	–\$406
Wednesday	\$672	–\$1,745

Make a table and graph each function. Use x values −2, −1, 0, 1, 2.

4. $y = x - 7$

5. $y = \frac{x}{2} - 1$

Problem Solving

10-9 Make a Graph

What You'll Learn

To solve problems by making a graph

. . . And Why

To better visualize the data in a problem

Check Skills You'll Need

For help, go to Lesson 10-8.

Complete the function table for the given rule.

1. Rule: Output = Input + 8

Input	Output
−6	■
0	■
8	■

2. Rule: Output = Input ÷ (−2)

Input	Output
−8	■
2	■
14	■

OBJECTIVE

Interactive lesson includes instant self-check, tutorials, and activities.

1 Making a Graph

When to Use This Strategy Making a graph can help you find relationships between data.

1 EXAMPLE Making a Graph — Real World

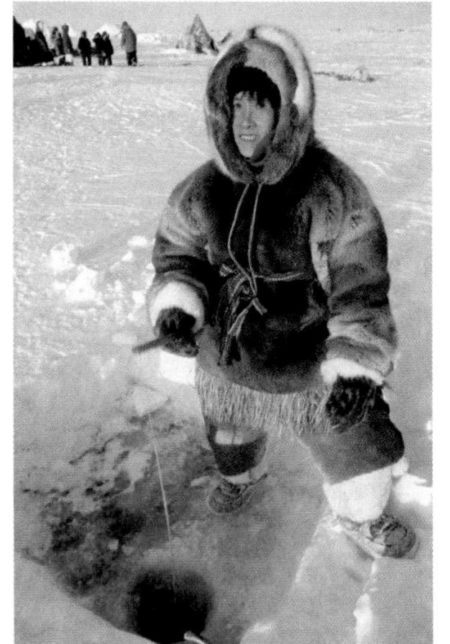

Temperature The average January temperature in Fairbanks, Alaska, is −23°C. Water freezes at 0°C (32°F) and boils at 100°C (212°F). Use a graph to estimate the average January temperature in degrees Fahrenheit in Fairbanks.

Read and Understand Water freezes at 0°C (32°F) and boils at 100°C (212°F). You need to find −23°C in degrees Fahrenheit.

Plan and Solve To approximate −23°C in degrees Fahrenheit, ***make a graph.*** You know two pairs of equivalent temperatures. Write the ordered pairs as (0, 32) and (100, 212).

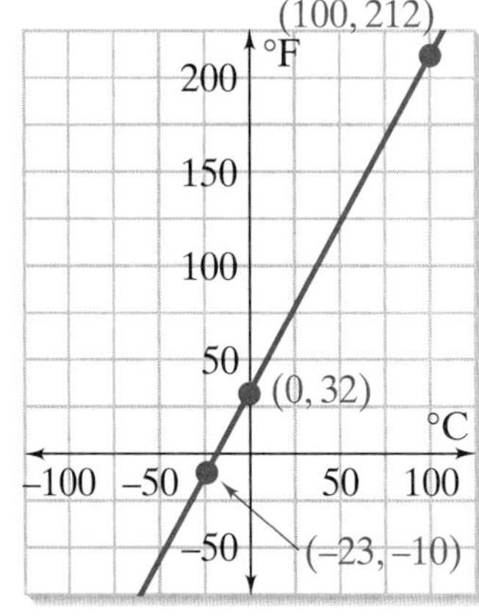

Connect the points with a line. The Fahrenheit temperature is about −10° when the Celsius temperature is −23°.

Look Back and Check Using number sense, since −23°C is less than 0°C and −10°F is less than 32°F, the answer is reasonable.

Check Understanding 1 Use the graph to estimate 22°C in degrees Fahrenheit.

EXERCISES

 For more practice, see *Extra Practice*.

A Practice by Example

Example 1 (page 533)

Need Help?
- Reread the problem.
- Identify the key facts and details.
- Tell the problem in your own words.
- Try a different strategy.
- Check your work.

Solve each problem by making a graph.

1. The water pressure at a depth of 100 feet in the ocean is 45 pounds per square inch. At a depth of 500 feet, the pressure is 225 pounds per square inch. What is the water pressure at a depth of 800 feet?

2. **Speed Limits** Mr. Zeller lives in New Zealand where speed limits are measured in kilometers per hour. While visiting the United States, Mr. Zeller drives along a road with a speed limit of 65 miles per hour. Use the signs below. Estimate 65 miles per hour in kilometers per hour.

3. A car slowed to a stop at a constant rate. After 5 seconds, the car was traveling 30 miles per hour. After 8 seconds, the car was traveling 12 miles per hour.
   a. How fast was the car moving before the driver applied the brakes?
   b. After how many seconds did the car come to a complete stop?

B Apply Your Skills

Strategies

Draw a Diagram
Make a Graph
Make an Organized List
Make a Table and Look for a Pattern
Simulate a Problem
Solve a Simpler Problem
Try, Check, and Revise
Use Logical Reasoning
Work Backward
Write an Equation

Choose a strategy to solve each problem.

4. **Music** Nate, Nellie, Nancy, and Ned sit in a row in the school orchestra. Each person plays one of the instruments shown below. Nate does not play a wind instrument. Nellie broke a string. Nancy sits next to the trumpet player. Which instrument does each person play?

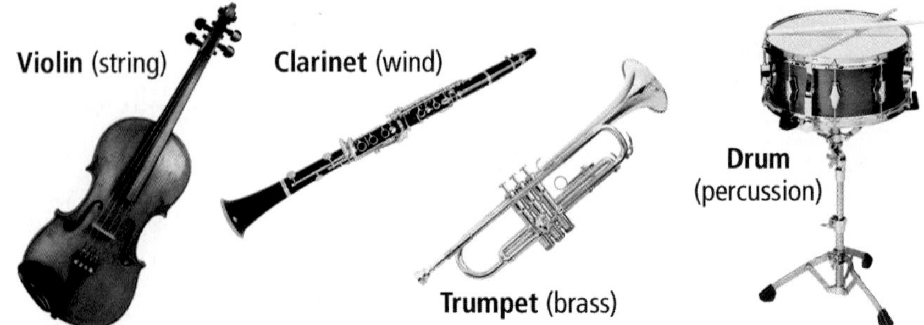

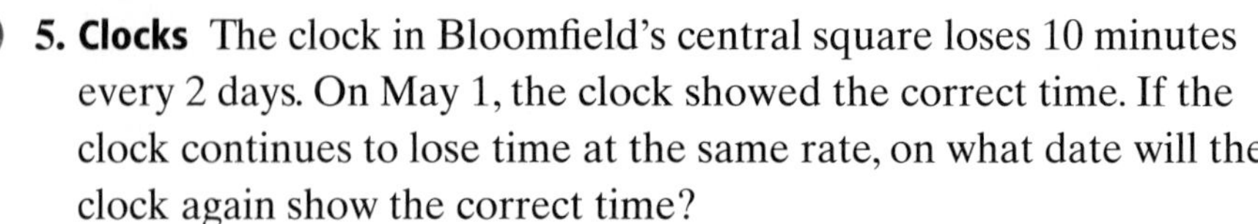

5. **Clocks** The clock in Bloomfield's central square loses 10 minutes every 2 days. On May 1, the clock showed the correct time. If the clock continues to lose time at the same rate, on what date will the clock again show the correct time?

Writing in Math

For help with writing to justify steps as in Exercise 9, see page 536.

6. **Writing in Math** At 10:00 A.M., Rick left camp on his bicycle riding at an average rate of 12 miles per hour. He traveled for 30 miles before he stopped. What time did he stop?

7. An ice cream parlor charges $2.40 for a 12-ounce shake and $3.60 for a 20-ounce shake. The parlor has just come out with a 16-ounce shake. What do you suggest the parlor should charge for the new size?

8. The average blink of an eye takes $\frac{1}{5}$ of a second. You blink 25 times per minute. If you travel at an average speed of 50 miles per hour for 12 hours, how many miles will you travel with your eyes closed?

9. **Stretch Your Thinking** Write 47 as the sum of 3 different prime numbers. How many different combinations are there?

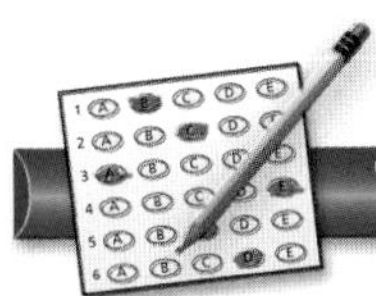

Test Prep

Multiple Choice

Use the coordinate plane at the right.

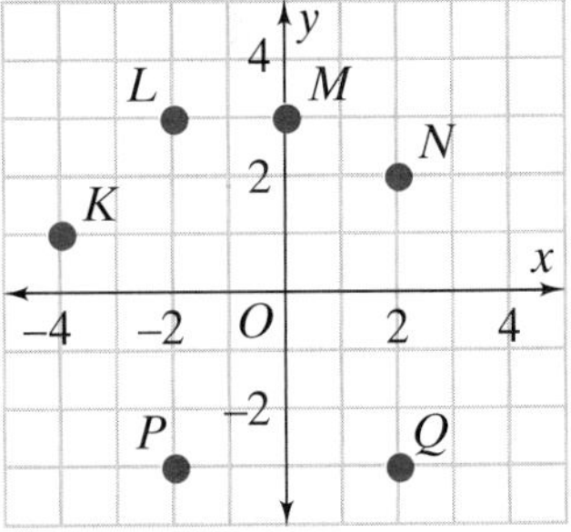

10. Which coordinates describes point *K*?
    - **A.** (4, 1)
    - **B.** (4, -1)
    - **C.** (-4, 1)
    - **D.** (-4, -1)

11. Which point is located at (0, 3)?
    - **F.** *L*
    - **G.** *P*
    - **H.** *Q*
    - **I.** *M*

12. Which point is 6 units right and 4 units up from point *Q*?
    - **A.** *N*
    - **B.** *M*
    - **C.** *K*
    - **D.** *L*

Short Response

13. Look at the number line at the right.

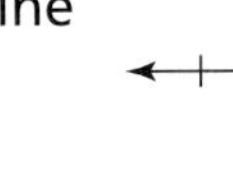

   a. Which point represents the opposite of point *S*?
   b. Which point represents the number with the greatest absolute value?

Take It to the NET
Online lesson quiz at **www.PHSchool.com**
Web Code: aaa-1009

Mixed Review

Lesson 10-1

Order the integers from least to greatest.

14. 4, −8, −10, 12 **15.** 0, 3, −6, 19 **16.** −1, 2, −3, 4

Lesson 8-4

Classify each triangle with the given side lengths by its sides.

17. 7, 7, 7 **18.** 4, 5, 12 **19.** 8, 9, 8

Writing to Justify Steps

For Use With Exercise 9, page 535

Some problems ask you to justify your steps. That means you must explain the reasons for going from one step to the next step. Some steps require a property you have learned. Other steps are procedures, like simplifying.

EXAMPLE

Here is one way you could solve Exercise 9 in Lesson 10-9, with the reason for each step.

6. **Writing in Math** At 10:00 A.M., Rick left camp on his bicycle riding at an average rate of 12 miles per hour. He traveled for 30 miles before he stopped. What time did he stop?

Rick traveled at the average rate of 12 per hour and he travels 30 miles. Let t stand for the time he travels. The equation $12t = 30$ represents this situation. the solve the equation. Then determine the time Rick stops.

Steps	Reasons
$12t = 30$	This is the equation to be solved.
$\frac{12t}{12} = \frac{30}{12}$	Divide each side by 12.
$t = 3\frac{1}{2}$	Simplify and write the fraction as a mixed number.
10:00	Starting time
+ 3:30	Write $3\frac{1}{2}$ hours as 3 hours and 30 minutes or 3:30.
1:30	Then add the times.

Rick will stop at 1:30. This is afternoon so it is 1:30 P.M.

EXERCISES

Justify each step.

1.
$$8 = 2x - 3$$
$$8 + 3 = 2x - 3 + 3$$
$$11 = 2x$$
$$\frac{11}{2} = \frac{2x}{2}$$

2.
$$\frac{1}{2}x = 15$$
$$2\left(\frac{1}{2}\right)x = 2 \cdot 15$$
$$x = 30$$

3. Ten pounds of potatoes cost \$2.55. How much will 6 pounds cost? Write and solve a proportion. Justify your steps.

Using a Variable

The problem-solving strategy ***write an equation*** can help you solve many problems when you are taking tests. Use a variable to represent the quantity that you are looking for. Then write an equation.

EXAMPLE

Admission to the county fair is \$4.50 per person. The Rodriguez family pays \$22.50 for admission to the fair. How many people are in the Rodriguez family?

Words	cost per person	times	number of people	=	total cost
↓	Let n = the number of people.				
Equation	4.50	·	n	=	22.50

$4.50n = 22.50$ ← **Write the equation.**

$\frac{4.50n}{4.50} = \frac{22.50}{4.50}$ ← **Divide both sides by 4.50.**

$n = 5$ ← **Simplify.**

There are 5 people in the Rodriguez family.

EXERCISES

Write and solve an equation for each situation.

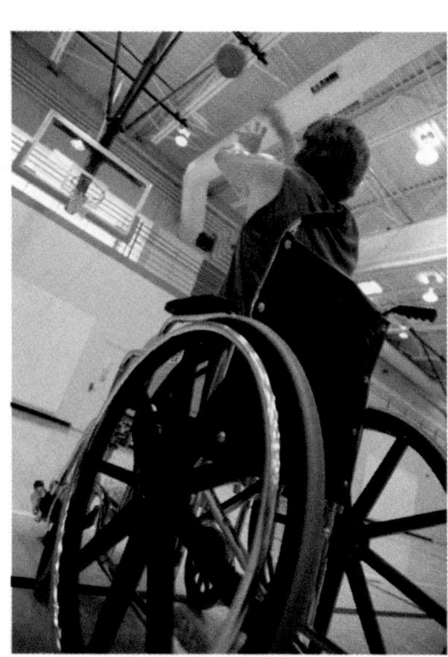

1. Stephanie scores 17 points in the first half of a basketball game. She scores 25 points in all during the game. How many points did she score in the second half of the game?

2. Suppose you pass out programs at a ballet. You have 178 programs twenty minutes before the ballet starts. You have 39 programs five minutes before the ballet starts. How many programs do you pass out during the 15 minutes?

3. Suppose you want to make double-decker peanut butter and jelly sandwiches. You need 3 pieces of bread for each sandwich. If you make 18 sandwiches, how many pieces of bread will you need?

4. Russell volunteers 36 hours at a local hospital. He volunteers over a period of 15 weekends. What is the average number of hours he volunteers each weekend?

Chapter 10

Chapter Review

Vocabulary

absolute value (p. 492)	**integers** (p. 491)	**origin** (p. 518)
coordinate plane (p. 518)	**opposites** (p. 491)	**quadrants** (p. 518)
function (p. 527)	**ordered pair** (p. 518)	

Reading Math: Understanding Vocabulary

Choose the vocabulary term that best completes each sentence.

1. A _?_ assigns one output value to each input value.
2. (8, −4) and (−2, −3) are examples of _?_.
3. The numbers −4, −2, −1, 0, and 3 are _?_.
4. _?_ are the regions of the coordinate plane.
5. −3 and 3 are _?_.

Take It to the NET
Online vocabulary quiz at **www.PHSchool.com**
Web Code: aaj-1051

Skills and Concepts

10-1 Objectives

- To graph integers on a number line
- To compare and order integers

Integers are the set of positive whole numbers, their opposites, and 0. The distance from 0 on a number line is the **absolute value** of a number.

Compare using < or >.

6. $|-5| \blacksquare |4|$ **7.** $-8 \blacksquare 12$ **8.** $4 \blacksquare |-9|$ **9.** $-12 \blacksquare -14$

Order from least to greatest.

10. −1, 1, 2, −2 **11.** 0, −4, 5, −6 **12.** −3, 5, −7, 9

10-2 and 10-3 Objectives

- To add integers with the same signs
- To add integers with different signs
- To subtract integers
- To solve equations with integers

The sum of two positive integers is positive. The sum of two negative integers is negative. The sum of integers with different signs is found by subtracting the lesser absolute value from the greater. The sum has the sign of the number with the greater absolute value.

You subtract an integer by adding its opposite.

Find each sum or difference.

13. $3 + 8$ **14.** $5 + (-9)$ **15.** $-4 + 2$ **16.** $-7 + (-6)$

17. $11 - 3$ **18.** $2 - (-6)$ **19.** $-7 - 4$ **20.** $-10 - (-2)$

10-4 and 10-5 Objectives

- To multiply integers
- To divide integers
- To solve equations

The product of two integers with the same sign is positive. The product of two integers with different signs is negative.

The quotient of two integers with the same sign is positive. The quotient of two integers with different signs is negative.

Find each product or quotient.

21. 4×9 **22.** $7 \times (-3)$ **23.** -5×2 **24.** $-6 \times (-8)$

25. $16 \div 4$ **26.** $25 \div (-5)$ **27.** $-32 \div 8$ **28.** $-49 \div (-7)$

10-6 Objectives

- To name coordinates
- To graph points on a coordinate plane

A **coordinate plane** is formed by the intersection of an x-axis and y-axis at the **origin.** An **ordered pair** identifies the location of a point. The x- and y-axes divide the coordinate plane into four regions called **quadrants.**

Graph each point on a coordinate plane.

29. $(0, 6)$ **30.** $(5, -4)$ **31.** $(-6, 1)$ **32.** $(-2, -3)$

10-7 Objectives

- To find profit and loss
- To draw and interpret graphs

The sum of a business's income and expenses is called a balance. A positive balance is a profit. A negative balance is a loss.

Use the table at the right.

33. Find the total balance for the four months.

34. Did Balloons Aloft have a profit or a loss during that time?

Balloons Aloft	
Month	**Profit/Loss**
January	–$985
February	$10,241
March	–$209
April	$17,239

10-8 and 10-9 Objectives

- To make a function table
- To graph functions
- To solve problems by making a graph

A **function** is a rule that assigns exactly one **output** value to each **input** value.

35. For the function rule "output = input × 5," what is the output for the input 8?

Make a table and graph each function. Use x-values $-2, -1, 0, 1,$ and 2.

36. $y = x + 3$ **37.** $y = 2x - 3$ **38.** $y = \frac{x}{4}$

39. Last year the ticket price for Fun Times Theme Park was $12. This year the price is $16. The rate of increase remains the same. Make a graph to find the ticket price in three years.

Chapter 10

Chapter Test

1. What integer represents 7°F below 0°?

2. Name the opposite of each integer.
   a. 89 b. −100

Compare using <, >, or =.

3. 18 ■ −24 4. −15 ■ −9 5. 27 ■ −27

6. Order the integers from least to greatest.
   3, −1, −13, 5, 0

7. **Writing in Math** Define *absolute value* and illustrate with a number line.

Find each sum.

8. 9 + (−4) 9. −13 + 6 10. −7 + (−5)

Find each difference.

11. 1 − (−7) 12. −2 − 8

13. −3 − (−3) 14. 3 − 9

15. Solve $d + 6 = -3$.

16. **Temperature** The temperature is 18°F at 1:00 A.M. The temperature falls 22 degrees by 6:00 A.M. Find the temperature at 6:00 A.M.

17. On a math quiz worth 50 points, a student misses 2 points on the first section, 3 points on the second, 2 points on the fourth, and 1 point on the last. Find the student's score.

Find each product.

18. 5 × (−4) 19. −3 × (−6) 20. −2 × 7

21. 9 ÷ (−3) 22. −5 ÷ (−5) 23. −12 ÷ 4

Use the coordinate plane for Exercises 24 and 25.

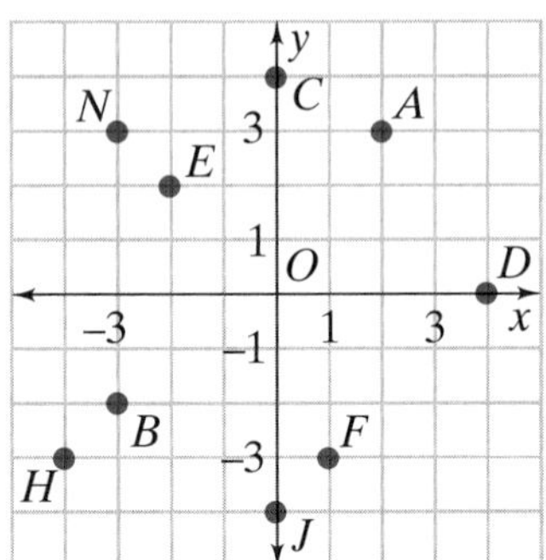

24. Name the point with the given coordinates.
    a. (0, 4) b. (−3, 3) c. (−4, −3)

25. Write the coordinates for each point.
    a. *A* b. *B* c. *F* d. *J*

26. Graph each point on a coordinate plane.
    a. (−2, −3) b. (4, −5) c. (2, 6)

27. a. Use the data below find Royale Bakery's profit or loss for each month.
    b. Graph the profit and loss data.

Income and Expenses for Royale Bakery

Month	Income	Expenses
Jan.	$1,314	–$828
Feb.	$2,120	–$120
Mar.	$1,019	–$1,285
Apr.	$1,438	–$765

28. Make a table and draw a graph for the linear function $y = x - 3$.

29. **Estimation** A mountain climber starts at 50 feet above sea level at 7:00 A.M. At 11:00 A.M., she is 210 feet above sea level. If she maintains a steady rate, estimate her height above sea level at 12:30 P.M.

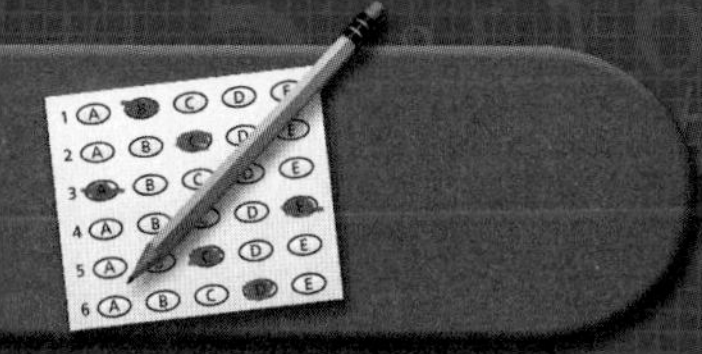

Test Prep

Multiple Choice

Choose the correct letter.

1. Evaluate the expression $b - a - 8$ when $a = 7$ and $b = 24$.
A. -25 **B.** -9 **C.** 9 **D.** 11

2. Which amount is the same as $1\frac{1}{2}$ pints?
F. 25 fluid ounces **G.** 3 cups
H. $\frac{3}{5}$ quart **I.** $\frac{1}{8}$ gallon

3. Suppose you purchase 9 peaches, 6 oranges, 12 pears, and 8 plums. What is the ratio of plums to pears?
A. $\frac{2}{3}$ **B.** 9 to 12 **C.** 12:8 **D.** 4:2

4. Find the median of the following set of data: 9, 19, 9, 17, 13, 14, 11, 9, 13.
F. 9 **G.** 10 **H.** $12\frac{2}{3}$ **I.** 13

5. Suppose you have a fresh lemonade stand. You spend $7 on the lemons, sugar, and cups. During the day, you sell 12 cups of lemonade for $.50 each. What is your profit or loss?
A. $-\$1$ **B.** $-\$.50$ **C.** $0 **D.** $1

6. Which of the following is the area of a circle with a diameter of 9 inches? Round to the nearest square unit.
F. 28 in^2 **G.** 57 in^2
H. 64 in^2 **I.** 254 in^2

7. Simplify: $-8 + 9 \div 3$.
A. $-\frac{1}{3}$ **B.** $\frac{1}{3}$ **C.** 5 **D.** -5

8. Which statement is false?
F. A square is always a rectangle.
G. Some rectangles are rhombuses.
H. All quadrilaterals are parallelograms.
I. A square is always a rhombus.

9. Which equation is NOT correct?
A. $\frac{3}{4} + 2\frac{1}{2} = 3\frac{1}{4}$ **B.** $3\frac{4}{5} - \frac{6}{8} = 3\frac{1}{20}$
C. $1\frac{7}{8} + 1\frac{5}{6} = 3\frac{17}{24}$ **D.** $5\frac{2}{5} - 2\frac{1}{3} = 3\frac{1}{10}$

10. Find the volume of a rectangular prism with the dimensions: $\ell = 10$ m, $w = 7$ m, $h = 8$ m.
F. $V = 25\ m^3$ **G.** $V = 56\ m^3$
H. $V = 70\ m^3$ **I.** $V = 560\ m^3$

11. The angles of 4 triangles have the following measures. Which of the triangles is obtuse?
A. 86°, 53°, 41° **B.** 89°, 45.5°, 45.5°
C. 123°, 32°, 25° **D.** 74°, 71°, 35°

Gridded Response

12. How many kilometers are in 120 meters?

13. Jack saves $32.75 from his newspaper delivery job. On Saturday, he spends $19.52 of his savings on a CD. How much does he have left?

Short Response

14. On a scale drawing, the scale shown is 1 inch to 10 feet. The length of a room is 2.5 inches on the drawing. Make a sketch and find the actual length of the room.

15. Write an integer to represent three degrees Fahrenheit below zero. Then graph the integer on a number line.

Extended Response

16. a. A parallelogram has a base of 9 inches and a height of 7 inches. What is its area?
b. The base and the height of the parallelogram are doubled. Is the area doubled? Explain.

Real-World Snapshots

Peaks and Valleys

Applying Integers Elevations in the United States vary from tens of thousands of feet above sea level to several hundred feet below sea level. Aerial photography and relief maps show these differences clearly.

Put It All Together

Data File **Use the information on these two pages and on page 489 to answer these questions.**

1. Which featured location has the highest elevation? The lowest elevation?
2. a. How much higher is the elevation of Vostok Station, Antarctica, than the elevation of Death Valley, California?
   b. How much higher is the elevation of New Orleans, Louisiana, than the elevation of Death Valley, California?
3. Which location has an elevation 5,512 feet lower than Colorado Springs, Colorado? Show your work.
   A. Colossal Cave, Arizona B. Detroit, Michigan
   C. Houston, Texas D. New Orleans, Louisiana
4. Which location has an elevation 16 feet higher than New Orleans, Louisiana? Show your work.
   A. Atlantic Ocean B. Death Valley, California
   C. Key West, Florida D. Long Island, New York
5. **Reasoning** Which of these places do you think has the highest elevation: Boston, Massachusetts; Denver, Colorado; Memphis, Tennessee? Explain.

Take It to the NET For more information about geography, go to **www.PHSchool.com**.
Web Code: aae-1053

Seattle, Washington

Mt. Whitney, California
Elevation: 14,495 feet
Highest point in the contiguous United States.

Las Vegas, Nevada

Death Valley, California
Elevation: −282 feet
Annual temperature: high 90.5°F, low 62.2°F
Lowest point in the contiguous United States.

Pacific Ocean
Elevation: Sea level (0 feet)

Detroit, Michigan
Elevation: 633 feet
Annual temperature: high 58.4°F, low 41°F
Boston, Massachusetts
Long Island, New York
Elevation: 16 feet
Annual temperature: high 61.2°F, low 43.5°F
Minneapolis, Minnesota
Denver, Colorado
Colorado Springs, Colorado
Elevation: 6,145 feet
Annual temperature: high 61.8°F, low 33.7°F
Chicago, Illinois
Washington, DC
New Orleans, Louisiana
Elevation: −8 feet
Annual temperature: high 78°F, low 59.6°F
Oklahoma City, Oklahoma
Memphis, Tennessee
Atlantic Ocean
Elevation: Sea level (0 feet)
Houston, Texas
Elevation: 96 feet
Annual temperature: high79.4°F, low 58.2°F
Key West, Florida Keys
Elevation: 8 feet
Annual temperature: high 73.2°F, low 82.9°F

CHAPTER 11

Exploring Probability

Lessons

Key Vocabulary

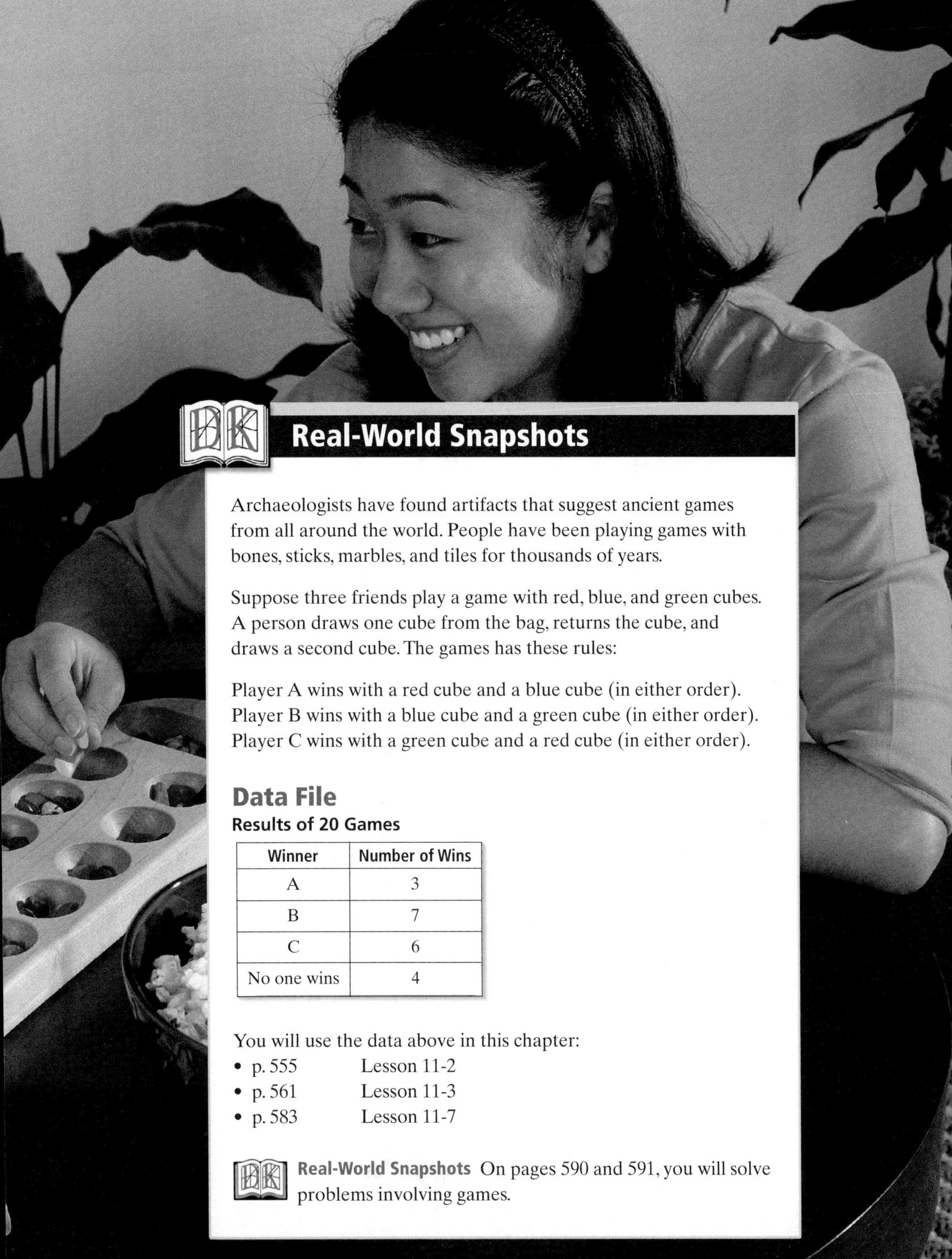

Real-World Snapshots

Archaeologists have found artifacts that suggest ancient games from all around the world. People have been playing games with bones, sticks, marbles, and tiles for thousands of years.

Suppose three friends play a game with red, blue, and green cubes. A person draws one cube from the bag, returns the cube, and draws a second cube. The games has these rules:

Player A wins with a red cube and a blue cube (in either order).
Player B wins with a blue cube and a green cube (in either order).
Player C wins with a green cube and a red cube (in either order).

Data File

Results of 20 Games

Winner	Number of Wins
A	3
B	7
C	6
No one wins	4

You will use the data above in this chapter:

- p. 555 Lesson 11-2
- p. 561 Lesson 11-3
- p. 583 Lesson 11-7

Real-World Snapshots On pages 590 and 591, you will solve problems involving games.

Chapter 11 Preview

Where You've Been

- In Chapters 4 and 5, you learned to write equivalent fractions, and to add, subtract, and multiply fractions.
- In Chapter 6, you learned to convert between decimals, fractions, and percents.

Where You're Going

- In Chapter 11, you will use decimals, fractions, and percents to find probabilities. You will find experimental probabilities and use simulations.
- Applying what you learn, you will make predictions about population.

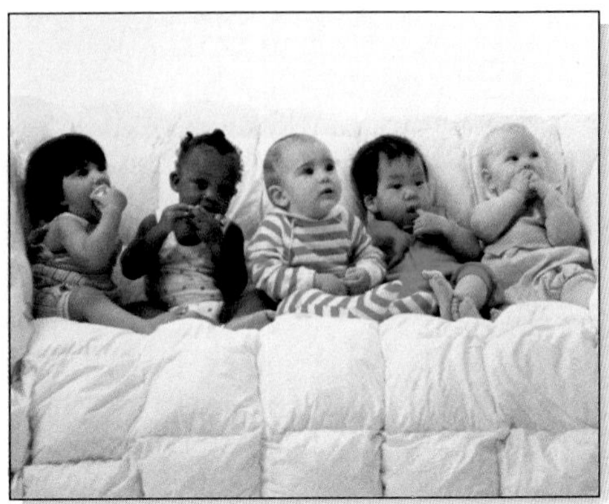

The birthrate in the entire world continues to decrease every year.

Instant self-check online and on CD-ROM

Diagnosing Readiness

For help, go to the lesson in green.

Subtracting Decimals (Lesson 1-5)

Find each difference.

1. $1 - 0.32$ **2.** $1 - 0.08$ **3.** $1 - 0.6$ **4.** $1 - 0.234$

Adding Fractions With Like Denominators (Lesson 4-2)

Find each sum.

5. $\frac{2}{5} + \frac{1}{5}$ **6.** $\frac{3}{6} + \frac{1}{6}$ **7.** $\frac{2}{8} + \frac{5}{8}$ **8.** $\frac{3}{10} + \frac{3}{10}$

Multiplying Fractions (Lesson 5-1)

Find each product.

9. $\frac{1}{2} \times \frac{5}{6}$ **10.** $\frac{3}{4} \times \frac{8}{9}$ **11.** $\frac{7}{10} \times \frac{5}{14}$ **12.** $\frac{2}{3} \times \frac{8}{9}$

Writing Equivalent Numerical Expressions (Lesson 6-6)

Write each fraction as a decimal and then as a percent.

13. $\frac{2}{8}$ **14.** $\frac{3}{9}$ **15.** $\frac{4}{5}$ **16.** $\frac{7}{10}$

Write each percent as a fraction in simplest form and as a decimal.

17. 13% **18.** 26% **19.** 10% **20.** 22%

11-1 Probability

What You'll Learn

To find the probability of an event

. . . And Why

To find the probability of a winning ticket, as in Example 2

✓ Check Skills You'll Need

For help, go to Lesson 6-6.

Write each number as a percent.

1. 0.32 **2.** $\frac{9}{25}$ **3.** $\frac{2}{5}$

4. $\frac{11}{50}$ **5.** 0.02 **6.** $\frac{17}{20}$

New Vocabulary

- equally likely outcomes
- event
- probability of an event

OBJECTIVE

 Interactive lesson includes instant self-check, tutorials, and activities.

1 Finding Probabilities of Events

If a coin is tossed once, there are two possible outcomes: heads or tails. An *outcome* is the result of an action. Outcomes that have the same chance of occurring are called **equally likely outcomes.**

Suppose you spin the pointer below once. If the arrow is equally likely to land on any of the 10 sections, the spin is random.

The 10 colored sections represent equally likely outcomes.

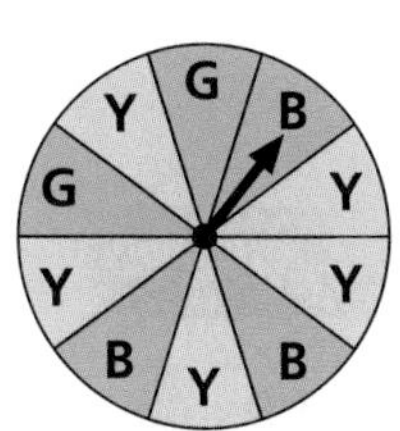

In 3 of the outcomes, the pointer lands on a blue section.

An **event** is an outcome or group of outcomes. The pointer landing on blue is an event.

The **probability of an event** is a number that describes how likely it is that the event will occur. For the spinner, the probability of landing on blue is 3 out of 10, or $\frac{3}{10}$.

Key Concepts — Probability of an Event

When outcomes are equally likely,

$$\text{the probability of an event} = \frac{\text{number of favorable outcomes}}{\text{total number of outcomes}}.$$

You can write $P(\text{event})$ for the phrase "probability of an event."

1 EXAMPLE Probability of an Event

Each face of a number cube displays one of the numbers 1 through 6. Find the probability of rolling an even number in one roll of a number cube.

There are 3 outcomes for the event "even" out of 6 equally likely outcomes.

$$P(\text{even}) = \frac{3}{6} \quad \begin{matrix}\leftarrow \text{outcomes with even numbers} \\ \leftarrow \text{total number of outcomes}\end{matrix}$$

$$= \frac{1}{2} \quad \leftarrow \text{Simplify.}$$

The probability of rolling an even number on the number cube is $\frac{1}{2}$.

Check Understanding 1 A number cube is rolled once. Find each probability.

a. $P(\text{odd})$ **b.** $P(5)$ **c.** $P(2 \text{ or } 6)$

d. **Reasoning** Is $P(3)$ different from $P(4)$? Explain.

All probabilities range from 0 to 1. The probability of rolling a 7 on a number cube is 0, which means that this is an *impossible* event. The probability of rolling a positive integer less than 7 is 1, which means this is a *certain* event.

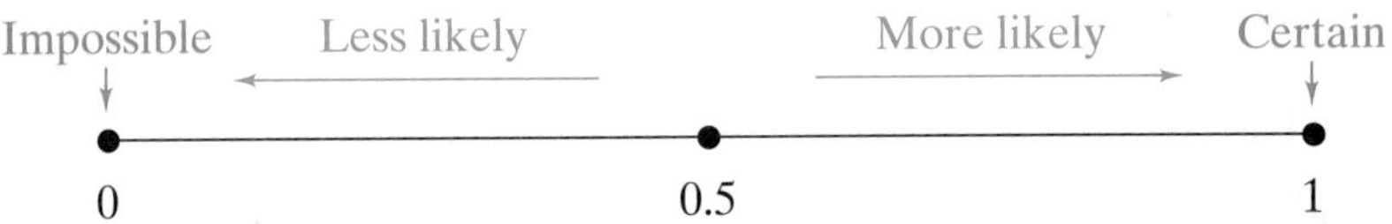

You can write probabilities as fractions, decimals, or percents.

2 EXAMPLE Real-World Problem Solving

School Fundraising Your class wants to raise money for a class trip. So you and your classmates sell 100 tickets for a drawing. You sell 11 tickets. A member of your class draws a ticket at random. Find the probability that the winning ticket will be a ticket you sold.

$$P(\text{winning ticket}) = \frac{11}{100} \quad \begin{matrix}\leftarrow \text{total number of tickets sold} \\ \leftarrow \text{number of tickets you sold}\end{matrix}$$

$$= 0.11, \text{ or } 11\%$$

There is a 11% probability that you sold the winning ticket.

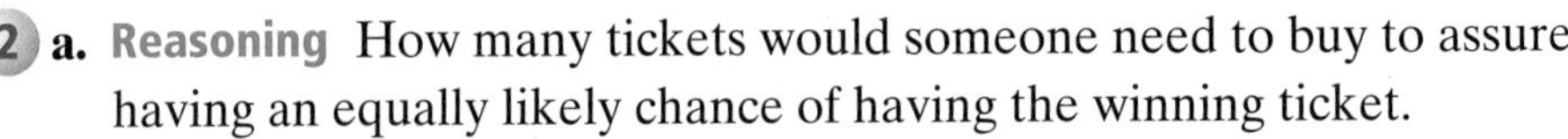

Check Understanding 2 **a.** **Reasoning** How many tickets would someone need to buy to assure having an equally likely chance of having the winning ticket.

b. In a bag of mixed nuts, 6 of 10 nuts are pecans. Find the probability of selecting a pecan at random. Write your answer as a fraction, a decimal, and a percent.

EXERCISES

For more practice, see *Extra Practice.*

A Practice by Example

Example 1 (page 548)

A jar contains 4 red marbles, 3 yellow marbles, 2 black marbles, and 1 green marble. You select a marble without looking. Find each probability.

1. P(red)

2. P(yellow)

3. P(black)

4. P(green)

5. P(black or red)

6. P(yellow or green)

7. P(orange)

8. P(yellow, red, or black)

9. P(red, blue, green, or black)

10. P(red, yellow, black, or green)

Example 2 (page 548)

Find the probability of each event. Write each answer as a fraction, a decimal, and a percent.

11. A spinner has equal sections of red, blue, pink, green, and yellow. You spin the spinner once and get blue or pink.

12. You roll a number cube and get a number greater than 3.

13. You write the letters A, B, C, D, E, and F on pieces of paper and select a letter that is a vowel at random.

14. Your name is selected at random from a list of names of 6 students.

15. Games A game has a square board divided into 4 equal sections numbered 1 through 4. You win when you toss a chip and it lands on the section numbered 4. What is the probability of winning when a toss lands on the board?

B Apply Your Skills

Ten cards are numbered 1 through 10. You select a card at random. Find each probability.

16. P(6)

17. P(even number)

18. P(1 or 2)

19. P(11)

20. P(a number less than 11)

21. Writing in Math For a game, is the probability of "not winning" always the same as "losing"? Explain.

22. Mental Math Is an event with a probability of $\frac{1}{2}$ *more* or *less* likely than an event with a probability of $\frac{2}{3}$? Explain.

23. Open-Ended Give an example of an impossible event and an example of a certain event.

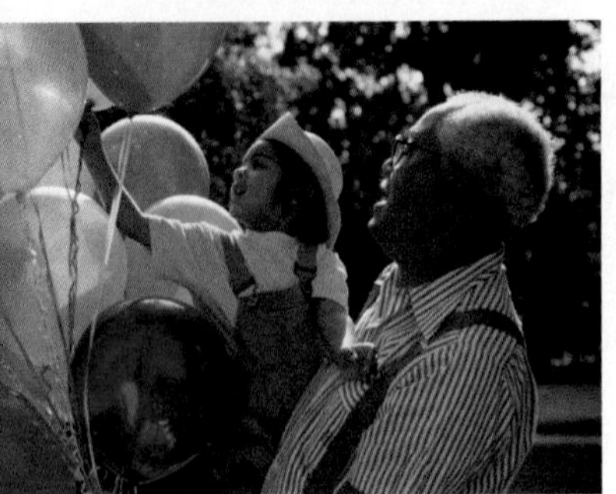

Real-World Connection

The girl chooses her favorite color when she selects the balloon. This is *not* a random event.

24. **Party** A package of 25 party balloons has 8 red, 6 blue, 6 green, and 5 yellow balloons.
    a. Find the probability of selecting a yellow balloon at random. Write your answer as a fraction, a decimal, and a percent.
    b. State whether the event "yellow balloon" is more or less likely than the event "green balloon."

Find each probability for one roll of a number cube.

25. P(multiple of 3)
26. P(factor of 8)
27. P(prime number)
28. P(multiple of 4)

29. Order the following outcomes from *most* likely to *least* likely.
    a. You flip a coin once and get tails.
    b. You roll a 5 on a number cube.
    c. You roll a 7 on a number cube.
    d. You select a 6 at random from a hat with the numbers 1 through 100 written on pieces of paper.

30. **Estimation** Suppose you spin the pointer once. Estimate each probability. Give your answer as a percent.
    a. The pointer lands on red.
    b. The pointer lands on green.
    c. The pointer lands on yellow.

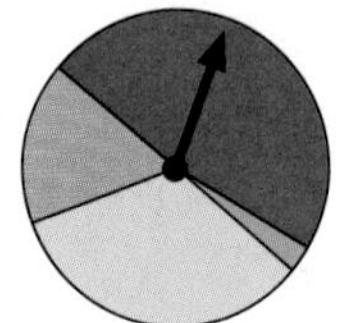

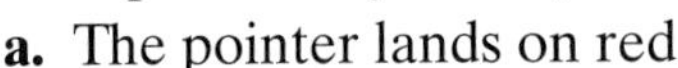

Each of the 26 letters in the English alphabet is put on a slip of paper. One slip is selected at random.

31. Find the probability that the letter comes before L in the alphabet.

32. Find the probability of selecting one of the letters in MISSISSIPPI.

33. **Reasoning** Which is more likely: selecting a letter from G through O, or from P through Z? Explain.

Reading Math

Icosahedron comes from the Greek words for "twenty" and "bases."

34. Suppose you roll an *icosahedron*, an object with 20 faces. All outcomes are equally likely. Each face is colored red, blue, yellow, or green.
    a. How many faces are colored with each color?
    b. In one roll, what is the probability that a green face will come up?

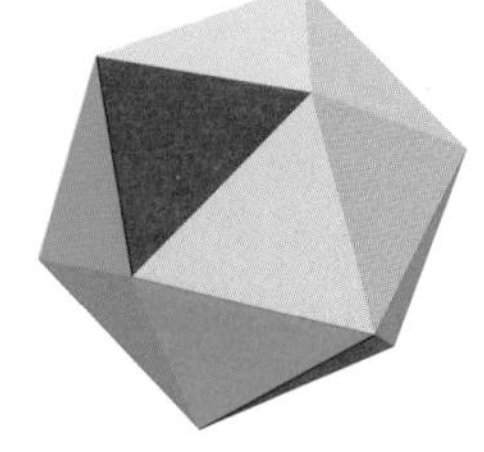

35. **Schedules** Volunteers use a spinner to determine job assignments at the local park. Each color indicates a different job. Sketch a four-color spinner with the following probabilities: $P(\text{Job } 1) = 25\%$, $P(\text{Job } 2) = 50\%$, $P(\text{Job } 3) = 10\%$, and $P(\text{Job } 4) = 15\%$.

Challenge

A bag contains red, green, and blue marbles. If you select a marble without looking, $P(\text{green}) = \frac{1}{3}$ and $P(\text{red}) = \frac{1}{2}$.

36. Find the probability of selecting a blue marble.

37. If there are 6 green marbles, how many marbles are there in all?

38. Twins In the United States, the probability that a child is a twin is about 2.9%. What is the probability that a child is *not* a twin? Write your answer as a fraction, decimal, and percent.

39. Stretch Your Thinking Karol is decorating a cube with seven colors of paint. She paints two dots of each color on each side of the cube. How many dots does she paint on the cube?

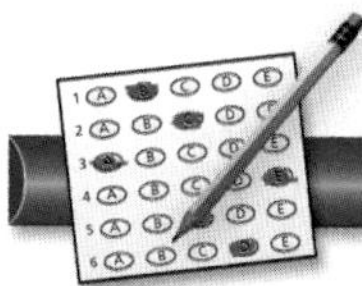

Test Prep

Gridded Response

For Exercises 40–44, a spinner has equal-sized sections numbered 1 through 30. Suppose you spin the pointer once.

40. What is the probability that the pointer lands on 2, 3, or 5?

41. What is the probability that the pointer lands on a multiple of 10?

Take It to the NET
Online lesson quiz at
www.PHSchool.com
Web Code: aaa-1101

42. What is the probability that the pointer lands on a prime number?

43. What is the probability that the pointer lands on an even number?

44. What is the probability that the pointer lands on a multiple of 5?

45. A bag contains 25 blue and yellow chips. There are 7 more yellow chips than blue chips. What is the probability of selecting a blue chip?

Mixed Review

Lesson 10-2

Find each sum.

46. $8 + 27$ **47.** $-5 + (-13)$ **48.** $10 + (-10)$

49. $-6 + 4$ **50.** $8 + (-8)$ **51.** $-7 + (-3)$

52. At 5 A.M., the temperature was $-3°$F. By noon, the temperature had risen $15°$F. What was the temperature at noon?

Extension

Odds

For Use With Lesson 11-1

When you roll a number cube, the probability that you will roll a 2 is $\frac{1}{6}$, or 1 out of 6.

You can describe your chances of rolling a 2 using odds.

> *Odds in favor* of an event is the ratio of the number of favorable outcomes to the number of unfavorable outcomes.
>
> *Odds against* an event is the ratio of the number of unfavorable outcomes to the number of favorable outcomes.

EXAMPLE Odds for an Event

a. In one roll of a number cube, what are the odds in favor of rolling a 2?

There is 1 favorable outcome.
There are 5 unfavorable outcomes.

The odds in favor of rolling a 2 are 1 to 5.

Ways to roll a 2	2
Ways *not* to roll a 2	1 3 4 5 6

b. What are the odds against rolling a 2?

The odds against rolling a 2 are 5 to 1.

EXERCISES

1. You roll a number cube once.
   a. What are the odds in favor of rolling an even number?
   b. What are the odds against rolling an even number?

2. A jar contains 6 marbles: 2 red, 2 blue, 1 yellow, and 1 green. You draw one marble at random.
   a. What are the odds in favor of drawing a blue marble?
   b. What are the odds against drawing a blue marble?

3. A store has a box of 1,000 tennis balls. Suppose the odds in favor of selecting a tennis ball marked "WIN" are 1 to 9. How many tennis balls are winners?

4. Algebra Suppose the odds in favor of an event are a to b. What is the probability of the event? (*Hint:* There are a favorable outcomes and b unfavorable outcomes. What is the total number of outcomes?)

11-2 Experimental Probability

What You'll Learn

To find experimental probabilities

. . . And Why

To decide whether a game is fair, as in Example 2

Check Skills You'll Need

For help, go to Lesson 3-4.

Write each fraction in simplest form.

1. $\frac{12}{20}$
2. $\frac{25}{50}$
3. $\frac{8}{30}$
4. $\frac{26}{40}$
5. $\frac{18}{30}$
6. $\frac{17}{51}$
7. $\frac{36}{45}$
8. $\frac{55}{88}$

New Vocabulary • experimental probability

Interactive lesson includes instant self-check, tutorials, and activities.

OBJECTIVE 1 Finding Experimental Probabilities

Investigation: Exploring Probabilities

Place 2 red cubes and 2 blue cubes in a bag. Suppose you draw 2 cubes out of the bag without looking.

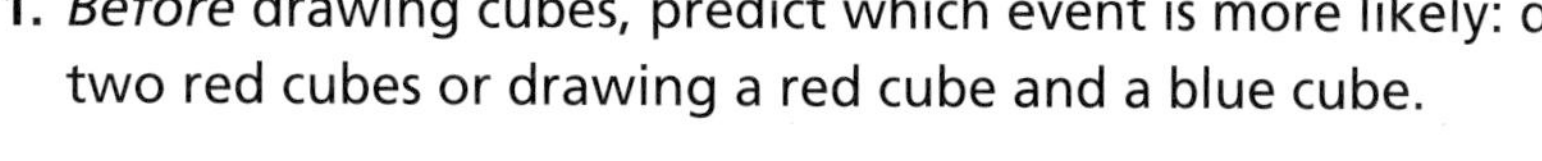

1. *Before* drawing cubes, predict which event is more likely: drawing two red cubes or drawing a red cube and a blue cube.

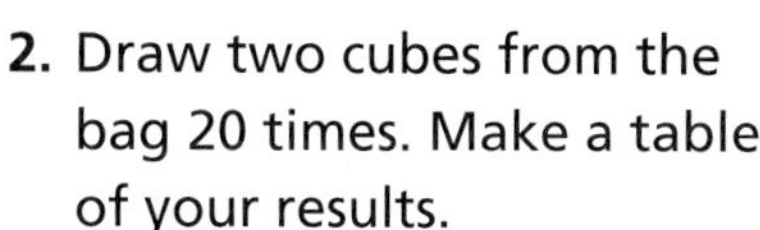

2. Draw two cubes from the bag 20 times. Make a table of your results.

Event	Number of Times Event Occurs	Probability
2 red	■	$\frac{■}{20}$
1 red 1 blue	■	$\frac{■}{20}$

3. a. Based on your results, was your prediction correct?
   b. To find the probability for each event find the ratio of the number of times the event occurs to 20.

Suppose you toss a ball of paper at a trash can. You toss it 12 times, and the ball of paper goes in 5 times. Each toss is a *trial*. To find an experimental probability, which is based on data you collect, use the following ratio.

Key Concepts **Experimental Probability**

experimental probability: $P(\text{event}) = \frac{\text{number of times an event occurs}}{\text{total number of trials}}$

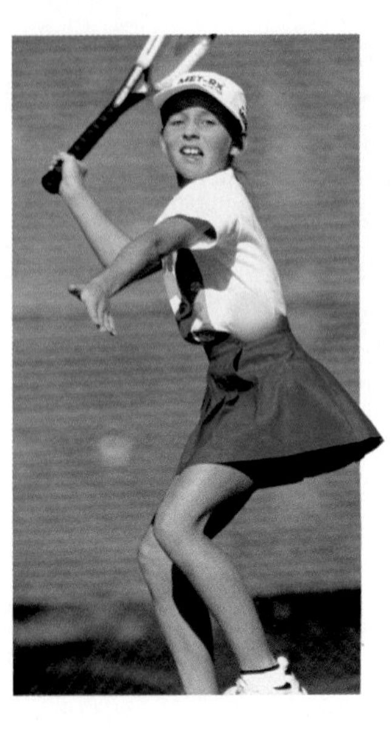

You can find the experimental probability when you compete in sports.

1 EXAMPLE Experimental Probability

Tennis In 20 tennis matches against Jennie, Ai-Ling wins 9 times.

a. What is the experimental probability that Ai-Ling wins a match?

$P(\text{Ai-Ling wins}) = \frac{9}{20}$ ← number of matches Ai-Ling wins / ← total number of matches

The experimental probability that Ai-Ling wins is $\frac{9}{20}$.

b. What is the experimental probability that Jennie wins a match?

$P(\text{Jennie wins}) = \frac{11}{20}$ ← number of matches Jennie wins / ← total number of matches

The experimental probability that Jennie wins is $\frac{11}{20}$.

Check Understanding 1 Franklin and Tom play 30 matches. Franklin wins 12 matches. What is the experimental probability that Franklin wins a match?

A *fair* coin or number cube generates equally likely outcomes. If coins, cubes, or spinners are unevenly made, they may *not* be fair.

2 EXAMPLE Analyzing Experimental Probability

Fair Games You and your friend want to play a game, but your only number cube is chipped. To make a fair game, you first roll the cube 60 times and record the results. Which of the following games seems fair? Explain.

Outcome	1	2	3	4	5	6
Number of Times Rolled	16	17	12	8	4	3

a. You win with a 6, and your friend wins with a 2.

The experimental probability of rolling a 2 is $\frac{17}{60}$. The experimental probability of rolling a 6 is $\frac{3}{60}$. Since the number cube strongly favors 2, the game seems to be unfair.

b. If the number is even, you win. If it is odd, your friend wins.

$17 + 8 + 3 = 28$ ← Add to find the number of trials for even.

$16 + 12 + 4 = 32$ ← Add to find the number of trials for odd.

So $P(\text{even}) = \frac{28}{60}$ and $P(\text{odd}) = \frac{33}{60}$. Since the probabilities are about the same, the game seems to be fair.

Check Understanding 2 In Example 2, suppose you win with a 1, 3, or 6, and your friend wins with a 2, 4, or 5. Is this game fair?

EXERCISES

For more practice, see *Extra Practice*.

A Practice by Example

Example 1 (page 554)

The table shows the results of students playing a video game. Find the experimental probability that each person wins.

Game Results

Player	Blake	Troy	Carla	Kate	Sara	Luis
Number of Wins	11	47	63	17	0	14
Number of times game is played	25	80	294	17	15	30

1. Carla **2.** Luis **3.** Kate

4. Sara **5.** Troy **6.** Blake

7. You toss a paper cup into the air 48 times. It lands on its side 36 times. Find the experimental probability that it lands on its side.

Example 2 (page 554)

Reasoning **Suppose Player A and Player B want to play a game with a number cube. The table below shows the results of tossing a number cube 80 times. Tell whether each game seems fair. Explain.**

Outcome	1	2	3	4	5	6
Number of Times Rolled	9	12	19	14	25	1

8. Player A wins if the number is even. Otherwise, Player B wins.

9. Player A wins if the number is 1, 2, or 3. Otherwise, Player B wins.

10. Player A wins if the number is 5 or 6. Otherwise, Player B wins.

B Apply Your Skills

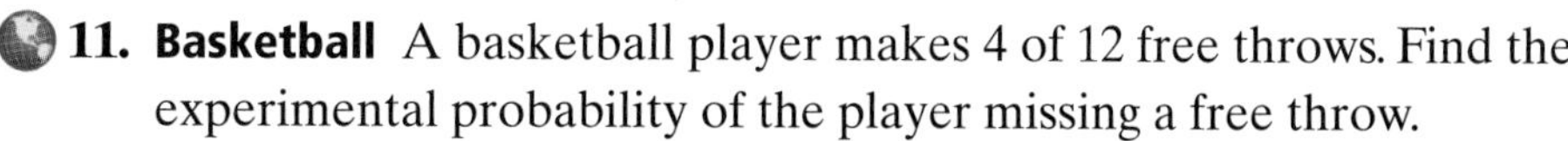

11. Basketball A basketball player makes 4 of 12 free throws. Find the experimental probability of the player missing a free throw.

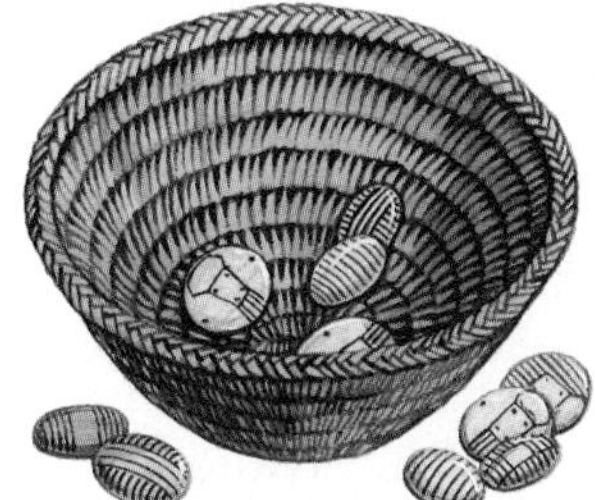

Real-World Connection

This basket is the type used by the Mandan peoples, who once lived along the banks of the Missouri River.

12. Fair Games The Mandan people played a game tossing decorated bone disks in a basket. Suppose Player A wins if the side with a decoration lands in the basket and faces up. Otherwise, Player B wins.

a. In 100 trials, $P(\text{A wins}) = \frac{30}{100}$ and $P(\text{B wins}) = \frac{70}{100}$. Does this seem to be a fair game?

b. Reasoning If the two players play the game the next day, will the experimental probabilities of winning be exactly the same? Explain.

13. a. Data File, p. 545 Find the experimental probability that Player A wins.

b. Find the experimental probability that Player B or Player C wins.

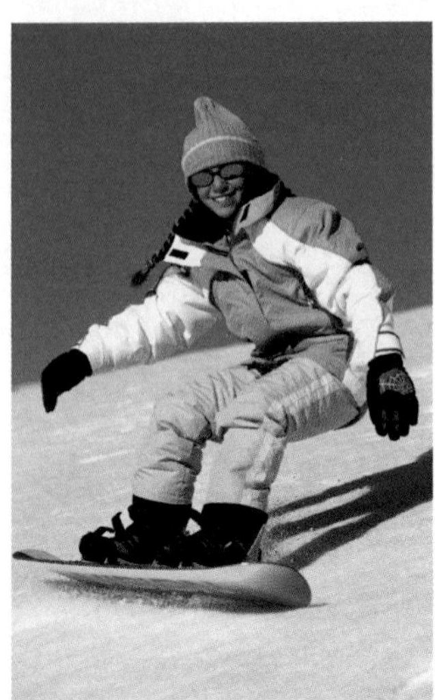

Real-World Connection

A good snowboarder knows how to use the snowboard's edges to increase speed.

14. a. **Snowboarding** You and a friend go snowboarding. You make it down the mountain before your friend 13 times out of 20. What is the experimental probability of you getting down the mountain first?
    b. What is the experimental probability of your friend being first?

15. **Reasoning** From the first 8 weeks of the school year, you find the experimental probability of having pizza on Friday is 100%. Explain what this means.

16. The table shows the results of five groups of students tossing the same coin.
    a. Find the experimental probability of getting heads for each group.
    b. Which group has results that most strongly suggest an unfair coin?
    c. Total the results and find the experimental probability of getting heads.

Group	H	T
A	11	9
B	8	12
C	13	7
D	10	10
E	6	14

Data Analysis **Carlos rolls 2 number cubes and finds the sum. He records the sums in the line plot below. Find each experimental probability.**

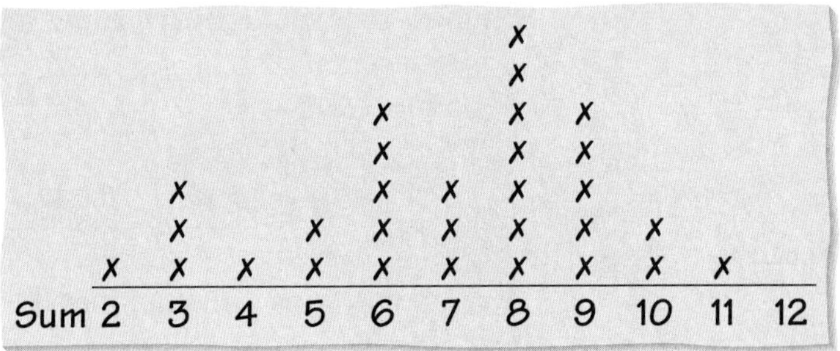

17. P(sum of 1)
18. P(sum of 3)
19. P(sum of 5)
20. P(sum of 7)
21. P(sum of 8)
22. P(sum of 12)

23. **Writing in Math** You and your friend want to play a game that uses a spinner with equal sections. Explain how you can use experimental probability to determine if the spinner is fair.

Data Collection **Roll a pair of number cubes 50 times. Record your results and find each experimental probability.**

24. P(1 and 1)
25. P(doubles)
26. P(even and even)
27. P(odd and odd)
28. P(2 and 3)
29. P(4 and 5)

Game Results	
A wins	卌 IIII
B wins	卌 卌 I
Times played	卌 卌 卌 卌

30. The table at the left shows the number of wins for two players after many games. Find the experimental probability of each player winning.

31. Geometry Lisa's dartboard has an area of 40 square inches. In the center is a triangle. In 50 throws that hit the board, Lisa hit the triangle 30 times. Estimate the area of the triangle and explain your answer.

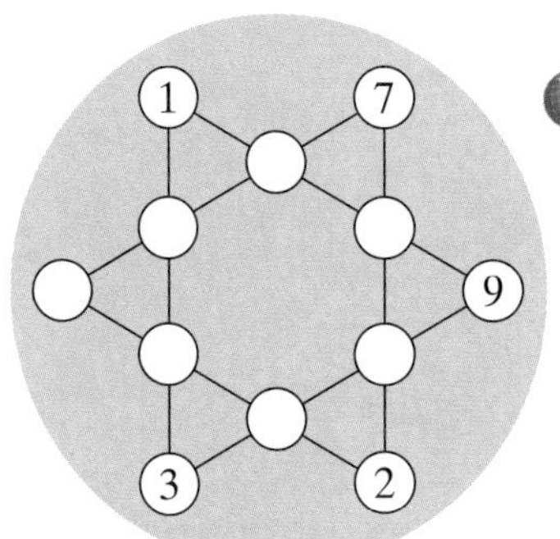

32. **Baseball** A baseball coach has to decide which player to put in as the designated hitter. Player A has 56 hits in 200 at bats. Player B has 48 hits in 160 at bats. Based on experimental probability, which player is more likely to get a hit?

33. Stretch Your Thinking Copy and complete the star at the left. Use each number from 1 through 12 only once. The sum of numbers on the six points of the star, and the sums on each of the six lines, must be 26.

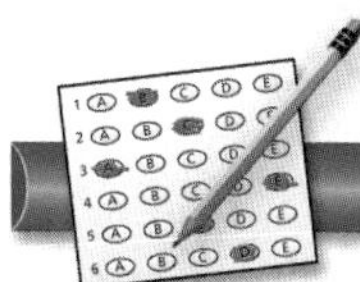

Test Prep

Multiple Choice

34. Which of the following probabilities is NOT equal to $\frac{14}{200}$?

A. 7% **B.** $\frac{7}{100}$ **C.** 0.07 **D.** 14%

35. A coin is tossed 50 times and comes up tails 23 times. What is the experimental probability of getting tails?

F. 23% **G.** $\frac{23}{100}$ **H.** $\frac{23}{50}$ **I.** 50%

Take It to the NET
Online lesson quiz at
www.PHSchool.com
Web Code: aaa-1102

36. A student rolls a number cube 40 times. The number 3 comes up eight times. What is the experimental probability of rolling a 3?

A. 8% **B.** 12.5% **C.** 0.20 **D.** $\frac{1}{4}$

Short Response

37. Tristan rolls a number cube 20 times. He rolls four 2's and three 4's. **(a)** What is the experimental probability of rolling a 2? **(b)** What is the experimental probability of rolling a 4? Explain each answer.

Mixed Review

Lesson 10-3

Find each difference.

38. $9 - (-3)$ 39. $-9 - 4$ 40. $20 - (-5)$

41. $-2 - (-12)$ 42. $16 - (-21)$ 43. $-4 - 17$

Lesson 8-7

Geometry **Tell whether the figures are *congruent* or *similar*.**

44. 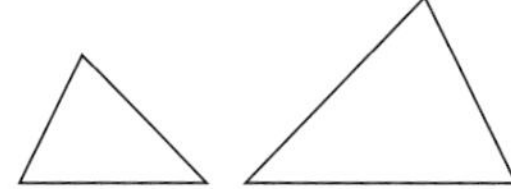

45. 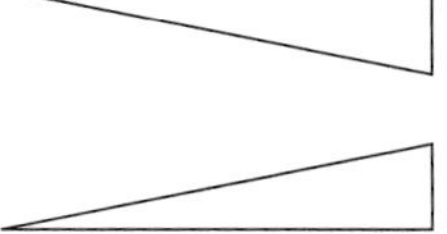

46.

11-3 Making Predictions From Data

What You'll Learn

To make predictions from probabilities

To make predictions based on a sample

. . . And Why

To make predictions from a sample, as in Example 2

Check Skills You'll Need

For help, go to Lesson 6-4.

Solve each proportion.

1. $\frac{2}{3} = \frac{4}{x}$ **2.** $\frac{n}{5} = \frac{10}{25}$ **3.** $\frac{12}{a} = \frac{6}{7}$

4. In a basket of apples, there are two green apples to every three red apples. If there are six green apples, how many red apples are there?

New Vocabulary • **population** • **sample**

Interactive lesson includes instant self-check, tutorials, and activities.

OBJECTIVE

1 Making Predictions From Probabilities

Investigation: Making Predictions

Suppose you place 8 blue cubes and 2 green cubes in a bag and you select one cube at random.

1. What is *P*(blue)? *P*(green)?
2. Suppose you draw a cube from the bag and replace it 20 times. How many times do you think you will draw a blue cube? Explain.
3. Select a cube and replace it 20 times. Record the color each time.
4. Did the number of blue cubes you obtained exactly match your prediction in Exercise 2? Explain why these answers might differ.

Probabilities can help you make predictions about the outcome of an experiment. However, they do not guarantee what will actually occur.

Need Help?
For help with multiplying fractions by whole numbers, go to Lesson 5-1.

To predict the number of times an event will occur, multiply the probability of the event by the total number of trials.

$$P(\text{event}) \times \text{total number of trials} = \text{number of predicted successes}$$

Suppose you flip a coin 10 times. To predict the number of times you get tails, multiply $\frac{1}{2} \times 10$. You would predict getting 5 tails in 10 trials.

Real-World Connection

The actual experimental probability of two male births in a row is about 27%.

1 EXAMPLE Making a Prediction From a Probability

In a family with 2 children, suppose there is a 25% chance that both of the children are boys. Out of 72 families, how many are likely to have 2 boys?

P(two boys)	×	number of families	=	number of families with two boys	
$\frac{1}{4}$	×	72	=	18	← Write 25% as $\frac{1}{4}$. Then multiply.

You can predict 18 families will have 2 boys.

Check Understanding 1 At an arcade, Juanita plays a game 20 times. She has a 30% probability of winning each game. How many times should she expect to win?

OBJECTIVE

2 Making Predictions Based on Samples

A **population** is a group about which you want information. A **sample** is a part of the population. You use a sample and proportions to make predictions about the population.

2 EXAMPLE Real-World  Problem Solving

Quality Control A company makes 15,000 toy robots. The company randomly selects a sample of 300 robots for inspection. This sample has 5 faulty robots. Predict how many of the 15,000 robots are faulty.

Words $\frac{\text{number of faulty toys in sample}}{\text{total number in sample}} = \frac{\text{number of faulty toys in production}}{\text{total number in production}}$

Let n = the number of faulty robots in the population.

Proportion $\frac{5}{300} = \frac{n}{15{,}000}$

$$\frac{5}{300} = \frac{n}{15{,}000}$$

$300n = 5 \cdot 15{,}000$ ← Write the cross products.

$300n = 75{,}000$ ← Simplify.

$\frac{300n}{300} = \frac{75{,}000}{300}$ ← Divide each side by 300.

$n = 250$ ← Simplify.

It is likely that about 250 toy robots are faulty.

Check Understanding 2 Suppose 1,000 toy robots are selected at random from 20,000 robots, and 54 are found faulty. How many of the 20,000 robots are likely to be faulty?

EXERCISES

For more practice, see *Extra Practice*.

Practice by Example

Example 1 (page 559)

The probability of winning a game is 40%. How many times should you expect to win if you play the following number of times?

1. 5 times

2. 10 times

3. 15 times

4. 30 times

5. 85 times

6. 120 times

Example 2 (page 559)

Write and solve a proportion to make each prediction. Exercise 7 has been started for you.

7. Tour On a field trip, 1,000 students visit the Kennedy Space Center in Florida. A teacher selects 70 students at random. They are asked, "Did you see the exhibit on rockets?" Of those questioned, 14 say that they did. Predict how many total students on the field trip saw the exhibit.

$$\begin{array}{r} \text{saw exhibit in sample} \rightarrow \\ \text{total in sample} \rightarrow \end{array} \frac{14}{70} = \frac{n}{1{,}000} \begin{array}{l} \leftarrow \text{total that saw exhibit} \\ \leftarrow \text{total in school} \end{array}$$

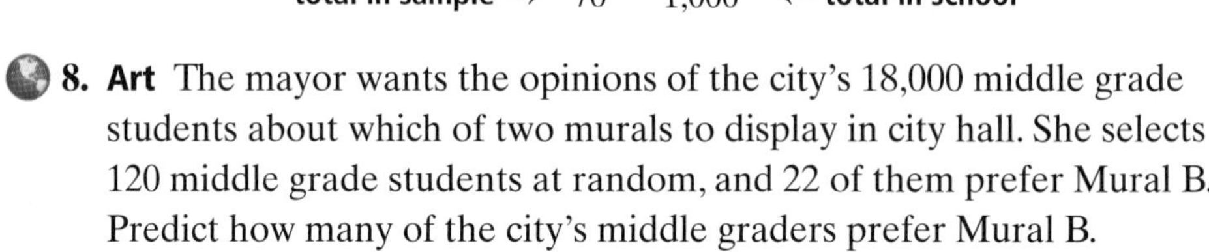

8. Art The mayor wants the opinions of the city's 18,000 middle grade students about which of two murals to display in city hall. She selects 120 middle grade students at random, and 22 of them prefer Mural B. Predict how many of the city's middle graders prefer Mural B.

Real-World Connection

Careers At the Kennedy Space Center, engineers show you how to use rocket equipment in space.

Use the following information to make a prediction. A company makes shirts, pants, belts, and T-shirts. It plans to ship 24,000 of each item. Before shipping, a sample of each product is tested. From each given sample, predict the number of items that are likely to have defects.

9. Of 500 shirts, 6 have defects.

10. Of 400 pants, 5 have defects.

11. Of 250 belts, 2 have defects.

12. Of 160 T-shirts, 3 have defects.

Apply Your Skills

In a survey, 1,580 parents were asked which trait they think is most desirable in their children. The table shows the results.

Trait	Probability of Response
Honest	42%
Good judgment	36%
Obeys parents	22%

13. Which trait is considered most desirable?

14. a. How many of the parents surveyed think "good judgment" is the most desirable trait?

b. How many think "honest" is the most desirable trait?

15. **Data File, p. 545** Suppose players A, B, and C play the game 30 times.
   a. How many times would you expect Player B to win?
   b. How many times would you expect Player C to win?

16. **Writing in Math** Why would a person take a random sample instead of counting or surveying the whole population?

Use the line plot at the right. A box of fruit snacks has many individual pieces. The line plot shows the result when 25 pieces are selected at random. For each box size, predict the number of each color in the box.

Fruit Pieces

blue	red	orange	yellow
		✗	
		✗	
		✗	
	✗	✗	
	✗	✗	
	✗	✗	✗
	✗	✗	✗
✗	✗	✗	✗
✗	✗	✗	✗
✗	✗	✗	✗

17. 200 pieces

18. 400 pieces

19. 250 pieces

20. 500 pieces

21. **Number Sense** Suppose you take a sample of 15 pieces and a sample of 60 pieces. Which sample is more likely to give you a prediction closer to the actual number of each color? Explain.

22. A sample of 100 gadgets is selected from the day's production of 5,000 gadgets. In the sample, 7 are defective. Predict the number of faulty gadgets in the day's production.

A computer dart game randomly selects points to represent darts being thrown. The areas of each section are as follows.

- black: 1 in.^{2}
- blue: 3 in.^{2}
- yellow: 5 in.^{2}
- red: 7 in.^{2}

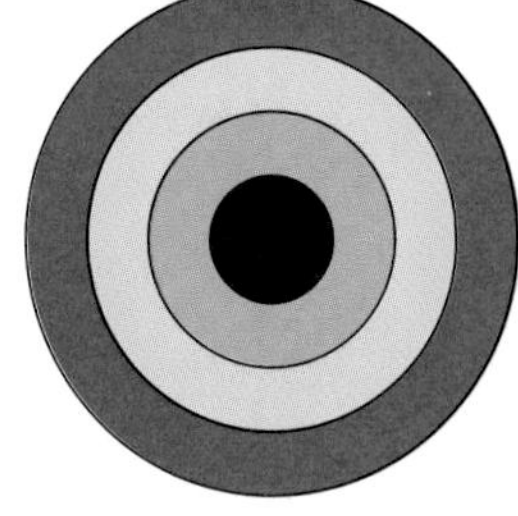

23. What is the probability that the point is in the yellow section?

24. What is the probability that the point is in the red or yellow section?

25. If the computer "throws" 1,000 darts, how many can you expect will "land" in the black area?

C Challenge

26. a. **Data Collection** Ask a sample of students from your school what type of music they listen to. Record your results.
   b. Find the total number of students in your school. Then make a prediction about the music preferences of students in your school.

27. **Stretch Your Thinking** Someone looking at a photo says, "Brothers and sisters have I none, but that man's father is my father's son." Explain how this can be true.

Test Prep

Reading Comprehension

Read the passage and answer the questions below.

Moviegoers Flock to See New Summer Blockbuster

Today movie fans got their first look at one of the year's most anticipated films. The movie took more than two years to produce. We surveyed 40 people who saw the movie and 38 of them said it was excellent. The film will open soon.

28. What is the experimental probability that a viewer thought the movie was excellent?

29. If there were 600 people in the theater, how many people are likely to think the movie was excellent?

Multiple Choice

30. A company has 20,000 hats in stock. In a random sample of 80 hats, 3 are defective. How many overall hats are likely to be defective?

A. 3 **B.** 80 **C.** 667 **D.** 750

Take It to the NET
Online lesson quiz at **www.PHSchool.com**
Web Code: aaa-1103

31. In a pet store's survey, 45 out of 60 people own at least one cat. How many out of 420 customers are likely to own at least one cat?

F. 7 **G.** 9 **H.** 315 **I.** 560

Mixed Review

Lesson 10-4

Algebra **Find each product.**

32. $10 \times (-8)$ **33.** -6×20 **34.** $16 \times (-1)$

35. $-24 \times (-4)$ **36.** $-7 \times (-12)$ **37.** -15×15

Checkpoint Quiz 1 — Lessons 11-1 through 11-3

Instant self-check quiz online and on CD-ROM

A number cube is rolled. Find each probability.

1. P(less than 3) **2.** $P(8)$ **3.** P(5 or 6)

4. A pencil is dropped 20 times. It points left 8 times. Find the experimental probability that it points left.

5. In a Patterstown survey, 40 out of 50 people say they eat lunch daily. The town has 35,000 people. Predict the number who eat lunch daily.

11-4 Simulate a Problem

What You'll Learn

To solve problems by simulation

. . . And Why

To simulate everyday situations, as in Example 1

Check Skills You'll Need

For help, go to Lesson 11-2.

Find the experimental probability that each person makes a basket during basketball practice.

1. Rachel makes 22 attempts and gets a basket 6 times.
2. Liam makes 30 attempts and gets a basket 8 times.

New Vocabulary • simulation

OBJECTIVE

Interactive lesson includes instant self-check, tutorials, and activities.

1 Solving a Problem by Simulation

When to Use This Strategy Sometimes it is difficult to collect data from an actual situation. Instead, you may be able to use a simulation.

A **simulation** of a real-world situation is a model used to find experimental probabilities. You can use number cubes, spinners, and computers to model real-world situations.

1 EXAMPLE Real-World Problem Solving

Newspaper Delivery Each day, Sue delivers Mrs. Rivers' newspaper sometime between 6:30 A.M. and 7:30 A.M. Mrs. Rivers leaves for work between 7:00 A.M. and 8:00 A.M. What is the probability that Mrs. Rivers will get her paper before she leaves for work?

Read and Understand Sue delivers the paper between 6:30 A.M. and 7:30 A.M. Mrs. Rivers goes to work between 7:00 A.M. and 8:00 A.M. You need to find the probability that Mrs. Rivers will get her paper before she goes to work.

Sue's Delivery Time

6:30
7:30

7:15 6:45

7:00

Time Mrs. Rivers Goes to Work

7:00
8:00

7:45 7:15

7:30

Plan and Solve You can't collect data from Sue and Mrs. Rivers. So, simulate the problem with a model. Assume each time is equally likely.

Use two spinners, like the ones at the left. One clock will simulate a random time from 6:30 A.M. to 7:30 A.M. The other clock will simulate a random time from 7:00 A.M. to 8:00 A.M.

Spin each spinner once to simulate what may happen on a given day. The table below shows the results for 28 days. For each day, circle the earlier time. If Time 1 is circled, Mrs. Rivers gets her paper.

Time 1 = Sue delivers paper. Time 2 = Mrs. Rivers leaves for work.		
Time 1, Time 2	**Time 1, Time 2**	**Time 1, Time 2**
(7:03), 7:55	(7:14), 7:16	(7:10), 7:18
(6:41), 7:02	(7:08), 7:27	7:21, (7:02)
(6:33), 7:16	(6:41), 7:59	(7:04), 7:46
(6:39), 7:28	(7:00), 7:08	7:09, (7:01)
7:24, (7:06)	(7:22), 7:52	(6:50), 7:28
(6:51), 7:18	(7:05), 7:54	(6:31), 7:52
(7:38), 7:45	(6:36), 7:48	(7:25), 7:27
(6:53), 7:31	(7:04), 7:13	(6:58), 7:34
(6:49), 7:16	(6:59), 7:07	7:23, (7:11)
(6:33), 7:55	(6:52), 7:27	(6:35), 7:57

In the 30 simulations, Mrs. Rivers receives the paper before leaving for work 26 times. So, $P(\text{paper before work}) = \frac{26}{30}$, or about 87%.

Look Back and Check The table below summarizes each delivery.

Summary of Delivery Results

Sue Delivers Paper	Mrs. Jones Leaves	Paper Received?
6:30 A.M. to 7:00 A.M.	7:00 A.M. to 7:30 A.M.	Yes
7:00 A.M. to 7:30 A.M.	7:00 A.M. to 7:30 A.M.	Sometimes
6:30 A.M.. to 7:00 A.M.	7:30 A.M. to 8:00 A.M.	Yes
7:00 A.M. to 7:30 A.M.	7:30 A.M. to 8:00 A.M.	Yes

The table shows that it is more likely that she will receive her paper. Since $P(\text{paper before work})$ is $\frac{26}{30}$, or about 87%, the answer is reasonable.

1 The forecast calls for a $\frac{2}{3}$ chance of rain in Detroit and a $\frac{1}{2}$ chance in Tampa. Find the experimental probability that it rains in both cities. Use two number cubes. Let 1, 2, 3, and 4 on one cube represent rain in Detroit. Let 1, 2, and 3 on the other cube represent rain in Tampa.

EXERCISES

For more practice, see *Extra Practice.*

A Practice by Example

Simulate and solve each problem. Show all your work.

Example 1 (page 563)

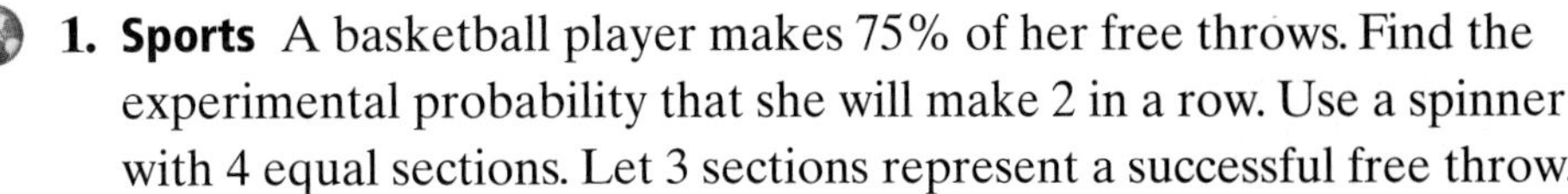

1. **Sports** A basketball player makes 75% of her free throws. Find the experimental probability that she will make 2 in a row. Use a spinner with 4 equal sections. Let 3 sections represent a successful free throw.

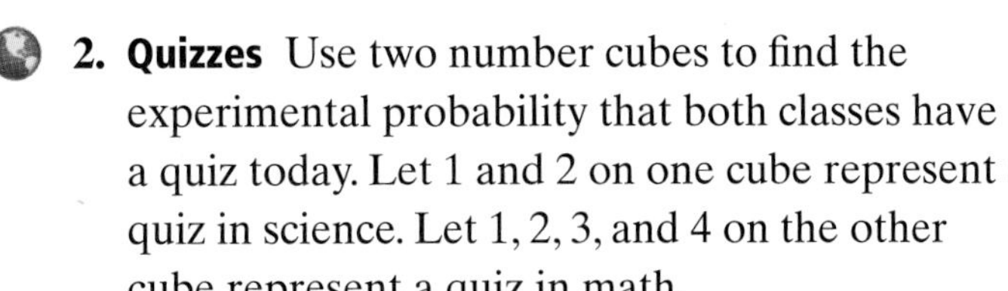

2. **Quizzes** Use two number cubes to find the experimental probability that both classes have a quiz today. Let 1 and 2 on one cube represent a quiz in science. Let 1, 2, 3, and 4 on the other cube represent a quiz in math.

Probability of a Quiz

Subject	Probability
Math	$\frac{2}{3}$
Science	$\frac{1}{3}$

Need Help?
- Reread the problem.
- Identify the key facts and details.
- Tell the problem in your own words.
- Try a different strategy.
- Check your work.

3. **Mail Delivery** Each day, Mr. Hill leaves his house for a walk between 11:00 A.M. and 12:00 P.M. Mr. Hill's mail is delivered between 10:20 A.M. and 11:20 A.M. Find the experimental probability that Mr. Hill will get his mail before he leaves. Use two spinners like those shown below.

Postal Delivery Time

10:20 / 11:20 (top), 10:35 (right), 10:50 (bottom), 11:05 (left)

Time Mr. Hill Goes for a Walk

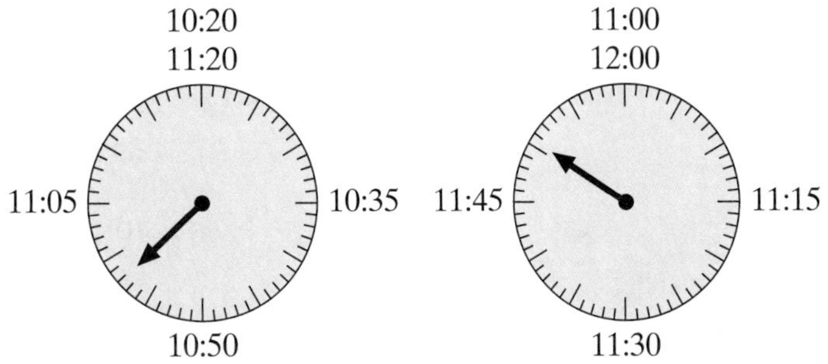

11:00 / 12:00 (top), 11:15 (right), 11:30 (bottom), 11:45 (left)

B Apply Your Skills

Choose a strategy to solve each problem.

Strategies
- Draw a Diagram
- Make a Graph
- Make an Organized List
- Make a Table and Look for a Pattern
- Simulate a Problem
- Solve a Simpler Problem
- Try, Check, and Revise
- Use Logical Reasoning
- Work Backward
- Write an Equation

4. A family expects to have 4 children. Assume that having a boy and having a girl are equally likely.
   a. How many coins can you use to simulate this situation?
   b. Find the experimental probability that 3 of the 4 children are girls.

5. Suppose you and a friend make a total of 33 pairs of gloves. Your friend makes twice as many pairs of gloves as you do. How many pairs do you and your friend each make?

6. **Writing in Math** Describe a situation where the strategy *simulate a problem* may be useful.

7. **Deli** Each time you visit a deli, they stamp a card for you with 1 of 3 kinds of stamps: soup, salad, or sandwich. When your card receives 8 stamps of one kind, they give you that item for free. What is the minimum number of visits you need to get one of each item for free?

 **8. Collecting** Each box of a cereal brand contains one of four prizes. A box costs $3.50. You want to collect all four prizes. What is the least amount of money you may need to spend to get all four prizes?

A jumping spider

9. a. Biology Jumping spiders can jump 40 times their body length. About how far in centimeters can a 15-millimeter spider jump?

b. Suppose another spider is 3 millimeters longer than the spider in part (a). About how far in centimeters can this spider jump?

10. Stretch Your Thinking How many squares of all sizes fit in a 5-by-5 square grid? Consider only squares that have integer side lengths.

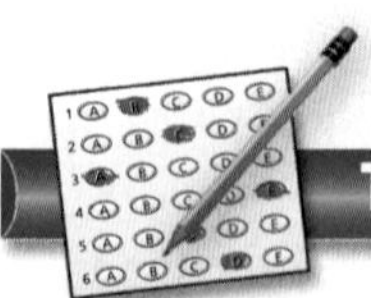

Test Prep

Multiple Choice

11. What is the expression 3.01 + 2.5 in simplest form?
A. 5.1 **B.** 5.15 **C.** 5.51 **D.** 5.6

12. What is the expression 8.4 − 1.7 in simplest form?
F. 17.4 **G.** 10.1 **H.** 7.3 **I.** 6.7

13. What is the expression 15 − 2 × 3 + 4 in simplest form?
A. 5 **B.** 13 **C.** 43 **D.** 91

14. What is the expression 4 + 8 × 6 − 1 in simplest form?
F. 71 **G.** 60 **H.** 51 **I.** 48

Take It to the NET
Online lesson quiz at **www.PHSchool.com**
Web Code: aaa-1104

15. What is the expression 20 + 10 ÷ 2 − 4 in simplest form?
A. 11 **B.** 16 **C.** 21 **D.** 29

Mixed Review

Lesson 10-6

Algebra **Name the point with the given coordinates.**

16. (2, 2) **17.** (2, −2)

18. (3, −4) **19.** (−3, −4)

20. (−2, 3) **21.** (−4, 4)

22. (−4, 1) **23.** (4, 3)

Lesson 9-1

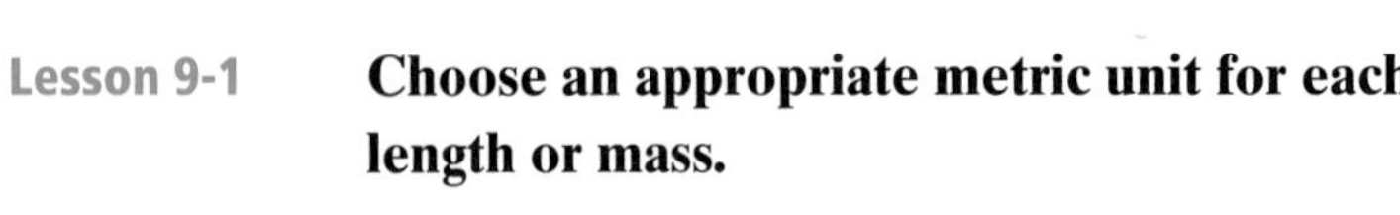

Choose an appropriate metric unit for each length or mass.

24. mass of a rock **25.** around your waist

Simulations

For Use With Lesson 11-4

You can use a spreadsheet, as shown below, to simulate events. Suppose you want to simulate 25 spins of a spinner with 5 equal parts numbered 1 to 5. You can make rows and columns of random integers from 1 to 5 by entering the following formula in each cell.

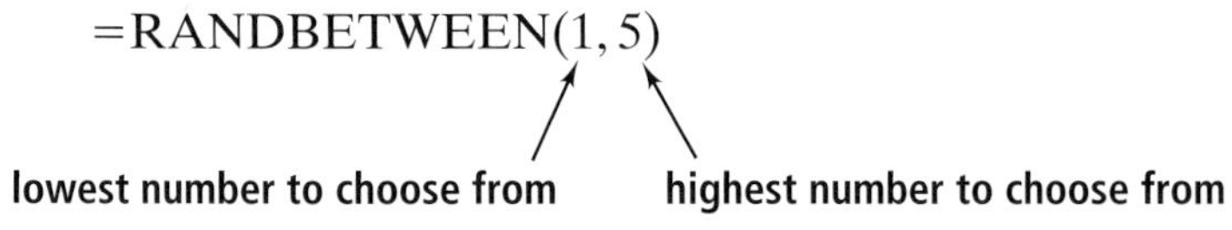

Random Numbers

	A	B	C	D	E	F
1	3	4	2	1	4	
2	2	4	4	2	4	
3	5	3	5	4	5	
4	4	3	1	4	2	
5	3	1	5	1	5	
6						
7						
8	Number of 3's:					
9	4					

You can use formulas to count results automatically. To count all the 3's in the 25 squares shown, enter the following formula.

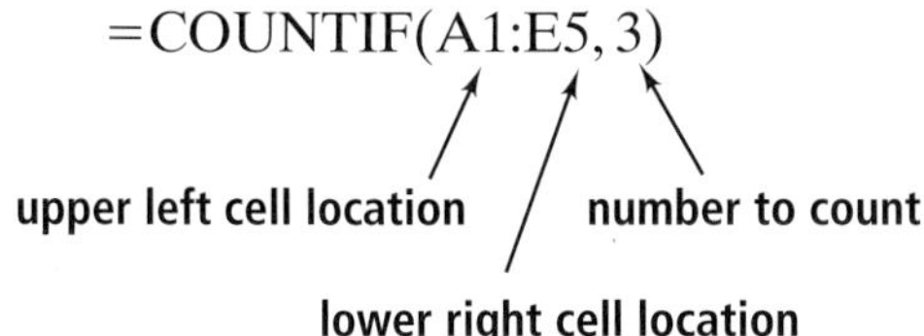

From the results, the experimental probability of spinning a 3 is $\frac{4}{25}$.

EXERCISES

1. Use the random numbers in the spreadsheet above. What is the experimental probability of spinning a 4?

2. **Basketball** Michelle plays basketball. Suppose she misses a free throw $\frac{1}{3}$ of the times she attempts one.
   a. To simulate the probability of a successful free throw, let 1 = misses, 2 = makes, and 3 = makes. Write a spreadsheet formula to generate the random numbers for this simulation.
   b. Write a spreadsheet formula to count the 1's automatically.
   c. Out of 30 numbers, how many 1's would you expect?
   d. Generate 30 random numbers from 1 to 3. Find the experimental probability that Michelle misses a free throw.

3. a. **Writing in Math** Suppose you take a test with three true-false questions. Describe a simulation to find the probability that you guess each answer correctly.
   b. Do the simulation you described in part (a). What is the probability that you get all three answers correct.

Tree Diagrams and the Counting Principle

What You'll Learn

To use tree diagrams

To use the counting principle

. . . And Why

To count a number of options, as in Example 2

✓ Check Skills You'll Need

For help, go to Lesson 11-1.

Suppose you roll a number cube once. Find each probability.

1. $P(1)$ **2.** $P(2 \text{ or } 5)$ **3.** $P(\text{less than } 7)$

4. $P(\text{prime})$ **5.** $P(0)$ **6.** $P(\text{odd})$

New Vocabulary

- tree diagram
- counting principle

OBJECTIVE 1

Interactive lesson includes instant self-check, tutorials, and activities.

1 Using Tree Diagrams

In Lesson 11-1, you found the probability of one event, like tossing a coin. You can use a **tree diagram** to find the probability of two or more events.

1 EXAMPLE Probabilities Using Tree Diagrams

Suppose you roll a number cube and then toss a coin. What is the probability that you will get an even number and tails?

Make a tree diagram to find all possible outcomes.

Number Cube	Coin	Outcome
1	H	1H
	T	1T
2	H	2H
	T	(2T)
3	H	3H
	T	3T
4	H	4H
	T	(4T)
5	H	5H
	T	5T
6	H	6H
	T	(6T)

The diagram shows 12 equally likely outcomes. There are 3 outcomes where an even number is paired with tails.

So $P(\text{even number, tails}) = \frac{3}{12}$, or $\frac{1}{4}$.

✓ **Check Understanding** 1 **a.** Find the probability of rolling a 2 and getting heads.

b. Number Sense How can you use your answer from part (a) to find the probability of rolling a 2 and getting tails?

OBJECTIVE

2 Using the Counting Principle

You can use the **counting principle** to find the number of outcomes.

Key Concepts — **Counting Principle**

Suppose there are m ways of making one choice and n ways of making a second choice. Then there are $m \times n$ ways to make the first choice followed by the second choice.

2 EXAMPLE Using the Counting Principle

Dessert A restaurant offers a dessert special. You can get one scoop of ice cream, a topping, and a cone for a reduced price. Use the menu at the left. How many different dessert specials can you order?

Use the counting principle to find the total number of specials.

Flavors		Toppings		Cones		Dessert specials
↓		↓		↓		↓
5	×	3	×	2	=	30

You can order 30 different dessert specials.

Check Understanding 2 Suppose you toss three coins once. What is the total number of outcomes?

You can use the counting principle to find probabilities.

3 EXAMPLE Finding a Probability

Club Officers The president and treasurer of a club are randomly chosen from the names shown. What is the probability that both are female?

President	Treasurer
Elaine	Pedro
Alan	Dina
Carolyn	Brian
Karen	

Find the number of outcomes where both officers are female, and the total outcomes.

President		Treasurer		Pairings	
3	×	1	=	3	←**number of all-female outcomes**
4	×	3	=	12	←**total number of outcomes**

$P(\text{both female}) = \frac{3}{12}$, or $\frac{1}{4}$

The probability that both officers are female is $\frac{1}{4}$.

Check Understanding 3 **Reasoning** How can you use a tree diagram for Example 3? Explain.

More Than One Way

Each lunch for a school field trip will have one sandwich (turkey, roast beef, or bologna), one fruit (orange or apple), and one dessert (cookie or muffin). The same number of each type of lunch will be made. Amanda and Zack would like to know the number of lunch choices.

Amanda's Method

I'm going to make a tree diagram to show all possible outcomes.

Sandwich	Fruit	Dessert	Outcome
Turkey	O	C	TOC
		M	TOM
	A	C	TAC
		M	TAM
Roast Beef	O	C	ROC
		M	ROM
	A	C	RAC
		M	RAM
Bologna	O	C	BOC
		M	BOM
	A	C	BAC
		M	BAM

The tree diagram shows 12 outcomes. So, there are 12 lunch choices.

Zack's Method

I'm using the counting principle to find all possible outcomes.

Sandwich		Fruit		Dessert		Lunches
3	×	2	×	2	=	12

There are 12 lunch choices.

Choose a Method

In the problem above, suppose there is a fourth sandwich choice (peanut butter). How many lunch choices are now available? Describe your method and explain why you chose it.

EXERCISES

For more practice, see *Extra Practice*.

Practice by Example

Example 1 (page 568)

The tree diagram below shows the possible outcomes for a family having three children. Find the probability of each event.

1. The oldest child is a girl.
2. The two youngest children are boys.
3. All three children are the same gender.
4. Two children are boys and one child is a girl.

Oldest	Middle	Youngest	Outcomes
B	B	B	BBB
		G	BBG
	G	B	BGB
		G	BGG
G	B	B	GBB
		G	GBG
	G	B	GGB
		G	GGG

Draw a tree diagram to find each probability.

5. A spinner has equal sections of red, blue, and green. You spin it twice. Find the probability of spinning blue and then red.
6. You toss a coin two times. Find the probability of getting heads on both tosses.
7. You toss a coin and then roll a number cube. Find the probability of getting heads and rolling a 3 or a 5.

Example 2 (page 569)

Use the counting principle to find the total number of outcomes.

8. You toss a coin four times.
9. You roll a number cube twice.
10. A cafeteria offers 4 soups, 4 salads, 8 main dishes, and 3 desserts. How many meals of soup, salad, main dish, and dessert are there?

Example 3 (page 569)

Find each probability using the counting principle.

11. You use a spinner like the one shown at the right. You spin it twice. Find the probability of landing on green twice.
12. You flip a coin twice. Find the probability of getting two heads.
13. You roll a number cube twice. Find the probability of getting an even number followed by an odd number.

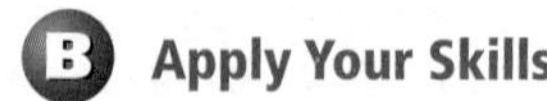

B Apply Your Skills

14. **Games** To play a game, you spin a spinner and take a card. The spinner has equal sections that tell you to move 1, 2, 3, or 4 spaces. The cards read *Free Turn*, *Lose a Turn*, or *No Change*. Find the probability that you move 3 spaces and lose a turn.

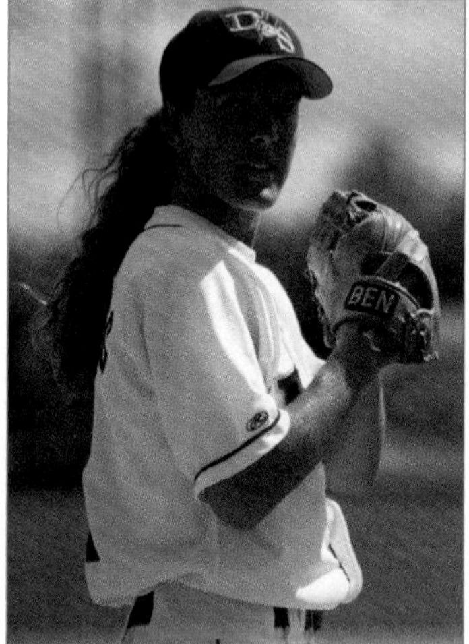

Real-World Connection

Ila Borders is the first woman to start a minor league baseball game.

15. **Baseball** A baseball team has starting and relief pitchers shown in the table. Suppose the team's coach selects a starter and a relief pitcher at random. What is the probability of selecting a starter and reliever that are both left-handed?

Pitchers on Baseball Team

Pitchers	Number
Left-Handed Starters	1
Right-Handed Starters	4
Left-Handed Relievers	2
Right-Handed Relievers	1

Choose a Method **Use a tree diagram or the counting principle to find each probability. Explain your choice.**

16. You roll a number cube three times. Find P(all odd).

17. Suppose you select a letter at random from A, B, and C. You replace the letter and select again. Find the probability of selecting an A twice.

18. **Writing in Math** Suppose you have five colors of cars to choose from in six different models. Describe the method you would use to find the number of different cars you can buy.

19. **Consumer Issues** The table below gives some choices available when you buy a computer. You want a monitor larger than 15 inches, but you do not want an adjustable keyboard. How many outcomes are left?

Keyboards	Monitors	Printers
Standard \$50	Color 15-in. \$369	Inkjet \$149
Extended \$90	Color 17-in. \$699	Color Inkjet \$369
Adjustable \$130	Color 19-in. \$1,399	Laser \$819

C Challenge

20. Suppose you spin the pointer three times.
    a. Draw a tree diagram showing all outcomes.
    b. How many outcomes are there in which each color appears exactly once?
    c. Find the probability that exactly two spins are the same color.

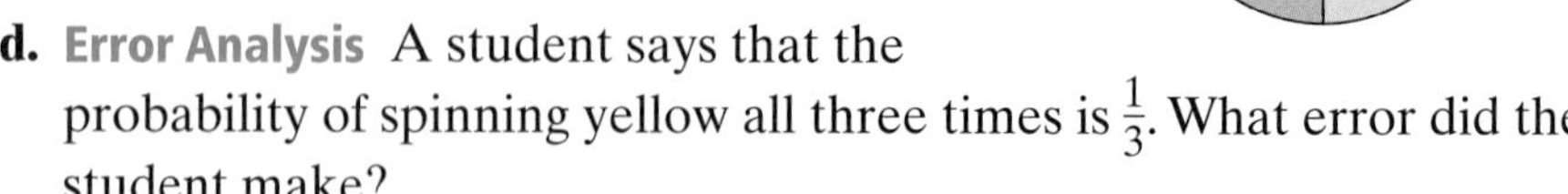

    d. **Error Analysis** A student says that the probability of spinning yellow all three times is $\frac{1}{3}$. What error did the student make?

21. **Stretch Your Thinking** Find the next four numbers in the pattern.

$$-1, 2, -2, 1, -3, \ldots$$

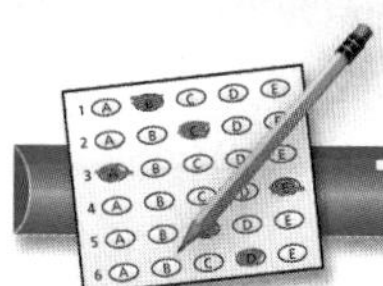

Test Prep

Multiple Choice

22. You roll a number cube and toss a coin. What is the total number of possible outcomes?

A. 2 **B.** 6 **C.** 12 **D.** 36

23. A store has 11 kinds of bagels and 5 kinds of spreads. How many different combinations of a bagel with 1 spread can be made?

F. 55 **G.** 16 **H.** 11 **I.** 5

24. Suppose you have more than one kind of shirt and more than one pair of jeans. Which of the following could NOT be the total number of outfits you can make?

A. 3 **B.** 6 **C.** 9 **D.** 12

Short Response

25. A store sells 4 flavors of frozen yogurt and 3 kinds of toppings.

a. Draw a tree diagram to find the possible outcomes of one flavor of yogurt with one topping.

b. Justify your answer in part (a) using the counting principle.

Mixed Review

Lesson 10-7

Read the table to find the profit or loss for each month.

Month	Income	Expenses
March	\$8,033	−\$10,203
April	\$9,625	−\$6,731
May	\$11,462	−\$5,220
June	\$6,028	−\$7,269

26. March **27.** April

28. May **29.** June

30. What is the total profit from March through June?

Lesson 9-4

31. **Geometry** Find the area of the figure below.

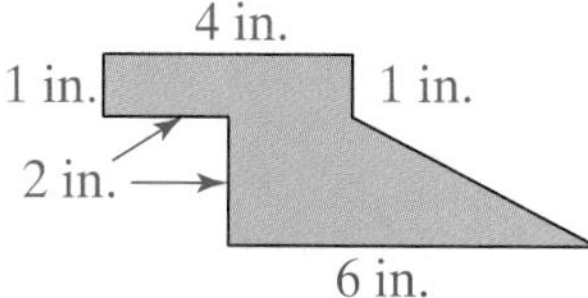

Lesson 8-5

Geometry **Write all the possible names for each quadrilateral. Then give the best name.**

32. 

33. 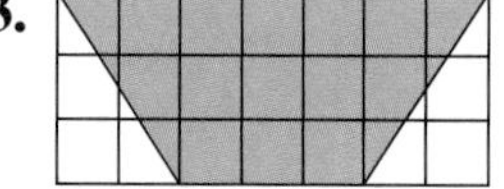

34. 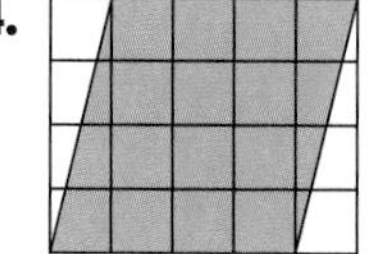

11-6 Exploring Permutations

What You'll Learn

To find permutations

To count permutations

. . . And Why

To find the number of arrangements, as in Example 3

For help, go to Skills Handbook page 658.

Simplify each expression.

1. 4×3 **2.** 10×9 **3.** 15×14

4. 20×19 **5.** $4 \times 3 \times 2$ **6.** $8 \times 7 \times 6$

New Vocabulary • permutation

Interactive lesson includes instant self-check, tutorials, and activities.

OBJECTIVE 1 Finding Permutations

Suppose a group of three people line up for a photograph.

1. How many arrangements are possible?
2. Represent each member of the group with a different letter. Make an organized list of all possible arrangements of the 3 letters. How many arrangements are in your list?

An arrangement of objects in a particular order is called a **permutation.** For the letters A and M, the permutations AM and MA are different because the orders of the letters are different.

1 EXAMPLE Using Organized Lists

Find the permutations of the letters in the word FLY.

Make an organized list. Use each letter exactly once.

FLY LFY YFL
FYL LYF YLF

Check Understanding 1 Make an organized list to find the permutations for the letters CAT.

You can also use a tree diagram to find permutations.

2 EXAMPLE Using a Tree Diagram

Find the two-digit permutations you can make with the digits 1, 3, 7, and 9.

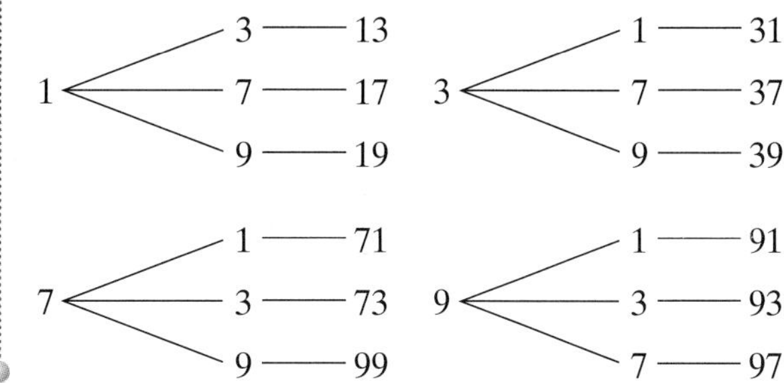

Check Understanding 2 Draw a tree diagram to find the 3-letter permutations of the letters PLAY. Here is how to start.

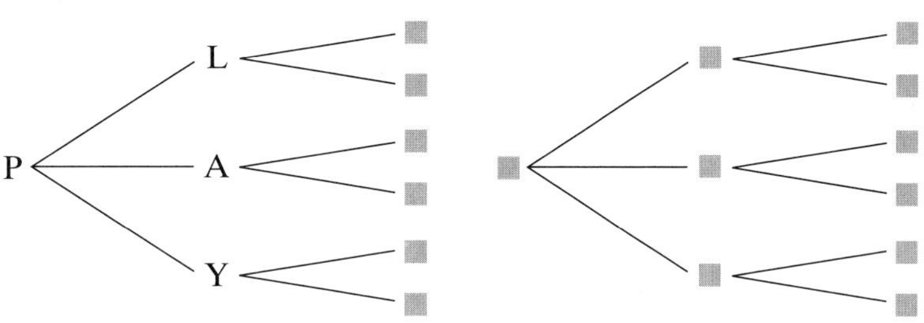

OBJECTIVE 2 Counting Permutations

You can think of permutations as selecting objects in some order. First select one object. Then select the second object. Then select the third, and so on. You can use the counting principle to count permutations.

3 EXAMPLE Applying the Counting Principle

Track and Field Suppose you are in the finals of the 50-meter dash with 4 other students. In how many different ways can all of you finish?

Find the product of the number of outcomes at each student's finish.

Five choices for first place		Four choices for second place		Three choices for third place		Two choices for fourth place		One choice for fifth place		Number of permutations
5	×	4	×	3	×	2	×	1	=	120

There are 120 different ways that you and 4 other runners can finish.

Check Understanding 3 In Example 3, suppose a new student enters the 50-meter dash. In how many different orders can all of you finish?

EXERCISES

For more practice, see *Extra Practice.*

A Practice by Example

Example 1 (page 574)

Make an organized list to find the permutations of each set of numbers or letters. Use each item exactly once.

1. the numbers 6, 7, 8, 9

2. the letters DOG

3. the numbers 5 and 6

4. the letters WORD

Example 2 (page 575)

Draw a tree diagram to find the permutations of each set.

5. the two-number permutations of the numbers 1, 2, 3, 4

6. the three-letter permutations of the letters BOLT

7. Movies Suppose you want to watch two movies. You have a movie with each of the following themes: drama, comedy, action, and sports. In how many orders can you watch two different movies?

Example 3 (page 575)

Use the counting principle to find the number of permutations of each set of letters.

8. the letters RED

9. the letters GAME

10. Public Speaking At a convention, five people will be giving speeches. In how many different orders can the five people give their speeches?

B Apply Your Skills

For the letters BEST, find the number of permutations for each exercise. Use the counting principle or a tree diagram.

11. two-letter permutations

12. three-letter permutations

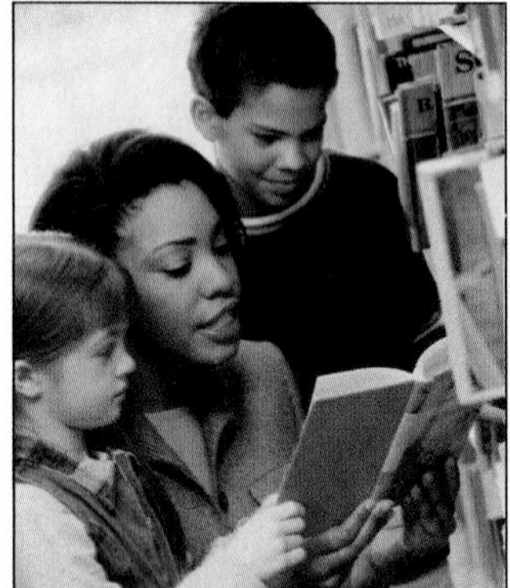

Real-World Connection
Careers Librarians assist people in finding information.

13. Libraries A library receives a new seven-volume set of nature books.
  a. In how many orders can the books be placed on a shelf?
  b. Suppose a new volume is added to the set. In how many orders can the books be placed on a shelf?

14. Fitness A body builder plans to do four different exercises in his workout. In how many ways can he complete his workout?

15. Error Analysis Ann says that the number of permutations of the letters in her name is 6. Explain her error.

16. The expression 4! is read "four factorial." You use factorial notation in math to show the product of all positive integers less than or equal to the given number. For example, $4! = 4 \times 3 \times 2 \times 1$, or 24. Find 5!.

17. **Writing in Math** Write a problem that you can solve by using the tree diagram shown.

red — white
red — blue
white — red
white — blue
blue — red
blue — white

18. **Olympics** In the bobsled competition, each team takes turns sledding down the track. Draw a tree diagram to show all possible orders in which the teams from Germany, Switzerland, and Italy can compete.

Reading Math
For help with Exercise 18, see p. 579.

Challenge

Use the cartoon below for Exercise 19.

The Born Loser *by Chip Sansom*

19. **Number Sense** Suppose the man knows that the phone number he needs includes one of each digit from 3 through 9. He also knows the correct seven-digit phone number starts with 639. The man decides to try each possible number until he reaches the phone company. At most, how many phone numbers will he have to try?

20. **Stretch Your Thinking** In a barnyard full of cows and chickens, there are 30 more legs than heads. If the ratio of cows to chickens is 4 to 3, how many cows are in the barnyard?

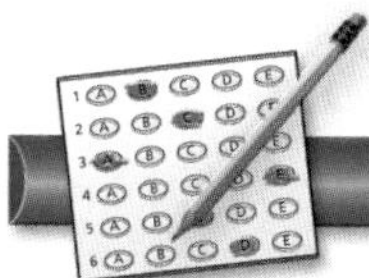

Test Prep

Multiple Choice

21. What is the expression $4 \times 3 \times 2 \times 1$ in simplest form?

A. 6 **B.** 12 **C.** 24 **D.** 48

22. What is the expression $5 \times 4 \times 3 \times 2 \times 1$ in simplest form?

F. 15 **G.** 120 **H.** 720 **I.** 840

23. How many ways can you arrange 6 video games on a shelf?

A. 12 **B.** 36 **C.** 120 **D.** 720

Take It to the NET
Online lesson quiz at **www.PHSchool.com**
Web Code: aaa-1106

Short Response

24. **a.** What are the permutations of the letters LIKE? Use each letter exactly once.
b. In part (a), what is the number of permutations? Use the counting principle to justify your answer.

Mixed Review

Lesson 10-7

Algebra **Complete each function table. Use the rule.**

25. Rule: Add 0.8.

Input	Output
−0.5	■
0.2	■
1.2	■

26. Rule: Multiply by −5.

Input	Output
−2	■
0	■
5	■

Lesson 9-3

Find the area of each square with the side *s* or the perimeter *P*.

27. $s = 3$ inches

28. $s = 2$ feet

29. $s = 3.5$ centimeters

30. $P = 4.4$ meters

31. $P = 20$ kilometers

32. $P = 2$ feet

Checkpoint Quiz 2 — Lessons 11-4 through 11-6

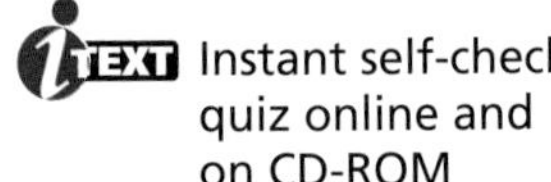

Suppose three coins are tossed. Use a tree diagram to find each probability.

1. *P*(exactly 1 tail)

2. *P*(exactly 2 heads)

3. *P*(3 tails)

4. *P*(all the same)

5. *P*(1 or more tails)

6. *P*(3 heads)

7. The probabilities of John and Sue winning different games are shown. Find the experimental probability that they both win. Use two number cubes to simulate the problem. Let 1, 2, and 3 on one cube represent "John wins." Let 1 and 2 on the other cube represent "Sue wins."

Game Probabilities

Name	Game	Probability
John	Game 1	$\frac{1}{2}$
Sue	Game 2	$\frac{1}{3}$

8. Find the permutations of the letters FUN. Use each letter exactly once.

9. Suppose you roll two number cubes once. Use the counting principle to find the probability of rolling a 4 on both cubes.

10. **Haircuts** Alicia wants to get her hair cut and dyed at a salon. The hair salon offers 10 different styles or haircuts. Also she has 6 different hair colors to choose from. How many different haircuts can she get?

Understanding Word Problems

For Use With Exercise 18, Page 577

Read the problem below. Then follow along with what Maya thinks as she solves the problem. Check your understanding by solving the exercises at the bottom of the page.

18. Olympics In the bobsled competition, each team takes turns sledding down the track. Draw a tree diagram to show all possible orders in which the teams from Germany, Switzerland, and Italy can compete.

What Maya Thinks	What Maya Writes
There are three ways to choose the team that will go first.	Germany Switzerland Italy
I see that, for each possible team that can go first, there are two teams left to go second. I will draw lines from the first teams to each of the second teams.	Germany < Switzerland, Italy Switzerland < Germany, Italy Italy < Germany, Switzerland
Finally, I see that the only remaining team must go third. I will draw lines from each of the second teams to the third teams.	Germany < Switzerland — Italy; Italy — Switzerland Switzerland < Germany — Italy; Italy — Germany Italy < Germany — Switzerland; Switzerland — Germany
Now I'll write my answer using the letters G, S, and I.	GSI, GIS, SGI, SIG, IGS, and ISG.

EXERCISES

1. What are the number of orders four cars that are red, blue, green, and black can be parked on a street?

2. Dan, Eugene, and Gabi are in line for movie tickets. Draw a tree diagram to show the number of ways they can stand in line.

11-7 Independent Events

What You'll Learn

To identify independent events

To find probabilities of compound independent events

. . . And Why

To find the probability of independent events, as in Example 3

Check Skills You'll Need

For help, go to Lesson 5-1.

Find each product.

1. $\frac{3}{4} \times \frac{3}{4}$
2. $\frac{2}{3} \cdot \frac{1}{7}$
3. $\frac{5}{9} \cdot \frac{2}{5}$
4. $\frac{2}{3} \times \frac{1}{9}$
5. $\frac{3}{8} \cdot \frac{2}{15}$
6. $\frac{5}{6} \cdot \frac{1}{2}$
7. $\frac{6}{11} \times \frac{7}{12}$
8. $\frac{5}{6} \times \frac{3}{10}$
9. $\frac{1}{4} \cdot \frac{4}{7}$

New Vocabulary • independent events • compound events

Interactive lesson includes instant self-check, tutorials, and activities.

OBJECTIVE 1 Identifying Independent Events

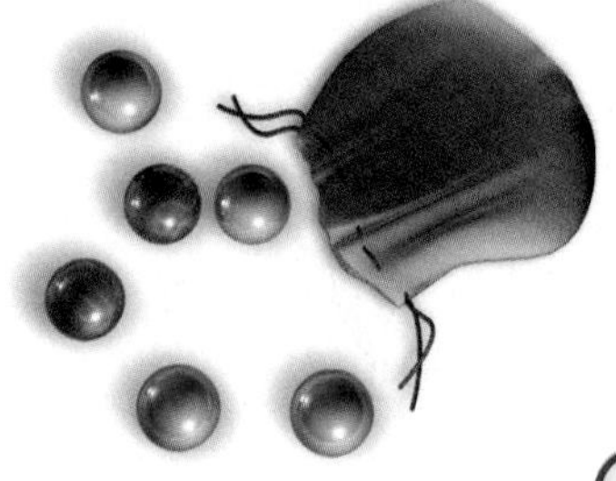

Suppose you draw a marble from a bag like the one at the left.

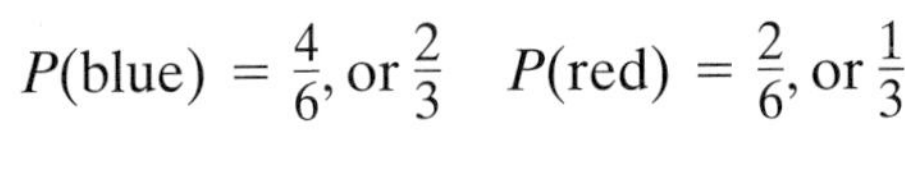
$$P(\text{blue}) = \frac{4}{6}, \text{ or } \frac{2}{3} \quad P(\text{red}) = \frac{2}{6}, \text{ or } \frac{1}{3}$$

When you return or *replace* the marble and draw again, the probabilities do not change. If the occurrence of one event does not affect the probability of another event, the two are **independent events.**

1 EXAMPLE Identifying Independent Events

Decide whether the given events are independent. Explain.

a. You toss a coin twice. The first toss is heads. The second toss is tails.

Independent: The first toss has no affect on the second toss.

b. You select a colored pen from a bowl of assorted colored pens. Your brother selects one after you.

Not independent: After you select one pen, there will be one less pen in the bowl. The first selection affects the second selection.

Check Understanding 1 Decide whether the events are independent. Explain your answers.

a. You select a card from eight cards. Without replacing it, you select another card.

b. You toss a coin and roll a number cube.

OBJECTIVE

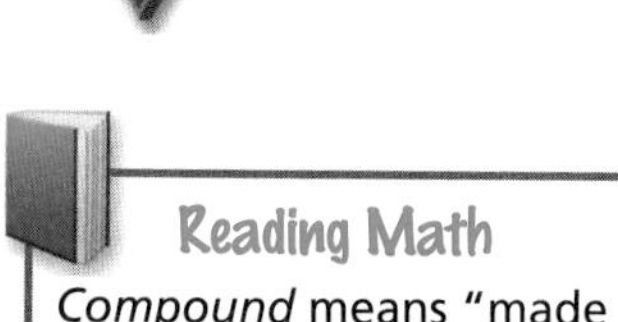

2 Finding Probabilities of Compound Independent Events

Reading Math

Compound means "made by combining parts."

A **compound event** consists of two or more separate events. When the events are independent, you can use a formula to find the probability.

Key Concepts | **Probability of Independent Events**

If A and B are independent events, then

$$P(A \text{ and } B) = P(A) \times P(B).$$

2 EXAMPLE Probability of Independent Events

Suppose you have a bag containing three red cubes and two yellow cubes. You draw a cube from the bag and put it back. Then you draw a second cube. Find the probability that both cubes are red.

The events are independent. The probability of drawing a red cube is $\frac{3}{5}$.

$$P(\text{red, then red}) = \frac{3}{5} \times \frac{3}{5} \quad \leftarrow \textbf{Use the formula.}$$

$$= \frac{9}{25} \quad \leftarrow \textbf{Multiply.}$$

The probability of drawing two red cubes is $\frac{9}{25}$.

Check Understanding 2 For the situation in Example 2, find P(yellow, then yellow).

You can multiply to find the probability of more than two events.

3 EXAMPLE Real-World Problem Solving

Quiz Show Three questions are asked during a quiz show. Each question has choices A, B, C, and D. Samantha guesses each answer at random. What is the probability that she answers all three questions correctly?

For each question, the probability of guessing the answer is $\frac{1}{4}$.

$$P(\text{three correct answers}) = \frac{1}{4} \times \frac{1}{4} \times \frac{1}{4}$$

$$= \frac{1}{64}$$

The probability of Samantha answering all three questions correctly is $\frac{1}{64}$.

Check Understanding 3 **Reasoning** Suppose the three questions were true-false questions. Would you multiply probabilities to find the probability that Samantha answers all three correctly? Explain your reasoning. Then find the probability.

EXERCISES

For more practice, see *Extra Practice*.

A Practice by Example

Example 1 (page 580)

Decide whether the events are independent. Explain your answers.

1. You have nickels and dimes in your pocket. You take out a dime at random and spend it. Then you take out a nickel at random.
2. You roll five number cubes and the numbers rolled are 1, 2, 3, 4, and 5.
3. At a soccer game, a coin is tossed that comes up heads. At the next game, the same coin is tossed and it comes up heads again.
4. A teacher selects a student to present his report. The teacher then selects another student.

Example 2 (page 581)

A bag contains 3 red, 5 blue, and 2 green marbles. Marbles are drawn twice, with replacement. Find the probability of each compound event.

5. both red
6. both green
7. both blue
8. red, then blue
9. blue, then red
10. red, then green

11. **Dining Out** A new gourmet restaurant offers a choice of 4 main courses and 3 desserts. If you randomly choose a main course and a dessert, what is the probability of choosing the chef's favorite main course and dessert?

Example 3 (page 581)

A number cube is rolled three times. Find the probability of each sequence of rolls.

12. even, even, odd
13. 3, 4, 5
14. all less than 5

B Apply Your Skills

15. **Biology** Assume two parents are equally likely to have a boy or a girl. Find the probability that they will have a girl and then have a boy.

Suppose you spin the pointer twice.

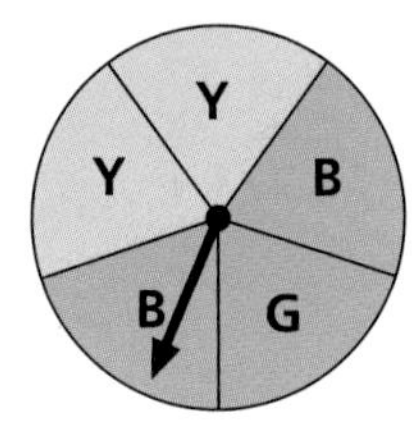

16. Is the outcome of the second spin independent of the outcome of the first spin? Explain.
17. **Choose a Method** Use a formula or draw a tree diagram to find the probability that the two spins will each be yellow.
18. **Writing in Math** Give an example of two events that are independent and two events that are not independent.

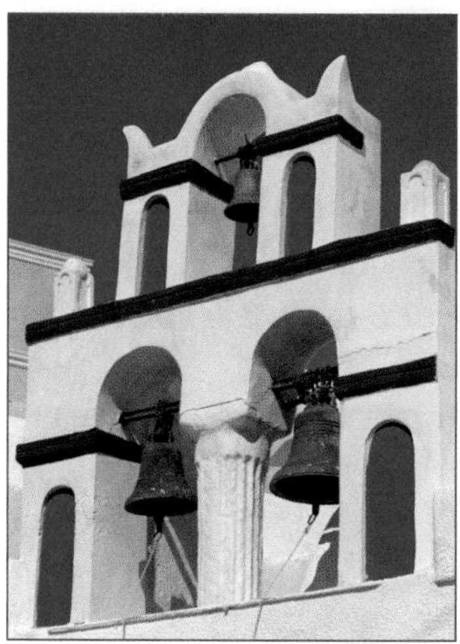

Real-World Connection

Bells are used for signaling local events and ringing intervals of time.

19. **Bells** Suppose one of three bells rings first each day. Each day the bells are rung in a random order. What is the probability that the same bell rings first three days in a row?

Use the two sets of letters below for Exercises 20–25. One letter is drawn from each set. Find each probability. (*Hint:* Assume Y is a vowel.)

H A P P Y   S U C C E S S

20. P(H and U)
21. P(Y and S)
22. P(P and C)
23. P(vowel and vowel)
24. P(consonant and E)
25. P(A and vowel)

26. **Data File, p. 545** Suppose there are equal numbers of red, blue, and green cubes in the bag.
    a. What is the probability of a player winning two games in a row?
    b. What is the probability of a player winning three games in a row?

Challenge

27. A bag of five apples contains three ripe apples and two rotten apples.
    a. If a ripe apple is selected first (and eaten), what is the probability that a second apple selected is rotten?
    b. If a rotten apple is selected first (and thrown away), what is the probability that a second apple selected is ripe?

28. **Stretch Your Thinking** Suppose n is an integer. When you add -1 to n, the sum is the opposite of the difference when you subtract -5 from n. What is the value of n?

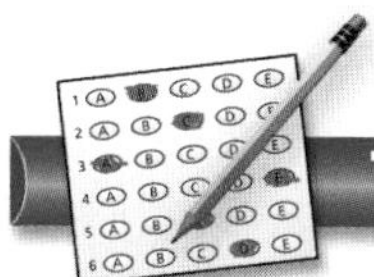

Test Prep

Multiple Choice

29. A coin is tossed twice. What is *P*(heads and heads)?
    A. 0 B. $\frac{1}{4}$ C. $\frac{1}{2}$ D. 1

30. A number cube is rolled twice. What is *P*(1 and 1)?
    F. $\frac{1}{2}$ G. $\frac{1}{6}$ H. $\frac{1}{12}$ I. $\frac{1}{36}$

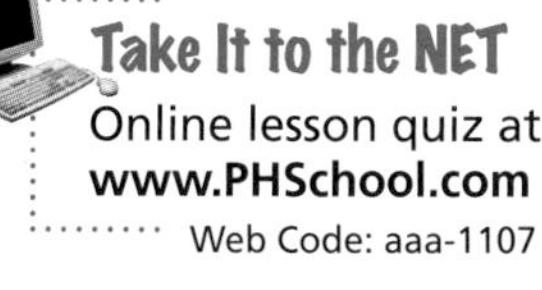

Take It to the NET
Online lesson quiz at **www.PHSchool.com**
Web Code: aaa-1107

31. A number cube is rolled twice. Which event is *least* likely to happen?
    A. same number B. odd, then even
    C. even, then even D. 3, then even

32. A spinner is divided into four equal sections labeled A, B, C, and D. What is the probability of spinning an A and then a D?
    F. $\frac{1}{8}$ G. $\frac{1}{4}$ H. $\frac{1}{3}$ I. $\frac{11}{2}$

33. A spinner is divided into equal sections with letters V, W, X, and Y. You spin the pointer twice. What is *P*(Y and Y)?

F. $\frac{1}{25}$ G. $\frac{1}{16}$ H. $\frac{1}{4}$ I. $\frac{1}{2}$

Extended Response

34. a. A marketer gets three types of answers when she visits a customer to make a sale. They are "yes," "no," and "maybe." Assume each answer is equally likely. Draw a tree diagram to show the possible outcomes when she visits two customers.

b. Suppose the probability that the marketer makes a sale is $\frac{1}{3}$. What is the probability of the marketer making a sale two times in a row? Justify your answer.

Mixed Review

Lesson 11-2

35. Pat makes 9 of 15 free throws. Find the experimental probability of Pat making a free throw.

36. Suppose you spin a pointer with four equal sections labeled A, B, C, and D. You spin the pointer nine times and get the letter C twice. What is the experimental probability of getting an A, B, or D?

Lesson 9-9

Find the volume of each rectangular prism.

37.

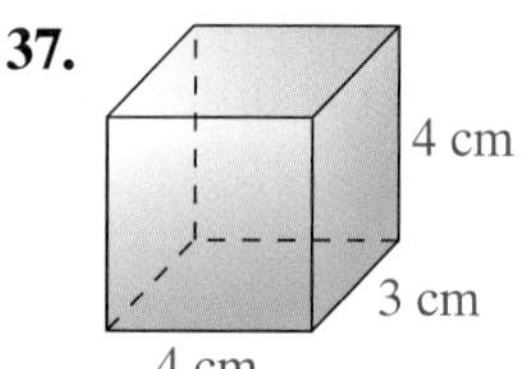

38.

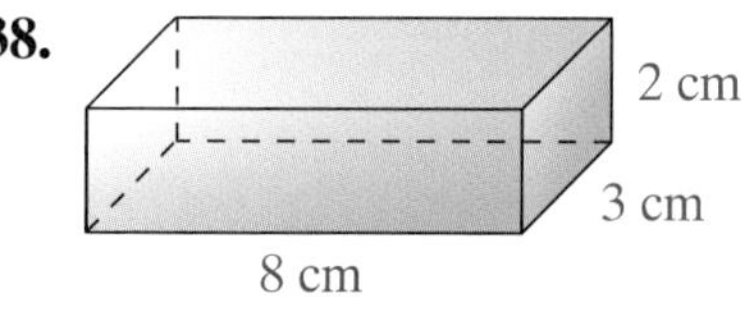

Math at Work

Board Game Designer

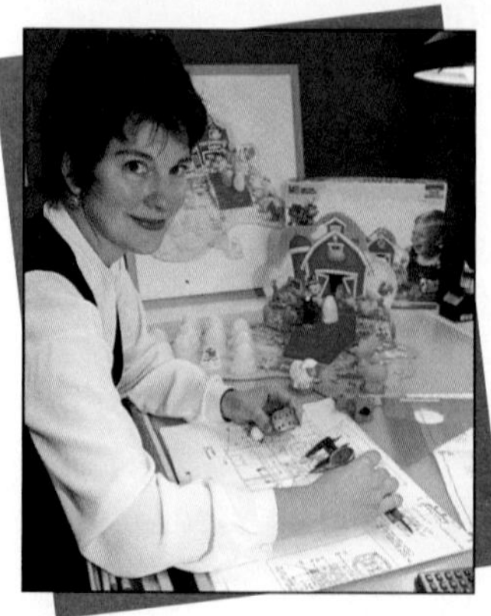

Board game designer is a career that could be just right for you if you love games. Game design requires an eye for color and a creative mind.

It also calls for mathematical skills. Many games involve the use of spinners or number cubes. That's where probability comes in. Data analysis is used to evaluate marketing information about a game.

Take It to the NET For more information about board game designers, go to **www.PHSchool.com**.

Web Code: aab-2031

Answering True-False Questions

A true-false question uses a statement that must be entirely true. Otherwise, the statement is false.

1 EXAMPLE

True or false? When a coin is tossed 21 times and heads comes up 9 times, the experimental probability of getting heads is $\frac{3}{7}$.

For this statement to be true, the ratio $\frac{\text{number of times an event occurs}}{\text{total number of trials}}$ must be equivalent to $\frac{3}{7}$. Since the experimental probability of $\frac{9}{21}$ equals $\frac{3}{7}$, the statement is true.

When words such as *all* or *always* are used, the statement may be true for many cases and false for just one.

2 EXAMPLE

True or false? The equation $|x| = x$ is always true.

This statement is true if x is positive or zero: $|3| = 3$. But it is false whenever x is negative: $|-5| \neq -5$. Since it is not always true, it is false.

EXERCISES

Determine whether each statement is true or false. Explain each answer.

1. When two number cubes are rolled once, P(1, then 2) is the same as P(6, then 6).

2. Joe, Sam, and Nate each toss a coin at the same time. The probability that they all get heads is $\frac{1}{16}$.

Use the letters shown for Exercises 3 and 4. Determine whether each statement is true or false. Explain each answer.

3. Suppose you select a letter at random from the letters at the right, replace it, and select again for a number of trials. You select an M 3 times out of 10. The experimental probability of selecting an M is $\frac{1}{4}$.

4. The probability of selecting an A at random is $\frac{1}{4}$.

Chapter 11 Chapter Review

Vocabulary

compound events (p. 581)
counting principle (p. 569)
equally likely outcomes (p. 547)
event (p. 547)
experimental probability (p. 554)
independent events (p. 580)
permutation (p. 574)
population (p. 559)
probability of an event (p. 547)
sample (p. 559)
simulation (p. 563)
tree diagram (p. 568)

Reading Math: Understanding Vocabulary

Choose the vocabulary term from the column on the right that best completes each sentence.

1. When tossing a coin, one possible __?__ is "heads."
2. __?__ have the same chance of occurring.
3. The __?__ can be used to find the number of outcomes in a compound event.
4. To make predictions about a population, you can use a(n) __?__ that represents that population.
5. One __?__ of the letters in CAT is TCA.

A. compound event
B. counting principle
C. equally likely outcomes
D. event
E. permutation
F. population
G. sample

Take It to the NET
Online vocabulary quiz at www.PHSchool.com
Web Code: aaj-1151

Skills and Concepts

11-1 and 11-2 Objectives

- To find the probability of an event
- To find experimental probabilities

An **event** is an outcome or group of outcomes. The **probability of an event** is the ratio

$$P(\text{event}) = \frac{\text{number of favorable outcomes}}{\text{total number of outcomes}}.$$

You can find probabilities by collecting data. For a series of trials, the **experimental probability** of an event is the ratio

$$P(\text{event}) = \frac{\text{number of times event occurs}}{\text{total number of trials}}.$$

A number cube is rolled once. Find each probability.

6. $P(5)$
7. $P(\text{even})$
8. $P(4, \text{or } 6)$

9. Noel and Kayla play a game 30 times. Noel wins 20 times. What is the experimental probability that Kayla wins? That Noel wins?

11-3 and 11-4
Objectives

- To make predictions from probabilities
- To make predictions based on a sample
- To solve problems by simulation

You can predict the number of times an event will occur by multiplying the probability of the event by the total number of trials. If you want to make predictions about a **population,** you can use a **sample** to gather the information you need. You can model many situations with a **simulation.**

10. Computers Out of 300 computers, 22 are defective. How many defective computers would you expect in a group of 30,000?

11. The probability of rain in San Francisco on a given day is $\frac{1}{6}$. The probability of rain in Miami is $\frac{5}{6}$. Use two number cubes to find the experimental probability of rain in both cities.

12. There are 3 kinds of soup and 2 kinds of salad on a menu. Describe how you could do a simulation to find the probability of selecting chicken soup and house salad if both are on the menu.

11-5 and 11-6
Objectives

- To use tree diagrams
- To use the counting principle
- To find permutations
- To count permutations

You can make an organized list, draw a tree diagram, or use the **counting principle** to find the number of arrangements, or **permutations,** of objects.

Make an organized list to find the permutations. Use each item once in each permutation.

13. the numbers 5, 6, 7, 8

14. the letters in the word PEN

15. Flags Suppose you want to make a flag with equal stripes colored red, blue, green, and white. Use the counting principle to find the number of ways you can order the colors.

11-7 Objectives

- To identify independent events
- To find probabilities of compound events

A **compound event** consists of two or more separate events. If A and B are independent events, you can find the probability of the compound event "A and B" with the formula

$$P(A \text{ and } B) = P(A) \times P(B).$$

Decide whether the events are independent. Explain your answers.

16. A roll of a number cube is 3. The fourth roll of the number cube is 6.

17. You draw a pink cube from a bag. Without replacing the pink cube, you draw a yellow cube.

A bag contains two red, four blue, and three green marbles. You draw marbles twice with replacement. Find each probability.

18. both green

19. green, then red

20. red, then blue

Chapter Test

1. Suppose you read in the newspaper that the probability of rain is 10%. Write this probability as a fraction and as a decimal.

2. **Simulation** On any day, suppose there is a probability of $\frac{1}{2}$ that you walk down a certain street to go to school. There is a probability of $\frac{1}{3}$ that a friend walks down the same street.
   a. Describe a simulation to find the experimental probability that both you and your friend walk down the same street today.
   b. Do your simulation to find the probability for part (a).

3. The shape at the right has numbered faces from 1 through 12. All outcomes are equally likely. Find each probability for one roll.

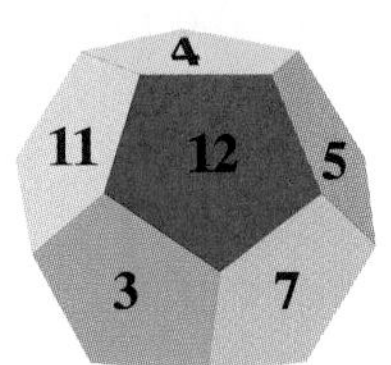

   a. P(even number)　b. P(prime)
   c. P(7 or 8)　d. P(13)

4. Pam and Tony play a game 20 times. Tony wins 7 times and Pam wins 13 times.
   a. Find the experimental probability that Pam wins.
   b. Find the experimental probability that Tony wins.
   c. **Writing in Math** If Pam and Tony play another 20 times, must the experimental probabilities be the same? Explain.

5. A ranch has 132 cows. You pick 32 of them at random and find that 18 of those cows have spots. Predict the number of cows on the ranch that have spots.

6. A bag contains blue and green chips. The probability of drawing a blue chip is $\frac{5}{12}$. Find P(green).

7. Make an organized list to find the two-digit permutations using the digits 2, 3, 4, and 5.

8. Use the counting principle to find the number of permutations of the letters GLACIER.

A bag contains four red, four blue, and three green cubes. Cubes are drawn twice with replacement. Find each probability.

9. P(blue, then green)
10. P(both red)
11. P(both green)
12. P(red, then blue)

13. Determine if the events are independent. Explain your answers.
    a. You roll two number cubes. One shows a 3. The other shows a 1.
    b. You draw a red marble from a bag containing red and yellow marbles. You do not put the marble back. You draw another red marble.

Suppose you spin the pointer three times.

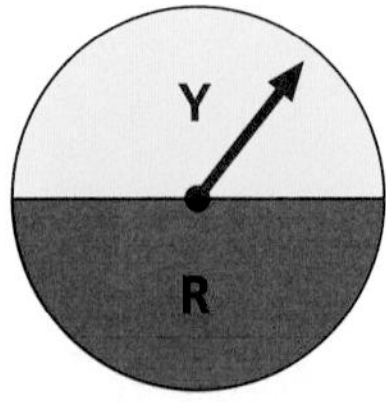

14. Make a tree diagram to show all possible outcomes.

15. Find P(yellow, then red, then yellow).

16. Suppose you roll a number cube twice. What is the probability of getting a 2 on the first roll and a 5 on the second roll?

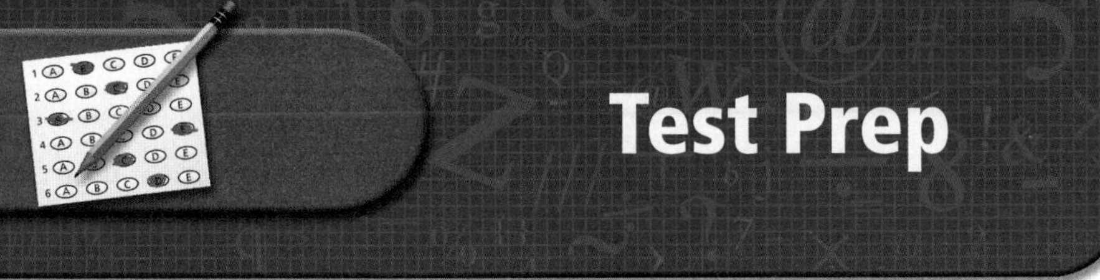

Test Prep

Reading Comprehension **Read each passage and answer the questions that follow.**

E-commerce In the future, purchasing items online is likely to become more popular than shopping at a store. During a recent year, the most popular items bought online were computer hardware goods.

Online sales for the year were as follows: 24% for computer hardware, 13% for clothing and footwear, 4% for music and videos, and 3% for toys and games.

1. Suppose a website that sells all types of goods receives 200 orders. How many sales would you expect to be for computer hardware goods?
   A. 4 **B.** 13 **C.** 24 **D.** 48

2. What is the probability, given as a fraction, that any computer sale during the year will be for clothing and footwear?
   F. $\frac{1}{24}$ **G.** $\frac{1}{13}$ **H.** $\frac{13}{100}$ **I.** $\frac{6}{25}$

3. What is the percentage of sales that will NOT be any of the items listed in the article?
   A. 56% **B.** 44% **C.** 37% **D.** 7%

4. Suppose an employee of an e-commerce company selects 20 orders at random. Of these, 4 are for clothing and footwear. In this sample, what is the experimental probability of a clothing or footwear order?
   F. 2.6% **G.** $\frac{13}{100}$ **H.** $\frac{1}{5}$ **I.** $\frac{4}{5}$

Sports Trends Are "ball" sports becoming less popular? From 1993 to 2000, the number of youths who play baseball went down from 23% to 12%. In that same period, the number of youths who play basketball decreased from 58% to 46%.

From 1993 to 2000, in-line skating participation increased from 17% to 30% and snowboarding participation rose by about 8%.

5. In 2000, what is the probability of a youth participating in in-line skating?
   A. 0.58 **B.** 0.46 **C.** 0.30 **D.** 0.17

6. About which sport are you NOT given enough information to find the probability of a youth playing the sport in 1993?
   F. baseball **G.** basketball
   H. in-line skating **I.** snowboarding

7. In 1993, suppose 300 youths were asked what sports they played. How many youths were likly to say basketball?
   A. 174 **B.** 138 **C.** 58 **D.** 46

8. Which sport discussed in the article had the largest percent decrease in participation?
   F. baseball **G.** basketball
   H. in-line skating **I.** snowboarding

Real-World Snapshots

Fair Chance?

Applying Probability Toss a ring onto a post, hit a target with a baseball, or pop a balloon with a dart. The real pleasure comes from playing the game, but how likely are you to win? Sometimes you can figure it out by using geometry and probability together.

Horseshoes

The game of horseshoes uses special shoes with a maximum weight of 2 pounds 10 ounces. A shoe must fall within 6 inches of the stake to score.

Heads or Tails?

A coin toss has two possible outcomes: heads or tails.

Milk-bottle array

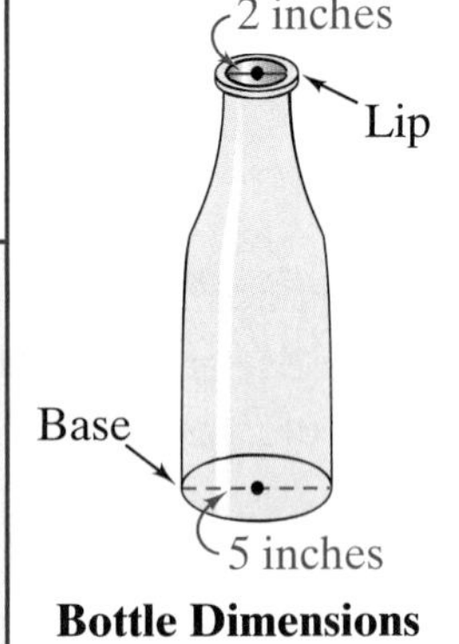

Bottle Dimensions

Put It All Together

At the school fair, the student council set up 100 old milk bottles in rows. The challenge is to throw a coin into one of the bottles. The game seems easy because there are so many bottles.

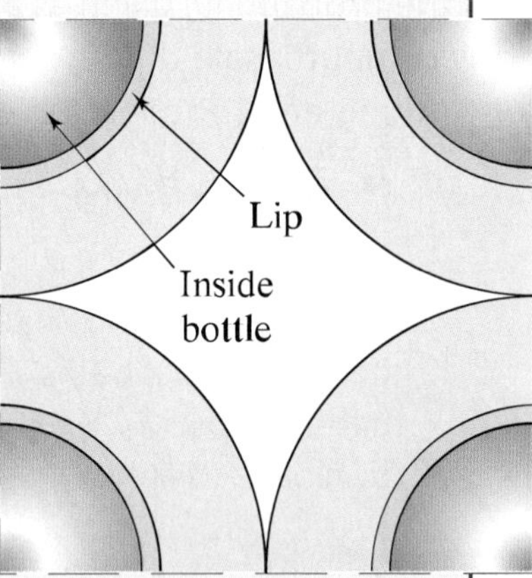

Top view of bottles

1. The square at the right shows part of the bottle array from above. Copy the diagram. Label as many dimensions as you can.
2. Since a coin can land anywhere within one of these square regions, the diagram shows the possible outcomes of each throw. What is the area of the square?
3. A favorable outcome is when a coin lands inside a bottle.
   - **a.** On your copy of the square, shade the regions in which the coin must land for a favorable outcome.
   - **b.** **Reasoning** If you made several copies of the square and put the shaded regions together, what shape would be shaded?
   - **c.** Find the area of the shaded part of your square.
4. **a.** Calculate the probability of winning the game. Write your answer as a percent.
   - **b.** Use your answer to part (a). How many tries would you expect it to take for you to win the game?
   - **c.** **Number Sense** It costs \$1 for three tries. The student council pays \$1.75 for each prize. If 50 people play, how much money can the student council expect to raise with this game? Show your work.

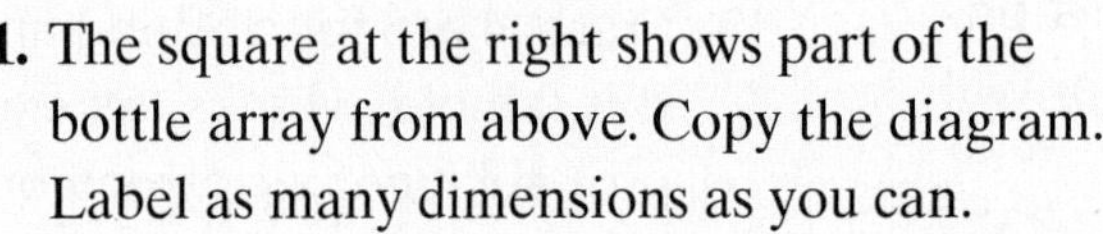

Carnival Games

Some schools use carnival games as fundraisers.

Take It to the NET For more information about games, go to **www.PHSchool.com**.
Web Code: aae-1153

Algebra

CHAPTER 12

Equations and Inequalities

Lessons

Key Vocabulary

- graph of an inequality (p. 602)
- hypotenuse (p. 622)
- inequality (p. 601)
- legs (p. 622)
- perfect square (p. 616)
- Pythagorean Theorem (p. 622)
- rational number (p. 617)
- solution of an inequality (p. 602)
- square root (p. 616)
- two-step equation (p. 596)

Real-World Snapshots

At night, human-made lights highlight the heavily populated and developed areas on Earth's surface. Lights consume energy in the form of electricity. Appliances in your home also consume energy. Some appliances consume more energy than others.

Data File

Energy Used by Appliances

Appliance	Average Monthly Energy Use (kilowatt-hours)
Dishwasher (air dry)	20
Dishwasher (cycle dry)	80
Dryer	100
Hair dryer	5
Microwave oven	25
TV (27-inch color)	110
VCR	4
Washer	10
Water heater	600

SOURCE: Boone REMC Electricity Utility Cooperative

You will use the data above in this chapter:

- p. 605 Lesson 12-2
- p. 613 Lesson 12-4

Real-World Snapshots On pages 634 and 635, you will solve problems involving electricity costs and light bulbs.

Chapter 12 Preview

Where You've Been

- In Chapter 2, you solved one-step equations. In Chapter 10, you added, subtracted, multiplied, and divided integers.

Where You're Going

- In Chapter 12, you will solve two-step equations and inequalities. You will also learn about square roots, rational numbers, and the Pythagorean Theorem.
- Applying what you learn, you will use inequalities to represent the training goals of a marathoner.

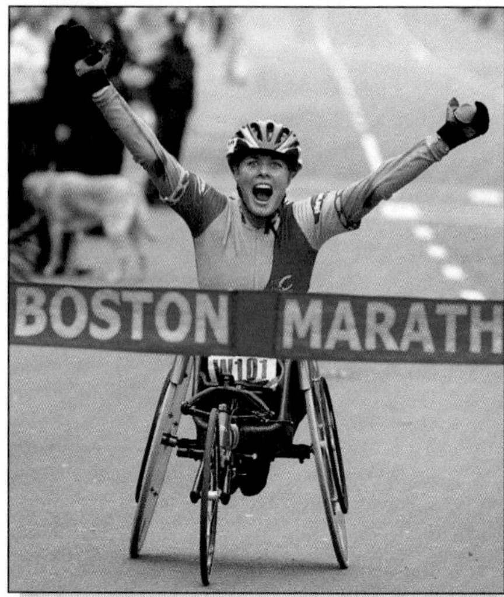

Edith Hunkeler won the Boston Marathon women's wheelchair division in 2002 with a time of 1:45:57.

Instant self-check online and on CD-ROM

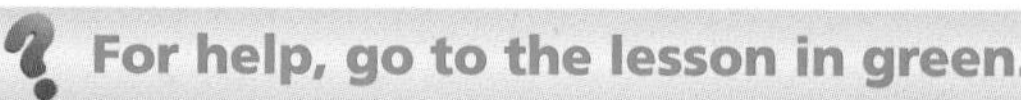

Diagnosing Readiness

For help, go to the lesson in green.

Algebra Solving Equations by Subtracting or Adding (Lesson 2-6)

Solve each equation.

1. $c + 9 = 34$ **2.** $a + 5 = -8$ **3.** $x - 2 = 6$

4. $y - 15 = 28$ **5.** $b - 21 = -11$ **6.** $p + 35 = 17$

Algebra Solving Equations by Dividing or Multiplying (Lesson 2-7)

Solve each equation.

7. $9x = 117$ **8.** $5r = 35$ **9.** $14z = 266$

10. $m \div 4 = 16$ **11.** $s \div 9 = 7$ **12.** $y \div 25 = 5$

Writing Exponents (Lesson 2-8)

Write each expression using an exponent. Name the base and the exponent.

13. $4 \times 4 \times 4$ **14.** 2×2 **15.** $1 \times 1 \times 1 \times 1$

16. $12 \times 12 \times 12 \times 12 \times 12 \times 12$ **17.** $8 \times 8 \times 8 \times 8 \times 8 \times 8 \times 8$

Comparing Integers (Lesson 10-1)

Compare using $<$ or $>$.

18. 4 ■ 8 **19.** −2 ■ −1 **20.** −100 ■ −101

Algebra

12-1 Solving Two-Step Equations

What You'll Learn

To solve two-step equations

. . . And Why

To find the cost of items bought, as in Example 2

Check Skills You'll Need

For help, go to Lesson 5-5.

Solve each equation.

1. $\frac{c}{3} = 5$

2. $\frac{n}{4} = 12$

3. $\frac{1}{7}x = 3$

4. $\frac{1}{8}y = 24$

New Vocabulary

- two-step equation

OBJECTIVE

Interactive lesson includes instant self-check, tutorials, and activities.

1 Solving Two-Step Equations

Suppose your dog has a litter of 3 puppies. To weigh the puppies, you put them together in a basket.

The empty basket weighs 2 pounds. The basket and puppies together weigh 14 pounds. You can solve the equation $3x + 2 = 14$ to find the average weight of each puppy. Algebra tiles can help you understand the solution.

$3x + 2 = 14$

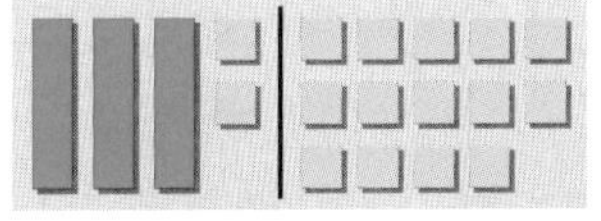

← **Model the equation.**

$3x + 2 - 2 = 14 - 2$

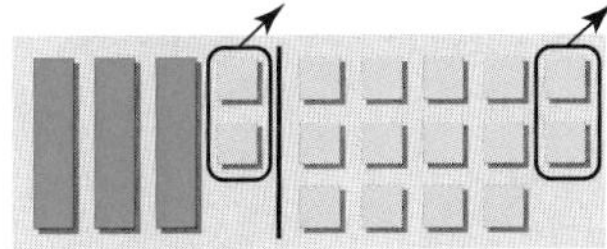

← **Remove 2 tiles from each side.**

$3x = 12$

← **Simplify.**

$\frac{3x}{3} = \frac{12}{3}$

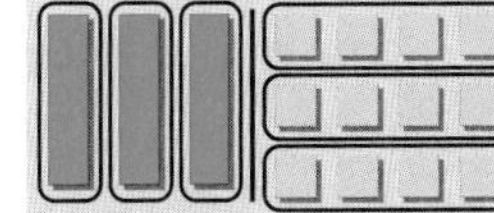

← **Divide each side into three equal groups.**

$x = 4$

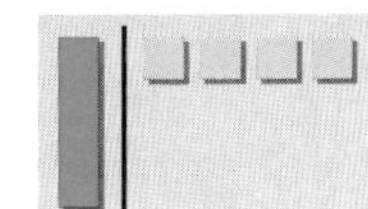

← **Simplify.**

A **two-step equation,** like $3x + 2 = 14$, is an equation containing two operations. To solve any two-step equation, begin by undoing the addition or subtraction, then undo the multiplication or division.

1 EXAMPLE Solving a Two-Step Equation

Solve $2y + 3 = 11$.

$$2y + 3 = 11$$

$$2y + 3 - 3 = 11 - 3$$ ← **Subtract 3 from each side to undo the addition.**

$$2y = 8$$ ← **Simplify.**

$$\frac{2y}{2} = \frac{8}{2}$$ ← **Divide each side by 2 to undo the multiplication.**

$$y = 4$$ ← **Simplify.**

Check $2y + 3 = 11$ ← **Check your solution in the original equation.**

$$2(4) + 3 = 11$$ ← **Substitute 4 for *y*.**

$$11 = 11 \checkmark$$ ← **The solution checks.**

Reading Math

$2y \div 2$ and $\frac{2y}{2}$ are each read "2*y* divided by 2." Both simplify to *y*.

✓ Check Understanding 1 Solve each equation. Check the solution.

a. $5x + 3 = 18$ **b.** $3x - 4 = 23$

c. **Mental Math** What is the solution to $2a - 1 = 11$?

2 EXAMPLE Real-World Problem Solving

Block Party Three neighbors are hosting a block party. They each purchase an \$8 carved watermelon and they split the cost for paper goods. If each person spends \$20, what was the total cost for the paper goods? Use *p* to represent the cost of the paper goods. Use the equation $\frac{p}{3} + 8 = 20$.

$$\frac{p}{3} + 8 = 20$$

$$\frac{p}{3} + 8 - 8 = 20 - 8$$ ← **Subtract 8 from each side to undo the addition.**

$$\frac{p}{3} = 12$$ ← **Simplify.**

$$3 \cdot \frac{p}{3} = 12 \cdot 3$$ ← **Multiply each side by 3 to undo the division.**

$$p = 36$$ ← **Simplify.**

The paper goods cost \$36.

Real-World Connection

Watermelon carving is an artistic way to display food.

✓ Check Understanding 2 Jim and Scott agree to split the cost to rent a moped. Scott pays the entire bill, considers the \$9 that he owes Jim, and tells Jim he now owes \$12. How much was the total bill? Use *m* to represent the cost to rent the moped. Use the equation $\frac{m}{2} - 9 = 12$.

More Than One Way

Solve $2b - 18 = 34$.

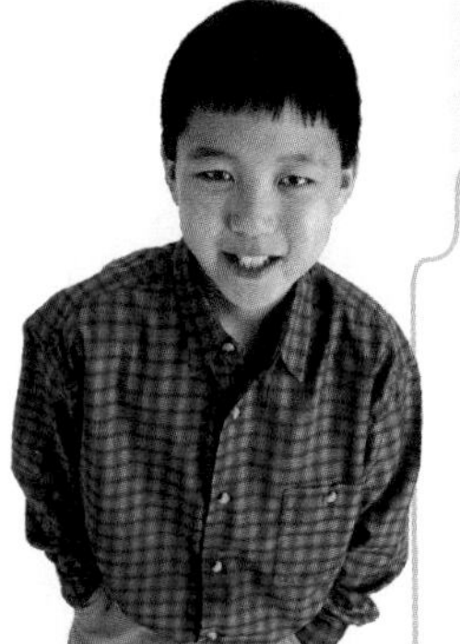

Michael's Method

First I'll add. Then I'll divide.

$$2b - 18 = 34$$
$$2b - 18 + 18 = 34 + 18 \quad \leftarrow \text{Add 18 to each side.}$$
$$2b = 52 \quad \leftarrow \text{Simplify.}$$
$$\frac{2b}{2} = \frac{52}{2} \quad \leftarrow \text{Divide each side by 2.}$$
$$b = 26 \quad \leftarrow \text{Simplify.}$$

Lauren's Method

Since each number in the equation is an even number, I'll begin by dividing each side of the equation by 2.

$$2b - 18 = 34$$
$$(2b - 18) \div 2 = 34 \div 2 \quad \leftarrow \text{Divide each side by 2.}$$
$$b - 9 = 17 \quad \leftarrow \text{Divide } 2b\text{, 18, and 34 by 2.}$$
$$b - 9 + 9 = 17 + 9 \quad \leftarrow \text{Add 9 to each side.}$$
$$b = 26 \quad \leftarrow \text{Simplify.}$$

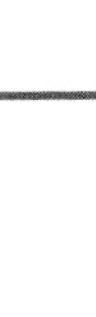

Need Help?

$(2b - 18) \div 2$

$= (2b - 18) \cdot \frac{1}{2}$

$= (2b \cdot \frac{1}{2}) - (18 \cdot \frac{1}{2})$

$= b - 9$

Choose a Method

Solve $5p + 75 = 245$. Describe your method and explain why you chose it.

EXERCISES

For more practice, see *Extra Practice*.

A Practice by Example

Example 1 (page 596)

Solve each equation. Exercises 1–3 have been started for you.

1. $2b + 4 = 12$
$2b + 4 - 4 = 12 - 4$

2. $3j - 6 = 12$
$3j - 6 + 6 = 12 + 6$

3. $\frac{a}{3} + 2 = 8$
$\frac{a}{3} + 2 - 2 = 8 - 2$

4. $2y + 5 = 9$

5. $2p + 13 = 3$

6. $5x + 7 = 22$

7. $\frac{a}{2} + 4 = 8$

8. $\frac{x}{3} + 2 = 5$

9. $\frac{n}{6} - 1 = 3$

Example 2 (page 596)  **10. Shopping** You want to buy a pair of pants and three shirts. You can spend \$90 on the items and still have enough money to pay the sales tax. If the pants you choose cost \$24, how much can you spend on each shirt? Use s to represent the cost of a shirt. Use the equation $24 + 3s = 90$.

11. Brendan orders a telephone for \$34 and some pens at \$2 each. Not including shipping or tax, his order totals \$46. How many pens did he order? Use p to represent the number of pens he ordered. Use the equation $34 + 2p = 46$.

B Apply Your Skills

Mental Math **Solve each equation.**

12. $2y + 1 = 11$ **13.** $5c + 15 = 30$ **14.** $4d - 12 = 8$

15. $3n - 1 = 17$ **16.** $\frac{w}{2} - 6 = 4$ **17.** $\frac{a}{5} + 7 = 12$

Choose the correct equation for each problem. Then use the equation to solve the problem.

18. Exercise It costs \$75 to join a health club, plus a monthly fee. Your uncle spends \$495 for his first year in the club. What is the monthly fee? Use m for the monthly fee.

A. $75 + 12m = 495$ **B.** $75 + 495 = 12m$

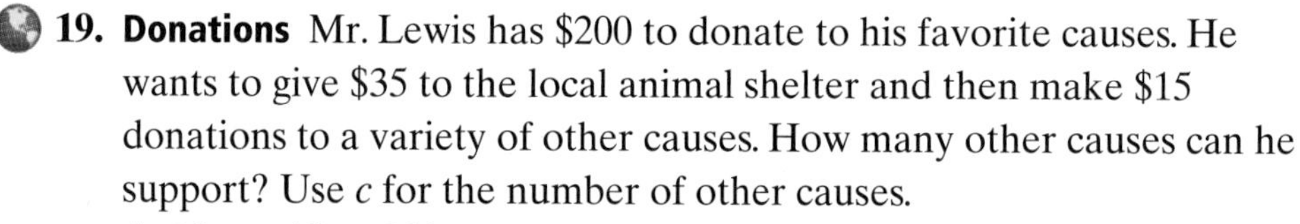

19. Donations Mr. Lewis has \$200 to donate to his favorite causes. He wants to give \$35 to the local animal shelter and then make \$15 donations to a variety of other causes. How many other causes can he support? Use c for the number of other causes.

A. $35c + 15 = 200$ **B.** $35 + 15c = 200$

20. Your brother buys 4 games. Each game costs the same amount. He uses a coupon for \$5 off the total purchase price, and owes the cashier \$30.80. How much does each game cost? Use c for the cost of one game.

A. $4c + 5 = 30.8$ **B.** $4c - 5 = 30.8$

21. Reading Beth is reading a 160-page book. She has already read 100 pages. If she reads 15 pages each day, how many days will it take her to finish the book? Use d for the number of days to finish.

A. $15d = 160$ **B.** $100 + 15d = 160$

Real-World Connection

Instead of money, you can donate your home as a foster home for an animal.

Solve each equation. Check the solution.

22. $9e + 5 = -4$ **23.** $7h + 12 = -9$ **24.** $3a + 8 = 2$

25. $2y - 3 = -11$ **26.** $-6 = 4b - 10$ **27.** $1 + \frac{g}{2} = -5$

28. Writing in Math How is solving $16e - 32 = 176$ different from solving $16e = 176$?

Real-World Connection

Careers A sales representative for a clothing manufacturer sells the latest fashions to retail stores.

29. Commission *Commission* is pay earned as a percent of sales. Suppose a sales representative receives a weekly base salary of \$250 plus a commission of 8% of her total weekly sales. At the end of one week, she earns \$410. What is her sales total for the week? Use s to represent the total sales. Use the equation $0.08s + 250 = 410$.

30. Suppose you save \$26 each week so you can buy a camcorder for \$260. So far, you have saved \$182. In how many more weeks will you have saved \$260? Use w to represent the number of weeks. Use the equation $26w + 182 = 260$.

Complete each function table given the rule.

31. Rule: Multiply by 2, then add 3.

Input	1	10	12
Output			

32. Rule: Divide by 3, then add 1.

Input	3	9	15
Output			

Write a rule for each function using two operations. Then complete the function table. (*Hint:* Multiply or divide first.)

33.

Input	Output
2	7
4	11
7	17
8	■
15	■

34.

Input	Output
6	−6
9	−5
15	−3
30	■
63	■

C Challenge

35. Error Analysis A student solves the equation $4 + \frac{m}{5} = 19$. Look at the solution at the right. What error does the student make?

$4 + \frac{m}{5} = 19$

$\frac{m}{5} = 15$

$m = 3$ ✗

Solve each equation.

36. $3x - \frac{5}{2} = \frac{7}{2}$

37. $\frac{a}{2} + \frac{2}{3} = 5\frac{1}{3}$

38. $8.25y - 3.5 = 36.5$

39. Stretch Your Thinking The perimeter of the figure below is 30.75 inches. Write an equation to represent the perimeter of the figure. Solve for x. (Note: The figure is not drawn to scale.)

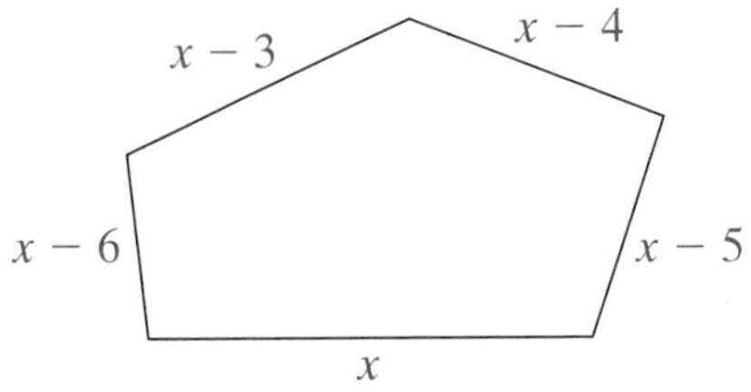

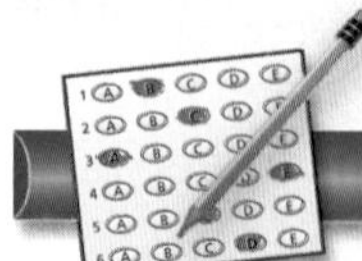

Test Prep

Gridded Response What is the solution of each equation?

40. $7x - 4 = 10$

41. $3x + 5 = 11$

42. $\frac{x}{4} + 2 = 10$

43. $\frac{x}{2} - 5 = 1$

Take It to the NET
Online lesson quiz at
www.PHSchool.com
Web Code: aaa-1201

44. Your sister buys 3 headbands. Each headband costs the same amount. She uses a \$2-off coupon and pays \$7 to the cashier. How much money does each headband cost? Use h to represent the cost of each headband. Use the equation $3h - 2 = 7$ to solve the problem.

Mixed Review

Lesson 11-1

A bag contains 3 red marbles, 2 green marbles, and 2 blue marbles. You pick one marble from the bag. Find the probability for each selection.

45. $P(\text{red})$

46. $P(\text{blue})$

47. $P(\text{yellow})$

Lesson 9-5

Find the unknown length for a circle with the given dimension.

48. $r = 12$ inches, $d = \blacksquare$

49. $d = 0.36$ meter, $r = \blacksquare$

Practice Game

What's My Rule?

How to Play

- Player A writes a rule for a two-step equation using only integers. The first step should use multiplication or division, and the second step should use addition or subtraction. Sample: To get y, multiply x by 5, and then subtract 3.
- Player B must figure out the rule. So Player B tells Player A a value for x. Player A responds with the correct y-value based on the rule. Player B records the x- and y- values in a function table like the one at the right.

x	y
2	7
−2	−13
0	−3

- If Player B provides an incorrect rule, the round ends. If Player B gives the correct rule, then Player B gets 1 point.
- Players take turns writing and determining the rules.
- The player with the most points wins.

12-2 Inequalities

What You'll Learn

To write inequalities

To identify solutions of inequalities

. . . And Why

To tell who can ride a roller coaster, as in Example 4

Check Skills You'll Need

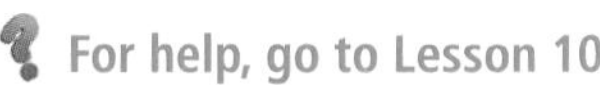
For help, go to Lesson 10-1.

Compare using < or >.

1. $-3 \blacksquare 6$ **2.** $4 \blacksquare -9$ **3.** $-2 \blacksquare -3$

4. $-94 \blacksquare -93$ **5.** $54 \blacksquare 47$ **6.** $1{,}001 \blacksquare 1{,}010$

New Vocabulary

- inequality
- graph of an inequality
- solution of an inequality

Interactive lesson includes instant self-check, tutorials, and activities.

OBJECTIVE 1 Writing Inequalities

Recall that an equation contains an equal sign, =. An **inequality** is a mathematical sentence that contains $<$, $>$, $\leq$, $\geq$, or $\neq$.

Symbol	Meaning
$<$	is less than
$>$	is greater than
$\leq$	is less than or equal to
$\geq$	is greater than or equal to
$\neq$	is not equal to

Some inequalities like $a < 8$ contain a variable. Real-world problems can sometimes be represented by inequalities.

1 EXAMPLE Writing an Inequality

Bison You must take less than 10 seconds to cross the field shown at the left. Otherwise, the bison may catch you! Write an inequality to express the time in which you must cross the field.

Words	time for you to cross field	is less than	time for bison to cross field
	Let t = your time to cross the field.		
Inequality	t	$<$	10

The inequality is $t < 10$.

Check Understanding 1 Most skydivers jump from an altitude of 14,500 feet or less. Write an inequality to express the altitude from which most skydivers jump.

The **graph of an inequality** shows all the solutions that satisfy the inequality. An open circle shows that the starting number is *not* included. A closed circle shows that the starting number *is* included.

2 EXAMPLE Writing Inequalities From Number Lines

Write an inequality for each graph.

a. −6 −5 −4 −3 −2 −1 0

Since the circle is open, use $<$ or $>$.
← Since the graph shows values greater than −3, use $>$.

$x > -3$

b. −3 −2 −1 0 1 2 3

Since the circle is closed, use $\leq$ or $\geq$.
← Since the graph shows values less than or equal to 0, use $\leq$.

$x \leq 0$

Check Understanding 2 Write an inequality for each graph.

a. −4 −3 −2 −1 0 1 2

b. 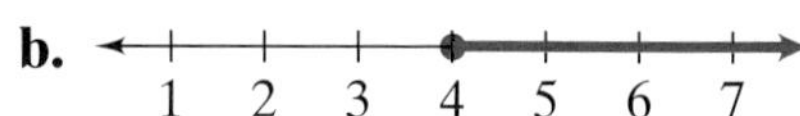

OBJECTIVE

2 Identifying Solutions of Inequalities

A **solution of an inequality** is any number that makes the inequality true. An inequality may have many possible solutions. Graphing an inequality on a number line can help you visualize all the solutions.

3 EXAMPLE Graphing Inequalities

Write an inequality to represent each situation. Then graph the inequality.

a. Karen rode her scooter more than 2 miles.

If k = Karen's distance, $k > 2$.

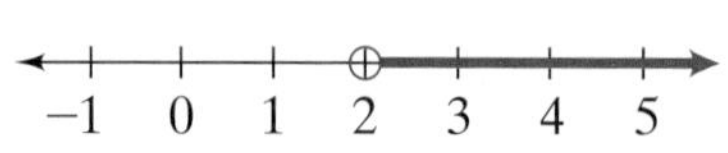

Use an open circle to show that the
← distance cannot include 2 miles.
Include all the numbers greater than 2.

b. The temperature was 3 degrees or less.

If t = the temperature, $t \leq 3$.

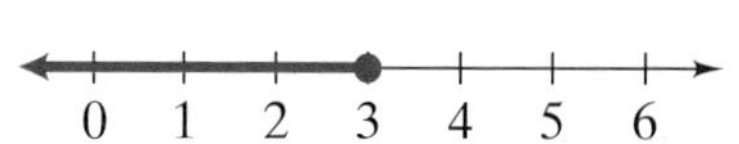

Use a closed circle to show that the
← temperature can include 3 degrees.
Include all the numbers less than 3.

Check Understanding 3 Write an inequality to represent the situation. Then graph the inequality. Linda spent at least 2 hours studying.

You can use an inequality to determine if someone or something meets a requirement.

Most park rides have safety rules based on age, height, or weight.

4 EXAMPLE Identifying Solutions of an Inequality 

Roller Coasters A person must be at least 48 inches to ride a certain roller coaster. Write an inequality to represent this requirement. Who of the following people can ride the roller coaster: Sally ($48\frac{1}{2}$ inches tall), Dean (48 inches tall), Kelsey ($46\frac{3}{4}$ inches tall)?

Words	person's height	is at least	48 inches	
	Let h = a person's height.			
Inequality	h	$\geq$	48	← **"At least" means $\geq$.**

To determine who can ride the roller coaster, find which heights are solutions of $h \geq 48$. Replace h with the height of each person. Then decide whether the inequality is true or false.

Sally	$48\frac{1}{2} \geq 48$	true
Dean	$48 \geq 48$	true
Kelsey	$46\frac{3}{4} \geq 48$	false

Sally and Dean are tall enough to ride the roller coaster.

Check Understanding 4 **a.** To be allowed into a certain jumping tent, you must be younger than 8 years old. Who of the following people can enter the jumping tent: Marissa (7 years, 11 months), Teagan (5 years), Ian (8 years, 3 months)?

b. **Reasoning** Are the solutions to $x < 3$ and $x \leq 3$ the same? Explain.

EXERCISES

 For more practice, see *Extra Practice.*

 **Practice by Example**

Example 1 (page 601)

Write an inequality for each situation.

1. There are more than 14 girls in the class.
2. No more than 45 students participated in the car-wash fundraiser.
3. Your sister had at least 15 people at her birthday party.
4. There were more than 15 ladybugs on the windowsill.
5. A sign on a bridge reads, "Maximum height of vehicles is 12 feet."
6. Cooking food at 165°F or higher will kill most bacteria.

Example 2 (page 602)

Write an inequality for each graph.

7. 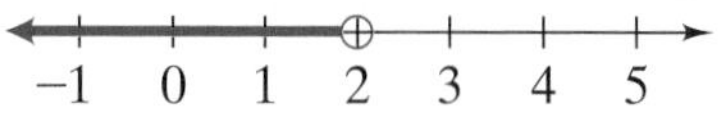

8. 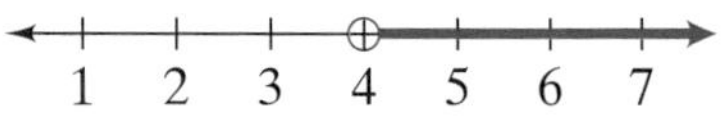

9. 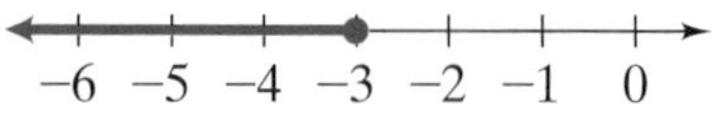

10. 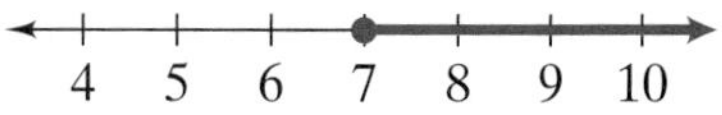

Example 3 (page 602)

Write an inequality to represent each situation. Then graph the inequality.

11. Four people or less are allowed on the ride at once.

12. The temperature never went below -2 degrees.

13. Kristen has less than three days to write her paper.

14. You must deposit at least $20 to open a bank account.

Example 4 (page 603)

15. CDs To buy a certain DVD, you must be at least 13 years old. Who of the following people can buy the DVD: Carl (12 years, 9 months), Cara (15 years, 4 days), Molly (13 years), Peter (8 years, 11 months)?

16. Playgrounds To ride on the playground animals, you must be under 50 pounds. Who of the following childen can ride the animals: Hugh (50 pounds), Paul (45 pounds), Andrea (25 pounds), Michelle (53 pounds), Tim (49 pounds)?

B Apply Your Skills

Tell whether each inequality is true or false.

17. $6 \leq 6$ **18.** $|-5| < 5$ **19.** $-4^2 < (-4)^2$ **20.** $0.05 > 0.5$

21. Football You must weigh 120 pounds or less to play in a junior football league. The table shows the weights of boys who would like to play. Which of the boys qualify to play?

Name	Weight
Aaron	118 lb
Steve	109 lb
Mark	131 lb
James	120 lb

Exercise 22

22. Highway Safety Write an inequality for the sign shown at the left.

23. Writing in Math Describe how to graph the inequality $x < -20$.

24. Replace ■ with $<$, $=$, or $>$ to make each statement true.
a. If $50 > b$, then b ■ 50.
b. If $a = b$ and $b < 50$, then a ■ 50.

25. Driving The minimum speed limit on an interstate is 50 miles per hour. The maximum speed limit is 65 miles per hour.
a. Write an inequality to describe a car that is going too slow.
b. Write an inequality to describe a car that is going too fast.

26. **Data File, p. 593** Write an inequality for an average monthly energy usage greater than 80 kwh. Which appliances have an average monthly energy usage greater than 80 kwh?

Challenge

27. **Number Sense** Graph the following inequality on a number line: $x \neq 4$.

28. **Stretch Your Thinking** Solve and graph $|x| < 2$.

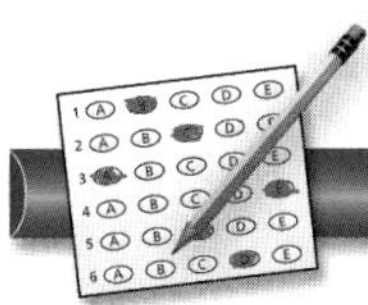

Test Prep

Reading Comprehension

Read the passage and answer the questions below.

A Career in Law Enforcement

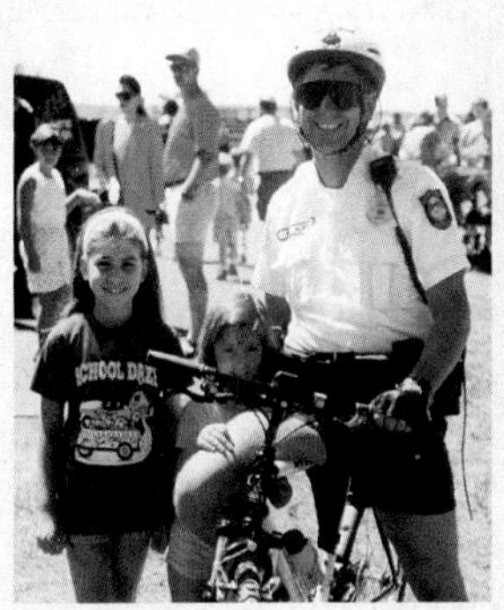

The work of police officers, detectives, and FBI agents seems exciting to many people. Individuals seeking a career in law enforcement must be citizens of the United States and must be at least 20 years of age at the time of appointment. Those seeking careers in federal law enforcement agencies, such as the FBI, must be at least 21 years of age, but less than 37.

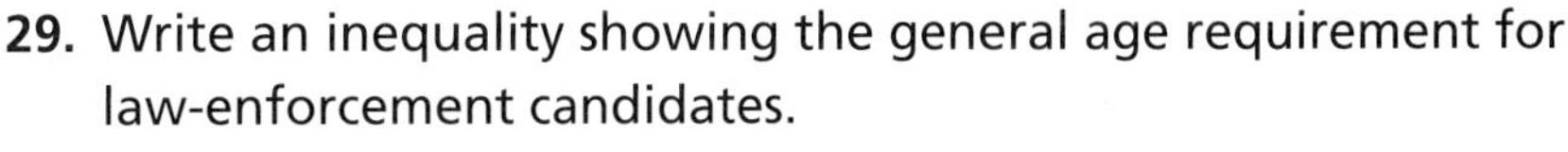

29. Write an inequality showing the general age requirement for law-enforcement candidates.

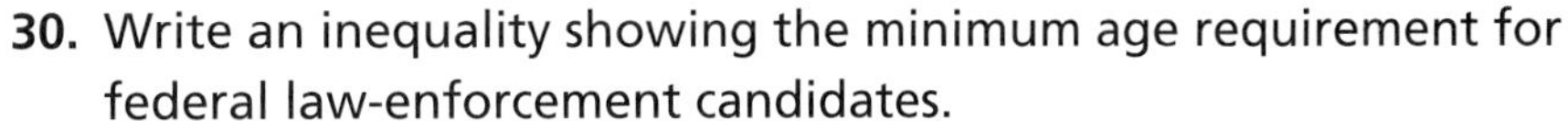

30. Write an inequality showing the minimum age requirement for federal law-enforcement candidates.

Take It to the NET
Online lesson quiz at
www.PHSchool.com
Web Code: aaa-1202

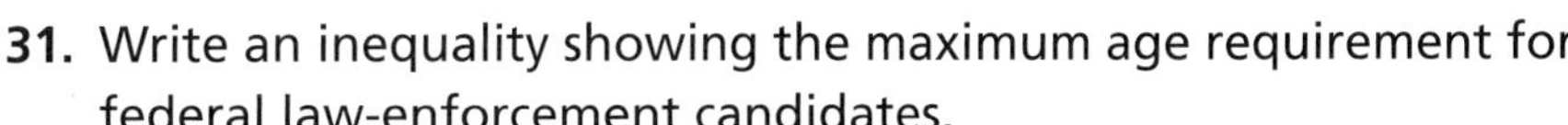

31. Write an inequality showing the maximum age requirement for federal law-enforcement candidates.

Multiple Choice

32. Which inequality does NOT have -2 as a solution?
A. $x \geq -2$ **B.** $x < -1$ **C.** $x > -1$ **D.** $x < 2$

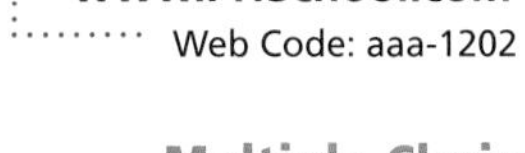

Mixed Review

Lesson 11-2

Find the experimental probability that each person wins.

33. Tom won a game 84 times and lost 24 times.

34. Rhonda played a game 222 times and won 88 times.

Lesson 9-10

35. You multiply a number by 6 and then subtract 4. The result is 38. Work backward to find the number.

Algebra

12-3 Solving One-Step Inequalities

What You'll Learn

To solve inequalities by adding or subtracting

. . . And Why

To determine how close you are to meeting a goal, as in Example 2

Check Skills You'll Need

For help, go to Lesson 2-6.

Solve each equation.

1. $y + 4 = -5$ **2.** $x + 6 = 9$ **3.** $b - 18 = 35$

4. $c - 5 = 16$ **5.** $3 + m = 10$ **6.** $-8 + c = 11$

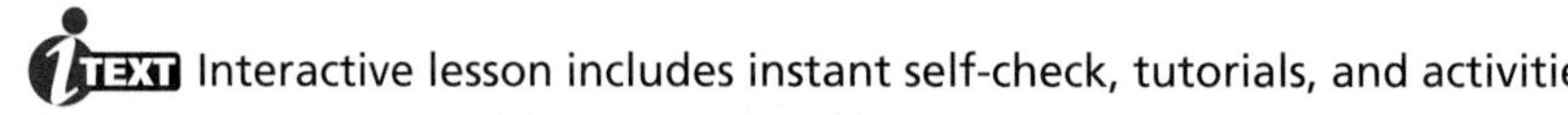
Interactive lesson includes instant self-check, tutorials, and activities.

OBJECTIVE 1

Solving Inequalities by Adding or Subtracting

To solve an inequality, use inverse operations to get the variable alone.

1 EXAMPLE Solving an Inequality by Adding

Solve $s - 7 < 3$.

$s - 7 < 3$

$s - 7 + 7 < 3 + 7$ ← **Add 7 to each side to undo the subtraction.**

$s < 10$ ← **Simplify.**

Check Understanding 1 Solve $u - 6 \leq 3$.

2 EXAMPLE Solving an Inequality by Subtracting

Real World

Running Suppose a marathon runner plans to run at least 55 miles this week. He has already run 42 miles. Write and solve an inequality to find how many more miles he needs to run in order to meet his goal.

Words	miles run	+	miles to run	is at least	55 miles
	Let m = the number of miles he still needs to run.				
Inequality	42	+	m	$\geq$	55

$42 + m \geq 55$

$42 + m - 42 \geq 55 - 42$ ← **Subtract 42 from each side.**

$m \geq 13$ ← **Simplify.**

The marathon runner needs to run at least 13 more miles this week.

Real-World Connection

Khalid Khannouchi set this world record for marathon running in 1999. He then beat it in 2002 with a time of 2.05.38.

✓ **Check Understanding** **2** A restaurant can serve a maximum of 115 people. There are already 97 people dining in the restaurant. Write and solve an inequality to find how many more people the restaurant can serve.

EXERCISES

For more practice, see *Extra Practice*.

A Practice by Example

Solve each inequality.

Example 1 (page 606)

1. $x - 2 \geq 5$ **2.** $z - 5 < 0$ **3.** $k - 21 > 1$

4. $j - 2 > -9$ **5.** $n - 96 < -58$ **6.** $s - 4 \leq 8$

Example 2 (page 606)

7. $r + 5 \geq 7$ **8.** $y + 12 \leq 11$ **9.** $w + 2 > -7$

10. $14 + d \leq 24$ **11.** $13 + f > 7$ **12.** $5 + g \leq 62$

13. Banks To avoid fees, you must have a minimum of \$250 in your bank account. You currently have \$143 in your account. Write and solve an inequality to find how much money you must deposit to avoid fees.

14. To get an A on a four-part test, Dana must score a minimum of 270 points. She scored 240 points on the first 3 parts of the test. What does she need to earn on the fourth part in order to receive an A?

B Apply Your Skills

For Exercises 15–19, write an inequality for each sentence or problem. Then solve the inequality.

15. Nine is less than or equal to a number n added to seven.

16. The sum of a number x and 5 is greater than 25.

17. The difference of a number a and 8 is less than 7.

18. 12 is greater than or equal to a number c minus 10.

19. Souvenirs Suppose you have \$15 to spend on souvenirs. You already bought the visor at the right. How much more money can you spend?

20. Writing in Math Without computing, how can you tell that $3n > 3n$ has no solutions?

Real-World Connection

A biplane is double winged. One wing is above and the other below the pilot.

21. **Flying** Mary is flying her plane at an altitude lower than its upper safety limit of 32,000 feet. To avoid a storm, she rises 2,500 feet without going above 32,000 feet. Write an inequality, and then use the inequality to find the maximum original altitude of the plane.

Mental Math Solve each inequality.

22. $c + 9 < 15$
23. $t - 6 > 24$
24. $q + 8 \leq 14$
25. $b - 3 > 12$
26. $c - 2 \leq 8$
27. $d + 4 \geq 12$

28. **Reasoning** What number is a solution to $y + 2 \geq 10$ but not to $y + 2 > 10$?

29. **Budgeting** Suppose you want to spend less than $30 total to buy two T-shirts and a pair of shorts. The shorts cost $13. Write and solve an inequality to find how much money you can spend on each T-shirt.

C Challenge

Solve each inequality.

30. $3d > 36$
31. $4p < 20$

32. **Stretch Your Thinking** A jar balances with a bottle on a scale. The same jar also balances with a mug and a plate. Three of these plates balance with two bottles identical to the first bottle. How many mugs identical to the first mug will balance the jar?

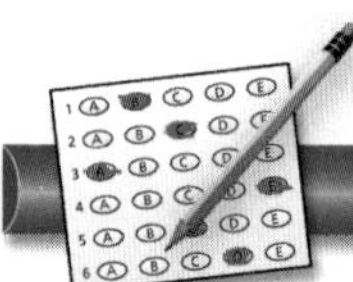

Test Prep

Multiple Choice

33. Which of the following operations would you use to get the variable in $x + 14 \leq 23$ alone on one side of the inequality?
    A. Add 14 to both sides.
    B. Subtract 14 from both sides.
    C. Add 23 to both sides.
    D. Subtract 23 from both sides.

34. What is the solution of $y - 6 \geq -3$?
    F. $y > -9$
    G. $y \geq 3$
    H. $y \leq -9$
    I. $y \leq 3$

35. What is the solution of $z + 3 > 4$?
    A. $z > 7$
    B. $z < 17$
    C. $z > 1$
    D. $z < 1$

Take It to the NET
Online lesson quiz at **www.PHSchool.com**
Web Code: aaa-1203

Short Response

36. Fifteen is subtracted from a number. The result is greater than 8.
    a. Write an inequality to describe the situation.
    b. What is the smallest integer value that is a solution for the inequality?

Mixed Review

Lesson 11-4

37. A quiz consists of four true-false questions. Use a simulation to find the experimental probability of guessing correctly on every question. Use four coins to model this situation. Let heads represent true and tails represent false.

Lesson 9-7

Name each figure.

38. 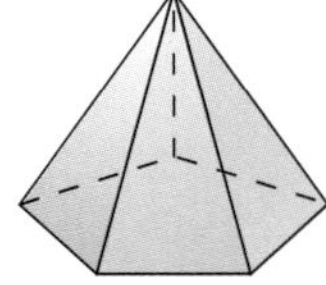

39. 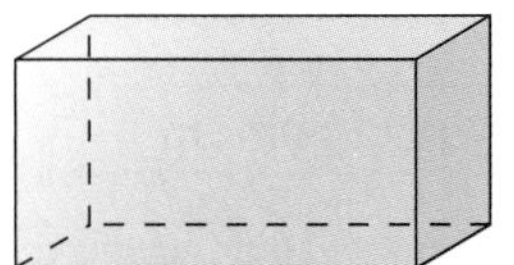

40. 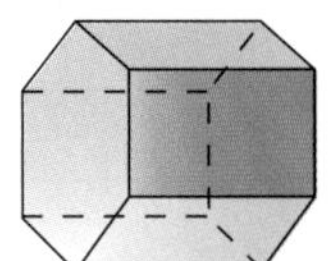

Lesson 8-9

Copy each diagram on graph paper and draw its reflection of the shape over the given line of reflection.

41. 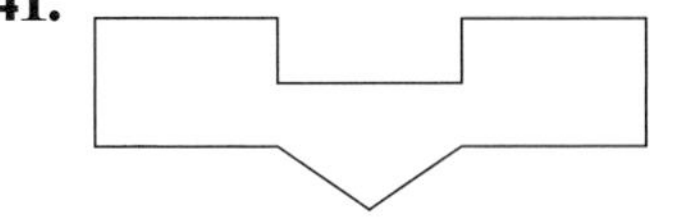

42. 

Checkpoint Quiz 1

Lessons 12-1 through 12-3

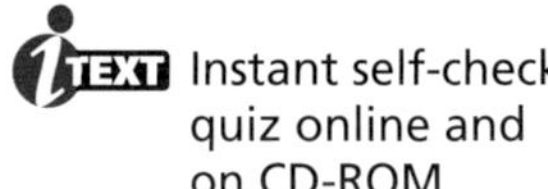

Instant self-check quiz online and on CD-ROM

Solve each equation.

1. $4t + 5 = 37$

2. $\frac{r}{2} - 8 = -4$

3. $5m - 8 = 57$

4. Tell whether each number is a solution to $x \leq -5$.

a. -8 **b.** -4 **c.** 3 **d.** 7

Graph the solution to each inequality on a number line.

5. $c > -2$

6. $d \leq 4$

7. $e < -4$

Solve each inequality.

8. $p + 8 < 3$

9. $n - 5 \geq 14$

10. Miguel sells coupon books. He earns $30 a day plus $2 for each book sold. Miguel would like to make a minimum of $65 each day. How many coupon books must he sell per day to earn the minimum?

Reading Math

Making Sense of Inequalities

For Use With Lesson 12-3

Inequalities can be expressed in three forms.

- as a word problem
- as a graph
- with symbols

Word Problem	Symbols	Graph
Sam ran less than 10 miles last week. How many miles could Sam have run?	$m < 10$	
At the book fair, books cost \$3 each. How many books can Jennifer buy without spending more than \$30?	$3b \leq 30$	
To win a contest, the band has to wash more than 50 cars. Students have already washed 30 cars. How many more cars must they wash to win the contest?	$c + 30 \geq 50$	

When you are working with inequalities, you can interchange the different forms shown above to help you understand and solve problems.

Sometimes, you will need to think of a situation that lends itself to a certain graph or set of symbols.

EXERCISES

Write entries that could appear in each row of the table below.

	Word Problem	Symbols	Graph
1.	Celia has \$20 in her savings account. How much does she need to deposit to have more than \$100 in the account?	?	?
2.	A pair of jeans costs more than \$15. How much could the jeans cost?	?	?
3.	?	$x < 10$	?
4.	?	?	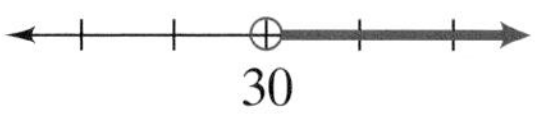

12-4 Comparing Strategies

What You'll Learn

To solve a problem using two different methods

. . . And Why

To compare strategies in problem solving, as in Example 1

✓ Check Skills You'll Need

For help, go to Lesson 2-7.

Solve each equation. Then check the solution.

1. $x \div 5 = 19$ **2.** $6y = 144$

3. $13b = 143$ **4.** $a \div 12 = 40$

5. $m \div 23 = 6$ **6.** $18p = 324$

OBJECTIVE

Interactive lesson includes instant self-check, tutorials, and activities.

1 Solving a Problem Using Two Different Methods

When to Use These Strategies You can ***draw a diagram*** to help you visualize the information given in a problem. This may help you understand and solve a problem. To clarify your thinking and provide a model of a problem, you can ***write an equation.***

You may use either of these strategies to solve the following problem.

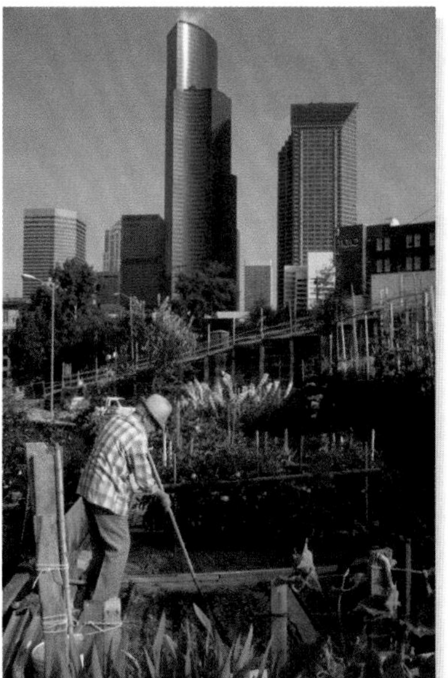

Real-World Connection

City land is sometimes available to neighborhoods for community gardening.

1 EXAMPLE Using Two Different Methods

Real World

Gardening A class is planning to plant a garden. The rectangular plot for the garden is 6 meters by 9 meters. The class wants to use 4 square meters of garden for each type of vegetable they plant. How many different vegetables can they plant?

Read and Understand The dimensions of the rectangular plot are 6 meters by 9 meters. Each vegetable will use 4 square meters of space. The goal is to find how many types of vegetables they can plant.

Plan and Solve

Method 1

Draw a diagram of the plot. Then divide the diagram into sections that are 4 square meters in size.

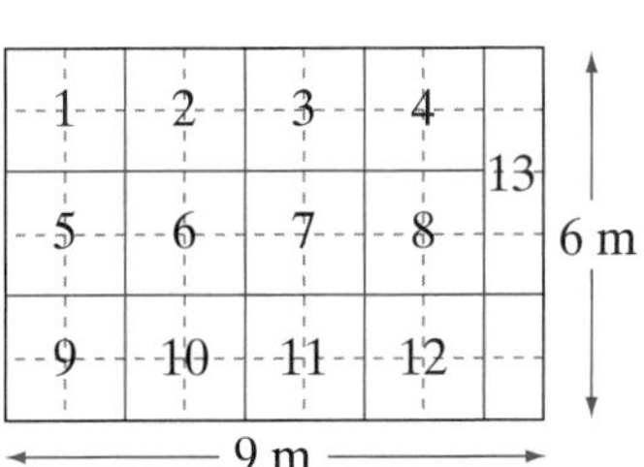

Thirteen sections of 4 square meters will fit in the plot. So, the class can plant 13 vegetables.

Method 2

Write and solve an equation.

Words	space for each vegetable	times	number of vegetables	equals	space available in garden

Let v = the number of vegetables the class can plant.

Equation	4	$\cdot$	v	$=$	54

$$4v = 54$$

$$\frac{4v}{4} = \frac{54}{4} \quad \leftarrow \text{Divide each side by 4.}$$

$$v = 13.5 \quad \leftarrow \text{Simplify.}$$

Since $v = 13.5$, the rectangular plot can be divided into 13.5 sections of 4 square meters. The half section only represents 2 square meters. The class can plant 13 different vegetables in the garden.

Look Back and Check There are 13 sections in the plot, and each section is 4 square meters. The total area used by the vegetables is 13×4, or 52 square meters. Since 52 square meters is only 2 square meters less than the size of the garden, the answer checks.

Check Understanding

1 a. **Reasoning** Look back at the two methods used to solve the example. Which method would you use? Why?

b. The length of a board is 54 inches. You cut the board into two pieces. One piece is 14 inches longer than the other. How long is each piece?

EXERCISES

For more practice, see *Extra Practice*.

A Practice by Example

Solve each problem by either drawing a diagram or writing an equation. Explain why you chose the method you did.

Example 1 (page 611)

1. **Baking** Tim is making granola bars. The top of each granola bar will be 2 inches by 3 inches. How many bars will he have if he bakes 3 batches, each in a 10-inch by 12-inch baking pan?

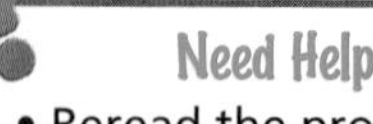

Need Help?
- Reread the problem.
- Identify the key facts and details.
- Tell the problem in your own words.
- Try a different strategy.
- Check your work.

2. **Carpet** A rectangular carpet is three times as long as it is wide. If the carpet was 3 meters shorter and 3 meters wider, it would be a square. What are the dimensions of the rectangular carpet?

3. **Biking** Suppose you bike along a 250-mile trail. You bike 40% of the distance the first day and 25% of the distance the second day. How many miles do you have to bike the third day to complete the trail?

B Apply Your Skills

Strategies

Draw a Diagram
Make a Graph
Make an Organized List
Make a Table and Look for a Pattern
Simulate a Problem
Solve a Simpler Problem
Try, Check, and Revise
Use Logical Reasoning
Work Backward
Write an Equation

Choose a strategy to solve each problem.

4. A pizza costs \$8.00. Each additional topping costs 75¢. If the total cost of the pizza is \$11.75, how many additional toppings are on the pizza?

5. Trisha buys 30 calendars for \$4 each. She then sells each calendar individually for a higher price. She earns \$165 in profit from selling all the calendars. What did she charge for each calendar?

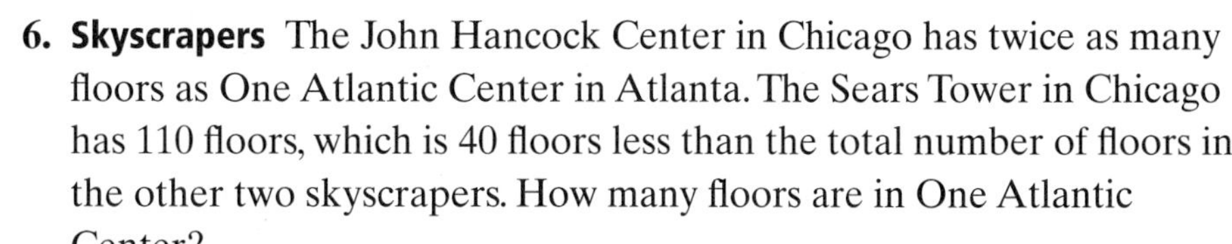

6. **Skyscrapers** The John Hancock Center in Chicago has twice as many floors as One Atlantic Center in Atlanta. The Sears Tower in Chicago has 110 floors, which is 40 floors less than the total number of floors in the other two skyscrapers. How many floors are in One Atlantic Center?

7. Dora and Kevin are making propellers for their model helicopters. Dora puts a number on her propeller. She notices that when she turns the propeller, she has the same number. Kevin would like to do the same thing to his propeller. What is the next greatest number that has this property?

8. **Data File, p. 593** Your neighbors use a water heater, microwave oven, TV, VCR, and hair dryer. Suppose they use the hair dryer four times as much as the average household, but they use the TV only half as much. What is the average monthly energy use for your neighbor's home?

9. One set of holiday lights blinks every 5 seconds. A second set of holiday lights blinks every 8 seconds. Assume the lights blink together when you first turn them on. How many times in one minute do the two sets of lights blink together?

10. **Writing in Math** Refer to Exercise 9. Suppose the first set of lights blinks every 6 seconds. Explain how this would change the answer.

11. **Yard Sale** Suppose you purchase a soccer ball at a yard sale for \$2. You then sell the ball to a friend for \$2.50. You buy the ball back for \$2.75 and then sell the ball for \$3.25. How much money do you make?

12. Packaging A book publisher ships its books packed in boxes. Each box is 12 inches long, 9 inches wide, and 8 inches high. If each book is 9 inches long, $7\frac{1}{4}$ inches wide, and $\frac{1}{2}$ inch thick, what is the maximum number of books the publisher can pack into each box?

13. Stretch Your Thinking An unknown number is divisible by 23 and 3. The two-digit number in the thousands and hundreds place is one less than the two-digit number in the tens and ones place. The unknown number is greater than 2,000, but less than 4,000. What is the unknown number?

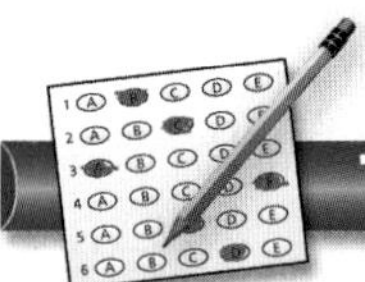

Test Prep

Multiple Choice

14. Which is a solution for $x \geq 7$?

A. -1 **B.** 5 **C.** 6 **D.** 7

15. The solution to which sentence is graphed at the right?

F. $x > -1$ **G.** $x < -1$ **H.** $x \geq -1$ **I.** $x \leq -1$

16. What is the solution of $6x + 9 = 81$?

A. 12 **B.** 13.5 **C.** 66 **D.** 72

Take It to the NET
Online lesson quiz at
www.PHSchool.com
Web Code: aaa-1204

17. What is the solution of $3x + 26 = -34$?

F. -20 **G.** $-2\frac{2}{3}$ **H.** $2\frac{2}{3}$ **I.** 20

Short Response

18. Chuck buys 6 herbs. He also buys a planting pot for \$7. The total cost of the herbs and pot is \$14.50.

a. Write an equation to determine how much each herb costs.

b. Solve your equation.

Mixed Review

Lesson 11-3

The probability of winning a game is 60%. How many times should you expect to win if you play each of the following number of times?

19. 5 times **20.** 20 times **21.** 75 times **22.** 150 times

Lesson 9-6

Find the area of each circle to the nearest tenth. Use 3.14 for π.

23. $r = 2$ in. **24.** $d = 4$ ft **25.** $r = 6$ m **26.** $d = 15$ km

Lesson 9-2

27. Cars A car is travelling at 40 kilometers per hour. How many meters per hour is this?

Exploring Squares

For Use With Lesson 12-5

You will need a geoboard and rubber bands.

Look at the geoboard at the right. Each side of the square is 1 unit long. The area is 1 square unit.

Activity

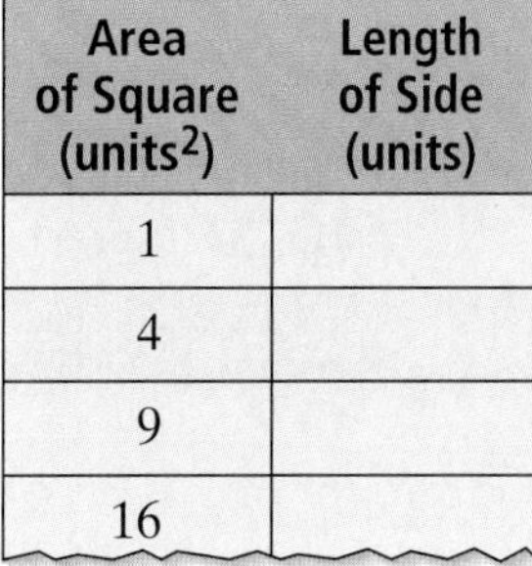

Area of Square (units^2)	Length of Side (units)
1	
4	
9	
16	

1. **a.** Use your geoboard to make squares with areas of 4, 9, and 16 square units.
   b. Copy the table at the right. Enter the length of a side for each square you made in part (a).

2. **a.** Look at your table. What pattern(s) do you notice?
   b. Continue the table for squares with areas of 25, 36, and 49 square units.

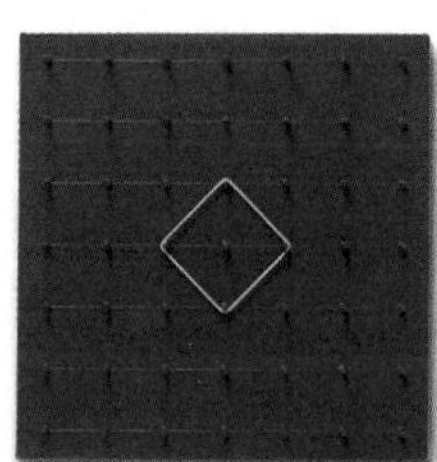

3. Make the figure shown at the right using your geoboard. The figure is a square with an area of 2 square units.
   a. Use your table to estimate the length of a side of this square.
   b. Recall that the formula for the area of a square is $A = s^2$. Use a calculator and the *Try, Check, and Revise* strategy. To the nearest hundredth, find the length of a side of a square with an area of 2 square units.

4. **a.** Use your calculator and the *Try, Check, and Revise* strategy. To the nearest hundredth, find the length of a side of a square with an area of 8 square units.
   b. How does the side length you found in Step 3(b) compare with your answer to Step 4(a)?

5. Use your geoboard to make a square with an area of 8 square units.

6. **Stretch Your Thinking** Use your geoboard to make a square with an area of 5 square units.

12-5 Exploring Square Roots and Rational Numbers

What You'll Learn

To find square roots

To classify numbers as rational

. . . And Why

To find the dimensions of a square, as in Example 3

Check Skills You'll Need

For help, go to Lesson 2-8.

Write each expression using an exponent. Name the base and the exponent.

1. 5×5 **2.** $6 \times 6 \times 6$ **3.** $4 \times 4 \times 4 \times 4 \times 4$

4. $999 \times 999 \times 999$ **5.** 72 **6.** 3.6×3.6

New Vocabulary

- square root
- perfect square
- rational number

OBJECTIVE

Interactive lesson includes instant self-check, tutorials, and activities.

1 Finding Square Roots

Reading Math

The expression $\sqrt{9}$ is read "the square root of 9."

The *square* of 3 is 3^2, or 9. The inverse of squaring is finding the square root. A **square root** of a given number is a number that, when multiplied by itself, is the given number. The square root of 9 is 3. In symbols, $\sqrt{9} = 3$. You will only find positive square roots in this course.

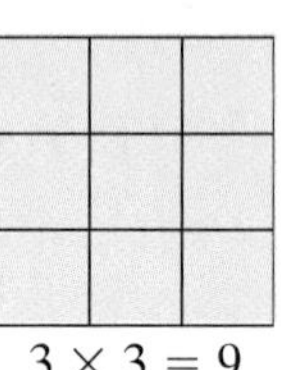
$3 \times 3 = 9$

1 EXAMPLE Finding Square Roots

a. Find $\sqrt{64}$.

Since $8 \times 8 = 64$, $\sqrt{64} = 8$.

b. Find $\sqrt{49}$.

Since $7 \times 7 = 49$, $\sqrt{49} = 7$.

Check Understanding 1 Find each square root. **a.** $\sqrt{4}$ **b.** $\sqrt{100}$

A **perfect square** is the square of a whole number. The number 64 is a perfect square because $64 = 8^2$. When finding the square root of a number that isn't a perfect square, you can use a calculator.

2 EXAMPLE Using a Calculator to Find a Square Root

Calculator Find $\sqrt{50}$ to the nearest tenth.

$\sqrt{50} \approx 7.071067812$ ← **On a calculator, press 2nd x^2 50 =.**

≈ 7.1 ← **Round to the nearest tenth.**

Check Understanding 2 Find each square root to the nearest tenth.

a. $\sqrt{7}$ **b.** $\sqrt{10}$ **c.** $\sqrt{24}$ **d.** $\sqrt{86}$

3 EXAMPLE Real-World Problem Solving

Board Games The square board has an area of 121 square inches. How long is each side of the game board?

The area of a square is found by squaring a side. So, find the square root of 121. Look for a number that is equal to 121 when it is squared.

Since $11^2 = 121$, $\sqrt{121} = 11$.

Each side of the game board is 11 inches long.

Check Understanding 3 How long is each side of a game board with an area of 81 square inches?

You can also estimate square roots of numbers that are not perfect squares. For example, notice that $\sqrt{3}$ is between $\sqrt{1}$ and $\sqrt{4}$.

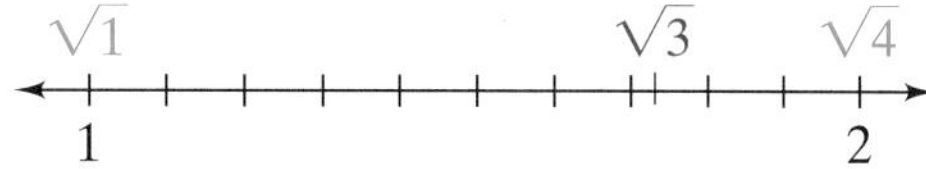

Thus, $\sqrt{3}$ is between 1 and 2.

4 EXAMPLE Approximating a Square Root

Tell which two consecutive whole numbers $\sqrt{5}$ is between.

$4 < 5 < 9$ ← **Find the perfect squares close to 5.**

$\sqrt{4} < \sqrt{5} < \sqrt{9}$ ← **Write the square roots in order.**

$2 < \sqrt{5} < 3$ ← **Simplify.**

$\sqrt{5}$ is between 2 and 3.

Check Understanding 4 **a.** **Number Sense** Is $\sqrt{5}$ closer to 2 or to 3? Explain.

b. Tell which two consecutive numbers $\sqrt{8}$ is between.

OBJECTIVE

2 Classifying Numbers as Rational

Need Help?
To review the terms *terminating* and *repeating*, see page 45.

A **rational number** is any number that can be written as a quotient of two integers, where the denominator is not 0. You can write any integer as a quotient with a denominator of 1, so all integers are rational numbers. Examples of rational numbers are 2 (or $\frac{2}{1}$), $\frac{4}{5}$, 0.38 (or $\frac{38}{100}$), −8 (or $\frac{-8}{1}$).

Rational numbers in decimal form either terminate or repeat.

5 EXAMPLE Identifying Rational Numbers

Tell whether each number is rational.

a. 6.7 — 6.7 is a terminating decimal. It is rational.

b. $8.\overline{9}$ — $8.\overline{9}$ is a repeating decimal. It is rational.

c. $\frac{1}{5}$ — $\frac{1}{5}$ is a quotient of integers. It is rational.

d. 3.262272228 . . . — This decimal does not repeat or terminate. It is not rational.

e. -10 — -10 is an integer. It is rational.

Check Understanding 5 Tell whether each number is rational.

a. 0.232323 **b.** $\frac{3}{8}$ **c.** 1.112111211112 . . .

The square root of a whole number is rational only when the whole number is a perfect square.

6 EXAMPLE Classifying Square Roots of Whole Numbers

Tell whether each number is rational.

a. $\sqrt{16}$ — 16 is a perfect square. $\sqrt{16}$ is rational.

b. $\sqrt{26}$ — $\sqrt{26}$ is between 5 and 6. It is not rational.

Check Understanding 6 Tell whether each number is rational.

a. $\sqrt{7}$ **b.** $\sqrt{36}$ **c.** $\sqrt{53}$ **d.** $\sqrt{121}$

EXERCISES

For more practice, see *Extra Practice*.

A Practice by Example

Example 1 (page 616)

Find each square root.

1. $\sqrt{1}$ **2.** $\sqrt{25}$ **3.** $\sqrt{81}$ **4.** $\sqrt{9}$

5. $\sqrt{16}$ **6.** $\sqrt{36}$ **7.** $\sqrt{100}$ **8.** $\sqrt{144}$

Example 2 (page 616)

Calculator **Find each square root to the nearest tenth.**

9. $\sqrt{21}$ **10.** $\sqrt{33}$ **11.** $\sqrt{50}$ **12.** $\sqrt{75}$

Example 3 (page 617)

13. **Patios** A square patio has an area of 169 square feet. How long is each side of the patio?

14. **Quilts** The area of a quilt is 36 square feet. How long is each side?

Example 4 (page 617)

Tell which two consecutive whole numbers the square root is between.

15. $\sqrt{2}$ 16. $\sqrt{6}$ 17. $\sqrt{28}$ 18. $\sqrt{18}$

19. $\sqrt{23}$ 20. $\sqrt{73}$ 21. $\sqrt{90}$ 22. $\sqrt{55}$

Examples 5, 6 (page 618)

Tell whether each number is rational.

23. $6.\overline{8}$ 24. $\frac{9}{11}$ 25. 0.10010001... 26. $-2\frac{1}{2}$

27. $\frac{7}{9}$ 28. 15 29. 6.2319743 30. $3\frac{1}{3}$

31. $\sqrt{4}$ 32. $\sqrt{9}$ 33. $\sqrt{49}$ 34. $\sqrt{18}$

35. $\sqrt{1}$ 36. $\sqrt{11}$ 37. $\sqrt{42}$ 38. $\sqrt{100}$

B Apply Your Skills

39. **Reasoning** Is $\sqrt{2}$ greater than 1? Is $\sqrt{2}$ greater than 2? Explain.

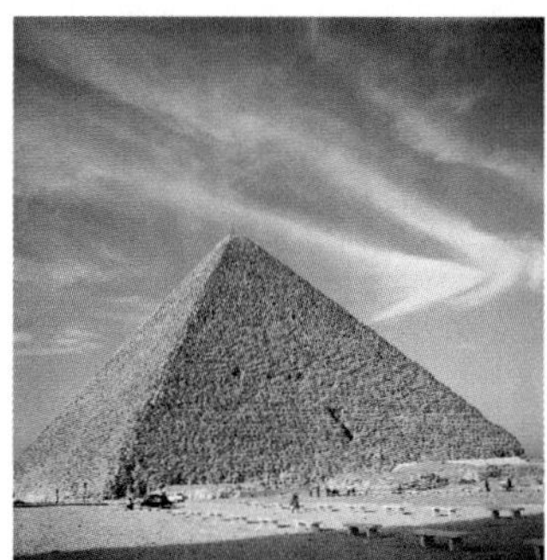

Real-World Connection

The Great Pyramid at Giza is the largest Egyptian pyramid.

40. **Egyptian Pyramids** The area of the square base of the Great Pyramid at Giza is 52,900 square meters. What is the length of each side of the square base of the pyramid?

Estimation **Estimate to the nearest whole number.**

41. $\sqrt{6}$ 42. $\sqrt{7}$ 43. $\sqrt{11}$ 44. $\sqrt{26}$ 45. $\sqrt{58}$

46. **Calculator** Use a calculator to evaluate each expression: $\sqrt{27}$, $\sqrt{9} \times \sqrt{3}$, and $3 \times \sqrt{3}$. What do you notice?

47. **Writing in Math** Find two consecutive whole numbers that have $\sqrt{29}$ between them. Explain how you chose the numbers.

C Challenge

48. **Number Sense** Find two perfect squares that have a sum of 100.

49. Simplify each expression.
   a. $(\sqrt{2})^2$ b. $(\sqrt{3})^2$ c. $(\sqrt{8})^2$ d. $(\sqrt{16})^2$
   e. **Number Sense** What do you get when you square the square root of a number?

50. **Stretch Your Thinking** Arrange the digits 1 through 9 in the bubbles in the triangle so the sum of the numbers along each side is 17.

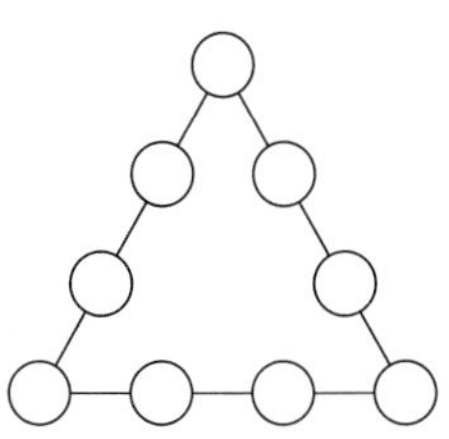

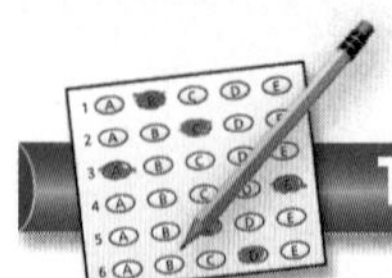

Test Prep

Multiple Choice

51. What is $\sqrt{196}$?

A. 12 **B.** 13 **C.** 14 **D.** 15

52. Between which consecutive whole numbers does $\sqrt{290}$ lie?

F. 7 and 8 **G.** 8 and 9 **H.** 17 and 18 **I.** 18 and 19

Take It to the NET
Online lesson quiz at **www.PHSchool.com**
Web Code: aaa-1205

53. A square afghan has an area of 3,600 square inches. How long is each side of the afghan?

A. 6 inches **B.** 5 feet
C. 60 square inches **D.** 50 feet

Short Response

54. The ceiling of a square room has an area of 256 square feet. What is the perimeter of the room? Justify your answer.

Mixed Review

Lesson 11-6

Find the number of possible permutations of each set of items.

55. the numbers 5, 6, and 7

56. the letters READ

Lesson 9-10

Work backward to solve each problem.

57. If you multiply a number by 9, and then subtract 16, the result is 56. What is the number?

58. Kayla gives Mike one-third of her pretzels. Mike gives Ronnie half of the pretzels he received from Kayla. Ronnie keeps 6 of the pretzels and gives 12 to Jeff. How many pretzels did Kayla give Mike?

Checkpoint Quiz 2 — Lessons 12-4 through 12-5

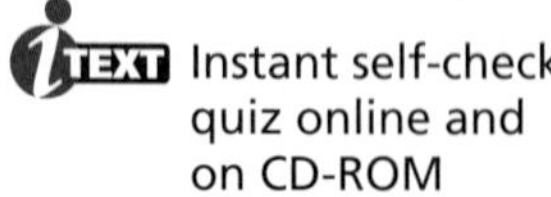

Instant self-check quiz online and on CD-ROM

1. A ribbon is 29 inches long. You cut the ribbon into two pieces so that one piece is 7.8 inches longer than the other. How long is each piece? Solve by either drawing a diagram or writing an equation. Explain why you chose the method you did.

Find each square root.

2. $\sqrt{121}$

3. $\sqrt{36}$

Tell whether each number is rational.

4. $\frac{1}{12}$

5. $\sqrt{169}$

Exploring Right Triangles

For Use With Lesson 12-6

Recall that a right triangle is a triangle with a right angle.

Activity

Step 1 Use centimeter grid paper to draw a right triangle. The right angle should be included between sides that are 3 centimeters and 4 centimeters long.

Step 2 Draw a 3-by-3 square along the side that is 3 centimeters long. Label the square A. Draw a 4-by-4 square along the side that is 4 centimeters long. Label the square B.

Step 3 Use another piece of the grid paper to make a square on the side opposite the right angle. Label the square C.

Step 1

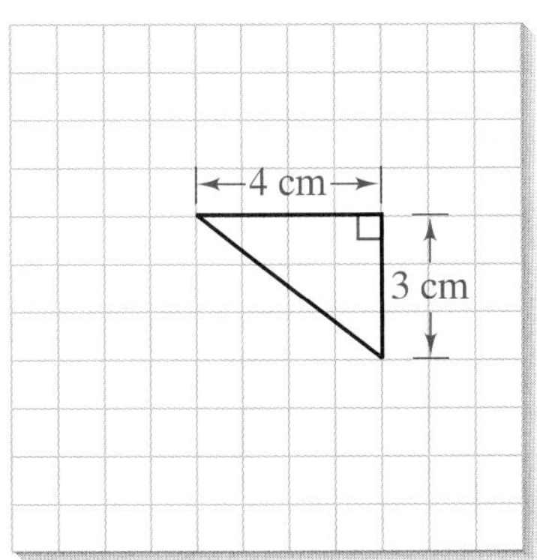

Step 2

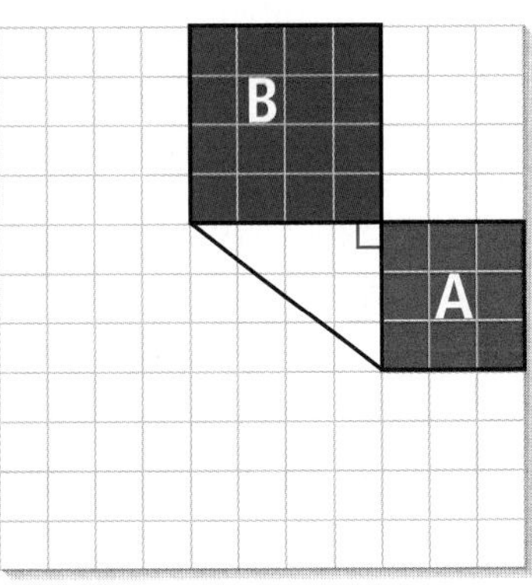

Step 3

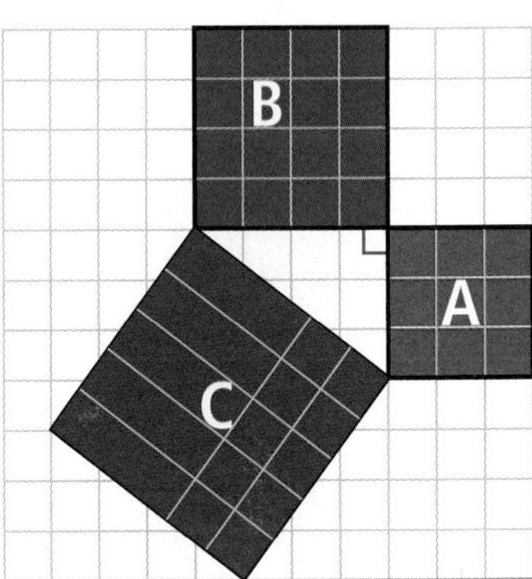

EXERCISES

1. Repeat the activity for the triangles shown in the table below. Copy and complete the table.

Sides of Triangle	Area of Square A	Area of Square B	Area of Square C
3, 4, 5	9	16	25
5, 12, ■	■	■	■
6, 8, ■	■	■	■
9, 12, ■	■	■	■

2. **Reasoning** Look at your table. What is the relationship between the areas of the two smaller squares (A and B) and the area of the largest square (C)?

12-6 Introducing the Pythagorean Theorem

What You'll Learn

To use the Pythagorean Theorem

. . . And Why

To find the height of a ramp, as in Example 2

For help, go to Lesson 12-5.

Find each square root.

1. $\sqrt{9}$ **2.** $\sqrt{64}$ **3.** $\sqrt{25}$

4. $\sqrt{36}$ **5.** $\sqrt{121}$ **6.** $\sqrt{625}$

New Vocabulary • legs • hypotenuse • Pythagorean Theorem

OBJECTIVE

1 Using the Pythagorean Theorem

Recall that a right triangle contains an angle measuring 90°. In a right triangle, the two shorter sides are called **legs.** The longest side, which is opposite the right angle, is called the **hypotenuse.**

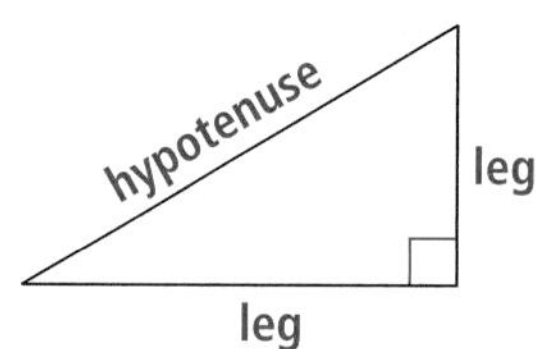

The symbol ⌐ in the triangle above indicates that the angle is a right angle. Notice that it forms a square using the sides of the angle.

The Pythagorean Theorem shows how the lengths of sides in a right triangle are related. The labels *a, b,* and *c* are commonly used to label the unknown lengths of sides in right triangles, but any labels can be used.

Key Concepts **Pythagorean Theorem**

In any right triangle, the sum of the squares of the lengths of the legs (a and b) is equal to the square of the length of the hypotenuse (c).

Arithmetic

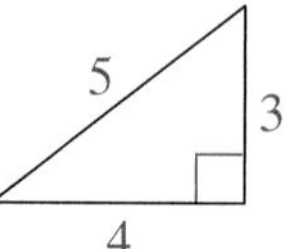

$3^2 + 4^2 = 5^2$

Algebra

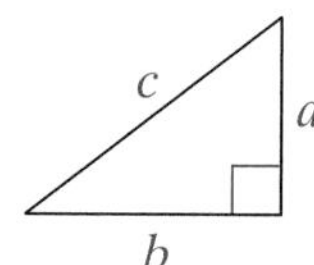

$a^2 + b^2 = c^2$

If you know the lengths of any two sides of a right triangle, you can use the Pythagorean Theorem to find the length of the other side.

1 EXAMPLE Finding the Length of a Hypotenuse

Test-Prep Tip
Sometimes you can draw a diagram to better understand a problem.

Find the length of the hypotenuse of the triangle.

$a^2 + b^2 = c^2$ ← **Write the Pythagorean Theorem.**

$9^2 + 12^2 = c^2$ ← **Substitute 9 for *a* and 12 for *b*.**

$81 + 144 = c^2$ ← **Square 9 and 12.**

$225 = c^2$ ← **Add.**

$\sqrt{225} = \sqrt{c^2}$ ← **Find the square root of each side.**

$15 = c$ ← **Simplify.**

The length of the hypotenuse is 15 units.

Check Understanding 1 **a.** Find the length of the hypotenuse of a triangle with legs of 12 inches and 16 inches.

b. **Reasoning** If both legs of a triangle are under 12 inches, will its hypotenuse always be less than your answer to part (a)?

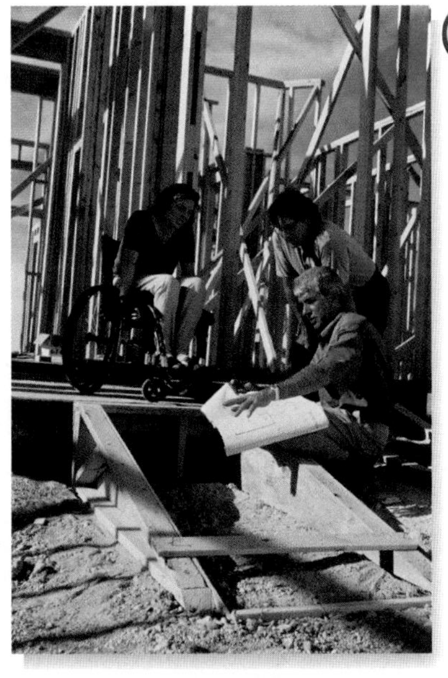

Real-World Connection
Ramps help people in wheelchairs get into buildings.

2 EXAMPLE Finding the Length of a Leg

Ramps A ramp forms part of the right triangle below. How high is the top of the ramp? Round to the nearest tenth.

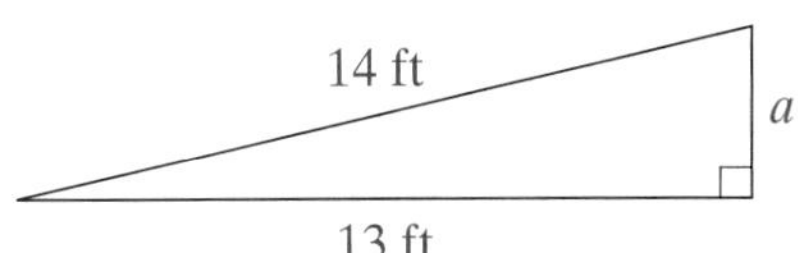

One leg has length 13 feet. The hypotenuse has length 14 feet.

$a^2 + b^2 = c^2$ ← **Write the Pythagorean Theorem.**

$a^2 + 13^2 = 14^2$ ← **Substitute 13 for *b* and 14 for *c*.**

$a^2 + 169 = 196$ ← **Square 13 and 14.**

$a^2 + 169 - 169 = 196 - 169$ ← **Subtract 169 from each side.**

$a^2 = 27$ ← **Simplify.**

$\sqrt{a^2} = \sqrt{27}$ ← **Find the square root of each side.**

$a \approx 5.196152423$ ← **Simplify**

The top of the ramp is about 5.2 feet high.

Check Understanding 2 A ramp is attached to a rental truck forming a right triangle. The base of the triangle is 10 feet and the hypotenuse is 11 feet. How high is the top of the ramp? Round to the nearest tenth.

For more practice, see *Extra Practice*.

A Practice by Example

Find the missing side length of each right triangle. Exercise 1 has been started for you.

Example 1 (page 623)

1. 7, 24, c

$$a^2 + b^2 = c^2$$
$$7^2 + 24^2 = c^2$$
$$49 + 576 = c^2$$

2.

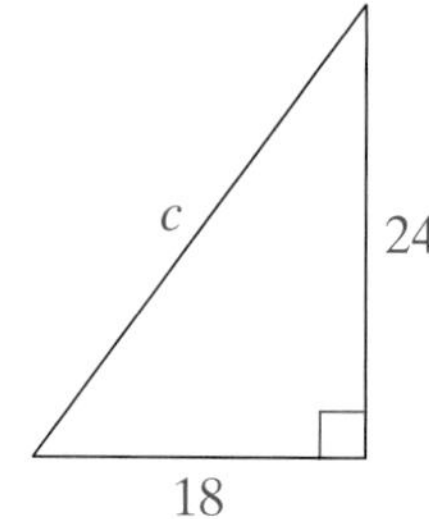

3. $a = 4, b = 3, c =$ ■

4. $a = 10, b = 24, c =$ ■

5. $a = 15, b = 12, c =$ ■

6. $a = 21, b = 20, c =$ ■

Example 2 (page 625)

7.

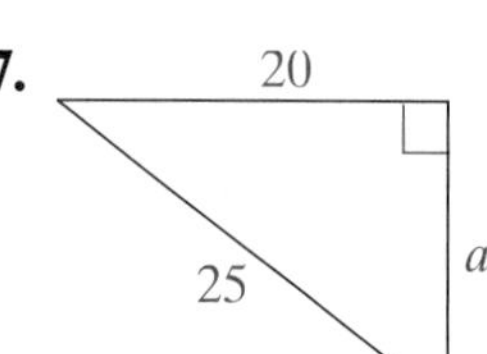

8.

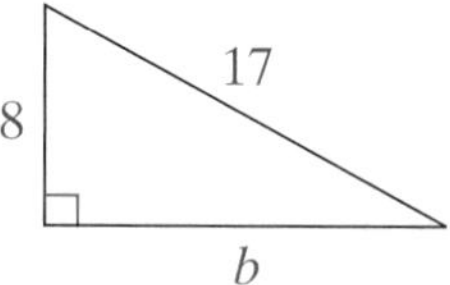

9. $a =$ ■, $b = 7, c = 9$

10. $a = 2, b =$ ■, $c = 5$

11. A 10-foot ladder leans against a building. The base of the ladder is 6 feet from the building. How high is the point where the ladder touches the building?

12. Flags Suppose you are sewing a Jamaican flag (like the one shown) that is 4 feet by 6 feet. How long will the yellow strip of fabric be? Round to the nearest tenth.

B Apply Your Skills

Find the missing side length of each right triangle. Round to the nearest tenth.

13. $a = 1.2, b = 0.5, c =$ ■

14. $a = 6, b = 3, c =$ ■

15. $a = 3, b =$ ■, $c = 17$

16. $a =$ ■, $b = 9, c = 12$

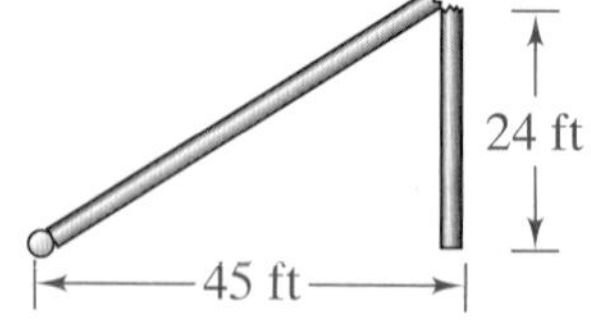

17. The broken pole at the left forms a right triangle with the ground. How tall was the pole before it was broken?

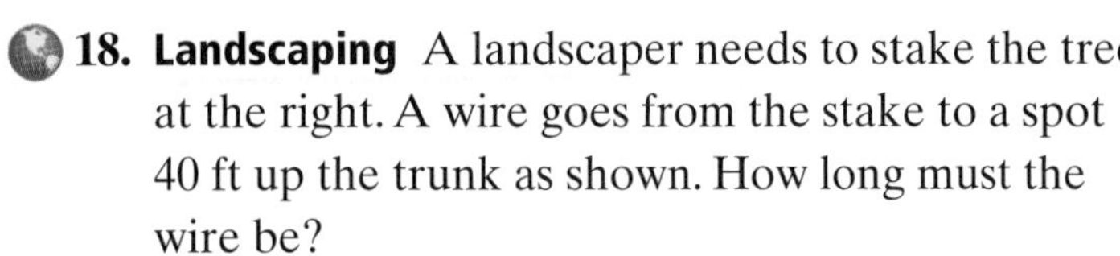

18. Landscaping A landscaper needs to stake the tree at the right. A wire goes from the stake to a spot 40 ft up the trunk as shown. How long must the wire be?

19. Number Sense A set of three whole numbers that are the lengths of the sides of a right triangle is called a Pythagorean triple. Tell whether each of the following is a Pythagorean triple.

a. $a = 9, b = 12, c = 15$
b. $a = 1, b = 2, c = 4$
c. $a = 5, b = 6, c = 11$
d. $a = 45, b = 24, c = 51$

In Exercises 21–23 you will be asked about diagonals. A *diagonal* of a rectangle connects opposite vertices like the one shown at the right.

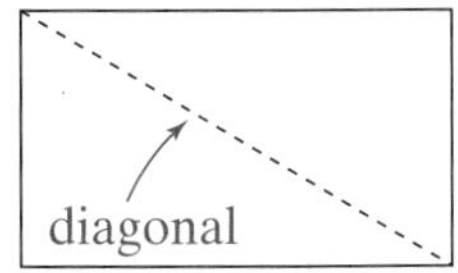

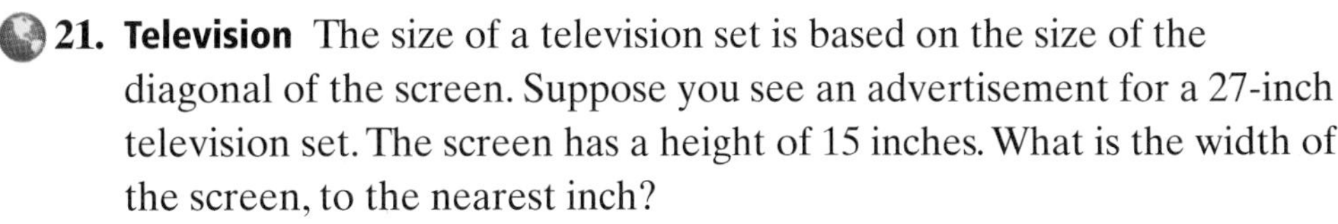

20. Framing Corey is constructing a picture frame. The length of the frame is 24 inches and the width is 10 inches. To make sure the frame has square corners, Corey measures the diagonal. What should be the length of the diagonal?

21. Television The size of a television set is based on the size of the diagonal of the screen. Suppose you see an advertisement for a 27-inch television set. The screen has a height of 15 inches. What is the width of the screen, to the nearest inch?

22. Quilting The diagonals for a quilting frame must be the same length to ensure the frame is rectangular. To the nearest tenth, what should the lengths of the diagonals be for a quilting frame 86 inches by 100 inches? Round to the nearest tenth of an inch.

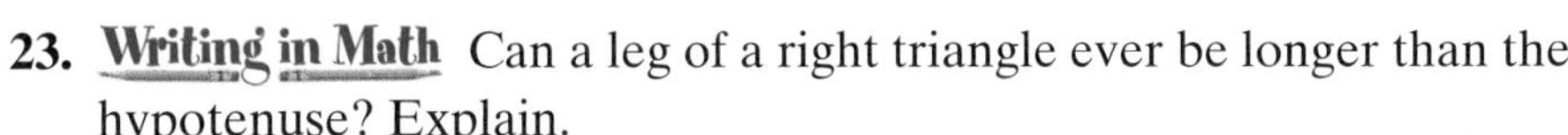

23. Writing in Math Can a leg of a right triangle ever be longer than the hypotenuse? Explain.

24. Algebra Use the Pythagorean Theorem to write an equation that expresses the relationship between the legs and the hypotenuse for the triangle at the right.

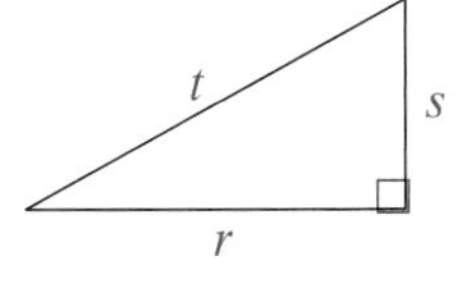

Challenge

25. Draw a triangle with a hypotenuse that is $\sqrt{2}$ inches long.

26. Number Sense What is the hypotenuse of a triangle whose legs are $\sqrt{9}$ and $\sqrt{16}$ inches long?

27. Stretch Your Thinking A door is 6 feet 8 inches tall and 3 feet wide. Suppose you need to fit a board that is 7 feet 3 inches wide through the doorway. Will it fit?

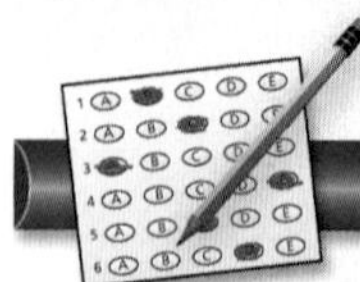

Test Prep

Multiple Choice

28. A right triangle has a leg measuring 9 feet and a hypotenuse measuring 15 feet. What is the length of the other leg in feet?

A. 12 **B.** 81 **C.** 144 **D.** 225

29. A rectangular park is 120 meters long and 40 meters wide. If a walk is built along a diagonal of the park, about how many meters long will the walk be?

F. 126 **G.** 400 **H.** 1,600 **I.** 14,400

30. Two girls walked along a 17-mile trail in a forest. They headed 5 miles due east and then 12 miles due north. If they were to make their own trail directly back to where they started, how long would the trail be?

A. 11 miles **B.** 13 miles **C.** 17 miles **D.** 34 miles

Extended Response

31. A surveyor needs to find the distance from point A to point B across the pond shown at the right. The surveyor sets a stake at point C so that $\angle B$ is a right angle. He measures the distance from point B to point C as 40 meters. The distance from point A to point C is 50 meters.

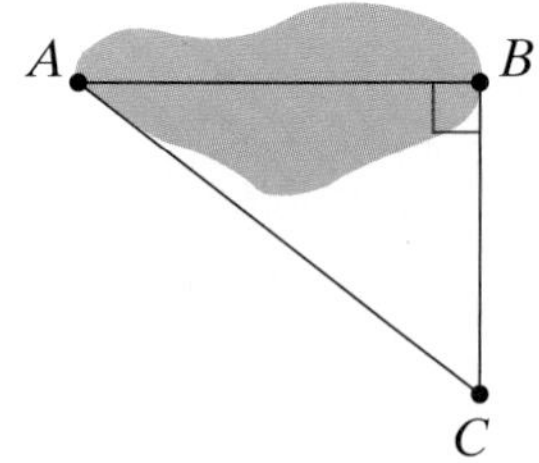

a. Write an equation relating the lengths of the triangle.

b. Explain in words how to solve the equation for the missing length. Then solve the equation.

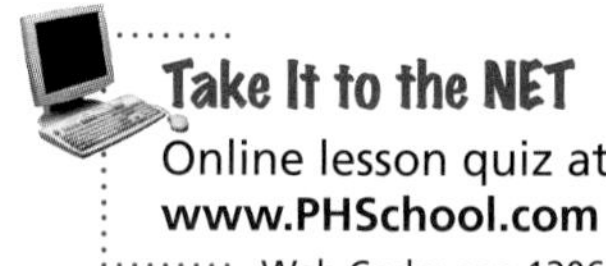

Online lesson quiz at **www.PHSchool.com**

Web Code: aaa-1206

Mixed Review

Lesson 11-7

A bag contains 3 red, 2 blue, and 1 green marble. Marbles are drawn twice with replacement. Find the probability of each compound event.

32. both blue

33. both red and blue

34. blue, then green

35. red, then *not* red

Lesson 10-1

Find each value.

36. $|0|$ **37.** $|-3|$ **38.** $|85|$ **39.** $|-84|$

Compare using $<$ or $>$.

40. 9 ■ 4 **41.** 5 ■ −5 **42.** −8 ■ 43 **43.** 1 ■ −6

Finding Multiple Correct Answers

In questions with multiple correct answers, determine whether each option is true or false. Then choose the answer with options that are all true.

EXAMPLE

Fewer than 35 students are at a birthday party. Let s be the number of students at the birthday party. Which numbers are reasonable values for s?

I. 24
II. 33.5
III. 35

A. I only **B.** I and II **C.** I and III **D.** II and III

Begin by drawing a graph. 32 33 34 35 36 37 38

Test each option.

I. 24 True; 24 is on the graph.
II. 33.5 False; you cannot have 33.5 people.
III. 35 False; 35 is not on the graph.

Since I is the only option that is true, the answer is A.

EXERCISES

1. Which numbers are solutions of $x \leq 0$?

I. -1
II. 0
III. 1

A. I only **B.** II only **C.** I and II **D.** I, II, and III

2. Which numbers are NOT solutions of $d \geq 2$?

I. 1
II. 2.5
III. 3

F. I only **G.** III only **H.** I and II **I.** I, II, and III

3. There are less than 4 boxes of cereal in the pantry. Let b be the number of cereal boxes in the pantry. Which numbers are reasonable values for b?

I. -4
II. 0
III. 4

A. I only **B.** II **C.** I and II **D.** I, II, and III

Chapter 12 Chapter Review

Vocabulary

graph of an inequality (p. 602)
hypotenuse (p. 622)
inequality (p. 601)
legs (p. 622)
perfect square (p. 616)
Pythagorean Theorem (p. 622)
rational number (p. 617)
solution of an inequality (p. 602)
square root (p. 616)
two-step equation (p. 596)

Reading Math: Understanding Vocabulary

Choose the vocabulary term from the column on the right that best completes each sentence. Not all choices will be used.

1. A(n) __?__ in decimal form terminates or repeats.
2. A(n) __?__ is the square of a whole number.
3. A(n) __?__ is a mathematical sentence using the symbol $<$, $>$, $\leq$, $\geq$, or $\neq$.
4. The inverse of squaring a number is finding the __?__.
5. The longest side of a right triangle is called the __?__.

A. hypotenuse
B. inequality
C. leg
D. perfect square
E. rational number
F. square root

Take It to the NET
Online vocabulary quiz at **www.PHSchool.com**
Web Code: aaj-1251

Skills and Concepts

12-1 Objective

- To solve two-step equations

A **two-step equation** is an equation containing two operations. To solve a two-step equation, undo the addition or subtraction, then undo the multiplication or division.

Solve each equation. Check the solution.

6. $3h + 6 = 15$ **7.** $2j - 4 = -2$ **8.** $\frac{f}{5} + 4 = 29$

12-2 Objectives

- To write inequalities
- To identify solutions of inequalities

An **inequality** compares expressions that are not equal. A **solution of an inequality** is any number that makes the inequality true.

State whether the given number is a solution of $x \leq -4$.

9. 4 **10.** -4 **11.** -2 **12.** -6

Graph each inequality.

13. $p > -4$ **14.** $h < 8$ **15.** $k \geq -5$ **16.** $g \leq 3$

12-3 Objectives

▼ To solve inequalities by adding or subtracting

To solve an inequality, get the variable alone on one side of the inequality.

Solve each inequality.

17. $q + 6 < 9$ **18.** $t - 7 < -2$ **19.** $v - 4 > 12$ **20.** $y + 9 \geq -11$

12-4 Objective

▼ To solve a problem using two different methods

You can solve a problem using different strategies.

Solve each problem by either drawing a diagram or writing an equation. Explain why you chose the method you did.

21. There are 35 people at a banquet. Three-fifths of the people are wearing black pants. How many people are wearing black pants?

22. A student cuts strips from a sheet that measures 60 inches by 80 inches Each strip is 2 inches by 13 inches. How many strips can the student cut?

12-5 Objectives

▼ To find square roots

▼ To classify numbers as rational

A **square root** of a number is a number that, when multiplied by itself, is the given number. A **perfect square** is the square of a whole number.

A **rational number** is a number that can be written as a quotient of two integers, where the divisor is not 0.

Find each square root. Round to the nearest tenth, if necessary.

23. $\sqrt{81}$ **24.** $\sqrt{24}$ **25.** $\sqrt{30}$ **26.** $\sqrt{144}$

Tell which two consecutive whole numbers each square root is between.

27. $\sqrt{6}$ **28.** $\sqrt{12}$ **29.** $\sqrt{21}$ **30.** $\sqrt{31}$

Tell whether each number is rational.

31. $0.\overline{3}$ **32.** $\sqrt{18}$ **33.** 0.123 **34.** $\sqrt{64}$

12-6 Objective

▼ To use the Pythagorean Theorem

The **Pythagorean Theorem** states that, given the triangle at the right, $a^2 + b^2 = c^2$.

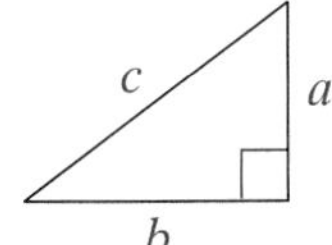

Find the missing side length of each right triangle. Round to the nearest tenth, if necessary.

35. $a = 6, b = 8, c = ■$ **36.** $a = 15, b = ■, c = 17$

37. $a = 1, b = 2, c = ■$ **38.** $a = ■, b = 6, c = 8$

Chapter 12 Chapter Test

Take It to the NET
Online chapter test at
www.PHSchool.com
Web Code: aaa-1252

Solve each equation. Check the solution.

1. $4u + 7 = 35$
2. $6r - 4 = 20$
3. $\frac{f}{3} + 5 = 20$
4. $\frac{n}{8} - 2 = -1$
5. An eraser and five pencils cost \$1.20. If the eraser costs \$.45, how much is each pencil?
6. Write an inequality for each situation.
   a. There are less than 6 hamsters in the cage.
   b. Fifty or more people are at the county fair.
7. Write an inequality for the graph below.

   −9 −8 −7 −6 −5 −4 −3

8. Tell whether each number is a solution of $c \leq -8$.
   a. 8 **b.** −7 **c.** −8 **d.** −10

Graph each inequality on a number line.

9. $w > -5$
10. $x \leq 4$
11. $y < 7$
12. $z \geq -12$
13. **Writing in Math** Is −9 a solution of the inequality $d \leq -9$? Explain.

Solve each inequality.

14. $j + 4 \geq 9$
15. $k - 6 < 2$
16. $s - 6 < 42$
17. $f + 2 \geq -1$
18. **Bank Fees** You have \$159 in a bank account. You need at least \$200 to avoid bank fees. Write and solve an inequality to find how much more money you should deposit.

Solve the problem by either drawing a diagram or writing an equation. Explain why you chose the method you did.

19. **Jogging** A person jogs 520 feet per minute. If the person continues to jog at the same rate, how far will the person jog in 30 minutes?
20. Your friend bought cream cheese for \$2.10 and bagels for \$.50 each. She spent a total of \$6.60. How many bagels did your friend buy?

Find the square root. Round to the nearest tenth, if necessary.

21. $\sqrt{25}$
22. $\sqrt{49}$
23. $\sqrt{60}$

Tell which two consecutive whole numbers each square root is between.

24. $\sqrt{5}$
25. $\sqrt{14}$
26. $\sqrt{97}$

Tell whether each number is rational.

27. $\sqrt{14}$
28. $5.\overline{5}$
29. $\frac{1}{13}$

Find the missing side length.

30.
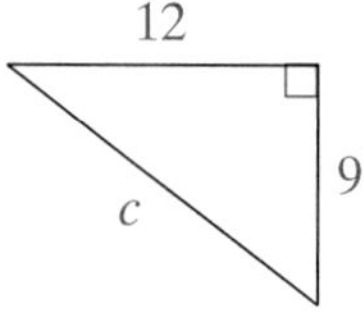

31.
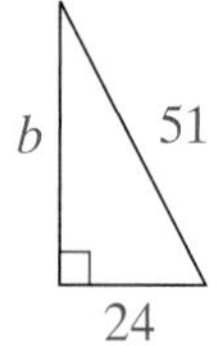

32. The solution to which inequality is represented by the graph below?

   −8 −7 −6 −5 −4 −3 −2

   A. $25 > y + 20$ **B.** $y - 5 < -10$
   C. $y - 15 > -20$ **D.** $y + 10 \geq -15$

Test Prep

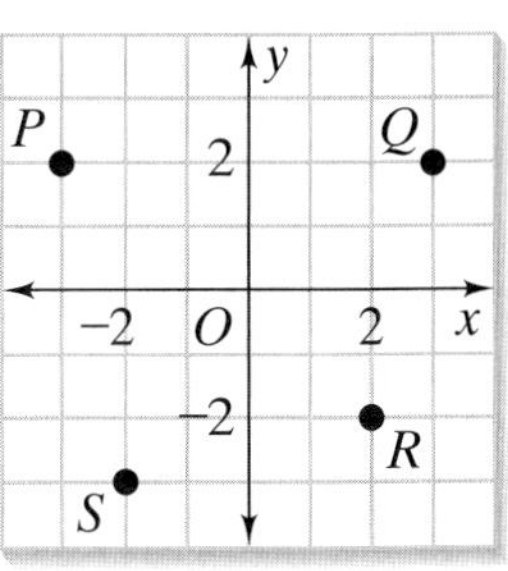

Multiple Choice

Choose the correct letter.

1. What operation would you perform first in the expression $3.9 + 4.1 \times 16 - 6 \div 4.8$?
A. Add 3.9 and 4.1.
B. Multiply 4.1 and 16.
C. Subtract 6 from 16.
D. Divide 10 by 4.8.

2. Four servers at a restaurant equally share $87.44 in tips. How much does each server receive?
F. $20.68 **G.** $20.86
H. $21.86 **I.** $22.86

3. Find the next two terms in the pattern: 2, 6, 12, 20, . . .
A. 24, 32 **B.** 28, 36
C. 30, 42 **D.** 32, 44

4. Solve the equation $0.2x = 46$.
F. 2.3 **G.** 9.2 **H.** 23 **I.** 230

5. Find the quotient $0.317 \div 0.08$.
A. 0.039625 **B.** 3.9625
C. 39.625 **D.** 396.25

6. Simplify the expression $4 + 6 \times (-3) - (-10) \div (-2)$.
F. -19 **G.** -10 **H.** 10 **I.** 19

7. Solve the equation $c + 3\frac{2}{3} = 7\frac{4}{5}$.
A. $3\frac{2}{15}$ **B.** $3\frac{7}{15}$ **C.** $4\frac{2}{15}$ **D.** $4\frac{7}{15}$

8. Estimate the product $7\frac{3}{8} \times 5\frac{3}{4}$.
F. 35 **G.** 40 **H.** 42 **I.** 48

9. Find the reciprocal of $4\frac{2}{5}$.
A. $\frac{5}{22}$ **B.** $\frac{1}{4}$ **C.** $\frac{5}{2}$ **D.** $2\frac{4}{5}$

10. What is the ordered pair for *P*?
F. (3, 2)
G. (−2, −3)
H. (2, −2)
I. (−3, 2)

11. Estimate the 8% sales tax for a sweater that costs $29.99.
A. $2.40 **B.** $20.40
C. $24.00 **D.** $240.00

12. Which of the following is NOT equivalent to 48%?
F. $\frac{48}{100}$ **G.** $\frac{24}{50}$ **H.** 0.048 **I.** 0.48

13. Which of the following is the most appropriate choice to display your height for each year since your birth.
A. circle graph **B.** line plot
C. bar graph **D.** frequency table

14. What is the value of cell D3 in the spreadsheet below?

	A	B	C	D
1	Test A	Test B	Test C	Mean
2	92	86	80	
3	79	82	82	
4	95	95	95	

F. 81 **G.** 86 **H.** 243 **I.** 285

15. Find the LCM of 20, 35, and 100.
A. 5 **B.** 10 **C.** 100 **D.** 700

16. You buy tape and seven boxes for $18.55. If the tape costs $2.10, how much is each box?
F. $.70 **G.** $2.35
H. $2.65 **I.** $2.95

17. Solve the proportion $\frac{2m}{21} = \frac{8}{35}$.

A. $1\frac{3}{5}$ B. $2\frac{2}{5}$ C. 7 D. 12

18. Which drawing shows a rotation of the face below?

F. 

G.

H. 

I. 

19. Which decimal is equivalent to $\frac{3}{8}$?

A. 0.037 B. 0.375 C. 0.38 D. 3.75

20. Solve $-9 + w < 12$.

F. $w < -21$ G. $w > -21$

H. $w < 21$ I. $w > 21$

21. What is 4.3 in words?

A. four and thirteen hundredths
B. four hundred and three
C. forty-three
D. four and three tenths

22. Which of the following is NOT true about the diagram below?

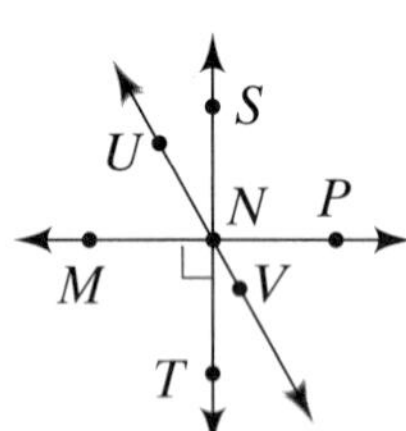

F. $\angle TNV$ is congruent to $\angle SNU$.
G. $\angle SNP$ is a right angle.
H. $\angle UNS$ is congruent to $\angle PNV$.
I. $\overleftrightarrow{ST}$ is perpendicular to $\overleftrightarrow{NP}$.

23. Which set of numbers is ordered from least to greatest?

A. $\frac{1}{2}, \frac{3}{4}, \frac{2}{3}, \frac{4}{5}, \frac{9}{10}$ B. $\frac{1}{2}, \frac{2}{3}, \frac{3}{4}, \frac{4}{5}, \frac{9}{10}$

C. $\frac{1}{3}, \frac{1}{2}, \frac{2}{3}, \frac{9}{10}, \frac{4}{5}$ D. $\frac{1}{4}, \frac{3}{10}, \frac{8}{5}, \frac{1}{2}, \frac{2}{3}$

Gridded Response

24. A bag contains 1 red marble, 1 yellow marble, and 1 green marble. Your friend choses the yellow marble. Your turn is next. If the yellow marble is NOT replaced in the bag, find the probability that you will choose the red marble.

25. Out of a sample of 125 CDs, 9 were found to have scratches. In a shipment of 5,000 CDs, how many would you predict will have scratches?

26. Find the surface area in square feet of the figure below.

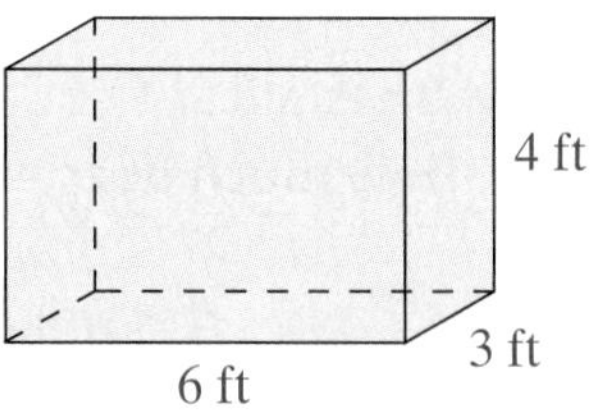

27. The probability of losing a particular game is 55%. Suppose you play this game 20 times. How many times would you expect to win the game?

28. Solve the equation $4j - 8 = 12$ for j.

29. Find the number of permutations of the letters in the word WYOMING.

30. Write 5.6×10^3 in standard form.

31. Simplify the expression $(16 - 8) \times 2 + (10 \div 100)$.

32. Evaluate the expression $j \div 10 + 8.3$ for $j = 11$.

33. Simplify the expression $3 \times 8 - 4 + 5$.

34. Find the measure in degrees of $\angle KLM$.

Short Response

Show your work.

35. No more than 12 students volunteered to work at the local food pantry.
   a. Write an inequality for this situation.
   b. Graph the solution on a number line.

36. a. Find $\sqrt{19}$.
   b. Is the $\sqrt{19}$ a rational number?

37. You and a friend walk along a 14-mile trail in a park. You head 8 miles due west and then 6 miles due south. If you make your own trail directly back to where you started, how long would the trail be?

38. The triangles below are congruent. Write two congruences involving corresponding parts of the triangles.

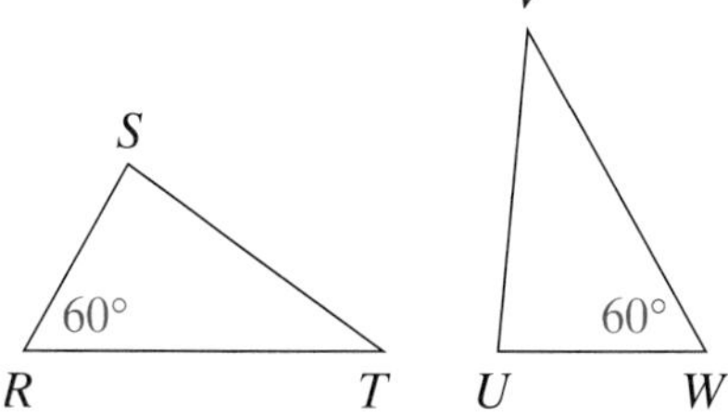

39. Write and then use an equation to find 43% of 87.

40. Sam works at a book store. When he punched in, the time clock read 3:15 P.M. When he punched out, the time clock read 7:45 P.M. He took a 15-minute break. How long did he work?

41. Solve $-\frac{b}{2} + 5 = 4$.

42. Solve $-\frac{k}{4} > 7$.

43. Find the prime factorization of 98 by using a factor tree.

44. A map with the scale 5 inches : 325 miles shows two landmarks that are 2 inches apart. How many miles apart are the landmarks?

Extended Response

45. Find the mean, median, and mode of the data in the line plot.

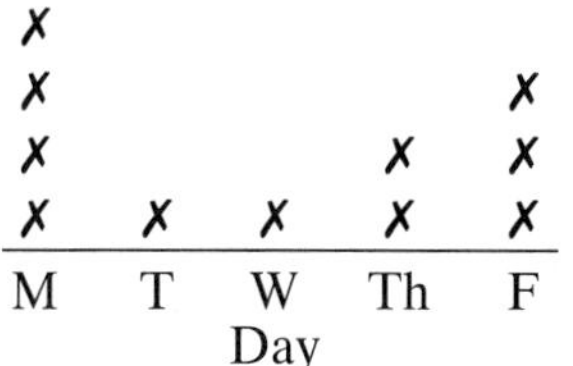

46. Three candy bars will cost you at least $1.83.
   a. Write an inequality for this situation.
   b. Solve the inequality.
   c. Graph the solution on a number line.

47. A rectangle measures 5 inches by 7 inches.
   a. What is the area of the rectangle?
   b. A 1-inch by 1-inch square is cut from each corner of the rectangle. What is the area of the new figure? Explain.

48. An open box is made by folding the sides of the net below.

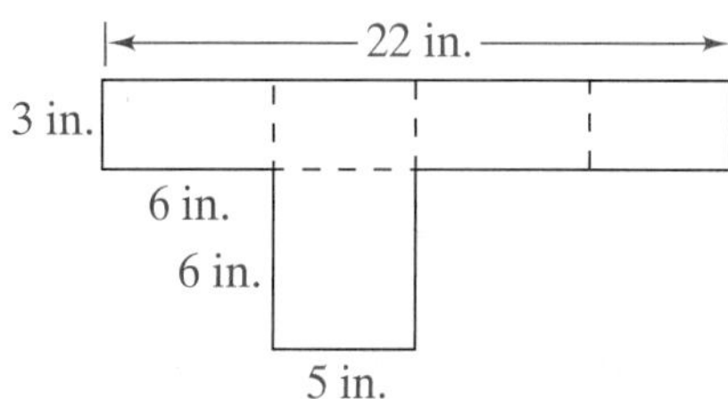

   a. Find the surface area of the open box.
   b. Now find the volume of the box.

49. The cost of your dinner is $18.64. You want to leave a 15% tip for the server.
   a. How much is the tip?
   b. What is the total cost of dinner, excluding any tax?

50. A store sells socks in two colors (gray or white), three sizes (small, medium, or large), and two fabrics (cotton or wool).
   a. Make a tree diagram to find the number of sock choices.
   b. If the store has one of every type of sock, what is the probability you will choose a wool sock at random?

Real-World Snapshots

A Bright Idea

Applying Equations Suppose you are changing the light bulbs in your bedroom. Regular (incandescent) light bulbs provide light, but they also get warm. Fluorescent light bulbs stay cool because they convert more energy into light. They cost more than regular bulbs, but they're cheaper to run. Should you replace your regular bulbs with fluorescent bulbs?

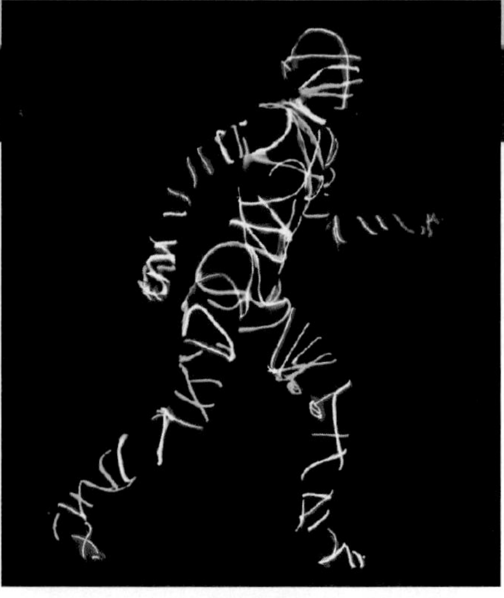

Neon Light

Colored glass tubes filled with neon gas glow when an electrical charge moves through the gas.

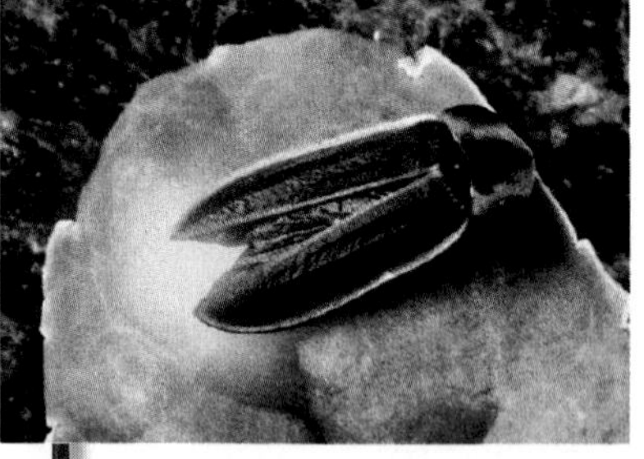

Fireflies

Fireflies, or lightning bugs, make light inside their bodies. The light can be any color from pale yellow to reddish green.

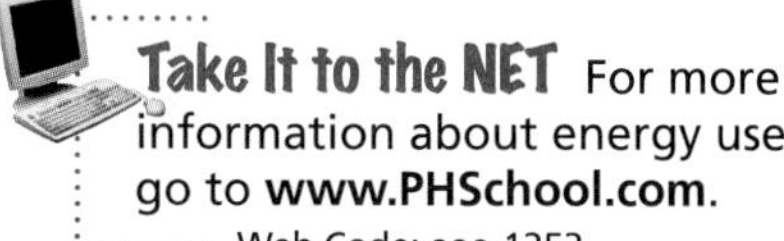

Take It to the NET For more information about energy use, go to **www.PHSchool.com**.
Web Code: aae-1253

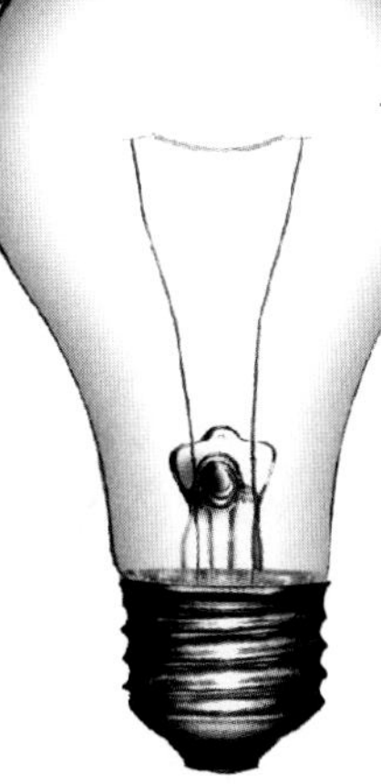

Incandescent light bulb
Cost: $1.80
Power: 100 watts per hour
Duration: 1,000 hours

Electricity costs $.15 per kilowatt-hour.

Fluorescent light bulb
Cost: $15.80
Power: 32 watts per hour
Duration: 10,000 hours

Fiber-Optic Light

Each hair-thin optical fiber has two layers of glass. Light travels from one end of the fiber to the other by bouncing along the sides of the fiber. A transparent colored disc between the light bulb and the fibers gives the fibers their color.

Put It All Together

1. How much more does a fluorescent light bulb cost than an incandescent light bulb?

2. a. How much power does each bulb use in 10 hours?

b. Divide your answer to part (a) by 1,000 to find the number of kilowatt-hours each bulb uses in 10 hours.

c. What is the cost of electricity for each bulb for 10 hours of use? Round your answer to the nearest cent.

3. Suppose the light is on for 10 hours each day.

a. How many of each type of bulb would you use in one year? (*Hint:* 1 year = 365 days)

b. How much would one year's supply of each type of bulb cost?

c. What is the cost of electricity for each bulb for one year? Round your answer to the nearest cent.

d. Calculate your total cost for each type of bulb for one year.

4. **Writing in Math** Which type of light bulb would you recommend to a friend? Explain.

Chapter Projects

Chapter 1 *Decimals*

Suppose your class is planning to honor someone special in the community or to congratulate a winning team. You need to decide when and where you will hold the event, how you will decorate, and what entertainment and refreshments you will provide. You may also need to decide how to raise funds for the celebration.

Plan a Celebration Your chapter project is to plan a celebration. You must decide how much it will cost and how much money each member of the class must raise. Your plan should include a list of supplies for the event and their costs.

Take It to the NET Go to **www.PHSchool.com** for information to help you complete your project.
Web Code: aad-0161

STEPPING STONES

Chapter 2 *Patterns and Variables*

Think about a historic building, such as one of the ancient pyramids or the Eiffel Tower. How many pieces of stone do you think were needed for the bottom of a pyramid compared to a layer near the top? Many buildings use mathematical patterns in their designs.

Building a Fort For this project, you will build a model of a simple fort. You will record the amounts of materials needed for each layer. You will look for patterns and write equations to describe the patterns.

Take It to the NET Go to **www.PHSchool.com** for information to help you complete your project.
Web Code: aad-0261

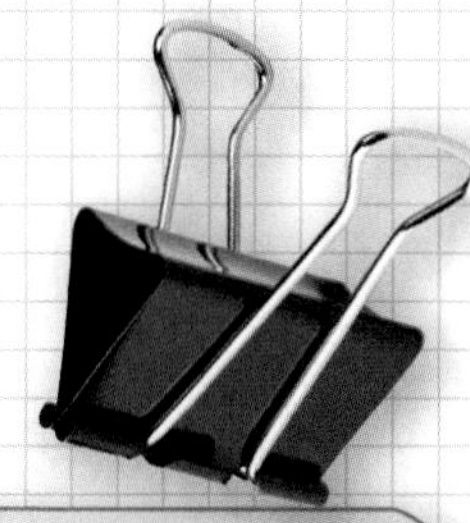

HOME COURT ADVANTAGE

Chapter 3 Number Theory and Fractions

In Malcolm's daydream, he floats in the air on the way to a slam dunk. In reality, he tosses pieces of paper into a wastebasket. He makes some shots, and he misses others.

Compare Basketball Statistics Your project will be to record and compare baskets attempted and baskets made by the players on your own imaginary basketball team. You can shoot baskets with a real basketball on a real court, or you can toss pieces of paper into a wastebasket.

Take It to the NET Go to **www.PHSchool.com** for information to help you complete your project.
Web Code: aad-0361

SEEing is Believing

Chapter 4 Adding and Subtracting Fractions

Have you ever conducted a science experiment? Scientists perform experiments to prove if an idea is correct or incorrect. You can prove if something is correct or not in math class, too.

Design a Demonstration You will learn ways to add fractions and mixed numbers with unlike denominators, but can you prove these techniques really work? Your goal is to prove that they do by giving several demonstrations.

Take It to the NET Go to **www.PHSchool.com** for information to help you complete your project.
Web Code: aad-0461

Crack It and Cook It!

Chapter 5 Multiplying and Dividing Fractions

Eating a hearty breakfast is a great way to start any day! You are probably familiar with pouring a bowl of cereal, making toast, or maybe even scrambling eggs. But have you ever made an omelet? An omelet recipe can be pretty simple—eggs, water, and maybe some salt or pepper. However, you can add other ingredients to this basic recipe to suit your taste. A cheese omelet is delicious. So is a bacon-and-tomato omelet. You might also add mushrooms, onions, and peppers.

Create a Recipe Put on your chef's hat. In this chapter project, you will write and name your own recipe for an omelet. Your final project will be a recipe that can feed everyone in your class.

Take It to the NET Go to **www.PHSchool.com** for information to help you complete your project.
Web Code: aad-0561

Planet of the Stars

Chapter 6 Ratios, Proportions, and Percents

When you look up at the stars in the sky, you may not think about how far away they are. Stars appear a lot closer than they really are. The same is true of planets. The huge distances between planets make it impossible for books to show how vast our solar system really is.

Make a Scale Model In this chapter project, you will make scale models of two planets. You will compare their sizes and distances from the sun and calculate the ratios involved in your scale model.

Take It to the NET Go to **www.PHSchool.com** for information to help you complete your project.
Web Code: aad-0661

ON YOUR OWN TIME

Chapter 7 Data and Graphs

RING!!! The last bell of the day has rung. You and your classmates will soon head in different directions. Some of your classmates are on the same team or in the same club as you. Some of them are not. Do you know how much time your classmates spend on their favorite activities? You could guess the answers to the last question, but a more accurate method of finding the answers would be to collect real data.

Conduct a Survey For this chapter project, you will survey 25 of your friends and classmates. You can choose the survey subject, such as how much time your classmates spend on sports. You will organize and graph the data. Then you will present your findings to your class.

Take It to the NET Go to **www.PHSchool.com** for information to help you complete your project.
Web Code: aad-0761

Puzzling Pictures

Chapter 8 Tools of Geometry

Do you remember putting together simple puzzles when you were younger? Puzzles designed for young children are often made of wood and have large pieces. The pieces have straight sides so that the child can put the puzzle together easily.

Create a Puzzle Think about one of your favorite pictures. How would it look as a puzzle? Your project is to make an attractive but challenging puzzle for your classmates. Include as many geometric shapes as you can.

Take It to the NET Go to **www.PHSchool.com** for information to help you complete your project.
Web Code: aad-0861

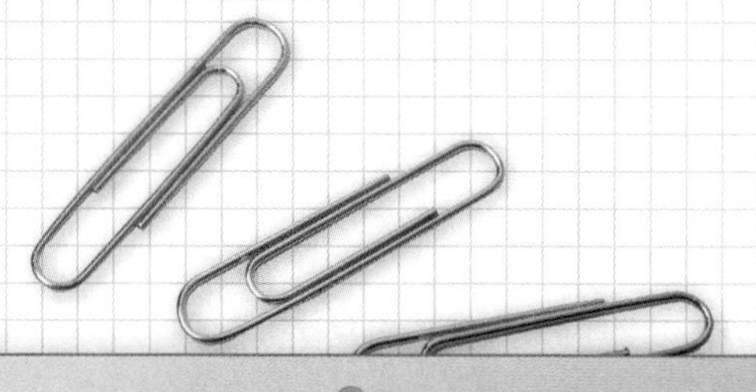

Go Fish

Chapter 9 Geometry and Measurement

Have you ever spent time gazing into an aquarium full of fish? You can get lost in thought as you look through the glass watching the fish. Many people enjoy having an aquarium because they feel peaceful while observing nature in this miniature form.

Design an Aquarium In this chapter project, you will design an aquarium for your classroom. You should consider how many fish you want in the aquarium. Also consider the size of each type of fish that you plan to place in the aquarium. As part of your final project, you will create a drawing of your proposed aquarium.

Take It to the NET Go to **www.PHSchool.com** for information to help you complete your project.
Web Code: aad-0961

The TIME of your life

Chapter 10 Integers

Do you know an older person who has lived an interesting life? That person could probably tell you a lot of stories about his or her life. You can tell stories about your life, too. You may not have lived as long, but there have been important events in your past, and there will be others in your future.

Draw a Time Line Your project will be to build a time line of your life—past, present, and future. Think about the time lines you have seen in your social studies classes. You will have a chance to apply math skills such as ratios, measurements, scale drawings, and integers.

Take It to the NET Go to **www.PHSchool.com** for information to help you complete your project.
Web Code: aad-1061

Chapter 11 *Exploring Probability*

Suppose you and a friend have to choose among three movies, and you can't make up your mind. Should you flip a coin? You'd probably agree that assigning "heads" to one movie, "tails" to the second, and "lands on edge" to the third would not give the third movie much of a chance. What should you do?

Design a Three-Choice System Your project will be to design a device or system that is equally fair to three different outcomes. You will test your system to make sure each outcome can be expected one third of the time over a large number of trials.

Take It to the NET Go to **www.PHSchool.com** for information to help you complete your project.
Web Code: aad-1161

WORKING for a Cause

Chapter 12 *Equations and Inequalities*

Have you ever participated in a fundraiser? Schools and sports clubs often use fundraisers as a way to pay for such things as equipment, trips, and camps. You have probably purchased candy bars, magazines, or wrapping paper to help a friend raise money.

Plan a Fundraiser In this chapter project, you will plan a fundraiser. You will choose a cause or charity, decide how much money you would like to raise, and determine the type of event to hold or the type of product to sell. As part of your final project, you will present a fundraising plan to your class.

Take It to the NET Go to **www.PHSchool.com** for information to help you complete your project.
Web Code: aad-1261

Chapter 1 Extra Practice

Lesson 1-1 and Lesson 1-2 Write each number in words.

1. 854
2. 10,059
3. 7,302
4. 1,205,807
5. 0.26
6. 0.3481
7. 72.053
8. 691.4

Write each number in standard form.

9. two hundred sixteen
10. two hundred twenty-two thousandths

Lesson 1-3 Order each set of decimals from least to greatest.

11. 0.2, 0.4, 0.7
12. 0.2, 0.02, 0.202, 0.002
13. 6.25, 6.05, 6.2, 6.025

Lesson 1-4 Use rounding, front-end estimation, or compatible numbers to estimate.

14. 5.32×2.01
15. $15.348 - 7.92$
16. $22.961 \div 3.6$
17. $728.6 + 36.09$

Lesson 1-5 First estimate and then find each sum or difference.

18. $1.14 + 9.3$
19. $3.541 + 1.333$
20. $5.45 - 2.8$
21. $4.11 - 2.621$

Lesson 1-6 Use Problem-Solving Plan to solve the problem.

22. A bag of popcorn costs \$2.35. A coupon will save you \$2.00 on 4 bags. How much will 5 bags cost before tax if you use the coupon?

Lesson 1-7 Find each product.

23. 1.8×4.302
24. $0.29(0.43)$
25. $7.4(930)$
26. $0.617 \cdot 0.09$

Lesson 1-8 Use mental math to find each product or quotient.

27. $3.85 \times 1{,}000$
28. $100 \cdot 2.7$
29. $93.1 \div 10$
30. $105 \div 1{,}000$

Lesson 1-9 Find each quotient. Identify each as a terminating or repeating decimal.

31. $8 \div 9$
32. $23 \div 25$
33. $348 \div 60$
34. $11 \div 16$

Lesson 1-10 Find the value of each expression.

35. $2 + 6 \times 3 + 1$
36. $(14 + 44) \div 2$
37. $3 + 64 \div 4 - 10$
38. $144 + 56 \div 4$

Chapter 2 Extra Practice

Lesson 2-1 Write the next three terms and write a rule to describe each number pattern.

1. 1, 4, 16, 64, . . . **2.** 2, 6, 18, 54, . . . **3.** 7, 11, 15, 19, . . . **4.** 80, 74, 68, 62, . . .

Lesson 2-2 Evaluate each expression for $n = 9$.

5. $n - 7$ **6.** $3n - 5$ **7.** $22 - 2n$ **8.** $4n \div 6$

Lesson 2-3 Write an expression for each word phrase.

9. 1 less than *b* **10.** *p* times 2 **11.** 4 more than *b* **12.** *n* divided by 2

Lesson 2-4 Use the strategy *Make a Table and Look for a Pattern.*

13. For \$3.00, Audrey buys a sandwich and milk for lunch. Suppose the amount she spends for lunch increases \$.10 each day. What will Audrey pay for lunch on the sixth day?

Lesson 2-5 Tell whether each equation is true or false.

14. $65 = 10 + 85$ **15.** $8 \times 6 = 48$ **16.** $1 \times 9.8 = 9.8$ **17.** $9 = 24 \div 3$

Use mental math to solve each equation.

18. $20 = y + 1$ **19.** $t - 10 = 24$ **20.** $a \div 3 = 3$ **21.** $178 = 10b$

Lessons 2-6 and 2-7 Solve each equation. Then check the solution.

22. $b + 4 = 7.7$ **23.** $c + 3.5 = 7.5$ **24.** $n - 1.7 = 8$ **25.** $8.4 = s - 0.2$

26. $15t = 600$ **27.** $62 = 2b$ **28.** $x \div 5 = 2.5$ **29.** $a \div 0.05 = 140$

Lesson 2-8 Write each number in expanded form using powers of 10.

30. 9,450 **31.** 72,003 **32.** 300,026 **33.** 8,120,432

Simplify each expression.

34. $7 + 5^2$ **35.** $(6 - 2)^3 \times 3$ **36.** 8^3 **37.** $9^2 + 2^2$

Lesson 2-9 Use the Distributive Property to simplify each expression.

38. 7×78 **39.** 3×19 **40.** 6×66 **41.** 4×47

Chapter 3

Extra Practice

Lesson 3-1 Test each number for divisibility by 2, 3, 5, 9, or 10.

1. 324 **2.** 2,685 **3.** 540 **4.** 114 **5.** 31 **6.** 981

Lesson 3-2 Tell whether each number is prime or composite.

7. 24 **8.** 49 **9.** 7 **10.** 81 **11.** 37 **12.** 29

Lesson 3-3 Find the GCF of each set of numbers.

13. 10, 30 **14.** 15, 18 **15.** 25, 35 **16.** 28, 36 **17.** 45, 72 **18.** 8, 12, 20

Lesson 3-4 Write each fraction in simplest form.

19. $\frac{6}{60}$ **20.** $\frac{3}{5}$ **21.** $\frac{27}{36}$ **22.** $\frac{40}{50}$ **23.** $\frac{3}{4}$ **24.** $\frac{42}{70}$

Lesson 3-5 Write each mixed number as an improper fraction. Write each improper fraction as a mixed number in simplest form.

25. $1\frac{7}{8}$ **26.** $2\frac{3}{5}$ **27.** $11\frac{1}{9}$ **28.** $\frac{25}{7}$ **29.** $\frac{39}{12}$ **30.** $\frac{12}{5}$

Lesson 3-6 Find the LCM of each set of numbers.

31. 4, 8 **32.** 6, 14 **33.** 15, 25 **34.** 20, 36 **35.** 3, 4, 12 **36.** 8, 10, 15

Lesson 3-7 Order each set of numbers from least to greatest.

37. $\frac{4}{7}, \frac{4}{5}, \frac{4}{9}$ **38.** $\frac{6}{16}, \frac{7}{16}, \frac{5}{16}$ **39.** $\frac{2}{3}, \frac{5}{6}, \frac{7}{12}$ **40.** $\frac{3}{4}, \frac{4}{6}, \frac{7}{9}$ **41.** $2\frac{3}{4}, 2\frac{1}{8}, 2\frac{1}{2}$ **42.** $\frac{5}{8}, \frac{3}{5}, \frac{9}{20}$

Lesson 3-8 Write each decimal as a fraction or mixed number in simplest form.

43. 1.25 **44.** 0.02 **45.** 0.32 **46.** 3.45 **47.** 0.175 **48.** 2.48

Write each fraction or mixed number as a decimal. Use a bar to indicate repeating digits.

49. $\frac{2}{3}$ **50.** $\frac{2}{5}$ **51.** $\frac{1}{4}$ **52.** $7\frac{5}{12}$ **53.** $4\frac{2}{3}$ **54.** $\frac{13}{8}$

Lesson 3-9 Use the strategy *Try, Check, and Revise* to solve the problem.

55. Reed pays $.40 for tolls twice a day. He must use exact change. How many quarters, nickels, and dimes does he need for five days?

Chapter 4

Extra Practice

Lesson 4-1 **Estimate each sum or difference. Use the benchmarks 0, $\frac{1}{2}$, and 1.**

1. $\frac{2}{3} + \frac{1}{8}$ **2.** $\frac{3}{5} + \frac{4}{7}$ **3.** $\frac{5}{6} - \frac{3}{8}$ **4.** $\frac{3}{8} - \frac{1}{3}$

Estimate each sum or difference.

5. $12\frac{3}{4} - 7\frac{4}{9}$ **6.** $5\frac{7}{9} + 9\frac{3}{5}$ **7.** $2\frac{1}{3} - 1\frac{6}{7}$ **8.** $6\frac{3}{10} + 4\frac{5}{8}$

Lessons 4-2 and 4-3 **Find each sum or difference.**

9. $\frac{5}{8} + \frac{1}{8}$ **10.** $\frac{4}{5} - \frac{2}{5}$ **11.** $\frac{11}{12} + \frac{5}{12}$ **12.** $\frac{7}{8} - \frac{3}{8}$

13. $\frac{5}{6} + \frac{2}{3}$ **14.** $\frac{7}{8} - \frac{3}{4}$ **15.** $\frac{3}{5} + \frac{5}{8}$ **16.** $\frac{3}{8} - \frac{1}{12}$

Lesson 4-4 **Find each sum.**

17. $6\frac{2}{3} + 1\frac{1}{2}$ **18.** $5\frac{7}{8} + 1\frac{3}{4}$ **19.** $8\frac{1}{4} + 3\frac{1}{3}$ **20.** $7\frac{3}{10} + 3\frac{1}{4}$

Lesson 4-5 **Find each difference.**

21. $7\frac{3}{8} - 1\frac{2}{3}$ **22.** $11\frac{1}{6} - 2\frac{3}{4}$ **23.** $7\frac{5}{6} - 2\frac{1}{10}$ **24.** $6\frac{1}{3} - 2\frac{1}{4}$

Lesson 4-6 **Solve each equation.**

25. $x + 6\frac{4}{9} = 8\frac{1}{9}$ **26.** $y + 2\frac{3}{8} = 8\frac{1}{5}$ **27.** $a + 9 = 12\frac{7}{9}$ **28.** $4\frac{5}{7} = b - 3\frac{1}{2}$

29. $c - 11\frac{2}{3} = 15$ **30.** $n + 4\frac{1}{2} = 5$ **31.** $m - 5\frac{3}{4} = 10\frac{1}{2}$ **32.** $p - 8\frac{1}{3} = 9\frac{1}{4}$

Lesson 4-7 **Find the elapsed time between each pair of times.**

33. from 3:45 P.M. to 5:15 P.M. **34.** from 8:10 P.M. to 11:55 P.M.

35. from 11:45 A.M. to 6:23 P.M. **35.** from 4:05 A.M. to 4:10 P.M.

37. from 3:25 P.M. to 5:02 P.M. **38.** from 8:10 A.M. to 11:55 A.M.

Lesson 4-8 **Use the strategy *Draw a Diagram* to solve the problem.**

39. All pies at a bakery are the same size. Apple pies are cut into eight pieces. Custard pies are cut into six pieces. Two slices of apple pie and three slices of custard pie are placed in a pie tin for a carry-out order. What fraction of the pie tin is filled?

Chapter 5 Extra Practice

Lesson 5-1 Find each product.

1. $\frac{1}{2}$ of $\frac{2}{3}$

2. $\frac{1}{3}$ of $\frac{1}{5}$

3. $\frac{7}{8} \times \frac{3}{4}$

4. $\frac{7}{6} \times 42$

Lesson 5-2 Find each product.

5. $7\frac{1}{2} \times 2\frac{2}{3}$

6. $6\frac{2}{3} \times 7\frac{1}{5}$

7. $5\frac{5}{8} \times 2\frac{1}{3}$

8. $12\frac{1}{4} \times 6\frac{2}{7}$

Lesson 5-3 Find each quotient.

9. $2 \div \frac{4}{5}$

10. $\frac{2}{3} \div \frac{2}{5}$

11. $\frac{1}{4} \div \frac{1}{5}$

12. $\frac{4}{11} \div 8$

Lesson 5-4 Estimate each quotient.

13. $12 \div 3\frac{1}{5}$

14. $7\frac{3}{7} \div 1\frac{2}{5}$

15. $41\frac{8}{10} \div 6\frac{1}{3}$

16. $36\frac{2}{7} \div 4\frac{3}{9}$

Find each quotient.

17. $2\frac{1}{4} \div \frac{2}{3}$

18. $4\frac{1}{2} \div 3\frac{1}{3}$

19. $2\frac{2}{5} \div \frac{2}{25}$

20. $5\frac{2}{3} \div 1\frac{1}{2}$

Lesson 5-5 Solve each equation. Check the solution.

21. $\frac{x}{4} = 8$

22. $\frac{a}{3} = 9$

23. $\frac{c}{7} = 24$

24. $\frac{m}{2} = 14$

25. $\frac{r}{4} = 3.5$

26. $\frac{t}{12} = 3$

27. $\frac{1}{3}y = 15$

28. $\frac{3}{4}w = 12$

Lesson 5-6 Use the strategy *Solve a Simpler Problem* to solve the problem.

29. You want to make a quilt that is 75 inches long and 50 inches wide. How many $6\frac{1}{4}$-inch squares do you need?

Lesson 5-7 Choose an appropriate unit for each measurement. Explain.

30. capacity of a bathtub

31. weight of a school bus

32. width of a computer monitor

33. weight of a pair of jeans

34. your height

35. capacity of a water pitcher

Lesson 5-8 Complete each statement.

36. 4 ft = ■ yd

37. 48 oz = ■ lb

38. 32 qt = ■ gal

39. 8,000 lb = ■ T

40. 10 lb = ■ oz

41. ■ ft = 60 in.

42. 64 cups = ■ pt

43. 9 mi = ■ ft

Chapter 6

Extra Practice

Lesson 6-1 Write three ratios equal to each ratio.

1. $\frac{30}{60}$ **2.** 5:15 **3.** 13 to 52 **4.** 10:77 **5.** 18 to 72

Lesson 6-2 Find each unit price. Round to the nearest cent. Then determine the better buy.

6. cereal: 12 ounces for $2.99
16 ounces for $3.59

7. rice: 8 ounce for $1.95
12 ounces for $2.89

Lesson 6-3 Do the ratios in each pair form a proportion?

8. $\frac{6}{30}, \frac{3}{15}$ **9.** $\frac{9}{12}, \frac{12}{9}$ **10.** $\frac{13}{3}, \frac{26}{6}$ **11.** $\frac{5}{225}, \frac{2}{95}$ **12.** $\frac{64}{130}, \frac{5}{10}$

Lesson 6-4 Solve each proportion.

13. $\frac{a}{50} = \frac{3}{75}$ **14.** $\frac{18}{b} = \frac{3}{10}$ **15.** $\frac{51}{17} = \frac{c}{3}$ **16.** $\frac{2}{16} = \frac{d}{24}$ **17.** $\frac{3}{45} = \frac{4}{g}$

Lesson 6-5 Use a map scale of 1 centimeter : 100 kilometers.

18. 3.5 cm **19.** 1.3 cm **20.** 0.7 cm **21.** 5 cm

Lesson 6-6 Write each percent as a decimal and as a fraction in simplest form.

22. 42% **23.** 96% **24.** 80% **25.** 1% **26.** 87% **27.** 88%

Write each decimal or fraction as a percent.

28. 0.18 **29.** 0.32 **30.** 0.05 **31.** $\frac{1}{4}$ **32.** $\frac{3}{4}$ **33.** $\frac{5}{8}$

Lesson 6-7 Find each answer.

34. 20% of 80 **35.** 15% of 22.5 **36.** 50% of 86 **37.** 90% of 100

Lesson 6-8 Estimate a 15% tip for each bill amount.

38. $34.90 **39.** $9.54 **40.** $17.50 **41.** $24.80 **42.** $15.21 **43.** $42.36

Lesson 6-9 Use the strategy *Write an Equation* to solve the problem.

44. Kennedy Middle School has 550 students. If the number of students increases by 8 percent, how many students will there be?

Chapter 7 Extra Practice

Lesson 7-1 Find the mean, median, and mode of each data set.

1. 23, 26, 22, 25, 22, 28, 22, 10 **2.** 14.2, 11.3, 12.0, 11.1, 13.0, 13.3 **3.** 36, 42, 58, 29, 45, 63, 57, 29

Lesson 7-2 Make a frequency table and a line plot for each set of data.

4. books read each month: 3, 1, 4, 2, 4, 1, 3, 2, 4, 4, 2, 1

5. words typed per minute: 65, 35, 40, 65, 40, 40, 55, 35, 35, 70, 35, 55

Lesson 7-3 Use the strategy *Make an Organized List* to solve the problem.

6. How many ways can you make $1 using quarters, nickels, and dimes?

Lesson 7-4 Use bar graph for Exercises 7–8.

Average Yearly Reading by Americans

Hours per Person

200
150
100
50
0

Magazines Newspapers Books

Print

7. What information is given on each axis?

8. What is the average yearly reading time for books?

Lesson 7-5 Use the circle graph for Exercises 10–11.

Malinda's Budget

Clothes
Food
Rent
Savings
Other
Insurance
Charity

9. What item accounts for the most money in Malinda's budget?

10. About what percent of her budget does Malinda use for rent?

Lesson 7-6 The spreadsheet below shows the number of medals the United States earned during the 2000 Summer Olympics.

11. a. What is the value in C2?
b. What does this number mean?

12. Write the formula for cell E2.

	A	B	C	D	E
1	Country	Gold	Silver	Bronze	Total
2	United States	39	25	33	■

Lesson 7-7 Make a stem-and-leaf plot for the set of data below.

13. test scores (percents): 86, 74, 72, 89, 69, 85, 78, 91, 77

Lesson 7-8 Use the line graph at the right.

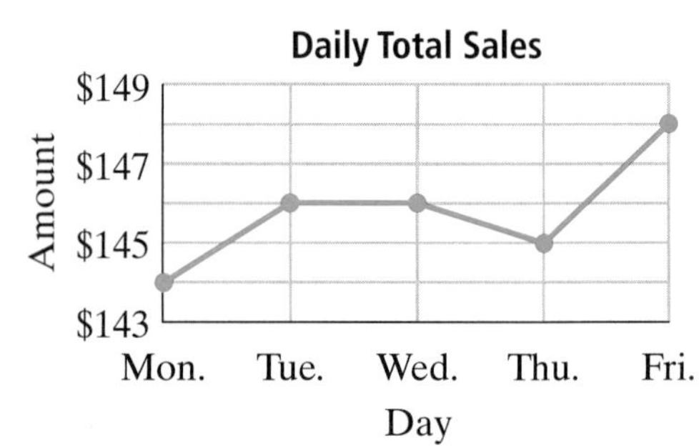

14. Explain why the graph is misleading.

15. Use the data to draw a graph that is not misleading.

Chapter 8

Extra Practice

Lessons 8-1 and 8-2 Use the diagram at the right for Exercises 1–8. Name each of the following.

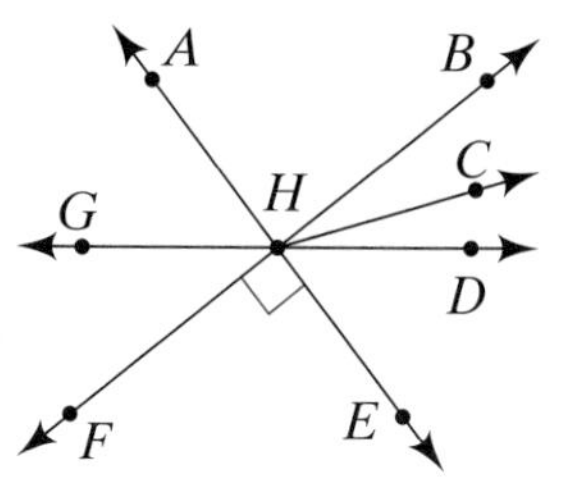

1. three collinear points **2.** six rays **3.** two perpendicular lines

Use a protractor to measure each angle. Classify each angle as *acute, right, obtuse,* or *straight*.

4. $\angle BHF$ **5.** $\angle FHC$ **6.** $\angle FHG$ **7.** $\angle CHD$ **8.** $\angle AHC$

Lesson 8-3 Find the complement and the supplement of each angle.

9. 28° **10.** 13.5° **11.** 56.3° **12.** 79° **13.** 85°

Lesson 8-4 Classify a triangle with the given side lengths.

14. 7 inches, 9 inches, 7 inches **15.** 3 feet, 3 feet, 3 feet **16.** 18 yards, 16 yards, 5 yards

Lesson 8-5 Classify each statement as *true* or *false*.

17. All octagons have eight sides. **18.** All rhombuses are squares. **19.** All squares are rectangles.

Lesson 8-6 Use the strategy of *Use Logical Reasoning* to solve the problem.

20. You have four pairs of pants, six T-shirts, and five vests. How many different outfits of pants, T-shirt, and vest can you wear?

Lesson 8-7 Each pair of figures appear to be *similar*. Confirm your answer by finding whether corresponding sides are proportional.

21.

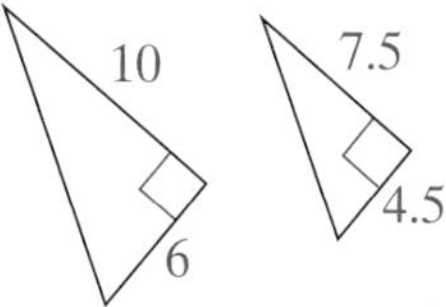

22.

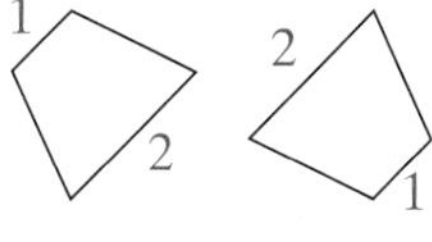

23.

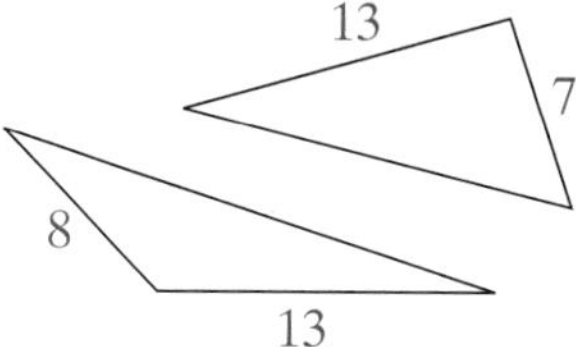

Lesson 8-8 Trace the figure at the right.

24. Draw all lines of symmetry in the figure.

Lesson 8-9 Copy the figure at the right on graph paper.

25. Draw its reflection over the given line of reflection.

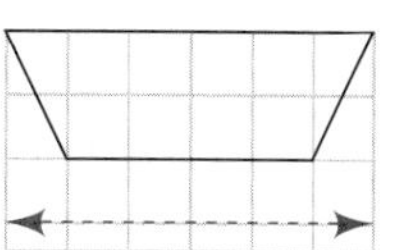

Chapter 9 Extra Practice

Lesson 9-1 Choose an appropriate metric unit of measure for each.

1. capacity of a shampoo bottle
2. mass of a television
3. length of your shoe

Lesson 9-2 Complete each statement.

4. 35 mm = ■ cm
5. 10.8 km = ■ m
6. ■ L = 2,400 mL
7. 1,008 g = ■ kg

Lesson 9-3 Each square represents 1 square centimeter. Estimate the area of each figure.

8. 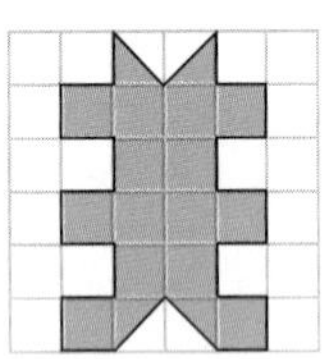

9. 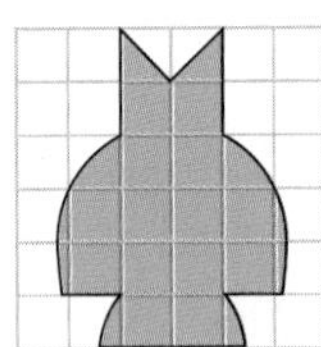

10. 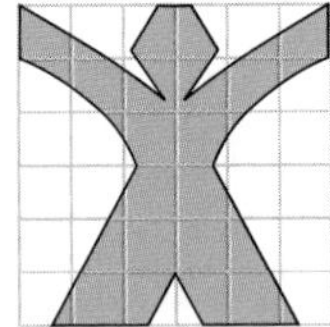

Lessons 9-3 and 9-4 Find the area of each figure.

11. 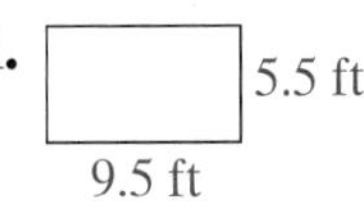

12. 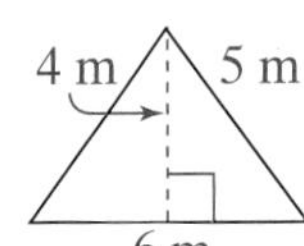

13. 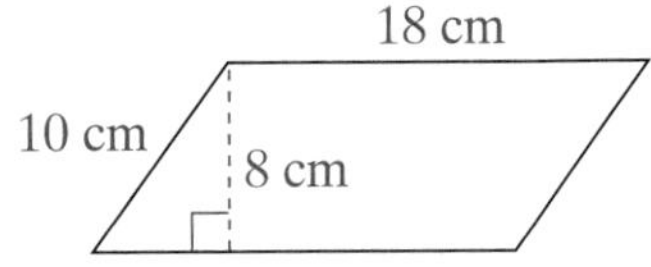

Lessons 9-5 and 9-6 Find the circumference and the area of a circle with the given diameter d or radius r. Round to the nearest whole number.

14. $d = 26$ yards
15. $d = 10.6$ feet
16. $r = 30$ inches
17. $r = 11$ miles
18. $d = 8.5$ meters

Lesson 9-7 Name each figure.

19. 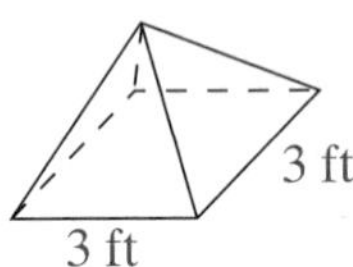

20. 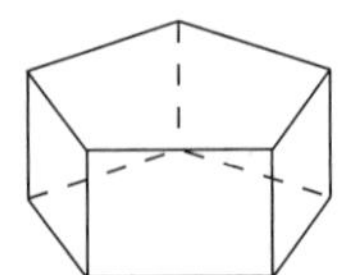

21. 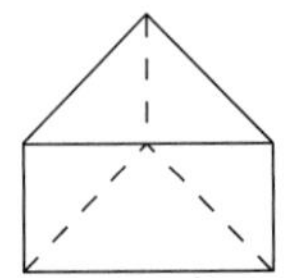

Lessons 9-8 and 9-9 Find the surface area and the volume of each rectangular prism with the given dimensions.

22. $\ell = 10$ ft, $w = 5$ ft, $h = 8$ ft
23. $\ell = 12$ m, $w = 16$ m, $h = 12$ m

Lesson 9-10 Use the strategy *Work Backward* to solve this problem.

24. If you multiply a number by 6 and then subtract 5, the result is 13. What is the number?

Chapter 10

Extra Practice

Lesson 10-1 Order from least to greatest.

1. $3, -1, 0, -2$
2. $4, -8, -5, 2$
3. $-6, 8, 7, -8$
4. $-1, -8, 0, 1$

Lesson 10-2 Find each sum.

5. $-3 + (-1)$
6. $-14 + 28$
7. $-72 + (-53)$
8. $-101 + 121$
9. $65 + (-5)$

Lesson 10-3 Find each difference.

10. $-3 - 1$
11. $4 - 8$
12. $31 - (-52)$
13. $-27 - (-27)$
14. $19 - (-18)$

Lesson 10-4 Find each product or quotient.

15. -8×5
16. $-4 \times (-9)$
17. $1 \times (-12)$
18. $93 \div (-3)$
19. $-68 \div 4$
20. $-5 \div (-2)$
21. $154 \div (-11)$
22. $-54 \div 9$

Lesson 10-5 Use the coordinate grid at the right for Exercises 23–30. Find the coordinates of each point.

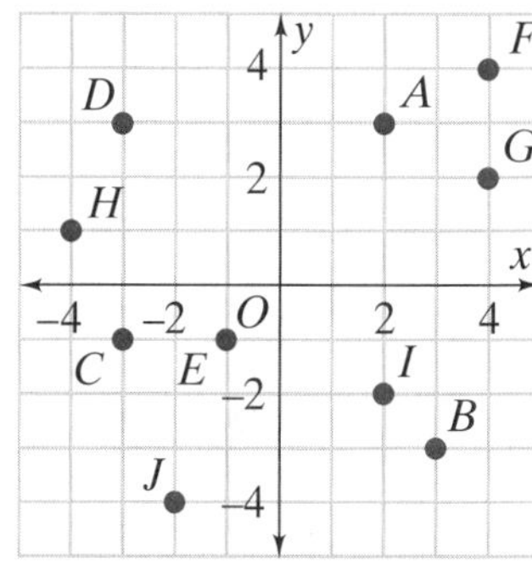

23. *A*
24. *B*
25. *C*
26. *D*

Name the point with the given coordinates.

27. $(4, 2)$
28. $(2, -2)$
29. $(-4, 1)$
30. $(-2, -4)$

Lesson 10-6 Look at the data for Snazzy Stuff. Find the profit or loss for each month.

31. January
32. March
33. May
34. Draw a line graph based on the profits and losses for Snazzy Stuff.

Snazzy Stuff

Month	Income	Expenses
Jan.	\$9,002	–\$4,000
Feb.	\$8,410	–\$5,113
Mar.	\$7,596	–\$6,333
Apr.	\$7,523	–\$7,641
May	\$7,941	–\$8,027
June	\$8,569	–\$6,299

Lesson 10-7 Make a function table and graph the function.

35. Kilometers are a function of meters.
36. Yards are a function of feet.

Lesson 10-8 Use the strategy *Make a Graph* to solve this problem.

37. A health bar charges \$1.76 for a 16-ounce shake and \$2.20 for a 20-ounce shake. What should the health bar charge for a 24-ounce shake?

Chapter 11 Extra Practice

Lesson 11-1 **A jar contains 2 red, 4 yellow, 3 green, and 5 blue marbles. You pick a marble without looking. Find each probability.**

1. P(yellow) **2.** P(green) **3.** P(red or blue) **4.** P(red, green, or blue)

Lesson 11-2 **Find the experimental probability that each person wins.**

5. Yelena won 168 of 196 games.

6. Chang played a game 43 times and did not lose a game.

Lesson 11-3 **The probability of winning a game is 80%. How many times should you expect to win if you play the following number of times?**

7. 4 **8.** 10 **9.** 30 **10.** 55 **11.** 125 **12.** 520

Write and solve a proportion to make the prediction.

13. In a school of 2,037 students, 500 were asked to name their favorite fruit. Apples were named by 325 students. Predict how many of the 2,037 students would name apples as their favorite fruit.

Lesson 11-4 **Use the strategy *Simulate a Problem* to solve the problem.**

14. The forecast calls for a $\frac{2}{3}$ chance of rain for each of the next three days. Find the experimental probability that it rains on two of the three days. Use three number cubes. Let 1, 2, 3, and 4 represent rain.

Lesson 11-5 **Use the counting principle.**

15. You flip a coin six times. Find P(three tails).

16. You roll a number cube two times. Find P(two odds).

Lesson 11-6 **Draw a tree diagram to find the permutations. Use each item exactly once.**

17. the numbers 6, 7, 8 **18.** the letters MATH

Lesson 11-7 **A bag contains 2 red, 6 blue, and 2 green marbles. Marbles are drawn twice with replacement. Find the probability of each compound event.**

19. blue, then red **20.** both blue **21.** both not green

Chapter 12 Extra Practice

Lesson 12-1 Solve each equation.

1. $2a + 8 = 26$
2. $3c + 2.5 = 29.5$
3. $5b - 13 = 17$
4. $7.5d - 7 = 53$
5. $4e - 1 = -93$
6. $\frac{f}{8} + 6 = 8$
7. $2 + 8g = 34$
8. $-4 + \frac{h}{4} = 4$

Lesson 12-2 Write an inequality for each graph.

9. −4 −3 −2 −1 0 1

10. 3 4 5 6 7 8

11. 

Write an inequality to represent each situation. Then graph the inequality.

12. The temperature stayed below 0°.
13. You must bring at least $5 to cover the cost of lunch.
14. A maximum of 12 people can sign up for the hiking trip.

Lesson 12-3 Solve each inequality.

15. $m + 8 < 14$
16. $n - 16 \geq 3$
17. $p + 9 \leq -5$
18. $q - 8 > 7$

Lesson 12-4 Use the strategy *Draw a Diagram* or *Write an Equation* to solve each problem. Explain why you chose the method you did.

19. There are 120 bicycles in a parade. Thirty-five percent of them have streamers. How many bicycles have streamers?
20. Your fabric is 10 feet by 8 feet. You want small strips that are 6 inches long and 4 inches wide. How many strips can you cut from the fabric?

Lesson 12-5 Find each square root.

21. $\sqrt{49}$
22. $\sqrt{81}$
23. $\sqrt{169}$
24. $\sqrt{484}$
25. $\sqrt{625}$
26. $\sqrt{900}$

Tell which two consecutive whole numbers the square root is between.

27. $\sqrt{3}$
28. $\sqrt{11}$
29. $\sqrt{17}$
30. $\sqrt{29}$
31. $\sqrt{51}$
32. $\sqrt{92}$

Lesson 12-6 Find the missing side length of each right triangle.

33. $a = 16, b = 30, c =$ ■
34. $a = 21, b =$ ■, $c = 35$
35. $a =$ ■, $b = 9, c = 15$

Skills Handbook

Place Value of Whole Numbers

The digits in a whole number are grouped into periods. A period has three digits, and each period has a name. Each digit in a whole number has both a place and a value.

Billions Period			Millions Period			Thousands Period			Ones Period		
Hundred billions	Ten billions	Billions	Hundred millions	Ten millions	Millions	Hundred thousands	Ten thousands	Thousands	Hundreds	Tens	Ones
9	5	1,	6	3	7,	0	4	1,	1	8	2

The digit 5 is in the ten billions place. So, its value is 5 ten billion, or 50 billion.

EXAMPLE

a. In what place is the digit 7?

millions

b. What is the value of the digit 7?

7 million

EXERCISES

Use the chart above. Write the place of each digit.

1. the digit 3 **2.** the digit 4 **3.** the digit 6

4. the digit 8 **5.** the digit 9 **6.** the digit 0

Use the chart above. Write the value of each digit.

7. the digit 3 **8.** the digit 4 **9.** the digit 6

10. the digit 8 **11.** the digit 9 **12.** the digit 0

Write the value of the digit 6 in each number.

13. 633 **14.** 761,523 **15.** 163,500,000 **16.** 165,417

17. 265 **18.** 4,396 **19.** 618,920 **20.** 204,602

21. 162,450,000,000 **22.** 7,682 **23.** 358,026,113 **24.** 76,030,100

25. 642,379 **26.** 16,403 **27.** 45,060 **28.** 401,601,001

Rounding Whole Numbers

Number lines can help you round numbers. On a number line, 5 is halfway between 0 and 10, 50 is halfway between 0 and 100, and 500 is halfway between 1 and 1,000. The accepted method of rounding is to round 5 up to 10, 50 up to 100, and 500 up to 1,000.

Round 2,462 to the nearest ten.

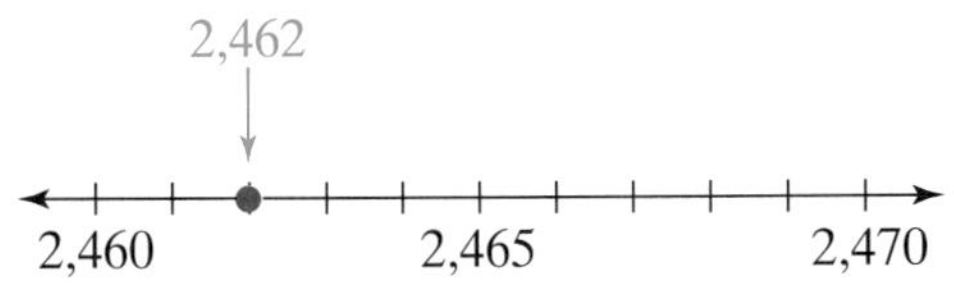

2,462 is closer to 2,460 than to 2,470.

2,462 rounded to the nearest ten is 2,460.

Round 247,451 to the nearest hundred.

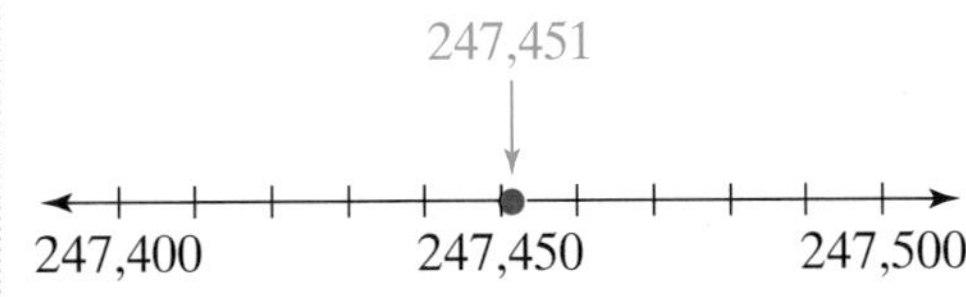

247,451 is closer to 247,500 than to 247,400.

247,451 rounded to the nearest hundred is 247,500.

EXERCISES

Round each number to the nearest ten.

1. 65 **2.** 832 **3.** 4,437 **4.** 21,024 **5.** 3,545

Round each number to the nearest hundred.

6. 889 **7.** 344 **8.** 2,861 **9.** 1,138 **10.** 50,549

11. 6,411 **12.** 88,894 **13.** 13,735 **14.** 17,459 **15.** 6,059

Round each number to the nearest thousand.

16. 2,400 **17.** 16,218 **18.** 7,430 **19.** 89,375 **20.** 9,821

21. 15,631 **22.** 76,900 **23.** 163,875 **24.** 38,295 **25.** 102,359

26. Describe a situation in which it is helpful to round data.

27. Explain how to round each of the numbers in Exercises 16–25 to the nearest ten thousand.

28. Suppose you round 31 to the nearest hundred. Is 0 a reasonable response? Explain your answer.

Adding Whole Numbers

When you add, line up the digits in the correct columns. You may need to regroup from one column to the next.

1 EXAMPLE

Add 463 + 58.

Step 1

$$\begin{array}{r} {}^{1} \\ 463 \\ +\ 58 \\ \hline 1 \end{array}$$

Step 2

$$\begin{array}{r} {}^{11} \\ 463 \\ +\ 58 \\ \hline 21 \end{array}$$

Step 3

$$\begin{array}{r} {}^{11} \\ 463 \\ +\ 58 \\ \hline 521 \end{array}$$

2 EXAMPLE

Find each sum.

a. 962 + 120

$$\begin{array}{r} 962 \\ +\ 120 \\ \hline 1{,}082 \end{array}$$

b. 25 + 9 + 143

$$\begin{array}{r} {}^{1} \\ 25 \\ 9 \\ +\ 143 \\ \hline 177 \end{array}$$

c. 3,887 + 1,201

$$\begin{array}{r} {}^{1} \\ 3{,}887 \\ +\ 1{,}201 \\ \hline 5{,}088 \end{array}$$

EXERCISES

Find each sum.

1. $\begin{array}{r} 45 \\ +\ 31 \\ \hline \end{array}$ **2.** $\begin{array}{r} 56 \\ +\ 80 \\ \hline \end{array}$ **3.** $\begin{array}{r} 25 \\ +\ 16 \\ \hline \end{array}$ **4.** $\begin{array}{r} 43 \\ +\ 29 \\ \hline \end{array}$ **5.** $\begin{array}{r} 66 \\ +\ 78 \\ \hline \end{array}$ **6.** $\begin{array}{r} 87 \\ +\ 35 \\ \hline \end{array}$

7. $\begin{array}{r} 81 \\ +\ 312 \\ \hline \end{array}$ **8.** $\begin{array}{r} 406 \\ +\ 123 \\ \hline \end{array}$ **9.** $\begin{array}{r} 207 \\ +\ 72 \\ \hline \end{array}$ **10.** $\begin{array}{r} 480 \\ +\ 365 \\ \hline \end{array}$ **11.** $\begin{array}{r} 217 \\ +\ 347 \\ \hline \end{array}$ **12.** $\begin{array}{r} 675 \\ +\ 329 \\ \hline \end{array}$

13. $\begin{array}{r} 2{,}051 \\ +\ 843 \\ \hline \end{array}$ **14.** $\begin{array}{r} 786 \\ +\ 4{,}109 \\ \hline \end{array}$ **15.** $\begin{array}{r} 5{,}227 \\ +\ 1{,}527 \\ \hline \end{array}$ **16.** $\begin{array}{r} 3{,}104 \\ +\ 2{,}698 \\ \hline \end{array}$ **17.** $\begin{array}{r} 5{,}337 \\ +\ 1{,}812 \\ \hline \end{array}$ **18.** $\begin{array}{r} 4{,}282 \\ +\ 7{,}518 \\ \hline \end{array}$

19. 78 + 56 **20.** 35 + 96 **21.** 105 + 71 **22.** 29 + 342 **23.** 654 + 103

24. 286 + 42 **25.** 55 + 77 **26.** 242 + 83 **27.** 32 + 68 **28.** 108 + 13

29. 589 + 318 **30.** 642 + 975 **31.** 2,308 + 451 **32.** 976 + 4,035

33. 8,228 + 1,024 **34.** 5,417 + 2,391 **35.** 6,470 + 9,828 **36.** 7,121 + 5,359

Subtracting Whole Numbers

When you subtract, line up the digits in the correct columns. Begin by subtracting the ones. Rename if the bottom digit is greater than the top digit. You may need to rename more than once.

1 EXAMPLE

Subtract 725 − 86.

Step 1

```
  115
  725
-  86
    9
```

Step 2

```
   11
  6 1 15
  725
-  86
   39
```

Step 3

```
   11
  6 1 15
  725
-  86
  639
```

2 EXAMPLE

Find each difference.

a. 602 − 174

```
   9
  5 10 12
  602
- 174
  428
```

b. 625 − 273

```
  5 12
  625
- 273
  352
```

c. 5,002 − 1,247

```
    9  9
  4 10 10 12
  5,002
- 1,247
  3,755
```

EXERCISES

Find each difference.

1. 81 − 37
2. 59 − 23
3. 41 − 19
4. 83 − 25
5. 99 − 78
6. 87 − 31

7. 707 − 361
8. 680 − 47
9. 240 − 63
10. 881 − 391
11. 517 − 287
12. 973 − 529

13. 7,411 − 583
14. 3,789 − 809
15. 6,508 − 2,147
16. 8,000 − 5,274
17. 3,003 − 1,998
18. 8,282 − 4,118

19. 78 − 19
20. 231 − 99
21. 901 − 65
22. 629 − 382
23. 918 − 133

24. 800 − 435
25. 403 − 122
26. 973 − 228
27. 721 − 119
28. 522 − 146

29. 642 − 223
30. 427 − 193
31. 444 − 345
32. 988 − 489
33. 601 − 425

Skills Handbook

Multiplying Whole Numbers

When you multiply by a one-digit number, multiply the one-digit number by each digit in the other number.

1 EXAMPLE

Multiply 294 × 7.

Step 1 Multiply 7 by the ones digit.

$$\begin{array}{r} {}^{2} \\ 294 \\ \times\ \ \ 7 \\ \hline 8 \end{array}$$

Step 2 Multiply 7 by the tens digit.

$$\begin{array}{r} {}^{6\,2} \\ 294 \\ \times\ \ \ 7 \\ \hline 58 \end{array}$$

Step 3 Multiply 7 by the hundreds digit.

$$\begin{array}{r} {}^{6\,2} \\ 294 \\ \times\ \ \ 7 \\ \hline 2{,}058 \end{array}$$

When you multiply by a two-digit number, first multiply by the ones. Then multiply by the tens. Add the products. Remember, 0 times any number is equal to 0.

2 EXAMPLE

Multiply 48 × 327.

Step 1 Multiply the ones.

$$\begin{array}{r} {}^{2\,5} \\ 327 \\ \times\ \ 48 \\ \hline 2{,}616 \end{array}$$

Step 2 Multiply the tens.

$$\begin{array}{r} {}^{1\,2} \\ 327 \\ \times\ \ 48 \\ \hline 2616 \\ +\ 1308 \\ \hline \end{array}$$

Step 3 Add the products.

$$\begin{array}{r} 327 \\ \times\ \ 48 \\ \hline 2616 \\ +\ 1308 \\ \hline 15{,}696 \end{array}$$

EXERCISES

Find each product.

1. 81×3 **2.** 47×2 **3.** 58×6 **4.** 678×5 **5.** 412×7 **6.** 326×4

7. 7 × 45 **8.** 62 × 3 **9.** 213 × 4 **10.** 8 × 177 **11.** 673 × 9

12. 5 × 41 **13.** 3 × 82 **14.** 94 × 6 **15.** 63 × 4 **16.** 58 × 3

17. 25×46 **18.** 62×88 **19.** 808×60 **20.** 409×70 **21.** 915×27 **22.** 312×53

23. 415 × 76 **24.** 500 × 80 **25.** 320 × 47 **26.** 562 × 18 **27.** 946 × 37

28. 76 × 103 **29.** 32 × 558 **30.** 371 × 84 **31.** 505 × 40 **32.** 620 × 19

Multiplying and Dividing Whole Numbers by 10, 100, and 1,000

Basic facts and patterns can help you when multiplying and dividing whole numbers by 10, 100, and 1,000.

$8 \times 1 = 8$	$5{,}000 \div 1 = 5{,}000$
$8 \times 10 = 80$	$5{,}000 \div 10 = 500$
$8 \times 100 = 800$	$5{,}000 \div 100 = 50$
$8 \times 1{,}000 = 8{,}000$	$5{,}000 \div 1{,}000 = 5$
Count the number of ending zeros.	**Count the zeros in the divisor.**
The product will have this many zeros.	**Remove this many zeros from the dividend. This number will be the quotient.**

Multiply or divide.

a. $77 \times 1{,}000$
$77{,}000$ ← **Insert three zeros.**

b. $430 \div 10$
43 ← **Remove one zero.**

EXERCISES

Multiply.

1. 85×10 **2.** 85×100 **3.** $85 \times 1{,}000$ **4.** $420 \times 1{,}000$ **5.** 420×100

6. 420×10 **7.** 603×100 **8.** 97×10 **9.** 31×100 **10.** 10×17

11. 100×56 **12.** $1{,}000 \times 4$ **13.** 13×10 **14.** 68×100 **15.** $19 \times 1{,}000$

Divide.

16. $3{,}200 \div 10$ **17.** $3{,}200 \div 100$ **18.** $32{,}000 \div 1{,}000$ **19.** $8{,}000 \div 100$ **20.** $8{,}000 \div 10$

21. $170 \div 10$ **22.** $45{,}000 \div 1{,}000$ **23.** $9{,}300 \div 10$ **24.** $90 \div 10$ **25.** $6{,}100 \div 100$

26. $7{,}900 \div 100$ **27.** $2{,}400 \div 10$ **28.** $240 \div 10$ **29.** $78{,}000 \div 1{,}000$ **30.** $9{,}900 \div 10$

Multiply or divide.

31. 76×100 **32.** $52 \times 1{,}000$ **33.** $370 \div 10$ **34.** 505×10 **35.** $6{,}200 \div 100$

36. $340 \div 10$ **37.** $14{,}000 \div 1{,}000$ **38.** 253×100 **39.** $3{,}700 \div 10$ **40.** 418×10

Dividing Whole Numbers

Division is the opposite of multiplication. So, you multiply the divisor by your estimate for each digit in the quotient. Then subtract. You repeat this step until you have a remainder that is less than the divisor.

EXAMPLE

Divide $23\overline{)1{,}178}$.

Step 1 Estimate the quotient.

$1{,}178 \div 23$ ← **The dividend is 1,178. The divisor is 23.**

$\downarrow \quad \downarrow$

$1{,}200 \div 20 \approx 60$ ← **Round 1,178 to the nearest hundred. Round 23 to the nearest ten.**

Step 2

$$\begin{array}{r} 6 \\ 23\overline{)1178} \\ -\ 138 \\ \hline \end{array}$$

← **Try 6 tens.**

← **6 × 23 = 138 You cannot subtract, so 6 tens is too much.**

Step 3

$$\begin{array}{r} 5 \\ 23\overline{)1178} \\ -\ 115 \\ \hline 2 \end{array}$$

← **Try 5 tens.**

← **5 × 23 = 115**

← **Subtract.**

Step 4

$$\begin{array}{r} 51\text{R}5 \\ 23\overline{)1178} \\ -\ 115\downarrow \\ \hline 28 \\ -\ 23 \\ \hline 5 \end{array}$$

← **Bring down 8.**

← **1 × 23 = 23**

← **Subtract. The remainder is 5.**

Step 5 Check your answer.

First compare your answer to the estimate. Since 51R5 is close to 60, the answer is reasonable.

Then find $51 \times 23 + 5$.

EXERCISES

Find each quotient. Check your answer.

1. $9\overline{)659}$ **2.** $9\overline{)376}$ **3.** $3\overline{)280}$ **4.** $8\overline{)541}$ **5.** $8\overline{)232}$

6. $1{,}058 \div 5$ **7.** $3{,}591 \div 3$ **8.** $5{,}072 \div 7$ **9.** $1{,}718 \div 4$ **10.** $3{,}767 \div 6$

11. $3{,}872 \div 17$ **12.** $19\overline{)1{,}373}$ **13.** $27\overline{)1{,}853}$ **14.** $4{,}195 \div 59$ **15.** $41\overline{)4{,}038}$

16. $2{,}612 \div 31$ **17.** $34\overline{)1{,}609}$ **18.** $1{,}937 \div 40$ **19.** $54\overline{)1{,}350}$ **20.** $1{,}824 \div 32$

21. **Writing in Math** Describe how to estimate a quotient. Use the words *dividend* and *divisor* in your description.

Zeros in Quotients

When you divide, after you bring down a digit you must write a digit in the quotient. In this example, the second digit in the quotient is 0.

EXAMPLE

Find 19)5,823.

Step 1

Estimate the quotient.

$$5{,}823 \div 19$$
$$\downarrow \quad \downarrow$$
$$5{,}800 \div 20 = 290$$

Step 2

$$\begin{array}{r} 3 \\ 19\overline{)5{,}823} \\ -\ 57 \\ \hline 1 \end{array}$$

Step 3

$$\begin{array}{r} 30 \\ 19\overline{)5{,}823} \\ -\ 57 \\ \hline 12 \\ -\ 0 \\ \hline 12 \end{array}$$

Step 4

$$\begin{array}{r} 306 \text{ R9} \\ 19\overline{)5{,}823} \\ -\ 57 \\ \hline 12 \\ -\ 0 \\ \hline 123 \\ -\ 114 \\ \hline 9 \end{array}$$

Step 5

Check your answer.
Since 306 is close to 290, the answer is reasonable.
Find 306 × 19 + 9.

EXERCISES

Find each quotient.

1. 7)212	**2.** 9)367	**3.** 3)271	**4.** 8)485	**5.** 6)483
6. 34)1,371	**7.** 19)1,335	**8.** 62)1,881	**9.** 54)1,094	**10.** 41)3,710
11. 282 ÷ 4	**12.** 143 ÷ 7	**13.** 181 ÷ 3	**14.** 400 ÷ 8	**15.** 365 ÷ 9
16. 1,008 ÷ 5	**17.** 3,018 ÷ 6	**18.** 4,939 ÷ 7	**19.** 1,682 ÷ 4	**20.** 3,647 ÷ 6
21. 2,488 ÷ 31	**22.** 3,372 ÷ 67	**23.** 1,937 ÷ 48	**24.** 4,165 ÷ 59	**25.** 1,686 ÷ 82

Reading Thermometer Scales

The thermometer at the right shows temperature in degrees Celsius (°C) and degrees Fahrenheit (°F).

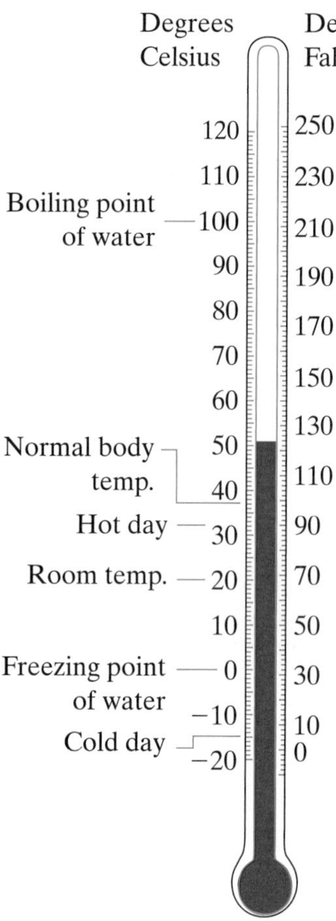

1 EXAMPLE

How do you read point *A* on the Celsius thermometer below?

Each 1-degree interval is divided into 10 smaller intervals of 0.1 degree each. The reading at point *A* is 36.2°C.

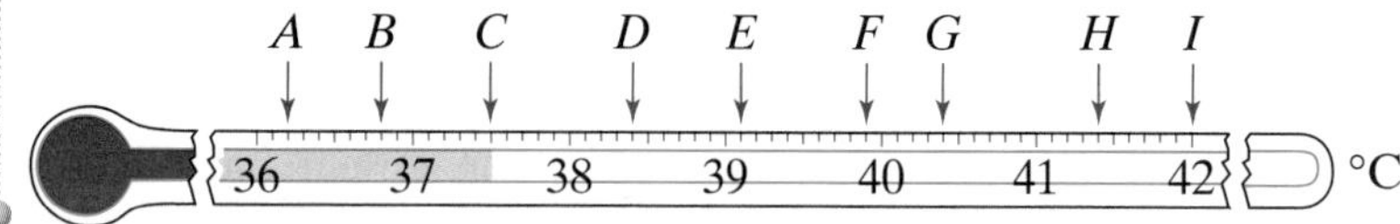

2 EXAMPLE

How do you read point *V* on the Fahrenheit thermometer below?

Each 1-degree interval is divided into 5 smaller intervals. Since 10 ÷ 5 = 2, each smaller interval represents 0.2 degree. Count by 0.2, beginning with 98.0. The reading at point *V* is 98.6°F.

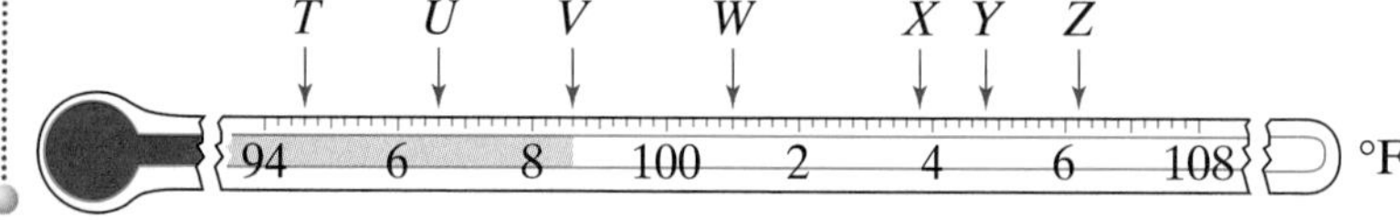

EXERCISES

Use the thermometers above to write the temperature reading for each point. Tell whether the reading is in degrees Celsius (°C) or degrees Fahrenheit (°F).

1. *B* **2.** *C* **3.** *D* **4.** *T* **5.** *U* **6.** *Z*

Use the thermometers above to name the point that relates to each temperature reading.

7. 40.4°C **8.** 42.0°C **9.** 39.9°C **10.** 104.8°F **11.** 101°F **12.** 103.8°F

Roman Numerals

The ancient Romans used letters to represent numerals. The table below shows the value of each Roman numeral.

I	V	X	L	C	D	M
1	5	10	50	100	500	1,000

Here are the Roman numerals from 1 to 10.

1	2	3	4	5	6	7	8	9	10
I	II	III	IV	V	VI	VII	VIII	IX	X

Roman numerals are read in groups from left to right.

If the value of the second numeral is the same as or less than the first numeral, add the values. The Roman numerals II, III, VI, VII, and VIII are examples in which you use addition.

If the value of the second numeral is greater than the first numeral, subtract the values. The Roman numerals IV and IX are examples in which you use subtraction.

EXAMPLE

Find the value of each Roman numeral.

a. CD

500 − 100

400

b. MXXVI

1,000 + 10 + 10 + 5 + 1

1,026

c. XCIV

(100 − 10) + (5 − 1)

90 + 4 = 94

EXERCISES

Find the value of each Roman numeral.

1. XI
2. DIII
3. XCV
4. CMX
5. XXIX
6. DLIX
7. MLVI
8. LX
9. CDIV
10. DCV

Write each number as a Roman numeral.

11. 15
12. 35
13. 1,632
14. 222
15. 159
16. 67
17. 92
18. 403
19. 1,990
20. 64

Estimating Lengths Using Nonstandard Units

Jan wanted to find a way to estimate lengths when she did not have any measuring tools. She measured her hand in several ways, the length of her foot and the length of her walking stride. Then she used these "natural units" as measuring tools.

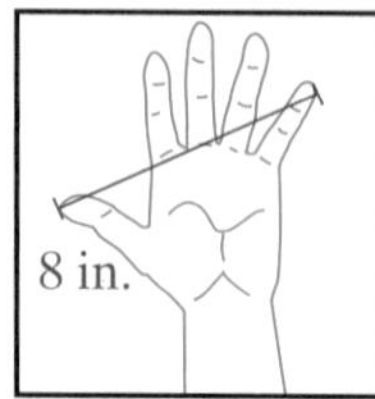

Span

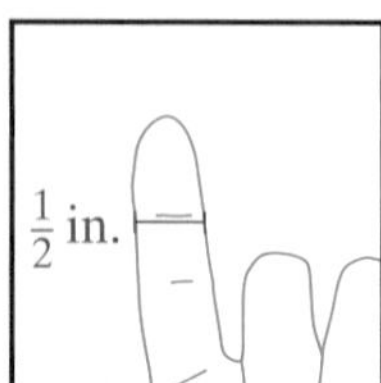

Finger width

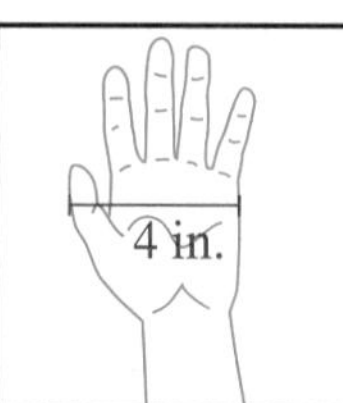

Hand

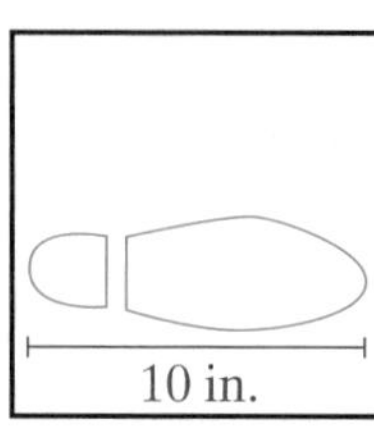

Heel to toe

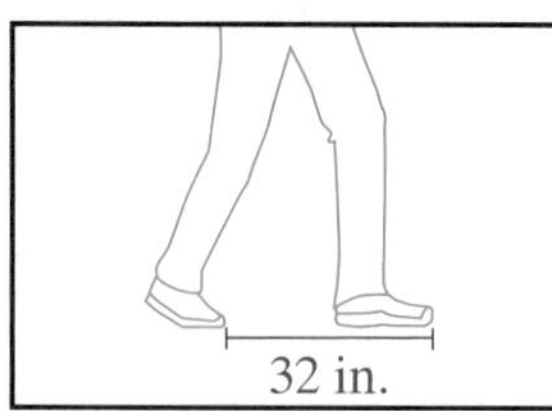

Stride

EXAMPLE

Jan used strides to measure the length of her room. She counted about 5 strides. What is the approximate length of the room?

1 stride ≈ 32 in.	← **Write the relationship between strides and inches.**
5 × 1 stride ≈ 5 × 32 in.	← **Multiply both sides by 5.**
5 strides ≈ 160 in.	← **Change strides to inches.**
160 in. ≈ (160 ÷ 12) ft	← **Change inches to feet.**
160 in. ≈ 13 ft	

The approximate length of the room is 13 feet.

EXERCISES

Measure your "finger width," "hand," "span," and "heel to toe." Use these natural units to find the indicated measure for each object. Then give the approximate measure in inches, feet, or yards.

1. thickness of a math book

2. height of a chair

3. height of a door

4. length of an eraser

5. height of your desk

6. length of a new pencil

7. distance across a room

8. thickness of a door

9. length of a chalkboard

10. **Open-Ended** Measure your stride. Then measure something such as a hallway in strides, and approximate the length in feet or yards. Tell what distance you measured.

Tables

Table 1 Measures

Metric	United States Customary
Length	**Length**
10 millimeters (mm) = 1 centimeter (cm) 100 cm = 1 meter (m) 1,000 mm = 1 meter 1,000 m = 1 kilometer (km)	12 inches (in.) = 1 foot (ft) 36 in. = 1 yard (yd) 3 ft = 1 yard 5,280 ft = 1 mile (mi) 1,760 yd = 1 mile
Area	**Area**
100 square millimeters (mm^2) = 1 square centimeter (cm^2) 10,000 cm^2 = 1 square meter (m^2)	144 square inches ($in.^2$) = 1 square foot (ft^2) 9 ft^2 = 1 square yard (yd^2) 4,840 yd^2 = 1 acre
Volume	**Volume**
1,000 cubic millimeters (mm^3) = 1 cubic centimeter (cm^3) 1,000,000 cm^3 = 1 cubic meter (m^3)	1,728 cubic inches ($in.^3$) = 1 cubic foot (ft^3) 27 ft^3 = 1 cubic yard (yd^3)
Mass	**Mass**
1,000 milligrams (mg) = 1 gram (g) 1,000 g = 1 kilogram (kg)	16 ounces (oz) = 1 pound (lb) 2,000 lb = 1 ton (t)
Liquid Capacity	**Liquid Capacity**
1,000 milliliters (mL) = 1 liter (L) 1,000 L = 1 kiloliter (kL)	8 fluid ounces (fl oz) = 1 cup (c) 2 c = 1 pint (pt) 2 pt = 1 quart (qt) 4 qt = 1 gallon (gal)

Time
60 seconds (s) = 1 minute (min) 60 min = 1 hour (h) 24 h = 1 day 7 days = 1 week (wk) 365 days ≈ 52 wk ≈ 1 year (yr)

Tables

Table 2 Reading Math Symbols

$+$	plus (addition)	p. 5
$=$	is equal to	p. 6
$>$	is greater than	p. 6
$<$	is less than	p. 6
$-$	minus (subtraction)	p. 17
$\times, \cdot$	times (multiplication)	p. 19
$\approx$	is approximately equal to	p. 19
$\div, \overline{)\ }$	divide (division)	p. 20
$\geq$	is greater than or equal to	p. 21
$\leq$	is less than or equal to	p. 21
$(\ )$	parentheses for grouping	p. 25
$\ldots$	and so on	p. 44
$^\circ$	degree(s)	p. 79
$\neq$	is not equal to	p. 84
$\stackrel{?}{=}$	Is the statement true?	p. 84
3^4	3 to the power 4	p. 99
$\frac{1}{4}$	reciprocal of 4	p. 230
$3 : 5$	ratio of 3 to 5	p. 269
%	percent	p. 293
*	multiply (in a spreadsheet formula)	p. 348
$\overline{AB}$	segment AB	p. 373
$\overrightarrow{AB}$	ray AB	p. 373
$\overleftrightarrow{AB}$	line AB	p. 373
$\angle ABC$	angle with sides BA and BC	p. 379
$\angle A$	angle with vertex A	p. 379
$\llcorner$	right angle (90°)	p. 380
P	perimeter	p. 441
ℓ	length	p. 441
w	width	p. 441
A	area	p. 441
b	base	p. 447
h	height	p. 447
C	circumference	p. 453
d	diameter	p. 453
π	pi; ≈ 3.14	p. 453
r	radius	p. 453
S.A.	surface area	p. 469
B	area of base	p. 472
V	volume	p. 472
-6	opposite of 6	p. 491
$\|5\|$	absolute value of 5	p. 492
$(2, 3)$	ordered pair with x-coordinate 2 and y-coordinate 3	p. 518
$P(\text{event})$	probability of the event	p. 548
$\sqrt{9}$	square root of 9	p. 616

Formulas and Properties

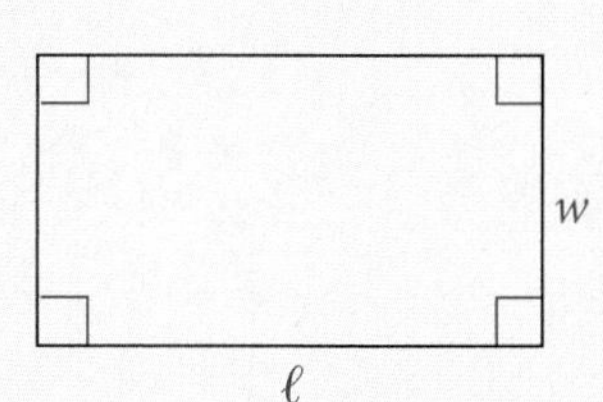

$P = 2\ell + 2w$, or $P = 2(\ell + w)$

$A = \ell \times w$

Rectangle

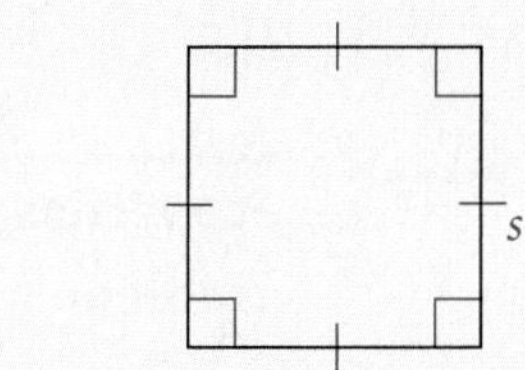

$P = s + s + s + s$, or $P = 4s$

$A = s \times s$, or $A = s^2$

Square

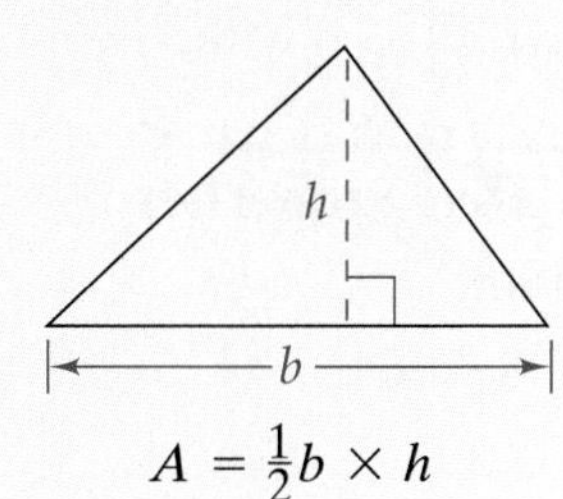

$A = \frac{1}{2}b \times h$

Triangle

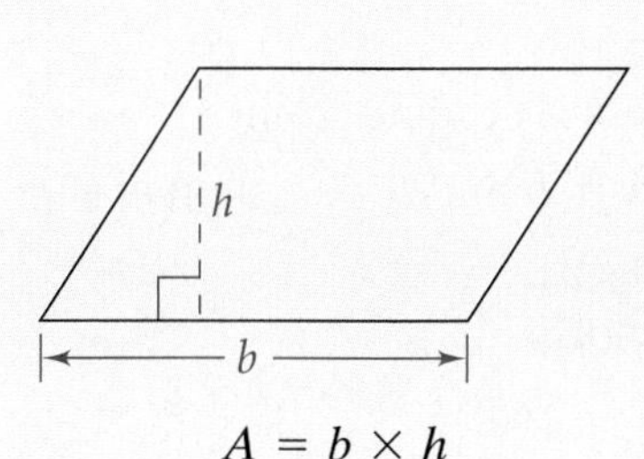

$A = b \times h$

Parallelogram

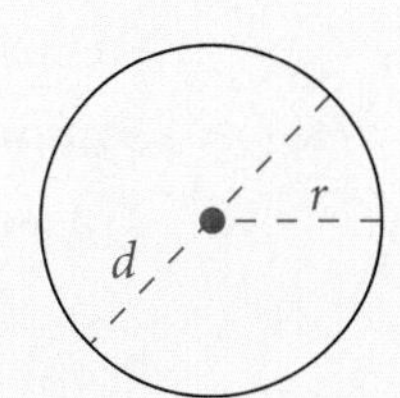

$C = 2\pi r$, or $C = \pi d$

$A = \pi r^2$

Circle

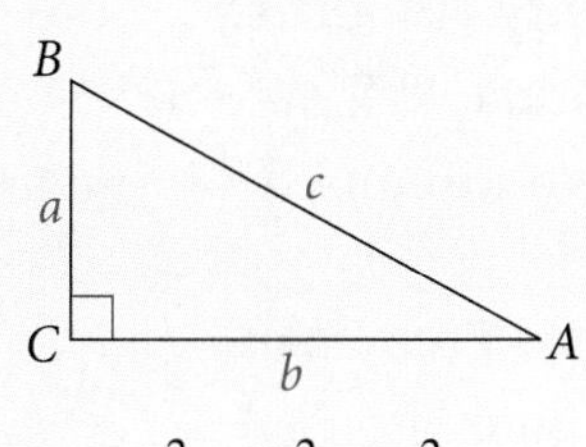

$a^2 + b^2 = c^2$

Pythagorean Theorem

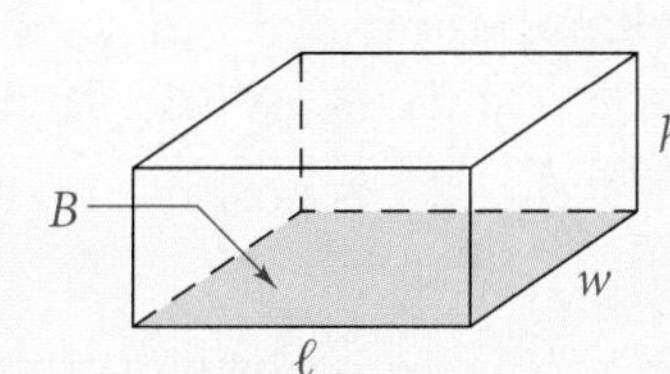

$V = B \times h$, or $V = \ell \times w \times h$

Surface Area (S.A.) =

$2(\ell \times w) + 2(\ell \times h) + 2(w \times h)$

Rectangular Prism

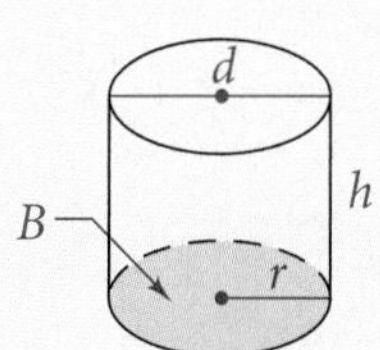

$V = B \times h$, or $V = \pi r^2 \times h$

Surface Area (S.A.) =

$2\pi r^2 + C \times h$

Cylinder

Properties of Numbers

Unless otherwise stated, the variables $a, b, c,$ and d used in these properties can be replaced with any number represented on a number line.

Associative Properties

Addition $(a + b) + c = a + (b + c)$

Multiplication $(a \cdot b) \cdot c = a \cdot (b \cdot c)$

Commutative Properties

Addition $a + b = b + a$

Multiplication $a \cdot b = b \cdot a$

Identity Properties

Addition $a + 0 = a$ and $0 + a = a$

Multiplication $a \cdot 1 = a$ and $1 \cdot a = a$

Inverse Properties

Addition

$a + (-a) = 0$ and $-a + a = 0$

Multiplication

$a \cdot \frac{1}{a} = 1$ and $\frac{1}{a} \cdot a = 1$ $(a \neq 0)$

Distributive Properties

$a(b + c) = ab + ac$

$a(b - c) = ab - ac$

Cross Products Property

If $\frac{a}{c} = \frac{b}{d}$, then $ad = bc$ $(c \neq 0, d \neq 0)$.

Zero-Product Property

If $ab = 0$, then $a = 0$ or $b = 0$.

Properties of Equality

Addition If $a = b$, then $a + c = b + c$.

Subtraction If $a = b$, then $a - c = b - c$.

Multiplication If $a = b$, then $a \cdot c = b \cdot c$.

Division If $a = b$, and $c \neq 0$, then $\frac{a}{c} = \frac{b}{c}$.

Substitution If $a = b$, then b can replace a in any expression.

Reflexive $a = a$

Symmetric If $a = b$, then $b = a$.

Transitive If $a = b$ and $b = c$, then $a = c$.

Properties of Inequality

Addition If $a > b$, then $a + c > b + c$.

If $a < b$, then $a + c < b + c$.

Subtraction If $a > b$, then $a - c > b - c$.

If $a < b$, then $a - c < b - c$.

Multiplication

If $a > b$ and c is positive, then $ac > bc$.

If $a < b$ and c is positive, then $ac < bc$.

Division

If $a > b$ and c is positive, then $\frac{a}{c} > \frac{b}{c}$.

If $a < b$ and c is positive, then $\frac{a}{c} < \frac{b}{c}$.

Note: The Properties of Inequality apply also to $\leq$ and $\geq$.

English/Spanish Illustrated Glossary

EXAMPLES

Absolute value (p. 492) The absolute value of a number is its distance from 0 on a number line.

Valor absoluto (p. 492) El valor absoluto de un número es su distancia del 0 en una recta numérica.

-7 is 7 units from 0, so $|-7| = 7$.

Acute angle (p. 380) An acute angle is an angle with a measure between 0° and 90°.

Ángulo agudo (p. 380) Un ángulo agudo es un ángulo que mide entre 0º y 90º.

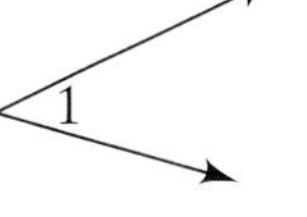

$0° < m\angle 1 < 90°$

Acute triangle (p. 392) An acute triangle has three acute angles.

Triángulo acutángulo (p. 392) Un triángulo acutángulo tiene tres ángulos agudos.

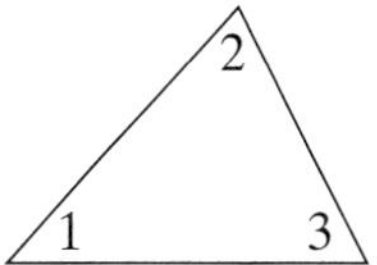

$\angle 1$, $\angle 2$, and $\angle 3$ are acute.

Addition Property of Equality (p. 91) The Addition Property of Equality states that if the same value is added to each side of an equation, the results are equal.

Propiedad aditiva de la igualdad (p. 91) La propiedad aditiva de la igualdad establece que si se suma el mismo valor a cada lado de una ecuación, los resultados son iguales.

Since $\frac{20}{2} = 10$, $\frac{20}{2} + 3 = 10 + 3$.
If $a = b$, then $a + c = b + c$.

Algebraic expression (p. 69) An algebraic expression is a mathematical phrase that uses variables, numbers, and operation symbols.

Expresión algebraica (p. 69) Una expresión algebraica es un enunciado matemático que usa variables, números y símbolos de operaciones.

$2x - 5$ is an algebraic expression.

Angle (p. 379) An angle is formed by two rays with a common endpoint called a vertex.

Ángulo (p. 379) Un ángulo está formado por dos rayos que tienen un punto final común llamado vértice.

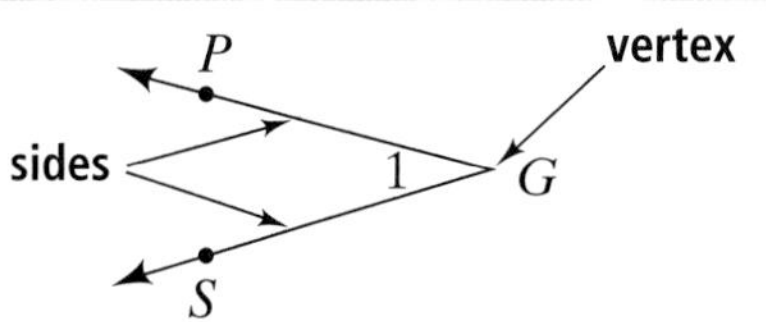

$\angle 1$ is made up of $\overrightarrow{GP}$ and $\overrightarrow{GS}$ with common endpoint G.

EXAMPLES

Angle bisector (p. 385) An angle bisector is a ray that divides an angle into angles of equal measure.

Bisectriz de un ángulo (p. 385) La bisectriz de un ángulo es un rayo que divide un ángulo en ángulos de igual medida.

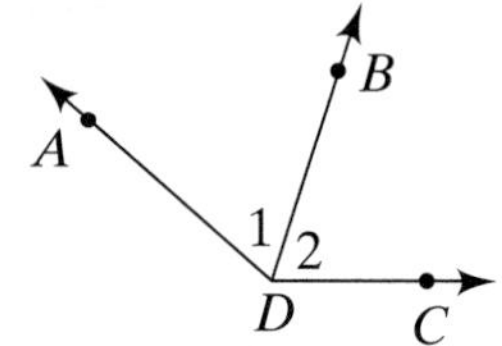

$\overrightarrow{DB}$ bisects $\angle ADC$, so $\angle 1 \cong \angle 2$.

Area (p. 440) The area of a figure is the number of square units it encloses.

Área (p. 440) El área de una figura es el número de unidades cuadradas que contiene.

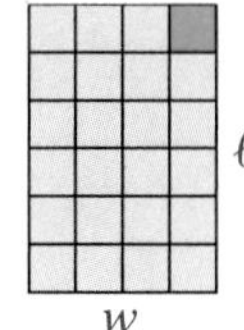

Each square equals 1 ft^2. With $\ell = 6$ ft and $w = 4$ ft, the area is 24 ft^2.

Associative Property of Addition (p. 25) The Associative Property of Addition states that changing the grouping of the addends does not change the sum.

Propiedad asociativa de la suma (p. 25) La propiedad asociativa de la suma establece que cambiar la agrupación de los sumandos no cambia la suma.

$(2 + 3) + 7 = 2 + (3 + 7)$

$(a + b) + c = a + (b + c)$

Associative Property of Multiplication (p. 36) The Associative Property of Multiplication states that changing the grouping of factors does not change the product.

Propiedad asociativa de la multiplicación (p. 36) La propiedad asociativa de la multiplicación establece que cambiar la agrupación de los factores no altera el producto.

$(3 \cdot 4) \cdot 5 = 3 \cdot (4 \cdot 5)$

$(a \cdot b) \cdot c = a \cdot (b \cdot c)$

Bar graph (p. 335) A bar graph uses vertical or horizontal bars to display numerical information.

Gráfica de barras (p. 335) Una gráfica de barras usa barras horizontales o verticales para mostrar información numérica.

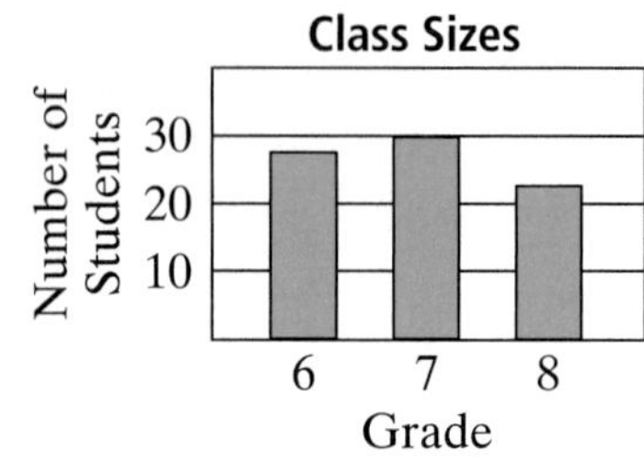

This bar graph represents class sizes for grades 6, 7, and 8.

EXAMPLES

Base (p. 99) When a number is written in exponential form, the number that is used as a factor is the base.

Base (p. 99) Cuando un número se escribe en forma exponencial, el número que se usa como factor es la base.

$5^4 = 5 \times 5 \times 5 \times 5$

↑ base

Bases of two-dimensional figures (p. 446, 447, 398) See *Parallelogram*, *Triangle*, and *Trapezoid*.

Bases de figuras bidimensionales (p. 446, 447, 398) Ver *Parallelogram*, *Triangle*, y *Trapezoid*.

Benchmark (p. 171) A benchmark is a convenient number used to replace fractions that are less than 1.

Punto de referencia (p. 171) Un punto de referencia es un número conveniente que se usa para reemplazar fracciones menores que 1.

Using benchmarks, you would estimate $\frac{5}{6} + \frac{4}{9}$ as $1 + \frac{1}{2}$.

Box-and-whisker plot (p. 356) A box-and-whisker plot is a graph that summarizes a data set using five key values. There is a box in the middle and "whiskers" at either side. The quartile values show how each fourth of the data is distributed.

Gráfica de caja y brazos (p. 356) Una gráfica de frecuencias acumuladas es un diagrama que resume un conjunto de datos usando cinco valores clave. Hay una caja en el centro y extensiones a cada lado. Los valores cuartiles muestran cómo se distribuye cada cuarto de los datos.

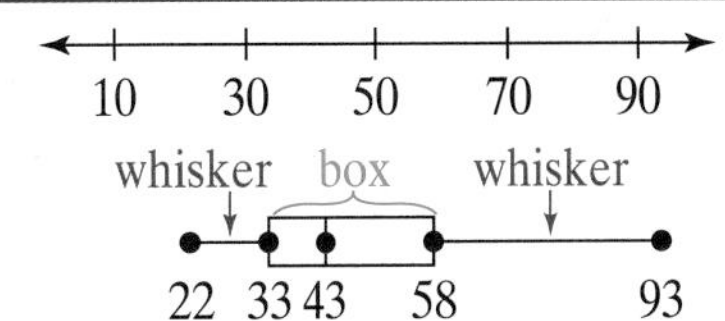

The box-and-whisker plot uses these data: 16 19 26 26 27 29 30 31 34 34 38 39 40.

The lower quartile is 26. The median is 30. The upper quartile is 36.

Capacity (p. 433) Capacity is a measure of the amount of space an object occupies.

Capacidad (p. 433) La capacidad es una medida de la cantidad de espacio que ocupa un objeto.

A juice bottle has a capacity of about 1 liter.

Cell (p. 347) A cell is a box in a spreadsheet where a row and a column meet.

Celda (p. 347) Una celda es una caja en una hoja de cálculo donde se unen una fila y una columna.

	A	B	C	D	E
1	0.50	0.70	0.60	0.50	2.30
2	1.50	0.50	2.75	2.50	7.25

Column C and row 2 meet at the shaded box, cell C2.

EXAMPLES

Center of a circle (p. 452) A circle is named by its center.

Centro de un círculo (p. 452) Un círculo es denominado por su centro.

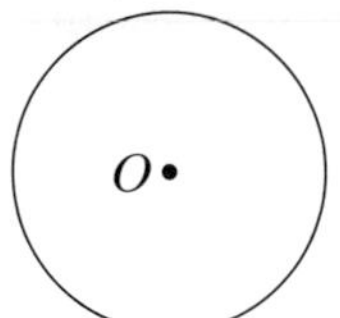

Circle O

Center of rotation (p. 416) The center of rotation is a fixed point about which a figure is rotated.

Centro de rotación (p. 416) El centro de rotación es un punto fijo alrededor del cual rota una figura.

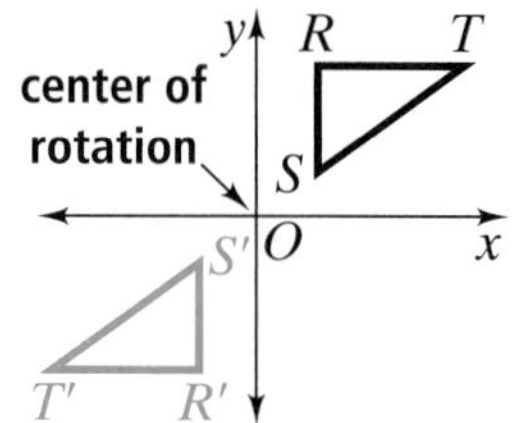

O is the center of rotation.

Chord (p. 452) A chord is a segment that has both endpoints on a circle.

Cuerda (p. 452) Una cuerda es un segmento que tiene ambos extremos sobre un círculo.

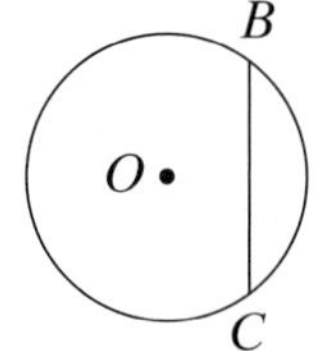

$\overline{CB}$ is a chord of circle O.

Circle (p. 452) A circle is the set of points in a plane that are all the same distance from a given point called the center.

Círculo (p. 452) Un círculo es el conjunto de puntos de un plano que están a la misma distancia de un punto dado llamado centro.

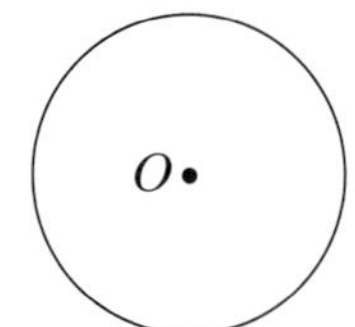

Circle graph (p. 341) A circle graph is a graph of data where a circle represents the whole.

Gráfica circular (p. 341) Una gráfica circular es una gráfica de datos donde un círculo representa el todo.

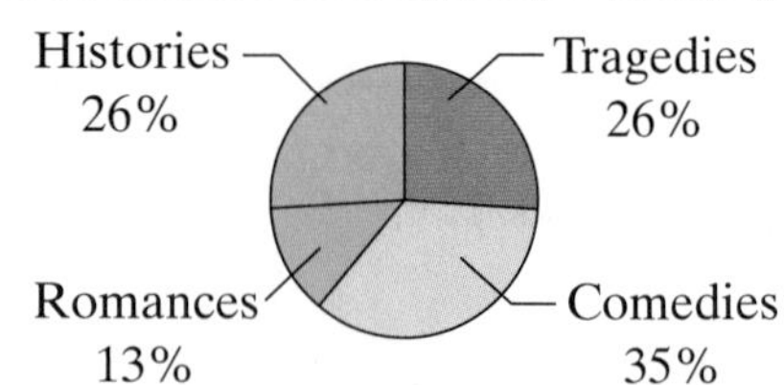

The circle graph represents the types of plays William Shakespeare wrote.

Circumference (p. 453) Circumference is the distance around a circle. You calculate the circumference of a circle by multiplying the diameter by π.

Circunferencia (p. 453) La circunferencia es la distancia alrededor de un círculo. La circunferencia de un círculo se calcula multiplicando el diámetro por π.

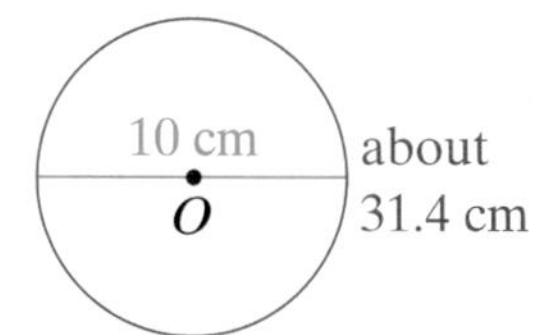

The circumference of a circle with a diameter of 10 cm is approximately 31.4 cm.

EXAMPLES

Collinear (p. 374) Points on the same line are collinear.

Colineal (p. 374) Los puntos que están en la misma recta son colineales.

B C R S

Points B, C, R, and S are collinear.

Common factor (p. 128) A factor that two or more numbers share is a common factor.

Factor común (p. 128) Un número que es factor de cada uno de dos o más números, es un factor común.

4 is a common factor of 8 and 20.

Common multiple (p. 143) A multiple shared by two or more numbers is a common multiple.

Múltiplo común (p. 143) Un número que es múltiplo de cada uno de dos o más números, es un múltiplo común.

12 is a common multiple of 4 and 6.

Commutative Property of Addition (p. 25) The Commutative Property of Addition states that changing the order of the addends does not change the sum.

Propiedad conmutativa de la suma (p. 25) La propiedad conmutativa de la suma establece que al cambiar el orden de los sumandos no se altera la suma.

$3 + 1 = 1 + 3$

$a + b = b + a$

Commutative Property of Multiplication (p. 36) The Commutative Property of Multiplication states that changing the order of the factors does not change the product.

Propiedad conmutativa de la multiplicación (p. 36) La propiedad conmutativa de la multiplicación establece que al cambiar el orden de los factores no se altera el producto.

$6 \cdot 3 = 3 \cdot 6$

$a \cdot b = b \cdot a$

Compass (p. 384) A compass is a geometric tool used to draw circles or arcs.

Compás (p. 384) Un compás es una herramienta que se usa en geometría para dibujar círculos o arcos.

Compatible numbers (p. 20) Compatible numbers are numbers that are easy to compute mentally.

Números compatibles (p. 20) Los números compatibles son números con los que se puede calcular mentalmente con facilidad.

Estimate $151 \div 14.6$.

$151 \approx 150, 14.6 \approx 15$

$150 \div 15 = 10$

$151 \div 14.6 \approx 10$

EXAMPLES

Complementary (p. 386) Two angles are complementary if the sum of their measures is 90°.

Complementario (p. 386) Dos ángulos son complementarios si la suma de sus medidas es 90°.

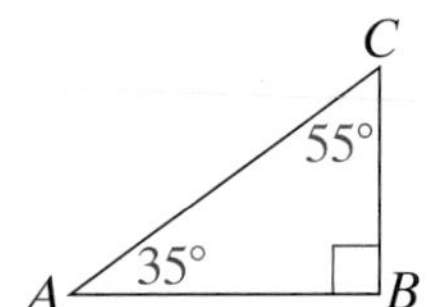

$\angle BCA$ and $\angle CAB$ are complementary angles.

Composite number (p. 124) A composite number is a whole number greater than 1 with more than two factors.

Número compuesto (p. 124) Un número compuesto es un número entero mayor que 1, que tiene más de dos factores.

24 is a composite number that has 1, 2, 3, 4, 6, 8, 12, and 24 as factors.

Compound event (p. 581) A compound event consists of two or more events. When the events are independent, the probability of a compound event is the product of the probabilities of each event.

Suceso compuesto (p. 581) Un suceso compuesto está formado por dos o más sucesos. Cuando los sucesos son independientes, la probabilidad de un suceso compuesto es el producto de las probabilidades de cada evento.

Suppose A and B are independent events. If $P(A) = \frac{1}{3}$ and $P(B) = \frac{1}{2}$, then $P(A \text{ and } B) = \frac{1}{3} \cdot \frac{1}{2} = \frac{1}{6}$.

Cone (p. 463) A cone is a three-dimensional figure with one circular base and one vertex.

Cono (p. 463) Un cono es una figura tridimensional con una base circular y un vértice.

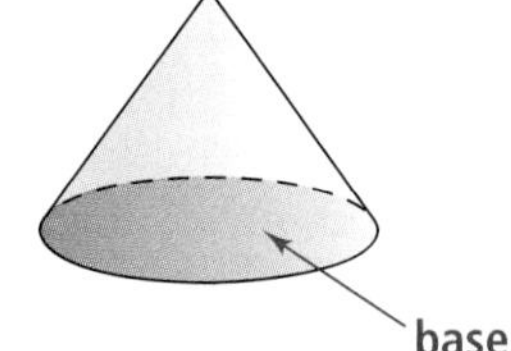

Congruent angles (p. 387) Congruent angles are angles that have the same measure.

Ángulos congruentes (p. 387) Los ángulos congruentes son ángulos que tienen la misma medida.

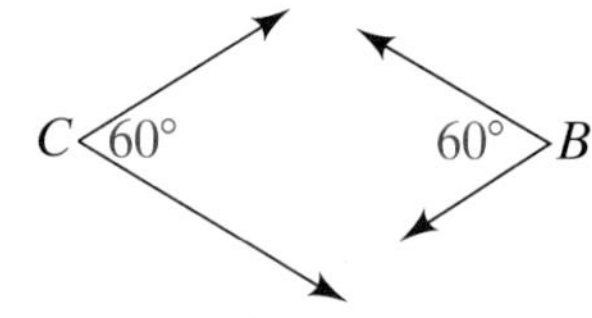

$\angle B \cong \angle C$

Congruent figures (p. 405) Congruent polygons are polygons with the same size and shape.

Polígonos congruentes (p. 405) Las figuras congruentes son segmentos congruentes que tienen el mismo tamaño y forma.

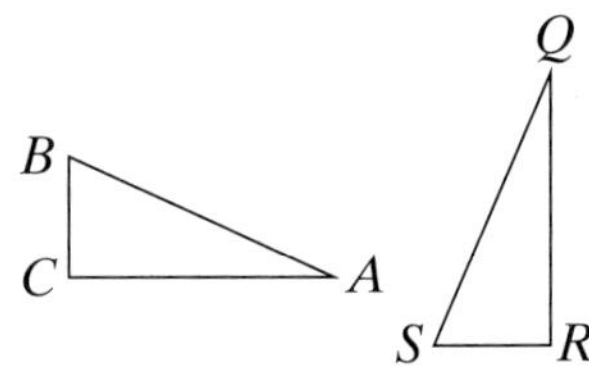

Triangle $ABC \cong$ Triangle QSR

EXAMPLES

Congruent segments (p. 393) Segments that have the same length are congruent segments.

Segmentos congruentes (p. 393) Los segmentos que tienen la misma longitud son segmentos congruentes.

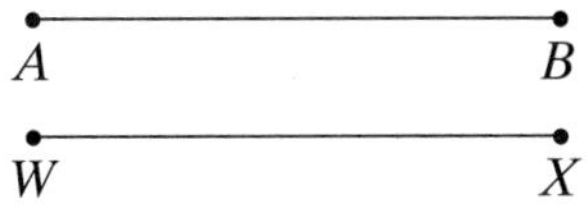

$\overline{AB}$ is congruent to $\overline{WX}$.

Conjecture (p. 64) A conjecture is a prediction that suggests what can be expected to happen.

Conjetura (p. 64) Una conjetura es una predicción que sugiere lo que se puede esperar que ocurra.

Every clover has three leaves.

Coordinate plane (p. 518) A coordinate plane is formed by a horizontal number line called the x-axis and a vertical number line called the y-axis.

Plano de coordenadas (p. 518) Un plano de coordenadas está formado por una recta numérica horizontal llamada eje de x y por una recta numérica vertical llamada eje de y.

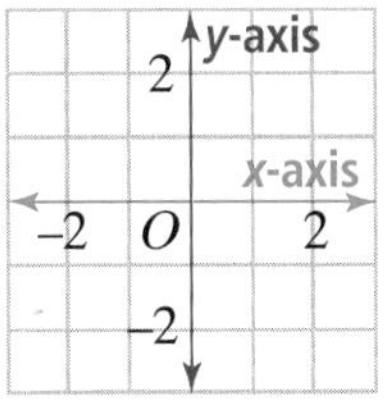

Corresponding parts (p. 405) The matching parts of similar figures are called corresponding parts.

Partes correspondientes (p. 405) Las partes que coinciden de figuras semejantes se llaman partes correspondientes.

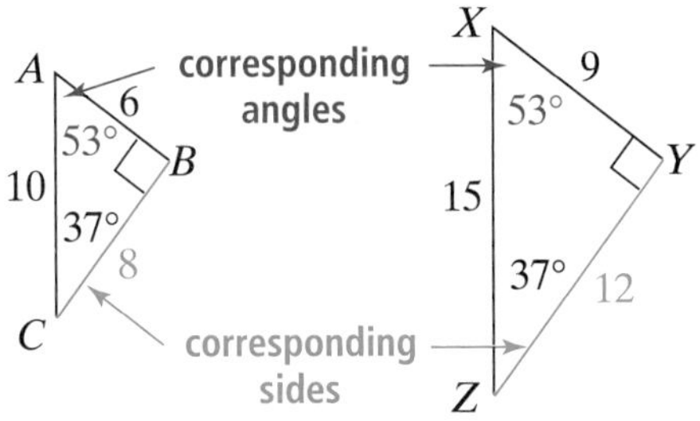

$\overline{AB}$ and $\overline{XY}$, $\overline{AC}$ and $\overline{XZ}$, $\overline{BC}$ and $\overline{YZ}$ are corresponding sides.

$\angle A$ and $\angle X$, $\angle B$ and $\angle Y$, $\angle C$ and $\angle Z$ are corresponding angles.

Counting principle (p. 569) If there are m ways of making one choice from a first situation and n ways of making a choice from a second situation, then there are $m \times n$ ways to make the first choice followed by the second.

Principio de conteo (p. 569) Si hay m maneras de hacer una elección para una primera situación y n maneras de hacer una elección para una segunda situación, entonces hay $m \times n$ maneras de hacer la primera elección seguida de la segunda.

Toss a coin and roll a standard number cube. The total number of possible outcomes is $2 \times 6 = 12$.

Cross products (p. 284) For two ratios, the cross products are found by multiplying the denominator of one ratio by the numerator of the other ratio.

Productos cruzados (p. 284) En dos razones, los productos cruzados se hallan al multiplicar el denominador de una razón por el numerador de la otra razón.

In the proportion $\frac{2}{5} = \frac{10}{25}$, the cross products are $2 \cdot 25$ and $5 \cdot 10$.

EXAMPLES

Cube (p. 462) A cube is a rectangular prism whose faces are all squares.

Cubo (p. 462) Un cubo es un prisma rectangular cuyas caras son todas cuadrados.

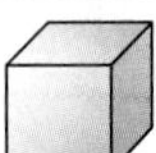

Cubic unit (p. 472) A cubic unit is a cube whose edges are one unit long.

Unidad cúbica (p. 472) Una unidad cúbica es un cubo cuyos lados tienen una unidad de longitud.

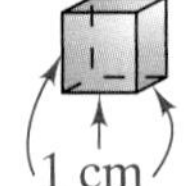

Cylinder (p. 463) A cylinder is a three-dimensional figure with two congruent parallel bases that are circles.

Cilindro (p. 463) Un cilindro es una figura tridimensional con dos bases congruentes paralelas que son círculos.

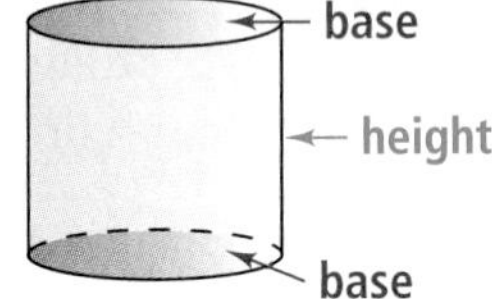

D

Decagon (p. 397) A decagon is a polygon with 10 sides.

Decágono (p. 397) Un decágono es un polígono que tiene 10 lados.

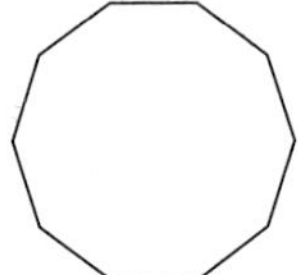

Degrees (p. 379) Angles are measured in units called degrees.

Grados (p. 379) Los ángulos se miden en unidades llamadas grados.

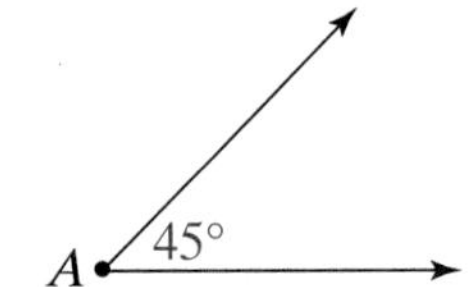

The measure of $\angle A$ is 45°.

Diameter (p. 453) A diameter is a segment that passes through the center of a circle and has both endpoints on the circle.

Diámetro (p. 453) Un diámetro es un segmento que pasa por el centro de un círculo y que tiene ambos extremos sobre el círculo.

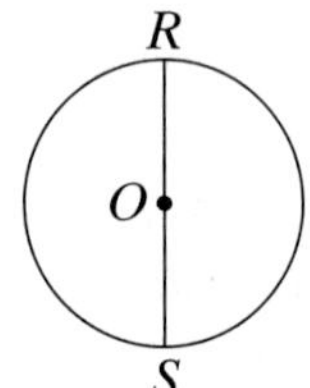

$\overline{RS}$ is a diameter of circle O.

Distributive Property (p. 105) The Distributive Property shows how multiplication affects an addition or subtraction: $a(b + c) = ab + ac$.

Propiedad distributiva (p. 105) La propiedad distributiva muestra cómo la multiplicación afecta a una suma o a una resta: $a(b + c) = ab + ac$.

$2\left(3 + \frac{1}{2}\right) = 2 \cdot 3 + 2 \cdot \frac{1}{2}$

$8(5 - 3) = 8 \cdot 5 - 8 \cdot 3$

EXAMPLES

Divisible (p. 119) A whole number is divisible by a second whole number if the first number can be divided by the second number with a remainder of 0.

Divisible (p. 119) Un número entero es divisible por un segundo número entero si el primer número se puede dividir por el segundo número y el residuo es 0.

16 is divisible by 1, 2, 4, 8, and 16.

Division Property of Equality (p. 95) The Division Property of Equality states that if both sides of an equation are divided by the same nonzero number, the results are equal.

Propiedad de división de la igualdad (p. 95) La propiedad de división de la igualdad establece que si ambos lados de una ecuación se dividen por el mismo número distinto de cero, los resultados son iguales.

Since $3(2) = 6$, $3(2) \div 2 = 6 \div 2$.
If $a = b$ and $c \neq 0$, then $\frac{a}{c} = \frac{b}{c}$.

Double bar graph (p. 340) A double bar graph is a graph that uses bars to compare two sets of data.

Gráfica de doble barra (p. 340) Una gráfica de doble barra es una gráfica que usa barras para comparar dos conjuntos de datos.

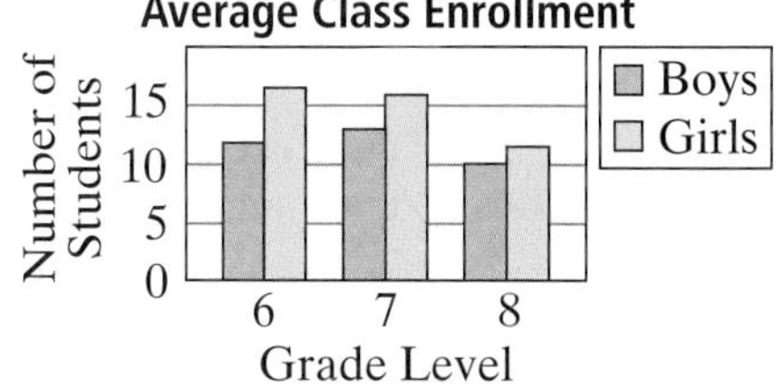

This double bar graph shows class size for grades 6, 7, and 8 for boys and girls.

Double line graph (p. 340) A double line graph is a graph that compares changes over time for two sets of data.

Gráfica de doble línea (p. 340) Una gráfica de doble línea es una gráfica que compara los cambios de dos conjuntos de datos a través del tiempo.

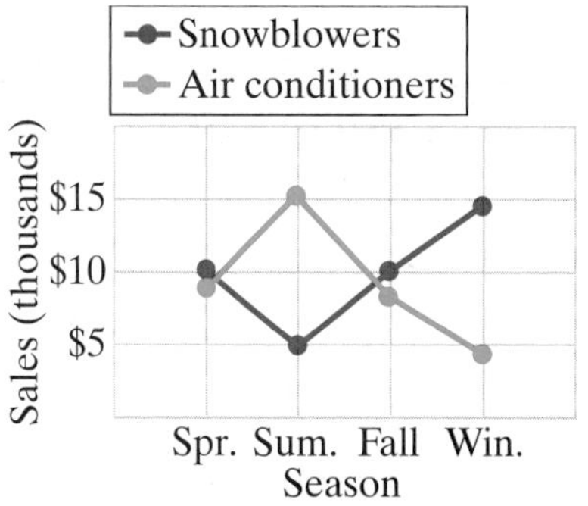

This double line graph represents seasonal air conditioner and snowblower sales for a large department store chain.

Edge (p. 462) An edge is a segment formed by the intersection of two faces of a three-dimensional figure.

Arista (p. 462) Una arista es un segmento formado por la intersección de dos caras de una figura tridimensional.

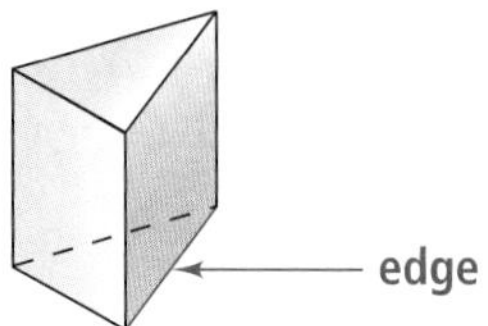

English/Spanish Glossary

EXAMPLES

Elapsed time (p. 202) The time between two events is elapsed time.

Tiempo transcurrido (p. 202) El tiempo que hay entre dos sucesos es el tiempo transcurrido.

The elapsed time between 8:10 A.M. and 8:45 A.M. is 35 minutes.

Equal ratios (p. 270) Equal ratios name the same number. Equal ratios written as fractions are equivalent fractions.

Razones iguales (p. 270) Las razones iguales indican el mismo número. Las razones iguales escritas como fracciones son fracciones equivalentes.

The ratios $\frac{4}{7}$ and $\frac{8}{14}$ are equal.

Equally likely outcomes (p. 547) Equally likely outcomes are outcomes that have the same chance of occurring.

Resultados igualmente probables (p. 547) Los resultados igualmente probables son resultados que tienen la misma posibilidad de ocurrir.

When a number cube is rolled once, the outcomes 1, 2, 3, 4, 5, and 6 are all equally likely outcomes.

Equation (p. 84) An equation is a mathematical sentence with an equal sign.

Ecuación (p. 84) Una ecuación es una oración matemática con un signo igual.

$27 \div 9 = 3$ and $x + 10 = 8$ are examples of equations.

Equilateral triangle (p. 393) An equilateral triangle is a triangle with three congruent sides.

Triángulo equilátero (p. 393) Un triángulo equilátero es un triángulo que tiene tres lados congruentes.

S L W

$\overline{SL} \cong \overline{LW} \cong \overline{WS}$

Equivalent fractions (p. 134) Equivalent fractions are fractions that name the same amount.

Fracciones equivalentes (p. 134) Las fracciones equivalentes son fracciones que indican la misma cantidad.

$\frac{1}{2}$ and $\frac{25}{50}$ are equivalent fractions.

Evaluating algebraic expressions (p. 69) To evaluate an algebraic expression, replace each variable with a number. Then follow the order of operations.

Evaluación de una expresión algebraica (p. 69) Para evaluar una expresión se reemplaza cada variable con un número. Luego se sigue el orden de las operaciones.

To evaluate the expression $3x + 2$ for $x = 4$, substitute 4 for x.

$3x + 2 = 3(4) + 2 = 14$

	EXAMPLES
Even number (p. 120) An even number is any whole number that ends with a 0, 2, 4, 6, or 8. **Número par (p. 120)** Un número par es cualquier número entero que termina en 0, 2, 4, 6 u 8.	20 and 534 are even numbers.
Event (p. 547) A collection of possible outcomes is an event. **Suceso (p. 547)** Un suceso es un grupo de resultados posibles.	In a game that includes tossing a coin and rolling a standard number cube, "heads and a 2" is an event.
Expanded form (p. 9) The expanded form of a number is the sum that shows the place and value of each digit. See also *Standard form.* **Forma desarrollada (p. 9)** La forma desarrollada de un número es la suma que muestra el lugar y valor de cada dígito. Ver también *Standard form.*	4.85 can be written in expanded form as $4 + 0.8 + 0.05$.
Experimental probability (p. 554) For a series of trials, the experimental probability of an event is the ratio of the number of times an event occurs to the total number of trials. $P(\text{event}) = \frac{\text{number of times an event occurs}}{\text{total number of trials}}$ **Probabilidad experimental (p. 554)** En una serie de pruebas, la probabilidad experimental de un suceso es la razón del número de veces que ocurre un suceso al número total de pruebas. $P(\text{suceso}) = \frac{\text{número de veces que ocurre un suceso}}{\text{número de pruebas}}$	A basketball player makes 15 baskets in 28 attempts. The experimental probability that the player makes a basket is $\frac{15}{28} \approx 54\%$.
Exponent (p. 99) An exponent tells how many times a number, or base, is used as a factor. **Exponente (p. 99)** Un exponente dice cuántas veces se usa como factor un número o base.	exponent $3^4 = 3 \times 3 \times 3 \times 3$ Read 3^4 as *three to the fourth power.*
Expression (p. 48) An expression is a mathematical phrase containing numbers and operation symbols. **Expresión (p. 48)** Una expresión es un enunciado matemático que contiene números y símbolos de operaciones.	The expression $24 - 6 \div 3$ contains two operations.
Exterior angles (p. 387) The angles outside two lines that are crossed by a transversal are called exterior angles. **Ángulos exteriores (p. 387)** Los ángulos que están fuera de las dos rectas cruzadas por una secante se llaman ángulos exteriores.	1 2 3 4 5 6 7 8 Angles 1, 2, 7, and 8 are exterior angles.

EXAMPLES

Face (p. 462) A face is a flat, polygon-shaped surface of a three-dimensional figure.

Cara (p. 462) Una cara es una superficie plana de una figura tridimensional que tiene la forma de un polígono.

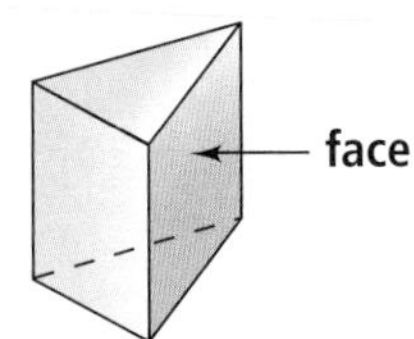

Factor (p. 123) A factor is a whole number that divides another whole number with a remainder of 0.

Divisor (p. 123) Un divisor es un número entero que divide a otro número entero y el residuo es 0.

1, 2, 3, 4, 6, 9, 12, 18, and 36 are factors of 36.

Factor tree (p. 124) A factor tree is a diagram that shows how a composite number breaks down into its prime factors.

Árbol de factores (p. 124) Un árbol de factores es un diagrama que muestra cómo se descompone un número compuesto en sus factores primos.

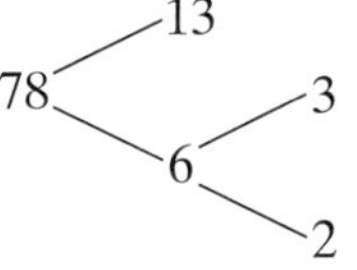

The prime factors of 78 are 2, 3, and 13.

Factorial (p. 576) A factorial is the product of all positive integers less than or equal to a number. The symbol for factorial is an exclamation point.

Factorial (p. 576) Un factorial es el producto de todos los enteros positivos menores o iguales que un número. El símbolo de factorial es un signo de cierre de exclamación.

$5! = 5 \times 4 \times 3 \times 2 \times 1 = 120$

Frequency table (p. 326) A frequency table lists each item in a data set with the number of times the item occurs.

Tabla de frecuencia (p. 326) Una tabla de frecuencia es una tabla que registra todos los elementos de un conjunto de datos y el número de veces que ocurre cada uno.

Household Telephones

Phones	Tally	Frequency
1	卌 |||	8
2	卌 |	6
3	||||	4

This frequency table shows the number of household telephones for a class of students.

Front-end estimation (p. 20) To use front-end estimation to estimate sums, first add the front-end digits. Then adjust by estimating the sum of the remaining digits. Add the two values.

Estimación de entrada (p. 20) Para estimar usando la estimación de entrada, primero se suman los dígitos de entrada. Luego se ajustan estimando la cantidad de los dígitos restantes. Finalmente, se suman las dos cantidades.

Estimate $3.09 + $2.99.

$**3**.09	→	$3.**09**
+$**2**.99		$2.**99**
$5		**about $1**

So, $3.09 + $2.99 ≈ 5 + 1, or $6.

EXAMPLES

Function (p. 527) A function is a relationship that assigns exactly one output value for each input value.

Función (p. 527) Una función es una relación que asigna exactamente un valor resultante a cada valor inicial.

Earned income i is a function of the number of hours worked h. If you earn \$6 per hour, then your income can be expressed by the function $i = 6h$.

G

Gram (p. 432) The standard unit of mass in the metric system is the gram.

Gramo (p. 432) La unidad de masa estándar en el sistema métrico es el gramo.

A paper clip has the mass of about 1 gram.

Graph of a function (p. 528) The graph of a function is the graph of all the points whose coordinates are solutions of the equation.

Gráfica de una función (p. 528) La gráfica de una función es la gráfica de todos los puntos cuyas coordenadas son soluciones a la ecuación.

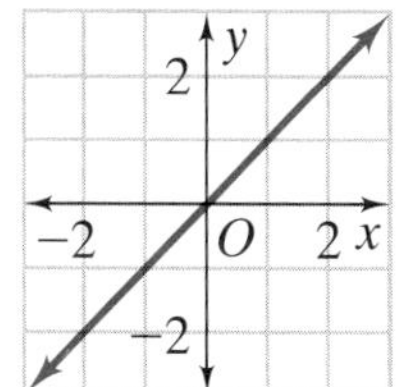

This is the graph of $y = x$.

Graph of an inequality (p. 602) The graph of an inequality shows all solutions that satisfy the inequality.

Gráfica de una designaldad (p. 568) La gráfica de designaldad muestra todas las soluciones que salisface la designaldad.

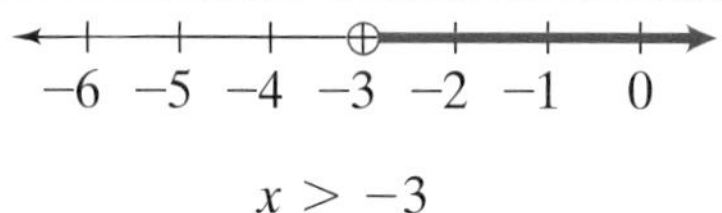

$x > -3$

Greatest common factor (GCF) (p. 128) The greatest common factor of two or more numbers is the greatest factor shared by all of the numbers.

Máximo común divisor (MCD) (p. 128) El máximo común divisor de dos o más números es el mayor divisor compartido con todos los números.

The GCF of 12 and 30 is 6.

H

Height of two-dimensional figures (p. 446, 447, 398) See *Parallelogram, Triangle,* and *Trapezoid.*

Altura de figuras bidimensionales (p. 446, 447, 398) Ver *Parallelogram, Triangle,* y *Trapezoid.*

EXAMPLES

Hexagon (p. 397) A hexagon is a polygon with six sides.

Hexágono (p. 397) Un hexágono es un polígono que tiene seis lados.

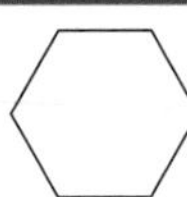

Histogram (p. 336) A histogram is a bar graph with no spaces between the bars. The height of each bar shows the frequency of data within that interval.

Histograma (p. 336) Un histograma es una gráfica de barras sin espacio entre las barras. La altura de cada barra muestra la frecuencia de los datos dentro del intervalo.

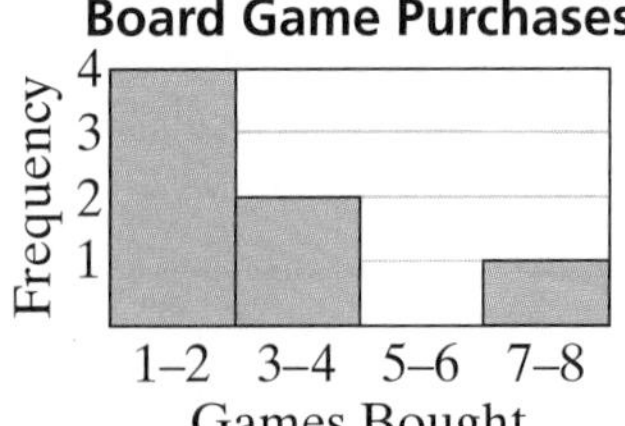

The histogram gives the frequency of board game purchases at a local toy store.

Hypotenuse (p. 622) In a right triangle, the hypotenuse is the longest side, which is opposite the right angle.

Hipotenusa (p. 622) En un triángulo rectángulo, la hipotenusa es el lado más largo, que es el lado opuesto al ángulo recto.

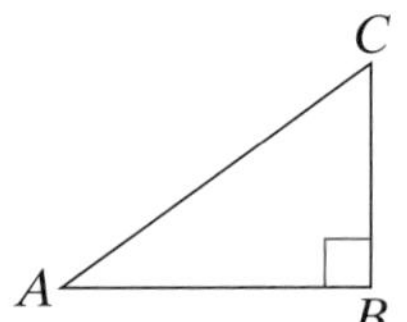

$\overline{AC}$ is the hypotenuse of $\triangle ABC$.

Identity Property of Addition (p. 25) The Identity Property of Addition states that the sum of 0 and a is a.

Propiedad de identidad de la suma (p. 25) La propiedad de identidad de la suma establece que la suma de 0 y a es a.

$0 + 7 = 7$

$a + 0 = a$

Identity Property of Multiplication (p. 36) The Identity Property of Multiplication states that the product of 1 and a is a.

Propiedad de identidad de la multiplicación (p. 36) La propiedad de identidad de la multiplicación establece que el producto de 1 y a es a.

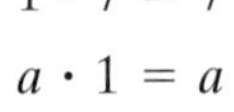

$1 \cdot 7 = 7$

$a \cdot 1 = a$

Image (p. 415) An image is the result of a transformation of a point, line, or figure.

Imagen (p. 415) Una imagen es el resultado de una transformación de un punto, una recta o una figura.

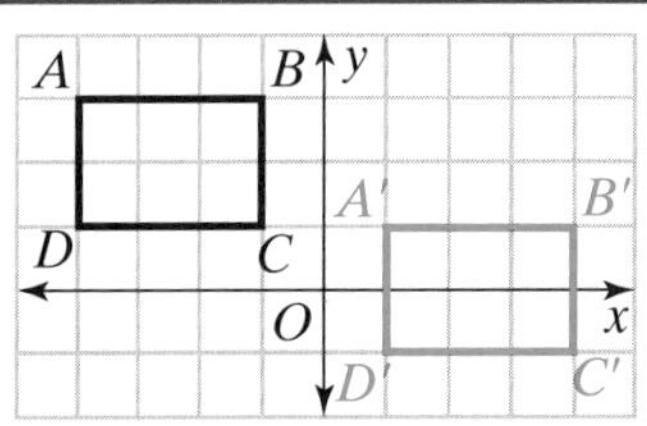

$A'B'C'D'$ is the image of $ABCD$.

	EXAMPLES
Improper fraction (p. 139) An improper fraction has a numerator that is greater than or equal to its denominator. **Fracción impropia (p. 139)** Una fracción impropia tiene un numerador mayor o igual que su denominador.	$\frac{24}{15}$ and $\frac{16}{16}$ are improper fractions.
Independent events (p. 580) Two events are independent events if the occurrence of one event does not affect the probability of the occurrence of the other. **Sucesos independientes (p. 580)** Dos sucesos son independientes si el acontecimiento de uno no afecta la probabilidad de que el otro suceso ocurra.	Suppose you draw two marbles, one after the other, from a bag. If you replace the first marble before drawing the second marble, the events are independent.
Inequality (p. 601) An inequality is a mathematical sentence that contains $<, >, \leq, \geq$, or $\neq$. **Desigualdad (p. 601)** Una desigualdad es una oración matemática que contiene los signos $<, >, \leq, \geq$, o $\neq$.	$x < -5$ $x > 8$ $x \leq 1$ $x \geq -11$ $x \neq 3$
Integers (p. 491) Integers are the set of positive whole numbers, their opposites, and 0. **Enteros (p. 491)** Los enteros son el conjunto de números enteros positivos, sus opuestos y el 0.	$\ldots -3, -2, -1, 0, 1, 2, 3, \ldots$
Interior angles (p. 387) The angles between two lines that are crossed by a transversal are called interior angles. **Ángulos interiores (p. 387)** Los ángulos que están entre dos rectas cruzadas por una secante se llaman ángulos interiores.	1 2 3 4 5 6 7 8 Angles 3, 4, 5, and 6 are interior angles.
Intersecting lines (p. 374) Intersecting lines lie in the same plane and have exactly one point in common. **Rectas que se intersectan (p. 374)** Las rectas que se intersectan y están en el mismo plano tienen exactamente un punto en común.	
Inverse operations (p. 90) Inverse operations are operations that undo each other. **Operaciones inversas (p. 90)** Las operaciones inversas son las operaciones que se anulan entre ellas.	Addition and subtraction are inverse operations.

EXAMPLES

Isosceles triangle (p. 393) An isosceles triangle is a triangle with at least two congruent sides.

Triángulo isósceles (p. 393) Un triángulo isósceles es un triángulo que tiene al menos dos lados congruentes.

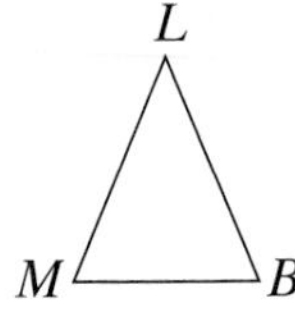

$\overline{LM} \cong \overline{LB}$

Least common denominator (LCD) (p. 148) The least common denominator of two or more fractions is the least common multiple (LCM) of their denominators.

Mínimo común denominador (MCD) (p. 148) El mínimo común denominador de dos o más fracciones es el mínimo común múltiplo (mcm) de sus denominadores.

The LCD of the fractions $\frac{3}{8}$ and $\frac{7}{10}$ is 40.

Least common multiple (LCM) (p. 143) The least common multiple of two numbers is the smallest number that is a multiple of both numbers.

Mínimo común múltiplo (MCM) (p. 143) El mínimo común múltiplo de dos números es el menor número que es múltiplo de ambos números.

The LCM of 15 and 6 is 30.

Legs of a right triangle (p. 622) The legs of a right triangle are the two shorter sides of the triangle.

Catetos de un triángulo rectángulo (p. 622) Los catetos de un triángulo rectángulo son los dos lados más cortos del triángulo.

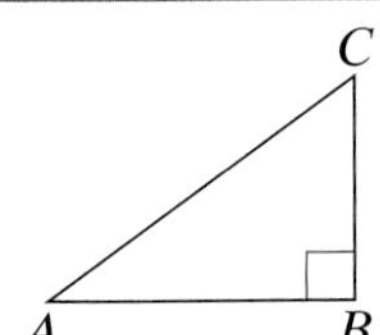

$\overline{AB}$ and $\overline{BC}$ are the legs of triangle ABC.

Line (p. 373) A line is a series of points that extends in two opposite directions without end.

Recta (p. 373) Una recta es una serie de puntos que se extiende indefinidamente en dos direcciones opuestas.

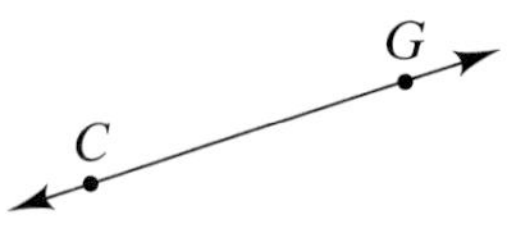

$\overleftrightarrow{CG}$ is shown.

Line graph (p. 336) A line graph is a graph that uses a series of line segments to show changes in data. Typically, a line graph shows changes over time.

Gráfica lineal (p. 336) Una gráfica lineal es una gráfica que usa una serie de segmentos de recta para mostrar cambios en los datos. Típicamente, una gráfica lineal muestra cambios a través del tiempo.

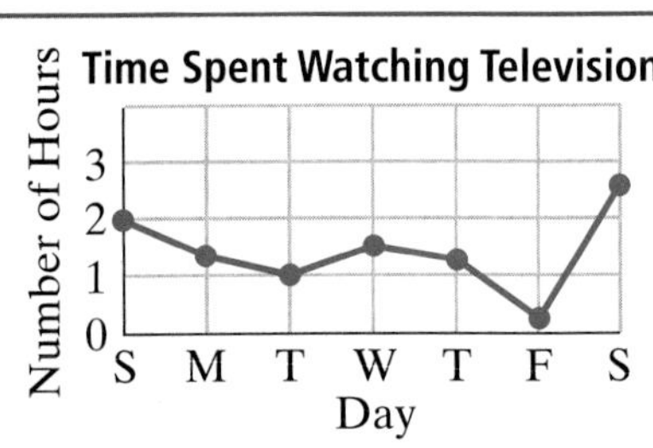

EXAMPLES

Line of reflection (p. 416) A line of reflection is a line over which a figure is reflected.

Eje de reflexión (p. 416) Un eje de reflexión es una recta sobre la cual se refleja una figura.

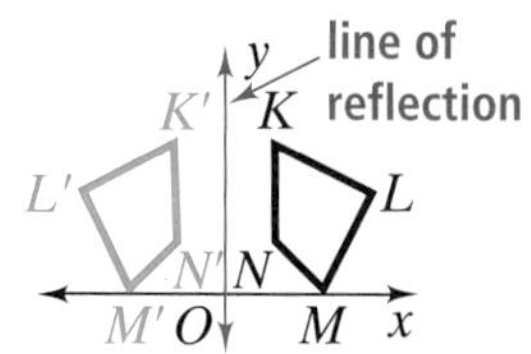

KLMN is reflected over the *y*-axis.

Line of symmetry (p. 410) A line of symmetry divides a figure into mirror images.

Eje de simetría (p. 410) Un eje de simetría divide una figura en imágenes reflejas.

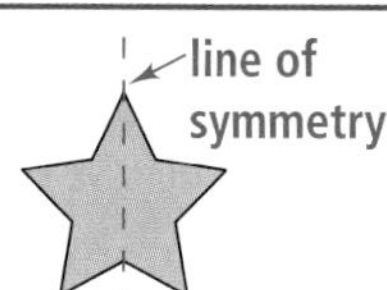

Line plot (p. 327) A line plot is a graph that shows the shape of a data set by stacking X's above each data value on a number line.

Diagrama de puntos (p. 327) Un diagrama de puntos es una gráfica que muestra la forma de un conjunto de datos agrupando X sobre cada valor de una recta numérica.

Pets Owned by Students

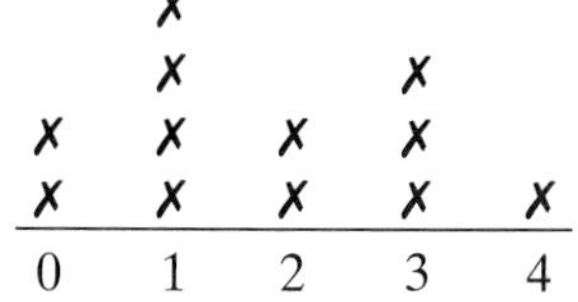

The line plot shows the number of pets owned by each of 12 students.

Liter (p. 433) The liter (L) is the standard unit of capacity in the metric system.

Litro (p. 433) El litro (L) es la unidad de capacidad estándar en el sistema métrico decimal.

A pitcher holds about 2 liters of juice.

M

Mass (p. 432) Mass is a measure of the amount of matter in an object.

Masa (p. 432) La masa es la medida de la cantidad de materia en un objeto.

A brick has a greater mass than a feather.

Mean (p. 322) The mean of a set of data values is the sum of the data divided by the number of data items.

Media (p. 322) La media de un conjunto de valores de datos es la suma de los datos dividida por el número de datos.

The mean temperature (°F) for the set of temperatures 44, 52, 48, 55, 61, and 67 is $\frac{44 + 52 + 48 + 55 + 61 + 67}{6} = 54.5$°F.

	EXAMPLES
Median (p. 323) The median of a data set is the middle value when the data are arranged in numerical order. When there is an even number of data values, the median is the mean of the two middle values. **Mediana (p. 323)** La mediana de un conjunto de datos es el valor del medio cuando los datos están organizados en orden numérico. Cuando hay un número par de valores de datos, la mediana es la media de los dos valores del medio.	A set of temperatures (°F) arranged in order are 44, 48, 52, 55, and 58. The median temperature is 52°F because it is the middle number in the set of data.
Meter (p. 431) The meter (m) is the standard unit of length in the metric system. **Metro (p. 431)** El metro (m) es la unidad de longitud estándar en el sistema métrico centesimal.	A doorknob is about 1 meter from the floor.
Metric system (p. 431) The metric system of measurement is a decimal system. Prefixes indicate the relative size of units. **Sistema métrico (p. 431)** El sistema métrico de medidas es un sistema decimal. Los prefijos indican el tamaño relativo de las unidades.	1 kilogram = 1,000 grams 1 centimeter = $\frac{1}{100}$ meter 1 milliliter = $\frac{1}{1,000}$ liter
Midpoint (p. 384) The midpoint of a segment is the point that divides the segment into two segments of equal length. **Punto medio (p. 384)** El punto medio de un segmento es el punto que divide el segmento en dos segmentos de igual longitud.	X M Y $XM = YM$. M is the midpoint of $\overline{XY}$.
Mixed number (p. 139) A mixed number is the sum of a whole number and a fraction. **Número mixto (p. 139)** Un número mixto es la suma de un número entero y una fracción.	$3\frac{11}{16}$ is a mixed number. $3\frac{11}{16} = 3 + \frac{11}{16}$.
Mode (p. 323) The mode of a data set is the item that occurs with the greatest frequency. **Moda (p. 323)** La moda de un conjunto de datos es el dato que sucede con mayor frecuencia.	The mode of the set of prices \$2.50, \$2.75, \$3.60, \$2.75, and \$3.70 is \$2.75.
Multiple (p. 143) A multiple of a number is the product of the number and any nonzero whole number. **Múltiplo (p. 143)** Un múltiplo de un número es el producto del número y cualquier número entero diferente de cero.	The number 39 is a multiple of 13.

EXAMPLES

Multiplication Property of Equality (p. 96) The Multiplication Property of Equality states that if each side of an equation is multiplied by the same number, the results are equal.

Propiedad multiplicativa de la igualdad (p. 96) La propiedad multiplicativa de la igualdad establece que si cada lado de una ecuación se multiplica por el mismo número, los resultados son iguales.

Since $\frac{12}{2} = 6$, $\frac{12}{2} \cdot 2 = 6 \cdot 2$.
If $a = b$, then $a \cdot c = b \cdot c$.

Net (p. 464) A net is a two-dimensional pattern that can be folded to form a three-dimensional figure.

Plantilla (p. 464) Una plantilla es un patrón bidimensional que se puede doblar para formar una figura tridimensional.

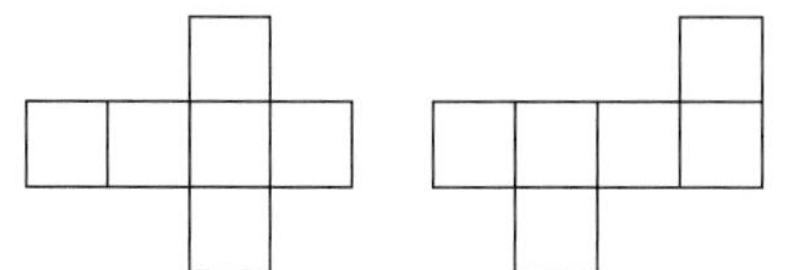

These are nets for a cube.

Numerical expression (p. 68) A numerical expression is an expression with only numbers and operation symbols.

Expresión numérica (p. 68) Una expresión numérica es una expresión que tiene sólo números y símbolos de operaciones.

$2(5 + 7) - 14$ is a numerical expression.

Obtuse angle (p. 380) An obtuse angle is an angle with a measure greater than 90° and less than 180°.

Ángulo obtuso (p. 380) Un ángulo obtuso es un ángulo que mide más de 90° y menos de 180°.

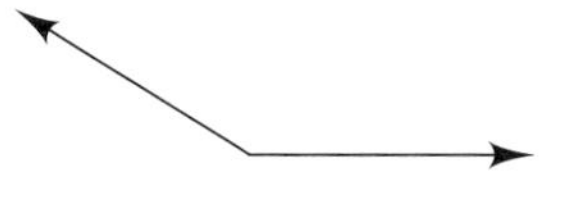

Obtuse triangle (p. 392) An obtuse triangle is a triangle with one obtuse angle.

Triángulo obtusángulo (p. 392) Un triángulo obtusángulo es un triángulo que tiene un ángulo obtuso.

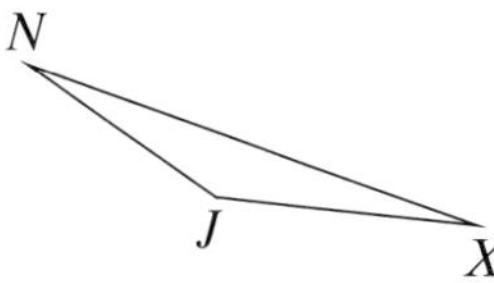

The measure of $\angle J$ is between 90° and 180°. Triangle NJX is an obtuse triangle.

Octagon (p. 397) An octagon is a polygon with eight sides.

Octágono (p. 397) Un octágono es un polígono que tiene ocho lados.

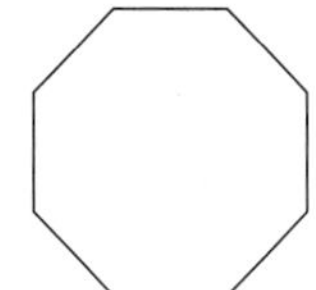

EXAMPLES

Odd number (p. 120) An odd number is a whole number that ends with a 1, 3, 5, 7, or 9.

Número impar (p. 120) Un número impar es un número entero que termina en 1, 3, 5, 7 ó 9.

43 and 687 are odd numbers.

Odds (p. 552) When outcomes are equally likely, odds are expressed as the following ratios.

odds *in favor of* an event = number of favorable outcomes : number of unfavorable outcomes

odds *against* an event = number of unfavorable outcomes : number of favorable outcomes

Posibilidades (p. 552) Cuando los resultados son igualmente posibles, las posibilidades se expresan como las siguientes razones.

posibilidades *en favor* de un suceso = número de resultados favorables : número de resultados desfavorables

posibilidades *en contra* de un suceso = número de resultados desfavorables : número de resultados favorables

You roll a standard number cube. The odds in favor of getting a 4 are $\frac{1}{5}$. The odds against getting a 4 are $\frac{4}{5}$.

Open sentence (p. 85) An open sentence is an equation with one or more variables.

Proposición abierta (p. 85) Una proposición abierta es una ecuación con una o más variables.

$b - 7 = 12$

Opposites (p. 491) Opposites are two numbers that are the same distance from 0 on a number line, but in opposite directions.

Opuestos (p. 491) Opuestos son dos números que están a la misma distancia del 0 en una recta numérica, pero en direcciones opuestas.

17 and −17 are opposites.

Ordered pair (p. 518) An ordered pair identifies the location of a point. The x-coordinate shows a point's position left or right of the y-axis. The y-coordinate shows a point's position up or down from the x-axis.

Par ordenado (p. 518) Un par ordenado identifica la ubicación de un punto. La coordenada x muestra la posición de un punto a la izquierda o derecha del origen. La coordenada y muestra la posición de un punto arriba o abajo del eje de x.

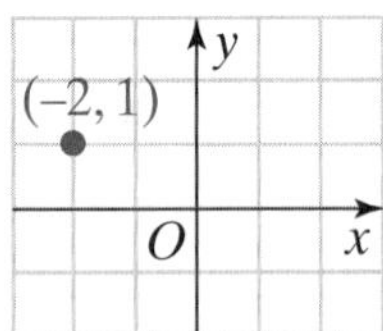

The x-coordinate of the point $(-2, 1)$ is -2, and the y-coordinate is 1.

EXAMPLES

Order of operations (pp. 48, 100)
1. Work inside grouping symbols.
2. Do all work with exponents.
3. Multiply and divide in order from left to right.
4. Add and subtract in order from left to right.

$2^3(7 - 4) = 2^3 \cdot 3 = 8 \cdot 3 = 24$

Orden de las operaciones (pp. 48, 100)
1. Trabaja dentro de los signos de agrupación.
2. Trabaja con los exponentes.
3. Multiplica y divide en orden de izquierda a derecha.
4. Suma y resta en orden de izquierda a derecha.

Origin (p. 518) The origin is the point of intersection of the x- and y-axes on a coordinate plane.

Origen (p. 518) El origen es el punto de intersección de los ejes de x y de y en un plano de coordenadas.

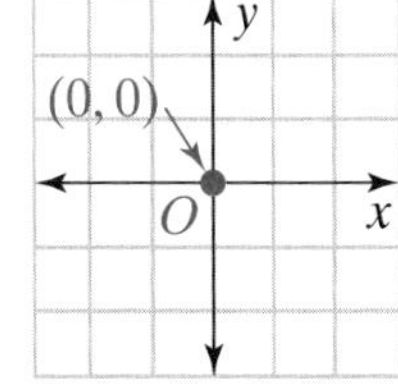

The ordered pair that describes the origin is (0, 0).

Outcome (p. 547) An outcome is any of the possible results that can occur in an experiment.

Resultado (p. 547) Un resultado es cualquiera de los posibles desenlaces que pueden ocurrir en un experimento.

The outcomes of rolling a standard number cube are 1, 2, 3, 4, 5, and 6.

Outlier (p. 322) An outlier is a data item that is much higher or much lower than the other items in a data set.

Valor extremo (p. 322) Un valor extremo es un dato que es mucho más alto o más bajo que los demás datos de un conjunto de datos.

An outlier in the data set 6, 7, 9, 10, 11, 12, 14, and 52 is 52.

Parallel lines (p. 374) Parallel lines are lines in the same plane that never intersect.

Rectas paralelas (p. 378) Las rectas paralelas son rectas en el mismo plano que nunca se intersectan.

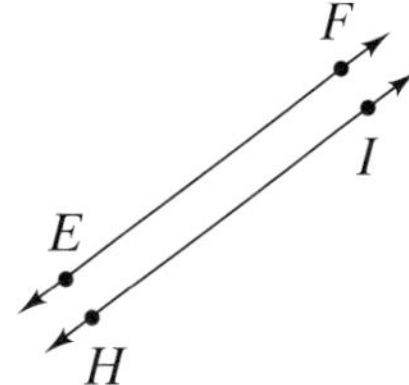

$\overleftrightarrow{EF}$ is parallel to $\overleftrightarrow{HI}$.

EXAMPLES

Parallelogram (p. 398) A parallelogram is a quadrilateral with both pairs of opposite sides parallel.

Paralelogramo (p. 398) Un paralelogramo es un cuadrilátero cuyos pares de lados opuestos son paralelos.

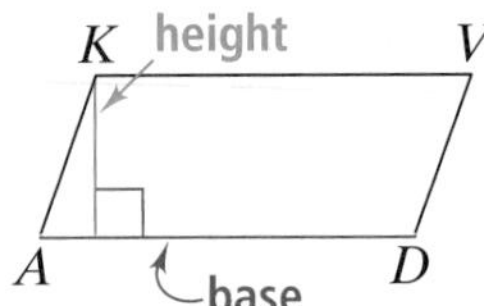

$\overline{KV}$ is parallel to $\overline{AD}$ and $\overline{AK}$ is parallel to $\overline{DV}$, so $KVDA$ is a parallelogram.

Pentagon (p. 397) A pentagon is a polygon with five sides.

Pentágono (p. 397) Un pentágono es un polígono que tiene cinco lados.

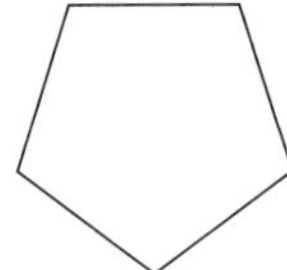

Percent (p. 294) A percent is a ratio that compares a number to 100.

Porcentaje (p. 294) Un porcentaje es una razón que compara un número con 100.

$\frac{25}{100} = 25\%$

Perfect square (p. 616) A perfect square is a number that is the square of an integer.

Cuadrado perfecto (p. 616) Un cuadrado perfecto es un número que es el cuadrado de un entero.

Since $25 = 5^2$, 25 is a perfect square.

Perimeter (p. 441) The perimeter of a figure is the distance around the figure.

Perímetro (p. 441) El perímetro de una figura es la distancia alrededor de la figura.

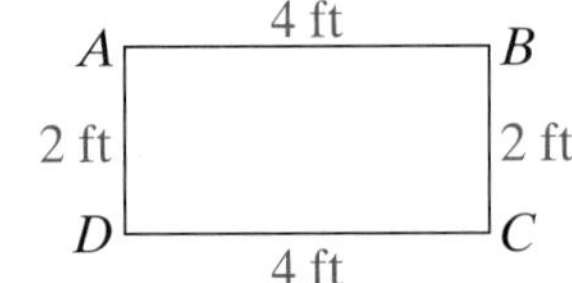

The perimeter of rectangle $ABCD$ is 12 ft.

Permutation (p. 574) A permutation is an arrangement of objects in a particular order.

Permutación (p. 574) Una permutación es un arreglo de objetos en un orden particular.

The permutations of the letters W, A, and X are WAX, WXA, AXW, AWX, XWA, and XAW.

Perpendicular bisector (p. 384) A perpendicular bisector is a segment bisector that is perpendicular to the segment.

Bisectriz perpendicular (p. 384) Una bisectriz perpendicular es una bisectriz de un segmento que es perpendicular a ese segmento.

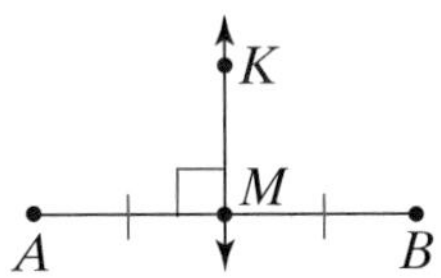

$\overleftrightarrow{MK} \perp \overline{AB}$, $AM = MB$. $\overleftrightarrow{MK}$ is the perpendicular bisector of $\overline{AB}$.

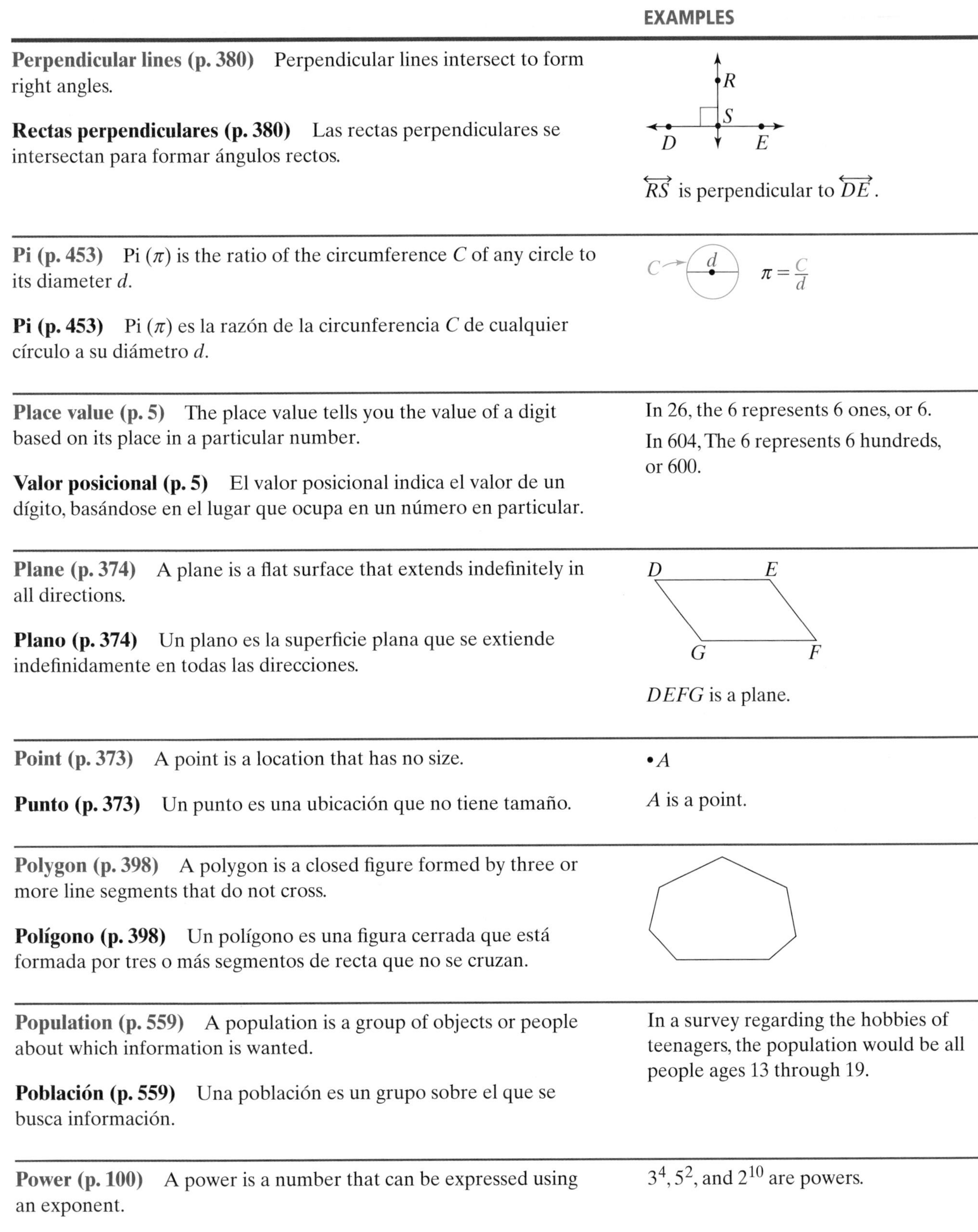

Perpendicular lines (p. 380) Perpendicular lines intersect to form right angles.

Rectas perpendiculares (p. 380) Las rectas perpendiculares se intersectan para formar ángulos rectos.

$\overleftrightarrow{RS}$ is perpendicular to $\overleftrightarrow{DE}$.

Pi (p. 453) Pi (π) is the ratio of the circumference C of any circle to its diameter d.

Pi (p. 453) Pi (π) es la razón de la circunferencia C de cualquier círculo a su diámetro d.

$\pi = \frac{C}{d}$

Place value (p. 5) The place value tells you the value of a digit based on its place in a particular number.

Valor posicional (p. 5) El valor posicional indica el valor de un dígito, basándose en el lugar que ocupa en un número en particular.

In 26, the 6 represents 6 ones, or 6.

In 604, The 6 represents 6 hundreds, or 600.

Plane (p. 374) A plane is a flat surface that extends indefinitely in all directions.

Plano (p. 374) Un plano es la superficie plana que se extiende indefinidamente en todas las direcciones.

DEFG is a plane.

Point (p. 373) A point is a location that has no size.

Punto (p. 373) Un punto es una ubicación que no tiene tamaño.

• *A*

A is a point.

Polygon (p. 398) A polygon is a closed figure formed by three or more line segments that do not cross.

Polígono (p. 398) Un polígono es una figura cerrada que está formada por tres o más segmentos de recta que no se cruzan.

Population (p. 559) A population is a group of objects or people about which information is wanted.

Población (p. 559) Una población es un grupo sobre el que se busca información.

In a survey regarding the hobbies of teenagers, the population would be all people ages 13 through 19.

Power (p. 100) A power is a number that can be expressed using an exponent.

Potencia (p. 100) Una potencia es un número que se puede expresar usando un exponente.

3^4, 5^2, and 2^{10} are powers.

EXAMPLES

Prime factorization (p. 124) Writing a composite number as the product of prime numbers is the prime factorization of the number.

Factorización en primos (p. 124) Escribir un número compuesto como el producto de sus factores primos es la factorización en primos del números.

The prime factorization of 12 is $2 \cdot 2 \cdot 3$, or $2^2 \cdot 3$.

Prime number (p. 124) A prime number is a whole number with exactly two factors, 1 and the number itself.

Número primo (p. 124) Un número primo es un entero que tiene exactamente dos factores, 1 y el mismo número.

13 is a prime number because its only factors are 1 and 13.

Prism (p. 462) A prism is a three-dimensional figure with two parallel and congruent faces that are polygons. These faces are called bases. A prism is named for the shape of its base.

Prisma (p. 462) Un prisma es una figura tridimensional que tiene dos caras paralelas y congruentes que son polígones. Estas curas se llaman bases. Un prisma recibe su nombre por la forma de su base.

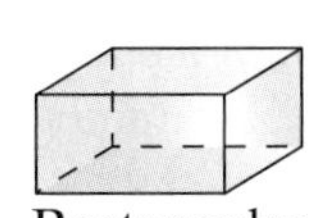
Rectangular Prism

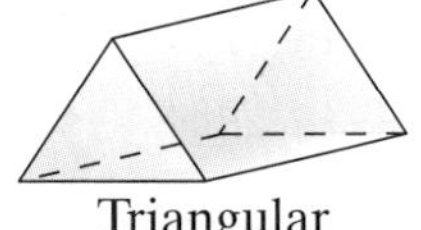
Triangular Prism

Probability of an event (p. 547) When outcomes are equally likely, the probability of an event is given by this formula:

$$P(\text{event}) = \frac{\text{number of favorable outcomes}}{\textit{total}\ \text{number of possible outcomes}}$$

See *Experimental probability.*

Probabilidad de un suceso (p. 547) Cuando los resultados son igualments posibles, la probabilidad de un suceso se da por esta fórmula:

$$P(\text{suceso}) = \frac{\text{número favorable de resultados}}{\text{número total de resultados posibles}}$$

Ver *Probabilidad experimental.*

Proper fraction (p. 139) A proper fraction has a numerator that is less than its denominator.

Fracción propia (p. 139) Una fracción propia tiene un numerador que es menos que su denominador.

$\frac{3}{8}$ and $\frac{11}{12}$ are proper fractions.

Proportion (p. 278) A proportion is an equation stating that two ratios are equal.

Proporción (p. 278) Una proporción es una ecuación que establece que dos razones son iguales.

$\frac{3}{12} = \frac{9}{36}$ is a proportion.

EXAMPLES

Pyramid (p. 463) A pyramid is a three-dimensional figure with triangular faces that meet at a vertex. Its base is a polygon. A pyramid is named for the shape of its base.

Pirámide (p. 463) Una pirámide es una figura tridimensional que tiene caras triangulares que coinciden en un vértice. Su base es un polígono. Una pirámide recibe su nombre por la forma de su base.

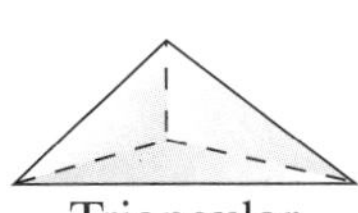
Triangular Pyramid

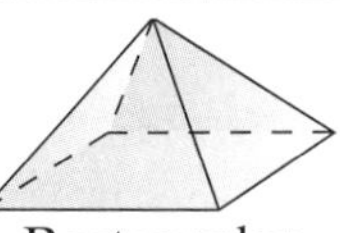
Rectangular Pyramid

Pythagorean Theorem (p. 622) In any right triangle, the sum of the squares of the lengths of the legs (a and b) is equal to the square of the length of the hypotenuse (c): $a^2 + b^2 = c^2$.

Teorema de Pitágoras (p. 622) En cualquier triángulo rectángulo, la suma del cuadrado de la longitud de los catetos (a y b) es igual al cuadrado de la longitud de la hipotenusa (c): $a^2 + b^2 = c^2$.

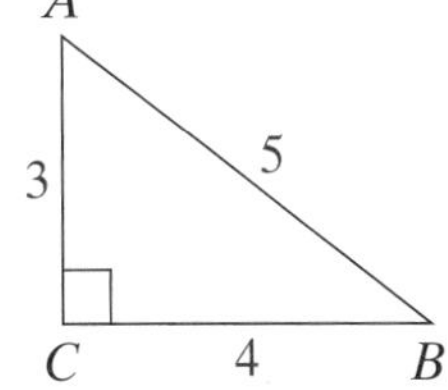

The right triangle has leg lengths 3 and 4 and hypotenuse length 5.

$$3^2 + 4^2 = 5^2.$$

Q

Quadrants (p. 518) The x- and y-axes divide the coordinate plane into four regions called quadrants.

Cuadrantes (p. 518) Los ejes de x y de y dividen el plano de coordenadas en cuatro regiones llamadas cuadrantes.

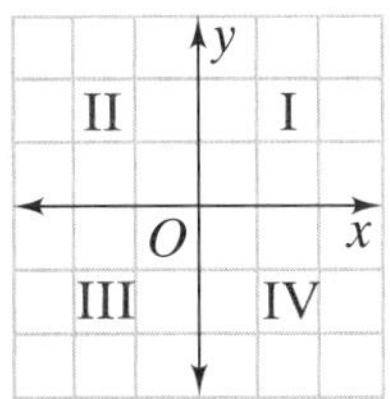

The quadrants are labeled I, II, III, and IV.

Quadrilateral (p. 398) A quadrilateral is a polygon with four sides.

Cuadrilátero (p. 398) Un cuadrilátero es un polígono que tiene cuatro lados.

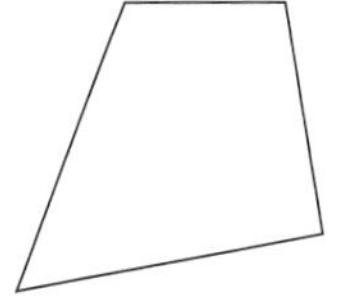

Quartiles (p. 356) Quartiles are three values that divide a data set into four equal parts.

- The *lower quartile* is the median of the lower half of the data.
- The *middle quartile* is the median of the data set.
- The *upper quartile* is the median of the upper half of the data.

Cuartiles (p. 356) Los cuartiles son los tres valores que dividen los datos de un conjunto en cuatro partes iguales.

- El *cuartil inferior* es la mediana de la mitad inferior de datos.
- El *cuartil medio* es la mediana del conjunto de datos.
- El *cuartil superior* es la mediana de la mitad superior de datos.

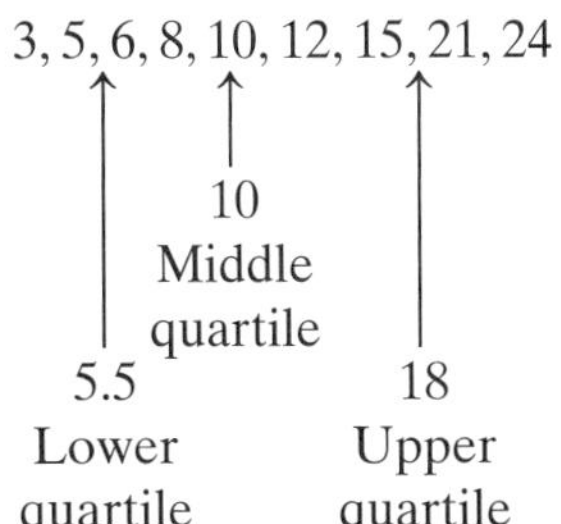

EXAMPLES

Radius (p. 452) A radius of a circle is a segment that connects the center to the circle.

Radio (p. 452) Un radio de un círculo es un segmento que conecta el centro con el círculo.

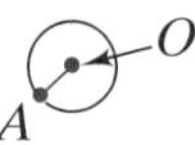

$\overline{OA}$ is a radius of circle O.

Range (p. 327) The range of a data set is the difference between the greatest and the least values.

Rango (p. 327) El rango de un conjunto de datos es la diferencia entre los valores mayor y menor.

Data set: 62, 109, 234, 35, 96, 49, 201
Range: $201 - 35 = 166$

Rate (p. 273) A rate is a ratio that compares two quantities measured in different units.

Tasa (p. 273) Una tasa es una razón que compara dos cantidades medidas en diferentes unidades.

Suppose you read 116 words in 1 minute. Your reading rate is $\frac{116 \text{ words}}{1 \text{ minute}}$.

Ratio (p. 269) A ratio is a comparison of two quantities by division.

Razón (p. 269) Una razón es una comparación de dos cantidades mediante la división.

There are three ways to write a ratio: 9 to 10, 9 : 10, and $\frac{9}{10}$.

Rational number (p. 617) A rational number is any number that can be written as a quotient of two integers where the denominator is not 0.

Número racional (p. 617) Un número racional es cualquier número que puede ser escrito como cociente de dos enteros, donde el denominador es diferente de 0.

$\frac{1}{3}$, -5, 6.4, 0.666 . . . , $-2\frac{4}{5}$, 0, and $\frac{7}{3}$ are rational numbers.

Ray (p. 373) A ray is part of a line. It has one endpoint and all the points of the line on one side of the endpoint.

Rayo (p. 373) Un rayo es parte de una linea. Tiene un extremo y todos los puntos de la recta a un lado del extremo.

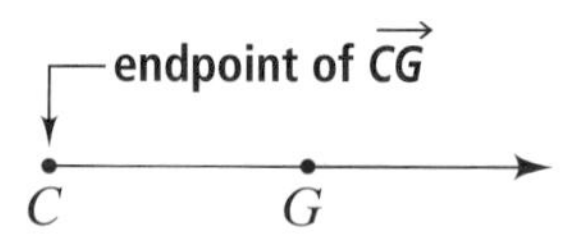

$\overrightarrow{CG}$ represents a ray.

Reciprocal (p. 230) Two numbers are reciprocals if their product is 1.

Recíproco (p. 230) Dos números son recíprocos si su producto es 1.

The numbers $\frac{4}{9}$ and $\frac{9}{4}$ are reciprocals.

Rectangle (p. 398) A rectangle is a parallelogram with four right angles.

Rectángulo (p. 398) Un rectángulo es un paralelogramo que tiene cuatro ángulos rectos.

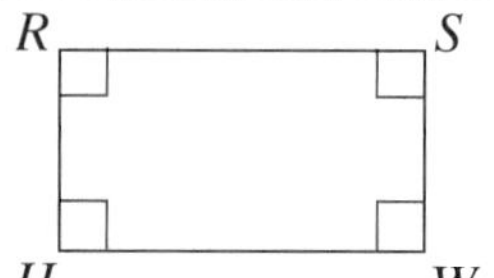

EXAMPLES

Reflection (p. 416) A reflection, or flip, is a transformation that flips a figure over a line of reflection.

Reflejo (p. 416) Un reflejo es una transformación que voltea una figura sobre un eje de reflexión.

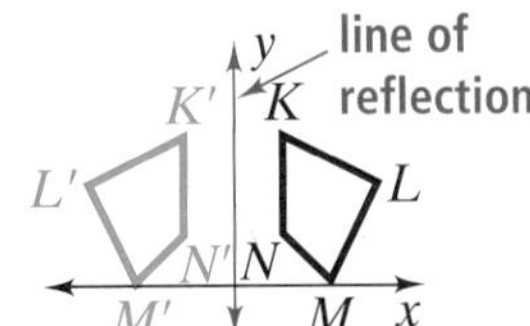

$K'L'M'N'$ is a reflection of $KLMN$ over the y-axis.

Repeating decimal (p. 44) A repeating decimal is a decimal that repeats the same digits without end. The repeating block can be one digit or more than one digit.

Decimal periódico (p. 44) Un decimal periódico es un decimal que repite los mismos dígitos interminablemente. El bloque que se repite puede ser un dígito o más de un dígito.

$0.888\ldots = 0.\overline{8}$

$0.272727\ldots = 0.\overline{27}$

Rhombus (p. 398) A rhombus is a parallelogram with four congruent sides.

Rombo (p. 398) Un rombo es un paralelogramo que tiene cuatro lados congruentes.

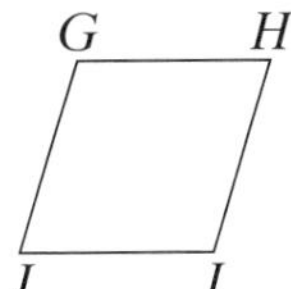

Right angle (p. 380) A right angle is an angle with a measure of 90°.

Ángulo recto (p. 380) Un ángulo recto es un ángulo que mide 90°.

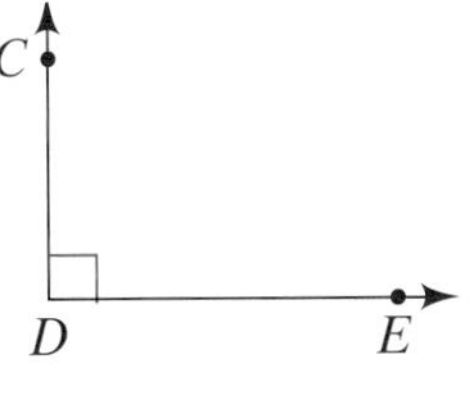

$m\angle D = 90°$

Right triangle (p. 392) A right triangle is a triangle with one right angle.

Triángulo rectángulo (p. 392) Un triángulo rectángulo es un triángulo que tiene un ángulo recto.

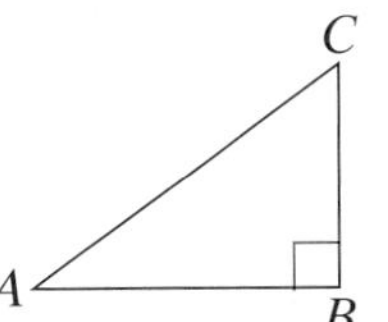

$\triangle ABC$ is a right triangle since $\angle B$ is a right angle.

Rotation (p. 416) A rotation is a transformation that turns a figure about a fixed point O, called the center of rotation.

Rotación (p. 416) Una rotación es una transformación que gira una figura sobre un punto fijo O, llamado centro de rotación.

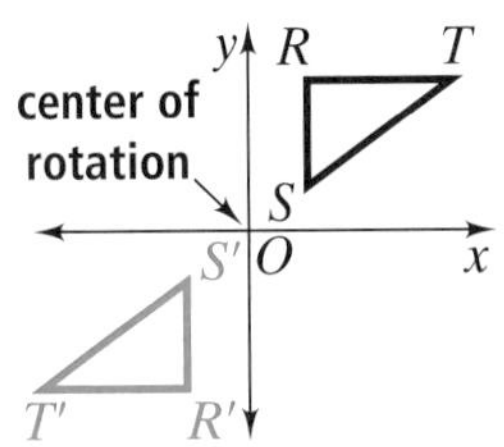

$\triangle RST$ has been rotated about the origin O to $\triangle R'S'T'$.

EXAMPLES

Sample (p. 559) A sample is a part of a population. You use a sample to make predictions about a population.

Muestra (p. 559) Una muestra es una parte de una población. Se usa una muestra para hacer predicciones acerca de una población.

Suppose 50 students out of the 700 students at a school are surveyed. The 50 students represent a sample population.

Scale (p. 288) A scale is the ratio that compares a length in a drawing to the corresponding length in the actual object.

Escala (p. 288) Una escala es la razón que compara la longitud en un dibujo con la longitud correspondiente en el objeto real.

A 25-mile road is 1 inch long on a map. The scale can be written three ways: 1 inch : 25 miles, $\frac{1 \text{ inch}}{25 \text{ miles}}$, 1 inch = 25 miles.

Scale drawing (p. 289) A scale drawing is an enlarged or reduced drawing of an object that is similar to the actual object.

Dibujo a escala (p. 289) Un dibujo a escala es un dibujo aumentado o reducido de un objeto que es semejante al objeto real.

Maps and floor plans are scale drawings.

Scalene triangle (p. 393) A scalene triangle is a triangle with no congruent sides.

Triángulo escaleno (p. 393) Un triángulo escaleno es un triángulo cuyos lados no son congruentes.

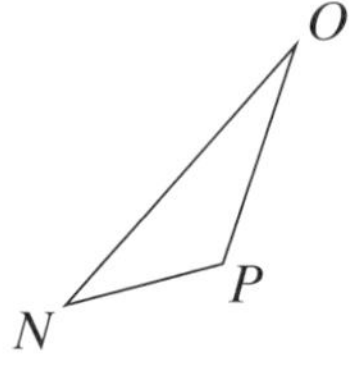

Scientific notation (p. 104) A number in scientific notation is written as the product of two factors. The first factor is a number greater than or equal to 1 and less than 10; the second factor is a power of 10.

Notación científica (p. 104) Un número en notación científica se escribe como el producto de dos factores. El primer factor es un número mayor o igual a 1 y menor que 10; el segundo factor es una potencia de 10.

37,000,000 is written as 3.7×10^7 in scientific notation.

Segment (p. 373) A segment is part of a line. It has two endpoints and all the points of the line between the endpoints.

Segmento (p. 373) Un segmento es parte de una linea. Tiene dos extremos y todos los puntos de la recta entre los puntos extremos.

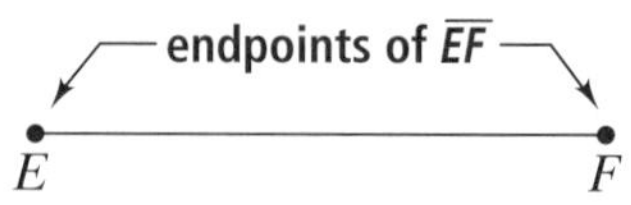

$\overline{EF}$ is a segment.

Similar figures (p. 406) Two figures are similar if their corresponding angles have the same measure and the lengths of their corresponding sides are proportional. The symbol ~ means "is similar to."

Figuras similares (p. 406) Dos figuras son semejantes si sus ángulos correspondientes tienen la misma medida y las longitudes de sus lados correspondientes son proporcionales. El símbolo ~ significa "es semejante a."

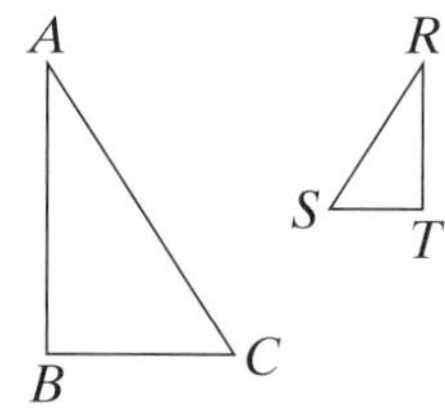

$\triangle ABC \sim \triangle RTS$

EXAMPLES

Simplest form (p. 135) A fraction is in simplest form when the numerator and denominator have no common factors other than 1.

Mínima expresión (p. 135) Una fracción está en forma simplificada cuando el numerador y el denominador no tienen otro factor común más que el 1.

The simplest form of $\frac{3}{9}$ is $\frac{1}{3}$.

Simulation (p. 563) A simulation of a real-world situation is a model used to find experimental probabilities.

Simulación (p. 563) Una simulación de una situación real es un modelo que se usa para hallar probabilidades experimentales.

A baseball team has equal chances of winning or losing the next game. You can use a coin to simulate the outcome.

Skew lines (p. 374) Skew lines lie in different planes. They are neither parallel nor intersecting.

Rectas cruzadas (p. 374) Las rectas cruzadas están en planos diferentes. No son paralelas ni se intersectan.

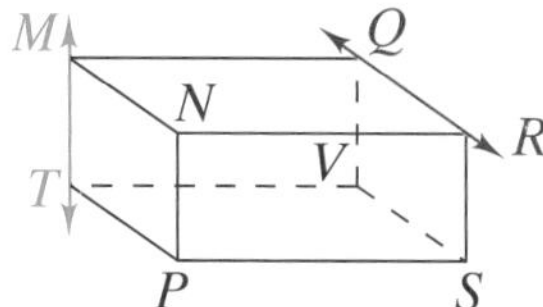

$\overleftrightarrow{MT}$ and $\overleftrightarrow{QR}$ are skew lines.

Solution (p. 85, 602) A solution is any value or values that makes an equation or inequality true.

Solución (p. 85, 602) Una solución es cualquier valor o valores que hacen que una ecuación o una desigualdad sea verdadera.

4 is the solution of $x + 5 = 9$.

7 is a solution of $x < 15$.

Sphere (p. 463) A sphere is the set of all points in space that are the same distance from a center point.

Esfera (p. 463) Una esfera es el conjunto de todos los puntos en el espacio que están a la misma distancia de un punto central.

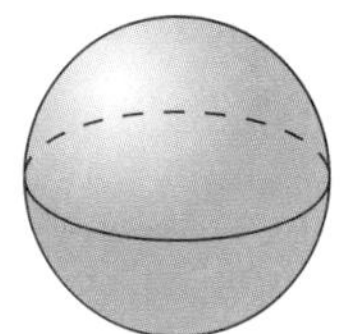

Spreadsheet (p. 347) A spreadsheet is a tool used for organizing and analyzing data. Spreadsheets are arranged in numbered rows and lettered columns.

Hoja de cálculo (p. 347) Una hoja de cálculo es una herramienta que se usa para organizar y analizar datos. Las hojas de cálculo se organizan en filas numeradas y columnas en orden alfabético.

	A	B	C	D	E
1	0.50	0.70	0.60	0.50	2.30
2	1.50	0.50	2.75	2.50	7.25

Column C and row 2 meet at cell C2.

Square (p. 398) A square is a parallelogram with four right angles and four congruent sides.

Cuadrado (p. 398) Una cuadrado es un paralelógramo que tiene cuatro ángulos rectos y cuatro lados congruentes.

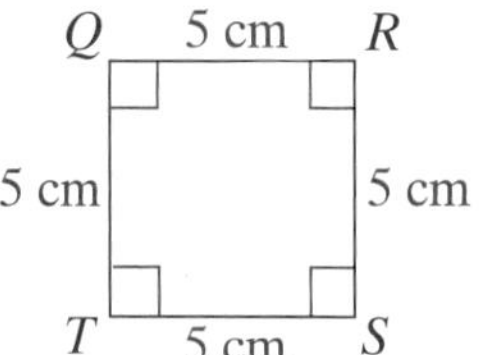

$QRST$ is a square. $\angle Q$, $\angle R$, $\angle S$, and $\angle T$ are right angles, and $\overline{QR} \cong \overline{RS} \cong \overline{ST} \cong \overline{QT}$.

English/Spanish Glossary

EXAMPLES

Square root (p. 616) Finding the square root of a number is the inverse of squaring a number.

Raíz cuadrada (p. 616) Hallar la raíz cuadrada de un número es el inverso de elevar un número al cuadrado.

$\sqrt{9} = 3$ because $3^2 = 9$.

Standard form (p. 9) A number written using digits and place value is in standard form. See also *Expanded form.*

Forma normal (p. 9) Un número escrito usando dígitos y valor posicional está escrito en forma normal. Ver también *Expanded form.*

2,174 is in standard form.

Stem-and-leaf plot (p. 352) A stem-and-leaf plot is a graph that uses the digits of each number to show the shape of the graph. Each data value is broken into a "stem" (digit or digits on the left) and a "leaf" (digit or digits on the right).

Diagrama de tallo y hojas (p. 352) Un diagrama de tallo y hojas es una gráfica en la que se usan los dígitos de cada número para mostrar la forma de la gráfica. Cada valor de los datos se divide en "tallo" (dígito o dígitos a la izquierda) y "hojas" (dígito o dígitos a la derecha).

stem	leaves
27	7
28	5 6 8
29	6 9
30	8

Key: 27 | 7 means 27.7

This stem-and-leaf plot displays recorded times in a race. The stems represent whole numbers of seconds. The leaves represent tenths of a second.

Straight angle (p. 380) A straight angle is an angle with a measure of 180°.

Ángulo llano (p. 380) Un ángulo llano es un ángulo que mide 180°.

The measure of $\angle TPL$ is 180°.

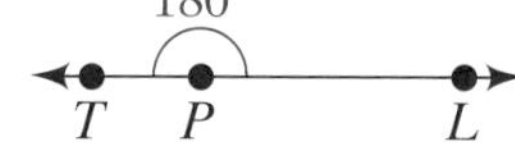

Subtraction Property of Equality (p. 90) The Subtraction Property of Equality states that if the same number is subtracted from each side of an equation, the results are equal.

Propiedad sustractiva de la igualdad (p. 90) La propiedad sustractiva de la igualdad establece que si se resta el mismo número a cada lado de una ecuación, los resultados son iguales.

Since $\frac{20}{2} = 10$, $\frac{20}{2} - 3 = 10 - 3$.
If $a = b$, then $a - c = b - c$.

Supplementary (p. 386) Two angles are supplementary if the sum of their measures is 180°.

Suplementario (p. 386) Dos ángulos son suplementarios si la suma de sus ángulos es 180°.

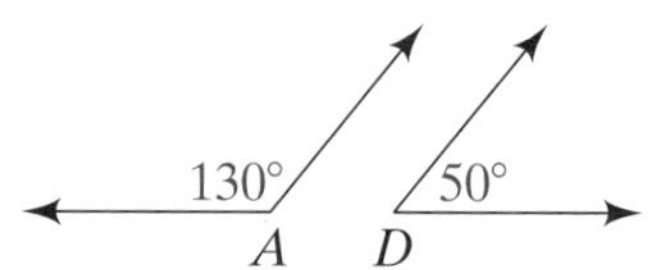

$\angle A$ and $\angle D$ are supplementary angles.

EXAMPLES

Surface area of a three-dimensional figure (p. 468) The surface area of a three-dimensional figure is the sum of the areas of all the surfaces.

Área total de una figura tridimensional (p. 468) El área total de una figura tridimensional es la suma de las áreas de todas sus superficies.

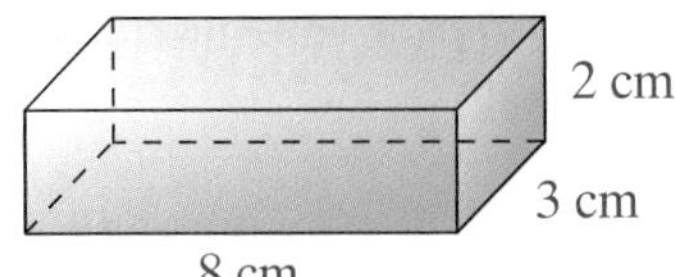

Term (p. 63) A term is a number in a pattern.

Término (p. 63) Un término es un número en un patrón.

6, 12, 24, 48, … The third term in this pattern is 24.

Terminating decimal (p. 44) A terminating decimal is a decimal that stops, or terminates.

Decimal exacto (p. 44) Un decimal finito es undecimal que termina.

Both 0.6 and 0.7265 are terminating decimals.

Three-dimensional figure (p. 462) Three-dimensional figures are figures that have length, width, and height.

Figura tridemensional (p. 462) Las figuras tridimensionales son figuras que tienen longitud, anchura y altura.

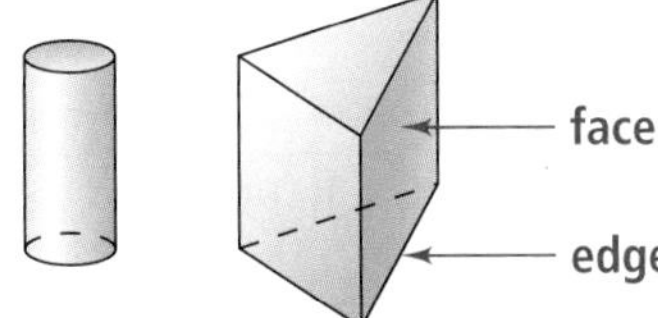

Transformation (p. 415) A transformation is a change in position, shape, or size of a figure. Three types of transformations that change position only are translations, reflections, and rotations.

Transformacion (p. 415) Una transformación es un cambio de posición, forma o tamaño de una figura. Tres tipos de transformaciones que cambian la posición son las traslaciones, los reflejos y las rotaciones.

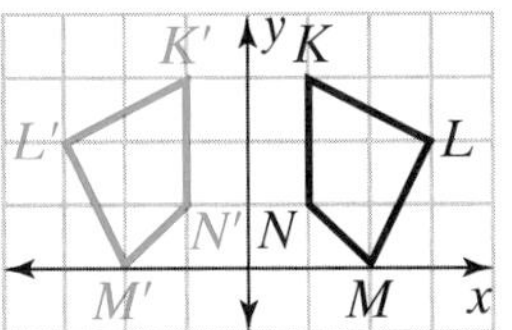

$K'L'M'N'$ is a reflection, or flip, of $KLMN$ across the y-axis.

Translation (p. 415) A translation is a transformation that slides each point of a figure the same distance and in the same direction.

Traslación (p. 415) Una traslación es una transformación que desliza cada punto de una figura la misma distancia y en la misma dirección.

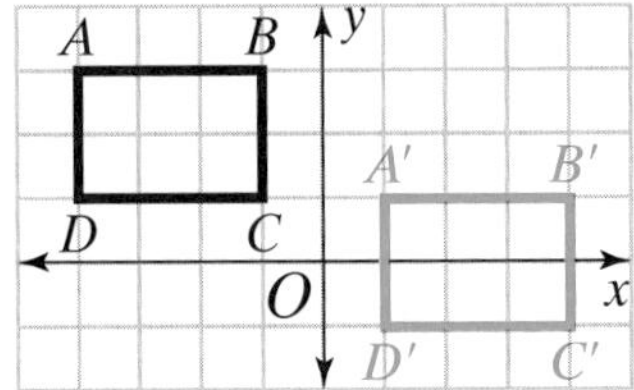

$A'B'C'D'$ is a translation of $ABCD$.

English/Spanish Glossary

EXAMPLES

Transversal (p. 387) A line that intersects two or more lines is called a transversal.

Secante (p. 387) Una recta que interseca a dos o más rectas se llama secante.

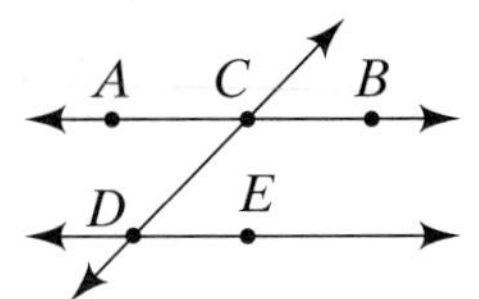

$\overleftrightarrow{CD}$ is a transversal.

Trapezoid (p. 398) A trapezoid is a quadrilateral with exactly one pair of parallel sides.

Trapecio (p. 398) Un trapecio es un cuadrilátero que tiene exactamente un par de lados paralelos.

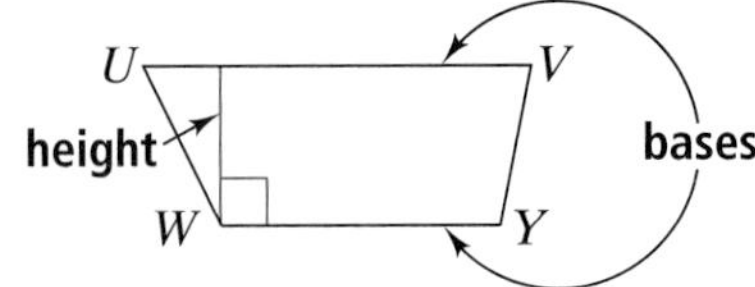

$\overline{UV}$ is parallel to $\overline{WY}$.

Tree diagram (p. 568) A tree diagram is an organized list of all possible combinations of items.

Diagrama en árbol (p. 568) Un diagrama en árbol es una lista organizada de todos los artículos.

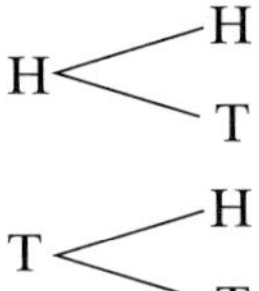

There are four possible outcomes for tossing two coins: HH, HT, TH, TT.

Triangle (p. 392) A triangle is a polygon with three sides.

Triángulo (p. 392) Un triángulo es un polígono que tiene tres lados.

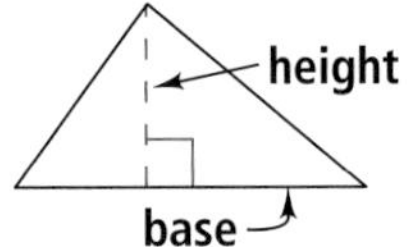

Two-step equation (p. 596) A two-step equation is an equation containing two operations.

Ecuación de dos pasos (p. 596) Una ecuación de dos pasos es una ecuación que contiene dos operaciones.

$2x + 3 = 10$

Unit price (p. 274) A unit price is a unit rate that gives the cost of one item.

Precio unitario (p. 274) Un precio unitario es una tasa unitaria que da el costo de un artículo.

$\frac{\$5.98}{10.2 \text{ fluid ounces}} = \$.59/\text{fluid ounce}$

EXAMPLES

Unit rate (p. 273) The rate for one unit of a given quantity is called the unit rate.

Tasa unitaria (p. 273) La tasa para una unidad de una cantidad dada se llama tasa unitaria.

If you drive 130 miles in 2 hours, your unit rate is $\frac{65 \text{ miles}}{1 \text{ hour}}$ or 65 mi/h.

Variable (p. 69) A variable is a letter that stands for a number. The value of an algebraic expression varies, or changes, depending upon the value given to the variable.

Variable (p. 69) Una variable es una letra que representa un número. El valor de una expresión algebraica varía, o cambia, dependiendo del valor que se le dé a la variable.

x is a variable in the equation $9 + x = 7$.

Vertex of an angle (p. 379) The vertex of an angle is the point of intersection of two sides of an angle or figure.

Vértice de un ángulo (p. 379) El vértice de un ángulo es el punto de intersección de dos lados de un ángulo o figura.

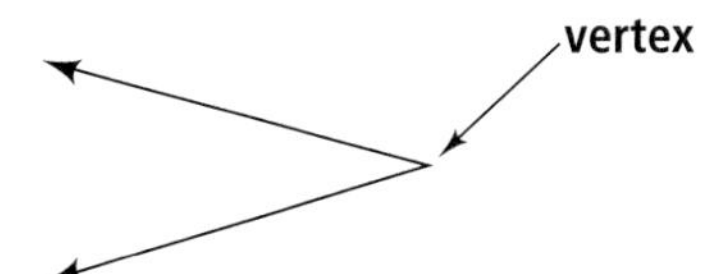

Vertical angles (p. 387) Vertical angles are formed by two intersecting lines. Vertical angles have equal measures.

Ángulos verticales (p. 387) Los ángulos verticales están formados por dos rectas que se intersectan. Los ángulos verticales son opuestos entre sí.

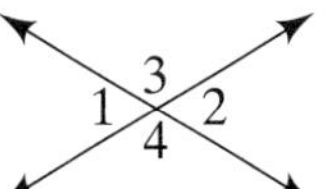

$\angle 1$ and $\angle 2$ are vertical angles, as are $\angle 3$ and $\angle 4$.

Volume (p. 472) The volume of a three-dimensional figure is the number of cubic units needed to fill the space inside the figure.

Volumen (p. 472) El volumen de una figura tridimensional es el número de unidades cúbicas que se necesitan para llenar el espacio dentro de la figura.

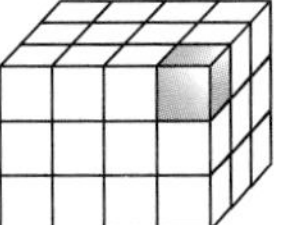

each cube = 1 in.^{3}

The volume of the rectangular prism is 36 in.^{3}.

x-axis (p. 518) The x-axis is the horizontal number line that, together with the y-axis, forms the coordinate plane.

Eje de x (p. 518) El eje de x es la recta numérica horizontal que, junto con el eje de y, forma el plano de coordenadas.

y-axis
2
x-axis
−2 O 2
−2

English/Spanish Glossary

EXAMPLES

x-coordinate (p. 518) The x-coordinate is the first number in an ordered pair. It tells the number of horizontal units a point is from the origin, 0.

Coordenada x (p. 518) La coordenada x es el primer número en un par ordenado. Indica el número de unidades horizontales a las que un punto está del orígen, 0.

The x-coordinate is -2 for the ordered pair $(-2, 1)$. The x-coordinate is 2 units to the left of the y-axis.

y-axis (p. 518) The y-axis is the vertical number line that, together with the x-axis, forms the coordinate plane.

Eje de y (p. 518) El eje de y es la recta numérica vertical que, junto con el eje de x, forma el plano de coordenadas.

y-axis
2
x-axis
−2 O 2
−2

y-coordinate (p. 518) The y-coordinate is the second number in an ordered pair. It tells the number of vertical units a point is from 0.

Coordenada y (p. 518) La coordenada y es el segundo número en un par ordenado. Indica el número de unidades verticales a las que un punto está del 0.

The y-coordinate is 1 for the ordered pair $(-2, 1)$. The y-coordinate is 1 unit up from the x-axis.

Zero pair (p. 496) The pairing of one "+" chip with one "−" chip is called a zero pair.

Par cero (p. 496) El emparejamiento de un signo "+" con un signo "−" se llama par cero.

Answers to Instant Check System™

Chapter 1

Diagnosing Readiness p. 4

1. 310 **2.** 7,530 **3.** 40 **4.** 60 **5.** 700 **6.** 1,990 **7.** 175 **8.** 145 **9.** 14,192 **10.** 3,027 **11.** 10,000 **12.** 1,392 **13.** 747 **14.** 4,544 **15.** 43,700 **16.** 25,000 **17.** 462 **18.** 1,856 **19.** 5 **20.** 17 **21.** 72 **22.** 32 **23.** 13 **24.** 73

Lesson 1-1 pp. 5–6

Check Skills You'll Need **1.** tens **2.** ones **3.** thousands **4.** hundred-millions

Check Understanding **1.** Twenty-six billion, two hundred and thirty-six million, eight-hundred and forty-six thousand and eighty dollars. **2a.** < **b.** 9,789; 9,897; 9,987

Lesson 1-2 pp. 9–10

Check Skills You'll Need **1.** twenty-eight **2.** eight thousand, six hundred and seventy-two **3.** six-hundred and twelve thousand, nine hundred and eighty **4.** fifty-eight million, twenty six thousand, one hundred and thirteen

Check Understanding **1a.** 3 + 0.1 + 0.04 + 0.001 + 0.0006 **b.** 0 + 0.8 + 0.06 + 0.005 **c.** 30 + 7 + 0.5 **d.** Yes; The zero in 6.207 is in the hundredth place and this value in expanded form is 0.00 **2a.** sixteen thousand, seven hundred two and three-tenths **b.** one thousand six hundred seventy and twenty-three hundredths **c.** one and sixty-seven thousand twenty-three hundred-thousandths **3a.** 9.587 **b.** the 5, since 0.5 > 0.007

Lesson 1-3 pp. 13–17

Check Skills You'll Need **1.** > **2.** > **3.** > **4.** > **5.** digits on the left

Check Understanding

1a. 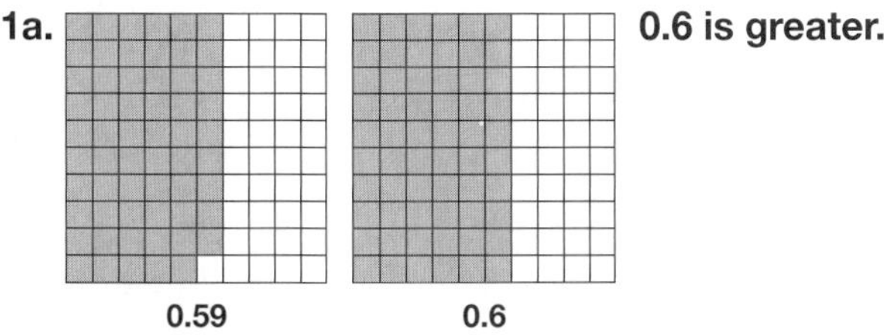

0.6 is greater.

b. 1.32 is greater. 3a. < **b.** > **c.** = **d.** Answers may vary. Sample: I would compare the values of numbers in similar places. In the hundredths place 1.697 has 9 hundredths. 1.697 > 1.679 **4a.** **2.**076, 2.6, 2.67, 2.76 **b.** 3.059, 3.46, 3.64

2a. 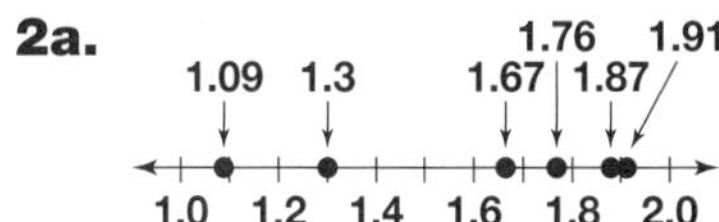

Lesson 1-3 pp. 16–17

Checkpoint Quiz 1 **1.** Answers may vary.

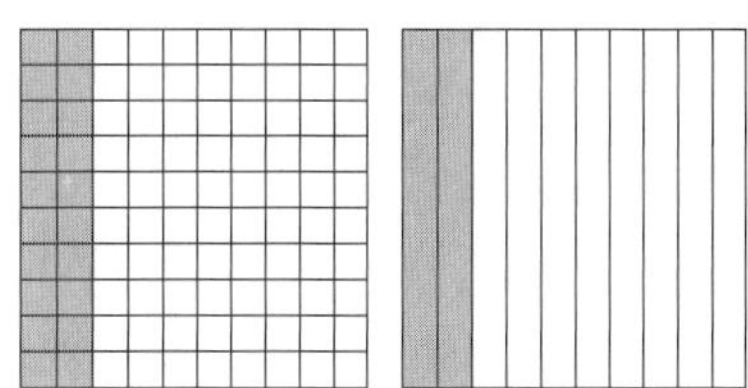

six trillion, eighty billion, four hundred five and thirty-one hundredths **2.** 10 + 2 + 0.0 + 0.03 + 0.005 **3.** 400.7 **4.** < **5.** 8.0, 8.05, 8.7, 9, 9.31

Lesson 1-4 pp. 19–20

Check Skills You'll Need **1.** 50 **2.** 65,330 **3.** 132,800 **4.** 30,910,000 **5.** 6,000 **6.** 15,345,000

Check Understanding **1a.** ≈ 32 **b.** ≈ 3 **c.** ≈ 112 **2a.** because 28 is divisible by 4 **b.** 250 **3a.** $22 **b.** $23; front end estimation makes sense because you will estimate higher instead of lower.

Lesson 1-5 pp. 25–27

Check Skills You'll Need **1.** 9 **2.** 10 **3.** 5 **4.** 1 **5.** 3 **6.** 3

Check Understanding **1.** 6; 6.16 **2a.** 13.9 **b.** 94 **c.** 9.4 **3a.** 2; 1.8 **b.** 7; 7.53 **c.** 0.3; 0.27 **d.** Answers may vary. Sample: Aligning the decimal points aligns all the places correctly. **4a.** 91; 91.2 **b.** 32; 31.68 **c.** 77; 77.084

Lesson 1-6 pp. 30–31

Check Skills You'll Need **1.** 62 **2.** 57 **3.** 24 **4.** 82 **5.** 77 **6.** 3,815

Check Understanding **1.** 0.16 s

Lesson 1-7 pp. 35–39

Check Skills You'll Need **1.** 147 **2.** 816 **3.** 21,607 **4.** 42,340

Check Understanding **1a.** 0.78 **b.** 21.85 **2a.** 0.06 **b.** 0.126 **c.** It is less than either factor. **3a.** 7.464 **b.** 57.984 **4a.** 23 **b.** 310 **c.** 333

Checkpoint Quiz 2 **1–4.** Answers may vary. Samples are given. **1.** 29 **2.** 60 **3.** 15 **4.** 9 **5.** 7.32 **6.** 8.26 **7.** 32.76 **8.** 1.42 **9.** 3.75 lb **10.** Answers may vary. Sample: Assoc. Prop. of Add.; 8(0.5) = 4 and 4(13.1) = 52.4

Lesson 1-8 pp. 40–41

Check Skills You'll Need **1.** 360 **2.** 3,600 **3.** 470 **4.** 47

Check Understanding **1a.** 342 **b.** 2.35 **c.** 55,200 **2a.** 5.342 **b.** 0.0235 **c.** 0.0552 **d.** Sample: To divide by 10,000, move the decimal point in the dividend four places to the left; 0.00073.

Lesson 1-9 pp. 43–45

Check Skills You'll Need **1.** 5 **2.** 32 **3.** 101 **4.** 27 **5.** yes **6.** no **7.** yes **8.** yes

Check Understanding **1a.** 1.52 **b.** 48.2 **c.** 0.144 **2a.** $0.\overline{66}$; repeating **b.** 0.25; terminating **c.** $0.\overline{18}$; repeating **3d.** 2 represents how many groups of 0.75 there are in 1.5 **4a.** 6.2 **b.** 108 **c.** 30.5

Lesson 1-10 pp. 48–49

Check Skills You'll Need **1.** = **2.** > **3.** > **4.** > **5.** < **6.** <

Check Understanding **1a.** 8 **b.** 11.7 **c.** 3 **d.** You would add before multiplying if the addition of two factors is done within parentheses and the multiplication is done outside of the parentheses. **2.** $46.85

Chapter 2

Diagnosing Readiness p. 62

1. 50 **2.** 7 **3.** 52 **4.** 42.15 **5.** 9.5 **6.** 5.1 **7.** 379 **8.** 3,040 **9.** 1.57 **10.** 26.5 **11.** 39 **12.** 17.2

Lesson 2-1 pp. 63–65

Check Skills You'll Need **1.** 0.0105, 0.105, 10.5 **2.** 3.1, 3.31, 3.331 **3.** 9.06, 9.09, 9.6 **4.** 0.602, 20.06, 26.0 **5.** 100.01, 100.1, 101.0 **6.** 0.35, 0.4, 0.99

Check Understanding **1a.** 41, 51 **b.** 24, 16 **c.** 57, 64 **d.** 22 tiles **2a.** 90, 75, 60, 45, 30, 15 **b.** 1, 3, 9, 27, 81, 243 **c.** 17, 36, 55, 74, 93, 112 **3a.** 2,401, 16,807, 117,649; the first term is 1; multiply each term by 7 to get the next term. **b.** 6.4, 5.2, 4; the first term is 10.0; subtract 1.2 from a term to get the next term. **c.** 32, 16, 8; the first term is 256; divide each term by 2 to get the next term.

Lesson 2-2 p. 68–70

Check Skills You'll Need **1.** 32 **2.** 19 **3.** 44.1 **4.** 4 **5.** 1 **6.** 7

Check Understanding

1a. 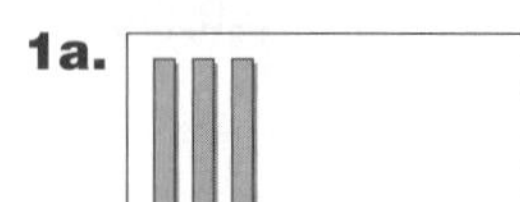 **b.** 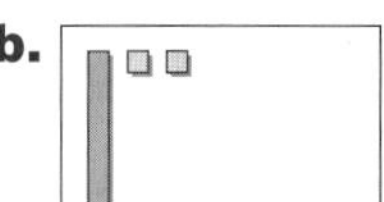

c. 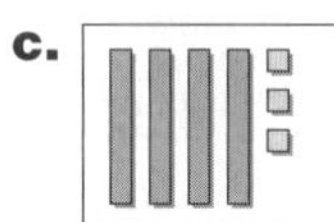

3a. Answers may vary. Sample is shown.

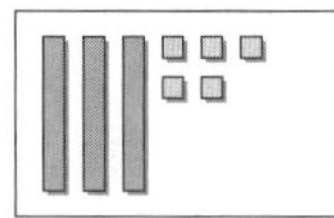

2a. 36 **b.** 5 **c.** 28 **d.** x was replaced by 7; 7 was multiplied by 4; 28 was subtracted from 56. **3.** $255

Lesson 2-3 pp. 74–78

Check Skills You'll Need **1.** 10 **2.** 1 **3.** 15 **4.** 30 **5.** 48 **6.** 11

Check Understanding **1a.** $5 \div y$ **b.** $6z$ **c.** $m + 3.4$ **2.** $h + 2$ **3.** Answers may vary. Samples are given. **a.** $n \div 2$ **b.** $n + 4$ **4a.** $b + 28$ **b.** 41

Checkpoint Quiz 1 **1.** 1,296; 7,776; 46,656; the first term is 1; multiply a term by 6 to get the next term. **2.** 225, 210, 195; the first term is 285; subtract 15 from a term to get the next term. **3.** 0.005, 0.0005, 0.00005; the first term is 50; divide a term by 10 to get the next term. **4.** 56 **5.** 9 **6.** 10.5 **7.** $17 - d$ **8.** ae **9.** $14 \div q$ **10a.** $5q + 3$ **b.** 63

Lesson 2-4 p. 80

Check Skills You'll Need **1.** 256; 1,024; 4.096 **2.** 35, 42, 49 **3.** 112, 224, 448 **4.** 52, 43, 34 **5.** 6.1, 7.2, 8.3 **6.** 5; 2.5; 1.25

Check Understanding **1.** No; For 10 tables, there are 64 seats, but for 20 tables there are 124 seats (not 128).

Lesson 2-5 pp. 84–85

Check Skills You'll Need **1.** 6 **2.** 4 **3.** 2 **4.** 16 **5.** 24 **6.** 5

Check Understanding **1a.** true **b.** false **c.** false **2a.** 9 **b.** 80 **c.** 1.2 **3a.–d.** Answers may vary. Samples are given. **3a.** 39 **b.** 6 **c.** 17.9

Lesson 2-6 — pp. 90–92

Check Skills You'll Need **1.** 9 **2.** 1 **3.** 70 **4.** 2 **5.** 9 **6.** 3

Check Understanding **1a.** 16 **b.** 105 **c.** 4.8 **2.** 9.8 lb **3a.** 81 **b.** 5.59 **c.** 6.4 **4.** t = temperature at 7:00 $t - 9 = 54$, $t = 63°$

Lesson 2-7 — pp. 95–98

Check Skills You'll Need **1–6.** Answers may vary. Samples are given. **1.** 7 **2.** 6 **3.** 16 **4.** 3 **5.** 8 **6.** 32

Check Understanding **1a.** 4 **b.** 2.7 **c.** 40 **2.** 865 cards **3a.** 200 **b.** 15 **c.** 1.58

Checkpoint Quiz 2 **1.** 13 **2.** 18.2 **3.** 2.2 **4.** 14.4 **5.** 10.8 **6.** 20 **7.** 8.4 **8.** 7 **9.** 5 **10.** x = change received; $x + 5.73 = 10.00$; $4.27

Lesson 2-8 — p. 99–101

Check Skills You'll Need **1.** 25 **2.** 0 **3.** 19.2 **4.** 10,000 **5.** 1 **6.** 2

Check Understanding **1a.** 3.94^2; 3.94; 2 **b.** 7^4; 7; 4 **c.** x^3; x; 3 **d.** No; 5^4 means $5 \times 5 \times 5 \times 5$ which is 625. 5×4 is 20. **2a.** $5 \times 10^4 + 5 \times 10^3 + 6 \times 10^2 + 0 \times 10^1 + 7 \times 1$ **b.** $3 \times 10^5 + 8 \times 10^4 + 0 \times 10^3 + 2 \times 10^2 + 5 \times 10^1 + 4 \times 1$ **3a.** 100,000 **b.** 19,683 **c.** 1.331 **d.** No; 2^5 means $2 \times 2 \times 2 \times 2 \times 2$ which is 32. 5^2 means 5×5 which is 25. **4a.** 6 **b.** 112 **c.** 14

Lesson 2-9 — pp. 105–106

Check Skills You'll Need **1.** 13.4 **2.** 17.3 **3.** 23.3 **4.** 16.5

Check Understanding **1a.** $3 \times (40 + 2) = (3 \times 40) + (3 \times 2) = 120 + 6 = 126$ **1b.** $5 \times (70 - 2) = (5 \times 70) - (5 \times 2) = 350 - 10 = 340$ **2a.** $14 **b.** Answers may vary. Sample: $5 \times (3 - .20) = 5 \times 3 - 5 \times .20 = 15 - 1 = 14$

Chapter 3

Diagnosing Readiness — p. 118

1. four tenths **2.** thirty-seven hundredths **3.** one and eight tenths **4.** two hundred five thousandths **5.** twenty and eighty-eight hundredths **6.** one hundred fifty thousandths **7.** 4.02, 4.2, 4.21 **8.** 0.033, 0.3, 0.33 **9.** 6.032, 6.203, 6.302 **10.** 0.8 **11.** 0.55 **12.** 19 **13.** 36.3 **14.** 132 **15.** $53.\overline{09}$ **16.** 3^3 **17.** 5^2 **18.** 2^6

Lesson 3-1 — pp. 119–121

Check Skills You'll Need **1.** 49 **2.** 41 **3.** 41.5 **4.** 145 **5.** 41 **6.** 50

Check Understanding **1a.** no **b.** yes **c.** $54 = 9 \times 6 = 9 \times (2 \times 3)$ **2a.** divisible by 2, 5, and 10 **b.** divisible by 5 **c.** divisible by none of these **d.** divisible by 2 **3a.** no **b.** yes **c.** yes **4a.** yes **b.** no **c.** yes **d.** $9 = 3 \times 3$

Lesson 3-2 — pp. 123–125

Check Skills You'll Need **1.** 2, 3, 5, 9, and 10 **2.** none **3.** 5 **4.** 2, 5, and 10 **5.** 2, 5, and 10 **6.** 2

Check Understanding **1.** 1, 2, 3, 6, 7, 14, 21, 42 **2a.** composite; $39 = 3 \times 13$ **b.** Prime; it has only two factors, 1 and 47. **c.** composite; $63 = 3 \times 21$ or $63 = 7 \times 9$ **3.** Answers may vary. Samples.

a. $28 = 2 \times 2 \times 7$

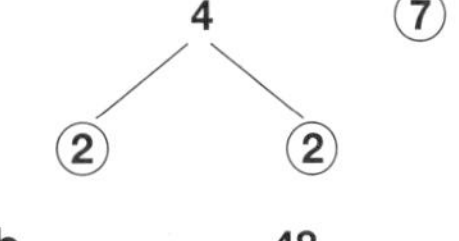

b. $48 = 2 \times 2 \times 2 \times 2 \times 3$

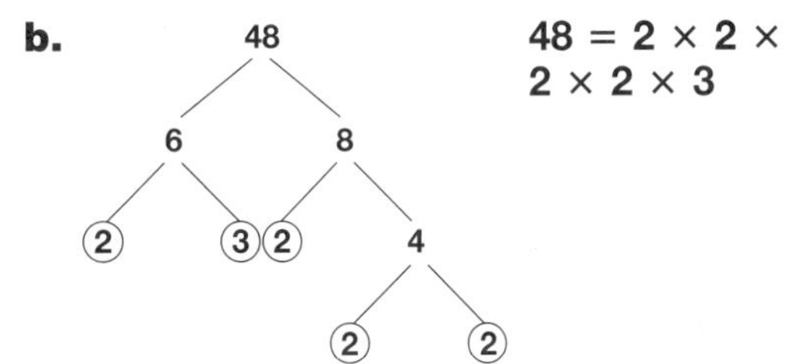

c. $125 = 5 \times 5 \times 5$

Lesson 3-3 — p. 129

Check Skills You'll Need **1.** $3 \times 3 \times 5$ **2.** 3×7 **3.** $3 \times 3 \times 11$ **4.** 3×31 **5.** 3×13 **6.** 2^7 **7.** 21 is not prime.

Check Understanding **1a.** factors of 6: 1, 2, 3, 6 factors of 21: 1, 3, 7, 21 GCF of 6 and 21: 3 **b.** factors of 18: 1, 2, 3, 6, 9, 18 factors of 49: 1, 7, 49 GCF of 18 and 49: 1 **c.** factors of 14: 1, 2, 7, 14 factors of 28: 1, 2, 4, 7, 14, 28 GCF of 14 and 28: 14 **d.** three from the set of 18 and five from the set of 30 **2a.** 2 24 54 3 12 27 4 9 GCF = 6 **b.** 3 18 27 36 3 6 9 12 2 3 4 GCF = 9 **3a.** $12 = 2 \times 2 \times 3$ $32 = 2 \times 2 \times 2 \times 2 \times 2$ GCF = 4 **b.** $18 = 2 \times 3 \times 3$ $42 = 2 \times 3 \times 7$ GCF = 6

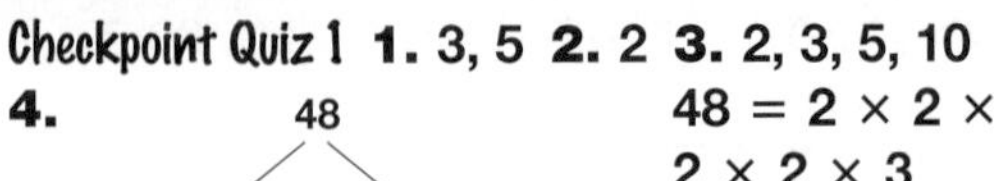

Checkpoint Quiz 1 **1.** 3, 5 **2.** 2 **3.** 2, 3, 5, 10

4. $48 = 2 \times 2 \times 2 \times 2 \times 3$

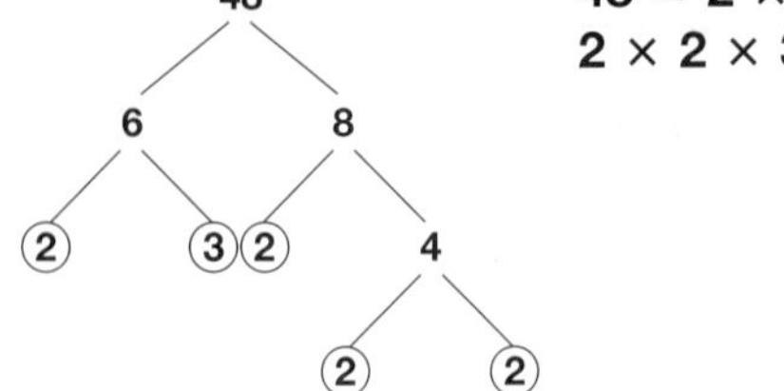

5. $80 = 2 \times 2 \times 2 \times 2 \times 5$

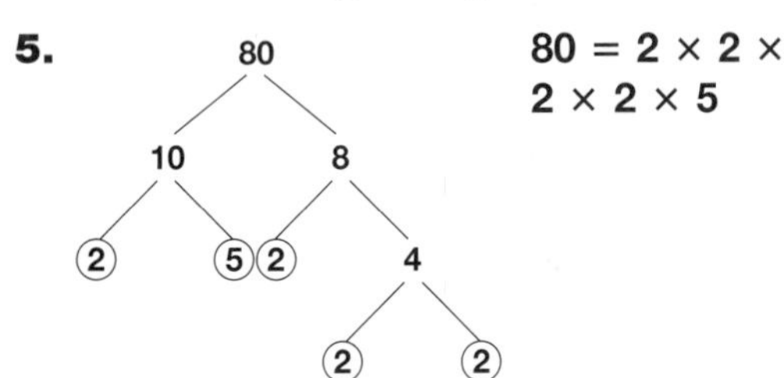

6. $1{,}000 = 2 \times 2 \times 2 \times 5 \times 5 \times 5$

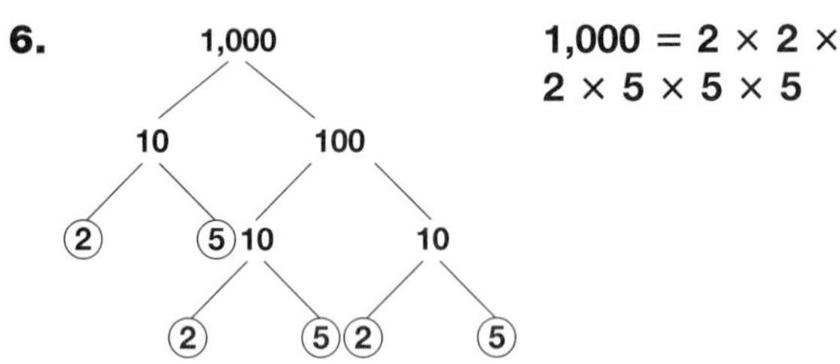

7. 5 **8.** 24 **9.** 3 **10.** 1, 2, 3, 6

Lesson 3-4 — pp. 134–136

Check Skills You'll Need **1.** 4 **2.** 5 **3.** 6 **4.** 1 **5.** 4 **6.** 7

Check Understanding **1a–c.** Answers may vary. Samples are given. **1a.** $\frac{2}{5}, \frac{8}{20}, \frac{12}{30}$ **b.** $\frac{10}{16}, \frac{15}{24}, \frac{25}{40}$ **c.** $\frac{1}{3}, \frac{4}{12}, \frac{6}{18}$ **2a.** $\frac{3}{4}$ **b.** $\frac{2}{7}$ **c.** $\frac{1}{5}$ **3a.** $\frac{7}{20}$ **b.** dog food and bird food; $42 + 18 = 60$, and $\frac{60}{120} = \frac{1}{2}$

Lesson 3-5 — pp. 139–141

Check Skills You'll Need **1.** $\frac{1}{3}$ **2.** $\frac{2}{3}$ **3.** $\frac{5}{16}$ **4.** $\frac{1}{17}$ **5.** $\frac{9}{10}$ **6.** There are 60 minutes in an hour, so compare 35 to 60 by using the fraction $\frac{35}{60}$. In simplest form, $\frac{35}{60}$ is $\frac{7}{12}$.

Check Understanding **1.** $\frac{25}{7}$ **2.** whole units **3a.** $4\frac{4}{9}$ **b.** $5\frac{1}{3}$ **c.** $5\frac{3}{4}$ **d.** $1\frac{2}{3}$

Lesson 3-6 — pp. 143–145

Check Skills You'll Need **1.** $2^4 \times 10^5$ **2.** 2^5 **3.** 5×19 **4.** $2^3 \times 5^4$ **5.** $2^4 \times 10^{13}$ **6.** 5^4

Check Understanding **1a.** 60 **b.** 12, 24, 36, 48, 60 **2.** 350

Lesson 3-7 — pp. 148–150

Check Skills You'll Need **1–9.** Answers may vary. Samples are given. **1.** $\frac{6}{14}, \frac{15}{35}$ **2.** $\frac{1}{3}, \frac{21}{63}$ **3.** $\frac{1}{5}, \frac{2}{10}$ **4.** $\frac{4}{6}, \frac{20}{30}$ **5.** $\frac{5}{6}, \frac{20}{24}$ **6.** $\frac{1}{6}, \frac{5}{30}$ **7.** $\frac{3}{4}, \frac{12}{16}$ **8.** $\frac{4}{10}, \frac{120}{300}$ **9.** $\frac{16}{10}, \frac{24}{15}$

Check Understanding **1a.** $<$ **b.** $=$ **c.** $>$ **d.** 40 min, 36 min; $\frac{2}{3}$ **2a.** $<$ **b.** $>$ **c.** $=$ **d.** Yes; $\frac{7}{8} = \frac{28}{32}$ and $\frac{28}{32} > \frac{27}{32}$. So $6\frac{7}{8} > 6\frac{27}{32}$. **3.** $2\frac{2}{3}, 2\frac{4}{5}, 2\frac{5}{6}$

Checkpoint Quiz 2 **1.** $\frac{2}{3}$ **2.** $\frac{3}{4}$ **3.** $\frac{1}{4}$ **4.** $\frac{16}{5}$ **5.** $1\frac{5}{8}$ **6.** 60 **7.** $\frac{1}{8}, \frac{3}{16}, \frac{1}{3}$ **8.** $<$ **9.** $>$ **10.** $>$

Lesson 3-8 — pp. 153–155

Check Skills You'll Need **1.** 1.5; terminating **2.** $0.\overline{6}$; repeating **3.** 1.6; terminating **4.** 0.375; terminating **5.** 0.3; terminating **6.** 0.24; terminating **7.** 0.24; terminating **8.** 0.2; terminating **9.** 3.2; terminating

Check Understanding **1a.** $\frac{3}{5}$ **b.** $\frac{7}{20}$ **c.** $3\frac{13}{100}$ **.** $7\frac{17}{20}$ **e.** The whole number you say first tells you the numerator, and the whole number that is read with "-th" at the end tells you the denominator. **2a.** 0.45 **b.** **3a.** $0.\overline{6}$ **b.** $0.1\overline{6}$ **c.** $0.\overline{45}$ **d.** $1.\overline{3}$ **e.** when the numerator is not divisible by 3

Lesson 3-9 — pp. 157–158

Check Skills You'll Need **1.** 10, 12, 14 **2.** 32, 64, 128 **3.** 54, 162, 483 **4.** 85, 80, 75 **5.** 21, 26, 31 **6.** 13, 21, 34

Check Understanding **1.** 20 adult tickets

Chapter 4

Diagnosing Readiness — p. 170

1. 2.59 **2.** 1.99 **3.** 6.22 **4.** $\frac{1}{2}$ **5.** $\frac{2}{5}$ **6.** $\frac{3}{4}$ **7.** $9\frac{2}{3}$ **8.** $5\frac{1}{4}$ **9.** $7\frac{1}{2}$ **10.** $\frac{26}{3}$ **11.** $\frac{23}{4}$ **12.** $\frac{151}{9}$ **13.** 72 **14.** 80 **15.** 210

Lesson 4-1 — p. 172

Check Skills You'll Need **1.** $>$ **2.** $<$ **3.** $=$ **4.** $<$ **5.** $>$ **6.** $<$

Check Understanding **1a.** $1\frac{1}{2}$ **b.** 1 **2a.** 14 **b.** 1

Lesson 4-2 p. 175

Check Skills You'll Need **1.** $\frac{1}{4}$ **2.** $\frac{1}{3}$ **3.** $\frac{4}{5}$ **4.** $\frac{4}{5}$ **5.** $\frac{2}{3}$ **6.** $\frac{3}{4}$

Check Understanding **1a.** $\frac{5}{6}$ **b.** $\frac{3}{5}$ **2a.** $1\frac{1}{8}$ **b.** $1\frac{2}{5}$ **3a.** $\frac{1}{5}$ **b.** $\frac{1}{2}$ **7.** $\frac{5}{6}$ **8.** $\frac{3}{7}$ **9.**

125
(5) 25
(5) (5)

Lesson 4-3 p. 180

Check Skills You'll Need **1.** 18 **2.** 36 **3.** 120 **4.** 240 **5.** 150 **6.** 60 **7.** 24. Explanations may vary. Sample: List multiples of 8: 8; 16; 24. List multiples of 12: 12; 24. The LCM is 24.

Check Understanding **1.** $\frac{7}{10}$ **2.** $1\frac{5}{12}$ h; $\frac{2}{3} + \frac{3}{4} \approx \frac{1}{2} + 1$; or $1\frac{1}{2}$ **3.** $\frac{1}{8}$ **4.** $\frac{1}{10}$

Checkpoint Quiz 1 **1.** $1\frac{1}{2}$ **2.** 1 **3.** $1\frac{1}{5}$ **4.** $\frac{1}{2}$ **5.** $1\frac{1}{4}$ **6.** $\frac{17}{30}$ **7.** $\frac{1}{2}$ **8.** $\frac{7}{10}$ **9.** $\frac{11}{18}$ of the class **10.** $1\frac{1}{6}$ c

Lesson 4-4 p. 185

Check Skills You'll Need **1.** $4\frac{1}{2}$ **2.** $3\frac{1}{3}$ **3.** $1\frac{1}{3}$ **4.** $2\frac{1}{2}$ **5.** $1\frac{3}{4}$ **6.** $2\frac{1}{2}$ **7.** $2\frac{2}{5}$ Explanations may vary. Sample: Divide 36 by 15. The quotient 2 is the integer of the mixed number. The remainder 6 is the numerator, and 15 is the denominator: $2\frac{6}{15}$. Reduce to $2\frac{2}{5}$.

Check Understanding **1.** Answers may vary. Sample: It doesn't matter because addition is commutative. **2a.** $6\frac{2}{15}$ h **b.** $2\frac{1}{3} + 3\frac{4}{5} \approx 3 + 3$, or 6 **3a.** $9\frac{3}{4}$ **b.** $19\frac{1}{8}$ **c.** $21\frac{4}{15}$ **4.** No; you need $3\frac{1}{4}$ c of milk, but you have only 3 c.

Lesson 4-5 p. 190

Check Skills You'll Need **1.** $1\frac{1}{2}$ **2.** $2\frac{2}{3}$ **3.** $4\frac{3}{5}$ **4–7.** Answers may vary. Samples are given. **4.** $\frac{5}{2}, \frac{10}{4}, \frac{15}{6}$ **5.** $\frac{30}{12}, \frac{45}{18}, \frac{60}{24}$ **6.** $\frac{48}{20}, \frac{72}{30}, \frac{96}{40}$ **7.** Divide 24 by 10. The quotient 2 is the integer of the mixed number. The remainder 4 is the numerator, and 10 is the denominator: $2\frac{4}{10}$. Reduce to $2\frac{2}{5}$.

Check Understanding **1a.** $\frac{11}{16}$ in. **b.** Yes. Answers may vary. Sample: 32 is the GCF of 8 and 4, so it is also a common denominator. **2a.** $1\frac{1}{3}$ **b.** $5\frac{3}{4}$ **3.** Answers may vary. Sample: If the benchmark of the first fraction is less than the benchmark of the second fraction, then rename before subtracting.

Lesson 4-6 p. 196

Check Skills You'll Need **1.** 26 **2.** 268 **3.** 3.8 **4.** 18.9 **5.** 0 **6.** 14.2

Check Understanding **1a.** $3\frac{2}{3}$ **b.** $11\frac{1}{4}$ **c.** $2\frac{3}{4}$ **2a.** $\frac{7}{12}$ **b.** $1\frac{5}{8}$ **c.** $\frac{1}{4}$ **3.** $1\frac{3}{4}$ in.

Lesson 4-7 p. 201

Check Skills You'll Need **1–6.** Answers may vary. Samples are given. **1.** $\frac{16}{60}$ **2.** $\frac{15}{60}$ **3.** $\frac{12}{60}$ **4.** $\frac{20}{60}$ **5.** $\frac{40}{60}$ **6.** $\frac{35}{60}$

Check Understanding **1.** 31 days **2.** 47 min **3a.** 9h 15 min **b.** Answers may vary. Sample: Adding 12 hours makes both times A.M. or both times P.M. so they can be subtracted. **4.** 5:20 P.M.

Checkpoint Quiz 2 **1.** $5\frac{5}{8}$ **2.** $4\frac{3}{4}$ **3.** $14\frac{5}{6}$ **4.** $5\frac{8}{9}$ **5.** $\frac{1}{2}$ **6.** $1\frac{2}{9}$ **7.** $\frac{3}{10}$ **8.** $\frac{12}{15}$ **9.** 6 h 47 min **10.** 9 h 43 min

Lesson 4-8 p. 206

Check Skills You'll Need **1–6.** Answers may vary. Samples are given. **1.** 6 **2.** 10 **3.** 11 **4.** 2 **5.** 19 **6.** 2

Check Understanding **1.** about 45 mats

Chapter 5

Diagnosing Readiness p. 218

1. 4 **2.** 5 **3.** 12 **4.** 112 **5.** 100 **6.** 5 **7.** 54 **8.** 0.6 **9.** 3 **10.** 12 **11.** 7 **12.** 3 **13.** 20 **14.** 6 **15.** 21 **16.** $\frac{3}{7}$ **17.** $\frac{2}{3}$ **18.** $\frac{1}{3}$ **19.** $\frac{3}{8}$ **20.** $\frac{1}{4}$ **21.** $\frac{3}{7}$ **22.** $\frac{2}{3}$ **23.** $\frac{7}{8}$ **24.** $\frac{3}{7}$

Lesson 5-1 p. 219

Check Skills You'll Need **1.** $\frac{1}{2}$ **2.** $\frac{3}{5}$ **3.** $\frac{2}{3}$ **4.** $\frac{9}{10}$ **5.** $\frac{3}{4}$ **6.** $\frac{3}{4}$ **7.** Answers may vary. Sample: Yes; the GCF of 9 and 16 is 1.

Check Understanding **1.** $\frac{2}{15}$ **2a.** $\frac{3}{20}$ **b.** $\frac{10}{63}$ **c.** When you add $\frac{3}{8}$ and $\frac{5}{8}$ you add numerators and keep the same denominator. When you multiply $\frac{3}{8}$

you multiply numerators and multiply denominators. **3a.** $\frac{28}{5} = 5\frac{3}{5}$ **b.** $\frac{40}{3} = 13\frac{1}{3}$ **c.** 8 **4.** $4\frac{1}{2}$ mi

Lesson 5-2 p. 224

Check Skills You'll Need **1.** 2 **2.** 13 **3.** 30 **4.** 8 **5.** 6 **6.** 6

Check Understanding 1a. 36 **b.** 56 **c.** 143 **d.** The actual product is greater than $80 \cdot \frac{1}{8}$, since $82\frac{5}{7} > 80$. So the actual product is greater than 10. $83 \cdot 0$ would give an estimate of 0, which is not realistic. **2a.** $3\frac{7}{16}$ **b.** $27\frac{1}{2}$ **c.** 18 **3.** $2\frac{5}{8}$ mi

Lesson 5-3 p. 230

Check Skills You'll Need **1.** 6 **2.** 4 **3.** $\frac{1}{5}$ **4.** 1 **5.** $\frac{1}{7}$ **6.** $\frac{4}{11}$

Check Understanding **1a.** $\frac{4}{3}$ or $1\frac{1}{3}$ **b.** $\frac{1}{7}$ 2a. $10\frac{2}{3}$ **b.** $31\frac{1}{2}$ **c.** $10\frac{1}{2}$ **3a.** $\frac{1}{12}$ **b.** $\frac{9}{20}$ **c.** $\frac{3}{11}$ **d.** Answers may vary. Sample: $\frac{2}{3}$ is between $\frac{1}{2}$ and 1. There are 2 fourths in $\frac{1}{2}$, and 4 fourths in 1. So there must be between 2 and 4 fourths in $\frac{2}{3}$. **4a.** $\frac{1}{32}$ **b.** $\frac{1}{150}$ **c.** Answers may vary. Sample: $\frac{1}{5}$ of the original piece.

Lesson 5-4 p. 236

Check Skills You'll Need **1.** 28 **2.** $23\frac{1}{3}$ **3.** $\frac{7}{24}$ **4.** $\frac{1}{6}$ **5.** $\frac{15}{16}$ **6.** $2\frac{8}{11}$ **7.** When you divide by a fraction, find its reciprocal and multiply by it.

Check Understanding **1a.** 7 **b.** 5 **c.** 10 **d.** Answers may vary. Sample: Round $59\frac{1}{2}$ to 60 and $6\frac{1}{4}$ to 6; then divide $60 \div 6 = 10$. **2a.** $\frac{13}{15}$ **b.** $3\frac{2}{5}$ **c.** $1\frac{1}{4}$c **3a.** 6 **b.** $2\frac{1}{20}$ **c.** When you divide a number by a greater number, the quotient is less than 1.

Checkpoint Quiz 1 **1.** 15 **2.** $23\frac{5}{8}$ **3.** 64 **4.** $\frac{1}{6}$ **5.** $1\frac{11}{21}$ **6.** $\frac{3}{5}$ **7.** $16\frac{1}{3}$ **8.** $2\frac{7}{30}$ **9.** 39 ft **10.** 24

Lesson 5-5 p. 242

Check Skills You'll Need **1.** $\frac{7}{30}$ **2.** $\frac{3}{11}$ **3.** $\frac{2}{5}$

Check Understanding **1a.** 30 **b.** 72 **2a.** 20 **b.** 25 **c.** 48 **3.** 10 boards

Lesson 5-6 p. 246

Check Skills You'll Need **1.** $1\frac{1}{2}$ **2.** $\frac{10}{27}$ **3.** 10 **4.** $\frac{25}{36}$ **5.** $6\frac{2}{5}$ **6.** $\frac{11}{12}$

Check Understanding **1.** 408 cards

Lesson 5-7 p. 250

Check Skills You'll Need **1.** > **2.** > **3.** > **4.** > **5.** < **6.** =

Check Understanding **1–3.** Answers may vary. Samples are given. **1a.** Inches; pencils are shorter than a foot. **b.** Feet or yards; small whales are twice as long as a man. **c.** Inches are a short unit of measure. Inches are too small to measure a walking distance. **2a.** Tons; even small whales are very large. **b.** Ounces; an ice cube weighs about the same as a slice of bread. **3a.** Gallons; a tanker truck holds more gasoline than can fit in a small bucket. **b.** Fluid ounces or cups; a serving of yogurt is less than a pint. **c.** Gallons; a bathtub can hold a few small buckets of water. **d.** Fluid ounces; a bottle of cough syrup holds less than a pint.

Lesson 5-7 p. 252

Checkpoint Quiz 2 **1.** $10\frac{1}{2}$ **2.** $\frac{2}{5}$ **3.** mile **4.** pound **5.** 6 markers

Lesson 5-8 p. 254

Check Skills You'll Need **1.** $25\frac{1}{2}$ **2.** $10\frac{1}{2}$ **3.** 24 **4.** $\frac{55}{78}$ **5.** $\frac{3}{8}$ **6.** $\frac{20}{27}$ **7.**

$\frac{3}{24} = \frac{1}{8}$

Check Understanding **1a.** $3\frac{3}{4}$ **b.** $4\frac{25}{36}$ **c.** $7\frac{1}{2}$ ft **2a.** $6\frac{1}{2}$ **b.** 4,500 **3.** 8 lb 1 oz.

Chapter 6

Diagnosing Readiness p. 268

1. 18 **2.** 7 **3.** 48 **4.** 132 **5.** 24 **6.** 42 **7.** 9 **8.** 16 **9.** $\frac{2}{5}$ **10.** $\frac{5}{11}$ **11.** $\frac{2}{3}$ **12.** $\frac{1}{3}$ **13.** > **14.** > **15.** > **16.** = **17.** $\frac{8}{21}$ **18.** $\frac{1}{2}$ **19.** $3\frac{8}{9}$ **20.** $4\frac{1}{8}$

Lesson 6-1 p. 269

Check Skills You'll Need **1.** $\frac{1}{3}$ **2.** $\frac{2}{3}$ **3.** $\frac{2}{9}$ **4.** $\frac{1}{16}$

Check Understanding **1a.** 2 to 4, 2:4, $\frac{2}{4}$ **b.** 2 to 6, 2:6, $\frac{2}{6}$ **2a–c.** Answers may vary. Samples are given. **2a.** 2 to 7, 4 to 14 **b.** 4 to 1, 8 to 2 **c.** 4 to 11, 12 to 33 **d.** 9 to 5 is a comparison of two numbers. $1\frac{4}{5}$ is not a comparison of two numbers. **3a.** 1:5 **b.** 10 to 9 **c.** $\frac{13}{1}$ **d.** 1 to 8

Lesson 6-2 p. 273

Check Skills You'll Need **1.** 4 **2.** 4 **3.** 5 **4.** 6 **5.** 25 **6.** 13

Check Understanding **1a.** 33 pages per hour **b.** 79 cents per pound **c.** $\frac{12 \text{ inches}}{1 \text{ foot}}$; it is the number of inches in 1 foot **2a.** $\frac{\$5.25}{1 \text{ hour}} = \frac{\$26.25}{5 \text{ hours}}$ **b.** $\frac{25 \text{ words}}{1 \text{ minute}} = \frac{250 \text{ words}}{10 \text{ minutes}}$ **3a.** \$.11 per ounce; \$.09 per ounce; the 32 ounce container **b.** \$.14 per minute; \$.09 per minute; the 15 minute plan **c.** AMV. Sample: it helps find the cheapter item.

Lesson 6-3 p. 278

Check Skills You'll Need **1.** $<$ **2.** $=$ **3.** $<$ **4.** $<$ **5.** $>$ **6.** $=$

Check Understanding **1a.** yes **b.** no **c.** no **2a.** 15 **b.** 6

Lesson 6-4 p. 283

Check Skills You'll Need **1.** 10 **2.** 6 **3.** 7 **4.** 12 **5.** 108 **6.** 56

Check Understanding **1.** Yes; the cross products are equal. **2a.** 15 **b.** 4 **c.** 5 **3a.** \$4.50 **b.** \$3.16

Lesson 6-5 p. 288

Check Skills You'll Need **1.** 20 **2.** 25 **3.** 6 **4.** 2 **5.** 1 **6.** 105

Check Understanding **1.** 1 in.:14 in. **2a.** about 450 mi **3.** 17 in.

Checkpoint Quiz 1 **1.** Answers may vary. Sample: $\frac{9}{20}, \frac{36}{80}$ **2.** \$2.85 **3.** \$17.50 **4.** no **5.** no **6.** yes **7.** 12 **8.** 78 **9.** \$16.20 **10.** 1 in.:36 ft

Lesson 6-6 p. 294

Check Skills You'll Need **1.** $\frac{6}{25}$ **2.** $\frac{2}{5}$ **3.** $\frac{3}{4}$ **4.** $\frac{1}{3}$ **5.** $\frac{79}{100}$

Check Understanding **1a.** 0.18 **b.** 0.02 **c.** 0.25 **2a.** $\frac{1}{25}$ **b.** $\frac{11}{20}$ **c.** $\frac{3}{4}$ **d.** $\frac{1}{5}$ **3a.** 52% **b.** 5% **c.** 50% **d.** slide the decimal two places to the left. **4a.** 5% **b.** **5.** about 7%

Lesson 6-7 p. 299

Check Skills You'll Need **1.** 18 **2.** 8 **3.** 15 **4.** 78 **5.** 85 **6.** 230 **7.** Answers may vary. Sample: Use cross products. $39 \times 40 = 100 \times x$; $1{,}560 = 100x$. Divide both sides by 100. The solution is 15.6.

Check Understanding **1.** 48 **2.** 10.92 **3a.** 5.6 **b.** 9 **c.** 18

Lesson 6-8 p. 303

Check Skills You'll Need **1.** 30 **2.** 120 **3.** 2,000 **4.** 40

Check Understanding **1a. b.** Answers may vary. Sample: High estimate; I may estimate too low and not have enough money. **2.** about \$6 **3a.** about \$28 **b.** High estimate; the original price was rounded up but the percent was kept at 40%

Checkpoint Quiz 2

1. 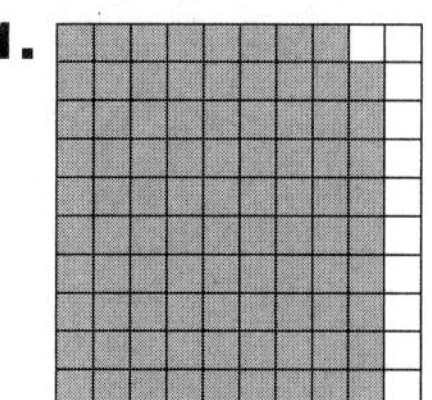

1. 0.74, $\frac{37}{50}$ **2.** 84% **3.** tax: \$0.75; 15.75 **4.** 110 **5.** 18

Lesson 6-9 p. 307

Check Skills You'll Need **1.** 5 **2.** 90 **3.** 4.5 **4.** 58 **5.** 22 **6.** 200

Check Understanding **1.** \$39.96

Chapter 7

Diagnosing Readiness p. 320

1. 0.12, 0.13, 0.21, 0.35, 0.45 **2.** 44, 45.01, 45.1, 46.01 **3.** 99.9, 100.80, 102, 124.32, 133 **4.** 0.22, 0.99, 2.5, 4.9, 7.04 **5.** 63.1 **6.** 423.9 **7.** 105.82 **8.** 25.87 **9.** 20.21 **10.** 1.06 **11.** 1.8 **12.** 14.203 **13.** 22.67 **14.** 4.03

Lesson 7-1 pp. 322–323

Check Skills You'll Need **1.** 27.5 **2.** 42.58 **3.** 59.35 **4.** 5.9 **5.** 8.55 **6.** 3.087

Check Understanding **1a.** 3.5 **b.** 22.4 **c.** 20 **d.** 57 **e.** 45. This is between 15 and 75. **2a.** 88 **b.** 27.5 **3.** apple

Lesson 7-2 pp. 326–327

Check Skills You'll Need **1.** blue and green **2.** 5.2; 5; 4, **3.** 2; 1.25; 0

Check Understanding **1a.**

Initial	Tally	Frequency
A	|	1
B	|	1
C	|	1
D	||	2
J	|	1
K	||	2
L	|||	3
P	|	1
S	|	1
D	|	1

b. The data items are letters, not numbers.
2a. 70 DVDs

b. Number of Phone Calls

```
 X
 X                 X
 X X               X
 X X             X X
 X X X X       X X X X
-----------------------
 0 1 2 3 4 5 6 7 8 9
      Phone Calls
```

3a. 32 **b.** 0.17 **c.** No; Explanations may vary. Sample: Add 10 to all data in the first set. The range stays the same, but the median increases by 10.

3.

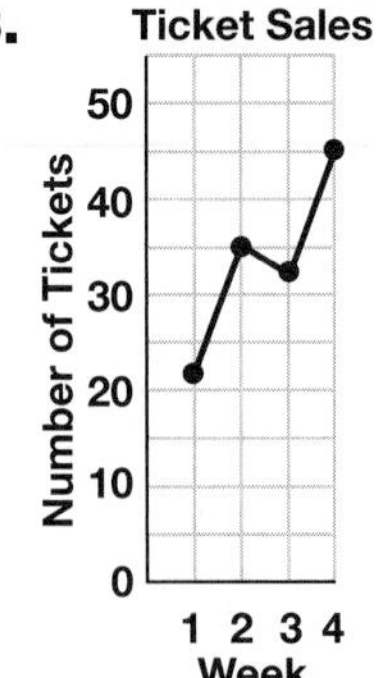

Lesson 7-3 pp. 332–334

Check Skills You'll Need **1.** 35, 42, 49 **2.** 13, 16, 19 **3.** 52, 43, 34 **4.** 324, 972, 2916

Check Understanding **1.** day 8

Checkpoint Quiz 1 **1.** 30; 30; 30; 26 **2.** 21 **3.** 21

4.

Grams of Fat	Tally	Frequency
0	𝍸 |||	8
1	𝍸 ||||	9
2	𝍸	5
3	|||	3

5. 10 ways

Lesson 7-4 pp. 335–336

Check Skills You'll Need

1. **2.**

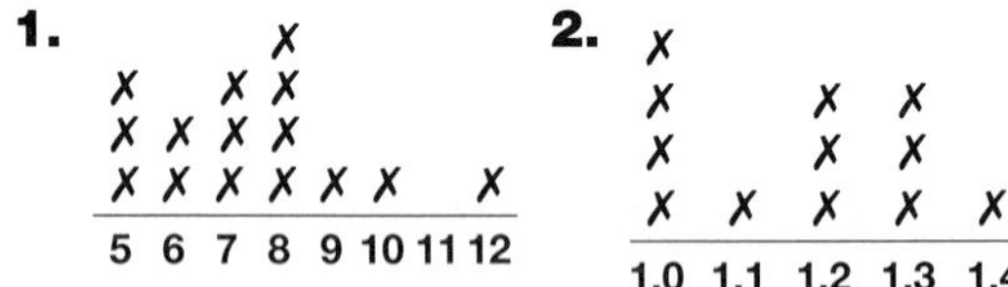

3.

```
 X        X    X    X       X
------------------------------------
10 11 12 13 14 15 16 17 18 19 21
```

Check Understanding

1.

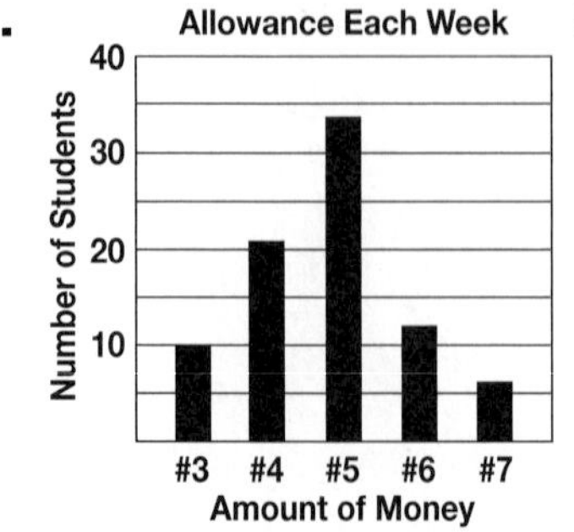

2. 12-15 hours

Lesson 7-5 pp. 341–342

Check Skills You'll Need **1.** 98 **2.** 104 **3.** 96 **4.** 88 **5.** 615 **6.** 136

Check Understanding **1a.** vinegar, cider, wine, juice, jelly, and apple butter **b.** 17%

2.

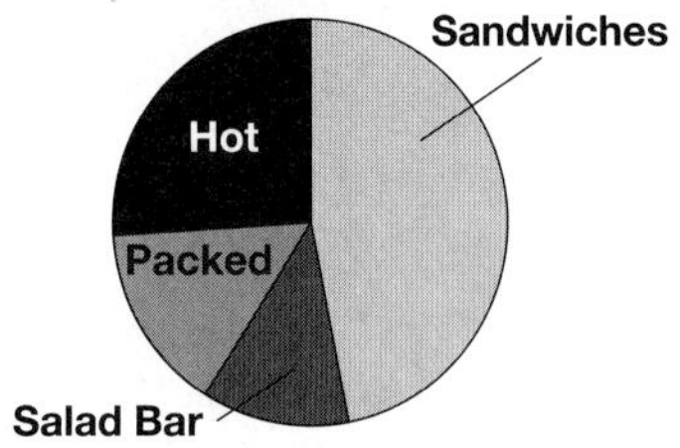

Lesson 7-6 pp. 347–350

Check Skills You'll Need **1.** $5x$ 2. $b - 7$ **3.** $52 - x$ **4.** $\frac{a}{9}$ **5.** xy **6.** $\frac{a}{b}$

Check Understanding **1a.** 30; the minutes of country music on disc 3 **b.** A2, B2, C2, D2; the minutes of rock/pop music on each disc **2a.** =B2+B3+B4 **b.** =D2+D3+D4

Checkpoint Quiz 2 **1.**

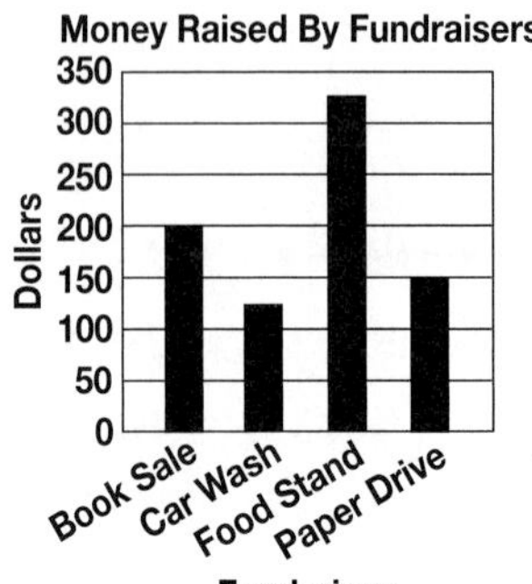

2. Money Raised by Fundraisers

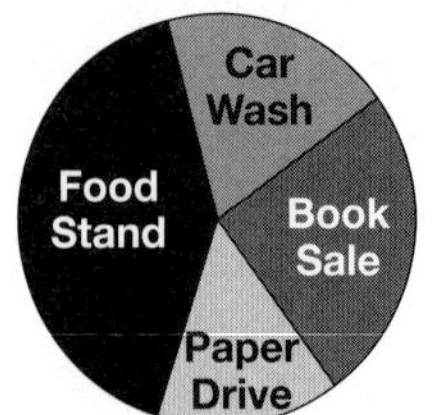

3. =B2+B3+B4+B5
4. $800

5.

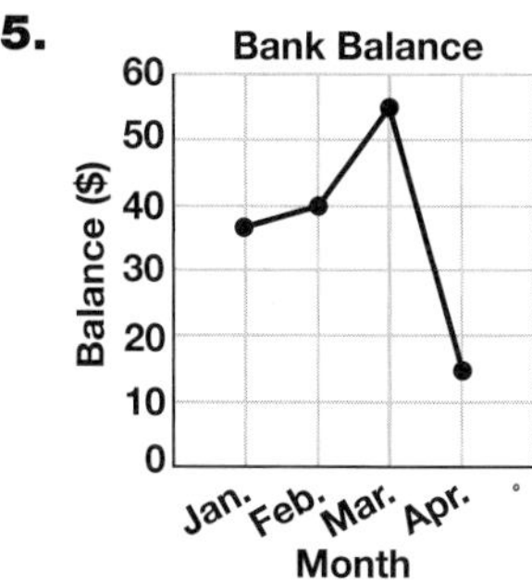

Lesson 7-7 pp. 352–353

Check Skills You'll Need **1.** 32 **2.** 15 **3.** 212 **4.** 5.2

Check Understanding **1a.** 3 **b.** Answers may vary. Sample: A stem-and-leaf plot organzies the lowest and highest data values. **c.** 35

2.

12	1 3 4 5 5 6 7
13	0 2 3 6 7 8 8
14	0 1 4 5
15	0 5
16	
17	
18	1

Legend: 12|3 means 123

Lesson 7-8 pp. 358–359

Check Skills You'll Need **1.** 55.5 **2.** 13.5 **3.** 131 **4.** 63.7 **5.** the data set in Exercise 4

Check Understanding

1a.

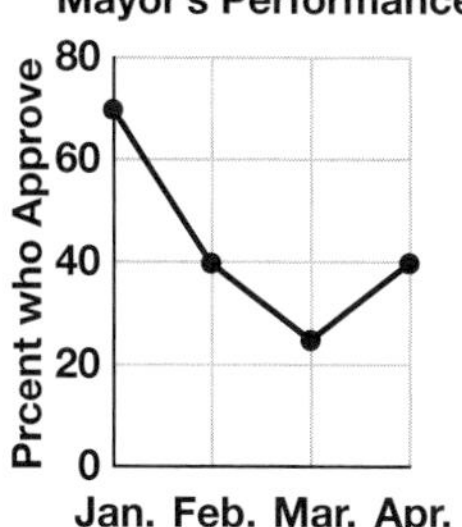

2a. two times taller **b.** 3 cars

c.

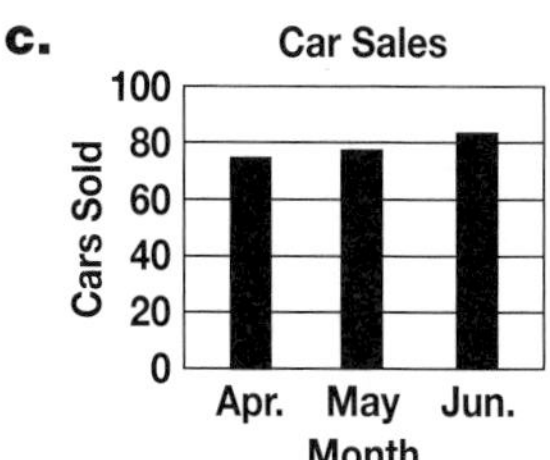

3a. $950,000 **b.** Median; the mode is the least data value. It occurs only twice, so its value is really too low to give a good idea of what a typical data value is.

Chapter 8

Diagnosing Readiness p. 372

1. 9 **2.** 9 **3.** 4 **4.** 10 **5.** 1.27 **6.** 59.5 **7.** 27.1 **8.** 17.5 **9.** 33.3 **10.** 12.07 **11.** Yes **12.** No **13.** No **14.** Yes **15.** No **16.** Yes

Lesson 8-1 p. 373

Check Skills You'll Need **1.** $2\frac{7}{8}$ in. **2.** 2 in. **3.** $3\frac{3}{8}$ in.

Check Understanding **1a.** Answers may vary. Samples are given. $\overrightarrow{VP}$, $\overrightarrow{MV}$ **b.** $\overline{VM}$, $\overline{VF}$, $\overline{MP}$ **c.** Answers may vary. Samples are given. $\overrightarrow{VM}$ is a ray that has vertex V and contains M. $\overrightarrow{MV}$ is a ray that has vertex M and contains V. **2a.** Answers may vary. Samples are given. Q, T, and M **b.** N, Q, and M **3a.** Answers may vary. Samples are given. W 37th and W 38th St. **b.** Broadway and W 40th St. **c.** No; all lines on the map represent streets in the same plane.

Lesson 8-2 p. 379

Check Skills You'll Need **1.** Answers may vary. Samples are given. $\overleftrightarrow{AC}$, $\overline{BE}$, $\overrightarrow{DB}$ **2.** No; they do not lie on the same line.

Check Understanding **1a.** 125° **b.** greater **2a.** Answers may vary. Sample: 60° **b.** acute

Lesson 8-3 p. 386

Check Skills You'll Need **1–4.** Check students' work.

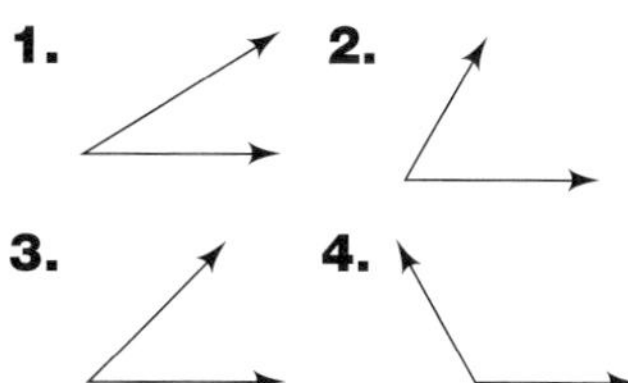

Check Understanding **1.** 37° **2.** 145° **3a.** $\angle 3$ and $\angle 6$ **b.** Answers may vary. Sample: $\angle 6$ and $\angle 2$

Checkpoint Quiz 1 **1–10.** Answers may vary. Samples are given. **1.** $\overleftrightarrow{LM}$ and $\overleftrightarrow{KN}$ **2.** $\overrightarrow{JP}$ and $\overrightarrow{NK}$ **3.** $\angle PJM$ **4.** $\angle PJK$ **5.** $\angle PJN$ **6.** $\angle LJM$ **7.** $\angle KJL$ and $\angle MJN$ **8.** $\angle PJN$ **9.** $\angle PJK$ and $\angle KJL$ **10.** $\angle LJN$ and $\angle NJM$

Lesson 8-4 p. 392

Check Skills You'll Need **1.** acute **2.** obtuse **3.** acute **4.** obtuse **5.** right **6.** acute **7.** obtuse **8.** straight

Check Understanding **1a.** acute triangle **b.** acute triangle **c.** No; an acute triangle has 3 acute angles. **2.** 50° **3a.** isosceles triangle **b.** scalene **4.** isoceles right triangle

Lesson 8-5 p. 397

Check Skills You'll Need **1–3.** Answers may vary. Samples are given. **1.** $\overline{DC}$ and $\overline{FG}$ **2.** $\overline{CB}$ and $\overline{GH}$ **3.** $\overline{FG}$ and $\overline{BC}$

Check Understanding **1a.** quadrilateral **b.** hexagon **c.** octagon **2a.** parallelogram, rectangle **b.** rectangle; Answers may vary. Sample: a rectangle has four right angles and two pairs of parallel lines. **c.** No; only rhombuses that have right angles are squares.

Lesson 8-6 p. 401

Check Skills You'll Need

1.

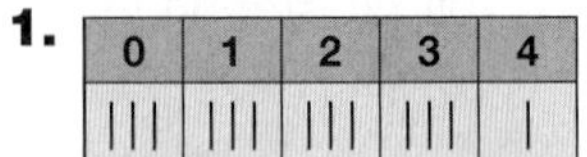

0	1	2	3	4
|||	|||	|||	|||	|

2.

75	|
80	|||
82	|
85	||
90	|||
100	||

3.

80	||
82	||
85	|
87	||
88	||
89	|

Check Understanding

1.

	a.	b.	c.	d.
a.	T	H	A	T
b.	H	E	X	A
c.	A	X	E	S
d.	T	A	S	K

2. Janna visited Jamaica. Georgine visited France. Tanika visited Peru.

Lesson 8-7 p. 405

Check Skills You'll Need **1.** isosceles **2.** isosceles **3.** scalene

Check Understanding **1a.** no **b.** yes **2.** b **3.** congruent and similar; all of their sides and angles are congruent.

Lesson 8-8 p. 410

Check Skills You'll Need **1.** yes **2.** yes

Check Understanding **1.** No; if you fold the figure along the line the two parts do not match.

2a. 1

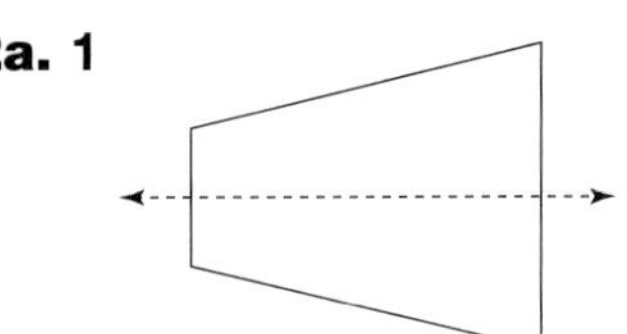

b. 4

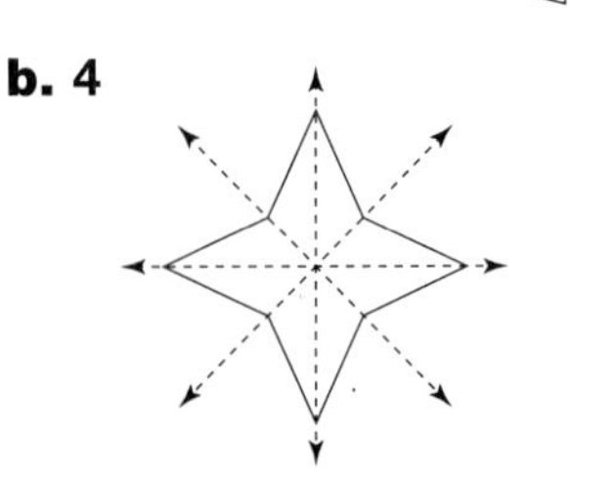

c. infinitely many; Any line that goes through the center of a circle is a line of symmetry.

Checkpoint Quiz 2 **1.** obtuse **2.** right **3.** acute **4.** isosceles **5.** scalene **6.** equilateral **7.** Answers may vary. Sample:

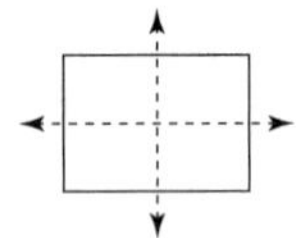

rectangle **8.** Fred is the teacher. Matt is the writer. Alison is the artist. **9.** B, C, and E **10.** B and E

Lesson 8-9 p. 415

Check Skills You'll Need

1. **2.**

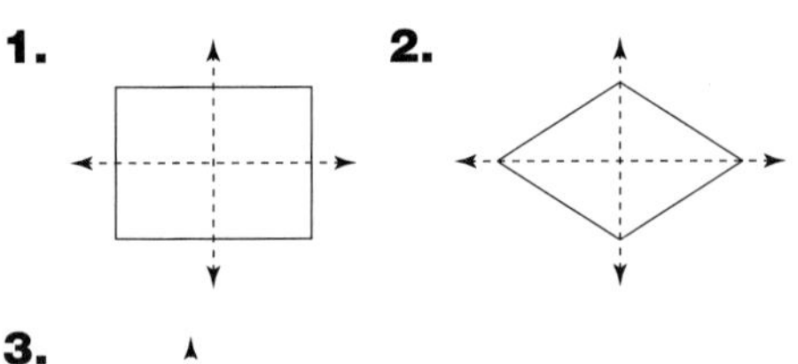

3.

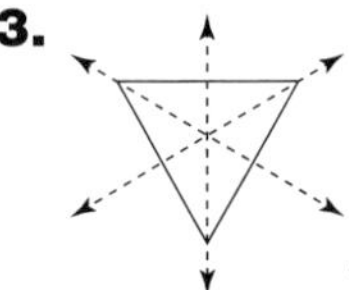

Check Understanding **1.** no

2a.

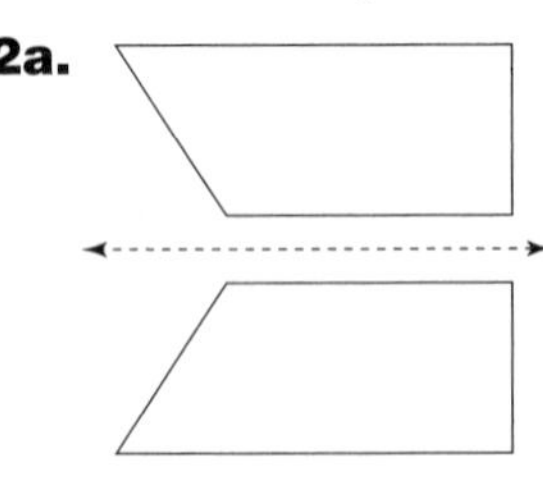

b.

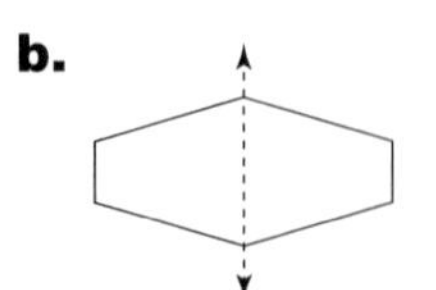

c. A reflection is called a flip because if you had the figure on paper you would flip it over to get the reflection. **3a.** no **b.** yes **c.** no

Chapter 9

Diagnosing Readiness p. 430

1. pounds; ounces are probably too small, and tons are much too large. **2.** gallons; A train's oil car holds a large amount of oil, so a large unit of capacity is appropriate **3.** pounds; Pianos vary in size and weight, but even a large, heavy grand piano usually weighs less than a ton. **4.** inches; The next larger unit is the foot, and almost everyone's hand length is less than a foot. **5.** 144 **6.** $3\frac{5}{6}$ **7.** $3\frac{5}{8}$ **8.** $2\frac{1}{4}$ **9.** 26 **10.** $1\frac{1}{2}$ **11.** rhombus **12.** isosceles triangle **13.** trapezoid

Lesson 9-1 pp. 431–433

Check Skills You'll Need **1.** ounces; A baseball weighs less than a pound. **2.** pounds; All desks will weigh more than a pound but much less than a ton. **3.** feet; A gym will be very long. You could use yards, but the length can be given more accurately using feet. **4.** pints; Many juice boxes and cartons hold more than a pint, but many are less than a quart. (Cups or fluid ounces would also be appropriate.)

Check Understanding **1.** millimeter **2a.** 20 mm or 2 cm **b.** 18 mm or 1.8 cm **c.** 79 mm or 7.9 cm **d.** millimeters; centimeters **3a.** kilograms **b.** kilograms **c.** milligrams **d.** milligrams **4a.** liters **b.** kiloliters **c.** milliliters

Lesson 9-2 pp. 436–437

Check Skills You'll Need **1.** 3,900 **2.** 53 **3.** 574 **4.** 0.07 **5.** 1.43 **6.** 980

Check Understanding **1a.** 150 mm **b.** 837,000 **c.** more than 5 mm; 1 m = 1,000 mm, so 5 m = 5,000 mm. **2a.** 500 m **b.** 7.5 cm **c.** To convert to a larger unit, divide. To convert to a smaller unit, multiply. **3a.** 0.1024 **b.** 4.52 **c.** 2.7 **4a.** 0.015 **b.** 0.386 **c.** 0.082

Lesson 9-3 pp. 440–443

Check Skills You'll Need **1.** 120 **2.** 2.56 **3.** 22 **4.** 29.8 **5.** 17 **6.** 100 **7.** To find $(36 \div 4)^2$, in parentheses first to get $(9)^2$. Then square 9 to get 81.

Check Understanding **1.** Answers may vary. Sample: about 144 square miles **2a.** A = 40 ft^2, P = 26 ft **b.** A = 88.8 cm^2, P = 38.8 cm **c.** For a cut parallel to the back wall, the area will be half of what it was, or 875 ft^2. The perimeter will be 70 ft less, or 120 ft. **3a.** 49 ft^2 **b.** 36 ft^2 **c.** Perimeter tells how far around and so is given in unit of length. Area tells how many square units a figure covers and so is given in square units.

Lesson 9-4 pp. 446–448

Check Skills You'll Need **1.** trapezoid **2.** parallelogram **3.** square

Check Understanding **1.** 40.18 $in.^2$ **2a.** 259.5 m^2 **b.** The area will double. **3a.** 16m^2 **b.** Answers may vary. Sample:

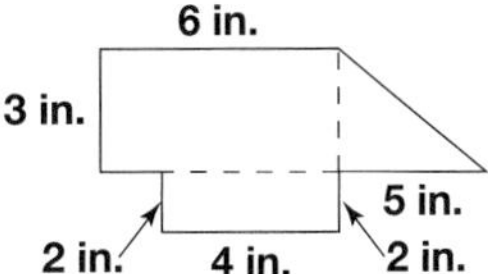

Checkpoint Quiz 1 **1.** milliliter **2.** gram **3.** centimeter **4.** 0.062 L **5.** 4,300 g **6.** 1.78 m **7.** P = 240 in., A = 3,456 $in.^2$ **8.** 72.25 cm^2 **9.** 1,000 ft^2 **10.** 78 m^2

Lesson 9-5 pp. 452–453

Check Skills You'll Need **1.** 4,898.4 **2.** 319.966 **3.** 307.406 **4.** 552.64 **5.** 226.08 **6.** 468.802 **7.** Less than 1; the product of two numbers both less than 1 is always less than 1.

Check Understanding **1.** $\overline{AC}$, $\overline{BD}$ **2a.** 4 cm **b.** 20 in. **c.** It would also be doubled. **3.** 42 cm

Lesson 9-6 pp. 456–457

Check Skills You'll Need **1.** 49 **2.** 25 **3.** 1,225 **4.** 144 **5.** 32 **6.** 175 **7.** 74 **8.** 1,225

Check Understanding **1a.** about 363 mi^2 **b.** about 108 cm^2 **c.** about 192 m^2 **d.** The actual area is greater than 75 ft^2 because π was rounded down. **2a.** about 0.20 yd^2 **b.** about 1.33 m^2 **c.** about 254.47 $in.^2$

Lesson 9-7 pp. 462–463

Check Skills You'll Need **1.** hexagon **2.** quadrilateral **3.** scalene obtuse triangle

Check Understanding **1a.** pentagonal prism **b.** rectangular prism **c.** triangular prism **d.** rectangle **2.** rectangular prism **3a.** cube **b.** triangular prism

Lesson 9-8 pp. 467–469

Check Skills You'll Need **1.** **2.** **3.** **4.** about 133 m^2 **5.** about 13 yd^2 **6.** about 5,027 mm^2

Check Understanding **1a.** A rectangular prism has three pairs of congruent faces. Find the areas of the front, right, and top faces, multiply each by 2, and find the sum. **b.** 216 cm^3 **2a.** A box has three pairs of congruent faces. The areas of the front and back sides are $\ell \times h$. The areas of the right and left sides are $w \times h$. The areas of the top and bottom sides are $\ell \times w$. **b.** 1728 m^2 **3a.** The areas of the top and bottom of the can are πr^2. The area around the can is the product of the height of the can and the distance around the can. The distance around the can is the circumference of the can, so the area around the can is Ch. **b.** 97 sq. in.

Lesson 9-9 pp. 470–471

Check Skills You'll Need **1.** 8 yd^2 **2.** 500 km^2

Check Understanding **1a.** 12 $units^3$ **b.** 48 $units^3$ **c.** The volume would double. **2.** 560 m^3 **3a.** about 42.4 $in.^3$ **b.** increasing the radius; the value of the radius is squared while the value of the height is not.

Checkpoint Quiz 2 **1.** 13 m **2.** 13 m^2 **3.** triangular pyramid **4.** cone **5.** octagonal prism **6.** 62 cm^2 **7.** 30 cm^2 **8.** 45.4 m^2 **9.** 210.1 m^2 **10.** 226.8 m^3

Lesson 9-10 pp. 477–478

Check Skills You'll Need **1.** 36 **2.** 7 **3.** 9 **4.** 68 **5.** 105 **6.** 14

Check Understanding **1.** 21 pencils

Chapter 10

Diagnosing Readiness p. 490

1. 39 **2.** 31 **3.** 100 **4.** 79 **5.** 31 **6.** 118 **7.** 6 **8.** 66 **9.** 4 **10.** 72 **11.** 15 **12.** 252 **13.** $<$ **14.** $>$ **15.** $=$ **16.** $\frac{1}{12}, \frac{1}{8}, \frac{1}{3}$ **17.** $\frac{4}{9}, \frac{7}{12}, \frac{5}{6}$ **18.** $\frac{1}{4}, \frac{1}{2}, \frac{6}{7}$

Lesson 10-1 pp. 491–493

Check Skills You'll Need **1.** $>$ **2.** $=$ **3.** $<$ **4.** $\frac{4}{3}, \frac{14}{9}, \frac{8}{5}$ **5.** $\frac{1}{4}, \frac{2}{5}, \frac{3}{6}$ **6.** $\frac{3}{8}, \frac{6}{15}, \frac{4}{5}$

Check Understanding

1. −2 −1 0 1 2

2. 10°F **3.** 55 **4a.** 7 **b.** 6 **c.** 100 **d.** The absolute values are the same as the positive integers. **5a.** $>$ **b.** $<$ **c.** $>$ **d.** Yes; negative numbers are always less than zero. **6a.** 0, 40, 70, 80, 110 **b.** −25, −10, −7, −3, −1 **c.** −62, −46, −35, −28, −16 **d.** −80, −42, −22, 40, 80 **e.** −67, −66, −64, 63, 65

Lesson 10-2 pp. 497–499

Check Skills You'll Need **1.** 50 **2.** 101 **3.** 434 **4.** 36 **5.** 812 **6.** 639 **7.** Answers may vary. Sample: 230

Check Understanding **1a.** −4 **b.** 22 **c.** −22 **2a.** 16 **b.** −9 **c.** −21 **d.** i. positive ii. negative **3a.** 3 **b.** 3 **c.** −2 **4a.** −3 **b.** −7 **c.** 9 **d.** 0 **e.** 0; the absolute value of both integers is the same positive number. The difference of identical numbers is zero. **5.** 2 ft

Lesson 10-3 pp. 503–505

Check Skills You'll Need **1.** 17 **2.** 31 **3.** 7 **4.** 0 **5.** 158 **6.** 180 **7.** Answers may vary. Sample: 40

Check Understanding **1a.** 0; backward; turn around; −2; −1 **b.** 4 **c.** −6 **d.** −2 **2a.** 12 **b.** −4 **c.** −8 **3.** 622 ft **4.** 9°F

Lesson 10-4 pp. 509–511

Check Skills You'll Need **1.** 576 **2.** 8 **3.** 252 **4.** 6 **5.** 540 **6.** 3 **7.** Divide both sides of the equation by 98.

Check Understanding **1a.** −42 **b.** 27 **c.** −15 **d.** 0 **e.** Answers may vary. Sample: The product of 4 and 2 is positive because the product of two integers with the same sign is always positive. $4 \times 2 = 8$. The product of 8 and −3 is negative because the product of two integers with different signs is always negative. $4 \times 2 \times (-3) = -24$ **2a.** −12 **b.** yes **3a.** −4 **b.** 18 **c.** −2 **4.** −2°F

Checkpoint Quiz 1 **1.** 4 **2.** −5 **3.** −8 **4.** −3 **5.** −2 **6.** −12 **7.** −16 **8.** −7 **9.** 7 **10a.** $c = -2 \times 10$ **b.** −20

Lesson 10-5 pp. 513–514

Check Skills You'll Need **1.** −2 0 **2.** 0 3

3. 0 **4.** 0 $\frac{1}{2}$ **5.** $-1\frac{1}{2}$ 0

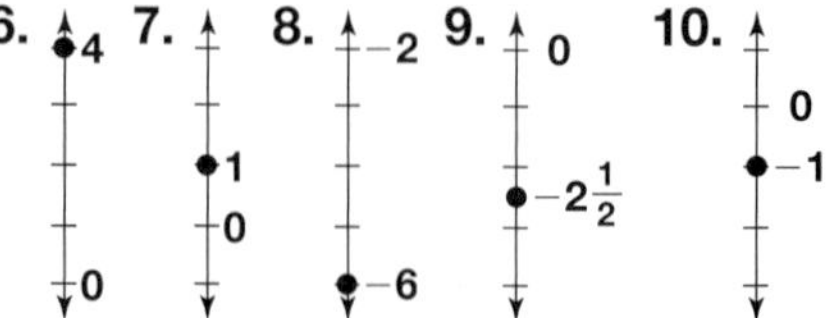

Check Understanding **1.** $C(1, 3)$, $D(-2, -3)$, $E(2, -2)$ **2a.** post office **b.** (−6, −1)

3a–d. 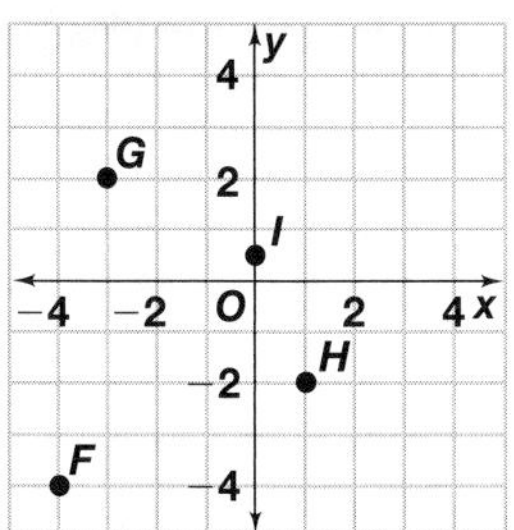

F lies in Quadrant III, *G* lies in Quadrant II, *H* lies in Quadrant IV, *I* lies on the *y*-axis between Quadrants I and II.

Lesson 10-6 pp. 518–519

Check Skills You'll Need **1.** 38 **2.** 9 **3.** −13 **4.** −28 **5.** −14 **6.** −6 **7.** −31 **8.** −59 **9.** 26 **10.** 18 **11.** 18 **12.** −6

Check Understanding **1a.** −\$2,886 **b.** \$821 **c.** −\$1,529 **d.** −\$337 **2a.** December; the point for December is the highest point above the *x*-axis. **b.** January; the point for January is the lowest point below the *x*-axis. **c.** Answers may vary. Sample: Many holidays take place at the end of the year. Many holiday-related gifts are purchased at this time.

Lesson 10-7 pp. 523–524

Check Skills You'll Need **1.** 11 **2.** 12 **3.** 6 **4.** 18 **5.** 43 **6.** 14 **7.** 50 **8.** 76 **9.** 33 **10.** 112

Check Understanding **1a.** 4, −6, 9 **b.** −10, −3.5, 5 **2a.** c = number of correct answers, s = score; $s = 2c$ **b.** 92 **3.** 21

More Than One Way \$52.50; Answers may vary. Sample: I substituted 45 for *x* in the equation and solved for *y*; I chose this method because it was easier than making a table or graph.

Lesson 10-8 pp. 527–528

Check Skills You'll Need **1.** 2; 8; 16 **2.** 2.5; −1; −7 **3.** $-9\frac{1}{2}$; $-2\frac{1}{2}$; $9\frac{1}{2}$

Check Understanding **1.** 64°F

Checkpoint Quiz 2

1–2. 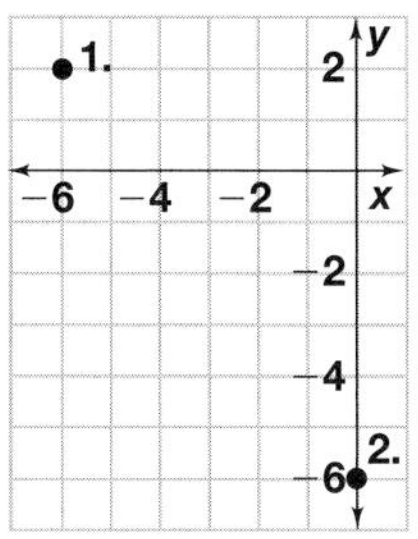

3. −\$1,293 **4.** 10; −7.5, −30 **5.** 28°F

Chapter 11

Diagnosing Readiness p. 546

1. 0.68 **2.** 0.92 **3.** 0.4 **4.** 0.766 **5.** $\frac{3}{5}$ **6.** $\frac{2}{3}$ **7.** $\frac{7}{8}$ **8.** $\frac{3}{5}$ **9.** $\frac{5}{12}$ **10.** $\frac{2}{3}$ **11.** $\frac{1}{4}$ **12.** $\frac{16}{27}$ **13.** 0.25; 25% **14.** $0.\overline{3}$; ≈ 33% **15.** 0.8; 80% **16.** 0.7; 70% **17.** $\frac{13}{100}$; 0.13 **18.** $\frac{13}{50}$; 0.26 **19.** $1\frac{1}{10}$; 1.10 **20.** $2\frac{1}{4}$; 2.25

Lesson 11-1 pp. 547–548

Check Skills You'll Need **1.** 32% **2.** 36% **3.** 67% **4.** 69% **5.** 2% **6.** 85% **7.** 80% **8.** 90% **9.** 4%

Check Understanding **1a.** $\frac{1}{2}$ **b.** $\frac{1}{6}$ **c.** $\frac{1}{3}$ **d.** Answers may vary. Sample: No; since each event is equally likely, the probabilities are the same. **2a.** certain **b.** likely **c.** unlikely **d.** impossible **e.** less; $\frac{1}{2} < \frac{2}{3}$ **3a.** $\frac{5}{7}$ **b.** 0% **c.** 0.66 **d.** Answers may vary. Sample: Unlikely; a likely probability is $> \frac{1}{2}$. So, 1 minus it is $< \frac{1}{2}$, or unlikely.

Lesson 11-2 pp. 553–554

Check Skills You'll Need **1.** $\frac{3}{5}$ **2.** $\frac{1}{2}$ **3.** $\frac{4}{15}$ **4.** $\frac{13}{20}$ **5.** $\frac{3}{5}$ **6.** $\frac{1}{3}$ **7.** $\frac{4}{5}$ **8.** $\frac{5}{8}$

Check Understanding **1a.** $\frac{3}{5}$ **b.** yes **c.** $\frac{5}{8}$ **2a.** Answers may vary. Sample: Sia could roll the number cube 120 times more and combine the data. **b.** Answers may vary. Sample: P(H) = $\frac{1}{2}$. $\frac{47}{100} \approx \frac{1}{2}$.

Lesson 11-3 pp. 558–559

Check Skills You'll Need **1.** 6 **2.** 2 **3.** 14 **4.** $6\frac{1}{4}$ **5.** 108 6. $5\frac{1}{2}$ 7. 9 green apples

Check Understanding **1.** 6 **2.** 60 toy robots

Checkpoint Quiz 1 **1.** $\frac{1}{3}$ **2.** 0 **3.** 66% **4.** $\frac{2}{5}$ **5.** 28,000 people

Lesson 11-4 pp. 563–564

Check Skills You'll Need **1.** $\frac{16}{25}$ **2.** $\frac{1}{2}$ **3.** $\frac{100}{173}$

Check Understanding **1a.** Check students' work. **b.** No; 75% × 6 is not an integer.

Lesson 11-5 pp. 586–569

Check Skills You'll Need

1. pants shirt 20 different combinations

1 — 1, 2, 3, 4
2 — 1, 2, 3, 4
3 — 1, 2, 3, 4
4 — 1, 2, 3, 4
5 — 1, 2, 3, 4

2. bread meat cheese

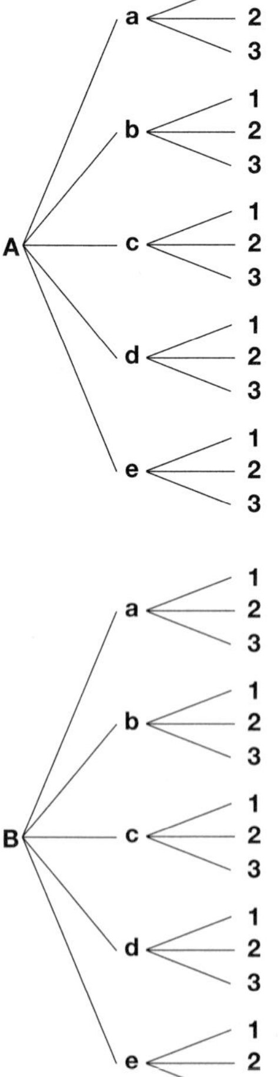

30 different sandwiches

Check Understanding **1a.** $\frac{1}{12}$ **b.** $\frac{1}{12}$ **c.** $\frac{1}{6}$ **2.** 8 **3a.** $\frac{1}{6}$ **b.** $\frac{1}{12}$

Lesson 11-6 pp. 574–575

Check Skills You'll Need **1.** 19 pennies; 14 pennies, 1 nickel; 9 pennies, 2 nickels; 9 pennies, 1 dime; 4 pennies, 3 nickels; 4 pennies, 1 nickel, 1 dime **2.** 18 different kinds

Check Understanding **1.** The order of the first letter of each column is the same as in the word PLAY. Then there are 3 choices for the second letter, 2 for the third letter and 1 for the last letter. **2a.** Answers may vary. Sample: A number cannot be repeated, so 3 is the only option.

b.

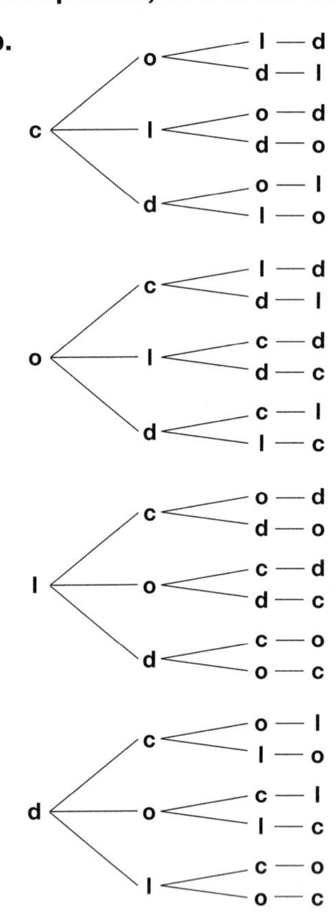

3. Answers may vary. Sample: It would take too much time and paper to draw a tree diagram. **4a.** 6 **b.** 720 **c.** 39,916,800 **d.** 9

Checkpoint Quiz 2 **1.** 25%; Answers may vary. Sample: Let 1, 3, 5 be rain and 2, 4, 6 be no rain. Toss the cube 50 or more times and record each outcome. Tally those outcomes in which both numbers are odd. Divide that number by the number of trials. **2.** Check students' work. Their probabilities should be near 41%. **3.** $\frac{7}{8}$ **4.** $\frac{1}{4}$ **5.** $\frac{1}{1,296}$ **6.** Use the initials M, E, S, and H.

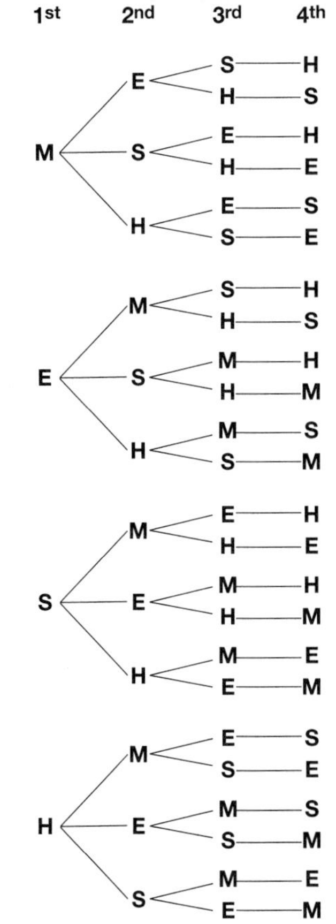

7. 120 permutations **8.** 5,040 **9.** 12
10. 39,916,800

Lesson 11-7 pp. 580–581

Check Skills You'll Need **1.** $\frac{9}{16}$ **2.** $\frac{2}{21}$ **3.** $\frac{2}{9}$ **4.** $\frac{2}{27}$ **5.** $\frac{1}{20}$ **6.** $\frac{5}{12}$ **7.** $\frac{7}{22}$ **8.** $\frac{1}{4}$ **9.** $\frac{1}{7}$

Check Understanding **1a.** Independent; the weather has no effect on the inauguration. **b.** Not independent; the number of points affects whether the team wins. **2.** $\frac{4}{25}$ **3.** Answers may vary. Sample: Yes; I'd multiply the probabilities for the three events because they are independent events.

Chapter 12

Diagnosing Readiness p. 594

1. 25 **2.** 13 **3.** 386 **4.** 43 **5.** 10 **6.** −18 **7.** 13 **8.** 7 **9.** 19 **10.** 64 **11.** 63 **12.** 125 **13.** 4^3; 4; 3 **14.** 2^4; 2; 2 **15.** 1^4; 1; 4 **16.** 12^6; 12; 6 **17.** 8^7; 8; 7 **18.** $<$ **19.** $<$ **20.** $>$

Lesson 12-1 pp. 595–596

Check Skills You'll Need **1.** 15 **2.** 48 **3.** 21 **4.** 3

Check Understanding **1a.** 9 **b.** 98 **c.** 3 **2.** $42

Lesson 12-2 pp. 601–603

Check Skills You'll Need **1.** $<$ **2.** $>$ **3.** $>$ **4.** $<$ **5.** $>$ **6.** $<$

Check Understanding **1.** Let a represent the altitude from which most skydivers jump. $a \leq 14{,}500$ **2a.** $x < -1$ **b.** $x \geq 4$ **3a.** $\ell \geq 2$ **b.** $t > \$10$ **4a.** Marissa; Taegan **b.** No. 3 is a solution to $x \leq 3$ but not to $x < 3$.

Lesson 12-3 pp. 606–607

Check Skills You'll Need **1.** 1 **2.** 3 **3.** 53 **4.** 4 **5.** 16.5 **6.** 19

Check Understanding **1.** $u \leq 9$ **2.** Let p = the number of additional people the restaurant can serve; $p + 97 \leq 115$, $p \leq 18$; The restaurant can serve at most 18 more people.

Checkpoint Quiz 1 **1.** 8 **2.** 8 **3.** 13 **4a.** yes **b.** no **c.** no **d.** no

5. 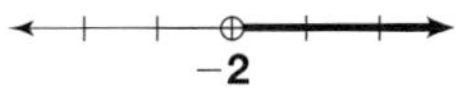

6. 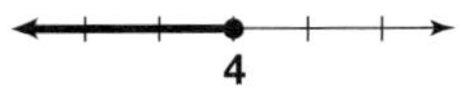

7. 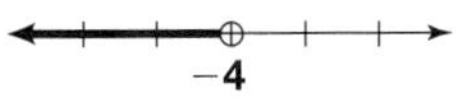

8. $p < -5$ **9.** $n > 6$ **10.** 18 coupon books

Lesson 12-4 pp. 611–612

Check Skills You'll Need **1.** 95 **2.** 24 **3.** 480 **4.** 11 **5.** 138 **6.** 18

Check Understanding **1a.** Answers may vary. Sample: I would use Method 2, because I have to spend less time thinking about possible sizes and shapes for the small sections for each vegetable. **b.** 20 in., 34 in.

Lesson 12-5 pp. 616–618

Check Skills You'll Need **1.** 5^2; 5, 2 **2.** 6^3; 6, 3 **3.** 4^5; 4, 5 **4.** 72^1; 72, 1 **5.** 999^3; 999, 3 **6.** 3.6^2; 3.6, 2

Check Understanding **1a.** 2 **b.** 6 **c.** 9 **d.** 10 **2a.** 2.6 **b.** 3.2 **c.** 4.9 **d.** 9.3 **3.** Find the square root of the area. **4.** Answers may vary. Sample: closer to 2; $2^2 = 4$ and $3^2 = 9$; 5 is closer to 4 than to 9, so the square root of 5 is closer to 2 than to 3. **5a.** rational **b.** rational **c.** rational **d.** rational **6a.** not rational **b.** not rational **c.** rational **d.** not rational

Checkpoint Quiz 2 **1.** 10.6 in. and 18.4 in. **2.** 14 **3.** 22 **4.** 36 **5.** 100 **6.** 24 in. **7.** rational **8.** rational **9.** rational

Lesson 12-6 pp. 622–623

Check Skills You'll Need **1.** 3 **2.** 8 **3.** 5 **4.** 6 **5.** 11 **6.** 25

Check Understanding **1a.** 15 **b.** 20 **2.** 13 mi

Selected Answers

Chapter 1

Lesson 1-1 pp. 6–7

EXERCISES **1.** 205; two hundred and five **3.** 508,310; five hundred and eight thousand, three hundred and ten. **5.** 7,000,002,031,000 **7.** < **9.** > **13.** 51,472; 51,572; 54,172; 57,142 **15.** 17,414; 17,444; 17,671; 18,242 **17.** ten-thousands **19.** thousands

25. ∩∩∩∩ II ∩∩∩∩; ∩∩∩ IIIII ∩∩ IIII

27. 2,198,000; 2,753,000; 2,739,000; 3,212,000; 3,304,000 **29.** >, > **31.** <, < **37.** 390 **39.** 2,129

Lesson 1-2 pp. 10–12

EXERCISES **1.** 500 + 30 + 0.3 + 0.04 **3.** 0.2 + 0.03 **9.** two and three tenths **11.** nine and five tenths **17.** 40.009 **19.** 0.0012 **21.** 8 + 0.2; eight and two tenths **23.** 90 + 1 + 0.09 + 0.001; ninety-one and ninety-one thousandths **25.** 0.20 **27.** 0.25 **29.** The value of each 2 is 10 times greater than the value of the 2 to its right. **31.** 4 tenths, or 0.4 **33.** 4 ten-thousandths, or 0.0004 **35.** $.006 **37.** $.053 **39.** 0.618 **47.** <

Lesson 1-3 pp. 16–17

EXERCISES

1.

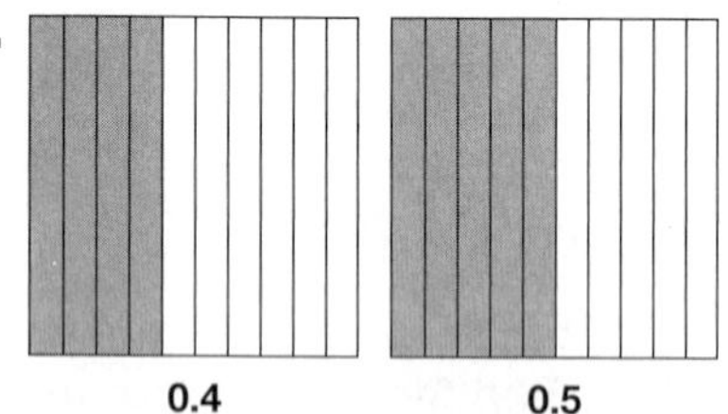

0.5 is greater.

3.

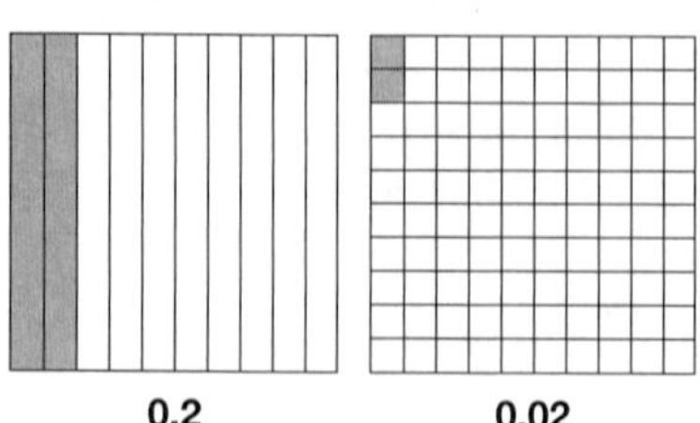

0.2 is greater.

5.

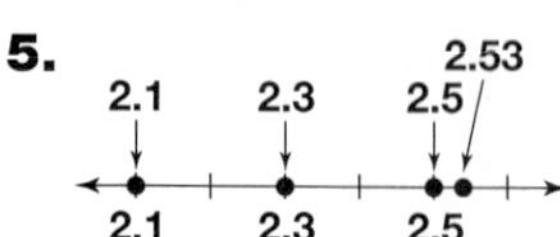

7.

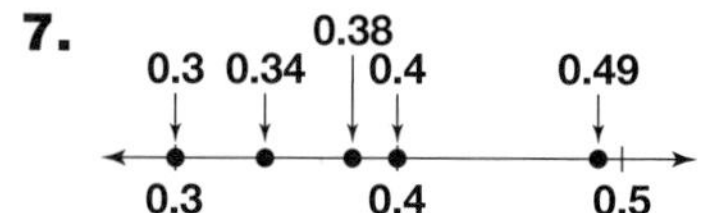

9. > **11.** > **15.** 13.7, 17.1, 17.7 **17.** 9.02, 9.024, 9.2, 9.209 **23.** 0.6595, 0.6095, 0.62 **25.** Alia; 11.88 < 11.9 **33.** 125 **35.** 10,136

Lesson 1-4 pp. 21–23

EXERCISES **1.** 37 **3.** 34 **9.** 600 **11.** 270 **17.** $15 **19.** $48 **21.** 9 **23.** 3.1 oz **25.** 1.9 oz **27.** 70 **29.** 2.320 **35.** 5 rounding; it is more accurate than using compatible numbers for subtraction. **37.** 83, rounding; it is more accurate than using compatible numbers for subtraction. **41a.** $9 **b.** I chose to round; 52 or 50 weeks in a year, 443.75 or 450 dollars. This uses compatible numbers to make division easier. **43.** 24 **45.** 15

Lesson 1-5 pp. 27–29

EXERCISES **1.** 4; 4 **3.** 9; 8.771 **7.** 9.7 **9.** 12.37 **13.** 18; 17.9 **15.** 5; 5.69 **21.** 2.72 m **23.** $270.15 **27.** > **29.** = **31.** 0; Ident. Prop. of Add. **33.** 7.5; Comm. Prop. of Add. **37a.** No; the value of the number he drew is 32,009 **39.** 0.66; yes; half is 0.5 and 0.66 > 0.5.

41.

Firewood/ Charcoal
Nuclear Power
Hydro (Water) Power
Other
Gas
Oil
Coal

51. 21,000 **53.** 0.1

Lesson 1-6 pp. 32–33

EXERCISES **1.** $26 **3.** 6:25 **5.** 15 min **7.** 12 teams **9a.** 6 cuts **b.** 27 pieces **c.** 1 piece **17.** 1.76 **19.** 1.71 **21.** tens **23.** hundreds

Lesson 1-7 pp. 37–39

EXERCISES **1.** 0.072 **3.** 173.6 **9.** 0.14 **11.** 0.15 **17.** 1,035 **19.** 14.4 **25.** $3.55 **27.** 2.8 **29.** 190 **35.** $50.00 **37.** 68.28 **39.** 56.414 **41.** 0.0064 **43.** 298.1973 **45.** 59.5 mi **47.** 483.48 million mi **49.** Incorrect, decimal should move left one place **51.** Incorrect; student performed addition **59.** < **61.** >

Lesson 1-8 pp. 41–42

EXERCISES **1.** 62 **3.** 92.5 **7.** 12.29 **9.** 1.617 **13.** < **15.** < **17.** 2.75 mph **19.** False; multiplying by 0.1 is the same as dividing by ten **21.** true

Lesson 1-9 pp. 45–47

EXERCISES **1.** 25.25 **3.** 7.2 **9.** $3.18 **11.** $0.\overline{54}$; repeating **13.** 0.76; terminating

19.

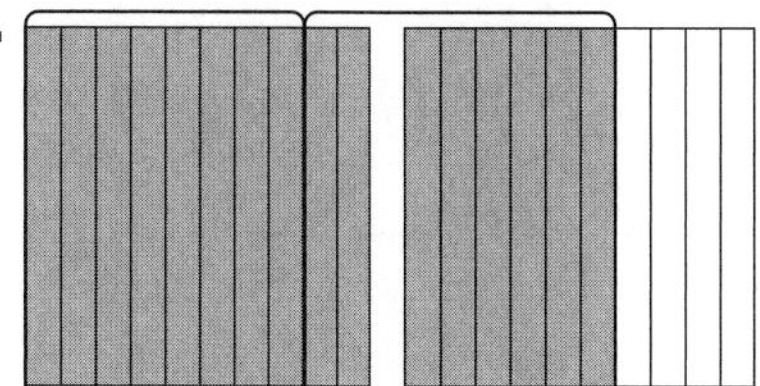

14

21.

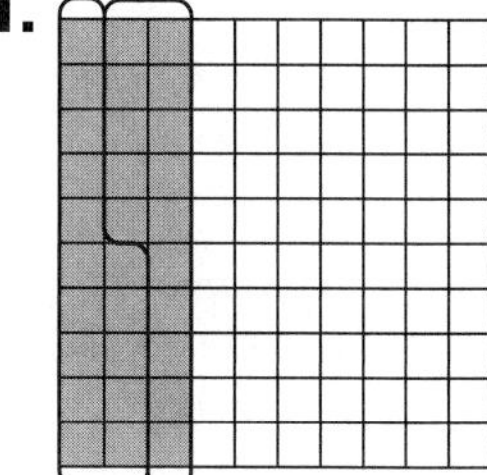

2

23. 73.75 **25.** 3.31 **29.** 0.8 **31.** 0.05 **33.** 20.30 **35.** 8.12 **37.** $4.95 **39.** 5; terminating **41.** 0.2; terminating **45.** 29.4 mi/gal **53.** 0.22675 **55.** 46.48

Lesson 1-10 pp. 49–51

EXERCISES **1.** 12 **3.** 60 **11a.** 1 × $.45 + 3 × $.95 + 2 × $.65 **b.** $4.60 **13.** 6 **15.** 7 **17.** 2 **19.** 0 **21.** = **23.** = **27.** C **29.** (11 − 7) ÷ 2 = 2 **31.** (7 − 2) × 2 − 1 = 9 **45.** 280 **47.** 0.00462

Chapter Review pp. 54–55

1. Comm. Prop. of Add. **2.** Order of Operations **3.** standard form **4.** repeating decimal **5.** Assoc. Prop. of Add **6.** 6,004,030 **7.** 6.043 **8.** five hundred twenty-five and five tenths; 500 + 20 + 5 + 0.5 **9.** five million, twenty-five; 5,000,000 + 20 + 5 **10.** five thousand, two hundred fifty-five ten-thousandths; 0.5 + 0.02 + 0.005 + 0.0005 **11.** five and twenty-five thousandths **12.** > **13.** < **14.** < **15.** > **16.** 0.06; 0.14; 0.4; 0.52 **17.** 23; 23.03; 23.2; 23.25 **18.** 9.04; 9.02; 9.24; 9.4 **19–22.** Answers may vary. Samples are given. **19.** 357 **20.** 1 **21.** 3 **22.** 6 **23.** 3.4 **24.** 0.17 **25.** 3.867 **26.** 7.4 **27.** $.48 **28.** 35.4 **29.** 2.02 **30.** 480 **31.** 9.18 **32.** 3.4 **33.** 0.9 **34.** 0.98127 **35.** 37 **36.** 0 **37.** 44.4

Chapter 2

Lesson 2-1 pp. 65–67

EXERCISES **1.** 18, 22 **3.** 81, 243 **5.** 7, 11, 15, 19, 23, 27, . . . **7.** 625; 3,125; 15,625; the first term is 1; multiply a term by 5 to get the next term. **9.** 6,000; 600, 60; the first term is 6,000,000, divide a term by 10 to get the next term. **11a.** 4:51, 5:52 **b.** 2:32, 3:17, 4:02, 4:47, 5:32 **13.** 6 **15.** 1,200 **19.** 189 **21.** 216 **27.** The computer looked at the difference between terms in a list to compute a pattern.

29.

37. 3; 3.2 **39.** 49; 49.21

Lesson 2-2 pp. 71–72

EXERCISES

1. **3.**

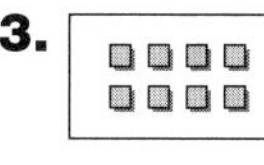

9. 20 **11.** 13

17.

Hour	Rental Fee
h	5 + 2*h*
1	7
2	9
3	11

19. 14 **21.** 4.8

31.

x	*x* + 6
1	7
4	10
7	13

33.

x	100 − *x*
20	80
35	65
50	50

45. 9, 3 **47.** 29.16 **49.** 0.0374

Lesson 2-3 pp. 76–78

EXERCISES **1.** *k* − 34 **3.** 50 + *d* **7.** 10 + 8*h* **9.** *n* − 3 **11.** *n* + 2 **13a.** *y* − 20 **b.** 7 years **15.** 11*n* **17a.** 10*w* **b.** 70 feet **19.** 3*j* + 12 **21.** Answers may vary. Sample: Your grandfather is 50 years older than you. The expression *y* + 50 relates his age to yours. **29.** 5.441 **31.** 3.149 **33.** 380

Lesson 2-4 pp. 81–82

EXERCISES **1.** 62 seats **3a.** 11 fence posts **b.** 10 fence posts **5.** 35 cars **7.** 9 pairs **9.** 132 in. **17.** 12c **19.** 4.5 + *n*

Lesson 2-5 pp. 86–88

EXERCISES **1.** false **3.** false **7.** 2 **9.** 0 **15.** 15 straps **23.** true **25.** yes **27.** no **29.** 20 lb **31.** false; 1 more than a number can never be equal to the number. **33.** true; (100 − 2) simplifies to 98. $98n = 98n$ **35.** 100 **37.** 500 **39.** No; $2x = 3x$ is true if $x = 0$. **55.** 324, 972, 2,916 **57.** 60 **59.** 16

Lesson 2-6 pp. 92–94

EXERCISES **1.** 26 **3.** 52 **11.** s = sale price of the jeans; $s + 4.99 = 29.97$ $s = \$24.98$ **13.** 11.4 **15.** 48 **21.** m = height of male giraffe; $m - 3.2 = 14.1$; 17.3 feet **23.** 8.3 **25.** 1.5 **29.** No; using estimation, 60 + 30 = 90, and 90 is not at all close to 31.8. **31.** Let c = approximate area of Cape Cod National Seashore; $c + 14{,}101 = 57{,}627$; 43,527 acres **41.** 37; 40; 43; 46; 49 **43.** 0 **45.** 24

Lesson 2-7 pp. 97–98

EXERCISES **1.** 20 **3.** 1.7 **11.** 32,000,000 square miles **13.** 441 **15.** 51,772 **21.** $2.99 per video **23.** 0.4096 **25.** 900 **29.** The teammate could not have scored half the goals because half of 41 is 20.5. It is impossible to score half of a goal. **41.** = **43.** 0.18

Lesson 2-8 pp. 101–103

EXERCISES **1.** 3^2; 3; 2 **3.** 9^3; 9; 3 **11.** $8 \times 10^4 + 3 \times 10^3 + 7 \times 10^2 + 9 \times 10^1 + 2 \times 1$ **13.** $6 \times 10^4 + 0 \times 10^3 + 2 \times 10^2 + 5 \times 10^1 + 1 \times 1$ **17.** 64 **19.** 15,625 **29.** 54,872 **31.** 60 **35.** 3 **37.** 1 **39a.** 10,000; 10^5; 100,000 **b.** The exponent tells the number of 0s in standard form. **c.** 10^7; 10,000,000; 10^8; 100,000,000 **41.** $3 \times 10^7 + 5 \times 10^6$ **43.** 27; 64; 125; 216 **45.** 2^7 **47.** 10^5 **49.** 80 **51.** 12 **61.** 1,123 **63.** 880 **67.** $<$ **69.** =

Lesson 2-9 pp. 107–108

EXERCISES **1.** $(4 \times 10) + (4 \times 8) = 40 + 32 = 72$ **3.** $8(20 + 8) = 8 \times 20 + 8 \times 8 = 160 + 64 = 224$ **7.** $27.00 **9.** 8.7 **11.** 9.5 **15.** 265 mi **17.** One way to find the total area is to find the area of each rectangle and then add the areas: $(6.8 \times 2.5) + (2 \times 2.5)$. Another way to find the total area is to multiply the total length of the rectangle by its width: $(6.8 + 2) \times 2.5$. **25.** false **27.** 32, 64

Chapter Review pp. 110–111

1. term **3.** base **7.** 55, 67, 79; the first term is 7; add 12 to a term to get the next term. **9.** 8 **11.** 42 **13.** 2 times a times b; 2 multiplied by ab. **15.** 28 laps **17.** true **19.** 5 **21.** 8 **23.** 7 **25.** 56 **31.** 128 **33.** 17 **35.** $7(20 + 8) = 140 + 56 = 196$ **37.** $(10 + 1)57 = 570 + 57 = 627$

Chapter 3

Lesson 3-1 pp. 119–121

EXERCISES **1.** yes **3.** yes **7.** 2, 5, and 10 **9.** 2 **11.** 2, 5, and 10 **13.** yes **15.** yes **19.** no **21.** yes **25.** Yes; since 1 + 1 + 4 = 6 and 6 is divisible by 3, 114 is divisible by 3. **27.** 3 and 9 **29.** 2 **35.** 4 **37.** 4 **39.** divisible by 2, 3, 4, 5, 6, and 10. **41a.** 30, 36, 42, 48 **b.** All are divisible by 6. **c.** Any number that is divisible by both 2 and 3 is also divisible by 6. **49.** 45 **51.** 16.2 **55.** 1 **57.** 11.5

Lesson 3-2 pp. 125–127

EXERCISES **1.** 1, 2, 4, 8 **3.** 1, 2, 3, 6, 9, 18 **9.** composite; $55 = 5 \times 11$ **11.** Prime; the only factors are 1 and 83.

17.

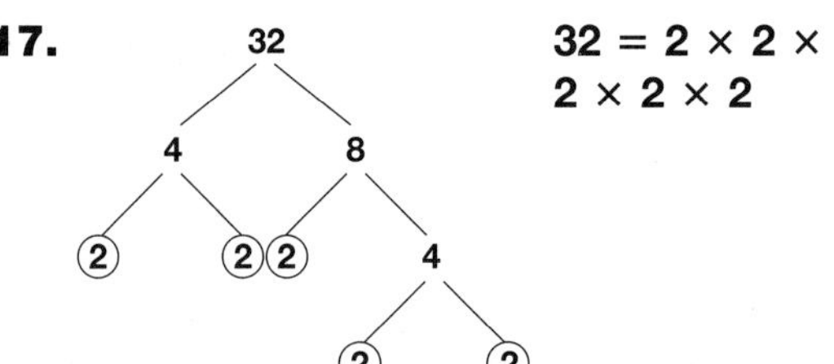

$32 = 2 \times 2 \times 2 \times 2 \times 2$

$42 = 2 \times 3 \times 7$

19.

75
3
25
5
5

$75 = 5 \times 5 \times 3$

25. 1,001 **27.** 1×36; 2×18; 3×12; 4×9; 6×6 **29.** $135 = 3 \times 3 \times 3 \times 5$ **31.** $210 = 2 \times 3 \times 5 \times 7$ **45.** 50 **47.** $>$ **49.** $<$

Lesson 3-3 pp. 129–131

EXERCISES **1.** factors of 14: 1, 2, 7, 14 factors of 35: 1, 5, 7, 35 GCF of 14 and 35: 7 **3.** factors of 26: 1, 2, 13, 26 factors of 34: 1, 2, 17, 34 GCF of 26 and 34: 2 **7.** 2 10 18 5 9 GCF = 2 **9.** GCF = 1 **13.** GCF = 22 **15.** GCF = 18

21. 140 **23.** 25 **27.** Brand B with 12 cards and Brand C with 15 cards **29.** 4 **31.** 10 **33.** 48; 1, 2, 3, 4, 6, 8, 12, 16, 24, 48 **39a.** 3 × \$1.25 + (\$4.50 ÷ 3) **b.** \$5.25

41. 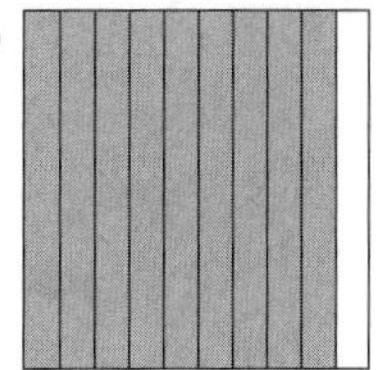 **43.** 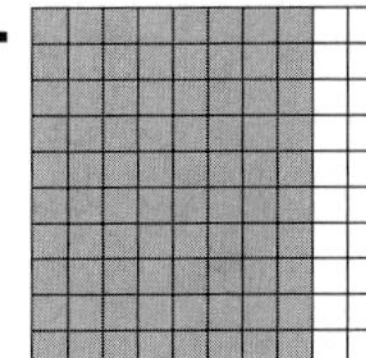

Lesson 3-4 pp. 136–137

EXERCISES **1.** $\frac{1}{2}, \frac{4}{8}$ **3.** $\frac{2}{3}, \frac{4}{6}$ **9.** **11.** $\frac{1}{2}$ **17.** $\frac{3}{5}$ **19.** no; $\frac{3}{4}$ **21.** no; $\frac{2}{3}$ **31.** The first engineer is recording time in minutes. The second engineer is recording fractions of an hour. **33.** To write a fraction in simplest form, divide the numerator and the denominator by their GCF. **35.** $\frac{8}{12}, \frac{3}{5}$; no **37.** $\frac{1}{2}$ **47.** 3 **49.** 150 **51.** 0.9 **53.** 20

Lesson 3-5 pp. 141–142

EXERCISES **1.** $\frac{23}{6}$ **3.** $\frac{23}{5}$ **12.** 5 **13.** $3\frac{2}{5}$ **15.** $2\frac{1}{4}$ **21.** $\frac{33}{7}$ **23.** $21\frac{1}{5}$ **29.** $1\frac{5}{16}$ inches; $1\frac{3}{4}$ inches **31.** $\frac{33}{2}$; $16\frac{1}{2}$ **33.** $\frac{106}{4}$; $26\frac{1}{2}$ **37.** $8\frac{1}{3}$; 9 **45.** false **47.** 26 **49.** 61

Lesson 3-6 pp. 145–146

EXERCISES **1.** 36 **3.** 60 **9.** 48 **11.** 72 **17.** 120th customer **19.** 84 **21.** 315 **29a.** 15 days **b.** If Monday is day 1, then the first time both items are picked up on a Sunday will be on day 91. **31a.** 2, 4, 5 **b.** 40 **33.** 120 **45.** 9.13, 9.2, 9.25, 9.26, 9.28 **47.** 4^4 **49.** 2^5

Lesson 3-7 pp. 150–152

EXERCISES **1.** < **3.** > **17.** $\frac{2}{3}, \frac{3}{4}, \frac{5}{6}$ **19.** $\frac{1}{8}, \frac{7}{40}, \frac{3}{10}$ **23.** the cherry-flavored drink **25a.** $\frac{1}{2}, \frac{1}{4}, \frac{1}{8}, \frac{1}{16}$

b. 𝅗𝅥 ♩ ♪ 𝅘𝅥𝅯

c. Yes; The note symbol that is "open" has the greatest value, and for the other symbols, the more flags there are, the less the value of the note. **27.** <, The numerators are equal, so the fraction with the lesser denominator is larger. **29.** > **31.** > **33.** true **35.** true **37.** In fractions with similar numerators, the fraction with the larger denominator is the smaller fraction.

47. $\frac{17}{3}$ **49.** $\frac{36}{21}$ or $\frac{12}{7}$ **51.** $\frac{3}{7}$ **53.** $\frac{3}{11}$

Lesson 3-8 pp. 155–156

EXERCISES **1.** $\frac{3}{10}$ **3.** $\frac{3}{4}$ **13.** 0.4 **15.** 0.375 **25.** 1.25 **27.** Write 0.125 as $\frac{125}{1,000}$. Divide numerator and denominator by 125 to express the fraction in simplest form as $\frac{1}{8}$. **29.** greater than **31.** equal to **33.** $4\frac{3}{4}$ lb, 4.75 lb **35.** 0.8, 0.87, $\frac{7}{8}$ **37.** \$6.625, \$8.50 **49.** 342 **51.** 20.5 **53.** 180 miles

Lesson 3-9 pp. 158–160

EXERCISES **1.** 48 juices **3.** 11 and 16

5.

7. 12:20 p.m. **9.** 24 sweatshirts **19.** ≠ **21.** ≠ **25.** 0.32 **27.** 10.5 **31.** p − 3

Chapter Review pp. 162–163

1. B **2.** D **3.** A **4.** C **5.** E **6.** 3 and 9 **7.** 3, 5, and 9 **8.** 2, 3, and 9 **9.** 2, 3, 5, 9, and 10 **10.** $28 = 2 \times 2 \times 7$, or $2^2 \times 7$ **11.** $51 = 3 \times 17$ **12.** $100 = 2 \times 2 \times 5 \times 5$, or $2^2 \times 5^2$ **13.** $250 = 2 \times 5 \times 5 \times 5$, or 2×5^3 **14.** 2 **15.** 2 **16.** 5 **17.** 8 **18.** No; $\frac{1}{4}$; Answers may vary. Sample: $\frac{2}{8}, \frac{3}{12}, \frac{10}{40}$ **19.** No; $\frac{2}{3}$; Answers may vary. Sample: $\frac{4}{6}, \frac{8}{12}, \frac{20}{30}$ **20.** yes **21.** yes **22.** $\frac{14}{3}$ **23.** $\frac{41}{5}$ **24.** $4\frac{1}{3}$ **25.** $9\frac{2}{3}$ **26.** 10 **27.** 18 **28.** 132 **29.** 140 **30.** $\frac{1}{6}, \frac{1}{4}, \frac{1}{2}$ **31.** $2\frac{1}{3}, 2\frac{2}{5}, 2\frac{4}{15}$ **32.** $\frac{17}{40}, \frac{5}{16}, \frac{7}{20}$ **33.** 0.1875 **34.** $6.208\overline{3}$ **35.** $\frac{3}{50}$ **36.** $4\frac{13}{25}$ **37.** 76 chicken dinners **38.** 2-36 exposure, 5-24 exposure

Chapter 4

Lesson 4-1 pp. 173–174

EXERCISES **1.** $\frac{1}{2}$ **3.** $1\frac{1}{2}$ **7.** 10 **9.** 5 **13.** about 4 ft **15.** $\frac{1}{2}$ **17.** $\frac{1}{2}$ **23.** about 4 in. **33.** 0.047 **35.** 0.006 **39.** $20h$ **41.** $s + 12$

Lesson 4-2 pp. 177–178

EXERCISES **1.** $\frac{1}{2}$ **3.** $\frac{2}{3}$ **9.** $\frac{2}{3}$ **11.** $\frac{1}{5}$ **17.** garden spider; $\frac{1}{2}$ in. **19.** $\frac{2}{6} + \frac{3}{6} = \frac{5}{6}$ **21.** $\frac{2}{3}$ **23.** $\frac{9}{20}$ **25.** $\frac{4}{5}$

39. **41.** **43.** 5

Lesson 4-3 pp. 182–184

EXERCISES **1.** $\frac{9}{10}$ **3.** $\frac{1}{2}$ **7.** $1\frac{23}{40}$ mi **9.** $\frac{1}{4}$ **11.** $\frac{9}{16}$ **15.** $\frac{5}{12}$ c **17.** $\frac{11}{15}$ **19.** $\frac{3}{10}$ **25a.** $1\frac{1}{2}$ in. **b.** $1\frac{7}{40}$ in. **27.** $\frac{9}{20}$ mi per min **29.** $\frac{1}{8}$ **43.** 11 **45.** 30 **47.** 16 **49.** 49 **51.** 720

Lesson 4-4 pp. 187–189

EXERCISES **1.** $6\frac{1}{6}$ **3.** $6\frac{5}{7}$ **5.** $4\frac{1}{4}$ lb **7.** $11\frac{1}{6}$ **9.** $4\frac{3}{8}$ **13.** $21\frac{1}{8}$ min **15.** $>$ **17.** $<$ **21.** $4\frac{1}{8}$ in. **23.** $8\frac{7}{8}$ **25.** 13 yd **35.** 360 mi **37.** 5

Lesson 4-5 pp. 192–194

EXERCISES **1.** $2\frac{3}{8}$ **3.** $1\frac{3}{8}$ **9.** $1\frac{1}{6}$ h **11.** $3\frac{3}{8}$ **13.** $6\frac{7}{10}$ **15.** $2\frac{2}{3}$ **17.** $1\frac{15}{16}$ in. **19.** $\frac{5}{6}$ **21.** $2\frac{1}{2}$ **29.** 6 in. **31.** 1 ft $5\frac{1}{2}$ in. **41.** $1\frac{1}{2}$ **43.** $\frac{4}{5}$ **47.** $\frac{2}{7}$ **49.** 2

Lesson 4-6 pp. 198–199

EXERCISES **1.** $3\frac{2}{5}$ **3.** $7\frac{1}{5}$ **7.** $1\frac{5}{42}$ **9.** $1\frac{17}{24}$ **13.** $\frac{7}{12}$ of the book **15.** $\frac{1}{4}$ **17.** $3\frac{17}{25}$ **21.** Sample: Let G ≠ length of Golden Gate Bridge; then $G \neq \frac{3}{10} \pm \frac{1}{2}$; $G \neq \frac{4}{5}$ mi **23.** Sample: Let R ≠ fraction of the class that chooses red; then $R \neq 1 - \frac{2}{5} - \frac{1}{3}$; $R \neq \frac{14}{15}$ **33.** $\frac{1}{4}$ **35.** $\frac{11}{12}$ **37.** $\frac{3}{10}, \frac{1}{2}, \frac{4}{7}, \frac{2}{3}$ **39.** $\frac{0}{5}, \frac{2}{11}, \frac{5}{9}, \frac{8}{7}$

Lesson 4-7 pp. 203–205

EXERCISES **1.** 90 min **3.** 482 min **7.** 1 h 10 min **9.** 5 h 46 min **13.** 9 h 47 min **15.** 29 min **17.** 1:00 P.M. **19.** 11:00 A.M. **31.** 36 **33.** −3.8

Lesson 4-8 pp. 207–208

EXERCISES Check students' diagrams. **1.** 55 **3.** 39 in. **5.** 18 lights **9.** 80 gifts **17.** $3\frac{1}{2}$ **19.** $13\frac{15}{16}$ **21.** $7\frac{7}{10}$

Chapter Review pp. 210–211

1. benchmark **11.** about 6 c **13.** $\frac{1}{2}$ **15.** $\frac{5}{9}$ **21.** $7\frac{1}{8}$ **23.** $6\frac{4}{5}$ **25.** $\frac{3}{7}$ **27.** $1\frac{1}{9}$ **31.** 3 h 41 min **33.** 8:10 P.M. **35.** 24 plants

Chapter 5

Lesson 5-1 pp. 222–223

EXERCISES **1.** $\frac{1}{12}$ **3.** 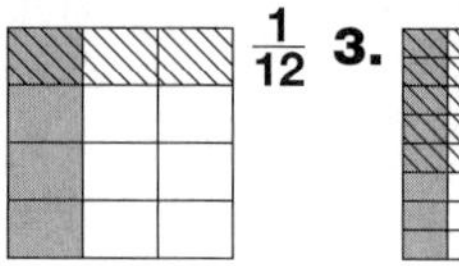 $\frac{5}{40} = \frac{1}{8}$

5. $\frac{3}{16}$ **7.** $\frac{11}{16}$ **15.** 22 **17.** $16\frac{1}{3}$ **21.** 11 23. 5 **29.** In the first and third fractions, divide denominator and numerator by the common factor 3. In the second and third fractions, divide numerator and denominator by the common factor 4. You get $\frac{2}{_1 3} \cdot \frac{4^1}{5} \cdot \frac{3^1}{4_1}$ or $\frac{2}{1} \cdot \frac{1}{5} \cdot \frac{1}{1}$. **31.** 10 **33.** $\frac{3}{5}$ **35.** $\frac{9}{20}$ **43.** $1\frac{1}{6}$ **45.** $\frac{8}{45}$ **51.** composite **53.** prime

Lesson 5-2 pp. 226–228

EXERCISES **1.** 4 **3.** 60 **7.** 65 **9.** $10\frac{1}{2}$ **17.** 5 in. by 5 in. **19.** 48 **21.** 18 **23.** No; the carpenter needs $6 \times 3\frac{1}{2} = 21$ ft of wood for the slats; two 10-ft boards are only 20 ft. **25.** 6 in. **27.** $104\frac{13}{15}$ **29.** $49\frac{5}{6}$

Lesson 5-3 pp. 232–234

EXERCISES **1.** $\frac{5}{2}$ **3.** $\frac{1}{11}$ **7.** $6\frac{2}{3}$ **9.** $11\frac{2}{3}$ **13.** $2\frac{2}{3}$ **15.** $7\frac{1}{3}$ **21.** $\frac{1}{4}$ **23.** $\frac{11}{12}$ **25.** $\frac{3}{16}$T **27.** $\frac{10}{11}$ **29.** $\frac{11}{27}$ **35.** 4 times more **37.** 36 **39.** $\frac{5}{12}$ **45.** 64 pieces **47.** 3 **49.** 2 **61.** 20 **63.** 15 **65.** 2, 3 67. 5

Lesson 5-4 pp. 238–240

EXERCISES **1.** 10 **3.** 11 **7.** 9 points **9.** $\frac{19}{20}$ **11.** $\frac{13}{16}$ ft **13.** $\frac{7}{16}$ **15.** $2\frac{2}{9}$ **19.** $\frac{5}{14}$ **21.** $\frac{2}{9}$ **29.** 24 strips **31.** 70 **33.** 5 **35.** 30 books **37.** $\frac{4}{11}$ **39.** $\frac{5}{18}$ **41.** $1\frac{1}{15}$ **43.** $2\frac{7}{9}$ **45a.** 80; 800; 80,000 **b.** As a gets larger $8 \div \frac{1}{a}$ also gets larger. **47.** $1\frac{1}{25}$ **49.** $\frac{7}{8}$ **61.** 9 **63.** 20 **65.** $2^4 \times 3^2$ **67.** $2^2 \times 3 \times 23$

Lesson 5-5 pp. 244–245

EXERCISES **1.** 36 **3.** 324 **11.** 15 **13.** 24 **17.** $7\frac{1}{2} \times p = 3$; $\frac{2}{5}$ lb **19.** 20 **21.** $\frac{4}{7}$ **27.** k is greater than 1 because the product is greater than the number multiplied by k. **29.** $\frac{8}{5}k = 12$; $7\frac{1}{2}$ mi **31.** about 300 mi **41.** $2\frac{1}{4}$ **43.** $21\frac{8}{9}$ **45.** $\frac{9}{100}$

Lesson 5-6 pp. 247–249

EXERCISES **1.** 7 classes **3.** 18 cuts **7a.** 1 in. **b.** 70 in. **9a.** Moe **11.** $79.20 **21.** $2\frac{1}{2}$ **23.** $\frac{20}{21}$ **27.** 6 **29.** 4

Lesson 5-7 pp. 252–253

EXERCISES 1–18. Answers may vary. Samples are given. **1.** Feet; lots are usually measured in feet. **3.** Inches; a license plate is a little longer than a foot-ruler. **5.** Pounds; one orange weighs less than a pound, so a bag of oranges would weigh more. **7.** Pounds; a bowling ball weighs more than a loaf of bread. **9.** Fluid ounces; a sample size bottle of shampoo holds less than a cup. **11.** Gallon; lawnmowers usually hold about 1 gallon of gas. **13.** > **15.** < **17.** about $13\frac{1}{3}$ times as heavy 27. $1\frac{1}{3}$ 29. 1 h 59 min

Lesson 5-8 pp. 256–257

EXERCISES **1.** 96 **3.** 66 **7.** about $\frac{1}{2}$ T **9.** 6 ft 7 in. **11.** 1 lb 1 oz **13.** = **15.** < **21.** 15 **23.** 68 **27.** $1\frac{8}{9}$, or 2 yd **35.** $5\frac{3}{14}$ **37.** $1\frac{7}{18}$ **39.** $5\frac{2}{3}$ **41.** $12\frac{3}{4}$

Chapter Review pp. 260–261

1. 12 **3.** 80 **5.** $\frac{3}{10}$ **7.** $\frac{2}{5}$ **13.** $\frac{1}{3}$ c **15.** 3 **17.** 2 **19.** $5\frac{2}{3}$ **21.** $\frac{8}{9}$ **27.** 25 **29.** $\frac{3}{4}$ **35.** tons **37.** $73\frac{1}{3}$ **39.** 6 **41.** >

Chapter 6

Lesson 6-1 pp. 271–272

EXERCISES **1.** 35 to 24, 35:24, $\frac{35}{24}$ **3.** 11 to 70, 11:70, $\frac{11}{70}$ **9.** 4:3 **11.** $\frac{1}{3}$ **17.** 700 **19.** 45 **25.** Divide each number by 8. **27.** 5:7 **29.** 4:2 **31.** 2:3 **45.** $\frac{15}{32}$ **47.** $\frac{1}{7}$

Lesson 6-2 pp. 275–276

EXERCISES **1.** 70 heartbeats per minute **3.** $6.50 per shirt **7.** 45 **9.** 225 **11.** $.95 per bagel; $.80 per bagel; 5 for $4.00 **13.** $.63 per lb; $.79 per lb; 3 lb for $1.89 **15.** 99 pages in 3 hr **17.** 33 mi in 3 hr **19a.** 85 jumps per min **b.** 288 jumps per min **c.** 203 jumps **31.** $\frac{6}{5}$ **33.** $2\frac{1}{20}$ **37.** $\frac{1}{14}$ **39.** $\frac{25}{33}$

Lesson 6-3 pp. 280–282

EXERCISES **1.** yes **3.** no **9.** 105 **11.** 114 **17.** 30 in. **19.** yes **21.** yes **23.** 14 in. **25.** 18 ft long × 14.25 ft wide **27.** 60 **29.** 168 **31.** The unit rates are not equal. **39.** $4\frac{4}{9}$ **41.** 6 **43.** 7,000 **45.** $1\frac{1}{4}$

Lesson 6-4 pp. 285–287

EXERCISES **1.** yes **3.** yes **7.** 63 **9.** 6.75 **15.** 28.8 oz **17.** no **19.** 1 **21.** 22 **25a.** 16.7 ft **b.** No, the ratios will be equal. **27.** 16 **29.** 32,815.41 ft **31.** 8,760 h **33.** Answers may vary. Sample: See if the product of 45 and 20 equals the product of 50 and 18. **35.** No; the unit rates are different. **45.** $\frac{1}{5}$ **47.** $\frac{4}{25}$

Lesson 6-5 pp. 290–292

EXERCISES **1.** 1 ft:25 ft **3.** 1 ft:20 ft **9.** 3 in. **11.** 1.125 in. **13.** 1.25 cm **15.** 40 cm **19a.** Reduce; the map is 4 cm wide and 3 cm high. For each centimeter on the map, I would draw 0.5 centimeter on my drawing. My drawing would measure 2 cm wide and 1.5 cm high. **21.** 5 in. **31.** 2 **33.** 2 **35.** 12 **37.** $49\frac{1}{2}$

Lesson 6-6 pp. 296–298

EXERCISES **1.** 0.15 **3.** 0.82 **10.** $\frac{7}{10}$ **13.** $\frac{1}{20}$ **21.** 17% **23.** 98% **31.** 60% **33.** about 27% **35.** about 63% **37.** about 7% **45.** 0.7, 70% **57.** 72.5% **69.** 18 **71.** 20

Lesson 6-7 pp. 301–302

EXERCISES **1–25.** Answers may vary. Samples are given. **1.** 7.2 **3.** 16.8 **9.** 30.6 **11.** 26.23 **15.** 32 **17.** 12.5 **19a.** about 39 people **21.** 152 **23.** 14 **27.** $10 **29.** $89.50 **31.** 10.23 **33.** 10.56 **41.** 2:5 **43.** $\frac{2}{3}$ **49.** $2\frac{1}{2}$ **51.** $8\frac{2}{5}$

Lesson 6-8 pp. 305–306

EXERCISES **1.** $1.96, $29.96 **3.** $1.05, $16.05 **5.** $6.30 **7.** $12 **9.** $24 **11.** $5.10 **13.** Florida: $4.80, $84.80 Georgia: $3.20, $83.20 Massachusetts: $4.00, $84.00 Tennessee: $5.60, $85.60 **15.** Florida: $.05, $.85 Georgia: $.03, $.83 Massachusetts: $.04, $.84 Tennessee: $.06, $.86 **19.** 45 **21.** 90 **33.** 1,488 times **35.** 130 min **37.** 380 min **39.** 180 **41.** 360

Lesson 6-9 pp. 308–309

EXERCISES **1.** 6,000,000 subscribers **3.** $79.90 **7.** $15 **9.** $13.25 **13.** 9,200,000 **15.** 1,250 t **23.** yes **25.** 44 **27.** 20

Chapter Review pp. 312–313

1. E **3.** C **7.** 15 to 8, 15:8, $\frac{15}{8}$ **9.** 15 to 46, 15:46, $\frac{15}{46}$ **11.** $\frac{3}{5}$ **13.** $\frac{5}{6}$ **15.** $12.50 **17.** no **19.** yes **21.** 354 **23.** ≈12.4 ft **25.** $\frac{3}{10}$, 0.3 **27.** $\frac{14}{25}$; 0.56 **29.** 60 **35.** 3 weeks

Chapter 7

Lesson 7-1 pp. 324–325

EXERCISES **1.** 10 **3.** 2 **7.** 0.5 **9.** 20.7 **11.** 8 **13.** 94 **15.** $2.09 **17.** 137; 13; no mode **19.** increase; decrease; stay the same; Explanations may vary. Sample: If a new value is added to a data set, and if the value is greater than/less than/equal to the mean of the original data set, the new mean will increase/decrease/stay the same. **21.** 240 **27.** 12 **29.** 10.8 **31.** 160 **33.** 30

Lesson 7-2 pp. 328–330

EXERCISES **1.**

Number of Days	Tally	Frequency
28	|	1
30	||||	4
31	~~||||~~ ||	7

3. Baseball Bat Lengths (in.)

```
     X  X
     X  X
     X  X
  X  X  X  X  X
  X  X  X  X  X
 28 29 30 31 32
  Length (in.)
```

5. 43,612 square miles **7.** 1.7 m

9.

Letter	Tally	Frequency
a	|||	3
b	|	1
c	||	2
d	|	1
e	|	1
f	|	1
g	~~||||~~ ||	7
h	||	2
i	|||	3
l	~~||||~~ ~~||||~~ |	11
n	||||	4
o	~~||||~~	6
p	|	1
r	||||	4
s	|	1
t	|	1
w	||||	4
y	~~||||~~	5

b. L is the mode. The letter L alone makes up about 19% of the letters in the name. **11.** frequency of letter grades on a test **13.** 11 students

15.

```
X
X   X X
X   X X
X X X X X X   X   X
1 2 3 4 5 6 7 8 9 10
```

17.

Number	Tally	Frequency
0	||||	4
1	~~||||~~ ||	7
2	~~||||~~	5
3	||	2
4	|	1

19. 3,953 meters **27.** 500 km **29.** 830 km **31.** $\frac{3}{10}$ **33.** $\frac{2}{9}$

Lesson 7-3 pp. 333–334

EXERCISES **1.** 12 ways **3.** 43 **5a.** $63 **b.** The numbers in the first list are 1 less than the corresponding numbers in the second list.; yes **c.** $1,023 **13.** 1 lb **15.** 8 oz **17.** $\frac{1}{16}$ **19.** $\frac{4}{5}$

Lesson 7-4 pp. 337–339

EXERCISES **1.**

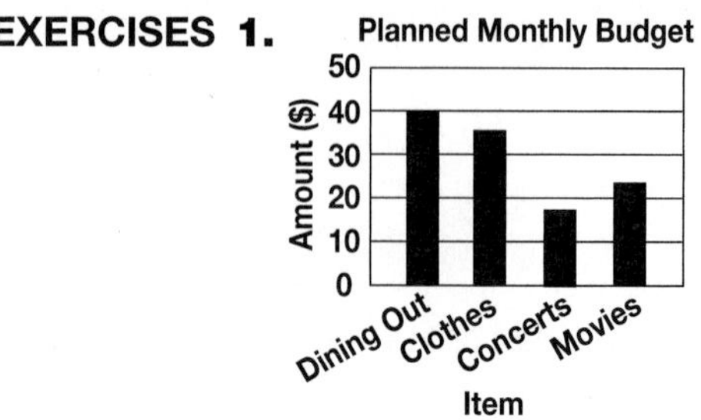

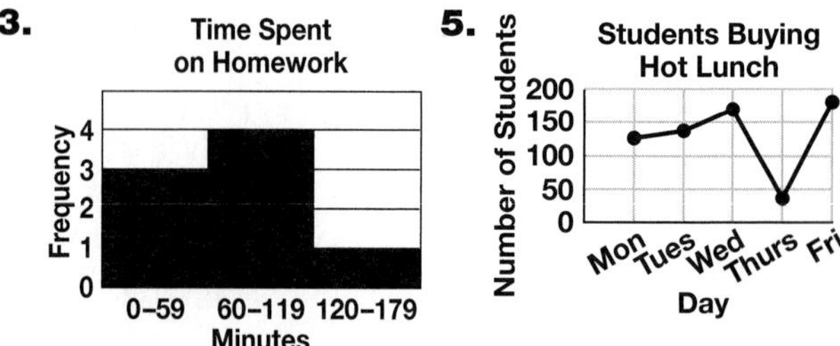

7a.

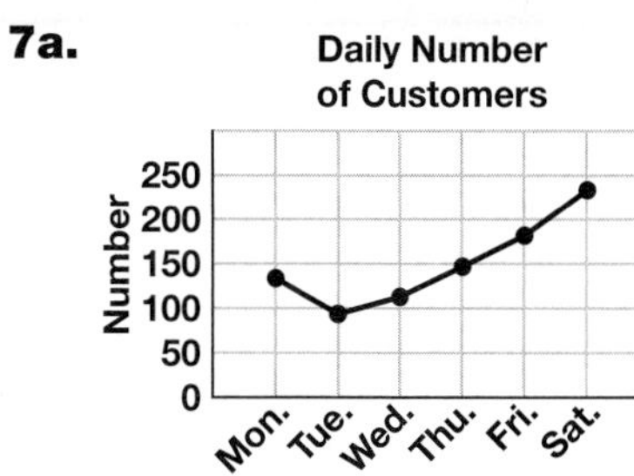

b. The daily number of customers increases, starting on Tuesday. **15.** 103 **17.** $48 **19.** $4 **21.** 10 to 18, 20 to 36, 25 to 45

Lesson 7-5 pp. 343–345

EXERCISES **1.** tennis **3.** 10%; tennis, volleyball, basketball, baseball, soccer

5. **7.**

11. **13.**

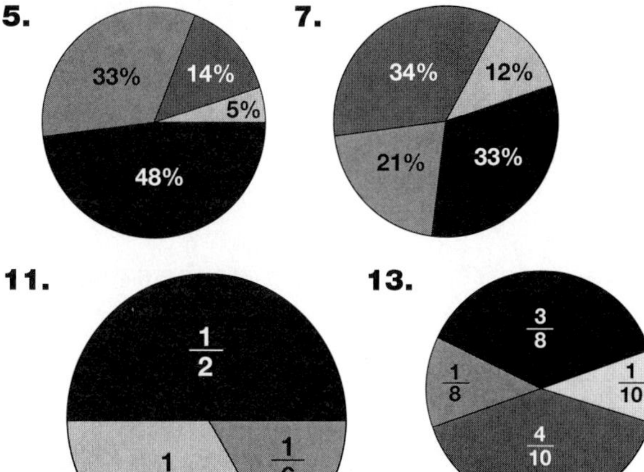

15a.

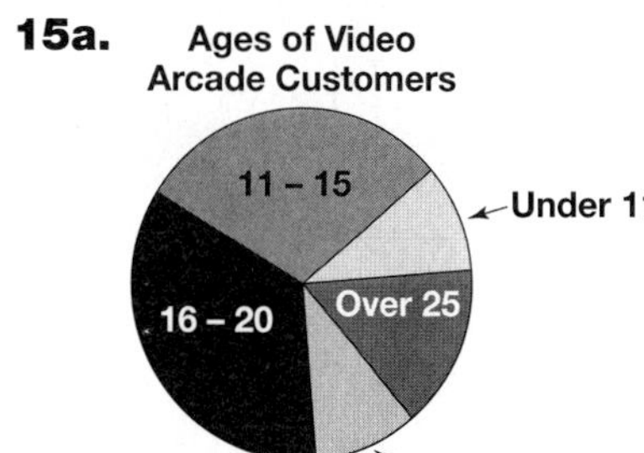

b. 60% **c.** No. Explanations may vary. Sample: You can find only the percent of customers 11 to 15 years old.

17. about 25% **23.** 12 **27.** 30 **29.** 5

Lesson 7-6 pp. 348–350

EXERCISES **1.** C2, C3, C4, C5, C6 **3.** B5, C5, D5, E5, F5 **5.** 100 **7.** 95 **9.** =B4+C4+D4 **11.** =C2−B2; 5 **13.** =E2+E3+E4 **21.** 4.5

Lesson 7-7 pp. 353–355

EXERCISES **1.** 88 **3.** none

5. Height of Tomato Plants (inches)

2	6 7 9
3	0 1 3 3 5 6 6
4	0 1

Key: 2|6 means 26 in.

7. Number of Jelly Beans in a Scoop

2	7 8
3	2 4 5 5 8
4	3 5 7 7
5	3 8
6	
7	6

Key: 2|5 means 25 jelly beans

9. Answers may vary. Sample: the median is the middle of all the leaves written in a row. The mode is the leaf which occurs most often for a given stem.

11a. Ages of people

0	9
1	1 2 2 2 2 3 3 5 5 6 9
2	0 1 3 4
3	5
4	0

b.

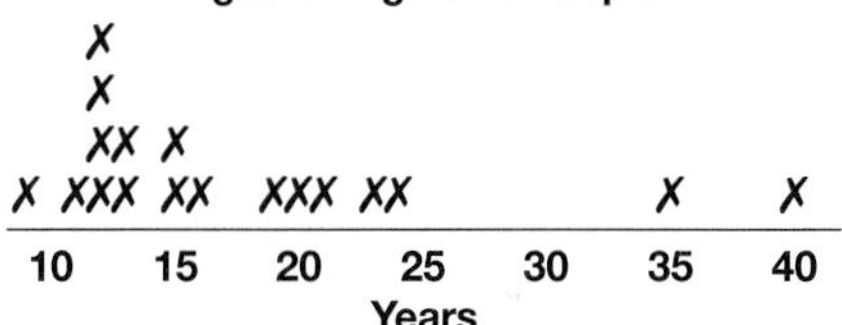

c. Line plot. Explanations may vary. Sample: the column with the most x's is the mode. **d.** Stem-and-leaf plot. Explanations may vary. Sample: the data with a stem of 1 and a leaf of 3 or more represent the teenagers. **19.** $59.40 **21.** no **25.** 53 1\3 OR 53.3

Lesson 7-8 pp. 360–362

EXERCISES **1a.** It looks like there was a dramatic decrease in phone sales. **b.** The vertical scale does not begin at 0. So, you are looking at just the top of the graph.

c.

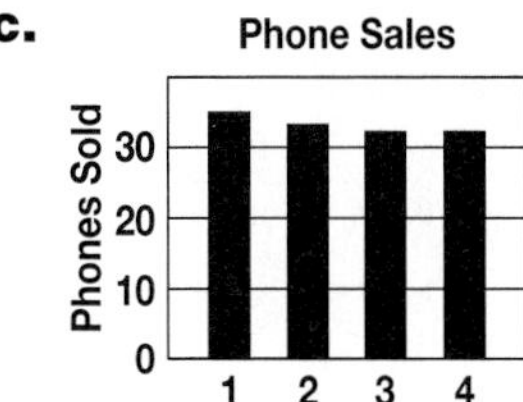

3a. The number of dogs in the animal shelter has increased at a steady rate from January to April. **b.** The intervals on the vertical axis are unequal.

Selected Answers

c. Dogs in Animal Shelter

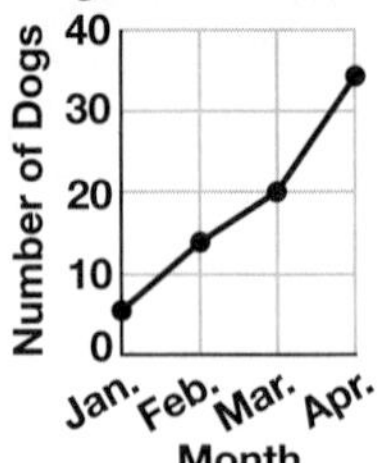

5. Answers may vary. Samples are given. **a.** She might point out that he had a high score that was much better than Allen's. **b.** He might point out that their median and mean scores were the same and that all his scores were higher than Jill's low score of 60. **7a.** mode **b.** mean **9.** The rises and falls of the values represented on the vertical axis seem more pronounced.
13. Graphs may vary. Samples are given.

a.

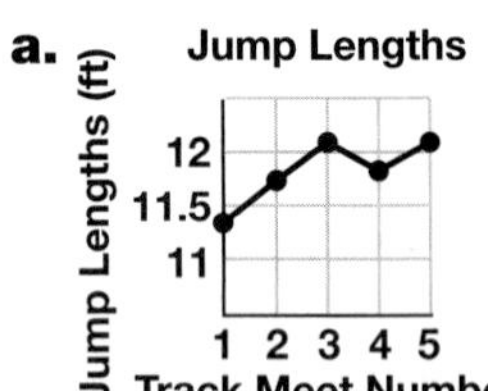

b.

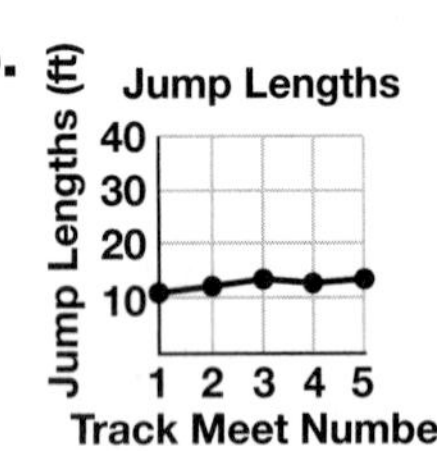

c. Both are misleading because the vertical scales were tampered with to create a specific type of impression. **21.** $6\frac{6}{7}$; 6; 6 **23.** $13\frac{1}{3}$; 13.5; 15 **25a.** 351 tiles **b.** Answers may vary. Sample: The floor has an area of 13 ft by 12 ft, or 156 ft^2. Each tile has an area of 2\3 by 2\3 ft, or 4\9 ft^2. Tara needs 156/4\9, or 351 tiles.

Chapter Review pp. 436–436

1. C **2.** A **3.** G **4.** F **5.** E **6.** 45, 49, 50 **7.** 6, 7, 9 **8.** 16, 15, 13

8.

Number of Times Vowels Occur		
Vowels	Tally	Frequency
A	𝍸𝍸𝍸 III	18
E	𝍸𝍸𝍸 III	18
I	𝍸𝍸	10
O	𝍸	5
U	𝍸	5
Y	III	3

9. 7.2, 7.5, 8

9. Number of Times Listed Words Appear

```
       X
X      X
X      X
X      X
X      X   X
X  X   X   X
the and a  of
```

Times Words Appear

10. 4 ways

11. Ticket Costs

Cost ($): 0, 10, 20, 30; Year: 1970, 1975, 1980, 1985, 1990

12.

13. Favorite Types of Books

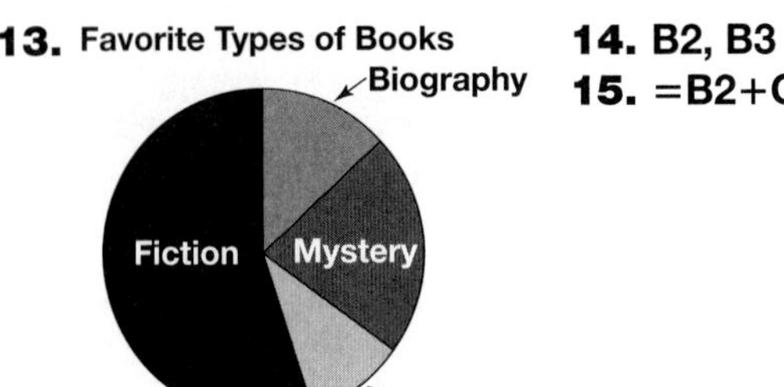

14. B2, B3 **15.** =B2+C2+D2

16.

3	01 41 67 79 88 99
4	65 79 79 83
5	07 12 43 48

Legend: 4|65 means 465

22.

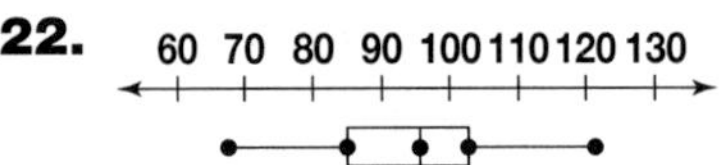

17. mean or median since they are the same
18. median

Chapter 8

Lesson 8-1 pp. 375–377

EXERCISES **1.** B **3.** D **5.** $\overline{HJ}$ **7.** $\overleftrightarrow{XY}$ **13.** *A*, *B*, and *C* **17.** noncollinear **23.** never **25.** never **41.** 520 **43.** .55; $\frac{11}{20}$ **45.** 0.5; $\frac{1}{20}$

Lesson 8-2 pp. 381–383

EXERCISES **1.** 120° **3.** 90° **7.** acute **9.** acute

13. **15.**

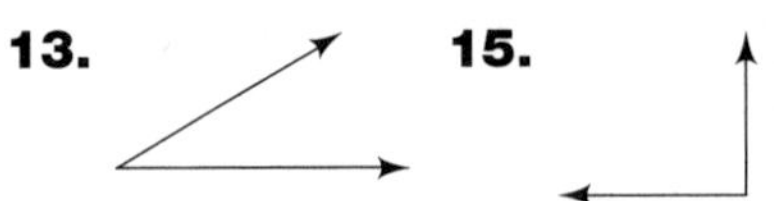

19. acute **23a.** 20° **b.** 70° **c.** 160° **d.** 120° **e.** 140° **f.** 90° **25.** ∠*AGD*, ∠*DGF*, ∠*CGE* **43.** yards **45.** miles **47.** No; you would need more than 18 cups.

Lesson 8-3 pp. 388–390

EXERCISES **1.** 78°; 168° **3.** 7°; 97° **7.** 64° **9.** $\overleftrightarrow{CE}$ **13.** sometimes **15.** never **17.** 50° **19.** 20° **21.** 85°; 95° **23.** An obtuse angle does not have a complement. **31.** 5 **33.** 9.6

Lesson 8-4 pp. 393–396

EXERCISES **1.** right **3.** obtuse **5.** right **7.** 25° **11.** isosceles **13.** isosceles **17.** isosceles, obtuse **19a.** sides $\frac{7}{8}$ in., $1\frac{1}{2}$ in., $1\frac{3}{4}$ in.; angles: 30°, 60°, 90° sides: $1\frac{1}{16}$ in., $1\frac{1}{16}$ in., $1\frac{1}{2}$ in; angles: 45°, 45°, 90° **b.** right; right **c.** scalene; isosceles **21.** No; an isosceles triangle has 2 congruent sides and an equilateral triangle has 3 congruent sides. **23.** acute scalene **25.** obtuse scalene

27. **29.**

37a. 50 **b.** 80 **39.** 66 mi **41.** 15 mi

Lesson 8-5 pp. 399–400

EXERCISES **1.** pentagon **3.** quadrilateral **5.** parallelogram, rectangle; quadrilateral, rectangle

11.

15. No **17.** All **25.** C3 **27.** 36%

Lesson 8-6 pp. 402–404

EXERCISES

1.

	a.	b.	c.	d.
a.	S	U	M	S
b.	U	N	I	T
c.	M	I	L	E
d.	S	T	E	M

3. Amy has a blue bike. Bill has a green bike. Chuck has a red bike. **5.** Sue **7.** 49 cards **9.** 68, 60. Start with 65. Subtract 2 for next term. Add the next consecutive number to the term. Subtract the next consecutive number from the term. **11a.** 360° **b.** 540°; 720° **c.** 900°; 1080° **d.** yes

17.

1	4, 6, 6, 6
2	3, 5, 8
3	3, 3, 7
4	2, 5

19. 4, 2

Lesson 8-7 pp. 407–409

EXERCISES **1.** yes **3.** yes **7.** no **9.** yes **11.** similar **13.** congruent; the window must be exactly the same size. **15.** C **17.** A and E, H and J **21.** 8 **29.** 0.75, 75% **31.** 2.5; 250%

Lesson 8-8 pp. 412–414

EXERCISES **1.** no **3.** yes

7. 2 **9.** 1

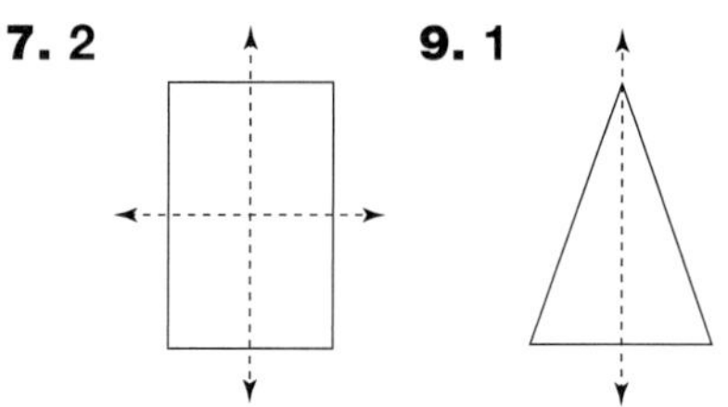

11. 2

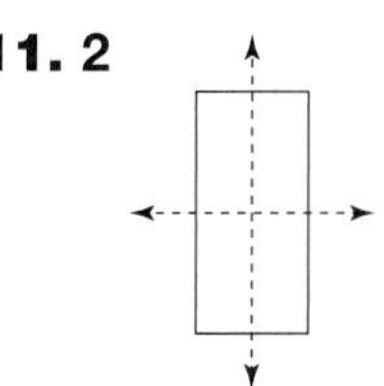

13. A, B, C, D, E, H, I, K, M, O, T, U, V, W, X, Y **17.** 3 **19.** 4 **31.** *A*, *C*, and *D*

Lesson 8-9 pp. 417–419

EXERCISES **1.** no **3.** yes

5. **7.**

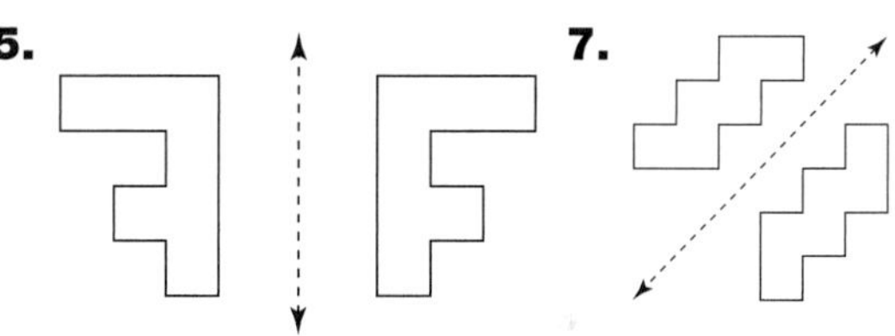

11. no **13.** yes **15.** Translations and reflections are alike because the figures stay the same size and shape. They are different because in a translation the object's orientation does not change, while in a reflection its orientation is reversed.

Translation

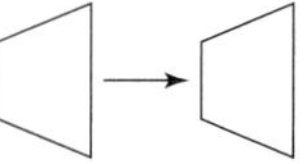

Reflection

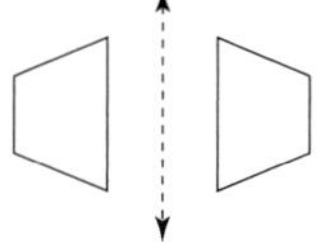

17. reflection **19.** reflection

21.

23. 180°

25.

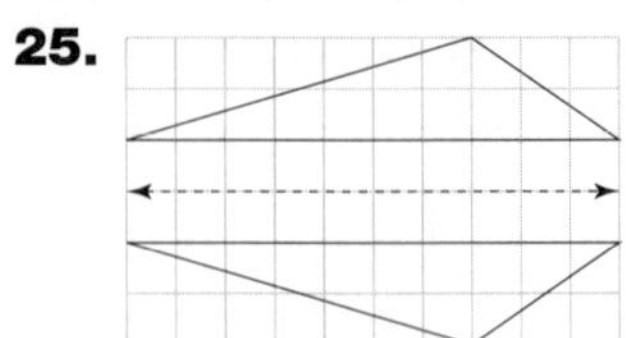

35. \$.30, \$4.05 **37.** $9\frac{1}{9}$ **39.** $7\frac{1}{3}$

Chapter Review pp. 422–423

1. obtuse **3.** perpendicular **9.** $\angle DEG$ and $\angle BEF$ **17.** similar

Chapter 9

Lesson 9-1 pp. 433–435

EXERCISES **1.** meters **3.** centimeters **7.** 12 mm or 1.2 cm **9.** 20 mm or 2cm **11.** 108 mm or 10.8 cm **13.** grams **17.** grams **19.** grams **23.** kiloliters **25.** milliliters **29.** true **31.** true **35.** true **37.** true **39.** Answers may vary. Sample: Move the table next to the wall and then determine how many desks stacked one on top of the other would reach to the ceiling. **41a.** Answers may vary. Sample: Use a piece of string whose width matches the width of the door. See how many times you can lay off end-to-end segments of that length from one end of the walk to the other end. **b.** Check student's work. **43.** Answers may vary. Sample: small insects such as a flea or mite **55.** 74°; 164° **57.** 27.5°; 117.5° **59.** 85 **61.** 528

Lesson 9-2 pp. 438–439

EXERCISES **1.** 1,300 m **3.** 4,700 mm **7.** 2.06 m **9.** 0.083 mm **13.** 610 **15.** 5,210,000 **17.** 5 **23.** 800g **25.** 240 m **27.** 0.007 g **33.** 1,000*x* grams **45a.** 2 L has 0.09 g of sugar as given, which is equal to 90 mg. **b.** 1 L has 45 mg of sugar, because this is half of the 2 L bottle. **c.** 1 mL has 0.045 mg of sugar because 1 mL is $\frac{1}{1,000}$ the 1 L amount. **d.** 80 mL has 3.6 mg of sugar because $80 \times 0.045 = 3.6$ [4] Each answer is correct and each explanation given [3] Each answer is correct but one or more explanations is missing [2] One of the parts (b), (c), or (d) is incorrect [1] Only part (a) and one of the other parts (b), (c), or (d) is correct. **47.** acute triangle equilateral triangle

Lesson 9-3 pp. 443–445

EXERCISES **1–8.** Answers may vary. Sample answers are given. **1.** 10 m^2 **3.** 15 m^2 **5.** 88 ft^2 **7.** 36 ft^2 **9.** P = 16 in., A = 16 $in.^2$ **15.** A = 0.375 m^2, P = 3.5 m **17.** 25 m^2 **21.** P = 17 cm; A = 17.5 cm^2 **23.** 0.1147 $in.^2$ **25.** P = 28.6 ft; A = 48.72 ft^2 **27.** P = 13 in.; A = $9\frac{13}{18}$ $in.^2$ **29.** P = 26.8 cm; A = 44.89 cm^2 **31.** The area increases from 13.5 $in.^2$ to 54 $in.^2$, which is 4 times the area of the original rectangle. **39.** D **41.** 75%

Lesson 9-4 pp. 448–450

EXERCISES **1.** 21 $unit^2$ **3.** 30 $unit^2$ **5.** 680 yd^2 **7.** 54 yd^2 **9.** 17.225 ft^2 **11.** 13 ft^2 **13.** 6 $unit^2$ **15.** 6 $unit^2$ **19.** The areas are the same. **21.** three \$1 items, four \$2 items, two \$5 items **25.** [2] a. 1 × 128, 2 × 64, 4 × 32, 8 × 16 b. 8 × 16; Spaces less than 8 ft wide are too narrow. [1] The answers are correct, but the explanation in part (b) is missing.

Lesson 9-5 pp. 454–455

EXERCISES **1.** $\overline{QR}$, $\overline{QS}$, $\overline{QT}$ **3.** $\overline{RT}$, $\overline{ST}$ **5.** 3.4 yd **7.** 0.125 km **9.** 157 mi **11.** 75 m **15.** about 2.45 km **17.** 405.2 m **19.** 3.13 m **21.** Answers may vary. Sample: The figure shows a circle with center Q and diameter $\overline{AB}$. The circle has two chords $\overline{AC}$ and $\overline{CB}$. **23.** 150.79632 in. **25.** 36 in^2 **33.** 41.7 **35.** 0.252

Lesson 9-6 pp. 458–459

EXERCISES **1–4.** Answers may vary. Samples are given. **1.** 432 ft^2 **3.** 12 $in.^2$ **7.** 13 yd^2 **9.** 147 m^2 **11.** about 50 $units^2$ **13.** about 177 ft^2 **15.** 27 mm^2 **17.** mi^2 **19.** 1 m^2 **21.** about 6,362 mi^2 **31.** 360 days

33.

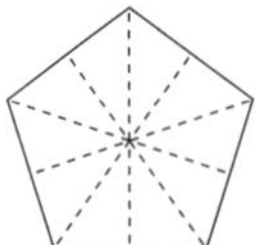

Lesson 9-7 pp. 464–466

EXERCISES **1.** triangular prism **3.** hexagonal prism **7.** cone **9.** triangular pyramid **13.** cone and cylinder **15.** hexagonal prism and hexagonal pyramid

23. trapezoidal prism; 6 faces, 8 vertices, 12 edges

25. Answers may vary. Sample: 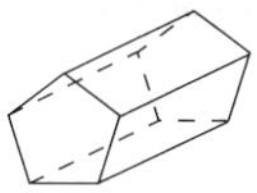

35. 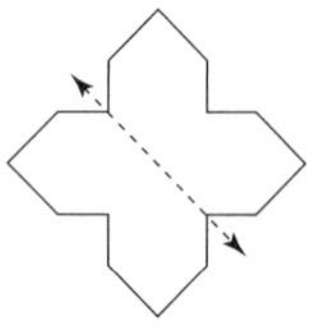 **37.** $14

Lesson 9-8 pp. 470–471

EXERCISES **1.** 450 cm^2 **3.** 132 $in.^2$ **5.** 22.5 cm^2 **7.** 216 ft^2 **11.** 14 cm^2 **13.** 28 cm^2 **15.** When each dimension of a rectangular prism is doubled, the area of each face is quadrupled. The surface area of the rectangular prism is 4 times as great. **17.** 243.8 $in.^2$ **19.** 24 cm^2 **21.** H

Lesson 9-9 pp. 474–476

EXERCISES **1.** 225 **3.** 48 **5.** 48 cm^3 **7.** 40 $in.^3$ **9.** 180 mm^3 **11.** 283.8 m^3 **15.** about 804.2 m^3 **17.** 70.2 ft^3 **19.** yes; Any face of a rectangular prism can be its base. **21.** 1 cm by 1 cm by 20 cm, 1 cm by 2 cm by 10 cm, 1 cm by 4 cm by 5 cm, 2 cm by 2 cm by 5 cm **23.** 1 cm by 1 cm by 54 cm, 1 cm by 2 cm by 27 cm, 1 cm by 3 cm by 18 cm, 1 cm by 6 cm by 9 cm, 2 cm by 3 cm by 9 cm, 3 cm by 3 cm by 6 cm **33.** G **35.** [4] a. 1 cm by 1 cm by 18 cm, 1 cm by 2 cm by 9 cm, 1 cm by 3 cm by 6 cm 2 cm by 3 cm by 3 cm b. 1 cm by 1 cm by 18 cm [3] Answer to part (b) and partial answer to part (a). [2] Answer to part (a) only. [1] Answer to part (b) only.

Lesson 9-10 pp. 478–480

EXERCISES **1.** 11 **3.** $32 **5.** $8 **7a.** answers to come **b.** answers to come **9.** 13 ticket buyers **11.** 6 minutes before the end of the 2-hour period **19.** [2] Diameter of tire ≈ 21.5 inches; The tire makes one complete circle every 68 inches, which is the tire's circumference. Divide 68 ÷ π to find the diameter. [1] Explanation is missing. **21.** 45.2 cm **23.** 79 cm **25.** no

Chapter Review pp. 482–483

1. B **2.** E **3.** C **4.** A **5.** F **6.** 300 **7.** 1.5 **8.** 57 **9a.** 40 $in.^2$ **b.** 45.6 m^2 **10.** Answers may vary. Sample: about 18 $unit^2$ **11.** 13.5 cm^2, 22 cm **12a.** $\overline{XV}$, $\overline{YW}$, $\overline{VW}$ **b.** $\overline{XV}$ **c.** $\overline{OV}$, $\overline{OX}$, $\overline{OY}$ **d.** about 30 in. **e.** 79 $in.^2$ **13a.** rectangular pyramid **b.** 5 faces, 8 edges, 5 vertices **14a.** 64 m^2 **b.** 28 m^3 **15.** 9:00 A.M.

Chapter 10

Lesson 10-1 pp. 493–495

EXERCISES

1. 

3. 

5. 8 **7.** 1 **9.** 4,418 **11.** 17 **13.** 0 **15.** > **17.** > **19.** −7, −3, −2, 0 **21.** −10, −6, 0, 5 **23.** Answers may vary. Sample: −4 **25.** Answers may vary. Sample: −5 **27.** −22, 22 **29.** −2,004; 2,004 **31a.** < **b.** > **41.** Answers may vary. Sample: Place 3 marks between 200 and 300 to divide the segment into 4 equal-size segments. The mark closest to 200 is the mark for 225. **43.** The dog and the three fifth graders will win.

Lesson 10-2 pp. 500–501

EXERCISES **1.** 10 **3.** −14 **7.** 7 **9.** 8 **13.** −45 **15.** negative **19.** −15.3 **21.** 5 **25.** 45°F **27.** =

29. 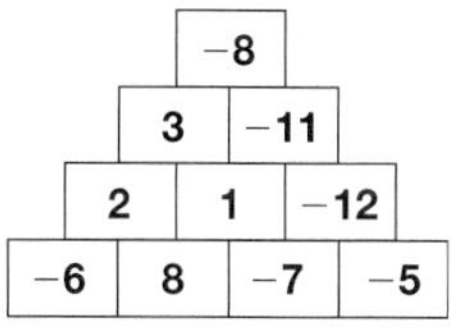

31. 1 **33.** 3 **35.** $\overline{JC}$, $\overline{JD}$, $\overline{JE}$, $\overline{JF}$, $\overline{JG}$, $\overline{JH}$ **37.** $\overline{CD}$, $\overline{DE}$, $\overline{EF}$, $\overline{FG}$, $\overline{GH}$, $\overline{HC}$

Lesson 10-3 pp. 505–508

EXERCISES **1.** 8 **3.** −3 **7.** −149 **9.** −4 **13.** −1 **15.** −43 **17.** 41.75 **21.** Answers may vary. Sample: Subtract an integer by adding its opposite. To subtract 26 from −15, add −26. −15 + (−26) = −41. **23.** 9 P.M., Dec. 31 **27.** 610°C **29a.** $323.59; $208.95; −$7.01; $535.86; $471.54; $479.89; $479.89 **b.** March 12; March 29 **31.** Friday **33.** G **35.** [2] **a.** $196 is added to the account. **b.** Subtract the sum of the bills from the sum of the checks. (OR equivalent explanation) [1] incorrect net result OR incorrect explanation **37.** $\overrightarrow{AB}$, $\overrightarrow{AD}$, $\overrightarrow{DE}$ **39.** B2 + C2 = D2

Lesson 10-4 pp. 511–512

EXERCISES **1.** 18 **3.** −14 **5.** −15 **7.** 84 **13.** −5 **15.** −5 **17.** −12 **19.** 350 **23.** 8 **31.** 16 **33.** −4,000 **35.** −4 **37.** −9

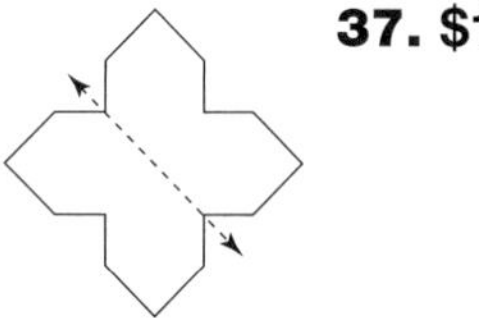

Lesson 10-5 pp. 515–516

EXERCISES **1.** (0, −3) **3.** (3, 3)

9–14.

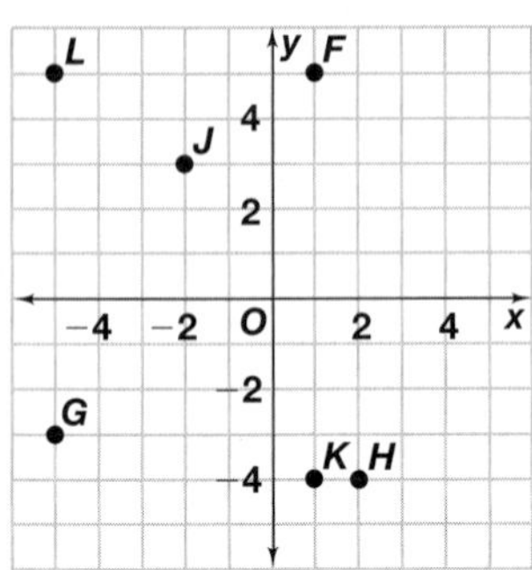

19. *A* **21.** *J* **23.** Answers may vary. Samples: **a.** Start at the origin. Move down the *y*-axis 8 units. **25.** (−8, −3) **27.** Check students' work. **35.** IV **37.** Their second coordinates are all 0; their first coordinates are all 0. **39.** Yes; answers may vary. Sample: The first coordinate tells you where to move along the *x*-axis and the second coordinate tells you where to move along the *y*-axis.

Lesson 10-6 pp. 520–521

EXERCISES **1.** −\$2,256 **3.** \$194

5.

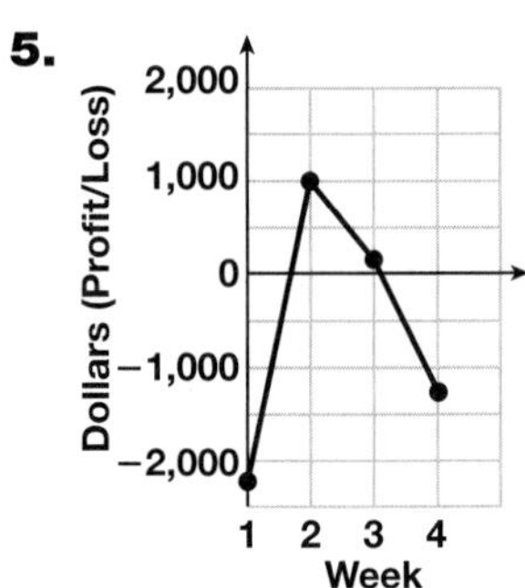

7. Week 2 **9.** \$10 **11.** −120 m **15.** As you move farther from the sun, the temperature decreases because less heat from the sun reaches the farther planets.

17.

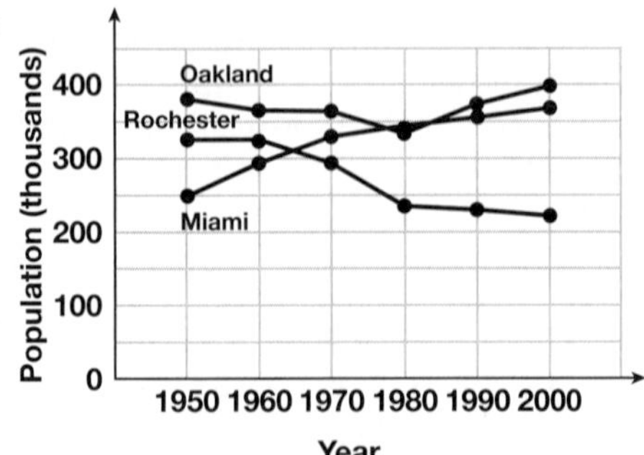

19. Rochester **21.** \$150

23.

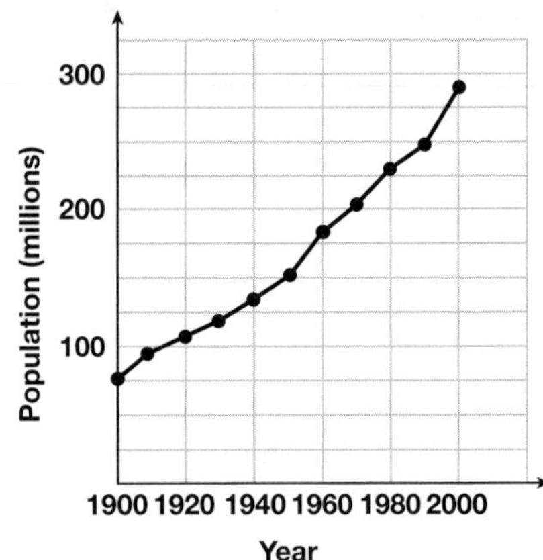

Predictions may vary. Sample: 315 million **25.** He made money; \$10 **27.** H

Lesson 10-7 pp. 524–526

EXERCISES **1.** −9; 27; 4 **3.** 24; −32; −72 **5.** $d = h \div 24$, where *d* is the number of days in *h* hours; table and graph may vary. Sample:

Hours	Days
24	1
72	3
120	5
168	7

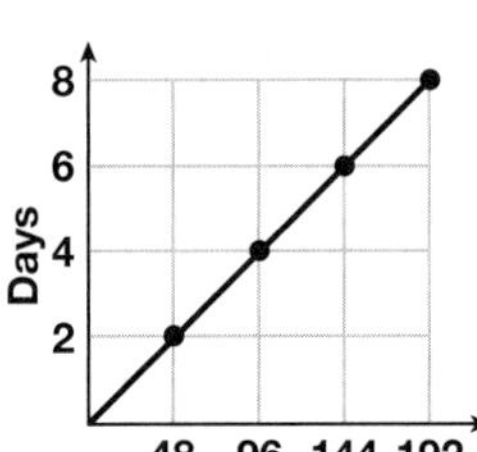

The line graph is solid because time is continuous. **7.** 5 days **9.** Graphs may vary. Sample:

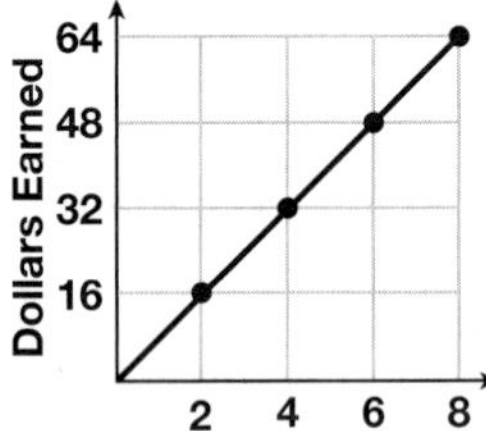

\$48

11. Add 2; 8; 9. **13a.** no **b.** yes **15.** 4; 5

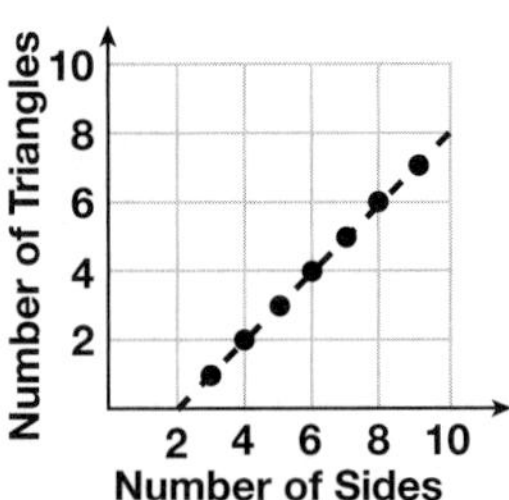

17.

x	−2	0	2	4
y	4	6	8	10

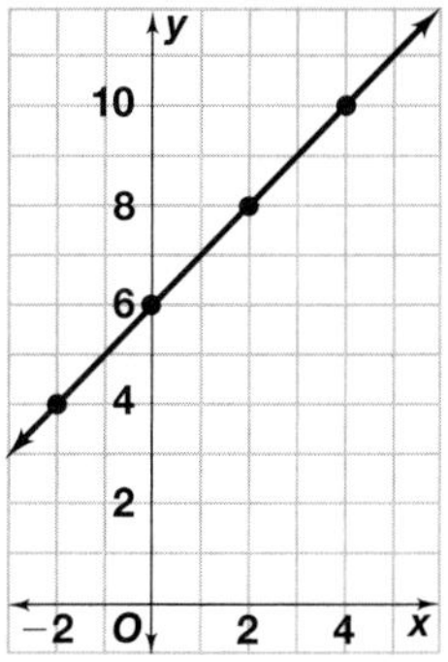

27. I

29. [2]

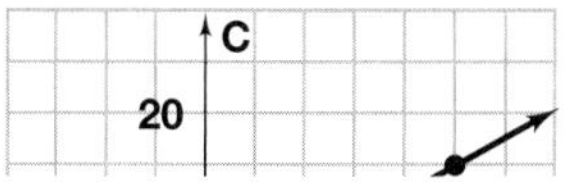

about −4°C

Lesson 10-8 pp. 530–532

EXERCISES **1.** 360 lb/ft^2 **3.** Estimates may vary. Sample: about 108 km/h **5a.** Job B **b.** Year 9 **c.** \$2,000 **7.** 981 miles **11.** Let a = my average score. $17a = -51$ Write the equation. $\frac{17a}{17} = \frac{-51}{17}$ Divide each side by 17. $a = -3$ Simplify. My average score per round is −3. **13.** [2] **a.** *Q* **b.** *P*; *R* **c.** 7; *Q* is 5 units to the left of *T*. So, subtract 5 from the coordinate of *T*, or 12. The coordinate of *Q* is 7. [1] incorrect points OR incorrect explanation **15.** G **19.** > **21.** −6, 0, 3, 19 **23.** equilateral **25.** isosceles **27.** acute

Chapter Review pp. 538–539

1. C **2.** A **3.** B **4.** F **5.** D

6–8. Graphs may vary. Samples are given.

6. 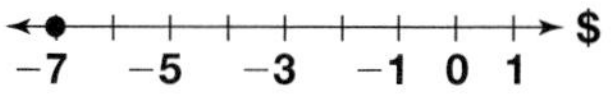

7. 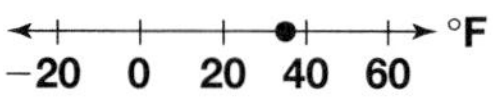

8. 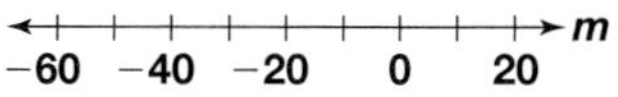

9. −2, −1, 1, 2 **10.** −4, 0, 5, |−6| **11.** −9, −7, −5, −3 **12.** −8, |−9|, 10, 11 **13.** 11 **14.** −4 **15.** −2 **16.** −13 **17.** 8 **18.** 8 **19.** −11 **20.** −8 **21.** I am winning by 7 strokes. **22.** 36 **23.** −21 **24.** −10 **25.** 48 **26.** 4 **27.** −5 **28.** −4 **29.** 7 **30.** 6 hr

31–34.

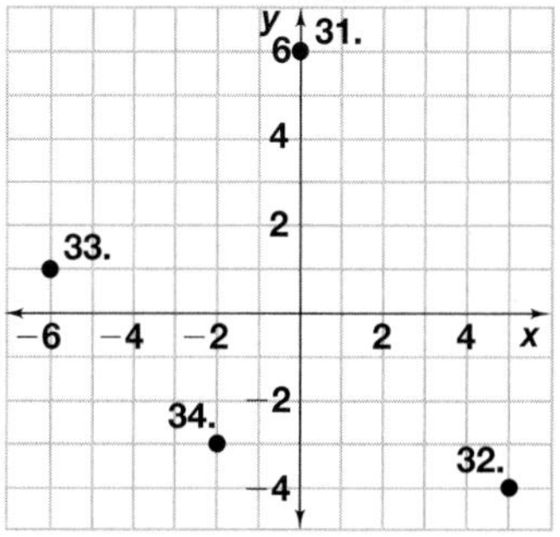

35.

36. \$26,286 **37–39.** Tables may vary. Samples are given.

37.

x	−3	−1	0	1
y	0	2	3	4

38.

x	0	1	2	3
y	−3	−1	1	3

39.

x	−3	1	3
y	0	2	3

40. For Ex. 37:

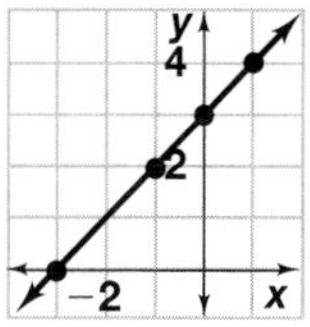

For Ex. 38:

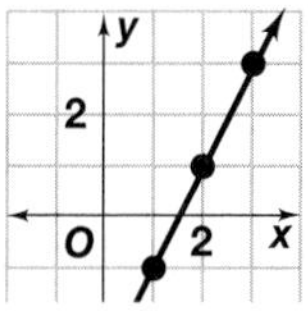

For Ex. 39:

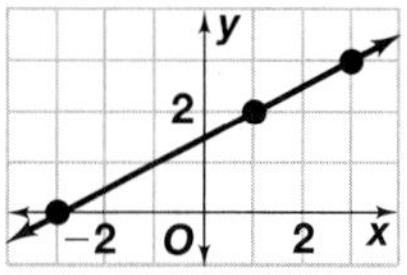

41.

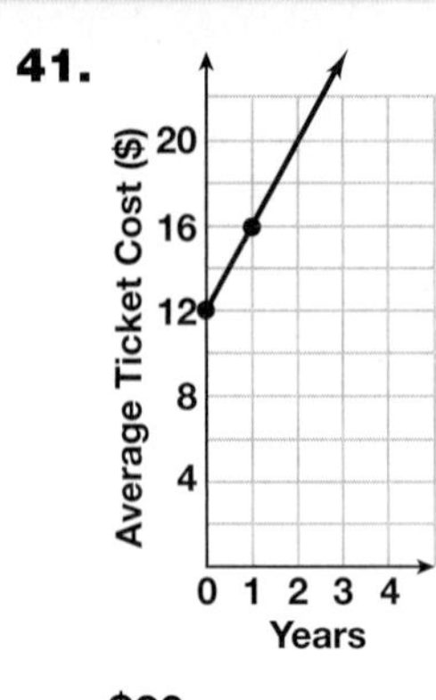

$20

Chapter 11

Lesson 11-1 pp. 549–551

EXERCISES **1.** $\frac{2}{5}$ **3.** $\frac{1}{5}$ **11.** $\frac{1}{365}$, ≈ 0.0027; ≈ 0%; unlikely **13.** $\frac{24}{25}$, 0.96, 96%; likely **15.** likely **17.** $\frac{1}{5}$ **19.** 50% **21.** 0.09 **23.** 1 **25.** 80% **27.** unlikely **29.** certain **31.** Answers may vary. Sample: c, b, e, a, d **33.** $\frac{5}{6}$ **35.** $\frac{1}{2}$ **47.** $1 - \frac{1}{n}$ **49.** $\frac{1}{5}$

Lesson 11-2 pp. 555–557

EXERCISES **1.** $\frac{7}{15}$ **3.** $\frac{33}{80}$ **7.** $\frac{3}{4}$ **9a.** $\frac{23}{50}$ **b.** Answers may vary. Sample: The probability of tossing heads is $\frac{1}{2}$. Since $\frac{23}{50}$ is close to $\frac{1}{2}$, the coin seems to be fair. **11.** $\frac{2}{5}$ **13a.** $\frac{9}{20}$ **b.** $\frac{11}{20}$ **15a.** Group A: $\frac{11}{20}$; Group B: $\frac{2}{5}$; Group C: $\frac{13}{20}$; Group D: $\frac{1}{2}$; Group E: $\frac{3}{10}$ **b.** E **c.** $\frac{12}{25}$ **d.** fair **17.** Answers may vary. Sample: Spin the spinner 100 times and record the results. Check whether every section is equally likely to be spun. **19.** $\frac{1}{10}$ **23.** 0 **25.** Check students' work. **27–32.** Check students' work. Probabilities should be close to those given. **27.** $\frac{1}{36}$ **39.** −13 **41.** 10 **45.** congruent

Lesson 11-3 pp. 560–562

EXERCISES **1.** 2 **3.** 6 **7.** 90 **9.** 400 **11.** $\frac{22}{30} = \frac{n}{150}$; 110 sixth graders **13.** $\frac{45}{60} = \frac{n}{420}$; 315 customers **15.** 300 **17.** 450 **19.** Answers may vary. Sample: The entire population could be too large or too dispersed to be surveyed. **21.** 284 parents **35.** I **37.** −120

Lesson 11-4 pp. 565–566

EXERCISES **1–4.** Check students' work. **5.** $14 **7.** no **17.** A **19.** Q

Lesson 11-5 pp. 571–573

EXERCISES **1.** $\frac{1}{2}$ **3.** $\frac{1}{4}$ **5.** spin 1 spin 2 $\frac{1}{9}$

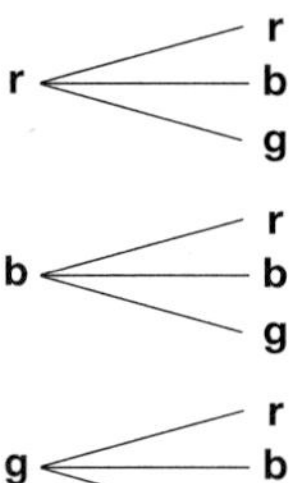

7. flip 1 flip 2 roll $\frac{1}{8}$

H — H: 1 2 3 4 5 6; T: 1 2 3 4 5 6
T — H: 1 2 3 4 5 6; T: 1 2 3 4 5 6

9. 32 outcomes **11.** 384 different meals **13.** $\frac{1}{32}$ **15.** $\frac{1}{4}$ **17.** $\frac{1}{12}$ **19–20.** Answers may vary. Samples are given. **19.** Counting Principle; it would take too much time and paper to draw a tree diagram. **27.** $\frac{5}{9}$ **29.** n^{20} outcomes **31.** D **33.** A

Lesson 11-6 pp. 576–578

EXERCISES **1.** 24 permutations **3.** 2 permutations **5.**

- 1
  - 2 — 3 — 4
  - 2 — 4 — 3
  - 3 — 2 — 4
  - 3 — 4 — 2
  - 4 — 2 — 3
  - 4 — 3 — 2
- 2
  - 1 — 3 — 4
  - 1 — 4 — 3
  - 3 — 1 — 4
  - 3 — 4 — 1
  - 4 — 1 — 3
  - 4 — 3 — 1
- 3
  - 1 — 2 — 4
  - 1 — 4 — 2
  - 2 — 1 — 4
  - 2 — 4 — 1
  - 4 — 1 — 2
  - 4 — 2 — 1
- 4
  - 1 — 2 — 3
  - 1 — 3 — 2
  - 2 — 1 — 3
  - 2 — 3 — 1
  - 3 — 1 — 2
  - 3 — 2 — 1

24 permutations

7. 24 permutations

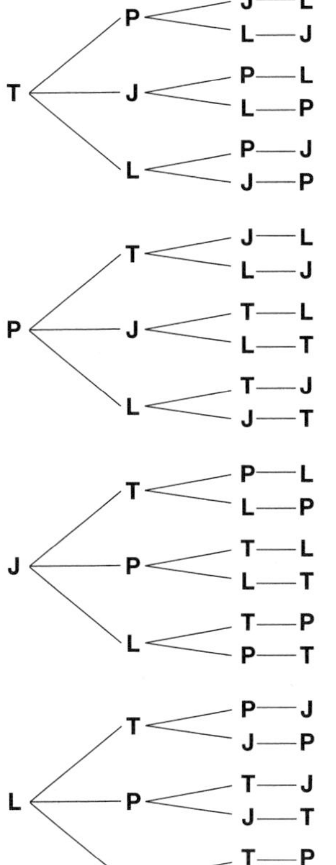

9. Let the 4 buyers be A, B, C, and D

prize 1 prize 2 prize 3 prize 4 24 possible ways

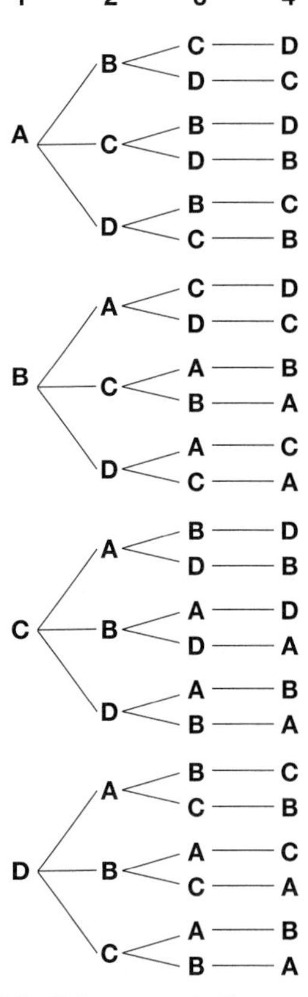

11. 24 permutations **13.** 120 orders **15.** 6 **17.** 362,880 **25.** 10 **27.** AIM **29a.** 5,040 ways **b.** $\frac{1}{5,040}$

Lesson 11-7 pp. 582–584

EXERCISES **1.** Not independent; The first pick affects the second because the number of dimes will be 1 less. **3.** Independent; The first toss does not affect the second toss. **5.** Dependent; The dish cannot break unless you take it out. **7.** Dependent; Eye color is genetic. **11.** $\frac{1}{4}$ **13.** $\frac{3}{20}$ **15.** $\frac{1}{10}$ **17.** $\frac{16}{25}$ **19.** $\frac{1}{216}$ **21.** $\frac{1}{216}$ **23.** $\frac{125}{216}$ **35.** the multiples of 4 **37.** 4, 8, and 12

Chapter Review pp. 586–587

1. complement of an event **2.** independent events **3.** equally likely outcomes **4.** sample **5.** permutations **6.** $\frac{1}{6}$ **7.** $\frac{1}{2}$ **8.** $\frac{1}{2}$ **9.** $\frac{5}{6}$ **10.** Noel: $\frac{2}{3}$; Kayla: $\frac{1}{3}$ **11.** 2,200 jelly beans **12.** $\frac{2}{25}$ **13.a.** 24 **b.** 720 **c.** 120 **14.** Answers may vary. Samples: **a.** independent; the first roll has no effect on the fourth roll. **b.** not independent; the second draw is affected by the first draw because you have not replaced the first cube. **15a.** $\frac{1}{9}$ **b.** $\frac{2}{27}$ **c.** $\frac{8}{81}$ **d.** $\frac{4}{81}$

Chapter 12

Lesson 12-1 pp. 597–600

EXERCISES **1.** 4 **3.** 18 **11.** 8 pens **13.** 3 **15.** 6 **19.** B **21.** B **23.** −3 **25.** −4 **29.** $2,000 **31.** −2; 4; 12 **33.** Rule: Multiply by 2, then add 3. 19; 33 **45.** $\frac{3}{7}$ **47.** 0 **49.** 0.18 m

Lesson 12-2 pp. 603–605

EXERCISES **1.** $g > 14$ **3.** $p \geq 15$ **7.** $x < 2$ **9.** $x \leq -3$ **11.** $p \leq 4$ **13.** $k < 3$ **15.** Cara, Molly **17.** true **19.** true **21.** Aaron, Steve, James **23.** Answers may vary. Sample: Use an open circle to exclude −20, and shade to the left of the open circle to show numbers less than 20. **25.** $w \leq 3$ **33.** $\frac{7}{9}$ **35.** 7

Lesson 12-3 pp. 607–609

EXERCISES **1.** $x \geq 7$ **3.** $k > 22$ **13.** Let d = the money you must deposit; $d + 143 \geq 250$, $d \geq 107$; You must deposit at least $107. **15.** Let n = the numbers; $n + 7 \geq 9$, $n \geq 2$; The number can be no less than 2. **17.** $a - 8 < 7$; $a < 15$ **19.** $7.01 **21.** $a + 2$; $500 \leq 32{,}000$; $a \leq 29{,}000$ft **23.** $t > 30$ **25.** $b > 4$ **29.** Let t = the cost of each T-shirt; $2t + 13 < 30$, $t < 8.5$; Each T-shirt must cost less than $8.50. **37.** Answers may vary. Sample: $\frac{1}{2}$ **39.** rectangular prism

Lesson 12-4 pp. 612–614

EXERCISES **1.** 24 years (assuming 364.25 days per year) **3.** 87.5 mi **7.** 100 floors **9.** 26 trees **11.** 2 times **19.** A **21.** [2] $6h + 7 = 14.5$ (OR equivalent number sentence); $1.25 [1] incorrect equation OR incorrect solution **23.** 12 **25.** 90

Lesson 12-5 pp. 618–620

EXERCISES **1.** 1 **3.** 7 **9.** 6.7 **11.** 8.7 **13.** 13 ft **15.** between 1 and 2 **17.** between 2 and 3 **23.** not rational **24.** rational **25.** not rational **39.** between 2 and 3 **41.** between 3 and 4 **43.** false **47.** 36 and 64 **55.** 24 **57.** 36 pretzels

Lesson 12-6 pp. 624–626

EXERCISES **1.** 35 **3.** 120 **11.** 8 ft **13.** 1.3 **15.** 16.7 **17.** $r^2 + s^2 = t^2$ **19.** 26 in. **21.** 12 units **23.** 75 ft **33.** [4] 6, 8, 10; 5, 12, 13; 9, 12, 15; I made a table showing the squares of the whole numbers from 1 to 15. Then I looked for squares that would have the sum of 100, 169, and 225 (10^2, 13^2, and 15^2 respectively); $6^2 + 8^2 = 36 + 64 = 100$, $5^2 + 12^2 = 25 + 144 = 169$, $9^2 + 12^2 = 81 + 144 = 225$ (OR equivalent explanation) [3] one error [2] two errors [1] three errors **35.** $\frac{1}{3}$ **37.** $\frac{1}{4}$ **39.** 3 **41.** 684 **43.** 84

Chapter Review pp. 628–629

1. B **2.** A **3.** D **4.** E **5.** F **6.** 3 **7.** 1 **8.** 8 **9.** 8 **10.** 125 **11.** 72 **12.** no **13.** yes **14.** no **15.** yes

16. −4 **17.** 8

18. −5 **19.** 3

20. $q < 3$ **21.** $r \geq 6$ **22.** $s > -11$ **23.** $t < 5$ **24.** $v > 4$ **25.** $w \leq 12$ **26.** $x \leq 6$ **27.** $y \geq -44$ **28.** 25 people **29.** 184 strips **30.** 14 **31.** 16 **32.** 22 **33.** 101 **34.** between 2 and 3 **35.** between 3 and 4 **36.** between 4 and 5 **37.** between 5 and 6 **38.** rational **39.** not rational **40.** rational **41.** rational **42.** 34 **43.** 28 **44.** 25

Extra Practice

Chapter 1 p. 642

1. one million, two hundred five thousand, eight hundred seven; 1,000,000 + 205,000 + 807 **3.** seventy-two and fifty-three thousandths; 70 + 2 + 0.05 + 0.003 **9.** 66.07

11. 1.05, 1.1, 1.35, 1.5
1.0 1.1 1.2 1.3 1.4 1.5

15. 15 − 8 = 7

17. 730 + 40 = 770 **19.** 2.65 **21.** 1.489 **23.** 7.7436 **25.** 0.05553 **27.** 3,850 **29.** 270 **31.** 0.8; repeating **33.** 5.8; terminating **35.** 21 **37.** 9

Chapter 2 p. 643

1. 256; 1,024; 4,096; the first term is 1. Multiply each term by 4. **3.** 23, 27, 31; the first term is 7. Add 4 to each term. **5.** 2 **7.** 4 **9.** $b - 1$ **11.** $b + 4$ **13.** $3.50 **15.** 34 **17.** 17.8 **19.** true **21.** false **23.** 11 **25.** 420 **31.** 192 **33.** 85 **35.** $9 \times 10^3 + 4 \times 10^2 + 5 \times 10^1$ **37.** $3 \times 10^5 + 2 \times 10^1 + 6 \times 1$ **39.** 57 **41.** 188

Chapter 3 p. 644

1. 2, 3, 9 **3.** 2, 3, 5, 9, 10 **7.** composite; 24 is divisible by 2 and 3 **9.** prime; 7 is only divisible by 1 and 7 **13.** $2 \times 2 \times 2 \times 2 \times 3$ **15.** $3 \times 3 \times 3 \times 5$ **19.** 10 **21.** 5 **25.** $\frac{1}{10}$ **27.** $\frac{3}{4}$ **31.** $\frac{15}{8}$ **33.** $\frac{100}{9}$ **37.** 8 **39.** 75 **43.** $\frac{4}{9}, \frac{4}{7}, \frac{4}{5}$ **45.** $\frac{7}{12}, \frac{2}{3}, \frac{5}{6}$ **49.** $1\frac{1}{4}$ **51.** $3\frac{9}{20}$ **55.** 7.146

Chapter 4 p. 645

1. $\frac{1}{2}$ **3.** 1 **5.** 6 **7.** 0 **9.** $\frac{3}{4}$ **11.** $1\frac{1}{3}$ **17.** $8\frac{1}{6}$ **19.** $11\frac{7}{12}$ **21.** $9\frac{1}{24}$ **23.** $5\frac{11}{15}$ **25.** $3\frac{1}{3}$ **27.** $3\frac{7}{9}$ **29.** 1 h 30 min **31.** 6 h 38 min **33.** 1 h 37 min **35.** $\frac{3}{4}$ of a tin

Chapter 5 p. 646

1. $\frac{1}{3}$ **3.** $\frac{1}{15}$ **5.** $\frac{1}{8}$ **7.** 24 **9.** 20 **11.** $14\frac{11}{16}$ **13.** $2\frac{1}{2}$ **15.** $\frac{1}{22}$ **17.** 4 **19.** 7 **21.** $3\frac{3}{8}$ **23.** 80 **29.** $490\frac{1}{5}$ **31.** tons **33.** pounds **37.** 3 **39.** 4

Chapter 6 p. 647

1. Answers may vary. Sample: $\frac{1}{2}$, 1:2, $\frac{3}{6}$.
3. Answers may vary. Sample: 1:4, $\frac{13}{52}$, $\frac{1}{4}$. **7.** no **9.** no **11.** 2 **13.** 9 **15.** 60 **19.** 500 km

21.

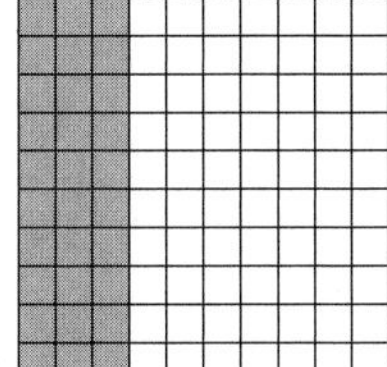

23.

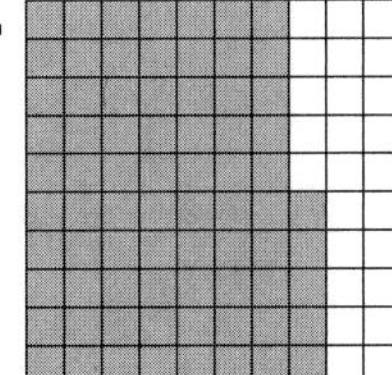

25.

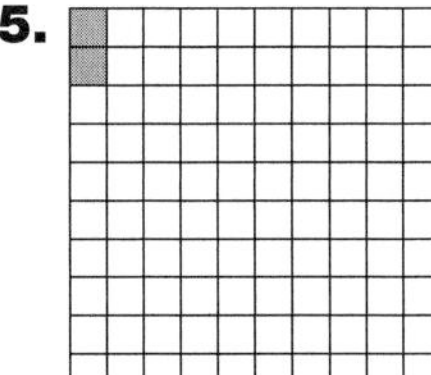

29. 0.01 **31.** 0.88 **35.** \$3.75

37. \$6.30 **39.** 3.375 **41.** 90

Chapter 7 p. 648

1. mean: 21.875 median: 22.5 mode: 22
3. mean: 44.875 median: 43.5 mode: 29

5.

wpm	Tally	Frequency
1	||||	4
2	|||	3
3	||	2
4	||	2
5	|	1

35 40 45 50 55 60 65 70

7. type of print **9.** 75–100 hours **11.** 25% **13.** = B2 + C2 + D2 **15a.** The vertical scale does not start at 0.

b.

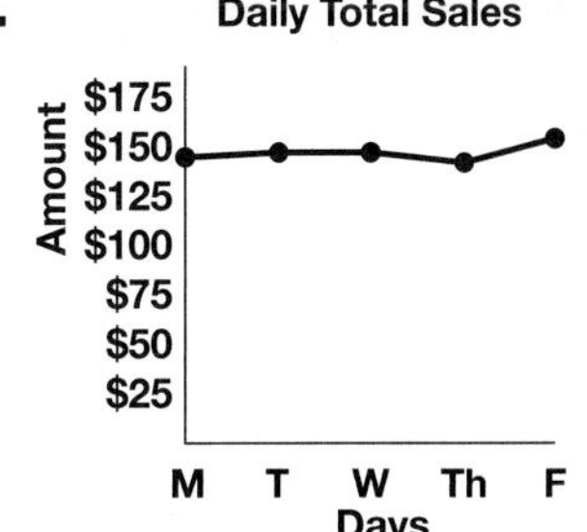

Chapter 8 p. 649

1. Answers may vary. Sample: G, H, D.
3. Answers may vary. Sample: $\overrightarrow{HA}$, $\overrightarrow{HB}$, $\overrightarrow{HC}$, $\overrightarrow{HD}$, $\overrightarrow{HE}$, $\overrightarrow{HF}$ **5.** obtuse **7.** acute **9.** complement: 62° supplement: 152° **11.** complement: 31.7° supplement: 123.7° **15.** equilateral **17.** true **19.** true **21.** similar **23.** neither

25.

Chapter 9 p. 650

1. oz **3.** in. **5.** 10,800 **7.** 1.008 **9.** 18 cm^2 **11.** 55.25 ft **13.** 144 cm **15.** circumference: 10.6π ft area: 28.09π ft^2 **17.** circumference: 22π ft area: 121π ft^2 **19.** square pyramid, 5 faces, 8 edges, 5 vertices **21.** triangular prism, 5 faces, 9 edges, 6 vertices **23.** 1,056 m^2

Chapter 10 p. 651

1. −2, −1, 0, 3 **3.** −8, −6, 7, 8 **5.** −4 **7.** −125 **11.** −4 **13.** 37 **15.** −40 **17.** −12 **23.** (2, 3) **25.** (−3, −1) **27.** G **29.** H **31.** \$5,002 **33.** −\$86

35. km = $\frac{m}{1,000}$;

m	1,000	1,500	2,000	2,500
km	1	1.5	2	2.5

Kilometers
Meters

37. \$2.64

Chapter 11 p. 652

1. $\frac{1}{7}$ **3.** $\frac{1}{2}$ **5.** 20% **7.** 0.66 **9.** $\frac{4}{4}$ **13.** 3 **15.** 24 **17.** 100 **19.** 1,332 **21.** $\frac{1}{2}$

Selected Answers

Chapter 12 p. 653

1. 7 **3.** 9 **9.** $x > -2$ **11.** $x \geq 1$ **13.** yes **15.** no

17. yes **19.** 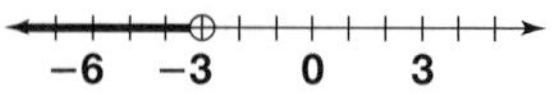

21. 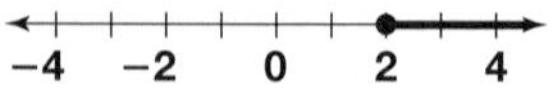 **23.** $m < 6$

27. $r > -8$ **29.** $t > 4$ **33.** 7 **35.** 13 **39.** yes
41. yes

Skills Handbook

1. ten millions **3.** hundred millions
5. hundred billions **7.** 30,000,000 **9.** 600,000,000
11. 900,000,000,000 **13.** 600 **15.** 60,000,000
17. 60 **19.** 600,000 **21.** 60,000,000,000 **23.** 6,000
25. 600,000 **27.** 60 **1.** 70 **3.** 4,440 **5.** 3,550
7. 300 **9.** 1,100 **11.** 6,400 **13.** 13,700 **15.** 6,100
17. 16,000 **19.** 89,000 **21.** 16,000 **23.** 164,000
25. 102,000 **1.** 76 **3.** 41 **5.** 144 **7.** 393 **9.** 279
11. 564 **13.** 2,894 **15.** 6,754 **17.** 7,149 **19.** 134
21. 176 **23.** 757 **25.** 132 **27.** 100 **29.** 907
31. 2,759 **33.** 9,252 **35.** 16,298 **1.** 44 **3.** 22
5. 21 **7.** 346 **9.** 177 **11.** 230 **13.** 6,828 **15.** 4,361
17. 1,005 **19.** 59 **21.** 836 **23.** 785 **25.** 281
27. 602 **29.** 419 **31.** 99 **33.** 176 **1.** 243 **3.** 348
5. 2,884 **7.** 315 **9.** 852 **11.** 6,057 **13.** 246
15. 252 **17.** 1,150 **19.** 48,480 **21.** 24,705
23. 31,540 **25.** 15,040 **27.** 35,002 **29.** 17,856
31. 20,200 **1.** 850 **3.** 85,000 **5.** 42,000 **7.** 60,300
9. 3,100 **11.** 5,600 **13.** 130l **15.** 19,000 **17.** 32l
19. 80 **21.** 17 **23.** 930 **25.** 61 **27.** 240 **29.** 78
31. 7,600 **33.** 37 **35.** 62 **37.** 14 **39.** 370
1. 73 R2 **3.** 93 R1 **5.** 29 **7.** 1,197 **9.** 429 R2
11. 227 R13 **13.** 68 R17 **15.** 98 R20 **17.** 47 R11
19. 25 **21.** Check students' work. **1.** 30 R2
3. 90 R1 **5.** 80 R3 **7.** 70 R5 **9.** 20 R14 **11.** 70 R2
13. 60 R1 **15.** 40 R5 **17.** 503 **19.** 420 R2
21. 80 R8 **23.** 40 R17 **25.** 20 R46 **1.** 36.8° C
3. 38.4° C **5.** 96.6° F **7.** G **9.** F **11.** W **1.** 11
3. 95 **5.** 29 **7.** 1,056 **9.** 404 **11.** XV
13. MDCXXXII **15.** CLIX **17.** XCII **19.** MCMXC

Index

Index

D

E

F

G

H

I

J

K

L

M

Q

R

S

T

U

Index

Acknowledgments

Staff Credits

The people who made up the *Prentice Hall Mathematics Courses 1, 2, and 3* team—representing design services, editorial, editorial services, market research, online services & multimedia development, production services, product services, project office, and publishing processes—are listed below. Bold type denotes the core team members.

Amy Acer, Leora Adler, Scott Andrews, Carolyn Artin, Barbara Bertell, Suzanne Biron, Stephanie Bradley, **Judith Buice,** Christine Cannon, Ronit Carter, Justin Collins, Bob Cornell, Patricia Crotty, Patrick Culleton, Carol Dance, Sheila DeFazio, Marian DeLollis, Jo DiGiustini, Delphine Dupee, Emily Ellen, **Janet Fauser,** Debby Faust, Suzanne Feliciello, Steve Fenton, Michael Ferrio, Jonathan Fisher, Barbara Hardt, Richard Heater, Kerri Hoar, Jayne Holman, Karen Holtzman, Kate House, Alan Hull, **Nancy Jones,** Judie Jozokos, Melissa Kent, Russ Lappa, Lisa LaVallee, Christine Lee, Carolyn Lock, Rebecca Loveys, Catherine Maglio, **Cheryl Mahan,** Barry Maloney, Chris Maniatis, **Tim McDonald**, Autumn Mellor, Eve Melnechuk, Terri Mitchell, Janet Morris, Sandra Morris, Kyai Mullei, **Cindy Noftle,** Marsha Novak, Greg Oles, Marie Opera, Jill Ort, Michael Oster, Christopher Ott, Steve Ouellette, Joan Paley, Dorothy Preston, Roberto Portocarrero, John Reece, Sandy Roedel-Baker, Rashid Ross, Irene Rubin, Alan Ruffin, Donna Russo, John Saxe, JoAnne Sgroi, Vicky Shen, Dennis Slattery, Lisa Smith-Ruvalcaba, **Nancy Smith,** Emily Soltanoff, Debby Sommer, David Spangler, Cynthia Speranza, Karen Swanson, Mark Tricca, Michael Vogel, Nate Walker, Lisa Walston, Roberta Warshaw, Matthew Wilson, Helen Young, **Carol Zacny**

Cover Design

Peter Brooks, Brainworx Studios

Cover Photos

t, PhotoDisc, Inc./Getty Images, Inc.; **b,** Wolfgang Kaehler/Corbis

Technical Illustration

New England Typographic Services

Photo Research

Sharon Donahue, Sue McDermott, Kathy Beaura Ringrose

Illustration

Brucie Rosch: 20, 90, 580
Daniel Collins: 527
Joel Dubin: 158, 160, 201, 226, 269, 289, 321, 326, 440, 468, 470, 473, 520, 534
John Edwards: 22, 29, 65, 151, 204, 270, 298, 398, 468, 478, 479, 525, 569, 604
Kenneth Batelman: 133, 141, 225, 235, 257, 309, 432, 473, 613
Precision Graphics: 77
Roberta Warshaw: 7, 17, 27, 49, 132, 178, 228
Trevor Johnston: 28, 94, 103, 132, 204, 223, 342, 345, 351
Wilkinson Studios: 251, 257
XNR Productions: 204, 233, 245, 289, 290, 440, 521

Photography

Front Matter: Pages vii, L. Clarke/Corbis; **viii,** Jerry Lodriguss/Photo Researchers, Inc.; **ix,** Bill Miles/Corbis; **x,** Tony Freeman/PhotoEdit; **xi,** Alan Linda Detrick/Grant Heilman Photography, Inc.; **xii,** AP Photo/The Grand Rapids Press, Lance Wynn; **xiii,** Gary Braasch/Getty Images, Inc.; **xiv,** Barros & Barros/Getty Images, Inc.; **xv,** Tim Thompson/Getty Images, Inc.; **xvi,** Myrleen Gerguson Cate/Photo Edit; **xvii,** Layne Kennedy/Corbis; **xviii,** Pete Saloutos/Corbis

Chapter 1: Pages 2–3, Andrew Leyerle/Dorling Kindersley; **4,** D. Young-Wolff/PhotoEdit; **5,** Joseph Nettis/Photo Researchers, Inc.; **7,** Frank Siteman/Rainbow; **10,** AP Photo/Tom Gannam; **11,** Royalty-Free/Getty Images, Inc.; **12,** David Young-Wolff/PhotoEdit; **14,** Carl Purcell/Photo Researchers, Inc.; **15 both,** Richard Haynes; **16,** Getty Images, Inc.; **18,** Robert Burke/Getty Images, Inc.; **21,** Lisette Le Bon/Superstock, Inc.; **22 l,** Tom Stack & Associates, Inc.; **22 r,** U.S. Bureau of Engraving and Printing; **26,** Bob Daemmrich/The Image Works; **28,** Spencer Grant/PhotoEdit; **31,** Reuters NewMedia Inc./Corbis; **32 t,** Russ Lappa; **32 b,** Syracuse Newspapers/The Image Works; **34,** Tony Freeman/PhotoEdit; **36,** L. Clarke/Corbis; **37,** www.SellPhotos.CA; **38,** Russ Lappa; **41,** James Watt/Animals Animals/Earth Scenes; **43,** Chad Slattery/Getty Images, Inc.; **45,** John Moore; **46,** Liaison/Getty Images, Inc.; **48,** Lori Adamski Peek/Getty Images, Inc.; **50 t,** John Moore; **50 b,** Mitch Kezar/Getty Images, Inc.; **53,** Jeff Affleck/SuperStock, Inc.; **58 t,** The British Museum/Dorling Kindersley; **58 bl,** The Science Museum/Dorling Kindersley; **58 br,** Russ Lappa; **59 tl,** The Science Museum/Dorling Kindersley; **59 tr,** Steve Gorton/Dorling Kindersley; **59 b,** Alistair Duncan/Dorling Kindersley

Chapter 2: Pages 60–61, Vanessa Vick/Photo Researchers, Inc.; **62,** Bryn Colton/Corbis; **64,** Michael Rosenfeld/Getty Images, Inc.; **66,** Jerry Lodriguss/Photo Researchers, Inc.; **67,** Phil Degginger/Color-Pics, Inc.; **69,** Benelux Press/Index Stock Imagery, Inc.; **70 both,** Richard Haynes; **72,** Tom Prettyman/PhotoEdit; **75,** Alan Thornton/Getty Images, Inc.; **77,** David Young-Wolff/PhotoEdit; **81,** Michael S. Yamashita/Corbis; **82,** Eyewire/Getty Images, Inc.; **85,** Russ Lappa; **87,** Grant Heilman Inc.; **91,** Image Source/SuperStock, Inc.; **93,** Russ Lappa; **93 b,** Marc Muench/Corbis; **93 t,** Getty Images, Inc.; **97,** Dianna Blell/Peter Arnold, Inc.; **100 both,** Russ Lappa; **107,** Chris Salvo/Getty Images, Inc.; **108,** Mark Richards/PhotoEdit; **109,** Mark Thayer; **114 l,** R. P. Meleski; **114 tr,** Baum/Dorling Kindersley; **114–115 b,** Carlyn Iverson/Absolute Science; **114–115,** Denis Scott/Stock Boston; **115 t,** Grace Davies/Omni-Photo Communications, Inc.

Chapter 3: Pages 116–117, Blair Seitz/Photo Researchers, Inc.; **117,** C Squared Studios/Getty Images, Inc.; **118,** Dennis MacDonald/PhotoEdit; **120,** Wally McNamee/Corbis; **122,** Mark Richards/PhotoEdit; **125,** Joanna McCarthy/SuperStock, Inc.; **126 both,** Richard Haynes; **128,** Österreichische Post AG; **130,** Jeff Greenberg/PhotoEdit; **133 l,** Russ Lappa; **133 ml,** Russ Lappa; **133 mr,** Russ Lappa; **133 r,** Russ Lappa; **133 tl,** Art Wolfe/Getty Images, Inc.; **133 tr,** Davies + Starr/Getty Images, Inc.; **135,** TSI Pictures/Getty Images, Inc.; **136,** Bettman/Corbis; **137,** David Young-Wolff/PhotoEdit; **139,** Mark Burnett/Stock Boston; **140,** Russ Lappa; **142,** Steve Cohen/Getty Images, Inc.; **143,** Tom Stewart/Corbis; **144,** Pictor/Uniphoto; **144 l,** Richard Haynes; **144 r,** Richard Haynes; **146,** Tony Freeman/PhotoEdit; **149,** Bill Miles/Corbis; **151,** Tim Ridley/Dorling Kindersley; **155 br,** Alan Schein Photography/Corbis; **155 l,** AP/Wide World Photos; **155 t,** Alan Schein Photography/Corbis; **157,** Bob Daemmrich/Stock Boston; **159,** Mary Kate Denny/PhotoEdit;

166 b, S. Wanke/Getty Images, Inc.; **166 t,** Geoff Brightling/ Dorling Kindersley; **167 bl,** Andy Crawford/Dorling Kindersley; **167 br,** Richard Megna/Fundamental Photographs; **167 ml,** Dave King/Dorling Kindersley; **167 t,** Dorling Kindersley; **167 tl,** Andy Crawford/Dorling Kindersley

Chapter 4: Pages 168–169, Mark C. Burnett/Photo Researchers, Inc.; **170,** Terry Cosgrove/Getty Images, Inc.; **172,** David Young-Wolff/PhotoEdit; **173,** Russ Lappa; **176,** Superstock, Inc.; **177,** NIBSC/Photo Researchers, Inc.; **178 t,** C Squared Studios/ Getty Images, Inc.; **178 bl,** John A. Rizzo/Getty Images, Inc.; **178 br,** David Toase/Getty Images, Inc.; **180,** Russ Lappa; **181,** Bob Daemmrich/Stock Boston; **183,** Faidley/Agliolol/ International Stock; **185,** Russ Lappa; **186,** Ronn Maratea/Image State; **188 t,** Tony Freeman/PhotoEdit; **188 b,** John Moore; **190,** Renee Lynn/Corbis; **192 both,** Richard Haynes; **193,** Tony Freeman/PhotoEdit; **198 t,** Adam Smith/Getty Images, Inc.; **198 b,** Frozen Images/The Image Works; **204,** Vicki Silbert/ PhotoEdit; **206,** Photo Edit; **207 l,** Pictor Uniphoto; **207 r,** Yuman/ The Image Works; **208,** Strauss/Curtis/Corbis; **214 t,** AP/Wide World Photos; **214 l,** AFP/Corbis; **214 r,** Russ Lappa; **215 t,** Robert Laberge/Getty Images, Inc.; **215 b,** AP/Wide World Photos

Chapter 5: Pages 216–217, The Image Works; **218,** Tom Stewart/ Corbis Stock Market; **219,** John Moore; **221,** Silver Burdett Ginn; **222,** Brian Parker/Tom Stack & Associates, Inc.; **224,** Guinness World Records, Ltd.; **226,** Richard Haynes; **227,** John Moore; **228 both,** Richard Haynes; **229,** John Moore; **232,** Alan Linda Detrick/Grant Heilman Photography, Inc.; **233 b,** John Moore; **233 t,** Silver Burdett Ginn; **236,** Dan McCoy/Rainbow; **237,** Russ Lappa; **239,** Ariel Skelley/Corbis Stock Market; **240,** Alan Oddie/ PhotoEdit; **243,** John Moore; **243,** Syracuse Newspapers/The Image Works; **246,** Owaki-Kulla/Corbis; **248 l,** Photodisc, Inc./ Getty Images, Inc.; **248 ml,** Photodisc, Inc./Getty Images, Inc.; **248 mr,** Photodisc, Inc./Getty Images, Inc.; **248 r,** Photodisc, Inc./ Getty Images, Inc.; **249,** John Moore; **250,** G. Biss/Masterfile Corporation; **252,** Past /Project Exploration; **255,** Bettmann/ Corbis; **256,** AP/Wide World Photos; **259,** David Young-Wolff/ PhotoEdit; **260,** 1995. Drabble by Kevin Fagan/United Feature Syndicate, Inc.; **264 b,** Annabelle Halls/Dorling Kindersley; **264 t,** James Muldowney/Getty Images, Inc.; **264–265,** Mike Powell/Getty Images, Inc.; **265 all,** James Jackson/Dorling Kindersley, Ltd.

Chapter 6: Pages 266–267, Tom Bean; **268,** Carl & Ann Purcell/ Corbis; **271,** Russ Lappa; **272,** Frederick M. Brown/Getty Images, Inc.; **274,** Russ Lappa; **275,** AP Photo/The Grand Rapids Press, Lance Wynn; **277,** Russ Lappa; **278,** SW Production/Index Stock Imagery, Inc.; **279,** American Honda Motor Co., Inc.; **280,** Richard Haynes; **281 t,** OMNI-Photo Communication Inc.; **281 b,** Tony Latham/Getty Images, Inc.; **282,** SuperStock, Inc.; **285,** Ken O'Donoghue; **286,** AP/Wide World Photos; **290,** Pictor Uniphoto; **295,** David Hanover/Getty Images, Inc.; **297,** The Academy of Natural Science/Corbis; **299,** Dennis MacDonald/PhotoEdit; **303,** Russ Lappa; **304,** Russ Lappa; **307,** Michael Spingler/AP/ Wide World Photos; **308,** Russ Lappa; **309,** Russ Lappa; **310,** Russ Lappa; **316 t,** Royal Tyrrell Museum/Alberta Community Development/Dorling Kindersley; **316–317 m,** Jim Channell/ Dorling Kindersley; **317 tl,** Jeffrey Sylvester/Getty Images, Inc.; **317 tr,** Andy Crawford/Dorling Kindersley; **317 m,** John Paul Endress; **317 br,** Brady

Chapter 7: Pages 318–319, Mack Henley/Visuals Unlimited; **320,** International Stock/ImageState; **323,** Dick Blume/Syracuse Newspaper/Image Works; **325,** Gary Braasch/Getty Images, Inc.; **327,** Craig Lovell/Corbis; **329,** Nancy Sheehan/PhotoEdit; **330,** Jane Burton/Dorling Kindersley; **332,** Ryan McVay/Getty Images, Inc.; **337,** Lon C. Diehl/PhotoEdit; **338 l,** AP/Wide World Photos; **338 ml,** Eddie Adams/Getty Images, Inc.; **338 mr,** Homer Sykes/Woodfin Camp & Associates; **338 r,** Pascal Volery Reuters/ Getty Images, Inc.; **343 both,** Richard Haynes; **344,** Bill Bachmann/Image Works; **347,** Spencer Grant/PhotoEdit; **349,** Bob Daemmrich/Stock Boston; **352,** Merritt Vincent/ PhotoEdit; **354,** Richard Cummins/Corbis; **359,** Stone/Getty Images, Inc.; **360,** Royalty-Free/Corbis; **369,** David Robbins/ Getty Images, Inc.

Chapter 8: Pages 370–371, Joseph Nettis/Photo Researchers, Inc.; **372,** Ronny Jaques/Photo Researchers, Inc.; **373,** Dennis Di Cicco/ Peter Arnold, Inc.; **375,** Barros & Barros/Getty Images, Inc.; **376,** Russ Lappa; **377,** William H. Mullins/Photo Researchers, Inc.; **379,** David Brooks/Corbis; **380,** Richard Haynes; **381,** Richard Haynes; **382,** Howie Garber/Animals Animals/Earth Scenes; **387,** George Shelley/Corbis; **388,** Peter Menzel/Stock Boston; **389 l,** Corbis; **389 r,** Russ Lappa; **394 both,** Russ Lappa; **395,** Russ Lappa; **395,** Rob Crandall/Stock Boston; **397 l,** S. Wanke/ PhotoDisc/Getty Images, Inc.; **397 m,** Ryan McVay/Getty Images, Inc.; **397 r,** Russel Illig/Getty Images, Inc.; **399,** Raphael Gaillarde/ Gamma Liaison/Getty Images, Inc.; **400,** AP/Wide World Photos; **403 l,** C Squared Studios/Getty Images, Inc.; **403 ml,** Siede Preis/ Getty Images, Inc.; **403 mr,** Siede Preis/Getty Images, Inc.; **403 r,** Siede Preis/Getty Images, Inc.; **403 b,** Tony Freeman/ PhotoEdit; **405,** W. Cody/Corbis; **407,** AP/Wide World Photos; **410,** Corel; **413 l,** Andrew J. Martinez/Photo Researchers, Inc.; **413 r,** Rod Planck/Photo Researchers, Inc.; **415,** Corbis; **416,** Suzanne & Nick Geary/Getty Images, Inc.; **418,** Dallas & John Heaton/Stock Boston; **420 b,** M.C. Escher © 2003 Cordon Art B.V.-Baarn-Holland; **420 t,** Russ Lappa; **426 b,** Paul Barton/ Corbis; **426 t,** Tony Freeman/PhotoEdit; **426–427 m,** David Jeffrey/ Getty Images, Inc.; **427 b,** PhotoEdit; **427 t,** Jim Hiss/Hispanic Business Inc.

Chapter 9: Pages 428–429, Jeff Greenberg/Peter Arnold, Inc.; **430,** Corbis; **431,** Ken O'Donoghue; **432,** Russ Lappa; **433,** Russ Lappa; **434,** Topham/The Image Works; **437,** NASA/Goddard Flight Center; **438,** Warren Bolster/Getty Images, Inc.; **441,** AP Photo/Elise Amendola; **442,** Richard Haynes; **443,** Richard Haynes; **444,** George McLean/Cardinal Spellman Philatelic Museum; **447,** Tim Thompson/Getty Images, Inc.; **449,** Tony Hopewell/Getty Images, Inc.; **453,** Tony Freeman/PhotoEdit; **454,** Digital Vision/Getty Images, Inc.; **455,** Bill Amend/ Universal Press Syndicate; **457,** Russ Lappa; **459,** Photo Researchers, Inc.; **463,** Bob Krist/Corbis; **465 bl,** Tony Freeman/ PhotoEdit; **465 br,** John Elk III/Stock Boston; **465 tl,** Tony Freeman/PhotoEdit; **465 tr,** R.M. Arakaki/International Stock; **468,** Alan Klehr/Getty Images, Inc.; **475,** Robin Weiner/WIREPIX/ The Image Works; **477,** Russell Illig/Getty Images, Inc.; **480,** Stephen Simpson/Getty Images, Inc.; **486 m,** Photo Courtesy of Northland College, Ashland, Wisconsin; **486 t,** Kim Sayer/Dorling Kindersley; **486–487 b,** Elfi Kluck/Index Stock Imagery, Inc.; **487 t,** Neil Setchfield/Dorling Kindersley

Chapter 10: Pages 488–489, Science VU/Visuals Unlimited; **491,** Neal Preston/Corbis; **493,** Tom Carter/PhotoEdit; **494,** Corbis; **499,** AP/Wide World Photo; **500,** Walter Bibikow/Index Stock Imagery/PictureQuest; **504,** Rid Catanach/Woods Hole Oceanographic Institution; **506,** Judith Canty/Stock Boston; **508,** John Moore; **509,** Tom Sanders/Corbis; **511,** Bob Daemmrich Photo, Inc.; **514 both,** Michael Schwartz/The Image Works; **517,** Spencer Grant/PhotoEdit; **520,** Myrleen Gerguson Cate/ Photo Edit; **523,** Susan Van Etten/PhotoEdit; **524,** Tom Stewart/ Corbis; **528,** Cary Wollinsky/Stock Boston; **529 both,** Richard Haynes; **531,** Sally & Derk Kuper; **533,** Yvette Californiardozo/ Index Stock Imagery/PictureQuest; **534 l,** Siede Preis/Getty Images, Inc.; **534 ml,** C Squared Studios/Getty Images, Inc.;

534 mr, C Squared Studios/Getty Images, Inc.; **534 r,** C Squared Studios/Getty Images, Inc.; **537,** Marc Romanelli/Getty Images, Inc.; **542 b,** Harald Sund/Getty Images, Inc.; **542 t,** Art Wolfe, Inc.; **542–543,** Planetary Visions, Ltd.; **543 bl,** David Muench/Getty Images, Inc.; **543 br,** Harvery Lloyd/Getty Images, Inc.; **543 ml,** Jeff Greenberg/Omni-Photo Communications, Inc.; **543 mr,** Getty Images/Eyewire, Inc.; **543 t,** Gery Randall/Getty Images, Inc.; **543 tr,** Peter Gridley/Getty Images, Inc.

Chapter 11: Pages 544–545, Richard Haynes; **546,** Anthea Sieveking/Petit Format/Photo Researchers, Inc.; **547,** Russ Lappa; **548 t,** Russ Lappa; **548 b,** David Young-Wolff/PhotoEdit; **550,** Elyse Lewin/Getty Images, Inc.; **553,** Russ Lappa; **554,** Tony Di Zinno/See Jane Run; **556,** Corbis; **559,** Paul Barton/Corbis; **560,** NASA/Dorling Kindersley Picture Library; **563,** Mark Burnett/ Stock Boston; **566,** Joe McDonald/Corbis; **570 both,** Richard Haynes; **572,** Layne Kennedy/Corbis; **574,** Getty Images, Inc.; **575,** Rudi Von Briel/PhotoEdit; **576,** EyeWire/Getty Images, Inc.; **577,** United Media/United Feature Syndicate, Inc.; **581,** Syracuse Newpaper/The Image Works; **583 l,** Ken Ross/Getty Images, Inc.; **583 r,** Russ Lappa; **584,** Courtesy of Milton Bradley Co.; **585,** Russ Lappa; **590 t,** C Squared Studios/Getty Images, Inc.; **590 b,** Al Francekevich/Corbis; **591,** MMI Flash! Light/Stock Boston

Chapter 12: Pages 592–593, Ron Brown/Superstock, Inc.; **594,** AFP Photo/Don Emmert/Corbis; **595,** Pete Saloutos/Corbis; **595,** Ron Brown/Superstock, Inc.; **596,** Gary Conner/PhotoEdit; **597 both,** Richard Haynes; **598,** Tom & Dee Ann McCarthy/Corbis; **599,** (ZF) T. Knsselmann/Masterfile; **600,** Richard Haynes; **601,** 1986 James Mayo/Chicago Tribune; **603,** Tony Freeman/ PhotoEdit; **604,** SuperStock, Inc.; **605,** Spokane Police Department; **606,** AP/Wide World Photos; **607,** Russ Lappa; **608,** Tim Thompson/Corbis; **611,** Bohemian Nomad Picturemakers/Corbis; **613,** David Young-Wolff/PhotoEdit; **616,** Ron Brown/Superstock, Inc.; **617,** Cynthia Hart Designer/Corbis; **619,** Roger Wood/Corbis; **623,** Zigy Kaluzny/Getty Images, Inc.; **625,** Jon Chomitz; **632 l,** Chris Bjornberg/Photo Researchers, Inc.; **632 t,** Tim Flach/ Getty Images, Inc.; **632–633 b,** Amanda Friedman/Getty Images, Inc.; **633 b,** General Electric Lighting; **633 t,** Davies & Starr/ Getty Images, Inc.